EARLY JEWISH LITERATURE

An Anthology

EARLY JEWISH LITERATURE

An Anthology

VOLUME 1

Scriptural Texts and Traditions •
Interpretive History • Romanticized Narrative •
Biblical Interpretation and Rewritten Scripture

Edited by

Brad Embry, Ronald Herms *&* Archie T. Wright

WILLIAM B. EERDMANS PUBLISHING COMPANY
GRAND RAPIDS, MICHIGAN

Wm. B. Eerdmans Publishing Co.
2140 Oak Industrial Drive N.E., Grand Rapids, Michigan 49505
www.eerdmans.com

Published 2018
Printed in the United States of America

27 26 25 24 23 22 21 20 19 18   1 2 3 4 5 6 7 8 9 10

ISBN 978-0-8028-9013-9 (vol. 1)
ISBN 978-0-8028-9014-6 (vol. 2)
ISBN 978-0-8028-6669-1 (set)

Library of Congress Cataloging-in-Publication Data

A catalog record for this book is available from the Library of Congress

To our mentors,

Loren T. Stuckenbruck and C. T. Robert Hayward

Contents

Preface

Description

This anthology presents a fresh introduction to an important or representative document from a period of history commonly referred to as the Second Temple period. Accompanying each introductory chapter is a translation of either the whole or representative parts of the document. This is to provide the reader with in-volume access to the primary material. The phrase "early Jewish literature" indicates that the material contained in this anthology is prerabbinic, though some of the traditions given expression in these documents, and indeed the texts themselves were known to the rabbis. Moreover, by the first centuries BCE and CE, Judaism was a highly variegated religion, represented by numerous and often conflicting expressions, albeit centered on certain shared characteristics. For instance, even though all Jewish groups held the Pentateuch in high regard, not all Jewish groups necessarily agreed on the interpretation of Leviticus. The literature produced during this period is emblematic of this variegation, which this anthology seeks to capture. Against this literature tapestry one might situate not only Judaism, but also Christianity, which could properly be labeled one more example of Judaism's diverse nature during this period.

Occasion and Rationale

EJL intends to do two things. The first is to introduce the reader to the literature of the period from 516/515 BCE to 70 CE, the Second Temple period. This period began with the reconstruction of the Jewish temple in Jerusalem by the Judeans who had returned from their exile in Persia and ended with the destruction of this temple by the Romans under the command of Titus in 70 CE. During this period, Judaism knew a literary productivity that surpassed in volume the material from the Hebrew Scriptures. Importantly, it was during this period that the Hebrew Scriptures began to take their shape as the authoritative body of literature that we are familiar with today. That is, not only was this period one of great literary vibrancy in its own right, but it also provided the context out of which the central texts for 3 major, world religions would begin their process of codification.

The second goal of this anthology is to provide the reader with a sense of why familiarity with this material might be important. Literary productivity of this extent and variety indicates a number of things. First, even though the material is called Jewish, its diversity underscores the breadth of Jewish religious expression during this period in both Palestine and the wider Diaspora. Judaism during this period was far from uniform. Because literature is in part a reflection of culture, an awareness of the literary nuances of a particular time period necessarily gives a sense of the diversity of the culture. This is acutely important in the sweep of general religious history owing to the fact that Christianity develops out of this cultural milieu.

Second, literature in the broadest sense of the term, which includes historical records as well as legendary, liturgical, and fictive creations, is the primary means by which we study this particular period. Contemporary scholarship on this era relies predominantly on literary artifacts, more so than archaeological data, to give shape to its historical reconstructions. This is because literary production and historical memory are oftentimes closely intertwined. For example, Josephus's history is also a story, a narrative, arguing for a particular point from a particular perspective (*see* Josephus). Thus, by approaching the historical period of 516/515 BCE–70 CE from the vantage of the literature that was produced, this anthology has in mind that the reader will begin to gain something of an insight into the complex and fascinating worldview of Judaism and the social, political, and theological mind of the early Jewish communities during this period.

Finally, the world of Second Temple period Judaism is the world of the New Testament. What was important to the various Jewish communities represented by this literature was also important, to one degree or another, to the earliest Christian communities. While not every text represented in *EJL* has a direct corollary to a document or passage in the New Testament, nearly every theme or motif that emerges in the New Testament can be identified within the Jewish literature of the Second Temple period. In this way, a study of the material presented in *EJL* should prove valuable to the study of the New Testament. Each introductory chapter aims to highlight points of the contact between New Testament texts and other, Jewish documents from this period.

Organization of the Texts

The emphasis on the literary landscape of this period is reflected in the arrangement of most of the material into literary genres. Each genre is based on form and theme. These genres attempt to capture something of the essential commonality between the documents that are grouped within them. At the beginning of each new genre, readers will find a brief explanation of its characteristics. The reader should be aware, however, that categorization of this type and nature rarely fully encompasses the document. For instance, many of the Qumran documents could have been grouped under the rubric "biblical interpretation," and 1 Enoch could be classified as a scriptural text or tradition. The categories and grouping decisions are not intended to be rigid. Rather, the categories and the texts that fill them represent an effort to provide the best sense of the literary shape and characteristics of a particular document. The introductory group "Scriptural Texts and Traditions" departs from the scheme of categorizing texts according to genre, however. In light of *EJL*'s interest in highlighting texts held to be authoritative for both Jews and Christians, it seemed appropriate here to begin with a selection of texts that eventually became authoritative for both of these communities. At the same time all of these texts could fit well into other areas of the anthology. For example, parts of Daniel certainly fit the "Apocalyptic Literature" genre and the selected Psalms certainly cohere with the later selection of "Psalms, Hymns, and Prayers."

While prioritizing the literary qualities and dimensions of this period, the editors also assume that readers will familiarize themselves with the history of this period through other resources. Even though the anthology has an introduction to the history of the Second Temple period, and the individual chapters contain excellent overviews of contextual background issues, *EJL* does not presume to replace comprehensive introductions to this period. Rather, readers ought to find that *EJL* functions well alongside other resources on this period. Thus, *EJL* can function as either a stand-alone, entry-level base text or as a supplement for more advanced studies on this literature and history.

Distinctives of the Anthology

So, what is the distinctive innovation of *EJL*? In a word, it is the range and breadth of literature that has been brought together in a single text. The editors, in consultation with a number of specialized scholars in the field, have collected a range of material into one anthology that has heretofore been scattered in a variety of sources. In this volume, one will read 1 Enoch alongside Josephus, not because these two share significant features, but because they both represent Jewish literature from the Second Temple period. What the reader will soon see, however, is that the various documents and authors, while at times widely divergent in terms of historical location, provenance, and orientation, do share many similarities. The hope is that this anthology will provide fresh insights into early Jewish and Christian studies by putting these various documents together in one collection. That is, in addition to offering fresh introductions to these documents, *EJL* hopes to stimulate fresh insights by placing texts typically isolated from one another into the same context.

Final Thoughts

One final word about the anthology concerns the emphasis on the relationship between the documents included and the New Testament. The focus of this anthology is not Christian origins, even though the origins of Christianity are to be found within the social and religious atmosphere of this period. Rather, *EJL* presumes that the primary influences, interests, and concerns of Jewish communities in the Second Temple period are best understood from a variety of vantage points and interests. As one reads, a number of shared characteristics often emerge between this body of literature and the New Testament. Since many of the documents contained in this anthology were concerned with the arrival of God's kingdom, with the intersection between Hellenistic and Jewish cultures, and with the effect that this intersection could have and was having on religious issues, the overlap between this material and the New Testament is to be expected and should be highlighted. Ideally, this project should provide the student with a platform from which to explore the continuation of Judaism and Christianity into the rabbinic and patristic periods. At a minimum, this volume seeks to place the two great faiths that either emerged or solidified during this period once more into conversation with one another over texts that speak to their shared concerns and worldviews. Perhaps, in this way, this anthology can contribute a little to the dialogue between these two great faiths.

BRAD EMBRY

Abbreviations

ABD	*Anchor Bible Dictionary*
ANRW	*Aufstieg und Niedergang der römischen Welt*
ATDA	Alte Testament Deutsch Apokryphen
ATDan	Acta Theologica Danica
BAR	*Biblical Archaeological Review*
BASOR	*Bulletin of the American Schools of Oriental Research*
BETL	Bibliotheca Ephemeridum Theologicarum Lovaniensium
BZNW	Beihefte zur Zeitschrift für die neutestamentliche Wissenschaft
CBQ	*Catholic Biblical Quarterly*
CBQMS	Catholic Biblical Quarterly Monograph Series
CD	Cairo *Damascus Document*
CEJL	Commentaries on Early Jewish Literature
CRINT	Compendia Rerum Iudaicarum ad Novum Testamentum
CSCO	Corpus Scriptorum Christianorum Orientalium
DDDB	*Dictionary of Deities and Demons in the Bible*
DJD	Discoveries in the Judaean Desert
DSD	*Dead Sea Discoveries*
HTR	*Harvard Theological Review*
HUCA	*Hebrew Union College Annual*
HUCM	Monographs of the Hebrew Union College
IOS	*Israel Oriental Society*
JAC	*Journal of Ancient Christianity*
JBL	*Journal of Biblical Literature*
JJS	*Journal of Jewish Studies*
JNES	*Journal of Near Eastern Studies*
JQR	*Jewish Quarterly Review*
JSHRZ	Jüdische Schriften aus hellenistisch-römischer Zeit
JSJ	*Journal for the Study of Judaism*
JSJSup	Journal for the Study of Judaism Supplement Series
JSOT	*Journal for the Study of the Old Testament*
JSOTSup	Journal for the Study of the Old Testament Supplement Series
JSP	*Journal for the Study of the Pseudepigrapha*

JSPSup	Journal for the Study of the Pseudepigrapha Supplement Series
JSQ	*Jewish Studies Quarterly*
JSS	*Journal of Semitic Studies*
JTS	*Journal of Theological Studies*
LSTS	Library of Second Temple Studies
NETS	*New English Translation of the Septuagint*
NovTSup	Novum Testamentum Supplements
NTOA	Novum Testamentum et Orbis Antiquus
NTS	*New Testament Studies*
OBO	Orbis Biblicus et Orientalis
OTL	Old Testament Library
PCW	Philo, L. Cohn and P. Wendland edition
PLCL	Philo, Loeb Classical Library edition
PsVTGr	Pseudepigrapha Veteris Testamenti Graece
PTSDSSP	Princeton Theological Seminary Dead Sea Scrolls Project
SAOC	Studies in Ancient Oriental Civilizations
SBLEJL	Society of Biblical Literature Early Judaism and Its Literature
SBLMS	Society of Biblical Literature Monograph Series
SBLSBS	Society of Biblical Literature Sources for Biblical Study
SBLSP	*Society of Biblical Literature Seminar Papers*
SBLSymS	Society of Biblical Literature Symposium Series
SBT	Studies in Biblical Theology
SNT	Supplements to Novum Testamentum
SP	Samaritan Pentateuch
STDJ	Studies on the Texts of the Desert of Judah
STh	*Studia Theologia*
StPB	Studia Post-Biblica
SVTP	Studia in Veteris Testamenti Pseudepigraphica
TSAJ	Texte und Studien zum antiken Judentum
VT	*Vetus Testamentum*
VTSup	Vetus Testamentum Supplements
WUNT	Wissenschaftliche Untersuchungen zum Neuen Testament

INTRODUCTION

Overview of Early Jewish Literature

The literature of the Second Temple period is far more extensive than the Hebrew Scriptures and the Christian New Testament combined. The volume of these writings presents a logistical difficulty for the student who is undertaking to read them for the first time since these texts are spread across numerous modern editions and multivolume sets. Students seeking an in-depth study of this field should obtain the Apocrypha (deuterocanonical books),[1] the Old Testament pseudepigrapha,[2] an edition of the Dead Sea Scrolls,[3] the writings of Philo of Alexandria (*see* Introduction to Philo of Alexandria),[4] the writings of Flavius Josephus (*see* Introduction to Flavius Josephus),[5] and the Greek Old Testament.[6] This list suggests only the major divisions of the literature.[7] In the chapters that

---

1. Michael D. Coogan, *The New Oxford Annotated Apocrypha*, 3rd ed. (Oxford: Oxford University Press, 2007); *The Apocrypha, NRSV Edition*, rev. ed. (Cambridge: Cambridge University Press, 1993).

2. James H. Charlesworth, *The Old Testament Pseudepigrapha*, 2 vols., The Anchor Yale Bible Reference Library (New Haven, Conn.: Yale University Press, 1983–85); R. H. Charles, *The Apocrypha and Pseudepigrapha of the Old Testament*, 2 vols. (Berkeley, Calif.: Apocryphile, 2004).

3. Florentino García Martínez and Eibert Tigchelaar, *The Dead Sea Scrolls Study Edition*, 2 vols. (Leiden: Brill, 1999); Michael Wise, Martin Abegg, and Edward Cook, *The Dead Sea Scrolls—Revised Edition: A New Translation* (New York: HarperCollins, 1996); Geza Vermes, *The Complete Dead Sea Scrolls in English* (New York: Penguin Classics, 2004).

4. David M. Scholer and Charles Duke Yonge, *The Works of Philo* (Peabody, Mass.: Hendrickson, 2006); *Philo of Alexandria*, Loeb Classical Library, 12 vols. (Harvard, Mass.: Harvard University Press, 1929–62).

5. William Whiston, *The Works of Josephus: Complete and Unabridged, New Updated Edition* (Peabody, Mass.: Hendrickson, 1980); *Flavius Josephus*, Loeb Classical Library, 13 vols. (Harvard, Mass.: Harvard University Press, 1926–65).

6. Alfred Rahlfs and Robert Hanhart, *Septuagint (Greek Edition)* (Stuttgart: Deutsche Bibelgesellschaft, 2006).

7. Although unable to be included in this collection of works due to space, additional Greco-Roman and early Christian authors may be included in a student's reading. These include Herodotus (480 BCE) and Thucydides (460 BCE); both these historians offer background information on the period, although primarily Greek. The historian Strabo (64 BCE) offers some account of Jewish life in the decades prior to Jesus. Roman historians include Tacitus (56 CE)

follow, sample texts from each collection identified above will be introduced and an accompanying English translation offered. This feature presents a strength of this anthology—direct engagement of these ancient texts by the reader. The six collections are not listed in any order of priority since the different collections developed for diverse authorial, geographic, and cultural reasons. In order to present a representative selection, *EJL* draws from each of these collections.

The Apocrypha

The first collection of the Second Temple period corpus is the Apocrypha, or **deuterocanonical** writings. The Apocrypha are understood as works that have a "hidden" character, in this case the "hidden books." The dating of the texts in the Apocrypha covers a period of roughly four hundred to five hundred years (fourth century BCE–late first century CE).[8] Along with other collections of texts, the Apocrypha provides details of a theological and historical bridge between the Hebrew Scriptures and the New Testament. The content of this material reveals how the authors transmitted the traditions of the Hebrew Bible through the Second Temple period as well as offering a window into the world of first-century Judaism within which Jesus and the authors of the New Testament lived. The books of the Apocrypha are a diverse collection of writings that have their own distinct historical settings, literary genres, content, and theological perspectives.

The collection of texts in the Apocrypha may be divided into three categories based on the particular Bible in which the books are included, as illustrated in the following table.

TEXTS IN THE APOCRYPHA BY CATEGORY

	Roman Catholic (Vulgate) Bible	Greek Bible	Slavonic Bible
The Prayer of Manasseh		•	•
1 Esdras		•	•
2 Esdras	*		•
Additions to Esther	•	•	•
Tobit	•	•	•

and Suetonius (60 CE). These works include testimonies of the Jews in the first century and describe Roman politics in the New Testament period. In addition, the fourth-century CE Christian historian Eusebius offers a description of Jewish history and culture in the days of the early church. Perhaps more important, he also preserved ancient authors' accounts of Jewish life in the closing centuries BCE. One should not overlook the contribution of what is identified as "rabbinic literature," which includes such works as the Mishnah, Tosephta, Babylonian Talmud, Jerusalem Talmud, and the various *targumim*. All of these writings preserved a record of early Jewish biblical interpretation—much of it influential for early Christian interpretation.

8. For a detailed introduction and discussion, see David DeSilva, *Introducing the Apocrypha: Message, Context, and Significance* (Grand Rapids: Baker Academic, 2004), or Daniel J. Harrington, *Invitation to the Apocrypha* (Grand Rapids: Eerdmans, 1999).

Judith	•	•	•
1 Maccabees	•	•	•
2 Maccabees	•	•	•
3 Maccabees		•	•
4 Maccabees		*	
Psalm 151		•	•
Wisdom of Solomon	•	•	•
Ecclesiasticus/Sirach	•	•	•
Baruch	•	•	•
Letter of Jeremiah	•	•	•
Additions to Daniel	•	•	•

*Appears in the appendix of this Bible.

The Apocrypha are contained in the following books and manuscripts:

1. The Septuagint (LXX)—except 2 Esdras
2. Codex Alexandrinus (A)—includes 3 and 4 Maccabees
3. Codex Vaticanus (B)—except 1 and 2 Maccabees and the Prayer of Manasseh
4. Codex Sinaiticus (‭א‬)
5. Codex Ephraemi Rescriptus (C)—includes Wisdom of Solomon and Ben Sira
6. Chester Beatty Papyri—fragments of Ben Sira
7. The Dead Sea Scrolls
8. The writings of church fathers

Scholarship has shown that the texts of the Apocrypha originated in a variety of locations, including Palestine, Alexandria, Antioch, and possibly Persia. These texts survive in Greek, Hebrew, and Aramaic, but it is likely that most were written in Hebrew or Aramaic. Their early existence among and acceptance by Christian communities is verified by the presence of the Apocrypha in the major manuscripts of the Greek translation of the Hebrew Bible—the LXX (*see* Greek Old Testament below)—in Codex Sinaiticus, Codex Vaticanus (fourth century), and Codex Alexandrinus (fifth century). It is yet unclear whether these texts were included in the Jewish LXX, which was in use in many Jewish communities throughout the Diaspora in the first century CE. What is likely is that these Jewish communities were using a sanctioned translation by Aquila or Theodotion, which did not contain the Apocrypha. This suggests that there may have been multiple versions of the Greek Old Testament circulating in the Mediterranean world. We know from arguments present in rabbinic writings that the Jewish rabbis rejected the inclusion of the Apocrypha in the Jewish canon as early as the late first century CE.

The question of the use or place of the Apocrypha in the Christian Bible began with a debate between the church fathers Jerome and Augustine. While translating the Greek LXX into the Latin Vulgate, Jerome made a division in the Christian Bible between the Hebrew Bible canon and the extra-biblical texts. Only those books he considered as ecclesiastical and those used for edifying the church were included in his canon. Conversely, Augustine argued for a much broader canon that included Tobit, Judith, 1 and 2 Maccabees, Wisdom of Solomon, and Ben Sira. Augustine writes in *De doctrina Christiana* 2.8.13:

> Now the whole canon of Scripture by which we say this judgment is to be exercised, is contained in the following books:—Five books of Moses, that is, Genesis, Exodus, Leviticus, Numbers, Deuteronomy; one book of Joshua, the son of Nun; one of Judges; one short book called Ruth, which seems rather to belong to the beginning of Kings; next, four books of Kings, and two of Chronicles—these not following one another, but running parallel, so to speak, and going over the same ground. The books now mentioned are history, which contains a connected narrative of the times, and follows the order of the events. There are other books which seem to follow no regular order, and are connected neither with the order of the preceding books nor with one another, such as Job, Tobit, Esther, Judith, the two books of Maccabees, and two of Ezra, which looks more like a sequel to the continuous regular history, which terminates with the books of Kings and Chronicles. Next are the Prophets, in which there is one book of the Psalms of David; and three books of Solomon—Proverbs, Song of Songs, and Ecclesiastes. For two books, one called Wisdom and the other Ecclesiasticus, are ascribed to Solomon from a certain resemblance of style, but the most likely opinion is that they were written by Jesus the son of Sirach. Still they are to be reckoned among the prophetical books, since they have attained recognition as being authoritative. The remainder are the books which are strictly called the Prophets: twelve separate books of the prophets which are connected with one another, and having never been separated, are reckoned as one book; the names of these prophets are as follows: Hosea, Joel, Amos, Obadiah, Jonah, Micah, Nahum, Habakkuk, Zephaniah, Haggai, Zechariah, and Malachi; then there are the four greater prophets, Isaiah, Jeremiah, Daniel, and Ezekiel. The authority of the Old Testament is contained within the limits of these forty-four books.[9]

Clearly, Augustine considered the Apocrypha as Scripture on par with the present Protestant canon; in fact, he went as far as to use the Wisdom of Solomon and Ben Sira in his discussion of the Trinity.

The debate has continued over the inclusion of the Apocrypha in the Christian Bible. The Protestant Reformation began in sixteenth-century Europe as an attempt to reform the tenets and customs of the Catholic Church. At stake were several core theological issues: the authority of Scripture alone (*sola scriptura*), an insistence that believers are saved by faith alone, and the notion that all believers are members of the holy priesthood. In an effort to curb what they perceived to be excesses of power and overemphasis on church tradition, the Reformers (in particular, Martin Luther) sought to reclaim Scripture as the primary source for faith and doctrine. This was done by generating new translations from original languages (Hebrew, Aramaic, and Greek) into regional languages (i.e., German, English) and by limiting their biblical canon to texts from the Jewish Scriptures

9. Translation courtesy of www.newadvent.org.

(Hebrew Bible/Old Testament) and traditional writings of the apostles (New Testament). In hindsight, one can see that while Protestant Christianity has largely retained this canonical difference from Catholic Christianity, there is some diversity among Protestants regarding the use and appreciation of the Apocrypha.

The books of the Apocrypha consist of a variety of genres, many of which are found in the canonized Hebrew Bible. They include such genres as historiography of early Judaism (200 BCE–100 CE) identified in texts such as 1 and 2 Maccabees (*see* 1 and 2 Maccabees)—which describe the Maccabean Revolt in 175-167 BCE. In addition, we see Jewish history retold in 1 Esdras, written in the second century BCE, which describes the Jewish return from exile in Babylon. A second genre is wisdom literature in which many of the books identify wisdom as knowledge and obedience to Torah. Some examples include Ben Sira (Sirach or Ecclesiasticus; *see* Ben Sira), written sometime between 219 and 196 BCE; the Wisdom of Solomon, written in the Diaspora sometime in the early first century CE; and the wisdom poetry of Baruch, the pseudepigraphic "scribe of Jeremiah," written sometime in the second or first century BCE.

A third genre is romanticized narrative. This genre includes the book of Tobit, which tells of Jewish piety in the Diaspora; scholars contend that it was written sometime between 250 and 175 BCE. A second book in the category is Judith, written in approximately 165 BCE, which details the heroics of a female military leader. A third selection is that of the Greek Additions to the Hebrew text of Esther, written sometime in the second century BCE. A similar text is identified as the Greek Additions to Daniel (*see* Additions to Daniel); like the Additions to Esther, scholars suggest it was written in the second century BCE.

A fourth genre has been identified as psalms and prayers of devotion. This genre is represented by the Prayer of Manasseh, which describes the boundless forgiveness of God; scholars suggest it was written between 200 BCE and 50 CE. A further example is LXX Psalm 151 (*see* LXX Psalm 151), which describes the occasion of David being chosen as king of Israel. The Apocrypha contains other miscellaneous material that is not easily identified with a specific genre. The Letter of Jeremiah is likely a polemic that describes the folly of Gentile religions, perhaps a critique of Hellenism during the second century BCE. A similar polemical posture is found in 3–4 Maccabees (although their dating is subject to debate). The apocalyptic text of 2 Esdras (*see* 4 Ezra [2 Esdras 3–14]), probably written around 95–96 CE, describes the destruction of Jerusalem and the second temple in 70 CE, but does so by employing the setting of the Babylonian destruction of the first temple. It may be that the main reason for rejection of these texts by Jews in the first century CE was their pseudepigraphic nature, although the observation has certainly been made that several texts in the Hebrew Bible canon are also, in fact, pseudepigraphical.

The books of the Apocrypha do offer an important picture of Judaism during the 200 BCE–100 CE period. Similar to the other material in this anthology, the Apocrypha provides a window through which to examine Jewish theology and ideology that helps us clarify some of the themes and issues present in the New Testament. Several major theological motifs of the New Testament such as messianic expectation, substitutionary atonement, afterlife, resurrection and immortality of the soul, angelology, and demonology are presented in the Apocrypha.

Figure 1. In 1947, two Bedouin shepherds in search of their goats stumbled across a cave in the cliffs near Khirbet Qumran and began one of the most significant archaeological discoveries in the field of religious studies. The photo shows what is now known as Cave 1, which held clay jars that contained the first set of Qumran Dead Sea Scrolls including, among others, the Community Rule (1QS), War Scroll (1QM), Thanksgiving Scroll (1QH), Great Isaiah Scroll (1QIsaa), Genesis Apocryphon (1QapGen), and Pesher Habakkuk (1QpHab). Photo courtesy of Brian Schultz.

These texts give the reader a contemporaneous view of Judaism rather than an antiquated Old Testament view. Finally, the texts of the Apocrypha illuminate Jewish life in the Diaspora, thus expanding our understanding of the social and religious contexts of the early Christian missionary movement.

The Dead Sea Scrolls

The second collection of writings from Second Temple period literature to be included in *EJL* is the Dead Sea Scrolls. Beginning in 1947, one of the most fascinating discoveries in relation to biblical studies was made at **Khirbet Qumran** in Palestine. According to some reports, two Bedouin shepherds came across a cave near the Dead Sea that housed clay jars containing (mostly fragmentary) ancient documents. Over the following decade, eleven such caves were found, containing documents dating from as early as the third century BCE to as late as the mid- to late first century CE.[10]

The caves in which the scrolls were discovered are located on the shores of the Dead Sea in what was then part of the Jordan territory, now modern-day Israel. The site of the discovery became known as Khirbet Qumran, and is located south of modern Jericho on the western shore of the Dead Sea toward the Herodian mountain fortress and palace of Masada (*see* Map of the Dead Sea Region, p. 40).

10. James VanderKam and Peter Flint, *The Meaning of the Dead Sea Scrolls: Their Significance for Understanding the Bible, Judaism, Jesus, and Christianity* (New York: HarperCollins, 2002); Timothy Lim, *The Dead Sea Scrolls: A Very Short Introduction* (Oxford: Oxford University Press, 2005).

Figure 2. Fortress Masada, the site of which is seen in an aerial view from the north, was the stronghold of Eliezar and the Zealots in the 60s CE. Todd Bolen/BiblePlaces.com

The distance from Jerusalem to Jericho is about 40 kilometers and the distance from Jericho to Qumran is roughly 32 kilometers. This desolate terrain would not have been easily traversed in the period in which the location was populated. The Dead Sea is the lowest point on the earth; it is approximately 79 kilometers long and 18 kilometers wide. It sits almost 427 meters below sea level with temperatures reaching 13 degrees Celsius in the winter and 46 degrees Celsius in the summer. These temperatures and extremely low humidity (averaging 31 percent) were key factors in the preservation of the scrolls in the caves for more than 2000 years.

Habitation of Khirbet Qumran

In 1949 the first excavation was made in an effort to tie the document caves to the nearby complex of buildings identified as Khirbet Qumran. However, the initial dig resulted in no significant connections being established. Excavations continued in the years following in which Roland de Vaux discovered three rooms from which containers similar to jars found in Cave 1 that contained the original scroll discovery were excavated. Other artifacts were discovered, including coins and other pottery. Further excavations continued under the supervision of de Vaux, who suggested that the inhabitants of the community appeared to reflect the description offered by Pliny the Elder. Pliny had proposed that this was the "headquarters" of the Essenes in his *Natural History* 5.73:

> From the west onward, Essenes flee the banks that harm; a group set apart and in the entire world beyond all others unique—without any women, stifling every

urge, without possessions, depending on palms. . . . Below them, there had been a town, Engedi, second to Jerusalem in fertility and the forest of palm-groves, but now another graveyard. Then follows Masada, a cliff fortress, and itself not very far from the Asphalt Lake.

It appears that Qumran was inhabited during various periods. There is evidence of walls and pottery dating from the eighth to seventh centuries BCE. Among this evidence, a potsherd was unearthed that is inscribed with Phoenician characters. An excavated deep circular cistern that was later used in the community's elaborate water system of aqueducts and reservoirs may also speak to a prolonged period of settlement of the site. Martin Noth has suggested that this period may be tied to 2 Chronicles 26:10 in which King Uzziah of Judah "built towers in the wilderness and hewed out many cisterns" (ca. 790–740 BCE; cf. Josh. 15:61).

The greatest interest of scholars centered on the Greco-Roman period (ca. 200 BCE–70 CE). De Vaux identified at least three distinct periods of settlement during this era.[11] The first period (Ia) most likely coincided with the rule of the Hasmoneans Simon Maccabeus (142–135 BCE) and Jonathan Hyrcanus I (135–104 BCE). He based his settlement theory on the discovery of a substantial number of coins bearing the images of Jonathan Hyrcanus I and Antiochus VII Sidetes. He

Figure 3. An elaborate system of reservoirs and aqueducts, like the one shown here, speaks to the possibility of a long habitation at Qumran in the eigth and seventh centuries BCE. Photo courtesy of Brian Schultz.

11. Stephen Pfann, *The Excavations of Khirbet Qumran and Ain Feshkha: Synthesis of Roland de Vaux's Field Notes*, Eng. ed. (Göttingen: Vandenhoeck & Ruprecht, 2003). See also James VanderKam and Peter Flint, *The Meaning of the Dead Sea Scrolls* (San Francisco: HarperCollins, 2002), p. 41.

argued that during this period the cistern (perhaps the one noted by Noth) was cleared and two *mikvaot* (immersion pools) were constructed.

The second period (Ib) identified by de Vaux coincided with the rule of other Hasmoneans, including Alexander Jannaeus. This phase suggests that a larger community was constructed, which included multistoried buildings, cisterns, and an elaborate aqueduct system to bring water from the Wadi Qumran during the rainy season. He argues that this stage of occupancy may have lasted until ca. 37 BCE, when it was halted due to an earthquake and fire.

A third Jewish phase (II) of settlement appears to have followed in which the complex was reconstructed (during the reign of Herod Archelaus) and reoccupied. It seems that this period lasted until approximately 68 CE, when it was occupied, according to de Vaux, by a Roman garrison (period III) probably on its way to Masada to capture Eliezer and the Zealots who were occupying the mountain stronghold. De Vaux bases this portion of his settlement theory on the discovery of "non-Jewish" coins dated from 67 to 73 CE.

A further important proposal comes from Jean-Baptiste Humbert and Jean-Luc Vesco of the École Biblique. Their proposal directly relates to the settlement of the Essenes at Qumran. Like de Vaux, they argue that the original occupation was likely attributed to Hasmoneans during the Hellenistic period, de Vaux's period Ia, but was destroyed in "either 57 BCE (by the Roman Gabinius) or in 31 BCE (by Herod)."[12] At this point, according to Humbert and Vesco, the site was taken over by Essenes and they constructed "the cultic center on the north side of the complex" that included an area for a sacrificial system. However, Humbert and Vesco suggest that only a dozen or so individuals occupied the site on a permanent basis.

Jodi Magness[13] argues that the Hasmonean "villa theory" put forth by Humbert and Vesco is dubious. She further suggests that de Vaux's period Ia never existed, contending instead that the settlement was likely established in the early first century BCE and that it was sectarian, most probably Essene. In addition, Magness maintains that the site was not abandoned following the earthquake; rather, the inhabitants repaired the structures and remained until roughly 9/8 BCE, when a fire forced them to leave.[14] The site was then likely reoccupied sometime during the reign of Herod Archelaus (4 BCE–6 CE). Magness's revised chronology is now the most widely recognized view in Qumran studies.

Further Scroll Discoveries

Expeditions were carried out around the area in which Cave 1 was discovered and other caves were found and were excavated beginning in 1951. What would prove to be one of the most important discoveries, Cave 4, was found in August 1952. This cave contained the largest quantity of manuscript material—pieces of some six hundred documents in all were found in Cave 4. The final Qumran cave

12. VanderKam and Flint, *Meaning*, p. 49.

13. Jodi Magness, "A Villa at Khirbet Qumran?" *Revue de Qumrân* 63 (1994): 397–419.

14. Jodi Magness, "The Chronology of the Settlement at Qumran in the Herodian Period," *Dead Sea Discoveries* 2 (1995): 58–65 (pp. 64–65).

Figure 4. 11Q19, the Temple Scroll, was found in 1956 in Cave 11, the last Qumran cave to be discovered to date. Supplied by the Estate of Yigel Yadin.

(at least for now), Cave 11, was discovered in 1956. It contained thirty-one texts, including some of the most important discoveries among the Qumran material, the Great Psalm Scroll, 11Q5, and the Temple Scroll, 11Q19–20.

Due to the extended period of time the scrolls were stored in the caves a great deal of deterioration occurred. Most of the Dead Sea Scrolls are fragments of larger scrolls where much of the original document has been lost. Some 30,000 fragments have been catalogued, which yield about 900 different texts. Most of the fragments have been dated between 200 BCE and the late first century CE. Three languages are found among the texts: Hebrew, Aramaic, and Greek.

The diverse content of the various documents does not allow one to categorize them into a single genre. Of the documents under consideration (we use the word "documents" cautiously, as much of the Qumran material is fragmentary, although they likely comprised a collection of documents at an early point), approximately one-third are copies of biblical texts from the Hebrew Bible. Fragments of every book in the Hebrew Bible except Esther have been found.[15] The remaining two-thirds of the texts are nonbiblical; however, the majority of these are religious in nature and closely related to a biblical text whether as a commentary (*pesharim*; *see* Introduction to *Pesharim*; *targumim*) or a biblical book that has been "rewritten." Some texts are previously known from the Old Testament pseudepigrapha or the Apocrypha such as Jubilees, 1 Enoch, or Ben Sira—these texts were previously known only in Greek or Ethiopic, but now appear in Hebrew or Aramaic. There are additional texts classified further as liturgical and legal texts from the community, magical texts (e.g., 4QHoroscope), and calendrical texts (texts describing the proper function and keeping of the heavenly feasts).

15. Although Sidnie White Crawford may suggest otherwise; see "Has Esther Been Found at Qumran? 4QProto-Esther and the Esther Corpus," *Revue de Qumrân* 17, nos. 1–4 D (1996): 307–25.

Some scrolls are directly related to the Qumran community and were likely authored by members of Qumran or other Essenes living outside the settlement.[16] These texts reveal how the members of the community lived their lives and formed their worldview. Two prime examples here include 1QS, identified as the Rule of the Community (*see* 1QS [Rule of the Community]) and the Damascus Document (*see* Damascus Document), which similarly describes how individuals were expected to live while part of the community. An interesting contrast occurs in the document identified as 4QMMT (*see* 4QMMT [Some Works of the Law])—this text describes the grievances against the wider Jewish community and priesthood in Jerusalem. Further, the document labeled the War Scroll (*see* 1QM [War Scroll]) foretells the coming battle between the forces of darkness and the Sons of Light—the eschatological battle that will restore the kingdom of God to Israel.

The discovery and eventual publication of the scrolls opened a window into life and religious thought in the Second Temple period never before seen by biblical scholars. As a result, new literary sources were unexpectedly accessible with which to examine the first-century CE Jewish world from which early Christianity would emerge (though the precise implications are an ongoing matter of debate). The scrolls reflect important theological perspectives, both sectarian and nonsectarian, including such issues as cosmology, purity (law), eschatology, and messianism.[17]

Flavius Josephus

The third collection of the Second Temple period corpus under consideration in this anthology is the writings of Flavius Josephus (*see* Introduction to Flavius Josephus). Josephus is considered a Jewish historian who was born during the reign of Emperor Gaius ca. 37 CE and lived until ca. 100 CE. The writings of Josephus comprise a complex collection of stories, which, at times, have been questioned by historians of first-century Palestine and Judaism as to their historical accuracy. He is best known for his comprehensive history of the Jewish people from the biblical period through the first century CE (*see* History of the Second Temple Period). He includes information about individuals, groups, customs, and geographical places, some of which are not referenced in other ancient texts, and so provides an important, though likely not unbiased, witness to the events and ideological currents within which early Christianity took shape.

In addition to the recounting of the rebellion of 66–70 CE, Josephus's writings provide a significant, extra-biblical account of the postexilic period, as well as the Maccabean and **Hasmonean** dynasties. Within these accounts he discusses religious and cultural features, including the Jewish high priesthood and Jewish sectarian groups such as Pharisees, Essenes, Sadducees, and Zealots—which he

16. *See* discussion in Gabriele Boccaccini, *Beyond the Essene Hypothesis: The Parting of the Ways between Qumran and Enochic Judaism* (Grand Rapids: Eerdmans, 1998).

17. George Brooke, *The Dead Sea Scrolls and the New Testament* (Minneapolis: Augsburg Fortress, 2005).

interestingly calls "philosophies." In addition, he describes several figures found in the New Testament narratives, including Pontius Pilate, Herod the Great, King Agrippa, John the Baptist, James the brother of Jesus, and Jesus of Nazareth (though this point is disputed). As such, he is an important source for the study of the context of early Christianity.

Josephus's description of history is presented in four major works: the *Jewish War* (covering the period 175 BCE–74 CE; see *War*); *Antiquities of the Jews* (creation to 66 CE; see *Antiquities*); *Life* (an appendix to *Antiquities*—his autobiography during the war against the Romans in the Galilee; see *Life*); and *Against Apion* (a refutation of anti-Jewish charges of Manetho, Apion, and others; see *Apion*). Further details of Josephus's life and writings will be offered below in the section covering his writings.

The Old Testament Pseudepigrapha

The fourth division of Second Temple period literature included in *EJL* is the Old Testament pseudepigrapha, which are defined as "falsely attributed works." Pseudepigrapha are texts that claim to be authored by well-known biblical figures from ancient Israel. However, these claims to authorship are questionable; better defined, the pseudepigrapha are works "whose real authors attributed them to figures of the past." The word "pseudepigrapha" (from the Greek: *pseudēs*, "lying" or "false," and *epigraphē*, "name," "inscription," or "ascription"; thus when combined these terms mean "false superscription or title") is the plural of "pseudepigraphon." The dating of the texts considered part of the pseudepigraphal collection could begin in the late fourth century BCE and reach to the late second century CE or early third century CE.

This literary convention is not limited to Second Temple period Jewish texts, but also appears among biblical texts. For example, few scholars would currently hold that the apostle Peter wrote the book of 2 Peter. Nevertheless, in cases where books belong to a religious canon, the question of whether or not a text is pseudepigraphical often elicits defensive reaction against perceived challenges to authenticity or trustworthiness and can become a matter of heated dispute. The value of such a text in its own right, which is a separate question for experienced readers of this literature, is often lost or diminished when entangled in the questions of canon.

Although the term "pseudepigraphon" literally means "false writing," it can more accurately be described as a literary work in which an unidentified author writes under a pseudonym. The name attributed to the writer is usually an ancient (even legendary) biblical figure long dead before the actual writing of the text. The primary purpose for this technique was to give the text greater authority in its receptor community and/or a wider hearing than otherwise possible. Unfortunately, and incorrectly, the term has often taken on the characterization that the writing itself contains false information or false accounts of events.

The primary issue concerning this particular corpus is one of authority of the text within a particular community rather than actual authorship. The authorship of the majority of the texts is attributed to individuals who would likely be considered "biblical heroes" of Israel such as prophets, kings, judges, patriarchs, and possibly matriarchs of the faithful community of Israel. The dating of a particular text (as will be discussed in each respective chapter below) will reveal the unlikelihood that a particular individual to whom the text is attributed was, in fact, the author. So, for example, Solomon did not write Psalms of Solomon, Enoch did not compose 1 Enoch, nor did Ezra write 4 Ezra. More recently, some scholars have argued that **pseudonymity** helps explain otherwise problematic features of some biblical texts such as certain epistles and Gospel traditions, as well as extra-biblical Christian literature.

The literary spectrum of the pseudepigrapha contains multiple genres, including narratives, hymns, apocalypses, oracles, prayers, and testaments. Apart from the inclusion of 1 Enoch and Jubilees in the Ethiopic canon, no individual book from this corpus is found in its entirety in the Hebrew or Christian Scriptures. There are nonetheless allusions to or quotes from the pseudepigrapha in the New Testament.

Several questions may be raised in relation to the use of a pseudonym in writing theological material. Were these authors being deliberately deceptive or dishonest? If so, what could they gain from it? It is highly unlikely that this practice was considered deceptive since some of the texts in question are quoted in the New Testament as authoritative. For example, in Jude 14–15 the author attributes these texts directly to the patriarch Enoch and not to an unknown author. This may tell us that the traditions found in 1 Enoch are much older than originally thought.

Finally, how can the value and significance of these pseudepigrapha to their communities be determined? Clearly, they reveal a great deal about events and conditions at the time of their writing. For example, the Animal Apocalypse of 1 Enoch gives an allegorical account of the Maccabean Revolt in 167 BCE. The book of Jubilees records a revelation reportedly given to Moses, which describes the beliefs of an observant Jew in the second century BCE. This text was circulated widely in the Second Temple period, suggesting that many Jewish communities may have been convinced by, and followed, the author's perspective. Significant theological and ideological motifs undertaken in the pseudepigrapha include cosmology, angelology, purity, eschatology and messianism, liturgical and ritual concerns, as well as resurrection and the fate of the dead.

Philo of Alexandria

The fifth collection of literary material in the Second Temple period corpus to be included in *EJL* is the work of Philo of Alexandria. Philo has been characterized as both a Jewish exegete and a Greek philosopher. His life and, in part, his writings are still shrouded in some mystery to contemporary scholars and students alike. His lifespan (20 BCE–50 CE) overlapped with three other significant figures of the Second Temple period—Jesus, Paul the apostle, and Flavius Josephus (see above). Josephus described Philo as a leading citizen in Alexandria during the late first century BCE and early first century CE. He writes that Philo's opinions in the community were held in high regard: "Philo, who stood at the head of the delegation of the Jews, a man held in the highest honor, brother of Alexander the

Alabarch, and no novice in philosophy, was prepared to proceed with a defense against the accusations."[18]

The collection of Philo's work is extensive, including ten volumes and two supplementary volumes in the Loeb Classical Library series. Nonetheless, David Runia maintains that there was little regard for Philo's work during his lifetime and contends that the majority of Jews "either ignored him or condemned him to silence."[19] However, despite the ambivalent response to his works by his contemporaries, the importance of Philo's writings for our understanding of Second Temple period Jewish and early Christian thought, perhaps particularly that of the apostle Paul, cannot be overstated. It should be noted that perhaps due to the insignificance of his work for the majority of Jews, Philo's writings survive due to their preservation by later Christian communities.

Philo is first and foremost an exegete of Jewish Scriptures to the Jews in the **Diaspora**. He is faithful to his Jewish traditions and offers a clear example of how a first-century CE Jew in the Diaspora was able to integrate his Jewish faith into the highly Hellenized social and cultural context of Alexandria. Perhaps the most interesting characteristic of Philo's work is his use of Greek philosophical language in his biblical commentaries and treatises. To this end, Philo interpreted the Law of Moses for the Jews of Alexandria in a manner compatible with Hellenistic thinking and Jewish exegesis. He employed the language of reason to examine the Scriptures in order to bring a deeper understanding of them to the Hellenistic Jewish community.[20] Consequently, no matter how "Greek" Philo may appear, he was in his own right a faithful Jew. Thus, his philosophy corresponded to his Judaism, or perhaps was formulated from Jewish thought.

However, Philo's philosophy was not his religion; it only served as a medium by which he explicated the biblical text. His favored interpretive tool for biblical exegesis was allegory. This convention may seem at first to reflect Philo's Greek tendencies, but Philo felt justified in using it because of its precedent in the Bible (*De plantatione* 36). His allegorical interpretation, however, must always be understood in the context of the biblical passage in question. It appears that Philo understood allegory as the true mystery by which one extracts the letter of the Torah.[21] In doing so, Philo attempted to make Judaism more accessible to his Greek community.

The second genre of Philo's writings is that of exegetical commentaries.[22]

---

18. *See* Josephus, *Antiquities* 18.259, and Philo's account in *Legatatio ad Gaium* of his journey to Rome as a member of the Jewish delegation appearing before the emperor.

19. *See* David T. Runia, *Philo in Early Christian Literature: A Survey*, Jewish Traditions in Early Christian Literature 44 (Minneapolis: Fortress, 1993), p. 17.

20. *See* Peder Borgen, *Philo of Alexandria, An Exegete for His Time*, NovTSup 86 (Leiden: Brill, 1997), p. 9. Borgen states that Philo has brought together Scripture and philosophical works, thus making his work pivotal in the history of thought.

21. R. Melnick, "On the Philonic Conception of the Whole Man," *JSJ* 11 (1980): 1–32.

22. *See Quaestiones et solutiones in Genesim, Quaestiones et solutiones in Exodum, Legatio ad Gaium, De cherubim, De sacrificiis Abelis et Caini, Quod deterius potiori insidiari soleaet, De posteritate Caini, De gigantibus, Quod Deus sit immutabilis, De agricultura, De plantatione, De ebrietate, De sobrietate, De confusione linguarum, De migratione Abrahami, Quis rerum divinarum heres sit, De congressu eruditionis gratia, De fuga et inventione, De mutatione nominum,* and *De somniis.*

These treatises may have been addressed to a wider Jewish population, who had a sophisticated knowledge of Scripture and philosophy. A third genre identified in Philo's works is his expository treatises.[23] These texts were likely directed to non-Jews who had little knowledge of Jewish practices, and for this reason Philo presented a rewritten Bible.[24] Additional details on the work of Philo will be offered below in the section covering his writings.

Greek Old Testament

Finally, in an anthology that introduces readers to early Jewish literature from several different collections (see above), the Greek versions of the Hebrew Bible (Christian Old Testament), and the legendary traditions that they spawned, also need some introduction. Though the organizing principle of *EJL* for early Jewish texts is on the basis of genre identification, Greek versions of the Hebrew Bible were, initially, the work of Jewish communities and were undertaken during the Second Temple period.[25]

As pointed out elsewhere in this anthology (*see* History of the Second Temple Period), this period found Jewish communities struggling mightily to reconcile the influence of the Hellenistic world with their religious and social convictions. Nowhere is this more poignant than in how they approached translation of their sacred texts from Hebrew into the **lingua franca** of their day, Greek. All translation is, to some degree, interpretation, and biblical texts are no exception. In some cases these Greek translations reflect the tension between literal reproduction of the Hebrew texts and the (perceived) need for theological clarification or expansion of them. In other instances a strategy for interpretation—what some might even call an "interpretive agenda"—is clearly present in ways not unlike the later *targumim* of post–Second Temple period rabbinic Judaism.

The term "Septuagint" (Latin: *septuaginta*, meaning "seventy" and designated by the Roman numeral LXX) commonly functions as a default expression for the Greek Old Testament. This, however, oversimplifies a more complex issue. Initially, in point of fact, only the translation of the Hebrew Pentateuch into Greek by Jews likely living in Alexandria, Egypt, is meant by this term. Certain traditions (*see* Letter of Aristeas) claimed that the translation was the product of seventy (or seventy-two) Jewish scholars working in a period of only seventy days. One can imagine how the Alexandrian intellectual climate could have stimulated such

23. *De opificio mundi, De Abrahamo, De Josepho, De Decalogo, De specialibus legibus, De virtutibus, De praemiis et poenis, De vita contemplativa, Hypothetica*, and *Vita Mosis*.

24. Two works that fall into this category are *Hypothetica*, which discusses Jewish law and the Essenes as a defense of the Jews, and *De vita contemplativa*, which discusses the lives of the Therapeutae in an attempt to impress the Jews by the work of the sect.

25. For full-length introductions to Greek versions of the Old Testament and the development of Septuagint traditions, see Jennifer M. Dines, *The Septuagint* (Edinburgh: T&T Clark, 2004); Karen Jobes and Moisés Silva, *Invitation to the Septuagint* (Grand Rapids: Baker Academic, 2000); Emmanuel Tov, "The Septuagint," in *Mikra: Text, Translation, Reading and Interpretation of the Hebrew Bible in Ancient Judaism and Early Christianity* (Assen: Van Gorcum, 1988), pp. 161–88; and Sidney Jellicoe, *The Septuagint and Modern Study* (Oxford: Clarendon, 1968).

a translation effort (see above for more detail on the Jewish theologian Philo), given the city's standing as a major center of both Jewish and Hellenistic traditions. Since this work significantly predates the extant manuscripts of the Hebrew **Masoretic Text (MT)**, these Greek versions may offer older readings than some MT traditions. In certain cases these Greek readings confirm versions of Hebrew texts found among the Dead Sea Scrolls against what we find in the MT. As such, these translations are not only an important opening into the dynamic scribal and textual world of early Judaism; they also function as literary testimonials to how some Diaspora Jews understood, expressed, and defended their faith. To this end, what we find in these Greek translations represents important Jewish interpretive traditions.

Eventually, the term "Septuagint" came to refer to the entire range of Greek Jewish Scriptures. These texts comprise both the canonical Hebrew Bible (though this was not yet fixed) and the Jewish literature now commonly referred to as the Apocrypha. At the same time, as both the scope of Hebrew Bible texts being translated and the geographic influence of these translations grew, the legendary account of their divinely inspired origins also flourished (*see* Letter of Aristeas and Philo's *Vita Mosis*).[26] While virtually no scholar accepts that this lofty account reflects historically accurate detail of actual events, its existence nevertheless shows the concern of Jews in the Second Temple period to validate and promote versions of sacred texts that could otherwise have been construed and dismissed as unacceptably compromised. Suffice it here to say that many Jewish communities (and later Greek-speaking Christian communities) accepted Septuagint traditions as authoritative biblical texts.

Ultimately, efforts continued to be made both to revise existing translations (what scholars refer to as **recensions**) and produce fresh Greek translations. Eventually a number of these "versions" circulated in Jewish (from the second century BCE) and Christian (from the first century CE) communities and were often referred to collectively as "Old Greek" or "Lucianic." Strong evidence exists to suggest that these communities made use of the range of Greek biblical texts available to them. Thus, it would be inaccurate to speak only of "one Greek Old Testament" as though a single, established text was universally used and its recovery was somehow possible. Several prominent versions emerged in the early centuries CE, including Aquila, Symmachus, and Theodotion (usually thought to come from Jewish origins). These are attested in Origen's *Hexapla*—an early type of "parallel Bible" in which several translation traditions may be seen alongside one another. Each version, in its own way, provides important information about the reception of these biblical traditions for certain groups in the Second Temple period and beyond. With the advent of full-scale Christian Bibles in the fourth and fifth centuries CE, these edited or collated biblical texts appeared alongside the New Testament in bound editions known as **codices,** of which the best attested are Codex Vaticanus (B), Codex Sinaiticus (‫א‬), and Codex Alexandrinus (A). Since the arrangement of the documents included in *EJL* is on the basis of genre, readers will encounter biblical and extra-biblical texts with LXX traditions or connections

---

26. *See* Letter of Aristeas, Josephus's *Antiquities* 12.2.1, and Philo's *Vita Mosis* 2.7 for this view of inspired translation—a view also accepted by many of the early church fathers.

of one form or another throughout the volume.[27] The earlier description of Catholic, Orthodox, and Protestant canons and their distinctive features is explained, in part, by the flexible and fluctuating nature of the LXX during this period.

In summary, a word should be said regarding the motivation and rationale for the emergence of the Septuagint in the Second Temple period. From the standpoint of Jews of this time, two dominant reasons appear to have driven these rich translation traditions: (1) to make their sacred texts accessible to the scattered Jewish people of the Diaspora for whom Greek had become the native language—Torah was to be the focal point of piety for people far removed from land and temple; and (2) to facilitate dialogue, defend distinctive Jewish practices, and promote the value of Jewish beliefs to the outside world (e.g., Philo describes the LXX as a "good gift" from the Jews to the wider world).[28] From within the earliest Christian communities, it should also be pointed out that theologians and scribes continued to preserve, use, and appropriate these translations of the Hebrew Bible as Christian Scripture. A cursory overview of New Testament quotations of Old Testament passages reveals that more than half reflect LXX traditions. In some cases where the LXX reading differed from the Hebrew text, the former was privileged over the latter; this means that significant features of early Christian biblical interpretation find their origins in LXX traditions.[29] Further, some scholars have argued that a case might be made for understanding Christian use of LXX traditions as a crucial point of transition and validation for these communities' self-understanding as the true representatives of Israel's religion in their own time. Such a judgment must ultimately be left in the hands of readers and, where appropriate, the chapters in *EJL* that deal with LXX material will aid in considering these claims further. Do not forget that though the LXX was preserved by Christians and became the Old Testament standard among a wide range of Christian communities for centuries, it is, first and foremost, a Jewish work. Thus, the value of the Greek versions of the Old Testament should not be underestimated as theological, social, and communal commentary from the Second Temple period and beyond.

As one can see from the brief descriptions above, a wide range of texts exists, whether complete or fragmentary, which represents the theological, social, and communal nature of the literature of the Second Temple period. The editors of this anthology believe that the texts represented here will offer new perspectives into the world of the Jewish (and early Christian) communities during this fertile, yet also volatile period in history. As a result, we anticipate that this work will act as a springboard into further studies of the greater corpus of Second Temple period literature.

ARCHIE T. WRIGHT AND RONALD HERMS

27. *See*, in particular, Dines, *Septuagint*, pp. 81–108.

28. *Vita Mosis* 2.47.

29. Craig Evans, *Ancient Texts for New Testament Studies* (Peabody, Mass.: Hendrickson, 2005), pp. 155–66; George Nickelsburg, *Jewish Literature between the Bible and the Mishnah*, 2nd ed. (Minneapolis: Augsburg Fortress, 2005), pp. 191–92.

History of the Second Temple Period

The history of the Second Temple period has its roots in the Assyrian and Babylonian exiles. The first exile began in 722 BCE when the armies of Shalmaneser V, the king of Assyria, overran the northern kingdom of Israel and large parts of the southern kingdom of Judea. As a result, Israel was sent into exile in Assyria and Media by Shalmaneser's successor, Sargon II (*see* Map of the Assyrian Exile, p. 33).[1] The second exile, involving Judah, began in 597 BCE when the Babylonian Empire, led by King Nebuchadnezzar, laid siege to Jerusalem and captured the city.[2] The Babylonian victory resulted in the deportation of King Jehoiachin (and his family), who was replaced by Zedekiah, the Babylonian-appointed king. Ignoring the advice of Jeremiah and other advisors (2 Kings 24:18–20), Zedekiah entered into an alliance with Egypt and Pharaoh Hophra and rebelled against Babylon. As a result, Nebuchadnezzar came against Jerusalem in 589 BCE (2 Kings 25:1), laying siege to the city for about thirty months; with full control of the city gained in 587/586, he sent the majority of the remaining population into exile in Babylon (*see* Map of the Babylonian Exile, p. 34). Following the capture of Zedekiah and those loyal to him, his sons were put to death and he was taken to Babylon and died there as a prisoner. In the years after the destruction of Jerusalem, a Babylonian-appointed governor, Gedaliah, ruled the province of Judah until he was assassinated, provoking most of the remaining Israelites to flee to Egypt. It is often argued that a final deportation of Judeans to Babylon took place in 582 BCE. These events began the period of Israel's history known as the "exilic period."

---

1. For a summary of this period, see James VanderKam, *An Introduction to Early Judaism* (Grand Rapids: Eerdmans, 2000); George Nickelsburg, *Jewish Literature between the Bible and the Mishnah*, 2nd ed. (Minneapolis: Fortress, 2005); Shaye Cohen, *From the Maccabees to the Mishnah*, 2nd ed. (Louisville: Westminster John Knox, 2006); Anthony Tomasino, *Judaism before Jesus: The Ideas and Events That Shaped the New Testament World* (Downers Grove, Ill.: InterVarsity, 2003).

2. Some scholars will argue that the Babylonian exile began around 604–601 BCE.

Life in Exile

The details of the life of the Judeans in Babylon can be partially reconstructed from various biblical texts such as Jeremiah, Ezekiel, Ezra, Nehemiah, and Daniel.[3] While the preponderance of Judean and Israelite exiles were sent to the east to Assyria and Babylon, an important minority went into exile in the west to Egypt. Chief among this group at an early stage was the prophet Jeremiah. It is likely that out of this group a later prominent Jewish community emerged in Egypt, which would produce a number of important Second Temple period texts (e.g., Philo's writings, Letter of Aristeas, Joseph and Aseneth). Nonetheless, the influence exerted on early Judaism by the Babylonian context is significant and became the primary literary setting for the biblical prophetic texts. These prophetic texts portray the struggles the Judeans faced in retaining and fostering their religious and cultural distinctiveness in the midst of the polytheistic context of Babylon. This particular era contributed significant features to the future development of early Judaism during the Second Temple period. It is likely during this period that the synagogue (among other noteworthy developments) first emerged as an institution in which the people assembled for cultic purposes in order to maintain a worshiping community of YHWH.[4] It is suggested that during the exile, or immediately thereafter, important stages of development of the final form of the subsequently canonized Deuteronomistic history (Deuteronomy–2 Kings) were completed.[5] Similarly, the writings of the "priestly" author who foresaw the return to Jerusalem and the reestablishment of the temple cult may well have taken final shape during this time. Ezekiel the prophet, perhaps as a member of this group of such "priestly" writers, proclaimed that the exile was YHWH's punishment for the idolatry and disobedience of the kings and the people of Judah. In the writings of Ezekiel, the reader discovers the hope of restoration and the return of God's glory to Jerusalem in the form of a Second Temple.[6]

Persian Period: Return from Exile

In 539 BCE the Persians, led by Cyrus the Great, conquered Babylon. One result, beginning in the 530s and continuing through the 520s, was that Cyrus allowed the Judeans to return to Jerusalem and Judea; in addition, the cultic vessels of the temple confiscated by Nebuchadnezzar were given to the Judean returnees

---

3. *See* Rainer Albertz, *Israel in Exile: The History and Literature of the Sixth c. BCE*, trans. John Bowden, SBLSBS 3 (Atlanta: SBL, 2003); John Bright, *A History of Israel*, 2nd ed. (Philadelphia: Westminster, 1971).

4. *See* George Nickelsburg, *Ancient Judaism and Christian Origins: Diversity, Continuity and Transformation* (Minneapolis: Fortress, 2003), p. 155; and Lee Levine, *The Ancient Synagogue: The First Thousand Years* (New Haven, Conn.: Yale University Press, 2000), pp. 22–23.

5. Nickelsburg, *Jewish Literature*, pp. 9–15.

6. *See* also (Second) Isaiah 40–55. Here one finds the mention of the restoration of the Davidic kingdom and suggestions of a future messianic figure that will help restore Israel.

led by Sheshbazzar.[7] Once in Judea, these returnees from exile encountered bitter opposition from those who had remained in the land (*see* Map of First-Century Palestine, p. 44). The events of the period in Jerusalem are reflected in the writings of Zechariah 9–14 (Second Zechariah), Isaiah 55–66 (Third Isaiah), Ezra 1–10, and Nehemiah 2–4 (as well as the apocryphal/deuterocanonical witness of 1 Esdras 6–9). It is clear from these works that the realities of resettlement did not match the hopes of those who had returned in the first wave of Judeans from Babylon. These unfulfilled high expectations of the returnees were on display in the yet unrestored temple and the clear factional divisions between those who had remained behind in Judea and those who had returned from Babylon.[8] The division between the righteous and the wicked found in Third Isaiah appears to reflect these conditions and subsequently set the foundation for related apocalyptic themes of Second Temple period literature found in 1 Enoch (*see* Introduction to 1 Enoch) and Daniel (although with some noteworthy missing components; *see* The Book of Daniel).[9] As a result, the literature of the future Jewish generations would reflect the hope for a restoration of the Davidic dynasty led by an "anointed" king of YHWH. These texts and others of the apocalyptic genre promote a perspective on the oppressed of Israel as YHWH's righteous ones who wait for the impending judgment and intervention of YHWH in the present troubles of Israel.

Following the little-known exploits of Sheshbazzar, Zerubbabel succeeded him as governor of Judah and the reconstruction of the temple began under his supervision. Zerubbabel had a staunch ally in his efforts to govern in the figure of Joshua, a Zadokite high priest. Alongside these two important figures in the reconstruction efforts of Jerusalem were the prophets Haggai and Zechariah. These two prophets legitimized the two "anointed" leaders of Judea and, as a result, the long-awaited construction of the temple began in approximately 515 BCE. Things did not go well for the early returnees, as many of those who were now living in the land did not want to see the temple rebuilt due to a conflict with the postexilic Jewish leaders (*see* 4 Ezra [2 Esdras 3–14]).[10] According to Ezra 4–6, it took approximately eighty to ninety years for the "children of the exile" to complete the Second Temple under the rule and permission of the Persian king Darius II (ca. 417 BCE). Following the completion of the temple, we find no mention of Zerubbabel in the historical writings of the Second Temple period. Alongside the previously mentioned texts of Haggai and Zechariah, one discovers in the writings of Malachi that due to the apparent infighting and loss of hope,

---

7. See Albertz, *Israel in Exile*, pp. 120–23.

8. This division among the Judeans is clearly spelled out in Isaiah 55–66, in which a separation will be made clear between the wicked and the righteous of the people. See Paul D. Hanson, *The Dawn of the Apocalyptic* (Philadelphia: Fortress, 1985).

9. *See* chapters below on texts specifically classified in this genre for the significant differences.

10. The term *Yehudi* occurs seventy-four times in the Hebrew Bible. The plural, *Yehudim*, appears first in 2 Kings 16:6 and in 2 Chronicles 32:18. In Jeremiah 34:9 we find the earliest singular usage of the word *Yehudi*, "Jew," being used. Originally the name referred to the territory allotted to the tribe descended from Judah, the fourth son of the patriarch Jacob. The term was translated into the Greek *Ioudaios* and Latin *Iudaeus*, from which the Old French term *giu*, which was derived after dropping the letter "d." This word was later adopted into English as the word "Jew."

the temple rituals began to collapse and betray a lack of commitment by the priesthood. This may be illustrated by their willingness to sacrifice unacceptable animals, their corrupt enactments of judgment, and their failure to uphold the rulings of Torah. Such realities highlight the importance of the rise of the figure of Ezra, the scribe of God.[11] Ezra is often represented as a reformer of Judaism with his sweeping proclamations against the practices of the Judeans, which brought about the public reading of the Torah of Moses in Nehemiah 8. It is suggested that during this same period the new governor of Judah, Nehemiah, arrived to see the great complacency that had enveloped the people. His task was to rebuild the city in order to provide protection for the people. Following a twelve-year period of governing, he briefly returned to Persia; soon afterward, he initiated further reforms that included such measures as institution of proper Sabbath practice, the outlawing of marriage to foreigners, and the payment of tithes to the temple. These efforts were undertaken to reestablish the distinct character of the people of YHWH among their pagan neighbors and renew their obedience to Torah. The return from exile marks the beginning of the period known as the "Persian period," which would last until approximately 333 BCE, at which time Alexander the Great, already moving through the Mediterranean world, conquered Persia and took control of the Fertile Crescent.

Hellenistic Period

The conquest of Persia and the occupation of the Fertile Crescent by Alexander the Great initiated the Hellenistic period. Soon after the conquest, the death of Alexander in 323 BCE brought about an approximately thirty-year period of infighting between his generals (the Diadochi, or "successors") known as the Wars of the Diadochi.[12] At the beginning of the conflicts, at least nine of the generals struggled for control of different parts of the empire. Following the power struggle between these generals, the eastern empire of Alexander was divided into the Ptolemaic (Egyptian) region and the Seleucid (Syrian) region with these two kingdoms continually vying for control of Palestine. The Ptolemaic Empire would rule Palestine from about 323 to 198 BCE, but relinquished control to the Seleucids in 198 BCE, who would then rule for approximately thirty-five years (note: the exact dating of these periods of each rule varies among scholars). During this time the region was a constant battleground for the two kingdoms.

The most determined of the Diadochi was Antigonus I Monophthalmus, who was the first of the generals to declare himself a king rather than a governor. Antigonus desired to unify the empire of Alexander the Great by defeating all the other generals; by 315 BCE, he was nearing his goal by unifying the eastern

11. *See* Ezra 7–10. For discussions on the shadowy figure of Ezra, see Lester Grabbe, *Judaism from Cyrus to Hadrian*, 2 vols. (Minneapolis: Fortress, 1995); Robert North, "Ezra," in *ABD*, 2:726–28; and various commentaries on the book of Ezra.

12. *See* John D. Montagu, *Battles of the Greek and Roman Worlds: A Chronological Compendium of 667 Battles to 31 BC, from the Historians of the Ancient World* (London: Greenhill, 2000); and Peter Green, *The Hellenistic Age: A Short History* (New York: Random, 2007).

PTOLEMAIC AND SELEUCID RULERS

Ptolemaic Rulers

Ptolemy I 323–305 satrap of Egypt
305–283 king of the empire
Ptolemy II 283–246
(267–259 joint rule)
Ptolemy III 246–221

Ptolemy IV 221–203
Ptolemy V 203–181/180
Ptolemy VI 180–145

Ptolemy VII 145

Ptolemy VIII 145–116

Cleopatra II in opposition 131–127

Cleopatra III 116–101
joint rule with Ptolemy IX 116–107
joint rule with Ptolemy X 107–101
Ptolemy IX (Soter II) 116–107 (with Cleo III)
Ptolemy X (Alexander I) 107–88

Soter II (Ptolemy IX) 88–81
Bernice III 81–80
Ptolemy XI 80
Ptolemy XII 80–58

Cleopatra V 58–55
Ptolemy XII 55–51
Cleopatra VII 51–30
joint rule with Ptolemy XIII 51–47;
Ptolemy XIV 47–44; Ptolemy XV 44–30
Arsinoe IV in opposition to Cleopatra VII
48–47

Seleucid Rulers

Seleucus I 312/311–305 satrap of Babylon
305–280 king of the empire

Antiochus I Soter 280–261
Antiochus II Theos 261–246
Seleucus II 246–226
Seleucus III 226–223
Antiochus III the Great 223–187

Seleucus IV 187–175
Antiochus IV Epiphanes 175–163
Antiochus V Eupator 163–162
Demetrius I 162–150
Alexander I Balas 150–145
Demetrius II (first reign) 145–138
Antiochus VI corule or in opposition 145–140?
Diodotus Trypho corule or in opposition
140?–138
Antiochus VII Sidetes 138
Demetrius II (2nd reign) 129–126
Alexander II 129–123 opposition to
Demetrius II
Cleopatra Thea corule 126–121 (murdered her
son Seleucus V)
Seleucus V corule? 126/125
Antiochus VIII 125–96 (murdered his mother
Cleopatra Thea)
Antiochus IX 114–96
opposition or corule to Antiochus VIII

Seleucus VI 96–95
Antiochus X 95–88
Demetrius III 95–87
opposition or corule to Antiochus X
Antiochus XI 95–92
opposition or corule to Antiochus X and
Demetrius III
Philip I 95–84/83
Antiochus XII 87/86–84/83
Tigranes I of Armenia 83–69

Seleucus VII 70s–60s?
Antiochus XIII 69–64
Philip II 65–63

Note: all dates are BCE.

regions of the empire under his rule. This action forced the remaining generals to join together in an attempt to defeat Antigonus.

Around 320 BCE Seleucus became the governor of the region of Babylon. However, by 315 BCE, he was forced to abscond to Egypt when Antigonus invaded. During this period, the remaining Diadochi (Cassander in Macedonia, Lysimachus in Thrace, and Ptolemy I in Egypt) joined forces in an effort to halt the advance of Antigonus. Ptolemy's armies defeated those of Antigonus at the Battle of Gaza, which permitted Ptolemy to advance northward. Ptolemy then gave his now ally Seleucus a tiny force of about one thousand soldiers in order to attempt to retake Babylon. On his journey northward, Seleucus amassed an additional three thousand men from the towns along the way and advanced on and captured Babylon. When the forces of Antigonus came to retake the city, to their surprise, Seleucus had hid his soldiers in the swamps around the city and launched a surprise attack during the night. He was victorious and those who survived from the attacking forces joined with Seleucus, giving him an army of 20,000, but he felt he was still not capable of fighting the armies of Antigonus in open battle. He chose instead to travel to the eastern provinces of the empire and captured them in short order.

Following about five years of on and off fighting, an unbrokered peace developed in 310 BCE among the remaining Diadochi (Cassander in Macedonia; Lysimachus in Thrace; Antigonus in the Near East, Anatolia, and portions of southern Greece; Seleucus in Mesopotamia and Persia; and Ptolemy in Egypt). In 307 BCE the Fourth Diadochi War broke out, ending the peace. As in previous wars, four of the Diadochi joined forces in an effort to defeat Antigonus. During the Battle of Ipsus, Antigonus was defeated and killed. The resulting victory saw the spoils of his kingdom divided among the remaining generals.

In 281 BCE Seleucus's army defeated and killed Lysimachus at the Battle of Corupedium due to an uprising within the provinces in Asia. Following this victory, Seleucus now ruled the region formerly controlled by Lysimachus; in addition he appeared ready to attack the kingdom of Macedon held by the sons of Antigonus. It seemed as if Seleucus was prepared to reunite the empire of Alexander, the dream held by all the Diadochi. Unfortunately, while Seleucus was traveling with Ptolemy I's son, Ptolemy Keraunos, the son stabbed Seleucus, killing him. Seleucus was succeeded in Asia by his son, Antiochus I. By 276 BCE, only three Diadochi remained; their territories included the Antigonids in Europe, the Seleucids in Asia, and the Ptolemies in Egypt. This division would continue for at least two more centuries despite continued warring among them. Although the empire of Alexander was never reestablished, the Hellenistic culture enveloped the Mediterranean world. A vast number of citizens from the three "kingdoms" remained in the Near East and Egypt, which helped establish Greek as the lingua franca of that part of the world and initiate the beginning of the Hellenistic Age. The beginning of the end of the kingdoms of the Diadochi came about with the emergence of the Roman and Parthian Empires in the second century BCE.

In 218 BCE the Seleucids, under the reign of Antiochus III, took control of Palestine. The results of the Battle of Raphia in 217 BCE restored power to the Ptolemies (Ptolemy IV), but the region rapidly changed hands again in approximately 198 BCE when Antiochus III defeated the Ptolemaic forces at Paneas. Initially, the

Seleucid rule proved auspicious for the Israelites, as Antiochus III declared that the Jews could restore the temple and self-rule according to the "laws of the fathers."[13] However, this favorable relationship was short lived when Antiochus IV Epiphanes came to power in approximately 175 BCE, ruling until 163 BCE. He initiated a practice of religious persecution against the Jews, highlighted by setting up an "abomination of desolation" in the temple (*see* The Book of Daniel and 1 and 2 Maccabees). This shift in the treatment of the Israelites was likely due in part to the growing power of Rome, which had inflicted a punishing defeat on the Seleucid armies at Magnesia in 190 BCE. In response to the demand for taxes from Rome, the rulers of the Seleucid kingdom attempted to remove the funds of the temple of Jerusalem (2 Maccabees 3). The once quiescent Jewish acceptance of the foreign rule would soon end with the Hasmonean rebellion in 167 BCE.[14]

Antiochus IV Epiphanes's proclamation against the Jews was highlighted by his attempt to Hellenize the population and the Jerusalem temple (1 Macc. 1:41–53) in order to unite his Seleucid kingdom with Palestine. Within the temple, he erected an altar to Zeus and demanded that Jews no longer obey the Torah. This prompted an armed resistance led by the family of Mattathias the Hasmonean and his son Judas Maccabeus (the Hammer). This revolt was known as the Maccabean Revolt (*see* 1 and 2 Maccabees). The Maccabees recaptured and rededicated the temple in 164 BCE; however, the Seleucids would continue their rule until about 141 BCE. At that point, the Hasmoneans established a (semi-) independent state under the watchful eye of the Seleucid kings until 63 BCE, at which time the Romans entered into the struggles of the **Levant.** During this roughly eighty-year period the Hasmoneans established an independent state of priests and kings, entered alliances with Rome against the Seleucids (1 Macc. 8), and built a kingdom that exceeded in size those of David and Solomon.

HASMONEAN RULERS

Judas Maccabeus	167–160
Jonathan Maccabeus	161–142
Simon Maccabeus	142–135
Jonathan Hyrcanus I	135–104
Aristobulus I	104–103
Alexander Jannaeus	103–76
Jonathan Hyrcanus II	76–66
Aristobulus II	66–63
Jonathan Hyrcanus II	63–40
Antigonus	40–37
Aristobulus III	36

Note: all dates are BCE.

13. *See* Josephus, *Antiquities* 12.138–44.

14. *See*, for example, Josephus, *Antiquities* 11–12. Josephus describes a letter between Alexander and the Judean high priest Aristeas in *Antiquities* 11.304–45; the translation of the LXX by scribes for the Ptolemaic rulers of Egypt in *Antiquities* 12.11–118; and the story of the Jewish tax collector Joseph, son of Tobias, in *Antiquities* 12.158–222. These stories perhaps reflect the respect the foreign leaders held (at least for a short time) for the religious practices of Israel—*Antiquities* 11.338.

From the Hellenistic to Roman Periods

The Hasmonean kingdom, however, was not entirely accepted by the wider Jewish populace. During the leadership of two Hasmoneans, Jonathan Hyrcanus I (135–104 BCE) and Alexander Jannaeus (103–76 BCE), many Jews voiced their discontentment with the way the state was being run. The primary complaint came from observant Jews who opposed the cultural and social Hellenization of Judaism as well as the political collaboration of the Maccabean aristocracy with their powerful neighbors and overlords. Because of the diminishing power of the Seleucids and the growing strength of the Hasmoneans, the emerging Roman Republic moved to control the Judean state.

In 63 BCE Rome ended the autonomous rule of the Hasmoneans when the Roman general Pompey's forces entered Jerusalem, removed the Hasmonean monarchy, and reinstated Jonathan Hyrcanus II as high priest.[15] These actions restricted the boundaries of the nation to Judea, Galilee, eastern Idumea, and the Transjordan. In essence, the former "Eretz Israel" was now a vassal state of Rome. This action did not go unopposed by the Jews in the land; episodes of rebellion repeatedly sprang up from the time of the Jonathan Hyrcanus II vassal state until the Bar Kochba Revolt in 132 CE.

During the Roman period, three specific divisions of rule in Palestine can be identified: (1) the vassal state of Jonathan Hyrcanus II (63–40 BCE); (2) the kingdom of the Herodians (37 BCE–6 CE); and (3) the Roman rule that included the period of the Roman prefects (6–44 CE). In addition to this, there was the rule of Herod Agrippa I (42–44 CE) and the period of the procurators (44–70 CE). During this time of heightened unrest, several members of the Hasmonean family attempted to regain control of the state but with little success. During frequent clashes between the Roman and Parthian Empires, Antigonus, the son of Aristobulus, gained enough support to be recognized as the Hasmonean king (40–37 BCE), but this renewed independence of the Judean state was short lived and likely served to exclude the Hasmoneans from any future role in the Roman vassal governance in Palestine. Following the short rule of Antigonus, the Idumean monarchy was established through the family of Antipater, who had negotiated his role with such Roman rulers as Pompey, Julius Caesar, Cassius,

---

15. Josephus, *Antiquities* 20.242-46: "When Alexander had been both king and high priest twenty-seven years, he departed this life, thus permitting his wife Alexandra to appoint the high priest; so she gave the high priesthood to Hyrcanus, but retained the kingdom herself for nine years, and then departed this life. For a similar period, her son Hyrcanus enjoyed the high priesthood; but after her death, his brother Aristobulus fought against him, and beat him, and deprived him of his principality; and he [Aristobulus] reigned as king and performed the office of high priest to God. However, when he had reigned three years, and as many months, Pompey came upon him, and not only took the city of Jerusalem by force, but put him and his children in bonds, and sent them to Rome. He [Pompey] also restored the high priesthood to Hyrcanus, and made him governor of the nation, but forbade him to wear a diadem. Hyrcanus ruled, besides his first nine years, twenty-four years more, until Barzapharnes and Pacorus, the generals of the Parthians, passed over Euphrates, and fought with Hyrcanus, and took him alive. They made Antigonus, the son of Aristobulus, king; and when he had reigned three years and three months, Sosius and Herod besieged him, and took him when Antony had him brought to Antioch, and he was slain there."

Mark Anthony, and Octavian. With the full support of the Roman legions, an Idumean known to history as Herod the Great would be appointed the vassal king of Judea from 37 to 4 BCE.[16]

Herodian Rule

Herod the Great established what would be a new social upper class that had no ties to the previous dynasties of the Hasmoneans. A problem facing Herod, however, was the appointment of a high priest. Unlike the Hasmoneans, who functioned as priest-kings, Herod was prevented from operating as priest because of his lineage. In an attempt to resolve the difficulty he turned to the Jews in the Diaspora, appointing a character named Hananel from Babylon, followed by a series of individuals from Egypt. All of these persons carried legitimate priestly lineage but were committed to Hellenization like Herod.[17] This action of Herod posed a significant change in the line of succession of the high priest; it was no longer an office passed from father to son, but one appointed by the reigning monarch.[18] In turn, the diminishing prestige of the office is reflected in the writing of various groups within Judaism during this period. Despite this corrupting of the office, the high priest still exerted significant power.

Despite his apparent concerns for the Jews in the Diaspora and his restoration of the Jerusalem temple, Herod's legacy remains his totalitarian reign that included the destruction of the community of sages[19] and the deportation of Jews into slavery. In addition, he is known to have established many building projects that were funded through a program of heavy taxation, a particular burden on the poorest citizens. An extremely paranoid individual, Herod killed many of the aristocracy, including numerous members of his immediate family, whom he suspected of plotting rebellion against his throne. Upon his death in 4 BCE, Herod's designated successor Archelaus was appointed king over Judea, Idumea, and Samaria. During the reign of Archelaus, disenchantment with Roman rule continued to grow. The literature of the period and the actions of the various rebel groups led by messianic figures marked a growing belief in the imminent intervention of YHWH in the political and religious turmoil of Israel. Alongside the rule of Archelaus, Herod's two brothers were given the powerful positions of tetrarchs in Galilee and Perea (Herod Antipas: 4 BCE–39 CE) and Golan, Trachon, and Batanea

16. *See* Peter Richardson, *Herod: King of the Jews and Friend of the Romans* (Minneapolis: Augsburg Fortress, 1996).

17. *See* Joachim Jeremias, *Jerusalem in the Time of Jesus* (Philadelphia: Fortress, 1975); Emil Schürer, *A History of the Jewish People in the Time of Jesus Christ*, 5 vols. (Peabody, Mass.: Hendrickson, 1994).

18. Josephus, *Antiquities* 15.22: "He [Herod the Great] also did other things in order to secure his government, which, in turn, occasioned sedition in his own family. He was cautious on how he made any illustrious person the high priest of God; as a result, he sent for an obscure priest out of Babylon, whose name was Ananelus, and he bestowed the high priesthood upon him."

19. B. Baba Bathra 3b–4a; Testament of Moses 6.2–6 (*see* Testament of Moses).

(Philip: 4 BCE–34 CE). Herod Antipas is identifiable for his role in the New Testament during the period of the life of Jesus.[20]

Period of the Prefects and Procurators: Beginnings of Rebellion

Roman association with certain Jews and their cooperation with the Romans are exemplified in the reigns of Herod the Great and his son Agrippa I, who reigned from 41 to 44 CE. However, following the death of the Herod the Great, the Romans shifted away from this mode of cooperation to one of direct rule by Roman prefects and procurators. Many Jews in Palestine viewed these individuals as brutal, corrupt, and incompetent, which often led to civil disobedience and social unrest. From the Roman perspective during this period, Judea was notoriously difficult to govern. Strong resistance against the Roman occupation began under the rule of Pontius Pilate in 26–36 CE and became increasingly hostile during the rule of Emperor Gaius Caligula from 37 to 41 CE. Caligula's ultimately unsuccessful attempt to erect a statue of himself in the Jerusalem temple became another example to many Jews of an "abomination of desolation."[21]

ROMAN PREFECTS

Coponius	6–9
Marcus Ambibulus	9–12
Annius Rufus	13–15
Valerius Gratus	15–26
Pontius Pilatus	26–36
Marcellus	36–38
Marullus	38–41
Judea ruled by King Agrippa I	41–44

ROMAN PROCURATORS

Cuspius Fadus	44–46
Tiberius Julius Alexander	46–48
Ventidius Cumanus	48–52
M. Antonius Felix	52–60
Porcius Festus	60–62
Albinus	62–64
Gessius Florus	64–66
Marcus Antonius Julianus	66–70

Note: all dates are CE.

20. *See* Morten H. Jensen, *Herod Antipas in Galilee*, WUNT 2.215 (Tübingen: Mohr Siebeck, 2006).

21. *See* Philo, *Legatio ad Gaium* 188, 203ff.; Josephus *Antiquities* 18.261; *War* 2.185–87. See also P. Bilde, "The Roman Emperor Gaius (Caligula)'s Attempt to Erect his Statue in the Temple of Jerusalem," *STh* 32 (1978): 67–93.

A growing undercurrent of unrest continued due to acute economic strife and prolonged ethnic and cultural tension between Jews and non-Jews (Josephus, *War* 2.277–43, 402–7, 418–20, 457, 531, 558). The leading Roman figure in these events was Gessius Florus (64–66 CE). He propagated insults of the Jewish religion and used military force against any group of Jews who did not follow his rule. During a conflict in Caesarea between Jews and Gentiles, Florus refused to support the Jews against the ensuing inflammatory remarks and actions. Instead, he plundered the Upper Market in Jerusalem, which resulted in the massacre of thousands of Jews, including women and children. Many of the Jewish nobility, including Agrippa II and his sister Berenice, attempted to intervene to prevent an uprising, but Florus ignored their pleas. Such escalating provocations triggered the "first great revolt" against the Roman rulers in 66 CE.[22]

In the midst of these internal struggles, proclamations of deliverance for Israel, often with messianic overtones, arose anticipating the recovery of freedom and prospect of becoming a "superpower" of the Levant. Initial success of the rebels forced the Roman general Vespasian to march into Galilee from his post in Syria in mid-67 CE. The strength of the Roman legions would methodically conquer the rebel forces by 68 CE and control most of the country with the exception of Jerusalem, Masada, and a few other rebel strongholds by that time. In 68 CE Emperor Nero allegedly committed suicide, which created a power vacuum in Rome and slowed considerably the ongoing war led by Vespasian. Nero's death created the opportunity for Vespasian to have himself proclaimed emperor in 69 CE.[23] Having consolidated his power in Rome, Vespasian sent his son Titus to Palestine to finish the job of subduing the rebels.

It is likely that during the Roman "cleansing" of Palestine several Jewish groups fought to wrest control of the temple (Josephus, *Life* 62; *Antiquities* 14.168; 20.200; Mark 14:53; Acts 4; 22:30).[24] Two main rebel groups in this struggle were the Sicarii and the Zealots. The Sicarii were Jewish "bandits" operating primarily during the revolts against Rome in 66–74 CE. It is generally thought that the group originated in Jerusalem and that it was named for the weapons it used—curved daggers. The Zealots comprised a revolutionary party established ca. 6 CE. In 64–66 CE they rebelled against Florus and the "treacherous" Jerusalem populace.

The Zealots repelled the Sicarii as they attempted to take control of Jerusalem in 66 CE; during the attack, the Sicarii sustained many casualties, including their leader Menahem. As a result, the remainder of the group fled to Masada and they remained there until 74 CE. Following a bloody struggle in 70 CE, Jerusalem was

---

22. *See* Josephus, *War*; Andrea Berlin, *The First Jewish Revolt: Archaeology, History, Ideology* (New York: Routledge, 2002).

23. Josephus, *War* 6.312–13: "What did the most to induce the Jews to start this war was an ambiguous oracle that was also found in their sacred writings, how, about that time, one from their country should become governor of the habitable earth. The Jews took this prediction to belong to them in particular, and many of the wise men were thereby deceived in their determination. Now this oracle certainly denoted the government of Vespasian, who was appointed emperor in Judea."

24. Anthony J. Saldarini, *Pharisees, Scribes and Sadducees in Palestinian Society* (Grand Rapids: Eerdmans, 1988).

Figure 5. The Arch of Titus was erected in Rome by Emperor Domitian to honor the memory and exploits of his late brother Titus, including his seige of Jerusalem in 70 CE. This relief from the arch shows spoils being taken from the temple.

captured, the temple was destroyed, and shortly thereafter (ca. 73–74 CE) the mountain fortress of Masada, occupied by the Sicarii, was taken, thus marking the commonly identified end of the Second Temple period.

Transition to the Rabbinic Period

Many scholars have argued that despite the destruction of the temple in 70 CE, the Second Temple period continued until the early second century. Such a reading contends that the end of the temple meant the end of the priesthood and the emergence of the power of the rabbinic sages. Along with this transformation came the official establishment of the Jewish synagogue and the transfer of authority from Jerusalem to Yavneh (*see* Map of First-Century Palestine, p. 44). However, it does not appear that the land of Palestine was devoid of Jews. Several scholars have argued that Jewish legal authority continued to function from Jerusalem, or at least in Palestine. That the aftermath of the fall of the temple brought devastation to the people of Israel is exemplified in the literature that followed in the late first century (*see* 2 Baruch and 4 Ezra [2 Esdras 3–14]). A leading rabbi at that time, Rabbi Yohanan ben Zakkai, who offered his opinions from Yavneh, attempted to convince Jewish communities to discontinue the ritual practices previously only performed at Jerusalem, that is, the sacrificial system.[25] Several rabbis followed ben Zakkai, including Gamaliel II; a number of other rabbis closely connected to this project, including Rabbi Akiva, played leading roles in the final revolt against Rome in 132 CE.

The task of these rabbinic leaders was to formalize Judaism, which included navigating the relationship between traditional Jews and Jewish Christians.

25. Shmuel Safrai, "New Research Concerning the Status and Actions of Rabban Yohanan ben Zakkai," in *G. Alon Memorial Volume* (Jerusalem: Magnes, 1970), pp. 203–26 (Hebrew).

Several rulings emerged from this period that attempted to delegitimize Jewish Christianity (in particular, *birkat ha-minim* by Gamaliel II).[26] During this period, the process of consolidation of Jewish **Halakhah** began in which the majority opinion became widely accepted in the community (e.g., M. Rosh ha-Shana 2.8–9; B. Berakhot 27b–28a). During the period of transition from a Jerusalem-centralized Judaism to one based on the school of Yavneh, two more revolts occurred against the Romans. The first transpired under the rule of Trajan (primarily outside Palestine—Egypt, North Africa, and Cyprus); the second took place under the hailed "messianic figure" of Bar Kochba in Judea from 132 to 135 CE. The resulting defeats of the Jewish resistance in these two episodes raised the status of the Jewish sages and their responsibility to reenvision forms of Judaism that could survive and flourish in the post–Second Temple period.[27] The rabbinic period began after the destruction of the Second Temple and is designated by the emergence of the Mishnah and the Babylonian and Jerusalem Talmudim.

FURTHER READING

Cohen, Shaye J. D. *From the Maccabees to the Mishnah*. 2nd ed. Louisville: Westminster John Knox, 2006.

Flusser, David, and Azzan Yadin. *Judaism of the Second Temple Period*, vol. 1, *Qumran and Apocalypticism*. Grand Rapids: Eerdmans, 2007.

Grabbe, Lester L. *A History of the Jews and Judaism in the Second Temple Period*, vol. 1, *The Persian Period (539–331 BCE)*. Edinburgh: T&T Clark, 2006.

———. *A History of the Jews and Judaism in the Second Temple Period*, vol. 2, *The Coming of the Greeks: The Early Hellenistic Period (335–175 BCE)*. Edinburgh: T&T Clark, 2011.

———. *An Introduction to Second Temple Judaism: History and Religion of the Jews in the Time of Nehemiah, the Maccabees, Hillel, and Jesus*. Edinburgh: T&T Clark, 2010.

Schiffman, Lawrence H. *From Text to Tradition: A History of Second Temple and Rabbinic Judaism*. Jerusalem: Ktav, 1991.

VanderKam, James C. *An Introduction to Early Judaism*. Grand Rapids: Eerdmans, 2000.

ARCHIE T. WRIGHT

26. *See* R. Kimelman, "*Birkat Ha-Minim* and the Lack of Evidence for an Anti-Christian Jewish Prayer in Late Antiquity," in *Jewish and Christian Self-Definition*, ed. E. P. Sanders (Philadelphia: Trinity Press International, 1990), pp. 226–44.

27. Peter Schafer, *Bar Kokhba War Reconsidered: New Perspectives on the Second Jewish Revolt Against Rome*, TSAJ 100 (Tübingen: Mohr Siebeck, 2003).

Maps

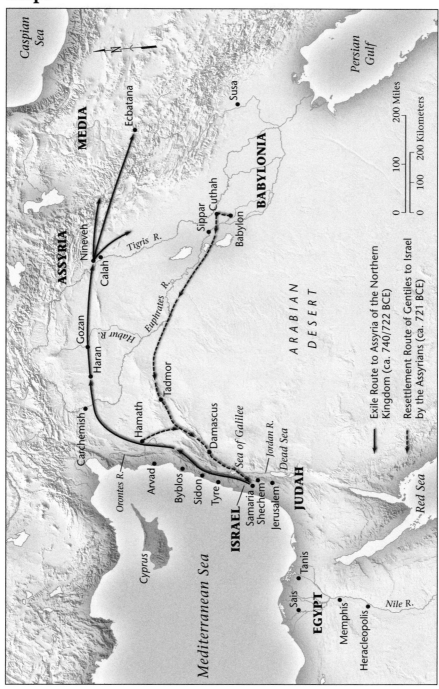

Map 1. Assyrian Exile, ca. 8th century BCE

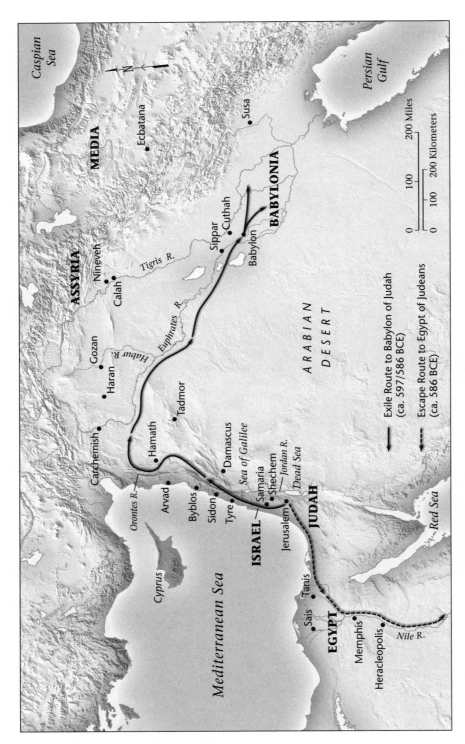

Map 2. Babylonian Exile, ca. 6th century BCE

34

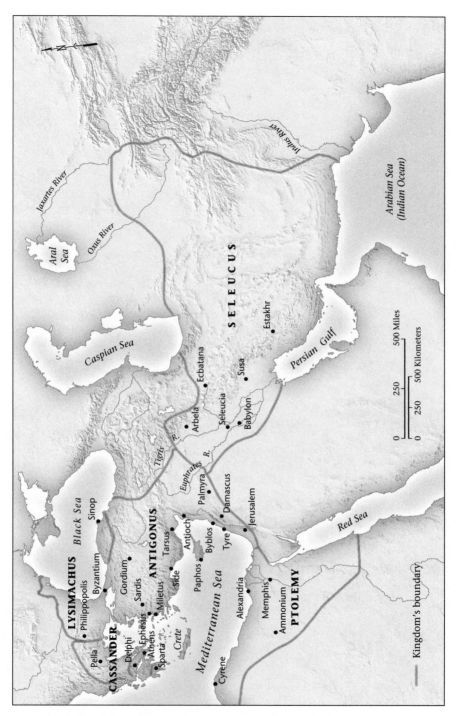

Map 3. The Near East Under the Diadochi, ca. late 4th to early 3rd centuries BCE

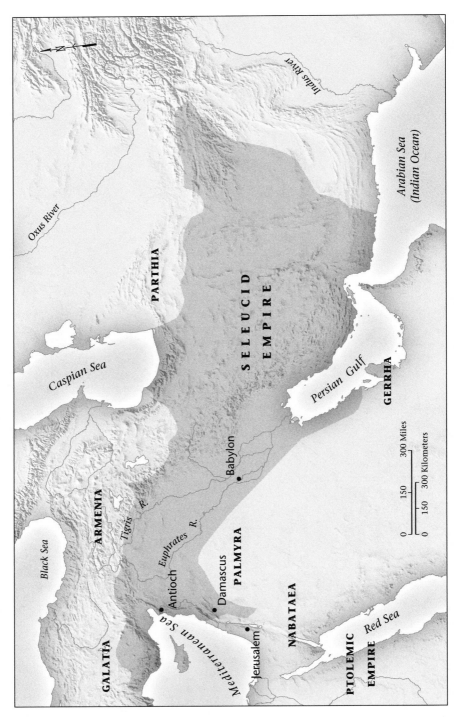

Map 4. The Seleucid Empire, ca. 3rd century BCE

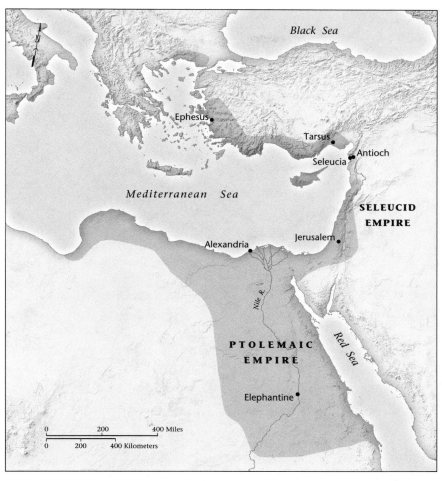

Map 5. The Ptolemaic Empire, ca. 2nd century BCE

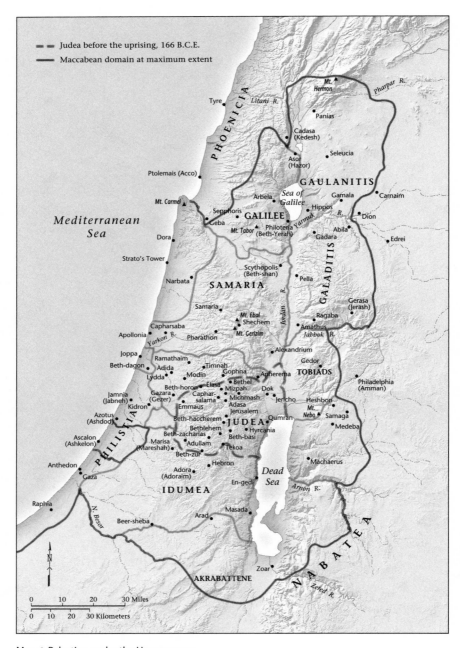

Map 6. Palestine under the Hasmoneans

Legend (on map):

- – – Judea before the uprising, 166 B.C.E.
- —— Maccabean domain at maximum extent

Labels (on map):

Mediterranean Sea

PHOENICIA

Litani R.

Mt. Hermon

Pharpar R.

Tyre

Panias

Cadasa (Kedesh)

Seleucia

Asor (Hazor)

Ptolemais (Acco)

GAULANITIS

Mt. Carmel

Arbela

Sea of Galilee

Gamala

Carnaim

Sepphoris

GALILEE

Hippos

Dion

Geba

Yarmuk R.

Abila

Mt. Tabor

Philoteria (Beth-Yerah)

Gadara

Edrei

Dora

Gadara

Strato's Tower

GALADITIS

Scythopolis (Beth-shan)

Pella

Narbata

SAMARIA

Gerasa (Jerash)

Samaria

Mt. Ebal

Shechem

Ragaba

Capharsaba

Mt. Gerizim

Amathus

Apollonia

Yarkon R.

Pharathon

Jabbok R.

Joppa

Ramathaim

Alexandrium

Beth-dagon

Adida

Gedor

Lydda

Modin

Timnah

Gophna

Apherema

TOBIADS

Beth-horon

Bethel

Elasa

Mizpah

Dok

Philadelphia (Amman)

Gazara (Gezer)

Caphar-salama

Michmash

Jericho

Heshbon

Jamnia (Jabneh)

Emmaus

Adasa

Jerusalem

Mt. Nebo

Samaga

Kidron

Beth-haccherem

Qumran

Azotus (Ashdod)

Bethlehem

JUDEA

Hyrcania

Medeba

Ascalon (Ashkelon)

Beth-zacharias

Beth-basi

Marisa (Mareshah)

Adullam

Tekoa

Beth-zur

Anthedon

Adora (Adoraim)

Hebron

Machaerus

Gaza

IDUMEA

En-gedi

Dead Sea

Arnon R.

Raphia

N A B A T E A

N. Besor

Beer-sheba

Arad

Masada

Zered R.

AKRABATTENE

Zoar

0   10   20   30 Miles

0   10   20   30 Kilometers

N

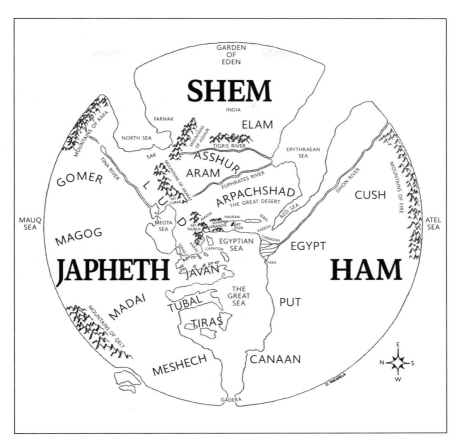

Map 7. The World at the Time of 1QapGen

Map 8. Dead Sea Region

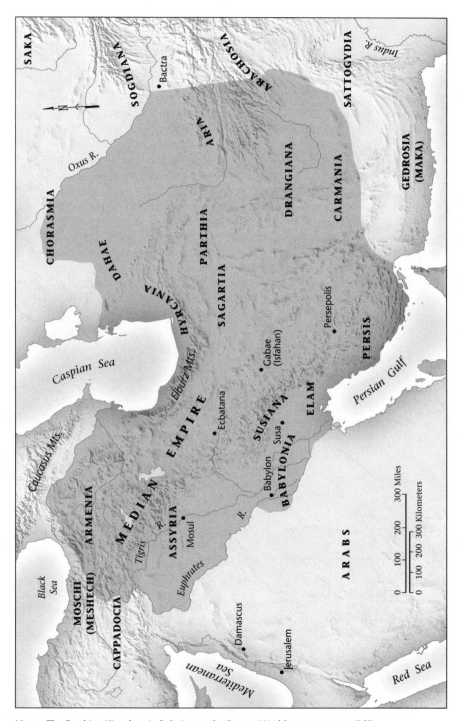

Map 9. The Parthian Kingdom in Relation to the Roman World, ca. 1st century BCE

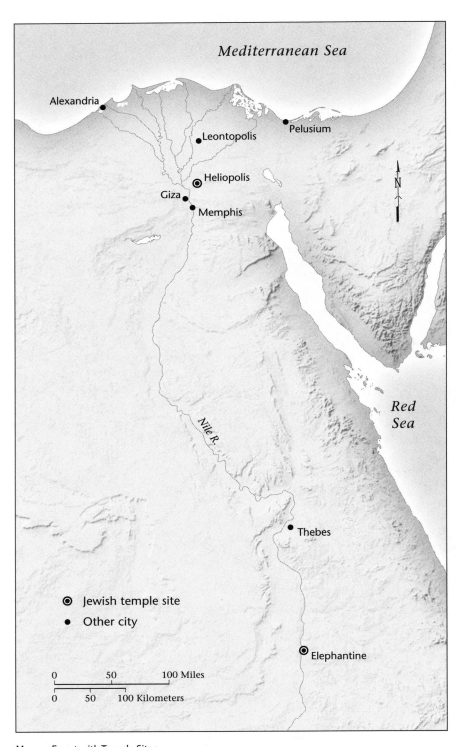

Map 10. Egypt with Temple Sites

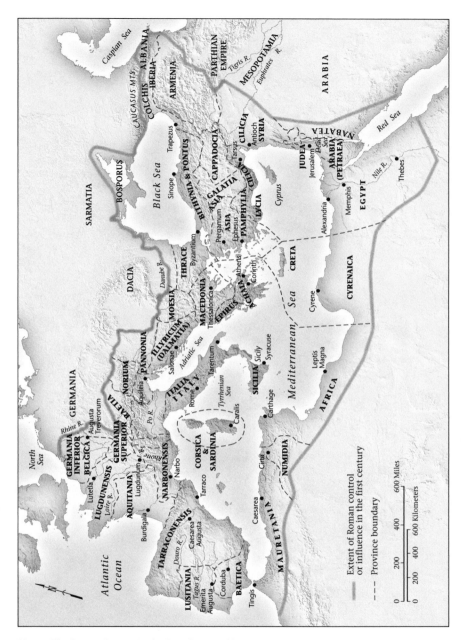

Map 11. The Roman Empire in the First Century CE.

Map 12. First-Century CE Palestine

1. Scriptural Texts and Traditions

The editors chose the category "Scripture," with some difficulty. Some of the literature that was written during the Second Temple period has found its way into the bodies of documents in use today by Jewish and Christian communities of faith and could be properly called "canonical". The editors have sought to avoid the term "canon" as a genre designator because the term, when used to define a cluster of texts, risks the error of anachronism. This should not imply that Jewish (and Christian) communities of this period lacked in their approach to some of the texts in this volume a sense of the authority of a particular text, such that the term "canon" may indeed be a useful measure. Rather, this is to suggest that matters of authority are characterized by a certain fluidity during this period to the point that allocating texts based on a "canonical status"— that is, a grouping of texts that coalesces around a certain sense of order or form, be it thematic to the contents or articulated through group dynamics and interests—seems difficult to accomplish well.

Instead, the editors have chosen to use the term "Scripture" to differentiate between Jewish documents written during this period, popular though they may have been, and Jewish documents written during this period that became canonical for the faith traditions that read the Hebrew Bible/Old Testament authoritatively. The editors wish to stress that many texts within this volume could qualify as scriptural in a broad sense. Much of the literature contained in this volume was very likely written by the authors in such a way that it might very well be considered "Scripture". That is, if not a "canonical consciousness" for many of the writings during this period, there may well have been a "scriptural consciousness," if by this designation we understand a text to function in such a capacity so as to explain, exhort, influence, or inspire a community whose faith and religious sensibilities were rooted in the traditions from the Hebrew Bible. By this calculus, many of the texts contained herein would qualify for the designation "Scripture."

At the same time, the term "Scripture" risks ambiguity without further qualification, as though to imply that all texts composed during this period may have been weighed and measured with an eye to their "canonical viability" qua Scripture. Such was certainly not the case, and some of the material contained in this volume was clearly never intended to attain such a status. As a result, the history of canonical formation, at the risk of being labeled anachronistic, ought to hold some sway over the delineation of these texts and those that we might refer to as scriptural. Regardless of whether this canonical tradition is committed to as an act of faith or as an act of historical reality, the point holds that some material was included within a canonical tradition and other material was not. In the end, the editors decided to include texts in this category that were most representative of the Jewish and Christian traditions of canon. There were discussions for including Tobit, for instance, which in the end was allocated to the category of "romanticized narrative" in part because it is not recognized in certain strands of Christianity (Protestantism) or in the Jewish community as canonical (see Preface).

In addition to the so-called canonical texts, the editors chose to incorporate biblical recensions found at Qumran in this section. This serves two purposes. First, these recensions provide an example of the tension between an established tradition articulated and underscored by thousands of years of tradition (the canonical text) and the dynamic nature of textual formation during this period (the recensions at Qumran). The examples of the biblical texts from Qumran highlight the recensionally complex situation of this period. As a result, the "pristine" form of Isaiah, for instance, requires that canonical versions of the text include a critical apparatus that takes these other recensions into consideration.

Second, this also provides an example of Jewish interests and commitments in the Second Temple period toward the literature of their spiritual heritage. The formation of libraries—either in the way of the act of writing itself or in the collection of books in circulation—is an important ideological stance taken by communities, signaling their commitment to their intellectual and spiritual heritage as the primary means of their survival and flourishing. The formation, tending, and keeping of books and knowledge in written form was a hallmark of this period and certainly helped lay the foundation for future commitments to formalized canons. The community at Qumran is an excellent example of this activity. The tendency to preserve primary literature (e.g., the Hebrew Bible for this volume) and the discussions that surrounded it (the secondary discourses in the way of books such as Tobit) is the very essence of both Jewish and Christian literary activity. Broadly, this is a scriptural activity.

BRAD EMBRY

The Book of Daniel

The book of Daniel is an early and distinctive example of Jewish apocalyptic literature (*see* Introduction to Apocalyptic Literature). The genre "apocalypse" is a category of revelatory literature that contains a narrative framework and describes a transcendent reality. This transcendent reality has temporal qualities—it deals with time and history and often the end of human history. This reality also has spatial features—it describes a heavenly world and its inhabitants. In the narrative framework of an apocalypse, a human visionary receives the revelation from a heavenly being, thereby making this transcendent reality known. But, in fact, Daniel (as it appears in the Hebrew Bible, without the Greek Additions) may be divided into two distinct halves representing different genres. The first half (chaps. 1–6) is court tales about the wise man Daniel and his friends, who are Judean exiles within the court of the foreign kings during the Babylonian and Persian periods. The second half of the book (chaps. 7–12) consists of the apocalyptic visions purportedly witnessed by Daniel. While in the first half of the book Daniel frequently interprets visions and dreams that the king sees, in the second half of the book it is Daniel's visions that must be interpreted, this time by an angelic figure. Despite significant differences in form, style, content, and even language (see further below), the two parts of the book are unified in various ways. The first court tale and the last vision sequence are connected by dating formulas (see 1:1; 10:1), indicating that seventy years have passed from the beginning of the book's events to its end—the length of the Babylonian exile according to Jeremiah 25:12.[1] These formulas create a bracketing structure for the entire book. Within this bracket, chapter 7 is the hinge that links the two halves. Chapters 7 and 2 are linked by their use of the four kingdoms motif and Aramaic, while chapters 7 and 8 share animal and horn imagery and use the apocalyptic dream and interpretation format. Finally, both halves of the book share a fundamental concern for divine rule over human history and the cosmos. Indeed, the book is an extended and developing

---

1. Jer. 25:12: "Then after seventy years are completed, I will punish the king of Babylon and that nation, the land of the Chaldeans, for their iniquity, declares the Lord, making the land an everlasting waste."

exploration of divine power in the light of Greek rule over Judea during the second century BCE.

Narrative Description

The narratives of chapters 1–6 may be divided into two basic types: contest and conflict stories. The contest tales (chaps. 1, 4, and 5) find Daniel and his friends (Shadrach, Meshach, and Abednego) in various situations where their abilities to reveal hidden knowledge are put to the test. Their loyalty to the Jewish God brings them success in every case. In the conflict stories of chapters 2, 3, and 6, Daniel and his friends face danger to life and limb as part of their service to the foreign king. In every case, however, God rescues the wise men from death. Shared features may be discerned among the tales, especially concerning the king and the status of the Jewish wise men. The king is often capricious, hubristic, blundering, and easily manipulated by self-interested parties. Nevertheless, at the end of most of the tales the king is also conciliatory—recognizing the wisdom and righteousness of the Jewish wise men and the superiority of the Jewish God. Though minorities in the king's court, the Jewish wise men excel in **mantic** or esoteric wisdom, surpassing the king's own men, and are promoted to ever-higher positions of power within the kingdom, thus elevating the status of the Jewish God in the foreign kingdom.

The visions of chapters 7–12 shift away from the court tales' conciliatory view of kingship. In each of these visionary sequences there is a review of history (depicted as a *vaticinium ex eventu*) and an anticipation of future events that present foreign kingship in ever more hostile terms. In chapter 7, foreign empires (Babylonian, Median, Persian, and Greek—the last including Alexander the Great and his various successors) are depicted as four beasts rising up from a chaotic sea. The beasts have wild and predatory features and are voracious in their rule. The fourth beast, which has ten horns plus a little horn, is especially vicious. The little horn speaks arrogantly—a symbol of **Antiochus IV Epiphanes.** But a heavenly court, over which the Ancient of Days is presiding, sits in judgment on the beasts and their power is destroyed. The Ancient of Days gives the dominion once enjoyed by the beasts to a heavenly figure, one who resembles a human (in contrast to the beasts) and who rides on the clouds (in contrast to the watery origins of the beasts). The dominion of this human-like being and the people who align themselves with the Most High will be everlasting.

In chapter 8, the empires are depicted as fierce domesticated and horned animals—a ram and a goat. Chapter 9 forgoes animal imagery and focuses primarily on the plight of the Jerusalem temple and its desecration by Antiochus IV Epiphanes. The last vision sequence, chapters 10–12, turns its focus to foreign kings and their squabbles over Judea. This detailed review of history telescopes the history of Alexander's successors into a series of encounters between the king of the north (the **Seleucid** kings culminating in Antiochus IV Epiphanes) and the king of the south (the **Ptolemies** in Egypt [*see* Map of the Seleucid Empire, p. 36; Map of the Ptolemaic Empire, p. 37]). The outrages perpetrated by the king of the north finally unleash an eschatological intervention. This is the point at which

Michael, the commander of the heavenly host, intervenes and delivers the righteous through a military intervention. There will also be a resurrection of some of the just and unjust deceased parties. The blaspheming king of the north will meet eternal punishments, while the wise and the righteous will enjoy elevation to everlasting brilliance along with the heavenly hosts.

THE FOUR KINGDOMS IN DANIEL

	Babylon/ Nebuchadnezzar	*Media*	*Persia*	*Greece*
Chap. 2	head of gold	chest and arms of silver	belly and thighs of bronze	legs and feet of iron/mixed iron
Chap. 7	lion with wings	bear	third beast like a leopard	fourth beast with ten horns and little horn
Chap. 8		first and shorter horn of the ram	second and longer horn of the ram	he-goat with long horn (Alexander the Great) and little horn
Chap. 11				kings of the north and south

Author/Provenance

Daniel seems to be the result of incremental development, but much about its growth remains unknown. The court narratives may have been authored separately in the eastern **Diaspora.** Little can be determined about the original authors of the court tales, but if the figure of Daniel is any indication, these authors were from a scribal group familiar with Mesopotamian mantic wisdom. Chapters 1–6 may have then circulated independently as a collection of tales before the second century BCE. During the second century, chapter 7 was added, completing a concentric ring structure in which chapters 2 and 7 comprise the outermost ring, chapters 3 and 6 form a ring within that, and chapters 4 and 5 are at the center. Chapters 8–12 were written and added on to the collection by a group that seems to refer to itself in Daniel 11:33 and 12:3 as the *maskilim,* or wise ones. This group was probably a scribal group among the elite of Judean society that was employed either by the aristocracy or by the local governing bureaucracy prior to Antiochus IV Epiphanes's reign. This group perceives itself as having access to esoteric or mantic wisdom, and they speak of themselves as righteous, as teachers of the masses, and as beleaguered—even martyred—by the events of the Maccabean Revolt. It is not clear that they seek political power as a group, though they present themselves as the means by which God's hidden presence in history may be discerned.

Date/Occasion

The court tales of chapters 1–6 cannot be dated precisely. The materials on which Daniel 4 draws were originally about the final Babylonian king, Nabonidus, and only later became associated with the more famous Nebuchadnezzar. Daniel 2 shows evidence of multiple stages of growth and **redaction,** the latest stage taking place around 252 BCE or shortly after (2:43 refers to one of two possible inter-dynastic marriages between the Seleucids and the Ptolemies). The view of the king and his relationship to God in the tales suggests that their function was tied to Diaspora life, when Judaism had to negotiate life among foreign nations, with all of its attractions and also its threats to Jewish distinctiveness. The court tales allow Judaism and the Jewish God to be visible, distinctive, and powerful in a situation where they would otherwise be peripheral, invisible, and subordinated.

In contrast to chapters 1–6, it is possible to date the apocalyptic materials in chapters 7–12 with more precision. Chapter 7 refers to Antiochus IV Epiphanes (the little horn) and his attempts to outlaw Jewish observances, sacrifices, and festivals (v. 25), but it does not speak of the desecration of the temple, which took place in late 167 BCE. Thus, it may have been written or edited in early 167 BCE. Chapters 8–12 are centrally concerned with the desolation of the temple, though on the whole they do not seem to know of its rededication (winter 164 BCE) or Antiochus IV Epiphanes's death (early 163 BCE). This places their composition in the three years between 167 and 164 BCE. The function of these materials is to encourage and strengthen the resistance toward the Seleucid king and his attempts to outlaw Judaism. The visions also offer a counter-story to the empire's narrative of foreign dominance.

Text, Language, Sources, and Transmission

Although the book of Ezra also contains Aramaic portions (4:8–6:18), Daniel's extensive bilingualism is curious among the canonical books. Daniel 2:4b–7:28 is written in Aramaic, which was the **lingua franca** of the **Hellenistic** world, while chapters 1:1–2:4a and 8–12 are in Hebrew. The Aramaic portions include the tales, with their conciliatory views of kingship, and Daniel 7, in which God commissions the foreign kings even as the perspective of conciliation is noticeably absent. Some commentators have argued that the Hebrew portions are translations of Aramaic originals, as there are some Aramaisms in these chapters and the Hebrew of these chapters is not always very good. While this is most likely the case for chapter 1, it is unlikely to be the case for chapters 8–12, which cannot be easily translated back into Aramaic. Since Hebrew was an insider language and distinctive to Judaism, these chapters were probably written in Hebrew by an Aramaic speaker or speakers for reasons tied to their function as resistance literature.

In addition to its preservation by the Jewish **Masoretes,** every chapter of Daniel is attested in fragmentary form in the Dead Sea Scrolls, the oldest fragment being 4QDan^c, which may be dated to within fifty years of the completion of

Daniel itself. On the whole, the fragments support or even clarify the consonantal text of the **Masoretic Text (MT)**. But a more complex relationship exists between the Hebrew text of Daniel and the Greek texts. There are two separate complete witnesses to Daniel in Greek. The Old Greek version of Daniel was translated no earlier than 100 BCE, but was rejected by early Christianity in favor of another Greek translation attributed to Theodotion (*see* Overview of Early Jewish Literature). The date of Theodotion-Daniel is not later than 180 CE and may well be earlier. Theodotion at times agrees with the Hebrew MT over and against the Old Greek, but both Theodotion and the Old Greek preserve a different ordering of the court tales from the Hebrew MT and, significantly, both contain additional materials that do not appear in the Hebrew (*see* Additions to Daniel).

Theology

The theological question with which Daniel wrestles has to do with God's power and presence within historical events, especially events relating to the foreign rule of Judea. While prophetic theology, including the **Deuteronomistic** theology of Jeremiah, often understands the Babylonian and Persian monarchs to be agents of divine power, bringing punishment or redemption to God's people according to God's intentions, this perspective cannot make sense of Judea's experience of Antiochus IV Epiphanes or Hellenistic rule more generally. The claim of Antiochus IV Epiphanes to be "God made manifest" is a hubristic one, and his criminalizing of Jewish practices seems inimical to God's purposes. While Deuteronomistic theology views history as the place in which God's power is demonstrated and God's presence is revealed, the Gentile rule of Hellenistic kings does not clearly disclose God's purposes for the Judean community. Nevertheless, Daniel argues that the foreign king and human history are still subject to divine sovereignty. The visions use an eschatological narrative in order to resolve the conundrum between the experiences of imperial rule and the power and presence of God. Within this narrative, the injustices of the little horn's rule and the tragedy of the community's experience may not be the direct work of God's mighty arm, and may not be commissioned directly by the Most High, but they are part of the divine plan for human history. The angelic messengers urge Daniel to see that the little horn's actions will be mitigated by the eschatological ending, at which point oppressive power will be punished, injustice will be reversed, and divine power will clearly be manifested in a new kingdom that will not be overthrown.

In order to illustrate God's power and presence, the visions make use of spatial dimensions of the universe as well as historical dimensions. Daniel sets much of its eschatological narrative within a cosmic framework, where heavenly dealings direct earthly outcomes. This cosmic view allows the reader to discern the otherwise hidden plan of God for the foreign king. In this cosmic vista, God is strikingly visible as the Ancient of Days in chapter 7, who brings order to chaotic waters and beasts at the time of judgment, just as God did in creation. But God is also strikingly invisible in both the cosmic and the historical vistas in chapters

8–12, where the angelic mediators and the scribal wise men become visibly brilliant instead (12:2–3).[2] Nevertheless, throughout these chapters, the actions of angels and faithful wise men revolve around knowing and understanding God's plans. For the community that models itself after Daniel, faithful action is none other than the work of discerning and making visible God's hidden workings.

Reception of Daniel in the Second Temple Period

Daniel, especially chapter 7, has had an enormous influence on the New Testament. The apocalyptic context of first-century CE Judaism was influenced by specific concepts and vocabulary found in Daniel, and this context is evident in the Gospels. The Synoptic Gospels pick up the reference to "one like a human being" who comes with the clouds of heaven (Dan. 7:13).[3] Turning the indefinite phrase for this angelic being into the title the "Son of Man," the Gospels refer to this future eschatological figure frequently (Mark 8:38;[4] 13:26; Matt. 13:24, 37; 16:28;[5] 19:28; 24:30; Luke 12:8–9). Moreover, the Gospels' language of God's kingdom as a foil to earthly political kingdoms probably invokes the four kingdoms that will be displaced by God's unending kingdom in Daniel 2 and 7. Mark 13:14[6] and Matthew 24:15[7] also borrow the phrase "desolating sacrilege" (Dan. 9:27)[8] to speak of Rome's interference with and destruction of the Jerusalem temple during the period 66–70 CE. Moreover, Daniel has fundamentally shaped the book of Revelation's apocalyptic imagination and its discourse against empire. Revelation borrows the language of Babylon to characterize Rome and uses Daniel's beastly adversaries to depict its own demonic and political enemies. Daniel contributes the imagery of the dragon in Revelation 12 (cf. Dan. 7:1–8) as well as the angelic commander Michael (Dan. 12:1) who battles the foe. The beast from the sea in Revelation 13, a symbol of Nero, has many of the same features as Antiochus IV Epiphanes, the fourth beast of Daniel 7. Finally, the language of resurrection,

2. Dan. 12:2–3: "Many of those who sleep in the dust of the earth will awake, some to everlasting life, and some to shame and everlasting contempt. Those who are wise will shine like the brightness of the sky, and those who lead many to righteousness, like the stars forever and ever."

3. Dan. 7:13: "As I watched in the night visions, I saw one like a human being coming with the clouds of heaven. And he came to the Ancient One and was presented before him."

4. Mark 8:38: "Those who are ashamed of me and of my words in this adulterous and sinful generation, of them the Son of Man will also be ashamed when he comes in the glory of his Father with the holy angels."

5. Matt. 16:27–28: "For the Son of Man is to come with his angels in the glory of his Father, and then he will repay everyone for what has been done. Truly I tell you, there are some standing here who will not taste death before they see the Son of Man coming in his kingdom."

6. Mark 13:14: "But when you see the desolating sacrilege set up where it ought not to be (let the reader understand), then those in Judea must flee to the mountains."

7. Matt. 24:15: "So when you see the desolating sacrilege standing in the holy place, as was spoken of by the prophet Daniel (let the reader understand)."

8. Dan. 9:27: "He will make a strong covenant with many for one week, and for half of the week he will make sacrifice and offering cease; and in their place will be an abomination that desolates, until the decreed end is poured out on the desolator."

which is so central to Paul's and the Gospels' depictions of Jesus, is indebted to Daniel 12 and its oracle of resurrection for the righteous and wise who have been martyred by the empire (*see* 1 and 2 Maccabees).

AMY C. MERRILL WILLIS

FURTHER READING

Collins, John J. *Daniel: A Commentary on the Book of Daniel*. Minneapolis: Augsburg, 1993.

Davies, Philip R. *Daniel*. Sheffield: JSOT, 1985.

Goldingay, John E. *Daniel*. Dallas: Word, 1988.

Newsom, Carol with Brennan W. Breed. *Daniel: A Commentary*, Louisville: Westminster John Knox, 2014.

Seow, C. L. *Daniel*. Louisville: Westminster John Knox, 2003.

ADVANCED READING

Collins, John J. *The Apocalyptic Imagination: An Introduction to Jewish Apocalyptic Literature*. 2nd ed. Grand Rapids: Eerdmans, 1998.

———. *The Apocalyptic Vision of the Book of Daniel*. Missoula: Scholars, 1977.

Davies, Philip R. "The Scribal School of Daniel." In *The Book of Daniel: Composition and Reception*, edited by John J. Collins and Peter W. Flint, 1:247–65. 2 vols. Leiden: Brill, 2001.

Humphreys, W. Lee. "A Lifestyle for the Diaspora: A Study of the Tales of Esther and Daniel." *JBL* 92 (1973): 211–23.

Newsom, Carol. "Rhyme and Reason: The Historical Résumé in Israelite and Early Jewish Thought." In *Congress Volume Leiden 2004*, edited by André Lemaire, pp. 215–33. Leiden: Brill, 2006.

Smith-Christopher, Daniel L. "Prayer and Dreams: Power and Diaspora Identities in the Social Setting of the Daniel Tales." In *The Book of Daniel: Composition and Reception*, edited by John J. Collins and Peter W. Flint, 1:266–89. 2 vols. Leiden: Brill, 2001.

Valeta, David. *Lions and Ovens and Visions, O My! A Satirical Analysis of Daniel 1–6*. Sheffield: Sheffield Phoenix, 2008.

Willis, Amy Merrill. *Dissonance and the Drama of Divine Sovereignty in the Book of Daniel*. New York: T&T Clark, 2010.

1.1 *from* Daniel

Daniel 2:31–45

[2:31] You, O king, were watching, and there was a vast image! That image was huge and its brightness was excessive. It rose before you and its appearance was terrible. [32] As for that statue, its head was of good gold, its breast and arms were of silver, its belly and thighs were of bronze, [33] its lower legs were of iron, its feet were partly of iron and partly of clay. [34] You were watching as a stone was broken off, not by human hands. It struck the image on its feet of iron and clay and it crushed them. [35] Then the iron, clay, bronze, silver, and gold were crushed altogether and became like chaff from the threshing floors of summer. Then the wind carried them away and no place for them was found. But the stone that struck the image became a huge mountain and it filled the whole earth. [36] This is the dream.

Now, we will declare its interpretation before the king: [37] You, O king, the king of kings, to whom the God of heaven has given the kingdom, the power, the might, and the honor [38] and has given into your hand humans, wherever they dwell, the beasts of the field, the birds of the sky, and has made you ruler over all of them—you are the head of gold. [39] After you, another kingdom will arise inferior to yours; then a third kingdom, of bronze, that will rule over all the earth. [40] The fourth kingdom will be strong as iron; because of this the iron will crush and grind everything. Like the iron, which crushes and grinds, it will crush and grind all these things. [41] Whereas you saw the feet and the toes, partly of potter's clay and partly of iron—the kingdom will be divided and it will not have the firmness of iron within it. Therefore, you saw the iron mixed with the clay. [42] And the toes of the feet, some of iron and some of clay—part of the end of the kingdom will be strong and part of it will be broken in pieces. [43] Whereas you saw the iron mixed with the clay, they will be mixed by means of human descendants but they will not cling to one another, just as the iron did not mix with the clay. [44] In the days of those kings, the God of heaven will establish a kingdom that will be forever. It will not be destroyed and the kingdom will not be left to another people. It will shatter and put an end to all of these kingdoms, but it will stand forever. [45] Therefore, you saw that from the mountain a stone was broken off, not by human hands, and it crushed the iron, the bronze, the clay, the silver, and the gold.

The great God has made known to the king what will happen after this. The dream is certain and its interpretation is trustworthy.

Translation by Amy C. Merrill Willis.

Daniel 4:1–34[a]

[4:1] I, Nebuchadnezzar, was at ease in my house and was flourishing in my palace. [2] Then I had a dream and it terrified me. The images and visions that came into my head as I was in bed alarmed me. [3] I issued a decree that all the wise men of Babylon should come before me in order to interpret the dream for me. [4] Then the magicians, the conjurers, the Chaldeans, and the astrologers came. I described the dream to them, but they could not give me an interpretation. [5] Finally, Daniel came before me, whose name, Belteshazzar, is like the name of my god and the spirit of the holy gods dwells in him. [6] "O Belteshazzar, chief of the magicians, I know that the spirit of the holy gods dwells in you, and there is no mystery that perplexes you. Interpret the dream vision that I saw. [7] As for the visions that I saw in my head while I was in my bed,

There was a tree in the middle of the earth and its height was great.

> [8] The tree grew tall and mighty and it was visible to the ends of the
> earth.
> Its leaves were beautiful, its fruit was abundant;
> it provided food for all.
> [9] Beneath its branches the wild animals found shade,
> The birds of the sky nested in its limbs,
> And from it all of the creatures were fed.

[10] "As I was watching the visions in my head while I was in my bed, a holy Watcher descended from heaven. [11] He called loudly and said,

> 'Cut down the tree and cut off its branches!
> Strip off its foliage and scatter its fruit;
> Let the beasts flee from beneath it
> and the birds from its branches.
> [12] Leave only the stump and its roots in the ground,
> and put an iron and bronze shackle on it in the grassy field.
> Let him be bathed with the dew of heaven,
> and let his lot be with the wild beasts.
> [13] Let his mind be changed from that of a human mind;
> Give him the mind of a beast instead.
> Let seven years pass over him!
> [14] The decree is in accordance with the word of the Watchers
> and the matter is ordered by the holy ones
> so that all living beings will know that the Most High rules over the
> kingdom of mortals.
> He gives it to whomever he pleases,
> and he sets even the lowliest person over it.'

[15] "This is the dream which I, King Nebuchadnezzar, saw. And you, Belteshazzar,

a. Follows the Aramaic versification and not the Greek.

tell me the interpretation, because none of the wise men of my kingdom were able to give me an interpretation. But you are able because the spirit of the holy gods is within you!"

[16] Then Daniel, whose name is Belteshazzar, was appalled for a moment and his thoughts alarmed him. The king said, "Do not let the dream and the interpretation alarm you." Belteshazzar said, "My lord, may the dream be for your foe and its interpretation for your enemy! [17] The tree that you saw, which was tall and strong and whose height reached to the heavens and its visibility was to the ends of the earth [18] and whose foliage was beautiful and its fruit abundant and was food for all, and beneath it dwelt the wild animals and in its branches lived the birds of the sky, [19] it is you, O king! You have grown great and strong; and your greatness reaches to the sky and your rule extends to the ends of the earth. [20] The king saw a holy Watcher descend from heaven who said, 'Cut down the tree and destroy it, leave only the stump and its roots in the ground and put an iron and bronze shackle on it in the grassy field. Let him be bathed with the dew of heaven and let his lot be with the wild beasts until seven years have passed over him.'

[21] "This is the interpretation, O king! The decree of the Most High has fallen upon my lord, the king. [22] You will be cut off from human company and your dwelling will be with the wild animals. You will eat the grass like cattle and the dew of heaven will bathe you. Seven years will pass you by until you acknowledge that the Most High is the sovereign ruler over the kingdom of mortals and he gives it to whomever he wishes. [23] Concerning the commands to leave the stump and the roots, your royal dominion will be reestablished when you acknowledge that heaven is the sovereign ruler. [24] Therefore, O king of kings, let my counsel be acceptable to you—cut away your sin by doing right and your iniquity by showing favor to the poor, thus your time of prosperity may be prolonged."

[25] All of this happened to King Nebuchadnezzar. [26] At the end of twelve months, the king was walking on the palace roof in Babylon. [27] The king said, "Is this not Babylon the great, which I have built as a royal house with my mighty power and for my glorious honor?" [28] The words were still in the mouth of the king when a voice came down from heaven: "Because of your words, Nebuchadnezzar, O king, the kingdom has passed away from you. [29] You will be cut off from human company and your dwelling will be with the wild animals. You will eat grass like the cattle. Seven years will pass over you until you acknowledge that the Most High is the sovereign ruler over the kingdom of mortals and he gives it to whomever he wishes." [30] At that moment the sentence was fulfilled concerning Nebuchadnezzar. He was cut off from human company and he ate grass like the cattle. His body was bathed with the dew of heaven. Then his hair grew long like eagle feathers and his nails became like bird claws.

[31] "At the end of the appointed time, I, Nebuchadnezzar, lifted my eyes to heaven and my intellect returned to me. I blessed the Most High. I praised the Eternal One, and I glorified him.

> His kingdom is an eternal kingdom
>> His sovereign rule is from generation to generation.
> [32] All who dwell on earth are of no account.
> He does whatever he pleases with the hosts of heaven

and all who live on the earth.
There is no one who can stay his hand
or say to him, 'What have you done?'

[33] "At that time, my intellect returned to me and my majesty and splendor were restored to me. My ministers and lords sought me out and I was reestablished over my kingdom. I was made exceedingly great. [34] Now I, Nebuchadnezzar, praise, extol, and glorify the King of Heaven. All of his works are truth and his ways are justice; and he is able to bring low those who walk proudly."

Daniel 7:1–28

[7:1] In the first year of Belshazzar, king of Babylon, Daniel saw a dream and visions in his head as he was sleeping. Then he wrote down the dream: [2] I was watching in my vision during the night and four winds of heaven were stirring up the Great Sea. [3] Four great beasts came up from the sea, each one different from the other. [4] The first was like a lion but it had the wings of an eagle. I was watching as its wings were plucked off and it was lifted from the ground. It was made to stand on feet like a human and a human mind was given to it. [5] Then there was another beast like a bear. It was lifted up on one side and three ribs were in its mouth between its teeth. It was commanded thus, "Arise! Devour much flesh!" [6] After this, I was watching and there was another one, like a leopard. It had four wings of a bird on its back and the beast had four heads. Dominion was given to it. [7] After this, I was watching in the visions of the night and there was a fourth beast, fearful and terrible and exceedingly mighty. It had large iron teeth that devoured and shattered. The remainder it crushed with its feet. It was different from all the beasts that were before it. It had ten horns. [8] As I was considering the beast with the horns, another little horn came up among them and three of the former horns were rooted up from before it. Eyes like the eyes of a human were in this horn and a mouth was speaking arrogantly.

[9] I was watching,
thrones were placed and one who was an Ancient of Days was seated.
His garment was like white snow, and the hair of his head was like
      pure wool.
His throne was flames of fire, its wheels were burning fire.
[10] A river of fire flowed and went forth from before him.
A thousand thousands were ministering to him
and a myriad of myriads were standing before him.
The court was seated and books were opened.

[11] I was watching from the time of the sound of the great words, which the horn was speaking, until the beast was killed and its body destroyed and given to the burning fire. [12] As for the rest of the beasts, their dominion was taken away but a prolonging of life was given to them for an appointed time.

¹³ I was watching in the visions of the night,
 one like a human came with the clouds of heaven.
  He came to the Ancient of Days and was brought before him.
¹⁴ He was given dominion, honor, and a kingdom.
 All the peoples, nations, and languages will serve him.
 His dominion is an everlasting dominion that will not pass away,
  and his kingdom will not be destroyed.

¹⁵ As for me, Daniel, my spirit was distressed on account of this and the visions of my head alarmed me. ¹⁶ I approached one of those who was standing there and I asked him the truth concerning all of this. He spoke to me and revealed the interpretation of the matters. ¹⁷ "As for these four great beasts, four kingdoms will be established on the earth. ¹⁸ But the holy ones of the Most High will receive the kingdom and they will possess the kingdom forever and ever."

¹⁹ But I wanted to make certain concerning the fourth beast, which was different from all of the others. It was exceedingly terrible. Its teeth were of iron and its claws of bronze. It was devouring and crushing and trampling the rest with its feet. I wanted to make certain concerning the ten horns that were in its head, and the other that came up and the three that fell out before it, ²⁰ and also concerning that horn with the eyes and a mouth that was speaking arrogantly. Its appearance was greater than that of its companions. ²¹ I was watching and that horn was making war with the holy ones. It was prevailing against them ²² until the Ancient of Days arrived and judgment was given to the holy ones of the Most High. The time arrived and the holy ones took possession of the kingdom.

²³ Thus he said,

 "Concerning the fourth beast,
 the fourth kingdom, which will be different from all of the kingdoms,
  will rule over the earth.
  It will devour the whole earth and will trample and crush it.
²⁴ As for the ten horns,
 ten kings will arise from its kingdom and another will arise after them.
  But he will be different from the former ones and he will bring down
   three kings.
²⁵ He will speak words against the Most High
 and he will wear out the holy ones of the Most High.
 He will think to alter the appointed seasons and laws.
 They will be given into his hand for a time, two times, and a half time.
²⁶ But the court will sit
 and his dominion will be removed for destruction and obliteration
  forever.
²⁷ The kingdom and the dominion, and the greatness of the kingdoms
  under all the skies
 will be given to the people of the holy ones of the Most High.
 Its kingdom is an eternal kingdom
  and all of the dominions will revere and obey it."

[28] Here is the end of the matter. As for me, Daniel, my thoughts greatly disturbed me and my face was downcast but I kept the matter in mind.

Daniel 8:1-27

[8:1] In the third year of the rule of Belshazzar, the king, a vision appeared to me, yes, to me, Daniel, after that which appeared to me at first. [2] I saw in the vision—when I saw it I was in the fortress of Susa, which is the province of Elam, and I was on the banks of the Ulai canal. [3] I lifted my eyes and looked, see! a ram was standing in front of the canal. He had two horns and they were high. One was loftier than the other with the higher one rising up behind the first. [4] I watched the ram charge toward the west and toward the north and toward the south. None of the beasts could stand before him. There was no one to deliver from his hand. He did whatever he wished and became mighty.

[5] I was thinking about this and look! a he-goat came over the entire earth from the west and he did not touch the ground. The goat had a conspicuous horn between his eyes. [6] He went to the ram who had the horns whom I saw standing by the canal and he ran toward him with the fury of his strength. [7] I saw him approach the ram. He was enraged against him and hit the ram. He shattered his two horns. There was no strength in the ram to stand against him. He threw him down to earth and trampled him. There was no one to deliver the ram from his hand.

[8] The he-goat became great, exceedingly so, but in his mightiness the great horn was broken. Four conspicuous ones grew up in its place, according to the four winds of the heavens. [9] From one of them a little horn grew out and it grew exceedingly great toward the south and the east and toward the beautiful land. [10] It became as great as the host of the heavens and made some of the host and some of the stars fall to the earth where he trampled them. [11] He became as great as the prince of the host, from whom the daily sacrifice was taken away and whose sanctuary was degraded. [12] A host was handed over, along with the daily sacrifice, in the course of transgression. The horn threw truth to the earth and in everything it did, it prospered.

[13] I heard one of the holy ones speaking. Then one holy one said to whomever it was who was speaking, "How long are the events of the vision to last—the daily sacrifice and the appalling transgression, the handing over of the host and sanctuary for trampling?"

[14] He said to him, "For 2,300 evenings and mornings; then the sanctuary will be made righteous."

[15] When I was watching the vision, I, Daniel, was trying to understand. Then there stood before me was one who looked liked a man. [16] I heard a human voice between the banks of the Ulai. He called, saying, "Gabriel, give this one an understanding of the vision." [17] He came near to where I was standing and when he came I was terrified and I fell on my face. He said to me, "Understand, mortal, that the vision concerns the time of the end."

[18] When he spoke to me, I fell into a heavy sleep on my face on the ground. But he touched me and made me stand. [19] He said, "I am informing you about that which is to happen at the end of the period of wrath, for it concerns the appointed

time of the end. ²⁰ The ram that you saw, which had the two horns, represents the kingdoms of Media and Persia. ²¹ The goat, the he-goat, is the king of Greece and the tall horn that was between its eyes is its greatest king. ²² Concerning the horn that was broken and the four that came up in its place, four Gentile kingdoms will arise but without his strength. ²³ After their kingdoms have come to an end, when their transgressions are complete, a king will arise, fierce-faced and skilled in double-dealing. ²⁴ His strength will be vast and he will cause immense destruction, succeeding in what he does. He will ruin the powerful and the holy ones. ²⁵ In his cunning, he will advance deceit with his hand and in his mind he will become great. Quietly, he will ruin many and will even stand up against the Chief of Chiefs. But without a hand he will be broken. ²⁶ The vision of the evening and the morning that has been revealed is true. As for you, keep secret the vision, for it concerns the future."

²⁷ I, Daniel, was undone and sick for days. Then I arose and did the king's work, but I was deeply disturbed because of the vision and had no understanding of it.

Daniel 11:1–12:4, 13

[The angel Gabriel said,]

¹¹:¹ As for me, in the first year of Darius the Mede, I arose to strengthen and protect him. ² Now I will declare to you a truth. See, three kings will yet arise out of Persia and the fourth one will grow far richer than all of them. When he grows strong on account of his riches, he will stir up all against the kingdom of Greece. ³ Then a warrior king will arise, who will rule over a great dominion and will do whatever he pleases. ⁴ But as it is rising in power, his kingdom will be shattered and it will be divided among the four winds of heavens. It will not go to his descendants nor will it continue to be as powerful as when he ruled, for his kingdom will be plucked up and will go to others besides these.

⁵ Then the king of the south will grow strong; but one of his officers will grow stronger than he and will rule over a kingdom larger than his. ⁶ After a time, they will unite and the daughter of the king of the south will go to the king of the north in order to make an equitable arrangement. But she will not be able to hold on to her power nor will his power endure. In time, she will be handed over, along with those who came with her, her child, and the one who supported her.

⁷ But a sprout from her roots will arise in his place and will advance against the army. He will enter the fortress of the king of the north and will take action against them. He will prevail. ⁸ Their gods, along with their idols and their precious vessels of silver and gold, he will take into captivity in Egypt. But then he will back down from the king of the north for some years. ⁹ Then the king of the north will enter the kingdom of the king of the south, only to return to his own land.

¹⁰ His sons will wage war and will assemble waves of great forces that will advance, flood, and overflow, waging war as far as the southern king's fortress. ¹¹ Enraged, the king of the south will go out and battle against him, against the king of the north. The latter will assemble another wave but these forces will be given into the hand of the king of south. ¹² After the force is carried off, the king

of the south will think highly of himself and will bring low tens of thousands but he will not prevail. [13] The king of the north will return and assemble a force greater than the previous one. After a time, he will advance with a large force and much equipment. [14] At that time, many will arise against the king of the south and some contentious men of your people will elevate themselves in order to fulfill a vision. But they will be overthrown. [15] The king of the north will advance, building up siege-works, and will seize a fortified city. The forces of the south will not stand, not even the elite among the troops; there will be no strength to withstand. [16] The advancing one will to do to him as he pleases, no one will be able to withstand him. He will occupy the beautiful land and all of it will be in his power. [17] Determined to advance with the strength of his entire kingdom, he will make an alliance with him [the king of the south] and will give to him his daughter as a wife in order to ruin him; but it will not prevail and it will not succeed for him. [18] He will turn his face to the coast and capture many but a captain will put an end to his reproach and will turn his reproach back onto him. [19] He will look to return to the safety of his own land, but he will stumble and fall and will not be found.

[20] One will arise in his place and he will send an official of royal eminence, but within a few days he will be broken, though not in anger or in battle. [21] In his place will arise a despicable man upon whom royal splendor was not bestowed. He will advance stealthily and seize the kingdom with smooth words. [22] Armies will be completely flooded and broken before him and also the prince of the covenant. [23] After an alliance is made with him, he will act deceitfully and rise to power with a small force. [24] Stealthily, he will advance into the wealthiest provinces and do what his fathers and fathers' fathers would not do: he will siphon off spoil, booty, and plunder to his supporters. He will continue to devise his plans against the fortified cities, but only for a time.

[25] Then he will rouse up his strength and set his mind against the king of the south with a great army. The king of the south will go to war with an even stronger army, but he will not prevail for others will devise plans against him. [26] Those who eat from the royal portions will break him. His army will be swept away in a flood and many will fall, fatally wounded. [27] The two kings, each with a mind for evil, will sit at one table and speak lies. Yet it will not succeed for there will be an end at the appointed time. [28] He will return to his land with much spoil and his mind set against the holy covenant. He will take measures but then return to his own land.

[29] At the appointed time, he will turn and advance toward the south. But this time it will not be like the first time. [30] Ships from Kittim will advance against him, and he will be forced to back down and turn back. He will rage against the holy covenant and lash out. Turning back, he will give his attention to those who have abandoned the holy covenant. [31] His forces will assemble and defile the sanctuary of the fortress, disrupt the daily sacrifice, and erect the desolating abomination. [32] The violators of the covenant he will seduce with smooth words, but the people who know their God will remain steadfast and will take action. [33] The wise ones of the people will instruct the many but they will be brought down by sword, flame, captivity, and plunder for many days. [34] In their stumbling, they will be helped a little, but many will join them insincerely, speaking smooth words. [35] Some of the wise ones will stumble so that they may be refined, purified, and made white until the time of the end, for the appointed time is still to come.

³⁶ The king will do as he pleases and he will exalt and elevate himself above every god; he will speak unbelievable things against the God of gods. But he will prosper until the period of wrath is completed, for what is determined will take place. ³⁷ He will not acknowledge the gods of his father or the gods adored by women. He will not acknowledge any of the gods for he will exalt himself above all. ³⁸ Instead, he will honor the god of fortresses; he will honor a god whom his fathers did not know with gold, silver, precious stones, and finery. ³⁹ He will deal with the strongest fortresses with the help of a foreign god—those whom he regards, he will honor and will cause them to rule over many people and divide the land for their wages.

⁴⁰ At the time of the end, he will fight a battle with the king of the south and the king of the north will storm against him with horses and riders and many ships. And he will advance through the lands, overtaking them like a flood. ⁴¹ He will enter the beautiful land and tens of thousands will fall, but some will escape his power—Edom, Moab, and the chiefs of the Ammonites. ⁴² He will also reach out his hand to other regions and the land of Egypt will not be able to escape. ⁴³ He will rule over stores of gold, silver, and every precious item. Egypt, Libya, and Ethiopia will be at his heel. ⁴⁴ Rumors from the east will terrify him, and he will go out in a great rage to exterminate and destroy many. ⁴⁵ He will pitch his pavilion tents between the sea and the beautiful holy mountain. There he will meet his end with no one to help him.

> ¹²:¹ At that time, Michael, the great prince, will arise,
>   the one who protects your people.
> It will be a time of distress such has not happened since the Gentiles
>   came to be
>   up to that time.
> At that time, your people will be delivered,
>   all those who have been written in the book.
> ² Many of those who sleep in the dust of the earth will awake;
>   some to everlasting life,
>   some to reproach and everlasting abhorrence.
> ³ But the wise ones will shine like the shining of the sky;
>   the ones who lead the many to righteousness will be like the stars
>   forever and ever.

⁴ But you, Daniel, stop up the words and seal up the book until the time of the end. At that time, many will roam back and forth so that knowledge may increase. . . . ¹³ As for you, go to your end. Then you will rest and you will rise to your reward at the end of the days.

Additions to Daniel and Other Danielic Literature

Many texts from antiquity show that Daniel was a popular figure in Second Temple Judaism, perhaps as early as the Persian period, and he is associated with several traditions found in the book of Daniel and other writings (*see* The Book of Daniel).

The biblical book of Daniel is not the focus of this chapter, but it will be helpful to comment briefly on scrolls containing it (or portions of it) among the Dead Sea Scrolls. Ten Daniel scrolls were discovered at Qumran (*see* Overview of Early Jewish Literature), two of which became known only in 2005. None have been found at other sites in the Judean Desert. Although these manuscripts are mostly very fragmentary, their number is significant and exceeds the totals for most books of the Hebrew Bible found at Qumran. Only the Psalms, Isaiah, and the books of the Pentateuch are represented by more scrolls among the Dead Sea Scrolls.

There are six more ancient compositions that feature Daniel. Three of these—known as the (Greek) Additions to Daniel—are familiar to modern scholars and other readers since they are among the **Apocrypha** in Roman Catholic and Orthodox Bibles and form part of the book of Daniel in the Septuagint (LXX; *see* Overview of Early Jewish Literature). They were later eliminated by the Protestant churches, which adopted the rabbinic Jewish canon of the Hebrew Bible for the Old Testament. The Prayer of Azariah in the Fiery Furnace and the Song of the Three Young Men is found between Daniel 3:23 and 3:24 as LXX Daniel 3:24–90, Susanna as LXX Daniel 13, and Bel and the Dragon as LXX Daniel 14. To these must be added three previously unknown texts, all written in Aramaic, that were discovered in Cave 4 at Qumran: The Prayer of Nabonidus (4Q242), Pseudo-Daniel A (4Q243–4Q244), and Pseudo-Daniel B (4Q245). These may conveniently be grouped as the Aramaic Additions to Daniel.

The existence of these six compositions strengthens the growing consensus among scholars that the book of Daniel is a composite work. Stories featuring Daniel were widely circulated well before the **Maccabean** (*see* 1 and 2 Maccabees) period, at least as early as the Hellenistic era (ca. 300–175 BCE), and contained elements dating perhaps as far back as the fifth century BCE. The three compositions preserved in the Septuagint can be traced back to Semitic originals, and the three found at Qumran can be dated to the second century BCE and earlier.

This chapter surveys the three Additions from the Septuagint and the three

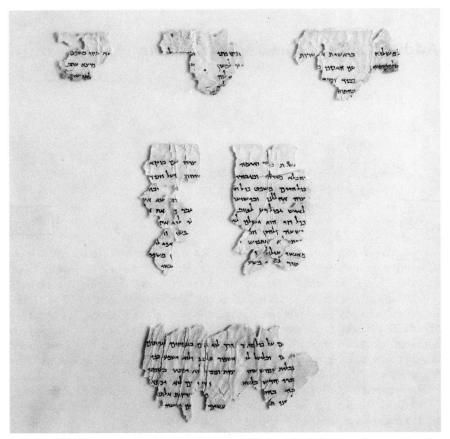

Figure 6. These fragments of scroll 4Q242, the Prayer of Nabonidus, belong to what are called the Aramaic Additions to Daniel. Courtesy Israel Antiquities Authority.

Aramaic Additions found among the Qumran scrolls, and comments on their settings and dates, connections to the book of Daniel, and provenance within later Judaism and the New Testament.

The six ancient compositions that feature Daniel discussed in this chapter speak to the dynamic and extensive history of the scriptural book of Daniel, and to the existence of a broader collection of "Daniel traditions" in the Second Temple period.

The three Greek Additions are all most likely of Semitic origin, although several borrow from preexisting traditions in Babylonian, Persian, or Egyptian literature. While they tend to be theologically diverse, and appear to largely have been circulated and collected independently from one another, they collectively exhibit a conflation of themes that emphasize religious purity, anti-idolatry polemics, political concerns within the Jewish state of the Hasmonean period, and, in some cases, internal religious conflicts also reflected in the apocalyptic section of scriptural Daniel. The Greek Additions have proven invaluable for reconstructing the history of the book of Daniel and its reception, and for providing additional insight into the religious, cultural, and political climate of early Judaism.

The three Aramaic Additions found at Qumran served to reinforce religious cohesion among the Qumran covenanters, or *yaḥad* movement.[1] The Prayer of Nabonidus attests to the adoption of a tradition into Jewish literature that promoted religious solidarity through the popular use of fabricated conversion tales amid the religious plurality of the Hellenistic world. It may also be related to an interest among the Essenes in healing.

Pseudo-Daniel A is similar to other apocalyptic works from the same period, and its heptadic perspective is closely connected to an apocalyptic worldview that was characteristic of the *yaḥad* movement. Features that situate this text quite firmly in this tradition include a highly schematized biblical chronology, the correct accounting of biblical history, and predictive prophecy. Pseudo-Daniel B was most likely a piece of propaganda against the conjoining of the offices of the high priest and the king in Judah. In keeping with the heptadic chronology of Daniel 9, the list in this text functions as a polemic against the high priesthood and rule of Jonathan Hyrcanus I or Alexander Jannaeus, and as a prediction of the end of days that would occur in his reign.

PETER W. FLINT AND C. J. PATRICK DAVIS

FURTHER READING

Collins, John J. *The Apocalyptic Imagination: An Introduction to Jewish Apocalyptic Literature*. 2nd ed. Grand Rapids: Eerdmans, 1999.

Davies, Philip R., George J. Brooke, and Phillip R. Callaway. *The Complete World of the Dead Sea Scrolls*. London: Thames & Hudson, 2002.

Flint, Peter W. "Non-Canonical Writings in the Dead Sea Scrolls: Apocrypha, Other Previously Known Writings, Pseudepigrapha." In *The Bible at Qumran: Text, Shape, and Interpretation*, edited by Peter W. Flint, pp. 80–123. Studies in the Dead Sea Scrolls and Related Literature 5. Grand Rapids: Eerdmans, 2000.

Garcia Martinez, Florentino. *The Dead Sea Scrolls Translated: The Qumran Texts in English*, pp. 288–89. 2nd ed. Grand Rapids: Eerdmans, 1996.

Harrington, Daniel J., S.J. *Invitation to the Apocrypha*. Grand Rapids: Eerdmans, 1999.

McLay, Timothy R. "Sousanna," "Daniel," and "Bel and the Dragon." In *The New English Translation of the Septuagint*, edited by Albert Pietersma and Benjamin W. Wright, pp. 986–1027. New York: Oxford University Press, 2007.

Nickelsburg, George W. E. *Jewish Literature between the Bible and the Mishnah*. 2nd rev. ed. Philadelphia: Fortress, 2005.

Sack, Ronald H. "Nabonidus (Person)." In *ABD*, 4:973–76.

VanderKam, James, and Peter Flint. *The Meaning of the Dead Sea Scrolls: Their Significance for Understanding the Bible, Jesus, and Christianity*. San Francisco: HarperCollins, 2002.

Vermes, Geza. *The Complete Dead Sea Scrolls in English*. 7th ed. Harmondsworth: Penguin, 2012.

Wise, Michael O., Martin G. Abegg, and Edward M. Cook. *The Dead Sea Scrolls: A New Translation*, pp. 340–45. Rev. ed. San Francisco: HarperSanFrancisco, 2005.

1. Some texts present history or the future in "heptads" or sevenfold "years" or periods, usually culminating with the end of days. The best-known example is in Dan. 9:24-27.

ADVANCED READING

Beyer, Klaus. *Die aramäischen Texte vom Toten Meer*. Göttingen: Vandenhoeck & Ruprecht, 1984.

Collins, John J. "242. 4QPrayer of Nabonidus ar." In *Qumran Cave 4, XVII: Parabiblical Texts, Part 3*, pp. 82–93. DJD 22. Oxford: Clarendon, 1996.

Collins, John J., and Peter W. Flint. "243–245. 4QPseudo-Daniel ar." In *Qumran Cave 4, XVII: Parabiblical Texts, Part 3*, pp. 95–164. DJD 22. Oxford: Clarendon, 1996.

Collins, John J., et al. *Daniel: A Commentary on the Book of Daniel*. Hermeneia. Minneapolis: Fortress, 1993.

Flint, Peter W. "Daniel in the Dead Sea Scrolls." In *The Book of Daniel: Composition and Reception*, edited by Peter W. Flint and John J. Collins, 2:329–67. The Formation and Interpretation of Old Testament Literature 2; Supplements to Vetus Testamentum 83. Leiden: Brill, 2001.

Flint, Peter W., and John J. Collins, eds. *The Book of Daniel: Composition and Reception*. 2 vols. The Formation and Interpretation of Old Testament Literature 2; Supplements to Vetus Testamentum 83. Leiden: Brill, 2001.

Knibb, Michael A. "The Book of Daniel in Its Context." In *The Book of Daniel: Composition and Reception*, edited by Peter W. Flint and John J. Collins, 1:16–35. The Formation and Interpretation of Old Testament Literature 2; Supplements to Vetus Testamentum 83. Leiden: Brill, 2001.

Moore, Carey A. *Daniel, Esther, and Jeremiah: The Additions*. Anchor Bible 44. New York: Doubleday, 1977.

Ulrich, Eugene. "Daniel, Book of: Hebrew and Aramaic Text." In *The Encyclopedia of the Dead Sea Scrolls*, edited by L. H. Schiffman and J. C. VanderKam, pp. 170–74. Oxford: Oxford University Press, 2000.

Vermes, Geza. "Essenes and Therapeutai." *Revue de Qumrân* 3 (1962): 495–504.

Wise, Michael O. "4Q245 (4QpsDanᶜ ar) and the High Priesthood of Judas Maccabaeus." *Dead Sea Discoveries* 12, no. 3 (2005): 313–62.

Introduction to the Prayer of Azariah in the Fiery Furnace and the Song of the Three Young Men

Narrative Description

The Prayer of Azariah in the Fiery Furnace and the Song of the Three Young Men consists of three parts: the Prayer (vv. 1–22 = LXX Dan. 3:24–45), a prose interlude describing the furnace (vv. 23–27 = LXX Dan. 3:46–50), and the Song (vv. 28–68 = LXX Dan. 3:51–90). The Prayer opens with Azariah, one of the three young men and a colleague of Daniel at court (cf. Dan. 1:6–7), delivering a penitential prayer that affirms the exile as just punishment for the sins of Israel:

> For you have executed true decrees, in accordance with everything you have caused to befall us, and upon the holy city of our fathers, Jerusalem. So in truth and judgment you have performed all of these things because of our sins. (v. 5 = LXX Dan. 3:28)

This confession indicts the nation for failing to obey God's laws and to keep his commandments (vv. 6–8 = LXX Dan. 3:29–30), thereby giving prominence to the Torah, a feature also found in some other Second Temple Jewish traditions. There follows an appeal for deliverance on the basis of the covenant promises (vv. 11–13 = LXX Dan. 3:34–36), on offering a "soul of contrition and a humbled spirit" (v. 16 = LXX Dan. 3:39), and on the basis of God's wonders and the glory of his name (vv. 19–22 = LXX Dan. 3:42–45).

The Song of the Three Young Men may be divided into two parts, the first (vv. 29–34 = LXX Dan. 3:52–56) a direct address to God, praising him in his residence in the Jerusalem temple (vv. 31–32 = LXX Dan. 3:53–55) and for his works in creation (vv. 33–34 = LXX Dan. 3:55–56). The second part (vv. 35–68 = LXX Dan. 3:57–90) calls on all the "works of the Lord" (v. 35 = LXX Dan. 3:57) to join in the song of blessing and in the repeated refrain, to "sing praise and exalt him forever."

The Prayer of Azariah in the Fiery Furnace and the Song of the Three Young Men survived only in the Septuagint and the **Peshitta**, or Syriac Bible, and was included in the early Christian canon of Scripture as part of the prophetic book of Daniel. It was inserted between Daniel 3:23 and 3:24 from the Hebrew Bible (where the entire chapter is in Aramaic). This section of the Aramaic text—beginning with verse 19—is part of the story of Daniel's three companions, Shadrach, Meshach, and Abednego, who were earlier identified with Hananiah, Mishael, and Azariah (cf. Dan. 1:6–7). The three were cast into a blistering hot furnace, to be executed for their failure to bow down and worship an idol erected by Nebuchadnezzar, king of Babylon (Dan. 3:1–23). In the scriptural Aramaic text, a curious gap may be detected in the flow of the narrative in verses 23–25a:

> [23] So these three men—Shadrach, Meshach, and Abednego—fell bound into the middle of the furnace of blazing fire. [24] Then Nebuchadnezzar the king was astonished and abruptly stood; he answered and said to his counselors, "Were there not three men, bound, and hurled into the middle of the fire?" They responded and said to the king, "Without a doubt, your majesty." [25] And he answered and said: "But look! I myself am seeing four men, loose and walking around, and they are unharmed!"

The break that appears between when the young men are thrown into the fire (v. 23) and Nebuchadnezzar's astonishment and mention of a fourth figure, "whose appearance is like that of an angel"[1] (v. 25b), is resolved through the insertion of the Prayer and then the Song.

Author/Provenance

The Prayer of Azariah in the Fiery Furnace and the Song of the Three Young Men is unattested in Hebrew and Aramaic, and there is no evidence that it formed part of the authoritative body of Scriptures (the term "canon" is anachronistic), for any sect within Judaism, with the apparent exception of **Hellenistic** Judaism. The text survives as part of Christian collections, in the Greek Septuagint, and in the Syriac Old Testament that was authoritative in the Eastern Orthodox Church.

The Prayer is classified as a "communal confession of sin and petition for mercy," which was typically popular among postexilic dispersed Jewish communities. Such confessions (also found in Dan. 9:1–19 and Bar. 1:15b–3:8) promoted **Deuteronomistic** ideals and the importance of Torah observance in the absence of an established temple service. The Song was a liturgical composition that appears closely related to so-called wisdom hymns in Psalm 148 and Job 38–41.

Date/Occasion

The Prayer, prose interlude, and Song are almost certainly not part of the original text of Daniel 3, and were not inspired by the existing narrative. The scholarly consensus is that they were preexisting, separate literary traditions, added to the tale of the furnace possibly because of the appearance of "Azariah" in the Prayer (v. 2 = LXX Dan. 3:25) and the names of all three (Hananiah, Azariah, and Mishael) in the Song (v. 66 = LXX Dan. 3:88). Themes related to religious

---

1. Literally, "a son of the gods."

oppression, the cessation of the temple services (v. 15 = LXX Dan. 3:38), and the portrayal of the king as wicked and unjust (v. 9 = LXX Dan. 3:32) suggest that the Prayer was composed during the Seleucid occupation under Antiochus IV Epiphanes (ca. 167–165 BCE; *see* The Book of Daniel), near in time to the compilation of the book of Daniel. The Song is more difficult to date, but seems to have been composed when the temple service was vibrant (third or late second century BCE). The setting for both compositions is most likely liturgical, but unlike the Prayer, the Song appears to assume that the temple services are still ongoing.

The Prayer and the Song were likely inserted as "pious embellishments" to a popular story, which is fairly characteristic of Second Temple Judaism.[2] Originally, both were liturgical texts perhaps used in the **Diaspora,** probably in the synagogue that developed outside Palestine. However, it is also possible that the Song originated in Palestine, and was once a part of the temple service.

Text, Language, Sources, and Transmission

The text survives in Greek and in Syriac, which is a form of Aramaic, but most scholars believe a Hebrew original to be at the heart of both the Prayer and the Song. The structure and themes in both suggest that they originated within Second Temple Judaism, and were viewed as authoritative by at least a few Jewish sects, most likely in the Diaspora.

Two versions of the Prayer and the Song survive in the **Old Greek** text of the Septuagint and in the **recension** of Theodotion, which became the standard text of the early church. Recovering the original Old Greek of the Prayer and the Song is complex and challenging; in many cases, Theodotion's text may represent the earliest rendering of the Semitic original. The translation below is based on Theodotion, but the footnotes highlight some important variant readings from the Old Greek of the Septuagint as found in the New English Translation of the Septuagint (NETS).

Reception of Additions to Daniel in the Second Temple Period

The Prayer and the Song forms a concise synopsis of three important themes and religious concerns during the mid-Second Temple period: the destructive impact of the exile, God's work in history among his chosen people, and God's supremacy over creation and the relationship between creation and worship.

The Prayer bears structural and thematic similarities with Daniel 9:4–19 as well as other postexilic Jewish traditions (cf. Ps. 106; Ezra 9:6–15; Neh. 1:5–11; 9:5–37; Bar. 1:15–3:8). It also reinforces an ongoing concern for the maintenance of Jewish

---

2. Other examples are the Additions to Esther, the Genesis Apocryphon from Qumran, and the superscriptions imposed on various other liturgical compositions from Scripture that connect them to biblical narratives: that is, LXX Ps. 3:1 and 2 Sam. 15:13–16; LXX Ps. 18:1 (= 2 Sam. 23); Ps. 54:1 and 1 Sam. 23:19–28; LXX Ps. 34:1 and 1 Sam. 21:11–16; LXX Lam. 1:1 and sections of Jeremiah.

religion and culture among communities that have been displaced and are geographically removed from Palestine and the temple. Emphasis is placed on God's mercies and his faithfulness to the Jewish people in a time of hardship brought about by foreign influence and persecution. The negative appraisal of the king as "the most wicked in all the earth" (v. 9 = LXX Dan. 3:32) and the suggestion that temple sacrifices have ceased (v. 16 = LXX Dan. 3:39) accord with the later portions of the book of Daniel, in which the survival of the covenant community of Israel was deemed crucial and achievable through strict observance of the law. As for the Song, its emphases on the Jerusalem temple and on the distinction of God from all creation are familiar themes from the period within other liturgical compositions.

The Prayer and the Song appears to have been popular and relevant in the early church, which led to their maintenance. The text is cited among the church fathers as early as the mid-second century CE by Justin Martyr (*1 Apologia* 46), Clement of Alexandria (*Eclogae propheticae* 1), and Tertullian (*De oratione* 15). A possible allusion in Hebrews 11:34, as part of a recounting of the biblical narrative, may demonstrate the importance of the story of the fiery furnace—which conceivably contained the Prayer and the Song—for the church in Antioch. The themes from the Prayer that focus on confession and exile would have been particularly popular among Christian communities, who envisioned themselves as a part of an ongoing exilic tradition (cf. James 1:1;[3] 1 Pet. 1:1).

PETER W. FLINT AND C. J. PATRICK DAVIS

---

3. James 1:1: "James, a servant of God and of the Lord Jesus Christ, to the twelve tribes in the dispersion, greetings."

1.2 The Prayer of Azariah in the Fiery Furnace and the Song of the Three Young Men

The Prayer of Azariah in the Fiery Furnace

1 (24) And they[a] were walking around in the midst of the fire, singing hymns
to God and blessing the Lord.[b] 2 (25)Then Azariah stood still,
praying as follows; opening his mouth[c] in the midst of the fire[d] he
said:

3 (26) "Blessed are you, O Lord, God of our ancestors,
praiseworthy and glorified is your name for eternity.

4 (27) For you are just in everything that you have done for us.
All your deeds are true and your ways are right, and all of your verdicts are true.

5 (28) For you have executed true verdicts in everything that you brought
upon us,
and upon Jerusalem, the holy city of our ancestors;
for in truth and judgment you brought about all these things because
of our sins.

6 (29) For we have sinned and behaved lawlessly by turning away from you,
and we have sinned in everything!

7 (30) And we failed to obey your commandments.
We have not observed or acted as you commanded us so that it may
go well for us.

8 (31) And now all that you have brought upon us,
and all that you have done to us, you have brought about in fair
judgment.

9 (32) And you delivered us into the hand of our enemies, lawless, hostile
traitors,
and to an unjust king, the most wicked in all the world.

10 (33) So now we are unable to open our mouth;
shame and disgrace have befallen your servants, and those who worship you.

a. That is, Hananiah, Mishael, and Azariah; cf. Dan. 2:17.
b. OG reads instead: "So, therefore, Hananias and Azarias and Misael prayed and sang hymns
to the Lord, when the king ordered them to be thrown into the furnace" (NETS).
c. OG adds: "and he acknowledged the Lord together with his companions" (NETS).
d. OG adds: "while the furnace was being heated exceedingly by the Chaldeans" (NETS).

Translation by Peter W. Flint, from Daniel 3:24–90 in Theodotion's Greek edition. Numerous
alternative readings are to be found in the Old Greek (OG). Since these variant readings are not
very numerous or complex for the Prayer of Azariah in the Fiery Furnace and the Song of the
Three Young Men, they are included in the footnotes. Inserted between Daniel 3:23 and 3:24,
Greek verses are given in parentheses.

11 (34)   Now[a] do not give us up completely for your name's sake,
          and do not annul your covenant.

12 (35)   And do not withdraw your mercy from us,
          for the sake of Abraham who was loved by you,
          and for the sake of your servant Isaac, and Israel, your holy one.

13 (36)   To them you promised to multiply their seed like the stars of the
          heavens,
          and like the sand on the shore of the sea.

14 (37)   For we, O Master, have become fewer than all the nations,
          and we are humbled today in all the world because of our sins.

15 (38)   And at this time there is no ruler, or prophet, or leader,
          no burnt offering, or sacrifice, or oblation, or incense,
          no place for making an offering to you and to find mercy.

16 (39)   But with a broken soul and a humbled spirit may we be accepted,

17 (40)   as though it were with burnt offerings of rams and bulls,
          or with tens of thousands of fat lambs.
          And let our sacrifice be like this before you today,
          and may it reach completion behind you,
          since no shame will come to those who place their trust in you.

18 (41)   And now we follow with our whole heart,
          and we fear you and we seek your face.

19 (42)   Do not put us to shame,
          but work among us in accordance with your kindness
          and according to the abundance of your mercy.

20 (43)   Also deliver us in accordance with your marvelous works,
          and bring glory to your name, O Lord.

21 (44)   Let all who do harm to your servants be put to shame,
          and may they be stripped of all might, and let their strength be
          crushed.

22 (45)   Let them know that you alone are the Lord God,
          and glorious over the entire world."

The Song of the Three Young Men

23 (46) Now the king's officials who cast them in did not stop stoking the furnace
with naphtha, pitch, flax, and small branches.[b] 24 (47) And the flames erupted
out of the furnace to a height of 49 cubits,[c] 25 (48) and burst forth and burned
whomever it found of the Chaldeans above the furnace. 26 (49) But the angel of
the Lord came down at that moment to be with those who were around Aza-

---

a. Not in the OG (thus also NETS).

b. OG instead reads: "And when they cast the three in all at once into the furnace, the furnace was red hot, sevenfold in its heat. And when they threw them in, those who threw them
in were over them, and those below them kept on stoking from underneath with naphtha and
pitch and tow and brushwood" (NETS).

c. Approximately 22.7 meters.

riah in the furnace, and he drove back the blazing fire out of the furnace. 27
(50) Then he made inside of the furnace something like a moist, whistling wind,
and the fire did not touch them at all, and it caused them no pain or distress.
28 (51) Then the three, as with one voice, praised and exalted and blessed God
in the furnace:

29 (52)   "Blessed are you, O Lord, God of our ancestors,
     and praiseworthy and highly exalted forever;
30   and blessed is your glorious, holy name,
     and to be highly praised and highly exalted forever![a]
31 (53)   Blessed are you, in the temple of your holy glory,
     and to be highly praised and highly glorified forever!
32 (55)   Blessed are you who look upon the depths, seated upon the cherubim,
     and to be praised and highly exalted forever.
33 (54)   Blessed are you, upon the throne of your kingdom,
     and to be highly praised and exalted forever!
34 (56)   Blessed are you, in the vault of heaven,
     and to be hymned and glorified forever!
35 (57)   Bless the Lord, all you works of the Lord,
     and sing praise and highly exalt him forever![b]
36 (59)   Bless the Lord, you heavens,
     and sing praise and highly exalt him forever!
37 (58)   Bless the Lord, you angels of the Lord,
     and sing praise and highly exalt him forever!
38 (60)   Bless the Lord, all you waters above the heavens,
     and sing praise and highly exalt him forever!
39 (61)   Bless the Lord, all you powers,
     and sing praise and highly exalt him forever!
40 (62)   Bless the Lord, you sun and moon,
     and sing praise and highly exalt him forever!
41 (63)   Bless the Lord, you stars of the heavens,
     and sing praise and highly exalt him forever!
42 (64)   Bless the Lord, every rainstorm and dew drop,
     and sing praise and highly exalt him forever!
43 (65)   Bless the Lord, all you winds,
     and sing praise and highly exalt him forever!
44 (66)   Bless the Lord, you fire and heat,
     and sing praise and highly exalt him forever!
45 (67)   Bless the Lord, you winter cold and summer heat,
     and sing praise and highly exalt him forever!
46 (68)   Bless the Lord, you dews and snowfalls,
     and sing praise and highly exalt him forever![c]

a. In the OG, verse 31 is omitted, and verse 32 (= 55) follows verse 33 (= 54) (thus also
NETS).
   b. In the OG, verse 36 (= 59) follows verse 37 (= 58) (thus also NETS).
   c. In the OG, verses 49–50 (= 73–74) follow verse 46 (= 68) (thus also NETS).

47 (71) Bless the Lord, night and day,
> and sing praise and highly exalt him forever!

48 (72) Bless the Lord, you light and darkness,
> and sing praise and highly exalt him forever!

49 (69) Bless the Lord, you icy pinnacles and cold,
> and sing praise and highly exalt him forever!

50 (70) Bless the Lord, you frost and snow,
> and sing praise and highly exalt him forever!

51 (73) Bless the Lord, you lightning and clouds,
> and sing praise and highly exalt him forever!

52 (74) Let the earth bless the Lord,
> and let it sing praise and highly exalt him forever!

53 (75) Bless the Lord, you mountains and hills,
> and sing praise and highly exalt him forever!

54 (76) Bless the Lord, all things that grow in the ground,
> and sing praise and highly exalt him forever![a]

55 (78) Bless the Lord, you seas and rivers
> and sing praise and highly exalt him forever!

56 (77) Bless the Lord, you springs of water,
> and sing praise and highly exalt him forever!

57 (79) Bless the Lord, you sea-monsters and all that swim in the waters,
> and sing praise and highly exalt him forever!

58 (80) Bless the Lord, all you winged creatures of the sky,
> and sing praise and highly exalt him forever!

59 (81) Bless the Lord, all you wild animals and livestock,[b]
> and sing praise and highly exalt him forever!

60 (82) Bless the Lord, you children of men,
> and sing praise and highly exalt him forever!

61 (83) Bless the Lord, O Israel,
> and sing praise and highly exalt him forever!

62 (84) Bless the Lord, you priests of the Lord,[c]
> and sing praise and highly exalt him forever!

63 (85) Bless the Lord, you servants of the Lord,
> and sing praise and highly exalt him forever!

64 (86) Bless the Lord, you spirits and souls of the righteous,
> and sing praise and highly exalt him forever!

65 (87) Bless the Lord, you who are pious and humble of heart,
> and sing praise and highly exalt him forever!

66 (88) Bless the Lord, Hananiah, Azariah, and Mishael,
> and sing praise and highly exalt him forever!
> For he has snatched us out of Hades, and saved us from the hand of death,

a. In the OG, verse 55 (= 78) follows verse 56 (= 77) (thus also NETS).

b. OG: "all you four-footed and wild animals of the earth."

c. For verse 62 (= 84), the OG reads, "Bless the Lord, you priests, servants of the Lord, and sing praise and highly exalt him forever!" and omits verse 63 (= 85) (thus also NETS).

and rescued us from the midst of the burning fiery furnace;
from the midst of the fire he has delivered us!

67 (89) Give thanks to the Lord, because he is kind,
for his mercy is forever!

68 (90) All you who worship the Lord, bless the God of gods!
Sing praise and proclaim thanks, for his mercy is forever![a]

a. OG reads "forever and ever and ever" (NETS).

Introduction to Susanna

Narrative Description

The tale of Susanna features the beautiful wife of Joakim, an upstanding and wealthy Jewish man living in exile. She is falsely accused of sexual impropriety by a pair of corrupt "elders," who are enamored by her appearance. The appeal of this story through its racy combination of sex and death would likely have added to its popularity and ensured its transmission in early Judaism. It conveys a moral message of sexual purity, obedience to the Torah, and the value of youth.

A pair of Jewish elders, men entrusted with settling disputes for the exiled communities,[1] would convene court in the house of Joakim, "the most highly regarded among them all" (LXX Dan. 13:4). These men become enraptured by his wife, Susanna, and conspire together to find her unattended and make her have sexual intercourse with them (LXX Dan. 13:8–14). When they finally catch Susanna alone, they issue her an ultimatum: "Consent to be with us. But if you refuse, we will testify against you that you were with a young man" (LXX Dan. 13:20b–21a). The virtuous Susanna is repulsed and cries out in alarm, for she would rather die "than to sin before the Lord!" (LXX Dan. 13:23). This commotion draws the attention of the household, at which point the two lecherous men claim they have discovered Susanna alone with a young man, engaged in acts of infidelity (LXX Dan. 13:27). The following day, the false elders testify against her in graphic detail in a court convened by the "synagogue" (Greek for "assembly," LXX Dan. 13:28–44), and Susanna is sentenced to death.

Fortunately for her, a young man named Daniel is present who is "aroused [in his] holy spirit" (LXX Dan. 13:45) to interject, for he cannot stomach the kangaroo court in process. He wisely advises the introduction of third-party testimony and a cross-examination of the two elders. The assembly perceives that God has revealed the truth to Daniel and has granted him the "privilege of age" (LXX Dan. 13:50), and so allows him to conduct the investigation. Daniel wisely separates the two accusers, and questions each more specifically on where they

---

1. The Septuagint version has people coming to Babylon "from other cities" to have their cases settled by these elders (v. 6).

witnessed Susanna's crime. When their stories contradict each other, Daniel calls for their execution: "The angel of God waits with sword in hand to cut you in two, so as to completely destroy you!" (LXX Dan. 13:59; cf. v. 55). Thus Susanna is vindicated, and the two bad and dangerous men are eliminated. In Theodotion's revision (translated in full below) the tale ends by emphasizing Susanna's virtue and Daniel's greatness before his people. In the Old Greek, however, the story of Susanna ends on a sermonic note:

> Because of this, the young are beloved by Jacob for their sincerity. As for us, let us watch over the young so they can become courageous sons. The young will worship, and there remains in them a spirit of knowledge and understanding forevermore. (v. 64)

Author/Provenance

Susanna is unattested in the Hebrew Bible, and appears to have not been included at any stage in the Jewish canon, with the apparent exception of **Hellenistic** Judaism. Nevertheless, a passage from the Babylonian Talmud suggests that it was known to the rabbis in the same context within the book of Daniel (cf. the Babylonian Talmud, Sanhedrin 93a). The talmudic tradition was cited by both Origen in his *Epistle to Africanus* and Jerome in his *Commentary on Jeremiah*. The story of Susanna itself found life within the early church, and is included in the Roman Catholic and Orthodox Old Testaments.

Date/Occasion

Many scholars agree that Susanna—like all the Additions to Daniel—was originally an independent composition. The Old Greek version of the story preserved in the Septuagint featured an anonymous Jewish hero who was distinguished by his virtue and youth, in sharp contrast to the wickedness of the elders. This older version of the story, which never identifies the young man as Daniel, appears unaware of the scriptural book of Daniel. It most likely predates the formation of the book, owing to a number of internal inconsistencies, and was eventually added to the Danielic collection only at a later date, based on the appearance of Daniel's name.[2]

Some scholars, however, hold that the story of Susanna more likely originated within Palestine, during a period of national independence after the mid-second century BCE. While the tale itself is difficult to date—and elements within it may date back into the Persian period—the lack of a court setting, the entirely internal national conflict, and the absence of any foreign cultural or religious pressure common to the other Additions suggests that it did not belong to the pre-**Hasmonean** period.[3]

---

2. *See* Michael Knibb, "The Book of Daniel in Its Context," in *The Book of Daniel*, ed. John J. Collins and Peter W. Flint (Leiden: Brill, 2001), pp. 26–28.

3. Carey A. Moore, *Daniel, Esther, and Jeremiah: The Additions*, Anchor Bible 44 (New York:

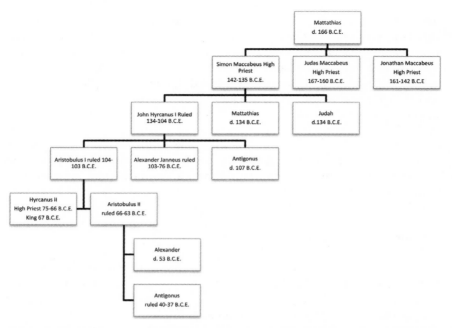

Figure 7. The story of Susanna may have been, in part, a critique of the leadership of the Hasmoneans, whose family tree is shown in this diagram. Diagram by Archie T. Wright

From its clear presentation as a moral tale, Susanna in its original setting was an instructive story for maturing young people and for encouraging obedience amid temptation.[4] The story may also be a cautionary tale about good leadership, in an era when the new independent Jewish state faced various novel challenges with regard to justice, politics, and religion. The role of the two elders in the story points to this, and likely has its roots in the letter of Jeremiah (in Jer. 29), which was written to the exiles in Babylon and warns against two specific "false prophets," Ahab son of Kolaiah and Zedekiah son of Maaseiah. The accusation: these men have "committed adultery with their neighbors' wives, and have spoken words in my name that were not true and which I did not command them" (Jer. 29:23).[5] This theme is similarly represented in a scroll from Qumran, 4QCatena B

Doubleday, 1977), pp. 91–92; George W. E. Nickelsburg, *Jewish Literature between the Bible and the Mishnah*, 2nd rev. ed. (Philadelphia: Fortress, 2005), p. 26.

4. Nickelsburg, *Jewish Literature*, p. 26.

5. Jer. 29:20–23: "But now, all you exiles whom I sent away from Jerusalem to Babylon, hear the word of the Lord: Thus says the Lord of hosts, the God of Israel, concerning Ahab son of Kolaiah and Zedekiah son of Maaseiah, who are prophesying a lie to you in my name: I am going to deliver them into the hand of King Nebuchadrezzar of Babylon, and he will kill them before your eyes. And on account of them this curse will be used by all the exiles from Judah in Babylon: 'The Lord make you like Zedekiah and Ahab, whom the king of Babylon roasted in the fire,' because they have perpetrated outrage in Israel and have committed adultery with their neighbors' wives, and have spoken in my name lying words that I did not command them; I am the one who knows and bears witness, says the Lord." Cf. also Jer. 5:8. Note also in Sus. 5 the vague recollection of the declaration of the Lord in Jer. 23:15: "from out of the prophets of Jerusalem pollution will spread."

(4Q182), fragment 1, lines 4–5, where false prophets are described as committing adultery and flocking to brothels: "They were well nourished, lusting stallions: each man neighing after his neighbor's wife."[6] This common thread (which may be traced back to Jer. 29) suggests that Susanna functioned in part to critique leadership, perhaps in the Hasmonean period that was frequently characterized by sectarianism and internal religious and political tensions revolving around the correct interpretation of the Torah (cf. LXX Dan. 13:62).

On another level, the placement of this story in the book of Daniel, and its association with the Jewish hero Daniel, serve to reinforce him as the main character of the whole book, and to provide background information regarding his prophetic insight and divine wisdom. In Theodotion's version, the story concludes: "And Daniel became great in the presence of the people from that day onward." While the tale most likely did not originate as part of the Daniel cycle,[7] it was assumed as part of the corpus because of its explanatory power for the protagonist's **mantic,** prophetic abilities.

Text, Language, Sources, and Transmission

The tale itself does not provide any indication that Susanna was translated from a Semitic original, and it was possibly composed in Greek. Some scholars, however, suggest that there was a Hebrew ***Vorlage*** owing to the simplicity of the language in Theodotion's version.[8] Speculation regarding the possibility of such a Semitic source must take into account more recent evidence from the Dead Sea Scrolls, where a version of the tale may have survived in an Aramaic scroll from Cave 4 (4Q551), but this is not certain (hence the epithet 4QDanSuz ar?). The mention of an old man and a court setting in a household in fragment 1, lines 2–5, suggests a possible connection to the tale of Susanna. However, owing to the very fragmentary nature of the text and the uncertainty of the allusion, such a connection is far from certain.[9]

As with the other Additions, two versions of Susanna have survived in the Old Greek text of the Septuagint and in Theodotion's recension, which became

---

6. 4Q182 (4QCatena B) i.4–5: "[. . . as is wr]itten about them in the book of [the prophet] Jere[miah:] [Jer. 5:7 Why should I have to forgive you?] Your [sons] have deserted me [. . .]"— trans. Garcia Martinez and Tigchelaar, *Dead Sea Scrolls Study Edition.* Cf. C. J. Patrick Davis, "Re-Presentation and Emerging Authority of the Jeremiah Traditions in Second Temple Judaism" (PhD diss, University of Manchester, 2009), pp. 137–38.

7. Many scholars argue to the contrary that the "Daniel" figure in Susanna more closely approximates the much more ancient, wise Daniel from Ezek. 14:14, 20; cf. Knibb, "Book of Daniel in Its Context," p. 27.

8. Moore, *Daniel, Esther, and Jeremiah*, pp. 82–83.

9. Peter W. Flint, "Non-Canonical Writings in the Dead Sea Scrolls: Apocrypha, Other Previously Known Writings, Pseudepigrapha," in *The Bible at Qumran: Text, Shape, and Interpretation*, ed. Peter W. Flint, Studies in the Dead Sea Scrolls and Related Literature 5 (Grand Rapids: Eerdmans, 2000), p. 114; K. Beyer, *Die aramäischen Texte vom Toten Meer* (Göttingen: Vandenhoeck & Ruprecht, 1984), pp. 224–25. Knibb, "Book of Daniel in Its Context," p. 24, n. 30, rejects 4Q551 as having any relationship to Susanna.

the standard text of the early church. The versions for Susanna are considerably different, even more so than the other Greek Additions or the two versions of Daniel. As with The Prayer of Azariah in the Fiery Furnace, the translation below is based on Theodotion. Since the alternative readings in the Old Greek are extensive and complex, very few are included in the footnotes. The Old Greek (Septuagint) translation may be found in NETS.

Theology

Despite the popularity of its themes around sex, death, and detection, the tale of Susanna does not sit well within the rest of the book of Daniel. Susanna is found at the beginning of Daniel in Septuagint manuscripts, but Jerome (ca. 347–420 CE) moved it to the end (as chap. 13), with a comment that it is not found in the Hebrew Bible. In addition to its use by Christians, Susanna may well have found an audience in postexilic Judaism, where purity and obedience remained ongoing concerns. The story possibly served as a cautionary tale about good leadership, and the importance of justice for those living in the Diaspora and subject to foreign powers.

PETER W. FLINT AND C. J. PATRICK DAVIS

1.3 Susanna

The Two Elders Are Attracted by Susanna's Beauty

[1]Now, there was a man living in Babylon whose name was Joakim. [2]He took a wife named Susanna, daughter of Hilkiah, a woman of exceptional beauty who feared the Lord. [3]Her parents, too, were righteous, and had trained their daughter according to the Law of Moses. [4]Now Joakim was very rich, and had a lovely garden attached to his house. And the Jews regularly consulted him because he was most highly regarded among them all.

[5]That year two elders from the people were appointed as judges. Concerning them the Lord had said: "Lawlessness has come from Babylon, from elders who were judges, who only seemed to govern the people."[a] [6]These men were often in Joakim's house, and all who had legal disputes would come to them.

[7]Now when the people left at noon, Susanna would go into her husband's garden to stroll. [8]Each day the two elders would watch her going in and walking about, and they began to lust after her. [9]And each perverted his mind and turned away his eyes, so as not to look to heaven or remember to make just decisions. [10]And they were both smitten[b] by her, but would not talk to one another of their distress [11]because they were ashamed to admit their burning desire, for they yearned to have sexual relations with her. [12]They would watch eagerly, day after day, to catch sight of her.

[13]One day,[c] they said to one another, "Let us go home, for it is lunchtime." So they left and parted from each other. [14]But turning back, they arrived at the same place, and when each questioned the other for the reason, they confessed their lust. Then together they arranged a time when they could find her alone.

The Two Elders Try to Force Themselves on Susanna

[15]Once, as they were watching for an opportune day, she came in as she usually did, but with only two servant girls; and she wanted to bathe in the garden because it was hot. [16]And there was no one else there except the two elders, who were hiding and watching her. [17]Then she said to the servant girls, "Bring me olive oil and lotions, and shut the garden doors so that I can bathe." [18]So they did as she instructed: they shut the garden doors and went out by the side doors to

a. Source unknown, but cf. Jer. 29:23.
b. Literally, "pierced to the heart."
c. Meaning implied; not extant in any of the versions.

Translation by Peter W. Flint, from Daniel B in Theodotion's Greek edition. Numerous alternative readings, many of them extensive or complex, are to be found the Old Greek (OG), but are generally not included in the footnotes.

fetch the items she had told them to get. But they did not see the elders because they were hiding.

[19] When the servant girls had left, the two elders stood up and raced toward[a] her. [20] They said, "Look, the garden doors are shut and no one can see us. We are burning with desire for you! So give in, and have intercourse with us. [21] But if you refuse, we will testify against you that a young man was with you, and it was for this reason that you sent the servant girls away from you."[b]

[22] Then Susanna groaned and said, "I am utterly trapped! For if I do this it will mean death for me; but if I do not, I cannot escape from your grasp. [23] It is better for me to not do it, and fall into your grasp, rather than to sin before the Lord!"

[24c] Then Susanna screamed in a loud voice, and the two elders shouted against her, [25] and one of them ran and opened the garden doors. [26] When the people in the house heard the cry in the garden, they hurried in through the side door to see what had happened to her. [27] But when the elders told their story, the servants felt highly ashamed since such a thing had never been said about Susanna.

The Two Elders Testify against Susanna

[28] And so, on the following day when the people gathered to meet her husband Joakim, the two elders came as well, filled with wicked intention against Susanna to have her executed. [29] Then in the presence of the people they said, "Send for Susanna, daughter of Hilkiah, who is Joakim's wife." So they sent for her, [30] and she arrived with her parents, her children, and all her relatives.

[31] Now Susanna was most refined and beautiful to behold. [32] And the lawless men ordered that she be unveiled (since she arrived veiled), in order to feast their eyes on her beauty. [33] So her companions and all those who saw her started crying.

[34] Then, standing in the midst of the people, the two elders laid their hands upon her head. [35] As she wept, Susanna looked up to heaven because her heart trusted the Lord. [36] The elders said, "As we were strolling alone in the garden, this woman entered with two servant girls, closed the garden doors, and dismissed the maids. [37] Then a young man, who was hiding there, came to her lay down with her. [38] We were in a corner of the garden, and when we saw this outrage, we ran toward them. [39] Although we witnessed them having sexual intercourse, we could not overpower the man because he was stronger than us, and so he opened the doors and escaped. [40] However, we managed to seize this woman, and asked who the young man was [41] —but she would not tell us. We testify to these things."

And the assembly believed them because they were elders of the people, as well as judges. So they condemned her to death. [42] Then Susanna cried out in a loud voice and said, "Eternal God! You are the one who knows secret things, and who is aware of all things before they happen. [43] You know that these men have

---

a. Literally, "raced after," "overwhelmed," or "overran."
b. Verses 20–21 are not in the OG (thus also NETS).
c. Verses 24–27 are not in the OG (thus also NETS).

testified falsely against me. And now I am about to die, even though I have done none of the things they have maliciously charged against me!"[a]

[44] And the Lord heard her cry.[b] [45] Then just as she was being led out to execution, God aroused the holy spirit of a young man whose name was Daniel, [46] and he shouted in a loud voice, "I want no responsibility for shedding this woman's blood!"[c]

Susanna Is Rescued by Daniel

[47] But all the people turned to him and said, "What is this that you are saying?" [48] Then he took his stand in their midst and replied, "How can you be such fools, you Israelites, that with no investigation and without establishing the facts you can condemn a daughter of Israel? [49] Go back to court, for these men have testified falsely against her!"[d]

[50] So all the people hurried back, and the other elders said to him, "Come, sit here among us and advise us since God has granted to you status of an elder."[e] [51] And Daniel said to them, "Separate them a good distance from one another, and I will question them."

[52] So they were separated from each other. Daniel summoned one of them and said to him, "You old fossil from wicked days, your sins have now caught up with you, which you committed in the past, [53] pronouncing unjust verdicts, condemning the innocent and acquitting the guilty, even though the Lord says, 'You will not put an innocent and the upright person to death.'[f] [54] Now then, if you really saw this woman, tell me this: Under what kind of tree did you witness them being intimate with one another?" And he replied, "Under a mastic tree." [55] Then Daniel said, "Truly you have lied at the expense of your own head! For the angel of God has received the sentence from God to cut you in two."

[56] Then Daniel had him removed and gave instructions to bring in the other, and said to him, "You offspring of Canaan and not of Judah! Beauty has beguiled you and lust has perverted your mind! [57] This is how you have been treating the daughters of Israel—and they were only intimate with you out of fear. But a daughter of Judah would not tolerate your wickedness! [58] Now then, tell me: Under what kind of tree did you catch them being intimate with one another?" And he replied, "Under an oak tree." [59] Then Daniel said, "Truly you have lied at the expense of your own head! For the angel of God is waiting with his sword in hand to split you in two, so as to completely destroy you both!"

[60] Then the whole assembly shouted in a great voice and blessed God, who saves those who hope in him. [61] And they took action against the two elders since

---

a. Verses 42–43 are not in the OG (thus also NETS).
b. Verse 44 is not in the OG (thus also NETS).
c. Verses 46–47 are not in the OG (thus also NETS).
d. Verse 49 is not in OG (thus also NETS).
e. Verse 50 is not in OG (thus also NETS).
f. Cf. Exod. 23:7; Ps. 94:20–21.

Daniel had convicted them from their own mouths of false testimony. And they did to them just as they had wickedly planned to do to their neighbor: [62] acting in accordance with the Law of Moses, they executed them. And so innocent blood was spared that day.

[63] Hilkiah and his wife praised God on account of their daughter Susanna, and so did her husband Joakim and all their relatives, for no shameful deed was discovered in her. [64] And Daniel had a great reputation among the people from that day on.

Introduction to Bel and the Dragon

Narrative Description

Bel and the Dragon forms the final chapter (chap. 14) of the Greek version of Daniel. It comprises two tales, the first in verses 1–22 and the second in verses 23–52, which may have once circulated independently. The main character is Daniel, who courts fate by questioning the divinity of two revered objects of worship in Babylon.

In the first tale, Daniel openly doubts—thereby mocking King Cyrus (v. 7)—that the idol Bel is in fact a living god that eats and drinks (vv. 5–7). The priests of Bel devise a test to prove that the enormous offerings of food and wine given to the "god" on a daily basis are actually consumed by him (vv. 10–12). Instead, through clever detective work (v. 14), Daniel reveals that the priests are actually stealing the provisions offered to Bel, and eating and drinking the food and wine with their families (vv. 15, 19–21). What is perhaps most interesting about this tale is its close connection to the documented practices of temple priests in the ancient world, who would engage in similar tactics in order to deceive worshipers (see, e.g., Aristophanes, *Plautus* 3.2).

In the second story, Daniel challenges the legitimate divinity of a fearsome creature that is worshiped by the Babylonians, a "dragon" or snake (Greek: *drakōn*, used in other writings of many fearsome animals, including snakes, sea creatures, and even wolves).[1] Daniel secures the king's permission to try to kill the dragon and, when he succeeds, the Babylonians are enraged (vv. 25–28). Fearing that the people will turn on him for the perception that he has "become a Jew" (vv. 28–30), King Cyrus seeks to placate the mob, and has Daniel thrown into a pit full of hungry lions (vv. 31–32). Daniel remains there unharmed for six days. Meanwhile, back in Jerusalem, the biblical prophet Habakkuk is commanded by the angel of the Lord to bring food to Daniel in Babylon (vv. 33–34). Habakkuk is transported by the angel to where Daniel is, and Daniel is nourished and revived as a result of his prayers (vv. 36–39). After seven days, Cyrus returns to the pit to mourn for Daniel (v. 40); when he happily discovers that

---

1. *See* Moore, *Daniel, Esther, and Jeremiah*, pp. 141–42.

God has saved him, he has those who sought Daniel harm thrown into the pit in Daniel's place (vv. 41–42).

Author/Provenance

Bel and the Dragon is not found in Hebrew and Aramaic, and there is no evidence that it was regarded as Scripture by any group within Judaism, with the apparent exception of **Hellenistic** Jews. It became part of Christian collections in the Greek Septuagint and in the Syriac Old Testament, which remain authoritative in the Eastern Orthodox Church.

These tales are addressed to Jewish communities living in the Diaspora, in cultures in which the worship of many different idols was commonplace, encouraging them to remain faithful to their Jewish heritage and obedient to God who would deliver them.

Date/Occasion

Bel and the Dragon bears many similarities to the rest of the court tales in the book of Daniel, but with some distinct differences. Most notably, the court settings in both of these stories have been deemphasized; Daniel's adversaries are Babylonian priests and the local crowds, as opposed to the sages and court officials. In addition, the **mantic**, otherworldly elements—with the exception of the Habakkuk tradition in verses 34–39—have been replaced with the more practical wisdom characteristic of the very ancient Words of Ahiqar (*see* The Book of Tobit).

The portrayal of religion and culture in the two stories suggests that they were composed during a period of foreign occupation. The sympathetic portrayal of the foreign king and the identification of Daniel as a priest in verse 1 suggest that it was composed before the Antiochene period (i.e., prior to the mid-second century BCE, after which many Jews opposed foreign kings and priestly rulers).[2]

The principal message behind Bel and the Dragon is a polemic against idolatry. This was a popular topic of concern throughout early Jewish literature, particularly for those communities living outside Palestine and amid cultures in which the worship of many different idols was normative (cf., e.g., the Letter of Jeremiah and Wis. 13:10–15:17; *see* Wisdom of Solomon). While the two stories once circulated independently, they appear to have been integrated together at a fairly early point in time, and the whole reads quite seamlessly as a unity with a consistent theme.[3]

The added, surprise elements in the second story are the divine intervention by the angel of the Lord and the aid of the biblical prophet Habakkuk; these indicate a well-developed angelology that was characteristic of mantic wisdom traditions. Finally, the peculiar element of Cyrus's alleged conversion in verse 28, coupled

---

2. Collins, *Daniel*, p. 418; Knibb, "Book of Daniel in Its Context," pp. 30–31.
3. Collins, *Daniel*, p. 409; Nickelsburg, *Jewish Literature*, pp. 26–27.

with the Babylonians' reaction, seems to indicate a climate of strong religious oppression. It may well have been included to help galvanize the collecting Jewish communities into having a stronger sense of solidarity with a well-developed "us" versus "them" group dynamic.

Text, Language, Sources, and Transmission

Both stories were almost certainly originally written in Hebrew or Aramaic, and were translated independently into Greek prior to their union.

Bel and the Dragon has survived only in Greek (in two versions: the Septuagint and Theodotion's recension). It is interesting to note a great deal of inconsistency between the versions for both stories. Whereas the story of Bel reads more seamlessly in Theodotion, the story of the dragon is much more effective from a literary point of view in the Old Greek of the Septuagint. These sharp differences testify to the independent origins of both stories as well as to the presence of distinct Semitic **Vorlagen** (i.e., parent texts) for each.

As with the other two Greek Additions, the translation of Bel and the Dragon below is based on Theodotion. Since the alternative readings in the Old Greek are extensive and complex, very few are included in the footnotes. The Old Greek (Septuagint) translation may be found in NETS.

It is difficult to locate the precise origins for either story, in large part owing to their historical inconsistencies and errors in their presentation of Babylonian and Egyptian religion.[4] Perhaps the most interesting feature of the second tale is its close literary and thematic relationship to the story of the lions' den in Daniel 6. It was previously assumed that the story of the dragon was secondary, and dependent on its counterpart in Daniel 6. More recently, however, some have recognized its survival in independent, parallel traditions that are represented separately in Daniel 6 and in Bel and the Dragon.[5]

Theology

Both stories are thematically connected via the point made by King Cyrus to Daniel: "You cannot deny that this is a living god" (v. 24; cf. v. 6). The purpose of both stories is to illustrate vividly the folly of foreign religion while amplifying the reality of the true God of Israel, who reveals to Daniel the truth about the Bel cult and miraculously rescues his faithful servant from harm.[6] In quite similar fashion to the other tales in scriptural Daniel 1–6, the supremacy of the Jewish God and the foolishness of idolatry are prominent features that drive both stories in Bel and the Dragon. Of further theological interest is the naturalistic worldview that comes through in Daniel's criticism and response to the idolatrous cults of Baby-

---

4. Knibb, "Book of Daniel in Its Context," pp. 29–30.

5. Compare Nickelsburg, *Jewish Literature*, pp. 27–28, with Collins, *Daniel*, pp. 263–64.

6. Daniel J. Harrington, *Invitation to the Apocrypha* (Grand Rapids: Eerdmans, 1999), p. 119; Nickelsburg, *Jewish Literature*, p. 27.

lon. His dependence on his own wits, in the first story to uncover the duplicitous activity of the priest of Bel and in the story of the dragon to kill the indomitable beast, is somewhat in contrast with the other tales in scriptural Daniel, where the hero regularly requests and receives divine intervention. However, this is balanced by the recognition in the story of the dragon that God is the source of strength and salvation; in the episode featuring Habakkuk, Daniel is the beneficiary of God's foresight and intervention.

Scholars have long recognized in Bel and the Dragon a close relationship to Isaiah 45–46, most notably in:

- Yahweh's address in 45:1 to Cyrus, the prediction that he will come to know him (45:3)
- the declarations of Yahweh's supremacy and his distinction as Creator (45:1–6, 18)
- the polemics against idolatry that dominate chapter 46[7]

Some have argued for a **midrashic** dependence of the stories on the prophecies of Jeremiah 51:34–35, 41.[8] Analogous stories to these tales appear elsewhere in Second Temple Jewish literature, most notably in a contemporary text, Jubilees 12 (*see* The Book of Jubilees) and in Josephus's *Against Apion* 1.22.201–4 (see *Apion*).

Among all the Additions, Bel and the Dragon perhaps carried the least significance in the mid- to late Second Temple period and beyond. While there are a few citations in the church fathers (e.g., Irenaeus, *Adversus haereses* 4.5.2; 4.26.3; Clement, *Stromata* 1.21; Tertullian, *De idololatria* 18), this text appears to have had limited popularity and appeal. This is most likely owing to its strong, and rather singular, theme of polemicizing against idolatry. This was probably not an ongoing concern for the church or for rabbinic Judaism after the destruction of the temple.

PETER W. FLINT AND C. J. PATRICK DAVIS

---

7. Nickelsburg, *Jewish Literature*, p. 27; Collins, *Daniel*, p. 218; Knibb, "Book of Daniel in Its Context," p. 31.

8. Moore, *Daniel, Esther, and Jeremiah*, pp. 122–23; Collins, *Daniel*, p. 218.

1.4 Bel and the Dragon

Daniel Confronts the Priests of Bel

[1]Now King Astyages was laid to rest with his ancestors, and Cyrus the Persian succeeded to his kingdom. [2]Daniel was a companion of the king, and was respected above all of his friends.

[3]The Babylonians had an idol named Bel, and every day they would spend on it twelve bushels of fine flour, forty sheep, and six measures of wine.[a] [4]And the king would worship it, and went every day to bow down to it. But Daniel would worship his God. Then the king said to him, "Why do you not bow down to Bel?" [5]He replied, "Because I do not worship idols made by human hands, but the living God who created heaven and earth and holds sovereignty over all living things."

[6]So the king said to him, "Does Bel not seem to you a living god? Do you not see how much he eats and drinks every day!" [7]But Daniel smiled and said, "Do not be taken in, O king, for this is merely clay inside and bronze outside, and it has never eaten or drunk anything."

[8]Then the king was infuriated. He summoned Bel's priests and said to them, "If you do not tell me who it is that devours these provisions, you will die. [9]But if you can prove that Bel devours *them*, then Daniel will die since he has spoken blasphemy against Bel!" And Daniel said to the king, "Let it be according to your pronouncement!"

[10]Now there were seventy priests of Bel, excluding their wives and children.[10]So the king went with Daniel into the temple[b] of Bel. [11]And the priests of Bel said, "Look, we are going outside. You, O king, personally lay out the food and mix the wine, then close the door and seal it with your signet ring. [12]When you return in the morning, if you do not find that everything has been eaten by Bel, we will die—otherwise, Daniel will, who is lying about us." [13](But they were unconcerned, for they had made underneath the table a concealed entrance through which they would regularly enter and consume the provisions.)[c]

[13]Then, after they went outside, the king laid out the food for Bel. [14]Daniel ordered his servants to bring ashes, and they spread these throughout the whole temple in the presence of the king alone. Then they went out, shut the door, and sealed it with the king's signet ring. And they left. [15]Now during the night the priests came, as they usually did, with their wives and children and devoured and drank everything.

a. About 246 liters.
b. Literally, "house."
c. Verse 13 is not in OG (thus also NETS).

Translation by Peter W. Flint, from Daniel 14 in Theodotion's Greek edition. Numerous alternative readings, many of them extensive or complex, are to be found the Old Greek (OG), but are generally not included in the footnotes.

[16] So early in the morning the king arose, along with Daniel, [17] and the king asked, "Are the seals intact, Daniel?" He replied, "They are intact, O king." [18] As soon as the doors were opened, the king looked at the table and shouted in a loud voice, "Bel! You are mighty! And there is no deceit in you; none whatever."

[19] But Daniel laughed and held on to the king to stop him from going inside. "Now look at the floor," he said, "and notice whom these footprints belong to!" [20] And the king replied, "I can see the footprints of men, women, and children."

[21] Then the king was angry, and arrested the priests and their wives and children. They showed him the hidden doors through which they would enter and *consume* what was on the table. [22] So the king put them to death, and handed Bel over to Daniel, who destroyed it as well as its temple.

Daniel Slays the Dragon

[23] Now in that place there was a great dragon, and the Babylonians worshiped it. [24] And the king said to Daniel, "Can you really claim that this is not a living god? So then, worship him!" [25] But Daniel replied, "I bow down only before the Lord my God, because he is the living God. [26] But grant me permission, O king, and I will kill the dragon without using a sword or club." The king responded, "I give you permission."

[27] So Daniel took resin, fat, and hair, and boiled them together and made cakes. Then he forced these into the dragon's mouth—and the dragon ate them and burst open! Then Daniel said to the king, "See what you have been worshiping!"[a]

[28] Now when the Babylonians learned about what happened they were very upset, and assembled against the king, saying, "The king has become a Jew! He has torn down Bel, killed the dragon, and slaughtered the priests!" [29] Then they came to the king, and said, "Surrender Daniel to us, otherwise we will kill you and your family!"[b] [30] Now the king saw that they were pressuring him; feeling compelled, he handed Daniel over to them.

Daniel in the Lions' Den

[31] Then they threw him into the lions' den, and he was there for six days. [32] There were seven lions in the den, and every day they had been fed[c] two human bodies[d] and two sheep. But now nothing was given to them, so that they would devour Daniel.

[33] Now the prophet Habakkuk[e] was in Judea. He had cooked a stew and had broken bread into a bowl, and was going into the fields to take it to the reapers.

a. Literally, "the objects of your worship."
b. Verse 29 is not in OG (thus also NETS).
c. Literally, "had been given to them."
d. These could be either corpses or living.
e. Greek "Hambakoum."

³⁴But an angel of the Lord said to Habakkuk, "Take the meal that you have to Babylon, to Daniel in the lions' den." ³⁵Habakkuk replied, "Sir,ᵃ I have not seen Babylon, and I know nothing about this den." ³⁶So the angel of the Lord took hold of the crown of his head, and carried him by his hair; with a great blast of his breathᵇ he set him down in Babylon, right over the den.

³⁷Then Habakkuk called out, saying, "Daniel! Daniel! Take the lunch that God has sent for you." ³⁸Daniel said, "Indeed, you have remembered me, O God! And you have not deserted those who love you." ³⁹So Daniel got up and ate. Then the angel of God immediately returned Habakkuk to his own place.

⁴⁰On the seventh day, the king came to grieve for Daniel. When he arrived at the den, he looked in—and there sat Daniel! ⁴¹The king shouted in a loud voice, "You are mighty, O Lord, the God of Daniel! There is no other except you!" ⁴²Then he pulled Danielᶜ out, but those who had plotted his ruin he hurled into the den, and they were immediately devoured in front of him.

a. Or, "Lord." The OG adds "God."
b. Alternatively, "by the power of his spirit," or "with the speed of his wind."
c. Literally, "him."

Introduction to the Prayer of Nabonidus

Narrative Description

Four Aramaic manuscripts, containing three compositions, among the Qumran scrolls have been classified as "Danielic"—that is, closely related to the text, themes, or narrative in the book of Daniel.

Although only a few fragments of the Prayer of Nabonidus remain, sufficient text survives to identify a personal prayer by Nabonidus, the last king of the Neo-Babylonian Empire who ruled from 556 to 539 BCE. The prayer is a confession of thankfulness to God for delivery from an illness or some sort of affliction through the aid of a Jewish "exorcist." Little survives of the final fragment (frag. 4), but it seems to affirm King Nabonidus's healing: "I became well. . . . The peace of [my] re[pose returned to me]."

Author/Provenance

The Prayer of Nabonidus is the earliest of the three Qumran texts of interest. While we have no clear indication of authorship, this text was most likely written in the Jewish Diaspora as a sort of apologetic for Judaism amid the religious plurality of the **Hellenistic** world. There is no evidence that it was composed by the Essenes, or *yaḥad* movement.

Date/Occasion

The Prayer of Nabonidus is connected to the tales in Daniel 1–6, and bears a parallel resemblance to the story of Nebuchadnezzar's madness in Daniel 4. For the final ten years of his reign, Nabonidus took leave of his position in Babylon and resided in Teima in Arabia. During this time, his son Belshazzar ruled as "coregent" in Babylon; he is the subject of one of the Daniel stories in Daniel 5.[1]

---

1. Cf. Ronald H. Sack, "Nabonidus (Person)," in *ABD*, 4:973–76.

While Nabonidus is not mentioned in the canonical book of Daniel, it was long presumed by scholars that the account in Daniel 4 was based on previously discovered Babylonian accounts of Nabonidus's self-imposed exile.[2]

When it was first published in 1956, the Prayer's preserved title in Aramaic, "The words of the prayer that Nabonidus, king of Babylon uttered," offered a more definitive link between the Babylonian record of Nabonidus and the story in Daniel 4. The text is particularly interesting because the Jewish "exorcist" in line 4, who may of course be compared to Daniel, is anonymous. Because of the Prayer's relationship to older Babylonian accounts and its lack of any mention of Daniel, most scholars date it before the final compilation of Daniel (165 BCE), and to the third century at least.

The Prayer of Nabonidus and its parallel tradition in Daniel 4 are almost certainly Judaized recensions of older Babylonian traditions, which are preserved in the Harran Inscription and in the Verse Account of Nabonidus. The adoption of this tradition into Jewish literature served to promote religious solidarity through the popular use of fabricated conversion tales. It has also been speculated that the appearance of the Prayer among the Qumran scrolls may be related to an interest among the Essenes (and their community at Qumran) in healing.[3]

Text, Language, Sources, and Transmission

Since this composition is introduced as the "words of the prayer," a large part must have been a prayer, which is no longer preserved. One helpful comparison is to the biblical prayer of Manasseh, made by an Israelite king while he was in distress: "God received his entreaty, heard his plea, and restored him again to Jerusalem and to his kingdom. Then Manasseh knew that the Lord indeed was God" (2 Chron. 33:12–13).[4] Second Chronicles also states that Manasseh's prayer may be found in the "Annals of the Kings of Israel" and in the "records of the seers" (11:18–19), which are now lost. However, a much later apocryphal prayer of Manasseh is found in the Septuagint and Vulgate.

The framework of an individual's psalm of praise, recounting affliction and deliverance and offering praise of the true God, is also found in Jonah 2. A broader

2. Dan. 4:25: "You will be driven away from human society, and your dwelling will be with the wild animals. You will be made to eat grass like oxen, you will be bathed with the dew of heaven, and seven times will pass over you, until you have learned that the Most High has sovereignty over the kingdom of mortals, and gives it to whom he will."

3. Peter W. Flint, "Daniel in the Dead Sea Scrolls," in *The Book of Daniel*, ed. John J. Collins and Peter W. Flint (Leiden: Brill, 2001), 2:335; cf. John J. Collins, "242. 4QPrayer of Nabonidus ar," in *Qumran Cave 4, Parabiblical Texts, Part 3*, ed. James VanderKam, DJD 22 (Oxford: Clarendon, 1996), p. 87; Geza Vermes, "Essenes and Therapeutai," *Revue de Qumrân* 3 (1962): 495–504.

4. 2 Chron. 33:12–13: "Therefore the Lord brought against them the commanders of the army of the king of Assyria, who took Manasseh captive in manacles, bound him with fetters, and brought him to Babylon. While he was in distress he entreated the favor of the Lord his God and humbled himself greatly before the God of his ancestors. He prayed to him, and God received his entreaty, heard his plea, and restored him again to Jerusalem and to his kingdom. Then Manasseh knew that the Lord indeed was God."

comparison of the Prayer of Nabonidus with the book of Job may also be made: in both cases, a stricken individual is restored by God and learns something in the process. Yet the Prayer and Daniel 4 extend beyond the simple wisdom tale by commonly featuring interest in the conversion of the Gentile king, thus lending to the story a propagandistic quality.

All three Qumran Additions to Daniel were written in, and have survived in, Aramaic. This further indicates the existence of a more extensive collection of Aramaic Daniel tales that circulated separately from the Hebrew portions of the book of Daniel. Some of these were included in the book (2:4–6:29), others were found at Qumran (the Prayer of Nabonidus, Pseudo-Daniel A and B), and possibly yet others are now lost.

Theology

Despite its poor preservation, the Prayer of Nabonidus contains themes pertaining to idolatry and the supremacy of the Jewish God in the exiled communities. It is noteworthy that amid this text's similarities to the story of Nebuchadnezzar's madness in Daniel 4, both Nebuchadnezzar and Daniel are absent from the Qumran text.

In their place is the later king Nabonidus, and instead of Daniel an otherwise unidentified Jewish exorcist (frag. 1, line 4). Most significantly, the Prayer of Nabonidus affirms the existence of this "mad king" tradition—and others like it—well prior to the mid-second century BCE when canonical Daniel was put together.

PETER W. FLINT AND C. J. PATRICK DAVIS

1.5 The Prayer of Nabonidus (4Q242)

Fragments 1, 2a–b, 3

[1]The words of the pr[ay]er that Nabonidus king of [Baby]lon, the[great] kin[g] uttered [when he was afflicted] [2]with a malignant disease at the command of G[o]d, in Teima, "[I, Nabonidus], was afflicted [with a malignant disease] [3]lasting seven years. *Then be[cause] G[od] set [his face on me, he healed me]*,[a] [4]and as for my sin, he forgave it. An exorcist—who was a Jew fr[om the community of the exiles—came to me, and said]: [5]'Make a proclamation and write it down in order to ascribe honor and gre[atn]ess to the name of [the Most High] G[od!' And so, I have written as follows]:

[6]I was afflicted with a ma[lignant] disease, [and remained] in Teima [at the command of the Most High God]. [7]For seven years [I] kept praying [*before*][b] the gods made of silver and gold, [bronze, iron], [8]wood, stone, and clay, because [I thou]ght that th[ey] were gods.

Fragment 4

[1]] without them *I became well.*[c] [2][. . .] for it he exch[an]ged. The peace of [my] re[pose returned to me . . .[3]. . .] my friends. I was not able [[4]. . .] how much you are like [. . .]

---

a. Alternative reconstructions have been proposed: "becoming like a beast, I prayed to the Most High" (Michael O. Wise, Martin G. Abegg, and Edward M. Cook, *The Dead Sea Scrolls: A New Translation*, rev. ed.[San Francisco: HarperSanFrancisco, 2005], p. 342); or "and was banished far [from men, until I prayed to the God Most High]" (Florentino Garcia Martinez, *The Dead Sea Scrolls Translated: The Qumran Texts in English*, 2nd ed. [Grand Rapids: Eerdmans, 1996], p. 289).

b. Or, "to all."

c. Or possibly, "I had a dream."

Translation by Peter W. Flint.

Introduction to Pseudo-Daniel A and B

Narrative Description

The three other Danielic manuscripts from Qumran contain fragments of two distinct compositions, each featuring the scriptural Daniel. In Pseudo-Daniel A (4Q243–4Q244, which overlap), Daniel appears in an imperial court setting before the Babylonian king Belshazzar, and at his behest reads from a book connected to Enoch (*see* Introduction to 1 Enoch). The reconstructed text reveals a recounting of the biblical narrative, beginning with the flood (4Q243, frag. 8, lines 2–3), continuing through the exodus (4Q243, frag. 12, lines 1–3) and the monarchic period past the Babylonian conquest of Jerusalem (4Q243, frag. 13 + 4Q244, frag. 12), and ending in a predictive prophecy of the future in the **Hellenistic** period. Pseudo-Daniel B (4Q245) contains a list of priests and kings from Israel that appears to have been written or copied by Daniel (frag. 1 i, lines 3–4).

Author/Provenance

The two Pseudo-Daniel compositions were composed either within the Qumran sectarian community, or by a group from the **Essenes,** or *yaḥad* movement, of whom the Qumran covenanters are the best-known group.

Pseudo-Daniel A (4Q243–4Q244) is particularly interesting since it bears generic similarities to other compositions that appear to have been very popular among the Qumran covenanters. Daniel was clearly a figure of considerable interest to them; as mentioned at the beginning of this chapter, ten biblical Daniel scrolls were discovered at Qumran, exceeding the totals for most other books of the Hebrew Bible (except for the Psalms, Isaiah, and the books of the Pentateuch).

The Qumran scrolls include many other texts that feature heptadic traditions, which closely approximate the apocalyptic discourse in Daniel 9.[1] Examples in-

---

1. Some texts present history or the future in "heptads" or sevenfold "years" or periods, usually culminating with the end of days. The best-known example is in Dan. 9:24–27.

clude the book of Jubilees, the Damascus Document 1:5–6, 4QAges of Creation A and B (4Q180–4Q181), the Apocalypse of Weeks (4Q247), the Calendar of Celestial Signs (4Q319), 4QCalendrical Document A (4Q320), the Apocryphon of Jeremiah C (4Q385a, 4Q387, 4Q388a, 4Q389, 4Q390, 4Q387a), and Melchizedek (11Q13), as well as the reference to Daniel 12:10 in the Florilegium (4Q174), 1–3 ii, lines 3–4. The heptadic perspective is closely connected to an apocalyptic worldview that appears to be characteristic of the *yaḥad* movement. A highly schematized biblical chronology, the correct accounting of biblical history, and predictive prophecy situate the larger Pseudo-Daniel text quite firmly within this tradition.

Date/Occasion

Pseudo-Daniel A (4Q243–4Q244) is difficult to date because of its fragmentary nature and the uncertainty of some personal names in the text. It is reasonably situated no earlier than the second century BCE, and dated no later than the arrival of **Pompey** in Jerusalem (ca. 60 BCE).[2] The list of priests and kings in Pseudo-Daniel B (4Q245) was most likely a piece of propaganda against the conjoining of the offices of the high priest and the king in Judah. Because it mentions **Simon,** who ruled as high priest in Jerusalem between 142 and 135 BCE, the most likely location of this text is during the reign of his successor, **Jonathan Hyrcanus I** (ca. 135–104 BCE), or of **Alexander Jannaeus** (103–76 BCE).[3]

Pseudo-Daniel A is similar to other apocalyptic works from the same period (*see* Introduction to Apocalyptic Literature), most notably 1 Enoch, Jubilees, the Damascus Document, and the Apocryphon of Jeremiah C (see below). These works commonly seek to legitimate a particular, theologized view of biblical history culminating in the emergence of an elite group from within fragmented Jewish religion in the second to first centuries BCE. As for the list of priests and kings in Pseudo-Daniel B, the naming of some priests and the fact that the priests and kings are presented separately are significant. This points to the list as a product of intra-priestly polemics that characterized the period, which likely served to validate the line of priests extending back to Abiathar, and to campaign for continued distinction between priesthood and crown in the independent state of Judah.

Text, Language, Sources, and Transmission

As mentioned with respect to the Prayer of Nabonidus above, the Aramaic Additions from Qumran—including Pseudo-Daniel A—were written in, and have

2. John J. Collins and Peter W. Flint, "243–245. 4QPseudo-Daniel ar," in *Qumran Cave 4, XVII: Parabiblical Texts, Part 3*, ed. James VanderKam (Oxford: Clarendon, 1996), pp. 137–38.

3. Collins and Flint, "243–245. 4QPseudo-Daniel ar," p. 158; cf. Michael O. Wise, "4Q245 (4QpsDan^c ar) and the High Priesthood of Judas Maccabaeus," *Dead Sea Discoveries* 12, no. 3 (2005): 359–61. *See* p. 26 for a chart of the Hasmonean rulers.

survived in, Aramaic. Thus a more extensive collection of Aramaic Daniel tales circulated separately from the Hebrew portions of the book of Daniel.

Theology

The smaller Pseudo-Daniel B (4Q245) features a list of priests and kings from Israel. It quite closely follows the listing of Zadokite priests in 1 Chronicles 5:27–41, but with the significant placement of Zadok and Abiathar together (col. i, line 7). With extensive reconstruction, the full text may well have totaled thirty-five priests (the number mentioned in frag. 3). Pseudo-Daniel B was composed in part as propaganda against those who saw fit to conjoin the throne of David with the Jerusalem temple priesthood. In keeping with the heptadic chronology of Daniel 9, the list seems to function as a polemic against the high priesthood and rule of Jonathan Hyrcanus I or Alexander Jannaeus, and as a calculated prediction of the onset of the end of days that would occur in his reign.[4]

PETER W. FLINT AND C. J. PATRICK DAVIS

---

4. Cf. Collins and Flint, "243–245. 4QPseudo-Daniel ar," p. 158; Wise, "4Q245 (4QpsDan^c ar) and the High Priesthood," pp. 359–61.

1.6 Pseudo-Daniel A (4Q243–4Q244)

Court Setting

1	. . . Daniel before . . .	(243, frag. 2)
2	. . . Belshazzar . . .	
3	. . . before the nobles of the king and the Assyrians (?) . . . of the king . . .	(244, frags. 1–3)
4	. . . He appointed . . .	
5	. . . and how . . .	
6	. . . O king, (or: the king) . . .	
7	. . . before . . .	(244, frag. 4)
8	. . . Daniel said . . .	
9	He asked Daniel saying "On account of [what] . . .	(243, frag. 1)
10	your God, and the number . . .	
11	he prayed . . .	
12	. . . there is . . .	(243, frag. 3)
13	. . . O King (or: the king). . .	
14	. . . Daniel . . .	(243, frag. 5)
15	. . . and in it was written . . .	(243, frag. 6)
16	. . . Daniel, who . . .	
17	. . . was found written . . .	

Primeval History

18	. . . Enoch . . .	(243, frag. 9)
19	. . . after the flood . . .	(244, frag. 8)
20	. . . Noah from (Mount) Lubar	
21	. . . a city . . .	
22	. . . a tower, its height . . .	(244, frag. 9)
23	. . . on the tower, and he sent (?) . . .	(243, frag. 10)
24	. . . to inspect the building . . .	
25	. . . and he scattered them . . .	(244, frag. 13)

From the Patriarchs to the Exile

26	. . . his reward . . .	(243, frag. 35)
27	. . . the land . . .	

Translation by Peter W. Flint. Arranged according to the transcription by John J. Collins and Peter W. Flint, "243–245. 4QPseudo-Daniel ar," in *Qumran Cave 4, XVII: Parabiblical Texts, Part 3*, DJD 22 (Oxford: Clarendon, 1996), pp. 133–51.

28	. . . Egypt, by the hand . . .	(243, frag. 11 col. ii)
29	. . . ruler in the land . . .	
30	. . . fo]ur hundred [years], and from . . .	(243, frag. 12)
31	. . . their [ ] and they will come out of . . .	
32	. . . their crossing the river Jordan . . .	
33	. . . and their children . . .	
34	. . . -el and Qa[hath . . .	(243, frag. 28)
35	. . . Phineha]s, Abish[ua . . .	
36	. . . from the tabernacle . . .	(243, frag. 34)
37	The Israelites chose their presence rather than [the presence of God]	(243, f. 13 + 244., f. 2)
38	[and they were] sacrificing their children to demons of error, and their God became angry at them and said to give them	
39	into the hand of Nebuchadnezzar [king of] Babylon, and to make their land desolate of them, which . . .	
40	. . . the exiles . . .	
41	. . . After] this it will be . . .	(243, frag. 14)
42	. . . hundred kin[gs	
43	. . . them in the midst of the p[eoples]	
44	. . . the Chaldeans . . . the children of [Israel?]	(243, frag. 7)
45	. . . the way of tr[uth]	
46	. . . [from] Israel men	(243, frag. 8)
47	. . . unchangeable	

Hellenistic Era

48	. . . will rule for years	(243, frag. 21)
49	. . . Balakros	
50	. . . y]ears	(243, frag. 19)
51	. . .]rhos son . . .	
52	. . .]os . . . years	
53	. . . they will speak . . .	
54	. . . a son and his name . . .	(243, frag. 22)
55	. . . to them two . . .	
56	. . . spoke . . .	
57	. . .]s son of M[. . .	(243, frag. 20)
58	. . . twenty years . . .	
59	. . . which . . .	

Eschatological Period

60	will oppress(?) [seven]ty years	(243, frag. 16)
61	with his great hand and he will save them . . .	
62	powerful . . . and the kingdoms of the peoples	

63	This is the h[oly] kingdom.	
64	... until ...	(243, frag. 25)
65	... and the land will be filled ...	
66	... all their decayed carcasses ...	
67	... those who l]eft the wa[y of truth ...	(243, frag. 33)
68	... the sons of] wickedness have led astray	(243, frag. 24)
69	... after this the elect (of ... ?) will be gathered ...	
70	... the peoples, and it will be from the day ...	
71	... and the kings of the peoples ...	
72	... they will be d]oing to the day ...	
73	... their numbers ...	(243, frag. 26)
74	... without number ...	
75	... Israel ...	

1.7 Pseudo-Daniel B (4Q245)

Fragment 1

Col. i [1][ ]*iah*[a] [2]] and what [3][. . .] Daniel [4][. . .] a book that was given [5][. . . Lev]i, Qahat [6][. . .] Bukki, Uzzi, [7][. . . Zado]k, Abiathar [8]Hi[l]kiah, [9][. . .] and Onias [10][. . . Jona]than, Simon, [11][. . .] and David, Solomon, [12][. . .] Ahazi[ah, Joa]sh, [13]] . . . [
   Col. ii [9]which [. . .]

Fragment 2

[2][. . .] for the end of wickedness [3][. . .] these are blind, and have wandered [4][. . . th]ese then will arise [5][. . .] the [h]oly, and they will return [6][. . .] wickedness

Fragment 3

[1][. . .] thirty fiv[e

---

a. Most likely a Hebraic name.

Translation by Peter W. Flint. Arranged according to the transcription by Collins and Flint, "243–245. 4QPseudo-Daniel ar."

The Great Isaiah Scroll and the Interpretation of Isaiah at Qumran

The focus of this chapter is the Great Isaiah Scroll (1QIsaᵃ) and other Isaiah scrolls along with the interpretation of biblical Isaiah in key nonbiblical scrolls found at Qumran (*see* Overview of Early Jewish Literature). The Great Isaiah Scroll was one of the first Dead Sea Scrolls discovered in Cave 1 at Qumran in 1947. It was found wrapped in a linen cloth and stored in a sealed clay jar. The scroll measures 734 centimeters long and 28 centimeters high and consists of 17 parchments that have been sewn together into a single scroll. It is considered the best preserved of all the biblical scrolls discovered at Qumran. The fifty-four columns contain all sixty-six chapters of the Hebrew version of the biblical Isaiah. The version of the text in 1QIsaᵃ is generally in agreement with the **Masoretic Text** (**MT**—the text that forms the basis of the Hebrew Bible), but it does contain some minor differences. Most of the differences are simply grammatical (e.g., spelling certain words with an extra letter that does not alter the pronunciation). However, it contains some variant readings, alternative spellings, scribal errors, and corrections. Prior to the discovery of the scroll, the Codex Leningrad, dated at 1000 CE, was the oldest known copy of the Hebrew Bible (including the book of Isaiah) in existence.

The prophet Isaiah is frequently cited in other Qumran scrolls as is the case in the writings of the New Testament. Thus, as can be seen, the book of Isaiah played a major role in the theology of Second Temple period Judaism. Two main issues arise from this assumption: (1) how do 1QIsaᵃ and the other Isaiah scrolls from the Judean Desert affect our understanding of the book of Isaiah? And (2) how was Isaiah used and interpreted by the *yaḥad* movement at Qumran?

The remains of twenty-two copies of Isaiah, most of them very fragmentary, were discovered in the Judean Desert. Twenty-one were located at Qumran: two in Cave 1 (1QIsaᵃ⁻ᵇ), eighteen in Cave 4 (4QIsaᵃ⁻ʳ), and one in Cave 5 (5Q3). The remaining Isaiah scroll was found at Murabbaʿat (MurIsa, or Mur 3). In addition, five or six *pesharim* on the book of Isaiah were discovered at Qumran (*see* Introduction to *Pesharim*). Five *pesharim* fragments were identified from Cave 4 (4Q161–4Q165 = 4QpIsaᵃ⁻ᶜ); an additional fragment from Cave 3 (3Q4 = 3QpIsa) is thought to be a part of another *pesher* on Isaiah (possibly on Isa. 1:1–2).

1QIsaᵃ has survived virtually intact; however, other Isaiah scrolls survived with a substantial amount of content (in descending order of quantity): 1QIsaᵇ, 4QIsaᵇ, and 4QIsaᶜ. Special attention should be given to 1QIsaᵇ (also known as the Hebrew University Isaiah Scroll), which preserves the MT ranging from Isaiah 7:22 to 66:24 with the majority of the extant text from the final third of Isaiah (chaps. 38–66). The **Herodian** script dates this manuscript to the third quarter of the first century BCE, and the text is generally close in content to that found in the MT.

The Great Isaiah Scroll preserves almost the entire contents of Isaiah, although portions of several verses were lost due to damage.[1] The original scroll is in two main sections: columns 1–27 (chaps. 1–33) and columns 28–54 (chaps. 34–66), which have been joined to make a single manuscript. It has been suggested that the manuscript was copied by one scribe in a typical hand from the middle of the **Hasmonean** period (ca. 125 BCE), with small additions and corrections by at least three more scribes. However, it should be noted that Emanuel Tov contends that there are two scribal hands present in 1QIsaᵃ. The first hand wrote columns 1–27 and the second hand columns 28–54.[2] Tov supports his contention by suggesting that the second scribe used a more complete orthography, emended additional gutturals, included individual scribal markings, and omitted more portions of the Isaiah text than the first scribe excluded.[3]

Author/Provenance

The popularity of Isaiah for the *yaḥad* movement and its use in certain **sectarian** scrolls offer many insights into life at Qumran. The community that wrote and collected the Qumran scrolls was deeply concerned about matters of ritual purity, correct observance of the religious calendar, priestly themes, and the legitimacy of the temple and the priesthood. Because they were at odds with the existing establishment with respect to the calendar—favoring a 364-day solar calendar over the official lunar one—and interpreted the Torah differently on several points, they broke communion with the ruling priests and practiced their religion apart from the temple, which they viewed as corrupt.

One major area of concern for this movement was their method of interpreting Scripture, which is illustrated by texts such as the Damascus Document (4Q266–4Q273; *see* Damascus Document), the Rule of the Community, and Some of the Works of the Law. The Qumranites' interpretation of Scripture located them in a long-standing tradition that they traced back to the prophets, through Moses, and ultimately to the beginning of time. The *yaḥad* saw itself as part of the biblical world, divinely ordained heirs of the Scriptures, and in continuity with figures and events of the past that formed their own sacred history. For them, the prophetic traditions preserved in Isaiah and other texts provided special insights into their

---

1. *See* Isa. 1:21, 23–26; 2:15, 17, 19–21; 5:10–14; 7:9–12, 14–15; 8:7; 10:13–14; 14:27, 29; 45:10–14.

2. *See* Emanuel Tov, *Hebrew Bible, Greek Bible, and Qumran,* TSAJ 121 (Tübingen: Mohr Siebeck, 2008), pp. 42–56.

3. Tov, *Hebrew Bible,* p. 50.

own circumstances. Thus several Scriptures such as Isaiah, and other previously known and unknown ancient compositions, were copied and recopied, and were the subject of ongoing commentary and discussion.

Authorship and Transmission of the Text of Isaiah

Most scholars agree that the book of Isaiah in the Jewish Scriptures is a complex composite work, having been written by at least three authors over the course of several centuries. Scholars divide the book into three main sections. The writing of First Isaiah, chapters 1–35, has been dated to just before the Assyrian occupancy of Jerusalem in the eighth century BCE. It is thought that this section contained the original oracles of the eighth-century prophet Isaiah, which were first disseminated orally before becoming the first edition. This section is followed by the "historical bridge," chapters 36–39. The section following the "bridge" is identified as Second Isaiah, which is dated to the exilic period following the Babylonian destruction of Solomon's temple in 587 BCE. It has been suggested that this section consisted of a series of prophecies that can be traced to the mid-sixth century BCE, written down, and attributed to Isaiah about 500 BCE. This section includes two possible collections, chapters 40–66, or as some scholars suggest, only chapters 40–55, with chapters 56–66 constituting Third Isaiah. Unfortunately, the Isaiah scrolls found in the Judean Desert do not include any relevant material that would assist with identifying the author or the dating of the various sections of biblical Isaiah. Nevertheless, the scrolls do impart valuable insight regarding the transmission and finalization of the book of Isaiah as a whole.

Date/Occasion

Paleographic analysis dates at least eighteen Isaiah scrolls to before the Common Era. The oldest is 1QIsa^a (125–100 BCE), and seven Cave 4 manuscripts were copied in the first half of the first century BCE (e.g., 4QIsa^f). Two of the Qumran Isaiah scrolls are classified as "Herodian" (30 BCE–70 CE, most notably, 1QIsa^b), one is placed in the middle third of the first century CE (4QIsa^c), and the sole manuscript from Murabba'at was copied at the very end of the Herodian period (MurIsa, ca. 70 CE). Thus, these scrolls contain the most ancient copies of the book of Isaiah (or portions of it) discovered to date, with the Great Isaiah Scroll (1QIsa^a) the oldest of them all.

As is evident by the substantial number of copies of the book of Isaiah found in the caves, the text was important to the *yaḥad* group at Qumran. This assumption is also evidenced by the five or possibly six *pesharim* (commentaries) on Isaiah along with references or allusions to Isaiah in many sectarian scrolls. At least twenty-one sectarian compositions, found in twenty-three scrolls, refer to Isaiah. Six more works (in eight scrolls) refer or allude to Isaiah; although they may not be strictly sectarian in origin, they at least seem to reflect the distinctive ideas of the *yaḥad*. Two Psalms scrolls from Cave 11 (11QPs^a [11Q5] and

11QPs[b] [11Q6]; *see* Psalms and Psalters at Qumran; *also see* LXX Psalm 151) are included here because they contain the "Plea for Deliverance," which alludes to Isaiah 38:19.

SECTARIAN COMPOSITIONS FOUND AT QUMRAN

Damascus Document (CD, 4QD[a]/4Q266, 4QD[b]/4Q267, 6QD/6Q15)
Rule of the Community (1QS)
Rule of the Blessings (1QSb/ 1Q28[b])
Habakkuk Pesher (1QpHab)
Hodayot (1QH[a])
War Scroll (1QM)
Isaiah Pesharim (3QpIsa/3Q4, 4QpIsa[a]/4Q161, 4QpIsa[b]/4Q162, 4QpIsa[c]/4Q163,
    4QpIsa[d]/4Q164, 4QpIsa[e]/4Q165)
Florilegium (4QFlor/4Q174)
Miscellaneous Rules (4Q265)
Sefer ha-Milḥamah (4Q285)
War Scroll-Like Text B (4Q471)
Self-Glorification Hymn (4Q471b)
Festival Prayers[c] (papPrFêtes[c]/4Q50)
Songs of the Sage[b] (4QShir[b]/4Q511)
Melchizedek (11QMelch/11Q13)

OTHER COMPOSITIONS THAT REFLECT THE *YAḤAD*'S IDEAS

Sapiential Work (4Q185)
Tanhumim (4Q176)
Catena (4Q177)
Barki Nafshi[a] (4Q434)
Barki Nafshi[d] (4Q437)
Messianic Apocalypse (4Q521)
Psalms Scrolls (11QPs[a]/11Q5, 11QPs[b]/11Q6)

Among these twenty-seven compositions, there are more than one hundred references or allusions to Isaiah or passages from the biblical text. At least ninety are clear references, whether in quotations using various formulas, representations of **pericopes**, or allusions to themes from Isaiah.

Several Qumran compositions refer to Isaiah in multiple ways, which combine to affirm its authoritative status for the author(s). For example, in the Damascus Document, Isaiah is cited in a direct quotation (CD 7:11–12 [Isa. 7:17]), in a more general reference (CD 14:1 [cf. Isa. 7:17]), and in a variety of allusions with no indication of a reference (CD 1:20 [cf. Isa. 24:5]; and 5:13–14 [cf. Isa. 50:11; 59:5]). In such cases, one should not assume that one method of referring to Isaiah reflects a higher level of authority than another; all may be considered reflective of the high status accorded to this book.

The citations of, and allusions to, Isaiah in the sectarian scrolls confirm its importance for the Qumran covenanters. This importance applies to virtually every part of scriptural Isaiah. Moreover, these references are found in texts through every period in the sectarians' history, which attests to the popularity and ongoing significance of Isaiah for the *yaḥad*.

Prominent imagery presented in these sectarian texts includes separation from outsiders, exile and return, the pain of childbirth, suffering and deliverance, and garden themes. Various texts that make use of Isaiah promote insider/outsider language directing those belonging to the *yaḥad* to live separately, recognize the formation of group identity through covenant keeping as an extension of the "biblical world," and describe the eschatological expectations of the end of days and the coming Messiah.

Text, Language, Sources, and Transmission

The book of Isaiah has long been considered the foremost book among the Hebrew Prophets. It cannot be identified with one single genre because it contains a rich array of prophetic and poetic materials, amid portions of historical narrative and apocalyptic discourses.

The Great Isaiah Scroll contains the entire text of the biblical book in Hebrew. However, 1QIsaᵃ uses a form of Hebrew that some scholars presume to be later, despite the fact that it is the oldest copy of Isaiah. The scroll is noted for its very full orthography (i.e., longer spellings being used for most words), and for what Emanuel Tov calls a "free approach" in the history of the transmission of scriptural texts.

In the light of the discovery of 1QIsaᵃ and the other Isaiah scrolls from Qumran and Murabbaʿat, one might ask, "What was the extent of the 'book of Isaiah' in the

Figure 8. Shown are columns 44–46 of 1QIsaiahᵃ, the first of the Great Isaiah Scrolls, which presents the most sncient division of this book to survive. Photo © The Israel Museum, Jerusalem.

ancient period, and was it divided into main sections?" Of all twenty-two Isaiah scrolls (including the one from Murabba'at), only five (1QIsaᵃ, 1QIsaᵇ, 4QIsaᵇ, 4QIsaᶜ, 4QIsaᵉ) preserve material from the two (or three) sections (chaps. 1–39 and 40–66), which raises three possibilities. One might suggest that all twenty-two Judean manuscripts originally contained Isaiah 1–66, but most are severely damaged. A second possibility is that some of the Isaiah scrolls originally contained only excerpts from the complete book of sixty-six chapters. A third option may suggest the book of Isaiah was compiled from smaller collections, some of which comprised the totality of certain scrolls.

As already mentioned, the Great Isaiah Scroll is divided into two sections, with columns 1 to 27 containing Isaiah 1–33 (ending with three blank lines) and columns 28 to 54 containing Isaiah 34–66. This bisection raises the live option of whether Isaiah comprised two books in its early (or earliest?) form, separated at the end of chapter 33. Therefore, while the Isaiah scrolls do not confirm the contents and divisions of "First and Second Isaiah" that have become conventional for scholars, 1QIsaᵃ presents the most ancient division of this book to survive (chaps. 1–33 and 34–66) and raises the possibility that very early on it consisted of smaller collections of text.

It is widely accepted among scholars of Isaiah that in the late Second Temple period at least three versions, or "editions," of the scriptural text were in circulation,[4] each with features of one of three later Bibles: the Masoretic Text (MT), the Samaritan Pentateuch, or the Septuagint (LXX; *see* Overview of Early Jewish Literature). The origin and development of these versions have been associated with Jewish groups or schools in Babylon, Palestine, and Alexandria, respectively. Several of the Qumran Isaiah scrolls are classified by Tov as "proto-Masoretic" (e.g., 1QIsaᵇ, 4QIsaᵃ⁻ᵇ, 4QIsaᵈ⁻ᵍ), but 1QIsaᵃ appears markedly different, containing (in addition to orthographic differences) thousands of variant readings against the MT. Because of its distinctive scribal features and lack of close correlation to the forms of Isaiah in the MT or the LXX, the textual form of 1QIsaᵃ may be described as "mixed."

Eugene Ulrich has proposed a theory of successive literary editions as a model for tracing and classifying the development of the text of various biblical books. These different literary editions occurred later in the compositional process of the Scriptures, which took place in several stages that were different for each book or set of books. Each new edition resulted from the creative efforts of some author or scribe who intentionally revised the edition (or passages) current in his time in the light of a new religious outlook or national challenge.

If 1QIsaᵃ indeed preserves the most ancient division of Isaiah that survives (chaps. 1–33 and 34–66), the Isaiah scrolls may bear witness to three early editions of the book: Edition 1 (Isa. 1–33), Edition 2 (Isa. 34–66), and the combined Edition 3 (Isa. 1–66). With its two—perhaps independent—halves, and its many divergences from the MT of Isaiah, 1QIsaᵃ may well represent a literary edition of the book that is distinct from other Isaiah scrolls (such as 1QIsaᵇ) that contain the same literary edition found in the MT.

---

4. Tov, *Hebrew Bible*, pp. 51–52.

With respect to the thousands of variant readings in 1QIsa^a, most are routine or minor (e.g., the addition of "and" or "the"), and many others are no better than or inferior to the corresponding readings in the Masoretic form of Isaiah. Nevertheless, there are still hundreds of textual readings in 1QIsa^a and the other Isaiah scrolls that will have to be considered seriously for establishing the most pristine or preferred reading of the biblical text. Even if most of these are not adopted in many English Bibles by the translation committees, scores will prove compelling enough to be incorporated in major translations, or at least indicated in the footnotes. Two examples may be given, the first from Isaiah 1–33 and the second from Isaiah 34–66.

Isaiah 21:8 in 1QIsa^a reads, "Then the *lookout* shouted: 'Upon a watchtower I stand, O Lord, continually by day, and at my post I am stationed throughout the night.'" In the MT, supported by the LXX, the verse begins "Then *a lion* (Hebrew: *'ryh*) shouted," which makes no sense in the context of what follows. A different word, *lookout* (Hebrew: *hr'h*) is found in 1QIsa^a, and supported by the Syriac Bible. Most scholars will have little difficulty in accepting the Qumran reading as original and superior, and thus incorporate it in Bible translations.[5]

A second example is found in Isaiah 49:24, which in 1QIsa^a reads, "Can they seize plunder from the mighty; can the captives of a *tyrant* be rescued?" In the MT, two minor differences are evident ("Can plunder *be seized*," "*and* can . . ."), but the reading of greatest interest is near the end of the verse: "can the captives of a *righteous person* (Hebrew: *ṣdyq*) be rescued?" In 1QIsa^a, supported by the Syriac Bible, the Vulgate, and (probably) the Septuagint, the key Hebrew term is different; 1QIsa^a reads *'ryṣ (tyrant)*. Most scholars now accept the Qumran reading as superior and likely original.[6]

Theology

Several themes in the book of Isaiah were attractive to the *yaḥad* movement and the Qumran community. As a group of Jews with priestly concerns, they were drawn to themes in Isaiah pertaining to the priesthood and the temple, and to its cosmological outlook. The Qumranites found Isaiah especially valuable for the hopeful exilic language in Second Isaiah (chaps. 40–60) and its proclivity toward eschatological and messianic interpretations.

Since the foundation of the Qumran community, Isaiah 40:3 was a critical text for their self-understanding, which can be understood in 1QS, column 8:11–14. The Rule then (1QS 8:15–16) interprets this passage to show the importance of

---

5. At least fifteen English Bibles have "lookout" or a similar word: CEB, ESV, GWORD, HCSB, ISV, NAB, NASB, NET, NIV, NJB, NLT-SE, NRSV, REB, RSV, and TNIV. The five main translations retaining the Masoretic reading "lion" are KJV, NKJV, ASV, CJB, and JPS.

6. An interesting case may be made, however, for retaining *ṣdyq* with the meaning "victor" (thus JPS). At least fourteen English Bibles have "tyrant" or similar wording: CEB, ESV, GWORD, ISV, NAB, NASB, NET, NIV, NJB, NLT-SE, NRSV, REB, RSV, and TNIV. Six translations retain "righteous person" with the MT: AMP, ASV, HCSB, JPS (with "victor"), KJV, and NKJV.

the study and correct interpretation of the Torah—which the *yahad* fiercely contested with adversarial groups of priests and Jewish leaders who controlled the temple.

Reception of the Great Isaiah Scroll in the Second Temple Period

The scriptural book of Isaiah (possibly in more than one form) was in circulation and accepted as authoritative from the beginning of the Second Temple period. Its popularity and broad appeal gave rise to several traditions of Isaiah that included his martyrdom in Lives of the Prophets, in the Martyrdom of Isaiah, later in Hebrews 11:37 in which he is the anonymous prophet who was "sawn in two," and in the Babylonian and Jerusalem Talmudim. Ben Sira also wrote of Isaiah's prophetic prowess (48:22–25) as part of his lengthy hymn devoted to the memory of Israel's ancestors.

Scriptural Isaiah was also influential because of the "Little Apocalypse" in Isaiah 24–27. This tradition served as a likely prototype (together with the "Night Visions" of Zech. 9–14) for later apocalyptic literature appearing in the late third and early second centuries BCE (*see* 1 Enoch; The Book of Daniel; and Sibylline Oracles). Furthermore, as evidenced in the *pesharim* dedicated to Isaiah and its frequent citation in the New Testament, this book became fertile ground for the development of a variety of messianic movements beginning in the second century BCE.

The Qumran community's reverence for the book of Isaiah resonates with the many citations and allusions in the New Testament. The messianic interpretations that the Gospel writers and others attached to Isaiah are reminiscent of the *yahad*'s handling of the book, especially in the Servant Songs of Isaiah 42–53. While both early Christianity and the Qumranites were eschatological, and harbored deeply engrained messianic ideals, we find their perspectives on the end of days and the deliverer who would accompany them frequently at odds.

Yet there are significant points of contact between the two, several of which were founded on similar understandings of Isaianic prophecies. For example, both groups perceived the "messenger of good" (Isa. 52:7[7] and 58:6[8]) as the same powerful, celestial messianic figure from Isaiah 61:2–3[9] (cf. 4Q521 frag. 2ii + 4.1–14[10]

7. Isa. 52:7: "How lovely on the mountains are the feet of the one who brings good news; who announces peace and brings good news of happiness; who announces salvation, saying to Zion, 'Your God is king.'"

8. Isa. 58:6: "Is this not the fast which I will choose, to loosen the bonds of wickedness, to undo the harness cords of a yoke, and to send forth the oppressed, and every yoke may be broken?"

9. Isa. 61:2–3: "To proclaim the favorable year of the Lord, and the day of vengeance of our God; to comfort all who mourn, to provide for the mourners of Zion; to give them a headdress instead of ashes, the oil of rejoicing instead of mourning, a mantle of praise instead of a fearful spirit. Calling them mighty trees of righteousness, the planting of the Lord, to manifest his glory."

10. 4Q521 f2ii+4:1–14: "[. . . For the hea]vens and the earth will listen to his Messiah [and all

[*see* Qumran Messianic Texts]; 11QMelch 2, lines 4–9, 14–17;[11] Matt. 11:5;[12] Luke 4:18–19; 7:22[13]). For the early Christians, these images from Isaiah applied to Jesus, but for the collectors and writers of the Qumran scrolls, they depict a future time when the "Messiahs of Aaron and Israel" (1QS 9:11)[14] would arrive to correct the injustices and inequities that they perceived as part of the **Hellenistic** Jewish world.

As was the case for the Qumran covenanters, Isaiah 40:3 plays a key role in all four Gospels—however, here it is prophesying John the Baptist's arrival and his mission to prepare the way of the Lord. Much may be said on how each gospel uses Isaiah 40:3 in its portrait of John and the expectation of Jesus; for example, all four Gospels use "in the wilderness" to denote John's location, whereas in Isaiah 40:3[15] and 1QS 8.12,[16] "in the wilderness" forms part of the proclamation itself. Unfortunately, space permits us to view the relevant texts and their rich details only in parallel columns.

w]hich are in them will not turn away from the commandments of the holy ones. Strengthen yourselves, seekers of the Lord, in his service. Will you not find the Lord in this, all who are enduring in their heart? For the Lord will attend to the pious and he will call the righteous by name. His spirit hovers over the humble and he will renew the faithful in his strength. For he will honor the pious upon the throne of his everlasting kingdom, releasing the ones who are bound, opening the eyes of the blind, raising up those who are be[nt down.] And for[ev]er I will hold fast [to] those [in w]aiting and in his faithfulness w[ill . . .] and the frui[t of] good [wor]ks will not be delayed for anyone and the Lord will do honorable things which have not been done, which he spoke. For he will heal the critically wounded, and the dead will live, he will send good news to the afflicted (Isa. 61:1), He will sati[sfy the poo]r, he will guide the uprooted, He will make the hungry rich."

11. 11QMelch. 2:4–9: "[Its interpretation refers] to the end of days and concerning the captives, just as [Isaiah said: "To proclaim the Jubilee to the captives" (Isa. 61:1). . .] just as [. . .] and from the inheritance of Melchizedek who [. . .] will return them to what is theirs. He will proclaim to them liberty, releasing them [from the debt] of all their iniquities. And this will be in the first week of the Jubilee following the ni[ne Jubile]es. The Da[y of Atone]ment will be the end of the tenth [Jubi]lee, when he will atone for all the Sons [of Light] and the lot of Melchizedek [. . .] This is the period for 'the year of Melchizedek's favor' (cf. Isa. 61:2)."

12. Matt. 11:5: "As they went away, Jesus began to speak to the crowds about John: 'the blind receive their sight, the crippled walk, the lepers are cleansed, the deaf hear, the dead are being raised, and the poor have good news brought to them.'"

13. Luke 4:18–19: "The Spirit of the Lord is upon me, because he has anointed me to bring good news to the poor. He has sent me to proclaim release to the captives and recovery of sight to the blind, to let the oppressed go free, to proclaim the acceptable year of the Lord."

Luke 7:22: "And answering, he said to them, 'Go and tell John what you saw and heard: the blind receive their sight, the lame walk, the lepers are being cleansed, the deaf are hearing, the dead are being raised, the good news is being brought to the poor.'"

14. 1QS 9.10–11: "They will be judged by the first judgments in which the men of the community began to be instructed, until the coming of the prophet and the Messiahs of Aaron and Israel."

15. Isa. 40:3: "A voice cries out: 'In the wilderness prepare the way of the Lord, make straight in the desert plain a highway for our God.'"

16. 1QS 8.12–14: "When these become the community in Israel they will separate themselves from the session of the men of deceit in order to depart into the wilderness to prepare the way of the Lord, as it is written: 'In the wilderness prepare the way of the Lord, make level in the desert a highway for our God.'"

Isa. 40:3–5	Mark 1:2–3	Matt. 3:1–3	Luke 3:3	John 1:21–23
		[1] In those days John the Baptist appeared in the wilderness of Judaea, proclaiming: [2] "Repent, for the kingdom of heaven is at hand."	[3] And [John] went into the entire region round about the Jordan, proclaiming baptism of repentance for the forgiveness of sins.	[22] Then they said to [John], "Who are you? Let us have an answer for those who sent us. What do you say about yourself?"
	[2] Just as it is written in the prophet Isaiah: "See, I am sending my messenger ahead of you, who will prepare thy way:	[3] For this is the one of whom the prophet Isaiah spoke when he said:	[4] As it is written in the book of the words of the prophet Isaiah,	
[3] The voice cries out: "In the wilderness prepare the way of the Lord, in the desert make straight a highway for your God. [4] Every valley will be lifted up, and every mountain and hill will be brought low, and the uneven ground will become level, and the rough places a plain. [5] Then the glory of the Lord will be revealed, and all humanity will see it together, for the mouth of the Lord has spoken."	[3] the voice of one crying out in the wilderness, 'Prepare the way of the Lord, make his paths straight.'"	"The voice of one crying out in the wilderness: 'Prepare the way of the Lord, make his paths straight.'"	"The voice of one crying out in the wilderness: 'Prepare the way of the Lord, make his paths straight. [5] Every valley will be filled, and every mountain and hill will be brought low, and the crooked will be made straight, and the rough ways made smooth, [6] and all flesh will see the salvation of God."	[23] He said, "I am the voice of one crying in the wilderness, 'Make straight the way of the Lord,' as the prophet Isaiah said."

Finally, mention must be made of an interesting reading in Isaiah 53:11, which describes the Suffering Servant. In the MT (as translated in the KJV), the first part of the verse reads (referring to the Servant): "He shall see of the travail of his soul, and shall be satisfied." However, all three Qumran scrolls preserving this portion (1QIsa^a, 1QIsa^b, and 4QIsa^d), as well the Septuagint, include the additional word "light": "Out of the suffering of his soul he will see *light*, and find satisfaction." This reading has messianic implications for New Testament studies, and transforms the meaning and exegesis of the verse (now with hints of life and even resurrection).[17]

17. It has been adopted in several modern English Bibles, including CEB, JB, NRSV, NIV, NEB, REB, and NAB. (Most other English translations follow the traditional MT, but in many cases the translators did not have access to the Cave 4 Isaiah scrolls, and did not fully realize the impact of the biblical scrolls for understanding the text of Scripture.)

Twenty-two copies of Isaiah were discovered in the Judean Desert, suggesting it was one of the most important books at Qumran. The Great Isaiah Scroll (1QIsa[a]) is the oldest copy of Isaiah in existence (125–100 BCE), and has survived virtually intact. This text is of great interest because of its advanced age, its complex use of the Hebrew language, its apparently "free approach" in transmitting the text, its division into two neat halves (chaps. 1–33 and 34–66), and its high number of variant readings.

The large number of copies of Isaiah in the Qumran scrolls, as well as the frequent citations of or allusions to the book in at least twenty-seven compositions that are sectarian or reflect the *yaḥad*'s distinctive ideas, confirm theories regarding the movement that collected them. This was an eschatological community who prioritized the study and correct interpretation of the Torah, and also had priestly concerns. Together with characteristic interpretations attached to the Isaiah prophecies in the Dead Sea Scrolls, the twenty-seven listed works show considerable agreement with New Testament writings in their handling of this important book.

Peter W. Flint

FURTHER READING

Abegg, Martin G., Peter W. Flint, and Eugene Ulrich. *The Dead Sea Scrolls Bible: The Oldest Known Bible Translated for the First Time into English.* San Francisco: HarperCollins, 1999.

Davies, Philip R., George J. Brooke, and Phillip R. Callaway. *The Complete World of the Dead Sea Scrolls.* London: Thames & Hudson, 2002.

VanderKam, James, and Peter W. Flint. *The Meaning of the Dead Sea Scrolls: Their Significance for Understanding the Bible, Jesus, and Christianity.* San Francisco: HarperCollins, 2002.

Wise, Michael O., Martin G. Abegg, and Edward M. Cook. *The Dead Sea Scrolls: A New Translation with Commentary.* 2nd ed. San Francisco: HarperCollins, 2005.

ADVANCED READING

Abegg, Martin G. "The Covenant of the Qumran Sectarians." In *The Concept of the Covenant in the Second Temple Period,* edited by Stanley E. Porter and Jacqueline C. R. de Roo, pp. 81–98. Leiden: Brill, 2003.

Brooke, George J. "On Isaiah at Qumran." In *"As Those Who Were Taught": The Interpretation of Isaiah from the LXX to the SBL,* edited by Claire Matthews McGinnis and Patricia K. Tull, pp. 69–85. SBLSymS 27. Atlanta: SBL, 2006.

———. "Types of Historiography in the Qumran Scrolls." In *Ancient and Modern Scriptural Historiography, L'historiographie Biblique, ancienne et moderne,* edited by G. J. Brooke and T. Römer, pp. 211–30. Bibliotheca ephemeridum theologicarum lovaniensium 207. Leuven: Leuven University Press, 2007.

Brownlee, William H. "The Literary Significance of the Bisection of Isaiah in the Ancient Scroll from Qumran." In *Trudy Dvardtsat Pyatogo Mezhdunarodnogo Kongressa Vostokokovedov,* pp. 431–47. Vol. 1. Moscow: Tzolatel'stvo Vostochnoi Literatary, 1962.

———. "The Manuscripts of Isaiah from which DSI[a] was Copied." *BASOR* 127 (1952): 16–21.

Flint, Peter W. "The Book of Isaiah in the Dead Sea Scrolls." In *The Bible as Book: The Hebrew Bible and the Judaean Desert Discoveries. Proceedings of the Conference Held at Hampton Court, Herefordshire, 18–21 June 2000,* edited by Edward D. Herbert and Emanuel Tov, pp. 229–53. London: British Library, 2002.

McGinnis, Claire Matthews, and Patricia K. Tull, eds. *"As Those Who Were Taught": The Interpretation of Isaiah from the LXX to the SBL.* SBLSymS 27. Atlanta: SBL, 2006.

Parry, Donald W., and Elisha Qimron. *The Great Isaiah Scroll (1QIsaᵃ)—A New Edition.* STJD 32. Leiden: Brill, 1999.

Tov, Emanuel. *Scribal Practices and Approaches Reflected in the Texts Found in the Judean Desert.* STDJ 54. Leiden: Brill, 2004.

Ulrich, Eugene. *The Dead Sea Scrolls and the Origins of the Bible.* Studies in the Dead Sea Scrolls and Related Literature. Grand Rapids: Eerdmans, 1999.

Ulrich, Eugene, and Peter Flint. *Qumran Cave 1.II: The Isaiah Scrolls.* 2 vols. DJD 32. Oxford: Clarendon, 2010.

1.8 *from* Great Isaiah Scroll (1QIsaᵃ)

^{1:1}The vision of Isaiah the son of Amoz, which he saw concerning Judah and Jerusalem in the days of Uzziah, Jotham, Ahaz, and Hezekiah, kings of Judah.

The Case against Judah: Rebellious Judah and Desolate Jerusalem

2 Hear, O heavens, and give ear, O earth;[a]
    for the Lord has spoken:
Children have I reared and brought up,
    but they have rebelled against me.
3 The ox knows its owner,
    and the donkey its master's crib,
[but] *Israel*[b] does not know,
    and[c] my people do not understand.
4 Ah, sinful nation,
    a people laden with iniquity,
offspring of evildoers,
    children who deal corruptly!
They have forsaken the Lord,
    they have despised the Holy One of Israel,
    they are utterly estranged.
5 Why will you still be struck down?
    Why will you continue to rebel?
The whole head is sick,
    and the whole heart faint.
6 From the sole of the foot even to the head,
    there is no soundness in it,
but bruises and sores
    and raw wounds;
they are not pressed out or bound up
    or softened with oil.
7 Your country lies desolate;

a. 1QIsaᵃ has the definite article, not in MT.
b. 1QIsaᵃ MT. *but Israel* 4QIsaʲ.
c. 1QIsaᵃ. Not in 4QIsaʲ MT.

Translation by Peter W. Flint and Eugene Ulrich. Footnotes indicate variant readings against other Isaiah scrolls, the Masoretic Text, and the Septuagint. For the complete Great Isaiah Scroll, see Peter W. Flint, *The Great Isaiah Scroll in Hebrew and English, with Variant Readings and Introduction* (Eerdmans, forthcoming). *Note:* for this translation, chapter numbers and subheadings are included to aid the reader by breaking up the text into smaller units.

> your cities are burned with fire;
> > in your very presence
> > > foreigners devour your land.
> > > *They have brought devastation upon it,*[a] as overthrown by foreigners.
> 8 And the daughter of Zion is left
> > like a booth in a vineyard,
> *and*[b] like a lodge in a cucumber field,
> > like a besieged city.
> 9 If the Lord of hosts
> > had not left us a few survivors,
> we should have been like Sodom,
> > and become like Gomorrah.

Summons to Reform: Turning from Evil and Doing Good

> 10 Hear the word of the Lord,
> > you rulers of Sodom!
> *And*[c] give ear to the teaching of our God,
> > you people of Gomorrah!
> 11 What to me is the multitude of your sacrifices?
> > says the Lord;
> I have had enough of burnt offerings of rams
> > and the fat of well-fed beasts;
> I do not delight in the blood of bulls,
> > or of lambs, or of goats.
> 12 When you come *to appear before my face,*[d]
> > who has required of you
> > this trampling of my courts?
> 13 Bring no more vain offerings;
> > incense is an abomination to me.
> New moon and Sabbath and the calling of convocations—
> > I cannot endure iniquity and *her*[e] solemn assembly.
> 14 Your new moons and your appointed feasts
> > my soul hates;
> they have become a burden to me;
> > I am weary of bearing them.
> 15 When you spread out your hands,
> > I will hide my eyes from you;
> even though you multiply prayers,
> > I will not listen;

a. 1QIsa[a]. *Devastated,* MurIsa MT LXX.
b. 1QIsa[a] LXX Syriac Vulgate. Not in MT Targum.
c. 1QIsa[a] Syriac. Not in MT LXX Targum Vulgate.
d. Or, *for my face to appear.*
e. 1QIsa[a]. Not in MT.

your hands are full of blood, *your fingers with iniquity.*^a

16 Wash yourselves; *and*^b make yourselves clean;
and^c remove the evil of your deeds from before my eyes;
cease to do evil,
17 learn to do good;
seek justice,
correct oppression;
bring justice to the fatherless,
plead the widow's cause.
18 Come now, and let us reason together, says the Lord:
though your sins are like scarlet,
they will be as white as snow;
though they *are like*^d crimson,
they will become like wool.
19 If you are willing and obedient,
you will eat the good of the land;
20 *but*^e if you refuse and rebel,
you will be eaten *by the sword;*^f
for the mouth of the Lord has spoken.

Isaiah Comforts Ahaz, King of Judah

7:1 In the days of Ahaz son of Jotham, son of Uzziah, king of Judah, Rezin king of Syria and Pekah son of Remaliah king of Israel came up to Jerusalem to wage war against it, but *they*^g could not mount an attack against it. ²When it was reported to the house of David, Syria is in league with Ephraim, *the heart*^h of his people shook as the trees of *the*ⁱ forest shake before *the*^j wind.

³And the Lord said to Isaiah, Go out to meet Ahaz, you and Shear-jashub your son, at the end of the aqueduct of the Upper Pool on the highway to Washerman's Field. ⁴And say to him, Be careful, be calm, do not be afraid, *and*^k do not lose heart because of these two smoldering stumps of torches, *because of*^l the fierce anger of Rezin and Syria and the son of Remaliah. ⁵Because Syria, with Ephraim and the son of Remaliah, has plotted evil against you, saying, ⁶Let us go up against

a. 1QIsaᵃ. Not in 4QIsaᶠ MT.
b. 1QIsaᵃ. Not in 4QIsaᶠ MT.
c. 1QIsaᵃ. Not in MT LXX.
d. 1QIsaᵃ LXX. *are red like* MT 4QIsaᶠ.
e. 1QIsaᵃ LXX Targum Syriac. Not in 4QIsaᶠ.
f. 1QIsaᵃ Targum Syriac. Not in MT. *(the) sword will devour you* LXX.
g. 1QIsaᵃ LXX. *he* MT.
h. 1QIsaᵃ. *his heart and the heart of his people* MT LXX.
i. 1QIsaᵃ. Not in MT.
j. 1QIsaᵃ. Not in MT.
k. 1QIsaᵃ LXX. Not in MT.
l. 7:4 1QIsaᵃ. Not in MT *(at)*.

Judah and alarm it, and let us conquer it for ourselves, and install the son of Tabeel as king in the midst of it, [7] thus says the Lord God:

> It will not take place,
>   and it will not happen.
> [8] For the head of Syria is Damascus,
>   and the head of Damascus is Rezin.
> And within sixty-five years
>   Ephraim will be too shattered to be a people.
> [9] And the head of Ephraim is Samaria,
>   and the head of Samaria is the son of Remaliah.
> If you do not stand firm in faith,
>   you will not stand firm at all.

A Sign for Ahaz: Immanuel

[10] Again the Lord spoke to Ahaz, [11] Ask a sign of the Lord your God: one as deep as Sheol or as high as heaven above. [12] But Ahaz said, I will not ask, and I will not put the Lord to the test. [13] And he said, Hear then, O house of David! Is it too little for you to try the patience of people, that you try the patience of my God also? [14] Therefore the *Lord*[a] himself will give you a sign. Behold, the young woman is with child and will give birth to a son, and *his name will be called*[b] Immanuel. [15] He will eat curds and honey when he knows enough to reject the wrong and choose the right. [16] For before the boy knows enough to reject the wrong and choose the right, the land whose two kings you dread will be deserted. [17] *And*[c] the Lord will bring upon you and upon your people and upon your father's house such days as have not come since the time that Ephraim broke away from Judah—the king of Assyria.

[18] On that day the Lord will whistle for flies that are at the source of Egypt's streams, and for bees that are in the land of Assyria. [19] And they will all come and settle in the steep ravines, and in the crevices of the rocks, and on all the thornbushes, and on all the pastures.

[20] On that day the Lord will shave with a razor that is hired beyond the river—with the king of Assyria—the head and the hair of your legs, and it will take off your beards also.

[21] In that day a man will keep alive a young cow and two sheep, [22] and because of the abundance of milk that they give, he will eat curds since *the one*[d] who is left in the land will eat curds and honey.

a. 1QIsa[a]. *Lord* MT.
b. 1QIsa[a]. *she will name him* MT LXX.
c. 1QIsa[a]. Not in MT.
d. 1QIsa[a] wrote *everyone* (= MT LXX), then deleted it.

²³ On that *day*ᵃ everyplace where there once were a thousand vines, worth a thousand shekels of silver, will become briers and thorns. ²⁴ With *bows*ᵇ and arrows people will come there, for all the land will be briers and thorns. ²⁵ And as for all the hills that used to be cultivated with a hoe, you will not come there for fear of *iron*ᶜ briers and thorns, but they will become a place where cattle are turned loose and where sheep tread.

The Fate of Creation

²⁴:¹   See, *the Lord*ᵈ is about to depopulate the land and devastate it;
           he will *turn it upside down*ᵉ and scatter its inhabitants.
² It will be the same as with people for priests,
           the same as with servants for their masters,
           as with maids for their mistresses,
       as with buyers for sellers,
           as with lenders for borrowers,
           as with creditors for debtors.
³ The earth will be utterly depopulated and completely laid waste—
           for the Lord has spoken this word.
⁴ The earth dries up and withers;
           the world languishes and fades away;
           *heaven fades away*ᶠ
           together with the earth.
⁵ The earth lies defiled
           beneath its inhabitants;
       for they have transgressed *the laws*,ᵍ
           violated the statutes,
           and broken the everlasting covenant.
⁶ For this reason a curse *consumes*,ʰ
           and its inhabitants are held guilty;
       for this reason the inhabitants of earth are ablaze,
           and few people are left.
⁷ The new wine dries up
           and the vine, *the oil*,ⁱ withers;
           all the merrymakers groan.
⁸ The gaiety of the tambourines has ended,

a. 1QIsaᵃ LXX. MT adds *will be.*
b. 1QIsaᵃ. *bow* MT LXX.
c. 1QIsaᵃ. Not in MT LXX.
d. 1QIsaᵃ MT. *the Lord* 4QIsaᶜ.
e. Or, *twist its surface.*
f. 1QIsaᵃ 4QIsaᶜ. *the heavens fade away* MT, cf. LXX.
g. 1QIsaᵃ MT. *the law* 4QIsaᶜ LXX.
h. 1QIsaᵃ. *consumes the earth* 4QIsaᶜ MT LXX.
i. 4QIsaᶜ. Not in 1QIsaᵃ MT LXX.

the noise of the jubilant has stopped,
and the mirth of the harp has ended.
9 No longer do they drink wine with singing,
and *beer*[a] is bitter to its drinkers.
10 The chaotic city lies broken down;
every house is closed up so that no one can enter.
11 There is an outcry in the streets over wine;
all cheer turns to gloom;
the gaiety of the earth is banished.
12 *Desolation*[b] is left in the city;
its gates lie battered into ruins.
13 So it will be on the earth
and among the nations,
just as when an olive tree is beaten,
or as gleanings when the grape harvest has ended.

Doxology and Impending Judgment

14 They raise their voices, *they shout for joy*;[c]
from *the west*[d] *they shout aloud*[e]
over the Lord's majesty.
15 Therefore, you *in the east*,[f] give glory to the Lord!
You in the coastlands of the sea,
give glory to the name of the Lord, the God of Israel!
16 From the ends of the earth we hear songs of praise:
"Glory to the Righteous One!"
But I say, "I am pining away,
I am pining away. Woe to me!
For treacherous people betray—
Treacherous people betray with treachery!"
17 Terror and pit and snare
are upon you, O inhabitants of the earth!
18 Whoever flees at the sound of terror
will fall into the pit,
and whoever climbs out of the pit
will be caught in the snare.
For the windows from above are opened,
and the foundations of earth shake.
19 The earth is utterly shattered,

a. Or, *strong drink.*
b. *And desolation* 1QIsa^a MT LXX.
c. 1QIsa^a MT. *and they shout* 4QIsa^c.
d. Literally, *the sea* 1QIsa^a MT, cf. LXX. *the day* 4QIsa^c.
e. 1QIsa^a MT. *and they cry out* 4QIsa^c.
f. 1QIsa^a MT. *in the east, in Aram* 4QIsa^c. Not in LXX.

    the earth is split apart,
    the earth is violently shaken.
20 *The earth*ª reels to and fro like a drunkard;
    it sways *and like a hut;*ᵇ
its transgression lies so heavy upon it,
    that it falls, never to rise again.
21 On that day the Lord will punish
    the host of the high ones *in heaven,*ᶜ
    and the kings of the earth on earth.
22 *They* ᵈ will be herded together
    *in a dungeon;*ᵉ
they will be shut up in prison,
    and after many days be punished.
23 Then the moon will be embarrassed
    and the sun ashamed,
for the Lord of hosts will reign
    on Mount Zion and in Jerusalem,
and before its elders there will be glory.

Praise for Deliverance

25:1 O Lord, you are my God;
    I will exalt you and praise your name,
for you have done marvelous things,
    plans made long ago in faithfulness and truth.
2 For you have made the city a heap of rubble,
    the fortified city a ruin;
the *foreigners' palace*ᶠ is no longer a city—
    it will never be rebuilt!
3 Therefore, strong peoples will glorify you;
    cities of ruthless nations will revere you.
4 For you have been a stronghold for the poor,
    a stronghold for the needy in his distress,
    a shelter from the storm and a shade from the heat—
for the blast of the ruthless is like a rainstorm beating against a wall,
5 and the noise of foreigners is like the heat of the desert.
Just as you subdue heat by the shade of clouds,
    so the victory songs of violent men will be stilled.
6 On this mountain the Lord of hosts will prepare for all peoples

a. 1QIsaª. *Earth* MT LXX.
b. 1QIsaª. *like a hut* MT (the better reading).
c. Literally, *on high.*
d. 1QIsaª. *And they* 4QIsaᶜ MT LXX.
e. 1QIsaª LXX. *like prisoners in a dungeon* 4QIsaᶜ MT.
f. 1QIsaª MT. *palace of arrogant people* MTmss LXX.

a banquet of rich food, a banquet of well-aged wines—
of rich food full of marrow, and of vintage and refined wines.

7 And on this mountain he will swallow up
the shroud that enfolds all peoples,
the veil that is spread over all nations—

8 *he has swallowed up*[a] death forever!
Then the Lord God will wipe away the tears from all faces,
and he will take away the disgrace of his people from all the earth—
for the Lord has spoken.

9 *And you will say*[b] on that day,
"See, *the Lord*[c]—this is our God!
We waited for him, and he saved us.
This is the Lord! We waited for him,
so let us rejoice, *and we will be glad*[d] in his salvation."

10 For the hand of the Lord will rest on this mountain,
but the Moabites will be trodden down beneath him,
just as straw is trodden down *in the slime of*[e] a manure pit.

11 And they will spread out their hands in the thick of it,
just as swimmers spread out their hands to swim,
but the Lord will bring down their pride,
together with the cleverness of their hands.

12 He brings down the high fortifications of your walls
and lays them low; *he will make them reach*[f] the ground, even to the
very dust.

Victory Song for Judah

26:1 On that day *one will sing this song*[g] in the land of Judah:
We have a strong city;
God makes victory
its walls and ramparts.[h]

2 Open *your gates,*[i]
so that the righteous nation that keeps faith may enter in.

3 You will keep *in perfect peace*[j]

a. 1QIsa^a MTms, cf. LXX. *And he will swallow up* MT (cf. Syriac, Theodotian, and 1 Cor. 15:54).

b. 1QIsa^a Syriac. *And he will say* 4QIsa^c MT. *And they will say* LXX.

c. 1QIsa^a. Not in MT LXX.

d. 1QIsa^a. *and let us be glad* MT.

e. Literally, *in the water of* 1QIsa^a MT. *in* MTqere. *with wagons* LXX.

f. Imperf. 1QIsa^a. *he casts them* (perf.) 4QIsa^c MT, which is more consistent with the preceding verbs.

g. 1QIsa^a. *this song will be sung* 1QIsa^b 4QIsa^c MT. *they will sing that song* LXX.

h. 4QIsa^c. *walls and ramparts* 1QIsa^a MT LXX (sing.).

i. 1QIsa^a. *the gates* MT LXX.

j. Literally, *peace, peace* 1QIsa^a MT. *peace* LXX Syriac.

him whose mind is fixed on you
because *he is in you.*[a]

4 Trust in the Lord forever,
for in *the Lord God*[b] you have an everlasting rock.

5 For *he has made drunk*[c]
the inhabitants of the height,
the lofty city.
He *lays it low*[d] to the ground
and casts it down to the dust.

6 *The feet of the oppressed trample it,*[e]
the footsteps of the needy.

7 The path of the righteous is level; *O Upright One,*[f]
you *bring to safety*[g] the way of *justice.*[h]

8 Yes, Lord, in the path of your judgments
we wait;[i]
your name and *your law*[j]
are *the soul's*[k] desire.

9 My soul yearns for you in the night;
my spirit within me searches for you.
For when your judgments are on the earth,
the inhabitants of the world learn righteousness.

10 If favor is shown to the wicked,
they do not learn righteousness;
even in a land of uprightness they act perversely
and do not perceive the majesty of the Lord.

11 O Lord, your hand is lifted up,
but they do not see it.
And let them see[l] your zeal for *your people*[m] and be put to shame—
yes, let the fire reserved for your enemies consume them!

12 Lord, you will *decide*[n] peace for us,
for you have indeed done all our achievements for us.

13 O Lord our God,

a. 1QIsa[a] 1QIsa[b] LXX. *he trusts in you* 4QIsa[c] MT.
b. 1QIsa[a] MT. *the Lord God* (lit. *Yah the Lord*) 4QIsa[b]. *the Lord, the Lord* LXX.
c. Meaning unclear (possibly similar to) MT 1QIsa[a]. *he has brought low* 1QIsa[b] 4QIsa[b] 4QIsa[c] MT LXX. *he has humbled and brought down* LXX.
d. 1QIsa[a] LXX. *He levels it, he levels it* MT.
e. 1QIsa[a] (but verb sing.) LXX. *The foot tramples it, the feet of the oppressed* MT.
f. 1QIsa[a] MT. *they go straight ahead* 4QIsa[c]. Not in LXX.
g. 1QIsa[a]. *make smooth* MT LXX *(prepare).*
h. 1QIsa[a] 4QIsa[c]. *the righteous* MT LXX (pl.).
i. 1QIsa[a] LXX. *we wait for you* MT.
j. 1QIsa[a]. *your renown* 4QIsa[c] MT, cf. LXX.
k. 1QIsa[a] MT. *my soul's* 4QIsa[b].
l. 1QIsa[a], cf. LXX. *Let them see* MT.
m. Literally, *the people* 1QIsa[a]. *people* MT.
n. 1QIsa[a]. *prepare* or *give* MT. *give!* LXX.

> other lords besides you have ruled over us,
>   but through you alone we acknowledge your name.
> ¹⁴ The dead will not live,
>   *and the departed spirits*[a] will not rise—
> to that end you punished and destroyed them
>   and *imprisoned*[b] all memory of them.
> ¹⁵ But you have enlarged the nation, O Lord,
>   *you have enlarged the nation.*[c] You have gained honor;
>   you have extended all the borders of the land.
>
> ¹⁶ O Lord, *they*[d] came to you in distress;
>   *they poured out their secret prayer*[e]
>   when *your chastenings were*[f] upon them.
> ¹⁷ Like a woman with child
>   writhes and cries out in her pangs
>   when she is near to giving birth,
> so were we because of you, O Lord.
> ¹⁸ We were with child, we writhed in pain,
>   but we gave birth only to wind.
> We have not won *your victory*[g] on earth,
>   Nor have the inhabitants of the world been born.
> ¹⁹ But your dead will live; their bodies will rise.
>   Those who live in the dust *will wake up and shout for joy!*[h]
> For your dew is like the dew of dawn,
>   and the earth will give birth to the dead.
> ²⁰ Come, my people, enter your rooms
>   and shut *your doors*[i] behind you.
> *Hide yourselves*[j] for a little while
>   until the fury has passed by.
> ²¹ *For*[k] see, the Lord is coming out from his place
>   to punish the inhabitants of the earth for their sins,
> and the earth will disclose the blood shed on it,
>   and will conceal its slain no longer.

a. 1QIsaᵃ LXX. *the departed spirits* 1QIsaᵃ corr MT.

b. 1QIsaᵃ. *wiped out* MT LXX.

c. 1QIsaᵃ MT. Not in MTms.

d. 1QIsaᵃ MT. *we* MTmss LXXmss. *I remembered you* LXX.

e. 1QIsaᵃ. *they poured out a magical prayer* 4QIsaᵇ MT.

f. 1QIsaᵃ. *your chastening was* MT LXX.

g. 1QIsaᵃ LXX. *victory* MT.

h. 1QIsaᵃ. *Wake up and shout for joy* (imperf.), *you* . . . MT. *(Those in the dust) will rejoice, for* . . . LXX.

i. 1QIsaᵃ MT. *your door* MTqere.

j. 1QIsaᵃ. *Hide yourself* MT.

k. 1QIsaᵃ. *For see,* MT LXX.

The Gathering and Redemption of Israel

27:1 On that day the Lord will punish with his fierce, mighty, and powerful sword Leviathan the gliding serpent, Leviathan the coiling serpent, and he will kill the dragon that is in the sea.

2 On that day,
A *fermenting*[a] vineyard, sing about it!
3 I, the Lord, watch over it;
    I water it continually.
    I guard it night and day
so that no one can harm it.
4 I am not angry.
If only it could give me briers *and thorns*[b] to battle!
    I would march against them,
    and[c] I would burn them all up.
5 Or else let it cling to me for protection;
    let it make peace with me,
    yes, let it make peace with me.

6 In days to come Jacob will root,
    and[d] Israel will blossom and sprout shoots
    and fill the whole world with fruit.
7 Has (the Lord) struck them down just as he struck down those who
    struck them?
    Or have they been killed just as *their killers* were killed?
8 *Measure by measure,*[e] by exile you contended with them;
    with his fierce blast he removed them, as on a day when the east
    wind blows.
9 By this, then, Jacob's guilt will be atoned for,
    and this will be the full fruitage of the removal of his sin:
when he makes all the altar stones
    like pulverized chalkstones,
    no Asherah poles or incense altars will be left standing.
10 For the fortified city stands desolate,
    a settlement abandoned and forsaken like the desert;
calves graze there,
    and there they lie down and strip its branches bare.
11 When its branches are dry, they are broken off
    and women come and make fires with them.
For this is a people who have no regard;

a. Apparent meaning 1QIsa[a]. *pleasant* MT LXX.
b. 1QIsa[a]. *thorns* MT.
c. 1QIsa[a]. Not in MT.
d. 1QIsa[a] LXX. Not in MT.
e. Or, *With war-cries.*

so the one who made them has no compassion on them,
and the one who created them will show them no mercy.

¹²On that day the Lord will thresh out the grain from the channel of the Euphrates to the Brook of Egypt, and you will be gathered in one by one, O people of Israel. ¹³And on that day a great trumpet will be sounded, and those who were perishing in the land of Assyria and those who were expelled to the land of Egypt will come and worship the Lord on his holy mountain at Jerusalem.

Comfort for God's People

40:1 Console, yes, console my people, says your God.
2 Speak tenderly to Jerusalem,
     and proclaim to her
 that her heavy service has been completed,
     that her penalty has been paid,
 that she has received from the Lord's hand
     double for all her sins.
3 A voice cries out:
 "In the wilderness prepare the way for the Lord;
     and[a] in the desert a straight highway for our God.
4 Every valley will be lifted up,
     and every mountain and hill will be lowered;
 the rough ground will become level,
     and the mountain ridges made a plain.
5 Then the glory of the Lord will be revealed,
     and all humanity will see it at once.
 For the mouth of the Lord has spoken."
6 A voice says, "Cry out!"
     So *I*[b] said, "What am I to cry out?"
 All humanity is grass,
     and all their loyalty is like the flowers of the field.
7 *Grass withers and flowers fade away*
     when the Lord's breath blows on them;
     surely the people are like grass.[c]
8 Grass withers and flowers fade away,
 when the Lord's breath blows on them,
     but *the word of our God*[d] will stand forever.

a. 1QIsaᵃ. Not in MT LXX.
b. 1QIsaᵃ LXX. *he* MT.
c. Entire verse 7 not in 1QIsaᵃ LXX, but in MT.
d. 1QIsaᵃ has *the word of our God* (= MT LXX) but marks *the word of* for deletion.

The Lord Is Coming with Power

⁹ Climb up a high mountain,
  messenger to Zion!
Lift up your voice with strength,
  messenger to Jerusalem!
  Lift it up, do not be afraid!
Say to the towns of Judah,
  "Here is your God!"
¹⁰ Look, the Lord God comes with power,
  and his arm rules for him.
Look, his reward is with him,
  and his payment accompanies him.
¹¹ Like a shepherd he tends his flock:
  he gathers the lambs in his arms
and carries them close to his heart,
  and gently leads the mother sheep.
¹² Who has measured *the waters of the sea*[a] in the hollow of his hand
  and marked off the heavens by *the width of his hand?*[b]
Who has enclosed the dust of the earth in a measuring bowl,
  or weighed the mountains in scales
  and the hills in a balance?
¹³ Who has fathomed the Spirit of the Lord,
  or as his counselor has taught *him?*[c]
¹⁴ With whom did he consult,
  to enlighten and instruct him on the path of justice?
  Or who taught him knowledge
 and showed him the way of wisdom?
¹⁵ *Look, the nations are like a drop from a bucket,*
 and are reckoned as dust on the scales.
 Look, he even lifts up the islands like powder!
¹⁶ *Lebanon would not provide enough fuel,*
  nor are its animals enough for a burnt offering.[d]
¹⁷ All the nations are as nothing before him,
  they are reckoned by him *as*[e] nothing and chaos.

a. 1QIsaᵃ LXX. *the waters* MT.

b. 1QIsaᵃ Syr. *a hand's width* MT LXX.

c. Refers to the *Spirit* in 1QIsaᵃ; refers to *the Lord* in MT.

d. Not written by original scribe of 1QIsaᵃ, added by a later scribe of 1QIsaᵃ; found in MT LXX.

e. 1QIsaᵃ LXX. *as less than* MT.

God Is Incomparable

18 To whom, then, will you *compare me—God?*[a]
  Or what image will you liken to *me?*[b]

19 An idol? A craftsman *makes the image,*[c]
    and a goldsmith overlays it with gold,
    and casts silver chains.

20 *The impoverished person, an offering,*[d]
    wood that will not rot;
  and he *chooses*[e] a skilled craftsman
  and[f] *seeks*[g] to set up an idol that will not topple.

21 Do you not know? Have you not heard?
    Has it not been told you from the beginning?
    Have you not understood from the foundations of *the*[h] earth?

22 He is the one who sits above the disk of the earth,
    and its inhabitants are like grasshoppers.
  He is the one who stretches out the heavens like a curtain,
    and spreads them like a tent to live in,

23 who brings princes to nothing,
    and makes the rulers of the earth like void.

24 No sooner are they planted, no sooner are they sown,
    no sooner *have*[i] their stems taken root in the earth;
  then[j] he blows on them, and they wither,
    and a tempest sweeps them away like stubble.

25 *To*[k] whom then will you compare me,
    and to whom should I be equal? says the Holy One.

26 Lift your eyes up to heaven and see:
    Who created all these?
  The One who leads out their starry host by number,
    calling them all by name
  because of his great might
    and *his*[l] powerful *strength,*[m]
    and[n] not one is missing.

a. 1QIsaᵃ. *compare God* MT, cf. LXX.
b. 1QIsaᵃ. *him* MT LXX.
c. 1QIsaᵃ, cf. LXX. *casts* MT.
d. MT, but Hebrew uncertain; not originally in 1QIsaᵃ but added later.
e. 1QIsaᵃ; in MT (cf. LXX), *chooses (wood)* goes with the preceding clause.
f. 1QIsaᵃ. Not in MT.
g. 1QIsaᵃ. MT reads with the preceding clause: *seeks (a skilled craftsman)*.
h. Implied in 1QIsaᵃ. Found in MT.
i. 1QIsaᵃ. *has* 4QIsaᵇ MT LXX.
j. 1QIsaᵃ. *and then* 4QIsaᵇ MT. Not in LXX.
k. 1QIsaᵃ. *And to* 4QIsaᵇ MT.
l. 1QIsaᵃ. Not in MT LXX.
m. 1QIsaᵃ LXX. *strong* MT (error).
n. 1QIsaᵃ. Not in MT LXX.

²⁷ Jacob, why do you say,
>> and Israel, why do you complain:
> "My lot is hidden from the Lord,
>> and my cause is ignored by my God"?

²⁸ Do you not know? Have you not heard?
> The Lord is the eternal God,
>> the Creator of the ends of the earth.
> He does not grow tired or weary;
>> *and*ᵃ his understanding cannot be fathomed.

²⁹ *The*ᵇ one who gives might to the faint,
>> will renew strength for the powerless.

³⁰ Even boys grow tired and weary
>> and young men collapse and fall,

³¹ but those who wait for the Lord will renew their strength.
>> *Then*ᶜ they will soar on wings like eagles;
> they will run and not grow weary;
>> they will walk and not grow tired.

The Lord's Servant

⁴²:¹ Here is my servant, whom I support,
>> my chosen one, in whom my soul delights.
> I have placed my Spirit upon him;
>> *and*ᵈ he will deliver *his*ᵉ justice to the nations.

² He will not shout or raise his voice,
>> or make it heard in the street.

³ A crushed reed he will not break,
>> and a fading *candle*ᶠ he will not *snuff out.*ᵍ
> He will bring forth justice for the truth.

⁴ *And*ʰ He will not grow faint or be crushed
>> until he establishes justice on the mainland,
>> and the islands *take ownership of*ⁱ his law.

⁵ This is what God says—*the God*ʲ
>> who created the heavens and stretched them out,
>> who spread out the earth and its produce,

a. 1QIsaᵃ, cf. LXX. Not in MT.
b. 1QIsaᵃ. Implied in MT.
c. 1QIsaᵃ. Not in MT LXX.
d. 1QIsaᵃ. Not in MT LXX.
e. 1QIsaᵃ. Not in MT LXX.
f. Literally, *linen wick.*
g. 1QIsaᵃ LXX. *quench it* MT.
h. 1QIsaᵃ. Not in 4QIsaʰ MT.
i. 1QIsaᵃ. *wait for* MT LXX (cf. 4QIsaʰ).
j. 1QIsaᵃ (but *the* was then erased to read *and*). *the Lord* MT.

who gives breath to the people upon it
and *life*[a] to those who walk in it:

6 *I*[b] have called you in righteousness,
I will take hold of your hand.
I will preserve you and appoint you
as *a covenant to the people,*[c]
as a light for the nations,

7 to open the eyes that are blind,
to bring out *those who are bound*[d] from their cells,
and[e] those sitting in darkness from prison.

8 *I the Lord am the one—and I will not give my name*[f] and glory to
another,
nor my praise to idols.

9 See, the former things have taken place,
and I am announcing *the*[g] new things—
before they spring into being
I am telling you about them.

Hymn to the Lord

10 Sing to the Lord a new song,
and[h] his praise from the ends of the earth,
you who sail down the sea and everything in it,
you islands and their inhabitants.

11 Let the desert *cry out,*[i]
its towns and the[j] villages where Kedar lives;
and[k] let those who live in Sela sing for joy.
Let them *shout aloud*[l] from the mountaintops.

12 Let them give glory to the Lord,
and declare his praise in the islands.

a. Literally, *spirit.*
b. 1QIsa[a]. *I the Lord* 4QIsa[h] MT. *I the Lord God* LXX.
c. 1QIsa[a] MT LXX. *an everlasting covenant* 4QIsa[h].
d. 1QIsa[a] (cf. LXX). *prisoners* 4QIsa[h] MT.
e. 1QIsa[a]. Not in 4QIsa[h] MT.
f. 1QIsa[a]. *I am the Lord, that is my name. I will not give* 4QIsa[h] MT LXX.
g. 1QIsa[a]. Not in 4QIsa[b] 4QIsa[h] MT LXX.
h. 1QIsa[a]. Not in 4QIsa[h] MT.
i. Singular 1QIsa[a] 4QIsa[h] LXX. Plural MT.
j. 1QIsa[a]. *and its towns, the* MT LXX.
k. 1QIsa[a]. Not in MT.
l. 1QIsa[a] (cf. LXX). *cry joyfully* MT.

The Lord as a Warrior

¹³ The Lord marches out like a warrior;
    he stirs up his rage like a man of war;
he makes his anger heard, he shouts aloud;[a]
    he declares his mastery over his enemies.
¹⁴ *Certainly*[b] I have stayed silent for a long time;
    I have kept still and held myself back.
Now, like a woman giving birth, I will cry out,
    I will gasp and pant at once.
¹⁵ I will devastate the mountains and hills,
    and dry up all their vegetation;
I will turn the rivers into islands,
    and dry up the ponds.
¹⁶ I will help the blind walk,
    and[c] on a road they do not know;
I will guide them
in paths they do not know.
I will turn the *dark places*[d] into light before them,
    and the rough places into level ground.
These are the things I will do,
    and I will not abandon them.
¹⁷ Those who trust in carved idols
will turn back *and*[e] be *completely disappointed,*[f]
    who say to metal images,
    "You are our gods."
¹⁸ Hear, you deaf people,
    and look up, you blind people, so you may see!
¹⁹ Who is blind except my servant,
    or deaf like my messenger I am sending?
Who is blind like the one committed to me,
    or blind like the Lord's servant?
²⁰ *You have seen*[g] many things, but *you pay no*[h] attention.
    His ears are *open,*[i] but he does not listen.
²¹ The Lord was pleased, for the sake of his vindication,
    that[j] he should magnify his law and make *it*[k] glorious.

a. 1QIsa^a. *He makes a war cry and shouts out his anger* MT.
b. 1QIsa^a. Not in MT.
c. 1QIsa^a. Not in MT.
d. 1QIsa^a (misspells the word). *Darkness* MT LXX.
e. 1QIsa^a. Not in MT.
f. 1QIsa^a MT LXX. *disappointed* MTms.
g. 1QIsa^a MT. *To see* (or, *He sees*) MTqere (thus RSV, NRSV).
h. 1QIsa^a MT LXX. *he pays no* MTmss (thus RSV, NRSV).
i. 1QIsa^a. *to open* (can mean, *are open*) MT.
j. 1QIsa^a. Implicit in MT.
k. 1QIsa^a. Implicit in MT.

22 But this is a people who have been robbed and plundered,
    all of them trapped in pits
    or hidden away in *prisons*.[a]
  They have become prey, with no one to rescue them;
    they have been made loot, with no one to say, "Send them back!"
23 Who is among you *that*[b] will hear,
    and[c] pay attention and listen for the time to come?
24 Who handed Jacob over to looters,
    and Israel to robbers?
  Was it not the Lord, against whom we have sinned?
    For they were not willing *to*[d] walk in his ways,
    and they would not obey his instruction.
25 So he poured upon him *the heat of his anger*,[e]
    the violence of war.
  It enveloped him in flames, but still he had no insight;
    it burned him up, but he did not take it to heart.

The Creator Redeems

43:1 But now this is what says the Lord says.
  the one who created you, Jacob,
    the one who formed you, Israel:
  Do not be afraid, because I have redeemed you.
    I have called you by name, you are mine.
2 When you pass through the waters, I will be with you;
    and through the rivers, they will not sweep over you.
  When you walk through fire you will not be scorched,
    and the flame will not set you ablaze.
3 *I*[f] am the Lord your God,
    the Holy One of Israel, your *Redeemer*.[g]
  And[h] I have given *Egypt as your ransom*,[i]
    Cush and *the people of Seba*[j] in exchange for you.
4 Since you are precious in my sight
    and honored, and because I love you,
  I give up people in your place,

a. 1QIsa[a] MT (cf. LXX). *prison* 4QIsa[g].
b. 1QIsa[a]. Not in 4QIsa[g] MT LXX.
c. 1QIsa[a]. Not in MT LXX.
d. 1QIsa[a]. Implicit in MT.
e. 1QIsa[a] LXX. *the heat, his anger* 4QIsa[g] MT.
f. 1QIsa[a]. *For I* 1QIsa[b] 4QIsa[g] MT LXX.
g. 1QIsa[a]. *Savior* MT LXX.
h. 1QIsa[a]. Not in MT.
i. 1QIsa[a]. *as your* ransom *Egypt* 1QIsa[b] MT LXX.
j. 1QIsa[a]. *Seba* 1QIsa[b] 4QIsa[g] MT.

and nations in exchange for your life.

5 Do not be afraid, for I am with you;
  I will bring your children from the east
  and gather you from the west.
6 I will say to the north, "Give them up!"
  and to the south, "Do not keep them back!"
  Bring[a] my sons from far away
  and my daughters from the ends of the earth—
7 everyone who is called by my name,
  whom I created for my glory,
  whom[b] I formed and made."
8 Bring out the people who are blind yet still have eyes,
  who are deaf yet still have ears!

Israel as God's Witness

9 Let all the nations be gathered together,
  and let the peoples be assembled.
  Who is there among them *that*[c] can declare this
  or *announce*[d] the former things?
  Let them produce their witnesses to prove them right,
  and let them *proclaim*[e] so people will say, "It is true."
10 You are my witnesses, declares the Lord,
  and my servant whom I have chosen,
  so that you may know and trust me
  and understand that I am *the one*.[f]
  Before me no God was formed,
  nor will there be one after me.
11 I, yes I, am the Lord,
  and apart from me there is no savior.
12 I have revealed and saved and proclaimed,
  when there was no foreign god among you—
  and you are my witnesses, declares the Lord.
13 *I am God; also*[g] from *ancient days*[h] I am the one.
  And there is no one who can deliver out of my hand;
  when I act, who can reverse it?

a. Masculine plural 1QIsaᵃ. Feminine plural MT.
b. 1QIsaᵃ MT. *and whom* 1QIsaᵇ.
c. 1QIsaᵃ. Not in MT LXX.
d. 1QIsaᵃ. *announce to us* MT. *announce to you* LXX.
e. 1QIsaᵃ. *hear* MT.
f. Or, *he.*
g. 1QIsaᵃ. *I am God. Yes,* MT (cf. LXX).
h. Or, *this day on.*

The Lord Will Do a New Thing

14 This is what the Lord says,
  your Redeemer, the Holy One of Israel:
For your sake I will send *to Babylon,*[a]
  and bring them all down as fugitives.
  And as for the Babylonians: their ringing cry will become lamentation.
15 I am the Lord, your Holy One,
  Creator of Israel, and your King.
16 This is what the Lord says—
  who makes a way through the sea,
  a path through the mighty waters,
17 who brings out chariots and horsemen,
    and[b] armies and warriors at the same time;
  they lie there, never to rise again,
    extinguished, snuffed out like a *candle:*[c]
18 *Do not remember*[d] the former things;
  do not dwell on things past.
19 See, I am about to carry out something new!
    And[e] now it is springing up—do you not recognize it?
I am making a way in the wilderness
  and *paths*[f] in the desert.
20 Wild animals, jackals and *owls,*[g] will honor me
because I *provide*[h] water in the desert
    and streams in the wilderness
to give drink to *my people, my chosen ones,*[i]
21 the people whom I formed for myself
and[j] so that they may *speak*[k] my praise.

The Lord Rebukes Israel

22 *And*[l] yet you did not call upon me, Jacob;
  indeed, you are tired of me, Israel!

a. 1QIsa[a], 4QIsa[b], and MT each spell differently.
b. 1QIsa[a] LXX. Not in MT.
c. Literally, *linen wick.*
d. Second-person singular 1QIsa[a]. Second-person plural MT LXX.
e. 1QIsa[a]. Not in MT.
f. 1QIsa[a]. *streams* MT LXX.
g. Or, *ostriches.*
h. 1QIsa[a]. *have provided* MT.
i. 1QIsa[a]. *my chosen people* MT.
j. 1QIsa[a]. Not in 4QIsa[g] MT.
k. 1QIsa[a]. *recount* 4QIsa[g] MT LXX.
l. 1QIsa[a] MT. Not in MTmss.

²³ You have not brought me your sheep for *a burnt offering*,ᵃ
nor have you honored me *with*ᵇ your sacrifices,
*nor have you made meal offerings for me*ᶜ —
yet I have not tired you about incense!
²⁴ *You*ᵈ have not bought me sweet cane with money,
nor have you satisfied me with the fat of your sacrifices.
You have only burdened me with your sins
and made me tired with your iniquities.
²⁵ I, I am the one
who blots out your *transgression*ᵉ for my own sake,
and I will *remember your sins no more.*ᶠ
²⁶ Recount the brief, let us argue the matter together;
present your case, so that you may be proved right.
²⁷ Your first ancestor sinned,
and your mediators rebelled against me.
²⁸ So I will disgrace the leaders of the temple,
and I will consign Jacob to total destruction
and Israel to contempt.

The Lord Reassures Israel

⁴⁴:¹ But now listen, Jacob my servant
and Israel whom I have chosen:
² This what the Lord says who made you,
and formed you from the womb, *who will help*ᵍ you:
Do not be afraid, Jacob my servant,
and Jeshurun whom I have chosen.
³ For I will pour water upon thirsty ground
and streams on parched land.
*Just so*ʰ will I pour my Spirit upon your offspring,
and my blessing upon your descendants.
⁴ *They*ⁱ *will spring up*ʲ *as among*ᵏ the green grass,
like willows by flowing streams.
⁵ One will say, "I belong to the Lord,"
and another will call himself by the name of Jacob;

a. 1QIsaᵃ. *your burnt offerings* MT.
b. Explicit in 1QIsaᵃ (cf. LXX). Implicit in MT.
c. 1QIsaᵃ. *I have not burdened you with grain offerings* 4QIsaᵍ MT. Not in LXX.
d. 1QIsaᵃ MT. *And you* 4QIsaᵍ.
e. 1QIsaᵃ. *transgressions* MT (cf. LXX).
f. 1QIsaᵃ. *not remember your sins* MT.
g. 1QIsaᵃ. MT reads *he will help.*
h. 1QIsaᵃ. Not in MT.
i. 1QIsaᵃ. MT LXX read *And they.*
j. 1QIsaᵃ and MT use different forms of the verb.
k. 1QIsaᵃ MTmss LXX Targ. MT reads *among.*

> still another will write on his hand, "the Lord's,"
> and adopt the name of Israel.

6 This is what the Lord says, the King of Israel
and its Redeemer—the Lord of hosts *is his name:*[a]
I am the first and I am the last;
and apart from me there is no God.
7 Who is like me? Let him proclaim
and declare it and lay it out for *himself*[b]
since he made[c] an ancient people.
And *let him speak*[d] future events;
let them tell him *what*[e] will happen.
8 Do not tremble, *and do not be afraid.*[f]
Did I not tell you and announce it long ago?
You are my witnesses.
Is there any God besides me?
There is no other Rock—I don't know any.

9 *Now,*[g] all the *forming of*[h] images means nothing, and the things they treasure are worthless. Their own witnesses cannot see; *they*[i] know not anything. And so they will be put to shame.

Absurdity of Idols Made by Craftsmen

10 Who would shape a god or cast an image that profits nothing? 11 To be sure, all associated with it will be put to shame; and as for the craftsmen, they are only human. Let them all gather together *and*[j] take their stand. *Then*[k] let them be in awe—they will be humiliated together.
12 The blacksmith prepares a tool and works in the coals, *and*[l] fashions an idol with hammers, working by the strength of his arm. He even becomes hungry and loses his strength; he drinks no water and grows faint. 13 The carpenter measures *it*[m] with a line; he traces its shape with a stylus, then fashions it with planes and shapes it with a compass. He makes the idol like a human figure, with human

---

a. 1QIsaᵃ. Not in MT LXX.
b. 1QIsaᵃ. MT LXX read *me*.
c. Or, *making him* 1QIsaᵃ. MT (cf. LXX) reads *Since I made* (Hebrew obscure).
d. 1QIsaᵃ. Not in 4QIsaᶜ MT (cf. LXX).
e. 1QIsaᵃ. MT reads *and what* 4QIsaᶜ.
f. 1QIsaᵃ MT (which misspells). Not in LXX.
g. 1QIsaᵃ. Not in MT LXX.
h. 1QIsaᵃ. MT LXX read *those who form*.
i. 1QIsaᵃ. MT LXX read *and they*.
j. 1QIsaᵃ LXX. Not in MT.
k. 1QIsaᵃ. Not in MT LXX.
l. 1QIsaᵃ. Not in MT LXX.
m. That is, the idol. 1QIsaᵃ LXX. Not in MT.

beauty, to dwell in a shrine. ¹⁴He cuts down cedars, or chooses a cypress tree or an oak, and lets it grow strong among the trees from the forest. Or he plants a cedar, and the rain makes it grow. ¹⁵ *He divides it up*ᵃ for people to burn. Taking part of it, he warms himself, makes a fire, and bakes bread. *Or perhaps*ᵇ he constructs a god and worships it; he makes it an idol and bows down to it. ¹⁶Half the wood he burns in the fire, *and*ᶜ *over*ᵈ that half *is meat so he may eat. He sits by its coals, warms himself,*ᵉ and says, "Ah! I am warm *in front of*ᶠ the fire." ¹⁷And the rest of it he makes into a *god. To blocks of wood he*ᵍ bows down and worships, prays to it and says, "Save me, for you are my god."

¹⁸They do not realize; they do not understand. For their eyes are plastered over so they cannot see; and their minds, too, so they cannot understand. ¹⁹No one stops to think; no one has the knowledge or understanding to think, yes *to think,*ʰ "Half of it I burned in the fire. I even baked bread on its coals, *and*ⁱ I roasted meat and ate it. *And*ʲ am I about to make *detestable things*ᵏ from what is left? Am I about to bow down to *blocks*ˡ of wood?" ²⁰He tends ashes; a deceived mind has led him astray. *It cannot be his life,*ᵐ nor can he say, "*There is a lie in my right hand*."ⁿ

> ²¹ Remember these things, Jacob,
>   *Israel,*ᵒ for you are my servant.
>   I have formed you; you are a servant to me.
>   *Israel,*ᵖ *you must not mislead me.* q

Israel Is Not Forgotten

> ²² I have wiped away your transgressions like a cloud
>   and your sins like mist.

a. 1QIsaᵃ. MT reads *It is.* LXX reads *so that it is.*

b. 1QIsaᵃ. MT reads *Also.*

c. 1QIsaᵃ LXX. Not in MT.

d. Not originally in 1QIsaᵃ, but added above the line.

e. 1QIsaᵃ. MT (cf. LXX) reads *eats meat he roasted as a roast and is satisfied. He also warms himself.*

f. 1QIsaᵃ. MT reads *I see.* LXX reads *and I have seen.*

g. *Blocks* is misspelled, or an error (for *to his Baals?*) in 1QIsaᵃ (see v. 19). MT (cf. LXX) reads *god, for his idol.*

h. Repeated in 1QIsaᵃ. Not in MT.

i. 1QIsaᵃ. Not in MT.

j. 1QIsaᵃ MT. Not in 4QIsaᵇ.

k. 1QIsaᵃ. 4QIsaᵇ MT LXX read *a detestable thing.*

l. 1QIsaᵃ. *a block* MT.

m. 1QIsaᵃ. 4QIsaᵇ MT (cf. LXX) read *He does not save his life.*

n. 1QIsaᵃ. 4QIsaᵇ MT (cf. LXX) read *"Is there not a lie in my right hand?"*

o. 1QIsaᵃ. 4QIsaᵇ MT LXX read *and Israel.*

p. 1QIsaᵃ MT. 4QIsaᵇ (cf. LXX) reads *and Israel.*

q. 1QIsaᵃ. 4QIsaᵇ MT read *you will not be forgotten by me.* LXX reads *do not forget me.*

Return to me; for I have redeemed you.
23 Shout for joy, you heavens, for the Lord has done it!
   Shout aloud, you depths of the earth!
Burst out with singing, you mountains,
   you forest and all your trees!
For the Lord has redeemed Jacob
   and will display his glory in Israel.
24 This is what the Lord says, your Redeemer
   and the one who formed you in the womb:
I am the Lord who has made everything,
   who alone stretched out the heavens,
   who spread out the earth—who was with me?—
25 who frustrates the omens of idle talkers
   and drives diviners mad,
   who turns back the wise
   and makes their knowledge *foolish*;[a]
26 who carries out the words of his servants
   and fulfills the predictions of his messengers;
who says of Jerusalem, "It will be lived in,"
   and of Judah's cities, "They will be rebuilt,"
   and of her ruins, "I will raise them up";
27 who says to the watery deep, "Be dry—
   I will dry up your rivers";
28 who says of Cyrus, "He is my shepherd,
   and he will carry out all that I please"—
he will say of Jerusalem, "Let it be rebuilt,"
   and of *my*[b] temple, "Let its foundations be laid again."

Cyrus Is the Lord's Instrument

45:1 This is what the Lord says to his anointed, Cyrus,
   whose right hand I have grasped
to subdue nations before him,
   as I *strip kings of their armor*,[c]
to open *doors*[d] before him
   and gates that cannot keep closed:
2 I myself will go before you,
   and *he*[e] will make the *mountains*[f] level;
I will shatter bronze doors

a. 1QIsaª 1QIsaᵇ 4QIsaᵇ LXX. Literally, *wise* MT.
b. 1QIsaª LXX. 4QIsaᵇ MT read *the*.
c. Literally, *expose the loins of kings*.
d. Plural 1QIsaª. Dual MT.
e. 1QIsaª. MT LXX read *I*.
f. 1QIsaª 1QIsaᵇ LXX. MT reads the *hills*.

and cut through iron bars.

³ I will give you *concealed treasures*[a]
and riches hidden in secret places,
so that you will know that it is I, the Lord,
the God of Israel, who calls you by name.

⁴ For the sake of Jacob my servant,
Israel[b] my chosen,
I have called you,
and he has established you with a name,[c]
although you have not acknowledged me.

⁵ I am the Lord, and *there is none else*
besides me: and there are no gods.[d]
I arm you, although you have not acknowledged me,

⁶ so that from *the sun's rising*[e] to the west
people may know that there is none besides me.
I am the Lord, and there is no other.

⁷ I form light and create darkness,
I make *goodness*[f] and create disaster.
I am the Lord, who does all these things.

⁸ *Shout,*[g] *you skies above and you clouds,*
and let righteousness stream down.[h]
The one who says to the earth, "Let salvation blossom,
and let righteousness sprout forth."[i]

⁹ Woe to the one who quarrels with his maker,
a mere potsherd with the potsherds of *the*[j] earth.
Woe to the one who says[k] *to the one forming him,*
"What are you making?"
or "Your work has no *human*[l] hands?"

¹⁰ Woe to *the*[m] one who says to his father,
"What are you begetting?"
or to a woman, "What are you giving birth to?"

---

a. Literally, *treasures of darkness.*

b. 1QIsaᵃ. MT LXX read *and Israel.*

c. 1QIsaᵃ. MT reads *I have called you by your name, given you a title.* LXX reads *I will call you by your name, and receive you.*

d. 1QIsaᵃ. MT (cf. 1QIsaᵇ) reads *there is no other: besides me there are no gods.*

e. That is, *the east.*

f. 1QIsaᵃ. MT reads *well-being.* LXX reads *peace.*

g. 1QIsaᵃ (cf. LXX). MT reads *Shower.*

h. 1QIsaᵃ. 1QIsaᵇ MT LXX read *Shower, you skies above, and let the clouds stream down righteousness.*

i. 1QIsaᵃ. 1QIsaᵇ 1QIsaᶜ(?) MT read *Let the earth open up, let them bear the fruit of salvation, and let righteousness sprout forth also. I the Lord have created it.*

j. 1QIsaᵃ. Implicit in MT.

k. 1QIsaᵃ. 1QIsaᵇ MT LXX read *Will clay say.*

l. 1QIsaᵃ. Not in MT LXX.

m. 1QIsaᵃ. Implicit in MT.

The Nations Will Help Restore Israel

¹¹ This is what *the Lord*^a says,
   the Creator of the signs:
Question me about my children?^b
   Or give me orders about the work of my hands?
¹² I myself made the earth
   and personally created humankind upon it.
My own hands stretched out the skies;
   I marshaled all their starry hosts.
¹³ I have aroused *him*^c in righteousness,
   and I will make all his pathways smooth.
It is he who will rebuild my city
   and set my exiles free,
but not for a price or reward,
   says the Lord of hosts.
¹⁴ This is what the Lord says:
The wealth of Egypt, and the merchandise of Ethiopia,
   those^d Sabeans, men of *great height*^e
—they will come over to you and will be yours;
   they will trudge behind you,
   coming over in chains they will bow down to you.
They will plead with you,
   "Surely God is in you; and there is
   no other God at all."
¹⁵ Truly you are a God who hides himself,
   O God of Israel, the Savior.
¹⁶ All of them will be put to shame, indeed, disgraced—
   the makers of idols will go off in disgrace together.
¹⁷ But Israel will be saved by the Lord
   with everlasting salvation;
you will not be put to shame or disgraced,
   never again.

The Lord Asserts Superiority over Idols

¹⁸ For this is what the Lord says,
   who created the heavens—

a. 1QIsa^a (originally). MT LXX read *the Lord, the Holy One of Israel.* 1QIsa^a (corrected: inserted above the line by a later scribe).

b. 1QIsa^a LXX (. . . *sons and daughters*). MT reads *and its creator: Question me of things to come about my children?*

c. That is, the Persian king Cyrus.

d. Literally, *and those* 1QIsa^a. MT LXX read *and those* (lit. *and the*).

e. Plural 1QIsa^a. MT reads *height* (sing.).

he is God
 and[a] the one who formed the earth and made it;
  and[b] he is the one who established it;
 he did not create it *for*[c] chaos,
  but formed it to be inhabited—
 I am the Lord and there is no other.

¹⁹ I did not speak in secret,
  from somewhere in a land of darkness;
 I did not say to Jacob's descendants,
  "Seek me in chaos."
 I, the Lord, speak truth,
  declaring what is right.

²⁰ Gather together and come;
  draw near *and enter,*[d]
  your fugitives from the nations.
 Those who carry around their wooden idols
  know nothing,
 nor do those who keep praying to a god
  that cannot save.

²¹ Explain and present a case,
  yes, let them take counsel together:
 Who announced this long ago,
  who declared it from the distant past?
 Was it not I, the Lord?
  And there is no other God besides me,
 a righteous God and Savior;
  and[e] there is none besides me.

²² Turn to me and be saved,
  all you ends of the earth.
  For I am God, and there is no other.

²³ By myself I have sworn,
  from my mouth has gone out integrity,
  a *promise*[f] that will not be revoked:
 "To me every knee will bow,
  and[g] every tongue will swear."

²⁴ "Only in the Lord," *one will say of me,*[h]
 "are victories and might."

---

a. 1QIsaª. Not in MT LXX.
b. 1QIsaª. Not in MT.
c. 1QIsaª LXX. Implicit in MT.
d. 1QIsaª. MT LXX read *together.*
e. 1QIsaª. Not in MT LXX.
f. Literally, *word.*
g. 1QIsaª. Not in MT.
h. 1QIsaª. MT reads *one said of me.* LXX reads *saying.*

To him *will come*[a]
> all who raged against him, and they will be put to shame.
25 In the Lord all the descendants of Israel
> will triumph and make their boast.

Exhortation for Zion to Awake and the Exiles to Return

52:1 Awake, awake,
> put on *strength*,[b] O Zion;
put on your beautiful garments,
> O Jerusalem, the holy city;
for the uncircumcised and the unclean will not enter *you*.[c]
2 Shake yourself from the dust; *and*[d] arise,
> *and*[e] sit on your throne, O Jerusalem;
loose the bonds from your neck,
> O captive daughter of Zion.

3 For this is what the Lord says: You were sold for nothing; and you will be redeemed without money.
4 For this is what *the Lord*[f] says: My people went down long ago into Egypt to sojourn there; the Assyrian, too, has oppressed them without cause.
5 Now therefore, *what*[g] am I doing here, says the Lord, seeing that my people are taken away without cause? Those who rule over them *are deluded*,[h] says the Lord, and continually, all the day long, my name is blasphemed. 6 Therefore my people will know my name; *in that day*[i] they will know that it is I who speaks; here am I.

7 How *beautiful*[j] upon the mountains
> are the feet of the one *who brings news of peace*,[k]
who announces good things, who announces salvation,[l]
> who says to Zion, "Your God reigns!"
8 Listen, your watchmen lift up *their voices*,[m]
> together they sing for joy;

a. Plural 1QIsaᵃ MTmss LXX. Singular MT.
b. 1QIsaᵃ. MT LXX read *your strength*.
c. 1QIsaᵃ. MT LXX read *you anymore*.
d. 1QIsaᵃ LXX. Not in 4QIsaᵇ MT.
e. 1QIsaᵃ. Not in MT LXX.
f. 1QIsaᵃ LXX. MT reads *the Lord God*.
g. 1QIsaᵃ LXX. Literally, *who* MT.
h. Meaning unclear 1QIsaᵃ. MT LXX read *wail*.
i. 1QIsaᵃ LXX. MT reads *therefore in that day*.
j. Literally, *they are beautiful* 1QIsaᵃ MTT LXXmss. Literally, *it is beautiful* 4QIsaᵇ.
k. 1QIsaᵃ. MT LXX read *who brings good news*.
l. 1QIsaᵃ. MT reads *who announces peace, who brings news of good things, who announces salvation* (cf. LXX).
m. Literally, *their voice* 1QIsaᵃ. Literally, *the voice* MT.

for in plain sight they will see
the return of the Lord to Zion *with compassion*.[a]

9 Break forth together *into singing*,[b]
you ruins of Jerusalem;
for the Lord has comforted his people,
and[c] he has redeemed Jerusalem.

10 The Lord has bared his holy arm
in the eyes of all the nations;
and all the ends of *the earth*[d] will see
the salvation of our God.

11 Depart, depart, go out from there,
touch no unclean thing;
go out from the midst of her, purify yourselves,
you who carry the vessels of the Lord.

12 For you will not go out in haste,
nor will you go in flight;
for the Lord will go before you;
and the God of Israel will be your rear guard.
He is called the God of all the earth.[e]

13 See, my servant will prosper,
and[f] he will be exalted and lifted up,
and will be very high.

14 Just as many were astonished *at you*[g]
—so was *he marred*[h] in his appearance, more than any human,
and his form beyond that of the sons of *humans*[i]—

15 so will he *startle*[j] many nations.
Kings will shut their mouths at him;
for what had not been told them they will see;
and what they had not heard they will understand.

The Suffering Servant

53:1 *Who*[k] has believed our message?
And *on whom*[l] has the arm of the Lord been revealed?

a. 1QIsa[a] (cf. LXX). Not in MT.
b. Literally, *sing for joy* (sing.) 1QIsa[a]. Literally, *sing for joy* (pl.) MT.
c. 1QIsa[a] LXX. Not in MT.
d. 1QIsa[a] LXX. MT reads *earth*.
e. 1QIsa[a]. Not in MT LXX.
f. 1QIsa[a]. Not in 1QIsa[b] 4QIsa[c] MT. LXX omits *(and) he will be exalted*.
g. 1QIsa[a] MT LXX. MTmss Syriac read *at him*.
h. Possibly *my marring* 1QIsa[a]. Literally, *marring of* MT.
i. Literally, *the human* 1QIsa[a] (cf. *the humans* LXX). Literally, *human* MT.
j. Or, *sprinkle*.
k. 1QIsa[a] 1QIsa[b] MT. LXX reads *Lord, who*.
l. 1QIsa[a] 1QIsa[b]. MT reads *on whom* (possible meaning).

2 For he grew up before him like a tender plant,
and like a root out of a dry ground;
he had no form *and he had no majesty*[a] that we should *look at him*,[b]
and no attractiveness that we should *desire him.*[c]

3 He was despised and rejected by others,
and[d] a man of sorrows, and *familiar*[e] with suffering;
and like one from whom people hide their faces
and[f] *we despised him*,[g] and we did not value him.

4 Surely he has borne our sufferings,
and carried our sorrows;
yet we considered him stricken,
and[h] struck down by God, and afflicted.

5 But he was wounded for our transgressions,
and[i] he was crushed for our iniquities,
and[j] the punishment that made us whole was upon him,
and by his bruises we are healed.

6 All we like sheep have gone astray,
we have turned, each of us, to his own way;
and the Lord has laid on him
the iniquity of us all.

7 He was oppressed and he was afflicted,
yet he did not open his mouth;
like a lamb that is led to the slaughter,
as[k] a sheep that before its shearers is silent,
so he *did not open*[l] his mouth.

8 From detention *and*[m] judgment *he was taken away*[n]
—and who can even think about his *descendants?*[o]
For he was cut off of the land of the living,
he was stricken[p] for the transgression of my people.

9 Then *they made*[q] his grave with the wicked,

a. 1QIsa[a]. 1QIsa[b] MT LXX read *and no majesty*.

b. 1QIsa[a] 1QIsa[b] MT LXX. 1QIsa[a] could also mean *look at ourselves*.

c. 1QIsa[a] MT LXX. 1QIsa[a] could also mean *desire ourselves*.

d. 1QIsa[a]. Not in 1QIsa[b] MT LXX.

e. Active (*knowing*) 1QIsa[a] LXX. Passive (*acquainted with*) MT). 1QIsa[b] is ambiguous.

f. 1QIsa[a] 1QIsa[b]. Not in MT LXX.

g. 1QIsa[a]. MT LXX read *he was despised*.

h. 1QIsa[a] (cf. LXX). Not in MT.

i. 1QIsa[a] LXX. Not in MT.

j. 1QIsa[a] 1QIsa[b]. Not in MT LXX.

k. 1QIsa[a]. MT LXX read *and as*.

l. 1QIsa[a]. MT reads *does not open*.

m. 1QIsa[a] MT. Not in 1QIsa[b].

n. 1QIsa[a] MT LXX. 1QIsa[b] reads *they took (him) away*.

o. Or, *future*.

p. 1QIsa[a]. Literally, *an affliction* MT.

q. 1QIsa[a]. 4QIsa[d] MT read *he made*. LXX reads *I will give*.

and with *rich people*[a] *in his death*[b]
—although he had done no violence,
    nor was any deceit in his mouth.

10 Yet the Lord was willing to crush him,
    and he made him suffer.[c]
Although you make his soul an offering for sin,
    and[d] he will see his offspring, *and*[e] he will prolong his days,
and the will of the Lord will triumph in his hand.

11 *Out of the suffering of his soul he will see light,*[f]
    and[g] *find satisfaction.*
And[h] *through his knowledge his servant,*[i] the righteous one,
    will make many righteous,
and he will bear their iniquities.

12 Therefore will I allot him a portion with the great,
    and he will divide the spoils with the strong;
because he poured out his life to death,
    and was numbered with the transgressors;
yet he bore *the sins*[j] of many,
    and made intercession for *their transgressions.*[k]

58:1 Shout aloud, do not hold back!
    Lift up your voice like a trumpet!
Declare to my people their *rebellions,*[l]
    and to the house of Jacob their sins.

2 *They*[m] seek me *day after day,*[n]
    and are eager to know my ways,
as if they were a nation that practices righteousness
    and has not forsaken the justice of their God.
They ask of me for just decisions;
    they are eager to draw near to God.

3 "Why have we fasted (they ask), but you do not see?
    Why have we humbled *ourselves,*[o] but you take no notice?"

a. Original reading, 1QIsa[a]. 1QIsa[a] (corrected) MT read *a rich man*.
b. Singular form 1QIsa[a] LXX. *in his deaths* (pl.) MT.
c. 1QIsa[a]. 4QIsa[d] MT read *he made (him) suffer*. LXX reads *with a blow*.
d. 1QIsa[a]. Not in MT LXX.
e. 1QIsa[a] 4QIsa[d]. Not in 1QIsa[b] MT.
f. 1QIsa[a] 1QIsa[b] 4QIsa[d] (cf. LXX). MT reads *He will see (some) of the suffering of his soul*.
g. 1QIsa[a] 4QIsa[d](?). Not in MT.
h. 1QIsa[a]. Not in 4QIsa[d] MT.
i. 1QIsa[a]. 4QIsa[d] MT read *my servant*.
j. 1QIsa[a] 1QIsa[b] 4QIsa[d] LXX. MT reads *the sin*.
k. 1QIsa[a] 1QIsa[b] 4QIsa[d] LXX. MT reads *the transgressors*.
l. 1QIsa[a] LXX. 1QIsa[b] MT read *rebellion*.
m. 1QIsa[a] 1QIsa[b] 4QIsa[d] LXX. MT reads *And they*.
n. Literally, *day and day* 1QIsa[a]. Literally, *day, day* 1QIsa[b] 4QIsa[d] MT.
o. 1QIsa[a] 1QIsa[b] LXX. MT reads *ourself*.

Look, on your fast day you serve your own interest
  and oppress all your workers.
4 Look, you fast only for quarreling, and *for*[a] fighting
  and for hitting with wicked fists.
You cannot fast as you do today
  and have your voice heard on high.
5 Is this the kind of fast that I have chosen,
   merely a day for a person to humble himself?
Is it merely for bowing down one's head like a bulrush,
   for lying[b] on sackcloth and ashes?
Is this what *you*[c] call a fast,
   an[d] acceptable day to the Lord?

6 Is not this *the*[e] fast *that*[f] I choose:
   to loose the bonds of injustice,
   and[g] to untie the cords of the yoke,
 and[h] to let the oppressed go free,
   and to break every yoke?
7 Is it not to share your bread with the hungry,
   and to bring the homeless poor into your house;
when you see the naked, to cover him *with clothing*,[i]
   and not to *raise yourself up*[j] from your own flesh and blood?
8 Then your light will break forth like the dawn,
   and your healing will spring up quickly;
and your vindication will go before you,
   and[k] the glory of the Lord will be your rear guard.
9 Then will you call, and the Lord will answer;
   you will cry for help, and he will say, Here I am.

If you do away with the yoke among you,
   and[l] pointing fingers, and malicious talk;
10 if you pour yourself out for the hungry
   and satisfy the needs of afflicted souls,
then your light will rise in darkness,
   and your night will be like noonday.

a. 1QIsa^b 1QIsa^a. Not in MT LXX.
b. 1QIsa^a 1QIsa^b. MT LXX read *and for lying*.
c. Plural 1QIsa^a 4QIsa^d LXX. Singular 1QIsa^b MT.
d. 1QIsa^a 1QIsa^b. MT reads *and an*.
e. 1QIsa^a. Not in 1QIsa^b MT LXX.
f. 1QIsa^a. Not in 1QIsa^b MT LXX.
g. 1QIsa^a. Not in 1QIsa^b MT LXX.
h. 1QIsa^a MT. Not in 1QIsa^b 4QIsa^d LXX.
i. 1QIsa^a. Not in 1QIsa^b MT LXX.
j. 1QIsa^a. 1QIsa^b MT read *hide yourself*. LXX reads *disregard*.
k. 1QIsa^a 1QIsa^b LXX. Not in MT.
l. 1QIsa^a LXX. Not in 1QIsa^b MT.

¹¹ And the Lord will guide you continually,
  and satisfy your soul in *parched places*,^a
  and *they will*^b strengthen your bones;
and you will be like a watered garden,
  like a spring of water,
  whose waters never fail.
¹² And your people will rebuild the ancient ruins;
  you will raise up *the age-old foundations*,^c
and *people will call you*^d Repairer of Broken Walls,
  Restorer of Streets to Live In.

¹³ If you keep your feet from trampling the Sabbath,
  from^e pursuing your own interests on my holy day,
if you call the Sabbath a delight
  and^f the Lord's holy day honorable;
and if you honor it by not going *your own ways*^g
  and^h seeking your own pleasure or speaking (idle) words—
¹⁴ then you will take delight in the Lord,
  *and he*ⁱ will make you ride upon the heights of the earth;
  and he^j will make you feast on the inheritance of your ancestor Jacob
    your father.
  Yes—the mouth of the Lord has spoken.

^{61:1} The spirit of *the Lord*^k is upon me,
  because the Lord has anointed me;
he has sent me to bring good news to the oppressed
  and^l to bind up the brokenhearted,
to proclaim freedom for the captives,
  and *release from darkness*^m for the prisoners;
² to proclaim the year of the Lord's favor,
  *the day*ⁿ of vengeance of our God;
  to comfort all who mourn;
³ to provide for those who grieve in Zion—

a. 1QIsa^a seems to spell the word incorrectly.
b. 1QIsa^a 1QIsa^b. MT reads *he will* MT. LXX reads *(and your bones) will be strengthened*.
c. Literally, *the foundations of many generations*.
d. 1QIsa^a. 1QIsa^b MT LXX read *you will be called*.
e. 1QIsa^a 4QIsaⁿ. Not in 1QIsa^b MT.
f. 1QIsa^a 1QIsa^b 4QIsaⁿ. Not in MT LXX.
g. 1QIsa^a 4QIsaⁿ MT. 1QIsa^b reads *your own way*.
h. 1QIsa^a. Not in 1QIsa^b MT.
i. 1QIsa^a 1QIsa^b 4QIsaⁿ LXX. MT reads *and I*.
j. 1QIsa^a LXX. 1QIsa^b 4QIsaⁿ MT read *and I*.
k. 1QIsa^a 1QIsa^b LXX. 4QIsa^m MT read *the Lord God*.
l. 1QIsa^a. Not in MT LXX.
m. Or, *release from prison*, or *opening of the eyes*.
n. 1QIsa^a LXXms. 4QIsa^b MT LXX read *and the day*.

to bestow on them a crown of beauty instead of ashes,
  the oil of gladness instead of mourning,
    a mantle of praise instead of a spirit of despair.
Then *people will call them*[a] oaks of righteousness,
  the planting of the Lord, in order to display his splendor.
⁴ They will rebuild the ancient ruins,
  they will restore the places long devastated;
they will build again the ruined cities,
  they will build again[b] the places devastated for many generations.

⁵ Strangers will stand and feed your flocks,
  and foreigners will work your land and dress your vines;
⁶ but as for you—you will be called priests of the Lord,
  and[c] you will be named ministers of our God.
You will feed on the wealth of the nations,
  and in their riches you will brag.
⁷ Instead of your shame you will receive double,
  and instead of disgrace people will shout with joy over *your
    inheritance;*[d]
therefore *you*[e] will inherit *a double portion in their land,*[f]
  everlasting joy will be *yours.*[g]

⁸ For I the Lord love justice, *and*[h]
  I hate robbery and iniquity;
I will faithfully *present your reward*[i]
  and make an everlasting covenant *with you.*[j]
⁹ *Your*[k] offspring will be known among the nations,
  and *your*[l] descendants among the peoples.
All who see them will acknowledge them,
  that they are an offspring the Lord has blessed.

¹⁰ I will heartily rejoice in the Lord,
  my soul will delight in my God;
for he has wrapped me in garments of salvation,
  he has arrayed me in a robe of righteousness,

a. 1QIsaᵃ. MT LXX read *they will be called.*
b. 1QIsaᵃ. Not in MT LXX.
c. 1QIsaᵃ. Not in MT LXX.
d. 1QIsaᵃ. MT reads *their inheritance.*
e. 1QIsaᵃ. MT (cf. LXX) reads *they.*
f. 1QIsaᵃ. MT reads *in their land a double portion* (word order).
g. 1QIsaᵃ. MT reads *theirs.* LXX reads *over their head.*
h. 1QIsaᵃ LXX. Not in MT.
i. 1QIsaᵃ. MT LX read *present their reward.*
j. 1QIsaᵃ. MT LXX read *with them.*
k. 1QIsaᵃ. MT LXX read *Their.*
l. 1QIsaᵃ. MT LXX read *their.*

just like a bridegroom, *like a priest*[a] with a garland,
    and like a bride adorns herself with her jewels.
11 For just as the soil brings forth its shoots,
    and as a garden makes what is sown in it spring up,
so the *Lord God*[b] will make righteousness and praise
    spring up before all the nations 62:1 *for Zion's sake.*[c]

a. 1QIsaᵃ. MT reads *decks himself like a priest*. LXX reads *decks me*.
b. 1QIsaᵃ. MT reads *the Lord God*. LXX reads *the Lord*.
c. Ends chap. 61 in 1QIsaᵃ. Begins chap. 62 in MT LXX.

Psalms and Psalters at Qumran

Approximately 1,000 scrolls were found in the Judean Desert, of which about 240—some 220 at Qumran—are classified as "biblical scrolls" (*see* Overview of Early Jewish Literature). While examining the contents and themes of biblical books is outside the bounds of this essay, the biblical scrolls are relevant because they are virtually the only surviving copies from the Second Temple period of books now comprising the Hebrew Bible. As such, some biblical scrolls offer important insights on the finalization and form of several scriptural books used in early Judaism and by Jesus and the New Testament writers. Only Deuteronomy (forty-one scrolls, with thirty-eight at Qumran) is represented by more copies than Psalms (forty, with thirty-eight at Qumran). This prominence highlights the importance of the Psalter among the *yaḥad,* or **Essene,** movement, whose most noteworthy center was at Qumran. As our earliest extant witnesses to the scriptural text of the Psalms, these scrolls hold significant implications for understanding the Psalms in the later Second Temple period and their finalization as a collection.

With the publication of 11QPs[a] in 1965, a heated debate ensued between James Sanders (who proposed that the Great Psalms Scroll contains the latter part of an authentic edition of the book of Psalms) and scholars such as Shemaryahu Talmon, G. H. Goshen-Gottstein, and Patrick Skehan (who proposed that 11QPs[a] is a liturgical collection secondary to the **Masoretic Text**, or **MT**). The resolution of this debate involves four questions, on which evidence was to come forward in the Psalms scrolls from Cave 4, one scroll from Cave 11 (11QPs[b]), and the second Psalms scroll from Masada (MasPs[b]).

1. Are there other Psalms scrolls that preserve the *distinctive arrangement* (sequence of Psalms) found in 11QPs[a]? At least eight Psalms scrolls diverge from the MT–150 Psalter in the ordering of contents (e.g., 4QPs[b]), but only two follow the arrangement in 11QPs[a]: 4QPs[e] (most probably Psalms 104→147→105 [→ indicates that a composition follows directly]) and 11QPs[b] (Psalms 141→133→144).
2. Are there other Psalms scrolls that preserve the *distinctive arrangement* (sequence of Psalms) found in the MT–150 Psalter? While many Psalms scrolls from Qumran contain material that corresponds with the MT–150 sequence

(e.g., Pss. 125–130 in 4QPs^e), these arrangements reflect the 11QPs^a-Psalter as well. In fact, no Psalms scroll from Qumran *unambiguously* confirms the MT–150 order. For such confirmation we must turn to Masada, where in MasPs^b Psalm 150 is directly followed by a blank column, thus denoting the end of that edition of the book of Psalms.

3. Do any other Psalms scrolls contain the *distinctive contents* (compositions absent from the MT–150 Psalter) found in 11QPs^a? Only two other Psalms scrolls contain such apocryphal compositions: 4QPs^f (the Apostrophe to Zion and the Eschatological Hymn and Apostrophe to Judah [which may be a single work]) and 11QPs^b (the Catena, the Plea for Deliverance, and the Apostrophe to Zion).

4. If 11QPs^a indeed contains the latter part of an authentic edition of the book of Psalms, are there any Psalms scrolls that preserve *earlier sections* of this larger Psalter (i.e., psalms prior to 93, the earliest one preserved in 11QPs^a in terms of the MT–150 numerical sequence)? 4QPs^e preserves text from Psalms 76–89, and 11QPs^b text from Psalms 77 and 78.

The evidence from the Psalms scrolls now indicates that at least three editions of the Psalms were in circulation in the late Second Temple period (or at least among the among the *yahad*, or Essene, movement):

Edition I: An early edition of the Psalter containing Psalms 1 or 2 to 72 or 89 (the cutoff point is not certain). The earliest and most complete example is 4QPs^a, which preserves text from Psalms 5–71.

Edition IIa: The 11QPs^a-Psalter, consisting of Edition I plus Psalms 101–151 as found in the Great Psalms Scroll (11QPs^a, 4QPs^e, and 11QPs^b), and including at least Psalm 93.

Edition IIb: The MT–150 Psalter, comprising Edition I plus Psalms 73 or 90 to 150 as found in the MT and the Septuagint. This arrangement is not *clearly* confirmed by any Qumran scroll, but only by one from Masada (MasPs^b, ending in Psalm 150). This larger Psalter, or parts of it, was most likely found in several Qumran scrolls as well, but these are too fragmentary for any firm conclusion to be reached.

The shape of the various Psalms scrolls from Qumran brings about the following reassessment of the development of the Psalter in the Second Temple period. The "book of Psalms" was put together in a first stage: Edition I. This was followed by two parallel stages: Editions IIa and IIb (both with Psalms 73 or 90 on, the precise cutoff point not being certain).

Authorship and Provenance

The Psalters found among the scrolls (11QPs^a-Psalter, the MT–150 Psalter, and perhaps others) are collections of material that were composed over several centuries by a variety of different authors and groups. Most psalms were **pseudonymously** attributed to famous biblical figures, notably David, who was remembered for establishing the temple service and the orders of personnel, with particular attention to the "service of song" (see 1 Chron. 25).

The Great Psalms Scroll, 11QPs[a], was arranged as a collection of Davidic psalms, and it appears to derive its authoritative status from this association. In David's Compositions (col. 27:2–11), David is renowned as a prophet who was gifted with divine predictive abilities, and who "composed through prophecy given him by the Most High" (27:1). The collection is clearly attributed to David, and it concludes with an account of his musical prowess, as one who wrote by divine gift 4050 songs (27:10).

Date/Occasion

The Psalms scrolls found at Qumran range in date from ca. 150 BCE (4QPs[a], 4QPs89) to ca. 68 CE (4QPs[c], 11QapocrPs), while the Nahal Hever Psalms scroll (5/6HevPs) and the Masada Psalms scrolls (MasPs[a-b]) are dated to the mid- to late first century CE.

The book of Psalms contains 150 (151 in Orthodox Bibles) poems, songs, or hymns, many of which were likely performed in the temple and religious services in Judaism from before the exile and into the Second Temple period. Of the 150 psalms in the Hebrew Psalter (the MT–150 Psalter), 126 are preserved in the Psalms scrolls from Qumran (including the Psalms commentaries, or *pesharim*) (*see* Introduction to *Pesharim*), most from the latter third of the book. Only five Qumran scrolls—1QPs[a], 4QPs[e], 4QPs[f], 11QPs[b], and 11QPs[d]—preserve material from both Psalms 1–89 and 90–150. Several other Psalms scrolls originally contained only small sections (e.g., 4QPs[g-h]) or individual psalms (5Q5, with Ps. 119).

One striking feature of the Psalms scrolls is that four found at Qumran (4QPs[f], 11QPs[a], 11QPs[b], 11QapocrPs) contain fifteen or sixteen psalms we would classify as apocryphal or extra-biblical. Seven of these were previously familiar to scholars or found in some early Bibles: Psalm 151 A and Psalm 151 B (*see* LXX Psalm 151) in the Septuagint (*see* Overview of Early Jewish Literature), Psalms 154 and 155 in a Syriac Psalter, David's Last Words (= 2 Sam. 23:1–7), the Catena (eight verses, seven of them from Ps. 118, but in a different order), and Ben Sira 51:13–30 (*see* Ben Sira). The other eight or nine compositions (the Eschatological Hymn and Apostrophe to Judah may be parts of the same one)—the Apostrophe to Judah, the Apostrophe to Zion, David's Compositions, the Eschatological Hymn, the Hymn to the Creator, the Plea for Deliverance, and Three Songs (or Incantations) against Demons—were unknown prior to the discovery of the scrolls.

Another interesting feature is several different arrangements of material in the Psalms scrolls. At least ten are arranged stichometrically (e.g., 4QPs[b] and MasPs[a]), twenty-one in prose format (e.g., 4QPs[a] and 11QPs[b]), and one (11QPs[a]) is a prose collection with a single piece written in **stichometric format.** These formats reinforce the view of many scholars that in the later Second Temple period there were several Psalters with varying liturgical functions.

Four Psalms scrolls are especially important for understanding the development and shape of the book of Psalms in the later Second Temple period: one from Cave 4 (4QPs[a], copied ca. 150 BCE), two from Cave 11 (11QPs[a] [ca. 30–50 CE] and 11QPs[b] [first half of the first century CE]), and one found at **Masada** (MasPs[b], second half of the first century BCE).

By far the largest manuscript is the Great Psalms Scroll (11QPsᵃ), which diverges radically from the MT–150 Psalter in two ways: by including eleven additional compositions and in its ordering of contents. Fifty compositions are preserved—with at least one more (Psalm 120) now missing—in the following order:

Psalm 101→102→103→109→118→104→147→105→146→148 [+ 120]→121→122 →123→124→125→126→127→128→129→130→131→132→119→135→136→Catena →145 (with postscript)→154→Plea for Deliverance→139→137→138→Ben Sira 51→ Apostrophe to Zion→93→141→133→144→155→142→143→149→150→ Hymn to the Creator→David's Last Words→David's Compositions→140→134 →151 A→151 B→blank column *[end]*

The Qumran Psalters probably had various liturgical functions connected with the *yaḥad*'s understanding of their role in the celestial temple of God. It is difficult to be specific regarding the purpose of each Psalter, but the contents of a few offer some important signals as to their function and usage. The Psalter in the Great Psalms Scroll (11QPsᵃ, also known as 11Q5) has been arranged according to its affirmation of David as the author, and includes a clear endorsement of the 364-day solar calendar: "And he wrote 3,600 psalms; and songs to sing before the altar over the whole-burnt perpetual offering every day, for all the days of the year—364" (col. 27:4–6).

Another Psalms scroll from Cave 11, 11QapocrPs (11Q11), contains three previously unknown deliverance psalms against demons, together with Psalm 91. Some scholars believe that this collection was a prayer book to accompany exorcisms or other rituals for combating illness or evil spirits (cf. 11QPsᵃ 27:9–10).

Figure 9. 11Q11, Apocryphal Psalms C, may have been a prayer book to accompany exorcisms or other rituals. Shown here is a fragment of column 5. Courtesy Israel Antiquities Authority

Text, Language, Sources, and Transmission

It cannot be proven that any of the Psalms collections in the scrolls were compiled at Qumran, although several Psalms scrolls were most likely copied there. What is certain, however, is that the Psalms scrolls were highly valued and used by the *yaḥad*, or Essene, movement, who wrote or collected the scrolls found at the site. These were probably scribes and priests, who were deeply concerned about matters of ritual purity, the correct observance of religious festivals, and the legitimacy of the temple and its personnel. The *yaḥad* were at odds with the **Pharisees** and temple establishment with regard to interpretation of the Torah as well as the correct calendar, favoring a 364-day solar calendar over the 354-day lunar calendar used at the temple in Jerusalem. Even before the Qumran community was established, the *yaḥad* broke communion with the ruling priests, and so were forced to practice their religion apart from the temple, which they viewed as corrupt. Much of their religious practice involved belief in a celestial, otherworldly temple of God in heaven, which they believed they could access through proper observance of the Torah and membership in their exclusive movement.

Not surprisingly, liturgy formed an integral part of everyday life for the *yaḥad* and the Qumran community. Accordingly, the Psalters and other liturgical texts (such as the Hodayot, Songs of the Sabbath Sacrifice, and the Festival Prayers) likely formed an important part of their own ritualized liturgies and religious observance. These texts were essential to their belief that they could participate in the services of the pure, holy temple of God in the heavens, alongside the angels.

Theology

The presence of various Psalters among the scrolls not only raises the issues of the provenance and shape of the Psalms in the Second Temple period, but also attests to a variety of functions for these texts that were not necessarily connected to the temple service. Prominent features in the compositions in the Great Psalms Scroll and other collections found at Qumran are largely connected to their programmatic nature.

Most notably, perhaps, the arrangement of texts in the 11QPsᵃ-Psalter based on Davidic authorship indicates some accordance with elements in the *yaḥad* movement's theology. This is very evident in David's Compositions (col. 27:2–11), which resonates with distinctive motifs found elsewhere in the Qumran **sectarian** scrolls, such as the 364-day solar calendar. The high importance attached to David, who wrote songs to sing daily before the altar over the whole-burnt perpetual offering for all 364 days of the year (col. 27:5–6), may be related to a similar programmatic endorsement of the class of Levitical priests whose services were traced directly to David in 1 Chronicles (1 Chron. 16:4–6, etc.). In addition, the characterization of David as a prophet (col. 27:11)—together with the Psalms *pesharim* (commentaries) and allusions among the sectarian scrolls to the Psalms as prophecies (cf. 4Q491, frag. 17.4)—accorded with the *yaḥad*'s professed connection to Israel's legendary king.

Reception of Psalms and Psalters at Qumran in the Second Temple Period

The Qumran Psalters draw attention to four features of interest concerning the New Testament. First, the presence of so many Psalms scrolls at Qumran (thirty-eight), as well as the many quotations of (or allusions to) the Psalms in the sectarian scrolls, attest to the importance of the Psalms for the *yaḥad* movement and the Qumran community. A similar prominence is evident in the New Testament, where the Psalms are quoted or alluded to more than eighty times.

Second, the Psalms were the model for several sectarian works composed by the *yaḥad* movement that were found at Qumran (notably the Hodayot, the Songs of the Sabbath Sacrifice, and the Festival Prayers). Very early Christian hymns were also modeled on the Psalms, such as Mary's Song (Luke 1:46–55), Zechariah's prophecy (Luke 1:68–79), and the early Christian hymn about Christ's humility and exaltation (Phil. 2:6–11).

Third, some distinctive readings among the Psalms scrolls are significant for New Testament exegesis. One is in Psalm 22, which is represented by two scrolls from Qumran (4QPs^f and 4QPs^w) and one from Nahal Hever (5/6HevPs). In this psalm, the Masoretic Text for verse 17 (v. 16 in English) is puzzling:

> For dogs are all around me; a company of evildoers encircles me.
> *Like a lion are* my hands and my feet.

In 1611 the King James Bible translated "*they pierced* my hands and my feet," following the Septuagint by using a verbal form instead of "like a lion." Some scholars, however, deemed this a corrupt reading in the Greek Bible's attempt to translate the difficult Hebrew "*Like a lion are* my hands and my feet," which makes little sense in the verse's context. Now the Psalms scroll from Nahal Hever—the only one to preserve the key Hebrew word in question—reads "*They have pierced* my hands and my feet," thus confirming that the Hebrew text used by the Septuagint translator indeed contained this reading, not the one in the MT.

In light of the Nahal Hever Psalms scroll and the Septuagint—which clearly affirm this reading in Hebrew before the destruction of the temple in 67 CE—many modern Bibles are correct to translate "*They have pierced* my hands and feet" (NASB, NIV, etc.), or "My hands and feet *have shriveled*" (NRSV). Since Psalm 22 is alluded to several times in the Gospels with reference to Jesus' crucifixion, this reading has significant connotations for Christian theology, which has interpreted this psalm as a prophetic foreshadowing of the crucifixion.[1]

Fourth, the 11QPs^a-Psalter, as preserved in the Great Psalms Scroll, accords with the New Testament perception of David as a prophet. The assertion in Da-

---

1. Ps. 22:1: "My God, my God, why have you forsaken me? Why are you so far from helping me, from the words of my groaning?"

Matt. 27:46: "And about three o'clock Jesus cried with a loud voice, 'Eli, Eli, lema sabachthani?' that is, 'My God, my God, why have you forsaken me?'"

Mark 15:34: "At three o'clock Jesus cried out with a loud voice, 'Eloi, Eloi, lema sabachthani?' which means, 'My God, my God, why have you forsaken me?'"

vid's Compositions that he "spoke through prophecy" (11QPs^a, col. 27:11) resonates with the evangelist's attribution of a "prophecy" concerning Jesus to David in Mark 12:36 (par. Matt. 22:43; Luke 20:41–42): "The Lord said to my Lord, 'Sit at my right hand.'" The Cave 11 text furthermore calls David "wise," "discerning and blameless in all his ways before God and humankind," and given a "discerning and brilliant spirit" by God (27:2–3). In two of the Synoptic accounts, the cited text from Psalm 110:1 is described as uttered by David "through the Holy Spirit" (Mark 12:36; Matt. 22:43).

The Psalters from Qumran, as well as the commentaries devoted to their interpretation (the *pesharim*), attest to the growing conviction in the later Second Temple period that Scripture, which included liturgies and ceremonial texts, was a source of cryptic knowledge and divine secrets that quite often contained meanings far deeper than those on the surface (*see* Introduction to Biblical Interpretation and Rewritten Scripture). In the case of the Psalms, for those in the *yaḥad* movement at Qumran and in early Christianity, special insight and knowledge were available through new interpretations of this ancient material, often in different contexts and as part of new reading traditions.

The book of Psalms was among the most popular in the Dead Sea Scrolls, as indicated by no fewer than forty-one individual manuscripts (with thirty-eight at Qumran) dating from about 150 BCE to the mid- to late first century CE. Several Psalms scrolls are dynamic, differ greatly from one another, and attest to at least three editions of the book of Psalms.

The earliest is Edition I, which contained Psalms 1 or 2 to 72 or 89 (the cutoff point is not certain), with 4QPs^a as the foremost example. Edition IIa is the 11QPs^a-Psalter, consisting of Edition I and Psalms 101–151 as found in the Great Psalms Scroll (11QPs^a, 4QPs^e, 11QPs^b) and including at least Psalm 93. Edition IIb is the MT–150 Psalter, comprising Edition I plus Psalms 73/90–150 as found in the MT and the Septuagint. Although this arrangement was most likely found in several scrolls, it is not *clearly* confirmed by any from Qumran, but only by MasPs^b, which ends with Psalm 150.

The presence of more than one Psalter among the scrolls suggests that some served specialized functions for the *yaḥad* community at Qumran. The 11QPs^a-Psalter appears to have been arranged to emphasize David's role as a prophet, and perhaps to elevate the Levitical class of priests. Furthermore, the small collection of exorcism psalms suggests that at least some such texts were used in deliverance rituals for combating evil forces. These Psalters and other liturgical texts (such as the Hodayot, the Songs of the Sabbath Sacrifice, and the Festival Prayers) likely formed an important part of the *yaḥad*'s ritualized liturgies and religious observance apart from the existing temple, which they viewed as corrupt and illegitimate.

The Psalms were also highly regarded by the *yaḥad* for their prophetic qualities, and were the subject of cryptic interpretation through running commentaries (the *pesharim*). In similar fashion to how the Psalms were treated in the early church, for the Qumran community they affirmed reverence for David as a prophet and functioned as channels for divine revelation.

PETER W. FLINT

FURTHER READING

Abegg, Martin, Peter Flint, and Eugene Ulrich. *The Dead Sea Scrolls Bible: The Oldest Known Bible Translated for the First Time into English*, pp. 505–89. San Francisco: HarperOne, 1999.

Davies, Philip R., George J. Brooke, and Phillip R. Callaway. *The Complete World of the Dead Sea Scrolls*. London: Thames & Hudson, 2002.

Sanders, James A. *The Dead Sea Psalms Scroll*. Ithaca, N.Y.: Cornell University Press, 1967.

VanderKam, James C. *The Dead Sea Scrolls Today*. 2nd rev. ed. Grand Rapids: Eerdmans, 2010.

VanderKam, James C., and Peter Flint. *The Meaning of the Dead Sea Scrolls: Their Significance for Understanding the Bible, Jesus, and Christianity*, pp. 120–28. San Francisco: HarperOne, 2002.

ADVANCED READING

Flint, Peter W. *The Dead Sea Psalms Scrolls and the Book of Psalms*. STDJ 17. Leiden: Brill, 1997.

———. "Five Surprises in the Psalms Scrolls." In *Flores Florentino: Dead Sea Scrolls and Other Early Jewish Studies in Honour of Florentino Garcia Martinez*, edited by Anthony Hilhorst, Émile Puech, and Eibert Tigchelaar, pp. 183–95. Supplements to the Journal for the Study of Judaism 122. Leiden: Brill, 2007.

———. "Psalms and Psalters in the Dead Sea Scrolls." In *The Bible and the Dead Sea Scrolls*, vol. 1, *Scripture and the Scrolls*, edited by James H. Charlesworth, pp. 233–72. Waco, Tex.: Baylor University Press, 2006.

Sanders, James A. *The Psalms Scroll from Qumran, Cave 11* (11QPs^a). DJD 4. Oxford: Clarendon, 1965.

1.9 The Eschatological Hymn and the Apostrophe to Judah

These two compositions are preserved in 4QPs ʲ (ca. 50 BCE). The Eschatological Hymn offers praise to God, but with an eschatological emphasis. The Apostrophe to Judah is likewise eschatological, but with a special focus on Judah. It is also highly anthological, containing many words and phrases known from other parts of the Hebrew Bible. Early editors, followed by most scholars, have treated these as two separate works; however, both may be parts of a single acrostic poem (each verse beginning with a successive letter of the Hebrew alphabet).

Eschatological Hymn

> [F]or he comes to judge [6]every ac[ti]on, to remove the wicked [7]from the earth,
> > [so that the children of] iniquity will not [8]be found.
> [And] the hea[v]ens [will give] their dew, [9]and there will be no searing dro[ught within] their borders.
> And the earth [10]will yield its fruit in its season, and will not [11]cheat of its [pro]duce.
> > The [12]fruit trees [will. . .] their vines, and [. . .] will not cheat of its [. . .[13]. . .]

Apostrophe to Judah

> [5]. . .Then let heavens and earth give praise together; [6]then let all the stars of twilight give praise!
> [7]Rejoice, O Judah, in your joy; [8]be happy in your happiness, and dance in your dance.
> [9]Celebrate your pilgrim feasts, fulfill your vows, for no longer is [10]Belial in your midst.
> > May your hand be lifted up! [11]May your right hand prevail!
> See, enemies will [12]perish, and all [13]evildoers will be scattered.
> > But you, O Lord, are forev[er]; [14]your glory will be forev[er and ev]er.
> [15]Praise the Lord!

Translation by Peter W. Flint. Adapted from Martin Abegg, Peter Flint, and Eugene Ulrich, *The Dead Sea Scrolls Bible: The Oldest Known Bible Translated for the First Time into English* (San Francisco: HarperOne, 1999), pp. 588–89.

1.10 Hymn to the Creator and *from* David's Compositions

Hymn to the Creator

This composition (only in 11QPs^a 26:9–15) is a wisdom psalm that praises God as Creator. It has clear affinities with Psalm 104 since both psalms draw on cosmic and creation themes from Genesis 1.

[1]Great and holy is the Lord, the holiest of holy ones for every generation.

[2]Majesty goes before him, and following him is the outpouring of many waters.

[3]Grace and truth surround his presence; truth and justice and righteousness are the foundation of his throne.

[4]Separating light from deep darkness, he established the dawn by the knowledge of his mind.

[5]When all his angels had witnessed it they sang aloud; for he showed them what they had not known:

[6]Crowning the hills with fruit, good food for every living being.

[7]Blessed be the one who makes the earth by his power, establishing the world in his wisdom.

[8]In his understanding he stretched out the heavens, and brought forth [wind] from his st[orehouses].

[9]He made [lightning for the rai]n, and caused mist[s] to rise [from] the end [of the earth].

from David's Compositions

This important piece forms a prose epilogue to the 11QPs^a-Psalter, although it is found in the second-last column (27) of 11QPs^a. It asserts that David is the author of the collection (and thus the 11QPs^a-Psalter), clearly implying that its arrangement and compositions were inspired by God himself. Note especially line 11: "All these he composed through prophecy. . . ." The numbers (e.g., 364, 52, and 30) show that this Psalter was arranged in accordance with the year, weeks, and months of the 364-day solar calendar, which was followed by the yaḥad movement at Qumran, rather than the lunar calendar, which had 354 days.

[2]And David, son of Jesse, was wise, and a light like the light of the sun, and literate, [3]and discerning and blameless in all his ways before God and humankind. And the Lord gave [4]him a discerning and brilliant spirit.

Translation by Peter W. Flint. Adapted from Abegg, Flint, and Ulrich, *The Dead Sea Scrolls Bible*, pp. 582–83.

And he wrote [5]3,600 psalms; and songs to sing before the altar over the whole-burnt [6]perpetual offering every day, for all the days of the year—364; [7]and for the offering of the Sabbaths—52 songs; and for the offering of the New [8]Moons and for all the Solemn Assemblies and for the Day of Atonement—30 songs. [9]And all the songs that he spoke were 446, and songs [10]for making music over the afflicted—4. And the total was 4,050.

[11]All these he composed through prophecy, which was given him from before the Most High.

1.11 Third Song (or Incantation) against Demons

*11QApocryphal Psalms (11QapocrPs, ca. 50–70 CE) preserves parts of four psalms for use in exorcisms of demons. Many scholars believe these to be the "four songs for making music over the afflicted" that are mentioned in David's Compositions in 11QPs*ᵃ*. The first three exorcism songs were unknown until the discovery of the Dead Sea Scrolls, but the fourth is found in modern Bibles as Psalm 91, which is connected with exorcisms of demonic forces in both rabbinic and church traditions. The third song, which is attributed to David, is poorly preserved but is clearly uttered against a demon or evil spirit. The reference to this demon's horns in line 7 is particularly interesting in view of popular notions that the devil has horns.*

(Col. 5) Superscription: ⁴A Psalm of David

Again[st. . .An incanta]tion in the name of the Lor[d. To be invoked at
   an]y time ⁵ to the heav[ens.
When] he comes to you at nig[ht], you will [say] to him:
   ⁶ "Who are you? [Withdraw from] humanity and from the offspring
   of the ho[ly one]s!
For your appearance is one of ⁷ [delu]sion, and your horns are horns
   of [illu]sion.
   You are darkness, not light, ⁸ [wicked]ness, not righteousness [. . .]
the commander of the army, the Lord [will send] you [down ⁹ into]
   deepest [Sheo]l,
   [. . .the] two bronze [ga]tes th[rough which n]o ¹⁰ light [can enter],
and [the] sun [will] not [shine for you] tha[t rises ¹¹ upon the] righteous to [. . .
   And] then you will say: [. . . ¹² . . . the right]eous, to come [. . .] for a
   de[mon] to harm him,
   [. . . ¹³ . . . of tr]uth from [. . .because] he has [righ]teousness to [. . . ¹⁴
   . . .] and. . ."

Translation by Peter W. Flint. Adapted from Abegg, Flint, and Ulrich, *The Dead Sea Scrolls Bible*, pp. 540–41.

LXX Psalm 151

Based on 1 Samuel 16–17, LXX Psalm 151 is part of the rewritten Scripture genre of the Second Temple period (*see* Introduction to Biblical Interpretation and Rewritten Scripture). As one of the longer titles of the Greek Psalter, the superscription of LXX Psalm 151 establishes three noteworthy matters. First, while the attribution of Davidic authorship to apocryphal psalms is well attested in the Second Temple period (e.g., the four apocryphal psalms of David in 11QPsApª, cols. 1–5), the emphasis placed on it in LXX Psalm 151 ("This psalm was written from David's own hand") is without parallel. Second, by employing the phrase "outside of *the number*," the author evidently recognized LXX Psalm 151 as a supplement to the previously established collection of 150 psalms of the Greek Psalter. Third, the final temporal clause of this title unifies the last two verses (vv. 6–7), whose origin is variously assessed (see the discussion of 11QPsalm 151 A + B below), with the rest of LXX Psalm 151.

LXX Psalm 151 is attested among all three of the important codices of the fourth and fifth centuries CE: Codex Vaticanus, Codex Sinaiticus, and Codex Alexandrinus (*see* Overview of Early Jewish Literature). The textual tradition of Psalm 151 is well preserved with only minor variants between these main codices. In selected manuscripts of the latter codex, the Odes of Solomon (*see* Odes of Solomon) were attached immediately after LXX Psalm 151. This psalm is attested in Greek, Latin, Coptic, Arabic, Ethiopic, and Armenian versions.

Regarding its position in the book of Psalms, both extant forms of Psalm 151 in the Septuagint and the Great Psalms Scroll (11QPsª) from Qumran (*see* Overview of Early Jewish Literature; Psalms and Psalters at Qumran) conclude a collection of psalms. Scholars postulate that one to three editions of the Psalter existed in the Second Temple period. This lack of unanimity in scholarship is, in no small measure, dependent on whether 11QPsª is viewed as an edition of a Second Temple period Psalter or a compilation of psalms (see below).

For Israel under Gentile rule, the biblical tradition of the heroic exploits of young David in 1 Samuel 16–17 became the object of midrashic interpretations in the Second Temple period. The motif of the unexpected rise of young David as an anointed leader appears to be an expression of Israel's messianic hopes of deliverance from Gentile hegemony in the Second Temple period (cf. "the foreigner," v. 6a).

Narrative Overview

This apocryphal psalm attributed to David rehearses his dramatic ascent from the apparent inconsequential position of a young shepherd to the role of the anointed deliverer of Israel. The motif of his older brothers as better suited leaders frames the first part of this psalm (vv. 1–5; cf. the repetitive resumption of the phrase "my brothers" in vv. 1 and 5). At the center of this literary framework in verses 1–5, the divine recognition and approval of the adolescent David are featured in verses 2–4. In addition to hearing of his musicianship (vv. 2–3), the God of Israel has set David apart from his brothers as an anointed leader of his people (v. 4).

After the hidden prospect of David's future leadership is established in verses 1–5, the beheading of Goliath by David with the enemy's own sword not only delivers Israel from the reproach of the enemy but it also climactically concludes this psalm (vv. 6–7). In verse 6, the author of LXX Psalm 151 summarizes the role of Goliath as both "a champion in the middle" and an idol worshiper. Regarding these features in verse 6, the author has paralleled two characteristics of the figure of Goliath, which are given uneven attention in his source (1 Sam. 16–17). While his role in the Philistine army was clearly stressed in the source of this author (17:4–51), the same amount of attention was not paid to Goliath's religious background ("the Philistine cursed David by his gods," v. 43b; cf. "uncircumcised Philistine," vv. 26, 36). By concluding this psalm with his deliverance of Israel from the enemy (LXX Ps. 151:7), the qualities of David's life recognized only by the Lord in verses 2–4 are now manifested to everyone. Consequently, LXX Psalm 151 concludes with the ironic reversals of the portraits in verses 1–5 of both young David and his ostensibly better qualified brothers. Even though other parts of this author's source were used in apocryphal psalms attributed to David in the Second Temple period (e.g., Syriac Psalms 152 and 153), Saul's relief from the torment of an evil spirit by David's musical performance (1 Sam. 16:14–23) and David's slaying of lions and bears (17:34–36) have been ignored in Psalm 151.

Author/Provenance/Date/Occasion

The publication of 11QPsᵃ in 1965 introduced scholars to the second of two extant text-forms of this psalm: (1) the Greek text-form of Psalm 151 of the Septuagint Psalter, and (2) the longer Hebrew composition of Psalm 151 in 11QPsᵃ of the Dead Sea Scrolls. The priority of these two text-forms remains a persistently debated topic among scholars. Is LXX Psalm 151 an abridgment of an older Hebrew text-form represented by 11QPsᵃ (col. 28:3–14), or is the latter Hebrew form a **recension** of a shorter, older Greek text-form of Psalm 151? The answers to these questions are inextricably connected with the differing perspectives of the provenance and reception of Psalm 151.

First, proponents of the priority of the Hebrew text-form of Psalm 151 contend that 11QPsᵃ is one stage in a long process of the composition of the biblical book of Psalms that ends in the first century CE. According to this theory, a Second Temple period scribe (an epitomist or amalgamist) truncated 11QPsalm 151A (col. 28:3–12 parallels LXX Psalm 151:1–5 broadly) and 11QPsalm 151B (col.

28:13–14 parallels LXX Psalm 151:6–7) to form the Hebrew source of LXX Psalm 151.[1] Even though LXX Psalm 151 is not a direct translation of 11QPsalm 151, the Greek text-form nevertheless depends on the complete amalgamation 11QPsalm 151 A + B. Due in part to his hypothesis of **Orphic** imagery in 11QPsalm 151 A (col. 28:2b–3), James A. Sanders initially identified this scribe as "a **Hellenized** Jew of the Palestine area" in the third century BCE.[2] Avoiding any claim to its detailed background, Peter W. Flint similarly dates 11QPsalm 151 to the pre-Qumran era along with the other psalms in 11QPs[a] not attested in the 150 psalms of the Masoretic Psalter.[3] According to Flint, 11QPsalm 151 was part of the 11QPs[a]-Psalter that was originally compiled prior to the inception of the Qumran era and was in all likelihood copied in this community. Consequently, advocates of the priority of the Hebrew text-form date the Hebrew text-form of Psalm 151 to the third century BCE or earlier.[4] According to this view, LXX Psalm 151 is interpreted as a later abridgment of this earlier Hebrew text-form of this psalm represented by 11QPsalm 151. Even though the Greek text-form is younger than that of 11QPsalm 151, according to Flint, to date LXX Psalm 151 more precisely than the third century BCE or earlier is impossible without an extensive reevaluation of the variants of the Greek Psalter and their relationship to the Dead Sea Scrolls.[5]

A second group of scholars characterizes 11QPsalm 151 as a later expansion of the older Greek text-form of Psalm 151. According to Menachem Haran, the scribe of the Hebrew version of 11QPsalm 151 enlarged the text-form of LXX Psalm 151 by utilizing forced, artificial, corrupt, and late expressions. Haran's examples of these late imitations of Biblical Hebrew are largely based on the ways that **parallelisms** and words in 11QPsalm 151 depart from the conventions of biblical poetry and language. These failed attempts at **archaizing Hebrew** appear exclusively "in those portions of the psalm which are not found in the LXX."[6] Consequently, the Hebrew version of Psalm 151 is viewed, in general, to be "expanded and derived" while the source of LXX Psalm 151 "reflects the original *extent* of the psalm" (i.e., seven verses).[7] Minus the expansions of 11QPsalm 151, the two text-forms become very similar without the late, imitative features of the Qumran scroll.[8]

Advocates of the priority of the Greek text-form have dated LXX Psalm 151 in both general and specific ways. According to Haran, LXX Psalm 151, which was "one of the late fruits of biblical literary output," was written before 11QPsalm 151 but not before the translation of the Greek Psalter (ca. early to mid-second cen-

1. James A. Sanders, *The Psalms Scroll of Qumran Cave 11*, DJD 4 (Oxford: Clarendon, 1965), pp. 59–63.

2. Sanders, *Psalms Scroll*, p. 63.

3. Peter W. Flint, *The Dead Sea Psalms Scrolls and the Book of Psalms*, STDJ 17 (New York: Brill, 1997), pp. 198–201.

4. Flint, *Dead Sea Psalms Scrolls*, pp. 176, 199, esp. n. 142.

5. Flint, *Dead Sea Psalms Scrolls*, p. 236.

6. Menachem Haran, "The Two Text-Forms of Psalm 151," *JSS* 39 (1988): 171–82 (p. 176).

7. Haran, "Two Text-Forms," p. 177, emphasis original.

8. Haran, "Two Text-Forms," p. 177. See also Mark S. Smith, "How to Write a Poem: The Case of Psalm 151A (11QPs[a] 28.3–12)," in *The Hebrew of the Dead Sea Scrolls and Ben Sira*, ed. T. Muraoka and J. F. Elwolde, STDJ 26 (Leiden: Brill, 1997), pp. 182–208 (pp. 186–87).

tury BCE).[9] Based on Haran's research, Natalio Fernández-Marcos has posited a more specific setting for LXX Psalm 151 during the Second Temple period. Even though the heroic deeds of the Maccabean era could plausibly be viewed as the background of this psalm, according to Fernández-Marcos, the emphasis placed on David as both a national hero and a victor over Goliath in LXX Psalm 151 fits the time of the **Hasmonean** rule (142–63 BCE).[10] Fernández-Marcos underscores that the aim of the patriotic reaction of the Hasmonean period "was to restore David's kingdom to its full extent."[11]

Text, Language, Sources, and Transmission

The disputed priority of the two extant text-forms of Psalm 151, which leads to differing assessments of its dating, provenance, and literary nature, can be illuminated further by a brief review of some of the underlying presuppositions in this debate. In defense of the priority of the Hebrew text-form of 11QPsalm 151, Flint rejects the assumption of the early reception of the Hebrew Psalter as canon in the Jewish world by proponents of the priority of the Greek text-form of Psalm 151.[12] In support of the latter view, however, Haran critiques the misreading of the long space that dominates line 12 by advocates of the priority of the text-form of 11QPsalm 151. According to Haran, instead of the assumption that this space indicates the combination of two psalms into one, its introduction by the scribe-copyist is more plausibly understood as the presentation of one psalm in two parts.[13] Haran also doubts that the eight nonbiblical psalms of 11QPs[a], half of which sound "imitative and secondary," were ever considered part of a canonical collection of psalms.[14]

Despite these persistent disagreements, the state of contemporary scholarship has progressed since the publication of the critical edition of 11QPs[a] in 1965. First, the continued study of both extant forms of Psalm 151 has nuanced the early consensus that the Hebrew text-form was more original than that of the Greek.[15] Second, since the David figure in 11QPsalm 151 is understood today to depend on the biblical but not the Hellenistic tradition,[16] the early

9. Haran, "Two Text-Forms," p. 178.

10. Natalio Fernández-Marcos, "David the Adolescent: On Psalm 151," in *The Old Greek Psalter: Studies in Honour of Albert Pietersma*, ed. Robert J. V. Hievert, Claude E. Cox, and Peter J. Gentry, JSOTSup 332 (Sheffield: Sheffield Academic Press, 2001), pp. 205–17 (p. 216).

11. Fernández-Marcos, "David," p. 216.

12. Flint, *Psalms Scrolls*, pp. 14, 226.

13. Haran, "Two Text-Forms," p. 181.

14. Menachem Haran, "11QPs[a] and the Canonical Book of Psalms," in *Minhah le-Nahum: Biblical and Other Studies Presented to Nahum M. Sarna in Honour of his 70th Birthday*, ed. Marc Brettler and Michael Fishbane, JSOTSup 154 (Sheffield: Sheffield Academic Press, 1993), pp. 193–201 (p. 199).

15. *See* James A. Sanders, "Psalms Scroll (11QPs[a]) Reviewed," in *On Language, Culture, and Religion: In Honor of Eugene A. Nida*, ed. Matthew Black and William A. Smalley (The Hague: Mouton, 1974), pp. 79–99 (p. 85).

16. Frank M. Cross, "David, Orpheus, and Psalm 151.3–4," *BASOR* 231 (1978): 69–71.

hypothesis that 11QPsalm 151 A may require an Orphic interpretation has been correctly set to rest.[17]

Reception of LXX Psalm 151 in the Second Temple Period

After generations of living under the oppression of Gentile **hegemony,** the account of the sudden ascendancy of adolescent David as the anointed victor over an arch-nemesis and idol worshiper became a compelling messianic motif in the Second Temple period. While no explicit reference is made to Psalm 151 in the New Testament, complementary portraits of David in the Hebrew Bible (e.g., the coronation of a Davidide in Ps. 2) were cited by the leaders of the earliest church as expressions of their messianic beliefs. The supplementation of Psalm 151 to the Greek Psalter, which corresponds to its final placement in 11QPsᵃ, also suggests that this psalm offered a credible expression of messianism under Rome in the late Second Temple period.

KEVIN L. SPAWN

FURTHER READING

Dines, Jennifer M. *The Septuagint.* London: T&T Clark, 2004.

Fernández-Marcos, Natalio. *The Septuagint in Context: Introduction to the Greek Version of the Bible.* Translated by W. Watson. Leiden: Brill, 2000.

Jobes, Karen H., and Moisés Silva. *Invitation to the Septuagint.* 2nd ed. Grand Rapids: Baker Academic, 2015.

Peters, Melvin K. H. "Septuagint." In *ABD*, 5:1093–1104.

Ulrich, Eugene. *The Dead Sea Scrolls and the Origins of the Bible.* Grand Rapids: Eerdmans, 1999.

ADVANCED READING

Cross, Frank M. "David, Orpheus, and Psalm 151.3–4." *BASOR* 231 (1978): 69–71.

Fernández-Marcos, Natalio. "David the Adolescent: On Psalm 151." In *The Old Greek Psalter: Studies in Honour of Albert Pietersma*, edited by Robert J. V. Hiebert, Claude E. Cox, and Peter J. Gentry, pp. 205–17. JSOTSup 332. Sheffield: Sheffield Academic Press, 2001.

Flint, Peter W. "The Book of Psalms in the Light of the Dead Sea Scrolls." *VT* 48 (1998): 453–72.

———. *The Dead Sea Psalms Scrolls and the Book of Psalms.* STDJ 17. Leiden: Brill, 1997.

———. "Noncanonical Writings in the Dead Sea Scrolls: Apocrypha, Other Previously Known Writings, Pseudepigrapha." In *The Bible at Qumran: Text, Shape, and Interpretation*, edited by Peter W. Flint, pp. 80–123. Grand Rapids: Eerdmans, 2001.

Haran, Menachem. "The Two Text-Forms of Psalm 151." *JJS* 39 (1988): 171–82.

———. "11QPsᵃ and the Canonical Book of Psalms." In *Minhah le-Nahum: Biblical and Other Studies Presented to Nahum M. Sarna in Honour of his 70th Birthday*, edited by Marc Brettler and Michael Fishbane, pp. 193–201. JSOTSup 154. Sheffield: Sheffield Academic Press, 1993.

17. Sanders, *Psalms Scroll*, pp. 61–63.

Sanders, James A. *The Psalms Scroll of Qumran Cave 11 (11QPsª)*. DJD 4. Oxford: Clarendon, 1965.

———. "Psalms Scroll (11QPsª) Reviewed." In *On Language, Culture, and Religion: In Honor of Eugene A. Nida*, edited by Matthew Black and William A. Smalley, pp. 79–99. The Hague: Mouton, 1974.

Smith, Mark S. "How to Write a Poem: The Case of Psalm 151 A (11QPsª 28.3–12)." In *The Hebrew of the Dead Sea Scrolls and Ben Sira: Proceedings of a Symposium Held at Leiden University 11–14 December 1995*, edited by T. Muraoka and J. F. Elwolde, pp. 182–208. STDJ 26. Leiden: Brill, 1997.

1.12 LXX Psalm 151

151:1 This psalm was written with David's own hand (even though it is
 outside the number),[a] after he fought Goliath in single combat.
I was small among my brothers
 and the youngest in my father's house;
I tended the sheep of my father.
2 My hands made a musical instrument;
my fingers tuned a harp.
3 But who will report this to my Lord?
 The Lord himself, he is the one who listens.
4 It was he who sent his messenger
 and took me from the sheep of my father
 and set me apart with his anointing oil.
5 My brothers were handsome and tall,
 but the Lord did not take delight in them.
6 I went out to meet the foreigner,
 and he cursed me by his idols.
7 But as for me, having drawn the sword from him,
I beheaded him and removed the reproach from the children of Israel.

---

a. That is, LXX Psalm 151 is "outside the number *of the 150 psalms of the Greek Psalter.*"

Translation by Kevin L. Spawn.

2. Interpretive History

Among the Second Temple period writings is the category of "interpretive history" into which fit several documents that recount Jewish history of the later Second Temple period (*see* History of the Second Temple Period). Some readers may wonder about the use of the term "interpretive" since it could imply something other than "actual" history. The premise here, for the *EJL* volume, is that all history or historiography is, to greater or lesser degrees, interpretive; in other words, there is inevitably a perspective and quite likely a set of commitments— religious or otherwise—that permeate any telling of events from the past. In the selections for this section, the contributors of each respective chapter make this case in much greater detail with some examples.

To begin, these narrative documents are invaluable for students of the Second Temple period for several reasons. First, in some cases they represent the only sources available to us for events of great significance to the Jewish people of the postexilic period. Second, the events of the second century BCE, which they recount often, provide valuable social and political context for other contemporaneous writings of the Second Temple period (literature found in other sections of *EJL*) and the subsequent New Testament writings. Third, these histories have, as part of their purpose, the goal of raising the sympathies of both their audience and outsiders toward the Jewish people, their plight, and their distinctive expressions of religious faith. This is what some scholars refer to as the "apologetic" or even, in the positive sense of the term, "pathetic" tone in these texts. Therefore, while it will become clear that not every detail of these histories can be taken at face value *as though it happened just that way,* nevertheless we are left with real artifacts of, and witnesses to, what these authors believed was the reality of their past and the lived experience of the Jewish people.

While not all "interpretive history" texts from the Second Temple period are included in *EJL*, readers will find chapters on two texts from the Maccabean era (1 and 2 Maccabees), an introduction to the Jewish historian Josephus, as well as the four extant texts from his writings (*Jewish War, Jewish Antiquities, Against Apion,* and the autobiographical *Life*). An important feature of these histories is their unapologetic, yet sometimes subconscious, subjectivity of perspective as they reflect the concerns of their authors and communities and influencing circumstances. Both Daniel Schwartz (Maccabean texts) and Steve Mason (Josephus) alert us to this characteristic of interpretive history in their introductions.

One final note: due to the length of the Josephus texts, readers will find abridged versions of these documents. The accompanying bibliographies provide information for full-length editions and translations of these texts.

RONALD HERMS

The Books of the Maccabees

It is not known whether 1 and 2 Maccabees originally bore titles, or, if they did, what the titles were. The conventional names, First and Second Book of Maccabees (or "of Maccabean affairs [Greek: *Makkabaika*]"), found in manuscripts cannot be original because "Maccabee" (Greek: *Makkabeus*), which may derive from the Hebrew *maqqevet,* "hammer" (e.g., Isa. 44:12), was originally the byname of a single individual, Judas Maccabeus (1 Macc. 2:4; 2 Macc. 5:27).[1] The use of the "Maccabees," in the plural, first appears in Christian texts, where it denotes the seven martyred brothers of 2 Maccabees 7. Origen records a Hebrew or Aramaic title for 1 Maccabees, transliterated as *Sarbēthsabanaiel,* which may mean "Book of the House of Those Who Rebelled against [or possibly, for] God" (see below). As for 2 Maccabees, there is some manuscript evidence for the title "Epitome of the Deeds of Judas Maccabaeus," but that fits only the latter half of the book.

Both books are works of history preserved in the Septuagint that recount, from very different points of view, the clash between the Jews of Judea and the Seleucid kingdom in the second century BCE (*see* Map of the Ptolemaic Empire, p. 37; Map of the Seleucid Empire, p. 36). That clash, in the midst of **Hellenization** and, eventually, royal decrees against the practice of Judaism, engendered a rebellion led in turn by several brothers of the **Hasmonean** family, of whom the first and the most famous was Judas Maccabeus. Within a few decades, these rebels succeeded in establishing an independent state, and their dynasty ruled Judea until the Roman takeover in 63 BCE.

First Maccabees, after a brief prologue (1:1–10) that begins with the arrival of Alexander the Great and ends with the rise of Antiochus IV Epiphanes in 175 BCE, is devoted to the history of the next forty years (175–135 BCE). After the first chapter reports the troubles under Antiochus, and the second chapter narrates the beginning of the Hasmonean rebellion, chapters 3–9 focus on Judas Maccabeus's leadership of the rebellion until his death in 160 BCE. Next, chapters 9–12 and 12–16 recount, respectively, the terms of two more brothers, Jonathan

---

1. 2 Macc. 5:27: "But Judas Maccabeus and about nine others withdrew to the wilderness to avoid sharing in defilement; there he and his companions lived like the animals in the hills, eating what grew wild."

Maccabeus (d. 142) and Simon Maccabeus (d. 135), who saw the growth of the Hasmonean state and its achievement of international recognition. The work ends with Simon Maccabeus's death and the succession to the throne of his son, Jonathan Hyrcanus I.[2]

Second Maccabees opens with two letters (chaps. 1–2) in which the Jews of Jerusalem invite those of Egypt to celebrate the festival of Hanukkah, which memorializes Judas Maccabeus's conquest of Jerusalem and rededication of the temple in 164 BCE. These letters, and an editor's preface (2:19–32; see below), are followed first by a prologue (chap. 3) on an episode in the days of Seleucus IV. Subsequently a detailed account of events under Antiochus IV Epiphanes (chaps. 4–9) is presented, followed by those of his son Antiochus V (chaps. 10–13). Next, the rule of Demetrius I is described (chaps. 14–15), and finally Judas Maccabeus's last major victory over a Seleucid general, **Nicanor,** in 161 BCE.[3] Thus, the book is, in its current form, an invitation to celebrate Hanukkah with a long attachment explaining the festival's historical background.

First Maccabees is a Judean work, as is indicated especially by the detailed attention the book gives to Judean and Palestinian geography. It is also conveyed by the original language of the work (see below) and, of course, by its pro-dynastic agenda. We may suppose someone close to the Hasmonean court, probably in Jerusalem, wrote 1 Maccabees.

As for 2 Maccabees, given its hybrid structure, two settings are to be considered. The letters with which it opens are from Jerusalem, and they invite the addressees to celebrate an eminently Jerusalemite holiday. Moreover, at least the first of the two letters (1:1–9) seems to be translated from Biblical Hebrew, and the views the letters convey are typical of Judean Judaism; note, for example, the assumption at 1:27 and 2:18[4] that it is terrible for Jews to be in exile and subject to foreign kings. The body of the book (chaps. 3–15), however, is a work of the **Hellenistic Diaspora.** This conclusion derives, first, from the notice at 2:23[5] that the present work is an abridgment of a longer work written by one Jason of Cyrene (Libya), which was part of the Ptolemaic kingdom. Second, it arises from the Greek language of the book and from the numerous ideas and values preserved in it that are typical of Jews of the Hellenistic Diaspora—for example, the assumption that Gentiles and their kings are usually full of respect for Jews (3:2–3; 4:35–37, 49; 5:16; etc.) and the insistence, in 5:19,[6] that God's choice of the Jewish people precedes his choice of the temple.

First Maccabees is meant to explain and to justify to readers how the Hasmoneans, in particular the Simonides, came to rule Judea. The first chapter de-

---

2. For a chart of the Hasmonean rulers, see p. 26.

3. For a chart of the rulers of the Hellenistic period, see p. 24.

4. 2 Macc. 1:27: "Gather together our scattered people, free those who are slaves among the Gentiles, look kindly on those who are despised and detested, and let the Gentiles know that you are our God." See also 2 Macc. 2:18.

5. 2 Macc. 2:23: "All this, detailed by Jason of Cyrene in five volumes, we will try to condense into a single book."

6. 2 Macc. 5:19: "The Lord, however, had not chosen the nation for the sake of the place, but the place for the sake of the nation."

scribes how terrible foreign rule is, while chapter 2 recounts the beginning of the rebellion by the founder of the Hasmonean dynasty, Mattathias, and it closes with a description of his death (not before his deathbed speech appoints Simon Maccabeus to be his successor).[7] The other chapters show how this family of men through whom salvation was given to Israel (5:62) fulfilled its mission, step by step.

STRUCTURE OF 1 MACCABEES

A. Chap. 1: the problem—foreign rule
B. Chaps. 2–16: the solution—Hasmonean rebellion and rule
   1. Chap. 2: Mattathias
   2. Chaps. 3–9: Judas Maccabeus
   3. Chaps. 9–12: Jonathan Maccabeus
   4. Chaps. 12–16: Simon Maccabeus (punctuated in chap. 14 by popular proclamation of Simonide rule)
   5. End of chap. 16: Simon Maccabeus is replaced by Jonathan Hyrcanus I

Second Maccabees contains different purposes in its different layers. The book's practical purpose, as suggested by the opening letters, is to urge the Jews of Egypt to celebrate Hanukkah by reminding them of the heroic story of the first major stage of the Hasmonean revolt. Presumably, this appeal was meant more generally to drum up Diaspora support for the Hasmonean dynasty. The body of the book (chaps. 3–15), however, has other purposes. First, it seems that the book was drawn up not to support Hanukkah, but, rather, to uphold an early Hasmonean festival, Nicanor's Day, which commemorated Judas Maccabeus's victory over Nicanor in 161 BCE. The manner in which the book focuses on Judas Maccabeus's two campaigns against Nicanor (chaps. 8 and 15), ending with the second campaign and the establishment of the festival (15:36), seems to make that purpose clear. Second, the book bolsters Jewish pride by telling the story of the Jewish *polis* (city), Jerusalem, and of the heroes who defended it against a barbarian attack on the city and its constitution. The use of such "political" language, which refers to Jewish institutions with vocabulary that pertains to the most respectable institution of the Hellenistic world, is widespread in the book, and it allows the Jews of the Hellenistic world, and their neighbors if they cared to read the book, to see that the Jews too were civilized people. A third purpose, which is even more prominent and pronounced in the book, is to make a religious point: that as long as the Jews observe divine law, God protects them. When they do not follow divine law, he ignores them (the biblical motif of God "turning his face away"—5:17); thus he allows foreign foes to have the upper hand against them. Once the Jews repent and seek atonement—which in this book happens via the martyrdoms reported at length in chapters 6–7—God is conciliated and from then on the Jews' fortunes are restored. This part of the message of 2 Maccabees is based on Deuteronomy 32, and 2 Maccabees 8:5 is, accordingly, the turning point of the entire book.

---

7. 1 Macc. 2:65: "Here is your brother Simeon who I know is a wise counselor; listen to him always, and he will be a father to you."

STRUCTURE OF 2 MACCABEES

A. Chaps. 1–2: introductory materials
1. Letters in which Jews of Judea invite Jews of Egypt to celebrate Hanukkah
2. Abridger's preface
B. Chap. 3: prologue—God protects the temple of Jerusalem
C. Chaps. 4–7: sin and atonement
1. Chap. 4: Jews sin by Hellenizing and ignoring the temple cult
2. Chap. 5: beginning of retribution: Antiochus IV Epiphanes's first attack on Jerusalem
3. Chaps. 6–7: intensified retribution: Antiochus IV Epiphanes's decrees against Judaism; accounts of martyrdom that work atonement
D. Chaps. 8–15: reconciliation
1. Chap. 8: Judas Maccabeus's first victories
2. Chap. 9: death of Antiochus IV Epiphanes
3. Chap. 10: Judas Maccabeus retakes Jerusalem and the temple; more fighting
4. Chap. 11: more fighting; Antiochus V Eupator revokes Antiochus IV Epiphanes's decrees against Judaism
5. Chaps. 12–13: more fighting
6. Chaps. 14–15: Judas Maccabeus first outwits the Seleucid general Nicanor and then defeats him

The Struggles for the Seleucid Throne

The rise of the Hasmonean dynasty, depicted in 1 Maccabees, was facilitated by protracted warfare over three decades between competing contenders for the Seleucid throne; several of them figure significantly in 1 and 2 Maccabees. The struggle divided the senior branch of the house, descended from Seleucus IV, and the junior branch, descended from Antiochus IV Epiphanes. The seed of the difficulties was sown upon the death of Seleucus IV in 175 BCE (2 Macc. 4:7). He was succeeded not by his son, Demetrius I (b. 186 BCE), who was too young at the time, but by his brother, Antiochus IV Epiphanes, who reigned until his death in 163 BCE (1 Macc. 6; 2 Macc. 9). At that point, a struggle began between Antiochus's young son, Antiochus V, who naturally expected to succeed his father and was supported by a powerful regent, Lysias, and Demetrius I, who naturally preferred to view Antiochus IV Epiphanes only as a stand-in for himself until he reached maturity. Demetrius won that first round of the struggle, killing Antiochus V and Lysias in 162 BCE (1 Macc. 7:1–4; 2 Macc. 14:1–2) and reigning without competition for a decade. However, in 153/152, Alexander I Balas appeared on the scene, claiming, probably falsely, to be another son of Antiochus IV Epiphanes. With the support of Rome, Ptolemy VI of Egypt (who gave Alexander his daughter in marriage), and Jonathan Maccabeus (whom he appointed high priest and invited to his wedding—1 Macc. 10:58–66), he waged war against Demetrius and defeated him (1 Macc. 10—150 BCE). Not long after, however, Demetrius's son Demetrius II resumed the struggle, Ptolemy VI shifted his support (and his daughter) to him, and in the ensuing war both Alexander I Balas and Ptolemy VI died (145 BCE), leaving Demetrius II alone on the throne (1 Macc. 10:67–11:19). At this point, however, an adventurer named Trypho attached himself to Alexander I Balas's young son, Antiochus VI, and managed to establish him as king, competing with Demetrius II for a few years—until, in 142, he killed Antiochus VI and began to reign in his stead still in competition with Demetrius II. Both of them met their downfall in 138 BCE: Demetrius was captured by the Parthians, while his brother, Antiochus VII Sidetes, succeeded him and drove Trypho into exile (1 Macc. 15:37–39). Antiochus VII Sidetes renewed Seleucid demands against the Hasmoneans (1 Macc. 15), which resulted in war (1 Macc. 16:1–10) and perhaps the scheming that led to Simon Maccabeus's death (1 Macc. 16:11–18).

Narrative Description

The story of 1 Maccabees is quite straightforward, and the frequent references to dates, that is, according to the Seleucid Era (S.E.), which began in 312/311 BCE, facilitate the narrative. After the opening chapter portrays the "problem" (foreign rule), which encompasses the depths of suffering by the end of chapter 1, chapter 2 provides the "solution" by introducing **Mattathias** and his sons and immediately proceeds to report the rebellion they initiated. When Mattathias dies at the end of chapter 2, he is replaced by Judas Maccabeus, who leads the rebellion in a series of victories reported in chapters 3–7, followed by the establishment of a treaty with Rome in chapter 8, and then by his defeat and death in chapter 9. At that point (160 BCE), Judas Maccabeus is replaced by his brother Jonathan Maccabeus, who, at first, essentially goes underground (chap. 9); however, in chapter 10, he is able to take advantage of a struggle in the Seleucid royal court and achieve a measure of international recognition. The new Seleucid king, **Alexander I Balas,** grants him the high priesthood (152 BCE—see 10:21) and even invites Jonathan Maccabeus as an honored guest at his own wedding to the daughter of **Ptolemy VI** of Egypt. When, however, as chapter 11 reports, Ptolemy and Alexander have a falling out and both die on the field of battle (145 BCE—11:15–19), Jonathan Maccabeus proceeds to hitch his wagon first to that of the new king, **Demetrius II,** and then to that of his competitors, **Antiochus IV Epiphanes** and **Trypho.** Chapter 12, in contrast, is the turning point for Jonathan Maccabeus. Although it begins with his diplomatic successes, vis-à-vis Rome and even Sparta, by the end he is betrayed and taken captive by Trypho. Consequently, chapter 13 depicts Simon Maccabeus's elevation to power (with finality when Jonathan Maccabeus is actually executed by Trypho—13:23), and the rest of chapter 13 and all of chapter 14 are devoted to his advances. He succeeds in enlarging the borders of the fledgling Jewish state, and Demetrius II agrees to give up all claims on tribute from Judea (taken as a granting of full independence in 142 BCE—13:41–42). A final success is the decision of a Jewish national assembly to install Simon Maccabeus and his descendants as rulers of Judea forever (140 BCE—chapter 14). After that climax of the story, the final two chapters implement its consequences. When a renewal of warfare and some internal difficulties lead to the death of Simon Maccabeus (135

BCE—16:13–14), he is succeeded in the book's final verses by his son, Jonathan Hyrcanus I. With the succession of a son instead of a brother, dynastic stability has been achieved and it indeed remains until the end of the dynasty; rule is retained by Simon Maccabeus's descendants.

Second Maccabees, in contrast, is organized not by the succession of Hasmonean leaders (of whom it focuses on only one, Judas) but, rather, by the Jews' status vis-à-vis God. After the first two prefatory chapters (letters and abridger's preface) and a prologue in chapter 3 that shows that God normally may be expected to protect the temple, even spectacularly, chapter 4 begins the real story by reporting sinful Jewish Hellenism in Jerusalem. In an explicit aside to his readers, the author announces that such disregard for the divine law would soon lead to trouble (4:16–17), and indeed it does. Namely, chapter 5 reports that Antiochus IV Epiphanes attacks Jerusalem, killing and enslaving tens of thousands and robbing the temple (an aside to readers reminds us this is punishment for sin—5:17–20). In chapter 6 things deteriorate when Antiochus IV Epiphanes also imposes decrees against the practice of Judaism. However, these troubles, explained didactically to readers (6:12–17), are met by heroic Jewish willingness to endure martyrdom, portrayed at length in chapters 6–7, rather than violate Jewish law; this action reconciles God to the Jews. The result is a complete reversal of the Jews' fortunes. In chapter 8 Judas Maccabeus earns his first victories. In chapter 9 Antiochus IV Epiphanes dies a horrible death by the hand of God. In chapter 10 Judas retakes Jerusalem and the temple, secures further victories, such that, in chapter 11, Antiochus's son and successor, Antiochus V and his regent, Lysias, abrogate all the decrees against Judaism, and make their peace with the Jews. For one reason or another this does not put an end to the fighting; it continues for a few more chapters, including during the reign of Demetrius I, who takes over the Seleucid throne in 162 BCE, and, inter alia, attempts to restore control over Judea (chap. 14). His effort to retake Judea, however, does not succeed; rather, in the showdown depicted in chapter 15, Judas defeats Demetrius I's general, Nicanor. At that point, the author announces that "since Nicanor's doings ended in this way, with the city remaining in the possession of the Hebrews from that time on, I will bring my story to an end here too" (15:37).

Authorship/Provenance

First Maccabees was obviously written by a Jew close to the Hasmonean throne. We can see that the author was very familiar with the Hebrew Bible, but also that, taken as he was by the achievements of the Hasmoneans, the author had little use both for martyrs and for God. Given the book's origin in the days of Jonathan Hyrcanus I, who according to both Josephus (*Antiquities* 13.296) and the rabbis (b. *Berakhot* 29a) became a Sadducee, it is perhaps relevant to cite, in this connection, Josephus's statement (*Antiquities* 13.173)[8] that the Sadducees

---

8. Josephus, *Antiquities* 13.173: "And for the Sadducees, they remove fate and say there is no such thing, and that the events of human affairs are not at fate's disposal; but they suppose

denied divine providence and held that men are themselves responsible for their well-being or misfortunes.

The authors (the original author and the so-called **epitomator** [2:19–32]) of the body of 2 Maccabees (as opposed to the opening letters) were Jews of the Hellenistic Diaspora. While the author shows some familiarity with the Hebrew Bible (he periodically alludes to it and quotes it explicitly in 7:6 and 10:26), he characteristically makes reference to Greek motifs, such as his use of **"Scythians"** as the archetypes of cruelty (4:47; 7:4 ["to Scythize a person's head" = scalping]) and his use of the oft-quoted *topos* of **Xerxes's** arrogance (Herodotus 7.22–24, 33–36; Isocrates, *Panegyricus* 89) to describe Antiochus IV Epiphanes (2 Macc. 5:21; 9:8).[9]

Date/Occasion

In general, both books apparently belong to the latter half, perhaps more specifically to the third quarter, of the second century BCE. First Maccabees ends with a reference to the accession to the throne of Jonathan Hyrcanus I in 135 BCE, but offers no details describing his years as ruler. It also seems (as Seth Schwartz has argued)[10] that the book's terribly hostile attitude toward Gentiles fits the early part of Jonathan Hyrcanus I's tenure rather than his later years when numerous Gentiles were associated with his regime. As for 2 Maccabees, since the letters seem to have been attached to the extant book, the dates mentioned in the first letter (1:7 refers to 169 SE [143/142 BCE] and 1:10 refers either to 148 or 188 SE [164/163 or 124/123 BCE]) offer a similar **terminus ad quem** for the book. Jason's original work, of course, would have been written even earlier—a point that corresponds to the fact that the work focuses only on the first stage of Hasmonean history

---

that all our actions are in our own power, so that we are the cause of what is good, and receive what is evil by our own folly."

9. Herodotus 7.24: "As far as I can judge, Xerxes gave the command for this digging out of pride, wishing to display his power and leave a memorial. They could have drawn their ships across the isthmus without any trouble, yet he ordered them to dig a canal from sea to sea, wide enough to float two galley ships abreast."

Isocrates, *Panegyricus* 88–89: "Then came the later expedition, which was led by Xerxes in person; he had left his royal residence, boldly taken command as general in the field, and collected about him all the hosts of Asia. What orator, however eager to overshoot the mark, has not fallen short of the truth in speaking of this king? He rose to such a pitch of arrogance that, thinking it a small task to subjugate Hellas, proposed to leave a memorial such as would suggest a more than human power. He did not stop until he had devised and compelled the execution of a plan whose fame is on the lips of all humankind—a plan by which, having bridged the Hellespont and channeled Athos, he sailed his ships across the mainland, and marched his troops across the main."

2 Macc. 5:21: "Antiochus carried off eighteen hundred talents from the temple and hurried back to Antioch, thinking in his arrogance that he could make the land navigable and the sea passable on foot, so carried away was he with pride."

10. Seth Schwartz, "Israel and the Nations Roundabout: 1 Maccabees and the Hasmonean Expansion," *JJS* 42 (1991): 16–38.

and, as we have seen, on a holiday, Nicanor's Day, which was later supplanted by Hanukkah. An early date for 2 Maccabees also accounts for the otherwise problematic fact that, although this book clearly views the temple of Jerusalem as the only legitimate Jewish temple, it nevertheless lionizes the high priest **Onias III** (3:1; 4:1-6; 15:12-14). Given the fact that, by the late 140s, Onias or his son of the same name had founded a Jewish temple in Egypt that competed with the one in Jerusalem, it is likely that 2 Maccabees was completed earlier.

Both works are historical monographs. First Maccabees is clearly a dynastic history—a work that both recounts the rise of a dynasty and justifies it. Second Maccabees has two interlocking foci. The basic structure focuses on the history of a city, Jerusalem, which is in an ideal situation at the opening of the story (3:1-3) and at the end of the story when it returns to an ideal situation (15:37). Beginning in chapter 8, however, the story focuses on Judas Maccabeus himself ("that man who was ever in body and soul the chief defender of his fellow citizens"—15:30)—the hero who saves the city. Beyond that, it is important to note that 2 Maccabees is written in the style of "pathetic" Hellenistic historiography that is meant to excite readers (see, e.g., 3:14-21 or 14:41-46). While the restrained style of 1 Maccabees is reminiscent of biblical historiography, 2 Maccabees has an explicit didactic religious message.

First Maccabees, composed in Hebrew, was obviously intended for the Jewish subjects of the Hasmonean kingdom. Second Maccabees, with its religious message, seems also to have been directed mainly at Jewish readers, but the explanations of Jewish concerns offered in a few passages (5:25; 7:1; 12:40) seem to indicate that Gentile readers are also contemplated—as may be expected of an author writing in Greek.

Text, Language, Sources, and Transmission

Although 1 Maccabees was preserved only in Greek and secondary translations made from it, Origen and Jerome testify that it was originally written in Hebrew, and that a substratum indeed shines through clearly in the book's syntax and vocabulary. The syntax frequently reflects typical Hebrew parataxis (finite verbs linked one to another by "and") and the vocabulary often slavishly reflects Hebrew idioms, such as "by the mouth of the sword," "was gathered up unto his fathers," "he answered and said," and the like. Moreover, the wording of 1 Maccabees often alludes to biblical phrases. Thus, for example, the references to the sinners who "allied themselves with the Gentiles" (1:15) and Mattathias's "zealous" response (2:24, 26) are meant to indicate to readers who know their Bible that Mattathias was a latter-day Phinehas (Num. 25:8-9) and that his descendants, therefore, were entitled to the high priesthood (Num. 25:11-13).[11] The references to the "descen-

---

11. 1 Macc. 2:24-26: "When Mattathias saw him, he was filled with zeal; his heart was moved and his just fury was aroused; he sprang forward and killed him upon the altar. At the same time, he also killed the messenger of the king who was forcing them to sacrifice, and he tore down the altar. Thus he showed his zeal for the law, just as Phinehas did with Zimri, son of Salu."

Num. 25:7-9: "When Phinehas son of Eleazar, son of Aaron the priest, saw it, he got up and

dants of Jacob" and the "Edomites" in 1 Maccabees 5:2–3 are meant to indicate to such readers that the enmity between the peoples was another cycle of the one that began in the days of the patriarchs. The references to people sitting calmly under vines and fig trees in the days of Simon (14:12) was meant to suggest that his days fulfilled biblical promises of messianic redemption (Mic. 4:4; Zech. 3:10).[12]

Second Maccabees, in contrast, was composed in Hellenistic Greek, with its typically involved periods and subordinate clauses. Apart from the introductory letters, only a few passages, of which the most salient is the lament at 5:13 (which evidently alludes to Deut. 32:25),[13] offer anything reminiscent of Semitic style.

Both texts survive in Greek and in translations made from the Greek. The main witnesses to the Greek text are the major uncial manuscripts of the Septuagint (see below). The ancient Latin translation is often valuable insofar as it testifies to more pristine readings of the Greek text, which underwent Lucianic revision in the third and fourth centuries CE. Josephus's paraphrase of 1 Maccabees is often valuable as well, whether his deviations from the extant Greek text derive from another text or, rather, indicate how an ancient reader understood the text as we have it. Thus, for example, in *Antiquities* 13.52 Josephus refers to forced labor where the Greek text of 1 Maccabees 10:33 mentions taxes.[14] This suggests that Josephus, who knew the Greek text reflected a Hebrew original, understood "taxes" here as representing the Hebrew *mas,* which refers to forced labor (e.g.,

---

left the congregation. Taking a spear in his hand, he went after the Israelite man into the tent, and pierced the two of them, the Israelite and the woman, through the belly. So the plague was stopped among the people of Israel. Nevertheless those that died by the plague were twenty-four thousand."

Num. 25:11–13: "Phinehas son of Eleazar, son of Aaron the priest, has turned back my wrath from the Israelites by manifesting such zeal among them on my behalf that in my jealousy I did not consume the Israelites. Therefore, say, 'I hereby grant him my covenant of peace. It will be for him and for his descendants after him a covenant of perpetual priesthood, because he was zealous for his God, and made atonement for the Israelites.'"

12. 1 Macc. 14:12: "Every one sat under his vine and fig tree, with no one to disturb them."

Mic. 4:4: "But they will all sit under their own vines and under their own fig trees, and no one will make them afraid; for the mouth of the Lord of hosts has spoken."

Zech. 3:10: "On that day, says the Lord of hosts, you will invite each other to come under your vine and fig tree."

13. 2 Macc. 5:13: "There was a massacre of young and old, a killing of women and children, a slaughter of young women and infants."

Deut. 32:25: "In the street the sword shall bereave, and in the chambers terror, for young man and woman alike, nursing child and old gray head."

14. 1 Macc. 10:33: "Every Jew who has been carried into captivity from the land of Judah into any part of my kingdom I set at liberty without ransom; and let all their taxes, even those on their cattle, be canceled." Josephus, *Antiquities* 13.52: "I also make free all those Jews who have been made captives and slaves in my kingdom. I also order that the beasts of the Jews not be pressed for our service; and let their Sabbaths, and all their festivals, and three days before each of them, be free from any imposition."

Exod. 1:11: "Therefore they set taskmasters over them to oppress them with forced labor. They built supply cities, Pithom and Rameses, for Pharaoh."

1 Kings 5:13: "King Solomon conscripted forced labor out of all Israel; the levy numbered thirty thousand men."

Exod. 1:11; 1 Kings 5:13). From this point of view, the Modern Hebrew translations of 1 Maccabees are also valuable insofar as they aspire, with the help of modern scholarship concerning Septuagintal usage, to recover the original text.

Next to nothing is known of the sources of either book. First Maccabees ends with an allusion to the annals of Jonathan Hyrcanus I's high priesthood ("Now the rest of the acts of John, his wars and the brave deeds he performed, his rebuilding of the walls, and all his achievements—these are recorded in the chronicle of his high priesthood, from the time that he succeeded his father as high priest") and that suggests there were such works available for the preceding Hasmoneans as well—but we have no knowledge about such works, and the phrase may be simply a literary embellishment reminiscent of such allusions in biblical historiography (e.g., 2 Kings 1:18; 14:18). In general, some of the accounts in 1 Maccabees are so colorful and circumstantial that it is often thought that they originate with eyewitnesses, but beyond general impressions little can be said securely. As for 2 Maccabees, it seems that Jason's original work was written within two or three decades of the events described, so there will not have been much need for sources. Nevertheless, it appears that some of the materials in 2 Maccabees have their own prehistory, especially the miracle account in chapter 3 and the martyrologies in chapters 6–7.

The official documents preserved in both books are a special category: 2 Maccabees has four (three Seleucid, one Roman) in chapter 11, 1 Maccabees has more than twice as many (mostly Seleucid, but also Roman, Judean, and even Spartan). Many of these are generally considered authentic, although especially in the case of 1 Maccabees, which preserved the original documents only via a double translation (the original Greek documents were translated into Hebrew when they were inserted into the book, and then the book was translated into Greek), the original text has not survived.

Both books were preserved unexceptionally, as part of the Septuagint. The standard editions, in the Göttingen Septuaginta, are based on the main uncial manuscripts (Sinaiticus, Alexandrinus, and Venetus for 1 Maccabees, the latter two for 2 Maccabees) and numerous miniscules. As mentioned above, the Old Latin tradition is also very valuable.

Theology

First Maccabees, a history of a human dynasty, evinces very little interest in God, theology, or religion in general. The first few chapters do include some prayers and some expressions of confidence that God will look out for those who are faithful to him (including Mattathias's long deathbed speech in 2:50–68), but such references become very rare by chapter 5. The book reports no miracles, no apparitions, and no revelations; there is no consciousness of Jewish sinfulness or of the notion that the Jews' suffering might be a result of sin. It views martyrs only as sufferers, attributing no efficacy to their death and, instead, contrasting ineffective martyrs with effective rebels (see esp. 2:39–41 and the move from 1:62–64 to 2:1). It mentions no notion of afterlife, and on three occasions (9:10; 12:1; 15:33–34) it explicitly says that things go right or wrong because of the "hour" *(kairos)*—whether that means "chance" or the "stars," it is far from any notion of divine providence. Indeed, after the first chapters, 1 Maccabees makes little reference to God altogether. This is all we would expect from a dynastic history of a sovereign state whose rulers were aware of their own accomplishments. Perhaps its content is just what is described by the title Origen cited: "Book of the House of Those Who Rebelled against God."

Second Maccabees is different on all these counts. It is full of prayers, apparitions (such as 3:24–28; 5:1–4; 10:29; 15), sin that causes suffering, martyrs who work atonement and thus stop suffering, explicit and underlined belief in resurrection (12:43–45), and references to God and his providence; nothing at all happens by chance. This is all we would expect from a Diasporan history: Jews abroad, who do not have their own army, can and must depend on God in a way that a dynasty of a sovereign state might find impossible or unnecessary.

Thus, these two books present the somewhat paradoxical situation; the one that was written in Biblical Hebrew betrays a highly unbiblical orientation concerning the Bible's prime values, while the one that was written in Hellenistic Greek adheres to them quite closely. Somewhat emblematic of this situation is the fact that the term "Judaism" first appears, in extant literature, in 2 Maccabees (2:21; 8:1; 14:38).

Reception of 1 and 2 Maccabees in the Second Temple Period

Virtually no evidence exists for readers of either book during the Second Temple period. However, both works survived, as part of the Septuagint, and not long after the destruction of the Second Temple other Jewish writers used both extensively. Josephus made widespread use of 1 Maccabees 1–13 in books 12–13 of his *Jewish Antiquities* (completed in the final decade of the first century CE), and the author of 4 Maccabees, perhaps around the same time as Josephus, used 2 Maccabees significantly in producing his philosophically oriented account of martyrdom in the days of Antiochus IV Epiphanes. It also seems that the author of the book of Hebrews used 2 Maccabees—compare Hebrews 11:35–38 to 2 Maccabees 7 and 10:6. Rabbinic tradition shows no knowledge of either work, just as in general it preserves little concerning the Hasmoneans.

DANIEL SCHWARTZ

FURTHER READING

Dancy, J. C. *A Commentary on I Maccabees.* Oxford: Blackwell, 1954.

Harrington, D. J. *First and Second Maccabees.* New Collegeville BIble Commentary. Old Testament, vol. 12. Collegeville, Minn.: Liturgical Press, 2012.

Nickelsburg, George W. E. "1 and 2 Maccabees—Same Story, Different Meaning." *Concordia Theological Monthly* 42 (1971): 515–26.

Schürer, Emil. *The History of the Jewish People in the Age of Jesus Christ (175 B.C.–A.D. 135).* Trans. and ed. Geza Vermes et al. 4 vols. Edinburgh: T&T Clark, 1973–87 (in particular see 1:17–19; 3:180–86, 531–37).

Tcherikover, Victor. *Hellenistic Civilization and the Jews*. Philadelphia: Jewish Publication Society, 1959.

Weitzman, S. *Surviving Sacrilege: Cultural Persistence in Jewish Antiquity*. Cambridge, Mass.: Harvard University Press, 2005.

ADVANCED READING

Bar-Kochva, B. *Judas Maccabaeus: The Jewish Struggle against the Seleucids*. Cambridge: Cambridge University Press, 1989.

Borchardt, F. *The Torah in 1 Maccabees: A Literary-Critical Approach to the Text*. Berlin: deGruyter, 2014.

Doran, R. *Temple Propaganda: The Purpose and Character of 2 Maccabees*. CBQMS 12. Washington, D.C.: Catholic Biblical Association of America, 1981.

Habicht, C. "Royal Documents in Maccabees II." *Harvard Series in Classical Philology* 80 (1976): 1–18.

Himmelfarb, M. "Judaism and Hellenism in 2 Maccabees." *Poetics Today* 19 (1998): 19–40.

Lichtenberger, Hermann. "History-Writing and History-Telling in First and Second Maccabees." In *Memory in the Bible and Antiquity: The Fifth Durham-Tübingen Research Symposium (Durham, September 2004)*, edited by S. C. Barton, L. T. Stuckenbruck, and B. G. Wold, pp. 95–110. WUNT 212. Tübingen: Mohr Siebeck, 2007.

Schwartz, D. R. *2 Maccabees*. CEJL. Berlin: De Gruyter, 2008.

Schwartz, S. "Israel and the Nations Roundabout: 1 Maccabees and the Hasmonean Expansion." *JJS* 42 (1991): 16–38.

Sievers, J. *Synopsis of the Greek Sources for the Hasmonean Period: 1-2 Maccabees and Josephus, War 1 and Antiquities 12–14*. Subsidia Biblica 20. Rome: Pontificio Istituto Biblico, 2001.

Van Henten, J. W. *The Maccabean Martyrs as Saviours of the Jewish People: A Study of 2 and 4 Maccabees*. JSJSup 57. Leiden: Brill, 1997.

Williams, D. S. "Recent Research in 1 Maccabees." *Currents in Research: Biblical Studies* 9 (2001): 169–84.

———. "Recent Research in 2 Maccabees." *Currents in Biblical Research* 2 (2003–4): 69–83.

———. *The Structure of 1 Maccabees*. CBQMS 31. Washington, D.C.: Catholic Biblical Association of America, 1999.

2.1 1 Maccabees

Alexander the Great

¹˙¹ After Alexander the Macedonian, Philip's son, who came from the land of Kittim, had defeated Darius, king of the Persians and Medes, he became king in his place, having first ruled in Greece. ² He fought many battles, captured fortresses, and put the kings of the earth to death. ³ He advanced to the ends of the earth, gathering plunder from many nations; the earth fell silent before him, and his heart became proud and arrogant. ⁴ He collected a very strong army and won dominion over provinces, nations, and rulers, and they paid him tribute.

⁵ But after all this he took to his bed, realizing that he was going to die. ⁶ So he summoned his noblest officers, who had been brought up with him from his youth, and divided his kingdom among them while he was still alive. ⁷ Alexander had reigned twelve years when he died.

⁸ So his officers took over his kingdom, each in his own territory, ⁹ and after his death they all put on diadems, and so did their sons after them for many years, multiplying evils on the earth.

Antiochus Epiphanes

¹⁰ There sprang from these a sinful offshoot, Antiochus Epiphanes, son of King Antiochus, once a hostage at Rome. He became king in the one hundred and thirty-seventh year of the kingdom of the Greeks.

¹¹ In those days there appeared in Israel transgressors of the law who seduced many, saying: "Let us go and make a covenant with the Gentiles all around us; since we separated from them, many evils have come upon us." ¹² The proposal was agreeable; ¹³ some from among the people promptly went to the king, and he authorized them to introduce the ordinances of the Gentiles. ¹⁴ Thereupon they built a gymnasium in Jerusalem according to the Gentile custom. ¹⁵ They disguised their circumcision and abandoned the holy covenant; they allied themselves with the Gentiles and sold themselves to wrongdoing.

¹⁶ When his kingdom seemed secure, Antiochus undertook to become king of the land of Egypt and to rule over both kingdoms. ¹⁷ He invaded Egypt with a strong force, with chariots, elephants, and cavalry, and with a large fleet, ¹⁸ to make war on Ptolemy, king of Egypt. Ptolemy was frightened at his presence and fled,

and many were wounded and fell dead. [19] The fortified cities in the land of Egypt were captured, and Antiochus plundered the land of Egypt.

Antiochus Persecutes the Jews

[20] After Antiochus had defeated Egypt in the one hundred and forty-third year, he returned and went up against Israel and against Jerusalem with a strong force. [21] He insolently entered the sanctuary and took away the golden altar, the lampstand for the light with all its utensils, [22] the offering table, the cups and bowls, the golden censers, and the curtain. The cornices and the golden ornament on the facade of the temple—he stripped it all off. [23] And he took away the silver and gold and the precious vessels; he also took all the hidden treasures he could find. [24] Taking all this, he went back to his own country. He shed much blood and spoke with great arrogance.

> [25] And there was great mourning throughout all Israel,
> [26] and the rulers and the elders groaned.
> Young women and men languished,
>   and the beauty of the women faded.
> [27] Every bridegroom took up lamentation,
>   while the bride sitting in her chamber mourned,
> [28] And the land quaked on account of its inhabitants,
>   and all the house of Jacob was clothed with shame.

[29] Two years later, the king sent the Mysian commander to the cities of Judah, and he came to Jerusalem with a strong force. [30] He spoke to them deceitfully in peaceful terms, and they believed him. Then he attacked the city suddenly, in a great onslaught, and destroyed many of the people in Israel. [31] He plundered the city and set fire to it, demolished its houses and its surrounding walls. [32] And they took captive the women and children, and seized the animals. [33] Then they built up the City of David with a high, strong wall and strong towers, and it became their citadel. [34] There they installed a sinful race, transgressors of the law, who fortified themselves inside it. [35] They stored up weapons and provisions, depositing there the plunder they had collected from Jerusalem, and they became a great snare.

> [36] The citadel became an ambush against the sanctuary,
>   and a wicked adversary to Israel at all times.
> [37] They shed innocent blood around the sanctuary;
> they defiled the sanctuary.
> [38] Because of them the inhabitants of Jerusalem fled away,
>   she became the abode of strangers.
> She became a stranger to her own offspring,
>   and her children forsook her.
> [39] Her sanctuary became desolate as a wilderness;
> her feasts were turned into mourning,

Her Sabbaths to shame,
her honor to contempt.
40 As her glory had been, so great was her dishonor:
her exaltation was turned into mourning.

Gentile Cults Exposed

41 Then the king wrote to his whole kingdom that all should be one people, 42 and abandon their particular customs. All the Gentiles conformed to the command of the king, 43 and many Israelites delighted in his religion; they sacrificed to idols and profaned the Sabbath.

44 The king sent letters by messenger to Jerusalem and to the cities of Judah, ordering them to follow customs foreign to their land; 45 to prohibit burnt offerings, sacrifices, and libations in the sanctuary, to profane the Sabbaths and feast days, 46 to desecrate the sanctuary and the sacred ministers, 47 to build pagan altars and temples and shrines, to sacrifice swine and unclean animals, 48 to leave their sons uncircumcised, and to defile themselves with every kind of impurity and abomination; 49 so that they might forget the law and change all its ordinances. 50 Whoever refused to act according to the command of the king was to be put to death.

51 In words such as these he wrote to his whole kingdom. He appointed inspectors over all the people, and he ordered the cities of Judah to offer sacrifices, each city in turn. 52 Many of the people, those who abandoned the law, joined them and committed evil in the land. 53 They drove Israel into hiding, wherever places of refuge could be found.

54 On the fifteenth day of the month Kislev, in the year one hundred and forty-five, the king erected the desolating abomination upon the altar of burnt offerings, and in the surrounding cities of Judah they built pagan altars. 55 They also burned incense at the doors of houses and in the streets. 56 Any scrolls of the law that they found they tore up and burned. 57 Whoever was found with a scroll of the covenant, and whoever observed the law, was condemned to death by royal decree. 58 So they used their power against Israel, against those who were caught, each month, in the cities. 59 On the twenty-fifth day of each month they sacrificed on the pagan altar that was over the altar of burnt offerings. 60 In keeping with the decree, they put to death women who had their children circumcised, 61 and they hung their babies from their necks; their families also and those who had circumcised them were killed.

62 But many in Israel were determined and resolved in their hearts not to eat anything unclean; 63 they preferred to die rather than to be defiled with food or to profane the holy covenant; and they did die. 64 And very great wrath came upon Israel.

Mattathias and His Sons

2:1 In those days Mattathias, son of John, son of Simeon, a priest of the family of Joarib, left Jerusalem and settled in Modein. 2 He had five sons: John, who was called Gaddi; [3] Simon, who was called Thassi; [4] Judas, who was called Maccabeus; [5] Eleazar, who was called Avaran; and Jonathan, who was called Apphus. [6] When he saw the sacrileges that were being committed in Judah and in Jerusalem, [7] he said:

> "Woe is me! Why was I born
>> to see the ruin of my people,
>> the ruin of the holy city—
> To dwell there
>> as it was given into the hands of enemies,
>> the sanctuary into the hands of strangers?
> [8] Her temple has become like a man disgraced,
>> her glorious vessels carried off as spoils,
>> Her infants murdered in her streets,
>> her youths by the sword of the enemy.
> [10] What nation has not taken its share of her realm,
>> and laid its hand on her spoils?
> [11] All her adornment has been taken away.
> Once free, she has become a slave.
> [12] We see our sanctuary laid waste,
>> our beauty, our glory.
> The Gentiles have defiled them!
> [13] Why are we still alive?"

[14] Then Mattathias and his sons tore their garments, put on sackcloth, and mourned bitterly.

[15] The officers of the king in charge of enforcing the apostasy came to the city of Modein to make them sacrifice. [16] Many of Israel joined them, but Mattathias and his sons drew together. [17] Then the officers of the king addressed Mattathias: "You are a leader, an honorable and great man in this city, supported by sons and kindred. [18] Come now, be the first to obey the king's command, as all the Gentiles and Judeans and those who are left in Jerusalem have done. Then you and your sons will be numbered among the King's Friends, and you and your sons will be honored with silver and gold and many gifts."

Mattathias Resists

[19] But Mattathias answered in a loud voice: "Although all the Gentiles in the king's realm obey him, so that they forsake the religion of their ancestors and consent to the king's orders, [20] yet I and my sons and my kindred will keep to the covenant of our ancestors. [21] Heaven forbid that we should forsake the law and the commandments. [22] We will not obey the words of the king by departing from our religion in the slightest degree."

[23] As he finished saying these words, a certain Jew came forward in the sight of all to offer sacrifice on the altar in Modein according to the king's order. [24] When Mattathias saw him, he was filled with zeal; his heart was moved and his just fury was aroused; he sprang forward and killed him upon the altar. [25] At the same time,

he also killed the messenger of the king who was forcing them to sacrifice, and he tore down the altar. ²⁶ Thus he showed his zeal for the law, just as Phinehas did with Zimri, son of Salu.

²⁷ Then Mattathias cried out in the city, "Let everyone who is zealous for the law and who stands by the covenant follow me!" ²⁸ Then he and his sons fled to the mountains, leaving behind in the city all their possessions.

²⁹ At that time many who sought righteousness and justice went out into the wilderness to settle there, ³⁰ they and their children, their wives and their animals, because misfortunes pressed so hard on them. ³¹ It was reported to the officers and soldiers of the king who were in the City of David, in Jerusalem, that those who had flouted the king's order had gone out to secret refuges in the wilderness. ³² Many hurried out after them, and having caught up with them, camped opposite and prepared to attack them on the Sabbath. ³³ The pursuers said to them, "Enough of this! Come out and obey the king's command, and you will live." ³⁴ But they replied, "We will not come out, nor will we obey the king's command to profane the Sabbath." ³⁵ Then the enemy attacked them at once. ³⁶ But they did not retaliate; they neither threw stones, nor blocked up their secret refuges. ³⁷ They said, "Let us all die in innocence; heaven and earth are our witnesses that you destroy us unjustly." ³⁸ So the officers and soldiers attacked them on the Sabbath, and they died with their wives, their children, and their animals, to the number of a thousand persons.

³⁹ When Mattathias and his friends heard of it, they mourned deeply for them. ⁴⁰ They said to one another, "If we all do as our kindred have done, and do not fight against the Gentiles for our lives and our laws, they will soon destroy us from the earth." ⁴¹ So on that day they came to this decision: "Let us fight against anyone who attacks us on the Sabbath, so that we may not all die as our kindred died in their secret refuges."

⁴² Then they were joined by a group of Hasideans, mighty warriors of Israel, all of them devoted to the law. ⁴³ And all those who were fleeing from the persecutions joined them and supported them. ⁴⁴ They gathered an army and struck down sinners in their wrath and the lawless in their anger, and the survivors fled to the Gentiles for safety. ⁴⁵ Mattathias and his friends went about and tore down the pagan altars; ⁴⁶ they also forcibly circumcised any uncircumcised boys whom they found in the territory of Israel. ⁴⁷ They put to flight the arrogant, and the work prospered in their hands. ⁴⁸ They saved the law from the hands of the Gentiles and of the kings and did not let the sinner triumph.

Mattathias's Final Words

⁴⁹ When the time came for Mattathias to die, he said to his sons: "Arrogance and scorn have now grown strong; it is a time of disaster and violent wrath. ⁵⁰ Therefore, my children, be zealous for the law and give your lives for the covenant of our ancestors.

⁵¹ "Remember the deeds that our ancestors did in their times,
and you will win great honor and an everlasting name.

52 Was not Abraham found faithful in trial,
    and it was credited to him as righteousness?
53 Joseph, when in distress, kept the commandment,
    and he became master of Egypt.
54 Phinehas our ancestor, for his burning zeal,
    received the covenant of an everlasting priesthood.
55 Joshua, for executing his commission,
    became a judge in Israel.
56 Caleb, for bearing witness before the assembly,
    received an inheritance in the land.
57 David, for his loyalty,
    received as a heritage a throne of eternal kingship.
58 Elijah, for his burning zeal for the law,
    was taken up to heaven.
59 Hananiah, Azariah, and Mishael, for their faith,
    were saved from the fire.
60 Daniel, for his innocence,
    was delivered from the mouths of lions.
61 And so, consider this from generation to generation,
    that none who hope in Heaven will fail in strength.
62 Do not fear the words of sinners,
    for their glory ends in corruption and worms.
63 Today exalted, tomorrow not to be found,
    they have returned to dust,
    their schemes have perished.
64 Children! Be courageous and strong in keeping the law,
    for by it you will be honored.

65 "Here is your brother Simeon who I know is a wise counselor; listen to him always, and he will be a father to you. 66 And Judas Maccabeus, a mighty warrior from his youth, will be the leader of your army and wage the war against the nations. 67 Gather about you all who observe the law, and avenge your people. 68 Pay back the Gentiles what they deserve, and observe the precepts of the law."

69 Then he blessed them, and he was gathered to his ancestors. 70 He died in the year one hundred and forty-six, and was buried in the tombs of his ancestors in Modein, and all Israel mourned him greatly.

Judas Maccabeus

3:1 Then his son Judas, who was called Maccabeus, took his place. 2 All his brothers and all who had joined his father supported him, and they gladly carried on Israel's war.

3 He spread abroad the glory of his people,
    and put on his breastplate like a giant.
He armed himself with weapons of war;

he fought battles and protected the camp with his sword.
4 In his deeds he was like a lion,
    like a young lion roaring for prey.
5 He pursued the lawless, hunting them out,
    and those who troubled his people he destroyed by fire.
6 The lawless were cowed by fear of him,
    and all evildoers were dismayed.
By his hand deliverance was happily achieved,
7 and he afflicted many kings.
He gave joy to Jacob by his deeds,
    and his memory is blessed forever.
8 He went about the cities of Judah
    destroying the renegades there.
He turned away wrath from Israel,
9 was renowned to the ends of the earth,
    and gathered together those who were perishing.

10 Then Apollonius gathered together the Gentiles, along with a large army from Samaria, to fight against Israel. 11 When Judas learned of it, he went out to meet him and struck and killed him. Many fell wounded, and the rest fled. 12 They took their spoils, and Judas took the sword of Apollonius and fought with it the rest of his life.

13 But Seron, commander of the Syrian army, heard that Judas had mustered an assembly of faithful men ready for war. 14 So he said, "I will make a name for myself and win honor in the kingdom. I will wage war against Judas and his followers, who have despised the king's command." 15 And again a large company of renegades advanced with him to help him take revenge on the Israelites.

16 When he reached the ascent of Beth-horon, Judas went out to meet him with a few men. 17 But when they saw the army coming against them, they said to Judas: "How can we, few as we are, fight such a strong host as this? Besides, we are weak since we have not eaten today." 18 But Judas said: "Many are easily hemmed in by a few; in the sight of Heaven there is no difference between deliverance by many or by few; 19 for victory in war does not depend upon the size of the army, but on strength that comes from Heaven. 20 With great presumption and lawlessness they come against us to destroy us and our wives and children and to despoil us; 21 but we are fighting for our lives and our laws. 22 He will crush them before us; so do not fear them." 23 When he finished speaking, he rushed suddenly upon Seron and his army, who were crushed before him. 24 He pursued Seron down the descent of Beth-horon into the plain. About eight hundred of their men fell, and the rest fled to the land of the Philistines. 25 Then Judas and his brothers began to be feared, and dread fell upon the Gentiles about them. 26 His fame reached the king, and the Gentiles talked about the battles of Judas.

Antiochus Is Angry

27 When King Antiochus heard these reports, he was filled with rage; so he ordered that all the forces of his kingdom be gathered, a very strong army. 28 He

opened his treasury, gave his soldiers a year's pay, and commanded them to be prepared for anything. ²⁹ But then he saw that this exhausted the money in his treasury; moreover the tribute from the province was small because of the dissension and distress he had brought upon the land by abolishing the laws which had been in effect from of old. ³⁰ He feared that, as had happened once or twice, he would not have enough for his expenses and for the gifts that he was accustomed to give with a lavish hand—more so than all previous kings. ³¹ Greatly perplexed, he decided to go to Persia and levy tribute on those provinces, and so raise a large sum of money.

³² He left Lysias, a noble of royal descent, in charge of the king's affairs from the Euphrates River to the frontier of Egypt, ³³ and commissioned him to take care of his son Antiochus until his return. ³⁴ He entrusted to him half of his forces, and the elephants, and gave him instructions concerning everything he wanted done. As for the inhabitants of Judea and Jerusalem, ³⁵ Lysias was to send an army against them to crush and destroy the power of Israel and the remnant of Jerusalem and efface their memory from the place. ³⁶ He was to settle foreigners in all their territory and distribute their land by lot. ³⁷ The king took the remaining half of the army and set out from Antioch, his capital, in the year one hundred and forty-seven; he crossed the Euphrates River and went through the provinces beyond.

³⁸ Lysias chose Ptolemy, son of Dorymenes, and Nicanor and Gorgias, powerful men among the King's Friends, ³⁹ and with them he sent forty thousand foot soldiers and seven thousand cavalry to invade and ravage the land of Judah according to the king's orders. ⁴⁰ Setting out with their whole force, they came and pitched their camp near Emmaus in the plain. ⁴¹ When the merchants of the region heard of their prowess, they came to the camp, bringing a huge sum of silver and gold, along with fetters, to buy the Israelites as slaves. A force from Edom and from Philistia joined with them.

Judas Prepares for Battle

⁴² Judas and his brothers saw that evils had multiplied and that armies were encamped within their territory. They learned of the orders which the king had given to destroy and utterly wipe out the people. ⁴³ So they said to one another, "Let us raise our people from their ruin and fight for them and for our sanctuary!"

⁴⁴ The assembly gathered together to prepare for battle and to pray and ask for mercy and compassion.

> ⁴⁵ Jerusalem was uninhabited, like a wilderness;
> not one of her children came in or went out.
> The sanctuary was trampled on,
>   and foreigners were in the citadel;
> it was a habitation for Gentiles.
> Joy had disappeared from Jacob,
>   and the flute and the harp were silent.

⁴⁶ Thus they assembled and went to Mizpah near Jerusalem, because formerly at Mizpah there was a place of prayer for Israel. ⁴⁷ That day they fasted and wore sackcloth; they sprinkled ashes on their heads and tore their garments. ⁴⁸ They unrolled the scroll of the law, to learn about the things for which the Gentiles consulted the images of their idols. ⁴⁹ They brought with them the priestly garments, the first fruits, and the tithes; and they brought forward the Nazirites who had completed the time of their vows. ⁵⁰ And they cried aloud to Heaven: "What will we do with these, and where will we take them? ⁵¹ For your sanctuary has been trampled on and profaned, and your priests are in mourning and humbled. ⁵² Now the Gentiles are gathered together against us to destroy us. You know what they plot against us. ⁵³ How will we be able to resist them unless you help us?" ⁵⁴ Then they blew the trumpets and cried out loudly.

⁵⁵ After this Judas appointed officers for the people, over thousands, over hundreds, over fifties, and over tens. ⁵⁶ He proclaimed that those who were building houses, or were just married, or were planting vineyards, and those who were afraid, could each return home, according to the law. ⁵⁷ Then the army moved off, and they camped to the south of Emmaus. ⁵⁸ Judas said: "Arm yourselves and be brave; in the morning be ready to fight these Gentiles who have assembled against us to destroy us and our sanctuary. ⁵⁹ It is better for us to die in battle than to witness the evils befalling our nation and our sanctuary. ⁶⁰ Whatever is willed in heaven will be done."

The Battle at Emmaus

⁴:¹ Now Gorgias took five thousand infantry and a thousand picked cavalry, and this detachment set out at night ² in order to fall upon the camp of the Jews in a surprise attack. Some from the citadel were his guides. ³ Judas heard of it and himself set out with his soldiers to attack the king's army at Emmaus ⁴ while these forces were still scattered away from the camp. ⁵ During the night Gorgias came into the camp of Judas, and found no one there; so he sought them in the mountains, saying, "They are fleeing from us."

⁶ But at daybreak Judas appeared in the plain with three thousand men; furthermore they lacked the helmets and swords they wanted. ⁷ They saw the army of the Gentiles, strong, with breastplates, and flanked with cavalry, and made up of experienced soldiers. ⁸ Judas said to the men with him: "Do not fear their numbers or dread their attack. ⁹ Remember how our ancestors were saved in the Red Sea, when Pharaoh pursued them with an army. ¹⁰ So now let us cry to Heaven in the hope that he will favor us, remember the covenant with our ancestors, and destroy this army before us today. ¹¹ All the Gentiles will know that there is One who redeems and delivers Israel."

¹² When the foreigners looked up and saw them marching toward them, ¹³ they came out of their camp for battle. The men with Judas blew the trumpet, and ¹⁴ joined the battle. They crushed the Gentiles, who fled toward the plain. ¹⁵ Their whole rear guard fell by the sword, and they were pursued as far as Gazara and the plains of Idumea, to Azotus and Jamnia. About three thousand of their men fell.

¹⁶ When Judas and the army returned from the pursuit, ¹⁷ he said to the people:

"Do not be greedy for plunder; for there is a fight ahead of us, [18] and Gorgias and his army are near us on the mountain. But now stand firm against our enemies and fight them. Afterward you can freely take the plunder."

[19] As Judas was finishing this speech, a detachment appeared, looking down from the mountain. [20] They saw that their army had been put to flight and their camp was burning. The smoke they saw revealed what had happened. [21] When they realized this, they completely lost heart; and when they also saw the army of Judas in the plain ready to attack, [22] they all fled to the land of the foreigners.

[23] Then Judas went back to plunder the camp, and they took much gold and silver, cloth dyed blue and marine purple, and great treasure. [24] As they returned, they were singing hymns and glorifying Heaven, "who is good, whose mercy endures forever." [25] Thus Israel experienced a great deliverance that day.

[26] But those of the foreigners who had escaped went and told Lysias all that had occurred. [27] When he heard it he was disturbed and discouraged, because things had not turned out in Israel as he intended and as the king had ordered.

Judas Prevails

[28] So the following year he gathered together sixty thousand picked men and five thousand cavalry, to fight them. [29] They came into Idumea and camped at Beth-zur, and Judas met them with ten thousand men. [30] Seeing that the army was strong, he prayed thus:

"Blessed are you, Savior of Israel, who crushed the attack of the mighty one by the hand of your servant David and delivered the foreign camp into the hand of Jonathan, the son of Saul, and his armor-bearer. [31] Give this army into the hands of your people Israel; make them ashamed of their troops and their cavalry. [32] Strike them with cowardice, weaken the boldness of their strength, and let them tremble at their own destruction. [33] Strike them down by the sword of those who love you, that all who know your name may sing your praise."

[34] Then they engaged in battle, and about five thousand of Lysias' army fell in hand-to-hand fighting. [35] When Lysias saw the tide of the battle turning, and the increased boldness of Judas, whose men were ready either to live or to die nobly, he withdrew to Antioch and began to recruit mercenaries so as to return to Judea with greater numbers.

Cleansing and Rededicating the Temple

[36] Then Judas and his brothers said, "Now that our enemies have been crushed, let us go up to purify the sanctuary and rededicate it." [37] So the whole army assembled, and went up to Mount Zion. [38] They found the sanctuary desolate, the altar desecrated, the gates burned, weeds growing in the courts as in a thicket or on some mountain, and the priests' chambers demolished. [39] Then they tore their garments and made great lamentation; they sprinkled their heads with ashes [40] and prostrated themselves. And when the signal was given with trumpets, they cried out to Heaven.

⁴¹ Judas appointed men to attack those in the citadel, while he purified the sanctuary. ⁴² He chose blameless priests, devoted to the law; ⁴³ these purified the sanctuary and carried away the stones of the defilement to an unclean place. ⁴⁴ They deliberated what ought to be done with the altar for burnt offerings that had been desecrated. ⁴⁵ They decided it best to tear it down, lest it be a lasting shame to them that the Gentiles had defiled it; so they tore down the altar. ⁴⁶ They stored the stones in a suitable place on the temple mount, until the coming of a prophet who could determine what to do with them. ⁴⁷ Then they took uncut stones, according to the law, and built a new altar like the former one. ⁴⁸ They also repaired the sanctuary and the interior of the temple and consecrated the courts. ⁴⁹ They made new sacred vessels and brought the lampstand, the altar of incense, and the table into the temple. ⁵⁰ Then they burned incense on the altar and lighted the lamps on the lampstand, and these illuminated the temple. ⁵¹ They also put loaves on the table and hung up the curtains. Thus they finished all the work they had undertaken.

⁵² They rose early on the morning of the twenty-fifth day of the ninth month, that is, the month of Kislev, in the year one hundred and forty-eight, ⁵³ and offered sacrifice according to the law on the new altar for burnt offerings that they had made. ⁵⁴ On the anniversary of the day on which the Gentiles had desecrated it, on that very day it was rededicated with songs, harps, lyres, and cymbals. ⁵⁵ All the people prostrated themselves and adored and praised Heaven, who had given them success.

⁵⁶ For eight days they celebrated the dedication of the altar and joyfully offered burnt offerings and sacrifices of deliverance and praise. ⁵⁷ They ornamented the facade of the temple with gold crowns and shields; they repaired the gates and the priests' chambers and furnished them with doors. ⁵⁸ There was great joy among the people now that the disgrace brought by the Gentiles was removed. ⁵⁹ Then Judas and his brothers and the entire assembly of Israel decreed that every year for eight days, from the twenty-fifth day of the month Kislev, the days of the dedication of the altar should be observed with joy and gladness on the anniversary.

⁶⁰ At that time they built high walls and strong towers around Mount Zion, to prevent the Gentiles from coming and trampling it as they had done before. ⁶¹ Judas also placed a garrison there to protect it, and likewise fortified Beth-zur, that the people might have a stronghold facing Idumea.

Gentiles Attack

5:1 When the nations round about heard that the altar had been rebuilt and the sanctuary restored as before, they were enraged. ² So they decided to destroy the descendants of Jacob who were among them, and they began to kill and eradicate the people. ³ Then Judas attacked the Edomites at Akrabattene in Idumea, because they were blockading Israel; he dealt them a heavy blow, humbled and despoiled them. ⁴ He also remembered the malice of the Baeanites, who had become a snare and a stumbling block to the people by ambushing them along the roads. ⁵ He forced them to take refuge in towers, which he besieged; he put them under the ban and burned down their towers along with all who were in them.

⁶ Then he crossed over to the Ammonites, where he found a strong army and a large body of people with Timothy as their leader. ⁷ He fought many battles with them, routed them, and struck them down. ⁸ After seizing Jazer and its villages, he returned to Judea.

⁹ The Gentiles in Gilead assembled to destroy the Israelites who were in their territory; these then fled to the stronghold of Dathema. ¹⁰ They sent a letter to Judas and his brothers saying: "The Gentiles around us have assembled against us to destroy us, ¹¹ and they are preparing to come and seize this stronghold to which we have fled. Timothy is the leader of their army. ¹² Come at once to rescue us from them, for many of us have fallen. ¹³ All our kindred who were in the territory of the Tobiads have been killed; the Gentiles have captured their wives, their children, and their goods, and they have slain there about a thousand men."

¹⁴ While they were reading this letter, suddenly other messengers, with garments torn, arrived from Galilee to deliver a similar message: ¹⁵ that "the inhabitants of Ptolemais, Tyre, and Sidon, and the whole of Gentile Galilee have joined forces to destroy us." ¹⁶ When Judas and the people heard this, a great assembly convened to consider what they should do for their kindred who were in distress and being attacked by enemies.

¹⁷ Judas said to his brother Simon: "Choose men for yourself, and go, rescue your kindred in Galilee; my brother Jonathan and I will go to Gilead."

¹⁸ He left Joseph, son of Zechariah, and Azariah, leader of the people, with the rest of the army in Judea to guard it. ¹⁹ He commanded them, "Take charge of these people, but do not join battle against the Gentiles until we return." ²⁰ Three thousand men were allotted to Simon to go into Galilee, and eight thousand men to Judas, for Gilead.

²¹ Simon went into Galilee and fought many battles with the Gentiles. They were crushed before him, ²² and he pursued them to the very gate of Ptolemais. About three thousand of the Gentiles fell, and he gathered their spoils. ²³ He took with him the Jews who were in Galilee and in Arbatta, with their wives and children and all that they had, and brought them to Judea with great rejoicing.

Judas Liberates Gilead

²⁴ Judas Maccabeus and his brother Jonathan crossed the Jordan and marched for three days through the wilderness. ²⁵ There they met some Nabateans, who received them peaceably and told them all that had happened to their kindred in Gilead: ²⁶ "Many of them are shut up in Bozrah, in Bosor near Alema, in Chaspho, Maked, and Carnaim"—all of these are large, fortified cities—²⁷ "and some are shut up in other cities of Gilead. Tomorrow their enemies plan to attack the strongholds and to seize and destroy all these people in one day."

²⁸ Thereupon Judas suddenly changed direction with his army, marched across the wilderness to Bozrah, and captured the city. He put every male to the sword, took all their spoils, and set fire to the city. ²⁹ He led his army from that place by night, and they marched toward the stronghold. ³⁰ When morning came, they looked ahead and saw a countless multitude, with ladders and machines for capturing the stronghold, beginning to attack. ³¹ When Judas perceived that the

struggle had begun and that the noise of the battle was resounding to heaven with trumpet blasts and loud shouting, [32] he said to the men of his army, "Fight for our kindred today." [33] He came up behind them with three columns blowing their trumpets and crying out in prayer. [34] When the army of Timothy realized that it was Maccabeus, they fled before him, and he inflicted on them a great defeat. About eight thousand of their men fell that day.

[35] Then he turned toward Alema and attacked and captured it; he killed every male, took spoils, and burned it down. [36] From there he moved on and took Chaspho, Maked, Bosor, and the other cities of Gilead.

[37] After these events Timothy assembled another army and camped opposite Raphon, on the other side of the wadi. [38] Judas sent men to spy on the camp, and they reported to him: "All the Gentiles around us have rallied to him, making a very large force; [39] they have also hired Arabians to help them, and have camped beyond the wadi, ready to attack you." So Judas went forward to meet them.

[40] As Judas and his army were approaching the flowing wadi, Timothy said to the officers of his army: "If he crosses over to us first, we will not be able to resist him; he will certainly defeat us. [41] But if he is hesitant and camps on the other side of the river, we will cross over to him and defeat him." [42] But when Judas reached the flowing wadi, he stationed the officers of the people beside it and gave them this order: "Do not allow anyone to encamp; all must go into battle." [43] He was the first to cross to the attack, with all the people behind him, and all the Gentiles were crushed before them. They threw away their arms and fled to the temple enclosure at Carnaim. [44] But Judas' troops captured the city and burned the temple enclosure with all who were in it. So Carnaim was subdued, and Judas met with no more resistance.

Returning to Jerusalem

[45] Then Judas assembled all the Israelites, great and small, who were in Gilead, with their wives and children and their goods, a very large company, to go into the land of Judah. [46] When they reached Ephron, a large and strongly fortified city along the way, they found it impossible to go around it on either the right or the left; they would have to march right through it. [47] But the people in the city shut them out and blocked up the gates with stones. [48] Then Judas sent them this peaceful message: "Let us cross your territory in order to reach our own; no one will harm you; we will only march through." But they would not open to him. [49] So Judas ordered a proclamation to be made in the camp that everyone should take up positions where they were. [50] When the men of the army took up their positions, he assaulted the city all that day and night, and it was delivered into his hand. [51] He put every male to the sword, leveled the city, took spoils, and passed through it over the slain.

[52] Then they crossed the Jordan to the great plain in front of Beth-shan; [53] and Judas kept gathering the stragglers and encouraging the people the whole way, until he reached the land of Judah. [54] They ascended Mount Zion in joy and gladness and sacrificed burnt offerings, because not one of them had fallen; they had returned in safety.

Defeat of Joseph and Zechariah

[55] In those days when Judas and Jonathan were in the land of Gilead, and Simon his brother was in Galilee opposite Ptolemais, [56] Joseph, son of Zechariah, and Azariah, the leaders of the army, heard about the brave deeds and the fighting that they were doing. [57] They said, "Let us also make a name for ourselves by going out and fighting against the Gentiles around us." [58] They gave orders to those of their army who were with them, and marched against Jamnia. [59] But Gorgias and his men came out of the city to meet them in battle. [60] Joseph and Azariah were routed and were pursued to the frontiers of Judea, and about two thousand Israelites fell that day. [61] It was a great setback for the people, because they had not obeyed Judas and his brothers, thinking that they would do brave deeds. [62] But they were not of the family through whom Israel's deliverance was given.

Victory at Hebron and Philiska

[63] The valiant Judas and his brothers were greatly honored in all Israel and among all the Gentiles, wherever their name was heard; [64] and people gathered about them and praised them.

[65] Then Judas and his brothers went out and attacked the Edomites in the land toward the south; he took Hebron and its villages, and he destroyed its strongholds and burned the towers around it. [66] He then set out for the land of the foreigners and passed through Marisa. [67] On that day some priests fell in battle who had gone out rashly to fight in their desire to do brave deeds. [68] Judas then turned toward Azotus in the land of the foreigners. He destroyed their altars and burned the carved images of their gods; and after plundering their cities he returned to the land of Judah.

Last Days of Antiochus

[6:1] As King Antiochus passed through the eastern provinces, he heard that in Persia there was a city, Elam, famous for its wealth in silver and gold, [2] and that its temple was very rich, containing gold helmets, breastplates, and weapons left there by the first king of the Greeks, Alexander, son of Philip, king of Macedon. [3] He went therefore and tried to capture and loot the city. But he could not do so, because his plan became known to the people of the city [4] who rose up in battle against him. So he fled and in great dismay withdrew from there to return to Babylon.

[5] While he was in Persia, a messenger brought him news that the armies that had gone into the land of Judah had been routed; [6] that Lysias had gone at first with a strong army and been driven back; that the people of Judah had grown strong by reason of the arms, wealth, and abundant spoils taken from the armies they had cut down; [7] that they had pulled down the abomination which he had built upon the altar in Jerusalem; and that they had surrounded with high walls both the sanctuary, as it had been before, and his city of Beth-zur.

⁸ When the king heard this news, he was astonished and very much shaken. Sick with grief because his designs had failed, he took to his bed. ⁹ There he remained many days, assailed by waves of grief, for he thought he was going to die. ¹⁰ So he called in all his Friends and said to them: "Sleep has departed from my eyes, and my heart sinks from anxiety. ¹¹ I said to myself: 'Into what tribulation have I come, and in what floods of sorrow am I now! Yet I was kindly and beloved in my rule.' ¹² But I now recall the evils I did in Jerusalem, when I carried away all the vessels of silver and gold that were in it, and for no cause gave orders that the inhabitants of Judah be destroyed. ¹³ I know that this is why these evils have overtaken me; and now I am dying, in bitter grief, in a foreign land."

¹⁴ Then he summoned Philip, one of his Friends, and put him in charge of his whole kingdom. ¹⁵ He gave him his diadem, his robe, and his signet ring, so that he might guide the king's son Antiochus and bring him up to be king. ¹⁶ So King Antiochus died there in the one hundred and forty-ninth year. ¹⁷ When Lysias learned that the king was dead, he set up the king's son Antiochus, whom he had reared as a child, to be king in his place; and he gave him the title Eupator.

Syria Attacks Again

¹⁸ Those in the citadel were hemming Israel in around the sanctuary, continually trying to harm them and to strengthen the Gentiles. ¹⁹ And so Judas planned to destroy them, and assembled the people to besiege them. ²⁰ So in the one hundred and fiftieth year they assembled and besieged the citadel, for which purpose he constructed platforms and siege engines. ²¹ But some of the besieged escaped, and some renegade Israelites joined them. ²² They went to the king and said: "How long will you fail to do justice and to avenge our kindred? ²³ We agreed to serve your father and to follow his orders and obey his edicts. ²⁴ And for this our own people have become our enemies; they have put to death as many of us as they could find and have seized our inheritances. ²⁵ They have acted aggressively not only against us, but throughout their whole territory. ²⁶ Look! Today they have besieged the citadel in Jerusalem in order to capture it, and they have fortified the sanctuary and Beth-zur. ²⁷ Unless you act quickly to prevent them, they will do even worse things than these, and you will not be able to stop them."

²⁸ When the king heard this he was enraged, and he called together all his Friends, the officers of his army, and the commanders of the cavalry. ²⁹ Mercenary forces also came to him from other kingdoms and from the islands of the seas. ³⁰ His army numbered a hundred thousand foot soldiers, twenty thousand cavalry, and thirty-two elephants trained for war. ³¹ They passed through Idumea and camped before Beth-zur. For many days they attacked it; they constructed siege engines, but the besieged made a sortie and burned these, and they fought bravely.

³² Then Judas marched away from the citadel and moved his camp to Beth-Zechariah, opposite the king's camp. ³³ The king, rising before dawn, moved his force hastily along the road to Beth-Zechariah; and the troops prepared for battle and sounded the trumpet. ³⁴ They made the elephants drunk on the juice of grapes and mulberries to get them ready to fight. ³⁵ The beasts were distributed along the phalanxes, each elephant having assigned to it a thousand men in coats of mail,

with bronze helmets on their heads, and five hundred picked cavalry. [36] These accompanied the beast wherever it was; wherever it moved, they moved too and never left it. [37] Each elephant was outfitted with a strong wooden tower, fastened to it by a harness; each tower held three soldiers who fought from it, besides the Indian driver. [38] The remaining cavalry were stationed on one or the other of the two flanks of the army, to harass the enemy and to be protected by the phalanxes. [39] When the sun shone on the gold and bronze shields, the mountains gleamed with their brightness and blazed like flaming torches. [40] Part of the king's army spread out along the heights, while some were on low ground, and they marched forward steadily in good order. [41] All who heard the noise of their numbers, the tramp of their marching, and the clanging of the arms, trembled; for the army was very great and strong.

[42] Judas with his army advanced to fight, and six hundred men of the king's army fell. [43] Eleazar, called Avaran, saw one of the beasts covered with royal armor and bigger than any of the others, and so he thought the king was on it. [44] He gave up his life to save his people and win an everlasting name for himself. [45] He dashed courageously up to it in the middle of the phalanx, killing men right and left, so that they parted before him. [46] He ran under the elephant, stabbed it, and killed it. The beast fell to the ground on top of him, and he died there. [47] But when Judas' troops saw the strength of the royal army and the ardor of its forces, they retreated from them.

Siege of the Temple

[48] Some of the king's army went up to Jerusalem to attack them, and the king established camps in Judea and at Mount Zion. [49] He made peace with the people of Beth-zur, and they evacuated the city, because they had no food there to enable them to withstand a siege, for that was a Sabbath year in the land. [50] The king took Beth-zur and stationed a garrison there to hold it. [51] For many days he besieged the sanctuary, setting up platforms and siege engines, fire-throwers, catapults, and mechanical bows for shooting arrows and projectiles. [52] The defenders countered by setting up siege engines of their own, and kept up the fight a long time. [53] But there were no provisions in the storerooms, because it was the seventh year, and the reserves had been eaten up by those who had been rescued from the Gentiles and brought to Judea. [54] Few men remained in the sanctuary because the famine was too much for them; the rest scattered, each to his home.

[55] Lysias heard that Philip, whom King Antiochus, before his death, had appointed to train his son Antiochus to be king, [56] had returned from Persia and Media with the army that accompanied the king, and that he was seeking to take over the government. [57] So he hastily decided to withdraw. He said to the king, the leaders of the army, and the soldiers: "We are growing weaker every day, our provisions are scanty, the place we are besieging is strong, and it is our duty to take care of the affairs of the kingdom. [58] Therefore let us now come to terms with these people and make peace with them and all their nation. [59] Let us grant them freedom to live according to their own laws as formerly; it was on account of their laws, which we abolished, that they became enraged and did all these things."

⁶⁰ The proposal pleased the king and the leaders; he sent peace terms to the Jews, and they accepted. ⁶¹ So the king and the leaders swore an oath to them, and on these terms the Jews evacuated the fortification. ⁶² But when the king entered Mount Zion and saw how the place was fortified, he broke the oath he had sworn and gave orders to tear down the encircling wall. ⁶³ Then he departed in haste and returned to Antioch, where he found Philip in control of the city. He fought against him and took the city by force.

Alcimus Assumes Control

⁷:¹ In the one hundred and fifty-first year, Demetrius, son of Seleucus, set out from Rome, arrived with a few men at a coastal city, and began to rule there. ² As he was entering the royal palace of his ancestors, the soldiers seized Antiochus and Lysias to bring them to him. ³ When he was informed of this, he said, "Do not show me their faces." ⁴ So the soldiers killed them, and Demetrius assumed the royal throne.

⁵ Then all the lawless men and renegades of Israel came to him. They were led by Alcimus, who desired to be high priest. ⁶ They made this accusation to the king against the people: "Judas and his brothers have destroyed all your friends and have driven us out of our land. ⁷ So now, send a man whom you trust to go and see all the destruction Judas has wrought on us and on the king's territory, and let him punish them and all their supporters."

⁸ So the king chose Bacchides, one of the King's Friends, who ruled the province of West-of-Euphrates, a great man in the kingdom, and faithful to the king. ⁹ He sent him and the renegade Alcimus, to whom he granted the high priesthood, with orders to take revenge on the Israelites. ¹⁰ They set out and, on arriving in the land of Judah with a great army, sent messengers who spoke deceitfully to Judas and his brothers in peaceful terms. ¹¹ But these paid no attention to their words, seeing that they had come with a great army.

¹² A group of scribes, however, gathered about Alcimus and Bacchides to ask for a just agreement. ¹³ The Hasideans were the first among the Israelites to seek peace with them, ¹⁴ for they said, "A priest of the line of Aaron has come with the army, and he will not do us any wrong." ¹⁵ He spoke with them peacefully and swore to them, "We will not seek to injure you or your friends." ¹⁶ So they trusted him. But he arrested sixty of them and killed them in one day, according to the words that he wrote:

> ¹⁷ "The flesh of your faithful,
>   and their blood they have spilled all around about Jerusalem,
>   and no one was left to bury them."

¹⁸ Then fear and dread of them came upon all the people, who said:

"There is no truth or justice among them; they violated the agreement and the oath that they swore."

¹⁹ Bacchides withdrew from Jerusalem and camped in Beth-zaith. He had many of the men who deserted to him arrested and some of the people. He killed them

and threw them into a great cistern. [20] He handed the province over to Alcimus, leaving troops to help him, while he himself returned to the king.

[21] Alcimus struggled to maintain his high priesthood, [22] and all those who were troubling the people gathered about him. They took possession of the land of Judah and caused great distress in Israel. [23] When Judas saw all the evils that Alcimus and those with him were bringing upon the Israelites, even more than the Gentiles had, [24] he went about all the borders of Judea and took revenge on the men who had deserted, preventing them from going out into the country. [25] But when Alcimus saw that Judas and his followers were gaining strength and realized that he could not resist them, he returned to the king and accused them of grave crimes.

Nicanor Attacks Jerusalem

[26] Then the king sent Nicanor, one of his honored officers, who was a bitter enemy of Israel, with orders to destroy the people. [27] Nicanor came to Jerusalem with a large force and deceitfully sent to Judas and his brothers this peaceable message: [28] "Let there be no fight between me and you. I will come with a few men to meet you face to face in peace."

[29] So he came to Judas, and they greeted one another peaceably. But Judas' enemies were prepared to seize him. [30] When he became aware that Nicanor had come to him with deceit in mind, Judas was afraid of him and would not meet him again. [31] When Nicanor saw that his plan had been discovered, he went out to fight Judas near Capharsalama. [32] About five hundred men of Nicanor's army fell; the rest fled to the City of David.

[33] After this, Nicanor went up to Mount Zion. Some of the priests from the sanctuary and some of the elders of the people came out to greet him peaceably and to show him the burnt offering that was being sacrificed for the king. [34] But he mocked and ridiculed them, defiled them, and spoke arrogantly. [35] In a rage he swore: "If Judas and his army are not delivered to me at once, when I return victorious I will burn this temple down." He went away in great anger. [36] The priests, however, went in and stood before the altar and the sanctuary. They wept and said: [37] "You have chosen this house to bear your name, to be a house of prayer and supplication for your people. [38] Take revenge on this man and his army, and let them fall by the sword. Remember their blasphemies, and do not let them continue."

[39] Nicanor left Jerusalem and camped at Beth-horon, where the Syrian army joined him. [40] But Judas camped in Adasa with three thousand men. Here Judas uttered this prayer: [41] "When they who were sent by the king blasphemed, your angel went out and killed a hundred and eighty-five thousand of them. [42] In the same way, crush this army before us today, and let the rest know that Nicanor spoke wickedly against your sanctuary; judge him according to his wickedness."

[43] The armies met in battle on the thirteenth day of the month Adar. Nicanor's army was crushed, and he himself was the first to fall in the battle. [44] When his army saw that Nicanor had fallen, they threw down their weapons and fled. [45] The Jews pursued them a day's journey from Adasa to near Gazara, blowing the trum-

pets behind them as signals. ⁴⁶ From all the surrounding villages of Judea people came out and outflanked them. They turned them back, and all the enemies fell by the sword; not a single one escaped.

⁴⁷ Then the Jews collected the spoils and the plunder; they cut off Nicanor's head and his right arm, which he had lifted up so arrogantly. These they brought and displayed in the sight of Jerusalem. ⁴⁸ The people rejoiced greatly, and observed that day as a day of much joy. ⁴⁹ They decreed that it should be observed every year on the thirteenth of Adar. ⁵⁰ And so for a few days the land of Judah was at rest.

The Fame of the Romans

⁸:¹ Judas had heard of the reputation of the Romans. They were valiant fighters and acted amiably to all who took their side. They established a friendly alliance with all who applied to them. ² He was also told of their battles and the brave deeds that they performed against the Gauls, conquering them and forcing them to pay tribute; ³ and what they did in Spain to get possession of the silver and gold mines there. ⁴ By planning and persistence they subjugated the whole region, although it was very remote from their own. They also subjugated the kings who had come against them from the far corners of the earth until they crushed them and inflicted on them severe defeat. The rest paid tribute to them every year. ⁵ Philip and Perseus, king of the Macedonians, and the others who opposed them in battle they overwhelmed and subjugated. ⁶ Antiochus the Great, king of Asia, who fought against them with a hundred and twenty elephants and with cavalry and chariots and a very great army, was defeated by them. ⁷ They took him alive and obliged him and the kings who succeeded him to pay a heavy tribute, to give hostages, and to cede ⁸ Lycia, Mysia, and Lydia from among their best provinces. The Romans took these from him and gave them to King Eumenes. ⁹ When the Greeks planned to come and destroy them, ¹⁰ the Romans discovered it, and sent against the Greeks a single general who made war on them. Many were wounded and fell, and the Romans took their wives and children captive. They plundered them, took possession of their land, tore down their strongholds, and reduced them to slavery even to this day. ¹¹ All the other kingdoms and islands that had ever opposed them they destroyed and enslaved; with their friends, however, and those who relied on them, they maintained friendship. ¹² They subjugated kings both near and far, and all who heard of their fame were afraid of them. ¹³ Those whom they wish to help and to make kings, they make kings; and those whom they wish, they depose; and they were greatly exalted. ¹⁴ Yet with all this, none of them put on a diadem or wore purple as a display of grandeur. ¹⁵ But they made for themselves a senate chamber, and every day three hundred and twenty men took counsel, deliberating on all that concerned the people and their well-being. ¹⁶ They entrust their government to one man every year, to rule over their entire land, and they all obey that one, and there is no envy or jealousy among them.

Judas Makes an Alliance with Rome

[17] So Judas chose Eupolemus, son of John, son of Accos, and Jason, son of Eleazar, and sent them to Rome to establish friendship and alliance with them. [18] He did this to lift the yoke from Israel, for it was obvious that the kingdom of the Greeks was subjecting them to slavery. [19] After making a very long journey to Rome, the envoys entered the senate chamber and spoke as follows: [20] "Judas, called Maccabeus, and his brothers, with the Jewish people, have sent us to you to establish alliance and peace with you, and to be enrolled among your allies and friends." [21] The proposal pleased the Romans, [22] and this is a copy of the reply they inscribed on bronze tablets and sent to Jerusalem, to remain there with the Jews as a record of peace and alliance:

[23] "May it be well with the Romans and the Jewish nation at sea and on land forever; may sword and enemy be far from them. [24] But if war is first made on Rome, or any of its allies in any of their dominions, [25] the Jewish nation will fight along with them wholeheartedly, as the occasion will demand; [26] and to those who wage war they will not give or provide grain, weapons, money, or ships, as seems best to Rome. They will fulfill their obligations without receiving any recompense. [27] In the same way, if war is made first on the Jewish nation, the Romans will fight along with them willingly, as the occasion will demand, [28] and to those who attack them there will not be given grain, weapons, money, or ships, as seems best to Rome. They will fulfill their obligations without deception. [29] On these terms the Romans have made an agreement with the Jewish people. [30] But if both parties hereafter agree to add or take away anything, they will do as they choose, and whatever they will add or take away will be valid.

[31] "Moreover, concerning the wrongs that King Demetrius is doing to them, we have written to him thus: 'Why have you made your yoke heavy upon our friends and allies the Jews? [32] If they petition against you again, we will enforce justice and make war on you by sea and land.'"

Judas Falls in Battle

[9:1] When Demetrius heard that Nicanor and his army had fallen in battle, he again sent Bacchides and Alcimus into the land of Judah, along with the right wing of his army. [2] They took the road to Galilee, and camping opposite the ascent at Arbela, they captured it and killed many people. [3] In the first month of the one hundred and fifty-second year, they encamped against Jerusalem. [4] Then they set out for Berea with twenty thousand men and two thousand cavalry. [5] Judas, with three thousand picked men, had camped at Elasa. [6] When they saw the great number of the troops, they were very much afraid, and many slipped away from the camp, until only eight hundred of them remained.

[7] When Judas saw that his army was melting away just as the battle was imminent, he was brokenhearted, because he had no time to gather them together. [8] In spite of his discouragement he said to those who remained: "Let us go forward to meet our enemies; perhaps we can put up a good fight against them." [9] They tried to dissuade him, saying: "We certainly cannot. Let us save our own lives

now, and come back with our kindred, and then fight against them. Now we are too few." ¹⁰ But Judas said: "Far be it from me to do such a thing as to flee from them! If our time has come, let us die bravely for our kindred and not leave a stain upon our honor!"

¹¹ Then the army of Bacchides moved out of camp and took its position for combat. The cavalry were divided into two squadrons, and the slingers and the archers came on ahead of the army, and in the front line were all the best warriors. Bacchides was on the right wing. ¹² Flanked by the two squadrons, the phalanx attacked as they blew their trumpets. Those who were on Judas' side also blew their trumpets. ¹³ The earth shook with the noise of the armies, and the battle raged from morning until evening.

¹⁴ When Judas saw that Bacchides was on the right, with the main force of his army, all the most stouthearted rallied to him, ¹⁵ and the right wing was crushed; Judas pursued them as far as the mountain slopes. ¹⁶ But when those on the left wing saw that the right wing was crushed, they closed in behind Judas and those with him. ¹⁷ The battle became intense, and many on both sides fell wounded. ¹⁸ Then Judas fell, and the rest fled.

¹⁹ Jonathan and Simon took their brother Judas and buried him in the tomb of their ancestors at Modein. ²⁰ All Israel wept for him with great lamentation. They mourned for him many days, and they said, ²¹ "How the mighty one has fallen, the savior of Israel!" ²² The other acts of Judas, his battles, the brave deeds he performed, and his greatness have not been recorded; but they were very many.

²³ After the death of Judas, the lawless raised their heads in every part of Israel, and all kinds of evildoers appeared. ²⁴ In those days there was a very great famine, and the country deserted to them. ²⁵ Bacchides chose renegades and made them masters of the country. ²⁶ These sought out and hunted down the friends of Judas and brought them to Bacchides, who punished and derided them. ²⁷ There was great tribulation in Israel, the like of which had not been since the time prophets ceased to appear among them.

Jonathan Becomes Leader

²⁸ Then all the friends of Judas came together and said to Jonathan: ²⁹ "Ever since your brother Judas died, there has been no one like him to lead us against our enemies, both Bacchides and those of our nation who are hostile to us. ³⁰ Now therefore we have chosen you today to be our ruler and leader in his place, to fight our battle." ³¹ From that moment Jonathan accepted the leadership, and took the place of Judas his brother.

³² When Bacchides learned of it, he sought to kill him. ³³ But Jonathan and his brother Simon and all who were with him discovered this, and they fled to the wilderness of Tekoa and camped by the waters of the pool of Asphar. ³⁴ [omitted].

³⁵ Jonathan sent his brother as leader of the convoy to implore his friends, the Nabateans, to let them deposit with them their great quantity of baggage. ³⁶ But the tribe of Jambri from Medaba made a raid and seized and carried off John and everything he had.

³⁷ After this, word was brought to Jonathan and his brother Simon: "The tribe

of Jambri are celebrating a great wedding, and with a large escort they are bringing the bride, the daughter of one of the great princes of Canaan, from Nadabath."
[38] Remembering the blood of John their brother, they went up and hid themselves
under cover of the mountain. [39] As they watched there appeared a noisy throng
with much baggage; then the bridegroom and his friends and kinsmen had come
out to meet them with tambourines and musicians with their instruments. [40] Jonathan and his party rose up against them from their ambush and killed them.
Many fell wounded; the rest fled toward the mountain; all their spoils were taken.
[41] Thus the wedding was turned into mourning, and the sound of their music into
lamentation. [42] Having taken their revenge for the blood of their brother, they
returned to the marshes of the Jordan.

[43] When Bacchides heard of it, he came on the Sabbath to the banks of the
Jordan with a large force. [44] Then Jonathan said to his companions, "Let us rise
up now and fight for our lives, for today is not like yesterday and the day before.
[45] The battle is before us, behind us are the waters of the Jordan, on either side of
us, marsh and thickets; there is no way of escape. [46] Cry out now to Heaven so that
you may be delivered from the hand of our enemies." [47] When they joined battle,
Jonathan raised his hand to strike Bacchides, but Bacchides backed away from
him. [48] Jonathan and those with him jumped into the Jordan and swam across to
the other side, but the enemy did not pursue them across the Jordan. [49] About a
thousand men on Bacchides' side fell that day.

[50] On returning to Jerusalem, Bacchides built strongholds in Judea: the Jericho fortress, as well as Emmaus, Beth-horon, Bethel, Timnath, Pharathon, and
Tephon, with high walls and gates and bars. [51] In each he put a garrison to harass
Israel. [52] He fortified the city of Beth-zur, Gazara, and the citadel, and put troops
in them and stores of provisions. [53] He took as hostages the sons of the leading
people of the country and put them in custody in the citadel at Jerusalem.

[54] In the one hundred and fifty-third year, in the second month, Alcimus ordered the wall of the inner court of the sanctuary to be torn down, thus destroying
the work of the prophets. But he only began to tear it down. [55] Just at that time
Alcimus was stricken, and his work was interrupted; his mouth was closed and he
was paralyzed, so that he could no longer utter a word or give orders concerning
his household. [56] Alcimus died in great agony at that time. [57] Seeing that Alcimus
was dead, Bacchides returned to the king, and the land of Judah was at rest for
two years.

The War Ends

[58] Then all the lawless took counsel and said: "Jonathan and those with him are
living in peace and security. Now then, let us have Bacchides return, and he will
capture all of them in a single night." [59] So they went and took counsel with him.
[60] When Bacchides was setting out with a large force, he sent letters secretly to
all his allies in Judea, telling them to seize Jonathan and his companions. They
were not able to do this, however, because their plan became known. [61] In fact,
Jonathan's men seized about fifty of the men of the country who were leaders in
the conspiracy and put them to death.

⁶²Then Jonathan and those with him, along with Simon, withdrew to Bethbasi in the wilderness; he rebuilt its ruins and fortified it. ⁶³When Bacchides learned of this, he gathered together his whole force and sent word to those who were in Judea. ⁶⁴He came and camped before Bethbasi, and constructing siege engines, he fought against it for many days.

⁶⁵Leaving his brother Simon in the city, Jonathan, accompanied by a small group of men, went out into the countryside. ⁶⁶He struck down Odomera and his kindred and the tribe of Phasiron in their encampment; these men had begun to attack and they were going up with their forces. ⁶⁷Simon and those with him then sallied forth from the city and set fire to the siege engines. ⁶⁸They fought against Bacchides, and he was crushed. They caused him great distress, because the enterprise he had planned was in vain. ⁶⁹He was enraged with the lawless men who had advised him to invade the province. He killed many of them and resolved to return to his own country.

⁷⁰Jonathan learned of this and sent ambassadors to agree on peace with him and to obtain the release of the prisoners. ⁷¹He agreed to do as Jonathan asked. He swore an oath to him that he would never try to do him any harm for the rest of his life; ⁷²and he released to him the prisoners he had previously taken from the land of Judah. Thereupon he returned to his own land and never came into their territory again. ⁷³Then the sword ceased from Israel. Jonathan settled in Michmash; he began to judge the people and he eliminated the renegades from Israel.

Alexander Epiphanes Revolts

¹⁰:¹In the one hundred and sixtieth year, Alexander Epiphanes, son of Antiochus, came up and took Ptolemais. They accepted him as king and he began to reign there. ²When King Demetrius heard of it, he mustered a very large army and marched out to engage him in battle. ³Demetrius sent a letter to Jonathan written in peaceful terms, to exalt him; ⁴for he said: "Let us be the first to make peace with him, before he makes peace with Alexander against us, ⁵since he will remember all the wrongs we have done to him, his brothers, and his nation."

⁶So Demetrius authorized him to gather an army and procure arms as his ally; and he ordered that the hostages in the citadel be released to him. ⁷Accordingly Jonathan went to Jerusalem and read the letter to all the people and to those who were in the citadel. ⁸They were struck with fear when they heard that the king had given him authority to gather an army. ⁹Those in the citadel released the hostages to Jonathan, and he gave them back to their parents. ¹⁰Thereafter Jonathan dwelt in Jerusalem, and began to build and restore the city. ¹¹He ordered those doing the work to build the walls and to encircle Mount Zion with square stones for its fortification, and they did so. ¹²The foreigners in the strongholds that Bacchides had built took flight; ¹³all of them left their places and returned to their own lands. ¹⁴Only in Beth-zur did some remain of those who had abandoned the law and the commandments, for it was a place of refuge.

¹⁵King Alexander heard of the promises that Demetrius had made to Jonathan; he was also told of the battles and brave deeds of Jonathan and his brothers and of the troubles that they had endured. ¹⁶He said, "Will we ever find another

man like him? Let us now make him our friend and ally." ¹⁷ So he sent Jonathan a letter written in these terms: ¹⁸ "King Alexander sends greetings to his brother Jonathan. ¹⁹ We have heard of you, that you are a mighty warrior and worthy to be our friend. ²⁰ We have therefore appointed you today to be high priest of your nation; you are to be called the King's Friend, and you are to look after our interests and preserve friendship with us." He also sent him a purple robe and a crown of gold. ²¹ Jonathan put on the sacred vestments in the seventh month of the one hundred and sixtieth year at the feast of Booths, and he gathered an army and procured many weapons.

Demetrius Writes Jonathan

²² When Demetrius heard of these things, he was distressed and said: ²³ "Why have we allowed Alexander to get ahead of us by gaining the friendship of the Jews and thus strengthening himself? ²⁴ I too will write them encouraging words and offer honors and gifts, so that they may support me." ²⁵ So he sent them this message: "King Demetrius sends greetings to the Jewish nation. ²⁶ We have heard how you have kept the treaty with us and continued in our friendship and not gone over to our enemies, and we are glad. ²⁷ Continue, therefore, to keep faith with us, and we will reward you with favors in return for what you do in our behalf. ²⁸ We will grant you many exemptions and will bestow gifts on you.

²⁹ "I now free you and exempt all the Jews from the tribute, the salt tax, and the crown levies. ³⁰ Instead of collecting the third of the grain and the half of the fruit of the trees that should be my share, I renounce the right from this day forward. Neither now nor in the future will I collect them from the land of Judah or from the three districts annexed from Samaria. ³¹ Let Jerusalem and her territory, her tithes and her tolls, be sacred and free from tax. ³² I also yield my authority over the citadel in Jerusalem, and I transfer it to the high priest, that he may put in it such men as he will choose to guard it. ³³ Every Jew who has been carried into captivity from the land of Judah into any part of my kingdom I set at liberty without ransom; and let all their taxes, even those on their cattle, be canceled.

³⁴ "Let all feast days, Sabbaths, new moon festivals, appointed days, and the three days that precede each feast day, and the three days that follow, be days of immunity and exemption for all Jews in my kingdom. ³⁵ No one will have authority to exact payment from them or to harass any of them in any matter.

³⁶ "Let thirty thousand Jews be enrolled in the king's army and allowances be given them, as is due to all the king's soldiers. ³⁷ Let some of them be stationed in the king's principal strongholds, and of these let some be given positions of trust in the affairs of the kingdom. Let their superiors and their rulers be chosen from among them, and let them follow their own laws, as the king has commanded in the land of Judah.

³⁸ "Let the three districts that have been added to Judea from the province of Samaria be annexed to Judea so that they may be under one rule and obey no other authority than the high priest. ³⁹ Ptolemais and its confines I give as a present to the sanctuary in Jerusalem for the necessary expenses of the sanctuary. ⁴⁰ I make a yearly personal grant of fifteen thousand silver shekels out of the royal rev-

enues, taken from appropriate places. ⁴¹ All the additional funds that the officials did not hand over as they had done in the first years will henceforth be handed over for the services of the temple. ⁴² Moreover, the dues of five thousand silver shekels that used to be taken from the revenue of the sanctuary every year will be canceled, since these funds belong to the priests who perform the services. ⁴³ All who take refuge in the temple of Jerusalem or in any of its precincts, because of money they owe the king, or because of any other debt, will be released, together with all the goods they possess in my kingdom. ⁴⁴ The cost of rebuilding and restoring the structures of the sanctuary will be covered out of the royal revenue. ⁴⁵ Likewise the cost of building the walls of Jerusalem and fortifying it all around, and of building walls in Judea, will be donated from the royal revenue."

⁴⁶ When Jonathan and the people heard these words, they neither believed nor accepted them, for they remembered the great evil that Demetrius had done in Israel, and the great tribulation he had brought upon them. ⁴⁷ They therefore decided in favor of Alexander, for he had been the first to address them peaceably, and they remained his allies for the rest of his life.

⁴⁸ Then King Alexander gathered together a large army and encamped opposite Demetrius. ⁴⁹ The two kings joined battle, and when the army of Demetrius fled, Alexander pursued him, and overpowered his soldiers. ⁵⁰ He pressed the battle hard until sunset, and Demetrius fell that day.

Alexander Makes a Treaty with Ptolemy

⁵¹ Alexander sent ambassadors to Ptolemy, king of Egypt, with this message: ⁵² "Now that I have returned to my realm, taken my seat on the throne of my ancestors, and established my rule by crushing Demetrius and gaining control of my country—⁵³ for I engaged him in battle, he and his army were crushed by us, and we assumed his royal throne—⁵⁴ let us now establish friendship with each other. Give me now your daughter for my wife; and as your son-in-law, I will give to you and to her gifts worthy of you."

⁵⁵ King Ptolemy answered in these words: "Happy the day on which you returned to the land of your ancestors and took your seat on their royal throne! ⁵⁶ I will do for you what you have written; but meet me in Ptolemais, so that we may see each other, and I will become your father-in-law as you have proposed."

⁵⁷ So Ptolemy with his daughter Cleopatra set out from Egypt and came to Ptolemais in the one hundred and sixty-second year. ⁵⁸ There King Alexander met him, and Ptolemy gave him his daughter Cleopatra in marriage. Their wedding was celebrated at Ptolemais with great splendor according to the custom of kings.

⁵⁹ King Alexander also wrote to Jonathan to come and meet him. ⁶⁰ So he went with pomp to Ptolemais, where he met the two kings and gave them and their friends silver and gold and many gifts and thus won their favor. ⁶¹ Some villainous men of Israel, transgressors of the law, united against him to accuse him, but the king paid no heed to them. ⁶² The king ordered Jonathan to be divested of his garments and to be clothed in royal purple; and so it was done. ⁶³ The king also had him seated at his side. He said to his magistrates: "Go with him to the center

of the city and make a proclamation that no one is to bring charges against him on any grounds or be troublesome to him for any reason." [64] When his accusers saw the honor paid to him according to the king's proclamation, and him clothed in purple, they all fled. [65] And so the king honored him, enrolling him among his Chief Friends, and he made him governor and chief of the province. [66] So Jonathan returned in peace and happiness to Jerusalem.

Jonathan Defeats Apollonius

[67] In the one hundred and sixty-fifth year, Demetrius, son of Demetrius, came from Crete to the land of his ancestors. [68] When King Alexander heard of it he was greatly troubled, and returned to Antioch. [69] Demetrius set Apollonius over Coelesyria. Having gathered a large army, Apollonius encamped at Jamnia. From there he sent this message to Jonathan the high priest:

[70] "You are the only one who resists us. I am laughed at and put to shame on your account. Why are you exercising authority against us in the mountains? [71] If you have confidence in your forces, come down now to us in the plain, and let us test each other's strength there; for the forces of the cities are on my side. [72] Inquire and find out who I am and who the others are who are helping me. People are saying that you cannot make a stand against us because your ancestors were twice put to flight in their own land. [73] Now you too will be unable to withstand our cavalry and such a force as this in the plain, where there is not a stone or a pebble or a place to flee."

[74] When Jonathan heard the message of Apollonius, he was provoked. Choosing ten thousand men, he set out from Jerusalem, and Simon his brother joined him to help him. [75] He encamped near Joppa, but the people of the city shut him out because Apollonius had a garrison in Joppa. When they attacked it, [76] the people of the city became afraid and opened the gates, and so Jonathan took possession of Joppa.

[77] When Apollonius heard of it, he drew up three thousand cavalry and a large force of infantry. He marched toward Azotus as though he were going on through, but at the same time he was advancing into the plain, because he had such a large number of cavalry to rely on. [78] Jonathan pursued him toward Azotus, and the armies engaged in battle. [79] Apollonius, however, had left a thousand cavalry in hiding behind them. [80] Jonathan discovered that there was an ambush behind him; his army was surrounded. From morning until evening they showered his troops with arrows. [81] But his troops held their ground, as Jonathan had commanded, while the enemy's horses became tired out.

[82] Then Simon brought forward his force, and engaged the phalanx in battle. Since the cavalry were exhausted, the phalanx was crushed by him and fled, [83] while the cavalry too were scattered over the plain. They fled to Azotus and entered Beth-dagon, the temple of their idol, to save themselves. [84] But Jonathan burned and plundered Azotus with its neighboring towns, and destroyed by fire both the temple of Dagon and those who had taken refuge in it. [85] Those who fell by the sword, together with those who were burned alive, came to about eight thousand.

⁸⁶ Then Jonathan left there and encamped at Askalon, and the people of that city came out to meet him with great pomp. ⁸⁷ Jonathan and those with him then returned to Jerusalem, with much spoil. ⁸⁸ When King Alexander heard of these events, he accorded new honors to Jonathan. ⁸⁹ He sent him a gold buckle, such as is usually given to King's Kinsmen; he also gave him Ekron and all its territory as a possession.

Ptolemy Rebels

¹¹:¹ Then the king of Egypt gathered forces as numerous as the sands of the sea-shore, and many ships; and he sought by deceit to take Alexander's kingdom and add it to his own. ² He set out for Syria with peaceful words, and the people in the cities opened their gates to welcome him, as King Alexander had ordered them to do, since Ptolemy was his father-in-law. ³ But when Ptolemy entered the cities, he stationed a garrison of troops in each one.

⁴ As they neared Azotus, they showed him the temple of Dagon destroyed by fire, Azotus and its suburbs demolished, corpses lying about, and the charred bodies of those burned in the war, for they had heaped them up along his route. ⁵ They told the king what Jonathan had done in order to denigrate him; but the king said nothing. ⁶ Jonathan met the king with pomp at Joppa, and they greeted each other and spent the night there. ⁷ Jonathan accompanied the king as far as the river called Eleutherus and then returned to Jerusalem.

⁸ And so King Ptolemy took possession of the cities along the seacoast as far as Seleucia by the sea, plotting evil schemes against Alexander all the while. ⁹ He sent ambassadors to King Demetrius, saying: "Come, let us make a covenant with each other; I will give you my daughter whom Alexander has married, and you will reign over your father's kingdom. ¹⁰ I regret that I gave him my daughter, for he has sought to kill me." ¹¹ He was criticizing Alexander, however, because he coveted his kingdom. ¹² After taking his daughter away, Ptolemy gave her to Demetrius and broke with Alexander; the enmity between them was now evident. ¹³ Then Ptolemy entered Antioch and assumed the crown of Asia; thus he set upon his head two crowns, that of Egypt and that of Asia.

¹⁴ Now King Alexander was in Cilicia at that time, because the people of that region had revolted. ¹⁵ When Alexander heard the news, he came against Ptolemy in battle. Ptolemy marched out and met him with a strong force and routed him. ¹⁶ When Alexander fled to Arabia to seek protection, King Ptolemy was triumphant. ¹⁷ Zabdiel the Arabian cut off Alexander's head and sent it to Ptolemy. ¹⁸ But three days later King Ptolemy himself died, and his troops in the strongholds were killed by the inhabitants of the strongholds. ¹⁹ Thus Demetrius became king in the one hundred and sixty-seventh year.

Jonathan's Diplomacy

²⁰ In those days Jonathan gathered together the people of Judea to attack the citadel in Jerusalem, and they set up many siege engines against it. ²¹ But some

transgressors of the law, enemies of their own nation, went to the king and informed him that Jonathan was besieging the citadel. [22] When Demetrius heard this, he was enraged; and as soon as he heard it, he set out and came to Ptolemais. He wrote to Jonathan to discontinue the siege and to meet him for a conference at Ptolemais as soon as possible.

[23] On hearing this, Jonathan ordered the siege to continue. He selected some elders and priests of Israel and put himself at risk. [24] Taking with him silver, gold, and apparel, and many other presents, he went to the king at Ptolemais, and found favor with him. [25] Although certain renegades of his own nation kept on bringing charges against him, [26] the king treated him just as his predecessors had done and exalted him in the presence of all his Friends. [27] He confirmed him in the high priesthood and in the other honors he had previously held, and had him enrolled among his Chief Friends.

[28] Jonathan asked the king to exempt Judea and the three districts of Samaria from tribute, promising him in return three hundred talents. [29] The king agreed and wrote a letter to Jonathan about all these matters as follows:

[30] "King Demetrius sends greetings to his brother Jonathan and to the Jewish nation. [31] We are sending you, for your information, a copy of the letter that we wrote to Lasthenes our Kinsman concerning you. [32] 'King Demetrius sends greetings to his father Lasthenes. [33] Upon the Jewish nation, who are our friends and observe their obligations to us, we have decided to bestow benefits because of the good will they show us. [34] Therefore we confirm their possession, not only of the territory of Judea, but also of the three districts of Aphairema, Lydda, and Ramathaim. These districts, together with all their dependencies, are hereby transferred from Samaria to Judea for those who offer sacrifices in Jerusalem in lieu of the royal taxes the king used to receive yearly from the produce of earth and trees. [35] From payment of the other things that would henceforth be due to us, namely, the tithes and taxes, as well as the salt tax, and the crown tax—from all these we grant them release. [36] Henceforth and forever not one of these provisions will ever be revoked. [37] See to it, therefore, that a copy of these instructions be made and given to Jonathan. Let it be displayed on the holy mountain in a conspicuous place.'"

Trypho Rebels

[38] When King Demetrius saw that the land was peaceful under his rule and that he had no opposition, he dismissed his entire army, each to his own home, except the foreign troops which he had hired from the islands of the nations. So all the soldiers who had served under his predecessors became hostile to him. [39] When a certain Trypho, who had previously supported Alexander, saw that all the troops were grumbling against Demetrius, he went to Imalkue the Arabian, who was raising Alexander's young son Antiochus. [40] Trypho kept urging Imalkue to hand over the boy to him, so that he might succeed his father as king. He told him of all that Demetrius had done and of the hostility his soldiers had for him; and he remained there for many days.

[41] Meanwhile Jonathan sent the request to King Demetrius to withdraw the

troops in the citadel from Jerusalem and from the other strongholds, for they were constantly waging war on Israel. ⁴²Demetrius, in turn, sent this word to Jonathan: "I will do not only this for you and your nation, but I will greatly honor you and your nation when I find the opportunity. ⁴³Now, therefore, you will do well to send men to fight for me, because all my troops have revolted."

⁴⁴So Jonathan sent three thousand good fighting men to him at Antioch. When they came to the king, he was delighted over their arrival. ⁴⁵The populace, one hundred and twenty thousand strong, massed in the center of the city in an attempt to kill the king. ⁴⁶So the king took refuge in the palace, while the populace gained control of the main streets of the city and prepared for battle. ⁴⁷Then the king called the Jewish force to his aid. They all rallied around him and spread out through the city. On that day they killed about a hundred thousand in the city. ⁴⁸At the same time, they set the city on fire and took much spoil. Thus they saved the king. ⁴⁹When the populace saw that the Jewish force controlled the city, they lost courage and cried out to the king in supplication, ⁵⁰"Extend the hand of friendship to us, and make the Jews stop attacking us and the city." ⁵¹So they threw down their weapons and made peace. The Jews thus gained honor in the eyes of the king and all his subjects, and they became renowned throughout his kingdom. Finally they returned to Jerusalem with much plunder.

⁵²But when King Demetrius was sure of his royal throne, and the land was peaceful under his rule, ⁵³he broke all his promises and became estranged from Jonathan. Instead of repaying Jonathan for all the favors he had received from him, he caused him much distress.

Trypho Takes Power

⁵⁴After this, Trypho returned and brought with him the young boy Antiochus, who became king and put on the diadem. ⁵⁵All the soldiers whom Demetrius had discharged rallied around Antiochus and fought against Demetrius, who was routed and fled. ⁵⁶Trypho captured the elephants and occupied Antioch. ⁵⁷Then young Antiochus wrote to Jonathan: "I confirm you in the high priesthood and appoint you ruler over the four districts, and to be one of the King's Friends." ⁵⁸He also sent him gold dishes and a table service, gave him the right to drink from gold cups, to dress in royal purple, and to wear a gold buckle. ⁵⁹Likewise, he made Jonathan's brother Simon governor of the region from the Ladder of Tyre to the borders of Egypt.

⁶⁰Jonathan set out and traveled through the province of West-of-Euphrates and its cities, and all the forces of Syria espoused his cause as allies. When he arrived at Askalon, the citizens welcomed him with pomp. ⁶¹But when he set out for Gaza, the people of Gaza shut him out. So he besieged it, and burned and plundered its suburbs. ⁶²Then the people of Gaza appealed to Jonathan, and he granted them terms of peace. He took the sons of their leaders as hostages and sent them to Jerusalem. He then traveled on through the province as far as Damascus.

⁶³Jonathan heard that the generals of Demetrius had come with a strong force to Kadesh in Galilee, intending to remove him from office. ⁶⁴So he went to meet

them, leaving his brother Simon in the province. ⁶⁵ Simon encamped against Beth-zur, attacked it for many days, and shut in the inhabitants. ⁶⁶ They appealed to him, and he granted them terms of peace. He expelled them from the city, took possession of it, and put a garrison there.

⁶⁷ Meanwhile, Jonathan and his army pitched their camp near the waters of Gennesaret, and at daybreak they went to the plain of Hazor. ⁶⁸ There the army of the foreigners met him on the plain. Having first detached an ambush in the mountains, this army mounted a frontal attack. ⁶⁹ Then those in ambush rose out of their places and joined in the battle. ⁷⁰ All of Jonathan's men fled; no one stayed except the army commanders Mattathias, son of Absalom, and Judas, son of Chalphi. ⁷¹ Jonathan tore his clothes, threw dust on his head, and prayed. ⁷² Then he went back to the battle and routed them, and they fled. ⁷³ Those of his men who were running away saw it and returned to him; and with him they pursued the enemy as far as their camp in Kadesh, and there they encamped. ⁷⁴ About three thousand of the foreign troops fell on that day. Then Jonathan returned to Jerusalem.

Jonathan Makes More Treaties

¹²:¹ When Jonathan saw that the time was right, he chose men and sent them to Rome to confirm and renew the friendship with the Romans. ² He also sent letters to the Spartans and other places to the same effect.

³ After reaching Rome, the men entered the senate chamber and said, "The high priest Jonathan and the Jewish people have sent us to renew the friendship and alliance of earlier times with them." ⁴ The Romans gave them letters addressed to authorities in various places, with the request to provide them with safe conduct to the land of Judah.

⁵ This is a copy of the letter that Jonathan wrote to the Spartans: ⁶ "Jonathan the high priest, the senate of the nation, the priests, and the rest of the Jewish people send greetings to their brothers the Spartans. ⁷ Long ago a letter was sent to the high priest Onias from Arius, who then reigned over you, stating that you are our brothers, as the attached copy shows. ⁸ Onias welcomed the envoy with honor and received the letter, which spoke clearly of alliance and friendship. ⁹ Though we have no need of these things, since we have for our encouragement the holy books that are in our possession, ¹⁰ we have ventured to send word to you for the renewal of brotherhood and friendship, lest we become strangers to you; a long time has passed since you sent your message to us. ¹¹ We, on our part, have unceasingly remembered you in the sacrifices and prayers that we offer on our feasts and other appropriate days, as it is right and proper to remember brothers. ¹² We likewise rejoice in your renown. ¹³ But many tribulations and many wars have beset us, and the kings around us have attacked us. ¹⁴ We did not wish to be troublesome to you and to the rest of our allies and friends in these wars. ¹⁵ For we have the help of Heaven for our support, and we have been saved from our enemies, and our enemies have been humbled. ¹⁶ So we have chosen Numenius, son of Antiochus, and Antipater, son of Jason, and we have sent them to the Romans to renew with them the friendship and alliance of earlier times. ¹⁷ We

have also ordered them to come to you and greet you, and to deliver to you our letter concerning the renewal of our brotherhood. ¹⁸ Therefore kindly send us an answer on this matter."

¹⁹ This is a copy of the letter that they sent to Onias: ²⁰ "Arius, king of the Spartans, sends greetings to Onias the high priest. ²¹ A document has been found stating that the Spartans and the Jews are brothers and that they are of the family of Abraham. ²² Now that we have learned this, kindly write to us about your welfare. ²³ We, for our part, declare to you that your animals and your possessions are ours, and ours are yours. We have, therefore, given orders that you should be told of this."

Jonathan's Campaigns

²⁴ Then Jonathan heard that the officers of Demetrius had returned to attack him with a stronger army than before. ²⁵ So he set out from Jerusalem and met them in the territory of Hamath, giving them no opportunity to enter his province. ²⁶ The spies he had sent into their camp came back and reported to him that the enemy were preparing to attack them that night. ²⁷ Therefore, when the sun set, Jonathan ordered his men to keep watch, with their weapons at the ready for battle, throughout the night; and he set outposts around the camp. ²⁸ When the enemy heard that Jonathan and his men were ready for battle, their hearts sank with fear and dread. They lighted fires in their camp and then withdrew. ²⁹ But because Jonathan and his men were watching the campfires burning, they did not know until the morning what had happened. ³⁰ Then Jonathan pursued them, but he could not overtake them, for they had crossed the river Eleutherus. ³¹ So Jonathan turned aside against the Arabians who are called Zabadeans, and he struck them down and plundered them. ³² Then he broke camp, marched on toward Damascus, and traveled through the whole region.

³³ Simon also set out and traveled as far as Askalon and its neighboring strongholds. He then turned to Joppa and took it by surprise, ³⁴ for he heard that its people intended to hand over the stronghold to the supporters of Demetrius. He left a garrison there to guard it.

³⁵ When Jonathan returned, he assembled the elders of the people, and with them he made plans for building strongholds in Judea, ³⁶ for making the walls of Jerusalem still higher, and for erecting a high barrier between the citadel and the city, to separate it from the city and isolate it, so that its garrison could neither buy nor sell. ³⁷ The people therefore gathered together to build up the city, for part of the wall of the eastern valley had collapsed. And Jonathan repaired the quarter called Chaphenatha. ³⁸ Simon likewise built up Adida in the Shephelah, and fortified it by installing gates and bars.

The Death of Jonathan

³⁹ Then Trypho sought to become king of Asia, assume the diadem, and do violence to King Antiochus. ⁴⁰ But he was afraid that Jonathan would not permit

him, but would fight against him. Looking for a way to seize and kill him, he set out and came to Beth-shan. ⁴¹Jonathan marched out to meet him with forty thousand picked fighting men and came to Beth-shan. ⁴²But when Trypho saw that Jonathan had arrived with a large army he was afraid to do him violence. ⁴³Instead, he received him with honor, introduced him to all his friends, and gave him presents. He also ordered his friends and soldiers to obey him as they would himself. ⁴⁴Then he said to Jonathan: "Why have you put all these people to so much trouble when we are not at war? ⁴⁵Now pick out a few men to stay with you, send the rest to their homes, and then come with me to Ptolemais. I will hand it over to you together with other strongholds and the remaining troops, as well as all the officials; then I will turn back and go home. That is why I came here."

⁴⁶Jonathan trusted him and did as he said. He dismissed his troops, and they returned to the land of Judah. ⁴⁷But he kept with him three thousand men, of whom he left two thousand in Galilee while one thousand accompanied him. ⁴⁸Then as soon as Jonathan entered Ptolemais, the people of Ptolemais closed the gates and seized him; all who had entered with him, they killed with the sword.

⁴⁹Then Trypho sent soldiers and cavalry to Galilee and the Great Plain to destroy all Jonathan's men. ⁵⁰These, upon learning that Jonathan had been captured and killed along with his companions, encouraged one another and went out in close formation, ready to fight. ⁵¹As their pursuers saw that they were ready to fight for their lives, they turned back. ⁵²Thus all Jonathan's men came safely into the land of Judah. They mourned Jonathan and those who were with him. They were in great fear, and all Israel fell into deep mourning. ⁵³All the nations round about sought to crush them. They said, "Now that they have no leader or helper, let us make war on them and wipe out their memory from the earth."

Simon Assumes Command

¹³:¹When Simon heard that Trypho was gathering a large army to invade and ravage the land of Judah, ²and saw that the people were trembling with terror, he went up to Jerusalem. There he assembled the people ³and exhorted them in these words: "You know what I, my brothers, and my father's house have done for the laws and the sanctuary; what battles and hardships we have seen. ⁴For the sake of this, for the sake of Israel, all my brothers have perished, and I alone am left. ⁵Far be it from me, then, to save my own life in any time of distress, for I am not better than my brothers. ⁶But I will avenge my nation and the sanctuary, as well as your wives and children, for out of hatred all the Gentiles have united to crush us."

⁷As the people heard these words, their spirit was rekindled. ⁸They shouted in reply: "You are our leader in place of your brothers Judas and Jonathan. ⁹Fight our battles, and we will do everything that you tell us." ¹⁰So Simon mustered all the men able to fight, and hastening to complete the walls of Jerusalem, fortified it on every side. ¹¹He sent Jonathan, son of Absalom, to Joppa with a strong force; Jonathan drove out the occupants and remained there.

Trypho Moves Against Simon

[12] Then Trypho moved from Ptolemais with a large army to invade the land of Judah, bringing Jonathan with him as a prisoner. [13] Simon encamped at Adida, facing the plain. [14] When Trypho learned that Simon had succeeded his brother Jonathan, and that he intended to fight him, he sent ambassadors to him with this message: [15] "It was on account of the money your brother Jonathan owed the royal treasury in connection with the offices that he held, that we have detained him. [16] Now send a hundred talents of silver, and two of his sons as hostages to guarantee that when he is set free he will not revolt against us, and we will release him."

[17] Simon knew that they were speaking deceitfully to him. Nevertheless, for fear of provoking much hostility among the people, he sent for the money and the boys, [18] lest the people say "Jonathan perished because I would not send Trypho the money and the boys." [19] So he sent the boys and the hundred talents; but Trypho broke his promise and would not release Jonathan.

[20] Next Trypho moved to invade and ravage the country. His troops went around by the road that leads to Adora, but Simon and his army moved along opposite him everywhere he went. [21] The people in the citadel kept sending emissaries to Trypho, pressing him to come to them by way of the wilderness, and to send them provisions. [22] Although Trypho got all his cavalry ready to go, there was a very heavy snowfall that night, and he could not go on account of the snow. So he left for Gilead. [23] When he was approaching Baskama, he had Jonathan killed and buried him there. [24] Then Trypho returned to his own land.

[25] Simon sent for the remains of his brother Jonathan, and buried him in Modein, the city of his ancestors. [26] All Israel bewailed him with solemn lamentation, mourning over him for many days. [27] Then Simon erected over the tomb of his father and his brothers a monument of stones, polished front and back, and raised high enough to be seen at a distance. [28] He set up seven pyramids facing one another for his father and his mother and his four brothers. [29] For the pyramids he devised a setting of massive columns, which he adorned with suits of armor as a perpetual memorial, and next to the armor carved ships, which could be seen by all who sailed the sea. [30] This tomb which he built at Modein is there to the present day.

Independance for Judea

[31] Trypho dealt treacherously with the young King Antiochus. He killed him [32] and became king in his place, putting on the crown of Asia. Thus he brought much evil on the land. [33] Simon, for his part, built up the strongholds of Judea, fortifying them all around with high towers, thick walls, and gates with bars, and he stored up provisions in the strongholds. [34] Simon also chose men and sent them to King Demetrius to obtain for the land an exemption from taxation, since Trypho did nothing but plunder. [35] King Demetrius replied favorably and sent him the following letter:

[36] "King Demetrius sends greetings to Simon, high priest and friend of kings, and to the elders and the Jewish people. [37] We have received the gold crown and

the palm branch that you sent. We are ready to make a lasting peace with you and to write to our officials to grant you exemption. [38] Whatever decrees we have made in your regard remain in force, and the strongholds that you have built you may keep. [39] We pardon any oversights and offenses committed up to now, as well as the crown tax that you owe. Any other tax that used to be collected in Jerusalem will no longer be collected there. [40] Any of you qualified for enrollment in our service may be enrolled. Let there be peace between us."

[41] Thus in the one hundred and seventieth year, the yoke of the Gentiles was removed from Israel, [42] and the people began to write in their records and contracts, "In the first year of Simon, great high priest, governor, and leader of the Jews."

Simon Captures Gazara and Frees the Citadel

[43] In those days Simon besieged Gazara and surrounded it with troops. He made a siege machine, brought it up against the city, and attacked and captured one of the towers. [44] Those in the siege machine leaped down into the city and a great tumult arose there. [45] Those in the city, together with their wives and children, went up on the wall, with their garments rent, and cried out in loud voices, begging Simon to grant them terms of peace. [46] They said, "Treat us not according to our evil deeds but according to your mercy." [47] So Simon came to terms with them and did not attack them. He expelled them from the city, however, and he purified the houses in which there were idols. Then he entered the city with hymns and songs of praise. [48] After removing from it everything that was impure, he settled there people who observed the law. He improved its fortifications and built himself a residence.

[49] The people in the citadel in Jerusalem were prevented from going out into the country and back to buy or sell; they suffered greatly from hunger, and many of them died of starvation. [50] They finally cried out to Simon, and he gave them terms of peace. He expelled them from the citadel and cleansed it of impurities. [51] On the twenty-third day of the second month, in the one hundred and seventy-first year, the Jews entered the citadel with shouts of praise, the waving of palm branches, the playing of harps and cymbals and lyres, and the singing of hymns and canticles, because a great enemy of Israel had been crushed. [52] Simon decreed that this day should be celebrated every year with rejoicing. He also strengthened the fortifications of the temple mount alongside the citadel, and he and his people dwelt there. [53] Seeing that his son John was now a grown man, Simon made him commander of all his soldiers, and he dwelt in Gazara.

Peace under Simon

14:1 In the one hundred and seventy-second year, King Demetrius assembled his army and marched into Media to obtain help so that he could fight Trypho. [2] When Arsaces, king of Persia and Media, heard that Demetrius had entered his territory, he sent one of his generals to take him alive. [3] The general went forth and attacked the army of Demetrius; he captured him and brought him to Arsaces, who put him under guard.

> [4] The land was at rest all the days of Simon,
>   who sought the good of his nation.
> His rule delighted his people
>   and his glory all his days.
> [5] As his crowning glory he took Joppa for a port
>   and made it a gateway to the isles of the sea.
> [6] He enlarged the borders of his nation
>   and gained control of the country.
> [7] He took many prisoners of war
>   and made himself master of Gazara, Beth-zur, and the citadel.
> He cleansed the citadel of its impurities;
> there was no one to withstand him.
> [8] The people cultivated their land in peace;
> the land yielded its produce,
>   the trees of the field their fruit.
> [9] Old men sat in the squares,
>   all talking about the good times,
>   while the young men put on the glorious raiment of war.
> [10] He supplied the cities with food
>   and equipped them with means of defense,
>   till his glorious name reached the ends of the earth.
> [11] He brought peace to the land,
>   and Israel was filled with great joy.
> [12] Every one sat under his vine and fig tree,
>   with no one to disturb them.
> [13] No attacker was left in the land;
> the kings in those days were crushed.
> [14] He strengthened all the lowly among his people
>   and was zealous for the law;
> he destroyed the lawless and the wicked.
> [15] The sanctuary he made splendid
>   and multiplied its furnishings.

Further Alliances with Rome and Sparta

[16] When people in Rome and even in Sparta heard that Jonathan had died, they were deeply grieved. [17] But when they heard that his brother Simon had become high priest in his place and was master of the territory and its cities, [18] they sent him inscribed tablets of bronze to renew with him the friendship and alliance that they had established with his brothers Judas and Jonathan. [19] These were read before the assembly in Jerusalem.

[20] This is a copy of the letter that the Spartans sent: "The rulers and the city of the Spartans send greetings to Simon the high priest, the elders, the priests, and

the rest of the Jewish people, our brothers. ²¹ The ambassadors sent to our people have informed us of your glory and renown, and we rejoiced at their coming. ²² In accordance with what they said we have recorded the following in the public decrees: Numenius, son of Antiochus, and Antipater, son of Jason, ambassadors of the Jews, have come to us to renew their friendship with us. ²³ The people have resolved to receive these men with honor, and to deposit a copy of their words in the public archives, so that the people of Sparta may have a record of them. A copy of this decree has been made for Simon the high priest."

²⁴ After this, Simon sent Numenius to Rome with a large gold shield weighing a thousand minas, to confirm the alliance with the Romans.

²⁵ When the people heard of these things, they said, "How will we thank Simon and his sons? ²⁶ He and his brothers and his father's house have stood firm and repulsed Israel's enemies, and so have established its freedom." So they made an inscription on bronze tablets, which they affixed to pillars on Mount Zion.

²⁷ The following is a copy of the inscription: "On the eighteenth day of Elul, in the one hundred and seventy-second year, that is, the third year under Simon the great high priest in Asaramel, ²⁸ in a great assembly of priests, people, rulers of the nation, and elders of the region, the following proclamation was made to us:

²⁹ "'Since there have often been wars in our country, Simon, son of the priest Mattathias, descendant of Joarib, and his brothers have put themselves in danger and resisted the enemies of their nation, so that their sanctuary and law might be maintained, and they have thus brought great glory to their nation. ³⁰ Jonathan rallied the nation, became their high priest, and was gathered to his people. ³¹ When their enemies sought to invade and ravage their country and to violate their sanctuary, ³² Simon rose up and fought for his nation, spending large sums of his own money to equip his nation's forces and give them their pay. ³³ He fortified the cities of Judea, especially the border city of Beth-zur, formerly the site of the enemy's weaponry, and he stationed there a garrison of Jewish soldiers. ³⁴ He also fortified Joppa by the sea and Gazara on the border of Azotus, a place previously occupied by the enemy; these cities he settled with Jews and furnished them with all that was necessary for their restoration. ³⁵ When the people saw Simon's fidelity and the glory he planned to bring to his nation, they made him their leader and high priest because of all he had accomplished and the justice and fidelity he had shown his nation. In every way he sought to exalt his people.

³⁶ "'In his time and under his guidance they succeeded in driving the Gentiles out of their country and those in the City of David in Jerusalem, who had built for themselves a citadel from which they used to sally forth to defile the environs of the sanctuary and inflict grave injury on its purity. ³⁷ In this citadel he stationed Jewish soldiers, and he strengthened its fortifications for the security of the land and the city, while he also built up the wall of Jerusalem to a greater height. ³⁸ Consequently, King Demetrius confirmed him in the high priesthood, ³⁹ made him one of his Friends, and conferred great honor on him. ⁴⁰ This was because he had heard that the Romans had addressed the Jews as friends, allies, and brothers, that they had received Simon's envoys with honor, ⁴¹ and that the Jewish people and their priests had decided the following: Simon will be their leader and high priest forever until a trustworthy prophet arises. ⁴² He will act as governor over them, and will have charge of the sanctuary, to make regulations concerning its

functions and concerning the country, its weapons and strongholds. [43] He will be obeyed by all. All contracts in the country will be written in his name, and he will be clothed in purple and gold. [44] It will not be lawful for any of the people or priests to nullify any of these decisions, or to contradict the orders given by him, or to convene an assembly in the country without his consent, to be clothed in purple or wear a gold buckle. [45] Whoever acts otherwise or violates any of these prescriptions will be liable to punishment.

[46] "'Thus all the people approved of granting Simon the right to act in accord with these decisions, [47] and Simon accepted and agreed to be high priest, governor, and ethnarch of the Jewish people and priests, and to have authority over all.'"

[48] It was decreed that this inscription should be engraved on bronze tablets, to be set up in a conspicuous place in the precincts of the sanctuary, [49] and that copies of it should be deposited in the treasury, where they would be available to Simon and his sons.

Antiochus Writes to Simon

[15:1] Antiochus, son of King Demetrius, sent a letter from the islands of the sea to Simon, the priest and ethnarch of the Jews, and to all the nation, [2] which read as follows:

"King Antiochus sends greetings to Simon, the high priest and ethnarch, and to the Jewish nation. [3] Whereas certain villains have gained control of the kingdom of our ancestors, I intend to reclaim it, that I may restore it to its former state. I have recruited a large number of mercenary troops and equipped warships. [4] I intend to make a landing in the country so that I may take revenge on those who have ruined our country and laid waste many cities in my kingdom.

[5] "Now, therefore, I confirm to you all the tax exemptions that the kings before me granted you and whatever other privileges they conceded to you. [6] I authorize you to coin your own money, as legal tender in your country. [7] Jerusalem and its sanctuary will be free. All the weapons you have prepared and all the strongholds you have built and now occupy will remain in your possession. [8] All debts, present or future, due to the royal treasury will be canceled for you, now and for all time. [9] When we establish our kingdom, we will greatly honor you and your nation and the temple, so that your glory will be manifest in all the earth."

[10] In the one hundred and seventy-fourth year Antiochus invaded the land of his ancestors, and all the troops rallied to him, so that few were left with Trypho. [11] Pursued by Antiochus, Trypho fled to Dor, by the sea, [12] realizing what troubles had come upon him now that his soldiers had deserted him. [13] Antiochus encamped before Dor with a hundred and twenty thousand infantry and eight thousand cavalry. [14] While he surrounded the city, his ships closed from the sea, so that he pressed it hard by land and sea and let no one go in or out.

Rome Supports Simon

[15] Meanwhile, Numenius and his companions came from Rome with letters containing this message to various kings and countries: [16] "Lucius, Consul of the

Romans, sends greetings to King Ptolemy. [17] Ambassadors of the Jews, our friends and allies, have come to us to renew their earlier friendship and alliance. They had been sent by Simon the high priest and the Jewish people, [18]and they brought with them a gold shield of a thousand minas. [19] Therefore we have decided to write to various kings and countries, that they are not to venture to harm them, or wage war against them or their cities or their country, and are not to assist those who fight against them. [20] We have also decided to accept the shield from them. [21] If, then, any troublemakers from their country take refuge with you, hand them over to Simon the high priest, so that he may punish them according to their law."

[22] The consul sent identical letters to Kings Demetrius, Attalus, Ariarthes and Arsaces; [23] to all the countries—Sampsames, the Spartans, Delos, Myndos, Sicyon, Caria, Samos, Pamphylia, Lycia, Halicarnassus, Rhodes, Phaselis, Cos, Side, Aradus, Gortyna, Cnidus, Cyprus, and Cyrene. [24] A copy of the letter was also sent to Simon the high priest.

[25] When King Antiochus encamped before Dor, he assaulted it continuously both with troops and with the siege engines he had made. He blockaded Trypho by preventing anyone from going in or out. [26] Simon sent to Antiochus' support two thousand elite troops, together with silver and gold and much equipment. [27] But he refused to accept the aid; in fact, he broke all the agreements he had previously made with Simon and became hostile toward him.

Antiochus Threatens Simon

[28] He sent Athenobius, one of his Friends, to confer with Simon and say: "You are occupying Joppa and Gazara and the citadel of Jerusalem; these are cities of my kingdom. [29] You have laid waste their territories, done great harm to the land, and taken possession of many districts in my kingdom. [30] Now, therefore, give up the cities you have seized and the tribute money of the districts you control outside the territory of Judea; [31] or instead, pay me five hundred talents of silver for the devastation you have caused and five hundred talents more for the tribute money of the cities. If you do not do this, we will come and make war on you."

[32] So Athenobius, the king's Friend, came to Jerusalem and on seeing the splendor of Simon's court, the gold and silver plate on the sideboard, and his rich display, he was amazed. When he gave him the king's message, [33] Simon said to him in reply: "It is not foreign land we have taken nor have we seized the property of others, but only our ancestral heritage which for a time had been unjustly held by our enemies. [34] Now that we have the opportunity, we are holding on to the heritage of our ancestors. [35] As for Joppa and Gazara, which you demand, those cities were doing great harm to our people and our country. For these we will give you a hundred talents." Athenobius made no reply, [36] but returned to the king in anger. When he told him of Simon's words, of his splendor, and of all he had seen, the king fell into a violent rage.

[37] Trypho had boarded a ship and escaped to Orthosia. [38] Then the king appointed Cendebeus commander-in-chief of the seacoast, and gave him infantry and cavalry forces. [39] He ordered him to encamp against Judea and to fortify Kedron and strengthen its gates, so that he could wage war on the people. Mean-

while the king went in pursuit of Trypho. ⁴⁰ When Cendebeus came to Jamnia, he began to harass the people and to make incursions into Judea, where he took people captive and massacred them. ⁴¹ As the king ordered, he fortified Kedron and stationed cavalry and infantry there, so that they could go out and patrol the roads of Judea.

John Defeats Cendebeus

¹⁶:¹ John then went up from Gazara and told his father Simon what Cendebeus was doing. ² Simon called his two oldest sons, Judas and John, and said to them: "I and my brothers and my father's house have fought the wars of Israel from our youth until today, and many times we succeeded in saving Israel. ³ I have now grown old, but you, by the mercy of Heaven, have come to maturity. Take my place and my brother's, and go out and fight for our nation; and may the help of Heaven be with you!"

⁴ John then mustered in the land twenty thousand warriors and cavalry. Setting out against Cendebeus, they spent the night at Modein, ⁵ rose early, and marched into the plain. There, facing them, was an immense army of foot soldiers and cavalry, and between the two armies was a wadi. ⁶ John and his people took their position against the enemy. Seeing that his people were afraid to cross the wadi, John crossed first. When his men saw this, they crossed over after him. ⁷ Then he divided his infantry and put his cavalry in the center, for the enemy's cavalry were very numerous. ⁸ They blew the trumpets, and Cendebeus and his army were routed; many of them fell wounded, and the rest fled toward the stronghold. ⁹ It was then that John's brother Judas fell wounded; but John pursued them until Cendebeus reached Kedron, which he had fortified. ¹⁰ Some took refuge in the towers on the plain of Azotus, but John set fire to these, and about two thousand of the enemy perished. He then returned to Judea in peace.

Simon and His Sons Are Killed

¹¹ Ptolemy, son of Abubus, had been appointed governor of the plain of Jericho, and he had much silver and gold, ¹² being the son-in-law of the high priest. ¹³ But his heart became proud and he was determined to get control of the country. So he made treacherous plans to do away with Simon and his sons. ¹⁴ As Simon was inspecting the cities of the country and providing for their needs, he and his sons Mattathias and Judas went down to Jericho in the one hundred and seventy-seventh year, in the eleventh month (that is, the month Shebat). ¹⁵ The son of Abubus gave them a deceitful welcome in the little stronghold called Dok which he had built. He served them a sumptuous banquet, but he had his men hidden there. ¹⁶ Then, when Simon and his sons were drunk, Ptolemy and his men sprang up, weapons in hand, rushed upon Simon in the banquet hall, and killed him, his two sons, and some of his servants. ¹⁷ By this vicious act of treachery he repaid good with evil.

John Succeeds Simon

[18] Then Ptolemy wrote a report and sent it to the king, asking him to send troops to help him and to turn over to him their country and its cities. [19] He sent other men to Gazara to do away with John. To the army officers he sent letters inviting them to come to him so that he might present them with silver, gold, and gifts. [20] He also sent others to seize Jerusalem and the temple mount. [21] But someone ran ahead and brought word to John at Gazara that his father and his brothers had perished, and "Ptolemy has sent men to kill you also." [22] On hearing this, John was utterly astounded. When the men came to kill him, he seized them and put them to death, for he knew that they sought to kill him.

[23] Now the rest of the acts of John, his wars and the brave deeds he performed, his rebuilding of the walls, and all his achievements—[24] these are recorded in the chronicle of his high priesthood, from the time that he succeeded his father as high priest.

2.2 2 Maccabees

A Letter to the Jews in Egypt

^{1:1} The Jews in Jerusalem and in the land of Judea send greetings to their kindred, the Jews in Egypt, and wish them true peace! ² May God do good to you and remember his covenant with his faithful servants, Abraham, Isaac, and Jacob, ³ give to all of you a heart to worship him and to do his will wholeheartedly and with a willing spirit, ⁴ open your heart to his law and commandments and grant you peace, ⁵ hear your prayers, and be reconciled to you, and never forsake you in time of adversity. ⁶ Even now we are praying for you here.

⁷ In the reign of Demetrius, the one hundred and sixty-ninth year, we Jews wrote to you during the height of the distress that overtook us in those years after Jason and his followers revolted against the holy land and the kingdom, ⁸ set fire to the gatehouse, and shed innocent blood. But we prayed to the Lord, and our prayer was heard; we offered sacrifices and fine flour; we lighted the lamps and set out the loaves of bread. ⁹ We are now reminding you to celebrate the feast of Booths in the month of Kislev. ¹⁰ Dated in the one hundred and eighty-eighth year.

A Letter to Aristobulus

The people of Jerusalem and Judea, the senate, and Judas send greetings and good wishes to Aristobulus, teacher of King Ptolemy and member of the family of the anointed priests, and to the Jews in Egypt. ¹¹ Since we have been saved by God from grave dangers, we give him great thanks as befits those who fought against the king; ¹² for it was God who drove out those who fought against the holy city. ¹³ When their leader arrived in Persia with his seemingly irresistible army, they were cut to pieces in the temple of the goddess Nanea through a deceitful stratagem employed by Nanea's priests. ¹⁴ On the pretext of marrying the goddess, Antiochus with his Friends had come to the place to get its great treasures as a dowry. ¹⁵ When the priests of Nanea's temple had displayed the treasures and Antiochus with a few attendants had come inside the wall of the temple precincts, the priests locked the temple as soon as he entered. ¹⁶ Then they opened a hidden trapdoor in the ceiling, and hurling stones at the leader and his companions, struck them down. They dismembered the bodies, cut off their heads, and tossed them to the people outside. ¹⁷ Forever blessed be our God, who has thus punished the impious!

A History of Nehemiah's Sacrifice

[18] Since we will be celebrating the purification of the temple on the twenty-fifth day of the month Kislev, we thought it right to inform you, that you too may celebrate the feast of Booths and of the fire that appeared when Nehemiah, the rebuilder of the temple and the altar, offered sacrifices. [19] For when our ancestors were being led into captivity in Persia, devout priests at the time took some of the fire from the altar and hid it secretly in the hollow of a dry cistern, making sure that the place would be unknown to anyone. [20] Many years later, when it so pleased God, Nehemiah, commissioned by the king of Persia, sent the descendants of the priests who had hidden the fire to look for it. [21] When they informed us that they could not find any fire, but only a thick liquid, he ordered them to scoop some out and bring it. After the material for the sacrifices had been prepared, Nehemiah ordered the priests to sprinkle the wood and what lay on it with the liquid. [22] This was done, and when at length the sun, which had been clouded over, began to shine, a great fire blazed up, so that everyone marveled. [23] While the sacrifice was being burned, the priests recited a prayer, and all present joined in with them. Jonathan led and the rest responded with Nehemiah.

[24] The prayer was as follows: "Lord, Lord God, creator of all things, awesome and strong, just and merciful, the only king and benefactor, [25] who alone are gracious, just, almighty, and eternal, Israel's savior from all evil, who chose our ancestors and sanctified them: [26] accept this sacrifice on behalf of all your people Israel and guard and sanctify your portion. [27] Gather together our scattered people, free those who are slaves among the Gentiles, look kindly on those who are despised and detested, and let the Gentiles know that you are our God. [28] Punish those who lord it over us and in their arrogance oppress us. [29] Plant your people in your holy place, as Moses said."

[30] Then the priests sang hymns. [31] After the sacrifice was consumed, Nehemiah ordered the rest of the liquid to be poured upon large stones. [32] As soon as this was done, a flame blazed up, but its light was lost in the brilliance coming from the altar. [33] When the event became known and the king of the Persians was told that, in the very place where the exiled priests had hidden the fire, a liquid was found with which Nehemiah and his people had burned the sacrifices, [34] the king, after verifying the fact, fenced the place off and declared it sacred. [35] To those whom the king favored, he distributed many benefits he received. [36] Nehemiah and his companions called the liquid nephthar, meaning purification, but most people named it naphtha.

Other Sacrifices

[2:1] In the records it will be found that Jeremiah the prophet ordered the deportees to take some of the fire with them as indicated, [2] and that the prophet, in giving them the law, directed the deportees not to forget the commandments of the Lord or be led astray in their thoughts, when seeing the gold and silver idols and their adornments. [3] With other similar words he exhorted them that the law should not depart from their hearts.

[4] The same document also tells how the prophet, in virtue of an oracle, ordered that the tent and the ark should accompany him, and how he went to the very mountain that Moses climbed to behold God's inheritance. [5] When Jeremiah arrived there, he found a chamber in a cave in which he put the tent, the ark, and the altar of incense; then he sealed the entrance. [6] Some of those who followed him came up intending to mark the path, but they could not find it. [7] When Jeremiah heard of this, he reproved them: "The place is to remain unknown until God gathers his people together again and shows them mercy. [8] Then the Lord will disclose these things, and the glory of the Lord and the cloud will be seen, just as they appeared in the time of Moses and of Solomon when he prayed that the place might be greatly sanctified."

[9] It is also related how Solomon in his wisdom offered a sacrifice for the dedication and the completion of the temple. [10] Just as Moses prayed to the Lord and fire descended from the sky and consumed the sacrifices, so also Solomon prayed and fire came down and consumed the burnt offerings. [11] Moses had said, "Because it had not been eaten, the purification offering was consumed." [12] Solomon also celebrated the feast in the same way for eight days.

[13] These same things are also told in the records and in Nehemiah's memoirs, as well as how he founded a library and collected the books about the kings and the prophets, the books of David, and the royal letters about votive offerings. [14] In like manner Judas also collected for us all the books that had been scattered because of the war, and we now have them in our possession. [15] If you need them, send messengers to get them for you.

[16] As we are about to celebrate the purification, we are writing: you should celebrate the feast days. [17] It is God who has saved all his people and has restored to all of them their inheritance, the kingdom, the priesthood, and the sacred rites, [18] as he promised through the law. For we hope in God, that he will soon have mercy on us and gather us together from everywhere under the heavens to his holy place, for he has rescued us from great perils and has purified the place.

Prologue

[19] This is the story of Judas Maccabeus and his brothers, of the purification of the great temple, the dedication of the altar, [20] the campaigns against Antiochus Epiphanes and his son Eupator, [21] and of the heavenly manifestations accorded to the heroes who fought bravely for the Jewish people. Few as they were, they plundered the whole land, put to flight the barbarian hordes, [22] regained possession of the temple renowned throughout the world, and liberated the city. They reestablished the laws that were in danger of being abolished, while the Lord favored them with every kindness. [23] All this, detailed by Jason of Cyrene in five volumes, we will try to condense into a single book.

[24] For in view of the flood of data, and the difficulties encountered, given such abundant material, by those who wish to plunge into accounts of the history, [25] we have aimed to please those who prefer simply to read, to make it easy for the studious who wish to commit things to memory, and to be helpful to all. [26] For us who have undertaken the labor of making this digest, the task, far from

being easy, is one of sweat and of sleepless nights. [27] Just so, the preparation of a festive banquet is no light matter for one who seeks to give enjoyment to others. Similarly, to win the gratitude of many we will gladly endure this labor, [28] leaving the responsibility for exact details to the historian, and confining our efforts to presenting only a summary outline. [29] As the architect of a new house must pay attention to the whole structure, while the one who undertakes the decoration and the frescoes has to be concerned only with what is needed for ornamentation, so I think it is with us. [30] To enter into questions and examine them from all sides and to be busy about details is the task of the historian; [31] but one who is making an adaptation should be allowed to aim at brevity of expression and to forgo complete treatment of the matter. [32] Here, then, let us begin our account without adding to what has already been said; it would be silly to lengthen the preface to the history and then cut short the history itself.

Heliodorus Arrives in Jerusalem

[3:1] While the holy city lived in perfect peace and the laws were strictly observed because of the piety of the high priest Onias and his hatred of evil, [2] the kings themselves honored the place and glorified the temple with the most magnificent gifts. [3] Thus Seleucus, king of Asia, defrayed from his own revenues all the expenses necessary for the liturgy of sacrifice.

[4] But a certain Simon, of the priestly clan of Bilgah, who had been appointed superintendent of the temple, had a quarrel with the high priest about the administration of the city market. [5] Since he could not prevail against Onias, he went to Apollonius of Tarsus, who at that time was governor of Coelesyria and Phoenicia, [6] and reported to him that the treasury in Jerusalem was full of such untold riches that the sum total of the assets was past counting and that since they did not belong to the account of the sacrifices, it would be possible for them to fall under the authority of the king.

[7] When Apollonius had an audience with the king, he informed him about the riches that had been reported to him. The king chose his chief minister Heliodorus and sent him with instructions to seize those riches. [8] So Heliodorus immediately set out on his journey, ostensibly to visit the cities of Coelesyria and Phoenicia, but in reality to carry out the king's purpose.

[9] When he arrived in Jerusalem and had been graciously received by the high priest of the city, he told him about the information that had been given, and explained the reason for his presence, and he inquired if these things were really true. [10] The high priest explained that there were deposits for widows and orphans, [11] and some was the property of Hyrcanus, son of Tobias, a man who occupied a very high position. Contrary to the misrepresentations of the impious Simon, the total amounted only to four hundred talents of silver and two hundred of gold. [12] It was utterly unthinkable to defraud those who had placed their trust in the sanctity of the place and in the sacred inviolability of a temple venerated all over the world.

Heliodorus Tries to Rob the Temple

¹³ But Heliodorus, because of the orders he had from the king, said that in any case this money must be confiscated for the royal treasury. ¹⁴ So on the day he had set he went in to take an inventory of the funds. There was no little anguish throughout the city. ¹⁵ Priests prostrated themselves before the altar in their priestly robes, and called toward heaven for the one who had given the law about deposits to keep the deposits safe for those who had made them. ¹⁶ Whoever saw the appearance of the high priest was pierced to the heart, for the changed complexion of his face revealed his mental anguish. ¹⁷ The terror and bodily trembling that had come over the man clearly showed those who saw him the pain that lodged in his heart. ¹⁸ People rushed out of their houses and crowded together making common supplication, because the place was in danger of being profaned. ¹⁹ Women, girded with sackcloth below their breasts, filled the streets. Young women secluded indoors all ran, some to the gates, some to the walls, others peered through the windows—²⁰ all of them with hands raised toward heaven, making supplication. ²¹ It was pitiful to see the populace prostrate everywhere and the high priest full of dread and anguish. ²² While they were imploring the almighty Lord to keep the deposits safe and secure for those who had placed them in trust, ²³ Heliodorus went on with his plan.

²⁴ But just as Heliodorus was arriving at the treasury with his bodyguards, the Lord of spirits and all authority produced an apparition so great that those who had been bold enough to accompany Heliodorus were panic-stricken at God's power and fainted away in terror. ²⁵ There appeared to them a richly caparisoned horse, mounted by a fearsome rider. Charging furiously, the horse attacked Heliodorus with its front hooves. The rider was seen wearing golden armor. ²⁶ Then two other young men, remarkably strong, strikingly handsome, and splendidly attired, appeared before him. Standing on each side of him, they flogged him unceasingly, inflicting innumerable blows. ²⁷ Suddenly he fell to the ground, enveloped in great darkness. His men picked him up and laid him on a stretcher. ²⁸ They carried away helpless the man who a moment before had entered that treasury under arms with a great retinue and his whole bodyguard. They clearly recognized the sovereign power of God.

Onias Prays for Heliodorus

²⁹ As Heliodorus lay speechless because of God's action and deprived of any hope of recovery, ³⁰ the people praised the Lord who had marvelously glorified his own place; and the temple, charged so shortly before with fear and commotion, was filled with joy and gladness, now that the almighty Lord had appeared. ³¹ Quickly some of the companions of Heliodorus begged Onias to call upon the Most High to spare the life of one who was about to breathe his last. ³² The high priest, suspecting that the king might think that Heliodorus had suffered some foul play at the hands of the Jews, offered a sacrifice for the man's recovery. ³³ While the high priest was offering the sacrifice of atonement, the same young men dressed in the same clothing again appeared and stood before Heliodorus. "Be very grateful to

the high priest Onias," they told him. "It is for his sake that the Lord has spared your life. ³⁴ Since you have been scourged by Heaven, proclaim to all God's great power." When they had said this, they disappeared.

³⁵ After Heliodorus had offered a sacrifice to the Lord and made most solemn vows to the one who had spared his life, he bade Onias farewell, and returned with his soldiers to the king. ³⁶ Before all he gave witness to the deeds of the most high God that he had seen with his own eyes. ³⁷ When the king asked Heliodorus what sort of person would be suitable to be sent to Jerusalem next, he answered: ³⁸ "If you have an enemy or one who is plotting against the government, send him there, and you will get him back with a flogging, if indeed he survives at all; for there is certainly some divine power about the place. ³⁹ The one whose dwelling is in heaven watches over that place and protects it, and strikes down and destroys those who come to harm it." ⁴⁰ This was how the matter concerning Heliodorus and the preservation of the treasury turned out.

⁴:¹ The Simon mentioned above as the informer about the funds against his own country slandered Onias as the one who incited Heliodorus and instigated the whole miserable affair. ² He dared to brand as a schemer against the government the man who was the benefactor of the city, the protector of his compatriots, and a zealous defender of the laws. ³ When Simon's hostility reached such a pitch that murders were being committed by one of his henchmen, ⁴ Onias saw that the opposition was serious and that Apollonius, son of Menestheus, the governor of Coelesyria and Phoenicia, was abetting Simon's wickedness. ⁵ So he had recourse to the king, not as an accuser of his compatriots, but as one looking to the general and particular good of all the people. ⁶ He saw that without royal attention it would be impossible to have a peaceful government, and that Simon would not desist from his folly.

Jason Becomes High Priest and Introduces Greek Customs

⁷ But Seleucus died, and when Antiochus surnamed Epiphanes succeeded him on the throne, Onias' brother Jason obtained the high priesthood by corrupt means: ⁸ in an interview, he promised the king three hundred and sixty talents of silver, as well as eighty talents from another source of income. ⁹ Besides this he would undertake to pay a hundred and fifty more, if he was given authority to establish a gymnasium and a youth center for it and to enroll Jerusalemites as citizens of Antioch.

¹⁰ When Jason received the king's approval and came into office, he immediately initiated his compatriots into the Greek way of life. ¹¹ He set aside the royal concessions granted to the Jews through the mediation of John, father of Eupolemus (that Eupolemus who would later go on an embassy to the Romans to establish friendship and alliance with them); he set aside the lawful practices and introduced customs contrary to the law. ¹² With perverse delight he established a gymnasium at the very foot of the citadel, where he induced the noblest young men to wear the Greek hat. ¹³ The craze for Hellenism and the adoption of foreign customs reached such a pitch, through the outrageous wickedness of Jason, the renegade and would-be high priest, ¹⁴ that the priests no longer cared

about the service of the altar. Disdaining the temple and neglecting the sacrifices, they hastened, at the signal for the games, to take part in the unlawful exercises at the arena. [15] What their ancestors had regarded as honors they despised; what the Greeks esteemed as glory they prized highly. [16] For this reason they found themselves in serious trouble: the very people whose manner of life they emulated, and whom they desired to imitate in everything, became their enemies and oppressors. [17] It is no light matter to flout the laws of God, as subsequent events will show.

[18] When the quinquennial games were held at Tyre in the presence of the king, [19] the vile Jason sent representatives of the Antiochians of Jerusalem, to bring three hundred silver drachmas for the sacrifice to Hercules. But the bearers themselves decided that the money should not be spent on a sacrifice, as that was not right, but should be used for some other purpose. [20] So the contribution meant for the sacrifice to Hercules by the sender, was in fact applied to the construction of triremes by those who brought it.

[21] When Apollonius, son of Menestheus, was sent to Egypt for the coronation of King Philometor, Antiochus learned from him that the king was opposed to his policies. He took measures for his own security; so after going to Joppa, he proceeded to Jerusalem. [22] There he was received with great pomp by Jason and the people of the city, who escorted him with torchlights and acclamations; following this, he led his army into Phoenicia.

Menelaus Becomes High Priest

[23] Three years later Jason sent Menelaus, brother of the aforementioned Simon, to deliver the money to the king, and to complete negotiations on urgent matters. [24] But after his introduction to the king, he flattered him with such an air of authority that he secured the high priesthood for himself, outbidding Jason by three hundred talents of silver. [25] He returned with the royal commission, but with nothing that made him worthy of the high priesthood; he had the temper of a cruel tyrant and the rage of a wild beast. [26] So Jason, who had cheated his own brother and now saw himself cheated by another man, was driven out as a fugitive to the country of the Ammonites. [27] But Menelaus, who obtained the office, paid nothing of the money he had promised to the king, [28] in spite of the demand of Sostratus, the commandant of the citadel, whose duty it was to collect the taxes. For this reason, both were summoned before the king. [29] Menelaus left his brother Lysimachus as his deputy in the high priesthood, while Sostratus left Crates, commander of the Cypriots.

[30] While these things were taking place, the people of Tarsus and Mallus rose in revolt, because their cities had been given as a gift to Antiochis, the king's concubine. [31] So the king hastened off to settle the affair, leaving Andronicus, one of his nobles, as his deputy. [32] Menelaus, for his part, thinking this a good opportunity, stole some gold vessels from the temple and presented them to Andronicus; he had already sold other vessels in Tyre and in the neighboring cities. [33] When Onias had clear evidence, he accused Menelaus publicly, after withdrawing to the inviolable sanctuary at Daphne, near Antioch. [34] Thereupon Menelaus

approached Andronicus privately and urged him to seize Onias. So Andronicus went to Onias, treacherously reassuring him by offering his right hand in oath, and persuaded him, in spite of his suspicions, to leave the sanctuary. Then, with no regard for justice, he immediately put him to death.

[35] As a result, not only the Jews, but many people of other nations as well, were indignant and angry over the unjust murder of the man. [36] When the king returned from the region of Cilicia, the Jews of the city, together with the Greeks who detested the crime, went to see him about the murder of Onias. [37] Antiochus was deeply grieved and full of pity; he wept as he recalled the prudence and noble conduct of the deceased. [38] Inflamed with anger, he immediately stripped Andronicus of his purple robe, tore off his garments, and had him led through the whole city to the very place where he had committed the outrage against Onias; and there he put the murderer to death. Thus the Lord rendered him the punishment he deserved.

Lysimachus Commits Sacrilege

[39] Many acts of sacrilege had been committed by Lysimachus in the city with the connivance of Menelaus. When word spread, the people assembled in protest against Lysimachus, because a large number of gold vessels had been stolen. [40] As the crowds, now thoroughly enraged, began to riot, Lysimachus launched an unjustified attack against them with about three thousand armed men under the leadership of a certain Auranus, a man as advanced in folly as he was in years. [41] Seeing Lysimachus' attack, people picked up stones, pieces of wood, or handfuls of the ashes lying there and threw them in wild confusion at Lysimachus and his men. [42] As a result, they wounded many of them and even killed a few, while they put all to flight. The temple robber himself they killed near the treasury.

[43] Charges about this affair were brought against Menelaus. [44] When the king came to Tyre, three men sent by the senate pleaded the case before him. [45] But Menelaus, seeing himself on the losing side, promised Ptolemy, son of Dorymenes, a substantial sum of money if he would win the king over. [46] So Ptolemy took the king aside into a colonnade, as if to get some fresh air, and persuaded him to change his mind. [47] Menelaus, who was the cause of all the trouble, the king acquitted of the charges, while he condemned to death those poor men who would have been declared innocent even if they had pleaded their case before Scythians. [48] Thus, those who had prosecuted the case on behalf of the city, the people, and the sacred vessels, quickly suffered unjust punishment. [49] For this reason, even Tyrians, detesting the crime, provided sumptuously for their burial. [50] But Menelaus, thanks to the greed of those in power, remained in office, where he grew in wickedness, scheming greatly against his fellow citizens.

[5:1] About this time Antiochus sent his second expedition into Egypt. [2] It then happened that all over the city, for nearly forty days, there appeared horsemen, clothed in garments of a golden weave, charging in midair—companies fully armed with lances and drawn swords; [3] squadrons of cavalry in battle array, charges and countercharges on this side and that, with brandished shields and bristling spears, flights of arrows and flashes of gold ornaments, together with armor of every sort. ⁴ Therefore all prayed that this vision might be a good omen.

Jason Tries to Regain Control

⁵ But when a false rumor circulated that Antiochus was dead, Jason gathered at least a thousand men and suddenly attacked the city. As the defenders on the walls were forced back and the city was finally being taken, Menelaus took refuge in the citadel. ⁶ For his part, Jason continued the merciless slaughter of his fellow citizens, not realizing that triumph over one's own kindred is the greatest calamity; he thought he was winning a victory over his enemies, not over his own people. ⁷ Even so, he did not gain control of the government, but in the end received only disgrace for his treachery, and once again took refuge in the country of the Ammonites. ⁸ At length he met a miserable end. Called to account before Aretas, ruler of the Arabians, he fled from city to city, hunted by all, hated as an apostate from the laws, abhorred as the executioner of his country and his compatriots. Driven into Egypt, ⁹ he set out by sea for the Lacedaemonians, among whom he hoped to find protection because of his relations with them. He who had exiled so many from their country perished in exile; ¹⁰ and he who had cast out so many to lie unburied went unmourned and without a funeral of any kind, nor any place in the tomb of his ancestors.

¹¹ When these happenings were reported to the king, he thought that Judea was in revolt. Raging like a wild animal, he set out from Egypt and took Jerusalem by storm. ¹² He ordered his soldiers to cut down without mercy those whom they met and to slay those who took refuge in their houses. ¹³ There was a massacre of young and old, a killing of women and children, a slaughter of young women and infants. ¹⁴ In the space of three days, eighty thousand were lost, forty thousand meeting a violent death, and the same number being sold into slavery.

The Temple Is Pillaged

¹⁵ Not satisfied with this, the king dared to enter the holiest temple in the world; Menelaus, that traitor both to the laws and to his country, served as guide. ¹⁶ He laid his impure hands on the sacred vessels and swept up with profane hands the votive offerings made by other kings for the advancement, the glory, and the honor of the place. ¹⁷ Antiochus became puffed up in spirit, not realizing that it was because of the sins of the city's inhabitants that the Sovereign Lord was angry for a little while: hence the disregard of the place. ¹⁸ If they had not become entangled in so many sins, this man, like that Heliodorus sent by King Seleucus to inspect the treasury, would have been flogged and turned back from his presumptuous act as soon as he approached. ¹⁹ The Lord, however, had not chosen the nation for the sake of the place, but the place for the sake of the nation. ²⁰ Therefore, the place itself, having shared in the nation's misfortunes, afterward participated in their good fortune; and what the Almighty had forsaken in wrath was restored in all its glory, once the great Sovereign Lord became reconciled.

²¹ Antiochus carried off eighteen hundred talents from the temple and hurried back to Antioch, thinking in his arrogance that he could make the land navigable and the sea passable on foot, so carried away was he with pride. ²² He left governors to harass the nation: at Jerusalem, Philip, a Phrygian by birth, and in character more barbarous than the man who appointed him; ²³ at Mount Gerizim, Andronicus; and besides these, Menelaus, who lorded it over his fellow citizens more than the others. Out of hatred for the Jewish citizens, ²⁴ the king sent Apollonius, commander of the Mysians, at the head of an army of twenty-two thousand, with orders to kill all the grown men and sell the women and children into slavery. ²⁵ When this man arrived in Jerusalem, he pretended to be peacefully disposed and waited until the holy day of the Sabbath; then, finding the Jews refraining from work, he ordered his men to parade fully armed. ²⁶ All those who came out to watch, he massacred, and running through the city with armed men, he cut down a large number of people.

²⁷ But Judas Maccabeus and about nine others withdrew to the wilderness to avoid sharing in defilement; there he and his companions lived like the animals in the hills, eating what grew wild.

Judaism Is Suppressed

⁶:¹ Not long after this the king sent an Athenian senator to force the Jews to abandon the laws of their ancestors and live no longer by the laws of God, ² also to profane the temple in Jerusalem and dedicate it to Olympian Zeus, and the one on Mount Gerizim to Zeus the Host to Strangers, as the local inhabitants were wont to be. ³ This was a harsh and utterly intolerable evil. ⁴ The Gentiles filled the temple with debauchery and revelry; they amused themselves with prostitutes and had intercourse with women even in the sacred courts. They also brought forbidden things into the temple, ⁵ so that the altar was covered with abominable offerings prohibited by the laws.

⁶ No one could keep the Sabbath or celebrate the traditional feasts, nor even admit to being a Jew. ⁷ Moreover, at the monthly celebration of the king's birthday the Jews, from bitter necessity, had to partake of the sacrifices, and when the festival of Dionysus was celebrated, they were compelled to march in his procession, wearing wreaths of ivy.

⁸ Following upon a vote of the citizens of Ptolemais, a decree was issued ordering the neighboring Greek cities to adopt the same measures, obliging the Jews to partake of the sacrifices ⁹ and putting to death those who would not consent to adopt the customs of the Greeks. It was obvious, therefore, that disaster had come upon them. ¹⁰ Thus, two women who were arrested for having circumcised their children were publicly paraded about the city with their babies hanging at their breasts and then thrown down from the top of the city wall. ¹¹ Others, who had assembled in nearby caves to observe the seventh day in secret, were betrayed to Philip and all burned to death. In their respect for the holiness of that day, they refrained from defending themselves.

God's Purpose Explained

[12] Now I urge those who read this book not to be disheartened by these misfortunes, but to consider that these punishments were meant not for the ruin but for the correction of our nation. [13] It is, in fact, a sign of great kindness to punish the impious promptly instead of letting them go for long. [14] Thus, in dealing with other nations, the Sovereign Lord patiently waits until they reach the full measure of their sins before punishing them; but with us he has decided to deal differently, [15] in order that he may not have to punish us later, when our sins have reached their fullness. [16] Therefore he never withdraws his mercy from us. Although he disciplines us with misfortunes, he does not abandon his own people. [17] Let these words suffice for recalling this truth. Without further ado we must go on with our story.

Eleazar Is Martyred

[18] Eleazar, one of the foremost scribes, a man advanced in age and of noble appearance, was being forced to open his mouth to eat pork. [19] But preferring a glorious death to a life of defilement, he went forward of his own accord to the instrument of torture, [20] spitting out the meat as they should do who have the courage to reject food unlawful to taste even for love of life.

[21] Those in charge of that unlawful sacrifice took the man aside, because of their long acquaintance with him, and privately urged him to bring his own provisions that he could legitimately eat, and only to pretend to eat the sacrificial meat prescribed by the king. [22] Thus he would escape death, and be treated kindly because of his old friendship with them. [23] But he made up his mind in a noble manner, worthy of his years, the dignity of his advanced age, the merited distinction of his gray hair, and of the admirable life he had lived from childhood. Above all loyal to the holy laws given by God, he swiftly declared, "Send me to Hades!"

[24] "At our age it would be unbecoming to make such a pretense; many of the young would think the ninety-year-old Eleazar had gone over to an alien religion. [25] If I dissemble to gain a brief moment of life, they would be led astray by me, while I would bring defilement and dishonor on my old age. [26] Even if, for the time being, I avoid human punishment, I will never, whether alive or dead, escape the hand of the Almighty. [27] Therefore, by bravely giving up life now, I will prove myself worthy of my old age, [28] and I will leave to the young a noble example of how to die willingly and nobly for the revered and holy laws."

He spoke thus, and went immediately to the instrument of torture. [29] Those who shortly before had been kindly disposed, now became hostile toward him because what he had said seemed to them utter madness. [30] When he was about to die under the blows, he groaned, saying: "The Lord in his holy knowledge knows full well that, although I could have escaped death, I am not only enduring terrible pain in my body from this scourging, but also suffering it with joy in my soul because of my devotion to him." [31] This is how he died, leaving in his death a model of nobility and an unforgettable example of virtue not only for the young but for the whole nation.

Seven Brothers Are Martyred

7:1a It also happened that seven brothers with their mother were arrested and tortured with whips and scourges by the king to force them to eat pork in violation of God's law. 2 One of the brothers, speaking for the others, said: "What do you expect to learn by questioning us? We are ready to die rather than transgress the laws of our ancestors."

3 At that the king, in a fury, gave orders to have pans and caldrons heated. 4 These were quickly heated, and he gave the order to cut out the tongue of the one who had spoken for the others, to scalp him and cut off his hands and feet, while the rest of his brothers and his mother looked on. 5 When he was completely maimed but still breathing, the king ordered them to carry him to the fire and fry him. As a cloud of smoke spread from the pan, the brothers and their mother encouraged one another to die nobly, with these words: 6 "The Lord God is looking on and truly has compassion on us, as Moses declared in his song, when he openly bore witness, saying, 'And God will have compassion on his servants.'"

7 After the first brother had died in this manner, they brought the second to be made sport of. After tearing off the skin and hair of his head, they asked him, "Will you eat the pork rather than have your body tortured limb by limb?" 8 Answering in the language of his ancestors, he said, "Never!" So he in turn suffered the same tortures as the first. 9 With his last breath he said: "You accursed fiend, you are depriving us of this present life, but the King of the universe will raise us up to live again forever, because we are dying for his laws."

10 After him the third suffered their cruel sport. He put forth his tongue at once when told to do so, and bravely stretched out his hands, 11 as he spoke these noble words: "It was from Heaven that I received these; for the sake of his laws I disregard them; from him I hope to receive them again." 12 Even the king and his attendants marveled at the young man's spirit, because he regarded his sufferings as nothing.

13 After he had died, they tortured and maltreated the fourth brother in the same way. 14 When he was near death, he said, "It is my choice to die at the hands of mortals with the hope that God will restore me to life; but for you, there will be no resurrection to life." 15 They next brought forward the fifth brother and maltreated him. 16 Looking at the king, he said: "Mortal though you are, you have power over human beings, so you do what you please. But do not think that our nation is forsaken by God. 17 Only wait, and you will see how his great power will torment you and your descendants."

18 After him they brought the sixth brother. When he was about to die, he said: "Have no vain illusions. We suffer these things on our own account, because we have sinned against our God; that is why such shocking things have happened.

---

a. Heb. 11:35-38: "Women received their dead by resurrection. Others were tortured, refusing to accept release, in order to obtain a better resurrection. Others suffered mocking and flogging, and even chains and imprisonment. They were stoned to death, they were sawn in two, they were killed by the sword; they went about in skins of sheep and goats, destitute, persecuted, tormented by the world was not worthy. They wandered in deserts and mountains, and in caves and holes in the ground."

¹⁹ Do not think, then, that you will go unpunished for having dared to fight against God."

²⁰ Most admirable and worthy of everlasting remembrance was the mother who, seeing her seven sons perish in a single day, bore it courageously because of her hope in the Lord. ²¹ Filled with a noble spirit that stirred her womanly reason with manly emotion, she exhorted each of them in the language of their ancestors with these words: ²² "I do not know how you came to be in my womb; it was not I who gave you breath and life, nor was it I who arranged the elements you are made of. ²³ Therefore, since it is the Creator of the universe who shaped the beginning of humankind and brought about the origin of everything, he, in his mercy, will give you back both breath and life, because you now disregard yourselves for the sake of his law."

²⁴ Antiochus, suspecting insult in her words, thought he was being ridiculed. As the youngest brother was still alive, the king appealed to him, not with mere words, but with promises on oath, to make him rich and happy if he would abandon his ancestral customs: he would make him his Friend and entrust him with high office. ²⁵ When the youth paid no attention to him at all, the king appealed to the mother, urging her to advise her boy to save his life. ²⁶ After he had urged her for a long time, she agreed to persuade her son. ²⁷ She leaned over close to him and, in derision of the cruel tyrant, said in their native language: "Son, have pity on me, who carried you in my womb for nine months, nursed you for three years, brought you up, educated and supported you to your present age. ²⁸ I beg you, child, to look at the heavens and the earth and see all that is in them; then you will know that God did not make them out of existing things. In the same way humankind came into existence. ²⁹ Do not be afraid of this executioner, but be worthy of your brothers and accept death, so that in the time of mercy I may receive you again with your brothers."

³⁰ She had scarcely finished speaking when the youth said: "What is the delay? I will not obey the king's command. I obey the command of the law given to our ancestors through Moses. ³¹ But you, who have contrived every kind of evil for the Hebrews, will not escape the hands of God. ³² We, indeed, are suffering because of our sins. ³³ Though for a little while our living Lord has been angry, correcting and chastising us, he will again be reconciled with his servants. ³⁴ But you, wretch, most vile of mortals, do not, in your insolence, buoy yourself up with unfounded hopes, as you raise your hand against the children of heaven. ³⁵ You have not yet escaped the judgment of the almighty and all-seeing God. ³⁶ Our brothers, after enduring brief pain, have drunk of never-failing life, under God's covenant. But you, by the judgment of God, will receive just punishments for your arrogance. ³⁷ Like my brothers, I offer up my body and my life for our ancestral laws, imploring God to show mercy soon to our nation, and by afflictions and blows to make you confess that he alone is God. ³⁸ Through me and my brothers, may there be an end to the wrath of the Almighty that has justly fallen on our whole nation."

³⁹ At that, the king became enraged and treated him even worse than the others, since he bitterly resented the boy's contempt. ⁴⁰ Thus he too died undefiled, putting all his trust in the Lord. ⁴¹ Last of all, after her sons, the mother was put to death. ⁴² Enough has been said about the sacrificial meals and the excessive cruelties.

Judas Maccabeus Revolts

8:1 Judas Maccabeus and his companions entered the villages secretly, summoned their kindred, and enlisted others who had remained faithful to Judaism. Thus they assembled about six thousand men. 2 They implored the Lord to look kindly upon this people, who were being oppressed by all; to have pity on the sanctuary, which was profaned by renegades; 3 to have mercy on the city, which was being destroyed and was about to be leveled to the ground; to listen to the blood that cried out to him; 4 to remember the criminal slaughter of innocent children and the blasphemies uttered against his name; and to manifest his hatred of evil.

5 Once Maccabeus got his men organized, the Gentiles could not withstand him, for the Lord's wrath had now changed to mercy. 6 Coming by surprise upon towns and villages, he set them on fire. He captured strategic positions, and put to flight not a few of the enemy. 7 He preferred the nights as being especially favorable for such attacks. Soon talk of his valor spread everywhere.

8 When Philip saw that Judas was gaining ground little by little and that his successful advances were becoming more frequent, he wrote to Ptolemy, governor of Coelesyria and Phoenicia, to come to the aid of the king's interests. 9 Ptolemy promptly selected Nicanor, son of Patroclus, one of the Chief Friends, and sent him at the head of at least twenty thousand armed men of various nations to wipe out the entire Jewish nation. With him he associated Gorgias, a general, experienced in the art of war. 10 Nicanor planned to raise the two thousand talents of tribute owed by the king to the Romans by selling captured Jews into slavery. 11 So he immediately sent word to the coastal cities, inviting them to buy Jewish slaves and promising to deliver ninety slaves for a talent—little anticipating the punishment that was to fall upon him from the Almighty.

Judas Prepares for Battle

12 When Judas learned of Nicanor's advance and informed his companions about the approach of the army, 13 those who were fearful and those who lacked faith in God's justice deserted and got away. 14 But the others sold everything they had left, and at the same time entreated the Lord to deliver those whom the ungodly Nicanor had sold before even capturing them. 15 They entreated the Lord to do this, if not for their sake, at least for the sake of the covenants made with their ancestors, and because they themselves invoked his holy and glorious name. 16 Maccabeus assembled his forces, six thousand strong, and exhorted them not to be panic-stricken before the enemy, nor to fear the very large number of Gentiles unjustly attacking them, but to fight nobly. 17 They were to keep before their eyes the lawless outrage perpetrated by the Gentiles against the holy place and the affliction of the humiliated city, as well as the subversion of their ancestral way of life. 18 He said, "They trust in weapons and acts of daring, but we trust in almighty God, who can by a mere nod destroy not only those who attack us but even the whole world." 19 He went on to tell them of the times when help had been given their ancestors: both the time of Sennacherib, when a hundred and eighty-five thousand of his men perished, 20 and the time of the battle in Babylonia against

the Galatians, when only eight thousand Jews fought along with four thousand Macedonians; yet when the Macedonians were hard pressed, the eight thousand, by the help they received from Heaven, destroyed one hundred and twenty thousand and took a great quantity of spoils. [21] With these words he encouraged them and made them ready to die for their laws and their country.

Nicanor Is Defeated

Then Judas divided his army into four, [22] placing his brothers, Simon, Joseph, and Jonathan, each over a division, assigning them fifteen hundred men apiece. [23] There was also Eleazar. After reading to them from the holy book and giving them the watchword, "The help of God," Judas himself took charge of the first division and joined in battle with Nicanor. [24] With the Almighty as their ally, they killed more than nine thousand of the enemy, wounded and disabled the greater part of Nicanor's army, and put all of them to flight. [25] They also seized the money of those who had come to buy them as slaves. When they had pursued the enemy for some time, they were obliged to return by reason of the late hour. [26] It was the day before the Sabbath, and for that reason they could not continue the pursuit. [27] They collected the enemy's weapons and stripped them of their spoils, and then observed the Sabbath with fervent praise and thanks to the Lord who kept them safe for that day on which he allotted them the beginning of his mercy. [28] After the Sabbath, they gave a share of the spoils to those who were tortured and to widows and orphans; the rest they divided among themselves and their children. [29] When this was done, they made supplication in common, imploring the merciful Lord to be completely reconciled with his servants.

Timothy and Bacchidas Are Defeated

[30] They also challenged the forces of Timothy and Bacchides, killed more than twenty thousand of them, and captured some very high fortresses. They divided the considerable plunder, allotting half to themselves and the rest to victims of torture, orphans, widows, and the aged. [31] They collected the enemies' weapons and carefully stored them in strategic places; the rest of the spoils they carried to Jerusalem. [32] They also killed the commander of Timothy's forces, a most wicked man, who had done great harm to the Jews. [33] While celebrating the victory in their ancestral city, they burned both those who had set fire to the sacred gates and Callisthenes, who had taken refuge in a little house; so he received the reward his wicked deeds deserved.

[34] The thrice-accursed Nicanor, who had brought the thousand slave dealers to buy the Jews, [35] after being humbled through the Lord's help by those whom he had thought of no account, laid aside his fine clothes and fled alone across country like a runaway slave, until he reached Antioch. He was eminently successful in destroying his own army. [36] So he who had promised to provide tribute for the Romans by the capture of the people of Jerusalem proclaimed that the

Jews had a champion, and that because they followed the laws laid down by him, they were unharmed.

God Punishes Antiochus

9:1 About that time Antiochus retreated in disgrace from the region of Persia. 2 He had entered the city called Persepolis and attempted to rob the temples and gain control of the city. Thereupon the people had swift recourse to arms, and Antiochus' forces were routed, so that in the end Antiochus was put to flight by the people of that region and forced to beat a shameful retreat. 3 On his arrival in Ecbatana, he learned what had happened to Nicanor and to Timothy's forces. 4 Overcome with anger, he planned to make the Jews suffer for the injury done by those who had put him to flight. Therefore he ordered his charioteer to drive without stopping until he finished the journey. Yet the condemnation of Heaven rode with him, because he said in his arrogance, "I will make Jerusalem the common graveyard of Jews as soon as I arrive there."

5 So the all-seeing Lord, the God of Israel, struck him down with an incurable and invisible blow; for scarcely had he uttered those words when he was seized with excruciating pains in his bowels and sharp internal torment, 6 a fit punishment for him who had tortured the bowels of others with many barbarous torments. 7 Far from giving up his insolence, he was all the more filled with arrogance. Breathing fire in his rage against the Jews, he gave orders to drive even faster. As a result he hurtled from the speeding chariot, and every part of his body was racked by the violent fall. 8 Thus he who previously, in his superhuman presumption, thought he could command the waves of the sea, and imagined he could weigh the mountaintops in his scales, was now thrown to the ground and had to be carried on a litter, clearly manifesting to all the power of God. 9 The body of this impious man swarmed with worms, and while he was still alive in hideous torments, his flesh rotted off, so that the entire army was sickened by the stench of his corruption. 10 Shortly before, he had thought that he could reach the stars of heaven, and now, no one could endure to transport the man because of this intolerable stench.

11 At last, broken in spirit, he began to give up his excessive arrogance, and to gain some understanding, under the scourge of God, for he was racked with pain unceasingly. 12 When he could no longer bear his own stench, he said, "It is right to be subject to God, and not to think one's mortal self equal to God." 13 Then this vile man vowed to him who would never again show him mercy, the Sovereign Lord, 14 that the holy city, toward which he had been hurrying with the intention of leveling it to the ground and making it a common graveyard, he would now set free; 15 that the Jews, whom he had judged not even worthy of burial, but fit only to be thrown out with their children to be eaten by vultures and wild animals—all of them he would make equal to the Athenians; 16 that he would adorn with the finest offerings the holy temple which he had previously despoiled, restore all the sacred vessels many times over, and provide from his own revenues the expenses required for the sacrifices. 17 Besides all this, he would become a Jew himself and visit every inhabited place to proclaim there the power of God. 18 But since his

sufferings were not lessened, for God's just judgment had come upon him, he lost hope for himself and wrote the following letter to the Jews in the form of a supplication. It read thus:

Antiochus's Last Acts

[19] "To the worthy Jewish citizens, Antiochus, king and general, sends hearty greetings and best wishes for their health and prosperity. [20] If you and your children are well and your affairs are going as you wish, I thank God very much, for my hopes are in heaven. [21] Now that I am ill, I recall with affection your esteem and goodwill. On returning from the regions of Persia, I fell victim to a troublesome illness; so I thought it necessary to form plans for the general security of all. [22] I do not despair about my health, since I have much hope of recovering from my illness. [23] Nevertheless, I know that my father, whenever he went on campaigns in the hinterland, would name his successor, [24] so that, if anything unexpected happened or any unwelcome news came, the people throughout the realm would know to whom the government had been entrusted, and so not be disturbed. [25] I am also bearing in mind that the neighboring rulers, especially those on the borders of our kingdom, are on the watch for opportunities and waiting to see what will happen. I have therefore appointed as king my son Antiochus, whom I have often before entrusted and commended to most of you, when I made hurried visits to the outlying provinces. I have written to him what is written here. [26] Therefore I beg and entreat each of you to remember the general and individual benefits you have received, and to continue to show goodwill toward me and my son. [27] I am confident that, following my policy, he will treat you with equity and kindness in his relations with you."

[28] So this murderer and blasphemer, after extreme sufferings, such as he had inflicted on others, died a miserable death in the mountains of a foreign land. [29] His foster brother Philip brought the body home; but fearing Antiochus' son, he later withdrew into Egypt, to Ptolemy Philometor.

Judas Purifies the Temple

[10:1] When Maccabeus and his companions, under the Lord's leadership, had recovered the temple and the city, [2] they destroyed the altars erected by the foreigners in the marketplace and the sacred shrines. [3] After purifying the temple, they made another altar. Then, with fire struck from flint, they offered sacrifice for the first time in two years, burned incense, and lighted lamps. They also set out the showbread. [4] When they had done this, they prostrated themselves and begged the Lord that they might never again fall into such misfortunes, and that if they should sin at any time, he might chastise them with moderation and not hand them over to blasphemous and barbarous Gentiles. [5] On the anniversary of the day on which the temple had been profaned by the foreigners, that is, the twenty-fifth of the same month Kislev, the purification of the temple took place. [6] The Jews celebrated joyfully for eight days as on the feast of Booths, remembering how, a little while before, they had spent the feast of Booths living like wild animals in the mountains and in caves. ⁷ Carrying rods entwined with leaves, beautiful branches, and palms, they sang hymns of grateful praise to him who had successfully brought about the purification of his own place. ⁸ By public decree and vote they prescribed that the whole Jewish nation should celebrate these days every year. ⁹ Such was the end of Antiochus surnamed Epiphanes.

The Reign of Antiochus Eupator

¹⁰ Now we will relate what happened under Antiochus Eupator, the son of that godless man, and will give a summary of the chief evils caused by the wars. ¹¹ When Eupator succeeded to the kingdom, he put a certain Lysias in charge of the government as commander-in-chief of Coelesyria and Phoenicia. ¹² Ptolemy, called Macron, had taken the lead in treating the Jews fairly because of the previous injustice that had been done them, and he endeavored to have peaceful relations with them. ¹³ As a result, he was accused before Eupator by the King's Friends. In fact, on all sides he heard himself called a traitor for having abandoned Cyprus, which Philometor had entrusted to him, and for having gone over to Antiochus Epiphanes. Since he could not command the respect due to his high office, he ended his life by taking poison.

Judas Defeats Idumea and Timothy

¹⁴ When Gorgias became governor of the region, he employed foreign troops and used every opportunity to attack the Jews. ¹⁵ At the same time the Idumeans, who held some strategic strongholds, were harassing the Jews; they welcomed fugitives from Jerusalem and endeavored to continue the war. ¹⁶ Maccabeus and his companions, after public prayers asking God to be their ally, moved quickly against the strongholds of the Idumeans. ¹⁷ Attacking vigorously, they gained control of the places, drove back all who were fighting on the walls, and cut down those who opposed them, killing no fewer than twenty thousand. ¹⁸ When at least nine thousand took refuge in two very strong towers, well equipped to sustain a siege, ¹⁹ Maccabeus left Simon and Joseph, along with Zacchaeus and his forces, in sufficient numbers to besiege them, while he himself went off to places where he was more urgently needed. ²⁰ But some of those in Simon's force who were lovers of money let themselves be bribed by some of those in the towers; on receiving seventy thousand drachmas, they allowed a number of them to escape. ²¹ When Maccabeus was told what had happened, he assembled the rulers of the people and accused those men of having sold their kindred for money by setting their enemies free to fight against them. ²² So he put them to death as traitors, and without delay captured the two towers. ²³ As he was successful at arms in all his undertakings, he destroyed more than twenty thousand in the two strongholds.
²⁴ Timothy, who had previously been defeated by the Jews, gathered a tremendous force of foreign troops and collected a large number of cavalry from Asia; then he appeared in Judea, ready to conquer it by force. ²⁵ At his approach,

Maccabeus and his companions made supplication to God, sprinkling earth upon their heads and girding their loins in sackcloth. ²⁶ Lying prostrate at the foot of the altar, they begged him to be gracious to them, and to be an enemy to their enemies, and a foe to their foes, as the law declares. ²⁷ After the prayer, they took up their weapons and advanced a considerable distance from the city, halting when they were close to the enemy. ²⁸ As soon as dawn broke, the armies joined battle, the one having as pledge of success and victory not only their valor but also their reliance on the Lord, and the other taking fury as their leader in the fight.

²⁹ In the midst of the fierce battle, there appeared to the enemy five majestic men from the heavens riding on golden-bridled horses, leading the Jews. ³⁰ They surrounded Maccabeus, and shielding him with their own armor, kept him from being wounded. They shot arrows and hurled thunderbolts at the enemy, who were bewildered and blinded, routed in utter confusion. ³¹ Twenty thousand five hundred of their foot soldiers and six hundred cavalry were slain.

³² Timothy, however, fled to a well-fortified stronghold called Gazara, where Chaereas was in command. ³³ For four days Maccabeus and his forces eagerly besieged the fortress. ³⁴ Those inside, relying on the strength of the place, kept repeating outrageous blasphemies and uttering abominable words. ³⁵ When the fifth day dawned, twenty young men in the army of Maccabeus, angered over such blasphemies, bravely stormed the wall and with savage fury cut down everyone they encountered. ³⁶ Similarly, others climbed up and swung around on the defenders; they put the towers to the torch, spread the fire, and burned the blasphemers alive. Still others broke down the gates and let in the rest of the troops, who took possession of the city. ³⁷ Timothy had hidden in a cistern, but they killed him, along with his brother Chaereas, and Apollophanes. ³⁸ On completing these exploits, they blessed, with hymns of grateful praise, the Lord who shows great kindness to Israel and grants them victory.

Lysias Invades Judea

^{11:1} Very soon afterward, Lysias, guardian and kinsman of the king and head of the government, being greatly displeased at what had happened, ² mustered about eighty thousand infantry and all his cavalry and marched against the Jews. His plan was to make their city a Greek settlement; ³ to levy tribute on the temple, as he did on the shrines of the other nations; and to put the high priesthood up for sale every year. ⁴ He did not take God's power into account at all, but felt exultant confidence in his myriads of foot soldiers, his thousands of cavalry, and his eighty elephants. ⁵ So he invaded Judea, and when he reached Beth-zur, a fortified place about five stadia from Jerusalem, launched a strong attack against it.

⁶ When Maccabeus and his companions learned that Lysias was besieging the strongholds, they and all the people begged the Lord with lamentations and tears to send a good angel to save Israel. ⁷ Maccabeus himself was the first to take up arms, and he exhorted the others to join him in risking their lives to help their kindred. Then they resolutely set out together. ⁸ Suddenly, while they were still near Jerusalem, a horseman appeared at their head, clothed in white garments and brandishing gold weapons. ⁹ Then all of them together thanked the merciful God,

and their hearts were filled with such courage that they were ready to assault not only human beings but even the most savage beasts, or even walls of iron. [10] Now that the Lord had shown mercy toward them, they advanced in battle order with the aid of their heavenly ally. [11] Hurling themselves upon the enemy like lions, they laid low eleven thousand foot soldiers and sixteen hundred cavalry, and put all the rest to flight. [12] Most of those who survived were wounded and disarmed, while Lysias himself escaped only by shameful flight.

[13] But Lysias was not a stupid man. He reflected on the defeat he had suffered, and came to realize that the Hebrews were invincible because the mighty God was their ally. He therefore sent a message [14] persuading them to settle everything on just terms, and promising to persuade the king also, and to induce him to become their friend. [15] Maccabeus, solicitous for the common good, agreed to all that Lysias proposed; and the king granted on behalf of the Jews all the written requests of Maccabeus to Lysias.

Peace Agreements with the Jews

[16] These are the terms of the letter which Lysias wrote to the Jews: "Lysias sends greetings to the Jewish people. [17] John and Absalom, your envoys, have presented your signed communication and asked about the matters contained in it. [18] Whatever had to be referred to the king I called to his attention, and the things that were acceptable he has granted. [19] If you maintain your loyalty to the government, I will endeavor to further your interests in the future. [20] On the details of these matters I have authorized my representatives, as well as your envoys, to confer with you. [21] Farewell." The one hundred and forty-eighth year, the twenty-fourth of Dioscorinthius.

[22] The king's letter read thus: "King Antiochus sends greetings to his brother Lysias. [23] Now that our father has taken his place among the gods, we wish the subjects of our kingdom to be undisturbed in conducting their own affairs. [24] We have heard that the Jews do not agree with our father's change to Greek customs but prefer their own way of life. They are petitioning us to let them retain their own customs. [25] Since we desire that this people too should be undisturbed, our decision is that their temple be restored to them and that they live in keeping with the customs of their ancestors. [26] Accordingly, please send them messengers to give them our assurances of friendship, so that, when they learn of our decision, they may have nothing to worry about but may contentedly go about their own business."

[27] The king's letter to the people was as follows: "King Antiochus sends greetings to the Jewish senate and to the rest of the Jews. [28] If you are well, it is what we desire. We too are in good health. [29] Menelaus has told us of your wish to return home and attend to your own affairs. [30] Therefore, those who return by the thirtieth of Xanthicus will have our assurance of full permission [31] to observe their dietary and other laws, just as before, and none of the Jews will be molested in any way for faults committed through ignorance. [32] I have also sent Menelaus to reassure you. [33] Farewell." In the one hundred and forty-eighth year, the fifteenth of Xanthicus.

[34] The Romans also sent them a letter as follows: "Quintus Memmius and Titus Manius, legates of the Romans, send greetings to the Jewish people. [35] What Lysias, kinsman of the king, has granted you, we also approve. [36] But for the matters that he decided should be submitted to the king, send someone to us immediately with your decisions so that we may present them to your advantage, for we are on our way to Antioch. [37] Make haste, then, to send us those who can inform us of your preference. [38] Farewell." In the one hundred and forty-eighth year, the fifteenth of Xanthicus.

Conflict with Joppa and Jamnia

[12:1] After these agreements were made, Lysias returned to the king, and the Jews went about their farming. [2] But some of the local governors, Timothy and Apollonius, son of Gennaeus, as also Hieronymus and Demophon, to say nothing of Nicanor, the commander of the Cyprians, would not allow them to live in peace and quiet.

[3] Some people of Joppa also committed this outrage: they invited the Jews who lived among them, together with their wives and children, to embark on boats which they had provided. There was no hint of enmity toward them. [4] This was done by public vote of the city. When the Jews, wishing to live on friendly terms and not suspecting anything, accepted the invitation, the people of Joppa took them out to sea and drowned at least two hundred of them.

[5] As soon as Judas heard of the barbarous deed perpetrated against his compatriots, he summoned his men; [6] and after calling upon God, the just judge, he marched against the murderers of his kindred. In a night attack he set the harbor on fire, burned the boats, and put to the sword those who had taken refuge there. [7] Because the gates of the town were shut, he withdrew, intending to come back later and wipe out the entire population of Joppa.

[8] On hearing that the people of Jamnia planned in the same way to wipe out the Jews who lived among them, [9] he attacked the Jamnians by night, setting fire to the harbor and the fleet, so that the glow of the flames was visible as far as Jerusalem, thirty miles away.

[10] When the Jews had gone about a mile from there in the march against Timothy, they were attacked by Arabians numbering at least five thousand foot soldiers and five hundred cavalry. [11] After a hard fight, Judas and his companions, with God's help, were victorious. The defeated nomads begged Judas to give pledges of friendship, and they promised to supply the Jews with livestock and to be of service to them in any other way. [12] Realizing that they could indeed be useful in many respects, Judas agreed to make peace with them. After the pledges of friendship had been exchanged, the Arabians withdrew to their tents.

[13] He also attacked a certain city called Caspin, fortified with earthworks and walls and inhabited by a mixed population of Gentiles. [14] Relying on the strength of their walls and their supply of provisions, the besieged treated Judas and his men with contempt, insulting them and even uttering blasphemies and profanity. [15] But Judas and his men invoked the aid of the great Sovereign of the world, who, in the days of Joshua, overthrew Jericho without battering rams or siege

engines; then they furiously stormed the walls. [16] Capturing the city by the will of God, they inflicted such indescribable slaughter on it that the adjacent pool, which was about a quarter of a mile wide, seemed to be filled with the blood that flowed into it.

Judas Defeats Timothy

[17] When they had gone on some ninety miles, they reached Charax, where there were certain Jews known as Toubians. [18] But they did not find Timothy in that region, for he had already departed from there without having done anything except to leave behind in one place a very strong garrison. [19] But Dositheus and Sosipater, two of Maccabeus' captains, marched out and destroyed the force of more than ten thousand men that Timothy had left in the stronghold. [20] Meanwhile, Maccabeus divided his army into cohorts, with a commander over each cohort, and went in pursuit of Timothy, who had a force of a hundred and twenty thousand foot soldiers and twenty-five hundred cavalry. [21] When Timothy learned of the approach of Judas, he sent on ahead of him the women and children, as well as the baggage, to a place called Karnion, which was hard to besiege and even hard to reach because of the difficult terrain of that region. [22] But when Judas' first cohort appeared, the enemy was overwhelmed with fear and terror at the manifestation of the all-seeing One. Scattering in every direction, they rushed away in such headlong flight that in many cases they wounded one another, pierced by the points of their own swords. [23] Judas pressed the pursuit vigorously, putting the sinners to the sword and destroying as many as thirty thousand men.

[24] Timothy himself fell into the hands of those under Dositheus and Sosipater; but with great cunning, he begged them to spare his life and let him go, because he had in his power the parents and relatives of many of them, and would show them no consideration. [25] When he had fully confirmed his solemn pledge to restore them unharmed, they let him go for the sake of saving their relatives.

Other Victories

[26] Judas then marched to Karnion and the shrine of Atargatis, where he killed twenty-five thousand people. [27] After the defeat and destruction of these, he moved his army to Ephron, a fortified city inhabited by Lysias and people of many nationalities. Robust young men took up their posts in defense of the walls, from which they fought valiantly; inside were large supplies of war machines and missiles. [28] But the Jews, invoking the Sovereign who powerfully shatters the might of enemies, got possession of the city and slaughtered twenty-five thousand of the people in it.

[29] Then they set out from there and hastened on to Scythopolis, seventy-five miles from Jerusalem. [30] But when the Jews who lived there testified to the goodwill shown by the Scythopolitans and to their kind treatment even in times of adversity, [31] Judas and his men thanked them and exhorted them to be well dis-

posed to their nation in the future also. Finally they arrived in Jerusalem, shortly before the feast of Weeks.

³² After this feast, also called Pentecost, they lost no time in marching against Gorgias, governor of Idumea, ³³ who opposed them with three thousand foot soldiers and four hundred cavalry. ³⁴ In the ensuing battle, a few of the Jews were slain. ³⁵ A man called Dositheus, a powerful horseman and one of Bacenor's men, caught hold of Gorgias, grasped his military cloak, and dragged him along by brute strength, intending to capture the vile wretch alive, when a Thracian horseman attacked Dositheus and cut off his arm at the shoulder. Then Gorgias fled to Marisa.

³⁶ After Esdris and his men had been fighting for a long time and were weary, Judas called upon the Lord to show himself their ally and leader in the battle. ³⁷ Then, raising a battle cry in his ancestral language, and with hymns, he charged Gorgias' men when they were not expecting it and put them to flight.

Atonement for the Dead

³⁸ Judas rallied his army and went to the city of Adullam. As the seventh day was approaching, they purified themselves according to custom and kept the Sabbath there. ³⁹ On the following day, since the task had now become urgent, Judas and his companions went to gather up the bodies of the fallen and bury them with their kindred in their ancestral tombs. ⁴⁰ But under the tunic of each of the dead they found amulets sacred to the idols of Jamnia, which the law forbids the Jews to wear. So it was clear to all that this was why these men had fallen. ⁴¹ They all therefore praised the ways of the Lord, the just judge who brings to light the things that are hidden. ⁴² Turning to supplication, they prayed that the sinful deed might be fully blotted out. The noble Judas exhorted the people to keep themselves free from sin, for they had seen with their own eyes what had happened because of the sin of those who had fallen. ⁴³ He then took up a collection among all his soldiers, amounting to two thousand silver drachmas, which he sent to Jerusalem to provide for an expiatory sacrifice. In doing this he acted in a very excellent and noble way, inasmuch as he had the resurrection in mind; ⁴⁴ for if he were not expecting the fallen to rise again, it would have been superfluous and foolish to pray for the dead. ⁴⁵ But if he did this with a view to the splendid reward that awaits those who had gone to rest in godliness, it was a holy and pious thought. ⁴⁶ Thus he made atonement for the dead that they might be absolved from their sin.

Antiochus Eupator Tries to Invade Judea

¹³:¹ In the one hundred and forty-ninth year, Judas and his men learned that Antiochus Eupator was invading Judea with a large force, ² and that with him was Lysias, his guardian, who was in charge of the government. They led a Greek army of one hundred and ten thousand foot soldiers, fifty-three hundred cavalry, twenty-two elephants, and three hundred chariots armed with scythes.

³ Menelaus also joined them, and with great duplicity kept urging Antiochus on, not for the welfare of his country, but in the hope of being established in office. ⁴ But the King of kings aroused the anger of Antiochus against the scoundrel. When the king was shown by Lysias that Menelaus was to blame for all the trouble, he ordered him to be taken to Beroea and executed there in the customary local method. ⁵ There is at that place a tower seventy-five feet high, full of ashes, with a circular rim sloping down steeply on all sides toward the ashes. ⁶ Anyone guilty of sacrilege or notorious for certain other crimes is brought up there and then hurled down to destruction. ⁷ In such a manner was Menelaus, that transgressor of the law, fated to die, deprived even of burial. ⁸ It was altogether just that he who had committed so many sins against the altar with its pure fire and ashes, in ashes should meet his death.

⁹ The king was advancing, his mind full of savage plans for inflicting on the Jews things worse than those they suffered in his father's time. ¹⁰ When Judas learned of this, he urged the people to call upon the Lord day and night, now more than ever, to help them when they were about to be deprived of their law, their country, and their holy temple; ¹¹ and not to allow this people, which had just begun to revive, to be subjected again to blasphemous Gentiles. ¹² When they had all joined in doing this, and had implored the merciful Lord continuously with weeping and fasting and prostrations for three days, Judas encouraged them and told them to stand ready.

¹³ After a private meeting with the elders, he decided that, before the king's army could invade Judea and take possession of the city, the Jews should march out and settle the matter with God's help. ¹⁴ Leaving the outcome to the Creator of the world, and exhorting his followers to fight nobly to death for the laws, the temple, the city, the country, and the government, he encamped near Modein. ¹⁵ Giving his troops the battle cry "God's Victory," he made a night attack on the king's pavilion with a picked force of the bravest young men and killed about two thousand in the camp. He also stabbed the lead elephant and its rider. ¹⁶ Finally they withdrew in triumph, having filled the camp with terror and confusion. ¹⁷ Day was just breaking when this was accomplished with the help and protection of the Lord.

¹⁸ The king, having had a taste of the Jews' boldness, tried to take their positions by a stratagem. ¹⁹ So he marched against Beth-zur, a strong fortress of the Jews; but he was driven back, checked, and defeated. ²⁰ Judas sent supplies to the men inside, ²¹ but Rhodocus, of the Jewish army, betrayed military secrets to the enemy. He was found out, arrested, and imprisoned. ²² The king made a second attempt by negotiating with the people of Beth-zur. After giving them his pledge and receiving theirs, he withdrew ²³ and attacked Judas' men. But he was defeated. Next he heard that Philip, who was left in charge of the government in Antioch, had rebelled. Dismayed, he negotiated with the Jews, submitted to their terms, and swore to observe all their rights. Having come to this agreement, he offered a sacrifice, and honored the sanctuary and the place with a generous donation. ²⁴ He received Maccabeus, and left Hegemonides as governor of the territory from Ptolemais to the region of the Gerrhenes. ²⁵ When he came to Ptolemais, the people of Ptolemais were angered by the peace treaty; in fact they were so indignant that they wanted to annul its provisions. ²⁶ But Lysias took the platform, defended

the treaty as well as he could, and won them over by persuasion. After calming them and gaining their goodwill, he returned to Antioch. That is the story of the king's attack and withdrawal.

14:1 Three years later, Judas and his companions learned that Demetrius, son of Seleucus, had sailed into the port of Tripolis with a powerful army and a fleet, 2 and that he had occupied the country, after doing away with Antiochus and his guardian Lysias.

Alcimus Denounces Judas

3 A certain Alcimus, a former high priest, who had willfully incurred defilement before the time of the revolt, realized that there was no way for him to be safe and regain access to the holy altar. 4 So he went to King Demetrius around the one hundred and fifty-first year and presented him with a gold crown and a palm branch, as well as some of the customary olive branches from the temple. On that day he kept quiet. 5 But he found an opportunity to further his mad scheme when he was invited to the council by Demetrius and questioned about the dispositions and intentions of the Jews. He replied: 6 "Those Jews called Hasideans, led by Judas Maccabeus, are warmongers, who stir up sedition and keep the kingdom from enjoying peace. 7 For this reason, now that I am deprived of my ancestral dignity, that is to say, the high priesthood, I have come here, 8 first, out of my genuine concern for the king's interests, and second, out of consideration for my own compatriots, since our entire nation is suffering no little affliction from the rash conduct of the people just mentioned. 9 When you have informed yourself in detail on these matters, O king, provide for our country and its hard-pressed people with the same gracious consideration that you show toward all. 10 As long as Judas is around, it is impossible for the government to enjoy peace." 11 When he had said this, the other Friends who were hostile to Judas quickly added fuel to Demetrius' indignation.

Nicanor Appointed Governor

12 The king immediately chose Nicanor, who had been in command of the elephants, and appointed him governor of Judea. He sent him off 13 with orders to put Judas to death, to disperse his followers, and to set up Alcimus as high priest of the great temple. 14 The Gentiles from Judea, who had fled before Judas, flocked to Nicanor, thinking that the misfortunes and calamities of the Jews would mean prosperity for themselves.

15 When the Jews heard of Nicanor's coming, and that the Gentiles were rallying to him, they sprinkled themselves with earth and prayed to him who established his people forever, and who always comes to the aid of his heritage by manifesting himself. 16 At their leader's command, they set out at once from there and came upon the enemy at the village of Adasa. 17 Judas' brother Simon had engaged Nicanor, but he suffered a slight setback because of the sudden appearance of the enemy.

[18] However, when Nicanor heard of the valor of Judas and his companions, and the great courage with which they fought for their country, he shrank from deciding the issue by bloodshed. [19] So he sent Posidonius, Theodotus, and Mattathias to exchange pledges of friendship. [20] After a long discussion of the terms, each leader communicated them to his troops; and when general agreement was expressed, they assented to the treaty. [21] A day was set on which the leaders would meet by themselves. From each side a chariot came forward, and thrones were set in place. [22] Judas had posted armed men in readiness at strategic points for fear that the enemy might suddenly commit some treachery. But the conference was held in the proper way.

[23] Nicanor stayed on in Jerusalem, where he did nothing out of place. He disbanded the throngs of people who gathered around him; [24] and he always kept Judas in his company, for he felt affection for the man. [25] He urged him to marry and have children; so Judas married and settled into an ordinary life.

[26] When Alcimus saw their mutual goodwill, he took the treaty that had been made, went to Demetrius, and said that Nicanor was plotting against the government, for he had appointed Judas, that conspirator against the kingdom, as his successor. [27] Stirred up by the villain's slander, the king became enraged. He wrote to Nicanor, stating that he was displeased with the treaty, and ordering him to send Maccabeus at once as a prisoner to Antioch. [28] When this message reached Nicanor he was dismayed and troubled at the thought of annulling his agreement with a man who had done no wrong. [29] However, there was no way of opposing the king, so he watched for an opportunity to carry out this order by a stratagem. [30] But Maccabeus, noticing that Nicanor was more harsh in his dealings with him, and acting with unaccustomed rudeness when they met, concluded that this harshness was not a good sign. So he gathered together not a few of his men, and went into hiding from Nicanor.

[31] When Nicanor realized that he had been cleverly outwitted by the man, he went to the great and holy temple, at a time when the priests were offering the customary sacrifices, and ordered them to surrender Judas. [32] As they declared under oath that they did not know where the man they sought was, [33] he stretched out his right arm toward the temple and swore this oath: "If you do not hand Judas over to me as prisoner, I will level this shrine of God to the ground; I will tear down the altar, and erect here a splendid temple to Dionysus."

[34] With these words he went away. The priests stretched out their hands toward heaven, calling upon the unfailing defender of our nation in these words: [35] "Lord of all, though you are in need of nothing, you were pleased to have a temple for your dwelling place among us. [36] Therefore, Holy One, Lord of all holiness, preserve forever undefiled this house, which has been so recently purified."

The Death of Razis

[37] A certain Razis, one of the elders of Jerusalem, was denounced to Nicanor as a patriot. A man highly regarded, he was called a father of the Jews because of his goodwill toward them. [38] In the days before the revolt, he had been convicted of being a Jew, and had risked body and soul in his ardent zeal for Judaism. [39] Ni-

canor, to show his disdain for the Jews, sent more than five hundred soldiers to arrest him. ⁴⁰ He thought that by arresting that man he would deal the Jews a hard blow.

⁴¹ But when the troops, on the point of capturing the tower, were forcing the outer gate and calling for fire to set the door ablaze, Razis, now caught on all sides, turned his sword against himself, ⁴² preferring to die nobly rather than fall into the hands of vile men and suffer outrages unworthy of his noble birth. ⁴³ In the excitement of the struggle he failed to strike exactly. So while the troops rushed in through the doors, he gallantly ran up to the top of the wall and courageously threw himself down into the crowd. ⁴⁴ But as they quickly drew back and left an opening, he fell into the middle of the empty space. ⁴⁵ Still breathing, and inflamed with anger, he got up and ran through the crowd, with blood gushing from his frightful wounds. Then, standing on a steep rock, ⁴⁶ as he lost the last of his blood, he tore out his entrails and flung them with both hands into the crowd, calling upon the Lord of life and of spirit to give these back to him again. Such was the manner of his death.

Nicanor Attacks Judas

¹⁵:¹ When Nicanor learned that Judas and his companions were in the territory of Samaria, he decided he could attack them in complete safety on the day of rest. ² The Jews who were forced to accompany him pleaded, "Do not massacre them so savagely and barbarously, but show respect for the day which the All-seeing has exalted with holiness above all other days." ³ At this the thrice-accursed wretch asked if there was a ruler in heaven who prescribed the keeping of the Sabbath day. ⁴ They replied, "It is the living Lord, the ruler in heaven, who commands the observance of the Sabbath day." ⁵ Then he said, "I, the ruler on earth, command you to take up arms and carry out the king's business." Nevertheless he did not succeed in carrying out his cruel plan.

⁶ In his utter boastfulness and arrogance Nicanor had determined to erect a public victory monument over Judas and his companions. ⁷ But Maccabeus remained confident, fully convinced that he would receive help from the Lord. ⁸ He urged his men not to fear the attack of the Gentiles, but mindful of the help they had received in the past from Heaven, to expect now the victory that would be given them by the Almighty. ⁹ By encouraging them with words from the law and the prophets, and by reminding them of the battles they had already won, he filled them with fresh enthusiasm. ¹⁰ Having stirred up their courage, he gave his orders and pointed out at the same time the perfidy of the Gentiles and their violation of oaths. ¹¹ When he had armed each of them, not so much with the security of shield and spear as with the encouragement of noble words, he cheered them all by relating a dream, a kind of waking vision, worthy of belief.

¹² What he saw was this: Onias, the former high priest, a noble and good man, modest in bearing, gentle in manner, distinguished in speech, and trained from childhood in all that belongs to excellence, was praying with outstretched arms for the whole Jewish community. ¹³ Then in the same way another man appeared, distinguished by his white hair and dignity, and with an air of wondrous and

majestic authority. [14] Onias then said of him, "This is a man who loves his fellow Jews and fervently prays for the people and the holy city—the prophet of God, Jeremiah." [15] Stretching out his right hand, Jeremiah presented a gold sword to Judas. As he gave it to him he said, [16] "Accept this holy sword as a gift from God; with it you will shatter your adversaries."

[17] Encouraged by Judas' words, so noble and capable of instilling valor and stirring young hearts to courage, they determined not merely to march, but to charge gallantly and decide the issue by hand-to-hand combat with the utmost courage, since city, sanctuary, and temple were in danger. [18] They were not so much concerned about wives and children, or family and relations; their first and foremost fear was for the consecrated sanctuary. [19] Those who were left in the city suffered no less an agony, anxious as they were about the battle in the open country. [20] Everyone now awaited the decisive moment. The enemy were already drawing near with their troops drawn up in battle line, their beasts placed in strategic positions, and their cavalry stationed on the flanks.

Judas Defeats Nicanor

[21] Maccabeus, surveying the hosts before him, the variety of weaponry, and the fierceness of their beasts, stretched out his hands toward heaven and called upon the Lord who works wonders; for he knew that it is not weapons but the Lord's decision that brings victory to those who deserve it. [22] Calling upon God, he spoke in this manner: "You, master, sent your angel in the days of King Hezekiah of Judea, and he slew a hundred and eighty-five thousand men of Sennacherib's camp. [23] And now, Sovereign of the heavens, send a good angel to spread fear and trembling ahead of us. [24] By the might of your arm may those be struck down who have blasphemously come against your holy people!" With these words he ended his prayer.

[25] Nicanor and his troops advanced to the sound of trumpets and battle songs. [26] But Judas and his troops met the enemy with supplication and prayers. [27] Fighting with their hands and praying to God with their hearts, they laid low at least thirty-five thousand, and rejoiced greatly over this manifestation of God's power. [28] When the battle was over and they were joyfully departing, they discovered Nicanor fallen there in all his armor; [29] so they raised tumultuous shouts in their ancestral language in praise of the divine Sovereign.

[30] Then Judas, that man who was ever in body and soul the chief defender of his fellow citizens, and had maintained from youth his affection for his compatriots, ordered Nicanor's head and right arm up to the shoulder to be cut off and taken to Jerusalem. [31] When he arrived there, he assembled his compatriots, stationed the priests before the altar, and sent for those in the citadel. [32] He showed them the vile Nicanor's head and the wretched blasphemer's arm that had been boastfully stretched out against the holy dwelling of the Almighty. [33] He cut out the tongue of the godless Nicanor, saying he would feed it piecemeal to the birds and would hang up the other wages of his folly opposite the temple. [34] At this, everyone looked toward heaven and praised the Lord who manifests himself: "Blessed be the one who has preserved undefiled his own place!" [35] Judas hung

Nicanor's head and arm on the wall of the citadel, a clear and evident sign to all of the Lord's help. 36 By public vote it was unanimously decreed never to let this day pass unobserved, but to celebrate the thirteenth day of the twelfth month, called Adar in Aramaic, the eve of Mordecai's Day.

Epilogue

37 Since Nicanor's doings ended in this way, with the city remaining in the possession of the Hebrews from that time on, I will bring my story to an end here too. 38 If it is well written and to the point, that is what I wanted; if it is poorly done and mediocre, that is the best I could do. 39 Just as it is unpleasant to drink wine by itself or just water, whereas wine mixed with water makes a delightful and pleasing drink, so a skillfully composed story delights the ears of those who read the work. Let this, then, be the end.

The Writings of Flavius Josephus

Josephus was a member of Jerusalem's hereditary priestly caste: an aristocrat, landowner, politician, ambassador, soldier, and writer. We know the year of his birth (37–38 CE; *Life* 5) but not that of his death (*see* Josephus, *Life*). Since he dates his major literary work to 93/94 CE (see below), but composed three volumes after that, he must have lived until at least 95/96 CE and possibly into the early second century CE. He was about twenty when Paul was being tried in Judea (late 50s CE) before being sent to Rome. Josephus himself traveled to Rome in 63/64 CE, on a mission to free some friends who had been sent to the emperor Nero in chains (*Life* 13–16)—just as the apostle Paul was. As a writer composing in the shadow of Jerusalem's fall (70 CE), Josephus was a contemporary of the Gospel writers.

In 66 CE, soon after his return to Judea from his successful Roman mission, war with Rome broke out. This conflict had begun because of local outrage over the behavior of successive governors in Judea, which combined with long-standing tensions between Judeans and their near neighbors in the coastal and inland (Decapolis) cities.

Josephus claims that many men of his class, including the chief-priestly commanders of the early war effort, were not rebel enthusiasts (*Life* 17–22). They were caught between their need to appear supportive of the people's anger and their own desire to wind down the conflict and reach peaceful terms with Rome. Because of his high social status, Josephus found himself leading part of the war effort: in Galilee, north of Judea proper, and Samaria. This was the first area the Roman legions struck when they arrived to quell the revolt in the spring of 67 CE. They had gathered from different provinces in the Roman colony of Ptolemais (modern-day Acco) on the coast. Once the Romans began their systematic subjection of Galilee under **Vespasian** and his son **Titus,** it was not long before Josephus had to surrender. He had found refuge in the strongest hilltop town available, Iotapata, but Vespasian and Titus besieged that town with three legions and thousands of auxiliary troops. After some weeks of this, they broke through Iotapata's defensive wall (*see* Map of First-Century Palestine, p. 44). While other leading men, hiding in a cave with Josephus, took their own lives so as not to face the shame of capture and risk of terrible abuse, Josephus claims that he avoided this fate because God had given him a message. As a priest he had been able to decipher from scriptural mysteries, illuminated by dream revelations, that Vespasian and Titus would soon rise to power in place of the current ruler Nero (*War* 3.350–54, 399–408).

According to the story, Vespasian kept his new prisoner in chains until Nero's death, when the rapid succession of other generals contending for power made him also a strong candidate, with the support of his many troops in Judea. In gratitude, he released Josephus, who then assisted Titus throughout the rest of the campaign: providing local intelligence, translating between local Aramaic and Greek, interviewing prisoners and refugees, and calling on the rebel leaders in Jerusalem to surrender (*Apion* 1.48–49). Jerusalem fell to the Romans in September 70 CE, and the following spring Josephus sailed to Rome with the conquering general Titus, not as a captured enemy general but as a free Roman citizen—his likely Latin name Titus Flavius Josephus complementing his Aramaic birth-name, Yoseph bar Mattityahu (Joseph son of Mattathias).

Josephus was not extremely well rewarded for his services, however. He received no prized land in Italy, no political rank in Rome (for himself or his children), and no place among the rulers' trusted counselors, as far as we know. It seems that he would have reported anything of this kind that had come his way because he does exuberantly list the benefits granted by the **Flavians:** Roman citizenship, some land in Judea to compensate for lost real estate in Jerusalem, some kind of financial maintenance, and at least initial accommodation in Vespasian's private house, from before his rise to power (*Life* 413–29). Josephus appears, then, to have been comfortable in Rome and, perhaps most important, protected from his enemies. Following the lead of many statesmen, in retirement from public life this thirty-five-year-old embarked on an energetic writing career. Over the next twenty-five or thirty years, he would write at least four works in thirty volumes.

For most ancient authors, even such famous ones as **Polybius** and **Tacitus,** we are missing large sections of their work. In Josephus's case, because his writing would be so highly valued by the early Christians as context for the New Testament, the four works mentioned were frequently copied and so have reached us more or less intact. His two main works are historical narratives, the *Jewish War* and the *Jewish Antiquities,* accounting for twenty-seven of the thirty volumes; the other three comprise his autobiography *(Life)* and a two-volume essay misleadingly known as *Against Apion.*

Author/Provenance

Older scholarship recognized the fairly high literary register of Josephus's writings, but could not believe that he—a Pharisee (as it was thought) from the provincial backwater of Judea—had the Greek education needed to produce such work. In the late nineteenth and early twentieth centuries, therefore, Josephus was widely thought to have borrowed, heavily and directly, from writers who were more talented. According to this view, he lifted most of the biblical paraphrase (*Antiquities* 1–11) and the sharp-witted polemic of *Apion* from more sophisticated Alexandrian-Jewish writers, while turning to Herod's learned aide Nicolaus of Damascus and official Roman sources for most of the *War* and the later volumes of the *Antiquities*. Josephus was viewed as essentially a copyist or anthologist of other people's work, a model also applied to many other ancient writers at the time. Even his own modest contributions, some scholars thought, owed more to the literary collaborators he briefly mentions in *Apion* 1.50 than to himself.[1]

Assumptions have changed nowadays, for many reasons. The old model of Josephus's writing procedure attributed the many contradictions and inconsistencies between the *War* and the *Antiquities/Life*, in their parallel coverage of the same material, to his use of different sources. Already in 1920 Richard Laqueur showed that the same kinds of differences that scholars found between (say) Josephus's two portraits of Herod, in the *War* and the *Antiquities,* which they attributed to different sources, were also apparent in his two versions of his own life story (in the *War* and the *Life*), and obviously *these* differences could not be explained by different sources—since his own life was the subject. Rather, Laqueur argued, Josephus was a "reason-endowed being like us," a creative writer in Greek who made the deliberate decision to retell his stories in different ways.

Second, scholars had to come to terms with ancient conceptions of history writing, which are very different from our own. Whereas we are bothered by conflicting accounts of the same events because we want to know *what really happened,* the Greco-Roman educational system aimed to produce men proficient in rhetoric, and this training emphasized the skill of telling the same story in very different ways. History writing was not an academic profession in antiquity, but was undertaken by men who shared this rhetorical education and the outlook that went with it. Getting at factual truth was not understood in the same way, or given the same priority, as in our world. Even the best ancient historians, such as **Thucydides,** say little if anything about *how they know* what they describe. They are mainly interested in talking about political morality and personal character, and in drawing different moral lessons from whatever material is available to them.

Third, and most important, since the 1980s we have had tools available for closely studying Josephus's language. First came the *Complete Concordance* (finished in 1983 [Brill]) and then a variety of electronic resources for searching his texts along with all other known Greek literature. With these remarkable tools, we no longer need to guess about what is Josephus's distinctive language and what might have been taken completely from a source. If we are wondering whether a certain passage was borrowed, we can test its language. If we find that it includes a number of terms and phrases that show up repeatedly in the *War,* but are hardly found in thousands of other ancient Greek texts, we may be confident that the person who wrote the *War* passage also wrote the passage we are wondering about (or that a later forger had the great skill to imitate the language of the work). It might well have *originated* in a written or oral source—in fact, anything outside Josephus's personal knowledge that he did not invent *must* have come from some such source—but it makes all the difference in the world to know that he wrote the account *as it stands*. It completely changes our view of him as an author, if he

---

1. Josephus, *Apion* 1.50: "Then, when I had leisure in Rome, and when all the work was prepared, having made use of some collaborators for the Greek language, I thus constructed my account of the events. So confident was I of its truthfulness that I decided to use as my witnesses, before everyone else, the commanders-in-chief during the war, Vespasian and Titus."

was personally capable of using cultured Greek and of thinking the sophisticated thoughts that we now read. This conclusion also has implications for our understanding of Greek education among Jerusalem's elite class.

This new kind of analysis allows us to explore similarities and differences between Josephus and other ancient writers. Those others include the great models of classical education, from centuries before his time, as well as his contemporaries at the end of the first century CE. Among the models, we find many parallels of language between Josephus and **Herodotus,** Thucydides, **Xenophon,** Polybius, **Diodorus of Sicily,** and **Dionysius of Halicarnassus.** He also seems well acquainted with the famous Greek tragedies (by **Aeschylus,** Sophocles, and Euripides) and the speeches of orators such as Demosthenes. There are surprisingly close parallels with Philo of Alexandria, a Jewish writer who died when Josephus was in his teens (*see* Philo of Alexandria), and with the contemporary Greek authors **Plutarch** and **Dio Chrysostom.** These last parallels have to do not only with elements of style (e.g., the new old-fashioned **Atticism**) and current vocabulary, but also subject matter. Josephus, Plutarch, and Dio Chrysostom were all political leaders concerned with managing affairs in their cities under Roman rule.

It emerges from all this that Josephus had the normal sort of education for young men in the Greek-speaking aristocracies of the eastern Mediterranean, and that he had fully absorbed the common values. As a member of Jerusalem's hereditary elite, he saw his task as, on the one hand, representing his people's traditions and concerns, but on the other hand, keeping the masses peaceful, productive, and loyal to Rome in spite of the inevitable humiliations of foreign domination. His works are all about these kinds of concerns: the Judean constitution and laws and the disastrous intersection of events that brought about Jerusalem's recent destruction. His assumptions, methods, and criteria are those taught by rhetorical education. He is concerned with exploring issues of personal and national *character:* not only distinguishing leaders who have the common good at heart from self-serving troublemakers (or "tyrants") who mislead the crowds for personal gain, but also typical groups in the rhetorical arsenal. These include the "hot-headed youths" who could be counted on to respond violently to any provocation (usually making everything worse), their wiser elders, the ever-present crowds of wailing women and children, and "bandits"—a term in Greek and Latin for those who occupy zones outside society and its laws. Like his contemporaries, Josephus frequently draws on these commonplaces, which were familiar to everyone who had received the standard rhetorical education.

For many of the ancient Jewish texts in this volume, especially the anonymous ones, we have no choice but to be cautious in making claims about their audiences. If we do not even know who wrote it, we can only try to place a text against various backgrounds to look for the best match. Josephus's works are different, partly because we are aware that Josephus wrote these works in Flavian Rome, partly because we know something about book production in Roman literary circles at the time, and partly because of his specific remarks about intended and real audiences.

First, we must rid our thinking of modern ideas about publication. Our assumptions depend on the existence of printing presses. I write this chapter in the privacy of my study, trying to *imagine* my "audience" but not expecting that I will ever meet them. When I am finished, I send my work electronically to editors in other cities, who send their completed volumes to the publisher in another city, where staff lay out the final book and secure thousands of identical copies from a printer before marketing the work to the "audiences" intended by authors, editors, and publisher. By the time the book reaches these audiences, it has long since left my hands and I have no control over sales, use, or interpretation.

In the Roman world the situation was nearly reversed because of the very different technologies available, which obviously did not include printing or digital communication. There were no publishing houses and no booksellers in our sense of the words—with stacks of identical warehoused copies. Every single book (a "book" being a long roll of papyrus sheets joined at the ends or a collection of such rolls) had to be written out by someone's hand. Because they were usually written without spaces between words or paragraphs, reading them visually was a tedious affair (privately reading letters or poems was different and common). But this was an oral culture in which texts were normally written and read *by speaking*. That is, authors normally dictated their work to slave-secretaries (as the apostle Paul dictated his letters), and on the other side of the communicative line, once they had been written they were usually read aloud. This reading might be private, in which case a wealthy person would have his slave read to him. We might compare modern audio books. For literary works, it was normal for an author to recite his new work, in draft, to ever-expanding groups of friends and associates, perhaps beginning with a dinner party and moving gradually to larger auditoriums. The Greek-Syrian writer **Lucian,** a couple of generations after Josephus, in his essay on history writing speaks always about *hearing* histories being read by their authors—and sometimes walking out in disgust at the bad writing.[2]

It was also common to share written sections of books with friends, to solicit their comment or correction, but again these would normally be read aloud by a slave. As we know from listening to audio books, or from reading our own writing aloud as a way of proofing it, sound adds a completely different dimension to words on a page. With oral presentation in mind, ancient writers were all the more careful to incorporate the principles of rhetoric into their compositions: constant variety (change of scene and type of material), excitement, creation and resolution of tension, vivid action scenes (especially bloody battles), the use of powerful speeches, and word pictures of exotic geographical settings or other pleasant scenes.

Therefore, producing a book in the Roman world was by definition a local and social matter, not something done in a private study and shipped abroad. This meant that the author's intended "audiences" were above all, in the literal sense, his physical hearers. He planned to face them and present his work to them. They would include friends, open-minded listeners interested in new compositions for entertainment, and the inevitable harsh-mind critics looking to expose others' weaknesses. This has all sorts of implications for understanding Roman-period literature. For example, when writers of the time talked about speaking "truth" in history, they were not so much referring to acquiring verifiable facts

---

2. Lucian, *How History Should Be Written* 5, 7, 10, 14, 28, 29, 40, 51.

and showing how they did that. They were talking more about the moral courage needed when addressing real audiences to avoid the temptation of flattering the powerful, especially if they happened to be sitting there in the audience (or they would likely hear about the recital from those who were present). The historian, everyone agreed, must be resolute in speaking about all parties' behavior *without fear or favor,* without flattering his friends[3] or those in a position to help his career or denigrating those who could hurt his career. Equally, the historian must avoid excessive denigration of the weak, or enemies, or those far away, who could do no harm to the author. Telling the truth meant, above all, fairness and *moral fearlessness.* Everyone talked about these values, but it was common for authors to profess fairness ("truthfulness") while still flattering the powerful and denigrating their enemies.

This is precisely the world we meet in the prologue to Josephus's *War.* He observes that at his time of writing, in the 70s CE, others *are collecting* and writing up stories about the recent Judean conflict (1.1–2, 7, 9), suggesting an ongoing activity that he has been hearing, not finished books read in his study. He remarks that "I am about *to speak*" to those who know his life story (1.22). He also implies that certain Greek intellectuals in Rome have been criticizing his work on the war—that is, before he writes this prologue—for his imperfections in using the Greek language (1.13, 16). We know from the Syrian writer Lucian, who also wrote Greek, that this kind of criticism was a favorite sport among native Greek literary men. This apparently means that Josephus has been reciting drafts of his work, in the expected way. The situation is a lively give-and-take in his adopted home city.

Throughout his works, Josephus shows that he is expecting an audience of Greek-speakers in the bilingual world capital where he lives. We need to remember that, unlike our world, in which ordinary folks have a great appetite for books and easy access to them in various forms, in Josephus's time those who had the education and leisure to attend literary recitals were a very small group. He characterizes the *War'*s audience as "Greeks and those Romans who did not march against us" (1.6). This may sound as though he were writing for everyone in the eastern Mediterranean. But he had no way of reaching them (there was not even a postal service), no way of mass-producing copies, and no bookstores or publisher. Most importantly, only a small fraction of even the Greek-speaking world had the education to appreciate the sort of work he was writing. The vast majority of the population was illiterate.

Like many writers, Josephus did hope that his writings would endure to be read by the "world," but his immediately expected audiences, the ones he says that he hoped to influence, were local. When he singles out "those Romans who did not fight in Judea" he is only being polite. When professors are invited to give public lectures to large audiences at other universities, academic specialists from the host institution will usually attend as a courtesy, and the speaker might acknowledge them by noting that the talk will not be new *for them* since they are specialists in

---

3. "His" because this was an exclusive male culture. There were powerful and wealthy women in Roman society, but their power was rarely exercised visibly in these literary circles. Rhetoric was almost by definition a male pursuit (for society's leaders) and those who taught oratory spoke often of manly kinds of gestures and voices.

the material. In the same way, Josephus is suggesting that, since he is only telling the facts about the recent war, those who were there have nothing to learn from him. But of course they *do* because of his unique access to both sides (*War* 1.1–3). In any case, when he finishes the *War* and presents a few slave-produced copies to associates, most of the recipients he names are those who *did* participate in the conflict. He mentions them because he cites them as witnesses to his truthfulness, as they know the truth and would object if he had lied (*Life* 361–63; *Apion* 1.50–51). But again, the recipients of these courtesy copies of the physical book were not the only audience he was trying to influence when he was "publishing"—that is, "making public"—his history. Those audiences, mentioned incidentally in the *War*'s prologue (1.1–2, 8–9, 13–16), appear to be all those involved in the literary give-and-take concerning the recent war: the authors promoting accounts he considers false, literary connoisseurs who will listen to anyone but mainly look for faults, powerful people who might be influenced by the other accounts, and Josephus's friends and supporters among both Judeans and upper-class Romans.

We actually know a few of the relevant names. For the *War,* Josephus claims that he shared drafts of specific volumes with Agrippa II, the great-grandson of Herod the Great, who (with his sister Berenice—Titus's lover) was often present in Rome during the 70s CE. Josephus and the king maintained a lively correspondence about his work, with occasional face-to-face consultations (*Life* 364–66). If these contacts were as supportive as Josephus claims, Agrippa II was a patron who would have helped promote Josephus's work, possibly inviting his distinguished friends to recitals.

Josephus dedicates all his later works to a Greek man of affairs named **Epaphroditus,** who cannot be confidently identified with other men of the same name. We first meet him when Josephus elaborately thanks him for his strong encouragement to complete the lengthy *Antiquities* (*Antiquities* 1.8–9; *Life* 430; *Apion* 1.1; 2.1, 278). There is no reason to imagine that Josephus's audiences changed significantly between the *War* and the later works, except that Agrippa II returned to his territories northeast of Judea. It seems easiest to understand Epaphroditus's encouragement over the *Antiquities* if he had been part of Josephus's circle also for earlier work. Moreover, the fact that Josephus often refers his later audiences to the *War*[4] suggests that they also know his first work.

In any case, Josephus consistently claims to write for Greek audiences in Rome. In *Antiquities* 1.9–12 he reflects that the sharing of excellent things with the Greek world is a Judean trait, begun by the high priest **Eleazar,** who three centuries earlier had sent scholars to translate the Septuagint in response to a Greek request (*see* Letter of Aristeas; Overview of Early Jewish Literature); Josephus is only continuing the practice now (cf. 20.262). In keeping with this implied audience, he is nearly always careful to explain even the most basic aspects of Judean culture—the major festivals, laws, Sabbath practice, and circumcision.[5] By contrast, he assumes his audience's knowledge of Roman politics, history, and personalities.[6]

---

4. *Antiquities* 1.4–7, 203; 13.72; 18.11; 20.258–59; *Life* 12, 27–28; *Apion* 1.46–54.

5. *War* 1.146, 152–53, 270; 2.1–5, 10, 155–56, 170, 313; 4.317; *Antiquities* 1.21–23, 33, 128–29; 3.317; 14.3; 17.254; *Life* 1–2, 7, 12, 26, 31, 65, 80, 128, 171, 269, 279, 321.

6. *War* 1.118, 127–28, 162, 183, 243, 400; 2.25, 247, 250–51; 4.40, 469; *Life* 13–16, 407–29.

This does not mean that fellow Judeans were somehow forbidden from attending his recitals or from reading his works, of course. No doubt many of his compatriots particularly enjoyed his work, and we have seen that he presented copies of the *War* to members of the Herodian family. In *Antiquities* 4.197 he self-consciously explains that he has taken the liberty of systematizing Moses' laws, in case one of his countrymen should come upon the narrative and criticize him for departing from Scripture. But even in conceding this, he is addressing a non-Judean Greek audience in Rome, of the sort represented by Epaphroditus and that circle.

We can see from the style and level of his work that Josephus expects a certain kind of literate, worldly-wise Greek-speaking audience, who will appreciate his efforts: the high register of vocabulary and sentence structure (NB: the *War*'s opening sentence is a demanding run of paired opposites—Greek: *men . . . de*— in 264 words), the magnificent speeches, the allusions to famous Greek authors (these are hidden treasures for the audience to find), the tragic tone of the *War* and clear allusions to Greek tragic plays, and the discussion of typical complexities faced by political leaders. All of this would be wasted on audiences lacking the appropriate background. It is not popular preaching for the street corner.

Text, Language, Sources, and Transmission

As we have seen, Josephus wrote in Greek. In the *War*'s prologue (1.3, 6), however, he tantalizingly mentions some earlier work of his on the same subject, in his native language. He remarks that he had written this for people living across the Euphrates in the east (the provisional frontier of the Roman Empire), including Judeans in the Parthian kingdom (roughly modern Iraq, Iran, Afghanistan, and Pakistan; *see* Map of the Parthian Kingdom in Relation to the Roman World, p. 41). Presumably, the language in question was Aramaic, rather than Hebrew, since Aramaic was spoken throughout the Parthian world. Unfortunately, we have no trace of this earlier writing on the war, which is not surprising since we have no literary remains from nearly five centuries of Parthian rule in the east. A once-popular suggestion that Josephus's Aramaic precursor survives in the thirteenth-century Old North Russian (or "Slavonic") version of the *War*, because that version includes some material not found in our Greek *War*, has now been almost universally rejected.

In any case, it is impossible to know how extensive this Aramaic version was, or how it corresponded to our *War*, which appears to be an original Greek production in that it is heavily influenced by other Greek literature, rhetorical norms, and current vocabulary (see above). It is possible that Josephus inflated some earlier "native" account so as to highlight his credentials as an exotic eastern eyewitness in the Greek *War*. He will not refer to the Aramaic version again, even when he comes to describe his procedure in writing the *War* (*Apion* 1.50). So the earlier version may have amounted to no more than a few letters to friends in the east, sent while this priest was still in Judea before and immediately after Jerusalem's fall.[7]

7. Many scholars have assumed that Josephus wrote and dispatched a full Aramaic account

As with other classical and biblical authors, we do not possess the Greek texts that Josephus wrote. What we have are manuscripts—of distinct sections of his corpus—dating from perhaps the ninth to the sixteenth centuries, long after he lived.[8] From the fifteenth century on the printing press began to make its mark, and from that time on we start to have exact copies of the many editions (and translations) of Josephus.

The handwritten manuscripts are the result of generations of recopying by hand, a process notorious for introducing small changes, which are compounded by subsequent copies. This means that we are dependent (as with most other ancient writings) on what are called *critical editions* of the Greek text. These are works created painstakingly by modern scholars, who compare the various Greek manuscripts, noticing where they differ, suggest which option they think Josephus most likely wrote, print that as the main text of Josephus, and indicate other possible readings in the notes below the main text.

In addition to the Greek manuscripts, we have two other valuable sources for figuring out what Josephus wrote: early citations of his work by Christian writers (especially **Eusebius** in the early fourth century, who quoted him extensively) and Latin translations of the *War* and the *Antiquities/Apion*, made in the fourth and sixth centuries, respectively. The fullest critical edition of Josephus's works that we have today, which takes all of these resources into account, was made in the late nineteenth century by the German scholar Benedictus Niese. In the intervening decades, many scholars have come to disagree with Niese's choices for the best reading, and various British, American, German, French, and Italian scholars have worked to update parts of the Greek text by offering what they consider better readings. But Niese's full edition remains the only complete one with extensive notes on variants. This is the Greek edition used as the basis for the major new English translation of Josephus, with the first comprehensive commentary, now being produced.[9]

So the student of Josephus must constantly remember not only that the ancient writer composed in a language very different from the English the student may be reading, which is unavoidably an interpretation of the Greek text, but also that the "Greek text" is not what Josephus wrote, but an approximation that we are constantly trying to improve. Differences among the Greek manuscripts are mostly

---

to the east *after arriving in Rome*. The urgency of such a work (it must have been written before the Greek, which was itself mostly completed in the 70s CE) suggested to Laqueur and Thackeray that it was Roman propaganda, commissioned to warn the Parthians against aggression. But there is no reason to think that Josephus wrote this Aramaic precursor *after* arriving in Rome, and hard to see why the Roman rulers would have him write something they could not read—especially since the Parthian ruling class all spoke Greek. In any case, a seven-volume history that opened with an elaborate study of Herod the Great and his succession woes, devoting a volume also to Josephus's brilliance as a general, and two more to the bloody internal strife inside Jerusalem (and the pollution of the holy sanctuary), would be closer to *torture* for eastern readers than to any sort of Flavian propaganda.

8. These are mostly written on parchment and bound in book (codex) form. There is one papyrus manuscript from the third century CE, but it contains only a few dozen words from *War* 2.

9. *See* Steve Mason's *Flavius Josephus: Translation and Commentary*, in the Advanced Reading.

trivial, it is true, but they can be significant. Compare, for example, my translation of *Antiquities* 20.262–65 in this volume with William Whiston's 1737 rendering of the same passage.[10] The differences are not only because of translation choices. Whiston's Greek text lacked any reference to Josephus's learning poetry or to the "elegance of styles" because these phrases did not appear in the Greek manuscript he used. It is open to debate, therefore, whether Josephus wrote those phrases or whether they crept into later copies of his writings because a scribe either was being careless or thought that Josephus must have written something of the kind, and so he "corrected" his source.

Reception of Josephus's Literary Works in the Second Temple Period

When scholars talk about "our sources" for first-century Judea, they nearly always mean Josephus's histories above all else. These provide the only narrative spine, so to speak, for the period from the **Hasmonean** revolt of the 160s BCE to the fall of Jerusalem and its aftermath in the 70s CE. Josephus's importance can be seen from the fact that, whereas we have many scholarly handbooks and guides to this period, we have very few (or only small sections of larger works) for the periods before 170 BCE and after 75 CE. When scholars say that there is not much evidence for those periods, they mean that we have nothing comparable to Josephus. In some respects, the archaeology is better for Judean life in the second and third centuries than for the pre-70 CE period, but it is still much harder to write that history without a Josephus. The descriptions we read in textbooks of institutions such as the Second Temple, the synagogue, and the priesthood; of Judea's political relations with neighboring peoples and with Rome; of Herod and his descendants; of Roman governors such as Pilate, Felix, and Gessius Florus; of groups such as Pharisees, Sadducees, and Essenes; of the laws and customs of the Judeans in the first century; and especially of the main events of the period such as the war against Rome—this comes almost entirely from Josephus (*see* History of the Second Temple Period).[11] Even when we study less historically oriented Judaean literature, from Jubilees and 4 Maccabees to the sectarian scrolls of Qumran, Josephus's narratives contribute greatly to the background matrix against which we read them (*see* Overview of Early Jewish Literature).

Now, this state of affairs presents both a trap and a challenge. The trap, which can ensnare even seasoned scholars, is the assumption that because Josephus

10. Whiston is readily available online, for example, at http://pace.mcmaster.ca (choose "Text and Commentary," then use pull-down menus to find the passage). The text I translate is favored by the Loeb Classical Library editor, Louis H. Feldman, based on manuscripts A and E.

11. Philo of Alexandria (*see* Introduction to Philo of Alexandria) mentions a few episodes in Judea of the 30s CE, connected with Pontius Pilate and the emperor Gaius Caligula, and the evidence of archaeology (including coins, inscriptions, and papyri) is extremely important, but Josephus provides the only continuous narrative. Rabbinic literature, which reached its present forms in the third to sixth centuries CE, contains many traditions about the first century, though nowadays these are used with great caution for historical purposes.

does not mention something, and so "there is no evidence for it," it *likely did not happen*. To make such a judgment would be a colossal error. Josephus wrote for his own reasons, and did not assume the burden of creating a video-like, proportional coverage of events in Judea, much as we would like one. We must not confuse his work with such a guide. This point becomes clear when archaeology shows us much that Josephus did not happen to mention, such as a second ramp at the siege of **Machaerus** or the large western palace on the summit of **Masada.** Although he describes these sites in some detail, he does not mention these items.

Even leaving aside archaeology, our historical imagination alone can reveal how much Josephus did not choose to explain, when we begin to ask questions about the background of the riots over Pilate's aqueduct, about Cestius Gallus's plan or strategy when he marched to (then abruptly withdrew from) Jerusalem in late 66 CE, or about the aims of those who fled to Masada during and after the war. Josephus cannot be faulted for any of this. The gaps in evidence that we face as historians are *our problem:* no one demanded that we investigate the ancient past! Josephus wrote about what he wanted to write about, for his own reasons at the time, and he apparently succeeded well. He could not say everything that could be said. Even video coverage is (notoriously) limited by time (it starts and stops somewhere) and vantage point. Most of what happened, in all the lives concerned and from all possible perspectives, he did not and could not write about.

Second, Josephus presents us with many challenges, partly because his interests, education, language, and categories were so different from ours. To take only some obvious examples, we easily describe him as writing about "Judaism" and "religious" matters. But these are modern Western categories that he did not know, and his categories were very different. No ancient word that even potentially corresponds to the English "Judaism" appears in Josephus's works or in any of those of his contemporaries, whether compatriots or outside observers such as Tacitus. There is a Greek word *Ioudaismos,* which looks like "Judaism," but it is restricted to 2 Maccabees (*see* 1 and 2 Maccabees) and its derivative 4 Maccabees, and it may mean something else. In any case, Josephus and his contemporaries talk rather about the "laws and ancestral customs" of the Judeans, using a variety of interchangeable Greek and Latin terms. These categories, however, applied to all peoples, whether defined by city (*polis*)—such as Romans, Athenians, Spartans, Ephesians, Palmyrenes, Ascalonites—or by ethnic region—Egyptians, Babylonians, Samarians, Syrians. They all had laws, customs, and traditions associated with their lawgivers, cities, temples, and rituals. There was no "Romanism" or "Egyptism" or "Ascalonism"—and therefore no Judaism either.

Similarly, the ancients had no word for what we call "religion," as a distinct part of life. The environment closest to what we do in our synagogues, churches, and mosques (i.e., reading authoritative texts, hearing talks, discussing the divine, devoting ourselves to introspection and moral living) was in the ancient world provided by the philosophical school or lecture hall. It was philosophy that called people to examine their lives; contemplate the nature of the divine; discuss the nature of the soul and possibility of an afterlife; and prepare themselves to handle grief, illness, and death. Thus Josephus describes Pharisees, Sadducees, and Essenes as Judaean "philosophical schools," even comparing them to **Pythagoreans** and **Stoics** (*Life* 11;[12] *Antiquities* 15.371[13]). In these and many other ways he constantly challenges us to rethink our categories when studying the ancient world.

These considerations are important also for students of the New Testament. Because there was no ready-made category of "religion" for the new Christian movements to step into, and Judean culture was a very different sort of thing—a famous nation with an old mother-city, temple, ancient lawgiver and constitution, hereditary priestly aristocracy, and sacrificial system—the early Christians faced a considerable struggle in trying to explain to the world exactly what they were. A part of Judean culture? A new philosophy based on their teacher? A club or voluntary association? Or a radically new group that cared nothing for the world's categories because it would all end soon?

Josephus is relevant for New Testament study in at least three other ways. First, everything just said about his importance for understanding ancient Judea applies also to the background of the Gospels and the book of Acts, which are largely set in the same region. Virtually every sentence in his works has potential value for New Testament study. His comprehensive paraphrase of the Bible (*Antiquities* 1–11) offers rich resources for comparison with New Testament biblical interpretation, and his postbiblical history focuses on a period contemporary with the lives of Jesus and the first Christian generation (to 70 CE). So the use of Josephus for general New Testament "background" is the most obvious and well-established way of using his narratives. The most famous academic reference work on ancient Jewish history, by Emil Schürer, was written precisely as background to the New Testament. But when scholarship took this approach (as clearly in Schürer's *History of the Jewish People in the Age of Jesus Christ*), Josephus's works were viewed as collections of facts and sources that could be individually pulled off, like tools from a peg-board, for application to the New Testament. Recent study of Josephus as a highly creative author immeasurably complicates that use. He is not a purveyor of neutral facts—no one can be since language requires choices and structures—but he is a creative writer.

Second, almost all of the significant groups, places, and individuals mentioned in the Gospels and the book of Acts appear in Josephus. Interestingly, Jesus' home of Nazareth—a village near the city of Sepphoris in Galilee—does not appear in Josephus while the larger city does not appear in the New Testament. This difference leads to an important observation: that the social status and outlooks of the New Testament authors are very different from Josephus's. He is a proud spokesman of the ancient priestly aristocracy, who varies from pity to contempt when he speaks of the vast majority of the population—the "rabble" or the "mob." He shows flashes of exasperation with the Pharisees, who use their support among

---

12. Josephus, *Life* 11 (trans. H. St. J. Thackeray, Loeb Classical Library): "Being now in my nineteenth year I began to govern my life by the rules of the Pharisees, a sect having points of resemblance to that which the Greeks call the Stoic school."

13. Josephus, *Antiquities* 15.371 (trans. Ralph Marcus, Loeb Classical Library): "And those who are called by us Essenes were also excused from this necessity. This is a group which follows a way of life taught to the Greeks by Pythagoras."

the masses to make life difficult for his ruling class. By contrast, the two-volume work known as Luke-Acts, though it shows the highest level of cultured Greek in the New Testament, takes a nearly opposite position. The poor Galilean villagers are Jesus' main concern. The author presents the Pharisees rather positively, as those most open to Jesus and Christian teaching, while portraying Josephus's powerful, temple-based priesthood in the bleakest terms, as the relentless persecutors of Jesus and the apostles.[14]

These differences of perspective make it all the more useful historically to compare the portraits in Luke-Acts and Josephus of the groups and individuals that turn up in both narratives: the Jerusalem court ("Sanhedrin"); the chief priests, Pharisees, and Sadducees; Herod, Antipas, Philip, Agrippa I, Agrippa II, Berenice, and Drusilla; the governors Pilate, Felix (married to Drusilla), and Festus; rebels such as Judas the Galilean, Theudas, the "Egyptian," and the remarkable **Sicarii.** All aspects of Judean and regional culture, the political atmosphere, and life around the temple can benefit from careful study of Josephus's presentations alongside, especially, Luke-Acts with its very different outlook. For example, Agrippa II and his sister Berenice are friends of Josephus, but come across as distant figures with whom Paul pleads in Acts 26. In considering such parallels we are no longer comparing Josephus's *facts* with New Testament writings, however; we are looking at two contemporary authors and their different portraits of the same people and events.

A third way in which Josephus is relevant for New Testament study is not as obvious as the first two, but may turn out to be the most valuable. Josephus's works reveal a man who is something of an outsider to Greco-Roman culture, trying nevertheless to show that he can use the tools and commonplaces of rhetorical education in presenting his people to that larger world. He does the expected things, emphasizing issues of character, changing his stories for the sake of interesting variety in the retelling, crafting speeches for his characters, and often winking mischievously at his audiences, who should appreciate (for example) the deceptive lengths to which he and some other Judean leaders went to in the hope of bringing the war to a good outcome. Traditionally, the New Testament texts have not been read in this way, with openness to rhetoric, wit, and irony. They have been read for their theology, ideas, and propositions. But were the Christian writers exempt from the rhetorical spirit of playfulness with language that pervades Greco-Roman literature and Josephus's works? In Josephus, it is often difficult to identify his earnest thoughts among the many twists and turns of his narratives, or in the speeches he creates for his various characters. Perhaps studying his use of the common rhetoric in fulfilling his aims as a historian can throw light on the contemporary efforts of those other outsiders to the main culture, the early Christians.

Josephus's thirty volumes of connected history are of unique value for the study of ancient Judea and Judean-Roman relations. This does not mean that they should

---

14. Contrast Josephus's Pharisees (*War* 1.110-14; *Antiquities* 13.288-98, 401-3; 17.41-45; 18.15, 18) with those of Luke (Luke 7:36; 11:37; 13:31; 14:1; 17:20; Acts 5:33-40; 15:5; 23:6; 26:5). For Josephus's kind of people, see Luke 22:50-54; Acts 4:1-5, 24.

be treated as some kind of authority or manual of facts. Rather, as fascinating examples of a cosmopolitan Judean leader trying to explain his people's culture and history to audiences in the world capital, they raise all sorts of questions for the study of other literature and history from Josephus's time: in Rome and in the provinces, among other Judeans, and by the early Christians.

STEVE MASON

FURTHER READING

Bilde, Per. *Flavius Josephus between Jerusalem and Rome: His Life, His Works and Their Importance*. Sheffield: JSOT, 1988.

Mason, Steve. *Josephus and the New Testament*. 2nd ed. Peabody, Mass.: Hendrickson, 2003.

———. "Will the Real Josephus Please Stand Up?" *BAR* 23, no. 5 (September–October 1997): 58–68.

Rajak, Tessa. *Josephus: The Historian and His Society*. 2nd ed. London: Duckworth, 2002.

Small, Jocelyn Penny. *Wax Tablets of the Mind: Cognitive Studies of Memory and Literacy in Classical Antiquity*. London: Routledge, 1997.

Thackeray, Henry St. John. *Josephus: The Man and the Historian*. 1929. Reprint, New York: Ktav, 1967. Online at http://pace=ancient.mcmaster.ca—"Scholarly Studies."

Winsbury, Rex. *The Roman Book: Books, Publishing and Performance in Classical Rome*. London: Duckworth, 2009.

ADVANCED READING

Cohen, Shaye J. D. *Josephus in Galilee and Rome: His Vita and Development as a Historian*. Leiden: Brill, 1979.

Den Hollander, William. *Josephus, the Emperors, and the City of Rome: From Hostage to Historian*. Leiden: Brill, 2014.

Feldman, Louis H. *Josephus's Interpretation of the Bible*. Berkeley: University of California Press, 1998.

Kelley, Nicole. "The Cosmopolitan Expression of Josephus's Prophetic Perspective in the Jewish War." *HTR* 97 (2004): 257–74.

Laqueur, Richard. *The Jewish Historian Flavius Josephus: A Biographical Investigation Based on New Critical Sources*. Ed. S. Mason. Trans. Caroline Disler. Toronto: York University, 2005. Translation of *Der Jüdische Historiker Flavius Josephus: ein biographischer Versuch auf neuer quellenkritischer Grundlage*. Giessen: Münchow, 1920. Online at http://pace=ancient.mcmaster.ca—"Scholarly Studies."

Leoni, Tommaso. "The Text of Josephus's Works." *JSJ* 40 (2009): 149–84.

Marincola, John. *Authority and Tradition in Ancient Historiography*. Cambridge: Cambridge University Press, 1997.

Mason, Steve, *A History of the Jewish War, AD 66-74*. New York: Cambridge University Press, 2016.

———. *Josephus, Judea, and Christian Origins: Methods and Categories*. Peabody, Mass.: Hendrickson, 2009.

Mason, Steve, ed. *Flavius Josephus: Translation and Commentary*. 12 vols. 9 published to date. Leiden: Brill, 2000-.

Parente, Fausto, and Joseph Sievers, eds. *Josephus and the History of the Greco-Roman Period*. Leiden: Brill, 1994.

Rodgers, Zuleika, ed. *Making History: Josephus and Historical Method.* Leiden: Brill, 2007.

Schwartz, Daniel R. *Reading the First Century: On Reading Josephus and Studying Jewish History of the First Century.* Tübingen: Mohr Siebeck, 2013.

Sievers, Joseph, and Gaia Lembi. *Josephus and Jewish History in Flavian Rome and Beyond.* Leiden: Brill, 2005.

Sterling, Gregory E. *Historiography and Self-Definition: Josephus, Luke-Acts, and Apologetic Historiography.* Leiden: Brill, 1992.

Introduction to the *Life*

Narrative Description

Josephus's *Life* covers his ancestry, education, family, and juvenile honors (1–12); early public achievements (13–16); public life (17–413); and domestic affairs (414–30). Like his major works, even this single volume shows many signs of symmetrical structuring. Both the opening and closing sections concern his personal relationships, including children; both involve trips to Rome by sea; both mention gifts received from the wives of emperors—Nero's Poppaea and Domitia; and both emphasize God's watchful protection of Josephus—from shipwreck and from accusers in Rome. There are two sections on Justus of Tiberias, near the beginning and near the end (36–42 and 336–67), and two strikingly similar revolts against Josephus's leadership, one at the one-quarter mark and one at the three-quarter mark of the story (84–103 and 271–308/335). Finally, the central panel of this work, more or less, is occupied by its only dream-revelation, in which God reassures Josephus about his divine mission (208–9).

Once again, however, the dramatic story proceeds on a different plane. The drama reaches its high point with the second Tiberian revolt against Josephus, after which the Jerusalem delegation returns home and Josephus has mastered his enemies (331–35, 368–72).

Date/Occasion

If we had only the evidence of the texts, we would date the *Life* immediately after the *Antiquities* (*see Antiquities*) to which it is bound, therefore to 93/94 CE or perhaps 95 CE to allow plenty of time for its writing. Josephus closes the *Life* expressing gratitude for benefits received from the emperor **Domitian** and his wife Domitia Longina (429). This would be a very puzzling way to end if he was writing after Domitian's death in 96 CE. He would not only be continuing to praise a dead ruler whose memory respectable Romans were trying to erase, but even worse, he would be failing to mention the kindness of the *current ruler* (Nerva or **Trajan**)—an ill-advised practice even under a relatively gentle monarch. If

Antiquities 20.267 is still introducing the *Life* (as 20.266 clearly is), when it speaks of briefly covering events of the war until the present day—the thirteenth year of Domitian—then the final sections of the *Life* would make perfectly good sense as a fulfillment of that expectation. Josephus would be writing while Domitian still rules and while Domitia's gifts are those of the emperor's wife. Incidental support for this natural conclusion is the similarity of phrasing between the last volume of *Antiquities* 20 and the *Life*: a number of phrases not found elsewhere in Josephus appear in these two volumes, which also share a similarly relaxed style after the frequent contortions of *Antiquities* 17–19.

ROMAN CAESARS DURING THE PALESTINE OCCUPATION

Augustus (Gaius Octavius)—Imperator Caesar Divi filius	40 BCE–14 CE
Tiberius (Tiberius Claudius Nero)	14 CE–37 CE
Caligula (Gaius Caesar Augustus Germanicus)	37–41 CE
Claudius (Tiberius Claudius Caesar Augustus Germanicus)	41–54 CE
Nero (Nero Claudius Caesar Augustus Germanicus)	54–68 CE
Galba (Servius Galba Imperator Caesar Augustus)	68–69 CE
Otho (Imperator Marcus Otho Caesar Augustus)	(Jan.) 69–(April) 69 CE
Vitellius (Aulus Vitellius Germanicus Imperator)	(April) 69–(Dec.) 69 CE
Vespasian (Imperator Titus Flavius Vespasianus Caesar)	69–79 CE
Titus (Imperator Titus Caesar Vespasianus Augustus)	79–81 CE
Domitian (Imperator Caesar Domintianus Augustus)	81–96 CE
Nerva (Imperator Nerva Germanicus Caesar Augustus)	96–98 CE
Trajan (Imperator Caesar Nerva Trajanus Augustus)	98–117 CE

The wrinkle is that Josephus appears to assume the death of Agrippa II. In *Life* 359 he chides Justus: "Why did you not bring your history into the open while **Vespasian** and **Titus,** the imperators who prosecuted the war, were still living, and while King Agrippa was still around[1] along with all those of his family—men attaining the highest level of Greek education?" A well-read and often reliable scholar named Photius, a church official in ninth-century Constantinople, in a large reference work he compiled, dated Agrippa II's death to the third year of Trajan (i.e., 100 CE). Because of that claim, many scholars used to insist that the *Life*, at least in its present form, could have been written only after 100 CE. In recent decades, however, many specialists have declined to give so much weight to Photius, given that he wrote some eight centuries later. They have preferred the evidence within the two works for keeping the *Life* close to *Antiquities* 20 as a published pair. Some have noted that even some passages in the *Antiquities*—17.28, appearing to suggest that Romans now rule Agrippa II's territory;

---

1. I would note that Josephus opts to use two very different verbs. The one relating to Vespasian and Titus clearly means that they are dead (not "living"), but the one relating to Agrippa is much more ambiguous (not "[getting] around," not "being here"). It could mean simply that Agrippa is no longer in Rome, as he was when Josephus brought out his work, having returned to his territories in Syria. Still, the absence of him and "all" his relatives may suggest that they are dead.

18.128, noting that within a century of Herod the Great's death (literally by 93 CE) almost all his descendants "have perished"—which was completed in 93/94 CE, might indicate that Agrippa II was gone.

One might think that inscribed archaeological remains would settle the question of Agrippa II's death date, but although we do have such evidence, scholars interpret it differently. Agrippa II's coins are the most potentially useful, but also the most notoriously complicated. His **Flavian** coin series bears dates as late as "Year 35." The problem is knowing what the king counted as Year 1. One possibility (56 CE) would place the latest coins in 91 CE, suiting the hypothesis that the king was dead by 93 CE. But another possibility (61 CE) would have him reigning and producing coins until at least 96 CE (when Flavian rule ended in Domitian's death)—which would bring us very close to Photius's 100 CE.

The majority of recent published scholarship on the matter favors the conclusion that Agrippa II was dead by about 93/94 CE, leaving it possible for the *Life* to have been completed shortly after the main *Antiquities*.

In the closing lines of his major work, the *Antiquities,* Josephus immodestly celebrates his achievement as something that hardly anyone else could have done (20.262–65).[2] He exploits the occasion to say that he will now give an account of his family and life achievements, hoping not to make others jealous and while there are people around who can verify his claims, and *after that* he will close his *Antiquities* (20.266). This turns out to be the introduction to his *Life,* which opens directly with his ancestry and education (1–12) before it moves quickly to his adult accomplishments. The *Life* itself closes with a final acknowledgment of **Epaphroditus,** "most excellent of men," a note that he is here closing the *Antiquities,* and an invitation to assess his character on the basis of this account (*Life* 430). Clearly, then, the *Life* was written as a biographical appendix to his major literary work, and it was understood that way by later readers.[3] After the arduous work of writing the master narrative, he says in effect, "Now let's talk about me!"

The same scholarly mentality that looked for hidden purposes in Josephus's *War* (allegedly Flavian propaganda; see *War*) and *Antiquities* (a work of repentance and reinstatement) produced the following explanation of the *Life*. Because Josephus twice attacks a literary rival named Justus of Tiberias, especially in a digression near the end (*Life* 336–67; cf. 40), it was thought that he must have written the short work as a response to Justus's account, which had harshly criticized Josephus's *War*. Justus's challenge bothered Josephus so much that he had to respond point by point. We may therefore assume that the whole *Life* replies to Justus, who must therefore have criticized Josephus's ancestry, education, early life, and everything else mentioned in the autobiography. Since Josephus often departs from what he had said in the *War,* wherever the two overlap it must be because Justus had exposed him and forced him to acknowledge the truth, or

2. Josephus, *Antiquities* 20.262–65: "And now I take heart from the consummation of my proposed work to assert that no one else, either Jew or Gentile, would have been equal to the task, however willing to undertake it, of issuing so accurate a treatise as this for the Greek world."

3. See Eusebius, *Historia ecclesiae* 3.10.8–11. Manuscript A includes a notation after *Life* 430 that this marks the "end of Josephus's *Jewish Antiquities*"—following the lead of his own words there.

something closer to it. Moreover, this would mean in turn that the *Life* could be used against the *War* to get a better idea of what actually happened during Josephus's Galilean command.

Now, there is no doubt that in the *Life* Josephus is irritated by Justus and denounces him thoroughly (*Life* 40–41),[4] but he is not the only one. Josephus denounces a number of enemies, most notably **John of Gischala** (*Life* 87–88).[5] It has been rightly observed that he takes on Justus only near the end, when he has finished most of what he wishes to say. He remarks there that he would like to break the narrative and address the claims of this Justus, who has written a book on the same material (*Life* 336). Therefore, if we read the work as Josephus wrote it, bearing in mind that in his other compositions he is clear about his reasons for writing, and if we ask ourselves how he could have expected his audiences to understand this autobiography, we must conclude that he did not expect them to think of it as a response to Justus. He gives his reasons for writing, gauche though they may be: he is very pleased with himself, on completing the *Antiquities*, and wants to share his personal story with his audiences.

The Justus-response theory based itself partly on the correct observation that this "autobiography" is a rather odd one (by modern standards) since it deals with the early and more recent parts of his life very quickly (1–16, 412–29), devoting itself almost entirely to the five months or so between his appointment to Galilee and the arrival of Vespasian's army there. The best explanation for such a narrow focus appears to be that this was the period Justus had attacked, and so Josephus needed to rebut him in detail.

But if we return to Josephus's stated purpose, we get a different picture. In his world, all biographies were seriously disproportionate. Consider the Gospels, which famously say either nothing (as Mark and John) or very little (as Matthew and Luke) about Jesus' ancestry, birth, and youthful achievement. They move directly on after a brief account of Jesus' birth to a very short period in his adult life. Even of that adult life, we hear very little, and what is related is quite episodic rather than a detailed and tightly connected narrative. Plutarch's *Lives* of famous Greeks and Romans, as well as **Suetonius's** biographies, are much the same in this respect. A man's character was thought to be the same throughout his life, though bad men sometimes disguised their "true natures" for a short time. It was already given in a person's bloodlines, combined with a personal "shape" that was his alone, and which might lead him to depart abruptly from his father's character. With these assumptions in view, it was normal to evaluate a man's ancestry, birth (particularly if accompanied by omens of greatness), and signs of childhood genius, and then to move directly to his public life as an adult. For

---

4. Josephus, *Life* 40–41: "But of this man's [Justus]'s general depravity and of the fact that to him and his brother our ruin was almost entirely due, I will adduce proof in the course of this narrative."

5. Josephus, *Life* 87–88: "On his arrival at Tiberias, John attempted to induce the inhabitants to abandon their allegiance to me and attach themselves to him; and there many who, ever craving for revolution, by temperament addicted to change and delighting in sedition, gladly responded to his invitation. In particular Justus and his father Pistus were eager to desert me and go over to John."

a man of affairs, his character was revealed by important political achievements (e.g., successful embassies to Rome) and administrative posts, but especially by military commands. Other relevant factors were one's circle of friends, their status, benefits received from the more powerful (a sign of recognition and status), and benefits given to less powerful dependents (indicating "greatness of soul" and of course justified wealth).

This is exactly the sort of material from which Josephus's *Life* is constructed. The obvious problem he faces is in the area of political and military achievement. In the *War*, where he wanted to show how tough and determined the Judean people were by nature, he included much about his exploits as resourceful commander, even in a losing cause that ended in surrender. That surrender was salvaged by a divine mission. Here, where the situation is Josephus's winning character, he wisely decides to end the story with the Romans' arrival, which allows him to show off a story of unbroken success—over his *internal Judean enemies*. These are all men of either bad character, such as John of Gischala, Justus, and the members of the Jerusalem delegation who tried to oust him from his post, or basically good men who allowed themselves to be fooled (and/or bribed) to join the opposition to him. No matter: in all cases Josephus was one step ahead of them, seeing through their ploys and using his inexhaustible resourcefulness, ruses, and deceptive oratory to keep them off balance—until the delegation finally returned, beaten and cowed, to Jerusalem (332).

As for military prowess, since he had no real victories to his credit, Josephus must resort to supposition and spin. For example, he claims in a summary to have taken several Galilean cities "by storm" (82), though his own narrative suggests that he barely hurt their feelings. Again, he claims that *he intimidated* Agrippa II's cavalry commanders, and that is why they would not face him in battle (120–21, 215, 406), though in reality they may have been unaware of his presence a few miles away or unwilling to chase him around the Galilean hills.

In any case, the five months or so between his appointment and Vespasian's arrival was the only period in which Josephus *could* plausibly describe a public life and quasi-military command as evidence of his character. His inclusion of the successful embassy to Rome (*Life* 13–16), somewhat humorously facilitated by a showman of the kind that young Nero was so enamored of, highlights his brilliant promise (and has nothing to do with Justus's criticisms). The story also allows him to show how he was favored by God—another standard ingredient of the excellent biography. He was one of only eighty who survived a shipwreck involving six hundred passengers, after swimming all night long, until he was taken on board a passing ship "by the provision of God" (*Life* 15). The rest of his career was marked by other displays of good character: incorruptible exercise of justice, restraint of his passions (63, 80–83), generosity, and clemency toward even violent enemies (103, 174, 244, 369). All of this was rounded out by the continued provision of God for his safety, the many benefits he received from the imperial family, and those he conferred on others (413–29). All of this should prove beyond doubt his remarkable character.

Steve Mason

2.3 from *Life*

Early Life (1.1–5.23)

1.1 Now in my case, my ancestry is rather distinguished, having originated with priests long ago. Just as the basis of noble birth is different among various [nations], so also among us membership in the priesthood is a certain proof of an ancestry's brilliance. ² Now in my case, my ancestry is not merely from priests; it is also from the first day-course of the twenty-four—an enormous distinction, this—and indeed, from the most elite of the divisions within this [course]. Further, I have a share of royal ancestry from my mother because the children of Asamonaeus, of whom she was a descendant, for a very long time served as high priests and exercised the kingship of our nation.

³ I will state the succession, then. Our patriarch was Simon, who was surnamed Psellus. This man lived in the period when the son of the high priest Simon served as high priest—he was the first of the high priests named Hyrcanus. ⁴ Simon Psellus had nine children. [One] of these was Matthias, known as "of Ephaeus." This man took for himself the daughter of the high priest Jonathan—the first of the children of Asamonaeus's ancestry to serve as high priest and the brother of Simon the high priest—into marriage. Then in the first year of Hyrcanus's rule, he [Matthias] had a child Matthias, surnamed Curtus. ⁵ From this man came Josephus, in the ninth year of Alexandra's rule; from Josephus, Matthias, in the tenth year of Archelaus's reign; and I from Matthias, in the first year of Gaius Caesar's *imperium*. I have three sons: Hyrcanus, the oldest, from the fourth year, Justus from the eighth year, and Agrippa from the ninth year of the *imperium* of Vespasian Caesar. ⁶ I thus present the succession of our ancestry as I have found it recorded in the public registers, sending a greeting to those who try to malign us.

²·⁷ My father Matthias was distinguished not because of his noble birth alone, but even more was he praised for his sense of justice, being a very eminent man among the Jerusalemites—in the greatest city we have.

⁸ Though jointly educated with a brother named Matthias—he had been born my full [brother] from both parents—I forged ahead into a vast wealth of education, gaining a reputation for excelling in both memory and insight. ⁹ While still a boy, really, about fourteen years old, I used to be praised by everyone because I loved studying: the chief priests and principal men of the city would often meet to understand the legal matters more precisely with my assistance.

¹⁰ When I was about sixteen years old, I chose to gain expertise in the philosophical schools among us. There are three of these, as we have often said: the first, Pharisees; the second, Sadducees; and the third, Essenes. In this way I intended to choose the best [school]—if I might examine them all. ¹¹ So I toughened myself and, after considerable effort, passed through the three of them. Yet

Translation by Steve Mason/Brill (modified). Republication of the Brill material courtesy of Koninklijke BRILL NV.

I did not regard even the resulting expertise sufficient for me. When I discovered that a certain man by the name of Bannus made his life in the desert, I became his devotee: wearing clothes [made] from trees, scavenging food that grew by itself, and washing frequently for purification—with frigid water, day and night! [12] When I had lived with him three years and so satisfied my longing, I returned to the city. Being now in my nineteenth year I began to involve myself in public life, deferring to the philosophical school of the Pharisees, which is quite like the one called Stoic among the Greeks.

[3.13] After my twenty-sixth year, indeed, it fell to me to go up to Rome for the reason that will be described. At the time when Felix was administering Judea, he had certain priests, close associates of mine and gentlemen, bound and sent to Rome on a minor and incidental charge, to submit an account to Caesar. [14] Wanting to find some means of rescue for these men, especially when I discovered that even in wretched circumstances they had not abandoned piety toward the deity but were subsisting on figs and nuts, I reached Rome after having faced many dangers at sea. [15] For when our ship was flooded in the middle of the Adriatic, we—being about six hundred in number—had to swim through the entire night. And when by the provision of God a Cyrenean ship appeared before us around daybreak, I and some others—about eighty altogether—overtook the rest and were taken on board. [16] After we had come safely to Dicaearcheia, which the Italians call Puteoli, through a friendship I met Aliturus: this man was a mime-actor, especially dear to Nero's thoughts and a Judean by ancestry. Through him I became known to Poppaea, the wife of Caesar, and then very quickly arranged things, appealing to her to free the priests. Having succeeded, with enormous gifts from Poppaea in addition to this benefit, I returned home.

[4.17] Now I was surprised already to find the beginnings of revolutions, with many [people] grandly contemplating defection from the Romans. So I tried to restrain the insurgents and charged them to think again. They should first place before their eyes those against whom they would make war—for not only with respect to war-related expertise but also with respect to good fortune were they disadvantaged in relation to the Romans—[18] and they should not, rashly and quite foolishly, bring upon their native places, their families, and indeed themselves the risk of ultimate ruin. [19] I said these things and was persistently engaged in dissuasive pleading, predicting that the outcome of the war would be utterly disastrous for us. I was not convincing, to be sure, because the frenzy of the desperadoes prevailed.

[5.20] I became anxious now that by saying these things constantly I might incur hatred and suspicion, as conspiring with the enemy, and I would risk being taken and done away with by them. Since the Antonia, which was a fortress, was already in their possession, I retreated into the inner temple. [21] After the removal of Menachem and the principal men of the bandit brigade, I came back out of the temple and held discussions with the chief priests and principal men of the Pharisees. [22] Extreme fear took hold of us as we saw the populace with weapons: we were unsure what we should do ourselves and were unable to halt the revolutionaries. Given the clear and present danger to ourselves, we said that we concurred with their opinions. But we counseled them to stand fast, even if the enemy soldiers had advanced, so that they should be given credit for justly taking up weapons in defense. [23] We did these things hoping that before long Cestius would come up with a large force and halt the revolution.

Brief Account of Justus of Tiberias, Enemy of Josephus (9.36–10.43)

[9.36] Justus son of Pistus, the principal man of the third bloc, although he kept pretending to be in doubt about the war, was actually longing for revolutionary activities, intending to manufacture power for himself out of the upheaval. [37] So he came along into the [city] center and tried to teach the mob that the city had always been the capital of Galilee since the times of Herod the Tetrarch, who was its builder, and who had wanted the city of the Sepphorites to submit to that of the Tiberians. They had not relinquished this primacy under King Agrippa the father, but it remained until Felix was put in charge of Judea. [38] Now, he was saying:

> "You yourselves just happen to have been given to the younger Agrippa as a gift from Nero! And because it submitted to Rome, Sepphoris immediately became the capital of Galilee, and both the royal bank and the archives, having been dismantled, are with them."

[39] These and many other things against King Agrippa he said to them, for the sake of provoking the populace to defection. He added:

> "Now is the time to take up weapons, after welcoming the Galileans as allies—for they are willing to begin, because of the hatred they have toward the Sepphorites for maintaining loyalty to the Romans—and with a large force to execute vengeance because of them."

[40] By saying these things, he won over the mob. For he was rather good at manipulating the populace and at overcoming the better arguments of disputants by craftiness and a kind of guile through words. In fact, he was well trained in the Greek sort of education, on the basis of which he audaciously took it upon himself to record also the history of these events—as if he could overcome the truth itself by means of this speech-craft. [41] But concerning this man—how sordid his life became and how he was, with his brother, the cause of almost complete ruin—we will explain as the story unfolds. [42] At that time, when he had persuaded the citizens to take up weapons and compelled many who did not so desire, Justus came out with all of these men and set fire to the villages of the Gadarenes and also of the Hippenes, which happened to lie on the frontier between Tiberias and the territory of the Scythopolitans.

[10.43] So Tiberias was in such straits as these.

Dabarittans' Robbery of the Wife of Agrippa II's Steward, and Josephus's Delicate Diplomacy (26.126–29.144)

[26.126] Some audacious young men of Dabarittan origin, having closely observed the wife of the king's administrator Ptolemy making her way through the Great

Plain, from territory subject to the royals into that occupied by the Romans, with considerable equipment and some mounted soldiers attending her for the sake of security, suddenly fell upon them. [127] They compelled the woman to flee, but seized everything that she was transporting and came into Tarichea, leading to me four mules loaded with clothes and gear. There was also a considerable stash of silver and some five hundred gold pieces.

[128] Wanting to preserve these things for Ptolemy, since he was a compatriot—and even robbing adversaries is proscribed by our laws—I said to those who had brought them that it was necessary to keep them so that the walls of Jerusalem might be repaired from their sale. [129] But the young fellows had a hard time accepting that they would not receive a share of the spoils as they had expected, and so they went into the villages around Tiberias and said that I was about to betray the territory to the Romans: [130] in claiming to keep what had been procured by the raid for the repair of the city walls of the Jerusalemites, I had employed a clever trick against them; I had really planned to return the seized goods to the "master." [131] In this respect, they did not mistake my intention. For once they had been released, I sent for the two principal men, Dassion and Jannaeus the son of Levis, who were established friends of the king at the highest level, and instructed them to take the gear from the raid and to conduct it to him. I threatened death as the penalty if they should report these matters to another person.

27.[132] Once the rumor had taken hold of the entire Galilee that their territory was about to be betrayed to the Romans by me, everyone was stirred up for my punishment. When the residents of Tarichea themselves supposed the young fellows to be telling the truth, they persuaded my bodyguards and armed soldiers to leave me sleeping and to go quickly to the hippodrome: there, with everyone, they would deliberate concerning the general. [133] A large crowd had already assembled beforehand when these men were persuaded and joined in. They were all making one sound: to discipline the man who had become a wretched traitor in relation to them. [134] Jesus the son of Sapphias, then the council president in Tiberias, a wretched person whose nature was to disrupt large affairs, a sedition-fomenter and revolutionary like no other, especially incited them. At that time he actually took the laws of Moyses into his hands and, having come forward into the [city] center, declared: [135] "If you are not able to hate Josephus for your own sakes, citizens, turn your attention to the ancestral laws, of which your foremost general was about to become a traitor. For the sake of these [laws], hate evil and punish such an insolent man!" 28.[136] When he had said these things, the mob applauded him. He gathered up some armed soldiers and hurried toward the house in which I was lodging, to dispose of me.

Not detecting anything in advance, before the disturbance I had turned in because of fatigue. [137] Now Simon, who had been entrusted with the protection of my person, and the only one who had stayed behind, when he saw the rush of the citizens, woke me up and apprised me of the impending danger. He thought it fitting that I should die nobly by my own hand, as a general, before my adversaries came to compel me or to kill me [themselves]. [138] Although he was saying these things, I, having entrusted my affairs to God, set out to meet the mob in advance. I put on black clothes, hung my sword from my neck, and went into the hippodrome—by a different route, on which I did not think any of the enemy would encounter me. When I suddenly appeared and fell facedown, wetting the dry ground with my tears, I seemed to everyone an object of pity. [139] Perceiving the mob's reversal, I tried to strengthen the disagreement in their opinions before the armed soldiers returned from the house. I conceded that I had committed an injustice—as they at least imagined—but I begged first to teach them for what purpose I was reserving the goods procured in the raid. Then I would die, if they should direct it. [140] As the mob was directing me to speak, however, the armed soldiers arrived and, when they observed me, they ran toward me to kill me. But the mob directed them to hold off, and they were persuaded—expecting that I would confess to them that I had kept the goods for the king, and that, after I had confessed the betrayal, they would dispose of me.

[29.141] When silence had come to everyone, then, I said:

> "Men, compatriots! I do not beg to avoid dying, if that is just. But at the same time I do want, before I should end my life, to indicate the truth to you. [142]For because I understood well that this city, so hospitable toward foreigners, was eagerly accommodating such men as these, who have left behind their native places and made common cause with our fortune, I wanted to construct walls from those goods about which there is such anger among us, spending thus on their building."

[143] At this, a noise went up from the Taricheans and their [resident] foreigners, who confessed their feelings of gratitude and gave themselves to cheering, whereas the Galileans and Tiberians continued in their feelings of anger. So a rift appeared among them, some promising to discipline me, but others to disregard. . . . [144] When I then announced that I would construct walls also for Tiberias and the other cities of theirs that needed them, and they had thus come to trust me, each person departed to his own home. And I too, having beyond all hope escaped the danger that I have described, returned home with my friends and twenty armed soldiers.

Introduction to the *Jewish Antiquities*

Narrative Description

Josephus's obvious interest in the temple and its priesthood provides the *Jewish Antiquities'* clearest structural criterion. The twenty-volume work falls neatly into two halves, the first ending with the fall of the first temple to the Neo-Babylonians (sixth century BCE), the second ending on the eve of the Second Temple's destruction, which it ominously anticipates (20.214, 218, 257–58). Josephus emphasizes the function of book 10 as a midpoint, by offering a preliminary summary of high priests and reiterating his philosophical (Stoic-like) theme of divine governance of human life *(pronoia)* against **Epicurean** philosophy there (10.277–81). Book 10 also features the biblical characters of the priestly prophet Jeremiah, who was branded a traitor for counseling submission to the Babylonians (10.114, 119, 125), and Daniel, who like Jeremiah foresaw all of the subsequent history through the fall of the Second Temple (10.79, 276). Since Josephus identifies himself as a sort of second Jeremiah (*War* 5.391–94) and especially values Daniel's acceptance of nations rising and falling under divine supervision, this makes an apt turning point for the whole composition.

There is some evidence that Josephus wanted not only to create this neat division but also, as in the *War*, to make the narrative move to and then away from the center as a fulcrum. A small example is the story of the Adiabenian family's adoption of Judean law in book 20, which includes reminiscences of book 1. These include an incidental and apparently unnecessary recollection of Noah's ark from the opening volume (20.24–26; cf. 1.90–92). Further, the jealousy of the Adiabenian prince Izates's brothers, because of their father's favor toward him (20.19), distinctly evokes the biblical story of Joseph and his brothers (2.9–10). It also seems that Israel's first king-tyrant, Saul, who dominates book 6 (in the middle of the first half), anticipates the tragically flawed tyrant Herod, who dominates—albeit at much greater length—the middle of the second half (books 14–17).

Date/Occasion

Josephus's *Antiquities* is the only one of his works to clearly mention its date: at the end, he says that he will append a brief account of events from the war "until this very day, which is the thirteenth year of the reign of Domitian Caesar and the fifty-sixth year of my own life" (20.267). Domitian's thirteenth year in power ran from 14 September 93 to 13 September 94 CE. Since Josephus was born in **Caligula's** first year (*Life* 5; see *Life*), which could be considered either 37 CE (the Roman year from January) or the regnal year from 18 March 37 to 17 March 38 CE, Josephus's fifty-sixth year fell in the range from March 92 to March 94 CE (*see* Introduction to Flavius Josephus). The overlap between these two calculations is the period from September 93 to March 94 CE.

Few things are so straightforward in academic research, however, and some scholars have argued that the *Antiquities* underwent multiple revisions. On this view, the passage to which the date is attached was a relatively *early* edition; Josephus further revised the work at least until 100 CE. Although the notion of multiple revisions is entirely likely, given the nature of ancient publication, the detection of traces from different revisions in the existing text, which has also been copied countless times since Josephus wrote it, is not likely to be convincing. Scholars generally agree today that the *Antiquities* may be considered a basically finished work from 93/94 CE.

Until the 1980s, given that the *War* (see *War*) was regarded as Josephus's collapse into Roman propaganda (and not read as a whole composition), the *Antiquities* and his later works appeared to mark an abrupt change of direction—toward enthusiastic defense and advocacy of Judean traditions. Great scholars such as Richard Laqueur, Henry St. John Thackeray, and many after them proposed a range of circumstances to explain the alleged change. Perhaps Josephus had lost his imperial support with the rise of the supposedly rejectionist Domitian and needed new sponsors. Perhaps he felt guilty about all his past life in propaganda as he got older, and wanted to make peace with both his tradition and his fellow Judeans. Perhaps he made a cynical calculation that his best chances for advancement now, having exhausted his Roman chances, lay in promoting the new Judean leadership in Yavneh (Jamnia) in Judea, which had become a seat of Jewish learning following the destruction of Jerusalem in 70 CE. Yavneh is where a number of prominent Jewish scholars, such as Johanan ben Zakkai, who was referred to as Nasi (Prince) or Rabban (Our Master), relocated after the destruction of Jerusalem.

All of these notions were put forward to explain how Josephus could have turned so abruptly from propaganda to obvious commitment to explicating his nation's beautiful laws and culture. But as we have come to jettison our old assumptions about Josephus's character and circumstances, and to focus instead on reading what he wrote, we have seen that the *War* does not serve the needs of Roman propaganda. This takes away the need to explain an alleged about-face between the *War* and the later works, and we are more willing to realize that Josephus himself assumed the *continuity* of his literary output.

For example, the *Antiquities* opens with a reflection on the *War*: in no way an apology for it, but a reiteration of what Josephus had said in the *War*'s prologue.

He recalls that he had felt compelled to write the earlier work because of the great importance of the events and because others were doing outrage to the truth (*Antiquities* 1–4; cf. *War* 1.1–9). Although he had thought of including the ancient history of his people in that work, he decided to keep the *War* a symmetrically balanced account, and postponed the treatment of more ancient history, including the whole political constitution of the Judeans, until now (1.5–7).

The main shift that Josephus suggests from the *War* to the *Antiquities* is one of environment. Whereas the *War*'s prologue shows him in verbal confrontation with anti-Judean stories in the shadow of the conflict, he claims to write the later and larger work from his own desire to make this excellent material available in Greek and, when his ambition and energy flagged, because of the insistent encouragement of **Epaphroditus** and his circle.[1] Remarkably enough, given the *War*'s more defensive posture, Josephus presents himself as wondering whether Judeans really ought to share so much of their treasure with the Greek world. He looks back to the model of the Septuagint (*see* Overview of Early Jewish Literature), the Greek translation of the Bible allegedly requested by the Greek king Ptolemy II (*see* Letter of Aristeas), as a supportive model for what he is doing. So, following his people's tradition of not jealously hoarding their excellent things, he has "yielded" to Epaphroditus's urging and completed the work (1.9).

Putting all this evidence together produces a two-sided picture of Josephus's context. On the one hand, the years 93–94 CE were precisely the time when it seems that Domitian's reign reached its low point (often called the "terror"), when he began executing even family members and formerly close friends on suspicion of treachery (**Suetonius,** *Lives of the Caesars* 10–15). This period would end with his assassination, a few days after the fifteenth anniversary of his accession (18 September 96 CE). On the other hand, Josephus describes a circle in Rome at this time that was keen to hear more about Judean law and custom. There had always been such interest among some Romans: L. Cornelius Alexander (nicknamed "Polyhistor"—researcher into everything) had written a book on the Judeans in the mid-first century BCE. But most of our evidence for such interest in Rome happens to come from the late first century CE, just when Josephus was writing.

These two sides come together in the later historian **Dio Cassius's** claim that some of the prominent people done away with by Domitian in 95 CE were charged with an "atheism" connected with having adopted Judean ways (67.14.1–3).[2] Similarly, he claims that Domitian's successor, Nerva, stopped hearing accusations of treason *or adopting the Judean way of life* (68.1.2). We do not know more about this intriguing connection, but all sorts of possibilities arise—for example, that exploration of foreign constitutions and cultures became a sort of outlet for those distressed about the state of Roman politics under an autocracy seen as tyrannical. Certainly Josephus's narrative could be construed as lending incidental encouragement to those who wanted the restoration of a senatorial

---

1. Epaphroditus ("Favorite of Aphrodite") was a common enough Greek name, and efforts to identify this figure with others of the same name have not proven decisive.

2. For other hints about Roman attraction to Judean ways in the late first and early second centuries CE, see **Tacitus,** *Histories* 5.5; Epictetus in Arrian, *Discourses of Epictetus* 2.9.20; Juvenal 14.96–106.

aristocracy and the removal of tyranny—though his main subject is Judean affairs. But we have no idea of how his writing in this vein connected with real individuals at the time.

Themes

The thematic groups established in the *War* continue in the *Antiquities*, but they take on new dimensions in light of the new context and different chronological focus. Although there are tragic elements in parts of the story, this is not an entire tragic history as the *War* is. Although political themes dominate the narrative, they are not so sharply focused on the scenario of political leaders desperate to prevent imminent catastrophe. The new and much larger work can afford to be more leisurely and reflective. We might identify, for convenience, five large thematic clusters.

First, Josephus is proud of the Judeans' great and unique antiquity. In the prologue (1.13) he claims that their recorded history extends back five thousand years to creation. We see throughout ancient literature a general assumption that "old is good." The Romans knew that their own civilization was not extremely old (they dated it to 753 BCE), but they derived it from somewhat older Greek roots, tracing their ancestor **Aeneas** to the Trojan War of a more distant past (twelfth century BCE?). The Greeks themselves recognized—as Josephus astutely observes in *Apion* 1.8—that the civilizations of Mesopotamia, Egypt, and Phoenicia were older and initially more accomplished than their civilization (see *Apion*). Although Judeans were widely thought to be a derivative culture from Egypt (a view supported by mangled versions of the Exodus story), Josephus writes the *Antiquities* in part to set that story straight, by claiming an uninterrupted history going back to the origin of the world.

In the process, the Judean lawgiver Moses becomes not merely a refugee from Egypt, as he was commonly imagined, but a member of the Hebrew people, who merely sojourned in Egypt. As a Hebrew, he far excelled his Egyptian peers in military leadership, and gave them their most brilliant successes while he was among them, at the same time showing them up and thereby incurring their undying hatred (*Antiquities* 2.238-55). He eventually left under divine direction to establish a new and superior political constitution for his own people in a new land.

Moses' laws are therefore the second major theme of the work, also emphasized in the prologue.[3] Josephus presents this "political constitution"—this terminology invites comparison with the constitutions of all others, Greek and Oriental—as unmatched in quality. That is because Moses carefully designed it to reflect the very laws of nature and the cosmos, which God had created (1.21-23). In Josephus's time, the issue of the best form of political life had been discussed for centuries, and the main options—along with their pitfalls—were well known: one-person rule, or monarchy, which tended almost invariably to tyranny and faced the serious problem of succession; governance by all citizens, or democracy,

---

3. Notice the constitutional language in, for example, *Antiquities* 1.5, 10, 114; 3.84, 213, 322; 4.3, 16, 22, 45, 146, 149, 198, 292, 302, 312; 5.132; 20.229, 251, 261.

the problem with which was that the "mob" was by definition impulsive and fickle, not suited to establishing rational policy; and finally, government by society's elite, or aristocracy, who achieved their status through birth into families of older wealth and were therefore schooled for leadership. The pitfall in this system was that these "oligarchs" would end up protecting their group or private interests to the detriment of the general populace.

Throughout *Antiquities* Josephus makes clear, though the Bible had not, that Moses was a firm supporter of "aristocracy" (4.223; cf. 4.184–87). The reasons are not explained but left implicit, namely: government by a "senate," in spite of possible abuse and challenge, avoids the much worse evils of both tyranny (5.338–39) and mob rule. An early challenge to Moses comes from another member of the aristocracy named Korah, who wants the high priesthood for himself (rather than for Moses' brother Aaron). Korah cleverly tries to turn this into a matter for democratic debate in an assembly of all citizens (4.12–62), but Moses proves that it was God who ordered their aristocratic system of government (on Korah's Rebellion, see Num. 16).

This does not mean that Judeans have always had aristocratic rule, even if it is the best way and was mandated by Moses. Josephus develops the Bible's brief story of the popular demand for a king during the prophet Samuel's days into a major constitutional crisis, with the aged prophet favoring "aristocracy, as something divine that renders happy those who use it as their constitution" (6.36). But he is forced by popular will and reluctant divine support to name a king. Sure enough, the first king—Saul—turns out to be the kind of tyrant Samuel had warned about (6.262–68), and he is followed by a line of other such kings before the fall of Jerusalem to the Babylonians (sixth century BCE).

Although the aristocracy is restored after the Babylonian exile (11.111), Josephus will spend several volumes describing Judea's most famous "tyrant," Herod, whose name was well known in the Roman world, and the disastrous effect that he and his successors had on Judea.[4] The most remarkable thing about the *Antiquities'* later volumes is that Josephus brings this entire constitutional issue right into the Romans' living room, so to speak. He describes, and has his characters present, all of the Roman emperors, from **Julius Caesar** to at least Gaius Caligula—leaving open the question of how recently this verdict extends—as tyrants.[5] He even writes a substantial speech for a Roman consul that praises aristocracy and rejects one-man rule (19.167–84; cf. 19.187).

In the prologue Josephus boldly invites his Roman audience to consider whether the constitution he is about to investigate at length does not offer the worthiest conception of God and human life (1.15). As he says there and insists throughout, God rewards *all* those who live in accord with it and punishes all who violate its precepts (1.14, 20)—not Judeans alone, but even rulers such as Gaius Caligula (*see* discussion of Pompey in Psalms of Solomon).

In Josephus's world, the context in which constitutional issues were discussed, and from which criticism of one-man rule historically emanated, was that of the philosophical schools. The assassins of Julius Caesar in 44 BCE, **Brutus** and

---

4. For example, Josephus, *Antiquities* 14.165; 16.1–4, 402–3; 17.304–8.
5. Josephus, *Antiquities* 18.169, 226; 19.2.

Cassius, had become heroes of **Stoic** lore, and members of the Stoic school continued to rail against emperors, sometimes at the cost of their lives. It fits with this that the third major thematic group in the *Antiquities* has to do with philosophy. Josephus remarks in the prologue that anyone who wants to explore the causes of each prescription in the Judean law would find it "extremely philosophical," though perhaps too much so for elaboration in this work (1.25); he hopes to return to the underlying philosophy in a later study—an ambition never fulfilled, unless the *Apion* covers that task.

Ancient philosophy was an extremely broad category, encompassing most of what we would call science, biology, astronomy, mathematics, psychology, political science, anthropology, sociology, theology, and religion—in addition to what we recognize as philosophy. All of this was united by *moral* questions. The pursuit of philosophy, whether figuring out how the world worked and what it was made of or deciding on the optimal form of government, was intended to produce human well-being (Greek: *eudaimonia*). Philosophy (rather than religion) was therefore the environment in which one learned to live right, with self-discipline, to "repent" if necessary of indulgent worldly ways, and to find the truth that brings inner calm and acceptance of life's trials—and of the ultimate challenge, death. Such well-being is precisely what Josephus promises as the outcome of following Judean law (1.14, 20), and he introduces the word *eudaimonia* some forty-seven times into his paraphrase of the Bible, though it did not appear in the Greek translation of the Bible. Daniel and his Hebrew friends, according to Josephus, follow a **Pythagorean**-like vegetarian diet (cf. Dan. 1:11–16),[6] which keeps their minds light and fresh so that they master the learning of both Hebrews and **Chaldeans** (10.193–94). Immediately after the Daniel story, he criticizes Epicurean philosophers, the favorite whipping posts of other ancient philosophers (10.277). It fits with all this that he describes Pharisees, Sadducees, and Essenes as Judea's philosophical schools (13.171–73; 18.12–25).

Accordingly, most of the major figures of the Bible become, in Josephus's hands, philosophers. Seth's descendants discover the orderly array of the planets (1.69) and Abraham reasons from their irregularity that there must be one ultimate God (1.155–56); Abraham also taught mathematics and science to the Egyptians (1.167–68). Moses was a uniquely gifted philosopher, surpassing in his understanding all who ever lived (4.328). Solomon, too, excelled even beyond the famous Egyptians: his knowledge covered the whole range of natural science and extended to cures and recipes for expelling demons (8.42–46). As for converts to the philosophical life: Josephus opens the story with the easterner Abraham,

---

6. Dan. 1:11–16: "But Daniel said to the overseer whom the commander of the officials had appointed over Daniel, Hananiah, Mishael, and Azariah, 'Please test your servants for ten days, and let us be given some vegetables to eat and water to drink. Then let our appearance be observed in your presence, and the appearance of the youths who are eating the king's choice food; and deal with your servants according to what you see.' So he listened to them in this matter and tested them for ten days. And at the end of ten days their appearance seemed better and they were fatter than all the youths who had been eating the king's choice food. So the overseer continued to withhold their choice food and the wine they were to drink, and kept giving them vegetables."

who both adopts monotheism himself and brings over the Egyptians to reorder their lives with the truth (1.161). He closes it (almost) with the stirring account of an eastern royal family, from Adiabene (modern-day Iraq), who courageously embrace the Judean constitution as their own (20.17–96).

Fourth, in the service of these constitutional and philosophical themes, but also in keeping with the tendencies of Roman (rhetorical) history writing, Josephus presents this long history as a kind of serial biography. That is, instead of working from one period to the next, and describing events that happened at each time, his story is about a succession of great figures, mostly men (exceptions include Deborah in book 5 and the **Hasmonean** Queen Alexandra in book 13). This format allows him to extract moral lessons from his characters, whether good or bad, and for this purpose, he typically supplies obituaries. The Bible itself had briefly indicated who, among the kings of the past, did or did not obey the divine will. However, Josephus's approach is much more expansive, rhetorical, and Greco-Roman. Using the general criteria of human virtue and vice, he elaborates the Bible's assessments and makes a noticeable effort at balance, mentioning both good and bad points.[7] Saul is a good example: although Josephus criticizes him harshly for disobeying divine commands and behaving with a tyrant's brutality (6.166, 378), he nevertheless gives him a remarkable send-off as a fine example of masculine virtue and contempt for death (6.344–50).

Finally, mixed in with all of these themes is that of the ancient temple and priesthood, which are so dear to our author and basic to his conception of Judean governance. The priests have always provided the core of the aristocracy—to which the government inevitably returns after its predictable experiments with monarchy spectacularly fail—for the two millennia since Moses and Aaron. They are the ones to whom the laws and constitution were entrusted by the lawgiver for safekeeping and skilled interpretation. Josephus is much concerned to follow the succession of high priests from Aaron all the way to his present day. He does this throughout the narrative, in a brief summary of high priests under the kings near the halfway point (*Antiquities* 10.151–53), and again in a complete final summary form near the end of the work (20.224–51).

STEVE MASON

---

7. For example, *Antiquities* 1.256, 346; 2.198–204; 4.327–31; 5.117–18, 253; 6.292–94; 7.37–38, 390–91.

2.4 from *Jewish Antiquities*

Prologue (1.1–26)

[1.1] I see among those wanting to compose histories that they do not have one and the same motive for their eagerness, but many reasons that differ greatly from one another. [2] Some, demonstrating their forcefulness with words and hunting the glory associated with this, charge ahead into this area of learning, while others, in currying favor with those to whom the writing relates, have undertaken the requisite labor even beyond their ability. [3] Then there are some who have been forced by the weight of events in which they happened to participate to cover these things in a lucid composition. And the magnitude of serviceable events lying buried in ignorance has prompted many others to bring out the history of them for common benefit. [4] Of the motives mentioned here, the final two have certainly applied to me, for after learning by hard experience about the war against the Romans that originated with us Judeans, the actions in it, and how the end turned out, I was forced to narrate it in detail because of those who in their writing were doing outrage to the truth.

[5] Now I have taken upon myself this present work supposing that it will appear to all the Greeks worthy of their eager attention; for it is going to encompass all of our ancient lore and plan of political life, translated from the Hebrew texts.

[6] I had actually intended earlier, when I was writing up the war, to explain who the Judeans were from the beginning and what fortunes they experienced, under what sort of lawgiver they were educated for piety and other training in virtue, and how many wars they had waged in times long ago, before they embarked unwillingly on this last one against the Romans. [7] But since the scope of such an account was too large, I separated that [*War*] by itself and made it a balanced composition, with its own beginnings and ending. With the passage of time, in the way familiar to those who are intent on committing themselves to great things, weariness and procrastination visited me, at the prospect of conveying such a vast subject in an idiom of language that is unaccustomed and foreign to us.

[8] But there were some people who, by their yearning for the history, urged me on, and most of all Epaphroditus: a man who has shown a love for every form of learning but finds particular joy in the experiences of public affairs—just as he himself has certainly been involved in the greatest affairs and many turns of fortune, in all of that exhibiting an astonishing strength in his nature and an unwavering preference for virtue. [9] Being won over by this man, as by someone always ready with friendly support for those who are able to produce something

Translation by Steve Mason (1.1–26; 20.262–67), Louis H. Feldman/Brill (2.39–60; 4.11–58; 4.196–239), Christopher T. Begg/Brill (6.35–54; 6.335–50; 8.42–56; 8.106–21), P. Spilsbury/Brill (10.186–215), and D. R. Schwartz/Brill (draft) (18.256–309). Republication of Brill material courtesy of Koninklijke BRILL NV.

useful or excellent, and feeling ashamed of myself if I should appear to find more joy in relaxation than in the labor involved in [producing] the most excellent things, I redoubled my enthusiasm.

In addition to these factors I have mentioned, I thought about (and not incidentally) whether, on the side of our forebears, they used to want to share such things as these, and on the side of the Greeks, whether some of them were keen to know about our affairs. ^(praef. 3) ¹⁰ So I found that, on the one side, the second of the Ptolemies, a king who was especially eager for learning and the collection of books, was singularly committed to rendering into the Greek language our law and the plan of the constitution within it. ¹¹ And on the other side, a man second to none in virtue among our high priests, Eleazar, did not begrudge the aforementioned king the enjoyment of this benefit, which he surely would have opposed had it not been an ancestral prohibition with us not to withhold excellent things. ¹² And I really thought it proper for me to imitate the magnanimity of the high priest, and to assume that even today there are many lovers of learning much like the king. For he did not yet set a precedent by obtaining all the record [i.e., Scripture]: those who were sent to Alexandria for the translation transmitted only the books of the law. ¹³ But the matters explained in the sacred texts are truly innumerable, seeing that five thousand years of history are included in them: all sorts of unexpected reversals, many twists of fortune in warfare as well as manly deeds of commanders, and upheavals in political life.

¹⁴ In general, someone would chiefly learn from this history, if he were willing to go right through it, that those who comply with the judgment of God and do not dare to contravene what has been excellently established as law, succeed in all things beyond belief, and happiness is set before them by God as reward, whereas to the extent that they abandon the precise observance of these [laws], productive things become unproductive, and whatever they eagerly pursue as a good thing turns into irremediable calamities. ¹⁵ And so now I appeal to those who will engage these volumes to cede their own judgment to God, and to test our lawgiver, as to whether he comprehended his nature worthily, having always been appropriate in the way he attributed his deeds to his power, and having kept the language concerning him pure from all the indecent mythology from other sources.

¹⁶ Certainly, given the length of time and antiquity involved, he had plenty of room for [writing] plausible falsehoods with impunity. For he was born two thousand years ago, a chronological era to which their [i.e., Greek] poets did not dare to trace back even the birth of the Gods, let alone the deeds or the laws of *men*.

¹⁷ As it proceeds, then, the story will make clear the precise details of what is in the records [Scriptures], following the proper sequence. For this is what I offered to do throughout this work, having neither added nor indeed left out anything.

¹⁸ Now, since nearly everything depends on the wisdom of our lawgiver Moyses, it is necessary for me to say a little about him beforehand, so that some of those who will read this should not be perplexed about how our story, containing the record concerning laws and deeds, has come to include such a large measure of natural science. ¹⁹ One must realize, therefore, that he [Moyses] considered it most important of all that the one who would order his life excellently and to establish law for others first understand the nature of God and, after becoming

one who contemplates—in the mind—his deeds, thus to imitate the best of all models and also try to follow it as far as possible. [20] For neither would the lawgiver himself ever acquire a good mind if he neglected this contemplation, nor would any of the things that were going to be written into the story of virtue have a good outcome for those receiving it, unless they had been taught before everything else that God, who is the Father and Master of all things and watches over all things, gives a happy life to those who follow him, but surrounds with great calamities those who go beyond the bounds of virtue.

[21] This being the lesson that Moyses wanted to teach his own citizens, he did not begin the composition of the laws with contracts and the rights of people in relation to one another, in the sort of way that others did, but he directed them upward, toward God and the construction of the world-order, and persuaded them that of God's works upon earth we humans are the most excellent. Once he had them submitting to a life of piety, he easily persuaded them about everything else. [22] The other legislators, taking their cue from the myths, transferred the shame of human failings to the gods in their accounts—and gave a great excuse to the wicked. [23] But our legislator, having shown that God possesses a virtue that is uncontaminated, thought that human beings should try to have a share in it, and those who do not think the same way or believe him he punished mercilessly.

[24] It is from this basic perspective that I invite readers to make their examination. To those who investigate in this way, nothing will appear either unreasonable or out of keeping with the magnificence and benevolence of God. For all things have their role in harmony with the nature of the universe: some things being put dexterously in riddles by the lawgiver; other things being formulated metaphorically [or allegorically], albeit with seriousness; but whatever it was advantageous to say straightforwardly, these things he put clearly as stated. [25] Now, for those who want to investigate the causes of each and every thing, that inquiry would be vast and rather too philosophical. So I postpone that for now, though if God should give us time I will attempt to write that work after this one.

[26] So I turn now to the narration of events, recalling first what Moyses said about the construction of the world-order. These things I have found recorded in the sacred books. It goes as follows.

Joseph and Potiphar's Wife (2.39–60)

[2.39]Pentephres, an Egyptian who was in charge of the cooks of the king Pharaothes, bought Iosepos when he was sold by the merchants. He held him in all honor and gave him the education that befits a free man and permitted him to enjoy a better way of life than the lot of a slave, and handed over to him the care of the affairs of his household.

[40] He had the benefit of these things, yet did not forsake the virtue that encompassed him, not even under the change of fortune, but he showed clearly that reason is able to overcome the difficulties in life, when it faces them with genuineness and does not merely accommodate itself to the successes of the time. [41] For his master's wife was disposed amorously to him because of his handsomeness and his adroitness in his doings, and she thought that if she would make this clear to

him she would easily persuade him to have intercourse, since he would consider it a stroke of luck that his mistress had solicited him. [42] She was looking at the outward bearing of his slavery at that time but not on the character that remained firm despite his change of fortune. And when she made clear her passion and addressed words to him with regard to sexual intercourse, he kept rejecting her request, judging that it would not be pious to grant to her such pleasure, in which there happened to be injustice and insolence toward the one who had bought him and had deemed him worthy of such honor.

[43] He kept on imploring her to prevail over her passion, setting before her the hopelessness of satisfying her desire, since this would cease when hope was not present, and he said that he himself would rather endure anything than to be obedient to this [request]. For, indeed, though it is necessary for one who is a slave to do nothing opposed to his mistress, the contradiction to such orders would have abundant excuse. [44] The fact that she did not expect Iosepos to oppose her increased her passion still more; and being terribly besieged by her wickedness she again by a second attempt strove to achieve her goal.

[45] Therefore, when a public festival was at hand, in which it was customary for women to come together frequently in the festal assembly, she feigned illness to her husband, while hunting for isolation and leisure to seek out Iosepos; and having obtained this opportunity, she addressed even more persistent words than the first, [46] that it would have been well for him to have yielded to her request from the beginning and to have refused nothing, both out of regard for the petitioner and for the extraordinary degree of the passion, owing to which she, though being a mistress, was forced to lower herself beneath her dignity; but even now by giving in better to sagacity he would remedy his senselessness in the past. [47] For if he were awaiting a second entreaty, this had come and with greater fervor, since she had feigned illness and had preferred the meeting with him to the festival and the festal assembly. And if, owing to distrust, he had rejected the first arguments, he should judge that her persistence in them was an indication that there was no evil intent. [48] He might expect both the advantage of his present blessings, in which he had participated, by acceding to her passion, and the enjoyment of greater ones if he would be obedient, but that there would be retaliation and hatred on her part if he should reject her request and should put his reputation for self-control above pleasing his mistress. [49] For this would not help him if she should turn to accuse him and should fabricate to her husband that he had made an attempt upon her, but Pentephres would rather give credence to her words than to his, even if they should be carried very far from the truth.

[50] Though the woman said these things and wept, neither did compassion persuade him not to be self-controlled nor did fear compel him, but he resisted her supplications and did not give in to her threats, and chose to suffer unjustly and to endure something more bitter rather than to enjoy the present by giving himself up to his emotions, for which he was conscious that he would justly perish. [51] He reminded her of her marriage and her conjugal union with her husband and exhorted her to have more regard for these than for the transitory pleasure of lust, which would later bring her regret that would be painful and would not remedy her sins, and fear of being discovered and the need to remain hidden if the wickedness should not be known. [52] On the other hand, association with her

husband afforded pleasure without danger and furthermore much self-confidence both before God and before men arising from her conscience; and by remaining morally pure she would command greater power over him and would exercise the authority of a mistress toward him, but not with the shame of being a partner in sin. Indeed, it was far better to have confidence in the known deeds of a life well lived than in wickedness kept secret.

[53] Saying these words and still more that were similar to them, he tried to restrain the impulse of the woman and to turn her passion into reasonableness. But she showed her fervor more impetuously, and throwing her hands upon him, she, abandoning hope of persuading him, wished to compel him. [54] When, however, Iosepos fled in rage leaving behind also his cloak, for indeed, while she held him, he threw this away and leaped from this room, she, having become very fearful lest he reveal this to her husband and being deeply hurt by his insolence, decided to anticipate him by falsely accusing Iosepos to Pentephres and in this manner to avenge her having been horribly despised. And she believed that to anticipate the accusation was both wise and womanish.

[55] She sat dejected and disconcerted, feigning, in her anger, that the grief at failing in her lust was due to an attempt at rape. And when her husband came and was dismayed at her appearance and asked the reason, she began the accusation of Iosepos and said, "May you die, my husband, or punish a wicked slave who wished to pollute your marriage-bed. [56] He, neither remembering what sort of person he was when he arrived in our house nor what he chanced upon through your generosity, showed no self-restraint; but he, who would have been ungrateful unless he had proven himself utterly good toward us, plotted to violate your wedlock and this on a festival, watching out for your absence. For, as much as he seemed restrained previously, he held his peace on account of fear of you and he was not well-disposed by nature. [57] His arrival, it seems, at undeserved and unexpected honor has made him such that he, who succeeded in obtaining the responsibility over and the administration of your possessions and in being preferred to the older servants, had the right also to lay hands on your wife."

[58] Having ceased from these words she showed him the cloak, as if he had left it behind when he was undertaking to rape her. Now Pentephres, being unable to disbelieve either his wife's weeping or the words with which she spoke and what he saw, and paying more attention to his passion for her, did not apply himself to the investigation of the truth.

[59] Giving to his wife credit for being sensible and having condemned Iosepos as wicked, he threw him into the dungeon of the criminals, but he was even more proud of his wife, bearing witness to her propriety and self-control. [60] Now Iosepos, putting everything concerning himself in the hands of God, did not apply himself to defending himself nor to a precise disclosure of what had happened, but in silence underwent the chains and the distress, being confident that God, knowing the reason for his misfortune and the truth, would be stronger than those who had bound him, and he straightway received proof of his providence.

Rebellion of Korah (4.11–58)

4.[11]But just as it happens with large armies, and especially in unfortunate situations, that they are unruly and disobedient, this also occurred to the Judeans. For numbering 600,000, and perhaps even in good circumstances not subordinated to their betters on account of their numbers, at that time even more influenced by their helplessness and their misfortune, they became very angry with each other and with their leader.

[12]Now such a sedition as we know has occurred neither among Greeks nor among barbarians took hold of them, from which Moyses, who was not resentful that he had come very close to being stoned to death by them, saved them when they were all in danger of perishing. [13]Nor did God fail to concern himself that they should suffer from misfortunes; but although they had acted outrageously against the lawgiver and the commandments, which he himself through Moyses had enjoined upon them, he rescued them from the misfortunes that would have resulted from their civil strife if he had not made provision. Now the civil strife and whatever measures Moyses instituted after this I will report in detail, after I have first narrated the cause from which it arose.

[14]Kores, a certain one of the Hebrews who was among the most distinguished both in ancestry and in wealth, an able speaker and most persuasive in dealing with crowds, seeing that Moyses was established in extraordinary honor, was hostile through envy, for he happened to be his fellow tribesman and kinsman, and was embittered because he was more deserving to enjoy this glory by virtue of his being wealthier and not inferior in ancestry.

[15]He inveighed against him among the Levites, who were his tribesmen, and especially among his kinsmen, saying that it was dreadful to overlook that Moyses was hunting to procure glory for himself and maliciously pretending to obtain this in the name of God. He said that he [Moyses] had given the priesthood to his brother Aaron contrary to the laws, not by the common decree of the multitude but by his own vote, [16]and that in the manner of tyrants he was conferring honors upon whomever he wished. He said that hidden outrage was actually more shocking than the use of force because it robbed of power not only those who were unwilling but those who were not even aware of the conspiracy. [17]For whoever is conscious of being worthy to obtain something seeks to attain it by persuasion and in that case without daring to use force, whereas those for whom it is impossible to be honored in accordance with justice, scheme with craft to attain it because, wishing to seem honest, they do not make use of force. [18]It was advantageous for the masses to punish such people while they still thought that they escaped notice and not to allow them to rise to power and to have obvious enemies. "What reason could Moyses offer for handing over the priesthood to Aaron and his sons? [19]For if God had judged that it was proper to hand over the honor to someone from the tribe of Levis, I am more deserving to obtain this, being on the same level as Moyses in ancestry, and superior in wealth and in age. But if it should go to the oldest of the tribes, the tribe of Roubelos would, of course, have the honor, with Dathames, Abirames, and Phalaos obtaining it, for they are the oldest of those belonging to this tribe, and powerful through abundance of wealth."

[20] Now in saying this, Kores wished to seem to care for the common good, but in fact he was manipulating to have the honor transferred by the multitude to himself. And he spoke these words insidiously to his tribesmen with fine-sounding pretext. [21] When his words gradually spread to the masses and when those who listened to them agreed with the slanders against Aaron, the whole army was filled up with them. Those who were arrayed with Kores were 250 of the foremost men, who were keen for removing the brother of Moyses from the priesthood and for dishonoring him [Moyses] himself. [22] The masses were provoked and bent on stoning Moyses, and they assembled in disorderly fashion with clamor and uproar; and standing before the tent of God they called aloud to drive out the tyrant and for the masses to be rid of their slavery to him who enjoined imperious decrees under the pretext of their coming from God.

[23] "For God, if, indeed, it was he who chose the one who was to be priest, would have appointed one who was worthy of the honor and would not have borne and assigned it to those who are inferior to many of us; and if he had decided to bestow it upon Aaron he would have arranged to have the multitude bestow it and would not have left it to his brother." [24] Moyses, however, though he had for a long time before known the slander of Kores and had seen the people being incited, was not alarmed, but being confident that he had counseled well concerning the matters, and knowing that his brother had obtained the priesthood in accordance with God's decision and not through his own favoritism, came into the assembly.

[25] Turning to the masses he uttered not a word; but to Kores he, who was skilled both in other respects and gifted by nature in dealing with the masses, shouted as loud as he could. "O Kores," he said, "both you and each of these," and he pointed at the 250 men, "seem worthy of honor, and I will not deprive all the throng of similar honor even if they are inferior to you in wealth and other merits. [26] And now the priesthood has been given to Aaron not because he was superior in wealth, for you surpass even both of us in magnitude of possessions; nor, indeed, is he superior in nobility of birth, for God made this status common for us by giving us the same forefather; nor in bestowing this was it because of brotherly love that I conferred upon my brother this that another would justly have deserved. [27] For even if I had granted this honor in disregard of God and the laws, I would not have passed over giving it to myself and offered it to another, inasmuch as I am more closely related to myself than is my brother and am more closely attached to myself than to him. Nor, indeed, would it have been sensible by exposing myself to the dangers resulting from an unlawful deed to grant to another the happiness arising through this. [28] I, however, am above doing malice; and God would not have overlooked his being disregarded nor your being ignorant of what you should do to be pleasing to him. But since he himself has designated the one who is to be high priest for him, he has freed us from the responsibility for this.

[29] But, indeed, Aaron, not having received this through my favor rather than in accordance with God's decision, offers it as a prize on which a legal claim may be made by those who wish it, nor does he deem himself worthy to be granted it on the ground that he had previously been chosen already to obtain it and to compete now for it. [30] Rather than keep this prize, he prefers to see that you are not engaging in sedition, although he happens to have it in accordance with your

will. For we were not mistaken in thinking that that which God gave he received with your consent also. [31] It would have been impious not to have accepted the honor when he offered it; and, on the other hand, to claim to have it for all time if God did not give him an assurance of security would have been altogether unreasonable. He himself will therefore judge again whom he wishes to offer the sacrifices to him on your behalf and to administer the religious rites. [32] For it would be absurd for Kores, who is striving for the honor, to take away from God this power of deciding to whom he should offer it. Therefore, cease from the civil strife and the tumult resulting from it, and in the morning let as many of you as lay claim to the priesthood bring a censer from his home with incense and fire and come here. [33] You, too, Kores, entrust the decision to God, and await his vote on these matters, and do not make yourself superior to God, but be present to be judged thus concerning the prize. Nor do I think that it is likely to give offense to accept Aaron as a competitor, since he is of the same family and cannot be reproached at all for his actions in his priesthood. [34] Therefore, on coming together, you will burn the incense in the presence of all the people; and when you have burned your incense, whosoever sacrifice God judges more pleasing, he will be elected priest for you, releasing me from the slander of having shown favoritism in conferring this honor upon my brother."

[35] When Moyses had said this, the masses ceased from both their uproar and their distrust of Moyses, and they consented to his proposals, for they also seemed good for the people. At that time, therefore, they dissolved the congress; but on the following day they gathered in assembly to be present at the sacrifice and at the judgment thereby of those competing with regard to the priesthood. [36] The assembly turned out to be tumultuous, with the masses being in high expectation of what would transpire. Some would have derived pleasure if Moyses had been convicted of doing malice; others, the prudent ones, if they had been released from troubles and tumult, for they feared that, if sedition should continue, the orderliness of their constitution might be further destroyed.

[37] All the crowd, by nature rejoicing in reviling those in authority and turning their opinion to whatever anyone said, cried out noisily. Moyses sent servants to Abirames and Dathames and bade them to come in accordance with what had been agreed and to await the sacrificial rites. [38] When they said that they would not heed the messengers and that they would not quietly allow Moyses to become powerful at the expense of all the people through malicious action, Moyses, hearing their reply, asked his chief counselors to accompany him and went off to Dathames's faction, not considering it to be shocking to go to these men who had behaved arrogantly. And they [the counselors] followed without offering any objection. [39] The people in Dathames's company, having learned that Moyses had come to them, together with the distinguished men of the masses, came forth, together with their wives and children, before their tents and kept looking to see what Moyses was about to do. Moreover, their servants were also around them, so that if Moyses should bring on some violence they would defend them.

[40] He, on coming near, lifted up his hands to heaven and cried out with a rather loud voice so that it might be audible to all the multitude, "O Lord," he said, "of what is in heaven and earth and sea, for you are a most worthy witness of what has been done by me, that all things are done in accordance with your will, and

that you contrived a device for their enterprises, taking pity on the Hebrews in all their dreadful circumstances, come and be a listener of these words of mine. [41] For neither action nor thought escapes your notice, so that you will not begrudge me the truth, placing before it the ingratitude of these men. Now you know more precisely the events prior to my birth, not by learning of them through hearsay but through seeing them and being present at them at the time when they occurred; but as for the events after this, which, although they know them clearly, these men unjustly suspect, be my witness of them. [42] After establishing a life free of cares through my manly virtue and through your will, and this [life] that my father-in-law Ragouelos left to me, I then abandoned the enjoyment of those good things and devoted myself to the hardships on behalf of these people. I then underwent great toils first for their freedom, and now for their salvation, ranging my enthusiasm against every dread.

[43] Now, therefore, when I am suspected of doing wrong by men whose survival is due to my exertions, it is fitting that you yourself—who showed me that fire at Sinai and at that time caused me to be a listener to your voice and an observer of as many miracles as that place permitted me to see; who instructed me to set out to Egypt and to reveal your will to these people; [44] who unsettled the prosperity of the Egyptians and offered us flight from slavery to them, and rendered the leadership of Pharaothes inferior to mine; who made the sea into dry land for us who were uninformed about the routes; who caused the sea, beaten back, to rise in waves for the destruction of the Egyptians; who generously granted to men who were naked the security of weapons; [45] who caused spoiled springs to flow so as to be drinkable, and devised drink to come for us from rocks when we were utterly without means; who, when we were at a loss for fruits from the earth, preserved us with food from the sea; who also sent down from heaven food that had not previously been reported; who proposed to us a conception of laws and an arrangement of a constitution—[46] come, Master of everything, be my judge and unbribable witness, that I have neither accepted a gift from any one of the Hebrews, approving of a perversion of justice, nor [persuaded by] wealth have I condemned poverty that deserved to win, nor have I, by enacting policies to harm the commonwealth, arrived at conceptions that were utterly alien to my habitual way of life, so as to give the priesthood to Aaron not through your urging but through my favoritism. [47] Demonstrate now also that all things are governed by your providence and that nothing happens by itself and that they come to their goal through your directed will, that you care for those who will assist the Hebrews, by executing vengeance on Abirames and Dathames, who reproach your insensibility as if you are overcome by my craft. [48] You will make your judgment clear against those who have raged madly against your dignity by removing them from life in no common way, nor should they die as appearing to have departed from life according to the law of humanity; but let there gape open around them, together with their family and their resources, the ground on which they tread.

[49] For this would be to all a demonstration of your power and instruction in moderation so that those who have impious opinions about you may fear that they will suffer the same result. For thus I would be found a good servant of what you decree. [50] But if they have made true accusations against me, may you

guard them unharmed from all misfortune, and may you inflict this destruction upon me that I have imprecated upon them. And having inflicted punishment upon the one who wished to do injustice to your people, henceforth granting harmony and peace, save the multitude that follows your ordinances, protecting them unscathed and without a share in punishment of those who have sinned. For you yourself know that it is not just that in payment for their crime all Israelites together should pay the penalty."

[51] When he had spoken these words and while he was weeping, suddenly the earth shook, and a tossing motion was agitated upon it, just as when a wave is tossed through the force of a wind and all the people are afraid; and after a crash and a frightful roar had burst forth against their tents, the earth sank and carried down into it all that was dear to them. [52] When they had thus been obliterated, so that some did not even know that they had been overtaken, after the ground had opened up around them, it came together again and was reestablished, so that not even if it had suffered something of what I have previously said was it evident to those who saw it. They perished in this way, serving as a demonstration of God's power.

[53] But one might bewail them not only for the misfortune, which also in itself is deserving of lament, but because their relatives rejoiced over those who had suffered thus. Completely forgetting those who had been arrayed with them, they confirmed the decision of what had happened; considering that Dathames and his company had perished as villains, they were not even grieving.

[54] Moyses called those who were contending for the priesthood in view of the testing of the priests, in order that, whosoever sacrifice God would receive with greater favor, that person should be elected. 250 men came together who were honored among the people both because of the virtue of their fathers and because of their own, in which they excelled even them [their fathers]; Aaron and Kores also came forth, and they all burned offerings on such incense altars as they happened to have brought with them.

[55] Now a fire blazed up of such a size that no one has recorded made by human hands, that has not issued forth from the earth through a subterranean current of burning heat and that has not been pushed out spontaneously through the force of winds, its matter having been rubbed against itself but of such a kind that God had ordered kindled, brilliant and extremely hot.

[56] All of them, both the 250 and Kores, were annihilated when it darted upon them, so that even their bodies vanished. Aaron alone remained alive, not at all harmed by the fire, because it was God who sent it to burn those whom it was necessary to burn. [57] When they had perished, Moyses, wishing that their punishment should be handed down to memory and that those who would exist in the future should learn of it, instructed Eleazar the son of Aaron to deposit their censers beside the bronze altar, [58] in order that it might be a reminder to those who would come afterward of what they had suffered because they thought that they could outwit the power of God. Aaron, no longer appearing to have the high priesthood by the grace of Moyses but by the decision of God which had become manifest, now securely enjoyed the honor with his sons.

4. Moses and Laws (4.196–239)

4.196 I wish first to describe the constitution, which is consonant with the renown of Moyses for virtue, and to convey to those reading, what sort of constitution it was at the beginning, and then to return to the narrative of the rest. Everything has been written as he left it. We have added nothing for embellishment, nor anything that Moyses has not left behind. 197 The arrangement of each topic according to its class has been innovated by us. For the writings were left by him in scattered condition, just as he ascertained each item from God. I considered it necessary to mention this beforehand, so that some blame may not be assigned to us for having erred by my fellow countrymen who encounter this text. 198 This is the arrangement of our laws that are relevant to the constitution. Those that he has left us pertaining to communal affairs and our relations with one another I have postponed for the account concerning customs and causes that, with God's help, lies ahead for us to compose after this undertaking.

199 Whenever you have acquired the land of the Chananaians and have leisure to enjoy the good things, choose from that time on to found cities. If you do this, your actions will be pleasing to God and you will have happiness that is established.

200 Let there be, in the fairest part of the land of the Chananaians, one holy city that is renowned for its excellence, whichever God selects for himself through prophecy; and let there be one temple in it and one altar of stones that are not hewn but chosen and joined together, which, smeared with whitewash, will be appealing and clean to view.

201 Let the access to this be not by steps but by a sloping ramp. In another city let there be neither an altar nor a temple, for God is one and the stock of the Hebrews one.

202 Let one who blasphemes be stoned and hanged for a day; let him be buried without honor and in obscurity.

203 Let them [the people] come together three times a year from the ends of the land that the Hebrews conquer, into the city in which they establish the temple, in order that they may give thanks to God for the benefits that they have received and that they may appeal for benefits for the future; and coming together and taking a common meal, may they be dear to each other.

204 For it is well that they not be ignorant of one another, being compatriots and sharing in the same practices. This will occur for them through such intermingling, instilling a memory of them through sight and association, for if they remain unmixed with one another they will be thought completely strangers to each other.

205 Let there be a selection by you of a tithe of fruits, apart from that which I ordered to be given to the priests and Levites, and let it be sold in its native regions, and let it serve for the feasts and the sacrifices in the holy city. For it is proper to enjoy, for the honor of the one who has given it, that which has grown from the land that God has granted them to possess.

206 From the wages of a woman who has prostituted herself do not offer sacrifices, for the Deity is not pleased with anything that comes from insolence,

nor could any shame be worse than that in bodies. Similarly, if someone should receive payment for the mating of a dog, whether a hunting-dog or a protector of flocks, he may not sacrifice from it to God.

²⁰⁷ Let no one blaspheme gods whom other cities believe in, nor rob foreign temples, nor take a treasure that has been consecrated to some god.

²⁰⁸ Let none of you wear a garment woven from wool and linen, for this has been designated for priests alone.

²⁰⁹ When the multitude has come together to the holy city for the sacrifices every seven years when the festival of Tabernacles is at hand, let the high priest, standing on a lofty platform from which he is audible, read the laws to everyone, and let neither a woman nor children nor even the slaves be prevented from hearing.

²¹⁰ For it is good that they [the laws] be inscribed in their souls, able to be guarded in memory and never to be obliterated. For thus they will not err, being unable to say that they are ignorant of what has been enacted in the laws; and the laws will have much power of action over the errant, since they announce to them beforehand what they will suffer, and since, through hearing, they will have inscribed in their souls what they direct,

²¹¹ so that through all time they will have within themselves their principle, by disregarding which they will have sinned and become subject to the penalty. Let your children also, in the first place, learn the laws, the lesson most beautiful and productive of happiness.

²¹² Twice each day, both at its beginning and when the time comes for turning to sleep, bear witness to God of the gifts that he granted them when they were delivered from the land of the Egyptians, since gratitude is proper by nature: it is given in return for those things that have already occurred and as a stimulus for what will be.

²¹³ They will also inscribe on their doorways the greatest of the benefits that God has bestowed upon them, and each will display them on his arms; and as many things as are able to show forth the power of God and his good will toward them let them display on the head and the arm, so that the favor of God with regard to them may be readily visible from all sides.

²¹⁴ In each city, let seven men rule who have previously displayed their virtue and their zeal for justice. For each office, let two assistants be given from the tribe of the Levites.

²¹⁵ Let those who have obtained the position of judging in the cities be held in every honor, so that when they are present no one be permitted to revile or to be overbold, since respect on the part of the people themselves for those in high position makes them more reverent, so as not to despise God.

²¹⁶ Let the judges be empowered to render opinions on the basis of what seems best to them, provided only that no one denounce them for having received money in corruption of justice or bring forth some other charge, according to which one convicts them of not having pronounced judgment well. For it is befitting to grant a favor neither because of gain nor because of rank in rendering judgments, but to put justice above all.

²¹⁷ For otherwise God would seem to be despised, judged weaker than those to whom someone, out of fear of strength, assigns his vote. For God's strength

is justice. Someone who shows favor to those who happen to be of rank makes them more powerful than God.

²¹⁸ If the judges do not understand how to decide about the matters that are lined up before them—and many such occurrences befall men—let them send the case up intact to the holy city and let the high priest and the prophet and the council of elders come together and decide what seems best.

²¹⁹ Let not one witness be trusted, but let there be three or, at the very least, two, whose credibility their previous way of life will attest. Let the testimony of women not be accepted because of the levity and boldness of their gender. Nor let slaves give testimony because of their ignobility of soul, since it is likely that they do not bear witness to the truth, whether because of gain or because of fear. And if someone bears false witness and is believed, let him, when convicted, suffer whatever the one against whom he bore false witness was going to suffer.

²²⁰ If, when a murder has been committed in any place and the one who did it is not found, and no one is suspected of having committed the slaying because of hatred, let them seek him with much diligence, offering rewards for information. But if there is no informer, let the officers of the cities near the place where the murder was committed and the council of elders come together and measure the ground from the place where the corpse lies.

²²¹ And whichever city is nearest, let the public officials in it buy a young cow and, conveying it to a ravine, to a place unsuited for plowing and plants, let them cut the cervical sinews of the cow.

²²² Taking water for washing the hands over the head of the cow, let the priests and the Levites and the council of elders of that city shout aloud that they have hands that are pure of the murder and that they neither did it nor were present when it was done, and that they call upon God to be merciful, that such a terrible misfortune may no longer occur in the land.

²²³ Now aristocracy and the life therein is best. Let not a longing for another government take hold of you, but be content with this. And having the laws as your masters do each thing according to them, for it is sufficient that God is your ruler. If, however, you should have a passion to have a king, let him be a compatriot, and let him always have a concern for justice and the other virtues.

²²⁴ Let him concede to the laws and to God their superiority of wisdom and let him do nothing apart from the high priest and the advice of the elders, and let him not have many wives, nor pursue an abundance of money or horses, since if he obtains them he will be full of contempt for the laws. If he should have a zeal for any of these, let him be prevented from becoming more powerful than is beneficial for you.

²²⁵ Let it not be permitted to move the boundary marks of your own land or those of others with whom you are at peace; and beware of removing God's pebble, as it were, which lies secure forever, since from there arise wars and seditions through the wish of those who are greedy to go further than the boundaries. For those who remove the boundary are not far also from transgressing the laws.

²²⁶ When one plants the soil, if the plants bring forth fruit before four years, let him neither offer firstfruits to God from it nor himself enjoy them. For this has not been borne by them in season; and since nature has used force in an untimely fashion, it is suitable neither for God nor for the owner himself to enjoy.

[227] But in the fourth year let him harvest all that has grown, for then it is at the right time; and having gathered it in, let him carry it to the holy city, and let him consume it, together with the tithe of the other fruit, feasting it with his friends and with orphans and widows. In the fifth year let him be master to enjoy his plantings.

[228] Do not sow the land that is planted with vines, for it is sufficient for it to raise this plant and to be freed from the toils of a plow. Plow the land with oxen, and lead no other animal with them under the yoke, but do the plowing even with them according to their own kinds. The seeds should be pure and unmixed; and do not sow two or three kinds together, for nature does not rejoice in association of dissimilar things.

[229] As to animals, do not lead those that are not of similar species. For from this there is fear that the dishonor for that which is of the same kind may pass over even to human practices, having taken its beginning from the previous treatment of small and trivial things.

[230] It is necessary that no such thing be permitted from which in imitation there may be some deviation from the rules in the constitution. There should not be a disregard of the laws even concerning chance matters, since they [the laws] know how to make provision for the blameless in those [circumstances].

[231] When reaping and gathering the crops do not glean, but leave behind some of the sheaves for those who are destitute of a livelihood, to be a godsend for their sustenance. Similarly, also at the harvest leave behind for the poor, the small grapes gleaned after the harvest and leave aside some of the fruit of the olive-groves for gathering by those who do not have their own to partake of.

[232] For great wealth will not adhere to the owners through such painstaking gathering on their part as much as gratitude will come from the needy. The Deity also will make the earth better disposed to the growing of fruits for those who care not only for their own advantage, but also have concern for the nourishment of others.

[233] Do not muzzle the mouths of oxen when they thresh the ears of corn on the threshing floor, for it is not right to bar from the fruit those who joined in the work and who have exerted themselves with regard to its production.

[234] Nor, when the autumn fruit is full ripe should you prevent those walking on the road from touching it, but allow them to fill themselves as if from their own, whether they happen to be natives or strangers, rejoicing at allowing them to partake of the fruits of the season; but let it not be permitted to them to carry anything away.

[235] Let not the vine-strippers bar those who encounter them from eating from what they are carrying to the winepresses, for it would be unjust to begrudge the good things that, in accordance with God's will, have come for our sustenance to those who desire to partake of them, when the season is at its height and is hastening to pass away.

[236] Indeed, it would be pleasing to God if they should invite some people, who hesitated out of shame to touch [the food]—both Israelites, as associates and owners, because of their blood tie, and foreign people who happen to have come from some other place—asking them to accept the gifts that God has provided for them in season.

237 One ought not to consider as expenses the things that someone, out of generosity, permits people to take, since God grants an abundance of good things not for the enjoyment of us alone, but also so that we may share them magnanimously with others, and wishes that in this way the special good will and the supply of happiness that he feels toward the Israelite people may also be shown to others, when from much excess [of ours] they partake of them.

238 Let one who acts against these things receive forty lashes minus one from the public whip, undergoing this shameful punishment because, being a slave to gain, he has done violence to his dignity.

239 For it is well for you, given that you have experienced sufferings in Egypt and in the wilderness, to show concern for those who are in a similar plight, and after receiving riches due to the compassion and providence of God, to apportion to those in need the same attitude arising from a similar feeling.

Clamor for Kingship, Samuel and Saul (6.35–54)

6.35 The people, however, resented the outrages that the prophet's sons were committing against their earlier form of government and constitution and ran together to him—he was residing in the city of Armatha. They spoke of the sons' transgressions and [added] that he, being already old and weakened by time, was no longer capable of administering their affairs as previously. 36 They asked and begged him to appoint someone as their king who would rule over the nation and punish the Palestinoi with the judgments they still had coming to them for their previous misdeeds.

Their words greatly grieved Samouel on account of his innate justice and hatred of kings. For he delighted intensely in aristocracy as something divine that renders blessed those who use it as their constitution. 37 In his agitation and distress over what had been said, he thought of neither food nor sleep; throughout the entire night he continued turning over thoughts about public affairs.

38 With things standing thus, the Deity appeared and admonished him not to be disturbed at what the crowd had requested in that they had rejected not him, but rather himself so that he alone might not rule as king. They had devised such deeds since the day when he brought them out of Egypt; it would not be long, however, before a painful change of mind would take hold of them by which, nonetheless, nothing would be undone of what was to be. "They would rather be convicted of having been contemptuous and taking ungrateful decisions regarding me and your prophesying. 39 I direct you, however, to appoint for them whomever I will nominate as king, once you have forewarned them of what calamities they will experience when ruled by kings and solemnly testified concerning the sort of change into which they are rushing."

40 When he heard these things, Samouel called the Judeans together at dawn and declared that he would appoint a king for them. He said, however, he must first precisely inform them of what would be with their kings and how many calamities they would get themselves into. "For know, first of all, that they will seize your sons by force and direct some of them to be their charioteers, others their horsemen and bodyguards. Others will be runners and commanders of

thousands and hundreds. They will also make them fashioners of weapons and chariot makers, and artificers of instruments, as well as farmers and caretakers of their own fields and diggers of vineyards. ⁴¹ There is nothing they [the sons] will not do, being directed in the manner of slaves purchased for money. Your daughters too they will designate as ointment makers and cooks and bakers, and will impose on them every work at which maids serve under compulsion, fearing blows and torture. They will take away your possessions and give these as gifts to their eunuchs and bodyguards, and will hand over your herds of cattle to their own entourage. ⁴² To sum up, you will be slaves to the king, together with all that is yours, along with your own servants. When he comes, he will remind you of my words and by your suffering these things [he will cause you], regretting your decision, to beg God to have mercy on you and grant you quick deliverance from your kings. He, however, will not accept your pleas; rather, turning a deaf ear, he will allow you to undergo judgment for your own folly."

⁴³ Yet even to these predictions of what would happen the crowd remained impervious and stubbornly refused to rid their minds of a decision that was already established in their thinking. For they did not allow themselves to be convinced by, nor to concern themselves with, the words of Samouel. Instead, they incessantly pressed him, requesting that he appoint the king right away, and give no thought to what would be. ⁴⁴ For it was a matter of necessity that they should have someone who would wage war along with themselves for the punishment of their enemies; nor was there anything improper about their having the same constitution as their neighbors who were ruled by kings.

Samouel, seeing that they had not been dissuaded by his previous words, but were persisting, said: "Let each one now go off to his home; I will summon you as needed, when I learn from God whom he is giving you as king."

⁴⁵ Now there was a certain man of the Benjamite tribe, well-born and of good character, named Keis. He had a son, a youth of outstanding appearance and tall in body; his intelligence and mind were superior to these visible [qualities.] He was called Saoul.

⁴⁶ Now this Keis, when some of his beautiful donkeys, in which he took greater pleasure than in any of his other possessions, wandered off from their pasture, sent out his son with a single attendant to look for the animals. Having gone round his father's tribe, he went to the others. Not meeting them in these, he decided to return, so as not to cause his father concern about himself for the future.

⁴⁷ When, however, they were opposite the city of Armatha, the attendant who followed him stated that there was a true prophet in it, and advised going to him; for through him they would find out what had become of the donkeys. [Saoul then] said that if they went to him, they had nothing to award him in exchange for his prophecy, for their provisions were already used up. ⁴⁸ But the servant stated that he had available the fourth of a shekel and would give him this (for they were in error, due to their ignorance that the prophet did not take recompense).

They went off and meeting up at the gates with some virgins who had come for water, questioned them about the prophet's house. They indicated this, and appealed to them to hurry before he reclined at the supper, for he was feasting many people and would recline prior to those who had been invited. ⁴⁹ The reason for Samouel's having brought many together for the feast at that time was this:

on the previous day God had informed him—who had been praying every day to God to foretell to him whom he was going to make king—that he would send a certain youth of the Benjamite tribe at this same hour. Samouel, sitting on the roof, was waiting for this time to come; once it arrived, he came down and went to the supper. [50] Upon his meeting Saoul, God indicated to him that this was the one who was to rule. Saoul approached Samouel and, having greeted him, asked him to inform him about the house of the prophet. For he stated that as a stranger he was ignorant [of this]. [51] Samouel then stated that he was [the prophet], and conducted him to the supper. As for the donkeys that he had been sent out to look for, these were safe, just as all things had been arranged to go well for himself. [Saoul] replied: "But I, O master, am inferior to this hope; my tribe is too small to produce kings, and my ancestral clan is humbler than the other ancestral clans. You, however, are joking and making a fool of me by speaking of things greater than what accords with my position."

[52] The prophet, however, conducted him to the meal and made him and his companion recline above those invited (who were seventy in number). He ordered the servers to set a kingly portion before Saoul. Then, when the bedtime hour approached, they arose and each went off to his own home, while Saoul and his attendant slept at the prophet's house.

[53] When it was day, Samouel roused him from his bed and accompanied him. Once they were outside the city, he directed him [Saoul] to make the attendant go on ahead, but himself to stay behind, for he had something to tell him in the other's absence.

[54] When Saoul had sent his companion off, the prophet took the holy oil and poured it on the youth's head and kissed him. "Know," he said, "that you have been appointed king by God against the Palestinoi and for vengeance on the Hebrews' behalf.

On King Saul near the End; Samuel Speaks through the Ventriloquist of Dor (6.335–50)

6.335 Samuel, seeing that his [Saoul's] change [of fortune] was now at an end, said: "It is pointless for you to wish to still learn from me, seeing that God has deserted you. But hear now that David must rule as king and be successful in war. You, however, will lose both your rulership and your life, [336] you who disobeyed God in the war against the Amalekites and did not keep his commands, just as I predicted to you while I was still alive. Know then that the people too will be subjected to the enemy, and that tomorrow you, having fallen in battle along with your sons, will be with me."

[337] When he heard these things, Saoul was rendered speechless by grief and sank down on the ground, either due to the pain that came upon him from what had been disclosed, or as a result of hunger—for he taken no nourishment the preceding day and night—and lay immobile, like a corpse.

[338] Once he, with difficulty, regained consciousness, the woman joined in pressing him to taste [something], requesting this as a favor from him in exchange for her risky mantic activity, this being something she was not permitted

to do because of her fear of him while she was ignorant of who he was, but which she had nevertheless undertaken and accomplished. In return for this she appealed to him [to permit her] to set a table with food for him, so that, having recovered his strength, he might return safely to his own camp. She compelled and helped persuade [Saoul], although he resisted and turned away completely in his dejection. ³³⁹ She had a single tame calf that she had undertaken to look after and feed in her house—for the woman was a day laborer and had to be satisfied with this as her only possession. Butchering the calf and preparing the meat, she set this before his servants and him. During the night Saoul then came to the camp.

³⁴⁰ It is just, however, to give credit to the woman for her friendly readiness because, even though she had been prevented by the king from exercising her craft that would had made things better and more abundant for her at home, and though she had never beheld him before, she did not hold it against him that her lore had been condemned by him. Nor did she turn away from him as a stranger and someone not of her acquaintance. ³⁴¹ Rather, she sympathized with and consoled him, and encouraged him [to do] what he himself was very reluctant [to do]; she likewise generously and humanely bestowed on him the only thing that she, in her poverty, had on hand. Nor did she do this in return for some past benefaction or striving after a future favor—for she was aware that he was about to die, even though it is but human nature either to do good to those who have previously shown friendly readiness or to exert oneself in advance for those from whom one might be able to benefit. ³⁴² It is noble therefore to imitate this woman and to do good to all who are in need and not expect a reward, nor suppose anything more fitting for the human race than this or that by anything else will we have God benevolent and conferring good things. But concerning this woman, it suffices to have reported these things.

³⁴³ But at this point I will say something that is advantageous to cities, peoples, and nations and of relevance for good persons, by which all will be moved to pursue virtue and be zealous for those things that are capable of conferring glory and an everlasting memory. In addition, I will cause kings of nations and rulers of cities to be inspired with a great desire and solicitude for noble deeds, incite them to confront dangers and death for their country's sake, and teach them to despise all that is terrible. ³⁴⁴ I find an occasion for such a word in Saoul, king of the Hebrews, for he, though he knew what was to happen and the death awaiting him—the prophet having foretold [this]—gave no thought to flight, nor was he so attached to life as to hand over his people to the enemy and thus dishonor the dignity of his kingship. ³⁴⁵ Instead, he thought it noble to expose himself, his house, and his sons to these dangers, to fall with them, fighting on behalf of those ruled by him. He likewise thought it better that his sons die as good men rather than to leave them behind, in uncertainty as to how they would turn out. For, as his successor and family he would thus have praise and an ageless memory.

³⁴⁶ He therefore seems to me a uniquely just, courageous, and prudent man, and if anyone has been or will be worthy of reaping the testimonial of virtue from all, it is he. For others go forth to battle in the hope that they will prevail and return safely. When such persons perform some splendid deed, it does not seem appropriate to me to call them courageous, however much they may have

been spoken of in histories and other writings. [347] Though these are justly praised, only those are justly said to be "great-souled," "greatly daring," and "despisers of terrors" who have imitated Saoul. For in the case of those who, not knowing what will happen to them in war, do not weaken in the face of it, but expose themselves to an uncertain future and are tossed about by it, this is still not bravery, however many deeds they may happen to perform. [348] Those, on the contrary, who anticipating nothing favorable in their minds, but instead foreseeing that they must die, and who suffer this [fate] while fighting, neither fearing nor being dismayed by the terror, but proceeding toward this as something foreknown—they, I judge, truly give evidence of courage. [349] This then is what Saoul did, thus showing that it is fitting for all who yearn for fame after their deaths to do these same things, whereby they will leave it behind for themselves. This is the case above all with kings, who, given the greatness of their rulership, are not allowed, not simply not to be a source of calamities to their subjects, but even to be only moderately kind [to them]. [350] I could say still more than this about Saoul and his greatness of soul, as a topic supplying us with a great deal of material, but in order that I not seem to exaggerate in my praise of him, I revert to the point from which I digressed to these matters.

Josephus on the Wisdom of Solomon (8.42–56)

[8.42] The intelligence and wisdom that God bestowed on Solomon was so great that he surpassed the ancients, and even the Egyptians, who are said to be superior to all in prudence, when compared with him proved to be not merely a little deficient, but completely unequal to the king's intelligence.

[43] He likewise exceeded and was superior in wisdom to those of his own time who had a reputation for cleverness among the Hebrews, whose names I will not pass over. They were Athan, and Haiman, Chalke, and Dardan, the sons of Hemaon. [44] He also composed 1,005 books of odes and songs, as well as 3,000 books of parables and allegories. For he spoke a parable about each kind of tree, from the hyssop to the cedar. In the same way he spoke of all the animals, those on the earth, those that swim, and those in the air. For there was nothing in nature of which he was ignorant or which he left unexamined. Rather, he investigated everything methodically and evidenced a remarkable knowledge of the peculiarities of things.

[45] God also enabled him to learn the technique against demons for the benefit and healing of humans. He composed incantations by which illnesses are relieved, and left behind exorcistic practices with which those binding demons expel them so that they return no more.

[46] And this same form of healing remains quite strong among us until today. For I became acquainted with a certain Eleazar of my own people, who, in the presence of Vespasian and his sons, along with their tribunes and a crowd of soldiers, delivered those possessed by demons. The method of healing is as follows:

[47] Bringing up to the nose of the demonized person a ring that had under its seal a root from among those prescribed by Solomon, he [Eleazar] would then draw out the demonic [presence] through the nostrils, as the man sniffed.

Upon the man's immediately falling down, he adjured the demonic [presence] not to return to him again, making mention of Solomon and likewise reciting the incantations he had composed. ⁴⁸ Eleazar, wishing to persuade and convince those present that he had this power, first placed a cup or foot basin filled with water a short distance away and ordered the demonic [presence], which was now outside the person, to knock these over, and so cause the spectators to realize that he had left the person. ⁴⁹ When this happened, the sagacity and wisdom of Solomon became evident through this. We felt bound to speak of these matters so that all might know the greatness of his nature and his closeness to God, and so that the king's preeminence in every sort of virtue should not hidden from any of those beneath the sun.

⁵⁰ When Heirom, the king of the Tyrians, heard that Solomon had succeeded to his father's kingship, he rejoiced exceedingly, for he had been a friend of David. Sending to him, he greeted him and congratulated him on the good things that were now his. Solomon, for his part, sent him a letter reading as follows:

⁵¹ King Solomon to King Heirom. Know that my father, although he wished to construct a sanctuary for God, was prevented by wars and continuous campaigns. For he did not cease subjugating his enemies until he had made them all payers of tribute. ⁵² I know that I have God to thank for the present peace, because of which I am free to build the house for God as I wish. For God announced to my father that this would happen under me. I therefore appeal to you to dispatch certain men along with my people to Mount Liban in order to cut timber, since the Sidonians are more proficient in felling trees than we are. I will pay your wood workers the wage you set.

⁵³ When he read the communication, Heirom was pleased with its requests. He wrote back to Solomon:

King Heirom to King Solomon. God is indeed worthy of praise, because he has entrusted your father's leadership to you, a wise man, having every virtue. For these [reasons] I will willingly be of service in regard to all your requests. ⁵⁴ Once many large cedar and cypress logs have been cut down by my men, I will send them down to the sea. I will also direct my men to assemble a raft and deliver this, sailing it to the place in your own country that you wish. Then your men will convey it to Hierosolyma. For your part, see to it that, in return for these things, you provide us with the wheat we need because we live on an island.

⁵⁵ Copies of these letters have endured until today, having been preserved not only in our records, but also in those of the Tyrians. Thus, if anyone should wish to learn about their reliability, upon his asking the keeper of the Tyrian archives he will find that what we have said agrees with what is in these. ⁵⁶ I have gone through these things in detail, then, wishing readers to know that we are speaking nothing but the truth. Nor are we trying to avoid research, or asking to be trusted immediately, by interlarding the history with persuasive and seductive items [with a view] to deception and delight; nor yet to remain unpunished, indulged, if we are violating what is appropriate to the work. Rather, we appeal for

no other accolade than that we are capable of setting forth the truth by means of demonstration and compelling proofs.

Solomon's Blessing and Prayer in Connection with the Temple (8.106–21)

8.106 Then when the priests had set everything in order around the ark and gone out, suddenly a dense cloud arose. Being neither dark nor filled with rain as in the winter season, but rather diffused and mild, this [cloud] made its way into the sanctuary. It so blinded the eyes of the priests that they did not recognize one another. At the same time, it conveyed to the minds of all the impression and opinion that God was descending into the sacred precinct and was willing to dwell in it.

107 While they were all thinking this thought, King Solomon arose—for he had been sitting—and spoke to God words he supposed appropriate to the divine nature and suitable to say to him. "We know," he said, "O Master, that you have an everlasting house, in those things you have devised for yourself, namely the heaven, the air, the earth, and the sea; you are spread throughout all these things, but are not encompassed by them. 108 I, however, have constructed this dedicated sanctuary for you, so that from it we may send up our prayers into the air, sacrificing and singing hymns and we may constantly be convinced that you are present and not far distant. For just as you look down upon everything and hear everything, you do not, even as you dwell here—as is possible for you to do—cease to be near to everyone. Rather, to each one who consults you, you are present night and day as a helper."

109 When he had made these prayers to God, he directed his words to the crowd, making clear the power and providence of God for them, in that, of all the things he had disclosed to David his father about the future, many had already come about, while the rest would do so. 110 [He further spoke] of how [God] had conferred his name on him even before he was born and foretold what he was to be called and that this king would build the sanctuary for him after the death of his father. He then requested that they, who saw that it had turned out in accordance with his prophecy, praise God and believe, on the basis of what they had already seen, that he would leave nothing undone in the future of what he had promised for their well-being.

111 Having said these things to the mob, the king again faced the sanctuary. He raised his right hand to the mob and said,

It is not possible for humans by their works to do God a favor, for the sake of the good things they have experienced. For the Deity requires nothing at all and is superior to any sort of recompense. But with that [capacity] by which we have been made by you superior to all other living beings, O Master, it is necessary for us to praise your majesty and thank you for your benefits to our house and the people of the Hebrews. 112 For with what else is it more appropriate for us to propitiate you when you are angry and displeased, and to render you well-disposed, than by the voice that we have from the air and that we know ascends through this [element] again? By means of this [voice] I therefore declare my thanks to you, first regarding my father, whom you advanced from obscurity to so great a glory, [113] and then for your having done everything on my behalf that you foretold until the present day. As for the future, I ask you to grant whatever the power of God [gives] to those who have been honored by you. [I also ask you] to prosper our house in everything, so that, as you promised to David, my father, both while he lived and at his death, the kingship will remain with us and that his family will retain it for countless descendants. Therefore, confer these things on me and award to all who are mine that virtue in which you rejoice.

[114] In addition to these things, I beg that you send forth a certain portion of your spirit to the sanctuary and cause it to dwell there, so that you may appear to be with us on earth. Now for you, of course, to whom the whole vault of heaven and everything that is beneath it is but a meager dwelling, this is no extraordinary sanctuary. Nevertheless, I appeal to you to preserve it undevastated by enemies as your own for all time and to care for it as a house that is your property.

[115] And if, when the people offend and then [are afflicted] with a certain evil blow from you on account of their offense, with fruitlessness of the soil, fatal pestilence, or any of those sufferings with which you bring retribution on those who transgress anything that is holy, they all flee for refuge and assemble at the sanctuary and beg and ask you to be saved, be attentive to them as if you were inside, acting mercifully to them and delivering them from their misfortunes.

[116] I do not, however, ask for this help from you for the Hebrews alone when they go astray. Rather, even if some should come from the ends of the inhabited world and from any country and turn to God in prayer and earnestly beseech that they obtain some good, be attentive and give [this] to them. [117] For thus all will learn that it was by your wish that this house was built by us for you and that we are not inhumane by nature or ill-disposed to those who are not compatriots. Rather, we wish that your help and the benefit of good things be common to all.

[118] Having said these things and thrown himself on the ground and paid homage until a late hour, Solomon arose and offered sacrifices to God, covering [the altar] with unblemished victims. He then found out very clearly that God willingly accepted the sacrifice. For fire, falling down from the air upon the altar in the sight of all, snatched away and consumed the entire sacrifice. [119] When this manifestation occurred, the people concluded that this disclosed that God's residence was to be in the sanctuary; they gladly paid homage, falling on the ground.

The king began to praise [God] and encouraged the crowd to do the same, seeing that they already had proofs of God's benevolence toward them. [120] [He also encouraged them to] pray that what [came] from him [God] would always turn out in the same way and that their minds would be preserved pure of all evil in justice and devotion and that they would continue to keep the commandments God had given them through Moyses. For thus the nation of the Hebrews would be happy and more blessed than the whole human race. [121] He appealed to them to remember that it was by the same [deeds] that they had obtained the present good things that they would get these confirmed and obtain greater and additional ones. For they should not only realize that they had received these things on account of their piety and justice, but also that they would preserve them in the same way. For it is not so great [a thing] for humans to obtain what they do not possess as to save what they have acquired and not offend to their own hurt.

Josephus on Daniel (10.186–215)

[10.186] When Nabouchodonosor the king of the Babylonians had taken the noblest of the Judean youths, including the relatives of their king Sacchias, who were admirable both for their bodily strength and for their beautiful appearance, he handed them over to the care of the tutors—after having some of them castrated. [187] And, treating them the same way he did others whom he had taken in the prime of life from whatever other nations he had subdued, he began to supply them with food from his own table as a regimen and to teach them the local ways and to instruct them in Chaldean literature. And so they began to be adept in the wisdom he directed them to study. [188] And among these there were four of the line of Sacchias, who were by nature both noble and good, of whom one was called Daniel, another Ananias, another Misael, and the fourth Azarias. These the Babylonian king renamed and ordered that they be called by different names. [189] So they called Daniel Baltasar, Ananias Sedrach, Misael Misach, and Azarias Abdenago. These, making progress because of their exceptional natural qualities and their enthusiasm for their studies and for wisdom, the king held in honor and continued favoring.

[190] But Daniel, along with his relatives, determined to discipline himself and to abstain from the food from the royal table and from all living things in general. Approaching Aschanes the eunuch who had been entrusted with their care, he appealed to him when receiving the food provided for them from the king to consume it himself, and to supply them instead with lentils and dates for sustenance and whatever other vegetarian food he might wish. For they were drawn to this regimen but disdained others. [191] And Aschanes said he was prepared to comply with their proposal, but suspected that when it was discovered by the king from the leanness of their bodies and the change in their appearance, which would be especially clear in comparison with the flourishing of the other youths—for their bodies and complexions would certainly change along with their regimen—they would be to blame for the danger and punishment he faced. [192] Therefore, since Aschanes was responding cautiously about this, they persuaded him to supply them with these foods for ten days as an experiment; if the condition of their bodies had not changed he should keep doing the same, since no further harm would be done to it. But if he should observe that they had grown thinner and were faring worse than the others, he could put them back on their former regimen. [193] And since not only did nothing harm them when supplied with that food, but their bodies were better fed and starting to get bigger than the others, it came about that those to whom the royal food was provided seemed to lack more, while those with Daniel seemed to be living in abundance and complete luxury. After that Aschanes began fearlessly to take for himself the food that the king habitually sent every day from his table to the youths, and continued to provide them with the food described above. [194] And so they readily mastered all

the learning among the Hebrews and the Chaldeans, their souls having become pure and uncorrupted for learning because of this [regimen], and their bodies having become more vigorous for hard work, for neither were the former dragged down and made heavy by a variety of foods, nor were the latter made softer by the same cause. And Daniel especially, already being sufficiently adept in wisdom, had applied himself zealously to the interpretation of dreams, and the Deity was becoming known to him.

[195] After the second year from the sack of Egypt, when King Nabouchodonosor had an amazing dream whose interpretation God himself made clear to him in his sleep, he forgot it when he got out of bed. So, after summoning the Chaldeans and the magi and the seers, and telling them that he had seen a certain dream and that he happened to have forgotten what he had seen, he directed them to tell him both what the dream was and its meaning. [196] But when they said that it was impossible for humans to discover this, and that if he would describe the details of the dream to them they would promise to explain its meaning, he threatened them with death unless they would tell the dream. And when they admitted that they were unable to do what was directed, he ordered all of them to be executed. [197] But when Daniel heard that the king had ordered all the wise men to be killed, and that along with them he and his relatives were also in danger, he approached Arioch, who was entrusted with the command of the king's bodyguards. [198] And when he asked to learn from him the reason why the king had ordered all the wise men and Chaldeans and seers to be executed, Daniel learned the matter about the dream, which, although he had forgotten, they had been ordered by the king to explain to him, and that when they had said that they were not able to do it they had enraged him. So Daniel appealed to Arioch to go in to the king and to ask for one night for the magi and to delay the execution for this long, for he hoped in that time to discover the dream by asking God. [199] Arioch reported to the king what Daniel was requesting. And he directed [him] to delay the execution of the magi until he knew [the outcome of] Daniel's undertaking.

Then, after retiring to his own house, the young man together with his relatives begged God all through the night to reveal the dream and to rescue from the king's anger the magi and the Chaldeans, along with whom they too would of necessity be destroyed, by displaying to him and making clear the vision that the king had seen in his sleep the previous night but had forgotten. [200] Then God, having mercy on those in danger and at the same time honoring Daniel for his wisdom, made known to him both the dream and its interpretation, so that the king too might learn from him what it meant. [201] And when Daniel came to know these things from God he arose joyfully and, telling it to his brothers, who had already despaired of life and whose thoughts were set on dying, he aroused them to cheerfulness and hope of life. [202] And after giving thanks with them to God for taking pity on their age, he went to Arioch at daybreak and asked him to take him to the king, for he wanted to explain to him the dream that, he related, he had seen two nights previously.

[203] When he entered the king's presence, Daniel first begged the king's leave that he should not esteem him wiser than the other Chaldeans and magi because none of them had been able to discover the dream whereas he himself was about to declare it. For this happened neither on the basis of skill nor because he had

worked out the meaning better than they, "but because God had mercy on us who were in danger of dying after I pleaded concerning my own life and that of my fellow nationals, and he made clear both the dream and its interpretation. [204] For no less than my distress that we ourselves had been condemned by you not to live was my concern about your own reputation, since you had thus unjustly condemned men to die, and these noble and good, of whom you ordered things not accessible to human wisdom—for you were demanding from them that which was from God. [205] In any case, while you were worrying about who will rule the world after you, you fell asleep, and because God desired to reveal to you all who will rule he showed you a dream like this: [206] you imagined seeing standing a huge image of a man, of which the head happened to be of gold, the shoulders and arms of silver, the belly and thighs of bronze, and the legs and feet of iron. [207] Then a stone that had been broken off from a mountain fell upon the statue and after knocking it down crushed it, leaving no part of it unbroken, so that the gold and the silver and the bronze and the iron became finer than flour; and when the wind blew more violently they were carried off by its force and scattered. But the stone grew so large that the whole earth seemed to have been filled by it. [208] So that is the dream that you saw, and its interpretation is in this vein: The golden head was indicating both you and the Babylonian kings who were before you. But the hands and the shoulders signify that your sovereignty is to be destroyed by two kings. [209] But a different one from the west wearing bronze will put down their rule, and yet another like iron will bring its power to an end, and this one will dominate everything because of the nature of iron—for it is stronger than gold and silver and bronze." [210] And Daniel also explained to the king about the stone, yet it seemed to me proper not to recount this, being obligated to record past events and things that have happened but not what is about to happen. But if anyone, anxious for precision, will not be deterred from being curious to the extent of even wishing to learn about the unexplained—what is to happen—let him make the effort to read the book of Daniel. He will find this among the sacred writings.

[211] And when King Nabouchodonosor heard these things and recognized the dream, he was amazed at Daniel's nature and, falling on his face, began to address Daniel in the manner in which they worship God; [212] he also ordered sacrifices as to a god. Moreover, having given him the name of his own god, he made him administrator of his whole kingdom along with his relatives, who because of jealousy and malice happened to fall into danger when they offended the king for the following reason. [213] After the king constructed a golden statue sixty cubits high and six wide and erected it in the great plain of Babylon and was about to consecrate it, he called together the leading citizens from the whole land that he ruled. First of all he ordered them, when they heard the signaling of the trumpet, to fall down at that time and to worship the statue; those who did not do this he threatened with being thrown into the furnace of fire. [214] So when everyone, upon hearing the signaling of the trumpet, worshiped the statue, Daniel's relatives, [to explain] not doing this, declared that they did not want to transgress the ancestral laws. They were convicted and immediately were thrown into the fire, but were saved by divine providence and, incredibly, escaped death. [215] The fire did not touch them and was too weak to burn the youths when it had them in it, I think,

because they were thrown into it when they had done no wrong and because God had prepared their bodies to be stronger so as not to be consumed by the fire. This commended them to the king as just and dear to God, for which reason afterward they continued being deemed worthy by him of all honor.

Gaius Caligula, Petronius, King Agrippa I, and the Statue (18.256–309)

18.256 As for Gaius—he managed affairs in the first and second year very magnanimously, and by practicing moderation he increased the affection of the Romans and their subjects toward him. But as time went by, the great size of the empire led him to stop thinking of himself as a human being and, making a god of himself, he presumed to conduct all affairs of state without any respect for the divine.

257 Thus, for example, when there was civic strife in Alexandria between Jews and Greeks residing there, three delegates chosen by each side came to Gaius. Among the Alexandrian delegates one was Apion, who terribly badmouthed the Jews, among other things claiming that they ignore the honors due the emperor. 258 Thus [he argued], of the subjects of Roman rule all had made altars and temples for Gaius, receiving him in all ways as they receive the gods; only these people consider it unrespectable to honor him with statues and to take oaths by his name. 259 After Apion spoke at length and harshly, hoping to arouse Gaius [against the Jews], as was indeed likely, Philo—the head of the Jewish delegation, a highly respected man who was the brother of Alexander the alabarch and not at all unfamiliar with philosophy—was about to turn to responding to the accusations. 260 But Gaius cut him off, demanding that he get himself away; he was very angry and it was obvious that he was going to do something terrible to them. Philo left, having thus been treated outrageously, and told the Jews who were with him that they should bolster their spirits. For although in word it was with them that Gaius was angry, in fact it was God that he had summoned against himself.

261 Gaius, taking it badly that the Jews alone so ignored him, sent out Petronius as the legate of Syria to replace Vitellius as ruler [there], ordering him to invade Judea with a large force; if they accept [Rome's demands] willingly, he should set up a statue of him in the sanctuary of God, but if they act out of folly, he should do the same after overcoming them in war. 262 And so Petronius, upon taking over in Syria, hastened to take care of the emperor's orders. Gathering together as many auxiliary troops as he could, he brought two legions of the Roman army to Ptolemais, planning to winter there so as to go off to war without delay when spring approached. He wrote to Gaius and told him what he planned to do, and the latter praised his energy and enjoined him not to hold back at all but, rather, to prosecute the war vigorously if they were not obedient.

263 But numerous myriads of Jews appeared before Petronius in Ptolemais, beseeching him not to force them into transgression and the violation of their ancestral law. 264 "If," they said, "you in any case are behooved to bring and erect the statue, do what has been decided upon only after first doing away with us. For we cannot stand by and watch as things happen that are forbidden to us by the dignity of our lawgiver and our forefathers, who adopted these [rules] as pertaining to virtue." 265 Petronius became angry and said: "If I were the emperor and had

taken into my mind to do these things on the basis of my own considerations, it would have been justified for you to speak that way. But since I have been ordered by the emperor [to do this] it is imperative to carry out his decisions, for there is a most irremediable punishment for disobeying them." [266] "Just as you think, O Petronius," said the Jews, "that it is impossible to disobey Gaius's orders, so too is it impossible for us to violate that which the law proclaims. Trusting in the virtue of God and in the labors of our ancestors, until now we have remained innocent of violation, and we would not dare to become so wicked that we would violate, out of fear of death, prohibitions that he thought bring us measures of goodness. [267] Rather, we will endure and face our fortunes while preserving our ancestral practices, risking what is set out for us, undertaking the worst things for the glory of God, firm in the belief that whatever happens there is hope because God will stand by us; because [we know that] Fortune tends to both sides in public affairs; [268] and because if we were to obey you it would bring upon us both great censure as being unmanly (for that would be seen to be the explanation for our violation of the law) as well as great wrath of God—who even in your judgment must be considered greater than Gaius."

[269] Petronius, seeing from their words how difficult it would be to overcome their will, and that it would not be within his power to carry out the dedication of the statue for Gaius without battle, and that there would be much killing, gathered his friends and the retinue that accompanied him and hurried to Tiberias, eager to become cognizant of the disposition of the Jews [there]. [270] Since the Jews, although they considered the danger of war against the Romans to be great, considered that of violating the Law to be even greater, numerous myriads again came out to confront Petronius when he came to Tiberias. [271] When they supplicated him not at all to subject them to such duress or to defile their city by the dedication of the statue, Petronius said: "Would you, then, go to war against Caesar, giving no thought to all that he can bring to bear or to your own weakness?" They said: "In no way will we fight, but we will die before we violate the laws." And lying upon their faces and proffering their throats for slaughter they said they were ready to be killed. [272] And they went on that way for forty days, all the time ignoring their fields although it was the sowing season—so great was their preference and firm decision to die eagerly rather than have to see the erection of the statue.

[273] With matters in this state, Aristobulus (King Agrippa's brother) and Helcias the Great and others who were of the most powerful of that house, along with the most prominent [Jews], came to see Petronius, appealing to him, [274] given the fact that he had seen the multitude's firm decision, not to bring it to desperation. Rather[, they urged him] to write Gaius about how implacable was their opposition to receiving the statue, that they had up and left their fields so as to sit and protest, and that while they did not want to go to war about it since they could not, they would gladly accept death rather than violate their regulations—the result being that the land remained unsown and so brigandage would flourish because of [the inhabitants'] inability to make the tribute payments. [275] Perhaps[, they urged,] Gaius might be moved to pity and neither be cruel in attitude nor contemplate devastating the people. But if [Gaius] persevered in his desire for war, then let [Petronius] undertake the project. [276] That was what Aristobulus's

people called upon Petronius to do. And Petronius, since Aristobulus's people were exerting so much pressure because their appeal was for great things, and they were using every possible tactic in their supplications, [277] and also beholding the Jews' decision to resist and thinking it terrible to bring death upon so many myriads of people in executing Gaius's madness, holding them guilty for their reverence to God and then living the rest of his life with an expectation of a terrible future, thought it much better to write Gaius and endure his implacable wrath at his not having immediately fulfilled his orders. [278] Perhaps[, he thought,] he might even convince him; but if the emperor remained in his original mania he would undertake the war against them—although if Gaius did turn some of his wrath against him it might be appropriate, for those who strive for virtue, to die for such a multitude of people. So he decided to deem his petitioners' request persuasive.

[279] Summoning to Tiberias the Jews, of whom numerous myriads came, he stood up in front of them and declared to them that the present military expedition had not been his idea, having been ordered by the emperor, whose wrath would be endured not with delay, but rather immediately, by anyone who was so bold as to disobey the orders. [He said:]

> And it is appropriate for someone who has attained such high an office by the emperor's approval not to oppose him in any way. [280] Nevertheless, I do not consider it right not to give up my safety and my honor so as you not be destroyed—you who are so many, [and] who are taking care of the virtue

> • of your law, which, it being your ancestral law, you consider it worth fighting for it,
> • and of God, who is above all authority and power—whose temple I would not be so bold as to overlook by allowing outrage to befall it at the behest of the ruling powers.

> [281] Rather, I am sending [a letter] to Gaius, explaining your opinions, also defending, in a fashion, the good arguments you put forward by which I, against my [original] opinion, was convinced. And let God—for his authority is greater than that of any human device or powers—give his support, ordaining both for you the preservation of the ancestral ways and, for himself, that he not fail, because of human decisions but against the wishes [of the Jews], to receive the usual honors [due him]. [282] And if Gaius becomes embittered and turns his implacable wrath toward me, I will endure any danger and any misery that visits my body and my fortune rather than look on as you, who are so many, are utterly destroyed for doing such good things. [283] So go away now, each of you to his own affairs, and work the land. And I myself will write to Rome, and neither I nor my friends will turn away from taking care of everything for you.

[284] Having said that and dissolved the assembly of the Jews, he asked the leaders to take care of what was needed for agriculture and to conciliate the people with optimism. Thus he, for his part, made an effort to raise the multitude's morale. And God, for his, demonstrated to Petronius his presence and that everything is in his control. [285] For just as Petronius finished his speech to the Jews,

God sent a heavy rain, which was against all human expectation—for that day had been clear since morning with nothing in the sky indicating rain. Moreover, the entire year had been afflicted by such a severe drought that it made people despair of any water at all from above, even when they saw the sky was cloudy. [286] As a result, when so much rain fell, which was unusual and against all expectation, it gave the Jews hope that Petronius could not possibly fail in his petition on their behalf. Petronius himself, moreover, was totally stunned by seeing with his own eyes God's care of the Jews; so bountifully had He displayed this apparition that not even those who in fact tended to hold the opposite position were left with any capacity to argue about it. [287] When writing Gaius he wrote about this along with all the rest, bringing everything and appealing in every way not to drive so many myriads of people into desperation; and [he explained] that if he killed them (for it would not happen without war that they would violate the regulation of their religion) he would both be denied the income normally received from them and be subjected to a curse as a deterrent for the next generation. [288] Moreover, the divine being that stands at their head had shown that its power was unimpaired, and had not left anything indicating any doubt about its power. This then, was how things stood with Petronius.

[289] Turning now to King Agrippa, who happened to be spending time in Rome—he was very closely befriended by Gaius. Once he made a dinner for him, with the intention of outdoing everyone both in expenditure and in supplying everything that is pleasurable, [290] so that none of the others, not even Gaius himself, believed he could even offer something equal to it, if he wanted to, not to mention outdoing it. So far did the man rise above himself in thinking out and supplying everything for the emperor. [291] Gaius was struck by his intelligence and munificence, such that in order to satisfy him he had forced himself to use an abundance of money even beyond his means, and he wanted to imitate Agrippa's ambitious undertaking for his pleasure. Therefore, when feeling free under the influence of wine and transformed into an especially cheerful mood, he said at the symposium when he had been called upon to drink:

> [292] Agrippa, already in the past I have seen the respect that you evince toward me and the great goodwill you demonstrated, even when you were beset by dangers on its account in the days of Tiberius. You never fail in any way to show goodness toward me, even beyond your means. Therefore, since it would be shameful for me to be behind you in enthusiasm, I would like now to make up for what I previously omitted. [293] Whatever gifts I have hitherto apportioned to you come to little. Anything, which can add you a measure of happiness, will be arranged for you with my enthusiasm and my strength.

Now he said that supposing that [Agrippa] would ask for a large territory bordering his own or the revenues of certain cities. [294] Agrippa, for his part, although he had prepared everything concerning which he wanted to make his request, did not reveal his intention. Rather, he immediately responded to Gaius that just as earlier it had not been in the anticipation of profit from him that he had served him against Tiberius's orders, so too now nothing of what he did in order to grant him pleasure was in return for any personal profits.

²⁹⁵ [He also said that] the gifts he had already received from Gaius were in fact great, beyond what he could hope for even when bold. "For even if they were less than what was in your power to give, they were greater than my intelligence and my dignity as recipient [deserved]." ²⁹⁶ Gaius, struck by his virtue, pressed him all the more to say what might make him happy if he granted it to him. He responded:

> Since, my lord, you have in your confidence [in me] proclaimed me worthy of your receiving gifts, I will not request anything that would make me happier, for I am already very distinguished by the things you have already granted me. ²⁹⁷ Rather, I will call upon you to [do something] that will bring you the reputation of piety and make the divine power your ally in all that you desire; as for me—it will give me the good reputation among those who learn of it, that I know that I would never fail to obtain your authority for anything I need. Namely, I request that you no longer contemplate erecting the statue that you ordered Petronius to bring into the temple of the Jews.

²⁹⁸ Although [Agrippa] was aware of the fact that it would be dangerous for him if Gaius decided not to accept the request and would do no other than get him killed, nevertheless, because he considered the matter of be of great significance (as it truly was) he decided to take the chance. ²⁹⁹ As for Gaius—being both beholden to Agrippa for his service of him, along with the fact that it would have been inappropriate if, in the sight of so many witnesses, he should immediately repent and break his promise about things that he himself had earnestly pushed Agrippa into requesting, ³⁰⁰ and also in awe of Agrippa's virtue, for he had given little thought to enlarging his own realm or income or power; rather, he had directed his attention to the general welfare, acting as if he were the ambassador of the laws and the divinity, he agreed and wrote to Petronius, praising him for having assembled the army and for what he had written him about them. ³⁰¹ "Now, however—if you have already set up the statue, let it stand. If, however, you have not yet made the dedication, do not trouble yourself about it anymore. Rather, dismiss the army and, as for you, go back to the affairs I originally sent you to take care of. For I no longer require the erection of the statue—thus showing grace to Agrippa, a man whom I honor so greatly that I cannot deny that which he needs and requests."

³⁰² Gaius wrote that to Petronius, however, before reading [Petronius's letter], from which he wrongly inferred that the Jews were hurrying into rebellion, as if their state of mind indicated nothing other than that they were threatening direct war against Rome. ³⁰³ He was very troubled [by that], as if they had dared to put his rule to the test. He was a man who was in all circumstances controlled by shame, one who overcame that which was better; and once he had decided to direct his rage against someone he rushed [into it] more than all others without imposing any control at all upon it. Rather, considering the pleasure he derived from his rage the criterion of happiness, he wrote to Petronius: ³⁰⁴ "Since you have considered whatever gifts the Jews have provided you to be weightier than carrying out my orders, and have in all ways lifted yourself up to give them pleasure in contravention of my orders, I order you to become your own judge and

consider what should be done to you, upon whom my wrath has descended—for you will be made into a paradigm, by all [who live] today and those who are later to come, for [the lesson that] the orders of a man who is emperor are never to be disobeyed."

305 That was the letter that he wrote to Petronius. But Petronius did not receive it while Gaius was still alive, for the ship that brought it was so delayed that Petronius first received a[nother] letter, from which he learned of Gaius's death. 306 For God was not about to forget the dangers that Petronius had undertaken in showing favor to the Jews and honor to him. Rather, by eliminating Gaius, angry at what he had dared to do in order to have himself worshiped, God discharged his debt [to Petronius]. And Rome and the entire regime too supported Petronius, especially the most dignified members of the Senate, for Gaius had turned his ungoverned wrath against them.

307 So he, on the one hand, died not long after he wrote Petronius the letter imposing death upon him; in the continuation of this work I will recount the circumstances in which he died, and the conspiracy against him. 308 As for Petronius, on the other hand: he first received the letter that informed him of Gaius's death, and not long after—the one commanding him to take his own life. He rejoiced at the good timing of the disaster that had overtaken Gaius 309 and marveled at God's providence, which with no delay, but rather immediately, remunerated him for having proffered both respect for the temple and aid to rescue the Jews. Thus it happened that, for Petronius, the danger of death was avoided in a way easier than possibly could have been imagined.

Josephus on Education and Introduction to the *Life* (20.262–67)

20.262 Encouraged by the completion of what I had projected [i.e., the body of the *Antiquities*], I would now say plainly that no other person who had wished to do so, whether a Judean or a foreigner, would have been able to produce this work so precisely for Greek speakers. 263 As my compatriots concede, I exceed them by far in the local education that we have, and I energetically pursued studies in Greek literature and poetry, after consolidating my familiarity with the grammar, granted that my traditional habit has frustrated precision in expression [*enunciation*]. 264 With us, they do not welcome those who have mastered the languages of many nations and deck out their speech with elegance of styles [*expressions, diction*], because they consider such a pursuit to be perfectly common—open not only to those who chance to be free citizens, but even to those of the domestic staff [i.e., slaves] who want it. No, they [my people] acknowledge *wisdom* only among those who clearly understand the legal precepts and are able to translate the power of the *sacred* literature. 265 So, although many have worked hard at this discipline, barely two or maybe three have succeeded, and they have soon reaped the benefits of their labors.

266 Perhaps it will not be a provocation to jealousy, or strike ordinary folk as gauche, if I review briefly both my own ancestry and the events of my life while there are still those living who can offer refutation or corroboration. 267 With these matters I will conclude the *Antiquities*, comprising 20 volumes and 60,000 lines,

and, should the Deity permit, I will again make mention, cursorily, of both the war and what has happened to us until the present day, which belongs to the thirteenth year of the rule of Domitian Caesar and, in my case, the fifty-sixth year from birth. [268] I have also conceived a plan to compose four volumes dealing with our—that is, Judeans'—opinions about God and his essence and about the laws: why, according to them, we are allowed to do some things and prevented from doing others.

Introduction to *Against Apion*

Narrative Description

Josephus offers a neat three-part statement of purpose in *Against Apion:* to expose lies, correct ignorance, and teach those open to the truth about the Judeans' origins and ancient past (1.3)—all this against the claim that Greek silence about the Judeans shows that they did not exist in ancient times. This is not yet a plan for the work, however. He comes closer to giving a plan in 1.4–5: he will first enlist the support of writers esteemed by the Greeks to confirm Judean antiquity, *then* expose the lies, and he will also explain why the Judeans have not been as widely mentioned by others. But even this is not a plan because the explanation of silence will be the *first* main item of the body (1.60–68), and that will come only after an unannounced digression, which tries to undermine the root assumption that Greeks should be considered authorities (1.6–59).

This alleged digression turns out to be one of the most valuable parts of the work and central to Josephus's theme: celebrating the unmatched Judean/priestly concern for preserving the ancient records and in the process describing Josephus's composition of his earlier works—as a living example of eastern priestly accuracy (1.47–56). After this digression, Josephus restates his plan for the remainder: to explain the Greek silence, cite outside evidence, and refute lies (1.58–59). Then again, after covering the first two of these, he will say yet again that he has one item left: to expose the lies of slanderers (1.219). But there is still a further twist, for once Josephus has finished the refutations he transitions neatly into a celebration of the Judean laws and their superiority over all other constitutions (2.145–86). Although he justifies this by saying in effect that "the best defense is a good offense" (2.147), and it certainly is connected organically with what goes before, this final section takes on a life of its own as he seeks to show that his nation's laws represent the finest examples of "piety, fellowship with each other, and humanity toward the world at large, and in addition to these, justice, endurance in the face of labors, and contempt for death" (2.146). Josephus's final summary in the closing paragraphs reprises this last part at length (2.291–95), showing that by the time he had written it, it had taken on independent importance. It is arguably the most memorable and sublime section of all Josephus's writing.

Not surprisingly, then, the *Apion* ends up having much the same "concentric" shape as Josephus's other works. Its opening and closing sections (1.1–218; 2.146–296) have many correspondences with each other: they both celebrate the unparalleled antiquity and unique virtues of the Judean constitution. The middle section—the last third of the first volume and first half of the second—attacks the Egyptian-Alexandrian slanderers and "convicts them on their own evidence" (1.219). If we ask why Josephus does not more clearly call the final section what it is—a panegyric or encomium (i.e., "piece in praise") of the Judean constitution that unfavorably compares others—we have at least one answer in his own comments. In criticizing Apion he says that the wise man is one who follows his own nation's laws and refrains from disparaging other people's (2.144)—something Apion failed to do. He later stresses that Judeans are accustomed to observe their laws and not criticize others' (2.237). By insisting on these points he leaves himself little room to maneuver, and this may explain why he insists that he is not about to present an encomium on Judean law (2.147), but is only trying another way to defend the Judeans from criticism—by speaking at length of their constitution's unmatched excellence.

So again, it seems that Josephus is writing for a basically well-disposed audience, eager to hear the bold Judean nobleman tear to shreds the standard rumors about Judean origins, while he reaches exultant heights describing the beauty of his culture, which he shares with others. With its unannounced finale, especially, the *Apion* ends up providing a fitting conclusion to Josephus's literary career, reprising the main themes of both the *War* and the *Antiquities*, though now in essay format.

Date/Occasion

Josephus's last known literary composition carries no indication of date, except that he must have written it sometime after the *Antiquities* (*see* Josephus, *Antiquities*). In its opening sentences, he summarizes the major work (1.1) and observes that some have rejected his account of the Judeans' great antiquity and independence because the most famous Greek historians have not mentioned them (1.2–3). For this reason, he has decided to write the present work: to convict the Judeans' accusers of falsehood, to correct the ignorance of others, and to instruct all who wish to know the truth about Judean antiquity (1.3, 5). This work is again dedicated, significantly, to the same **Epaphroditus** (1.1; 2.1) who had encouraged Josephus to complete the *Antiquities*, and when he speaks of writing for those "who want to know the truth" (1.3) the phrase recalls the Greek "lovers of learning" gathered around Epaphroditus (*Antiquities* 1.12). It also fits with Josephus's closing tribute to Epaphroditus, at the end of the *Apion*, as one "who loves the truth" and provides an avenue to others who "want to know" (2.296).[1]

This opening explanation of the context raises, then, an interesting problem.

---

1. Josephus, *Against Apion* 2.296: "To you, Epaphroditus, who is a devoted lover of truth, and for your sake to any who, like you, wish to know the facts about our race, I beg to dedicate this and the preceding book."

Much of the following work will be devoted to attacking Greek (mainly Alexandrian) critics of Judean antiquity, though the writers in question are all long dead (*see* Letter of Aristeas). Is Josephus, then, trying to enter the fray with certain anonymous but still-living defamers of the Judeans, or is he writing for those who are already disposed to listen: people such as those connected with Epaphroditus? Several considerations support the latter option.

First, as we all know from experience, in cases of sharp differences of political and religious opinion, partisan groups—say, American liberals and conservatives, critics and supporters of Israel, environmentalists and their detractors—speak mostly to their own people, even when constructing formidable arguments against the other side. Members of the group are hugely impressed by these arguments, and wish the "other side" could hear them, but in reality, the mental framework and assumptions of each group are so different that they would not likely be impressed even if they did hear the others' claims.

In the case of Josephus's *Apion*, we need to recognize that ancient "publication" meant first of all gathering a physical audience willing to listen. We have plenty of evidence that audiences for literary works were often willing to be challenged, for example, in **Lucian**'s going to hear historical works that he ended up disliking, or in Josephus's own remarks about those who criticized his efforts (*War* 1.13; *see* Josephus, *War*). Roman literary culture included a large measure of entertainment. It was not simply a matter of going to hear ideological soulmates. Therefore, we should imagine such audiences for Josephus: some, such as Epaphroditus and his friends, facilitating Josephus's work and perhaps finding venues for him to speak with larger groups of potentially interested but less committed hearers. If we take the three groups that Josephus claims to address—slanderers, those possibly affected by their slander, and those eager for the truth—and if we assume the slanderers to be the dead writers he confronts in this work, then we are left with an audience comprising sympathetic and at least open-minded people—albeit with room for the sort of carping critics who appear in *War* 1.13–16. It is hard to imagine that fierce ideological denouncers of the Judeans, if there were such people in Rome, would come along to hear Josephus in the first place. If they did, they would not likely be moved by his arguments, which expect a more "tractable" audience.

Finally, both the content and the tone of Josephus's criticisms of the dead literary slanderers—his highly selective content, reconfigured on his terms, and his tone of ridicule and mockery—would presumably be effective only with an audience willing to be moved in his direction. In the case of *Apion*, Josephus is merciless in ridicule; he wonders whether it is even worthwhile to reply to the clownish and ignorant ramblings of such a detestable man (2.3–4). He finally delights in Apion's painful death from an ulcer of the genitals—he who had mocked Judean circumcision, which we are led to think might have spared him (2.143). This would all have been entertaining for the right sort of audience, but it would hardly have impressed the Alexandrians whom Josephus lampoons with *Apion* or any Egyptians visiting Rome: "These frivolous and utterly senseless specimens of humanity, accustomed from the first to erroneous ideas about the Gods, incapable of imitating the solemnity of our theology" (1.225).

In form, this is a two-volume essay, departing from Josephus's usual historical narratives. It was known in antiquity as "On the Antiquity of the Judeans." The familiar title, *Against Apion,* is a misnomer, because Apion is only the last in a series of slanderers targeted. Further, there is much more in the essay than the promised refutation of slander, and Josephus appears to be addressing much the same group that has always formed his audience. He will now regale them with a triumphant statement on Judean antiquity and a witty, stinging rebuttal of those dead literary enemies.

Themes

The thematic clusters we have gleaned from the main narratives are all collected here in summary form. The five thousand-year antiquity of Judean history covered by the sacred records (as in the *Antiquities*) is the most obvious and overriding theme. Whereas the *Antiquities* had invited the audience to assess the Judean constitution, Josephus goes further here and advantageously compares it with other systems, whether real (Athenian and Spartan) or ideal (Plato's *Republic*). He shows not only that the Judean constitution excels above all others (2.164–65, 170, 184–88), but that Pythagoras and Plato imitated Moses (e.g., 1.162, 2.257), and those who have roughly comparable high standards cannot live up to them as the Judeans do (2.273).

The word "aristocracy," so prominent in the *Antiquities*, does not appear here because again Josephus goes further, pushing past the generic language of all aristocracies. Focusing now on the priestly nature of the governing Senate (already described in the *Antiquities*), which administers these laws emanating from God, he coins the durable word "**theocracy**" for the Judean kind of aristocracy, elevating it to a unique level (2.160–66 [esp. 165], 170, 185–88).

Similarly, the noun "philosophy" no longer needs to appear in the *Apion* because it is obvious that the whole discussion is a philosophical one. The wisdom *(sophia)* of the laws is mentioned frequently, and Josephus places Moses alongside **Anaxagoras, Pythagoras, Thales,** Plato, and Aristotle (1.14, 162, 164, 176, 182; 2.14, 168). Indeed, "those of the Greeks who philosophized" (Josephus uses the verb) were the first imitators of the Judeans, holding *Mosaic* views of both God and human virtue (2.280–81). The moral-philosophical values listed above (piety, humanity, courage, etc.) pervade the work. "Contempt for death," which was the acid test of all claims to philosophical truth, figures especially prominently in the *Apion* as a distinctive and ongoing Judean trait, *unlike* the long-faded Spartan reputation—as the recent war has illustrated (1.43; 2.146, 218–19, 232–34, 271–72, 294). So here we come full circle, returning to the most basic issues of national character that Josephus had tried to illustrate by means of narrative in the *War*.

Finally, Josephus's featured themes of fellowship and humanity are illustrated in ways that cap the whole thrust of the *Antiquities,* which began with Abraham's quest for intellectual and moral truth. Other nations such as the Athenians and Spartans, granted that their constitutions had some noble elements, selfishly guarded them for their own citizens, to keep them from corruption, Josephus claims. The Judeans, he says, have found a more productive path: they certainly keep their laws from contamination, by living apart from others and not permitting dilution, but nevertheless they "receive with pleasure" those who wish to come and live under their laws (2.258–61). Just as in the *Antiquities* Josephus had pointed out the Judeans' tradition of ungrudgingly keeping their excellent things from others (1.10–11), and described in detail the successful adoption of Judean laws by foreign royals (20.17–96), so here he emphasizes Moses' insistence that, while the laws must be kept pure, they are also thrown open ungrudgingly to all those who want to share and live under them (2.209–10). On a slightly different plane, he closes the body of this section with broad claims about the universal attraction and at least partial adoption of Judean laws and customs (2.281–86).

If we imagine the circle of Greeks around Epaphroditus eager to hear more from Josephus about his nation's laws and culture, we can only conclude from the *Antiquities'* eagerness to share the Judeans' excellent things and the *Apion's* insistence on both the superiority of this constitution and its availability to foreigners who choose to adopt it, that Josephus strongly encouraged Epaphroditus's group in their interests.

STEVE MASON

2.5 from *Against Apion*

Prologue (1.1–5)

[1.1] Through my treatise on *Ancient History*, most eminent Epaphroditus, I consider that, to those who will read it, I have made it sufficiently clear concerning our people, the Judeans, that it is extremely ancient and had its own original composition, and how it inhabited the land that we now possess; for I composed in the Greek language a history covering 5,000 years, on the basis of our sacred books. [2] However, since I see that a considerable number of people pay attention to the slanders spread by some out of malice, and disbelieve what I have written on ancient history, but adduce as proof that our people is of more recent origin that it was not thought worthy of any mention by the most renowned Greek historians, [3] I thought it necessary to write briefly on all these matters, to convict those who insult us as guilty of malice and deliberate falsehood, to correct the ignorance of others, and to instruct all who wish to know the truth on the subject of our antiquity. [4] I will employ as witnesses for my statements those judged by the Greeks to be the most trustworthy on ancient history as a whole, and I will show that those who have written about us slanderously and falsely are convicted by themselves. [5] I will try also to explain the reasons why not many Greeks made mention of our nation in their histories; at the same time, however, I will draw attention to those who have not passed over the history which relates to us for those who are, or feign to be, ignorant.

On Judean Scripture ("Canon") and His Own Writings (1.37–56)

[1.37] Naturally, then, or rather necessarily—seeing that it is not open to anyone to write of their own accord, nor is there any disagreement present in what is written, but the prophets alone learned, by inspiration from God, what had happened in the distant and most ancient past and recorded plainly events in their own time just as they occurred—[38] among us there are not thousands of books in disagreement and conflict with each other, but only twenty-two books, containing the record of all time, which are rightly trusted. [39] Five of these are the books of Moyses, which contain both the laws and the tradition from the birth of humanity up to his death; this is a period of a little less than 3,000 years. [40] From the death of Moyses until Artaxerxes, king of the Persians after Xerxes, the prophets after Moyses wrote the history of what took place in their own times in thirteen books; the remaining four books contain hymns to God and instructions for people on

Translation by John Barclay/Brill. Republication of Brill material courtesy of Koninklijke BRILL NV.

life. [41] From Artaxerxes up to our own time every event has been recorded, but this is not judged worthy of the same trust, since the exact line of succession of the prophets did not continue.

[42] It is clear in practice how we approach our own writings. Although such a long time has now passed, no one has dared to add, to take away, or to alter anything; and it is innate in every Judean, right from birth, to regard them as decrees of God, to remain faithful to them and, if necessary, gladly to die on their behalf. [43] Thus, to date many have been seen, on many occasions, as prisoners of war suffering torture and all kinds of deaths in theaters for not letting slip a single word in contravention of the laws and the records associated with them. [44] What Greek would suffer this on behalf of his own writings? He will not face the slightest injury even to save the whole body of Greek literature from obliteration! [45] For they regard these as stories invented at the whim of their authors, and they are right to think this even with regard to the older authors, since they see some of their contemporaries daring to write accounts of events at which they were not present and about which they have not troubled to gain information from those who know the facts. [46] In fact, even in relation to the war that happened recently to us, some have published works under the title of histories without either visiting the sites or going anywhere near the action; rather, concocting a few things on the basis of misinformation, they have given it the name of "history" with the complete shamelessness of a drunk.

[47] I, on the other hand, have written a truthful account of the whole war and its individual details, having been present myself at all the events. [48] For I was in command of those we call "Galileans" for as long as it was possible to resist, and after being captured lived among the Romans as a prisoner. When they had me under guard, Vespasian and Titus compelled me to be continually in attendance on them, initially bound; then, when I was released, I was sent from Alexandria with Titus to the siege of Jerusalem. [49] During that time none of the action escaped my knowledge: for I watched and carefully recorded what happened in the Roman camp, and I alone understood what was reported by deserters. [50] Then, when I had leisure in Rome, and when all the work was prepared, having made use of some collaborators for the Greek language, I thus constructed my account of the events. So confident was I of its truthfulness that I decided to use as my witnesses, before everyone else, the commanders-in-chief during the war, Vespasian and Titus. [51] For I presented the books to them first of all; after them I sold copies to many Romans who had fought with them in the war, and to many of our own people, men also steeped in Greek wisdom, among whom were Julius Archelaus, the most distinguished Herod, and the most renowned King Agrippa himself. [52] These all bore witness that I had carefully safeguarded the truth, and they would not have held back or kept silent if, out of ignorance or bias, I had altered or omitted any of the facts.

[53] But certain despicable characters have attempted to libel my history, thinking they have been set an exercise, as are boys at school, of an extraordinary form of accusation and libel. They ought to know that it is incumbent on the person who promises to give others an account of true occurrences that he first himself acquire an accurate knowledge of these, either by having followed events or by gaining information from those who know about them. [54] This I consider I

have accomplished very well in both my works: the *Ancient History*, as I said, I translated from the sacred writings, being a priest by ancestry and steeped in the philosophy contained in those writings; [55] and I wrote the history of the war having been personally involved in many events, an eyewitness of most of them, and not in the slightest deficient in my knowledge of anything that was said or done. [56] So how could one consider other than reckless those who have attempted to challenge my truthfulness—who, even if they claim to have read the field notes of the commanders-in-chief, were certainly not present in the affairs on our side as well, in the opposite camp?

Polemic against Apion (2.8–32)

[2.8] That our fathers were neither Egyptians by descent nor expelled from there because of bodily injury or any other such afflictions, I think I have already demonstrated not merely adequately but more than adequately. [9] I will mention briefly the material that Apion adds. [10] In the third book of his *Aegyptiaca* he says this:

> Moyses, as I heard from the elders of the Egyptians, was a Heliopolitan, who, being pledged to his ancestral customs, used to build open-air prayer houses in line with whatever circuits the sun had, and used to turn them all toward the east; for that is also the orientation of Heliopolis. [11] In place of obelisks he set up pillars, under which there was the base of a sundial sculptured in relief; this had the shadow of a statue cast upon it, in such a way that this went round in accordance with the course of the sun as it travels continuously through the air.

[12] Such is the amazing statement of the "scholar." Its falsity does not need to be argued, but is quite evident from the facts. For neither did Moyses himself, when he constructed the first tent for God, place in it any such sculptured object, nor did he instruct his successors to make one. And Solomon, who later constructed the sanctuary in Jerusalem, refrained from any such curiosity of the kind that Apion has fabricated. [13] He says that he heard from the "elders" that Moyses was a Heliopolitan; evidently, being younger himself, he has trusted those who, because of their age, knew Moyses and were his contemporaries! [14] With regard to the poet Homer, though he is a "scholar" he would not be able to say with confidence what his homeland was, nor with regard to Pythagoras, who lived just about "yesterday or the day before"; but with regard to Moyses, who preceded these men by such a vast number of years, he gives his opinion with such ease, trusting the report of elders, that he is clearly telling lies.

[15] With respect to the date at which he says Moyses led out the lepers, the blind, and those whose feet were crippled, the precise "scholar" is in complete agreement, I should imagine, with his predecessors. [16] In fact, Manetho says that the Judeans left Egypt during the reign of Tethmosis, 393 years before Danaus's flight to Argos, Lysimachus when Bocchoris was king, that is, 1,700 years ago, and Molon and some others as seems good to them. [17] Apion, being of course the most reliable of them all, fixed the date of the exodus precisely during the seventh Olympiad, and in its first year, the year in which, he says, the Phoenicians founded

Karchedon [Carthage]. He certainly added this reference to Karchedon thinking it would be very clear evidence of his veracity, not realizing that he was incorporating something that refuted himself. [18] For if one may believe the Phoenician records concerning the colony, King Eiromos is there recorded as having lived more than 150 years before the founding of Karchedon. Concerning this man, I earlier provided proofs from the Phoenician records [19] that Eiromos was a friend of Solomon who built the sanctuary in Jerusalem, and contributed much toward the construction of the sanctuary. But Solomon himself built the sanctuary 612 years after the Judeans left Egypt.

[20] Having guessed, for the number of those expelled, the same figure as Lysimachus (he says there were 110,000), he offers an amazing and persuasive reason for how, he says, the *sabbaton* got its name. [21] When they had traveled for six days, he says, they contracted swellings in the groin and for this reason rested on the seventh day, after arriving safely in the land that is now called Judea; and they called that day *sabbaton,* preserving the Egyptian language, for the Egyptians call the inflammation of the groin *sabbatōsis.* [22] Would not anyone either laugh at such nonsense or alternatively detest the effrontery in writing such things? Obviously, all 110,000 contracted such inflammation of the groin! [23] But if they were blind and lame and sick in every way, such as Apion says they were, they would not have been able to make even one day's journey! And if they were able to cross an extensive desert and, moreover, defeat those who opposed them, all taking part in the fight, they were not afflicted en masse with groin swellings after the sixth day. [24] For it is not natural for such a thing to happen to those on a march; many thousands in army units march at a steady pace continuously for many days. Nor is it likely that such a thing should happen by chance—that would be the most absurd notion of all. [25] This amazing Apion stated previously that they arrived in Judea in the course of six days, but says otherwise that Moyses, having ascended the mountain between Egypt and Arabia called Sinaeus, was hidden for forty days, and descended from there to give the Judeans the laws. But how was it possible for the same people both to remain for forty days in the desert, a waterless place, and to cross all the intervening distance in six days? [26] The linguistic transposition regarding the naming of the *sabbaton* reflects gross effrontery or terrible ignorance. For *sabbo* and *sabbaton* are very different from each other. [27] According to the language of Judeans, *sabbaton* means rest from all work, while among Egyptians *sabbo,* as he says, means an inflammation in the groin.

[28] Such are some of the things that the Egyptian Apion has invented concerning Moyses and the departure of the Judeans from Egypt being more imaginative than the others. And why should we be amazed if he lies about our ancestors, claiming that they were Egyptians by descent? [29] He used to lie about himself in the opposite direction. Although he was born at an oasis of Egypt and was, as one might say, the original Egyptian, he disowned his true homeland and people, and, while falsely claiming to be an Alexandrian, acknowledges the depravity of his people. [30] Understandably, then, those whom he hates and wishes to insult he calls "Egyptians"; for if he had not considered Egyptians utterly worthless, he would not himself have deserted his own people. Those who think highly of their own homelands are proud to be named after them, and censure those who improperly lay claim to that origin. [31] In relation to us, Egyptians are affected in

one of two ways: they either boost themselves by claiming kinship with us, or they drag us by association into their poor reputation. [32] But the noble Apion seems to want to present his slander of us to the Alexandrians as a kind of payment for the citizenship given to him. Knowing their hatred of the Judeans who live among them in Alexandria, he sets out to insult those Judeans, and to include all the rest, in both cases lying shamelessly.

In Praise of the Judean Constitution (2.164–98)

[2.164] There are infinite varieties in individual customs and laws among humanity as a whole, but in summary one may say: some have entrusted the power of government to monarchies, others to the rule of the few, others again to the masses. [165] But our legislator took no notice of any of these, but instituted the government as what one might call—to force an expression—a "theocracy," ascribing to God the rule and power [166] and, persuading everyone to look to him as the cause of all good things, both those that are common to all humanity and those that they themselves received when they prayed in difficulties, and that neither any deed nor anything that anyone thought in private could escape his attention, [167] he represented him as single and uncreated and immutable through all eternity, more beautiful than any mortal form, known to us by his power, but as to what he is like in essence, unknown. [168] That the wisest among the Greeks were taught these ideas about God, after he [Moyses] provided their original expression, I refrain from speaking about now; but that they are excellent and fitting in relation to the nature and majesty of God they have abundantly testified. For Pythagoras, Anaxagoras, Plato, and, after him, the Stoic philosophers practically all seem to have thought in this way about the nature of God.

[169] These, however, confined their philosophy to a few and did not dare to disclose the truth of their doctrine to the masses, who were in the grip of opinions. But our legislator, by putting deeds in harmony with words, not only won consent from his contemporaries but also implanted this belief about God in their descendants of all future generations, [such that it is] unchangeable. [170] The reason is that, by the very shape of the legislation, it is always employable by everyone, and has lasted long. For he did not make piety a part of virtue, but recognized and established the others as parts of it—that is, justice, moderation, endurance, and harmony among citizens in relation to one another in all matters. [171] For all practices and occupations, and all speech, have reference to our piety toward God; he did not leave any of these unscrutinized or imprecise.

All education and custom construction is of two kinds: one instructs by means of words, the other through training in character. [172] Other legislators were divided in their opinions, choosing one kind and omitting the other, as each saw fit: thus, the Lacedaemonians and Cretans used to conduct their education through customs, not words, whereas the Athenians and almost all the rest of the Greeks used to issue instruction on what should or should not be done through laws, but neglected to accustom people to these through deeds. [173] But our legislator combined both forms with great care: he neither left character training mute nor allowed the words from the law to go unpracticed. Rather, starting right from the beginning of their nurture and from the mode of life practiced by each individual in the household, he did not leave anything, even the minutest detail, free to be determined by the wishes of those who would make use of [the laws], [174] but even in relation to food, what they should refrain from and what they should eat, the company they keep in their daily lives, as well as their intensity in work and, conversely, rest, he set the law as their boundary and rule, so that, living under this as a father and master, we might commit no sin either willfully or from ignorance.

[175] He left no pretext for ignorance, but instituted the law as the finest and most essential teaching material; so that it would be heard not just once or twice or a number of times, he ordered that every seven days they should abandon their other activities and gather to hear the law, and to learn it thoroughly and in detail. That is something that all [other] legislators seem to have neglected. [176] Most people are so far from living in accordance with their own laws that they hardly even know them; it is only when they do wrong that they learn, from others, that they have transgressed the law. [177] Even those who hold their most important and most powerful political offices admit their ignorance, for they appoint as overseers for the administration of affairs those who profess expertise in the laws. [178] Were anyone of us to be asked about the laws, he would recount them all more easily than his own name. So, learning them thoroughly from the very first moment of consciousness, we have them, as it were, engraved on our souls; it is rare to find a transgressor, and impossible to gain exemption from punishment.

[179] It is this above all that has created our remarkable concord. For holding one and the same conception of God, and not differing at all in lifestyle or customs, produces a very beautiful harmony in [people's] characters. [180] Among us alone one will hear no contradictory statements about God, such as is common among others—and not just what is spoken by ordinary people as the emotion grips them individually, but also in what has been boldly pronounced among certain philosophers, some of whom have attempted to do away with the very existence of God by their arguments, while others eliminate his providence on behalf of humankind. [181] Nor will one see any difference in our living habits: we all share common practices, and all make the same affirmation about God, in harmony with the law, that he watches over everything. As for the habits of daily life: that everything should have piety as its goal, one could gather even from women and slaves.

[182] In fact, this is the origin of the charge that some have raised against us, that we have produced no inventors of novel deeds or words. Others consider it honorable not to remain faithful to any ancestral customs, and those who most dare to transgress these customs they acknowledge for their "skillful ingenuity." [183] We, on the contrary, have taken the sole expression of both wisdom and virtue to consist in doing or thinking absolutely nothing contrary to the laws as originally promulgated. It would be reasonable to take that as evidence that the law was extremely well laid down; for the test of experience shows up those that do not have this quality as needing amendment.

[184] For us, who are convinced that the law was originally laid down in accordance with God's will, it would not be pious to fail to maintain it. What part of it would one change? What finer law could one invent? What could one bring from elsewhere as an improvement? What about the whole structure of the constitution? [185] What could be finer or more just than [a structure] that has made God

governor of the universe, that commits to the priests in concert the management of the most important matters, and, in turn, has entrusted to the high priest of all the governance of the other priests? [186] These the legislator initially appointed to their office not for their wealth or because they were superior by any other fortuitous advantage; but whoever of his generation surpassed others in persuasiveness and moderation, these were the people to whom he entrusted, in particular, the worship of God. [187] That involved close supervision of the law and of the other life habits; for the priests have been appointed as general overseers, as judges in disputes, and with responsibility for punishing those condemned. [188] So, what regime could be more holy than this? What honor could be more fitting to God, where the whole mass [of people] is equipped for piety, the priests are entrusted with special supervision, and the whole constitution is organized like some rite of consecration? [189] The practices that other people are unable to maintain over the space of a few days, under the name of "mysteries" and "rites of consecration," we maintain with great joy and unalterable determination for all time.

[190] What, then, are the proclamations and prohibitions? They are simple and well known. The first, at the head, speaks about God, that God encompasses all things, perfect and blessed, self-sufficient and sufficing for all, that he is the beginning, middle, and end of all things; he is evident through his works and acts of grace, and more apparent than anything else, but in form and greatness beyond our description. [191] For every material, however costly, is unworthy to form his image, and skill unskilled in imagining his likeness. We have seen nothing comparable, nor can we imagine it, nor is it holy to represent it. [192] We see his works: light, heaven, earth, sun and moon, rivers and sea, the birth of animals, the production of crops. These God made without hands, without effort, without needing any assistants, but when he willed beautiful things, they at once beautifully came to be. All must follow him, and worship him by exercising virtue; for this is the form of worship of God that is most holy.

[193] One temple of the one God—for like is always attracted to like—common to all people as belonging to the common God of all. The priests will continuously offer worship to him, and the one who is first by descent will always be at their head. [194] He, together with the other priests, will sacrifice to God, will safeguard the laws, will adjudicate in disputes, and will punish those who are convicted. Whoever disobeys him will pay a penalty as if he were sacrilegious toward God himself. [195] We offer sacrifices not for our gratification or drunkenness—for that is undesirable to God and would be a pretext for violence and lavish expenditure—but such as are sober, orderly, well-behaved, so that, especially when sacrificing, we may act in sober moderation. [196] And at the sacrifices we must first offer prayers for the common welfare, and then for ourselves; for we were born for communal fellowship, and the person who sets greater store by this than by his own personal concerns would be especially pleasing to God. [197] And let appeal be made to God through prayer, and request, not that he might give good things—for he has given them of his own accord and made them available to everyone—but that we might be able to receive them, and when we have them, to keep them. [198] In view of the sacrifices, the law has decreed purifications after a funeral, after childbirth, after sexual union with a woman, and from many other causes, which it would take a long time to describe. Such is our doctrine concerning God and his worship, and the law is one and the same.

Introduction to the *Jewish War*

Narrative Description

Even if Josephus faced a delay in producing book 7 of his *Jewish War*, which is possible, it was not an afterthought but part of the structure he had envisaged all along. In the opening lines of the narrative (1.31–33) Josephus mentions a temple built by a refugee high priest in Leontopolis, Egypt, and promises that he will speak about this further in the proper place (*see* Map of Egypt with Temple Sites, p. 42). But he does not mention it again until the end of book 7 (7.420–36), when he is about to describe its end in 73 or 74 CE. Many other features of book 7—an "Antiochus" based in Antioch (like the Seleucid king of book 1) who tries to end the practice of Judean customs (7.46–53), a royal figure named Antiochus IV Epiphanes (7.219–44; *see* The Book of Daniel; Introduction to the History of the Second Temple Period), the story of **Antony** and **Cleopatra** (7.300–303), and the description of current Parthians by the old-fashioned name "Medes" (7.245–46)—recall book 1, the only place where they have appeared before. All of this creates a sense that the long narrative begun in the first book is closing in on a matching conclusion. It suggests a kind of "ring composition," in which the story moves first toward the center and then away from it. Is there such a matching structure, in fact?

In general terms, yes. For example, only near the beginning of book 2 and the end of book 6 does Josephus refer to a festival called *Pascha* (Passover), where many sacrifices are made (2.10; 6.423). Other parallels concern the "piling up" of corpses (2.30; 6.259, 431), the five modes of death experienced by fighters on the temple colonnade (2.49–50; 6.181), his only two descriptions of souls as composed of pure "ether" (2.154–56; 6.47), and the only two occurrences of the word "pseudoprophet"—both connected with "signs" (2.261; 6.285). Stepping further inside the ring, Josephus surrenders to Vespasian and Titus near the end of book 3, and is released from his chains near the end of book 4.

These parallels focus our attention on the middle of book 4. Does something of great significance happen there? It does. Josephus first gives an elaborate description of the entry of **Idumeans** (allies of the **Zealots**) into Jerusalem (4.224–304), and then has them leave again in disgust (4.354). In between, what creates their

328

disgust is that they are persuaded by the Zealots to murder the distinguished chief priests who have led the war effort to that point, Ananus and Jesus (4.314–17).[1] Josephus clearly makes this the turning point of his whole story. He says that these outrageous murders began "the taking of the city" and "the fall of the Judean republic" (4.318–21). In book 7, similarly, surveying the whole war in retrospect he will describe this as the end of the Judean constitution and the beginning of desperate lawlessness (7.267). So clearly, he winds up the narrative toward this central panel, in order to let it unravel from there on. This concentric movement exists alongside the more standard dramatic plot, which builds to its climax with the fall of Jerusalem at the end of book 6.

THE HIGH PRIESTHOOD DURING THE PERIOD OF THE ROMAN OCCUPATION (63 BCE–70 CE)

Jonathan Hyrcanus II	76–66 BCE
Aristobulus II	66–63
Jonathan Hyrcanus II (restored)	63–40
Antigonus	40–37
Ananelus	37–36
Aristobulus III	36
Ananelus (restored)	36–30
Joshua ben Fabus	30–23
Simon ben Boerhus	23–5
Matthias ben Theophilus	5–4
Joazar ben Boethus (Sadducee)	4
Eleazar ben Boethus (Sadducee)	4–3
Joshua ben Sie	3 BCE–6 CE
Joazar ben Boethus (?)	6 CE
Ananus ben Seth	6–15
Ishmael ben Fabus	15–16
Eleazar ben Ananus	16–17
Simon ben Camithus	17–18
Joseph Caiaphas	18–36
Jonathan ben Ananus	36–37
Theophilus ben Ananus	37–41
Simon Cantatheras ben Boethus (Sadducee)	41–43
Matthias ben Ananus	43
Elioneus ben Simon Cantatheras (Sadducee)	43–44
Jonathan ben Ananus (restored)	44
Josephus ben Camydus	44–46
Ananias ben Nebedeus	46–52

1. Josephus, *War.* 4.314–17: "The Idumeans . . . went in search of the chief priests, it was for them that the main rush was made, and they were soon captured and slain. Then standing over their dead bodies, they scoffed Ananus for his patronage of the people. . . . They actually went so far as to cast out the corpses without burial, although the Jews are so careful about funeral rites that even malefactors who have been sentenced to crucifixion are taken down and buried before sunset."

Jonathan	52–56
Ishmael ben Fabus	56–62
Joseph ben Ananus	63
Joshua ben Damneus	63
Joshua ben Gamaliel	63–64
Mattathias ben Theophilus	65–66
Phannias ben Samuel	67–70

Two other observations confirm that Josephus had such a concentric pattern in mind while composing the *War*, though he does not spell it out, but leaves it for skilled audiences to notice. (This kind of pattern was common in ancient literature.) First, at the beginning of the *Antiquities* (1.7), where he is describing his decision to omit ancient history from the *War*, he claims that he wanted to keep the earlier work proportional on its own terms, with the beginning matching the end. He uses a verb related to our noun "symmetry," saying in effect that he "measured off" the beginning and the end so that they would match. The verb was used most often in architectural contexts to indicate matching columns or the like.

Second, however, if we count all the words in the *War* and find *their* midpoint, it would actually come about three-quarters of the way through book 3, not in book 4. This is because Josephus has deliberately created seven books of unequal size. Book 1, at nearly 30,000 words, is far longer than the others. Books 6 and 7 nearly match each other, at just under 12,500 words each. The others average about half the size of book 1, except for book 2, which falls in between (22,470 words). Obviously, Josephus could have combined books 6 and 7 and still had a volume smaller than book 1. This shows that he really wanted a seven-book structure (like Julius Caesar's *Gallic Wars*; like Caesar, Josephus refers to himself in the third person). He stuffs book 1 as full as possible (mostly with material on Herod), but confines it there so that he can maintain the symmetry of the volumes, with the narrative fulcrum sitting in the middle of book 4.

Even though they are not at all comparable in size, then, books 1 and 7 correspond to each other in providing, respectively, the remote background (including Herod's rebuilding of the city) and then the aftermath to the fall of Jerusalem. Book 2 covers the seventy years from Herod's death in 4 BCE to the outbreak of war in 66 CE, including the complex interplay of the war's causes, the failure of the governor in Syria to stop the revolt at an early point, Josephus's appointment, and his initial activities in Galilee. Book 3 opens with the Roman legions' arrival and is dominated by their Galilean campaign, near the end of which Josephus surrenders. At the center, book 4 is the most diverse, or chaotic, in keeping with the atmosphere of turmoil it seeks to create. It moves from the Romans' final subjection of Galilee with the fall of Gischala (home of one of the two main rebel leaders, who then heads to Jerusalem), through the crisis that sees the deaths of the city's honorable leading men, to the outbreak of savage rivalry and civil war in the doomed city. All of this Josephus artfully compares (4.545) with the civil war in Rome at the same time (following Nero's death).

Book 5 sets up two contrasting themes: the civil war and its horrors inside Jerusalem, including the famine it generated (5.1–38), and the arrival of Titus's forces outside to press the siege (5.39–97). Josephus moves back and forth, in part to ask whether the Judeans' actions toward each other, as they ostensibly fought for "freedom" from Rome, were any worse than those of their ostensible enemies outside. Book 6 takes this contrasting pair to a higher level of intensity (e.g., with an episode of desperate cannibalism in the city) before the resolution that comes with the burning and capture of the city. Book 7 covers a wide range of aftereffects, from the reactions of Judea's hostile neighbors, the triumph in Rome, and the capture of the final strongholds (**Herodium, Machaerus,** and **Masada**) in the years after 70 CE. The closure of that temple in Egypt, it turns out, results from Roman concern over some militants who have escaped to Egypt from Judea.

Date/Occasion

Josephus later claims (*Life* 361; see *Life*) that, unlike one of his critics who brought out a history of the war twenty years later, when many important witnesses were long dead, he had presented "the volumes" to **Vespasian** and **Titus** "when the events were barely out of view"—therefore, soon after the conflict ended with Masada's fall in 73 or 74 CE (also *Apion* 1.50–51; see *Apion*) (*see* Map of the Dead Sea Region, p. 40; Introduction to Flavius Josephus). The last datable event in Josephus's *War* is Vespasian's dedication of the Forum of Peace (7.158), alongside the main Roman forum, in 75 CE (**Dio Cassius** 65/66.15.1). Since Vespasian died on 23 June in 79 CE, the *War*'s completion has usually been dated between 75 and 79 CE. Some scholars have argued for a slightly later date, at least for the last volume or two, noting, for example, that Josephus mentions only Titus (ruled 79–81 CE) as authorizing support for his work (*Life* 363). Some have detected shifts in the language of book 7, and argued that its alleged flattery of Domitian (7.85–88) along with other historical allusions indicate a completion date for book 7 in Domitian's reign (81–96 CE).

There is, however, no decisive reason to abandon the 75–79 CE range. That Titus alone supported the publicizing of Josephus's *War* is not surprising, even if his father was still alive when it came out. Pliny the Elder dedicated his work to Titus alone in 77 CE, while Vespasian was still emperor. Titus reportedly had stronger literary interests than his father (**Suetonius,** *Lives of the Caesars* 3). And the reasons offered for dating book 7 to Domitian's reign are rather subjective. We must take seriously Josephus's repeated insistence that (in contrast to his rival) he presented his completed *War* to Vespasian and Titus, who were both in a position to expose its errors if these had been significant. It would be hard for him to rest so much on that point if everyone knew that much of his work was actually later.

After his surrender Josephus's life became entwined with Rome's new **Flavian** rulers (*see* Introduction to Flavius Josephus). But how so? The natural (and still common) suspicion that he therefore became their literary mouthpiece does not explain the actual content of his works. The Flavians were important for Roman history because they put the government on a new and stable footing after Nero's suicide in June 68 CE ended the century-long Julio-Claudian dynasty. Nero had become emperor at only sixteen years of age. His fourteen-year reign was widely seen as a travesty of Roman values, the absurd outcome of a dynastic system of succession: this indulgent boy artiste had no right to the status of "first man" *(princeps)* in the Roman Senate. In the bloody civil war that followed his death, three senators asserted their claims to power, each claiming experience of high military command—the most important proof of masculine capability in Rome— and the loyalty of many legions. When two of those contenders had fallen and the third had an unsteady grip on power, Vespasian used his military and political support to join the fray, and by the end of 69 CE (having left the Judean conflict to his son) he had defeated his last rival.

Vespasian's victory turned out to be momentous because, with two sons ready as successors and given that the next long-ruling emperor, Trajan (reigned 98–117 CE), would be the son of one of Vespasian's commanders, the new dynasty stabilized rule for decades to come, leading to the famously peaceful and happy second century.

In all of this, the war in Judea played a fundamental role. Not only did it give Vespasian and Titus the direct practical support of the eastern legions; it also solidified the image of the Flavians, who had no long history in high Roman politics, as "real men" of the old school who could keep the respect of the Senate and the people. They were the antithesis of the juvenile mother-killer and singer Nero. In order to emphasize their achievements in Judea, the Flavians took what was the suppression of a revolt in the provinces—there had been several of these in the first century—and transformed it into the defeat of a foreign enemy who had dared to wage war against Rome, the Judeans. Vespasian and Titus celebrated this victory over an eastern menace (evoking the great Augustus's earlier alleged victories over the Parthians) in a huge triumphal procession, an unprecedented series of victory coins, a new Temple of Peace, and several monumental buildings (including the Coliseum) and arches in Rome.

Did Josephus, who was living in Rome while all this was going on, use his writing to contribute still further to the Flavians' euphoria? The way he tells it, they did not need him as a spokesman. He opens his *War* by describing the many accounts by other writers that have just these traits: "Whereas *they* want to portray the Romans as great, they always vilify and denigrate the Judean side" (1.7). But Josephus finds an opening here for a uniquely positioned eyewitness such as himself, who knew the Judean side intimately and even fought against the Romans, but was also forced to watch from the Roman side through the end, and has now achieved a measure of respectability in the capital (1.2–3). Without undermining the rulers' achievement, but indirectly enhancing it, he finds a way to put his own people in a better light than their current reputation as defeated losers and enemies would suggest. The fundamental purpose of his work will be to balance the record (1.9). This will mean showing that the Judeans have an excellent and admirable character. What counted as good character in the Roman world was essentially manliness—courage, willingness to face death as men rather than breaking ancestral laws—and that is the picture Josephus wants to create. An implicit message, of course, is that the author himself is a wise judge of character, who knows all about human affairs and foibles.

Themes

A seven-volume narrative covering nearly 250 years, filled with character studies, geographical and philosophical digressions, speeches, and much else, does not have a single thesis, like an essay. Rather, it has dozens of themes and language patterns that keep turning up to give the whole story a unified atmosphere. Perhaps the best we can do is to group some of these themes in clusters (for convenience—they cannot be isolated from each other), of which I would specify four.

First and most fundamental are those themes that have to do with the Judean national character. Josephus has a range of terms connected with maleness, courage, endurance, daring, risk, hardiness, and contempt for death, and he has many passages in which the Romans must frankly recognize the indomitable spirit and daring of the Judeans (e.g., 4.89–90; 5.315–16; 6.11–14, 42–44). An important point here is that this national trait is present no matter how foolish or destructive the political choices of the Judeans in question may be. We see this particularly in Josephus's final remarks on the **Sicarii** (knife-assassins) who fled to Egypt. Although he repudiates them as insanely murderous and self-destructive (7.410–16), he also dwells on their astonishing imperviousness to torture—a virtue shared even by their children (7.417–19). The same contrast appears in the Masada story and many others.

Second, Josephus has a large number of themes related to managing the *polis* (city)—political themes of the kind that contemporary authors discussed often. In his portrait, society is rightly led by elders who go by many names (principals, first men, the powerful, the leaders, and the best); the mass of people, by contrast, are not distinguished individually. They are the "people" or, more often, the "rabble," the "mob." As everyone knew, the main task of a statesman like Josephus was to steer this rabble, making sure that they felt their needs were being met and their complaints adequately addressed. This was done while neutralizing the influence of others ("revolutionaries," "innovators," "enchanters," "tyrants") who would use fancy speech to make impossible promises of "freedom," and get the masses excited about better prospects for the future, though this could only lead to a harsher slavery under Rome. The rebels' program was one of madness or insanity, and was (Josephus claims) usually motivated by a quest for personal power and wealth at the expense of the common good.

Third, Josephus frames all of this in the familiar language of tragedy. His *War* as a whole is a deeply tragic story, concerning the fall of one of the most fortunate cities to the lowest depths (1.11). As in tragedy, the movement of Fate cannot be halted in spite of the characters' best efforts, and many of them unwittingly make the situation worse (as Oedipus unknowingly killed his father and married his mother). The story is also filled with tragic figures who are rapidly undone, in spite of their great ability and achievements in some cases: Herod (book 1), Simon of Scythopolis (2.469–76), Josephus himself (cf. 3.393–95), the leaders Ananus and Jesus, many of the aristocrats, the elegant woman driven to cannibalism (6.201–19), and the final inhabitants of Masada (7.320–401). Already in the prologue, Josephus introduces the tragic language of misfortune, mourning, lamentation, calamity, wailing, and dirge, not to mention the tragic hallmarks of fear and pity (1.11–12), and they reappear often in the story.

Classical tragedy (such as Sophocles's *Oedipus* or **Aeschylus's** *Oresteia*) often has to do with an act of serious pollution or defilement *(miasma)* in the city, a violation of natural and divine law that needs purging. This is the fourth set of themes that runs throughout the *War*. The most sacred precincts of the temple are in Josephus's account the scene of the most heinous acts of pollution, as the human blood shed by Judean compatriots mixes with the blood of their animal sacrifices. This defilement so offends the Deity that he abandons his own shrine in order to allow the Romans to purge it by fire.

Nowhere does Josephus merely report facts in neutral language. Nor could he have done so if he had wanted. Language requires choices, and he opts for highly charged language, full of resonance for his educated ancient audiences.

STEVE MASON

2.6 from *Jewish War*

Prologue (1.1–30)

[1.1] With respect to the war of Judeans against Romans—the greatest ever joined, not only of those in our times, but almost the greatest even of those about which we have received report, where cities have clashed with cities or nations with nations—those who were not actually present at the events, but are collecting random and incoherent tales through the report of others, are writing them up sophist-like, [2] while others who were there are misrepresenting the events, through either flattery toward the Romans or hatred toward the Judeans. So their compositions consist of denunciation in some cases and encomium in others, but nowhere the precision of history. [3] For this reason I, Josephus son of Matthias, a priest from Jerusalem, who myself fought against the Romans at first and eventually happened to be among them by necessity, have set myself the task of providing a narrative in the Greek language, for those under the Roman *imperium,* having reworked what I had formerly written up in my ancestral language and sent to the upper barbarians.

[4] With what I have called this greatest instability, among the Romans domestic affairs were becoming diseased, while the revolutionary element of the Judeans reached its peak in those turbulent times, in terms of number and also in resources, so that in the excess of disorders the fate of the regions to the east was uncertain: some were in hope of their acquisition, others in anxiety over their possible loss. [5] And whereas Judeans hoped that their compatriot element beyond the Euphrates would be swept up together in the war with themselves, in the case of the Romans the neighboring Gauls were becoming restive, and the Celtic world was not quiet either. Everything was filled with disorders after the death of Nero. While the opportunity induced many to seek sovereignty, the military were craving change in the hope of gain. [6] So I considered it absurd to stand by and watch the truth about such momentous events being obfuscated [here in Rome] while even the Parthians and Babylonians, the most remote of the Arabs, our own compatriot element over the Euphrates, and Adiabenians should know precisely—through my diligence—why the war began, through what mutations it proceeded, and the way in which it came to an end, whereas Greeks and those Romans who had not marched against us should not know these things, but be left reading either flatteries or fictions.

[7] Moreover, they dare to entitle those books "histories," in which they present nothing sound and seem to me at least to miss their target. For although they want to portray the Romans as great, they always vilify and denigrate the Judean side. [8] I really do not see how those who have conquered insignificant people

---

Translation by Steve Mason (1.1–30; 3.340–61, 383–408; 6.193–219; 7.320–36) and Steve Mason/Brill (modified) (2.117–66; 2.169–77; 2.342–505). Republication of Brill material courtesy of Koninklijke BRILL NV.

should seem to be great. And they respect neither the length of the war nor the mass of the army that exhausted itself on the Roman side, nor the greatness of the generals, who sweated so much in the vicinity of Jerusalem. I suppose that, by denigrating their [the generals'—now the imperial family's] achievement, they regard them too as unworthy!

⁹ I certainly had no intention of contending with those who heap praise on the Romans' deeds by exaggerating those of my compatriots. No, I go through the actions of both sides with precision, though on top of the events I do overlay language related to my personal disposition, and I have permitted my own feelings to mourn over the calamities of my native place. ¹⁰ That domestic factional strife brought it down, and that the Judean tyrants drew both the Romans' unwilling hands and the fire upon the shrine, Titus Caesar—the very one who destroyed it— is witness. Toward the populace, kept under guard by the insurgents, he showed pity throughout the entire war. Often, deliberately postponing the capture of the city, he gave opportunity, even during the siege, for a change of mind on the part of those responsible.

¹¹ Now, in case anyone would unjustly find fault with the things we say by way of accusation against the tyrants and their bandit element, or our groaning over the misfortunes of our native place, let him grant indulgence for such emotion beyond the "law of history." For what happened was that our city, of all those subject to the Romans, reached the most complete happiness, and then in turn fell into the worst of calamities. ¹² At any rate, the unfortunate things that have happened to all [nations] since time immemorial pale, in my view, in comparison with what has happened to the Judeans. And since no foreigner was the cause of these things, it was not possible to keep control over one's lamentations. If, however, anyone should be too rigid a judge for compassion, let him assign the facts to the history, the expressions of mourning to its writer.

¹³ And yet I myself might fairly criticize the storytellers among the Greeks who have positioned themselves as judges of these events of such moment that have happened in their own times, which expose the ancient wars as paltry by comparison, while abusing those who rival them for honor—in relation to whom, even if they prove superior in speech-craft, they are inferior in choice [of subject]. They themselves write the history of the Assyrians and Medes, as if these events had been less well reported by the ancient historical writers! ¹⁴ And yet in the same measure they are unequal to those men with respect to ability at writing, they are also their inferiors in judgment. For each of those [ancient] men was keen to write of his own times, where their presence at the events made the report vivid; lying, among those who were knowledgeable, was a shameful thing. ¹⁵ Certainly, at any rate, placing in a memorial matters not previously treated historically, and putting together the affairs of one's own times for those who come afterward, is worthy of praise and acknowledgment. The industrious man is not the one who merely remodels another person's arrangement and order, but the one who, by speaking of recent things, also establishes the body of the history in a distinctive way.

¹⁶ For my part, it is through the greatest expenditures and exertions that I, albeit a foreigner, present to Greeks and also Romans this memorial of achievements. As for the native Greeks, when it comes to profits or lawsuits, the mouth

immediately bursts open and the tongue is let loose; but when it comes to history, where one must speak the truth and may only assemble the facts through much exertion, they stand muzzled, having allowed feebler men to write—and those who do not even know the deeds of the leaders. Let the truth of history, then, be honored among us, since among the Greeks it has been neglected.

[17] To speak of ancient things in the case of the Judeans, actually—who some of these were, how they up and fled from the Egyptians, what sort of country they encountered while they were wandering, how many places they seized in sequence, and how they found themselves displaced—I considered to be untimely now and in any case redundant, seeing that many Judeans before me have recounted the deeds of our ancestors with precision, and certain Greeks have changed those things into their native language without veering much from the truth. [18] So just where both the historical writers of this group and our own prophets finished, from there I will establish the beginning of my account.

Now, although I will go through the matters related to the war in my own time with greater detail and with as much nuance as I am able, those that occurred before my age I will pass over concisely: [19] that Antiochus, the one called Epiphanes, having taken Jerusalem by storm and having held it down for three years and six months, was expelled from the region by the sons of Asamonaeus; after that, that the descendants of these men, by generating factions in pursuit of the kingship, drew the Romans and Pompey into their affairs; that Herod [the son] of Antipater utterly destroyed their sovereignty, after enlisting Sossius; [20] further, how after the demise of Herod the people fell into sedition, when Augustus was ruling the Romans and Quintilius Varus was in the region; how, in the twelfth year of Nero's rule the war erupted—and what had happened under Cestius—and what the Judeans under arms encountered in the first assaults; (praef. 8) [21] further, how they walled the neighboring settlements, and how Nero, becoming anxious for the whole situation because of the blunders of Cestius, placed Vespasian in charge of the war; that this man with the older of his sons invaded the region of the Judeans; what sort of Roman army and allied forces he employed in attacking all of Galilee, and that he took her cities—some devastatingly, by storm, and some through surrender.

[22] At that point I will go through: the discipline of the Romans at war and the training of the legions; the proportions and physical character of each of the two Galilees; the boundaries of Judea and also the distinctive features of the region, both the lakes and the streams there; and the sufferings of those taken captive in each city, with precision, just as I saw or suffered them—for I will not conceal any of my own calamities, since I am about to speak to those who know them.

[23] After that, though matters are already going hard for the Judeans, Nero dies and Vespasian, while striking at Jerusalem, is drawn away by the imperial power; also the signs that occurred concerning this event—and him—and the upheavals at Rome; [24] and how he, reluctantly, is acclaimed *imperator* by the soldiers, and when he has withdrawn to Egypt to take on the administration of the world, things among the Judeans erupted in factional strife, and the tyrants rose up over them, and the differences these men had with one another.

[25] And that Titus having set out from Egypt a second time invaded the region, how and where and how many forces he assembled, and how the city was faring

as a result of the factional strife when he arrived, what strikes he made and how many embankments, the encirclements provided by the three walls and the measurements of these, also the strength of the city and the disposition of the temple and the shrine; [26] still further, all the measurements of these and of the altar, with precision; also some of the festival customs and the seven purities and the public services of the priests, still further the garments of the priests and of the high priest, and of what sort was the holy place of the shrine, neither concealing nor embellishing anything of what was actually found there.

[27] After that I will go through in detail the savagery of the tyrants toward their compatriots and the consideration of the Romans toward foreigners, and how many times Titus, longing to save the city and the shrine, appealed to the insurgents to reach terms. But I discriminate among the sufferings and calamities of the populace: how much they were afflicted by the war, how much by the factional strife, and how much by the famine, before they were taken captive. [28] I will neglect neither the unfortunate cases of the deserters nor the punishments of the prisoners of war, how the shrine was set on fire against Caesar's will and how many of the temple treasures were seized, the capture of the entire city and the signs and wonders prior to this, and the imprisonment of the tyrants, the mass of those reduced to slavery and what fortune each of them was allotted; [29] that, whereas the [other] Romans went out against the remnants of the war and brought down the defenses of the outposts, Titus went over the whole region and restored order; his return to Italy and the triumph.

[30] All these things I have covered in seven volumes [or scrolls]: I have left nothing, no occasion for blame or accusation, to those who know the events and who were present in the war: indeed, I wrote for those who love the truth, not with an orientation to pleasure. I will take this as the beginning of the narrative, which I also took similarly for the summaries [above].

Judea Becomes a Province; Three Philosophical Schools (2.117–66)

2.117 When the territory of Archelaus had been marked off for a province, Coponius, a procurator from the equestrian order among the Romans, was sent. He had received from Caesar an authority that went as far as the death penalty. [118] In his [term] a certain Galilean man by the name of Judas incited the locals to rebellion, lambasting them if they were going to put up with paying tribute to Romans and tolerate mortal masters after God. This man was a sophist of his own peculiar school, which had nothing in common with the others.

[119] For three forms of philosophy are pursued among the Judeans: the members of one are Pharisees, of another Sadducees, and the third, who certainly are reputed to cultivate seriousness, are called Essenes; although Judeans by ancestry, they are even more mutually affectionate than the others. [120] Whereas these men shun the pleasures as vice, they consider self-control and not succumbing to the passions virtue. And although there is among them a disdain for marriage, adopting the children of outsiders while they are still malleable enough for the lessons they regard them as family and instill in them their principles of character: [121] without doing away with marriage or the succession resulting from it, they

nevertheless protect themselves from the wanton ways of women, having been persuaded that none of them preserves her faithfulness to one man.

[122] Since they are despisers of wealth—their communal stock is astonishing—one cannot find a person among them who has more in terms of possessions. For by a law, those coming into the school must yield up their funds to the order, with the result that in the whole group neither the humiliation of poverty nor the superiority of wealth is detectable, but the assets of each one have been mixed in together, as if they were brothers, to create one fund for all.

[123] They consider olive oil a stain, and should anyone be accidentally smeared with it he scrubs his body, for they make it a point of honor to remain hard and dry, and to wear white always.

The curators of the communal affairs are elected by hand and they are indivisible, each for all without division.

[124] No one city is theirs, but they settle amply in each. And for those school members who arrive from elsewhere, all that the community has is laid out for them in the same way as if they were their own things, and they go in and stay with those they have never even seen before as if they were the most intimate friends. [125] For this reason they make trips without carrying any baggage at all—though armed on account of the bandits. In each city a steward of the order appointed specially for the visitors is designated quartermaster for clothing and amenities.

[126] Dress and also deportment of body: [they are] like children being educated with fear. They replace neither clothes nor footwear until the old set is ripped all over or worn through with age. [127] Among themselves they neither shop for nor sell anything, but each one, after giving the things that he has to the one in need, takes in exchange anything useful that the other has. And even without this return giving, the transfer to others—from whomever they wish—is unhindered.

[128] Certainly toward the Deity they have uniquely pious observances. Before the sun rises, they say nothing on mundane things, but only certain ancestral prayers to him, as though begging him to come up. [129] After these things, they are dismissed by the curators to the various crafts that they have each come to learn, and after they have worked strenuously until the fifth hour they are again assembled in one area, where they belt on linen covers and wash their bodies in frigid water. After this purification they gather in a private hall, into which none of those who hold different views may enter: now pure themselves, they approach the dining room as if it were a sort of sanctuary. [130] After they have seated themselves in silence, the baker serves the loaves in order, whereas the cook serves each person one dish of one food. [131] The priest offers a prayer before the food, and it is forbidden to taste anything before the prayer; when he has had his breakfast again he says a concluding prayer. So, while starting and also while finishing, they honor God as the sponsor of life. At that, laying aside their clothes as if they were holy, they apply themselves to their labors again until evening.

[132] They dine in a similar way: when they have returned, they sit down with the visitors, if any happen to be present with them, and neither yelling nor disorder pollutes the house at any time, but they yield conversation to one another in order. [133] And to those from outside, the silence of those inside appears as a kind of shiver-inducing mystery. The reason for this is their continuous sobriety

and the rationing of food and drink among them—[eating only] to the point of fullness.

¹³⁴ As for other areas, although there is nothing that they do without the curators' having ordered it, these two things are matters of personal prerogative among them: rendering assistance and mercy. For helping those who are worthy, whenever they might need it, and also extending food to those who are in want are indeed left up to the individual. But in the case of the relatives, such distribution is not allowed to be done without [permission from] the managers.

¹³⁵ Of anger, [they are] just controllers; as for temper, [they are] able to contain it; of fidelity, masters; of peace, servants.

And whereas everything spoken by them is more forceful than an oath, swearing itself they avoid, considering it worse than the false oath; for the person who is unworthy of belief without God's help they declare to be already convicted.

¹³⁶ They are extraordinarily keen about the compositions of the ancients, selecting especially those connected with the benefit of soul and body. On the basis of these and for the treatment of diseases, roots, apotropaic materials, and the special properties of stones are investigated.

¹³⁷ To those who are eager for their school, the entryway is not straightforward, but they prescribe a regimen for the person as he remains outside for a year, giving him a little hatchet in addition to the aforementioned waist covering and white clothing. ¹³⁸ Whenever he should give proof of his self-control during this period, he approaches nearer to their regimen and indeed shares in the purer waters for purification, though he is not yet received into the functions of communal life. For after this demonstration of endurance, the character is tested for two more years, and only after he has thus been shown worthy is he reckoned into the group.

¹³⁹ Before he may touch the communal food, however, he swears dreadful oaths to them: first, that he will observe piety toward the Deity; then, that he will maintain just actions toward humanity; that he will harm no one, whether by his own deliberation or under order; that he will hate the unjust and contend together with the just; ¹⁴⁰ that he will always maintain faithfulness to all, especially to those in control, for without God it does not fall to anyone to hold office, and that, should he hold office, he will never abuse his authority—outshining his subordinates, whether by dress or by some form of extravagant appearance; ¹⁴¹ always to love the truth and expose the liars; that he will keep his hands pure from theft and his soul from unholy gain; that he will neither conceal anything from the school members nor disclose anything of theirs to others, even if one should apply force to the point of death.

¹⁴² In addition to these, he swears that he will impart the precepts to no one otherwise than as he received them, that he will keep away from banditry, and that he will preserve intact their school's books and the names of the angels. With such oaths as these they completely secure those who join them.

¹⁴³ Those they have convicted of sufficiently serious errors they expel from the order. And the one who has been reckoned out often perishes by a most pitiable fate. For, constrained by the oaths and customs, he is unable to partake of food from others. Eating grass and in hunger, his body wastes away and perishes. ¹⁴⁴ That is why they have actually shown mercy and taken back many

in their final gasps, regarding as sufficient for their errors this ordeal to the point of death.

¹⁴⁵ Now with respect to trials, [they are] just and extremely precise: they render judgment after having assembled no fewer than a hundred, and something that has been determined by them cannot be appealed.

There is a great reverence among them for—next to God—the name of the lawgiver, and if anyone insults him he is punished by death.

¹⁴⁶ They make it a point of honor to submit to the elders and to a majority. So if ten were seated together, one person would not speak if the nine were unwilling.

¹⁴⁷ They guard against spitting into middles or to the right side and against applying themselves to labors on the seventh days in a way distinct from all other Judeans: for not only do they prepare their own food one day before, so that they might not kindle a fire on that day, but they do not even dare to transport a container or go to relieve themselves.

¹⁴⁸ On the other days they dig a hole of a foot's depth with a trowel (this is what that small hatchet given by them to the neophytes is for) and wrapping their cloak around them completely, so as not to offend the rays of God, they relieve themselves into it [the hole]. ¹⁴⁹ After that, they haul back the excavated earth into the hole. When they do this, they pick out for themselves the more deserted spots. Even though the secretion of excrement is certainly a natural function, it is customary to wash themselves off after it as if they have become polluted.

¹⁵⁰ They are divided into four classes, according to their duration in the training, and the later joiners are so inferior to the earlier joiners that if they should touch them, the latter wash themselves off as if they had mingled with a foreigner.

¹⁵¹ [They are] long-lived, most of them passing 100 years—as a result, it seems to me at least, of the simplicity of their regimen and their orderliness. Despisers of terrors, triumphing over agonies by their wills, considering death (if it arrives with glory) better than deathlessness. ¹⁵² The war against the Romans proved their souls in every way: during it, while being twisted and also bent, burned and also broken, and passing through all the torture-chamber instruments, with the aim that they might insult the lawgiver or eat something not customary, they did not put up with suffering either one: not once gratifying those who were tormenting them, or crying. ¹⁵³ Smiling in their agonies and making fun of those who were inflicting the tortures, they would cheerfully dismiss their souls, since they were going to get them back again.

¹⁵⁴ For the view has become tenaciously held among them that whereas our bodies are perishable and their matter impermanent, our souls endure forever, deathless: they get entangled, having emanated from the most refined ether, as if drawn down by a certain charm into the prisons that are bodies. ¹⁵⁵ But when they are released from the restraints of the flesh, as if freed from a long period of slavery, then they rejoice and are carried upward in suspension. For the good, on the one hand, sharing the view of the sons of Greece they portray the lifestyle reserved beyond Oceanus and a place burdened by neither rain nor snow nor heat, but which a continually blowing mild west wind from Oceanus refreshes. For the base, on the other hand, they separate off a murky, stormy recess filled with unending retributions.

¹⁵⁶ It was according to the same notion that the Greeks appear to me to have

laid on the Islands of the Blessed for their most courageous men, whom they call heroes and demigods, and for the souls of the worthless the region of the impious in Hades, in which connection they tell tales about the punishments of certain men—Sisyphuses and Tantaluses, Ixions and Tityuses—establishing in the first place the [notion of] eternal souls and, on that basis, persuasion toward virtue and dissuasion from vice. [157] For the good become even better in the hope of a reward also after death, whereas the impulses of the bad are impeded by anxiety, as they expect that even if they escape detection while living, after their demise they will be subject to deathless retribution. [158] These matters, then, the Essenes theologize in relation to the soul, laying down an irresistible bait for those who have once tasted of their wisdom.

[159] There are also among them those who profess to foretell what is to come, being thoroughly trained in holy books, various purifications, and concise sayings of prophets. Rarely if ever do they fail in their predictions.

[160] There is also a different order of Essenes. Though agreeing with the others about regimen and customs and legal matters, it has separated in its opinion about marriage. For they hold that those who do not marry cut off the greatest part of life, the succession. Moreover, if all were to think the same way, the line would very quickly die out. [161] To be sure, testing the brides in a three-year interval, once they have been purified three times as a test of their being able to bear children, they take them in this manner; but they do not continue having intercourse with those who are pregnant, demonstrating that the need for marrying is not because of pleasure, but for children. Baths are taken by the women wrapping clothes around themselves, just as by the men in a waist covering. Such are the customs of this order.

[162] Now, of the former two schools, Pharisees, who are reputed to interpret the legal matters with precision, and who constitute the first school, attribute everything to Fate and indeed to God: [163] although doing and not doing what is right rests mainly with the human beings, Fate also assists in each case. Although every soul is imperishable, only that of the good passes over to a different body, whereas those of the vile are punished by eternal retribution. [164] Sadducees, the second order, do away with Fate altogether and place God beyond both the committing and the contemplating of evil: [165] they claim that both the honorable and the despicable [courses of action] reside in the choice of human beings, and that it is according to the judgment of each person to embrace either of these. The survival of the soul, the punishments and rewards in Hades—they do away with them. [166] And whereas Pharisees are mutually affectionate and cultivate concord in relation to the community, Sadducees have a rather harsh disposition even toward one another: encounters with their peers are as uncouth as those with outsiders.

This is what I had to say concerning those among the Judeans who philosophize.

Pontius Pilate (2.169–77)

[2.169] When he had been sent to Judea as procurator by Tiberius, Pilate introduced into Jerusalem—by night, concealed—the images of Caesar, which are called "standards." [170] After daybreak this stirred up a huge disturbance among the Judeans. For those who were close to the sight were shocked at their laws' having been trampled—for they think it fitting to place no representation in the city—and [in addition] to the indignation of those in the city, the citizenry from the countryside streamed together en masse. [171] They rushed to Pilate in Caesarea and kept begging him to take the standards out of Jerusalem and to preserve their ancestral customs. But when Pilate refused, they fell down around his residence, prone, and held out motionless for five days and nights alike.

[172] On the next [day], Pilate sat on a tribunal platform in the great stadium and, after summoning the rabble as though truly intending to answer them, gave the soldiers a signal, according to a scheme, to encircle the Judeans with weapons. [173] As the infantry column was positioned around three-deep, the Judeans were speechless at the unexpectedness of the sight. After saying that he would cut them to pieces if they would not accept Caesar's images, Pilate nodded to the soldiers to bare their swords. [174] The Judeans, just as if by an agreed signal, fell down en masse, bent their necks to the side, and shouted that they were ready to do away with themselves rather than transgress the law. Pilate, who was overwhelmed by the purity of their superstition, directed [his men] immediately to carry the standards out of Jerusalem.

[175] After these [events] he set in motion a different kind of disturbance by exhausting the sacred treasury—it is called the *corbonas*—on a water conduit; it conducted [water] from 400 *stadia* away. At this there was indignation among the rabble, and when Pilate was present at Jerusalem they stood around his tribunal platform and kept yelling at [him]. [176] But because he had foreseen their disturbance, he had mixed in among the rabble soldiers-in-arms, but concealed in civilian clothes. He had prohibited them from using the sword, but had directed them instead to beat with sticks those who had begun screaming. So he gave the agreed signal from the tribunal-platform. [177] Many Judeans were lost from being hit by the blows, but many others from having been trampled under by their very own [people] in the escape. Given the calamity of those who had been taken, the beaten down rabble became silent.

Speech of Agrippa (2.342–405)

[2.342] Now the rabble of the Judeans rounded on both the king and the chief priests and kept clamoring that they send emissaries to Nero against Florus, and that they not, by holding their silence about such great slaughter, leave a suspicion of rebellion on themselves; for if they did not take the lead and identify the one who had begun this [i.e., Florus], they would appear to have begun with the weapons themselves. [343] And they were clear that they were not about to acquiesce if anyone should block the embassy.

For Agrippa, hand-selecting Florus's accusers was bound to produce a grudge, whereas standing by and watching the Judeans become inflamed for war did not seem to be in his interest either. [344] After summoning the rabble into the *xystus* and placing his sister Bernice alongside him, in plain view atop the Hasmonean residence—this was above the *xystus* at the transition to the Upper City, where a bridge connected the temple to the *xystus*—Agrippa spoke as follows:

[345] "If I saw all of you rushing to make war on the Romans, and not the purest and sincerest [element] of the populace preferring to make peace, I would neither have come to you here nor dared to give advice; for every speech in the service of doing what is necessary is pointless whenever the consensus of all those listening is for the worse [course]. [346] But seeing that some are provoked by an age [in life] inexperienced in the evils that accompany war, some by an irrational hope for freedom, and a few by a certain greed and—should matters become confounded—the [prospect of] profit from those who are weaker; in order that these very ones might be recalled to their senses and reverse course, and that the good might not share the harvest of the bad counsel of a few, I reckoned that I ought to gather you all together in the same place, to say what I consider to be advantageous.

[347] Now, let no one create disorder for me if what he hears is not to his liking! For those who have begun rushing irremediably into the rebellion, it remains possible also after my exhortation to hold the same views, whereas on my side the speech falls through—also for those who wish to hear [it]—if there is not silence from everyone.

[348] Although, then, I know that many are waxing tragic on the abuses by the procurators, and with encomia on freedom, before scrutinizing who you are, and against whom you take it upon yourselves to make war, I will first unravel this entanglement of justifications. [349] For if, on the one hand, you are avenging yourselves on those causing injury, why do you treat *freedom* as sacred? If, on the other hand, you consider it intolerable to be a slave, then [leveling] blame at the governors is superfluous; being a slave would be equally shameful even if they were showing restraint!

[350] But examine closely how slight the case is—even according to each of these [arguments]—for making war. First, as for the accusations against the procurators: it is necessary to cultivate, and not goad, the authorities. [351] Whenever you fashion great echoes of scandal from these minor shortcomings, it is to your own detriment that you prosecute the objects of scandal; after leaving off harming you covertly, and with shame, they ruin you openly. Nothing repels the blows as well as tolerating them, and to those who cause injury the quiet [disposition] of those being injured becomes a distraction.

[352] Stipulate that the underlings of the Romans are incorrigibly harsh. In no way do *all* Romans injure you—certainly not Caesar, against whom you are choosing war. For it is not [the case] that any worthless [fellow] has come as a result of instruction from them; nor, at any rate, are those from the west looking closely upon those in the east. It is by no means easy there to hear quickly from here. [353] Indeed, it is perverse to make war against many because of one person; because of trivial causes against those who are so great—and when they do not even know what we are blaming them for!

[354] There might indeed be a swift redress of our complaints, for the same procurator does not remain in perpetuity, and it is likely that the successors to come will be more restrained. Once the war has been set in motion, however, it is not easy either to put it aside or to sustain it without calamities.

[355] Certainly, the longing for freedom now is untimely; it *was* necessary to struggle in the past for the sake of not throwing it away. The experience of slavery is indeed harsh, and the struggle not to initiate this is just. [356] Yet the one who has

once been subdued and then resists is not a freedom lover but an obstinate slave. At that time, accordingly, when Pompey was setting foot in the region, it was necessary to do everything for the sake of not admitting the Romans. [357] But our forebears and their kings—much better positioned than you, in finances, in bodies, and in souls—did not hold out against a small fraction of the Roman force. And you, who have inherited the [art of] submitting as a tradition, who are so inferior in your affairs to those who first submitted, *you* are setting yourselves against the entire *imperium Romanum?*

[358] Even the Athenians—those who at one time handed over their city even to fire for the freedom of the Greeks; those who pursued like a runaway on a single ship the arrogant Xerxes, who had sailed across land and made a footpath across the sea, not yielding to the depths but leading the army that was broader than Europe; having broken Asia so mighty near tiny Salamis—they are now slaves to the Romans, and the orders from Italy administer the governess of Greece.

[359] And the Lacedaemonians, after Thermopylae, Plataea, and Agesilaus's having explored Asia, are fond of the same masters; [360] and the Macedonians, though still conjuring up Philip and envisioning their domination of the world being disseminated by Alexander, tolerate such a great reversal and make obeisance before those to whom fortune has passed over.

[361] But myriads of nations that are full of very bold talk in connection with 'freedom' nevertheless yield. Do you alone scorn to be slaves to those who have subdued everything? In what sort of army, in what sort of weapons are you trusting? Where is your force that will seize the Roman seas, and where are the treasuries that will quite suffice for the offensives?

[362] Do you believe, as it seems, that you are setting this war in motion against Egyptians or against Arabs? Will you not take into full view the Roman *imperium?* Will you not take the measure of your own feebleness? Were not our [people] often weaker even than those of the nearby nations, whereas their [the Romans'] strength is invincible across the world? [363] But indeed they sought something rather more than even this. For the whole Euphrates in the east did not suffice at all for them, nor the northerly Ister, or again southerly Libya, which had been explored all the way to the uninhabited parts, and Gadeira to the west; but they sought another world beyond Oceanus, and they brought over their weapons all the way to the previously unexplored Britons.

[364] What, then? Richer than the Galatians, are you? Tougher than the Germans? More intelligent than the Hellenes? More numerous than all [others] throughout the world? What *is* that persuading something that propels you against the Romans? [365] 'Being a slave is painful!' someone will say. How much more for the Hellenes? They, who take first place in nobility of all those under the sun, and who apportion among themselves such a great region, give way to six *fasces* of the Romans; to such a number the Macedonians also [give way], whose responsibility to contend for freedom has greater justice than yours.

[366] And what about the 500 cities of Asia? Do they not, without a garrison, make obeisance before one governor and the consular *fasces?*

Why is it necessary to mention Heniochians as well as Colchians and the people of the Taurians, Bosporans, and the nations dwelling around the Pontus and the Maeotis? [367] Whereas in the past no master of their own was recognized among them, now they are subject to 3,000 armed troops, and 40 long ships pacify the formerly unnavigable and wild sea.

³⁶⁸ How much do Bithynia and Cappadocia and the Pamphylian nation, Lycians and also Cilicians, have to say in behalf of 'freedom' as they are subject to tribute—without weapons?

So, what? The Thracians, who have seized a region five days in breadth and seven in length, more rugged than yours—and more secure by a long way, driving back attacking armies with its deep frost: do they not submit to 2,000 Roman guards? ³⁶⁹ And after these the Illyrians, inhabiting the [region] all the way to Dalmatia, cut off by the Ister: do they not give way to only two legions, alongside which they themselves drive back the assaults of the Dacians? ³⁷⁰ And the Dalmatians, who so often bucked the yoke for freedom—and for this [purpose] alone always marshaled their strength to rebel again, whenever they had been subdued in those days: do they not now keep quiet under one legion of Romans?

³⁷¹ But in truth, if indeed great stimuli might understandably provoke some people toward rebellion, it should obviously have been the Galatians, who have been walled off by nature thus: from the east by the Alps, to the north by the Rhenus River, in the south by the Pyrenean Mountains, and by Oceanus to the west. ³⁷² But even still, having been enclosed by such great defenses, and abounding with 305 nations, and having the springs of prosperity, as one might say, in the country itself, and with their goods flooding nearly the whole world, they tolerate being Romans' revenue and serving as paymaster for their very own, domestic prosperity. ³⁷³ And they put up with this not because of any softness in aspirations or lack of nobility—they who for eighty years persevered with a war in behalf of freedom—but in connection with the Romans' power, and after being astonished at their fortune, which brings them success more than their weapons. Surely that is why they are slaves under 1,200 soldiers, when they very nearly have more cities than that!

³⁷⁴ Nor, with the Iberians, did the gold that was being dug up suffice at all for the war in behalf of freedom; nor, for the Ares-mad peoples of the Lusitanians and Cantabrians, did such a great distance by land and sea from the Romans [suffice]; nor did neighboring Oceanus, though inflicting a surging tide that is frightening even to the locals. ³⁷⁵ Rather, after extending their weapons beyond the Pillars of Heracles and traversing the Pyrenean Mountains through the clouds, the Romans enslaved these people also. As a garrison—of those who were thus hard to fight and living so far away—one legion sufficed.

³⁷⁶ Who among you has not learned, by hearsay, about the horde of Germans? No doubt you have often seen the strength and size of their bodies, since Romans have their captives everywhere. ³⁷⁷ But these men, although they apportion among themselves a boundless land, and have aspirations bigger than their bodies, as well as the soul that holds death in contempt and tempers that are more violent than those of the wildest beasts, have the Rhine as a boundary to their impulse. Being dominated by eight legions of Romans, those who have been conquered are slaves, while their nation as a whole is preserving itself by fleeing.

³⁷⁸ Now, you who rely on the walls of Jerusalem, consider also the 'wall' of the Britons, for the Romans sailed [there] and enslaved even those people who are surrounded by Oceanus and inhabit an island no smaller than the world of our parts, and four legions closely guard such a big island.

³⁷⁹ And why is it necessary to say much when even the Parthians, that most bellicose people, ruling so many nations and having equipped themselves with so large a force, send hostages to the Romans, and in Italy it is possible to see—with 'peace' as justification—the nobility from the east serving in slavery?

³⁸⁰ While nearly everyone under the sun is making obeisance before the Romans' weapons, will you alone go to war, not considering the end of the Carthaginians, who, though boasting the great Hannibal and their nobility from the Phoenicians, fell beneath the right hand of Scipio? ³⁸¹ Neither Cyreneans (Laconians by ancestry), nor Marmaridae (the people extending all the way to the parched land), nor the Syrtes—frightening even to those hearing [about them]—nor Nasamones, or yet Maurians or the countless mass of Nomads, have checked the Romans' exploits. ³⁸² They have subdued this entire third portion of the world, the nations of which are not easily enumerated, marked off by the Atlantic Sea and also the Pillars of Heracles, and distributed the countless Ethiopians all the way to the Red Sea. ³⁸³ But quite apart from their annual harvests, which feed the masses in Rome for eight months, they are in addition subject to tribute of every kind, and they hand over their prepared tax levies for the uses of the imperial power, considering none of the orders to be an outrage as you do, even though one legion remains with them.

³⁸⁴ And why is it necessary to show you examples of the Romans' power from afar, when it is easy with neighboring Egypt? ³⁸⁵ Although extending all the way to Ethiopia and Arabia Felix, and being a harbor for the Indic [region], and having 7,500,000 people—aside from those inhabiting Alexandria—as may be clearly proven from the tax levy on each head, it does not scorn the Roman *imperium*. And yet what a great spur for rebellion it has in Alexandria, on account of both mass of men and wealth, and given its size; ³⁸⁶ yet although its length is a good thirty *stadia* and its breadth not less than ten, it hands over to the Romans more in one month than the yearly tax from you—and, besides the money, grain for Rome for four months. And it is walled off on every side: by impassable deserts, harborless seas, rivers, or marshes. ³⁸⁷ But none of these has been found stronger than Romans' fortune, and two legions stationed in the city bridle deeper Egypt together with the nobility of the Macedonians.

³⁸⁸ Which allies, then, will you take in? From the uninhabited [region]? Certainly all those in the inhabited earth are Romans, unless someone extends his hopes beyond the Euphrates and supposes that his compatriots from Adiabene are joining the defense. ³⁸⁹ But they will not embroil themselves in so serious a war for an irrational cause; nor would the Parthian grant permission to any who had decided so badly, for he shows concern for the armistice with the Romans, and he will regard it as violating that treaty if one of those under him moves against the Romans.

³⁹⁰ Finally, then, one must resort to the alliance of God. But this too has been formed up on the side of the Romans—for without God it is impossible to put together such a formidable empire.

³⁹¹ And consider how the purity of your cultic practice [will be] hard to manage, even if you were to make war on easy victims; and how, as you are compelled to violate those things for the sake of which you more fervently put your hope in God as an ally, you will actually turn him away. ³⁹² Certainly, by observing the customs

of the seventh [days] and initiating no activities whatsoever, you will easily be conquered, just as your ancestors were by Pompey, who made these days, on which those who were under siege were inactive, especially active for the siege. [393] If you are violating the ancestral law in the [context of] war, on the other hand, I do not know on what basis you will press the contest further, when your one keen desire is not to relinquish any of the ancestral [laws]. [394] How will you call upon the Deity for defense when you have willfully violated your attentiveness toward him?

All those who take war upon themselves have come to trust in either divine or human help. But whenever probability cuts it off on both [sides], those who make war are choosing evident capture. [395] What in fact prevents you from executing your children and women with your own hands, and from incinerating this most exceptionally beautiful homeland? For in behaving madly in this way, at least you will spare yourselves the scandal of defeat.

[396] Friends, as long as the boat is still at the dock, it is noble—noble!—to consider beforehand the approaching winter storm and not to be led back into the middle of squalls, to perish: whereas those who fall into terrible [circumstances] from *unseen* [causes] are at least to be pitied, the one who has rushed into *foreseen* destruction attracts only scandal. [397] But in case perhaps anyone supposes that you will be making war according to articles of agreement, and that the Romans will show restraint after taking control of you, and will not, as an example to the other nations, both incinerate the holy city and do away with your entire people: well, you will find no place of refuge, if you have survived, with everyone having—or afraid to have—Romans as masters.

[398] And the danger is not only for those who are here, but also for those residing in the other cities; for there is no population across the world that does not have a share of ours. [399] Upon your going to war, their foes will massacre all of them, and because of the bad counsel of a few men every city will be filled with Judean slaughter. To be sure, pardon will come to those who have done this; but if it should not be done, ponder how impious [it would be] to turn weapons against those who are so humane. [400] So let compassion reach into you, if not for the children and women, at least for this mother city and the sacred precincts. Spare the temple and keep for yourselves the shrine along with the holy [things]. For the Romans will no longer hold back after taking control over these, when they have been shown ingratitude after sparing them before.

[401] For my part, I call to witness your holy [places], the sacred messengers of God, and our common homeland, that I betrayed nothing of what conduces to your safety. You, if you have resolved on what is necessary, will hold the peace in common with me, whereas if you have been led on by your tempers you will face the peril without me."

[402] When he had said such things as these he cried over [them], along with his sister, and he halted much of the rush with the tears. Yet they kept shouting out that they were at war not with the Romans but with Florus, because of what they had suffered. [403] At this King Agrippa declared:

"But these actions are of people already at war with the Romans: you have not given your tribute to Caesar and you severed the colonnades of the Antonia! [404] You will off-load the responsibility for the rebellion if you reattach these [colonnades] and also pay your tax levies. For the fortress is certainly not Florus's; nor will you be giving the goods to Florus."

405 The populace was persuaded by these [words] and, with the king and Bernice, went up into the temple and began the rebuilding of the colonnades. The leaders and the council members, having been assigned to the villages, collected the taxes. And quickly the forty talents—for that is how much remained [owing]—were gathered.

Josephus's Surrender at Iotapata (3.340–62, 383–408)

In July 67 CE the Romans have concluded their siege of the Galilean hilltop town of Iotapata, where Josephus as Galilean "commander" had taken refuge, by breaking in and massacring everyone they find.

3.340 As the Romans were searching for Josephus, because of their own rage and in view of their commander's [Vespasian's] keen ambition[a]—his capture was considered the biggest part of the war—they inspected both the dead and those who had tried to conceal themselves. 341 But as the city is being taken, he takes advantage of some otherworldly assistance, extricates himself from the middle of the enemy, and leaps down into a deep cistern, to which a wide cave was adjoined at the side, invisible to those above. 342 There he discovers forty of the distinguished men in hiding, and a provision of supplies capable of satisfying them for quite a few days. 343 In the daylight hours he would keep himself back, as the enemy had systematically taken over everywhere, but at night, after going up, he would search for an escape route and scrutinize the guards. But with every place being kept under watch from every direction, because of him, so that there was no way to go undetected, he would descend again into the cave.

344 For two days, then, he conceals himself. But on the third day, after a woman who was with them was captured, he is exposed. Vespasian immediately and enthusiastically sends two tribunes, Paulinus and Gallicanus, having directed them to give Josephus their pledge of safety [*lit. right hands*] as a way of persuading him to come up.

345 When they arrived, they duly made their appeal to the man and also gave him assurances of safety, but they could not persuade him. 346 For he inferred from these things—not, however, from the civil nature of those making the appeals—the probability that someone who had done so much [against the Romans] would suffer. He was afraid that he was being summoned for retribution, until Vespasian sends a third tribune to him: Nicanor, an acquaintance and longtime associate of Josephus. 347 When this fellow reached him, he expatiated on the innate kindness of Romans toward those they have once taken under their power, and how on account of his virtue [*or military prowess*] he was much more admired

a. The verb is hard to translate with one English word. It denotes a strong desire to do something because of the honor associated with it, often in contexts of rivalry for honor (here perhaps because Josephus was the enemy commander).

than hated by the commanders. [348] The general [Vespasian] was eager to have him brought back not for retribution—for that could be exacted if he did *not* come forward—but because he had deliberately chosen to rescue such a superior man. [349] He added that if Vespasian were laying a trap he would not have sent a friend, in order to present the noblest activity as a pretext for the most despicable—friendship for treachery; nor would he himself [Nicanor] have agreed to come on a mission to trick a man who was his friend.

[350] While Josephus was in two minds, even about Nicanor, the military in their rage were charging ahead to burn out the cave, but their marshal [Vespasian] restrained them because of his ambition to take this man alive. [351] As Nicanor stayed where he was insistently pleading, and Josephus detected the threats of the enemy mob, a memory visited him of those nighttime dreams through which God had indicated to him in advance the coming calamities of the Judeans and what was going to happen in connection with the Romans' kings.[a] [352] He was also competent at interpreting dreams and at putting together the ambiguous sayings of the Deity, for he was quite familiar with the prophecies in the sacred writings, since he was both a priest himself and a descendant of priests. [353] In that moment he became ecstatic and plucked out from his recent dreams their dreadful visions, and offers to God a concealed prayer: [354] "Since you, who created the tribe of Judeans, have seen fit to crush it," he said, "and fortune [*or luck*] has completely passed over to the Romans, and you selected my soul to speak about what is to come, I voluntarily give my hands to the Romans [in surrender] and live. I testify, however, that I am no traitor but your servant."

[355] Having spoken these things he was in the process of surrendering to Nicanor. But when those Judeans who shared his underground refuge realized that he was yielding to those who were making the appeals, they surrounded him en masse [356] and shouted:

> Surely the ancestral laws, which God promulgated, must be groaning in terrible mourning—the God who planted souls in Judeans that hold death in contempt! [357] Do you love life, Josephus, and can you bear to see daylight as a slave? How quickly you have lost track of yourself! How many others you persuaded to die for the sake of freedom! [358] Well, it is certainly a false reputation for manliness [*or courage*] you have had—and a false one for intelligence, too, if you have hopes of rescue from those against whom you have waged war in this way, or if you wish to be rescued by them, should it [their offer] prove real. [359] But if the fortune [*or luck*] of the Romans has showered you with forgetfulness of yourself, concern for our ancestral glory falls to us. We give you the use of [our] right hand and sword. If you go willingly, you die as general of the Judeans; if unwillingly, you will die as a traitor.

[360] While they were saying this, they held out their swords and threatened that they would do away with him if he surrendered to the Romans. [361] Josephus,

---

a. Roman autocrats ("emperors" we call them) absolutely rejected the label of king (Latin: *rex*) at this time, though they were often known by the equivalent term *(basileus)* in the Greek-speaking provinces.

afraid of their assault but also regarding it as a betrayal of God's commands if he should die before their transmission, in this moment of necessity began to reason philosophically with them. [362] "Why are we being so murderous toward our own selves, dear companions?" he said. "Why are we splitting apart that closest pair, body and soul? . . ."

Here follows a lengthy speech on the evils of suicide. Arguments made by others, for suicide and against Josephus, are challenged (363–65). Killing themselves to avoid being killed by Romans is illogical (366–68). Suicide is unnatural and contrary to divine law (369–78). The honorable course is to preserve life when the chance is there, and if the Romans prove faithless they can then die with clear consciences (379–82).

[383] Josephus said many things such as these aimed at dissuading them from suicide. [384] But in their rejectionist mood they had blocked their hearing, and having long since consecrated themselves for death they were furious at him. Running at him with sword in hand, each from a different angle, they abused him for his cowardice, and it was clear that each one was on the verge of striking him. [385] But he, calling one by name, staring at another in his general's pose, grasping the hand of another, and embarrassing another with an appeal, and by thus separating out the many kinds of perils in this moment of necessity he blocked the iron [sword] in all cases from the slaughter—just as wild animals do when surrounded, always turning to face the one who touches them. [386] Respecting their general even in these extreme calamities, their right hands became weak, their swords glanced away from the target, and many—while attacking—spontaneously let go of their broadswords.

[387] Even in these desperate straits he was not lacking in ideas, but trusting in God the protector, he put his safety at risk thus. [388] "Well then, if dying is a given," he said, "let's get on with it and allow the lot to decide the order in which we slaughter one another. [389] Let the one first selected fall to the next one [chosen], and in this way fortune [*or luck*] will make its way through all of us, and each one will not be brought down by his own right hand.[a] It would be unfair if, when the others were gone, someone should change his mind and be saved." He seemed trustworthy enough, having said these things, and after persuading them he received a lot with them. [390] The one selected would present his victim neck to the one after him—on the premise that the general would die shortly, too, because they regarded death with Josephus more pleasant than life itself. [391] But he was left—whether one should say by fortune [*or luck*] or by the provision of God—together with one other man. Being keen neither to be condemned by the lot nor to pollute his right hand with the murder of a compatriot, he persuades the other in an act of trust to live.

[392] So escaping the war with the Romans—and with his own people—in this way, he was led by Nicanor to Vespasian. [393] The Romans all ran to see the spectacle of him, and with the mob pressing in around the general there was a many-sided clamor: some were thrilled that he had been taken, others were threatening him, and others were forcing their way to see him up close. [394] Those far away were shouting for the enemy to be punished, but among those nearby the memory

a. This provides a loophole, given Josephus's recent speech against suicide.

of his accomplishments came to mind, and a sense of amazement at this reversal. [395] Of the commanders there was none who, even if he had formerly been enraged, did not then relent at the sight of him. [396] The extraordinary perseverance of Josephus in the face of calamities affected Titus in particular, along with compassion because of his [young] age. Recalling that this was the one he had been fighting all along, and seeing him now [with his fate] lying in his adversaries' hands, he reflected on the capacity of fortune [or luck], and how abrupt is the turn of war, and how in human affairs nothing at all is certain. [397] From this basis he [Titus] brought over most of them to his view, to have pity for Josephus, and indeed he had the largest role with his father in his [Josephus's] preservation.[a] [398] All the same, Vespasian ordered him to be watched with the tightest security, for he was going to send him soon to Nero.

[399] When Josephus heard this, he said that there was something he wished to discuss with him [Vespasian] alone. When the latter had dismissed all the others except his son Titus and two of friends, [400] he said:

> "Although you suppose, Vespasian, that you have taken a mere prisoner in this Josephus, I have in fact come to you as a messenger of things to come; for if I were not being sent on a mission by God, I knew the custom of the Judeans, how it is proper for generals to die. [401] You're sending me to Nero—but why? [. . . text missing . . . Perhaps: Not even] the successors after Nero and before you will endure. *You* are Caesar,[b] Vespasian, and *imperator*,[c] you and this son of yours. [402] Bind me now even more securely, and keep me for yourself [i.e., don't send me to Nero]. For you are master not only of *me*, Caesar, but even of the earth and sea and the entire human race. For my part, I beg for a much harsher custody, as retribution, if I am found being frivolous in relation to God."

[403] When he had said these things, Vespasian was inclined not to believe him: he assumed that Josephus was cunningly inventing them with a view to his preservation. [404] But after a while he turned to belief, as God was already stirring him toward ultimate power and showing him by different signs the power of the scepter. [405] He also found out that Josephus had been exactly right about other matters. For the second of the two friends present at these closed proceedings remarked that he wondered—if these words were not mere nonsense designed to keep away the acts of rage headed his way—how he should have failed to prophesy either

a. If it took Titus's pity and intercession to spare his life, it seems that Josephus's fears were justified and Nicanor's appeals to Roman kindness and admiration for the prisoner were indeed mere words.

b. This was the family name (sometimes by adoption) of rulers from Julius Caesar to Nero Caesar. After Nero, it had become such an established way of indicating the ruler, who held no clear office, that it became a title. It is the word from which we get "Kaiser," "Tsar," "Czar," and similar terms.

c. In Rome's macho military culture, this traditional title of conquering generals became in the first century the exclusive property of the ruling family, matching their exclusively superior *imperium* (the right and power to command obedience). These Latin terms are the origin of our "emperor" and "empire," though they had somewhat different connotations from the English descendants.

the matters related to the capture of the Iotapatans or his own imprisonment. [406] But Josephus affirmed that he did predict to the Iotapatans that they would be taken captive—*on the forty-seventh day* [from then]—and that he himself would be taken alive by the Romans. [407] When Vespasian investigated and found out from the prisoners in private that they were true, he thus began to believe also the things pertaining to himself. [408] Therefore, although he did not release Josephus from custody and chains, he expressed his affection by presenting him with clothing and the other valuables, and he continued to treat him with respect, and Titus cooperated fully in honoring him.

Famine and Cannibalism in Jerusalem (6.193–219)

[6.193] Now, of those throughout the city who were wasting away from the famine, a countless number were falling [dead], and the horrible sufferings that occurred were indescribable. [194] In each house, if even some shadow of food should appear, there was war: the closest relatives raised their hands against one another, snatching away the miserable scraps needed for the soul's survival. [195] Not even the dying were trusted to truly be in want, but the robbers searched even those who were expiring in case someone had food in the fold of his cloak, and was faking his own death. [196] Those who were gaping from hunger would stagger around like raving dogs, and go off rattling and smashing doors the way that drunks do, and in their confusion would burst into the same house two or three times in a single hour. [197] Necessity was bringing *everything* to the mouth [*lit. to the teeth*], and they were collecting—and degrading themselves to eat—items that even dumb animals consider disgusting. Finally, they did not hold themselves back from belts and sandals; they stripped off and chewed even the leather skins from their shields. [198] For some, food was a tuft of withered grass: a few people were collecting this and selling the tiniest bundle for four Attic drachmas.

[199] But why should I speak about the shameless behavior brought on by the famine in relation to inanimate objects? For I am about to describe an act of a sort that has not been reported among either Greeks or barbarians—terrible to relate, incredible to hear. [200] I certainly would not want to seem, to people living in later times, to be inventing monstrous tales here. In fact, I would gladly have bypassed this calamity, if I did not have countless witnesses among people of my own time. Anyway, I would be paying a cold compliment to my homeland if I wormed my way out of giving a statement of the events that she suffered.

[201] Among those residing across the Jordan was a certain woman by the name of Maria, whose father was Eleazar, from the village of Bethezuba—the name signifies "house of hyssop"—eminent by virtue of both ancestry and wealth, who had fled to Jerusalem with the rest of the mass, and so was now under siege. [202] The tyrants had already ransacked the rest of her possessions, which she had packed up and brought with her from Peraea, and the armed thugs were grabbing whatever was left of her valuables—and any food she had thoughtfully preserved—when they burst in on a daily basis. [203] So a fearsome indignation possessed the little woman, and by constantly abusing and cursing the plunderers, she kept trying to provoke their anger against her.

[204] Yet no one would, whether in rage or out of pity, actually do away with her, and she grew tired of finding bread for other people—in any case it was now impossible to find food anywhere. The famine worked its way through her inner organs and bone marrow, and still more than the famine her anger was ablaze. [205] So she took the combined counsel of rage and necessity and proceeded [to an act] contrary to nature.

Now, she had an infant who was breast-feeding. She took him and said:

> "Miserable baby, given this war and famine and civil strife, what should I preserve you for? [206] [Life] among the Romans would mean slavery, should we survive until they come, but famine is precluding even slavery, and the insurgents are harsher than both. [207] So come: be food to me, to the insurgents an avenging fury,[a] and to the living a story [Greek: *mythos*]—the only item missing from the calamities of the Judeans."

[208] After saying this, she kills her son. After that she roasts him and devours one half. The rest she concealed and guarded.

[209] Presently the insurgents appeared and, when they caught the smell of the illicit sacrifice, they threatened that if she did not show them what she had prepared, they would cut her throat on the spot. But she had kept a good portion for them, she said—and disclosed the remainder of the child. [210] Terror and stupefaction seized them immediately, and they froze at the sight. But she said, "This is my own natural child, my own issue. [211] Eat, for I have feasted! Don't be softer than a woman, or more compassionate than a mother! Now if you are going to be all pious and repulsed by my sacrifice, leave the rest to me as well, since I have already feasted on half of it!" At this they went out, trembling—[212] cowards in this one instance only, though indeed scarcely conceding even this food to the mother. The entire city was presently filled with [the story of] the abomination, and as each one brought this horrible suffering before his mind's eye, he shuddered as though it had been ventured by himself. [213] And so among those facing the famine there was a keen desire for death, with blessings uttered on those who had gone ahead [i.e., already died], before hearing or seeing such evils.

[214] The horrible suffering was quickly reported to the Romans. Some of them did not believe it, while others were moved to pity, but for most it had the effect of increasing their hatred of the nation. [215] Caesar [Titus] absolved himself also of this before God, declaring that he had offered the Judeans peace and self-government, as well as amnesty for all everything they had committed:

> Whereas they are choosing civil strife in place of harmony, [216] war in place of peace, famine instead of plenty and prosperity, and with their own hands they set fire

---

a. This story is filled with allusions to classical tragedy, and these are capped by this reference to the avengers of Aeschylus's famous trilogy, the *Oresteia*. The furies are beings who relentlessly pursue those guilty of shedding familial blood (there, a son's killing of his mother and her lover, in retribution for her murder of his father and the father's paramour). Here the sense may be that the infants' ghosts will relentlessly pursue the insurgents inside Jerusalem who have caused such a desperate act.

to the sacred precinct that was being carefully preserved by us: they deserve such food! [217] Certainly, this abomination of child-eating [Greek: *teknophagia*] must be covered over by the fall of the homeland itself, and a city must not be allowed to remain in the civilized world, for the Sun to look upon, in which mothers eat thus. [218] Granted, such food is less fitting for mothers than for the fathers, who even after such horrible sufferings continue in arms.[a]

[219] As he said these things, he had in mind also the desperate condition of these men, for it was no longer possible to bring to reason those who had already suffered everything that, in order *not* to suffer, men with ordinary common sense would reform their ways.

Masada (7.320–406)

The Romans have apparently made quick work of besieging Masada, the last fortress remaining several years after Jerusalem's fall and the war's end (7.304–19). They have completed a ramp up the western side and used a battering ram to open a breach in the stone wall on the summit, finally setting ablaze the emergency wooden wall built by the defenders inside that one. Although the fire temporarily blew back against the Romans, it is now burning up the wooden reinforcement, and night has fallen. The Romans will rush onto the summit at first light tomorrow.

[7. 320] There was no way, however, that Eleazar would contemplate a dash himself; nor was he about to allow anyone else to do so. [321] When he saw that the wall was being consumed by the flame, and was unable to think up another means of either rescue or showing strength, but had set before his eyes what the Romans—if they got control—were going to do to them and to their wives and children, he resolved on death for all of them. [322] Once he had judged this to be the best course in the present circumstances, he gathered the most manly of his companions and urged them on to the deed with such words as these:

[323] "We determined long ago, good men, that we would be slaves neither to the Romans nor to anyone else except God, for he alone is the true and just Master of humanity. Now the moment of truth has arrived, which demands that we realize our ideal with actions. [324] So let us not bring shame on ourselves—we who in the past would not tolerate even a slavery that carried no danger[b]—by choosing now, along with slavery, the implacably cruel retribution that would come if we should find ourselves alive in Roman hands, for we were the first of all to revolt and are the last ones waging war against them.

[325] But I reckon that God has given us this favor, of being able to die nobly and freely, which was not the case with others, who were taken in spite of their hopes.

a. That is, the stubborn men should have to eat their children as punishment for their intransigence.

b. That is, they had rebelled against the political concept of "slavery to Rome," not the real kind with physical abuse that awaits them now.

³²⁶ With us it is clear that daybreak will mean capture, but we have the free choice of an honorable death beside those who are dearest to us. Neither can our enemies prevent this, though they are vowing to take us alive by all means, nor can we still defeat them by fighting.

³²⁷ We should perhaps have figured out the judgment of God immediately, back at the beginning when we wanted to pursue resistance for the sake of our freedom—and yet things were so tough from each other, still worse from our enemies—and realized that the tribe of the Judeans, his ancient friend, he had now condemned. ³²⁸ For had he remained well disposed to us, or even moderately disaffected, he would not have stood by and watched the destruction of so many people, or offered his holiest city to the enemies' fire and demolition.

³²⁹ Now of course, *we* hoped to come through, we alone of the Judean people having preserved our freedom—like we were sinless before God and had not even participated in anything [. . . text missing . . .]. We who taught others! ³³⁰ Well, then, look how he convicts us of futility for having expected such things, bringing upon us this doom amid terrors, which overrides our hopes. ³³¹ For even the impregnable nature of this fortress has not proven to be our rescue. But since we have plenty of food, a stack of weapons, and an abundance of other equipment, it is perfectly obvious that it is *by God himself* that we have been deprived of rescue. ³³² The fire that was being driven against the enemy did not turn back of its own will, against the wall that we had carefully prepared. This is [divine] wrath for all the injustices that we brazenly committed, in our madness, against our compatriots. ³³³ So let us suffer the punishments for these things not from the Romans, who are so hostile, but from God—that is, by means of our own hands. These [punishments] are certainly more tolerable than the other kind.

³³⁴ Let our wives die unmolested, and our children without experience of slavery. After [killing] them, we may provide each other with this noble favor, an excellent funerary monument, with our having preserved our freedom. ³³⁵ Before that, though, we should destroy both our goods and the fortress by fire, for the Romans will be the ones grieving, I know very well, when they cannot control our bodies and also fail to get any gain! ³³⁶ We should leave only our food provisions untouched, for these will testify that we died not because we were overcome by want, but just as we determined from the beginning, we chose death before slavery."ᵃ

³³⁷ This is what Eleazar said. He did not affect the opinions of those present in the same way, however. Although some were eager to comply and all but filled with pleasure, considering this death to be excellent, ³³⁸ pity for their wives and families got into the softer men. Seeing in each other also the certain and vivid reality of their own ends, by their tears they signaled their lack of agreement with the proposition.

³³⁹ When he saw these people acting like cowards, and their souls collapsing at the scale of the plan, Eleazar became afraid that this lot would, with their howling and crying, cause those who had heard his words with resolve also to behave like women. ³⁴⁰ So he did not relax his appeal, but raised himself up and, full of great purpose, made an effort with more brilliant words—on the immortality of the soul.

a. With this sentence (note the same verb), Eleazar closes the circle begun at 7.323.

Here follows a lengthy philosophical discourse on suicide. Life, not death, is the calamity for humanity; only death brings freedom (341–48). Death is like sleep (349–50). The Indians kill themselves all the time (351–57). Anyway, God has obviously decreed our destruction, not having intervened to save us Judeans or Jerusalem (358–77). Only shame now awaits us if we live; surrender, humiliation, abuse of ourselves and our families, and a reputation for lack of courage (378–88).

³⁸⁹ He wanted to keep going with his exhortations, but they all cut him off and rushed to do the deed. Filled with some uncontrollable urge, indeed possessed by spirits, they went off, each man struggling to get ahead of the other, supposing this to be a demonstration of his courage and prudence, that he not be seen among the last [to act]. So great was the desire [Greek: *erōs*] for slaughter—of wives and of children and of themselves—that overcame them. ³⁹⁰ And when it came to the deed itself they were not cowed, as one might have imagined, but they pursued intently the resolve they had found while listening to Eleazar's words, though certainly emotion and tender affection toward their own remained with them all, but reason, which had seemed to offer the best counsel for those dearest to them, won out.

³⁹¹ So [two things happened together:] they hugged and greeted their wives, and took their children in their arms, planting final kisses on them and welling up with tears. ³⁹² At the same time, as though it were being done by the hands of complete strangers, they carried out the plan on which they had resolved, having the image of the atrocities they would suffer from their enemies as consolation for the necessity of this killing. ³⁹³ And in the end, no one was found to be unequal to such daring, but all of them ran through their closest relations. Miserable victims of necessity, for whom the killing of their wives and children with their own hands seemed the least of evils!

³⁹⁴ No longer able to bear their distress, and considering it an injustice to those who had been dispatched if they should remain alive even for a short time, they quickly heaped up all their property in one spot and tossed fire into it. ³⁹⁵ Then, choosing by lot ten from among them all to serve as slaughterers [*or butchers*], and each man laying himself down where his wife and children were lying, and wrapping his arms around them, they presented their victim necks ready to those who were executing this miserable service.

³⁹⁶ When these men had unwaveringly slaughtered everyone [else], they opted for the same convention of the lot for each other, such that the one selected would kill the other nine and then dispatch himself after all. In this way they were all showing the same daring, with no difference from one to another in what they were either doing or suffering. ³⁹⁷ Finally, then, they showed their victim necks. The one man who was last looked around at the mass of those lying around him, in case there was someone left who still needed his hand in completing the slaughter. When he knew that all had been dispatched, he created a big fire in the royal precincts and, with a supreme thrust of the hand drove his sword all the way through himself, and fell near his family members.

³⁹⁸ They all died imagining that nothing having a soul among them was left to fall into the Romans' hands. ³⁹⁹ But an old woman, along with another who surpassed most women in prudence and education (she was a relative of Elea-

zar), and five children, had hidden in those underground spaces that collected drinking water through the ground, to conceal themselves while the minds of the others were occupied with the slaughter. [400] Those others numbered nine hundred and sixty with women and children counted in. [401] This horror occurred on the fifteenth of the month of Xanthicus [= Jewish Nisan].

[402] Now the Romans, still anticipating a fight, had equipped themselves by dawn and, after fashioning access routes to bridge up the distance from the earthworks, by means of ladders, they began making their assaults. [403] Seeing none of the enemy, however, but only an ominous desolation on all sides, a fire within, and silence, they were at a loss to put together what had happened. Finally they cried in a loud voice, as if releasing a projectile, in case they might be able to call out one of those inside.

[404] The sound of this shouting reached the little women, and so they came up to ground level from their underground places and informed the Romans of all that had happened as it had fallen out, with the second one mentioned [Eleazar's relative] narrating clearly both what was said and the way in which it was done. [405] They [the Romans] did not readily commit themselves to her report, by any means, disbelieving the scale of the daring involved. They took it upon themselves to extinguish the fire and cut their way through to where they were inside the royal precincts. [406] Now coming upon the mass of those who had been slaughtered, they took no pleasure as [one normally would] over an enemy, but rather admired the nobility of the plan and the unwavering contempt for death shown by so many through these actions.

3. Romanticized Narrative

Following the Babylonian exile, Jewish communities produced a significant amount of narrative literature describing various settings of the biblical Israelite history. Many of the works located in this section of the *EJLA* could fit, and indeed have been located by others, in other genre categories. One such example would be the book of Tobit, which is defined by some as wisdom literature.

The texts within this collection tend to describe crisis periods of Israel's history (e.g., the Babylonian or Assyrian exiles) or social contexts that presented ethical and moral challenges for Israelites. Often included are known historical figures (e.g., Nebuchadnezzar, Cyrus, Antiochus IV Epiphanes), biblical patriarchs or prophets (e.g., Abraham, Moses, the Twelve Patriarchs, Ezra, Isaiah, Jeremiah), and various accounts and themes that replicate known biblical narratives. Typically, these "new" narratives include expansions, contractions, and omissions of the biblical ones. They may also seek to idealize certain "historical" moments in order to explain how something in the biblical narrative could happen and retain its Jewish flavor (e.g., Joseph's marriage to an Egyptian) or to authenticate contemporary Jewish religious practices that may have been a source of some debate (such as the use of the Greek Old Testament). Several scholars argue that these texts fall into the category "rewritten Scripture"; however, discussion of this issue pertaining to the various documents organized under this heading is left to each individual contributor. Questions surrounding the historicity (and chronology) of some of these texts have been raised in previous scholarship and will be addressed in the particular chapters.

Another name often given to the works collected here as romanticized narratives is "Jewish novellas." The editors prefer the title "romanticized narrative" because it more comprehensively captures the nature of this material as expansions or elaborations, for the sake of glorifying the Jewish past, than does the term "novella." This category includes such works as Greek Additions to Esther, Greek Additions to Daniel, Tobit, Judith, and Joseph and Aseneth, as well as the works anthologized here. There has been much debate as to the nature of this genre of literature—was it considered to reflect historical events or was it purely fiction? It is quite possible that the literature was considered a subgenre of history or localized history and was read or understood as stories that were grounded in real events.

It is also possible to argue more correctly that some of these books straddle both historical narrative and wisdom literature (e.g., Tobit). These texts can contain sayings like those found in wisdom literature as well as standard wisdom topics: devotion to the law; the intercessory function of angels; reverence toward parents; purity of marriage; respect for the dead; and the value of almsgiving, prayer, and fasting (*see* Introduction to Wisdom Literature).

Imaginary or romanticized settings, entertaining plots, successful conclusions, and heroic female characters often mark the content of the texts under discussion. Inspiration for these features likely arose out of Israelite biblical and oral traditions, ancient Near Eastern traditions, or Greek narrative traditions. One characteristic of the genre is the treatment of an unknown and marginal character of the ancient past. In addition, these texts often contain obviously implausible royal figures such as "Darius the Mede," "Esther, queen of Persia" (there was no known Persian queen), and "Nebuchadnezzar, king of the Assyrians" (Nebuchadnezzar was king of Babylon).

Some interesting characteristics can be identified in this literature. The texts exhibit real interest in the domestic setting of the story and the moral values of the characters. The narrative usually includes a chaos or crisis episode, which is then followed by resolution to the crisis. This chaos often centers on a threat that focuses on one protagonist from the story at a time; the protagonist is usually a devout individual who is involved in a confrontation with a powerful antagonist. He or she often has the burden of delivering (rescuing) the extended family (community) in the midst of turmoil. These texts also promote a sense of suffering—even martyrdom—for the main characters, whereby some event or revelation has convinced the protagonist that it was worth dying for God.

These selected texts served as "handbooks of discipline of the self, even a narrative discipline of self-formation."[1] Within these romanticized narratives, the authors identified a set of coded obstacles—adultery, idolatry, foreign rule—along with models and patterns for overcoming them that could both inspire and facilitate healthy discussions of these tensions.

The primary texts chosen as representative of this section are the book of Tobit, the Letter of Aristeas, Joseph and Aseneth, and the Life of Adam and Eve.

Archie T. Wright

---

1. See Lawrence M. Wills, "Jewish Novellas in a Greek and Roman Age: Fiction and Identity," *JSJ* 42 (2011): 164–65.

The Book of Tobit

The book of Tobit has an unusual setting: its main protagonist, Tobit, is an exile from the northern kingdom of Israel, which has been taken captive to Nineveh by the Assyrians. Much of the story also takes place in Media, and most particularly in the city of Ecbatana (modern-day Hamedan, in northwest Iran), where other members of Tobit's extended family are living (*see* Map of the Assyrian Exile, p. 33). The book has a profound interest in Jerusalem, however, and in the restoration of a united Israel: its Jewish characters are not typical of the apostate north depicted in the biblical histories, but are pious victims of circumstance. Correspondingly, they still enjoy the protection of God, and the narrative is centered on the angel Raphael's mission to resolve the serious problems faced by Tobit and his young relative Sarah, who have each been driven to despair. The narrative also serves as a vehicle, though, for extensive prayers, praises, and instructions.

Tobit is well attested among the manuscripts from Qumran (*see* Overview of Early Jewish Literature), and medieval Jewish versions of the book have survived, suggesting that it may have remained popular, at least in certain circles or communities, for many centuries. It never became authoritative in Judaism, however, and its absence from the Jewish canon, noted by St. Jerome in the prologue to his translation of the book, led subsequently to its rejection from the Protestant canon and its classification as apocryphal (*see* Overview of Early Jewish Literature). It remains, however, a part of the Roman Catholic, Orthodox, and other Christian canons.

Narrative Description

The textual history of Tobit is complicated, as we will see below, and although the broad outline of the story is consistent between the different versions, some details and aspects of the presentation vary. These differences are especially visible in the first few verses: 1:1–2 introduces Tobit with a genealogy that varies enormously between texts, and a note that explains how he was taken captive from Thisbe in the Galilee (a complicated, and again, rather variable description of Thisbe's geographical position suggests that it may have been no better known to the original readership than it is now. The first part of the story follows in 1:3–3:6, and in the earliest versions of the book, Tobit himself narrates this section.

After an initial claim that he has been righteous throughout his life and charitable toward his fellow exiles, Tobit looks back to his younger days in Israel, when his tribe, Naphtali, was separated from Judah and Jerusalem, and other members of the tribe would sacrifice "on all the mountains of Galilee to the bull-calf that Jeroboam the king of Israel had made in Dan" (1:5). Recognizing that it was Jerusalem that had been divinely appointed for all the tribes, Tobit traveled there instead, and he offers a detailed account of the offerings that he used to take. On reaching manhood, he married Anna, from within his own extended family, and they had a son, Tobias. After that, the family was taken into exile, where Tobit again demonstrated his piety by avoiding the food of the Gentiles, which his other compatriots used to eat. God gave him favor with the Assyrian king, however, and although he was a captive, he prospered, working in Media on the king's behalf: he notes that on one trip he deposited with one Gabael a considerable sum of money—ten talents of silver—in Media; this will become significant later in the story.

Tobit's fortunes change with the death of this first king, who is called Enemessar in the Greek text (1:15). The roads to Media become too dangerous for travel, and the new king **Sennacherim** is unsympathetic to Jews when he has been forced to retreat from Judah after an unsuccessful invasion.[1] Tobit's charity toward his fellow exiles has always included burial of the unclaimed dead, and this now becomes a risky activity, when he starts to steal away the bodies of Sennacherim's victims. After an informer tells the king, Tobit has to go into hiding and all his possessions are confiscated. Tobit is only able to return to Nineveh following Sennacherim's assassination, when the next king puts **Ahiqar**, the son of Anael, in charge of internal affairs. Ahiqar is a close relative of Tobit, and is able to intercede on his behalf.[2] Things rapidly go wrong again, however, when Tobit's charitable instincts lead him to send Tobias out to find a pious pauper, with whom he may share his ample dinner (2:2). Tobias finds instead a corpse, which he feels obliged to retrieve and bury. As he is sleeping outside in the courtyard afterward, birds nesting on the wall above drop excrement into his eyes, which become affected by white spots. Medical attention only makes these worse, and Tobit is ultimately left completely blind. Unable to work, he has to be supported out of Anna's earnings. His piety then gets him in trouble once more, when he suggests that a kid she has been given by a client might in fact be stolen, and in the face of his anger she asks what has happened to the charity and righteousness that used to define him (2:14).

At this point in the story, Tobit is in despair and wishes to die. He is not alone in this, however: far away in Ecbatana, Sarah, the daughter of Raguel, has also

---

1. 2 Kings 19:36: "Then King Sennacherib of Assyria left, went home, and lived at Nineveh."

2. Tobit 1:22: "Then Ahiqar petitioned on my behalf, and I returned to Nineveh, for Ahiqar had been the chief cupbearer, and in charge of the seal and of administration and finance in the time of Sennacherim, king of Assyria, and Sacherdonos appointed him a second time. But he was my nephew, and of my kin." Translated by Weeks.

reached the point that she wishes to die, and 3:7–15 tells her story more briefly: the demon Asmodeus has killed each of the seven men married to her before they could consummate the marriage, and she is now being accused by her maids of killing them. Simultaneously, Tobit and Sarah both pray to God for death, and their prayers are heard. To deal with their situations, the angel Raphael is sent to restore Tobit's sight and to release Sarah from the attentions of the demon; the solution to each problem is to involve marrying Sarah to Tobit's son Tobias (3:16–17). As Raphael is dispatched, Tobit and Sarah return from the place where they had prayed.

The rest of the story plays out accordingly. Having prayed for death, Tobit remembers the money he had deposited in Media many years before, and summons Tobias to tell him about it. He offers him teaching, mostly about the need to honor his mother after he has gone, about the benefits of charity, and about the need to marry within his own tribe (4:3–19), but he then arranges for Tobias to go and fetch the money. A guide is needed, so Tobias is sent out to find one, and immediately bumps into Raphael, who has disguised himself as Azarias, another distant relative. When Tobit learns that he is family, which seems more important to him than Azarias's qualities as a guide, he is delighted and dispatches them immediately, to Anna's distress.

The first key event in their journey occurs when Tobias and Raphael reach the River Tigris on their first night (6:2–6). A fish attacks Tobias (it tries to eat him in some later versions, but only nibbles his feet in the earliest telling). At Azarias/Raphael's urging, Tobias catches it and kills it, removing the gallbladder, heart, and liver. As they go on, Azarias/Raphael explains that the heart and the liver can be burned to make a smoke that drives away demons, while the gallbladder will heal white spots on a man's eyes. Later in the journey, as they approach Media, he then tells Tobias that they will have to stop overnight at the house of Raguel. He explains that Tobias is related to Raguel, and that Raguel's daughter Sarah has no relative eligible to marry her closer than Tobias himself, who therefore stands not only to gain a beautiful girl for his wife, but also to inherit all that is Raguel's since she is an only child. When Tobias expresses some reservations, having already heard the story of Sarah's troubles, his fears are calmed by Azarias/Raphael's advice to drive away the demon using the fish innards, and by the time they reach Raguel's house, he is quite smitten with the idea of marrying Sarah.

After the initial introductions, to Raguel, his wife Edna, and Sarah, which result in a warm welcome for Tobias when his relationship to Tobit is discovered, the matter of marriage is broached over dinner (7:1–9), and Raguel gives Sarah to the insistent Tobias despite warning him of the precedents. He is sufficiently pessimistic to have a grave dug during the night, but Tobias has followed the advice given to him, burned the fish parts, and prayed with Sarah to God; when a maid investigates in the morning, Tobias and Sarah are both alive (8:13–14). Asmodeus, driven to Egypt, has been bound there by Raphael. A delighted Raguel insists on throwing a lengthy wedding party, keeping Tobias with him for two weeks, during which Raphael, as Azarias, goes and collects the money from Gabael in nearby Rages, bringing him back to join the feast. Raguel would continue longer, but Tobias is worried about his father and insists on returning (10:7–9). He sets off for home with his new bride and with half of Raguel's wealth.

Tobias hurries ahead with his guide as they near Nineveh (11:1), and is seen by the now desperate Anna. As Tobit stumbles trying to get out of the door to meet him, this offers an opportunity for Tobias to make use of the fish gall, which he puts into Tobit's eyes, healing them. It is a newly invigorated Tobit, possessed once again of his sight, who makes his way to meet Sarah at the city gate, praising God as he goes. Another long wedding party follows (11:18), after which Tobit suggests that they should pay the guide who had served Tobias so well, and it is agreed that they should offer him a generous bonus of half the wealth with which they had returned. Azarias, however, summons Tobit and Tobias to meet him secretly (12:6), and he reveals to them both his true story and the plan that has been worked out through the preceding events. He disappears, but urges Tobit to write a record of what has happened. Chapter 13 then consists largely of a prayer by Tobit, on the theme of punishment and mercy: Israel, which has been punished, should turn to God and look for restoration; Jerusalem faces destruction, but can expect also a great and glorious rebuilding.

Finally, and almost by way of a postscript, Tobit gives another speech in 14:3–11—a second deathbed speech since his first proved premature (*see* Introduction to Testamentary Literature). Confident that prophetic predictions about the fall of **Nineveh** (*see* Map of the Assyrian Exile, p. 33) are accurate, he urges Tobias to take his family away. Israel and Judah are also to be destroyed and become desert for a while before their eventual restoration (at which point, all the Jews will return to Jerusalem and all the peoples of the world will fear God, according to 14:6–7). Tobit dies at a great age, with a final commendation of charity and condemnation of injustice, in 14:11. Tobias waits until after his mother has died too, and then returns to Raguel's house, where he cares for his parents-in-law until they die. When he finally reaches the end of his own life, and the book concludes, Nineveh has itself been destroyed, and its population has been carried off to Media.

Author/Provenance

The main events of the story are supposed to have happened in Assyria and Media during the seventh century BCE. Even allowing that some details may have become obscured in the course of transmission, it is not clear that the author really knew very much about either the period or the place: his understanding of the Assyrian monarchy, for instance, is sketchy (Sennacherib did not succeed Shalmaneser as 1:15 claims), and his geographical knowledge is misleading—Rages is much more than the two-day trip from Ecbatana suggested in 5:6, and Raphael might have needed his angelic powers to get there and back (with servants and camels) well inside the fourteen days of Tobias's wedding feast (9:2–6). The work is perhaps supposed to be identified with the book Raphael told Tobit to write (12:20), but the actual provenance and authorship are unknown.

Date/Occasion

It is generally supposed that the book was actually composed at some point between the late fourth and early second century BCE, and probably in the later part of this period. Attempts to tie it to specific situations have not generally won wide acceptance, and it is not clear what audience was intended. At most, perhaps, we can say that it seems to address the situation of **Diaspora** communities, and was perhaps composed within such a community (although probably not the one within which it is set).

Text, Language, Sources, and Transmission

The textual problems surrounding Tobit are notoriously complicated. Briefly, the work was composed in either Aramaic or Hebrew (probably the former), and versions in both languages have been found at Qumran (4Q196–4Q200). Perhaps quite early on, it was translated into Greek from a text very like the Qumran ones, but by the time of our earliest complete manuscripts, an unrevised text (commonly known as G2) had been replaced almost entirely by an extensively revised version (G1). The only major manuscript to preserve the original is Codex Sinaiticus, but Sinaiticus has inherited a text that had been badly corrupted by scribal errors and omissions (*see* Overview of Early Jewish Literature). To an extent this can be "repaired," in some places more confidently than in others, by reference to the revised text, to the surviving Old Latin translations based on the original Greek, and to a few chapters of unrevised text which is found in one other manuscript (ms. 319). The common revised text G1, and a less well known, independent revision preserved in the Georgian for the second half of the book only in Syriac and in a few quite late Greek manuscripts (G3) can also offer guidance, as can the Qumran versions. The translation offered below is based on comparison of those sources with Sinaiticus, and although necessarily speculative in a few places, it probably offers something much closer to the original G2 text than do the usual translations of G1 or Sinaiticus. The relationship between the medieval Hebrew and Aramaic versions and the early text has not yet been established clearly. The Vulgate is often implicated in that discussion because St. Jerome claimed to have used an Aramaic text for his translation, which has points of contact with some of the later materials, but it is more likely that they have been influenced by his readings than he by theirs.

Theology

It has been common in recent scholarship to describe Tobit as **Deuteronomic,** but it lacks most of the concerns associated specifically with Deuteronomic theology. The law is important (e.g., 1:8; 6:13)—although it is difficult to pin down a biblical basis for the insistence on intermarriage within a tribe (4:12–13) or the threat of death for Raguel if he gives Sarah to someone other than Tobias (6:13). The book places far more weight, though, on such matters as charity and burial of the dead, which largely define Tobit's own behavior, and have more to do with personal piety and community service than legal obligation. In the closing chapters, which are sometimes thought to include major additions to the text, there is a strong emphasis on the future restoration of Jerusalem and Israel, which is eschatological in character, but tied to the book's perception that its story offers an insight into the mercifulness of God. If there is a single, simple message, it is that Jews in exile must retain their personal piety and their religious or ethnic integrity, helping each other and trusting God until such time as he will restore them to Jerusalem. Setting aside its central concerns, the book's interest in angels and demons, and, indeed, its portrayal of angels carrying memos to God[3] seem to reflect a relatively late, and perhaps somewhat popular understanding. It also has a strong interest in prophecy, and 14:4, in particular, is keen to emphasize that every word of prophecy will find its fulfillment at the right time.

Reception of Tobit in the Second Temple Period

Tobit is not clearly cited in the New Testament, although the book was known and quoted by church fathers from the second century on. Suggested resemblances to various passages tend to be very vague or untenable, and, in particular, the description of Raphael's eventual disappearance may resemble the ascension narratives simply because of the similar subject matter. The book is interesting, though, as a source of insight into early Jewish piety, prayer, and praise at a personal level—aspects of Judaism that have not always received due attention in considerations of the background to early Christianity.

STUART WEEKS

FURTHER READING

Di Lella, Alexander A. "Tobit." In *A New English Translation of the Septuagint and Other Greek Translations Traditionally Included under that Title,* edited by Albert Pietersma and Benjamin Wright, pp. 456–77. New York: Oxford University Press, 2007.

Jacobs, Naomi S. "Tobit, Book of." In *The Eerdmans Dictionary of Early Judaism,* edited by John J. Collins and Daniel C. Harlow, pp. 1314–15. Grand Rapids: Eerdmans, 2010.

Moore, Carey A. "Tobit, Book of." In *ABD,* 6:585–94.

Otzen, Benedikt. *Tobit and Judith.* Guides to Apocrypha and Pseudepigrapha. London: Sheffield Academic Press, 2002.

Perrin, Andrew B. "An Almanac of Tobit Studies: 2000-2014." *Currents in Biblical Research* 13 (2014): 107–42.

Stuckenbruck, Loren, and Stuart Weeks. "Tobit." In *The T&T Clark Companion to the Septuagint,* edited by James K. Aitken, pp. 237-60. Bloomsbury: T&T Clark, 2015.

ADVANCED READING

Bredin, Mark, ed. *Studies in the Book of Tobit: A Multidisciplinary Approach.* Library of Second Temple Studies 55. London: T&T Clark, 2006.

3. Tobit 12:12: "And now, when you prayed, and Sarah, I presented the memorial of both your prayers before the glory of the Lord, and when you used to bury the dead, likewise." Translation by Weeks.

Corley, J., and V. Skemp, eds. *Intertextual Studies in Ben Sira and Tobit.* CBQMS 38. Washington, D.C.: Catholic Biblical Association of America, 2005.

Fitzmyer, Joseph A. *Tobit.* CEJL. Berlin: De Gruyter, 2003.

Littman, Robert J. *The Book of Tobit in Codex Sinaiticus.* Septuagint Commentary Series. Leiden: Brill, 2008.

Moore, Carey A. *Tobit: A New Translation with Introduction and Commentary.* Anchor Bible 40A. New York: Doubleday, 1996.

Xeravits, Géza G., and József Zsengellér, eds. *The Book of Tobit: Text, Tradition, Theology.* JSJSup 98. Leiden: Brill, 2005.

3.1 Tobit

[1:1] The book of the words of Tobit, son of Tobiel, son of Ananiel, son of Adouel, son of Gabael, from the seed of Asiel, from the tribe of Naphthali, [2] who was taken captive in the days of Enemessar,[a] the king of the Assyrians, out of Thisbe, which is to the right of Kedesh-of-Naphthali, in the upper Galilee, above Asser[b] beyond the western side, on the left of Phogor.

[3] I, Tobit, walked in ways of truth and in righteous deeds all the days of my life, and performed many acts of charity toward my brothers and my people, who came with me into captivity to the land of the Assyrians, to Nineveh. [4] And when I was in my country, in the land of Israel, and when I was a younger man, all the tribe of Naphthali, my ancestor, were in secession from the house of David, and from Jerusalem, a city that had been selected from all the tribes of Israel for sacrificing by all the tribes of Israel; and the temple of God's dwelling was sanctified and built in it, for all generations of time.

[5] And all my brothers, the house of Naphthali, my ancestor, sacrificed on all the mountains of Galilee to the bull-calf that Jeroboam, the king of Israel, had made in Dan, [6] while I, all alone, would go frequently to Jerusalem on the feast days, as is prescribed for all Israel in an eternal commandment, holding the first fruits, and the first products, and the tithes of the produce, and the first shearings of the flocks. [7] And I would give them to the priests, the sons of Aaron, before the altar. And the tithe of grain, and of wine, and of oil, and of figs and of pomegranates, and of the remaining fruits I would give to the sons of Levi, who minister in Jerusalem. And I would tithe the second tithe in money every six years, and go and spend it in Jerusalem each year, [8] and I would give it to the orphans and to the widows, and to proselytes who were attached to the sons of Israel. I would take and give to them in the third year, and we would consume these things according to the commandment commanded about them in the law of Moses, and according to the instructions that Deborah gave—the mother of Ananiel, our ancestor—for my father left me an orphan and died. [9] And when I had become a man, I took a wife, Anna, from the seed of our lineage, and had a son by her, and called his name Tobias.

[10] After being taken captive to Assyria, and while I was held in captivity at Nineveh, all of my brothers and the members of my race used to eat Gentiles' food, [11] but I kept myself safe from eating the Gentiles' food. [12] And when I remembered my God in my whole self, [13] then the Most High gave me grace and favor in the eyes of Enemessar; and I used to procure everything useful for him, [14] and I would go to Media and do his procurement there until he died. And I deposited

a. Shalmaneser: that name is in fact attested in the Latin texts, but may be a correction there in the light of 2 Kings 17:3–6; 18:9–11.

b. Hazor?

Translation by Stuart Weeks.

ten talents of silver with Gabael, the brother of Gabri, in the land of Media. [15] But when Enemessar died, and his son Sennacherim[a] reigned in his place, then the roads of Media became unsafe, and I was no longer able to travel to Media.

[16] In the days of Enemessar, I had performed many charitable acts for my brothers, from my race: [17] I would give my food to the hungry and clothes to the naked, and if I observed anyone of my race dead and cast out behind the wall of Nineveh, I would bury him. [18] And if Sennacherim killed someone when he retreated fleeing from Judea—in the days of the sentence that the King of Heaven executed on him because of the blasphemies that he had blasphemed—I did the burying. For he killed many of the children of Israel in his anger, and I would steal their bodies and do the burying, while Sennacherim sought them and did not find them. [19] And a certain somebody from the residents of Nineveh went and informed the king about me, that I was burying them, and I hid. And when I realized that the king knew about me, and that I was being sought for execution, I was afraid and made a getaway. [20] Then all the things that belonged to me were seized, and I was left with nothing that had not been confiscated for the royal revenues, except Anna, my wife, and Tobias, my son.

[21] But not forty-five days had passed when his two sons killed him and fled to the mountains of Ararat, and his son Sacherdonos[b] ruled in his place. And he put Ahiqar, the son of Anael, my brother, in charge of all the auditing of his kingdom, and he held power over the whole internal administration. [22] Then Ahiqar petitioned on my behalf, and I returned to Nineveh, for Ahiqar had been the chief cupbearer, and in charge of the seal and of administration and finance in the time of Sennacherim, king of Assyria, and Sacherdonos appointed him a second time. But he was my nephew, and of my kin.

[2:1] And under King Sacherdonos I returned to my home, and my wife Anna was returned to me, along with my son Tobias. And on our feast day Pentecost, which is the Holy of Weeks, there was a fine dinner for me, and I lay down to dine. [2] And the table was set for me, and I saw there were many dishes. So I said to my son Tobias, "Lad, go round, and any pauper you should find from our brethren, from the Ninevite captives, who remembers God with all his heart, then bring him and he will share my meal with me; and, look, I will wait for you, lad, until you come." [3] And Tobias went to seek some pauper from our brethren, and returning he said, "Father!" And I said to him, "Here I am, lad." Then replying, he said to me, "Father, look! One of our race has been killed and cast into the marketplace, and he has just this moment been strangled!" [4] And jumping up, I left the dinner before I'd tasted it and picked him up from the street. And I put him in one of the outhouses until the sun should set and I could bury him. [5] Returning, therefore, I washed myself and ate my food with mourning. [6] And I remembered the word of the prophet, such things as Amos had spoken at Bethel, saying, "Your feasts will be turned to mourning, and all your songs to lamentation,"[7] and I wept. And when the sun had set, I went off and, after some digging, I buried him. [8] And my neighbors made fun, saying, "Is he still not afraid? For he has already been sought for execution for doing this and run away—but look, he is burying the

a. Sennacherib.
b. Esarhaddon.

dead again!" ⁹ And that night I washed myself after burying him, and went to my courtyard and lay down against the courtyard wall, with my face uncovered because of the heat. ¹⁰ But I had not been aware that there were sparrows in the wall above me, and their droppings lodged in my eyes while warm and brought on white spots. And I went to the doctors to be treated, and the more they smeared me with medicines, the more my eyes were blinded by the white spots, until the onset of total blindness. And I was incapacitated in my eyes for four years, and all my relatives and friends grieved over me. Ahiqar cared for me for two years, before his departure to Elymais.

¹¹ And during that time, my wife Anna was employed at women's tasks, ¹² making wool and weaving, and she supported me out of her earnings. And she would dispatch (her products) to those who were in charge of them, and they would pay her the fee. And on the seventh day of Dystros, she finished a piece of weaving and sent it to those in charge. Then they gave her the whole fee, and also gave her a kid from the goats for the pot. ¹³ And when the kid came in toward me, it began to bleat, and I called her in, and said, "Where is this kid that is bleating from? Stolen, perhaps? Give it back to its owners, for we don't have the right to eat anything stolen!" ¹⁴ And she replied and said to me, "It has been given to me as a gift, on top of my pay." But I did not believe her, and said all the more, "Return it to the owners!"—and I got red in the face at her over this. Then in reply she said to me, "And where are your good deeds? Where are your righteous actions? Look, these are the things associated with you!"

³:¹ And becoming distressed of spirit and sighing, I wept and went to my courtyard, and began to pray, sobbing: ² "You are just, Lord, and all your deeds are just and all your ways are mercy and truth. You judge forever. ³ And now you, Lord, be mindful of me and look upon me. And do not punish me for my sins, and for the oversights by me and my forebears. They sinned before you ⁴ and disobeyed your commandments. And you gave us over to plunder and captivity and death, and to be a cautionary tale and a byword, and a target of abuse for all those peoples among whom you scattered us. ⁵ And now your judgments are many: they are fair with regard to me, so far as the sins by me and my forebears are concerned, for we did not enact your commandments and did not walk properly before you. ⁶ And now deal with me according to your pleasure, and order that my breath be taken, so that I might be released from the surface of the earth and become earth—as it is better for me to die rather than live, for I have heard false reproaches and am much grieved. Lord, command, therefore, that I be released from this hardship; let me go to the eternal place. And do not turn your face away from me, for it is better for me to die, rather than see so much hardship in my life, and to hear reproaches no more."

⁷ On that very day, it happened likewise to Sarah, the daughter of Raguel, who was in Ecbatana of Media, that she too was hearing reproaches—from her father's maids. ⁸ For she had been given in marriage to seven husbands, and Asmodeus, the evil demon, killed them before they had sex with her, as one is supposed to with wives. And the maids said to her, "You are the one smothering your husbands: look, you have already been given to seven husbands, and have enjoyed not a single one of them! ⁹ Why do you punish us? Is it about your husbands because they have died? Go with them! And may we never see from you a son or daughter!"

¹⁰ On that day she was distressed in spirit and wept; and going to her father's upper floor, she wanted to hang herself. Then she thought again, and said, "Let no one ever reproach my father and say, 'You had a single beloved daughter, and she hanged herself,' nor let me bring down my father's old age to Hades through grief. It would be better for me not to strangle myself, but rather to beg the Lord that I might die, and that I and my father might no longer hear any reproach." ¹¹ At that very time, having spread her hands toward the window, she prayed, and said, "Blessed are you, merciful Lord God, and blessed your holy and honorable name for all eternity: may all your works bless you always. ¹² And now, Lord, with my face upon you, and with my eyes I have looked up: ¹³ give the word for me to be released from the earth, and for me to hear reproaches no more. ¹⁴ You know, Master, that I am clean of all uncleanliness of man ¹⁵ and have not defiled my own name, nor the name of my father in the land of my captivity. I am an only child to my father, and he has no other child that might be his heir, nor does he have any close relative or kinsman for whom I might keep myself or be a wife for some son. Seven have perished already, so what point is there for me in living? And if it does not seem good to you to kill me, then give the order, and pay attention to me, and take pity on me, so that I don't have to listen to reproach anymore."

¹⁶ At that very time the prayer of each was heard in the presence of the glory of the great God. ¹⁷ And Raphael was sent to heal them both: Tobit, by removing the white spots from his eyes, so that he might see the light of the sky, and Sarah, the daughter of Raguel, by giving her as wife to Tobias, the son of Tobit, and by releasing the evil demon Asmodeus from her. For by inheritance it fell to Tobias to take possession of her, before anyone else who wanted to take her. At the same moment, Tobit returned from his courtyard to his house, and Sarah, the daughter of Raguel, she too went down from the upper floor.

^{4:1} On that day, Tobit remembered the money, which he had deposited with Gabael in Rages of Media. ² And he said in his heart, "Look, I have requested death. Why don't I call my son Tobias, and let him know about this money before I die?" ³ Then he called his son, and he came to him. And he said, "Son!" And he said, "Here I am, father!" and he said, "Son, when I die, bury me properly. And honor your mother, and do not abandon her for all the days of her life, and do what pleases her, and do not cause her spirit to be distressed by any deed. ⁴ Remember, lad, for she experienced many dangers on your behalf when you were in her womb. And when she dies, bury her with me in a single grave.

⁵ And for all your days, lad, be mindful of God, and do not be willing to sin and transgress his commandments. Do what is right all the days of your life, and do not walk in the ways of iniquity. ⁶ For when you are doing truth there will be success for all your deeds, as for all who are doing what is right. ⁷ Give charity according to your circumstances, lad, and do not turn your face away from any poor man—and then the face of God will not be turned from you. ⁸ Do so according to what you have, lad. If you have plenty, give charity from that, and if you have little, give charity in line with that little. And do not be afraid, lad, when you are giving charity, ⁹ for you are saving up a good nest egg for yourself against a day of need. ¹⁰ For charity delivers from death, and does not let one depart into the darkness. ¹¹ Charity is a good gift to all who do it, before the Most High.

¹² Keep yourself, lad, from all sexual misconduct. At the first opportunity, take

a wife from the seed of your forebears. And do not take a wife from outside, who is not of the tribe of your forebears. For we are children of prophets, and true-born children of prophets. The first prophet was Abraham, then Isaac and Jacob, our forebears of old. Remember, lad, that these all took wives from among their relatives, and were blessed in their children—and their seed will inherit the earth. ¹³ And now, lad, love your relatives, and do not be disdainful in your heart of the daughters of the sons of your people, so that you do not take one of them. For in disdain is destruction and much disorder. And in idleness, there is loss and great want: idleness is mother to starvation.

¹⁴ As for every person who works with you, give him his pay daily, and don't let a person's pay stop over with you. And your pay will not stop over, if you serve God truly. Take care for yourself, lad, in all your doings, and be well bred in all your conduct. ¹⁵ And whatever you hate, do to nobody else. And may no evil travel with you on any of your path. ¹⁶ Give of your food to someone who is hungry, and of your clothes to the naked. Use for charity whatever you have in surplus: lad, may your eye not be grudging when you give to charity. ¹⁷ Pour out your food and your wine on the grave of the righteous, and do not give it to sinners. ¹⁸ Seek advice from every wise man, and do not be disdainful when there is value in all advice. ¹⁹ Bless God on every occasion, and ask of him that your ways may be straight and all your paths and plans prosper. For no nation has good counsel, but by gift of the Lord himself. And whom he wants to, he exalts, and whom he wants to, he lowers to Hades below. And now, lad, remember these commands of mine, and let them not be erased from your heart.

²⁰ And now, lad, let me inform you that I deposited ten talents of silver with Gabael, who is the son of Gabri in Rages of Media. ²¹ And do not be apprehensive, lad, because we have become poverty-stricken. You possess much wealth if you fear God and flee all sin, and do what is good before the Lord your God."

^{5:1} Then, replying, Tobias said to his father Tobit, "All that you have commanded me I will do, father. ² But how will I be able to get it from him? He does not know me, and I do not know him. What sign should I give to him so that he will recognize me, and trust me, and give me the money? And I do not know the roads to Media, so as to travel there." ³ Then, replying, Tobit said to his son Tobias, "He gave me his note of hand, and he took my note of hand and tore it in two: I kept one part, and put the other with the money. And now look, it's twenty-six years since I deposited this money. So now, lad, seek for yourself some trustworthy person who will travel with you, and we will give him a wage. Get this money from him while I'm alive!"

⁴ Then Tobias went out to seek a man who would go with him to Media, who would be acquainted with the route. And going out, he found the angel Raphael standing in front of him, and he did not know that he was an angel of God. ⁵ And he said to him, "Where are you from, young man?" And he replied to him and said, "From the children of Israel, your relatives, and I have come here to work." And he said to him, "Do you know the way to get to Media?" ⁶ And he said to him, "I know many, and I'm acquainted with all the roads. I have traveled often to Media, and lodged with Gabael, our brother, who lives in Rages of Media. And it is a distance by road of two standard days from Ecbatana to Rages—for it lies in the hill country, Ecbatana in the midst of the plain." ⁷ And he said to

him, "Wait, young man, until I can go in and tell my father. For I need you to journey with me, and I will pay you." [8] And he said to him, "Look, I'll wait for you—just don't be long." [9] And going in, Tobias told Tobit his father, and said to him, "Look, I have found a man from our brethren, the children of Israel, who will go with me." And he said to him, "Call the man for me, so that I may know what his ancestry is, and from what tribe he is, and whether he is trustworthy, that he might go with you, lad."

[10] And Tobias went out and called him, and said to him, "Young man! Come in! Father is calling you!" And he went in to him, and Tobit greeted him first. Then he said to him, "Many happy greetings to you!" But, replying, Tobit said to him, "What is there for me still to greet happily? I am a man with no function in my eyes, and I do not see the light of the sky, but lie in darkness, like the dead who no longer perceive the light. Living, I am among the dead: I hear the voice of people, and don't see them." And he said to him, "Take courage! Your healing by God is close at hand! Take courage!" And Tobit said to him, "My son Tobias wishes to travel to Media. If you are able to accompany him, and guide him, then I will pay you, brother." And he said, "I will be able to travel with him, and I am familiar with all the roads, and have often gone to Media, and crossed all its plains and hills; and I know all its roads."

[11] And he said to him, "Brother, of what lineage are you, and from what tribe? Tell me, brother." [12] And he said, "What need have you of a tribe or lineage? Are you looking for a hired man to travel with your son, or for a tribe and lineage?" And he said to him, "I wish to know the facts of what your family is, brother, and what your name is." [13] And he said to him, "I am Azarias, son of Ananias the older, from your brethren." [14] And he said to him, "May you be well and safe, brother, and do not be irritated, brother, by my wishing to know the truth about your lineage. And you happen to be my relative, and you are from a fine and good family. I used to know Ananias and Nathanias, the two sons of Semelios the older, and they used to travel with me to Jerusalem, and worship with me there. And these men, our fine brethren, did not go astray. You are from good stock, brother, and may you come welcome!"

[15] And he went on, saying, "I am going to give you a fee of a drachma per day, and expenses for you, just as for my son. And do travel along with him, [16] then I will give you a bonus to your pay." And he said to him, "I will travel along with him, and do not fear: we will go safely and return safely to you, for the road is secure."

[17] And he said to him, "Bless you, brother." And he called his son and said to him, "Lad, get ready and go out with your brother. And may God who is in heaven bring you both there safely, and bring you back to me well, and may his angel accompany you in peace." Then he prepared things needed for the road, and he went out to set off on his journey. And he kissed his father and mother, and Tobit said to him, "Travel safely!"

[18] And his mother wept, and said to Tobit, "Why is it that you have sent away our son? Is he not the staff of our hand, and does he not go in and go out before us? [19] May he not attain money for the money,[a] but may it become what our son

a. The text is obscure, and probably corrupt.

disdains. [20] What is given us to live by the Lord is sufficient for us." [21] And he said to her, "Have no concern. Our son will travel safely, and come back to us safely, and your eyes will see him on the day when he comes to you safely. Have no concern, do not be afraid for him, sister. [22] For a good angel will accompany him and his journey will be made easy, and he will return safely." [6:1] And she was silent, not weeping.

[2] And the boy went out, and the angel with him; and the dog went out with him and traveled with them. And they traveled together, and the first night came upon them. Then they spent the night at the River Tigris. [3] And the boy went down to wash his feet in the River Tigris, and a large fish, leaping up from the water, tried to swallow the boy's foot, and the boy cried out. [4] And the angel said to him, "Catch and control the fish!" And the boy controlled the fish, and dragged it onto the land. [5] And the angel said to him, "Cut up the fish, and take out the gallbladder, and the heart, and the liver, and set them aside with you. And throw away the entrails. For it is useful as medicine—the gallbladder, and the heart, and the liver." [6] And the boy cut up the fish and collected the gallbladder, and the heart, and the liver, and he roasted some of the fish, and ate, and took some for the journey, and he put aside some of it salted.

And they both journeyed together until they were approaching Media. [7] And then the boy questioned the angel, and said to him, "Azarias, brother, what is the medicinal property in the heart, and in the liver of the fish, and in the gallbladder?" [8] And he said to him, "The heart and the liver of the fish: make smoke from them in the presence of a man or woman who has contact from a demon or unclean spirit, and it will flee away from them, every contact—and they will not hang around them ever again. [9] And the gallbladder: anoint the eyes of a man who has white spots growing upon them, or puff on them, on the white spots, and they will heal."

[10] And when they had got to Media, and were already approaching Ecbatana, [11] Raphael said to the boy, "Tobias, brother." And he said to him, "I'm here," and he said to him, "We have to spend tonight in the household of Raguel; and the man is your relative, and he has a beautiful daughter, whose name is Sarah. [12] And he has no male child or any daughter other than just Sarah. And you are her next of kin: you are first in line to inherit her, and her father's things, and to take her as a wife. And the girl is intelligent and courageous and very beautiful, and her father loves her. Whatever he possesses, he gives to her, and so her father's inheritance is destined for you. [13] It is right for you to take her. And now listen to me, brother, and speak about the girl tonight, so that we may get her as a bride for you. And when we return from Rages, we will have her wedding. And I know that Raguel will not be able to withhold her from you because he knows that if he were to give her to another man he would become liable to death, according to the judgment of the book of Moses, when he is aware that it is fitting as an inheritance for you, above every man, to take his daughter. And now listen to me, brother, and we will speak about the girl tonight and get her betrothed to you. And when we return from Rages, we will take her and lead her away with us to your home."

[14] Then Tobias said to Raphael in response, "Azarias, brother, I've heard that she has already been given to seven husbands, and that they died in their wedding chambers, the night they approached her—and they *died!* And I've heard people

saying that a demon kills them. ¹⁵ And now I am afraid of this demon. For he does no harm to her, but he kills anyone who wants to get close to her. I am my father's only child: let me not die and drag down the life of my father and mother to their grave through grief for me, when they have no other child to bury them."

¹⁶ And he said to him, "Do you not recall your father's admonishments, that he told you to take a wife from your father's household? And now listen to me, brother: do not worry about this demon, but take her. And I know that tonight she will be given to you as a wife. ¹⁷ And when you enter the wedding chamber, take some of the liver of the fish and the heart, and place them on the embers of the incense-burners, and there will be a smell. ¹⁸ And the demon will catch the smell and flee, and will never anymore appear around her. And when you are about to be with her, you must both first get up and pray, and ask the Lord of heaven for there to be mercy and salvation upon you. Do not be afraid, for she has been set apart for you from eternity. And you will save her, and she will go with you, and I expect that you will have children by her, and they will be like siblings for you. Have no concern." And when Tobias heard the words of Raphael, and that she was a sister to him from the seed of his father's household, he loved her very much, and his heart became extremely attached to her.

⁷:¹ And when he arrived at Ecbatana, he said to him, "Azarias, brother, take me straight off to Raguel, our brother!" And he led him, and they went to the house of Raguel. And they found him sitting by the door of the courtyard, and they greeted him first. And he said to them, "Many greetings, brothers, enter in peace." And he led them into his house. ² And he said to his wife Edna, "How alike this young man is to Tobit, my relative!" ³ And Edna questioned them, and said to them, "Where are you from, brothers?" And they said to her, "From the children of Naphthali: we are some of those held captive in Nineveh." ⁴ And she said to them, "Do you know Tobit, our brother?" And they said to her, "We know him." And she said to them, "Is he well?" ⁵ And they said to her, "He is well, and living." And Tobias said, "He is my father." ⁶ And Raguel jumped up and kissed him and wept. ⁷ And he spoke, and said to him, "Bless you, lad! The son of a fine and good father! Oh, what a terrible business, that a righteous and charitable man should be blinded!" And falling upon the neck of Tobias, his relation, he wept. ⁸ And his wife Edna wept for him, and their daughter Sarah wept, she too. ⁹ And they welcomed them warmly, and killed a ram from the flock.

And when they had cleansed themselves, and washed, and lain down to dine, Tobias said to Raphael, "Azarias, brother, speak to Raguel about giving me my sister Sarah." ¹⁰ And Raguel heard what was said, and said to the boy, "Eat and drink and spend tonight happily since there is no man other than you suitable to take my daughter Sarah. Furthermore, I do not have the power to give her to a man other than you, for you are my next of kin. But I will point out to you the plain truth, lad: ¹¹ I have given her to seven husbands from among our brethren, and they all died the night they approached her. So now, lad, eat and drink, and the Lord will deal with you." But Tobias said, "I'm not going to eat or drink from now on until you discuss my concerns." And Raguel said, "I am doing so: she has been given to you according to the decree of the book of Moses, and she is decreed from heaven to be given to you. Receive your sister: from now on you are her brother, and she is your sister; she is given to you from this day and forever.

And the Lord of heaven will make straight the way for you both tonight, lad—and may he bring mercy and peace upon you." [12] And Raguel summoned his daughter Sarah, and she came to him. And taking her hand, he handed her over to him, and said, "Receive—according to the law, and according to the decree written in the book of Moses, about giving you your wife. Keep—and take her away to your father, keeping her safe. And may the God of heaven make straight the way for you, in peace." [13] And he summoned her mother, and said to fetch a scroll for him to write a written document of marriage, and about how he was giving her to him as wife, according to the decree of the law of the book of Moses. And her mother fetched (it), and he wrote and set a seal. [14] From that moment they began to eat and drink.

[15] And Raguel summoned his wife Edna, and said to her, "Sister, prepare the other chamber, and take her there." [16] And she proceeded to furnish the room, as he had told her. Then she took her there, and wept over her. And she wiped away the tears, and said to her: [17] "Be brave, daughter. May the Lord of heaven give you joy in place of your grief! Be brave, daughter." And she left.

[8:1] And when they had finished eating and drinking, they wanted to go to bed. And they led the young man out, and took him to the chamber. [2] And Tobias remembered the words of Raphael, and took the liver of the fish, and the heart, from the bag that he was holding; and he put them on the embers of the incense-burners. [3] And the smell of the fish was repellent, and the demon ran away to the upper parts of Egypt. Then Raphael went and bound him there, and tied him up immediately.

[4] Then they went out, and closed the door of the chamber. And Tobias got up from the bed and said to her, "Sister, get up! Let us pray and ask the Lord to bring mercy and salvation upon us!" [5] And she got up, and they began to pray and to ask for salvation for themselves. And he started by saying, "Blessed are you, Lord, the God of our fathers, and blessed your name for all the ages of time. And may the heavens bless you, and all your creation. [6] You made Adam and gave him an assistant, a support—Eve his wife. And from the two came the seed of humans. And you said that it was not right for the man to be alone, 'let us make for him an assistant like him.' [7] And now, Lord, I take this, my sister, not in lust but in sincerity. Ordain that there may be mercy for me and her, and that we may grow old together, and give us children with blessing." [8] And they said with each other, "Amen. Amen." [9] And they went to bed for the night.

But getting up, Raguel summoned the household servants to him, and they went out and dug a grave. [10] For he said, "Just in case he should die, and we become an object of ridicule and reproach. . . ." [11] And when they finished digging the grave, Raguel went to the house, and he summoned his wife. [12] And he said, "Send one of the maidservants, and let her go in and see whether he is alive or has died, so that we may bury him without anyone knowing." [13] And Edna sent the maidservant, and they lit the lamp, and opened the door, and she went in, and found them lying and sleeping together. [14] And coming out, the maidservant told them that he was alive, and nothing was wrong. [15] And they blessed the God of heaven, and he said, "Blessed are you, God, with every holy and pure blessing; may your holy angels bless you, and your elect bless you for all ages. [16] Bless you for making me happy, and because things did not turn out for me as I expected;

rather, you dealt with us according to your great mercy. ¹⁷ Bless you for being merciful to two only children. Show them mercy, Master, and salvation, and fulfill their life with mercy and happiness." ¹⁸ Then he told his servants to fill in the grave before it should be sunset.

¹⁹ And he told his wife to make many loaves. And going to the herd, he took two oxen and four rams, and gave the order for them to be slaughtered; and they began to make the preparations. ²⁰ And he summoned Tobias, and put him under oath, saying to him, "You may not move from here for fourteen days, but will stay here, eating and drinking with me, and cheer the troubled spirit of my daughter. ²¹ And take half straight away of as much as belongs to me, then depart to your father with my best wishes: the other half belongs to the two of you when I and my wife die. Be of good cheer, lad: I am your father, and Edna is your mother: we are yours and your sister's, from now forever. Be happy, lad!"

⁹·¹ Then Tobias summoned Raphael and said to him, ² "Azarias, brother, take with you four household servants and two camels, and travel to Rages, and go to the house of Gabael, and give the note of hand to him. Get the silver, and bring him with you to the wedding. ³ For you know that father is going to be counting the days, and if I delay for a single day, I will cause him a lot of pain. ⁴ But you see what Raguel swore—and I cannot break his oath." ⁵ Then Raphael traveled—along with the four servants and the two camels—to Rages of Media, and lodged with Gabael, and gave him his note of hand, and told him about Tobias, the son of Tobit, how he had taken a wife, the daughter of Raguel, and how he was inviting him to the wedding. And getting up, he counted out for him the moneybags with their seals, and they agreed on them. ⁶ Then they got up early together, and went to the wedding. And they went to the home of Raguel and found Tobias reclining at table. And he jumped up and greeted him, and he wept and blessed him, and said to him, "May the Lord who has given you peace bless you, you fine and good son of a fine and good man, righteous and a doer of good deeds. May the Lord give the blessing of heaven to you, and to your wife, and to your father and to your mother, and to the father and to the mother of your wife. Blessed be God, for I have seen my cousin Tobit, his very image!"

¹⁰·¹ But each day after day, Tobit was calculating the days: how many it would take him to travel, and within how many he would return. And when the days were up, and his son was not there, ² he said, "Perhaps he has been detained there, or perhaps Gabael has died, and nobody is giving him the silver." ³ And he began to grieve. ⁴ But his wife Anna said, "My son is lost, and belongs no more among the living: why is he late?" And she began to weep and to mourn her son, and said, ⁵ "Woe is me, child, for I let you, the light of my eyes, travel away." ⁶ And Tobit said to her, "Calm down, and don't worry, sister: he is well, and surely something is keeping them busy there. And the man who is traveling with him is trustworthy, and one of our brothers. Do not grieve for him, sister—he will be here shortly." ⁷ But she said to him, "Be quiet—get away from me, and don't deceive me: my son is lost!" And rushing out, she looked up and down the road by which her son had left each day, and could be persuaded by no one. And when the sun set, she would go in and mourn and weep the whole night, and get no sleep.

And when the fourteen days of the wedding that Raguel had promised to provide for his daughter came to an end, Tobias went in to him, and said, "Send me out, for I know that my father and my mother believe that they will never see me again. And now I ask you, father, that you send me on my way, so I can travel to my father. I have told you already how I left him." [8] And Raguel said to Tobias, "Stay, lad, stay with me, while I send messengers to your father Tobit, and they will tell him about you." [9] And he said to him, "No! I am asking you to send me on my way from here to my father." [10] And getting up, Raguel handed over to Tobias his wife Sarah and the half of his belongings, servants and maidservants, oxen and sheep, donkeys and camels, clothing and silver, and goods. [11] And he sent them on their way with his best wishes, and bade him goodbye, and said to him, "Farewell, lad, have a safe return. May the Lord of heaven smooth the way for you all and for your wife Sarah, and may I see from you both children before I die!" [12] And he said to his daughter Sarah, "Depart to your father-in-law, for from now on they are your parents, as if they had given birth to you. Go in peace, daughter: let me hear good things about you for so long as I live." And taking his leave, he let them go. And Edna said to Tobias, "My child and beloved brother, may the Lord carry you back, and may I see your children while I am alive, and those of my daughter Sarah before I die. In front of the Lord, I entrust my daughter to you, to be held in trust. Do not cause her any grief all the days of your life. Lad, go in peace. From now, I am your mother, and Sarah a sister. May we all find our way smooth together for all the days in our life." And she kissed them both, and sent them off faring well. [13] And Tobias went away from Raguel faring well, and rejoicing, and blessing the Lord of heaven and earth, the king of all, because he had made his path smooth. And he blessed Raguel and his wife Anna, and said, "May it fall to me to honor them all the days of their life."

[11:1] And they traveled until they neared Haran, which is opposite Nineveh. [2] Raphael said, "Don't you know how we left your father? [3] Let us hurry ahead of your wife and prepare the house for their coming." [4] And they both traveled together. And he said to him, "Put the gall in your hands." And the dog went with them, behind him.

[5] And Anna sat, looking up and down her son's route. [6] And she caught sight of him coming, and said to his father, "Look! your son is coming, and the man who was traveling with him!"

[7] And Raphael said to Tobias, before he drew near to his father, "I know that his eyes will be opened: [8] Coat the gall of the fish on his eyes, and the medicine will shrink and peel the white spots from his eyes, and your father will recover his sight, and will see light."

[9] And Anna ran up and fell on the neck of her son, and said to him, "I have seen you, lad: now I can die!" And she wept. [10] Then Tobit got up, and stumbled with his feet, and went out the door of the courtyard. And Tobias went on toward him. [11] And the gall of the fish was in his hand, and he blew into his eyes, and took him, and said, "Don't worry, father." And he put the medicine on him and it stung. [13a] And with each of his hands, he peeled from the corners of his eyes, and he saw his son and fell on his neck. [14] And he wept, and said to him, "I have seen you, son, the light of my eyes!" And he said, "Blessed be God, and blessed his great name, and blessed all his holy angels. May his name be holy forever.

---

a. 11:12 appears only in the G1 version (see above).

¹⁵ For he has punished me and had mercy on me, and look, I see Tobias my son!" And Tobit went in rejoicing and praising God with all his voice. And Tobias told his father that his journey had been made smooth, and that he had brought the silver, and how he had taken Sarah, the daughter of Raguel, as a wife, and that, look, she was coming, and was close to the gate of Nineveh.

¹⁶ And he went out to meet his daughter-in-law, rejoicing and praising God, toward the gate of Nineveh. And those in Nineveh, seeing him walking, and striding through with all his strength, and with nobody guiding him by the hand, were amazed. ¹⁷ And Tobit declared before them how God had had mercy on him, and how he had opened his eyes. Then Tobit drew near to Sarah, the wife of his son Tobias, and he blessed her and said to her, "May you come in welcome, daughter—and blessed be your God who brought you to us, daughter, and blessed your father and your mother, and blessed Tobias my son, and blessed you. Enter your home welcome, in blessing and joy! Enter, daughter!" On that day, there was joy among all the Jews who were in Nineveh. ¹⁸ And Ahiqar and Nabad, his nephew, came rejoicing to Tobit. And the wedding feast was celebrated for seven days with joy, and many gifts were given.

¹²:¹ And when the wedding feast was completed, Tobit called his son Tobias and said to him, "Lad, see to giving the fee to the man who traveled with you; we should give him something beyond the fee." ² And he said to him, "Father, how much pay will I give? I wouldn't hurt myself by giving him half of the possessions, which he brought back with me. ³ For he has guided me safely, and healed my wife, and brought the money with me, and healed you. How much more pay should I give him?" ⁴ And Tobit said to him, "It would be right for him, lad, to take half of everything that he came holding." ⁵ And he summoned him, and said, "Take half of all that you came holding for your pay, and depart with my best wishes."

⁶ Then he called the two secretly, and said to them, "Bless God, and give thanks to him before all the living for what he has done with you, good things for the blessing of God and praising of his name in hymns. Show the words about the deeds of God to all humans with honor, and do not hesitate to give thanks to him. ⁷ It is best to hide a king's secret, but honorable to give thanks for and to reveal the works of God. Do what is good, and evil will not find you. ⁸ Prayer is good with fasting, and charity with justice better than both. A little with justice is better than a lot with injustice: it is better to do charity than to hoard up gold. ⁹ For charity rescues from death, and it purges every sin. Those who do charity are fed full of life, ¹⁰ but those who do sin and injustice are enemies of their own life.

¹¹ I will show you all the truth, and will hide no word from you: I already showed you, and said, 'It is best to hide the secret of a king, and to reveal the works of God gloriously.' ¹² And now, when you prayed, along with Sarah, I presented the memorial of both your prayers before the glory of the Lord, and when you used to bury the dead, likewise. ¹³ And when you did not hesitate to get up and leave your meal, and went and laid out the corpse, ¹⁴ then I was sent to you to test you, and at the same time God sent me to heal you and Sarah, your daughter-in-law, also. ¹⁵ I am Raphael, one of the seven holy angels who are present and go in before the glory of God."

¹⁶ And the two men were agitated, and fell on their faces, and were afraid.

[17] And he said to them, "Do not be afraid! Peace be with you! Bless God for all the age! [18] I, when I was with you, was not acting on my own account, but by the will of God: bless him, every day praise him in hymns. [19] And you observed me, that I did not eat or drink anything, but it was an illusion observed by you. [20] And now bless the Lord on the earth, and give thanks to God. Look, I am ascending to him who sent me. Write down all the things which have happened to you." And he ascended. [21] And they got up, and were no longer able to see him. [22] And they blessed and praised God in hymns, and gave thanks to him for these great deeds and wonders of his, as the angel of God had appeared to them.

[13:1] Then Tobit spoke and wrote a prayer in praise, and he said, "Blessed be God, living forever, as his kingdom is for all time. [2] For he punishes and shows mercy, he pushes down to Hades below, and he pulls back up from great destruction, and there is nothing that escapes his hand. [3] Give thanks to him, sons of Israel, before the peoples, for he scattered you among them, [4] and recount his greatness there. And exalt him before everyone alive, seeing as he is our Lord, and he is our God, and he is our father, and he is God for all the ages. [5] He will punish you for your sins, and will show mercy to all of you, and will gather you out of all the peoples, wherever you have been scattered among them. [6] Whenever you turn to him with all your heart and with all your soul, to do truth before him, then he will turn to you, and will hide his face from you no longer. And now observe what he did with you, and give thanks to him with all your voice, and bless the Lord of righteousness, and exalt the king of the ages. I, in the land of my captivity, give thanks to him and make known his strength and greatness to a nation of sinners. Turn, sinners, and do righteousness before him: who knows if he might favor you, and be charitable to you? [7] I, and my soul, shall speak joy to the king of heaven, and my soul will rejoice all the days of my life. [8] May all chosen ones bless the Lord, and may all praise his greatness; let them speak with hymns of joy and give thanks to him. [9] Jerusalem, holy city, he will punish you for the deeds of your hands. [10] Give thanks to the Lord properly, and bless the king of ages, so that again your tabernacle will be built for you with joy, and may he cheer within you all the captives and may he love within you all those who suffer, for all the generations of the age. [11] A bright light, you will shine into all the farthest parts of the earth. Many peoples from afar will migrate to you from all the ends of the earth, to your holy name. And holding gifts in their hands for the king of heaven, generations of generations will give exultation in you, and the name of the 'chosen' for all the generations of the age. [12] Cursed be all those who reject you, and all who blaspheme you; cursed are all who hate you and all who speak a harsh word; cursed are all those who raze you and pull down your walls; and all who ruin your towers, and set fire to your houses. And blessed are all those forever who build you. [13] Be happy and rejoice at the sons of the righteous, for all will be gathered together and bless the Lord of the age. [14] Happy those who love you, and happy those rejoicing in your peace; and happy all the people who grieved for you, for all your punishments, as they will rejoice in you, and see all your joy forever. [15] My soul blesses the Lord, the great king, [16] for Jerusalem will be built again as his home for all the ages. I should be happy were a remnant of my seed to exist to see your glory and give thanks to the king of heaven. And the doors of Jerusalem will be built with lapis lazuli and emerald, and with precious stone all your walls. The towers of Jerusalem will be built with gold, and their battlements with pure gold. ¹⁷ The streets of Jerusalem will be laid with carbuncle, and with stone of Ophir. ¹⁸ And the doors of Jerusalem will speak hymns of exultation, and all her houses say, 'Alleluia! Blessed be the God who exalts you, and blessed for all ages' because in you they will bless the holy name forever and beyond."

¹⁴:¹ And the words of Tobit's thanksgiving were brought to a close. And he died in peace at the age of one hundred and twelve years, and was buried honorably in Nineveh. ² And he was fifty-eight years old when he became impaired in his eyes, and after he could see again, he lived for fifty-four years in prosperity and did charitable deeds, and he still continued to bless God, and to give thanks for the greatness of God.

³ And when he was dying, he summoned his son Tobias and his seven sons, and commanded him, saying, "Lad, take your sons away, ⁴ and flee to Media, for I believe in the word of God about Nineveh, that all will be and will happen to Ashur and Nineveh, and whatever things the prophets of Israel said, whom God sent, all those will happen, and nothing will be left out from all the sayings, and all will come to pass at their proper times. And it is in Media that there will be safety, rather than among the Assyrians or in Babylon. Therefore I know and trust that all things that God has said will be fulfilled and will be, and no saying will escape from the words. And our brothers who are dwelling in the land of Israel will all be scattered and taken captive from the good land, and all the land of Israel will be a desert, and Samaria and Jerusalem will be a desert, and the house of God, which is in it, will be burned down, and will be desert for a time.

⁵ Then once more, God will have mercy on them, and God will return them to the land of Israel. And once more they will build the house, but not as the first one, until the occasion when the occasion of times will be fulfilled. And after these things, they will return from their captivity, all of them, and will build Jerusalem with honor, and the house of God will be built in it, and it will be built for all time, just as the prophets of Israel have spoken about it. ⁶ And all the peoples who are in the whole world will all turn and fear God in truth, and set aside all their idols that mislead them, false in their misleadingness.ᵃ ⁷ And they will bless God forever in righteousness. All the sons of Israel who are saved in those days, sincerely mindful of God, will be brought together and come to Jerusalem, and they will dwell forever in that day with safety, and all justice will be among them. And those who love God truly will rejoice, and those doing wrong and injustice will be absent from the entire world. ⁹ᵇ And now, children, I charge you: serve God in truth, and do what is pleasing to him, and see that doing righteousness and charity will be associated with your children, and that they may be mindful of God and bless his name on every occasion sincerely and with all their might. ⁸ And now you, lad, leave Nineveh, and do not remain here. ¹⁰ On the day you bury your mother with me, on that very day, do not stay overnight within its borders. For I see that much injustice exists in it, and much deceit is accomplished in it, and they have no shame. See, lad, what Nadab did to Ahiqar, who was raising

a. The text and meaning are uncertain.

b. The verse numbers are drawn from another Greek tradition (G1, see above), which presents this material in reverse order.

him: was he not brought down to the ground alive? And God repaid the dishonor to his face, and Ahiqar went out to the light, while Nadab went into the eternal darkness, for he sought to kill Ahiqar. By doing charity, he escaped from the deadly trap, which Nadab had set for him, while Nadab fell into the deadly trap, and it destroyed him. [11] And now, lad, see what charity does, and what injustice does, that it destroys. And look, my life is failing."

And they laid him on the bed, and he died, and was buried with honor. [12] And when his mother died, Tobias buried her with his father, and he went away, along with his wife, to Media. And he lived in Ecbatana with Raguel, his father-in-law. [13] And he cared for them in old age honorably, and buried them in Ecbatana of Media. And he inherited the house of Raguel and of Tobit, his father. [14] And he died at the age of one hundred and seventeen years, gloriously. [15] And he saw and heard before he died the destruction of Nineveh, and saw its captive population led to Media, which Achiacharos, the king of Media, had captured. And he blessed God for all that he had done to the children of Nineveh and Assyria; before dying, he rejoiced about Nineveh, and blessed the Lord God forever. Amen.

The Letter of Aristeas

The Letter of Aristeas has been located under the general rubric "romanticized narrative" because the document tells the story of the translation of the Hebrew Scriptures into Greek in the middle of the third century BCE under the auspices of Ptolemy II (283–246 BCE). This story is certainly legendary, a point of fact that does not necessarily set the letter at a remove from the general description of "historiography" as understood within the context of early Jewish literature. This expanded notion of "legendary historiography" might fit nicely with Aristotle's contention that poetry is a "higher thing" than history (*Poetics* 9), and the Letter of Aristeas reads very well as a series of idealized statements rather than a simple itemization of events.

The Letter of Aristeas is not organized by chapters and verses, but by 322 "lines." The modern designation "letter" follows from the work's title, which is simply "Aristeas to Philocrates," and Josephus would refer to it as the "Book of Aristeas" (*Antiquities* 12.100). Some scholars suggest "letter" to be a misrepresentation of the document's genre, preferring instead to call it an "epistle." Still others have suggested that the Letter of Aristeas defies easy literary description as it is given over in places to a variety of literary forms: romantic reconstructions, homilies, dialogues, and narration. What is clear, however, is that the Letter of Aristeas was written as a piece of Jewish propaganda organized around the core story of the translation. Of course, letter writing—of an epistolary nature—was certainly popular in the ancient world among Jews with a Hellenistic background (see, for example, the apostle Paul) as a rhetorical form intended to influence people. In this way, "epistle" does suit the content better, but perhaps it is best to conceive of the document simply as an account. This is particularly important if the Letter of Aristeas proves to have been intended for a wide audience (and not just "Philocrates").

The Letter of Aristeas is most commonly associated with the story of the translation of the law book of the Jews into Greek (*see* Overview of Early Jewish Literature). When the LXX is referred to in the Letter of Aristeas, it has the Torah/Pentateuch in mind, and not the whole of the Hebrew Scriptures. The Letter of Aristeas is the story of this translation, but as will be discussed below, this is hardly the focal point for the author. Instead, the purpose of the story is to enhance the attractiveness of Judaism, and consequently the Jews, to a Hellenistic audience. Given its story-like qualities, the basic shape of the Letter of Aristeas is easily recognizable.

Narrative Structure of the Letter of Aristeas

1. Lines 1–8: Introduction from Aristeas to Philocrates.
2. Lines 9–11: The need for a translation—Demetrius of Phalerum, Ptolemy's librarian, proposes to secure the law book of the Jews for the Alexandrian library.
3. Lines 12–27: Aristeas counsels Ptolemy to free the Jews in Egypt from slavery; Ptolemy's favorable response, which is divinely compelled.
4. Lines 28–33: Details of the translation—capable Jewish translators needed.
5. Lines 34–50: The interchange between Ptolemy and Eleazar, the high priest in Jerusalem, regarding the arrangements for translators to be sent to Alexandria to undertake the project.
6. Lines 51–120: Details of the deputation to Jerusalem: descriptions of Ptolemy's gifts, Jerusalem, the temple and its function.
7. Lines 121–71: Eleazar's thoughts regarding the translators and the superiority of Jewish Law, pointing to the rule of the Jewish God over all things.
8. Lines 172–300: The arrival of the translators in Alexandria and the banquet held by the king, where the translators are questioned by Ptolemy.
9. Lines 301–16: The translation is done—it is accepted by the king and Jewish population in Alexandria, and is considered divinely ordained.
10. Lines 317–22: The departure of the translators, who were richly compensated and the closing statements from Aristeas to Philocrates.

As the divisions attest, the story of the translation of the law of the Jews occupies a relatively minor part in the Letter of Aristeas (parts 2, 4, 9 = 25 lines). The story that surrounds and occurs in between these sections of the actual translation is dominated by two primary agendas: (1) emphasizing the austerity, grandeur, and superiority of Jewish religion and customs over pagan expressions (lines 51–171) and (2) the compatibility of Jewish thought (morally and ethically) with Hellenistic philosophy/religion (lines 172–300). While unmistakably organized around the event of the translation, the Letter of Aristeas is far more a treatise on the superiority of Jewish religion and an appeal for mutual respect between Jew and Gentile.

Narrative Description

Aristeas begins his story by referring to his "mission" (line 1), which Philocrates has been eager to learn. Aristeas is clearly presented as a Gentile, speaking of the Jews as another people group, but as a Jewish sympathizer, relating to Philocrates that the mission afforded him an "opportunity of pleading with the king on behalf of the Jewish captives" (lines 4–5).

Introductions aside, Aristeas's story tells of the impetus for the translation. The librarian Demetrius had been charged with the task of collecting all of the books of the world at the library at Alexandria (line 9), expanding the collection from 200,000 books to 500,000. In this report, Demetrius remarks that the law book of the Jews is worth representation in the library, but that it is in a foreign tongue and therefore requires translation. The king then orders a letter to be sent to the Jewish high priest Eleazar in Jerusalem in order to arrange for this translation (lines 10–11).

The need for Jewish help provides an opportunity for Aristeas to appeal to Ptolemy regarding the Jews enslaved in Egypt. In this appeal, two features stand out. First, while his precise standing is unknown, Aristeas is clearly in the company of the king, suggesting that he is a ranking courtier (lines 9, 12, 14 [mention of Aristeas by name—line 40]). Second, Aristeas is at pains to reconcile Jewish and Hellenistic religious and philosophical mores. In lines 15–16 he notes that the Jews "worship the same God, the Lord and Creator of the universe, as all other men, as we ourselves, O king, though we call him by different names, such as Zeus or Dis." This statement reveals the intentions of the Letter of Aristeas, which is clearly apologetic of Jewish identity and religious practices and directed toward a Gentile audience. Others are also presented as Jewish sympathizers (Sosibius and Andreas, chief bodyguards—line 19 [see also line 12]). Together, they persuade the king that the emancipation of the slaves will not only be an act of goodwill toward the Jewish people of Palestine and Jerusalem from whom the king is seeking help, but also toward the God of the Jews who is both the "supreme God" and the one who has "greatly honored" Ptolemy in the first place (line 19).

Ptolemy and Eleazar then exchange letters, through which a deputation is appointed to go to Jerusalem to receive the translators. As an act of goodwill, Ptolemy has gifts made for the temple: a table and sets of bowls. The description of these elements is decidedly influenced both by biblical tradition and with deference to Jewish religious practices (lines 54–56). Aristeas is sent along with the deputation and provides an account of the trip to Jerusalem in lines 83–120. The land of Jerusalem is described with specific details being given to the performance of the **cult** in Jerusalem. The scene of the temple ministrations, the appearance of the curtain and the high priest, and the location of Jerusalem "in the center of the country" present the Jewish religion in a mythical light that would not have been lost on a Hellenistic audience familiar with oracular locations such as Delphi. Interpretive presentations of this variety were not uncommon in Second Temple Jewish literature, with the two major Jewish historians, Philo[1] and Josephus,[2] presenting the Jewish cult in a similar way.

---

1. Philo, *De specialibus legibus* 1.66: "We ought to look upon the universal world as the highest and truest temple of God, having for its most holy place that most sacred part of the essence of all existing things, namely, the heaven; and for ornaments, the stars; and for priests, the subordinate ministers of his power, namely, the angels, incorporeal souls, not beings compounded of irrational and rational natures, such as our bodies are, but such as have the irrational parts wholly cut out, being absolutely and wholly intellectual, pure reasoning, resembling the unit." Translation by Yonge.

2. Josephus, *Antiquities* 3.179–84: "Now here one may wonder at the ill will which men

Eleazar dispatches a select group of Jews, who are described as moderates in outlook and fluent in both Jewish and Greek literature (lines 121–22). Prior to their departure, Aristeas relates two events. The first is Eleazar's concern and anxiety about the safe return of the translators (lines 123–27). The second is Eleazar's response to a question regarding Jewish dietary laws, in which he explains that they are allegorical. The prohibitions and regulations surrounding Jewish dietary laws are set in place for the purpose of aiding in the pursuit of **virtue.** "Cud-chewing" is described as "nothing else than that reminiscence of life and existence" (line 154).

Upon their arrival in Egypt, the Jewish deputation is invited to a feast where each is questioned in turn by the king (lines 187–300). This section reads like a **catechetical** manual and the narrative plays out with each response satisfying the king in every way. In the end, the whole assembly and the Greek philosophers in attendance glowingly endorse the Jewish contingent (line 296).

The translation of the Jewish law occupies only twenty-two lines at the end of the story (lines 301–22). The translators, seventy-two in all, take seventy-two days

---

bear to us, and which they profess to bear on account of our despising that Deity which they pretend to honor; for if anyone should consider the fabric of the tabernacle, and take a view of the garments of the high priest, and of those vessels which we make use of in our sacred ministration, he will find that our legislator was a divine man, and that we are unjustly reproached by others; for if anyone should without prejudice, and with judgment, look upon these things, he will find they were all made in way of imitation and representation of the universe. When Moses distinguished the tabernacle into three parts, and allotted two of them to the priests, as a place accessible and common, he denoted the land and the sea, these being of general access to all; but he set apart the third division for God, because heaven is inaccessible to men. And when he ordered twelve loaves to be set on the table, he denoted the year, as distinguished into so many months. By branching out the candlestick into seventy parts, he secretly intimated the **Decani,** or seventy divisions of the planets; and as to the seven lamps upon the candlesticks, they referred to the course of the planets of which that is the number. The veils, too, which were composed of four things, they declared the four elements; for the fine linen was proper to signify the earth, because the flax grows out of the earth; the purple signified the sea, because that color is dyed by the blood of a sea shellfish; the blue is fit to signify the air; and the scarlet will naturally be an indication of fire. Now the vestment of the high priest which was made of linen, signified the earth; the blue denoted the sky, being like lightning in its pomegranates, and the noise of the bells resembled thunder. And for the ephod, it showed that God had made the universe of four elements; and as for the gold interwoven, I suppose it related to the splendor by which all things are enlightened. He also appointed the breastplate to be placed in the middle of the ephod, to resemble the earth, for that has the very middle place of the world. And the girdle which encompassed the high priest, signified the ocean, for that goes round about and includes the universe. Each of the sardonyxes declares to us the sun and the moon; those, I mean, that were in the nature of buttons on the high priest's shoulders. And for the twelve stones, whether we understand the months by them, or whether we understand the number of the signs of that circle which the Greeks call the **Zodiac,** we will not be mistaken in their meaning. And for the miter, which was of a blue color, it seems to me to mean heaven; for how otherwise could the name of God be inscribed upon it? That it was also illustrated with a crown, and that of gold also, is because of that splendor with which God is pleased. Let this explication suffice at present, since the course of my narration will often, and on many occasions, afford me the opportunity of enlarging upon the virtue of our legislator." Translation by Whiston.

to complete the translation with the Letter of Aristeas inserting the appositive to this "just as if this had been arranged of set purpose" (line 307). The translation is then presented to the Jewish population in Alexandria by Demetrius. The translation is acclaimed by one and all and a curse is put upon anyone who might in the future seek to make any alteration to it, thereby underwriting its austerity and sanctity (line 311). In reflecting on the translation, which is a revelation to King Ptolemy, he expresses his pleasure with the translation and is awestruck by the Jewish law.

Author/Provenance

There is no good reason for supposing that Aristeas, as he is presented in the Letter of Aristeas, was either the author of the work or a real person. The Aristeas from the letter is too familiar with Jewish customs and practices to have been a Gentile. It is more likely that the author of the Letter of Aristeas was an Alexandrian Jew, who was familiar with Jewish practices and with Hellenistic sensibilities, and who may have been a courtier in Ptolemy's service. His immediate context was the realpolitik of Jewish-Hellenistic interactions, which makes the Letter of Aristeas more of an overture to détente and mutual respect between Jew and Greek than a story of the legendary origins of the Greek Scriptures. It should also be added that the Letter of Aristeas endorses Jewish religious practices as superior to their Hellenistic counterparts. The law book of the Jews is described as "sacred and of divine origin" by the librarian, which brooks no objection from the king. While apologetic of Jewish religious practices, the Letter of Aristeas promotes Jewish ideas as not only consonant with Hellenistic philosophical traditions, but superior to them.

Date/Occasion

Scholarly consensus tends to view a range from 200 to 150 BCE for composition. Like other Jewish histories of this period, the Letter of Aristeas is an exercise in chronological hodgepodge and a precise date is difficult to pinpoint. The author allegedly is writing in the late third century BCE. The LXX was used as early as 200 BCE, making the composition of the Letter of Aristeas possible by that time. The letter places Demetrius as a contemporary of Ptolemy II. But Demetrius was exiled by Ptolemy II, having served under the latter's father. There is no mention of the **Seleucid Empire** in the account, and Eleazar acts with autonomy suggestive of a level of independence not likely under Seleucid control. Some scholars, however, suggest that the Letter of Aristeas was written as a way of soothing tensions between the Jewish and Hellenistic cultures during the period of the Seleucid incursions under **Antiochus IV Epiphanes** (175–163 BCE). Since there is no mention of Rome, it is likely that the Letter of Aristeas was written prior to 63 BCE. Failure to mention the Seleucid Empire could reflect the social and political realities of life under **Hasmonean** rule (140–63 BCE), but this would make Eleazar, who was high priest in the early Hellenistic period, an anachronism in addition to Demetrius. The story might also be a narrative tale intended to defend the LXX in the face of mounting calls for a return to the Hebrew version.

Text, Language, Sources, and Transmission

The Letter of Aristeas was originally written in Greek with twenty-three manuscripts remaining. The oldest extant copies are from the eleventh to fifteenth centuries CE, though the current textual tradition likely goes back to the second to third centuries CE. The first witnesses to the Letter of Aristeas are Philo (20 BCE–40 CE?) and Josephus (37/38–100 CE), and the letter shares a number of similarities in style and outlook with the works of these two historians. References to the Letter of Aristeas appear in the rabbis (e.g., b. Megillah 9a),[3] but the tale was not particularly well received in rabbinic Judaism generally. As a story that defends the authenticity and accuracy of the Greek translation, the Letter of Aristeas became an important document for the early Christian church, which used the LXX as its "Old Testament." Through the first four centuries CE, church fathers continued to elaborate the story. One elaboration, perhaps initiated by **Irenaeus** (200 CE), was that the translators were separated from one another to undertake their translation. The separate translations were found to be identical, which only added to the element of divine intervention and revelation in the formation of the LXX.

Theology

There is much to suggest that the Letter of Aristeas is both an apologetic of the Jewish religion and a piece of propaganda intended to enhance relationships between Jew and Gentile; it is simultaneously an overture for friendship between Jew and Gentile in the **Ptolemaic Empire** and an assertion of the supremacy of the God of the Jews over the philosophical system of the Greeks. The story of the emancipation of the Jewish slaves in the Letter of Aristeas reminds the reader of the exodus account from the Hebrew Bible, where the Israelites are freed from Egyptian slavery and receive the revelation of the law at Sinai (Exod. 12–15—emancipation; Exod. 19–23—giving of the law). Aristeas's story contains these two features as well, and it is perhaps no accident then that the temple and priesthood, their services, designs, and function also occupy a significant section of the Letter of Aristeas (lines 83–99), as such are also features in Exodus (Exod. 25–31 and 35–40).

---

3. b. Megillah 9a: "As it was taught in a *baraita*: In happened with King Ptolemy, that he gathered seventy-two elders, and gathered them in seventy-two houses, and did not reveal to them the purpose for which he had gathered them, and he went in to visit each of them, one by one, and he said to them, 'Write for me the Torah of Moshe your teacher.' The Holy One, Who is Blessed, gave to the heart of each of them, one by one, wisdom, and all of them arrived at a single understanding even in difficult passages or those which might lend themselves to heretical interpretation if not translated with care." See also Midrash Rabbah on Exodus 5.

Reception of the Letter of Aristeas in the Second Temple Period

Insofar as the New Testament writings use the LXX as their text for referring to the Hebrew Scriptures, and the Letter of Aristeas provides a theoretical basis for the austerity of the LXX, it is easy to see the church fathers' rationale for holding the Letter of Aristeas in such high regard. Thus, the Letter of Aristeas is far more important to the literary foundations of the early church than it is to any direct, explicit intertextual reference in the New Testament writings. On occasion, however, scholars have taken note of the similarities between the Letter of Aristeas and some New Testament writings, particularly the Gospel of Luke. In both, temple and prayer are significant features, and banqueting becomes an important theological canvas upon which key features of the author's agenda are laid out.

BRAD EMBRY

FURTHER READING

Hadas, Moses, ed. and trans. *Aristeas to Philocrates: Letter of Aristeas.* Eugene, Ore.: Wipf & Stock, 2007.

Honigman, Sylvie. *The Septuagint and Homeric Scholarship in Alexandria: A Study in the Narrative of the Letter of Aristeas.* London: Routledge, 2003.

Jellicoe, Sidney. *The Septuagint and Modern Study.* Ann Arbor, Mich.: Eisenbrauns, 1978.

Meecham, Henry G. *The Letter of Aristeas: A Linguistic Study with Special Reference to the Greek Bible.* Manchester: Manchester University Press, 1935.

Nickelsburg, George W. E. *Jewish Literature between the Bible and the Mishnah: A Historical and Literary Introduction.* Philadelphia: Fortress, 1981.

VanderKam, James C. *An Introduction to Early Judaism.* Grand Rapids: Eerdmans, 2001.

Wasserstein, Abraham, and David J. Wasserstein. *The Legend of the Septuagint: From Classical Antiquity to Today.* New York: Cambridge University Press, 2006.

Wright, Benjamin G., III. *Praise Israel for Wisdom and Instruction: Essays on Ben Sira and Wisdom, the Letter of Aristeas and the Septuagint.* JSJSup 131. Leiden: Brill, 2008.

ADVANCED READING

Hacham, Noah. "The *Letter of Aristeas*: A New Exodus Story?" *JSJ* 36 (2005): 1–20.

Hayward, C. T. R. *The Jewish Temple: A Non-Biblical Source Book.* London: Routledge, 1996.

Jellicoe, Sidney. "St. Luke and the Letter of Aristeas." *JBL* 80 (June 1961): 149–55.

Johnson, Sara Raup. *Historical Fictions and Hellenistic Jewish Identity: Third Maccabees in Its Cultural Context.* Berkeley: University of California Press, 2004.

Orlinsky, Harry M. "The Septuagint as Holy Writ and the Philosophy of the Translators." *HUCA* 46 (1975): 89–114.

Tcherikover, V. "The Ideology of the Letter of Aristeas." *HTR* 51 (April 1958): 59–85.

3.2 Letter of Aristeas

[1] Since I have collected material for a memorable history of my visit to Eleazar, the high priest of the Jews, and because you, Philocrates, as you lose no opportunity of reminding me, have set great store upon receiving an account of the motives and object of my mission, I have attempted to draw up a clear exposition of the matter for you, for I perceive that you possess a natural love of learning, [2] a quality which is the highest possession of humans—to be constantly attempting "to add to his stock of knowledge and acquirements" whether through the study of history or by actually participating in the events themselves. It is by this means, by taking up into itself the noblest elements, that the soul is established in purity, and having fixed its aim on piety, the noblest goal of all, it uses this as its infallible guide and so acquires a definite purpose. [3] It was my devotion to the pursuit of religious knowledge that led me to undertake the embassy to the man I have mentioned. He was held in the highest esteem by his own citizens and by others for both his virtue and his majesty and who had in his possession documents of the highest value to the Jews in his own country and in foreign lands for the interpretation of the divine law; for their [4] laws are written on leather parchments in Jewish characters. This embassy I undertook with enthusiasm, having first of all found an opportunity of pleading with the king on behalf of the Jewish captives who had been transported from Judea to Egypt by the king's father, when he first obtained possession of this city and conquered the land of Egypt. It is worthwhile that I should tell [5] you this story too since I am convinced that you, with your disposition toward holiness and your sympathy with men who are living in accordance with the holy law, will all the more readily listen to the account which I purpose to set forth, since you yourself have lately come to us from the island and are anxious to hear everything that tends to build up the soul. [6] On a former occasion, I too sent you a record of the facts that I thought worth relating about the Jewish race—the record [7] which I had obtained from the most learned high priests of the most learned land of Egypt. As you are so eager to acquire the knowledge of those things that can benefit the mind, I feel it incumbent upon me to impart to you all the information in my power. I should feel the same duty toward all who possessed the same disposition, but I feel it especially toward you since you have aspirations which are so noble, and since you are not only my brother in character no less than in blood but are one with me as well in the pursuit of goodness. [8] For neither the pleasure derived from gold nor any other of the possessions that are prized by shallow minds confers the same benefit as the pursuit of culture and the study which we expend in securing it. But that I may not weary you by a too lengthy introduction, I will proceed at once to the substance of my narrative.

[9] Demetrius of Phalerum, the president of the king's library, received vast sums

Translation by R. H. Charles, *The Apocrypha and Pseudepigrapha of the Old Testament in English* (Oxford: Oxford University Press, 1913). Edited by Joshua Williams. Republication courtesy of Wesley Center Online (wesley.nnu.edu).

of money for the purpose of collecting together, as far as he possibly could, all the books in the world. By means of purchase and transcription, he carried out, to the best of his ability, the purpose of the king. On one occasion when I was present he was asked how many thousand books are there in the library [10] and he replied, "More than two hundred thousand, O king, and I will make an endeavor in the immediate future to gather together the remainder also, so that the total of five hundred thousand may be reached. I am told that the laws of the Jews are worth transcribing and deserve a place in [11] your library." "What is to prevent you from doing this?" replied the king. "Everything that is necessary has been placed at your disposal." "They need to be translated," answered Demetrius, "for in the country of the Jews they use a peculiar alphabet (just as the Egyptians, too, have a special form of letters) and speak a peculiar dialect. They are supposed to use the Syriac tongue, but this is not the case; their language is quite different." And the king when he understood all the facts of the case ordered a letter to be written to the Jewish high priest that his purpose (which has already been described) might be accomplished.

[12] The time had come to press the demand, which I had often laid before Sosibius of Tarentum and Andreas, the chief of the bodyguard, for the emancipation of the Jews who had been transported from Judea by the king's father.[13] For when by a combination of good fortune and courage he had brought his attack on the whole district of Coele-Syria and Phoenicia to a successful issue, in the process of terrorizing the country into subjection, he transported some of his foes and others he reduced to captivity. The number of those whom he transported from the country of the Jews to Egypt amounted to no less than a hundred thousand. Of these he armed thirty thousand picked men and settled them in garrisons in the country districts. (And even before this time large numbers of Jews had come into Egypt with the Persians, and in an earlier period still others had been sent to Egypt to help Psammetichus in his campaign against the king of the Ethiopians. But these were nothing like so numerous as the captives whom Ptolemy the son of Lagus transported.) [14] As I have already said, Ptolemy picked out the best of these, the men who were in the prime of life and distinguished for their courage, and armed them, but the great mass of the others, those who were too old or too young for this purpose, and the women too, he reduced to slavery, not that he wished to do this of his own free will, but he was compelled by his soldiers who claimed them as a reward for the services which they had rendered in war. Having, as has already been stated, obtained an opportunity for securing their emancipation, I addressed the king with the following arguments. "Let us not be so unreasonable as to allow [15] our deeds to give the lie to our words. Since the law which we wish not only to transcribe but also to translate belongs to the whole Jewish race, what justification will we be able to find for our embassy while such vast numbers of them remain in a state of slavery in your kingdom? In the perfection and wealth of your clemency release those who are held in such miserable bondage, since as I have been at pains to discover, the God who gave them their law is the God who maintains your kingdom. They worship the same God—the Lord and Creator of the universe, as all other men, as we ourselves, O king, though we call him by different names, such as Zeus or [16] Dis. This name was very appropriately bestowed upon him by our first ancestors in order to signify

that he through whom all things are endowed with life and come into being, is necessarily the Ruler and Lord of the universe. Set all humankind an example of magnanimity by releasing those who are held in bondage."

[17] After a brief interval, I was offering up an earnest prayer to God that he would so dispose the mind of the king that all the captives might be set at liberty—(for the human race, being the creation of God, is swayed and influenced by him). Therefore with many prayers I called upon him who rules the heart that the king might be constrained to grant my request. For I had [18] great hopes with regard to the salvation of the men since I was assured that God would grant a fulfillment of my prayer. For when humans from pure motives plan some action in the interest of righteousness and the performance of noble deeds, Almighty God brings their efforts and purposes to a successful issue. The king raised his head and looking up at me with a cheerful countenance asked, "How many thousands do you think they will number?" Andreas, who was standing near, replied, "A little more than a hundred thousand." "It is a small boon indeed," said the king, "that Aristeas asks of us!" [19]Then Sosibius and some others who were present said, "Yes, but it will be a fit tribute to your magnanimity for you to offer the enfranchisement of these men as an act of devotion to the supreme God. You have been greatly honored by Almighty God and exalted above all your forefathers in glory and it is only fitting that you should render to him the greatest thank offering in your power." Extremely pleased with these arguments he gave orders that an addition should be [20] made to the wages of the soldiers by the amount of the redemption money, that twenty drachmas should be paid to the owners for every slave, that a public order should be issued, and that registers of the captives should be attached to it. He showed the greatest enthusiasm in the business, for it was God who had brought our purpose to fulfillment in its entirety and constrained him to redeem not only those who had come into Egypt with the army of his father but any who had come before that time or had been subsequently brought into the kingdom. It was pointed out to him that the ransom money would exceed four hundred talents.

[21] I think it will be useful to insert a copy of the decree, for in this way the magnanimity of the king, who was empowered by God to save such vast multitudes, will be made clearer and more [22] manifest. The decree of the king ran as follows: "All who served in the army of our father in the campaign against Syria and Phoenicia and in the attack upon the country of the Jews and became possessed of Jewish captives and brought them back to the city of Alexandria and the land of Egypt or sold them to others—and in the same way any captives who were in our land before that time or were brought hither afterward—all who possess such captives are required to set them at liberty at once, receiving twenty drachmas per head as ransom money. The soldiers will receive [23] this money as a gift added to their wages, the others from the king's treasury. We think that it was against our father's will and against all propriety that they should have been made captives and that the devastation of their land and the transportation of the Jews to Egypt was an act of military wantonness. The spoil that fell to the soldiers on the field of battle was all the booty which they should have claimed. To reduce the people to slavery in addition was an act of absolute injustice. [24]Wherefore since it is acknowledged that we are accustomed to render justice to all men and especially

to those who are unfairly in a condition of servitude, and since we strive to deal fairly with all men according to the demands of justice and piety, we have decreed, in reference to the persons of the Jews who are in any condition of bondage in any part of our dominion, that those who possess them will receive the stipulated sum of money and set them at liberty and that no man will show any tardiness in discharging his obligations. Within three days after the publication of this decree, they must make lists of slaves for the officers appointed to carry out our will, 25 and immediately produce the persons of the captives. For we consider that it will be advantageous to us and to our affairs that the matter should be brought to a conclusion. Anyone who likes may give information about any who disobey the decree on condition that if the man is proved guilty he will become his slave; his property, however, will be handed over to the royal treasury."

26 When the decree was brought to be read over to the king for his approval, it contained all the other provisions except the phrase "any captives who were in the land before that time or were brought hither afterward," and in his magnanimity and the largeness of his heart the king inserted this clause and gave orders that the grant of money required for the redemption should be deposited in full with the paymasters of the forces and the royal bankers, and so the matter was decided and the 27 decree ratified within seven days. The grant for the redemption amounted to more than six hundred and sixty talents; for many infants at the breast were emancipated together with their mothers. When the question was raised whether the sum of twenty talents was to be paid for these, the king ordered that it should be done, and thus he carried out his decision in the most comprehensive way. 28 When this had been done, he ordered Demetrius to draw up a memorial with regard to the transcription of the Jewish books. For all affairs of state used to be carried out by means of decrees and with the most painstaking accuracy by these Egyptian kings, and nothing was done in a slipshod or haphazard fashion. And so I have inserted copies of the memorial and the letters, the number of the presents sent and the nature of each, since every one of them excelled in 29 magnificence and technical skill. The following is a copy of the memorial: "The memorial of Demetrius to the great king. 'Since you have given me instructions, O king, that the books which are needed to complete your library should be collected together, and that those which are defective should be repaired, I have devoted myself with the utmost care to the fulfillment of your wishes, 30 and I now have the following proposal to lay before you. The books of the law of the Jews (with some few others) are absent from the library. They are written in the Hebrew characters and language and have been carelessly interpreted, and do not represent the original text as I am 31 informed by those who know; for they have never had a king's care to protect them. It is necessary that these should be made accurate for your library since the law that they contain, inasmuch as it is of divine origin, is full of wisdom and free from all blemish. For this reason literary men and poets and the mass of historical writers have held aloof from referring to these books and the men who have lived and are living in accordance with them, because their 32 conception of life is so sacred and religious, as Hecataeus of Abdera says. If it pleases you, O king, a letter will be written to the high priest in Jerusalem, asking him to send six elders out of every tribe—men who have lived the noblest life and are most skilled in their law—that we may find out the points in which the majority of

them are in agreement, and so having obtained an accurate translation may place it in a conspicuous place in a manner worthy of the work itself and your purpose. May continual prosperity be yours!'"

[33] When this memorial had been presented, the king ordered a letter to be written to Eleazar on the matter, giving also an account of the emancipation of the Jewish captives. And he gave fifty talents weight of gold and seventy talents of silver and a large quantity of precious stones to make bowls and vials and a table and libation cups. He also gave orders to those who had the custody of his coffers to allow the artificers to make a selection of any materials they might require for the purpose, and that a hundred talents in money should be sent to provide sacrifices for the temple and [34] for other needs. I will give you a full account of the workmanship after I have set before you copies of the letters. The letter of the king ran as follows:

[35] "King Ptolemy sends greeting and salutation to the High Priest Eleazar. Since there are many Jews settled in our realm who were carried off from Jerusalem by the Persians at the time of their [36] power and many more who came with my father into Egypt as captives—large numbers of these he placed in the army and paid them higher wages than usual, and when he had proved the loyalty of their leaders he built fortresses and placed them in their charge that the native Egyptians might be intimidated by them. And I, when I ascended the throne, adopted a kindly attitude toward all [37] my subjects, and more particularly to those who were citizens of yours—I have set at liberty more than a hundred thousand captives, paying their owners the appropriate market price for them, and if ever evil has been done to your people through the passions of the mob, I have made them reparation. The motive which prompted my action has been the desire to act piously and render unto the supreme God a thank offering for maintaining my kingdom in peace and great glory in the entire world. Moreover those of your people who were in the prime of life I have drafted into my army, and those who were fit to be attached to my person and worthy of the confidence of the [38] court, I have established in official positions. Now since I am anxious to show my gratitude to these men and to the Jews throughout the world and to the generations yet to come, I have determined that your law will be translated from the Hebrew tongue which is in use among you [39] into the Greek language, that these books may be added to the other royal books in my library. It will be a kindness on your part and a regard for my zeal if you will select six elders from each of your tribes, men of noble life and skilled in your law and able to interpret it, that in questions of dispute we may be able to discover the verdict in which the majority agree, for the investigation is of the highest possible importance. I hope to win great renown by the accomplishment of this [40] work. I have sent Andreas, the chief of my bodyguard, and Aristeas—men whom I hold in high esteem—to lay the matter before you and present you with a hundred talents of silver, the firstfruits of my offering for the temple and the sacrifices and other religious rites. If you will write to me concerning your wishes in these matters, you will confer a great favor upon me and afford me a new pledge of friendship, for all your wishes will be carried out as speedily as possible. Farewell."

[41] To this letter Eleazar replied appropriately as follows: "Eleazar the high priest sends greetings to King Ptolemy his true friend. My highest wishes are for your

welfare and the welfare of Queen Arsinoe your sister and your children. I also am well. I have received your letter and am greatly [42] rejoiced by your purpose and your noble counsel. I summoned together the whole people and read it to them that they might know of your devotion to our God. I showed them too the cups which you sent, twenty of gold and thirty of silver, the five bowls and the table of dedication, and the hundred talents of silver for the offering of the sacrifices and providing the things of which the [43] temple stands in need. These gifts were brought to me by Andreas, one of your most honored servants, and by Aristeas, both good men and true, distinguished by their learning, and worthy in every way to be the representatives of your high principles and righteous purposes. [44]These men imparted to me your message and received from me an answer in agreement with your letter. I will consent to everything that is advantageous to you even though your request is very unusual. For you have bestowed upon our citizens great and never to be forgotten benefits in many [45] (ways). Immediately therefore I offered sacrifices on behalf of you, your sister, your children, and your friends, and all the people prayed that your plans might prosper continually, and that Almighty God might preserve your kingdom in peace with honor, and that the translation of the [46] holy law might prove advantageous to you and be carried out successfully. In the presence of all the people I selected six elders from each tribe, good men and true, and I have sent them to you with a copy of our law. It will be a kindness, O righteous king, if you will give instruction that as soon as the translation of the law is completed, the men will be restored again to us in safety. Farewell."

[47] The following are the names of the elders: Of the first tribe, Joseph, Ezekiah, Zachariah, John, Ezekiah, Elisha. Of the second tribe, Judas, Simon, Samuel, Adaeus, Mattathias, Eschlemias. Of [48] the third tribe, Nehemiah, Joseph, Theodosius, Baseas, Ornias, Dakis. Of the fourth tribe, Jonathan, Abraeus, Elisha, Ananias, Chabrias. . . . Of the fifth tribe, Isaac, Jacob, Jesus, [49] Sabbataeus, Simon, Levi. Of the sixth tribe, Judas, Joseph, Simon, Zacharias, Samuel, Selemias. Of the seventh tribe, Sabbataeus, Zedekiah, Jacob, Isaac, Jesias, Natthaeus. Of the eighth tribe, Theodosius, Jason, Jesus, Theodotus, John, Jonathan. Of the ninth tribe, Theophilus, Abraham, [50]Arsamos, Jason, Endemias, Daniel. Of the tenth tribe, Jeremiah, Eleazar, Zachariah, Baneas, Elisha, Dathaeus. Of the eleventh tribe, Samuel, Joseph, Judas, Jonathes, Chabu, Dositheus. Of the twelfth tribe, Isaelus, John, Theodosius, Arsamos, Abietes, Ezekiel. They were seventy-two in all. Such was the answer which Eleazar and his friends gave to the king's letter.

[51] I will now proceed to redeem my promise and give a description of the works of art. They were wrought with exceptional skill, for the king spared no expense and personally superintended the workmen individually. They could not therefore scamp any part of the work or finish it off negligently. [52] First of all I will give you a description of the table. The king was anxious that this piece of work should be of exceptionally large dimensions, and he caused inquiries to be made of the Jews [53] in the locality with regard to the size of the table already in the temple at Jerusalem. And when they described the measurements, he proceeded to ask whether he might make a larger structure. And some of the priests and the other Jews replied that there was nothing to prevent him. And he said that he was anxious to make it five times the size, but he hesitated lest it should prove

useless [54] for the temple services. He was desirous that his gift should not merely be stationed in the temple, for it would afford him much greater pleasure if the men whose duty it was to offer the fitting [55] sacrifices were able to do so appropriately on the table which he had made. He did not suppose that it was owing to lack of gold that the former table had been made of small size, but there seems to have been, he said, some reason why it was made of this dimension. For had the order been given, there would have been no lack of means. Wherefore we must not transgress or go beyond the proper [56] measure. At the same time he ordered them to press into service all the manifold forms of art, for he was a man of the most lofty conceptions and nature had endowed him with a keen imagination which enabled him to picture the appearance which would be presented by the finished work. He gave orders too, that where there were no instructions laid down in the Jewish Scriptures, everything should be made as beautiful as possible. When such instructions were laid down, they were to be carried out to the letter.

[57] They made the table two cubits long (one cubit broad) and one and a half cubits high, fashioning it of pure solid gold. What I am describing was not thin gold laid over another foundation, but the whole [58] structure was of massive gold welded together. And they made a border of a hand's breadth round about it. And there was a wreath of wave-work, engraved in relief in the form of ropes marvelously [59] wrought on its three sides. For it was triangular in shape and the style of the work was exactly the same on each of the sides, so that whichever side they were turned, they presented the same appearance. Of the two sides under the border, the one that sloped down to the table was a very [60] beautiful piece of work, but it was the outer side that attracted the gaze of the spectator. Now the upper edge of the two sides, being elevated, was sharp since, as we have said, the rim was three-sided, from whatever point of view one approached it. And there were layers of precious stones on it in the midst of the embossed cord-work, and they were interwoven with one another by an inimitable artistic [61] device. For the sake of security they were all fixed by golden needles that were inserted in [62] perforations in the stones. At the sides they were clamped together by fastenings to hold them firm. On the part of the border round the table that slanted upward and met the eyes, there was wrought a pattern of eggs in precious stones, elaborately engraved by a continuous piece of fluted relief-work, closely [63] connected together round the whole table. And under the stones which had been arranged to represent eggs the artists made a crown containing all kinds of fruits, having at its top clusters of grapes and ears of corn, dates also and apples, and pomegranates and the like, conspicuously arranged. These fruits were wrought out of precious stones, of the same color as the fruits themselves, and [64] they fastened them edgeways round all the sides of the table with a band of gold. And after the crown of fruit had been put on, underneath there was inserted another pattern of eggs in precious stones, and other fluting and embossed work, that both sides of the table might be used, according to the wishes of the owners and for this reason the wave-work and the border were extended [65] down to the feet of the table. They made and fastened under the whole width of the table a massive plate four fingers thick, that the feet might be inserted into it, and clamped fast with linchpins that fitted into sockets under the border, so that whichever side of the table people preferred, might be used. Thus it became manifestly clear that the

work was intended to be used [66] either way. On the table itself they engraved a winding pattern, having precious stones standing out in the middle of it, rubies and emeralds and an onyx too and many other kinds of stones which excel [67] in beauty. And next to the winding pattern there was placed a wonderful piece of network, which made the center of the table appear like a rhomboid in shape, and on it a crystal and amber, as it is called, [68] had been wrought, which produced an incomparable impression on the beholders. They made the feet of the table with heads like lilies, so that they seemed to be like lilies bending down beneath the table, and the parts that were visible represented leaves that stood upright. [69]The basis of the foot on the ground consisted of a ruby and measured a hand's breadth high all round. It had the appearance of a shoe and was eight fingers broad. Upon it the whole expanse of the foot rested. [70] And they made the foot appear like ivy growing out of the stone, interwoven with acanthus and surrounded with a vine that encircled it with clusters of grapes, which were worked in stones, up to the top of the foot. All the four feet were made in the same style, and everything was wrought and fitted so skillfully, and such remarkable skill and knowledge were expended upon making it true to nature, that when the air was stirred by a breath of wind, movement was imparted to the leaves, and [71]everything was fashioned to correspond with the actual reality which it represented. And they made the top of the table in three parts like a triptychon, and they were so fitted and dovetailed together with spigots along the whole breadth of the work, that the meeting of the joints could not be seen or even discovered. The thickness of the table was not less than half a cubit, so that the whole work [72] must have cost many talents. For since the king did not wish to add to its size, he expended on the details the same sum of money that would have been required if the table could have been of larger dimensions. And everything was completed in accordance with his plan, in a most wonderful and remarkable way, with inimitable art and incomparable beauty.

[73] Of the mixing bowls, two were wrought (in gold), and from the base to the middle were engraved with relief work in the pattern of scales, and between the scales precious stones were inserted with [74] great artistic skill. Then there was a winding pattern a cubit in height, with its surface wrought out of precious stones of many colors, displaying great artistic effort and beauty. Upon this there was a mosaic, worked in the form of a rhombus, having a netlike appearance and reaching right up to the [75] brim. In the middle, small shields that were made of different precious stones placed alternately and varying in kind, not less than four fingers broad, enhanced the beauty of their appearance. On the top of the brim there was an ornament of lilies in bloom, and intertwining clusters of grapes were [76] engraven all round. Such then was the construction of the golden bowls, and they held more than two firkins each. The silver bowls had a smooth surface, and were wonderfully made as if they were intended for looking glasses, so that everything which was brought near to them was reflected even more [77] clearly than in mirrors. But it is impossible to describe the real impression that these works of art produced upon the mind when they were finished. For when these vessels had been completed and placed side by side, first a silver bowl and then a golden, then another silver, and then another golden, the appearance they presented is altogether indescribable, and those who came to see [78] them were not able to tear

themselves from the brilliant sight and entrancing spectacle. The impressions produced by the spectacle were various in kind. When men looked at the golden vessels, and their minds made a complete survey of each detail of workmanship, their souls were thrilled with wonder. Again when one wished to direct his gaze to the silver vessels, as they stood before him, everything seemed to flash with light round about the place where he was standing, and afforded a still greater delight to the onlookers. So that it is really impossible to describe the artistic beauty of the works. [79] The golden vials they engraved in the center with vine wreaths. And about the rims they wove a wreath of ivy and myrtle and olive in relief work and inserted precious stones in it. The other parts of the relief work they wrought in different patterns, since they made it a point of honor to [80] complete everything in a way worthy of the majesty of the king. In a word it may be said that neither in the king's treasury nor in any other, were there any works that equaled these in costliness or in artistic skill. For the king spent no little thought upon them, for he loved to gain glory for the [81] excellence of his designs. For oftentimes he would neglect his official business, and spend his time with the artists in his anxiety that they should complete everything in a manner worthy of the place to which the gifts were to be sent. So everything was carried out on a grand scale, in a manner [82] worthy of the king who sent the gifts and of the high priest who was the ruler of the land. There was no stint of precious stones, for not less than five thousand were used and they were all of large size. The most exceptional artistic skill was employed, so that the cost of the stones and the workmanship was five times as much as that of the gold.

[83] I have given you this description of the presents because I thought it was necessary. The next point in the narrative is an account of our journey to Eleazar, but I will first of all give you a description of the whole country. When we arrived in the land of the Jews we saw the city situated [84] in the middle of the whole of Judea on the top of a mountain of considerable altitude. On the summit the temple had been built in all splendor. It was surrounded by three walls more than seventy cubits high and in length and breadth corresponding to the structure of the edifice. All the buildings [85] were characterized by a magnificence and costliness quite unprecedented. It was obvious that no expense had been spared on the door and the fastenings, which connected it with the doorposts, and [86] the stability of the lintel. The style of the curtain too was thoroughly in proportion to that of the entrance. Its fabric owing to the draught of wind was in perpetual motion, and as this motion was communicated from the bottom and the curtain bulged out to its highest extent, it afforded a pleasant [87] spectacle from which a man could scarcely tear himself away. The construction of the altar was in keeping with the place itself and with the burnt offerings that were consumed by fire upon it, and the approach to it was on a similar scale. There was a gradual slope up to it, conveniently arranged for the purpose of decency, and the ministering priests were robed in linen garments, down to their [88] ankles. The temple faces the east and its back is toward the west. The whole of the floor is paved with stones and slopes down to the appointed places, that water may be conveyed to wash away the [89] blood from the sacrifices, for many thousand beasts are sacrificed there on the feast days. And there is an inexhaustible supply of water, because an abundant natural spring gushes up from within the temple area. There are moreover

wonderful and indescribable cisterns underground, as they pointed out to me, at a distance of five furlongs all round the site of the temple, and each of them has countless pipes [90] so that the different streams converge together. And all these were fastened with lead at the bottom and at the sidewalls, and over them a great quantity of plaster had been spread, and every part of the work had been most carefully carried out. There are many openings for water at the base of the altar that are invisible to all except to those who are engaged in the ministration, so that all the blood of the sacrifices which is collected in great quantities is washed away in the twinkling of an [91] eye. Such is my opinion with regard to the character of the reservoirs and I will now show you how it was confirmed. They led me more than four furlongs outside the city and bade me peer down toward a certain spot and listen to the noise that was made by the meeting of the waters, so that the great size of the reservoirs became manifest to me, as has already been pointed out.

[92] The ministration of the priests is in every way unsurpassed both for its physical endurance and for its orderly and silent service. For they all work spontaneously, though it entails much painful exertion, and each one has a special task allotted to him. The service is carried on without interruption—some provide the wood, others the oil, others the fine wheat flour, others the spices; others [93] again bring the pieces of flesh for the burnt offering, exhibiting a wonderful degree of strength. For they take up with both hands the limbs of a calf, each of them weighing more than two talents, and throw them with each hand in a wonderful way onto the high place of the altar and never miss placing them on the proper spot. In the same way the pieces of the sheep and also of the goats are wonderful both for their weight and their fatness. For those, whose business it is, always select the beasts that are without blemish and specially fat, and thus the sacrifice which I have described [94] is carried out. There is a special place set apart for them to rest in, where those who are relieved from duty sit. When this takes place, those who have already rested and are ready to assume their duties rise up spontaneously since there is no one to give orders with regard to the arrangement of [95] the sacrifices. The most complete silence reigns so that one might imagine that there was not a single person present, though there are actually seven hundred men engaged in the work, besides the vast number of those who are occupied in bringing up the sacrifices. Everything is carried out with [96] reverence and in a way worthy of the great God.

We were greatly astonished, when we saw Eleazar engaged in the ministration, at the mode of his dress, and the majesty of his appearance, which was revealed in the robe that he wore and the precious stones upon his person. There were golden bells upon the garment which reached down to his feet, giving forth a peculiar kind of melody, and on both sides of them there were pomegranates [97] with variegated flowers of a wonderful hue. He was girded with a girdle of conspicuous beauty, woven in the most beautiful colors. On his breast he wore the oracle of God, as it is called, on which twelve stones, of different kinds, were inset, fastened together with gold, containing the names of the leaders of the tribes, according to their original order, each one flashing forth in an indescribable way [98] its own particular color. On his head he wore a tiara, as it is called, and upon this in the middle of his forehead an inimitable turban, the royal diadem full of glory with the name of God inscribed in sacred letters on a plate of gold . . . having been judged worthy to wear these emblems in the [99] ministrations. Their appearance created such awe and confusion of mind as to make one feel that one had come into the presence of a man who belonged to a different world. I am convinced that any one who takes part in the spectacle which I have described will be filled with astonishment and indescribable wonder and be profoundly affected in his mind at the thought of the sanctity which is attached to each detail of the service.

[100] But in order that we might gain complete information, we ascended to the summit of the neighboring citadel and looked around us. It is situated in a very lofty spot, and is fortified with many towers, which have been built up to the very top of immense stones, with the object, as we were informed, of [101] guarding the temple precincts, so that if there were an attack, or an insurrection, or an onslaught of the enemy, no one would be able to force an entrance within the walls that surround the temple. On the towers of the citadel engines of war were placed and different kinds of machines, and the position was [102] much higher than the circle of walls which I have mentioned. The towers were guarded too by most trusty men who had given the utmost proof of their loyalty to their country. These men were never allowed to leave the citadel, except on feast days and then only in detachments. Nor did they permit any [103] stranger to enter it. They were also very careful when any command came from the chief officer to admit any visitors to inspect the place, as our own experience taught us. They were very reluctant to [104] admit us—though we were but two unarmed men—to view the offering of the sacrifices. And they asserted that they were bound by an oath when the trust was committed to them, for they had all sworn and were bound to carry out the oath sacredly to the letter, that though they were five hundred in number they would not permit more than five men to enter at one time. The citadel was the special protection of the temple and its founder had fortified it so strongly that it might efficiently protect it.

[105] The size of the city is of moderate dimensions. It is about forty furlongs in circumference, as far as one could conjecture. It has its towers arranged in the shape of a theater, with thoroughfares leading between them; now the crossroads of the lower towers are visible but those of the upper [106] towers are more frequented. For the ground ascends since the city is built upon a mountain. There are steps too which lead up to the crossroads, and some people are always going up and others down, and they keep as far apart from each other as possible on the road because of those who [107] are bound by the rules of purity, lest they should touch anything which is unlawful. It was not without reason that the original founders of the city built it in due proportions, for they possessed clear insight with regard to what was required. For the country is extensive and beautiful. Some parts of it are level, especially the districts that belong to Samaria, as it is called, and which border on the land of the Idumeans, other parts are mountainous, especially (those which are contiguous to the land of Judea). The people therefore are bound to devote themselves to agriculture and the cultivation of the soil that by this means they may have a plentiful supply of crops. In this way [108] cultivation of every kind is carried on and an abundant harvest reaped in the whole of the aforesaid land. The cities that are large and enjoy a corresponding prosperity are well populated, but they neglect the country districts, since all men are inclined to a life of enjoyment, for every one has a natural tendency toward

the pursuit of pleasure. [109]The same thing happened in Alexandria, which excels all cities in size and prosperity. Country people by migrating from the rural districts and settling [110]in the city brought agriculture into disrepute: and so to prevent them from settling in the city, the king issued orders that they should not stay in it for more than twenty days. And in the same way he gave the judges written instructions, that if it was necessary to issue a summons against any one [111]who lived in the country, the case must be settled within five days. And since he considered the matter one of great importance, he appointed also legal officers for every district with their assistants, that the farmers and their advocates might not in the interests of business empty the granaries of the [112]city, I mean, of the produce of husbandry. I have permitted this digression because it was Eleazar who pointed out with great clearness the points that have been mentioned. For great is the energy which they expend on the tillage of the soil. For the land is thickly planted with multitudes of olive trees, with crops of corn and pulse, with vines too, and there is abundance of honey. Other kinds of fruit trees and dates do not count compared with these. There are cattle of all kinds in [113]great quantities and a rich pasturage for them. Wherefore they rightly recognize that the country districts need a large population, and the relations between the city and the villages are properly [114]regulated. A great quantity of spices and precious stones and gold is brought into the country by the Arabs. For the country is well adapted not only for agriculture but also for commerce, and the [115]city is rich in the arts and lacks none of the merchandise which is brought across the sea. It possesses too suitable and commodious harbors at Askalon, Joppa, and Gaza, as well as at Ptolemais that was founded by the king and holds a central position compared with the other places named, being not far distant from any of them. The country produces everything in abundance, [116]since it is well watered in all directions and well protected from storms. The river Jordan, as it is called, which never runs dry, flows through the land. Originally (the country) contained not less than sixty million acres—though afterward the neighboring peoples made incursions against it—and six hundred thousand men were settled upon it in farms of one hundred acres each. The river like the Nile rises in harvest-time and irrigates a large portion of the land. Near the district belonging to the people of [117]Ptolemais it issues into another river and this flows out into the sea. Other mountain torrents, as they are called, flow down into the plain and encompass the parts about Gaza and the district of [118]Ashdod. The country is encircled by a natural fence and is very difficult to attack and cannot be assailed by large forces, owing to the narrow passes, with their overhanging precipices and deep ravines, and the rugged character of the mountainous regions which surround all the land. [119]We were told that from the neighboring mountains of Arabia copper and iron were formerly obtained. This was stopped, however, at the time of the Persian rule, since the authorities of the time spread [120]abroad a false report that the working of the mines was useless and expensive, in order to prevent their country from being destroyed by the mining in these districts and possibly taken away from them owing to the Persian rule, since by the assistance of this false report they found an excuse for entering the district.

I have now, my dear brother Philocrates, given you all the essential information upon this subject [121]in brief form. I will describe the work of translation in the sequel. The high priest selected men of the finest character and the highest culture, such as one would expect from their noble parentage. They were men who had not only acquired proficiency in Jewish literature, but had studied most [122] carefully that of the Greeks as well. They were specially qualified therefore for serving on embassies and they undertook this duty whenever it was necessary. They possessed a great facility for conferences and the discussion of problems connected with the law. They espoused the middle course—and this is always the best course to pursue. They abjured the rough and uncouth manner, but they were altogether above pride and never assumed an air of superiority over others, and in conversation they were ready to listen and give an appropriate answer to every question. And all of them carefully observed this rule and were anxious above everything else to excel each other in [123] its observance, and they were all of them worthy of their leader and of his virtue. And one could observe how they loved Eleazar by their unwillingness to be torn away from him and how he loved them. For besides the letter which he wrote to the king concerning their safe return, he also earnestly [124] besought Andreas to work for the same end and urged me, too, to assist to the best of my ability and although we promised to give our best attention to the matter, he said that he was still greatly distressed, for he knew that the king out of the goodness of his nature considered it his highest privilege, whenever he heard of a man who was superior to his fellows in culture and wisdom, to [125] summon him to his court. For I have heard of a fine saying of his to the effect that by securing just and prudent men about his person he would secure the greatest protection for his kingdom, since such friends would unreservedly give him the most beneficial advice. And the men who were [126] now being sent to him by Eleazar undoubtedly possessed these qualities. And he frequently asserted upon oath that he would never let the men go if it were merely some private interest of his own that constituted the impelling motive—but it was for the common advantage of [127] all the citizens that he was sending them. For, he explained, the good life consists in the keeping of the enactments of the law, and this end is achieved much more by hearing than by reading. From this and other similar statements it was clear what his feelings toward them were.

[128] It is worthwhile to mention briefly the information that he gave in reply to our questions. For I suppose that most people feel a curiosity with regard to some of the enactments in the law, [129] especially those about meats and drinks and animals recognized as unclean. When we asked why, since there is but one form of creation, some animals are regarded as unclean for eating, and others unclean even to the touch (for though the law is scrupulous on most points, it is specially scrupulous on such [130] matters as these) he began his reply as follows: "You observe," he said, "what an effect our modes of life and our associations produce upon us; by associating with the bad, humans catch their depravities and become miserable throughout their life; but if with the wise and prudent, they find [131] the means of escaping from ignorance and amending their lives. Our lawgiver first of all laid down the principles of piety and righteousness and inculcated them point by point, not merely by prohibitions but by the use of examples as well, demonstrating the injurious effects of sin and the [132] punishments inflicted by God upon the guilty. For he proved first of all that there is only one God and that his power is manifested throughout the universe, since every place is filled with

his sovereignty and none of the things which are wrought in secret by men upon the earth escape his knowledge. For all that one does and all that is to come to pass in the future are manifest to [133] him. Working out these truths carefully and having made them plain he showed that even if one should think of doing evil— to say nothing of actually effecting it—[134]he would not escape detection, for he made it clear that the power of God pervaded the whole of the law. [135]Beginning from this starting point he went on to show that all humankind except ourselves believe in the existence of many gods, though they themselves are much more powerful than the beings whom they vainly worship. For when they have made statues of stone and wood, they say that they are the images of those who have invented something useful for life and they worship them, though [136] they have clear proof that they possess no feeling. For it would be utterly foolish to suppose that any one became a god in virtue of his inventions. For the inventors simply took certain objects already created and by combining them together, showed that they possessed a fresh utility: they [137] did not themselves create the substance of the thing, and so it is a vain and foolish thing for people to make gods of men like themselves. For in our times there are many who are much more inventive and much more learned than the men of former days who have been deified, and yet they would never come to worship them. The makers and authors of these myths think that they are [138] the wisest of the Greeks. Why need we speak of other infatuated people, Egyptians and the like, who place their reliance upon wild beasts and most kinds of creeping things and cattle, and worship them, and offer sacrifices to them both while living and when dead?

[139] "Now our lawgiver being a wise man and specially endowed by God to understand all things, took a comprehensive view of each particular detail, and fenced us round with impregnable ramparts and walls of iron, that we might not mingle at all with any of the other nations, but remain pure in body and soul, free from all vain imaginations, worshiping the one Almighty God above the whole [140] creation. Hence the leading Egyptian priests, having looked carefully into many matters and being cognizant with (our) affairs, call us 'men of God.' This is a title that does not belong to the rest of humankind but only to those who worship the true God. The rest are people not of God but of meats and drinks and clothing. For their whole disposition leads them to find solace in these things. [141] Among our people such things are reckoned of no account, but throughout their whole life their [142] main consideration is the sovereignty of God. Therefore lest we should be corrupted by any abomination, or our lives be perverted by evil communications, he hedged us round on all sides by [143] rules of purity, affecting alike what we eat, or drink, or touch, or hear, or see. For though, speaking generally, all things are alike in their natural constitution, since they are all governed by one and the same power, yet there is a deep reason in each individual case why we abstain from the use of certain things and enjoy the common use of others. For the sake of illustration I will run over one or two [144] points and explain them to you. For you must not fall into the degrading idea that it was out of regard to mice and weasels and other such things that Moses drew up his laws with such exceeding care. All these ordinances were made for the sake of righteousness to aid the quest for virtue and [145] the perfecting of character. For all the birds that we use are tame and distinguished by their cleanliness, feeding on various kinds of grain

and pulse, such as for instance pigeons, turtledoves, [146] locusts, partridges, geese also, and all other birds of this class. But the birds which are forbidden you will find to be wild and carnivorous, tyrannizing over the others by the strength which they possess, and cruelly obtaining food by preying on the tame birds enumerated above and not only so, but [147] they seize lambs and kids, and injure human beings too, whether dead or alive, and so by naming them unclean, he gave a sign by means of them that those, for whom the legislation was ordained, must practice righteousness in their hearts and not tyrannize over any one in reliance upon their own strength nor rob them of anything, but steer their course of life in accordance with justice, just as the tame birds, already mentioned, consume the different kinds of pulse that grow upon the earth [148] and do not tyrannize to the destruction of their own kindred. Our legislator taught us therefore that it is by such methods as these that indications are given to the wise, that they must be just and effect nothing by violence, and refrain from tyrannizing over others in reliance upon their own [149] strength. For since it is considered unseemly even to touch such unclean animals, as have been mentioned, on account of their particular habits, ought we not to take every precaution lest our own [150] characters should be destroyed to the same extent? Wherefore all the rules which he has laid down with regard to what is permitted in the case of these birds and other animals, he has enacted with the object of teaching us a moral lesson. For the division of the hoof and the separation of the claws are intended to teach us that we must discriminate between our individual actions with a view [151] to the practice of virtue. For the strength of our whole body and its activity depend upon our shoulders and limbs. Therefore he compels us to recognize that we must perform all our actions with discrimination according to the standard of righteousness—more especially because we have [152] been distinctly separated from the rest of humankind. For most other men defile themselves by promiscuous intercourse, thereby working great iniquity, and whole countries and cities pride themselves upon such vices. For they not only have intercourse with men but they defile their own [153] mothers and even their daughters. But we have been kept separate from such sins. And the people who have been separated in the previously mentioned way are also characterized by the lawgiver as possessing the gift of memory. For all animals 'which are cloven-footed and chew the cud' [154] represent to the initiated the symbol of memory. For the act of chewing the cud is nothing else than the reminiscence of life and existence. For life is wont to be sustained by means of food [155] wherefore he exhorts us in the Scripture also in these words, 'Thou shalt surely remember the Lord that wrought in thee those great and wonderful things.' For when they are properly conceived, they are manifestly great and glorious; first the construction of the body and the disposition of the [156] food and the separation of each individual limb and, far more, the organization of the senses, the operation and invisible movement of the mind, the rapidity of its particular actions and its discovery of the [157] arts, display an infinite resourcefulness. Wherefore he exhorts us to remember that the aforesaid parts are kept together by the divine power with consummate skill. For he has marked out every [158] time and place that we may continually remember the God who rules and preserves (us). For in the matter of meats and drinks he bids us first of all offer part as a sacrifice and then forthwith enjoy our meal. Moreover, upon our garments he has given us a symbol of remembrance, and in like manner he has ordered us to put the divine oracles upon our gates and doors as a remembrance of [159] God. And upon our hands, too, he expressly orders the symbol to be fastened, clearly showing that we ought to perform every act in righteousness, remembering (our own creation), and above all the [160] fear of God. He bids men also, when lying down to sleep and rising up again, to meditate upon the works of God, not only in word, but by observing distinctly the change and impression produced upon them, when they are going to sleep, and also their waking, how divine and incomprehensible [161] the change from one of these states to the other is. The excellence of the analogy in regard to discrimination and memory has now been pointed out to you, according to our interpretation of 'the cloven hoof and the chewing of the cud.' For our laws have not been drawn up at random or in accordance with the first casual thought that occurred to the mind, but with a view to truth and the [162] indication of right reason. For by means of the directions that he gives with regard to meats and drinks and particular cases of touching, he bids us neither to do nor listen to anything thoughtlessly, [163] nor to resort to injustice by the abuse of the power of reason. In the case of the wild animals, too, the same principle may be discovered. For the character of the weasel and of mice and such [164] animals as these, which are expressly mentioned, is destructive. Mice defile and damage everything, not only for their own food but even to the extent of rendering absolutely useless to human beings whatever [165] it falls in their way to damage. The weasel class, too, is peculiar: for besides what has been said, it has a characteristic which is defiling: it conceives through the ears and brings forth through the [166] mouth. And it is for this reason that a like practice is declared unclean in men. For by embodying in speech all that they receive through the ears, they involve others in evils and work no ordinary impurity, being themselves altogether defiled by the pollution of impiety. And your king, as we are informed, does quite right in destroying such people." [167] Then I said, "I suppose you mean the informers, for he constantly exposes them to tortures and to [168] painful forms of death?" "Yes," he replied, "these are the men I mean, for to watch for human beings' destruction is an unholy thing. And our law forbids us to injure anyone either by word or deed. My brief account of these matters ought to have convinced you that all our regulations have been drawn up with a view to righteousness, and that nothing has been enacted in the Scripture thoughtlessly or without due reason, but its purpose is to enable us throughout our whole life and in all our actions [169] to practice righteousness before all men, being mindful of Almighty God. And so concerning meats and things unclean, creeping things, and wild beasts, the whole system aims at righteousness and righteous relationships between human beings."

[170] He seemed to me to have made a good defense on all the points; for in reference also to the calves and rams and goats which are offered, he said that it was necessary to take them from the herds and flocks, and sacrifice tame animals and offer nothing wild, that the offerers of the sacrifices might understand the symbolic meaning of the lawgiver and not be under the influence of an arrogant self-consciousness. For he who offers a sacrifice makes an offering also of his own soul in all its moods. [171] I think that these particulars with regard to our discussion are worth narrating and on account of the sanctity and natural meaning of the

law, I have been induced to explain them to you clearly, Philocrates, because of your own devotion to learning.

[172] And Eleazar, after offering the sacrifice, and selecting the envoys, and preparing many gifts for the [173] king, dispatched us on our journey in great security. And when we reached Alexandria, the king was at once informed of our arrival. On our admission to the palace, Andreas and I warmly greeted [174] the king and handed over to him the letter written by Eleazar. The king was very anxious to meet the envoys, and gave orders that all the other officials should be dismissed and the envoys [175] summoned to his presence at once. Now this excited general surprise, for it is customary for those who come to seek an audience with the king on matters of importance to be admitted to his presence on the fifth day, while envoys from kings or very important cities with difficulty secure admission to the court in thirty days—but these men he counted worthy of greater honor, since he held their master in such high esteem, and so he immediately dismissed those whose presence he regarded as superfluous and continued walking about until they came in and he was able to welcome them. [176] When they entered with the gifts which had been sent with them and the valuable parchments, on which the law was inscribed in gold in Jewish characters, for the parchment was wonderfully prepared and the connection between the pages had been so effected as to be invisible, the king as soon [177] as he saw them began to ask them about the books. And when they had taken the rolls out of their coverings and unfolded the pages, the king stood still for a long time and then making obeisance about seven times, he said: "I thank you, my friends, and I thank him that sent you still more, and [178] most of all God, whose oracles these are." And when all the envoys and the others who were present as well, shouted out at one time and with one voice, "God save the king!" he burst into tears of joy. For his exaltation of soul and the sense of the overwhelming honor that had been [179] paid him compelled him to weep over his good fortune. He commanded them to put the rolls back in their places and then, after saluting the men, said, "It was right, men of God, that I should first of all pay my reverence to the books for the sake of which I summoned you here and then, when I had done that, to extend the right hand of friendship to you. It was for this reason that I [180] did this first. I have enacted that this day, on which you arrived, will be kept as a great day and it will be celebrated annually throughout my lifetime. It happens also that it is the anniversary of [181] my naval victory over Antigonus. Therefore I will be glad to feast with you today. Everything that you may have occasion to use," he said, "will be prepared in a befitting manner and for me also with you." After they had expressed their delight, he gave orders that the best quarters near the citadel should be assigned to them, and that preparations should be made for the banquet. [182] And Nicanor summoned the lord high steward, Dorotheus, who was the special officer appointed to look after the Jews, and commanded him to make the necessary preparation for each one. For this arrangement had been made by the king and it is an arrangement which you see maintained today. For as many cities (as) have (special) customs in the matter of drinking, eating, and reclining, have special officers appointed to look after their requirements. And whenever they come to visit the kings, preparations are made in accordance with their own customs, in order that there may be no discomfort to disturb the enjoyment of their visit. The same precaution

was taken in the case of the Jewish envoys. Now Dorotheus who was the patron appointed to look after Jewish guests was [183] a very conscientious man. All the stores that were under his control and set apart for the reception of such guests, he brought out for the feast. He arranged the seats in two rows in accordance with the king's instructions. For he had ordered him to make half the men sit at his right hand and the rest behind him, in order that he might not withhold from them the highest possible honor. When they had taken their seats he instructed Dorotheus to carry out everything in [184] accordance with the customs that were in use among his Jewish guests. Therefore he dispensed with the services of the sacred heralds and the sacrificing priests and the others who were accustomed to offer the prayers, and called upon one of our number, Eleazar, the oldest of the Jewish priests, to offer prayer instead. And he rose up and made a remarkable prayer. "May Almighty [185] God enrich you, O king, with all the good things which he has made and may he grant you and your wife and your children and your comrades the continual possession of them as long as you live!" At these words a loud and joyous applause broke out which lasted for a considerable time, and then [186] they turned to the enjoyment of the banquet which had been prepared. All the arrangements for service at table were carried out in accordance with the injunction of Dorotheus. Among the attendants were the royal pages and others who held places of honor at the king's court.

[187] Taking an opportunity afforded by a pause in the banquet the king asked the envoy who sat in the seat of honor (for they were arranged according to seniority), how he could keep his kingdom [188] unimpaired to the end. After pondering for a moment he replied, "You could best establish its security if you were to imitate the unceasing benignity of God. For if you exhibit clemency and inflict mild punishments upon those who deserve them in accordance with their deserts, you will [189] turn them from evil and lead them to repentance." The king praised the answer and then asked the next man how he could do everything for the best in all his actions. And he replied, "If one maintains a just bearing toward all, he will always act rightly on every occasion, remembering that every thought is known to God. If you take the fear of God as your starting point, you will never miss the goal."

[190] The king complimented this man, too, upon his answer and asked another how he could have friends like-minded with himself. He replied, "If they see you studying the interests of the multitudes over whom you rule; you will do well to observe how God bestows his benefits on the [191] human race, providing for them health and food and all other things in due season." After expressing his agreement with the reply, the king asked the next guest how in giving audiences and passing judgments he could gain the praise even of those who failed to win their suit. And he said, "If you are fair in speech to all alike and never act insolently or tyrannically in your treatment of [192] offenders. And you will do this if you watch the method by which God acts. The petitions of the worthy are always fulfilled, while those who fail to obtain an answer to their prayers are informed by means of dreams or events of what was harmful in their requests and that God does not smite them according to their sins or the greatness of his strength, but acts with forbearance toward them."

[193] The king praised the man warmly for his answer and asked the next in order how he could be invincible in military affairs. And he replied, "If he did not trust

entirely to his multitudes or his warlike forces, but called upon God continually to bring his enterprises to a successful issue, while [194] he himself discharged all his duties in the spirit of justice." Welcoming this answer, he asked another how he might become an object of dread to his enemies. And he replied, "If while maintaining a vast supply of arms and forces he remembered that these things were powerless to achieve a permanent and conclusive result. For even God instills fear into the minds of humans by granting reprieves and making merely a display of the greatness of his power."

[195] This man the king praised and then asked the next what is the highest good in life. And he answered, "To know that God is Lord of the universe, and that in our finest achievements it is not we who attain success but God who by his power brings all things to fulfillment and leads us to the goal."

[196] The king exclaimed that the man had answered well and then asked the next how he could keep all his possessions intact and finally hand them down to his successors in the same condition. And he answered, "By praying constantly to God that you may be inspired with high motives in all your undertakings and by warning your descendants not to be dazzled by fame or wealth, for it is God who bestows all these gifts; humans never by themselves win the supremacy."

[197] The king expressed his agreement with the answer and inquired of the next guest how he could bear with equanimity whatever befell him. And he said, "If you have a firm grasp of the thought that all men are appointed by God to share the greatest evil as well as the greatest good, since it is impossible for one who is a man to be exempt from these. But God, to whom we ought always to pray, inspires us with courage to endure."

[198] Delighted with the man's reply, the king said that all their answers had been good. "I will put a question to one other," he added, "and then I will stop for the present: that we may turn our attention [199] to the enjoyment of the feast and spend a pleasant time." Thereupon he asked the man, "What is the true aim of courage?" And he answered, "If a right plan is carried out in the hour of danger in accordance with the original intention. For all things are accomplished by God to your advantage, O king, since your purpose is good."

[200] When all had signified by their applause their agreement with the answer, the king said to the philosophers (for not a few of them were present), "It is my opinion that these men excel in virtue and possess extraordinary knowledge, since on the spur of the moment they have given fitting answers to these questions which I have put to them, and have all made God the starting point of their words."

[201] And Menedemus, the philosopher of Eretria, said, "True, O king—for since the universe is managed by providence and since we rightly perceive that man is the creation of God, it follows [202] that all power and beauty of speech proceed from God." When the king had nodded his assent to this sentiment, the speaking ceased and they proceeded to enjoy themselves. When evening came on, the banquet ended.

[203] On the following day they sat down to table again and continued the banquet according to the same arrangements. When the king thought that a fitting opportunity had arrived to put inquiries to his guests, he proceeded to ask further questions of the men who sat next in order to those who [204] had given answers

on the previous day. He began to open the conversation with the eleventh man, for there were ten who had been asked questions on the former occasion. When silence was [205] established, he asked how he could continue to be rich. After a brief reflection, the man who had been asked the question replied, "If he did nothing unworthy of his position, never acted licentiously, never lavished expense on empty and vain pursuits, but by acts of benevolence made all his subjects well disposed toward himself. For it is God who is the author of all good things and [206] him humankind certainly must obey." The king bestowed praise upon him and then asked another how he could maintain the truth. In reply to the question he said, "By recognizing that a lie brings great disgrace upon all men, and more especially upon kings. For since they have the power to do whatever they wish, why should they resort to lies? In addition to this you must always remember, O king, that God is a lover of the truth."

[207] The king received the answer with great delight and looking at another asked, "What is the teaching of wisdom?" And the other replied, "As you wish that no evil should befall you, but to be a partaker of all good things, so you should act on the same principle toward your subjects and offenders, and you should mildly admonish the noble and good. For God draws all men to himself by his benignity."

[208] The king praised him and asked the next in order how he could be the friend of humanity. And he replied, "By observing that the human race increases and is born with much trouble and great suffering: wherefore you must not lightly punish or inflict torments upon them, since you know that the life of a human is made up of pains and penalties. For if you understood everything you would be filled with pity, for God also is full of pity."

[209] The king received the answer with approbation and inquired of the next, "What is the most essential qualification for ruling?" "To keep oneself," he answered, "free from bribery and to practice sobriety during the greater part of one's life, to honor righteousness above all things, and to make friends of people of this type. For God, too, is a lover of justice."

[210] Having signified his approval, the king asked another, "What is the true mark of piety?" And he replied, "To perceive that God constantly works in the universe and knows all things, and no one who acts unjustly and works wickedness can escape his notice. As God is the benefactor of the whole world, so you, too, must imitate him and be void of offense."

[211] The king signified his agreement and asked another, "What is the essence of kingship?" And he replied, "To rule oneself well and not to be led astray by wealth or fame to immoderate or unseemly desires, this is the true way of ruling if you reason the matter well out. For all that you really need is yours, and God is free from need and yet also gracious. Let your thoughts be such as become a man, and desire not many things but only such as are necessary for ruling."

[212] The king praised him and asked another man how his deliberations might be for the best. And he replied, "If he constantly set justice before him in everything and thought that injustice was equivalent to deprivation of life. For God always promises the highest blessings to the just."

[213] Having praised him, the king asked the next how he could be free from disturbing thoughts in his sleep. And he replied, "You have asked me a question which is very difficult to answer, for we cannot bring our true selves into play

during the hours of sleep, but are held fast in these [214] by imaginations that cannot be controlled by reason. For our souls possess the feeling that they actually see the things that enter into our consciousness during sleep. But we make a mistake if we suppose that we are actually sailing on the sea in boats or flying through the air or traveling to other regions or anything else of the kind. And yet we actually do imagine such [215] things to be taking place. So far as it is possible for me to decide, I have reached the following conclusion. You must in every possible way, O king, govern your words and actions by the rule of piety that you may have the consciousness that you are maintaining virtue and that you never choose to gratify yourself at the expense of reason and never by abusing your power do [216] despite to righteousness. For the mind mostly busies itself in sleep with the same things with which it occupies itself when awake. And he who has all his thoughts and actions set toward the noblest ends establishes himself in righteousness both when he is awake and when he is asleep. Wherefore you must be steadfast in the constant discipline of self."

[217] The king bestowed praise on the man and said to another, "Since you are the tenth to answer, when you have spoken, we will devote ourselves to the banquet." And then he put the question, [218] "How can I avoid doing anything unworthy of myself?" And he replied, "Look always to your own fame and your own supreme position, that you may speak and think only such things as are [219] consistent therewith, knowing that all your subjects think and talk about you. For you must not appear to be worse than the actors, who study carefully the role, which it is necessary for them to play, and shape all their actions in accordance with it. You are not acting a part, but are really a king, since God has bestowed upon you a royal authority in keeping with your character."

[220] When the king had applauded loud and long in the most gracious way, the guests were urged to seek repose. So when the conversation ceased, they devoted themselves to the next course of the feast.

[221] On the following day, the same arrangement was observed, and when the king found an opportunity of putting questions to the men, he questioned the first of those who had been left over [222] for the next interrogation, "What is the highest form of government?" And he replied, "To rule oneself and not to be carried away by impulses. For all men possess a certain natural bent of mind. [223] It is probable that most men have an inclination toward food and drink and pleasure, and kings a bent toward the acquisition of territory and great renown. But it is good that there should be moderation in all things. What God gives, that you must take and keep, but never yearn for things that are beyond your reach."

[224] Pleased with these words, the king asked the next how he could be free from envy. And he after a brief pause replied, "If you consider first of all that it is God who bestows on all kings glory and great wealth and no one is king by his own power. All people wish to share this glory but cannot, since it is the gift of God."

[225] The king praised the man in a long speech and then asked another how he could despise his enemies. And he replied, "If you show kindness to all people and win their friendship, you need fear no one. To be popular with all people is the best of good gifts to receive from God."

[226] Having praised this answer the king ordered the next man to reply to the question how he could maintain his great renown. And he replied, "If you are

generous and large-hearted in bestowing kindness and acts of grace upon others, you will never lose your renown, but if you wish the aforesaid graces to continue to be yours, you must call upon God continually."

²²⁷ The king expressed his approval and asked the next to whom ought a man to show liberality. And he replied, "All men acknowledge that we ought to show liberality to those who are well disposed toward us, but I think that we ought to show the same keen spirit of generosity to those who are opposed to us that by this means we may win them over to the right and to what is advantageous to ourselves. But we must pray to God that this may be accomplished, for he rules the minds of all men."

²²⁸ Having expressed his agreement with the answer, the king asked the sixth to reply to the question to whom ought we to exhibit gratitude. And he replied, "To our parents continually, for God has given us a most important commandment with regard to the honor due to parents. In the next place he reckons the attitude of friend toward friend for he speaks of 'a friend that is as your own soul.' You do well in trying to bring all men into friendship with yourself."

²²⁹ The king spoke kindly to him and then asked the next, "What is it that resembles beauty in value?" And he said, "Piety, for it is the preeminent form of beauty, and its power lies in love, which is the gift of God. This you have already acquired and with it all the blessings of life."

²³⁰ The king in the most gracious way applauded the answer and asked another how, if he were to fail, he could regain his reputation again in the same degree. And he said, "It is not possible for you to fail, for you have sown in all people the seeds of gratitude which produce a harvest of goodwill, ²³¹ and this is mightier than the strongest weapons and guarantees the greatest security. But if any man does fail, he must never again do those things that caused his failure, but he must form friendships and act justly. For it is the gift of God to be able to do good actions and not the contrary."

²³² Delighted with these words, the king asked another how he could be free from grief. And he replied, "If he never injured any one, but did good to everybody and followed the pathway of ²³³ righteousness, for its fruits bring freedom from grief. But we must pray to God that unexpected evils such as death or disease or pain or anything of this kind may not come upon us and injure us. But since you are devoted to piety, no such misfortune will ever come upon you."

²³⁴ The king bestowed great praise upon him and asked the tenth, "What is the highest form of glory?" And he said, "To honor God, and this is done not with gifts and sacrifices but with purity of soul and holy conviction, since all things are fashioned and governed by God in accordance with his will. Of this purpose you are in constant possession as all can see from your achievements in the past and in the present."

²³⁵ With a loud voice the king greeted them all and spoke kindly to them, and all those who were present expressed their approval, especially the philosophers. For they were far superior to them [the philosophers] both in conduct and in argument, since they always made God their starting point. After this the king to show his good feeling proceeded to drink to the health of his guests.

²³⁶ On the following day the same arrangements were made for the banquet, and the king, as soon as an opportunity occurred, began to put questions to

the men who sat next to those who had already responded, and he asked the first, "Is wisdom capable of being taught?" And he said, "The soul is so constituted that it is able by the divine power to receive all the good and reject the contrary."

237 The king expressed approval and asked the next man, "What is it that is most beneficial to health?" And he said, "Temperance, and it is not possible to acquire this unless God create a disposition toward it."

238 The king spoke kindly to the man and asked another, "How can a man worthily pay the debt of gratitude to his parents?" And he said, "By never causing them pain, and this is not possible unless God dispose the mind to the pursuit of the noblest ends."

239 The king expressed agreement and asked the next how he could become an eager listener. And he said, "By remembering that all knowledge is useful, because it enables you by the help of God in a time of emergency to select some of the things which you have learned and apply them to the crisis which confronts you. And so the efforts of human beings are fulfilled by the assistance of God."

240 The king praised him and asked the next how he could avoid doing anything contrary to law. And he said, "If you recognize that it is God who has put the thoughts into the hearts of the lawgivers that the lives of men might be preserved, you will follow them."

241 The king acknowledged the man's answer and asked another, "What is the advantage of kinship?" And he replied, "If we consider that we ourselves are afflicted by the misfortunes that fall upon our relatives and if their sufferings become our own, then the strength of kinship is 242 apparent at once, for it is only when such feeling is shown that we will win honor and esteem in their eyes. For help, when it is linked with kindliness, is of itself a bond that is altogether indissoluble. And in the day of their prosperity we must not crave their possessions, but must pray God to bestow all manner of good upon them."

243 And having accorded to him the same praise as to the rest, the king asked another how he could attain freedom from fear. And he said, "When the mind is conscious that it has wrought no evil, and when God directs it to all noble counsels."

244 The king expressed his approval and asked another how he could always maintain a right judgment. And he replied, "If he constantly set before his eyes the misfortunes that befall men and recognized that it is God who takes away prosperity from some and brings others to great honor and glory."

245 The king gave a kindly reception to the man and asked the next to answer the question of how he could avoid a life of ease and pleasure. And he replied, "If he continually remembered that he was the ruler of a great empire and the lord of vast multitudes, and that his mind ought not to be occupied with other things, but he ought always to be considering how he could best promote their welfare. He must pray, too, to God that no duty might be neglected."

246 Having bestowed praise upon him, the king asked the tenth how he could recognize those who were dealing treacherously with him. And he replied to the question, "If he observed whether the bearing of those about him was natural and whether they maintained the proper rule of precedence at receptions and councils, and in their general intercourse, never going beyond the bounds of

²⁴⁷ propriety in congratulations or in other matters of deportment. But God will incline your mind, O king, to all that is noble." When the king had expressed his loud approval and praised them all individually (amid the plaudits of all who were present), they turned to the enjoyment of the feast.

²⁴⁸ And on the next day, when the opportunity offered, the king asked the next man, "What is the grossest form of neglect?" And he replied, "If one does not care for his children and devote every effort to their education. For we always pray to God not so much for ourselves as for our children that every blessing may be theirs. Our desire that our children may possess self-control is only realized by the power of God."

²⁴⁹ The king said that he had spoken well and then asked another how he could be patriotic. "By keeping before your mind," he replied, "the thought that it is good to live and die in one's own country. Residence abroad brings contempt upon the poor and shame upon the rich as though they had been banished for a crime. If you bestow benefits upon all, as you continually do, God will give you favor with all and you will be accounted patriotic."

²⁵⁰ After listening to this man, the king asked the next in order how he could live amicably with his wife. And he answered, "By recognizing that womankind are by nature headstrong and energetic in the pursuit of their own desires, and subject to sudden changes of opinion through fallacious reasoning, and that their nature is essentially weak. It is necessary to deal wisely with them ²⁵¹ and not to provoke strife. For the successful conduct of life the steersman must know the goal toward which he ought to direct his course. It is only by calling upon the help of God that men can steer a true course of life at all times."

²⁵² The king expressed his agreement and asked the next how he could be free from error. And he replied, "If you always act with deliberation and never give credence to slanders, but prove for yourself the things that are said to you and decide by your own judgment the requests which are made to you and carry out everything in the light of your judgment, you will be free from error, O king. But the knowledge and practice of these things is the work of the divine power."

²⁵³ Delighted with these words, the king asked another how he could be free from wrath. And he said in reply to the question, "If he recognized that he had power over all even to inflict death upon them, if he gave way to wrath, and that it would be useless and pitiful if he, just because he was lord, ²⁵⁴ deprived many of life. What need was there for wrath, when all were in subjection and no one was hostile to him? It is necessary to recognize that God rules the whole world in the spirit of kindness and without wrath at all, and you," said he, "O king, must of necessity copy his example."

²⁵⁵ The king said that he had answered well and then inquired of the next man, "What is good counsel?" "To act well at all times and with due reflection," he explained, "comparing what is advantageous to our own policy with the injurious effects that would result from the adoption of the opposite view, in order that by weighing every point we may be well advised and our purpose may be accomplished. And most important of all, by the power of God every plan of yours will find fulfillment because you practice piety."

²⁵⁶ The king said that this man had answered well, and asked another, "What is philosophy?" And he explained, "To deliberate well in reference to any question

that emerges and never to be carried away by impulses, but to ponder over the injuries that result from the passions, and to act rightly as the circumstances demand, practicing moderation. But we must pray to God to instill into our mind a regard for these things."

257 The king signified his consent and asked another how he could meet with recognition when traveling abroad. "By being fair to all men," he replied, "and by appearing to be inferior rather than superior to those among whom he was traveling. For it is a recognized principle that God by his very nature accepts the humble. And the human race loves those who are willing to be in subjection to them."

258 Having expressed his approval at this reply, the king asked another how he could build in such a way that his structures would endure after him. And he replied to the question, "If his creations were on a great and noble scale, so that the beholders would spare them for their beauty, and if he never dismissed any of those who wrought such works and never compelled others to minister to his 259 needs without wages. For observing how God provides for the human race, granting them health and mental capacity and all other gifts, he himself should follow his example by rendering to all a recompense for their arduous toil. For it is the deeds that are wrought in righteousness that abide continually."

260 The king said that this man, too, had answered well and asked the tenth, "What is the fruit of wisdom?" And he replied, "That one should be conscious in himself that he has wrought no evil 261 and that he should live his life in the truth, since it is from these, O mighty king, that the greatest joy and steadfastness of soul and strong faith in God accrue to you if you rule your realm in piety." And when they heard the answer they all shouted with loud acclaim, and afterward the king in the fullness of his joy began to drink to their health.

262 And on the next day the banquet followed the same course as on previous occasions, and when the opportunity presented itself the king proceeded to put questions to the remaining guests, and 263 he said to the first, "How can a man keep himself from pride?" And he replied, "If he maintains equality and remembers on all occasions that he is a man ruling over men. And God brings the proud to nothing and exalts the meek and humble."

264 The king spoke kindly to him and asked the next, "Whom ought a man to select as his counselors?" And he replied, "Those who have been tested in many affairs and maintain unmingled goodwill toward him and partake of his own disposition. And God manifests himself to those who are worthy that these ends may be attained."

265 The king praised him and asked another, "What is the most necessary possession for a king?" "The friendship and love of his subjects," he replied, "for it is through this that the bond of goodwill is rendered indissoluble. And it is God who ensures that this may come to pass in accordance with your wish."

266 The king praised him and inquired of another, "What is the goal of speech?" And he replied, "To convince your opponent by showing him his mistakes in a well-ordered array of arguments. For in this way you will win your hearer, not by opposing him, but by bestowing praise upon him with a view to persuading him. And it is by the power of God that persuasion is accomplished."

267 The king said that he had given a good answer, and asked another how he

could live amicably with the many different races who formed the population of his kingdom. "By acting the proper part toward each," he replied, "and taking righteousness as your guide, as you are now doing with the help of the insight which God bestows upon you."

268 The king was delighted by this reply, and asked another, "Under what circumstances ought a man to suffer grief?" "In the misfortunes that befall our friends," he replied, "when we see that they are protracted and irremediable. Reason does not allow us to grieve for those who are dead and set free from evil, but all grieve over them because they think only of themselves and their own advantage. It is by the power of God alone that we can escape all evil."

269 The king said that he had given a fitting answer and asked another how reputation is lost. And he replied, "When pride and unbounded self-confidence hold sway, dishonor and loss of reputation are engendered. For God is the Lord of all reputation and bestows it where he will."

270 The king gave his confirmation to the answer, and asked the next man, "To whom ought men to entrust themselves?" "To those," he replied, "who serve you from goodwill and not from fear or self-interest, thinking only of their own gain. For the one is the sign of love, the other the mark of ill will and time serving. For the one who is always watching for his own gain is a traitor at heart. But you possess the affection of all your subjects by the help of the good counsel which God bestows upon you."

271 The king said that he had answered wisely, and asked another, "What is it that keeps a kingdom safe?" And he replied to the question, "Care and forethought that no evil may be wrought by those who are placed in a position of authority over the people, and this you always do by the help of God who inspires you with grave judgment."

272 The king spoke words of encouragement to him, and asked another, "What is it that maintains gratitude and honor?" And he replied, "Virtue, for it is the creator of good deeds, and by it evil is destroyed, even as you exhibit nobility of character toward all by the gift which God bestows upon you."

273 The king graciously acknowledged the answer and asked the eleventh (since there were two more than seventy) how he could in time of war maintain tranquility of soul. And he replied, "By remembering that he had done no evil to any of his subjects, and that all would fight for him in return for the benefits which they had received, knowing that even if they lose their lives, you will care for those 274 dependent on them. For you never fail to make reparation to any—such is the kindheartedness with which God has inspired you." The king loudly applauded them all and spoke very kindly to them and then drank a long draught to the health of each, giving himself up to enjoyment, and lavishing the most generous and joyous friendship upon his guests.

275 On the seventh day much more extensive preparations were made, and many others were present from the different cities (among them a large number of ambassadors). When an opportunity occurred, the king asked the first of those who had not yet been questioned how he could avoid 276 being deceived by fallacious reasoning. And he replied, "By noticing carefully the speaker, the thing spoken, and the subject under discussion, and by putting the same questions again after an interval in different forms. But to possess an alert mind and to be

able to form a sound judgment in every case is one of the good gifts of God, and you possess it, O king."

277 The king loudly applauded the answer and asked another, "Why is it that the majority of people never become virtuous?" "Because," he replied, "all are by nature intemperate and inclined to 278 pleasure. Hence, injustice springs up and a flood of avarice. The habit of virtue is a hindrance to those who are devoted to a life of pleasure because it enjoins upon them the preference of temperance and righteousness. For it is God who is the master of these things."

279 The king said that he had answered well, and asked, "What ought kings to obey?" And he said, "The laws, in order that by righteous enactments they may restore the lives of men. Even as you by such conduct in obedience to the divine command have laid up in store for yourself a perpetual memorial."

280 The king said that this man, too, had spoken well, and asked the next, "Whom ought we to appoint as governors?" And he replied, "All who hate wickedness, and imitating your own conduct act righteously that they may maintain a good reputation constantly. For this is what you do, O mighty king," he said, "and it is God who has bestowed upon you the crown of righteousness."

281 The king loudly acclaimed the answer and then looking at the next man said, "Whom ought we to appoint as officers over the forces?" And he explained, "Those who excel in courage and righteousness and those who are more anxious about the safety of their men than to gain a victory by risking their lives through rashness. For as God acts well toward all, so too you in imitation of him are the benefactor of all your subjects."

282 The king said that he had given a good answer and asked another, "What man is worthy of admiration?" And he replied, "The man who is furnished with reputation and wealth and power and possesses a soul equal to it all. You yourself show by your actions that you are most worthy of admiration through the help of God who makes you care for these things."

283 The king expressed his approval and said to another, "To what affairs ought kings to devote most time?" And he replied, "To reading and the study of the records of official journeys, which are written in reference to the various kingdoms, with a view to the reformation and preservation of the subjects. And it is by such activity that you have attained to a glory which has never been approached by others, through the help of God who fulfills all your desires."

284 The king spoke enthusiastically to the man and asked another how ought a man to occupy himself during his hours of relaxation and recreation. And he replied, "To watch those plays which can be acted with propriety and to set before one's eyes scenes taken from life and enacted 285 with dignity and decency is profitable and appropriate. For there is some edification to be found even in these amusements, for often some desirable lesson is taught by the most insignificant affairs of life. But by practicing the utmost propriety in all your actions, you have shown that you are a philosopher and you are honored by God on account of your virtue."

286 The king, pleased with the words that had just been spoken, said to the ninth man, "How ought a man to conduct himself at banquets?" And he replied, "You should summon to your side men of learning and those who are able to give you useful hints with regard to the affairs of your kingdom and the lives of your

subjects (for you could not find any theme more suitable or more [287] educative than this) since such men are dear to God because they have trained their minds to contemplate the noblest themes—as you indeed are doing yourself—since all your actions are directed by God."

[288] Delighted with the reply, the king inquired of the next man, "What is best for the people, that a private citizen should be made king over them or a member of the royal family?" And he [289] replied, "He who is best by nature. For kings who come of royal lineage are often harsh and severe toward their subjects. And still more is this the case with some of those who have risen from the ranks of private citizens, who after having experienced evil and borne their share of [290] poverty when they rule over multitudes turn out to be crueler than the godless tyrants. But, as I have said, a good nature which has been properly trained is capable of ruling, and you are a great king, not so much because you excel in the glory of your rule and your wealth but rather because you have surpassed all in clemency and philanthropy, thanks to God who has endowed you with these qualities."

[291] The king spent some time in praising this man and then asked the last of all, "What is the greatest achievement in ruling an empire?" And he replied, "That the subjects should continually dwell in a state of peace, and that justice should be speedily administered in cases of dispute. [292] These results are achieved through the influence of the ruler, when he is a man who hates evil and loves the good and devotes his energies to saving the lives of human beings, just as you consider injustice the worst form of evil and by your just administration have fashioned for yourself an undying reputation, since God bestows upon you a mind which is pure and untainted by any evil."

[293] And when he ceased, loud and joyful applause broke out for some considerable time. When it stopped the king took a cup and gave a toast in honor of all his guests and the words that they had uttered. Then in conclusion he said, "I have derived the greatest benefit from your presence. [294] I have profited much by the wise teaching which you have given me in reference to the art of ruling." Then he ordered that three talents of silver should be presented to each of them, and appointed one of his slaves to deliver over the money. All at once shouted their approval, and the banquet became a scene of joy, while the king gave himself up to a continuous round of festivity.

[295] I have written at length and must crave your pardon, Philocrates. I was astonished beyond measure at the men and the way in which on the spur of the moment they gave answers that [296] really needed a long time to devise. For though the questioner had given great thought to each particular question, those who replied one after the other had their answers to the questions ready at once and so they seemed to me and to all who were present and especially to the philosophers to be worthy of admiration. And I suppose that the thing will seem incredible to those who will [297] read my narrative in the future. But it is unseemly to misrepresent facts which are recorded in the public archives. And it would not be right for me to transgress in such a matter as this. I tell the story just as it happened, conscientiously avoiding any error. I was so impressed by the force of their utterances, that I made an effort to consult those whose business it was to make [298] a record of all that happened at the royal audiences and banquets. For it is the custom, as you know, from the moment the king begins to transact business

until the time when he retires to rest, for a record to be taken of all his sayings and doings—a most excellent and useful arrangement. [299] For on the following day the minutes of the doings and sayings of the previous day are read over before business commences, and if there has been any irregularity, the matter is at once set right. [300] I obtained therefore, as has been said, accurate information from the public records, and I have set forth the facts in proper order since I know how eager you are to obtain useful information.

[301] Three days later Demetrius took the men and passing along the seawall, seven stadia long, to the island, crossed the bridge, and made for the northern districts of Pharos. There he assembled them in a house, which had been built upon the seashore, of great beauty and in a secluded situation, and invited them to carry out the work of translation, since everything that they needed for the purpose [302] was placed at their disposal. So they set to work comparing their several results and making them agree, and whatever they agreed upon was suitably copied out under the direction of Demetrius. [303] And the session lasted until the ninth hour; after this they were set free to minister to their physical [304] needs. Everything they wanted was furnished for them on a lavish scale. In addition to this Dorotheus made the same preparations for them daily as were made for the king himself—for thus he had been commanded by the king. In the early morning they appeared daily at the court, and [305] after saluting the king went back to their own place. And as is the custom of all the Jews, they washed their hands in the sea and prayed to God and then devoted themselves to reading and [306] translating the particular passage upon which they were engaged, and I put the question to them, "Why it was that they washed their hands before they prayed?" And they explained that it was a token that they had done no evil (for every form of activity is wrought by means of the hands) since in their noble and holy way they regard everything as a symbol of righteousness and truth.

[307] As I have already said, they met together daily in the place that was delightful for its quiet and its brightness and applied themselves to their task. And it so chanced that the work of translation was completed in seventy-two days, just as if this had been arranged of set purpose.

[308] When the work was completed, Demetrius collected together the Jewish population in the place where the translation had been made, and read it over to all, in the presence of the translators, who met with a great reception also from the people, because of the great benefits which they had [309] conferred upon them. They bestowed warm praise upon Demetrius, too, and urged him to have the whole law transcribed and present a copy to their leaders. [310] After the books had been read, the priests and the elders of the translators and the Jewish community and the leaders of the people stood up and said, that since so excellent and sacred and accurate a translation had been made, it was only right that it should remain as it was and no [311] alteration should be made in it. And when the whole company expressed their approval, they bade them pronounce a curse in accordance with their custom upon anyone who should make any alteration either by adding anything or changing in any way whatever any of the words that had been written or making any omission. This was a very wise precaution to ensure that the book might be preserved for all the future time unchanged. [312] When the matter was reported to the king, he rejoiced greatly, for he felt that the design that he had

formed had been safely carried out. The whole book was read over to him and he was greatly astonished at the spirit of the lawgiver. And he said to Demetrius, "How is it that none of the historians or the poets have ever thought it worth their while to allude to such a wonderful [313] achievement?" And he replied, "Because the law is sacred and of divine origin. And some of those who formed the intention of dealing with it have been smitten by God and therefore desisted from [314] their purpose." He said that he had heard from Theopompus that he had been driven out of his mind for more than thirty days because he intended to insert in his history some of the incidents from the earlier and somewhat unreliable translations of the law. When he had recovered [315] a little, he besought God to make it clear to him why the misfortune had befallen him. And it was revealed to him in a dream, that from idle curiosity he was wishing to communicate sacred truths to common humanity, and that if he desisted he would recover his health. I have heard, too, from the lips [316] of Theodektes, one of the tragic poets, that when he was about to adapt some of the incidents recorded in the book for one of his plays, he was affected with cataract in both his eyes. And when he perceived the reason why the misfortune had befallen him, he prayed to God for many days and was afterward restored. [317] And after the king, as I have already said, had received the explanation of Demetrius on this point, he did homage and ordered that great care should be taken of the books, and that they should [318] be sacredly guarded. And he urged the translators to visit him frequently after their return to Judea, for it was only right, he said, that he should now send them home. But when they came back, he [319] would treat them as friends, as was right, and they would receive rich presents from him. He ordered preparations to be made for them to return home, and treated them most munificently. He presented each one of them with three robes of the finest sort, two talents of gold, a sideboard weighing one talent, all the furniture for three couches. [320] And with the escort he sent Eleazar ten couches with silver legs and all the necessary equipment, a sideboard worth thirty talents, ten robes, purple, and a magnificent crown, and a hundred pieces of the finest woven linen, also bowls and dishes, and two golden beakers to be dedicated to God. [321] He urged him also in a letter that if any of the men preferred to come back to him, not to hinder them. For he counted it a great privilege to enjoy the society of such learned men, and he would rather lavish his wealth upon them than upon vanities. [322] And now Philocrates, you have the complete story in accordance with my promise. I think that you find greater pleasure in these matters than in the writings of the mythologists, for you are devoted to the study of those things that can benefit the soul and spend much time upon it. I will attempt to narrate whatever other events are worth recording, that by perusing them you may secure the highest reward for your zeal.

Joseph and Aseneth

Joseph and Aseneth is a **Hellenistic** romance that recounts the conversion of the Egyptian woman Aseneth to the God of Israel, her marriage to the patriarch Joseph, and the social and religious conflicts surrounding that conversion and marriage. Genesis 41:45,[1] 41:50–52,[2] and 46:20[3] provide the biblical point of departure for this fictional tale by referring in passing to Joseph's marriage to Asenath (LXX Aseneth), daughter of the Egyptian priest Potiphera (LXX Pentephres). As a Jewish (some think Jewish-Christian) writing from the Greco-Roman period, the work is now often included in the Old Testament pseudepigrapha (*see* Overview of Early Jewish Literature) and is recognized to be important for the study of early Judaism and Christian origins.

Narrative Description

The story falls into two distinct parts. The first (chaps. 1–21) begins with Aseneth, the beautiful virgin daughter of Pentephres, priest of Heliopolis and chief of Pharaoh's noblemen, secluded in luxurious penthouse quarters to avoid all suitors. Joseph, who is touring Egypt to gather grain, announces plans to dine in Pentephres's house. Aseneth arrogantly refuses her father's suggestion that she be given to Joseph in marriage, but when Joseph arrives she is awestruck by his beauty and falls madly in love with him. However, as "a man who worships God," Joseph will have nothing to do with a strange woman polluted by idolatry. After praying for Aseneth's conversion, Joseph departs, promising to return in a week. In the

---

1. Gen. 41:45: "Pharaoh gave Joseph the name Zaphenath-paneah; and he gave him Asenath daughter of Potiphera, priest of On, as his wife. Thus Joseph gained authority over the land of Egypt."

2. Gen. 41:50–52: "Before the years of famine came, Joseph had two sons, whom Asenath daughter of Potiphera, priest of On, bore to him. Joseph named the firstborn Manasseh, 'For,' he said, 'God has made me forget all my hardship and all my father's house.' The second he named Ephraim, 'For God has made me fruitful in the land of my misfortunes.'"

3. Gen. 46:20: "To Joseph in the land of Egypt were born Manasseh and Ephraim, whom Asenath daughter of Potiphera, priest of On, bore to him."

meantime, Aseneth retires to her penthouse, goes into mourning, and utterly repudiates her idols. Following soliloquies in which she expresses reluctance to address the God from whom she is alienated by reason of her idol worship, her defilement from food tainted by idolatry, and her blasphemy against God's son Joseph, Aseneth musters courage and prays a lengthy prayer of confession and repentance in which she turns to God for mercy and refuge. She is then visited by a "man from heaven" who provides heavenly acknowledgment of her conversion and describes the blessings that accrue to her. Foremost among these are life and immortality, in which she participates symbolically by eating from a mysterious honeycomb that is said to be the same immortal food as that eaten by the angels in paradise. The heavenly visitor also announces that Aseneth will be Joseph's bride and changes her name to "City of Refuge," making her the prototypical proselyte. When Joseph returns and learns that she has renounced idolatry, he embraces and kisses the gloriously transformed Aseneth. The couple marries amid elaborate festivities, and from their union Manasseh and Ephraim are born.[4]

In the second part of the double novella (chaps. 22–29), Pharaoh's son becomes jealous of the couple and enlists the aid of some of Joseph's brothers (the sons of the handmaids Bilhah and Zilpah) to murder Joseph and abduct Aseneth. The plot fails because of timely divine intervention and support for the couple by some of Joseph's other brothers (especially Simeon, Levi, and Benjamin). Pharaoh's son is mortally wounded during the conflict, and when the grief-stricken Pharaoh also dies, Joseph becomes king of Egypt.

Author/Provenance

Despite a recent revival of the old view that Joseph and Aseneth is a Christian composition,[5] authorship by a non-Christian Jew best accounts for all the data.[6] The very problem in the biblical text for which the story of Aseneth's conversion offers a solution—the patriarch's marriage to an Egyptian woman—is a problem to the Jewish conscience. The ethnic particularism in Aseneth's physical profile in 1:5 ("And she bore no resemblance to the virgins of the Egyptians but was in every respect like the daughters of the Hebrews. And she was tall like Sarah and lovely like Rebecca and beautiful like Rachel") is possible in a Christian work but more likely in a Jewish one. The same is true of 8:5–7, where the separation between the leading characters is couched in both religious and ethnic terms: intimacy between a worshiper of God and anyone defiled by eating idol-tainted food, or

---

4. The names of the two sons of Joseph and Aseneth derive from the biblical narrative (Gen. 41:50–52). According to Gen. 48:5, Jacob blessed these two grandsons and elevated them to equal status with his own sons. Manasseh and Ephraim thus became eponymous ancestors of two of the tribes of Israel, and the "house of Joseph" received a double portion in the territorial division. In time the tribe of Ephraim gained such importance that its name became synonymous with that of the northern kingdom of Israel.

5. See especially Ross Kraemer, *When Aseneth Met Joseph: A Late Antique Tale of the Biblical Patriarch and His Egyptian Wife, Reconsidered* (New York: Oxford University Press, 1998).

6. John Collins, "Joseph and Aseneth: Jewish or Christian?" *JSP* 14 (2005): 97–112.

anyone outside the tribe and kindred, is taboo. Aseneth converts to the "Lord God of Joseph" (6:6), the "Lord God of my [Joseph's] father Israel" (8:9), the "Lord, the Most High God of the mighty Joseph" (11:7), and the "God of the Hebrews" (11:10), and the author is as concerned with her incorporation into the family of Jacob as with her acceptance by God (22:3–10). All of this suggests Jewish rather than Christian authorship. The designation of Joseph as the "son of God" and the absence of any hint of baptism in a story of conversion likewise weigh against Christian authorship. Certainly there is nothing distinctively Christian in the work. The affinities with Late Antique Christian sources that have been noted are all very general; the closer linguistic and thematic affinities are with the writings of **Diaspora** Jews in the Hellenistic era.

The work is of unknown provenance but makes most sense if composed in Egypt. The persistent vilifying of Egyptian idolatry and its polluting effect gives the impression that the Egyptian setting of the story reflects not merely the biblical framework but also the milieu in which the author and his community actually lived. In addition, Egyptian elements are discernible in various individual motifs, such as the depiction of Joseph in terms reminiscent of the solar deity Re and the portrayal of Aseneth in terms that evoke the image of the Egyptian goddess Neith. Nevertheless, the provenance remains uncertain; Syria and other locations have also been proposed as possibilities.

Date/Occasion

The date of the work is also uncertain. Dependence on the Septuagint (*see* Overview of Early Jewish Literature) means that it cannot have been composed prior to ca. 100 BCE. A work in which Gentile conversion to Judaism is a realistic possibility must have been composed before **Hadrian's** measures against Judaism in 132–135 CE. If an Egyptian provenance is assumed, Joseph and Aseneth must have been written before the great Jewish revolt under **Trajan** in 115–117 CE that resulted in the decimation of Egyptian Jewry. A more specific date within these broad limits is difficult to determine, but the conciliatory attitude toward Gentiles fits better before than after 70 CE, and in Egypt such an outlook fits better before than after the pogrom against Alexandrian Jews in 38 CE. The absence of any allusion to the Romans and the depiction of Egypt as an independent country with rulers favorably disposed toward Jews may reflect the **Ptolemaic** period in Egypt before the Roman takeover in 30 BCE, but this is by no means certain. Lexical considerations and the relationship between this work and other Greek romances are likewise inconclusive as criteria for dating. The alleged affinities with Late Antique Christian sources that lead some to date the work to the third or fourth century CE,[7] as has been noted above, are very general and afford no basis for such a late dating of the work. In sum, while a precise date cannot be determined, composition sometime within a century or so on either side of the turn of the eras seems probable.[8]

---

7. Kraemer, *When Aseneth Met Joseph*, pp. 225–44.

8. See the summaries of the evidence in Randall Chesnutt, *From Death to Life: Conversion*

Text, Language, Sources, and Transmission

Joseph and Aseneth was almost certainly composed in Greek. Semitisms abound, but no more than in other products of Greek-speaking Hellenistic Judaism. Frequently used words that have no Semitic equivalents (such as *athanasia*, "immortality," and *aphtharsia*, "incorruption") argue decidedly for a Greek original.

The text is extant in sixteen Greek manuscripts and numerous versional witnesses in Syriac, Armenian, Latin, Slavonic, and Ethiopic. Of the two principal forms of the story, one about two-thirds as long as the other, the longer version lies closer to the original according to the careful work of the leading textual expert,[9] although a number of modern studies have been based on the short recension, in part because of the lack of a critical edition of the long text until quite recently. The translation that follows is based on Burchard's 2003 critical edition of the long version.

Theology

Although other scenarios have been proposed,[10] a reasonable glimpse of the likely setting and purpose of the work emerges if we assume that the characters and tensions in the narrative reflect something of the real milieu in which Joseph and Aseneth was written. On this basis, we can infer a setting in which Jews lived in dynamic tension with Gentiles and struggled to maintain a distinctive Jewish identity, and where table fellowship and intermarriage with Gentiles, including marriage between a convert to Judaism and a born Jew, were pressing issues. According to 8:5-7, it is improper for the man whose mouth blesses the living God and partakes of life-giving food to kiss a strange woman whose mouth blesses dead and deaf idols and eats their polluted food. That the ethnic and religious dichotomy expressed here is not merely literary but a real one in the author's community is evidenced by the further interdiction against the woman who worships God kissing a strange man. Nothing in the story line calls for this additional interdiction; there is no Israelite woman in the story for whom **exogamy** is a possibility. The generalization from the specific case at hand to a related situation beyond what is represented in the narrative suggests that threats to Jewish identity from intermarriage and food defiled by idolatry dominated the author's religious and social landscape. Emphasis on the exalted status of the true convert and internecine conflicts in the second part of the narrative after

in *Joseph and Aseneth,* JSPSup 16 (Sheffield: Sheffield Academic Press, 1995), pp. 80–85; and Collins, "Joseph and Aseneth," pp. 109–12.

9. Christoph Burchard, "Zum Text von 'Joseph und Aseneth,'" *JSJ* 1 (1970): 3–34; "Joseph and Aseneth," in *The Old Testament Pseudepigrapha,* ed. James H. Charlesworth, 2 vols. (Garden City, N.Y.: Doubleday, 1983–85), 2:177–247; Randall D. Chesnutt, "The Text of *Joseph and Aseneth* Reconsidered," *JSP* 14 (2005): 83–96.

10. Gideon Bohak, *Joseph and Aseneth and the Jewish Temple in Heliopolis,* Early Judaism and Its Literature 10 (Atlanta: Scholars, 1996); and Kraemer, *When Aseneth Met Joseph.*

Joseph marries Aseneth suggest that the perception of the Gentile convert was also a point of contention.[11]

Opinion varies on the purpose of the work. Some consider it missionary propaganda designed to win Gentile converts to Judaism, while others maintain that it was written for Jewish readers to address intramural issues.[12] The assumption that readers are familiar with the patriarchal narratives and can understand other allusions to Scripture makes it likely that the author envisioned primarily Jewish readers, or at least those who already stood very close to Judaism. The repeated use of the formula "it is not proper for a man (woman) who worships God to . . ." (8:5, 7; 21:1; 23:9, 12; 29:3) and the other ways of defining conduct befitting "those who worship God" (23:10; 28:5, 7) likewise point to an intramural aim.

The exalted estimation of the convert and artful placement of her on a par with those who belong to the people of God by birth suggests that a primary purpose was to enhance the status of converts within the Jewish community. The prototypical convert is shown to be a beneficiary of all the blessings and privileges of the people of God and thus worthy to be received fully into that community and to be a suitable mate for one born into that community. God's chief angel even makes an appearance to provide heavenly endorsement of the leading character's conversion and marriage. The author also extols Israel's religion and warns against exogamy and idolatry, perhaps to show that the openness to converts is no concession to idolatry and its corrupting effect and no threat to a distinctive Jewish identity. Because Aseneth was unacceptable as a wife for Joseph until she renounced her idols, her story implies no concession to idolatry. Neither is **endogamy** compromised; Aseneth could marry a "son of God" only because she had become a "daughter of the Most High" (6:3, 5; 18:11; 21:4). Neither does full acceptance of the convert dilute the blessed status of the people of God; these blessings are in fact articulated at length, but with the emphasis that the one who converts enjoys them as fully as the one born into the people of God. Membership in the people of God according to this work is not even determined by ethnic descent but by acknowledgment of the true God and is characterized by "proper" conduct. Thus the true convert is on par with those born into the community, and the latter must engage in "proper" conduct in order to retain God's favor. "Proper" conduct entails not only avoiding contamination from idolatry but also treating those both within and without the community with magnanimity and respect in situations of conflict (8:5; 21:1; 23:9, 12; 29:3; see also 28:5, 14).

Reception of Joseph and Aseneth in the Second Temple Period

Nothing is known of the fate of Joseph and Aseneth in later Jewish tradition, but on the assumption of Jewish authorship, the work is quite important for the study of Judaism around the turn of the eras and has received considerable attention in recent years from specialists in this area. It provides a rare narrative glimpse of conversion to Judaism in the Greco-Roman period, with unparalleled insights

11. Chesnutt, *Death to Life*, pp. 97–117.
12. See the survey of views in Chesnutt, *Death to Life*, pp. 20–64, 256–65.

into the theological, social, and ritual dimensions of such a conversion. It also affords a prime example of Diaspora Jews opposed to intermarriage and determined to eat apart from idolaters and avoid impure food. Of particular interest in this connection is the use of meal language—specifically, the life-giving bread, cup, and ointment of those who worship God in contrast to the defiling food, drink, and ointment of idolaters—as consummate expressions of Jewish identity. The ethics declared appropriate and inappropriate for "those who worship God," the central role of a woman in the story, the Jewish deployment of the novelistic genre, and the understanding of God's fatherhood and other aspects of the prayers embedded in the narrative are but a few examples of what this work has to say about early Judaism.

Joseph and Aseneth was more popular in Christian tradition, where translations into several languages were generated over the centuries and where influence on literature, iconography, drama, and liturgy has been considerable. Indeed, the text was transmitted to us exclusively by Christian copyists. It is important for the New Testament and Christian origins in numerous ways: in addition to those features that make it pertinent for the study of Judaism are the eucharistic associations of the meal language, the designation of Joseph as the "son of God" as this relates to New Testament Christology, and the new creation and death-to-life images for conversion.

RANDALL D. CHESNUTT

FURTHER READING

Burchard, Christoph. "Joseph and Aseneth." In *The Old Testament Pseudepigrapha*, edited by James H. Charlesworth, 2:177–247. 2 vols. Garden City, N.Y.: Doubleday, 1983–85.

Collins, John J. *Between Athens and Jerusalem: Jewish Identity in the Hellenistic Diaspora.* 2nd ed. Grand Rapids: Eerdmans, 1999 (pp. 230–39).

———. "Joseph and Aseneth: Jewish or Christian?" *JSP* 14 (2005): 97–112.

Humphrey, Edith M. *Joseph and Aseneth.* Guides to Apocrypha and Pseudepigrapha. Sheffield: Sheffield Academic Press, 2000.

Nickelsburg, George W. E. *Jewish Literature between the Bible and the Mishnah.* 2nd ed. Minneapolis: Fortress, 2005 (pp. 332–38).

ADVANCED READING

Bohak, Gideon. *Joseph and Aseneth and the Jewish Temple in Heliopolis.* Early Judaism and Its Literature 10. Atlanta: Scholars, 1996.

Burchard, Christoph. *Gesammelte Studien zu Joseph und Aseneth.* Studia in Veteris Testamenti Pseudepigrapha 13. Leiden: Brill, 1996.

———. *Joseph und Aseneth.* Pseudepigrapha Veteris Testamenti Graece 5. Leiden: Brill, 2003.

———. "The Text of Joseph and Aseneth Reconsidered." *JSP* 14 (2005): 83–96.

———. *Untersuchungen zu Joseph und Aseneth: Überlieferung-Ortsbestimmung.* WUNT 8. Tübingen: Mohr, 1965.

———. "Zum Text von 'Joseph und Aseneth.'" *JSJ* 1 (1970): 3–34.

Chesnutt, Randall D. *From Death to Life: Conversion in Joseph and Aseneth.* JSPSup 16. Sheffield: Sheffield Academic Press, 1995.

Kraemer, Ross S. *When Aseneth Met Joseph: A Late Antique Tale of the Biblical Patriarch and His Egyptian Wife, Reconsidered.* New York: Oxford University Press, 1998.

Philonenko, Marc. *Joseph et Aséneth: Introduction, text critique, traduction et notes.* StPB 13. Leiden: Brill, 1968.

Sänger, Dieter. *Antikes Judentum und die Mysterien: Religionsgeschichtliche Untersuchungen zu Joseph und Aseneth.* WUNT 2.5. Tübingen: Mohr, 1980.

Standhartinger, Angela. *Das Frauenbild im Judentum der hellenistischen Zeit: Ein Beitrag anhand von "Joseph und Aseneth."* Arbeiten zur Geschichte des antiken Judentums und des Urchristentums 26. Leiden: Brill, 1995.

3.3 *from* Joseph and Aseneth

[1:1] And in the first year of the seven years of abundance, in the second month, on the fifth day of the month, Pharaoh sent Joseph out to tour all the land of Egypt. [2] And Joseph went in the fourth month of the first year, on the eighteenth day of the month, into the region of Heliopolis, and he was gathering the grain of that country like the sand of the sea.

[3] And there was a man in that city, a satrap of Pharaoh, who was ruler of all Pharaoh's satraps and nobles. And this man was very rich and prudent and kind, and he was Pharaoh's advisor because he was more understanding than all Pharaoh's nobles. And the man's name was Pentephres, priest of Heliopolis. [4] And he had a daughter, an eighteen-year-old virgin, who was tall and lovely and beautiful in appearance more than all the virgins in the land. [5] And she bore no resemblance to the virgins of the Egyptians but was in every respect like the daughters of the Hebrews. And she was tall like Sarah and lovely like Rebekah and beautiful like Rachel. And that virgin's name was Aseneth. [6] And the fame of her beauty spread throughout all that land and even to the far reaches of the world. And all the sons of the nobles and the satraps and all the kings—all of them young and mighty—sought to marry her, and there was great contention among them over Aseneth, and they tried to fight with each other over her.

[7] And Pharaoh's firstborn son heard about her and pled with his father to give her to him as a wife. And his firstborn son said to Pharaoh, "Father, give me Aseneth, the daughter of Pentephres, priest of Heliopolis, for a wife." [8] And his father Pharaoh said, "Why do you seek a wife who is inferior to you, when you are king of all the land of Egypt? [9] Behold, is not the daughter of Joakim, king of Moab, pledged to you, and is she not a queen and very beautiful? Take her as your wife."

[2:1] And Aseneth disdained and scorned all men, and she was haughty and arrogant toward everyone. And no man had ever seen her because Pentephres had a very large and high tower adjoining his house, and at the top of that tower was an upper story that had ten rooms. [2] And the first room was large and magnificent, covered with purple stones, and its walls were faced with colorful precious stones. And the ceiling of that room was of gold. [3] And within that room the countless gold and silver gods of the Egyptians were fastened to the walls. And Aseneth worshiped all of them and feared them and offered sacrifices to them daily. [4] And the second room contained Aseneth's adornments and chests, and in it was much gold and silver and clothing interwoven with gold and choice costly stones and fine linens and the adornments of her virginity. [5] And the third room was Aseneth's storeroom, and in it were all the good things of the land. [6] And seven virgins had the remaining seven rooms, each occupying one room. And these attended Aseneth, and they were all the same age, born on the same night as Aseneth, and she loved them very much. And they were very beautiful

---

Translation by Randall D. Chesnutt.

like the stars of heaven, and no man had ever had contact with them, not even a male child.

[*7–12 Next are described the windows in Aseneth's room, her luxurious bed where her virginity was strictly maintained, and the beautiful courtyard that surrounded the house.*]

3:1 And in the first year of the seven years of abundance, in the fourth month, on the eighteenth day of the month, Joseph came into the region of Heliopolis and was gathering the abundant grain of that country. 2 And as he drew near to that city Joseph sent ahead of him twelve men to Pentephres the priest, saying, "I will stay with you because it is midday and time to eat, and the sun's heat is burning, and I will cool off in the shade of your house." 3 And Pentephres heard this and rejoiced greatly and said, "Blessed is the Lord God of Joseph because my lord Joseph considered me worthy to come to us." 4 And Pentephres called the man who was over his household and said to him, "Hurry and get my house ready and prepare a great dinner, for Joseph, the mighty one of God, is coming to us today."

5 And Aseneth heard that her father and mother had arrived from the field of their inheritance and she rejoiced and said, "I will go and see my father and mother, for they have arrived from the field of our inheritance." For it was the harvest season. 6 And Aseneth hurried into her room where her robes lay and put on a linen robe, the color of hyacinth and interwoven with gold, and she girded herself with a golden sash, and she put bracelets on her hands and feet, and she put golden coverings on her feet, and around her neck she put valuable adornments and costly stones that were hanging on all sides. And the names of the gods of the Egyptians were engraved everywhere on the bracelets and the stones, and the faces of all the idols were represented on them. And she put a tiara on her head and bound a diadem around her temples and covered her head with a veil.

4:1 And she hurried down the stairs from the upper story and came to her father and mother and greeted them and kissed them. And Pentephres and his wife rejoiced greatly over their daughter Aseneth, for they saw her adorned as God's bride.

[*4:2–6 After a joyful reunion, Aseneth prepared to hear what her father had to say.*]

4:7 And her father Pentephres said to her, "Joseph, the mighty one of God, is coming to us today. And he is ruler of all the land of Egypt, and Pharaoh the king has appointed him king over all the land, and he is supplying grain for all the land and saving it from the impending famine. And Joseph is a man who worships God, and wise, and a virgin today like you; and Joseph is a man mighty in wisdom and understanding, and the spirit of the Lord is upon him, and the grace of the Lord is with him. 8 Now come, my child, and I will give you to him as a wife, and you will be his bride, and he will be your groom forever."

9 And when Aseneth heard these words from her father, much red sweat poured over her face and she was enraged and looked askance at her father with her eyes and said, "Why does my lord and father speak such words as these, to hand me over as a captive to a man who is a foreigner and a fugitive and one sold into slavery? 10 Is this not a shepherd's son from the land of Canaan, and was he not caught in the very act of lying with his mistress, and did his lord not throw him into a dark prison, and did Pharaoh not bring him out of prison because he

interpreted his dream just as aged Egyptian women interpret? [11] No, I will rather be married to the king's firstborn son because he is king of all the land of Egypt." [12] Upon hearing this Pentephres was ashamed to speak further to his daughter Aseneth about Joseph, for she had answered him rashly and with haughtiness and anger.

[5:1] And a young man from Pentephres's retinue burst in and said, "Behold, Joseph is standing before the doors of our court." [2] And Aseneth fled from her father and mother's presence when she heard them say these words about Joseph, and she went up to the upper story and entered her room and stood by the large window that faced east in order to see Joseph enter her father's house. [3] And Pentephres and his wife and all his family went out to meet Joseph. [4] And the gates of the court that faced east were opened, and Joseph entered, standing on the chariot of Pharaoh's second-in-command. And harnessed to it were four horses that were white like snow and had golden bridles, and the whole chariot was constructed of pure gold. [5] And Joseph was dressed in a special white tunic, and the robe wrapped around him was purple, made of fine linen interwoven with gold, and a golden crown was on his head, and around the crown were twelve choice stones, and above the stones were twelve golden sunbeams. And a royal staff was in his left hand, and in his right hand he had an olive branch extended. And there was much fruit on it, and in the fruit was much olive oil. [6] And Joseph entered the court, and the gates of the court were closed. And every strange man and woman remained outside the court, for the guards of the gates drew in and closed the doors, and all the strangers were shut out. [7] And Pentephres and his wife and all his family, except their daughter Aseneth, came and bowed down before Joseph, with their faces to the ground. And Joseph got down from his chariot and greeted them with his right hand.

[6:1] And Aseneth saw Joseph on his chariot and she was deeply disturbed and her soul was crushed and her knees were weakened and her whole body trembled and she was terribly afraid. And she groaned and said in her heart,

[2] "What will I, the wretched one, do now?
Did I not speak and say that Joseph, the shepherd's son from Canaan, is coming?
And now, behold, the sun from heaven has come to us in his chariot
and has entered our house today,
and shines in it like light upon the earth.
[3] But I, the foolish and rash one, have disdained him,
and I have spoken evil words about him,
and I did not know that Joseph is God's son.
[4] For what person on earth will produce such beauty,
and what woman's womb will give birth to such light?
I am wretched and foolish because I have spoken evil words to my father about
   him.
[5] And now where will I go and hide from his presence
so that Joseph, God's son, may not see me,
for I have spoken evil things about him?
[6] And where will I go and hide,
because he sees every concealed thing

and nothing hidden escapes his notice because of the great light that is in him?
⁷ And now have mercy on me, Lord God of Joseph,
for I have spoken evil words against him in ignorance.
⁸ And now let my father give me to Joseph as a handmaid and a servant,
and I will serve him forever."

⁷:¹ And Joseph entered Pentephres's house and sat upon the throne. And they washed his feet and prepared a table for him by itself, for Joseph would not eat with the Egyptians because this was an abomination to him. ² And Joseph raised his eyes and saw Aseneth looking in. And Joseph spoke to Pentephres and his whole family, saying, "Who is that woman standing at the window in the upper story? Now let her leave this house." For Joseph was afraid and said, "This woman must not harass me too." ³ Because all the wives and daughters of the nobles and satraps of all the land of Egypt harassed him in order to lie with him, and at the sight of Joseph all the wives and daughters of the Egyptians suffered badly because of his beauty. ⁴ But Joseph disdained them, and the emissaries whom the women sent to him with gold and silver and valuable gifts Joseph sent back with threats and insults, for Joseph said, "I will not sin before the Lord God of my father Israel or in the face of my father Jacob." ⁵ And Joseph always had before his eyes the face of his father Jacob, and he remembered his father's commands. For Jacob said to his son Joseph and all his sons, "My children, guard carefully against associating with a strange woman, for association with her is destruction and corruption." ⁶ For this reason Joseph said, "Let that woman leave this house."

⁷ And Pentephres said to him, "My lord, that one whom you saw standing in the upper story is not a strange woman but our daughter, a virgin who despises every man, and there is no other man who has ever seen her besides you only today. And if you wish, she will come and greet you, for our daughter is like a sister to you." ⁸ And Joseph rejoiced greatly that Pentephres had said, "She is a virgin who despises every man." And Joseph said to himself, "If she is a virgin who despises every man, surely she will not harass me." And Joseph said to Pentephres and all his family, "If she is your daughter and a virgin, let her come because she is my sister and I love her from this day as my sister."

⁸:¹ And Aseneth's mother went up to the upper story and brought her to stand before Joseph. And Pentephres said to his daughter Aseneth, "Greet your brother, for he is also a virgin, as you are today, and he despises every strange woman, even as you do every strange man." ² And Aseneth said to Joseph, "Greetings, my lord, blessed by God Most High." ³ And Joseph said to Aseneth, "May the Lord God, who gives life to all things, bless you." ⁴ And Pentephres said to his daughter Aseneth, "Come and kiss your brother." ⁵ And as Aseneth came to kiss Joseph, Joseph extended his right hand and put it on her chest between her two breasts, and her breasts were already standing forth like lovely apples. And Joseph said, "It is not proper for a man who worships God, who blesses with his mouth the living God and eats blessed bread of life and drinks a blessed cup of immortality and is anointed with blessed ointment of incorruption, to kiss a strange woman, who blesses with her mouth dead and dumb idols and eats bread of strangling from their table and drinks a cup of treachery from their libation and is anointed with ointment of destruction. ⁶ Rather, a man who worships God will kiss his

mother and the sister born from his mother and the sister from his tribe and family and the wife who shares his bed, who bless with their mouths the living God. ⁷ Likewise, it is not proper for a woman who worships God to kiss a strange man, for this is an abomination before the Lord God."

⁸ And when Aseneth heard these words from Joseph, she was deeply disturbed and very sad, and she groaned and looked intently at Joseph with her eyes opened, and her eyes were filled with tears. And Joseph saw her and had great mercy on her and was himself disturbed, for Joseph was gentle and merciful and one who feared God. ⁹ And he raised his right hand and put it on her head and said:

"Lord God of my father Israel,
the Most High, the Mighty One of Jacob,
who gives life to all things,
and calls them from darkness into light,
and from deception into truth,
and from death into life;
you, Lord, bless this virgin,
and renew her with your spirit,
and form her anew with your hidden hand,
and make her alive again with your life,
and let her eat your bread of life,
and let her drink your cup of blessing,
and count her among your people whom you chose before all things came into
      being,
and let her enter your rest that you prepared for your chosen ones,
and let her live in your eternal life forever."

[⁹:¹⁻¹⁰:⁹ *Aseneth rejoiced over Joseph's blessing but retired to her penthouse to lament her separation from Joseph and the Most High God because of her idolatry. Joseph departed, promising to return in a week. In the meantime the distraught Aseneth fasted and wept. In preparation for repentance, she gathered ashes from the fireplace, took out her black mourning garment, isolated herself even from her seven beloved virgin attendants, withdrew to her private room, and bolted the door.*]

¹⁰:¹⁰ And Aseneth hurried and took off her royal linen robe that was interwoven with gold and put on the black mourning garment; and she loosened the golden sash and tied a rope around herself and set aside the headdress from her head and the diadem and the bracelets from her hands and feet and put everything on the floor. ¹¹ And she took her choice robe and the golden sash and the headdress and the diadem, and she threw everything out for the poor through the window that faced north. ¹² And Aseneth hurried and took all her gods that were in her room, both the gold and silver ones that were countless, and she smashed them to pieces and threw all the idols of the Egyptians out for the needy and the beggars through her upper-story window that faced north. ¹³ And Aseneth took her royal dinner and the fattened animals and the fish and the meat from the heifer and all the sacrifices of her gods and the vessels of wine for their libation and threw everything out through the window that faced north and gave everything

to the strange dogs. For Aseneth said to herself, "By no means should my dogs eat from my dinner and from the sacrifice of the idols; rather, let the strange dogs eat them."

[¹⁰:¹⁴⁻¹¹:³ᵃ *Aseneth poured ashes on the floor, loosed her hair and sprinkled ashes on her head, beat her breast, and wept bitterly until morning. Mud from Aseneth's tears and the ashes covered the floor. After seven days of self-abasement, Aseneth, weakened and scarcely able to move, sat before the east-facing window with continued gestures of mourning and silently bemoaned her miserable state.*]

¹¹:³ᵇ "What will I, the lowly one, do,
or where will I go;
with whom will I take refuge,
or what will I say—
I, a virgin and an orphan and desolate and forsaken and despised?
⁴ For all have come to despise me,
and among these are my father and my mother,
for I, too, have come to despise their gods, and I destroyed them,
and I gave them up to be trampled under people's feet.
⁵ And for this reason my father and my mother and all my family have come to
    despise me and have said,
'Aseneth is not our daughter, for she destroyed our gods.'
⁶ And all people despise me,
for I, too, have come to despise all men and all those who sought to marry me.
And now in this humiliation of mine, all have come to despise me,
and they rejoice over this affliction of mine.
⁷ And the Lord, the Most High God of the mighty Joseph, despises all who wor-
    ship idols,
for he is a jealous and frightening God toward all who worship strange gods.
⁸ For this reason he has come to despise me as well,
for I, too, worshiped dead and dumb idols,
and blessed them, ⁹ and ate from their sacrifice,
and my mouth is defiled from their table,
and I am not bold enough to call upon the Lord God of heaven, the Most High,
    the Almighty One of the mighty Joseph,
for my mouth is defiled from the sacrifices of the idols.
¹⁰ But I have heard many say
that the God of the Hebrews is a true God and living God
and a merciful God and compassionate and patient and very forbearing and
    kind
and does not count the sin of a lowly person
nor expose the lawless deeds of an afflicted person at the time of that one's
    affliction.
¹¹ Therefore I, too, will be bold
and turn to him
and take refuge in him
and confess all my sins to him
and pour out my request before him.

[12] Who knows whether he might see my humiliation and have mercy on me?
Perhaps he will see this desolation of mine and have compassion for me,
[13] or see that I am an orphan and protect me,
for he is the father of the orphans and protector of the persecuted and helper of
the afflicted.
[14] I will be bold and cry out to him."

[[15-19] *In a second soliloquy Aseneth further lamented her desolate and orphaned
state. Defiled from the sacrifices of the Egyptian gods, she was loath to invoke the
name of the Most High God. At last she mustered courage and addressed God as
follows.*]

[12:1] "Lord God of the ages,
who created all things and gave them life,
who gave the breath of life to all your creation,
who brought the invisible things out into the light,
[2] who made the things that exist and that appear out of those that do not appear
and do not exist,
who raised up the heaven and laid its foundation on a dome on the back of the
winds,
who laid the earth's foundation on the waters,
who placed great stones on the watery abyss.
And the stones will not sink
but are like oak leaves on top of the waters,
and they are living stones,
and they hear your voice, Lord,
and they keep your commandments that you commanded them,
and from your ordinances they do not deviate,
but do your will to the end.
Because you, Lord, spoke and they were made alive,
because your word, Lord, is life for all your creatures.
[3] To you I come for refuge, Lord,
and to you I will cry out, Lord,
to you I will pour out my plea,
to you I will confess my sins,
and to you I will reveal my transgressions.
[4] Spare me, Lord,
because I have sinned much before you.
I have transgressed and committed sacrilege,
and I have spoken evil and unspeakable things before you.
[5] My mouth is defiled from sacrifices to idols
and from the table of the gods of the Egyptians.
I have sinned, Lord,
before you I have sinned much in ignorance,
and I have worshiped dead and deaf idols.
And now I am not worthy to open my mouth to you, Lord.
And I, Aseneth, daughter of Pentephres the priest, the virgin and queen,

who was at one time pompous and arrogant and prospering in my riches beyond all people,
am now an orphan and desolate and forsaken by all people.
⁶ To you I come for refuge, Lord,
and to you I bring my plea,
and to you I will cry out.
⁷ Rescue me before I am seized by those who persecute me.
⁸ For as a frightened young child flees to his father,
and the father extends his hands and picks him up from the ground
and embraces him against his chest,
and the child clasps his hands around his father's neck
and sighs relief from his fear
and rests upon his father's chest,
while the father smiles at his childish trouble,
so you also, Lord, reach out your hands to me as a father who loves his child,
and pick me up from the ground.
⁹ For, behold, the wild old lion pursues me,
for he is the father of the gods of the Egyptians,
and his children are the gods of those obsessed with idols.
And I have come to despise them
because they are the lion's children,
and I threw all of them away from me and destroyed them.
¹⁰ And their father the lion fiercely pursues me.
¹¹ But you, Lord, rescue me from his hands,
and deliver me from his mouth,
lest he carry me away like a lion and tear me to pieces,
and throw me into the flaming fire,
and the fire throw me into the tempest,
and the tempest enshroud me in darkness and throw me out into the depths of
  the sea,
and the great eternal sea monster swallow me,
and I perish forever.
¹² Rescue me, Lord, before all this comes upon me.
Rescue me, Lord, the desolate and solitary one,
for my father and mother have disowned me and said,
'Aseneth is not our daughter,'
for I destroyed and shattered their gods and came to despise them.
¹³ And now I am an orphan and desolate,
and I have no other hope except in you, Lord,
and no other refuge besides your mercy, Lord,
for you are the father of orphans and a protector of the persecuted and a helper
  of the afflicted.
¹⁴ Have mercy on me, Lord,
and keep watch over me, the chaste virgin who is forsaken and an orphan,
for you, Lord, are a sweet and good and kind father.
¹⁵ What father is as sweet as you, Lord?
And which one is as quick in mercy as you, Lord?

And which one is as patient toward our sins as you, Lord?
For behold, all the gifts of my father Pentephres that he has given to me for an
     inheritance are temporary and vanishing,
but the gifts of your inheritance, Lord, are incorruptible and eternal."

[¹³:¹⁻¹⁵ *Aseneth continued her penitent prayer. She recounted her repudiation of the idols that she had worshiped in ignorance and appealed to God for compassion and pardon for her idolatry and her blasphemy against God's son, Joseph, whom she promised to love and serve forever.*]

¹⁴:¹ And as Aseneth finished confessing to the Lord, behold, the morning star arose out of heaven in the east, and Aseneth looked and rejoiced and said, "So then the Lord has heard my prayer, for this star arose as an angel and a herald of the light of the great day." ² And Aseneth kept looking and behold, near the morning star the heaven was split open, and a great and indescribable light appeared. ³ And Aseneth looked and fell on her face on the ashes. And a man came to her out of heaven and stood over Aseneth's head. ⁴ And he called her and said, "Aseneth, Aseneth." ⁵ And she said, "Who is it who calls me, for the door of my room is closed and the tower is high; so then how has someone come into my room?" ⁶ And the man called her a second time and said, "Aseneth, Aseneth." ⁷ And she said, "Here I am, Lord; tell me who you are." ⁸ And the man said, "I am the ruler of the Lord's house and commander of all the army of the Most High. Arise and stand on your feet and I will speak my words to you."

⁹ And Aseneth raised her head and looked, and behold, there was a man like Joseph in every respect, with the robe and the crown and the royal staff, except that his face was like lightning, and his eyes were like sunshine, and the hairs of his head were like the fiery flame of a burning torch, and his hands and feet were like iron shining from a fire, and sparks were flying from both his hands and his feet. ¹⁰ And Aseneth looked and fell on her face at his feet on the ground. And Aseneth was terribly afraid, and every part of her trembled. ¹¹ And the man said to her, "Have courage, Aseneth, and do not be afraid, but arise and stand on your feet and I will speak my words to you." ¹² And Aseneth arose and stood on her feet. And the man said to her, "Proceed directly to your second room and take off your black mourning garment, and remove the sackcloth from your waist, and shake those ashes from your head, and wash your face and your hands with living water, and put on a new untouched fine linen robe, and gird your waist with the new double sash of your virginity. ¹³ And come to me and I will speak my words to you."

¹⁴ And Aseneth hurried and went into her second room where the chests of her adornments were, and she opened her coffer and took out a new fine untouched linen robe, and she took off the black mourning garment, and took the sackcloth from her waist, and put on her fine untouched linen garment, and girded herself with the double sash of her virginity, one sash around her waist and the other sash on her chest. ¹⁵ And she shook the ashes from her head and washed her hands and face with living water. And she took an untouched fine linen veil and covered her head.

¹⁵:¹ And she went to the man in her first room and stood before him. And the man said to her, "Now take the veil off your head. And why have you done this?

For you are a chaste virgin today, and your head is like that of a young man." ² And Aseneth took the veil off her head.

And the man said to her, "Have courage, Aseneth, chaste virgin. Behold, I have heard all the words of your confession and prayer. ³ Behold, I have also seen the humiliation and affliction of your seven days of deprivation. Behold, from your tears and these ashes much mud has formed before your face. ⁴ Have courage, Aseneth, chaste virgin. For behold, you name has been written in the book of the living in heaven; at the beginning of the book, as the first of all, your name was written by my finger, and it will not be erased forever. ⁵ Now behold, from this day you will be renewed and formed anew and made alive again, and you will eat blessed bread of life and drink a blessed cup of immortality and be anointed with blessed ointment of incorruption. ⁶ Have courage, chaste virgin. Behold, I have given you this day as a bride to Joseph, and he will be your groom forever.

⁷ "And your name will no longer be called Aseneth, but your name will be City of Refuge, for in you many nations will take refuge in the Lord God Most High, and under your wings many peoples will be sheltered when they trust in the Lord God, and within your walls those who devote themselves to God Most High in the name of Repentance will be kept safe. For Repentance is in heaven as an extremely beautiful and good daughter of the Most High. And she pleads with God Most High on your behalf every hour and on behalf of all who repent in the name of God Most High because he is the father of Repentance, and she is the overseer of all virgins and loves you greatly and makes requests for you every hour to the Most High, and for all who repent she has prepared a place of rest in the heavens. And she will renew all who repent, and she will attend them forever and ever. ⁸ And Repentance is extremely beautiful, a pure virgin and always laughing, and she is kind and gentle. And for this reason the Father Most High loves her, and all the angels respect her. And I love her greatly because she is also my sister. And because she loves you virgins, I also love you.

⁹ "And behold, I am going away to Joseph, and I will speak all my words about you to him. And Joseph will come to you today, and he will see you, and he will rejoice over you and love you, and he will be your groom, and you will be his bride forever. ¹⁰ And now hear me, Aseneth, chaste virgin, and put on your wedding robe, the ancient and first robe that has been stored in your room from the beginning, and put all your wedding ornaments around yourself as a good bride, and go meet Joseph. For behold, he is coming to you today and he will see you and rejoice."

¹¹ And as the man finished speaking these words, Aseneth rejoiced greatly over all his words and she fell at his feet and bowed down before him, with her face to the ground, and said to him, ¹²"Blessed is the Lord your God, the Most High, who sent you to rescue me from the darkness and to lead me from the foundations of the abyss, and blessed is your name forever. ¹²ˣ What is your name, Lord? Tell me, in order that I may sing your praises and glorify you forever." And the man said to her, "Why do you seek this name of mine, Aseneth? My name is in the heavens in the book of the Most High, written by the finger of God at the beginning of the book above all because I am ruler of the house of the Most High. And all the names written in the book of the Most High are unspeakable, and no one in this

world is allowed either to say or to hear them because those names are great and wonderful and extremely praiseworthy."

[*13-15 Aseneth's heavenly visitor accepted her invitation to stay and dine with her.*]

16:1 And Aseneth hurried and set a new table before him and proceeded to bring him bread. And the man said to her, "Now bring me a honeycomb also." 2 And Aseneth stood still and was sad, for she did not have a honeycomb in her storeroom. 3 And the man said to her, "Why do you stand still?" 4 And Aseneth said, "Now I will send a lad to the country estate, for the field of our inheritance is near, and he will quickly bring you a honeycomb from there and I will set it before you, Lord." 5 And the man said to her, "Go ahead and enter your storeroom and you will find a honeycomb lying on the table. Pick it up and bring it here." 6 And Aseneth said, "Lord, there is no honeycomb in my storeroom." 7 And the man said, "Go ahead and you will find it."

8 And Aseneth entered her storeroom and found a honeycomb lying on the table. And the comb was large and white like snow and full of honey. And that honey was like dew from heaven, and its scent was like the scent of life. 9 And Aseneth marveled and said to herself, "So then did this comb come from the mouth of this man? For its scent is like the scent of this man's mouth." 10 And Aseneth took that honeycomb and brought it to the man and put it on the table that she had prepared before him.

And the man said to her, "Why did you say, 'There is no honeycomb in my storeroom'? And behold you have brought a marvelous honeycomb." 11 And Aseneth was afraid and said, "Lord, I never had a honeycomb in my storeroom, but you spoke and it came to be. Surely this has come from your mouth because its scent is like the scent of your mouth."

12 And the man smiled at Aseneth's understanding. 13 And he called her to himself and extended his right hand and took hold of her head and shook her head with his right hand. And Aseneth was afraid of the man's hand because sparks flew from his hand as from molten iron. And Aseneth looked, fixing her eyes intently on the man's hand. 14 And the man looked and smiled and said, "Blessed are you, Aseneth because the unspeakable mysteries of the Most High have been revealed to you; and blessed are all who devote themselves to the Lord God in repentance because they will eat from this comb. For this comb is the spirit of life, and the bees of the paradise of delight have made this from the dew of the roses of life that are in God's paradise. And all the angels of God and all the chosen ones of God and all the sons of the Most High eat from it because this is the comb of life, and everyone who eats from it will not die forever."

15 And the man extended his right hand and broke off a small piece of the honeycomb. And he ate, and with his hand he put what was left into Aseneth's mouth and said to her, "Eat," and she ate. 16 And the man said to Aseneth, "Behold, you have eaten bread of life and drunk a cup of immortality and been anointed with ointment of incorruption. Behold, from this day your flesh teems with flowers of life from the land of the Most High, and your bones will be strengthened like the cedar trees of God's paradise of delight, and untiring powers will surround you, and your youth will not see old age, and your beauty will not fail you forever. And you will be like a fortified mother city for all who take refuge in the name of the Lord God, the king of the ages." 16x And the man extended his right hand

and touched the comb where he had broken it, and it was restored and filled out, and immediately it became intact as it was at the beginning. [17] And again the man extended his right hand and put his finger on the edge of the comb that was facing east and dragged it to the edge facing west, and the path of his finger became like blood. And he extended his hand a second time and put his finger on the edge of the comb facing north and dragged it to the edge facing south, and the path of his finger became like blood. [17x] And Aseneth stood on his left side and watched everything the man did.

And the man said to the comb, "Come." [17y] And the bees arose from the cells of that comb, and the cells were countless, ten thousands of ten thousands and thousands of thousands. [18] And the bees were white like snow, and their wings were like purple and hyacinth and scarlet and linen garments interwoven with gold, and golden diadems were on their heads, and they had sharp stingers but harmed no one. [19] And all those bees swarmed around Aseneth from her feet to her head. And other bees were great and chosen like their queens, and they arose from the marred part of the comb and swarmed around Aseneth's face and made a comb on her mouth and lips like the comb that lay before the man. [20] And all those bees ate from the comb that was on Aseneth's mouth. And the man said to the bees, "Now go away to your place." [21] And all the bees arose and flew away into heaven. [22] And those who wanted to harm Aseneth fell to the ground and died. And the man extended his staff over the dead bees and said to them, "You also arise and go away to your place." [23] And the bees that had died arose and went away into the court adjoining Aseneth's house and dwelt in the fruit trees.

[[17:1–18:5a] *After assuring Aseneth that all of his words to her were as trustworthy as those about the honeycomb, the man from heaven caused the honeycomb to disappear. At Aseneth's request, he blessed her seven virgin attendants, calling them "seven pillars of the City of Refuge." He then departed in a fiery chariot. Aseneth again lamented her presumptuous language and prayed for mercy for having assumed in ignorance that it was a man rather than God who had visited her. Upon hearing of Joseph's imminent return, Aseneth ordered her steward to prepare a great meal. The steward, saddened by Aseneth's emaciated appearance from her seven days of deprivation and mourning, prepared the meal.*]

[18:5b] And Aseneth remembered the man and his command, and she hurried and entered her second room where the chests of her adornments were, and she opened her large coffer and took out her first robe, the wedding robe that was like lightning in appearance, and put it on. [6] And she girded herself with a golden royal sash that had precious stones. And on her hands she put golden bracelets, and on her feet golden coverings, and she put precious ornaments around her neck, on which countless costly precious stones were hanging. And she put a golden crown on her head, and on the crown, in front of her brow, was a large stone the color of hyacinth, and around the large stone were six costly stones. And with a veil she covered her head like a bride and took a scepter in her hand.

[7] And Aseneth remembered the words of her steward, for he had said to her, "Your face is emaciated." And she groaned and was very sad and said, "Woe to me, the lowly one because my face is emaciated. Joseph will see me and disdain me." [8] And she said to her companion who was raised with her, "Bring me pure water from the spring, and I will wash my face." [9] And she brought pure water

from the spring and poured it into the basin. And Aseneth leaned forward to wash her face and saw her face in the water. And it was like the sun, and her eyes were like a rising morning star, and her cheeks were like the fields of the Most High, and in her cheeks was a redness like a son of man's blood, and her lips were like a rose of life coming forth from its bud, and her teeth were like warriors lined up for battle, and the hair of her head was like a vine in God's paradise prospering with its fruit, and her neck was like a variegated cypress tree, and her breasts were like the mountains of God Most High. ¹⁰ And when Aseneth saw herself in the water she was astonished at the sight and rejoiced greatly and did not wash her face, for she said, "Lest I wash off this great beauty."

¹¹ And her steward came to say to her, "All things are prepared as you ordered." And when he saw her he was alarmed and stood speechless for a long time, and he was greatly afraid and fell at her feet and said, "What is this, my princess, and what is this great and wonderful beauty? Has the Lord God of heaven perhaps chosen you as a bride for his firstborn son Joseph?"

¹⁹:¹ And while they were still saying this, a lad came and said to Aseneth, "Behold, Joseph is standing at the doors of our court." ² And Aseneth hurried and went downstairs from the upper story with the seven virgins to meet Joseph, and she stood at the entrance to the house. ³ And Joseph entered into the court and the gates were closed, and all strangers remained outside.

⁴ And Aseneth went out through the entrance to meet Joseph, and Joseph saw her and was astonished at her beauty and said to her, "Who are you? Tell me quickly." ⁵ And she said to him, "I am your handmaid Aseneth, and all the idols I have thrown away from me and they were destroyed. And a man came to me from heaven today and gave me bread of life and I ate, and a cup of blessing and I drank. And he said to me, 'I have given you as a bride to Joseph today, and he will be your groom forever.' And he said to me, 'Your name will no longer be called Aseneth, but your name will be called City of Refuge, and the Lord God will reign over many nations forever because in you many nations will take refuge in the Lord God Most High.' ⁶ And the man said to me, 'I will go to Joseph as well and speak in his ears my words about you.' ⁷ And now, my lord, you know whether that man has come to you and spoken to you about me."

⁸ And Joseph said to Aseneth, "Blessed are you by God Most High, and your name will be blessed forever, for the Lord God has laid the foundation of your walls in the highest, and your walls are unbreakable walls of life, for the sons of the living God will dwell in your City of Refuge, and the Lord God will reign over them forever. ⁹ Because that man came to me and spoke to me words such as these about you. And now come to me, chaste virgin; why do you stand far from me?"

¹⁰ And Joseph extended his hands and called Aseneth with a wink of his eyes. And Aseneth also extended her hands and ran to Joseph and fell against his chest. And Joseph embraced her and Aseneth embraced Joseph, and they greeted each other for a long time, and both came to life again in their spirit. ¹¹ And Joseph kissed Aseneth and gave her a spirit of life, and he kissed her a second time and gave her a spirit of wisdom, and he kissed her a third time and gave her a spirit of truth.

²⁰:¹ And they hugged each other for a long time and clasped their hands with a tight grip.

And Aseneth said to Joseph, "Come, my lord, and enter into our house, for I have prepared our house and made a great dinner." ² And she grasped his right hand and led him into her house and seated him on the throne of her father Pentephres. And she brought water to wash his feet. ³ And Joseph said, "Now let one of the virgins come and wash my feet." ⁴ And Aseneth said to him, "No, my lord because from now on you are my lord and I am your handmaid. And why do you say this—that another virgin should wash your feet? For your feet are my feet and your hands my hands and your soul my soul, and no other woman will ever wash your feet." ⁵ And she insisted and washed his feet. And Joseph observed her hands, and they were like hands of life, and her fingers were delicate like the fingers of a scribe writing swiftly. And after this Joseph grasped her right hand and kissed it, and Aseneth kissed his head and sat on his right side.

⁶ And her father and mother and all her family came from the field of their inheritance. And they saw Aseneth appearing as light, and her beauty was like heavenly beauty. And they saw her sitting with Joseph and dressed in a wedding garment. ⁷ And they were astonished at her beauty and they rejoiced and gave glory to God who gives life to the dead. And after this they ate and drank and celebrated.

[²⁰:⁸⁻²²:⁹ *Pentephres proposed a great wedding feast, and Joseph departed to gain Pharaoh's approval of the marriage. Pharaoh gladly obliged and solemnized the marriage of this "firstborn son of God" and "daughter of the Most High." The couple married amid elaborate festivities, and from their union Manasseh and Ephraim were born. Then follows a long psalm by Aseneth with the repeated refrain, "I have sinned, Lord, I have sinned; before you I have sinned much." Here Aseneth confessed again her arrogant and idolatrous past and reveled in her acceptance by God, her marriage to Joseph, and her sharing in the bread of life and cup of wisdom.*

When the years of abundance ended and the famine began, Jacob and his family moved to Egypt. Aseneth met Jacob, whom she considered "like a father and god" to her, and received his blessing. Then the conflict that dominates the second part of the double novella begins to unfold.]

²²:¹⁰ And after this they ate and drank. And Joseph and Aseneth went to their house. ¹¹ And Joseph's brothers Simeon and Levi, the sons of Leah, alone accompanied them; but the sons of Zilpah and Bilhah, handmaids of Leah and Rachel, did not accompany them, for they envied them and were hostile toward them. ¹² And Levi was on Aseneth's right side and Joseph on her left. ¹³ And Aseneth grasped Levi's hand. And Aseneth loved Levi greatly above all Joseph's brothers because he was one who devoted himself to the Lord, and he was a man of understanding and a prophet of the Most High and one whose eyes had keen vision, and he saw letters written in heaven by the finger of God, and he knew the unspeakable things of God Most High and revealed them to Aseneth privately because Levi himself loved Aseneth very much and saw her place of rest in the highest, and her walls like unbreakable eternal walls, and her foundations laid on a rock of the seventh heaven.

²³:¹ And as Joseph and Aseneth passed by, Pharaoh's firstborn son saw them from the wall. And he saw Aseneth and was disturbed and very irritated and became sick because of her beauty. And he said, "It will not be so!" ² And Pharaoh's son sent messengers and called Simeon and Levi to him. And the men came to

him and stood before him. And Pharaoh's firstborn son said to them, "I know today that you are mighty men above all men on the earth, and with these right hands of yours the city of the Shechemites was overthrown, and with these two swords of yours thirty thousand warriors were cut down. [3] And behold, today I will take you as my comrades, and I will give you much gold and silver and servants and handmaids and houses and a great inheritance. Only do this thing and have mercy on me, for I have been terribly insulted by your brother Joseph, for he took for himself my wife Aseneth, who was pledged to me from the beginning. [4] And now, come help me and we will fight against your brother Joseph and I will kill him with my sword and I will have Aseneth as a wife and you will be brothers and faithful friends to me. [5] Only do this thing. But if you hesitate to do this thing and disdain my plan, behold, my sword is prepared against you." [6] And at the same time that he was saying this he unsheathed his sword and showed it to them.

But when the men, Simeon and Levi, heard this, they were very disturbed, for Pharaoh's son had spoken to them in a tyrannous manner. [7] And Simeon was a rash and bold man, and he intended to lay his hand on the handle of his sword and draw it from its sheath and strike Pharaoh's son, for he had spoken harsh things to them. [8] And Levi saw the intention of his heart, for Levi was a man who was a prophet, and he saw keenly with both his mind and his eyes, and he read what is written in the heart of men. And Levi stepped with his foot on Simeon's right foot and pressed down on it and signaled to him to cease from his anger. [9] And Levi said quietly to Simeon, "Why are you so enraged toward this man? And we are men who worship God and it is not proper for us to repay evil for evil."

[10] And Levi spoke to Pharaoh's son boldly. With a cheerful face and without the least bit of anger, but in gentleness of heart, he said to him, "Why does our lord speak things such as these? And we are men who worship God, and our father is a friend of God Most High, and Joseph our brother is like the firstborn son of God. [11] And how will we do this evil thing and sin before our God and our father Israel and our brother Joseph? [12] And now, hear my words. It is not proper for a man who worships God to harm another person in any way. And if someone wants to harm a man who worships God, no man who worships God aids him, for there is no sword in his hands. [13] And you, guard against speaking any more things such as these about our brother Joseph. But if you persist in this evil plan of yours, behold, our swords are drawn in our right hands before you."

[23:14–25:8 *Simeon and Levi drew their swords in defiance of Pharaoh's son and departed. Rebuffed by Simeon and Levi, Pharaoh's son found willing accomplices in Dan and Gad, sons of Bilhah and Zilpah, handmaids of Jacob's wives. Alleging that Joseph intended to kill these half-brothers and their offspring after Jacob's death, Pharaoh's son arranged an elaborate scheme in which he would assassinate his father while the sons of Bilhah and Zilpah ambushed Aseneth's entourage as she traveled to the family estate for the harvest. The four sons of Bilhah and Zilpah, each with five hundred fighting men, set the ambush for Aseneth and her escort of six hundred fighting men. After assassinating his father, Pharaoh's son was to take fifty archers on horseback and position himself to capture the fleeing Aseneth, and the sons of Bilhah and Zilpah were to kill Joseph and his children. Pharaoh's son was unable to gain access to his father's room to kill him, but the plot to abduct Aseneth and murder Joseph proceeded. Naphtali and Asher, the younger sons of Bilhah and Zilpah, tried to dissuade their brothers from the murderous plot, but Dan and Gad refused to "die like women" and persisted in the conspiracy.*]

26:1 And Aseneth arose early in the morning and said to Joseph, "I will go, just as you have said, to the field of our inheritance. And my soul is anxious, for you are separating yourself from me." 2 And Joseph said to her, "Have courage, and do not be afraid, but go, for the Lord is with you and he himself will guard you like the apple of his eye from every evil deed. 3 For I, too, will go forth to supply grain, and I will give bread to all the people, and all the land will surely not perish from the presence of the Lord." 4 And Aseneth went on her way, and Joseph went away to supply grain.

5 And Aseneth and the six hundred men with her came to the place of the brook. And suddenly those who were lying in wait burst forth from their ambush and engaged Aseneth's men in battle and cut them down with the edge of the sword and killed all of her forerunners. And Aseneth fled ahead with her carriage.

6 And Levi, Leah's son, knew all these things in the spirit as a prophet, and he announced Aseneth's danger to his brothers, the sons of Leah. And each one took his sword and put it on his thigh, and they took their shields and put them on their arms, and took their spears in their right hands and hunted for Aseneth in rapid pursuit.

7 And Aseneth fled ahead, and behold, Pharaoh's son and fifty horsemen with him met her. 8 And Aseneth saw him and was afraid and very troubled, and her whole body trembled. And she called on the name of the Lord her God.

27:1 And Benjamin sat on Aseneth's left side in her carriage. And Benjamin was a big and strong and princely eighteen-year-old lad, and he had unspeakable beauty and strength as of a lion's cub, and he feared the Lord greatly. 2 And Benjamin bounded down from the carriage and took a round stone from the brook, and with all his strength he hurled it at Pharaoh's son and struck his left temple and wounded him gravely. 3 And Pharaoh's son fell from his horse onto the ground half-dead. 4 And Benjamin bounded up onto a rock and said to Aseneth's carriage driver, "Give me stones from the brook." 5 And he gave him fifty stones. And Benjamin hurled the fifty stones and killed the fifty men who were with Pharaoh's son. And all the stones penetrated their temples.

6 And Leah's sons, Reuben and Simeon, Levi and Judah, Issachar and Zebulon, hunted down the men who had been lying in wait for Aseneth and fell upon them suddenly and cut them all down; and the six men killed two thousand.

7 And their brothers, the sons of Bilhah and Zilpah, fled from their presence and said, "We have been destroyed by our brothers, and Pharaoh's son has died by the hand of the lad Benjamin, and all who were with him have been destroyed single-handedly by the lad Benjamin. 8 And now come, let us kill Aseneth and Benjamin and flee into this thicket of reeds." 9 And they came upon Aseneth having their swords drawn and covered with blood. 10 And Aseneth saw them and was greatly afraid and said,

"Lord my God,
who made me alive again,
who rescued me from idols and the corruption of death,

who said to me, 'Your soul will live forever,'
rescue me from the hands of these evil men.'"

¹¹ And the Lord God heard Aseneth's voice, and immediately their swords fell from their hands on the ground and were burned to ashes.

²⁸:¹ And the sons of Bilhah and Zilpah saw this great thing and they were greatly afraid and said, "The Lord is fighting against us for Aseneth." ² And they fell on their faces to the ground and bowed down before Aseneth and said, "Have mercy on us, your servants, for you are our princess and queen. ³ And we have done evil things against you and our brother Joseph, and the Lord has repaid us according to our deeds. ⁴ And now we, your servants, beg you, have mercy on us and rescue us from the hands of our brothers, for they have come as avengers of the insult done to you, and their swords are against us. ⁵ And we know that our brothers are men who worship God and do not repay anyone evil for evil. ⁶ What remains is for you to be merciful to your servants before them, princess." ⁷ And Aseneth said to them, "Have courage and do not be afraid of your brothers, for they are men who worship God and fear God and respect every man. But go into this thicket of reeds until I appease them with regard to you and put an end to their anger, for you have acted audaciously against them. Therefore, have courage and do not be afraid. Besides, the Lord will judge between me and you." ⁸ And Dan and Gad and their brothers fled into the thicket of reeds.

And behold, Leah's sons came running like three-year-old deer against them. ⁹ And Aseneth came down from the carriage that was her shelter and tearfully greeted them with her right hand. And they fell down and bowed down to her on the ground and wept with a loud voice; and they were seeking their brothers, the sons of their father's handmaids, to do away with them. ¹⁰ And Aseneth said to them, "I beg you, spare your brothers and do not do them evil for evil, for the Lord protected me from them and shattered their swords from their hands, and behold they melted on the ground like wax in front of a fire. And this is enough for them—that the Lord fights against them for us. ¹¹ And you, spare them, for they are your brothers and your father Israel's blood."

¹² And Simeon said to her, "Why does our princess speak good things on behalf of her enemies? ¹³ No, rather let us cut them down with our swords, for they were first to plot evil things against us and our father Israel and our brother Joseph—indeed twice already—and today against you, our princess and queen." ¹⁴ And Aseneth extended her right hand and touched Simeon's beard and kissed him and said, "By no means, brother, will you do evil for evil to your neighbor. You will give to the Lord the right to avenge their insult. And they are your brothers and the offspring of your father Israel, and they fled far from your presence. What remains is for you to grant them pardon."

¹⁵ And Levi came to her and kissed her right hand and knew that she wanted to save the men from their brothers' anger so that they would not kill them. ¹⁶ And they were nearby in the thicket of reeds. ¹⁷ And their brother Levi knew it and did not announce it to his brothers, for he was afraid that in their anger they might cut them down.

²⁹:¹ And Pharaoh's son arose from the ground and sat up and spat blood from his mouth, for the blood from his temple dripped down over his mouth. ² And

Benjamin ran up to him and took his sword and drew it from its sheath because Benjamin did not have a sword on his thigh. And he was about to strike the chest of Pharaoh's son. ³ And Levi ran up to him and grasped his hand and said, "By no means, brother, will you do this deed, for we are men who worship God and it is not proper for a man who worships God to repay evil for evil or to trample on one who has fallen or to afflict his enemy to death. ⁴ And now, return your sword to its place and come, help me, and we will heal him of his wound; and if he lives he will be our friend after this and his father Pharaoh will be like a father to us." ⁵ And Levi raised Pharaoh's son up from the ground and washed the blood from his face and tied a bandage around his wound and put him on his horse and conveyed him to his father Pharaoh and described all these things to him. ⁶ And Pharaoh arose from his throne and bowed down before Levi on the ground and blessed him.

⁷ And on the third day Pharaoh's son died from the wound from the lad Benjamin's stone. ⁸ And Pharaoh grieved much for his firstborn son, and from the grieving he became sick; and Pharaoh died at the age of one hundred and nine years and left his diadem to Joseph. ⁹ And Joseph reigned in Egypt forty-eight years, and after this Joseph gave the diadem back to Pharaoh's younger child, who was still nursing when Pharaoh died. And Joseph was like a father to Pharaoh's younger son in the land of Egypt all the days of his life.

The Life of Adam and Eve

When Constantin von Tischendorf devoted twenty-three pages in the mid-1800s to Greek manuscripts about Adam and Eve, he played Pandora to a culture that for two thousand years had been fascinated with its ancestral parents. Tischendorf wrested from obscurity fascinating stories that offer a fuller account of the life of Adam and Eve than Genesis 1–5. Here in the open was a tantalizing tale of brother-murder (1–4), a heroic but failed quest to retrieve the oil of mercy from paradise to alleviate human pain (5–14), two autobiographical accounts of temptation and fall (7–8 and 15–30), and a vivid depiction of divine forgiveness (31–43).

While Tischendorf simply took his manuscripts' heading—a revelation (apocalypse) of Moses—as the text's title, probably a better title is the Life of Adam and Eve (the Greek version, which features here, is the Greek Life of Adam and Eve). Whatever it is called, this text contains elements of enormous importance. It demonstrates how deeply early Jewish authors drank of Greco-Roman culture. In the final scene, for example, an angel plucks Adam's corpse from the earth and washes it in the **Acherusian Sea**. This symbolizes the Greek Life of Adam and Eve, where a key figure of Judaism and Christianity is purified in mysterious Greek waters. The text contains as well the earliest known Jewish or Christian autobiographical narrative of a woman, the *first* woman no less. No less fascinating is that she lays the blame for the first sin at Adam's feet; in his account, Adam lays the blame at her feet!

The Life of Adam and Eve is preserved in several versions (see below), and its purpose differs according to which version is read. The dominant purpose of the Greek Life of Adam and Eve is to reinterpret Genesis 1–5 in order to provide hope for its readers by presenting Adam as a forgiven sinner who endures the pain of existence, faces death with uncertainty, but receives mercy after death. The purpose of the Latin version, in contrast, is to present readers with a perfect penitent, a righteous Adam who receives mercy not just after but also during life.

Narrative Description

The Greek Life of Adam and Eve can be divided into four well-ordered sections, each of which can be encapsulated in a word: **patrimony,** pain, **parenesis,** and pardoning.

1. *Patrimony* (1:1–5:3; retelling Gen. 4:1–5:5). Long after the births of Cain and Abel, in a dream—a nightmare, really—Eve learns of the murder of Abel by Cain. Patrimony, however, does not belong to Cain, to whom Adam must not, God commands, reveal the mystery that Adam knows. God promises instead that Seth will be born to replace Abel. As life goes on, Adam—he is given credit, not Eve—bears thirty sons and thirty daughters. After this flurry of births, Adam falls into an unknown condition and gathers his children around him in traditional testamentary fashion.

2. *Pain* (6:1–14:2). Adam proposes that Seth and Eve should travel to paradise, beg God to send an angel into paradise to retrieve the oil of mercy, and return with the oil to alleviate Adam's inscrutable suffering. This story (6:1–2; 9:1–3; 13:1–14:2) is interrupted twice, first by Adam's autobiographical recollection of the first sin (6:3–8:2), then by a wild animal, which attacks Seth and accuses Eve of initiating, with her greed, the dominion of the wild animals (10:1–12:2). The scene ends when the archangel Michael denies Seth's request, so he and his mother return incapable of relieving Adam's duress.

3. *Parenesis* (14:3–30:1; retelling Gen. 3:1–24). After Seth and Eve return from paradise, Adam again indicts Eve, providing an occasion for her to reveal her own perspective on the first sin in what might be called Eve's testament. Eve recounts, in a flourish of biblical and unbiblical elements, the envy of the devil; the entrance of the serpent, the devil's tool, into paradise; Eve's inability to resist the devil's trickery; Eve's taking of the fruit; Eve's ability to persuade Adam to eat; God's awesome entry into paradise on a chariot; the curses; and the expulsion of the first pair from paradise, despite angelic pleas for mercy.

Striking about Eve's autobiography is that it functions as parenesis (ethical instruction). Eve ends her testament: "Now therefore, my children, I have disclosed to you the way in which we were deceived. And you yourselves—guard yourselves so as not to disregard what is good" (30:1). Yet Eve does more than simply warn her children. She tells the same story of deceit, with five identical steps, in the case of the serpent, herself, and Adam. In each case:

a. The deceiver approaches and arouses desire (16:1; 18:1; 21:1).
b. The deceiver invites the soon-to-be deceived to follow (16:3; 18:1; 21:3).
c. The soon-to-be deceived hesitates, saying, "I fear lest the Lord/God be angry with me" (16:4; 18:2; 21:4).
d. The deceiver responds with the words "fear not," accompanied by a part-truth intended to allay fear (16:5; 18:3–4; 21:4).
e. The deceived gives in (17:1; 19:3; 21:5).

This pattern is repeated with variations to reinforce, in a parenetic pattern, how Eve's children can resist evil and hold to what is good. The deception of the serpent outlines the basic elements in the process of deception (16). The deception of Eve exposes the inner turmoil of the process (18–19). The deception of Adam, marked by brevity, indicates how easily the unguarded victim falls prey to deception (21).

A stunning dimension of Eve's autobiography is how self-serving it is. Eve may have committed the first sin, but a slew of elements indicate her innocence:

the devil entered Adam's region, not hers; the devil looked just like an angel; Eve resisted the devil's deceptive wiles, unlike Adam, who succumbed immediately to Eve; and Adam alone, in her version, claims responsibility. "I alone have sinned," Adam confesses (27:2).

4. *Pardoning* (31:1–43:4). Following Eve's testament, Adam attempts to assuage Eve's anxiety by promising her a shared destiny with him. Eve then confesses her sin repeatedly and is subsequently instructed by an angel to watch Adam's ascent. While she is watching, God's chariot arrives in paradise, replete with an entourage consisting of angels, the sun, and the moon. Seth explains to Eve what she sees, including the inability of the sun and the moon to shine in the presence of God. The story continues with the burial of Adam's body and the sealing of his tomb until the burial of Eve should take place. Eve is then buried, and the archangel Michael delivers final instructions about burial to Seth.

Author/Provenance

The question of place of origin is equally inscrutable. Jan Dochhorn, who thinks that the Greek Life of Adam and Eve was originally written in Hebrew, notes several correspondences with the book of Jubilees (*see* The Book of Jubilees), which was found among the Dead Sea Scrolls. He proposes, therefore, a Palestinian provenance. Other proposals range from Egypt to Rome. There is no consensus whatsoever about the place of origin.

Date/Occasion

Possible dates of origin are equally erratic, ranging seven hundred years, from 100 BCE to 600 CE. Scholars who favor a Jewish origin tend to date the Greek Life of Adam and Eve earlier in this period; scholars who favor a Christian origin tend to date it in the second to fourth centuries CE. It has recently been argued that pivotal features of Paul's argument in Romans 1 exhibit uniquely rich correspondences with the Greek Life of Adam and Eve.[1] This does not demand that the Greek Life of Adam and Eve in its entirety was already written by the mid-first century CE, but it does suggest that Paul may have used some portion of this narrative—either written or oral—in the construction of his argument.

Text, Language, Sources, and Transmission

Precious little is known about the origin of this narrative—if it was a single narrative at all rather than a collection of separate stories.

Some scholars (e.g., Dochhorn) regard the Greek Life of Adam and Eve as a composition that was written in Hebrew and then translated into Greek. Others

---

1. Jack Levison, "Adam and Eve in Romans 1.18–25 and the Greek *Life of Adam and Eve*," *NTS* 50 (2004): 519–34.

(e.g., Michael Stone, Johannes Tromp, and M. de Jonge) are convinced that the Greek is natural and that there is no need to suppose that it translates an original Hebrew composition. Debate festers around whether the Greek Life of Adam and Eve contains authentic Hebraisms—Greek that looks like it must have been translated from Hebrew—such as the occurrence of a different word order (e.g., in Hebrew, the verb precedes the subject).

This intractable question surfaces in all interpretations of the Greek Life of Adam and Eve, though without resolution. Those who propose a Jewish origin note that it contains few if any Christian elements. Further, Dochhorn believes it is a Jewish text in part because the author of the Hebrew original solved biblical problems that arise in the Hebrew Bible but not in the Septuagint. In contrast, Tromp points to alleged indications of a Christian origin: Adam's incense offerings reflect Christian worship practices (29:4; 33:4; 38:2); the triangular seal on Adam's tomb (42:1—"After these words God made a triangular seal and sealed the tomb in order that no one might do anything to him [Adam] for six days, when his rib would return to him") is reminiscent of the seal on Jesus' tomb (Matt. 27:66—"So they went with the guard and made the tomb secure by sealing the stone"), and the triangular shape of the "seal" may reflect the Trinitarian dimension of baptism, in which Christians were believed to receive the "seal" of the spirit; Adam's being washed in the Acherusian Sea (37:3—"And when the angels had said these outcries, look, one of the six-winged seraphim came and seized Adam—into the Acherusian Lake—and washed him clean three times, and led him into the presence of God"), while traceable ultimately to Greco-Roman literature, reflects as well Christian belief that sinners could be cleansed in the Acherusian Sea (Apocalypse of Peter 14; Apocalypse of Paul 22). The tentative quality of observations on both sides of the debate demonstrates how difficult it can be to decide whether a text was composed in a Jewish or Christian community during this period. Recently, scholars have pointed out that the border between Judaism and Christianity was porous; it may not always be wise to drive a wedge between a Jewish or Christian origin. The Greek Life of Adam and Eve may reflect a community that saw itself as *both* Jewish and Christian rather than as Jewish *or* Christian.

Manuscripts of the Greek Life of Adam and Eve, which date from the eleventh to the seventeenth centuries, fall into three versions, with significant variations. For instance, one Greek version, represented principally by manuscripts R and M, contains a story of Adam and Eve's acts of penitence: Adam heads to the Jordan River and Eve to the Tigris, where Satan disguises himself as an angel and tricks Eve into coming out of the river before her penitence is complete (29:7-13; see the translation in italics). Although this story occurs in only one Greek version, it is found as well in several other languages, including Georgian, Armenian, and Latin. In these versions, the penitence of Adam and Eve in the Jordan and Tigris Rivers occurs at the beginning of the story—not later, as in the Greek version of manuscripts R and M. This detailed account of penitence, set at the start of the story in these versions, creates a different narrative altogether, in which Adam receives mercy while he is still alive because of his penitence. One other version, in a Slavonic translation, follows the Greek more closely, though with its own distinctive features, such as an initial statement of Adam's dominion over the animals in paradise—something absent from other versions.

Theology

Shades of an intimate and compassionate God in Genesis 2–3 are struck from the record of the Greek Life of Adam and Eve. So, for example:

1. God does not walk in the cool of the garden, as in the Bible; in the Greek Life of Adam and Eve, God travels instead on a magnificent chariot throne.
2. God does not encounter the first couple face to face; in the Greek Life of Adam and Eve, God is accompanied by the archangel Michael and an entourage of heavenly courtesans who do God's bidding.
3. God is omniscient. The biblical question, "Where are you?" (Gen. 3:9), which suggests that God may not know where Adam and Eve are hiding, is replaced by an exclamation point of omniscience: "Adam, where have you gone into hiding, thinking that I will not find you? A building will not be hidden from the one who built it, will it?" (23:1).
4. God is not compassionate; in the Greek Life of Adam and Eve God is just. There is no sewing of garments for the first couple in a moment of compassionate care prior to their expulsion; instead, God vilifies the compassionate angels when they stop driving Adam out of paradise with the indictment, "Why did you stop throwing Adam out of paradise? The sinful act is not mine, is it, or did I hand down a sentence wickedly?" (27:4).

Reception of the Greek Life of Adam and Eve in the Second Temple Period

Perhaps the most striking feature of the Greek Life of Adam and Eve is that it diverges wildly from Genesis 2:4–5:3 even while it purports to proffer a narrative about Adam and Eve. There is much here that is not drawn from the Bible, not least the placement of the story of Adam and Eve in a theological context that delays mercy to the day of resurrection.

The Greek Life of Adam and Eve also offers a fabulous look at significant twists and turns in postbiblical interpretations of Genesis 2:4–5:3. For example, paradise is divided into a male and a female portion, indicating that there was no sexual intercourse between animals or humans prior to expulsion (15). Again, blood does not cry out from the mouth of the ground when Cain murders Abel, as in Genesis 4:10; instead, the mouth of Cain vomits Abel's blood (2:3).

Some interpretations correspond to New Testament letters: Eve rather than Adam is the source of sin and death (14:2; 32:1–2; cf. 2 Cor. 11:3; 1 Tim. 2:4); Satan disguises himself as an angel (17:1—"And immediately he became suspended next to the walls of paradise. And when the angels of God ascended to worship, then Satan was transformed into [the] appearance of an angel and praised God with hymns—just like the angels"; cf. 2 Cor. 11:13–14—"For such boasters are false apostles, deceitful workers, disguising themselves as apostles of Christ. And no wonder! Even Satan disguises himself as an angel of light"); God is the "father of lights" (36:3—"And Seth says to her, 'Their light has not moved away, but they are not able to shine in the presence of the Light of the Whole

Creation, the Father of Lights, and on this account the light has been hidden from them'"; cf. James 1:17—"Every generous act of giving, with every perfect gift, is from above, coming down from the Father of lights, with whom there is no variation or shadow due to change"); paradise is located in the third heaven (37:5—"Take him up into paradise, as far as the third heaven, and leave him there until that intensely frightful day of cosmic ordering, which I will accomplish in the world"; cf. 2 Cor. 12:2—"I know a person in Christ who fourteen years ago was caught up to the third heaven—whether in the body or out of the body I do not know; God knows"); and desire is the root of all sin (19:3—"When he had extracted from me the oath, then he came and placed upon the fruit which he gave to me the venom of his wickedness [[this is of desire. For desire is of all sin.]] And after having bent the branch to the ground, I took from the fruit, and I ate"; cf. Rom. 7:7—"What then should we say? That the law is sin? By no means! Yet, if it had not been for the law, I would not have known sin. I would not have known what it is to covet if the law had not said, 'You will not covet'"). Even more convincing are two exchanges in Romans 1:18–25[2] that correspond to the Greek Life of Adam and Eve: the exchange of God's glory for mortality (14:2; 21:1–6;[3] and 39:1–3); and the exchange of natural for unnatural (10:1–12:2).[4] Is it

2. Rom. 1:21–25: "For though they knew God, they did not honor him as God or give thanks to him, but they became futile in their thinking, and their senseless minds were darkened. Claiming to be wise, they became fools; and they exchanged the glory of the immortal God for images resembling a mortal human being or birds or four-footed animals or reptiles. Therefore God gave them up in the lusts of their hearts to impurity, to the degrading of their bodies among themselves, because they exchanged the truth about God for a lie and worshiped and served the creature rather than the Creator, who is blessed forever! Amen."

3. Life of Adam and Eve 21:1–6: "And I cried out at that very hour, saying, 'Adam, Adam, where are you? Get up, come to me, and I will show you an enormous mystery.' But when your father came, I spoke to him words of lawlessness, which brought us down from intense glory. For when he came, I opened my mouth, and the devil was speaking, and I began to give harsh counsel to him, saying, 'Come, my lord Adam, listen to me and eat from the fruit of the tree [about] which God said to us not to eat from it, and you will be as God.' And answering, your father said, 'I am frightened that perhaps God will be angry with me.' But I myself said to him, 'Stop being frightened, for when you eat, you will be knowledgeable [about] good and evil.' And then after having quickly persuaded him, he ate, and his eyes were opened, and he became aware of his nakedness. And he said to me, 'Oh, evil woman, what did you bring about among us? You have estranged me from the glory of God.'" — trans. Levison

4. Life of Adam and Eve 10:1–12:2: "And Seth went, and Eve, into the regions of paradise. And Eve saw her son and a wild animal battling with him. And Eve wept, saying, 'Ah me! Ah me! Because if I come to the day of the resurrection, all who have sinned will curse me, saying, "Eve did not keep the command of God."'" And she said to the wild animal, 'Oh, you evil wild animal, aren't you yourself frightened of doing battle with the image of God? How was your mouth opened? How have your teeth become strong? How did you not remember your submission—that in the past you submitted to the image of God?' Then the wild animal cried out, saying, 'Oh, Eve, your greed is not about us, nor your weeping, but about you, since the dominion of the wild animals came to be from you. How was your mouth opened to eat from the tree about which God commanded you not to eat from it? For this reason also our natures were altered. Now, therefore, you will not be able to endure [it] if I begin to cross-examine you.' Seth said to the wild animal, 'Shut your mouth and be quiet, and move away from the image of

possible that Paul is dependent for his interpretation of the story of Adam and Eve, not directly on Genesis 1–5, but on the version of the story we discover in the Greek Life of Adam and Eve?

JOHN R. LEVISON

FURTHER READING

Anderson, Gary, and Michael E. Stone, eds. *A Synopsis of the Books of Adam and Eve.* 2nd ed. SBL Early Judaism and Its Literature 17. Atlanta: Scholars Press, 1999.

Johnson, M. D. "Life of Adam and Eve." In *The Old Testament Pseudepigrapha,* edited by James H. Charlesworth, 2:249–95. 2 vols. Garden City, N.Y.: Doubleday, 1985.

Levison, John R. "Adam and Eve, Literature concerning." In *Dictionary of New Testament Backgrounds,* edited by Craig Evans and Stanley Porter, pp. 1–6. Downers Grove, Ill.: InterVarsity, 2000.

Nickelsburg, George W. E. *Jewish Literature between the Bible and the Mishnah.* 2nd ed. Minneapolis: Augsburg Fortress, 2005 (pp. 327–32).

Stone, Michael E. *A History of the Literature of Adam and Eve.* SBL Early Judaism and Its Literature 3. Atlanta: Scholars Press, 1992.

Tromp, Johannes. *The Life of Adam and Eve and Related Literature.* Sheffield: Sheffield Academic Press, 1997.

Wells, L. S. A. "The Books of Adam and Eve." In *The Apocrypha and Pseudepigrapha of the Old Testament,* edited by R. H. Charles, 2:123–54. 2 vols. Oxford: Clarendon, 1913.

ADVANCED READING

Anderson, Gary A. "Adam and Eve in the 'Life of Adam and Eve.'" In *Biblical Figures Outside the Bible,* edited by Michael E. Stone and Theodore A. Bergren, pp. 7–32. Harrisburg, Pa.: Trinity Press International, 1998.

———, Michael E. Stone, and Johannes Tromp, eds. *Literature on Adam and Eve.* Leiden: Brill, 2000.

Dochhorn, Jan. *Die Apokalypse des Mose: Text, Übersetzung, Kommentar.* Tübingen: Mohr Siebeck, 2005.

Levinson, John R. "Adam and Eve in Romans 1.18–25 and the Greek *Life of Adam and Eve.*" In *The Pseudepigrapha and Christian Origins: Essays from the Studiorum Novi Testamenti Societas,* edited by Gerbern Oegema and James H. Charlesworth, pp. 87–101. Jewish and Christian Texts in Contexts and Related Studies 4. New York: T&T Clark/Continuum, 2008. Reprinted from *New Testament Studies* 50 (2004): 519–34.

———. "The Exoneration of Eve in the Apocalypse of Moses 15–30." *JSJ* 20 (1989): 135–50.

———. *Portraits of Adam in Early Judaism: From Sirach to 2 Baruch.* JSPSup 1. Sheffield: Sheffield Academic, 1988.

———. *Texts in Transition: The Greek Life of Adam and Eve.* SBL Early Judaism and Its Literature 16. Atlanta: Scholars, 2000.

Tromp, Johannes. *The Life of Adam and Eve in Greek: A Critical Edition.* Leiden: Brill, 2005.

God until [the] day of judgment.' Then the wild animal said to Seth, 'Look I am moving away from the image of God.' And he went into his tent."—trans. Levison

3.4 Life of Adam and Eve

THE NARRATIVE AND WAY OF LIFE
OF ADAM AND EVE, THE FIRST-FORMED,
REVEALED BY GOD TO MOSES HIS SERVANT
WHEN HE RECEIVED THE TABLETS OF THE LAW FROM HIS HAND,
HAVING BEEN TAUGHT BY THE ARCHANGEL MICHAEL[a]

Lord, bless!

1:1 This is the narrative of Adam and Eve.

After they went out from paradise, 2 Adam took Eve his wife and returned to the east and remained there for eighteen years and two months. 3 Eve became pregnant and gave birth to two sons, *Unenlightened,* who was called Cain, and *Amilabes,* who was called Abel.

2:1 Now after these things, Adam and Eve were together. And while they were sleeping Eve said to her lord, Adam, 2 "My lord, I myself saw in a dream this very night the blood <of Abel> my son [[Amilabes who is called Abel]] being thrust into the mouth of Cain, his brother, and he drank it mercilessly. And he begged him to leave him a bit of it. 3 But he did not listen to him, but he gulped it down whole. And it did not remain in his belly, but it went out of his mouth. 4 And Adam said, "Getting up, let's go and see what it is that has happened to them. I am afraid that the enemy is doing battle somehow against them."

3:1 And as both went, they found Abel murdered by the hand of Cain his brother. 2 And God says to Michael the archangel, "Say to Adam, 'The mystery that you know do not reveal to Cain your son because he is a son of anger. But stop grieving. For I will give to you in his stead another son. This one will disclose to you everything that you will do. But you—do not say anything to him.'" 3 God said these things to his archangel. And Adam kept the word in his heart, with him as well as Eve, although they felt grief about Abel their son.

4:1 And after these things, Adam knew his wife, and she became pregnant and gave birth to Seth. 2 And Adam says to Eve, "Look, we gave birth to a son in Abel's stead, whom Cain murdered. Let's give glory and an offering to God."

---

a. This translation is based on the Greek edition produced by Johannes Tromp. Two large segments in italics are questionable (in chaps. 13 and 29) in terms of the original text, but too important to omit. Some marks ([[and]]; < and >) are an indication of uncertain texts. Simple brackets ([and]) contain English words I have added to the Greek just to make the English translation more comprehensible for modern readers. As to my translation method, I have followed the Greek closely, even when the word order is odd or the tenses are irregular. For instance, the Greek text frequently switches back and forth between past and present tenses; despite its awkwardness, I have chosen to preserve this shift in tenses.

Translation by John R. Levison.

⁵:¹ And Adam produced thirty sons and thirty daughters. And Adam lived nine hundred and thirty years, ² and, having fallen into disease [and] crying out with a loud voice, he says, "Let all my sons come to me so that I may see them before I die." ³ And all gathered (for the world was settled in three regions) ⁴ and Seth his son said to him, "Father, what is disease?" ⁵ And he says, "My children, much pain grips me." And they say to him, "What is your pain and disease?"

⁶:¹ And Seth, answering, says to him, "You don't remember, do you, father, paradise from which [fruits] you used to eat—and you grieved? ² If this is so, reveal [it] to me, and I myself will go and bring to you fruit from paradise. For I will place excrement upon my head, and I will weep and pray, and my Lord will hear me and will send his angel, and I will bring to you so that the pain will leave you." ³ Adam says to him, "No, my son Seth, but disease and pains, I have." Seth says to him, "And how did they come to you?"

⁷:¹ And Adam said to him: "When God made us, both me and your mother, through whom I am also dying, he gave to us every plant in paradise, but about one he commanded us not to eat from it, through which also we are dying. ² And the hour for the angels who were guarding your mother to ascend and to worship the Lord drew near. And the enemy gave to her and she ate from the tree, knowing that I was not very near her—nor the holy angels. ³ Then she gave also to me to eat.

⁸:¹ "And God was angry with us. And coming into paradise, the Authoritative One called me with a frightful voice, saying, 'Adam, where are you? And why do you hide yourself from my face? A building cannot be hidden from the one who built it, can it?' ² And he says, 'Since you disregarded my covenant and my command you disobeyed, I have inflicted upon your body seventy blows. The first disease of a blow: violence to the eyes. The second [is a disease of] a blow to hearing—and in this way, one after the other, all the blows to your body will follow closely behind.'"

⁹:¹ And saying these things to his sons, Adam groaned deeply and said, "What will I do because I am in deep grief?" ² And Eve wept, saying, "My lord, Adam, get up, give to me half of your disease, and I will endure it because on account of me this has happened to you, on account of me you are meeting with troubles." ³ And Adam said to Eve, "Get up and go with our son Seth to the vicinity of paradise, and place earth upon your heads and weep, begging God to have compassion upon me and send his angel into paradise and give to me from the tree in which the oil flows from it, and [so that] you may bring [it] to me and I may anoint myself and be free from my disease."

¹⁰:¹ And Seth went, and Eve, into the regions of paradise. And Eve saw her son and a wild animal battling with him. ² And Eve wept, saying, "Ah me! Ah me! Because if I come to the day of the resurrection, all who have sinned will curse me, saying, 'Eve did not keep the command of God.'" ³ And she said to the wild animal, "Oh, you evil wild animal, aren't you yourself frightened of doing battle with the image of God? How was your mouth opened? How have your teeth become strong? How did you not remember your submission—that in the past you submitted to the image of God?"

¹¹:¹ Then the wild animal cried out, saying, "Oh, Eve, your greed is not about us, nor your weeping, but about you, since the dominion of the wild animals came to be from you. ² How was your mouth opened to eat from the tree about which God

commanded you not to eat from it? For this reason also our natures were altered. Now, therefore, you will not be able to endure [it] if I begin to cross-examine you."

¹²:¹ Seth says to the wild animal, "Shut your mouth and be quiet, and move away from the image of God until [the] day of judgment." ² Then the wild animal says to Seth, "Look, I am moving away from the image of God." And he went into his tent.

¹³:¹ But Seth went with his mother Eve into the vicinity of paradise. And they wept, begging God to send his angel and to give to them the oil of mercy. ² And God sent Michael the archangel, and he said to him, "Seth, man of God, stop laboring, praying with this pleading about the tree in which flows the oil, in order to anoint your father Adam—³ which will not take place for you now. *But in the ends of times when all flesh from Adam until that great day will be raised, who will be a holy people, ⁴ then to them will be given all (the) joy of paradise, and God will be in their midst, ⁵ and they will no longer be sinning before him because the evil heart will be taken from them and a heart that understands for itself the good will be given to them—to worship God alone.* ⁶ But you yourself go again to your father since the measure of his life has been fulfilled—within three days. And when his soul comes out, you are about to see its frightful ascent."

¹⁴:¹ And having said these things, the angel went away from them. And Seth came, and Eve, into the tent where Adam was lying. ² And Adam says to Eve, "Oh, Eve, what did you bring about among us? You have brought upon us enormous anger, which is death's exercise of dominion over all of our race." ³ And Adam says to Eve, "Call all our children and the children of our children, and reveal to them the manner of our sinful neglect."

¹⁵:¹ Then Eve says to them: "Listen, all my children and the children of my children, and I will reveal to you how the enemy deceived us. ² And it just so happened that we were tending paradise, each of us the portion allotted to him, whatever region [was] from God, and I myself tended in my allotment—south and west. ³ And the devil went into the allotment of Adam, where the wild animals were (since God had divided the wild animals; all the males he had given to your father, and all the females he had given to me).

¹⁶:¹ "And the devil spoke to the serpent, saying, 'Get up. Come to me.' And, having gotten up, he went to him. ² And the devil says to him, 'I hear that you are shrewder than all the wild animals. <Listen to me> and I will become friends with you. ³ Why are you eating from the weeds of Adam and not from paradise? Get up and come, and let us make him to be thrown out of paradise, as also we were thrown out through him.' ⁴ The serpent says to him, 'I am frightened that perhaps the Lord will be angry with me.' ⁵ The devil says to him, 'Stop being frightened. Become a tool for me, and I myself will speak through your mouth one word aimed at deceiving them.'

¹⁷:¹ "And immediately he became suspended next to the walls of paradise. And when the angels of God ascended to worship, then Satan was transformed into [the] appearance of an angel and praised God with hymns—just like the angels. ² And as I peeped out of the wall, I saw him—similar to an angel. And he says to me, 'Are you Eve?' And I said to him, 'I am.' And he says to me, 'What are you doing in paradise?' ³ And I said to him, 'God placed us [here] to tend and to eat from it.' ⁴ The devil answered through the mouth of the serpent, 'You are doing well. But you are eating from every plant, aren't you?' ⁵ And I said, 'Yes, from all

of them we are eating, except one only, which is well inside paradise, about which God commanded us, "Do not eat from it, since with death you will die."'

18:1 "Then the serpent says to me, 'God lives—because I grieve for you [two], for I do not want you to be ignorant. Come therefore and eat and consider the value of the tree.' ² But I said to him, 'I am frightened that perhaps God will be angry with me, just as he said to us.' ³ And he says to me, 'Stop being frightened. For when you eat, your eyes will be opened, and you will be as gods, knowing what is good and what is evil. ⁴ And because God knows this, that you will be just like him, he bore a grudge against you and said, "Do not eat from it." ⁵ But you, turn your attention to the plant, and you will see intense glory.' But I was frightened to take from the fruit, and he says to me, 'Come, I will give [it] to you. Follow me.'

19:1 "And I opened, and he entered inside into paradise. And he passed through ahead of me. And after walking a bit, he turned and says to me, 'Because I have changed my mind, I will not give to you to eat, unless you swear to me that you [will] give [it] also to your husband.' ² But I myself said to him, 'I don't know with what kind of oath I will swear to you. Nevertheless, what I know I say to you: By the throne of the Authoritative One and the cherubim and the tree of life, I will give also to my husband.' ³ When he had extracted from me the oath, then he came and placed upon the fruit which he gave to me the venom of his wickedness [[this is of desire. For desire is of all sin]]. And after having bent the branch to the ground, I took from the fruit, and I ate.

20:1 "And at that very hour my eyes were opened, and I knew that I was naked of the righteousness with which I had been clothed. ² And I wept, saying, 'What did you bring about, that I have been estranged from my glory?' ³ And I began to weep about the oath. And that one got down from the plant and became invisible. ⁴ And I was searching in my region for leaves so that I could hide my shame, and I did not find [any]. For the leaves had fallen off all the plants of my region, except for the fig alone. ⁵ And having taken the leaves from it, I made for myself loincloths.

21:1 "And I cried out at that very hour, saying, 'Adam, Adam, where are you? Get up, come to me, and I will show you an enormous mystery.' ² But when your father came, I spoke to him words of lawlessness, which brought us down from intense glory. ³ For when he came, I opened my mouth, and the devil was speaking, and I began to give harsh counsel to him, saying, 'Come, my lord Adam, listen to me and eat from the fruit of the tree [about] which God said to us not to eat from it, and you will be as God.' ⁴ And answering, your father said, 'I am frightened that perhaps God will be angry with me.' But I myself said to him, 'Stop being frightened, for when you eat, you will be knowledgeable [about] good and evil.' ⁵ And then after having quickly persuaded him, he ate, and his eyes were opened, and he became aware of his nakedness. ⁶ And he says to me, 'Oh, evil woman, what did you bring about among us? You have estranged me from the glory of God.'

22:1 "And at that very hour we heard the archangel Michael sounding the trumpet and calling the angels and saying, ² 'These things says the Lord, "Come with me into paradise and hear the sentence with which I am going to sentence Adam."' And when we heard the archangel sounding the trumpet, we said, 'Look, God is coming into paradise to sentence us.' And we were frightened, and we hid. ³ And God came into paradise mounted upon a cherubim-throne, and the angels were praising him with hymns. And when God entered, the plants of Adam's allotment sprouted—and all of mine. [4] And the throne of God was established firmly where the tree of life was.

23:1 "And God called Adam, saying, 'Adam, where have you gone into hiding, thinking that I will not find you? A building will not be hidden from the one who built it, will it?' [2] Then answering, your father said, 'Not, my Lord, are we hiding from you because we think that we cannot be found by you, but I am frightened because I am naked, and I stood in awe of your power, Authoritative One.' [3] God says to him, 'Who made known to you that you are naked, unless you disregarded my command—to keep it?' [4] Then Adam remembered the word that I had spoken to him, 'Free of danger from God I will make you.' [5] And having turned to me, he said, 'Why did you do this?' And I said, 'The serpent deceived me.'

24:1 "And God says to Adam, 'Since you disobeyed my command and listened to your wife, cursed is the earth on your account. [2] You will work it, and it will not give its produce. Thorny and prickly plants it will sprout for you, and with [the] sweat of your face you will eat your bread. And you will be in various diseases, [having been] oppressed by bitterness, [and] you will not taste sweetness— [3] [having been] oppressed by burning heat and constrained by cold. And wild animals, which you used to rule, will rise up in revolt against you with anarchy because my command you did not keep.'

25:1 "And having turned toward me, the Lord says, 'Since you yourself listened to the serpent and disobeyed my command, you will be in various diseases, and in unendurable pains [2] you will give birth to children [[in many ways]]. And in one hour you will come to give birth and you will lose your life from your intense bodily anguish and childbirth pains. [3] And you will confess and say, "Lord, Lord, save me, and I will not return to the sin of the flesh." [4] On account of this, on the basis of your words I will sentence you—on account of the enmity that the enemy placed in you. And having turned again to your husband, (and) he himself will rule you.'

26:1 "And after he had said these things to me, he said to the serpent with intense anger, saying to him, 'Since you did this and became an ungrateful tool, so that you could deceive the careless of heart, cursed are you from all domestic animals. [2] You will be deprived of your food, which you used to eat, and dust you will eat all the days of your life. Upon your breast and your belly you will go, lacking both your hands and feet. [3] There will be left to you neither ear nor wing nor one body part of these with which you enticed with your wickedness and caused them to be thrown out of paradise. [4] And I will place enmity between you and between their seed. And he himself will (closely) watch your head, and you the heel of that one, until the Day of Judgment.'

27:1 "Having said these things, he commands his angels for us to be thrown out of paradise. [2] And while they were driving us out and wailing out loud, your father Adam begged the angels, saying, 'Allow me a little [time] so that I may beg God to have compassion and show me mercy, for I only sinned.' [3] And they themselves stopped driving him out. And Adam cried out with weeping, saying, 'Forgive me, Lord, what I have done.' [4] Then God says to his angels, 'Why did you stop throwing Adam out of paradise? The sinful act is not mine, is it, or did I hand down a sentence wickedly?' [5] Then the angels, having fallen upon the earth, worshiped the Lord, saying, 'You are just, Lord, and you hand down fair sentences.'

28:1 "And having turned toward Adam, he said, 'I will not allow you from now on to be in paradise.' ² And answering, Adam said, 'Lord, give to me from the plant of life so that I may eat before I am thrown out.' ³ Then the Lord spoke to Adam, 'You will not take now from it. For it was determined that the cherubim and the fiery sword which revolves should guard it on your account so that you may not taste from it and be immortal forever. ⁴ And you have the enmity that the enemy placed in you. But when you go out of paradise, if you guard yourself from all wickedness—as if longing to die—again, when the resurrection happens, I will raise you, and (it) will be given to you from the tree of life, and you will be immortal forever.'

29:1 "And having said these things, the Lord commanded his angels for us to be thrown out of paradise. ² And your father wept in the presence of the angels in paradise, and the angels say to him, 'What do you want us to do for you, Adam?' ³ And answering, your father said to the angels, 'Look, you are throwing me out. I beg you: Allow me to take away fragrances out of paradise so that, after I go out, I may present an offering to God, so that God will hear me.' ⁴ And having approached, the angels said to the Lord, 'Jael, eternal King, command that incenses of fragrance from paradise be given to Adam.' ⁵ And God commanded that it be allowed to Adam that he should take fragrances and seeds for his sustenance. ⁶ And having left him, the angels brought four kinds: saffron, spikenard, aromatic cane, and cinnamon—and other seeds for his sustenance. And having taken these, he went out of paradise. And we came to be upon the earth. ⁷ *And it happened that we grieved for seven days, and after the seven days we were hungry, and I said to Adam, 'Get up and give thought to food for us so that we can eat and live so that we will not die, (so that) we will be raised and encircle the earth—if in this way God will hear us.' And we got up and passed through all that earth, and we did not find.* ⁸ *And again Eve said to Adam, 'Get up, lord, and destroy me, so that I may take leave from your face and the face of God and from the angels, so that they will stop being angry with you through me.'* ⁹ *Then, having answered, Adam said to Eve, 'Why do you remember this evil, that I should commit murder and bring death to my side, or how can I lay a hand upon the image of God, which [God] formed—but let us do penitence for forty days so that God will have compassion on us and give to us food better than the wild animals.* ¹⁰ *And I myself, on the one hand, will do (this) for forty days [[and four]], but you yourself, on the other hand, fast for thirty-four days because you yourself were not formed on the sixth day, in which God made his creation. But get up and go into the Tigris River, and take this stone and place [it] under your feet and stand still, clothed in water up to the neck, and stop speech from leaving your mouth, and praying to God, for we are worthless, and our lips are not clean; but, keeping silent, immersed in water, cry out to God with your whole heart.'* ¹¹ *And Adam went into the Jordan, and the hair of his head spread out, and he screamed with a loud voice, saying, 'To you, I say, to the water of the Jordan River: stand still and pray.' And at once all the wild animals and all the birds and all the creeping animals in the earth and sea and all the angels and all the works of God encircled Adam as a wall around him, weeping and praying to God on Adam's behalf that God might hear him.* ¹² *But the devil, not having found a passage to Adam, went to the Tigris River, to Eve, and having taken an angelic appearance, and stood before her weeping, and his tears were flowing*

upon the earth and upon his robe, and he says to Eve, 'Get up out of the water and
stop this weeping, for God has heard your prayer because also we angels and all his
works begged God on your [and Adam's] behalf.' [13] *And having said these things,*
he deceived us, and I got out of the water.

30:1 "Now therefore, my children, I have disclosed to you the way in which
we were deceived. And you yourselves—guard yourselves so as not to disregard
what is good."

31:1 And having said these things in the presence of her sons, while Adam was
sleeping in his disease (he had one additional day to go out of his body), [2] and Eve
says to Adam, "Why are you dying, and I live? Oh, how much time do I have to
spend after your death? Reveal [it] to me." [3] Then Adam says to Eve, "Stop giving
thought to these matters. For you will not be much longer than I, but we are both
alike about to die. And you will be placed into my burial place. And when I die,
leave me alone, and let no one touch me until an angel says something about me.
[4] For God will not forget me but will search [his] own tool that he formed. Get
up instead. Pray to God until I give back my spirit into the hands of the one who
has given it to me since we do not know how we will meet the one who made us,
whether he will be angry with us or turn around to show us mercy."

32:1 Then she got up and went outside. And having fallen upon the earth, she
said repeatedly,

> [2] "I sinned, God,
> I sinned, father of all,
> I sinned against you.
> I sinned against your chosen angels,
> I sinned against the cherubim,
> I sinned against your immovable throne,
> I sinned, Lord,
> I sinned much,
> I sinned in your sight,
> And all sin because of me has come about in the creation."

[3] While Eve was still praying, look, the angel of humanity came to her, and
made her stand up, saying, [4] "Get up, Eve, from your penitence. For, look, Adam
your husband has gone out from his body. Get up and see his spirit being carried
up to the one who made him in order to meet him."

33:1 And having gotten up, Eve placed her hand onto her face, [2] and having
looked closely into heaven, she saw a chariot of light coming by four radiant
eagles, which it was not possible that they were birthed from a belly, or to speak
about their glory, or to see their face—and angels bringing the chariot. [3] And
when it came [to] where your father Adam was lying, the chariot stood still and
the seraphim between your father and the chariot. [4] And I myself saw golden incense altars and three libation bowls, and, look, all the angels with frankincense
and the incense altars came with great speed to the altar and were breathing into
them, and the smoke of the incense hid the heavenly firmaments. [5] And the angels
prostrated themselves to God, crying out and saying, "Jael, Holy One, forgive,
because he is your image and the handiwork of your holy hands."

34:1 And I, Eve, saw two enormous and frightful mysteries in the presence of God. And I wept for fright and cried out to my son Seth, saying, 2 "Get up, Seth, from the body of your father, and come to me, and see things that no eye of anyone has ever seen, and they are begging on behalf of your father, Adam."

35:1 Then Seth got up and went to his mother, and he says to her, "Why are you weeping?" 2 And she says to him, "Look up with your eyes, and see the seven heavenly firmaments standing open and how the body of your father lies upon [its] face and all the holy angels with him praying for him and saying, "Forgive him, Father of the Whole Creation, because he is your image." 3 And, therefore, my child Seth, what is [this] to me? And when will [he] be handed over into the hands of our invisible God? 4 And who are, my son Seth, the two Ethiopians who stand by at the prayer for your father?"

36:1 And Seth says to his mother, "These are the sun and the moon, and they are prostrating themselves and praying for my father, Adam." 2 And Eve says to him, "And where is their light, and why have they become black looking?" 3 And Seth says to her, "Their light has not moved away, but they are not able to shine in the presence of the Light of the Whole Creation, the Father of Lights, and on this account the light has been hidden from them."

37:1 And while Seth was saying these things to his mother Eve, look, the angel sounded the trumpet, and all of the angels who were lying upon [their] faces got up. And they cried out with a frightful sound, saying, 2 "Blessed be the Glory of the Lord by all his works because he has shown mercy to one formed by his hands, Adam." 3 And when the angels had said these outcries, look, one of the six-winged seraphim came and seized Adam—into the Acherusian Lake—and washed him clean three times, and led him into the presence of God. 4 And he spent three hours, lying. And after these things, the Father of the Whole Creation, [who was] seated upon his throne, stretched out his hand and took Adam up and handed him over to the archangel Michael, saying, 5 "Take him up into paradise, as far as the third heaven, and leave him there until that intensely frightful day of cosmic ordering, which I will accomplish in the world." 6 Then Michael took Adam up and left him where God had said to him, and all the angels were praising with an angelic hymn, marveling at the forgiving of Adam.

38:1 And after the [[coming]] joy of Adam, the archangel Michael cried out to the Father on account of Adam. 2 And the Father said to him that all the angels should be gathered in the presence of God, each according to his rank, and all the angels were gathered, some (on the one hand) holding incense altars in their hands and others (on the other hand) holding lyres and libation bowls and trumpets. 3 And, look, the Lord of Armies mounted up, and four winds were moving him, and the cherubim holding the winds in check, and the angels from heaven leading him forward, and they came upon the earth, where the body of Adam was. [[4 And they came into paradise, and all the plants of paradise were set in motion, so that all human beings who had been birthed from Adam dozed off from the fragrance, apart from Seth alone because he happened to be facing (the) mountain of God—from that place in the direction of the body of Adam.]]

39:1 And he was terribly grieved about him, and God says to him, "Adam, why did you do this? If you had kept my command, those who brought you down into this place would not have rejoiced. 2 Nevertheless, I say to you that their joy I will

459

transform into grief, and your grief I will transform into joy. And I will restore you to your dominion, and I will seat you on the throne of the one who deceived you. ³ And that one will be thrown into this place so that he may see you seated upon it. Then he himself will be condemned—and those who listened to him—and he will be grieved when he sees you sitting upon his throne."

⁴⁰:¹ After these things, God said to the archangel Michael, "Go away into paradise in the third heaven, and bring three linen cloths—silken and of fine linen." ² And after having been led in, God commanded the archangel Michael—and Gabriel and Uriel—to bury the body of Adam, speaking in this way: "Spread out the linen cloths and cover the body of Adam. And, having brought oil from the oil of fragrance, pour (it) out upon him." And they did as God had commanded. And the three high-ranking angels buried him. ³ And when they had finished burying Adam, God said that the body of Abel should also be led in. And having brought other linen cloths, they buried him, ⁴ since he had been unburied since the day when Cain, his brother, had murdered him. And although Cain had wanted very much to hide him, he was unable because his body sprang up from the earth. ⁵ And a voice came out of the earth, saying, "Another formed one will not be hidden in the earth until the time when the first formed one, which was taken away from me, should leave to me the dust from which it was taken." And the angels had taken, at that time, and placed it upon the rock until Adam, his father, would be buried. ⁶ And God commanded, after the burial of Adam and Abel, to take the two up into the regions of paradise, into the place where God had taken up dust and formed Adam, and made the place for the two of them to be dug. ⁷ And God sent seven angels into paradise, and they brought many fragrances and placed them in the earth. And after these things, they took the two bodies and buried them in the place [into] which they themselves had dug and built.

⁴¹:¹ And God called Adam and said, "Adam. Adam." The body answered from the earth and said, "Look, I, Lord." ² And the Lord says to him, "I said to you, 'Earth you are and into earth you will go away.' Again the resurrection I am promising to you. I will raise you in the resurrection with every race of human beings which (is) from your seed."

⁴²:¹ And after these words, God made a triangular seal and sealed the tomb so that no one could do anything to him during the six days until his rib would be returned to him. ² Then the Lord and the angels went into their place. ³ And Eve, she herself, when the six days were fulfilled, fell asleep. And while she was still living, she wept about Adam's sleep. For she did not know where he had been placed since when the Lord came to paradise to bury Adam, all fell asleep until God gave the command to bury Adam—except Seth alone—and no one upon the earth knew except for his son Seth. ⁴ And Eve prayed, weeping, that she would be buried in the place where Adam her husband was. ⁵ And after she finished the prayer, she says, "Lord, Authoritative One, God of All Virtue, stop estranging me from the body of Adam, from which you took me up from his body parts, ⁶ but consider even me—this worthless sinner—worthy to enter with his tent-dwelling. As I was with him in paradise, both of us, without being separated from one another, ⁷ as in the (act of) sinful neglect, having been deceived, we sinfully neglected your command without being separated—so also now, Lord, stop sep-

arating us." **8** And after she prayed, having looked up into heaven, she groaned, beating her breast and saying, "Oh, God of All, receive my spirit."

43:1 And Michael came and taught Seth how to bury Eve. And three angels went and took her body up and buried it where the body of Adam—and of Abel—was. **2** And after these things, Michael spoke to Seth, saying, "In this way bury every person who dies until [the] day of the resurrection." **3** And after he gave the regulation, he said to him, "Beyond six days, stop grieving. And on the seventh day, leave off and rejoice about it, because in it God and we, the angels, rejoice with the just soul that vanishes from earth." **4** Having said these things, the angel ascended into heaven, praising and saying, "Alleluia! Holy, holy, holy Lord!"

TO (THE) GLORY OF GOD THE FATHER.
AMEN.

4. Biblical Interpretation and Rewritten Scripture

The classifications "biblical interpretation" and "rewritten Scripture" are perhaps the most telling categories of the literature from the Second Temple period.[1] How individuals or communities during this period were interpreting and rewriting Scripture reveals significant aspects of the worldviews that were held among the various Jewish sects. In addition, the category "biblical interpretation" crosses over the lines of several other classifications in this volume such as "apocalyptic literature" (*see* Introduction to Apocalyptic Literature), for example, 1 Enoch (*see* Introduction to 1 Enoch) and the War Scroll (*see* War Scroll [1QM]), and "romanticized narrative" (*see* Introduction to Romanticized Narrative), for example, the Life of Adam and Eve (*see* the Life of Adam and Eve) and Tobit (*see* The Book of Tobit).

The Qumran scrolls (*see* Overview of Early Jewish Literature) contain the most recognizable texts of biblical interpretation among the corpus of Second Temple period literature. These include the pesharim (*see* Introduction to *Pesharim*), targumim, and those texts identified as rewritten Scripture. At least eighteen *pesharim* commenting on the biblical text have been found in the Qumran library: fourteen on the prophets, three on the Psalms, and one unidentified.[2] Among

---

1. See Molly M. Zahn, *Rethinking Rewritten Scripture: Composition and Exegesis in the 4QReworked Pentateuch Manuscripts* (Leiden: Brill, 2011), pp. 1–2; idem, "Genre and Rewritten Scripture: A Reassessment," *JBL* 131, (2012): 271–88; Geza Vermes, *Scripture and Tradition in Judaism: Haggadic Studies,* 2nd ed., StPB 4 (Leiden: Brill, 1973); Moshe J. Bernstein, "'Rewritten Bible': A Generic Category Which Has Outlived Its Usefulness?" *Textus* 22 (2005): 169–96; Anders Klostergaard Petersen, "Rewritten Bible as a Borderline Phenomenon—Genre, Textual Strategy, or Canonical Anachronism?" in *Flores Florentino: Dead Sea Scrolls and Other Early Jewish Studies in Honour of Florentino Garcia Martinez,* ed. Anthony Hilhorst et al., JSJSup 122 (Leiden: Brill, 2007), pp. 285–306; James C. VanderKam, "The Wording of Biblical Citations in Some Rewritten Scriptural Works," in *The Bible as Book: The Hebrew Bible and the Judaean Desert Discoveries,* ed. Edward D. Herbert and Emanuel Tov (London: British Library, 2002), pp. 41–56 (pp. 42–43); Anders Klostergaard Petersen, "Rewritten Bible," in *The Bible as Book: The Hebrew Bible and the Judaean Desert Discoveries,* ed. Edward D. Herbert and Emanuel Tov (London: British Library, 2002), pp. 286–88.

2. The following texts are identified in the category *pesharim*: 1QpHab, 1QpMic,

these eighteen documents, three categories of *pesharim* have been differentiated: (1) a continuous *pesher* that contains verse-by-verse commentary on an entire biblical book (e.g., Habakkuk Pesher; *see* Habakkuk Pesher [1QpHab]); (2) a thematic *pesher* that contains quotations from various biblical texts that are grouped together under a specific topic (*see* Melchizedek [11Q13], Florilegium [4Q174]); and (3) an isolated *pesher* that includes commentary on one or two verses from the Jewish Scriptures combined with terminology found in a larger composition (e.g., CD 19.7–9 on Zech. 13:7; 1QS 8.12b–16 on Isa. 40:3). Each of these forms of interpretation found in the scrolls legitimizes the author's interpretation by linking the method in question to texts already recognized as sacred by the community; at the same time, an author could claim a fresh revelation of the biblical text.

A *pesher* was considered inspired, which implied a religious authority similar to that of the Hebrew Scriptures; however, the *pesher* was "not regarded as equal in authority to the text being interpreted." Further, the biblical prophecies present in the *pesher* were interpreted under the premise that the interpreter's community was living out its days on the brink of the eschaton. The author of a given *pesher* operated with the conviction that the prophets of the Hebrew Bible predicted his present times and the role of his community in them. This understanding imposed either a double meaning on the prophetic text or it suggested that the Second Temple period interpreter was ignoring or bypassing the implied setting of the biblical book. As such, interpreters saw their interpretation of the prophecy as the true, divinely inspired word; nonetheless, they were careful to distinguish commentary from the sacred text.

A further set of texts of interpretation includes *targumim*, which offer a running commentary on the biblical narrative that often includes an expansion of the biblical text (e.g., 4QTargumJob). The above-mentioned genres include several subcategories in each—such concepts as paraphrastic translation and anthological writings are included in this area. The third category of interpretative texts from the Second Temple period is "rewritten Scripture," in which the author/interpreter expanded, rearranged, or conflated the biblical text before him.

Any text that falls into one of these categories offers the reader a window into understanding the worldviews of the various Jewish (and early Christian) groups that flourished during the Second Temple period. Of particular importance to the authors of these texts was the inspiration they were granted by the divine (holy) spirit in interpreting or rewriting the biblical text. The "inspired interpretation" implied in these texts denotes a specific hermeneutical approach that suggests true meaning is inaccessible to the average reader of the biblical texts. Therefore, the "inspired interpreter" has a special insight that not all individuals share. One of the primary purposes of the *pesharim,* or the texts identified as rewritten Scripture, was to establish religious doctrines of the community that had scriptural precedent. In many instances, interpreters read the biblical text in a way that supported their views on a particular issue. This method helped the community retain the relevance of the text to its particular needs—social, political, and theological.

1QpZeph, 1QpPs, 3QpIsa, 4QpIsa^a–e, 4QpHos^a–b, 4QpMic, 4QpNah, 4QpZeph, 4QpPs^a–b, and 4QpUnid.

Several principles of biblical interpretation can be discerned from the various documents of the corpus of the Second Temple period literature. In several cases, it is apparent that a given community believed itself to represent the generation in which God would once again visit Israel. As such, members of a particular community understood that God revealed his eschatological purpose to the biblical prophets, but it remained a mystery until interpreted by their community (leaders). For example, the interpreters from Qumran looked to their current circumstances in order to understand properly the message of the prophets. Often variant readings of a particular text were chosen in order to bend the text to the community's situation. If a text did not readily address their situation, the interpreter could offer an allegorical interpretation of the passage; as a result, many biblical prophecies were reinterpreted to apply a given passage to the "end-time" perspective of the interpreter.

The primary texts (along with two general introductions) chosen as representative for this section include 1QpHab (Habakkuk Pesher), 11Q13 (Melchizedek), 4Q174 (Florilegium) and 4Q175 (Testimonia), the book of Jubilees, 1QapGen (Genesis Apocryphon), 4Q158, 4Q364–67 (Reworked Pentateuch), 11Q19–20 (Temple Scroll), and Philo of Alexandria's *On the Creation of the World, On the Giants, On the Decalogue,* and *On the Life of Moses.*

ARCHIE T. WRIGHT

The *Pesharim*

Found among the Dead Sea Scrolls, the *pesharim* are distinctive commentaries on specific biblical books (*see* Overview of Early Jewish Literature). The term *pesharim* is the plural form of the Hebrew word *pesher,* which means "interpretation." Scriptural interpretation in the *pesharim* includes three components: (1) a citation of the biblical text (**lemma**), (2) an introductory formula containing some form of the term *pesher* (e.g., "the interpretation of the passage" or "its interpretation"), and (3) an interpretation.

Two types of Qumran documents employ the *pesher* formula. The first group—called "continuous *pesharim*"—consists of running commentaries that follow the sequence of a given biblical book: a portion of the biblical text (the length of which may vary) is quoted followed by its interpretation; after that, the next portion of the biblical text is quoted followed by its interpretation; and so on. The second group—called "thematic *pesharim*"—comprises documents that juxtapose scriptural quotations and interpretations that pertain to a certain theme (*see* Florilegium [4Q174]; Melchizedek [11Q13]). The term *pesharim* without a qualifier typically refers to thematic *pesharim*. Following the seminal work of Maurya P. Horgan,[1] it has become customary to ascribe seventeen documents to this group of texts: three *pesharim* on the Psalms (1QpPs [1Q16], 4QpPs^a [4Q171], 4QpPs^b [4Q173]), six on Isaiah (3QpIsa [3Q4], 4QpIsa^a [4Q161], 4QpIsa^b [4Q162], 4QpIsa^c [4Q163], 4QpIsa^d [4Q164], 4QpIsa^e [4Q165]), two on Hosea (4QpHos^a [4Q166], 4QpHos^b [4Q167]), two on Micah (1QpMic [1Q14], 4QpMic [4Q168]), one on Nahum (4QpNah [4Q169]), one on Habakkuk (1QpHab), and two on Zephaniah (1QpZeph [1Q15], 4QpZeph [4Q170]).

---

1. Maurya P. Horgan, *Pesharim: Qumran Interpretations of Biblical Books,* CBQMS 8 (Washington, D.C.: Catholic Biblical Association, 1979); idem, "Pesharim," in *Hebrew, Aramaic, and Greek Texts with English Translations,* vol. 6B:, *Pesharim, Other Commentaries, and Related Documents,* ed. James H. Charlesworth, PTSDSSP 6B (Tübingen: Mohr Siebeck, 2002), pp. 1–193.

Author/Text/Date

All of the *pesharim* were composed in Hebrew by anonymous members of the Qumran community. What is most peculiar about these documents is that only one extant copy of each of them has been found. Even when there are several commentaries on the same prophetic book their contents never overlap. Although it is possible that the *pesharim* are **autographs**,[2] scribal corrections and spacing in some of the manuscripts suggest that at least some of them are copies.[3] Based on **paleography**, the manuscripts can be dated to the **Hasmonean** (ca. 140–ca. 63 BCE) and **Herodian** (37 BCE–70 CE) periods. The dating of the actual compositions depends on how one sees their relationship to the historical events to which they refer. It appears that most of the *pesharim* were composed during the first century BCE, though for some of them a slightly earlier or later date is also possible.

Genre

The *pesharim* are examples of biblical commentaries that contain explicit exegesis of Scripture. In contrast to the Second Temple exegetical writings that belong to the category "rewritten Scripture" (*see* Introduction to Biblical Interpretation and Rewritten Scripture), which blend text and interpretation, the *pesharim* are characterized by a "citation plus comment" form and a relatively stable base text. *Pesharim* predate, as early as the second century BCE, the systematic practice of biblical interpretation in the form of commentaries, which would eventually become dominant in rabbinic and Christian literature.[4]

Exegetical Techniques

The purpose of the *pesharim* is to apply Scripture to the experience of the members of the Qumran community, who interpreted recent and current events as fulfilled prophecy. The exegetical techniques they employ include wordplay (i.e., **paronomasia**, **polyvalence**, reordering of consonants, different vocalization), **allegorization**, and **atomization**. The authors frequently single out individual words or short phrases and apply them to contemporary events on the basis of their linguistic features or allegorical potential. In some cases, the new application

2. See Jósef T. Milik, *Ten Years of Discovery in the Wilderness of Judaea*, trans. John Strugnell, SBT 26 (London: SCM, 1959), p. 41; Frank Moore Cross, *The Ancient Library of Qumran and Modern Biblical Studies*, rev. ed., Anchor Books (Garden City, N.Y.: Doubleday, 1961), pp. 114-15.

3. See Horgan, *Pesharim*, pp. 3-4.

4. See Markus Bockmuehl, "The Dead Sea Scrolls and the Origins of Biblical Commentary," in *Text, Thought, and Practice in Qumran and Early Christianity*, ed. Ruth A. Clements and Daniel R. Schwartz (Leiden: Brill, 2009), pp. 3-29. Bockmuehl notes that "the gradual move from 'rewriting' via implicit exegesis to formally explicit commentary documents the emergence of a conviction that the text is now a given" (p. 6).

corresponds to the original context of the lemma. In most cases, however, various components of the biblical passages are applied to a new situation without regard to their original literary and historical contexts.[5]

To the modern reader, the rules that govern scriptural interpretation in the *pesharim* may seem arbitrary, but for the members of the Qumran community they were quite persuasive. For example, the "wicked one" and the "righteous one" from Psalm 37:32 ("The wicked one is watching for the righteous one and he is seeking to kill him") are interpreted as the "Wicked Priest" and "Teacher of Righteousness" from the Qumranites' own experience (4QpPs[a], frags. 1–10, 4.8: "Its interpretation concerns the Wicked [Prie]st who is wat[ching out] for the Right[eous One and he is seeking] to kill him"—A. Wright). The prophetic critique in Habakkuk 2:8a, "you have plundered many nations," is related to "the last priests of Jerusalem, who amass wealth and profit from the plunder of the peoples" (1QpHab 9.4–5). Individual words or phrases sometimes have different referents. For example, the "lion" from Nahum 2:12b (MT, "Where is the den of the lions, and the feeding place of the young lions, where walks the lion, lioness, and lion's cub, with nothing to frighten [them]? The lion tore enough for his cubs and killed [enough] for his lionesses, and filled his dens with prey, and his lairs with torn flesh"—A. Wright) is identified with "Demetrius, King of Greece, who sought to enter Jerusalem on the advice of the Seekers-After-Smooth-Things" (4QpNah, frags. 3–4, 1.2) and the "lion" from Nahum 2:13a (MT—see above) with **Alexander Jannaeus** (4QpNah, frags. 3–4, 1.4–7).

Pesharim and Qumran History

Given their tendency to relate biblical prophecies to the Qumranites' **sectarian** experience, the *pesharim* could be used for reconstructing the history of the Qumran community.[6] However, only the Nahum Pesher mentions the names of recognizable historical personalities—Demetrius and Antiochus (4QpNah, frags. 3–4, 1.2–3)—that presumably refer to **Demetrius III** and **Antiochus IV Epiphanes**. In all other cases, the *pesharim* use sobriquets, such as Teacher of Righteousness, Man of the Lie, Wicked Priest, House of Absalom, Kittim, Seekers-After-Smooth-Things, Ephraim, and Manasseh. This figurative language complicates the identification of the persons and the events to which the commentaries allude. Moreover, the events they mention are not narrated in chronological order but sporadically.

What can be said with certainty is that the Teacher of Righteousness was the unique recipient of divine revelation (1QpHab 7.4–5). God established him to build a congregation (4QpPs[a], frags. 1–10, 3.15–17); the House of Absalom did not support him when he came into conflict with the Man of the Lie (1QpHab 5.9–12) who deceived many (4QpPs[a], frags. 1–10, 1.26–27) and joined the traitors

---

5. See Horgan, *Pesharim*, pp. 244–47; Timothy H. Lim, *Pesharim* (London: Sheffield Academic Press, 2002), pp. 27–39.

6. See James H. Charlesworth, *The Pesharim and Qumran History: Chaos or Consensus?* (Grand Rapids: Eerdmans, 2002), pp. 17–118.

who did not accept the interpretations of the Teacher of Righteousness (1QpHab 2.1–10). The Wicked Priest abandoned God, violated God's statutes for wealth (1QpHab 8.8–13), dealt wickedly with the Poor Ones (1QpHab 12.2–6), and defiled the sanctuary (1QpHab 12.7–10). He tried to murder the Teacher of Righteousness by ambush (4QpPs[a], frags. 1–10, 4.8–10); he pursued him to his place of exile when, following a different calendar, he celebrated the Day of Atonement (1QpHab 11.4–8). The Wicked Priest was eventually delivered into the hands of his enemies (1QpHab 9.9–12) and punished with a horrible disease (1QpHab 9.1–2; *see* Habakkuk Pesher [1QpHab]).

The identification of some of the groups mentioned in the *pesharim* is fairly straightforward. The term "Kittim" regularly refers to the Romans. The Seekers-After-Smooth-Things is a standard Qumran sobriquet for the **Pharisees**. Ephraim and Manasseh most likely refer to the Pharisees and the **Sadducees**, respectively. Other sobriquets, however, are much more difficult to decipher. One of the most challenging questions is the identity of the Wicked Priest, the archenemy of the Teacher of Righteousness. Geza Vermes argues that this is a sobriquet for Jonathan,[7] while Frank Moore Cross believes that it refers to his brother Simon,[8] both of whom were Hasmonean priests. According to the Groningen hypothesis, the Wicked Priest is a title that refers to not one but six different high priests—**Judas Maccabeus**, Alcimus, Jonathan Maccabeus, Simon Maccabeus, **Jonathan Hyrcanus I**, and Alexander Jannaeus.[9] All such reconstructions can be only tentative. The *pesharim*, by their very nature, do not offer reliable historical reports but present the actual events as the members of the Qumran community perceived them. Thus, they provide information not only about the events that occurred but also about the group that interpreted them.[10] In some cases, the chronological distance between the actual events and their mention in the *pesharim* spans almost a century. Some passages might even reflect more than one stage in the transmission process, which further complicates historical reconstruction.

Theology

Jewish exegetical writings from the Second Temple period rarely explain their hermeneutical principles (**emic** [insider] perspective), so that in most cases scholars have to uncover them from the outside (**etic** perspective). With the Qumran *pesharim*, however, we are in a privileged position because the Habakkuk Pesher (1QpHab) provides an emic viewpoint on the concept of *pesher*.

---

7. Geza Vermes, *The Dead Sea Scrolls: Qumran in Perspective* (London: Collins, 1977), p. 11.

8. Frank Moore Cross, *The Ancient Library of Qumran*, 3rd ed. (Sheffield: Sheffield Academic Press, 1995), p. 115.

9. Florentino Garcia Martinez and A. S. van der Woude, "A 'Groningen' Hypothesis of Qumran Origins and Early History," *Revue de Qumrân* 14 (1990): 521–42. For a critique, see Timothy H. Lim, "The Wicked Priests of the Groningen Hypothesis," *JBL* 112 (1993): 415–25.

10. See Jutta Jokiranta, "Pesharim: A Mirror of Self-Understanding," in *Reading the Present in the Qumran Library: The Perception of the Contemporary by Means of Scriptural Interpretations*, ed. Kristin De Troyer and Armin Lange, SBLSymS 30 (Atlanta: SBL, 2005), p. 27.

At the beginning of column 7, the author explains that "God told Habakkuk to write down the things that are going to come upon the last generation, but the fulfillment of the period he did not make known to him" (1QpHab 7.1–2). This assertion clarifies the view of the biblical text: the prophet was an original recipient of divine revelation and wrote it down faithfully, but he did not understand its true meaning because the prophetic message referred to the future time that remained undisclosed to him. In line 3 the *pesherist* quotes Habakkuk 2:2b—"And when it says, 'so that he can run who reads it'"—which is followed in lines 4–5 by an interpretation introduced with the *pesher* formula: "its interpretation concerns the Teacher of Righteousness, to whom God made known all the mysteries of the words of his servants the prophets." These lines clarify that God revealed the true meaning of the text to the Teacher of Righteousness. As a unique recipient of divine revelation about the textual meaning, the Teacher of Righteousness acted as the only authorized interpreter of the text.

The interpretations of biblical prophecies that were revealed to the Teacher of Righteousness, and perhaps to a close circle of his followers, were most likely transmitted orally until they were recorded, along with other interpretative traditions of the Qumran community, in the *pesharim* and other related works. The authors of the *pesharim* believed that they were living in the final period of history, which had been, albeit inadvertently, prophesied about by the biblical prophets. The phrase "the latter days" occurs more than thirty times in the entire Qumran corpus. The Habakkuk Pesher also indicates that the Qumranites expected a certain delay of the completion of this last period of history (1QpHab 7.7, 12). However, they interpreted this apparent prolongation to mean that the future had already been set in motion and that their own history was part of it. Not surprisingly, then, they applied the various prophecies uttered by Isaiah, Hosea, Micah, Nahum, Habakkuk, and even David (because the Qumranites believed that he had composed the Psalms "through prophecy given to him by the Most High" [11Q5 27:11]) to the recent or current events that were taking place in their own community.

The most remarkable feature of the *pesharim* is their presumption that the text of Scripture is a mysterious entity that can be understood properly only through special revelation given to a uniquely gifted interpreter. The closest analogy to this kind of interpretation outside Qumran is found in the interpretation of dreams and visions in the Aramaic section of the book of Daniel (*see* The Book of Daniel). A dream or a vision remains a mystery for the recipient until an interpreter receives a revelation that deciphers its meaning (Dan. 5:12, 16–17, 26; 7:16). In the Qumran *pesharim,* the mysterious content is supplied not by a dream or a vision, but by a biblical text. Yet, as in Daniel, the meaning of the text cannot be perceived by ordinary means, such as rational faculties, but only through special divine revelation to a chosen individual.

This type of exegesis could be rightly called revelatory and inspired[11] because it presumes that only a select few are capable of understanding it. Since it is based on the assumption that the only truth is the revealed truth, it is not intended to convince outsiders. Such interpretation is typical for sectarian communities

11. See Lim, *Pesharim*, p. 35.

whose experiences have been shaped decisively by separation and alienation from a larger group. Its primary task is to justify the community's existence and its sectarian worldview and to strengthen it in its struggle against external and internal opponents.[12]

Pesharim and the Rabbinic *Midrashim*

Since the *pesharim* provide the earliest examples of biblical commentary, a literary genre that became dominant in rabbinic times, the exegetical techniques they employ are sometimes compared to those in the rabbinic *midrashim*.[13] There are, however, significant differences between the hermeneutical principles that govern biblical interpretation in these two literary corpora. Interpretative techniques are more transparent in the *midrashim* than in the *pesharim*. The *pesharim* offer only one reading of a scriptural passage, while the *midrashim* typically offer several interpretations of a given text. The *pesharim* apply Scripture to the history of the Qumran community, while the *midrashim* show little desire to relate biblical texts to current events.[14]

Reception of *Pesharim* in the Second Temple Period

Formally, the New Testament writings are quite different from the *pesharim* because they comprise neither continuous nor thematic commentaries on the biblical books and do not employ the *pesher* formula. Behind these formal differences, however, lie some striking similarities. Like the *pesharim*, the New Testament writings frequently quote Scripture and claim that biblical prophecies have been fulfilled in the career of Jesus and the emergence of the early church. They also frequently employ exegetical techniques resembling those found in the *pesharim*, such as allegorization and atomization of the text. Therefore, a study of the *pesharim* can shed light on the use of Scripture by early Christian interpreters who, like the Qumranites, believed they were living in the last days and interpreted their sacred texts in light of their own experiences.

The *pesharim* are running commentaries on the Psalter and on selected prophetic books. Their distinctive characteristic is the "citation plus comment" form, in which a quotation from Scripture is followed by a commentary that is intro-

---

12. Jokiranta ("Pesharim," pp. 24–25) notes the propensity of the authors of the *pesharim* to identify all kinds of enemies of the community. She concludes that "the reader of the pesharim gains the impression that the Scriptures were all about the community and its adversaries— Scripture is dualistic in its sharp division between the two groups, and the world is manifested as a place of struggle and dichotomy."

13. See George J. Brooke, *Exegesis at Qumran: 4QFlorilegium in Its Jewish Context* (Sheffield: JSOT, 1985), pp. 154–55, 283–92.

14. See Gary G. Porton, "Defining Midrash," in *The Study of Ancient Judaism*, vol. 1:, *Mishnah, Midrash, Siddur*, ed. Jacob Neusner, South Florida Studies in the History of Judaism 49 (Atlanta: Scholars, 1992), pp. 75–77, 79–81.

duced with a formula including the Hebrew word *pesher*. The interpretation is tied to the text of Scripture through a series of identifications for the purpose of contemporary application. This actualizing interpretation has a revelatory character because it presumes that the meaning of an otherwise mysterious portion of Scripture has been divinely disclosed to the Teacher of Righteousness, the interpreter par excellence. The *pesharim* reflect the sectarian self-understanding of the Qumran community and they should be used with caution for reconstructing its history.

LIDIJA NOVAKOVIC

FURTHER READING

Berrin, Shani. "Qumran Pesharim." In *Biblical Interpretation at Qumran*, edited by Matthias Henze, pp. 110–33. Grand Rapids: Eerdmans, 2005.

Brooke, George J. "The Pesharim and the Origins of the Dead Sea Scrolls." In *Methods of Investigation of the Dead Sea Scrolls and the Khirbet Qumran Site: Present Realities and Future Prospects*, edited by John J. Collins et al., pp. 339–53. Annals of the New York Academy of Sciences 722. New York: New York Academy of Sciences, 1994.

———. "Qumran Pesher: Toward the Redefinition of a Genre." *Revue de Qumrân* 10 (1979–81): 483–503.

Dimant, Devorah. "Pesharim, Qumran." In *ABD* 5:244–51.

Jokiranta, Jutta. "Pesharim: A Mirror of Self-Understanding." In *Reading the Present in the Qumran Library: The Perception of the Contemporary by Means of Scriptural Interpretation*, edited by Kristin De Troyer and Armin Lange, pp. 23–34. SBLSymS 30. Atlanta: SBL, 2005.

Nitzan, Bilhah. "The Pesher and Other Methods of Instruction." In *Mogilany 1989: Papers on the Dead Sea Scrolls Offered in Memory of Jean Carmignac, Part II: The Teacher of Righteousness, Literary Studies*, edited by Zdzusław J. Kapera, pp. 209–20. Cracow: Enigma, 1991.

ADVANCED READING

Bengtsson, Håkan. *What's in a Name? A Study of Sobriquets in the Pesharim*. Uppsala: Uppsala University Press, 2000.

Charlesworth, James H. *The Pesharim and Qumran History: Chaos or Consensus?* Grand Rapids: Eerdmans, 2002.

Horgan, Maurya P. *Pesharim: Qumran Interpretations of Biblical Books*. CBQMS 8. Washington, D.C.: Catholic Biblical Association, 1979.

Jokiranta, Jutta. *Social Identity and Sectarianism in the Qumran Movement*. STDJ 105. Leiden: Brill, 2012.

Lim, Timothy H. *Pesharim*. Companion to the Qumran Scrolls 3. London: Sheffield Academic Press, 2002.

Patte, Daniel. *Early Jewish Hermeneutic in Palestine*. SBLDS 22. Missoula: Scholars, 1975.

Wacholder, Ben Zion. "The Righteous Teacher in the Pesherite Commentaries." *HUCA* 73 (2002): 1–27.

Introduction to the Habakkuk Pesher

The Habakkuk Pesher (1QpHab) was among the first seven scrolls that were discovered in 1947 in Cave 1 at Qumran (*see* Overview of Early Jewish Literature). Upon its initial, though hasty, evidentiary publication in 1948,[1] its distinctiveness and significance for understanding Jewish scriptural interpretation during the Second Temple period was quickly recognized; these issues in particular generated numerous studies of its content and exegetical techniques. Although **pesharim** on other biblical books were discovered later, the Habakkuk Pesher is still the most investigated of all the Qumran commentaries (*see* Introduction to *Pesharim*). It owes its preeminence among the *pesharim* not only to its chronological priority but also to its length and relative completeness. The document is composed of thirteen columns written on golden-brown leather. Each column consists of seventeen lines, with the exception of column 13, which has only four lines. The text of most columns is well preserved except for column 1, which contains only the ends of the lines, and column 2, which is damaged in the center. In addition, the last two or three lines of each column are missing due to deterioration of the bottom of the scroll.

Narrative Description

Like other continuous pesharim, the Habakkuk Pesher alternates between **lemma** and commentary following the order of the book of Habakkuk. Each comment is introduced with a *pesher* formula. The author sometimes repeats a portion of the

---

1. For the first translation of 1QpHab, see William H. Brownlee, "The Jerusalem Habakkuk Scroll," *BASOR* 112 (1948): 8–18. For subsequent corrections, see idem, "Further Light on Habakkuk," *BASOR* 114 (1949): 9–10; idem, "Further Corrections of the Translation of the Habakkuk Scroll," *BASOR* 116 (1949): 14–16; idem, *The Text of Habakkuk in the Ancient Commentary from Qumran*, SBLMS 11 (Philadelphia: Society of Biblical Literature and Exegesis, 1959). For the **editio princeps**, see idem, "The Habakkuk Commentary," in *The Dead Sea Scrolls of St. Mark's Monastery*, vol. 1: *The Isaiah Manuscript and the Habakkuk Commentary*, ed. Millar Burrows et al. (New Haven, Conn.: American Schools of Oriental Research, 1950), pp. xix–xxi and pls. lv–lxi.

lemma that has already been quoted, introducing it with either "for this is what it says" or "and when it says." The biblical quotations in the document presume a stable base text, which sometimes differs from the **Masoretic Text (MT)** and can thus be used in text-critical studies. It seems that in some cases, however, the author has intentionally altered the wording of the citations to suit his own purposes.[2]

The Habakkuk Pesher applies the prophecies of Habakkuk to the contemporary circumstances of the Qumran community. Specific events to which it refers include the conflicts of the **Teacher of Righteousness** with the **Wicked Priest** and with the **Man of the Lie**, which are usually dated to the second century BCE, and the Roman occupation of Judea, which took place during the first century BCE. Yet, even though these references appear to be somewhat haphazard, it is possible to discern an overarching structure within the Habakkuk Pesher. The first seven columns relate the prophecies about the coming of the **Chaldeans** from Habakkuk 1 to the coming of the **Kittim**, along with sporadic references to an intracommunal conflict between the Teacher of Righteousness and the Man of the Lie. Columns 8 through 12 apply the woes against the evildoers in Habakkuk 2 to the Wicked Priest, again alongside sporadic references to tensions within the community. The commentary ends with a description of the doom of idolatrous nations.

The author of the Habakkuk Pesher typically applies Scripture to the historical context of his community by identifying individual persons and groups from Habakkuk's prophecies (especially if they are vague) with those of his own time. He then provides additional information about their contemporary circumstances, which may or may not have basis in the biblical text. Those portions of the citations that have no relevance for the present are frequently ignored. What emerges is a portrait of a community and its original leader—the Teacher of Righteousness—that is endangered by various internal and external opponents. The community's self-presentation includes the following descriptions: they are the "Men of Truth" in 1QpHab 7.9–14a:

> [9] Habakkuk 2:3b: "If it is made to delay, wait for it, for it will surely come and it will not [10] delay." *(vacat)* Its interpretation concerns the *Men of Truth,* [11] those who carry out the Torah, whose hands do not lose heart in the works of [12] the truth by the stretching out of the final period against them, for [13] all of God's periods will come according to their fixed order, as he decreed [14] for them in the mysteries of his discernment.

They are the "elect of God" in 1QpHab 10.9–13:

> [9] The interpretation of the passage concerns the Preacher of Falsehood, who caused many to err, [10] building a worthless city by bloodshed and raising up a congregation in falsehood [11] for the sake of its glory causing many to grow weary in the service

2. See Timothy H. Lim, "Eschatological Orientation and the Alteration of Scripture in the Habakkuk Pesher," *JNES* 49 (1990): 185–94; idem, *Pesharim,* Companion to the Qumran Scrolls 3 (London: Sheffield Academic Press, 2002), pp. 54–63.

of deception and teaching them [12] with w[o]rks of deception, their trouble will be in vain; so that they will come [13] to the judgments of fire, because they blasphemed and reproached the *elect of God*.

They are the "Poor Ones" in 1QpHab 12.2–3:

> [2] The interpretation of the passage concerns the Wicked Priest—to pay him [3] his recompense as much as he dealt out upon the *Poor Ones*.

The Poor Ones are those who observe the Torah. They are tireless in the service of the truth and persevere despite the delay of the end (5.5–8; 7.10–12; 12.4–5), and because of their loyalty to the Teacher of Righteousness, God will save them from judgment (7.17–8.3: "[7.17] [. . . Habakkuk 2:4b: "but the righteous person by his faithfulness will live."] [8.1] Its interpretation concerns all those who carry out the Torah in the House of Judah, whom [2] God will rescue from the house of judgment on account of their tribulation and their faithfulness [3] to the Teacher of Righteousness"). Moreover, they will eventually judge all the nations and convict the wicked (5.4–5: "[4] but into the hand of his chosen one God will give the judgment of all the nations. And by their reproach [5] all the wicked of his people will incur guilt [by those] who kept his commandments"). The Teacher of Righteousness himself is presented as the recipient of divinely revealed interpretations of biblical prophecies who has conveyed them to other members of the community (7.4–5; 2.8–10).

Much more space, however, is devoted to the descriptions of the community's opponents. They are sometimes described in general terms as the wicked ones who reject the Torah and do not keep the commandments (1.10; 2.14–15; 5.5) or simply as idolaters (12.12–14; 13.1–4). More often, however, they are identified with certain individuals and groups from the community's experience. According to 1QpHab 1.16–2.3a:

> [1.16] Habakkuk 1:5: "Look among the nations and observe] [17] [gaze at each other and be astonished, for a work is being accomplished in your days that you would not believe if] [2.1] it were told." *(vacat)* [The interpretation of the passage concerns] the faithless ones together with the Man of [2] the Lie for (they did) not [believe in the words of] the Teacher of Righteousness from the mouth of [3] God.

The Teacher of Righteousness was opposed from within by a Man of the Lie (2.1–2), who rejected the Torah (5.10–12). Those who supported the Man of the Lie are simply called "traitors" (2.1–2). The same passage also mentions the "traitors to the new covenant" (2.3) and the "traitors at the latter days" who are the "ruthless ones of the covenant" (2.5–6). These could be additional designations for the same group or references to different groups. Not only the derogatory term "traitors" but also the actions ascribed to them—being unfaithful or unbelieving—suggest that they originally belonged to the Teacher of Righteousness's community.

1QpHab 5.9–12 mentions another group, called the "House of Absalom," which also participated in the conflict between the Man of the Lie and the Teacher of Righteousness. Yet, unlike the traitors, who took sides and actively supported the Man of the Lie, the House of Absalom remained passive and did not support the Teacher of Righteousness. Another epithet—the Spouter of the Lie—appears in 1QpHab 10.9–13 and may refer to the same person as the Man of the Lie. This passage is more elusive regarding the cause of a rift within the community, but it provides more information about the establishment of a rival congregation. The Spouter of the Lie caused many to go astray, built a "city of emptiness" with bloodshed, established a congregation with falsehood, and reviled the elect of God. The commentary concludes with the verdict that this whole endeavor will be for naught because it was based on deceit and eventually will be judged by fire.

The author of the Habakkuk Pesher identifies the Kittim and the Wicked Priest as the two major external opponents of the community and describes each of them more elaborately than he does any other group. The Kittim dominate the first half of the document. They are swift, strong in battle, and able to destroy many (2.10b–13: "[10]Habakkuk 1:6a: "For behold I am raising up the [11]Chaldeans, that fierce [and rash]ly acting nation." *(vacat)* [12]Its interpretation is about the Kittim, w[ho are fier]ce, swift and strong [13]in battle, so as to destroy many"). They come from a distance to annihilate the people and to plunder the cities of the land (3.1, 9–11). All the nations stand in fear and dread of them (3.4–5). All their plans are to do evil and to deceive the people (3.5–6). They burn with rage (3.12–13), mock the leaders of other nations, and deride their military fortifications (4.2–3, 5–6). Their military success serves as God's judgment on the iniquities of the people (4.8–9). Yet they themselves commit injustices and ruin the land (4.10–13). They sacrifice to their standards and revere their weapons (6.3–5). They impose their yoke and forced service on the nations to impoverish them (6.6–8). They show no compassion even to the most vulnerable groups, such as the elderly, women, and children (6.8b–12a): "[8]Habakkuk 1:17: 'Therefore he will draw out his net, continuing [9]to kill nations, and he will not spare (any).' *(vacat)* [10]Its interpretation concerns the Kittim, who destroy many with the sword—[11] young men, adult men and old men, women and children—even on the child in [12]the womb they have no mercy."

The Wicked Priest is not mentioned before column 8. After an initial period in office that was approved by the author of the *pesher* (8.9), the Wicked Priest became arrogant and strayed from God's statutes for the sake of wealth (8.10–13, 16–17). He pursued the Teacher of Righteousness to his house of exile on the Teacher's **Yom Kippur** (11.4–8), walked in the ways of drunkenness (11.12–15), dealt wickedly with the members of the community (12.2–6, 9–10), committed abominable deeds in Jerusalem, and defiled God's sanctuary (12.7–10). God punished him with a horrible malady (9.1–2) and gave him into the hands of his enemies (9.10–12). Inserted between these two references to God's judgment on the Wicked Priest is a brief description of God's judgment on the last priests of Jerusalem, whose wealth, gathered through plundering the peoples, will eventually be given into the hands of the army of the Kittim in 1QpHab 9.3–7a:

> [3]Habakkuk 2:8a: "For you have plundered many nations, but all the remainder of the peoples will [4]plunder you." *(vacat)* Its interpretation concerns the last priests [5]of Jerusalem, who gathered up wealth and unjust gain from the plunder of the peoples; [6]but toward the last days their wealth together with their plunder will be given into the hand of [7]the army of the Kittim.

The characterizations of these groups and individuals provide very little information for precise historical reconstruction, but a number of theories about their identity have nevertheless been proposed. While the Kittim undoubtedly refer to the Romans, the identities of other parties, including the fiercely debated identity of the Wicked Priest, remain elusive.[3] What should be kept in mind, however, is that as much as these coded references point to events that had taken place in the community's past, they also mirror the community's experience at the time of the composition of the document. The faithful are endangered not only by external enemies, embodied by the Kittim and the Wicked Priest, but also by internal adversaries, embodied by the Man of the Lie and the traitors.[4] As a result, the character traits of the main actors in the Habakkuk Pesher contribute to the community's self-understanding and reinforce its sectarian identity.

Author/Provenance

The handwriting in the Habakkuk Pesher betrays two different hands. The first scribe wrote the first eleven columns and stopped in line 13 of column 12. The second scribe resumed with the word "which" in line 13, finished column 12, and added four more lines in column 13. With this ending, the Habakkuk Pesher offers a continuous commentary on the first two of Habakkuk's three chapters.[5]

Date/Occasion

Since both scribes wrote in a **Herodian** script, the document is usually dated to the second half of the first century BCE. One of the scroll's distinctive characteristics is its use of paleo-Hebrew script for the **Tetragrammaton**. Also, there are several X-shaped marks throughout the document, which could support the theory that this manuscript is a copy of an earlier composition.[6]

---

3. See William H. Brownlee, "The Wicked Priest, the Man of Lies, and the Righteous Teacher: The Problem of Identity," *JQR* 73 (1982): 1–37; A. S. van der Woude, "Wicked Priest or Wicked Priests? Reflections on the Identification of the Wicked Priest in the Habakkuk Commentary," *JJS* 33 (1982): 349–59; Timothy H. Lim, "The Wicked Priest or the Liar?" in *The Dead Sea Scrolls in Their Historical Context,* ed. Timothy H. Lim (Edinburgh: T&T Clark, 2000), pp. 45–51; James H. Charlesworth, *The Pesharim and Qumran History: Chaos or Consensus?* (Grand Rapids: Eerdmans, 2002), pp. 80–118.

4. Cf. Jutta Jokiranta, "Pesharim: A Mirror of Self-Understanding," in *Reading the Present in the Qumran Library: The Perception of the Contemporary by Means of Scriptural Interpretation,* ed. Kristin De Troyer and Armin Lange, SBLSymS 30 (Atlanta: SBL, 2005), pp. 31–33.

5. For various explanations of why Hab. 3 is absent from the Habakkuk Pesher, see Brownlee, *Text of Habakkuk,* pp. 91–95; idem, *The Midrash Pesher of Habakkuk: Text, Translation, Exposition with an Introduction,* SBLMS 24 (Missoula: SBL, 1979), p. 219; J. G. Harris, *The Qumran Commentary on Habakkuk,* Contemporary Studies in Theology 9 (London: Mowbray, 1966), pp. 7–8.

6. Cf. Hanan Eshel, "The Two Historical Layers of Pesher Habakkuk," in *Northern Lights on the Dead Sea Scrolls: Proceedings of the Nordic Qumran Network 2003-2006,* ed. Anders Klostergaard Petersen et al., STDJ 8 (Leiden: Brill, 2009), pp. 108–9.

Theology

Scriptural interpretation in the Habakkuk Pesher is guided by several key theological convictions. The first and foremost among them is the belief that God is in control of history. Time is divided into periods that will occur according to their fixed order as determined by God's sovereign decree. Even if it seems at the moment that the last period is being delayed, the faithful can be reassured that the end will surely come (*see* 1QpHab 12.2–3). At that time, God will execute judgment and punish the enemies of his chosen ones, including the Wicked Priest (9.9–12; 10.12–13; 11.14–15; 12.5–6). The expectation of divine retribution offers consolation to those who suffer in the present and reassures them that God's justice will eventually prevail. It encourages the members of the Qumran community to persevere in their Torah observance and not to grow weary in their commitment to truth and justice. Internal conflicts within the community are presented as tests for distinguishing those who have remained faithful to the teaching of the Teacher of Righteousness from those who have deserted him. In this way, internal divisions are redefined as the necessary afflictions of the chosen ones.[7]

Reception of the Habakkuk Pesher in the Second Temple Period

Although there is no direct relationship between the Habakkuk Pesher and the New Testament writings, this document offers important comparative material for studying scriptural interpretation in early Christian communities. One of the most interesting examples is the interpretation of Habakkuk 2:4 ("The righteous will live by his faith") in 1QpHab 7.17–8.3 and in the letters of the apostle Paul. While the author of the *pesher* applies this text to the members of his own community—called the "House of Judah"—who observe the law and are faithful to the Teacher of Righteousness, Paul uses it to argue just the opposite, namely, that "no one is justified before God by the law" (Gal. 3:11; cf. Rom. 1:17). Paul bases his interpretation on a quotation of Habakkuk 2:4 that does not include the possessive pronoun "his,"[8] which enables him to associate justification with faith and to contrast it with (works of) the law because "the law does not rest on faith" (Gal. 3:12). In addition, the Habakkuk Pesher addresses the problem of dashed hopes that were caused by a delay of the end time, which can shed light on early Christians coping with a delay of the *parousia*. This Qumran document also supplies important background material for a study of the sectarian nature of early Christian communities, including intracommunal tensions and divisions, such as those reflected in the Johannine literature[9] and the letters of Paul.[10]

---

7. See Jokiranta, "Pesharim," pp. 32–33.

8. Compare a different version of Hab. 2:4 in Heb. 10:37–38: "For yet 'in a very little while, the one who is coming will come and will not delay; but my righteous one will live by faith. My soul takes no pleasure in anyone who shrinks back.'"

9. See 1 John 2:18–19; 3 John 9–10.

10. See 1 Cor. 1:10–12; 11:18–19.

COMPARISON OF "THE RIGHTEOUS SHALL LIVE BY FAITH"

Hab. 2:4: "And a righteous person shall live in his or her steadfast faith."	1QpHab 7.17–8.3a: "7.17 [. . . Hab. 2:4b: 'but the righteous person by his faithfulness will live.'] 8.1 Its interpretation concerns all those who carry out the Torah in the House of Judah, whom 2 God will rescue them from the house of judgment on account of their tribulation and their faithfulness 3 to the Teacher of Righteousness."	Gal. 3:11: "The righteous person will live according to faith."	Rom. 1:17: "As it is written, 'but the righteous person will live according to faith.'"

The Habakkuk Pesher is a prime example of Qumran scriptural commentaries called "continuous *pesharim*." It provides insights into Qumran hermeneutics, theology, and history. It also offers a glimpse into the community's self-understanding and identity formation in relation to its external and internal foes. As such, it is one of the most valuable Jewish documents for illuminating our understanding of the variegated nature of Judaism during the Second Temple period.

LIDIJA NOVAKOVIC

FURTHER READING

Bernstein, Moshe J. "Pesher Habakkuk." In *The Encyclopedia of the Dead Sea Scrolls*, edited by Lawrence H. Schiffman and James C. VanderKam, 2:647–51. 2 vols. Oxford: Oxford University Press, 2000.

Brooke, George J. "The Kittim in the Qumran Pesharim." In *Images of Empire*, edited by Loveday Alexander, pp. 135–59. JSOTSup 122. Sheffield: Sheffield Academic Press, 1991.

Brownlee, William H. "The Wicked Priest, the Man of Lies, and the Righteous Teacher: The Problem of Identity." *JQR* 73 (1982): 1–37.

Bruce, F. F. "The Dead Sea Habakkuk Scroll." *Annual of Leeds University Oriental Society* 1 (1958–59): 5–24.

Eshel, Hanan. "The Two Historical Layers of Pesher Habakkuk." In *Northern Lights on the Dead Sea Scrolls: Proceedings of the Nordic Qumran Network 2003–2006*, edited by Anders Klostergaard Petersen et al., pp. 107–17. STDJ 8. Leiden: Brill, 2009.

ADVANCED READING

Brownlee, William H. *The Midrash Pesher of Habakkuk: Text, Translation, Exposition with an Introduction.* SBLMS 24. Missoula: SBL, 1979.

———. *The Text of Habakkuk in the Ancient Commentary from Qumran.* SBLMS 11. Philadelphia: Society of Biblical Literature and Exegesis, 1959.

Elliger, Kurt. *Studien zum Habakkuk-Kommentar vom Toten Meer.* Tübingen: Mohr Siebeck, 1953.

Harris, J. G. *The Qumran Commentary on Habakkuk.* Contemporary Studies in Theology 9. London: Mowbray, 1966.

Horgan, Maurya P. *Pesharim: Qumran Interpretations of Biblical Books.* CBQMS 8. Washington, D.C.: Catholic Biblical Association, 1979.

Silberman, Lou H. "Unriddling the Riddle: A Study in the Structure and Language of the Habakkuk Pesher (1QpHab)." *Revue de Qumrân* 3 (1961–62): 323–64.

4.1 Habakkuk Pesher (1QpHab)

Column 1

¹ [The burden that Habakkuk the prophet saw: How long, Yahweh,] have
I cried out for help, but you do not

² [hear? (Hab. 1:1–2a) . . . the expec]tation of the generation of

³ [. . . to co]me upon them.

⁴ [I cry out to you "Violence!" but you do not save. (Hab. 1:2b) . . . Its
interpretation is that] they [c]ry out against

⁵ [. . . Why do you make me see evil, and] do you gaze at [tri]bulation?
(Hab. 1:3a)

⁶ [. . .] God with oppression and treachery.

⁷ [And destruction and violence are before me; and there is strife, and
contention arises. (Hab. 1:3b)] (vacat)

⁸ [. . .] and strife

⁹ [. . . qu]arrel, and [. . .] is

¹⁰ [. . .] Therefore the Torah is numbed,

¹¹ [and judgment does not go forth to victory. (Hab. 1:4a) Its interpretation is] that they rejected the Torah of God.

¹² [. . . For the wicked surrou]nd the righteous. (Hab. 1:4b)

¹³ [. . .] is the Righteous Teacher.

¹⁴ [. . . Th]erefore the judgment goes forth

¹⁵ [perverted. (Hab. 1:4b) Its interpretation . . .] and not [. . .]

¹⁶ [. . . Look, O traitors, and] s[ee;]

¹⁷ [and wonder (and) be amazed, for I am doing a deed in your days that
you would not believe if]

Column 2

¹ it were told. (Hab. 1:5) (vacat) [. . .] the traitors together with the Man of

² the Lie for (they did) not [. . .] the Righteous Teacher from the mouth of

³ God. And it concerns the trait[ors to] the new [covenant,] f[o]r they were
not

⁴ faithful to the covenant of God [. . .] his holy name.

⁵ And thus (vacat) the interpretation of the passage [concerns the trai]tors
at the latter

⁶ days. They are the ruthless [ones of the cove]nant who will not believe

⁷ when they hear all that is going to co[me up]on the last generation from
the mouth of

⁸ the priest, to whom God gave into [his heart discernme]nt to interpret all

Translation by Archie T. Wright. Bold type indicates quotation from Habakkuk.

9 the words of his servants the prophets [whom] by their hand God enumerated

10 all that is going to come upon his people and up[on . . .] **For now I am raising up the**

11 **Chaldeans, that bitter [and ha]sty nation.** (Hab. 1:6a) *(vacat)*

12 Its interpretation concerns the Kittim, w[ho ar]e swift and strong

13 in battle, so as to destroy many [. . .] in the dominion of

14 the Kittim, and the wick[ed ones . . .], and they will not be faithful

15 to the statutes of [Go]d [. . .]

16 [. . . **who go through the breadth of the land**]

17 [**to take possession of dwelling places that are not theirs.** (Hab. 1:6b) . . .]

Column 3

1 and by (way of) the level plain they come to smite and to loot the cities of the land.

2 For this is what it says: **To take possession of dwelling places not their own. Fearful**

3 **and terrible are they. From them goes out their judgment and dignity.** (Hab. 1:6b–7)

4 Its interpretation concerns the Kittim, fear and dread of whom are upon all

5 the nations. And by design all their plans are to do evil, and with cunning and deceit

6 they will deal with all the peoples. **And their horses are swifter than leopards and more fierce**

7 **than the wolves of the evening. They paw the ground, and their riders spread out from a distance.**

8 **They fly like the eagle, (which) hastens to devour all. They come for violence. The horror**

9 **of their faces is an east wind.** (Hab. 1:8–9a) *(vacat)* Its inter[pretation] concerns the Kittim, who

10 trample the land with [their] horses and with their beasts. And from a distance

11 they come, from the islands of the sea, to devour all the peoples like an eagle

12 and there is no satiety. And with rage th[ey] gr[ow hot, and with] burning anger and fury

13 they speak with all [. . . Fo]r this is what it

14 says: **The horro[r of their faces is an east wind. And they gather] captives [like sa]nd.** (Hab. 1:9a–9b)

15 Its [interpreta]tion [. . .]

16 [. . .]

17 [. . . **And at kings**]

Column 4

1   **they scoff, and princes are to them a laughing matter.** (Hab. 1:10a) *(vacat)* Its interpretation is that
2   they mock great ones and they despise honored ones; kings
3   and princes they mock, and they scoff at a great people. **And they**
4   **laugh at every fortress, and they heap up earthen mounds to capture it.** (Hab. 1:10b)
5   Its interpretation concerns the rulers of the Kittim, who despise
6   the fortifications of the peoples and laugh with derision at them;
7   and with many (people) they surround them to capture them. And with terror and dread
8   they are given into their hand, and they tear them down, because of the iniquity of those who dwell
9   in them. **Then they changed, a wind, and they passed by, and these made their power**
10 **their God.** (Hab. 1:11) *(vacat)* Its interpretation [con]cerns the rulers of the Kittim,
11 who, in the council of [their] guilty house, pass by, each man
12 before his neighbor. [Their] rulers come [on]e after another
13 to ruin the l[and, **and] these [made] their power their God.** (Hab. 1:11b)
14 Its interpretation [. . . al]l the peoples
15 [. . .]
16 [. . . **Are you not from of old,**]
17 [**Yahweh, my holy God? We will not die. Yahweh,**]

Column 5

1   **for judgment you have set him up, and a rock as his reprover you have established. (You are) too pure of eyes**
2   **to look on evil, and to gaze at tribulation you are not able.** (Hab. 1:12–13a)
3   The interpretation of the passage is that God will not destroy his people by the hand of the nations,
4   but into the hand of his chosen God will give the judgment of all the nations. And by means of their rebuke
5   all the wicked ones of his people will be convicted (by those) who have kept his commandments
6   in their distress. For this is what it says: **(You are) too pure of eyes to look**
7   **on evil.** (Hab. 1:13a) *(vacat)* Its interpretation is that they did not whore after their eyes in the time of
8   wickedness. **Why do you heed traitors, but are silent when a**
9   **wicked one swallows up one more righteous than he?** (Hab. 1:13b) *(vacat)* Its interpretation concerns the house of Absalom

10 and the men of their counsel, who were quiet at the rebuke of the Righteous Teacher

11 and did not support him against the Man of the Lie *(vacat)* who rejected

12 the Torah in the midst of all their counsel. **And you make humanity like the fish of the sea,**

13 **like creeping things to rule over it. He brings everythi[ng] up [with the fis]hhook and drags it into his net.**

14 **And he gathers it in [his] se[ine. Therefore he sacrifi]ces to his net; therefore he is glad**

15 **[and shouts for jo]y, [and he burns incense to his fishing net, for on account of them] his portion grows fat**

16 **[and his food is rich.** (Hab. 1:14–16) Its interpretation . . .]

17 [. . .]

Column 6

1 the Kittim, and they increase their wealth with all their booty

2 like the fish of the sea. And when it says, **Therefore he sacrifices to his net**

3 **and burns incense to his seine,** (Hab. 1:16a) *(vacat)* its interpretation is that they

4 sacrifice to their standards, and their weapons of war are

5 the objects of their reverence. **For on account of them his portion grows fat and his food is rich.** (Hab. 1:16b)

6 Its interpretation is that they divide their yoke and

7 their forced service—their food—upon all the peoples year by year

8 to lay waste many lands. **Therefore he draws his sword continually**

9 **to slaughter nations, and he has no compassion.** (Hab. 1:17) *(vacat)*

10 Its interpretation concerns the Kittim, who destroy many with the sword

11 —young men, strong men and old men, women and toddlers—and on the fruit of

12 the womb they have no compassion. **At my station will I stand,**

13 **and I will post myself at my fortification, and I will watch to see what he says**

14 **to me and what [he answers regar]ding my objection. And Yahweh did answer me,**

15 **[and he said: "Write the vision and make it pl]ain upon the tablets so that he can run**

16 **[who reads it."** (Hab. 2:1–2) Its interpretation . . .]

17 [. . .]

Column 7

1 and God told Habakkuk to write down the things that are going to come upon

2 the last generation, but the fulfillment of the period he did not make known to him.

3 *(vacat)* And when it says, **so that he can run who reads it,** (Hab. 2:2b)

4 its interpretation concerns the Teacher of Righteousness, to whom God made known

5 all the mysteries of the words of his servants the prophets. **For there is yet a vision**

6 **concerning the appointed time. It testifies to the period, and it will not deceive.** (Hab. 2:3a)

7 Its interpretation is that the last period will be prolonged, and it will be greater than anything

8 of which the prophets spoke, for the mysteries of God are awesome.

9 **If it tarries, wait for it, for it will surely come and it will not**

10 **be late.** (Hab. 2:3b) *(vacat)* Its interpretation concerns the men of truth,

11 those who observe the Torah, whose hands do not grow slack in the service of

12 the truth, when the last period is drawn out for them, for

13 all of God's periods will come according to their fixed order, as he decreed

14 for them in the mysteries of his prudence. **Now [his soul] is heedless, not upright**

15 **[within him.** (Hab. 2:4a)] *(vacat)* Its interpretation is that they double upon them

16 [. . . and] they will n[ot] find favor at their judgment [. . .]

17 [. . . **And the righteous man will live by his faithfulness.** (Hab. 2:4b)]

Column 8

1 Its interpretation concerns all those who observe the Torah in the House of Judah, whom

2 God will save from the house of judgment on account of their tribulation and their fidelity

3 to the Righteous Teacher. **And moreover, wealth betrays a haughty man, and**

4 **he is unseemly, who opens his soul wide like Sheol; and like death he cannot be sated.**

5 **And all the nations are gathered about him, and all the peoples are assembled to him.**

6 **Do not all of them raise a taunt against him and interpreters of riddles about him,**

7 **who say: "Woe to the one who multiplies what is not his own! How long will he weigh himself down with**

8 **debt?"** (Hab. 2:5–6) *(vacat)* Its interpretation concerns the Wicked Priest, who

9 was called by the true name at the beginning of his standing, but when he ruled

¹⁰ in Israel, his heart became large, and he abandoned God, and betrayed the statutes for the sake of

¹¹ wealth. And he stole and amassed the wealth of the men of violence who had rebelled against God,

¹² and he took the wealth of peoples to add to himself guilty iniquity. And the abominable

¹³ ways he pursued with every sort of unclean impurity. **Will it not be [. . .], that your cre[di]tors**

¹⁴ **will arise? And will those who make you tremble awake, and will you become their booty?**

¹⁵ **For you have plundered many nations, but all the rest of the peoples will plunder you.** (Hab. 2:7–8a)

¹⁶ The inte[rpretation of the passage] concerns the priest, who rebelled

¹⁷ [and transgre]ssed the statutes of [God . . . but they will pl]under him [. . .]

Column 9

¹ his injury on account of wicked judgments. And horrors of evil

² diseases were at work in him, and acts of vengeance on his carcass of flesh. And when

³ it says, **For you have plundered many nations, but all the rest of the peoples will**

⁴ **plunder you,** (Hab. 2:8a) *(vacat)* its interpretation concerns the last priests

⁵ of Jerusalem, who amass wealth and profit from the plunder of the peoples;

⁶ but in latter days their wealth together with their plunder will be given into the hand of

⁷ the army of the Kittim. *(vacat)* For they are the rest of the peoples.

⁸ **On account of human bloodshed and violence (done to) the land, the town, and all its inhabitants.** (Hab. 2:8b)

⁹ Its interpretation concerns the [Wi]cked Priest, whom—because of wrong done to the Teacher of Righteousness

¹⁰ and the men of his counsel—God gave into the hand of his enemies to humble him

¹¹ with disease for annihilation in bitterness of soul, beca[u]se he had acted wickedly

¹² against his chosen ones. **Woe to the one who makes an evil profit for his house, setting**

¹³ **his nest on high to be delivered from the reach of evil. You have planned shame**

¹⁴ **for your house, the ends of many peoples and (even) the threads of your own [sou]l, for**

¹⁵ **a ston[e] will cry out from the wall, [and] stucco from the framework will give an[swer.** (Hab. 2:9–11)]

16 [The interpretation of the passa]ge concerns the pr[iest,] who [. . .]
17 [. . .]

Column 10

1 so that its stones are (built up) by oppression and the stucco of its framework by robbery. And when
2 it says **cutting off many peoples and (even) the threads of your own
soul,** (Hab. 2:10b)
3 its interpretation: This is the house of judgment when God will give
4 his judgment in the midst of many peoples, and from there he will bring
him up for judgment,
5 and in their midst he will condemn him as guilty and with a fire of brim-
stone he will punish him. **Woe**
6 **to the one who builds a city with blood and founds a town on iniquity.
Are not**
7 **these from Yahweh of Hosts? Peoples toil for fire**
8 **and nations grow weary for nothing.** (Hab. 2:12–13) *(vacat)*
9 The interpretation of the passage concerns the Spouter of the Lie, who
caused many to err,
10 building a city of emptiness with bloodshed and establishing a congregation with falsehood
11 for the sake of its glory making many toil in the service of emptiness and
saturating them
12 with w[o]rks of falsehood, with the result that their labor is for nothing;
so that they will come
13 to the judgments of fire, because they reviled and reproached the elect of
God.
14 **For the earth will be filled with the knowledge of the glory of Yahweh,
as the waters**
15 **cover the sea.** (Hab. 2:14) [. . .] *(vacat)* The interpretation of the passage
[is that]
16 when they return [. . .]
17 [. . . Spouter of]

Column 11

1 the Lie, and afterward the knowledge will be revealed to them, like the
waters of
2 the sea, in abundance. **Woe to him who gives his neighbors to drink,
mixing in**
3 **his poison, indeed, making (them) drunk in order that he might look
upon their feasts.** (Hab. 2:15)
4 *(vacat)* Its interpretation concerns the Wicked Priest, who
5 pursued the Righteous Teacher—to swallow him up with his poisonous

6 vexation—to his house of exile. And at the end of the feast, (during) the repose of

7 the Day of Atonement, he appeared to them to swallow them up

8 and to make them stumble on the fast day, their restful Sabbath. **You will be sated**

9 **with shame rather than glory. Drink then, you yourself, and totter.**

10 **The cup of Yahweh's right hand will come around to you, and disgrace (will come)**

11 **upon your glory.** (Hab. 2:16) *(vacat)*

12 Its interpretation concerns the priest whose shame prevailed over his glory,

13 for he did not circumcise the foreskin of his heart, but he walked in the ways of

14 inebriety in order that the thirst might be consumed, but the cup of the wrath of

15 [Go]d will swallow him up, ad[d]ing [t]o [all] his [s]ha[me] and a wound

16 [. . .]

17 [. . . **For the violence to Lebanon will cover you and the assault of beasts**]

Column 12

1 **will destroy. On account of human bloodshed and violence (done to) the land, the town and all who inhabit it.** (Hab. 2:17)

2 The interpretation of the passage concerns the Wicked Priest—to pay him

3 his due inasmuch as he dealt wickedly with the Poor Ones; for "Lebanon" is

4 the Council of the Community, and the "beasts" are the simple ones of Judah, those who observe

5 the Torah—(he it is) whom God will condemn to complete destruction

6 because he plotted to destroy completely the Poor Ones. And when it says, **On account of the bloodshed of**

7 **the town and violence (done to) the land,** (Hab. 2:17b) its interpretation: the "town" is Jerusalem,

8 where the Wicked Priest committed abominable deeds and defiled

9 God's sanctuary. And "violence (done to) the land" (refers to) the cities of Judah, where

10 he stole the wealth of the Poor Ones. **What profit does an idol bring, when its maker has hewed (it),**

11 **a molten statue and an image of falsehood? For the maker relies on the things he makes,**

12 **fashioning mute idols.** (Hab. 2:18) The interpretation of the passage concerns all

13 the idols of the nations, which they have made so that they may serve them and bow down

14 before them, but they will not save them on the day of judgment. **Woe,**
15 **wo[e to the one who says] to the wood, "Wake up!" "A[rise!"] to a**
 silent [st]one.
16 **[Is this a teacher? Behold, it is overlaid with gold and silver, yet no]**
17 **[breath is in it. But Yahweh is in his holy temple;]**

Column 13

1 **all the land keeps silent before him.** (Hab. 2:19–20) Its interpretation
 concerns all the nations
2 who have served the stone and the wood, but on the day of
3 judgment God will destroy completely all who serve the idols
4 and the evil ones from the land.

The Melchizedek Scroll

Among the finds from Qumran Cave 11 (*see* Overview of Early Jewish Literature) were fifteen parchment fragments belonging to three successive columns. On account of the unfortunate condition of the document, we do not know its original length or where the surviving columns appeared within the overall work. The composition is written in Hebrew with the full **orthography** common to other scrolls from the Qumran library. The **paleographical** style is indicative of late **Hasmonean** or early **Herodian** book hand (50–25 BCE), although J. T. Milik ventured that the archaic form of the some of the letters suggests it originated slightly earlier, perhaps 75–50 BCE.

Narrative Description

The work reflects the **sectarian** penchant to divide history into periods with the fragments from the document describing the tenth and final Jubilee. The best-preserved text is column 2, which presents an eschatological description of the end of days by means of a thematic *pesher* (*see* Introduction to *Pesharim*) on Leviticus 25, Deuteronomy 15, Isaiah 52:7 and 61:1–3, and Psalms 7:8–9 and 82:1–2. It describes a hoped-for redemption that will free the Sons of Light from the dominion of the Sons of Belial. At the center of God's redemptive initiative is the figure of Melchizedek, who is described in a role similar to that of the Prince of Lights (1QS 3.20;[1] *see* Rule of the Community [1QS]; CD 5.18;[2] *see* Damascus Document [CD]) and the archangel Michael (1QM 17.6–7;[3] *see* War Scroll [1QM]). The narrative concludes with a description of the annihilation of Belial and his lot. Accordingly, the editors (F. Garcia Martinez, E. J. C. Tigchelaar, and A. S. Van

---

1. 1QS 3.20: "In the hand of the Prince of Lights is authority over all the Sons of Righteousness; they will walk in the ways of light." —trans. Wright

2. CD 5.18: "Moses and Aaron by the hand of the Prince of Lights and Belial caused Jannes to rise up." — trans. Wright

3. 1QM 17.6–7: "And he sent everlasting help to the lot of his redeemed by the power of the mighty angel for the dominion of Michael in an everlasting light." —trans. Wright

der Woude) suggest that the presentation indicates that the columns belong near the conclusion of the composition.

Theology

Belief in the return of Melchizedek is also heard outside the Qumran library. According to a Jewish legend preserved in 2 Enoch, his priestly father—the apocryphal Nir—is told that the child is to be taken to paradise to escape the coming flood in the generation of Noah: "For the time is now very near when I will let loose all the waters over the earth, and all that is on the earth will perish; and I will give him a place of honor in *another* [ms. J: *last*] generation, and Melchizedek will be chief priest in that generation" (2 Enoch 23:34).

The events surrounding the advent of Melchizedek closely resemble the day of deliverance and vindication expected at the coming of the Messiah of Aaron and Israel in the Damascus Document. The appearance of Melchizedek occurs in the tenth Jubilee inaugurated on the Day of Atonement: "And this thing will [occur] in the first week of the Jubilee that follows the nine Jubilees. And the Day of Atonement is the e[nd of the] tenth [Ju]bilee, when all the sons of [Light] and men of the lot of Mel[chi]zedek *will be atoned*" (11Q13 2.8). In a similar collocation, the advent of the priestly Messiah is accompanied by atonement in CD 14.19: "Until the appearance of the Messiah of Aaron and Israel and their [the community's] *iniquity will be atoned*." This combination is repeated on several occasions in the Dead Sea Scrolls where redemption occurs with atonement. "Then God will make *atonement* for them, and they will experience his *deliverance* because they have trusted in his holy name" (CD 20.34; cf. CD 4.9b–10a—"According to the covenant that God established with the first ones to atone concerning their sins; thus, God will atone on account of them"— trans. Wright).

Melchizedek's return in 11Q13 coincides with the dawning of the redemptive era in the final Jubilee. Column 2 opens with a combined citation of Leviticus 25:13 ("In this year of Jubilee you will return, every one of you, to your property") and Deuteronomy 15:2 ("And this is the manner of the remission: every creditor will remit the claim that is held against a neighbor, not exacting it of a neighbor who is a member of the community, because the Lord's remission has been proclaimed"— trans. Wright); both are concerned with the Jubilee year. The significance of the Jubilee for the author is twofold. According to Leviticus 25:10, it is in that year that the people of God "will proclaim liberty in the land." The time of redemption is also related to the fact that this year will be a time of the "Lord's remission" (Deut. 15:2). While the biblical verse speaks of a remission of debts, the sectarian spiritual interpretation of "remission" is shaped by the fact that redemption will be inaugurated on the "Day of Atonement [Lev. 25:9] at the end of the tenth Jubilee" (11Q13 2.7). Thus, the tenth Jubilee begins with atonement for past iniquities, and culminates in redemption with divine vengeance on Belial and his lot.

The two themes of deliverance and atonement and their coincidence during the tenth Jubilee in 11Q13 belong to a larger complex of eschatological ideas built on a chronological determinism that is not unique to Qumran. Central to it is the expectation that the Day of Redemption and judgment will occur in the final Jubilee. Periodization and the belief in a Jubilee redemption can be seen in other Qumran works (e.g., 4Q390), as well as in literature belonging to broader streams of thought that resemble the thinking at Qumran, for example, Jubilees 50:4[4] (*see* The Book of Jubilees), 1 Enoch 10:11–12[5] (*see* Book of Watchers [1 Enoch 1–36]), and 1 Enoch 91:11–19 and 93:3–10 (*see* Apocalypse of Weeks).

The beginnings of a Jubilee redemptive chronology are already visible in the Chronicler's reinterpretation (2 Chron. 36:21)[6] of Jeremiah's prophecy (Jer. 25:11–12)[7] in light of the sabbatical years of Leviticus 26:34–35.[8] Even closer to the present document, the periodic Jubilee structure together with atonement for iniquity is heard in Daniel 9:24: "*Seventy weeks of years . . .* to finish transgression, to put an end to sin, and *to atone for iniquity,* to bring an everlasting righteousness, to seal both vision and prophet" (cf. 11Q13 2.18–19: "And the messenger is the anointed one of the spirit about whom Dan[iel spoke, 'To seal both vision and prophet, and to anoint a most holy place.' The 'messenger who brings] good news, who annou[nces salvation' of whom it is written, ['to proclaim the year of the Lord's favor, the day of vengeance of our God']"—trans. Notley; *see* The Book of Daniel).

Finally, employing the same periodic Jubilee scheme, the Greek Testament of Levi 16–18 portrays a priestly redeemer coming during the final Jubilee (*see* Introduction to Testaments of the Twelve Patriarchs). The testament's periodic structure has been corrupted and doubtless has felt the influence of a later Christian hand. However, Milik is correct in his assessment that behind the Greek Testament of Levi is a pre-Christian periodic structure that is derived from a Jubilee chronological complex similar to that witnessed in 4Q180–81. In the Greek Testament of Levi we hear elements that also resemble closely the Qumran presentation of Melchizedek: "You have heard concerning the

---

4. Jub. 50:4: "For this reason, I have ordained for you the year-weeks and the years and the Jubilees: there are forty-nine Jubilees from the days of Adam until this day, and one week and two years: and there are yet forty years left for learning the commandments of the Lord until they pass over into the land of Canaan, crossing the Jordan to the west." — trans. VanderKam

5. 1 En. 10:12: "And when their sons have been slaughtered and they see the destruction of their loved ones, bind them seventy generations in the valleys of the earth until the day of their judgment and consummation of days; until the completion of the eternal judgment." —trans. Wright

6. 2 Chron. 36:21: "To fulfill the word of the Lord by the mouth of Jeremiah, until the land had enjoyed its Sabbaths. All the days of its desolation it kept the Sabbath until seventy years were complete." —trans. Wright

7. Jer. 25:11–12: "This whole land will become a ruin and a waste, and these nations will serve the king of Babylon seventy years. Then after seventy years are completed, I will punish the king of Babylon and that nation, the land of the Chaldeans, for their iniquity, says the Lord, making the land an everlasting waste." —trans. Wright

8. Lev. 26:34–35: "Then the land will enjoy its Sabbath years as long as it lies desolate, while you are in the land of your enemies; then the land will rest, and enjoy its Sabbath years. As long as it lies desolate, it will have the rest it did not have on your Sabbaths when you were living on it." —trans. Wright

seventy weeks [ten Jubilees], hear also concerning the priesthood . . . For in each *Jubilee* there will be a priesthood . . . then [in the final Jubilee] will the Lord raise up a new priest . . . He will execute a *righteous judgment* upon the earth . . . his star will rise [cf. Num. 24:17;[9] 4Q175 11–12;[10] *see* Florilegium (4Q174) and Testimonia (4Q175)] in heaven like a *king* . . . In his priesthood *will sin come to an end* . . . And *Belial* will be bound by him [cf. Testament of Levi 17:1–2;[11] *see* Introduction to Testamentary Literature; Testament of Levi 18:1, 3, 9, 12; 11Q13 2.25; Testament of Moses 10:1;[12] *see* Testament of Moses; Jubilees 50:5[13]]."

What we witness in all of these works is a hope that through the hands of a divinely appointed human figure—most often portrayed as an exalted priest—the nation will experience atonement and deliverance. The introduction of the notion of atonement into a discussion about the Day of Redemption, of course, stems from the fact that the Jubilee is inaugurated by the blowing of the trumpet on the Day of Atonement (Lev. 25:9: Then you will have the trumpet sounded loud; on the tenth day of the seventh month—on the day of atonement—you will have the trumpet sounded throughout all your land"). Thus, the Qumran sectarians looked to the day when iniquity would be atoned, resulting in deliverance and vindication for the community before their adversaries. That is precisely what is intended in the last line of 11Q13, column 2, where we hear again of both the deliverance brought by Melchizedek and the blowing of the trumpet of the Jubilee (11Q13 2.25): "[Melchizedek, who will del]iv[er them from the po]wer of Belial (cf. Testament of Levi 18:12;[14] Testament of Moses 10:1). Concerning what Scripture says, 'Then you shall have the trumpet [sounded loud; in] the [seventh m]o[nth' (Lev. 25:9)."[15]

9. Num. 24:17: "I see him but not now; I behold him but not imminently; a star will march out from Jacob; a tribe will rise up from Israel and smite the borders of Moab and destroy the sons of Seth." —trans. Wright

10. 4Q175 12–13: "I behold him but not near; a star will come forth from Jacob, and a scepter will arise from Israel, and batter the brow of Moab, and destroy all the sons of tumult." —trans. Kugler.

11. Testament of Levi 17:1–2: "And because you have heard concerning the seventy weeks, hear also concerning the priesthood, for in each Jubilee there will be a priesthood. In the first Jubilee the first anointed to the priesthood will be great, and he will speak to God as to a father, and his priesthood will be completely true to the Lord, and in the day of his joy he will arise for the salvation of the world." —trans. Kugler

12. Testament of Moses 10:1: "And then his kingdom will appear before every creature of his and then the Devil will know his end, and sadness will be taken away with him."—trans. Wright and White

13. Jub. 50:5: "And the Jubilees will pass, until Israel is cleansed from all guilt of fornication, uncleanness, pollution, sin, and error, and dwells with confidence in all the land, and there will no longer be a Satan or an evil one, and the land will be cleansed from that time eternally." —trans.VanderKam

14. Testament of Levi 18:12: "And Belial will be bound by him and he will give power to his children to trample on the wicked spirits."—trans. Kugler

15. Lev. 25:9: "Then you shall have the trumpet sounded loud; on the tenth day of the seventh month—on the day of atonement—you shall have the trumpet sounded throughout all your land." —NRSV

The proclamation of liberty in Leviticus 25:10[16] allowed the author to introduce Isaiah 61:1, in which liberty is also proclaimed. This period of redemption is called the "year of Melchizedek's favor" (11Q13 2.9), alluding to Isaiah 61:2, the "year of the Lord's favor and the vengeance of our God," and anticipates Melchizedek's role in executing divine vengeance. He arises to accomplish the *vengeance of God's judgments* in a fashion very similar to that of the priestly redeemer of the Testament of Moses 10:2–3 ("Then the hands of his angel will be filled up, he will be set up on high, he will defend them on the spot from their enemies. For the Heavenly One will arise from his kingly throne; and he will depart from his holy dwelling-place with displeasure and wrath on account of his sons" —trans. Wright and White).

Throughout 11Q13, the author utilizes words and phrases from Isaiah 61:1–3 that are then combined with other verbally connected Hebrew Scriptures:

> A spirit of the Lord God is upon me, because the Lord anointed me, he sent me to make known the good news to the oppressed ones, to wrap up the wounds of the broken hearted, to proclaim to the captive ones, "Freedom," to the imprisoned ones, "Release," to proclaim the year of favor from the Lord and the day of vengeance from our God, to comfort all the mourners, to provide for the mourners of Zion, to give them a headdress instead of ash, oil of gladness instead of mourning, a cloak of praise instead of a dull spirit, and they will be called the pillars of righteousness, a planting of the Lord to glorify him. —trans. Wright

Psalm 82:1 is cited in 11Q13 2.10 to take advantage of the parallel occurrence of Elohim:

> Elohim stands in the Divine Assembly;
> he will judge in the midst of the Elohim.

In Biblical and Postbiblical Hebrew, the term "Elohim" may be used to signify a human figure in the role as judge, without any suggestion that this figure is a divine being (e.g., Exod. 18:9; 22:7, 8 [Eng. 22:8, 9], 28; 1 Sam. 2:25; cf. LXX, Targum Onqelos, and Mekilta. R. Ish. on Exod. 21:6).

Contrary to Van der Woude's suggestion, which was based on a late medieval Jewish text, Psalm 82:1 is not intended to identify Melchizedek as a celestial being (i.e., the archangel Michael). Unfortunately, scholarship has not fully recognized the implications of Y. Yadin's correction of Van der Woude's earlier mistaken reading of the **lacuna** at the beginning of line 9: *hô'h (hu)* [. . .]. According to Van der Woude's proposed reconstruction (*hô'h hōqq [hu hoqeq]*, "He is the Rod"; cf. CD 6.9), the metaphor is to be identified with Melchizedek, who thus becomes the subject of line 9 and serves as the ***nomen regens*** of the construct chain. Since Yadin, however, there has been scholarly consensus that the lacuna should read *hô'h hqsl (hu haqats):* "It is the (final) period." Horton recognized the significance

---

16. Lev. 25:10: "And you shall hallow the fiftieth year and you shall proclaim liberty throughout the land to all its inhabitants. It shall be a jubilee for you: you shall return, every one of you, to your property and every one of you to your family." —NRSV

of this change by observing that grammatically Psalm 82:1 in 11Q13 2.10 must be understood to describe the *nomen regens* of the construct chain and the subject of line 9.

The purpose of the citation of Psalm 82:1 is therefore not to identify Melchizedek as a celestial being at all, but to define the nature of the final period, that is, "Concerning it the Song of David says. . . ." This period has just been described as a time for "the administration of judgment" in which the eschatological priest will play a role. Nothing in the thematic *pesher* indicates that Melchizedek signifies anyone other than the historical figure of Genesis 14:18-20 ("And Melchizedek king of Salem brought out bread and wine; now he was a priest of the Most High God. He blessed him and said, 'Blessed is Abram by the Most High God, maker of heaven and earth; and blessed is the Most High God, who has delivered your enemies into your hand!' And he gave him one tenth of everything"—trans. Wright). Instead, Psalm 82:1 serves simply as a literary device for introducing the **dramatis personae** that belong to the community's hope for imminent redemption and revenge against its enemies.

According to the collective sectarian thought at Qumran, Melchizedek would not be the only instrument of divine judgment. Rather, he sits among the "Divine Assembly," an epithet for the community that appears elsewhere in the Dead Sea Scrolls (1QM 1.10;[17] 1QH[a] 5.25[18]). In the War Scroll (1QM 4.9),[19] the title is inscribed on the ensign of the Qumran community in preparation for the eschatological battle. Because of the structural parallelism of Psalm 82:1 in which the Divine Assembly is also called Elohim, the title's singular appearance in the Hebrew Scriptures provided the author of 11Q13 with an opportunity to describe both Melchizedek and the Qumran community in their future roles as Elohim.

The author has ingeniously fused the structural parallelism inherent in both Isaiah 61:2 and Psalm 82:1 to create a bifocal presentation in which Melchizedek and the community will be executors of divine judgment on the Day of Vengeance. Mention of the Divine Assembly from Psalm 82:1 led to the introduction of Psalm 7:8-9[20] (Eng. 7:7-8), which includes the appellation for the community's adversaries—the Assembly of the Nations—and the motif of divine judgment. The author presents Melchizedek enthroned over them—"Over [the Assembly of the Nations] be seated on high" (11Q13 2.6-7; Ps. 7:8)—but once again this does not mean that the king of Salem is a celestial being. Similar enthronement depictions of historical figures are witnessed in ancient Jewish literature (e.g., Ezekiel the Tragedian 67-76; *Antiquities* 2.233-34; Exod. Rab. 1:26; 3 En. 12:1-5).

---

17. 1QM 1.10: "For this day has been determined by him from the past times as the war of annihilation for the Sons of Darkness. On it (this day) the assembly of the gods and the congregation of men will draw near to one another for great destruction." —trans. Wright

18. 1QH[a] 5.25: ". . .] all your works before you created them with the host of your spirits and the assembly of [the gods] . . . your holy expanse [and all]." —trans. Wright

19. 1QM 4.9: "Rule of the banners of the congregation. When they come out to battle they will write on the first banner, 'God's congregation.'" —trans. Wright

20. Ps. 7:8-9: "Let the congregation of the peoples surround you and return over it to the place on high. Let the Lord judge the peoples; judge me, Lord, according to my righteousness and according to my integrity that is upon me." —trans. Wright

Instead, the priestly figure is seated above the Assembly of the Nations to execute divine judgment.

COMPARISON OF 11Q13 2.9; ISAIAH 61:2; PSALM 82:1

	11Q13 2.9	Isaiah 61:2	Psalm 82:1
Melchizedek:	(A) The year of Melchizedek's favor	(A) The year of the Lord's favor	(A) Elohim stands in the Divine Assembly
Community:	(B) The day of vengeance of the Saints of God	(B) The day of vengeance of our Elohim	(B) He will judge in the midst of Elohim.

The whole episode resembles Psalm 110, where we hear reference both to Melchizedek and to one seated in judgment: "The Lord says to my lord: 'Sit at my right hand, until I make your enemies your footstool'" (110:1). The notion that Melchizedek himself would be the eschatological judge seems to be the fruit of a creative exegesis of the consonantal text of Psalm 110. Like the author of the book of Hebrews, the Qumran community read Psalm 110 to concern Melchizedek himself: "You are a priest forever, *according to my words (al divrati)*, O Melchizedek!" (Ps. 110:4;[21] cf. Heb. 7:3[22]). Consequently, in the following verse the Dead Sea sect and other early Jewish interpreters understood the consonantal reading of *adoni* to signify not the Lord (i.e., *Adonai*) as vocalized by the Masoretes, but the human figure (i.e., *adoni*) already mentioned in the opening verse: "My lord [*adoni*] is at your [the Lord's] right hand" (Ps. 110:5).

This ancient, **non-Masoretic reading** of Psalm 110:5 presents the seated description identical to that of Psalm 110:1: "The Lord (YHWH) said to my lord (*adoni*), 'Sit at my right hand.'" It is not the Lord who is seated at the right hand to execute judgment in the following verse (110:6), but the appointed human redeemer (*adoni*), or as he is identified in the non-Masoretic reading of Psalm 110:1-5 and 11Q13—Melchizedek: "He will execute judgment among the nations, filling them with corpses; he will shatter chiefs over the wide earth" (Ps. 110:6). So we hear in 11Q13 2.13 that Melchizedek will "render the vengeance of God's judgment." In effect, through Melchizedek *God will judge the nations*, a description that closely resembles the intermediary role of the redeemer figure in Psalm 110:6, who likewise *will judge the nations*.

Reception of 11Q13 in the Second Temple Period

11Q13 presents poignant areas of interest for readers of the New Testament. Most obvious is the figure of Melchizedek and his role in the redemptive expectations

21. Ps. 110:4: "The Lord has sworn and will not change his mind, 'You are a priest forever according to the order of Melchizedek.'" —NRSV

22. Heb. 7:3: "Without father, without mother, without genealogy, having neither beginning of days nor end of life, but resembling the Son of God, he remains a priest forever." —NRSV

of the Qumran community. We have noted that undergirding the presentation of Melchizedek in the Dead Sea document is a creative reading of Psalm 110. Only through such a non-Masoretic reading—"You are *a priest forever*, according to my words, O Melchizedek!"—could the New Testament author describe the king of Salem—"He is *a priest forever*" (Heb. 7:3). Additionally, David Flusser noted that only in 11Q13 and the New Testament epistle do we find together Melchizedek, the Messiah, and the Son of Man/Judge of the end of days.

The Qumran periodization of redemptive history, particularly its expression of a hoped-for Jubilee redemption, may likewise be reflected in the New Testament. Both the wording of John the Baptist's preaching (i.e., "a baptism for *remission of sins*") and Jesus' reading of Isaiah 61:1–2 in the Nazareth synagogue may echo these contemporary expectations. Milik suggested that a ten-Jubilee structure may even be witnessed in the genealogy of Jesus with its seventy-six names in Luke 4:23–38. "If one deducts the first six patriarchs, one finds again in the era of the patriarch Enoch the beginning of a computation of seventy generations— exactly the same, therefore, as *1 Enoch* 10:12."[23]

11Q13 is a thematic *pesher* that describes the redemptive hopes of the Qumran congregation. While the work shares some similarities with other writings from the Dead Sea Scrolls and Jewish literature of Late Antiquity, its presentation has no exact parallel. The author divides history into periods and sees its culmination in the advent of Melchizedek in the tenth and final Jubilee. At that time, the sins of the Sons of Light will be atoned and the wicked punished. According to 11Q13, the biblical figure Melchizedek will play a central role in the deliverance of God's elect and the execution of righteous judgment on the congregation's adversaries. The expectation of a future role for the king of Salem is likely derived from a non-Masoretic reading of Psalm 110:4 in which Melchizedek himself is ascribed with an eternal priesthood and, accordingly, in verses 5–7 identified with the one who sits at the Lord's right hand to mete out divine retribution. The author uses the structural parallelism of Psalm 82:1 and Isaiah 61:2 to complete his eschatological portrait with a bifocal presentation in which Melchizedek and the congregation together execute judgment on the Day of Vengeance.

R. Steven Notley

FURTHER READING

Brooke, G. "Melchizedek." In *ABD*, 4:687–88.

Collins, J. J. *The Scepter and the Star: The Messiahs of the Dead Sea Scrolls and Other Ancient Literature*. New York: Doubleday, 1995 (pp. 161–63).

Flusser, D. "Melchizedek and the Son of Man." In *Judaism and the Origins of Christianity*, pp. 186–92. Jerusalem: Magnes, 1988.

Steudel, A. "Melchizedek." In *Encyclopedia of the Dead Sea Scrolls*, edited by L. H. Schiffman and J. C. VanderKam, 1:534. 2 vols. Oxford: Oxford University Press, 2000.

VanderKam, J., and P. Flint. *The Meaning of the Dead Sea Scrolls*. New York: Harper-Collins, 2002 (pp. 224–25).

23. J. T. Milik, *The Books of Enoch: Aramaic Fragments of Qumran Cave 4* (Oxford: Clarendon, 1976), p. 257.

ADVANCED READING

De Jonge, M., and A. S. van der Woude. "11QMelchizedek and the New Testament." *NTS* 12 (1965–66): 301–26.

Delcor, M. "Melchizedek from Genesis to the Qumran Texts and the Epistle to the Hebrews." *JSJ* 2 (1971): 115–35.

Fitzmyer, J. A. "Further Light on the Melchizedek from Qumran Cave 121." *JBL* 86 (1967): 25–41.

García Martínez, F., E. J. C. Tigchelaar, and A. S. Van der Woude. *Discoveries in the Judaean Desert XXIII, Qumran Cave 11, II (11Q2–18, 11Q20–31)*. Oxford: Clarendon, 1988 (pp. 221–41).

Horton, F. L. *The Melchizedek Tradition*. Society of New Testament Studies Monograph Series. Cambridge: Cambridge University Press, 1976.

Kobelski, P. *Melchizedek and Melchiresa*. CBQMS 10. Washington, D.C.: Catholic University Press, 1981.

Milik, J. T. *The Books of Enoch: Aramaic Fragments of Qumran Cave 4*. Oxford: Clarendon, 1976.

———. "Milki-sedeq et Milki-resa." *JJS* 23 (1972): 95–144.

Notley, R. S. "The Eschatological Thinking of the Dead Sea Sect and the Order of Blessing in the Christian Eucharist." In *Jesus' Last Week: Jerusalem Studies in the Synoptic Gospels*, pp. 121–38. Jewish and Christian Perspectives Series 11. Leiden: Brill, 2005.

Sanders, J. A. "The Old Testament in 11QMelchizedek." *Journal of the Ancient Near Eastern Society of Columbia University* 5 (1973): 373–82.

Van der Woude, A. S. "Melchisedek als himmlische Erlösergestalt in den neugefundenen eschatologischen Midraschim aus Qumran-Höhle IX." *Old Testament Studies* 14 (1965): 354–73.

Yadin, Y. "A Note on Melchizedek and Qumran." *Israel Exploration Journal* 15 (1965): 152–54.

4.2 *from* Melchizedek (11Q13)

11Q13 2.2–25

[2.2] And concerning that which is said, "In [this] year of Jubilee [you will return, every one of you, to your property" (Lev. 25:13), and likewise what is said,] "And this [3] [is the manner of the remission:] Every creditor will remit the claim that is held [against a neighbor, not exacting it of a neighbor who is a member of the community, because] God's remission [has been proclaimed]" (Deut. 15:2). [4] [Its interpretation refers] to the end of days and concerning the captives, just as [Isaiah said: "To proclaim the Jubilee to the captives" (Isa. 61:1) . . .] just as [. . .] [5] and from the inheritance of Melchizedek who [. . .] [6] will return them to what is theirs. He will proclaim to them liberty, releasing them [from the debt] of all their iniquities. And this will be [7] in the first week of the Jubilee following the ni[ne Jubile]es. The Da[y of Atone]ment will be the end of the tenth [Jubi]-lee, [8] when he will atone for all the Sons [of Light] and the lot of Melchizedek [. . .] [9] This is the period for the "year of Melchizedek's favor" (cf. Isa. 61:2) and his hos[ts with] the holy ones of God for the administration of judgment, as it is written [10] concerning it in the Songs of David, "Elohim sits in the Divi[ne Assembly], he will judge in the midst of the Elohim" (Ps. 82:2). And concerning it, Scripture says, "Over it [11] be seated in the highest heaven. God will judge the peoples" (Ps. 7:7–8). Concerning which Scripture sa[ys, "How long will you jud]ge unjustly, and show partiality to the wicked? Selah" (Ps. 82:2). [12] Its interpretation concerns Belial and the spirits of his lot [because they have re]belled against the laws of God to [. . .] [13] Melchizedek will execute the vengeance of God's judg[ments in that day and de]liver [them from the hand] of Belial and the hand of the spi[rits of his lot]. [14] And with the aid of all the Oaks of [Righteousness] (Isa. 61:3) [. . .] all the sons of God [. . .] [15] This is the Day of [Peace/Salvation] that [is spoken by I]saiah the prophet, who said, "[How] beautiful upon the mountains are the feet of the messenger who announces peace, who brings [16] [good] news, [who announces salva]tion, who [sa]ys to Zion, 'Your Elohim [reigns]'" (Isa. 52:7). [17] Its interpretation: the "mountains" [are] the prophets [. . .] [18] And the "messenger" is the "anointed one of the spirit" about whom Dan[iel spoke, "To seal both vision and prophet, and to anoint a most holy place" (Dan. 9:24). The "messenger who brings] [19] good news, who annou[nces salvation" of whom it is written, ["to proclaim the year of the Lord's favor, the day of vengeance of our God,] [20] to comfort those who [mourn" (Isa. 61:2). Its interpretation:] He will instruct them in all the periods of the age [. . .] [21] in truth [. . .] [22] [. . .] and before [23] by the judgments of God, as it is written concerning him, ["who says to Zi]on, 'Your Elohim reigns'" (Isa. 52:7). Zion is [24] [the Assembly of all the Sons of Righteousness,] who uphold the covenant and turn away from walking in the way of the people. "Your

---

Translation by R. Steven Notley.

Elohim" is [25] [Melchizedek who will de]liver [them from the ha]nd of Belial about which it is said, "Then you will have the trumpet [sounded loud; in] the seventh month" (Lev. 25:9).

Florilegium and Testimonia

Among the Dead Sea Scrolls (*see* Overview of Early Jewish Literature) a number of *pesharim* ("interpretations of scripture") were discovered that organize selected biblical passages around a particular theme. 4Q174 and 4Q175 are two of the best examples of these "thematic *pesharim*" and have attracted considerable attention, especially because of interest in anointed figures. Both documents contain collections of scriptural citations that serve to communicate expectations about salvation in the end time for Israel. Although 4Q174 is known by other names, the title Florilegium, a Latin term that literally means "gathering of flowers," is especially descriptive of this anthology. Because 4Q174 contains the phrase "the last days" the editor of this document and also of 4Q175, John Allegro, first referred to it as the "eschatological midrash." Allegro named 4Q175 Testimonia and unlike "eschatological midrash" this title for 4Q175 has endured. A *testimonia*, which is also a Latin term, is often used to describe various classical works that survive only in part, or contain a list of prooftexts, or provide a list of works cited. In this introduction these two documents will simply be referred to as Florilegium and Testimonia (*see* Introduction to Biblical Interpretation and Rewritten Scripture; Introduction to *Pesharim*).

Florilegium (4Q174)

Narrative Description

Before its discovery at Qumran, Florilegium was entirely unknown. A major concern of Florilegium is the captivity of Israel. Israel's captivity, a pivotal event that left untold trauma in its wake and that is reflected in a wide range of literature from the period, is attributed in this document to the ultimate adversarial character: Belial and the Sons of Belial (*see* Melchizedek [11Q13]). A time is anticipated when the situation of ongoing captivity will be set straight and the elect of the elect, a remnant community that is the faithful of Israel, will be restored and the wicked will be judged. Restoration is also conceived of by means of the metaphor of "planting." When considering the future, the author is particularly interested in a select number of passages that are interpreted in connection with an end-time period, or eschaton. These passages are 2 Samuel 7 (related to Exod. 15:17–18 because of a common interest in Israel as something that will be "planted"), Psalm 2 (related to 2 Sam. 7 because of interest in a "son"), and Deuteronomy 33.

Part of Israel's restoration—recall that captivity begins with the destruction of the first temple and the group behind this document likely does not accept that the Second Temple is legitimate or indicates that restoration took place—is rebuilding the temple and raising up anointed ones. The anointed ones in the fragment are found in 1.19 (citing Ps. 2:2: "The kings of the earth set themselves, and the rulers take counsel together, against the Lord and his anointed") which refers to the community, and in 1.11 the "Seeker of the Torah" is understood by many as an anointed priestly figure. The Seeker of the Torah stands alongside the royal offspring of David in 1.11 ("forever, I will be to him a father and he will be to me a son"; cf. 2 Sam 7:12–14); he is the sprout of David, the one standing with the Seeker of the Torah.

Florilegium envisages a future temple that is expressed with a Hebrew phrase that has been interpreted in more than one way: *Miqdash Adam* (1.6). On the one hand, this may be translated in relation to the proper name of the first man Adam. On the other hand, one may understand "humanity" (Hebrew: *adam*) more generally. Thus, several translations offered are "sanctuary of Adam," "human sanctuary," or a "sanctuary *among* humanity." If one understands this as a "sanctuary of Adam," then the author would seem to conceive of the eschaton as a time when the world will be restored to Eden at the beginning of creation (sometimes referred to by the German phrase *Urzeit ist Endzeit*—"the beginning is the end"). This community would then have understood that when restoration comes it will be a return to this time of paradise in the garden. Such a notion would find resonances elsewhere in literature from Qumran, especially references to the "glory of Adam" as a reward for the upright (*see* CD 3.20;[1] *see* Damascus Document [CD]). If the Hebrew *adam* is understood as "humanity" instead, this then would fit well with the idea that the community is a sanctuary, such as what one finds in the Rule of the Community (8.5–10; *see* Rule of the Community [1QS]).

Date, Provenance, and Genre

The style of writing dates this manuscript to the late first century BCE. Annette Steudel has suggested that in its original form Florilegium was six columns long; compare this with the length of the Rule of the Community found in Cave 1, which is eleven columns long.[2] What actually remains from Florilegium are twenty-six fragments, the largest of which preserves parts of columns 1–2. If this is not the original autograph, which would then allow for an earlier date of com-

---

1. CD 3.20: "The people who cling to him are destined for eternal life and all human glory will be accorded to them." —trans. Wacholder

2. A. Steudel, *Der Midrasch zur Eschatologie aus der Qumrangemeinde (4QMidrEschata, b): Materielle Rekonstruktion, Textbestand, Gattung und Traditionsgeschichte Einordnung des durch 4Q174 ("Florilegium") und 4Q177 ("Catena") repräsentierten Werkes aus den Qumranfunden*, STDJ 13 (Leiden: Brill, 1994), pp. 5–22.

position, then references to the community's experiences would be internal and perhaps align themselves with a date similar to Habakkuk Pesher (*see* Habakkuk Pesher [1QpHab]) and a conflict with a **Hasmonean** high priest. That this document is to be located among the so-called **sectarian** compositions is clear from the reference to the council of the yaḥad ("community") in 1.17.[3] The community is also referred to with the sectarian terminology "Sons of Light" in 1.8.

The genre of Florilegium is best described as thematic *pesher* rather than as anthology. Unlike continuous *pesharim*, which provide a running commentary on a particular book (e.g., Habakkuk Pesher), the thematic *pesharim* organize passages from multiple sources around a common topic. While an anthology collects excerpts, Florilegium goes beyond simply gathering passages. The concern of the author, which is the lens through which the passages are interpreted, is his community and how they have suffered and await a time of restoration and vindication. Therefore, the selected passages communicate about the present situation and more recent history of the community.

Reception of Florilegium in the Second Temple Period

Several aspects of Florilegium have attracted the attention of New Testament scholars. First, if *Miqdash Adam* is understood as a reference to the community as a temple, this concept is reflected in 2 Corinthians 6:14–7:1, where the church is discussed as a temple.[4] Second, 2 Samuel 7 and Psalm 2 are referred to, both individually and together, in the New Testament in regard to Jesus' sonship. Finally, many of the writings in the New Testament, from the Gospels to the book of Hebrews, have been interpreted against the backdrop of ongoing exile and the restoration of Israel in the eschaton. Florilegium provides insights into how one community conceived of Israel as remaining in captivity and attributed this to the activity of an ultimate adversary. In Mark's Gospel, Jesus' ministry begins

---

3. The scholarly consensus regarding the Qumran scrolls is that they most likely represented part of a library of ancient religious documents that belonged to the inhabitants of the site nearby. Most frequently, this collection is divided into three categories, scrolls that (1) are part of the Hebrew Bible in our own time; (2) belong to the Qumran "sectarian" group; and (3) should be viewed as reflecting Jewish religiosity more broadly than the so-called sectarian group. Delineating whether certain scrolls are best categorized as either (2) or (3) is not always straightforward. Nondisputed, for the most part, sectarian documents are the Rule of the Community (1QS), Habakkuk Pesher (1QpHab), War Scroll (1QM), Thanksgiving Hymns (1QH[a]), and the Damascus Document (CD). A comparison of themes and language found in another scroll with these core documents helps scholars to adjudicate where scrolls best belong. Other methods and criteria for categorizing scrolls have also been developed. Locating a document in one of these categories potentially has a significant influence on how one understands the breadth of influence a document's ideas may have had on Jewish thought in the period.

4. This section of 2 Corinthians is thought by many to be a later addition (or "interpolation"). These few sentences have attracted considerable attention not only because the community is a temple, but also the question is asked (6:15): "What accord has Christ with Belial?" This is the only place in the New Testament where "Belial" occurs and yet is frequent in early Jewish literature as a title for the ultimate antagonist.

with him being tempted by Satan (1:12–13: "And the Spirit immediately drove him out into the wilderness. He was in the wilderness forty days, tempted by Satan; and he was with the wild beasts; and the angels waited on him"), and after a confrontation from which Jesus leaves victorious, he then proceeds to set the way straight by confronting the demonic and unclean spirits. Restoration is therefore associated with overthrowing Belial or a synonymous character.

Testimonia (4Q175)

Narrative Description

Four biblical passages frame Testimonia, and the author has conveniently placed these in four separate paragraphs, each with a space and hooklike stroke to divide them. Central to interpreting Testimonia is to assess how these four passages relate to one another. The first citation is found in the Hebrew Bible (MT) in Deuteronomy 5:28–29[5] and 18:18–19,[6] but Testimonia is actually following Exodus 20:21 ("And the people stood afar off, and Moses drew near unto the thick darkness where God [was]") in the Samaritan Pentateuch (*see* Reworked Pentateuch [4Q158, 4Q364–67]). The author is citing a tradition from the Samaritan Pentateuch that merges these two passages from Deuteronomy. After this first paragraph, the following two passages cited, found in the second and third paragraphs, are straightforwardly from Numbers 24:15–17[7] and Deuteronomy 33:8–11.[8]

The last passage in Testimonia clearly reflects Joshua 6:26 ("Joshua then pronounced this oath, saying, 'Cursed before the Lord be anyone who tries to build

---

5. Deut. 5:28–29: "The Lord heard your words when you spoke to me, and the Lord said to me, 'I have heard the words of this people, which they have spoken to you; they are right in all that they have spoken. If only they had such a mind as this, to fear me and to keep all my commandments always, so that it might go well with them and with their children forever!'"—NRSV

6. Deut. 18:18–19: "I will raise up for them a prophet like you from among their own people; I will put my words in the mouth of the prophet, who will speak to them everything that I command. Anyone who does not heed the words that the prophet will speak in my name, I myself will hold accountable."—NRSV

7. Num. 24:15–17: "So he uttered his oracle, saying, 'The oracle of Balaam son of Beor, the oracle of the man whose eye is clear, the oracle of one who hears the words of God, and knows the knowledge of the Most High, who sees the vision of the Almighty, who falls down, but with his eyes uncovered: I see him, but not now; I behold him, but not near—a star shall come out of Jacob, and a scepter shall rise out of Israel; it will crush the borderlands of Moab, and the territory of all the Shethites.'"—NRSV

8. Deut. 33:8–11: "And of Levi he said, 'Give to Levi your Thummim, and your Urim to your loyal one, whom you tested at Massah, with whom you contended at the waters of Meribah; who said of his father and mother, 'I regard them not'; he ignored his kin, and did not acknowledge his children. For they observed your word, and kept your covenant. They teach Jacob your ordinances, and Israel your law; they place incense before you, and whole burnt offerings on your altar. Bless, O Lord, his substance, and accept the work of his hands; crush the loins of his adversaries, of those that hate him, so that they do not rise again.'"—NRSV

this city— this Jericho! At the cost of his firstborn he will lay its foundation, and at the cost of his youngest he will set up its gates!'"), but it should likely not be referred to as a "citation," but rather an interpretation of Joshua 6:26 that was circulating in the period. This interpretation of Joshua 6:26 is also found in the Apocryphon of Joshua (4Q379 22 2.7–14), a manuscript that may be dated considerably earlier than Testimonia, and when Testimonia 21–23 uses Joshua 6:26 the adaptations and changes are the same as those found in the Apocryphon of Joshua.[9] To explain this interpretive tradition by concrete example, Testimonia and the Apocryphon of Joshua begin their citation of Joshua 6:26 and then stop near the middle in order to add a statement about the accursed one being a "man of Belial." Another addition is found at the conclusion of the citation where comments occur that are found in only these two Dead Sea Scrolls. Such observations indicate a common way of thinking about Joshua 6:26 and many have suggested that Testimonia is actually quoting the Apocryphon of Joshua as a source. Hanan Eshel has presented a theory that the relationship between Testimonia and the Apocryphon of Joshua (i.e., that Testimonia is quoting the Apocryphon) may not be as straightforward as many have considered.

That the author conceives of himself and his community as living in an end-time period and enduring persecution as a righteous community is suggested by the particular use of these four biblical citations. The first three paragraphs of Testimonia take up passages to portray three messianic figures. Exodus 20:21 (= Deut. 5:28–29, 18:18–19) refers to the raising up of a prophet like Moses. Numbers 24:15–17 is concerned with the expectation of royal and priestly messiahs collectively (cf. CD 7.18–21; 1QM 11.6; 1QSb 5.27, which also cite Numbers 24; *see* War Scroll). Deuteronomy 33:8–11 is about a future high priest like Aaron.

The author then moves on from these three biblical citations to the accursed one who belongs to Belial and his two sons. A number of attempts have been made to identify to whom this prophetic utterance is supposed to refer. Modern interpreters have suggested nearly every Hasmonean ruler possible; among them two stand out as more convincing: (1) Simon (143–135 BCE) and his sons Judas and Mattathias; and (2) Jonathan Hyrcanus I (135–104 BCE) and his sons Aristobulus and Alexander Janaeus (*see* 1 and 2 Maccabees). The man of Belial identified as a corrupt Hasmonean preceded by an expectation of messianic figures underscores the interpretation of this manuscript as a work concerned with the fulfillment and expectation of the community in the eschaton.

---

9. Apocryphon of Joshua (4Q379) 22 2.7–9: "At the time when Joshua finished praising and offering psalms of thanksgiving, he said, 'Cursed be the man who builds this city, by his firstborn he will establish it and by his youngest will he set up its gates,'"—trans. Wold. Testimonia 21–23: "At the time when Joshua finished praising and offering psalms of thanksgiving, he said, 'Cursed be the man who builds this city, by his firstborn he will establish it and by his youngest will he set up its gates; and behold, an accursed man, one of Belial.'" Josh. 6:26: "Joshua then pronounced this oath, saying, 'Cursed before the Lord be anyone who tries to build this city—this Jericho! At the cost of his firstborn he will lay its foundation, and at the cost of his youngest he will set up its gates!'"—trans. Wold.

Date, Provenance, and Genre

Testimonia is among the best preserved documents from Qumran. It is written in Hebrew on a single sheet of parchment and survives nearly intact, with only the bottom right-hand corner missing. The handwriting is mid-Hasmonean and allows the manuscript to be dated to about 100 BCE.

There are several good reasons that Testimonia should be located among sectarian compositions. The worldview of the document fits well with core sectarian compositions and especially the Rule of the Community. The eschatological figures found in both are the same (1QS 9.11: "until the prophet comes and the messiahs of Aaron and Israel"). Noteworthy too is that the same scribe who copied the Rule of the Community also copied Testimonia (i.e., handwriting is the same). However, the same scribe also copied other works, not all of which may be sectarian; these are 1QSa, 1QSb, 4Q53 and also corrections to the Great Isaiah Scroll (*see* The Great Isaiah Scroll and the Interpretation of Isaiah at Qumran). Therefore, the observation that the same scribe who copied the Rule of the Community also transcribed Testimonia does not necessarily lead to the judgment that Testimonia is sectarian. Another interesting detail is that Testimonia has a number of spelling mistakes and is oddly arranged, leading to a theory that the scribe did not copy it, but rather authored it. Testimonia may be located among the sectarian corpus, and if this is not the case then it preserves traditions that were in broader circulation in which the sectarians participated.

Reception of Testimonia in the Second Temple Period

Traditions related to messianic figures in Testimonia are developed within early Christianity. In the case of messiahs relating to the figures of prophets, priests, or kings in New Testament writings, each of these are taken up. Jesus is related to a prophet in the transfiguration (Luke 9:35; Matt. 17:5; Mark 9:7), and one could note the proclamation of the audience in the Fourth Gospel (John 6:14: "When the people saw the sign that he had done, they began to say, 'This is indeed the prophet who is to come into the world.' When Jesus realized that they were about to come and take him by force to make him king, he withdrew again to the mountain by himself") and Stephen's speech in Acts 7:37 ("This is the Moses who said to the Israelites, 'God will raise up a prophet for you from your own people like *he raised up* me'"). While Jesus as a royal Messiah is well known, the book of Hebrews is unique in its presentation of Jesus as a priestly messiah (see Heb. 4:14–5:10, esp. vv. 5–6[10]).

Both Florilegium and Testimonia as collections of prooftexts shed light on the use of anthologies in Antiquity. When the New Testament collects prooftexts, scholars have often questioned whether they were indebted to anthologies that were already in circulation. Both of these documents provide clear indication that early Christian authors were aware of and indebted to scriptural antholo-

---

10. Heb. 5:5–6: "So also Christ did not glorify himself in becoming a high priest, but was appointed by the one who said to him, 'You are my Son, today I have begotten you'; as he says also in another place, 'You are a priest forever, according to the order of Melchizedek.'"

gies. The particular interests of Florilegium and Testimonia, such as messianism and future restoration and redemption, witness to the growth of ideas that went on to develop further and are eventually reflected in the writings of earliest Christianity.

BENJAMIN WOLD

FURTHER READING

Brooke, George J. "Florilegium." In *Encyclopedia of the Dead Sea Scrolls*, edited by L. Schiffman and J. VanderKam, 1:297–98. 2 vols. Oxford: Oxford University Press, 2000.

Charlesworth, J. H., and H. W. Rietz, eds. *Dead Sea Scrolls: Hebrew, Aramaic, and Greek Texts with English Translation*, vol. 6B:, *Pesharim and Related Documents*. Tübingen: Mohr Siebeck, 2002 (pp. 312–19).

Flint, P., and J. VanderKam. *The Meaning of the Dead Sea Scrolls: Their Significance for Understanding the Bible, Judaism, Jesus and Christianity*. London: T&T Clark, 2002 (pp. 221–23).

Lübbe, J. "A Reinterpretation of 4Qtestimonia." *Revue de Qumrân* 12 (1986): 187–97.

Steudel, Annette. "Testimonia." In *Encyclopedia of the Dead Sea Scrolls*, edited by L. Schiffman and J. VanderKam, 2:936–38. 2 vols. Oxford: Oxford University Press, 2000.

ADVANCED READING

Brooke, George J. *4QFlorilegium in its Jewish Context*. JSOTSup 29. Sheffield: Sheffield University Press, 1985.

Dimant, Devorah. "4QFlorilegium and the Idea of the Community as Temple." In *Hellenica et Judaica: Hommage à V. Nikiprovetzky*, edited by A. Caquot et al., pp. 165-89. Leuven: Peeters, 1986.

Eshel, H. "The Historical Background of the Pesher Interpreting Joshua's Curse on the Rebuilder of Jericho." *Revue de Qumrân* 15/59 (1992): 409–20.

Fitzmyer, J. A. "4QTestimonia and the New Testament." In *Essays on the Semitic Background of the New Testament*, pp. 59–89. London: Chapman, 1971.

Newsom, C. "4Q378-379: 4QApocryphon of Joshuaa-b." In *Qumran Cave 4, XVII: Parabiblical Texts, Part 3*, edited by J. VanderKam, pp. 237–88. DJD 22. Oxford: Oxford University Press, 1996.

Schwarz, Daniel R. "The Three Temples of 4QFlorilegium." *Revue de Qumrân* 10/37 (1979): 83–91.

4.3 Florilegium (4Q174)

¹·¹ [. . .] enemy ["and] a son of perdition [will not aga]in [harm him as the first time, from the day that ² [I appointed judges] over my people Israel" (2 Sam. 7:10–11); this is the house that [. . .] [. . . in] the last days, as it is written in the scroll of ³ [. . . "a sanctuary, O Lord, y]our hand established it, YHWH reigns forever" (Exod. 15:17–18); and that is the house that will not enter into it ⁴ [. . . forever] and ever, and the Ammonite and Moabite and foreigner and son of a stranger and sojourner, forever and ever, for my holy ones are there ⁵ [. . .] [. . .] forever, he will always be seen upon it, and the godless will not make it desolate again, as they made the sanctuary of Israel desolate the first time ⁶ by their sin and instructed to build for him a sanctuary of man (Hebrew: *Miqdash Adam*) to make offerings in it to him, ⁷ (being) before him works of the law, for he said to David: "I will give rest to you from all of your enemies" (2 Sam. 7:11); that is, he will give rest to them from all ⁸ the Sons of Belial who cause them to stumble and to destroy the[m] when they came with the cunning of Belial to cause the Sons of Light ⁹ to stumble and to devise against them wicked devices to [his] life to Belial in straying [. . .] ¹⁰ [and] YHWH told you that he will build a house for you, and "I will raise up your seed after you and establish the throne of his kingdom ¹¹ forever, I will be to him a father and he will be to me a son" (2 Sam. 7:12–14); he is the sprout of David, the one standing with the Seeker of the Torah who ¹² [. . .] in Zion in the last days, as it is written: "and I will raise up the fallen tent of David" (Amos 9:11); it is ¹³ the fallen tent of David that will arise to save Israel. ¹⁴ A midrash: "Blessed is the man who does not walk in the council of wicked ones" (Ps. 1:1); the interpretation of this thin[g . . .] turning from the way [. . .] ¹⁵ which is written in the scroll of Isaiah the prophet about the end of days, it will be "as a strong [hand and he instructed me not to walk in the way] ¹⁶ of this people" (Isa. 8:11); and they are those about whom it is written in the scroll of Ezekiel the prophet: they will not defile themselves any longer ¹⁷ with their [i]d[o]ls (cf. Ezek. 37:23; 44:10), they are the Sons of Zadok and the men of their council [. . .] after them to the council of the *yaḥad*. ¹⁸ "Why do the nations rage and the people plot a vain thing, the kings of the earth set themselves and the rulers take council together against YHWH and ¹⁹ [his anointed/*messiah*" (Ps. 2:1–2), the in]terpretation of this thing [. . . na]tions and the [. . .] chosen of Israel in the last days.

²·¹ It is the time of testing that co[mes . . . J]udah to complete [. . .] ² Belial, and will remain [. . . m]embership, and they will complete the whole Torah [. . .] ³ Moses, it is the [. . . whic]h is written in the scroll of Daniel the prophet, for the wicked to act wickedly [. . .] ⁴ᵃ and the righteous [. . . and "will be mad]e white and pure" and "a people knowing God will seize" the [. . .] (cf. Dan. 12:10) ⁴ . . . [. . .] after the [. . .] that to them [. . .]

Translation by Benjamin Wold.

4.4 Testimonia (4Q175)

[1] And the Lord spoke to Moses saying, "I have heard the sound of the words [2] of this people that they spoke to you, they are right in all they have spoken. [3] O that they had such a heart in them to fear me and to keep all [4] my commandments always so that it would be well with them and their children forever" (Deut. 5:28–29). [5] "I will raise up a prophet for them, from the midst of their brothers, like you; and I will place my word [6] in his mouth and he will speak to them all that I command, and anyone [7] that does not listen to my words that the prophet speaks in my name, I [8] will require it of him" (Deut. 18:18–19).

[9] And he took up his oracle and spoke, "The utterance of Balaam the son of Beor, and the utterance of the man [10] whose eyes are open, the utterance of the one who hears the words of God and understands the knowledge of the Most High who [11] sees the vision of the Almighty, falls down and eyes wide open: I see him, but not now, [12] I behold him but not near, a star will come forth from Jacob, and a scepter will arise from Israel, and batter the [13] brow of Moab, and destroy all the sons of tumult" (Num. 24:15–17).

[14] "And of Levi he said, Give to Levi your Thummim, and Urim to your faithful one whom [15] you tested at Massah, and with whom you contended at the waters of Meribah, the one who said of his father [16] and mother 'I knew them not' and does not recognize his brothers, and does not know [17] his children, for they have observed your word and kept your covenant, they will cause your decrees to shine for Jacob, [18] and your law to Israel, they will place incense before you, and a whole burnt offering upon your altar, [19] bless his substance, O Lord, and accept the work of his hand, strike the loins of those who rise up against him, and of those who hate him [20] that they do not rise again" (Deut. 33:8–11).

[21] At the time when Joshua finished praising and offering psalms of thanksgiving, [22] he said, "Cursed be the man who builds this city, by his firstborn [23] he will establish it and by his youngest will he set up its gates" (Josh. 6:26); and "Behold, an accursed man, one of Belial, [24] is about to become a fowl[er's sn]are to his people and a terror to all his neighbors and will arise [25] [. . .] the two of them will be violent vessels and they will return and build [26] this city and will raise up walls and towers to make it an evil stronghold, [27] [great wickedness] in Israel and a horrible thing in Ephraim and Judah [28] [. . . and] they will perform ungodly things in the land and great disgrace among the sons of [29] [Jacob and will shed bl]ood like water upon the ramparts of the Daughter of Zion and within the borders of [30] Jerusalem" (Josh. 6:26).

Translation by Benjamin Wold.

The Book of Jubilees

The book of Jubilees describes itself in the prologue and first chapter as the angelic dictation to Moses from the heavenly tablets the day after the "first law" was given to Moses (Exod. 24). This revelation retells the basic story of Genesis and the first half of Exodus, with frequent additions, deletions, summaries, and alternate versions of stories. Jubilees infuses Genesis and Exodus with other books, including Leviticus, Deuteronomy, Isaiah, Psalms, and the Book of Watchers (*see* Book of Watchers [1 Enoch 1–36]). Besides solving interpretive problems, Jubilees traces legal issues, including the festival calendar, to Genesis and asserts the eternality of the laws, originating well before Sinai and enduring forever after. The introduction suggests its contents will cover "all time," but in fact Jubilees makes only short predictions of the progress of history after Moses. It seems the laws and calendar described in Jubilees are for all time, not that all events of history are recorded in Jubilees.

Author/Provenance

Most scholars believe the book of Jubilees, as we have it, is the work of a single author who drew on and reworked multiple sources. The author valued synthesis of received traditions more than originality. The attempt to reconcile traditions and interpretations in tension left certain seams in the final product. The work is complex and uses different rhetorical and literary styles, but coheres thoroughly in substance. It is possible, as some scholars believe, that different individuals are responsible for different sections, but they must have been very like-minded individuals.

The author leaves no autobiographical statements, but it stands to reason that the author had himself and his work in mind in describing the commission of the Levites: "[Jacob] gave all his books and the books of his fathers to his son Levi so that he could preserve them and renew them for his sons until today" (Jub. 45:16). The book also praises Levi and priests at length. Jubilees treats Levi as a priest and generally does not distinguish between priests and Levites, so there is a lack of evidence by which to speculate if the author was a priest. The author's ideas generally fit with what little we know about the **Hasidim.** In later times, the **Essenes** would agree with Jubilees on many issues (*see* History of the Second Temple Period). It stands to reason that Jubilees influenced the Essenes, but that does not mean that the author identified with this or any sect. The emphasis on Jewish unity indicates the author predates or resists such sectarian divisions.

There have been no thorough studies of the social setting of Jubilees, but some elements may be consistent with the results of sociological studies of Ben Sira, earlier in the second century (*see* Ben Sira). The book both promotes and reflects thorough study, and is so complex that sustained instruction would have been necessary to appreciate it fully. The emphasis on choosing a proper wife may have been particularly salient for adolescent males. The repeated descriptions of learning to read and write function primarily to reinforce the authority, antiquity, and reliability of the written word, going back to the heavenly tablets. Secondarily, however, the many instances of angels and parents teaching must reflect the circumstance of the author in some way, perhaps even an academic calendar in Jub. 12:27 ["He took his fathers' books (they were written in Hebrew) and copied them. From that time, he began to study them, while I was telling him everything that he was unable (to understand). He studied them throughout the six rainy months"—trans. Vanderkam], where Abraham studies during the six rainy months. It would be impossible to speak precisely of "schools" in Jubilees. If anything, the imagery of teaching "all Israel" and lack of elitism would suggest a more public form of instruction than what Ben Sira seems to reflect. This issue remains a desideratum for future study.

Date/Occasion

Jubilees is part of the flourishing of literary activity around the time of the Maccabean Revolt. The book reflects the **Hellenistic** crisis and at least some of the events under the reign of Antiochus IV Epiphanes (175–163 BCE), such as the crisis over the high priesthood, civil war, and invasion. A comparison with 1 Maccabees shows many parallels and echoes with events of the 160s BCE, perhaps up to the peaceful retreat of the **Seleucid** army in 159. Jubilees seems to be unaware of Jonathan's consolidation of the high priesthood and kingship in 152, although some scholars believe the book, or its final form, was completed shortly before the oldest known copy of the book from the last quarter of the second century BCE. Even though the book is not an account of recent events, the Maccabean Revolt significantly influences the ideas of the book. Consequently, the book can be compared to other responses to the revolt, such as the Animal Apocalypse (*see* Animal Apocalypse [1 Enoch 85–90]), Daniel (*see* The Book of Daniel), and 1–2 Maccabees (*see* 1 and 2 Maccabees).

If, as seems likely, the book was composed between 159 and 152 BCE, it gives us special insight into the transitional period in Judaism in which there is no recorded high priest (called the *intersacerdotium*), the **Hasmonean** dynasty had not yet been established, Seleucid political presence was reduced, and Judea was recovering from devastating war and famine. It stands to reason that this was a time of reconstruction in which Jubilees' proposals on theological and legal (including calendrical) issues were made in a relative vacuum. This would explain the lack of **sectarian** polemic against other Jews, and strong emphasis on Jewish unity. Within a matter of decades, powerful voices would develop in Judaism and reject the positions in Jubilees. Those who continued to accept the legitimacy of Jubilees would become marginalized. Consequently, Jubilees is central to understanding the development of Jewish sectarianism in the Hasmonean period, and should probably be viewed as representative of the early cusp of views that were not yet marginalized or suppressed by a dominant authority.

Jubilees seems to assume an audience that already accepts the authority of the Torah and the importance of following it according to one interpretation or another. For example, part of the debate about circumcision is not whether to practice it, but whether it could be rescheduled from the eighth day (presumably for reasons such as Sabbath or illness). Even if the firsthand audience consisted of religious Jews, the book also responds indirectly to the Hellenistic assimilationists whose position is described in 1 Maccabees 1:11–15:

> In those days certain renegades came out from Israel and misled many, saying, "Let us go and make a covenant with the Gentiles around us, for since we separated from them many disasters have come upon us." This proposal pleased them, and some of the people eagerly went to the king, who authorized them to observe the ordinances of the Gentiles. Therefore, they built a gymnasium in Jerusalem, according to Gentile custom, removed the marks of circumcision, and abandoned the holy covenant. They joined with the Gentiles and sold themselves to do evil. (NRSV)

Several of the emphases in Jubilees can be understood as responses to this position. First, Jubilees calls for absolute separation from Gentiles, and specifically rejects the suggestion of a covenant between Isaac and the Philistines in Genesis. Jubilees also rejects "since we separated" by insisting that Israel was separated from all the other nations by God from the first week of creation, and is destined to remain separated forever. Jubilees 1 and 23 explain "disasters" as punishment for failure to separate from Gentiles. The Gentile gymnasium (which included nude athletics) and forgoing of circumcision are emphatically rejected in Jubilees.

Text, Language, Sources, and Transmission

Jubilees was written in Hebrew. Fourteen Hebrew copies were found near Qumran (*see* Overview of Early Jewish Literature; see especially DJD 13 [1994]). Although these manuscripts preserve only a small portion of the complete work, they support the general reliability of the Ethiopic (**Ge'ez**) version. From Hebrew, the work was copied into Greek and perhaps Syriac, and from Greek into Latin and Ethiopic. Citations are preserved in several Greek and Syriac works, and part of one Latin copy has survived. Twenty-seven copies, some going back to about the fourteenth century, were preserved in Ethiopic and were used to produce J. C. VanderKam's definitive critical text and English translation (1989), which is used in this introduction and reader. R. H. Charles's translation (1902, 1917) is widely available in the public domain. A translation by O. S. Wintermute also appears in *The Old Testament Pseudepigrapha* (1985).

Theology

Jubilees adapts the portrayal of God in Genesis and Exodus to maintain God's absolute omniscience, omnipotence, and transcendence. For example, God went through no process of discovery or learning in finding a partner for Adam or determining the wickedness of Sodom. God does not have partners in creation, such as angels or elements of creation bringing forth other elements of creation. God is removed from unbecoming deeds, such as trying to kill Moses and hardening Pharaoh's heart. Jubilees also establishes at length God's perfect justice. Sinners are warned before their judgment. The punishment for crimes is fixed and absolute (although Israel has the opportunity for atonement). Judgment is not delayed or deferred until a final day of judgment. Jubilees often makes use of angels and demons, adapted from the tradition exemplified by the Book of the Watchers, in order to maintain God's transcendence and justice. **Mastema**, a figure resembling the accuser (*satan*) in the prologue to Job, takes on the unbecoming roles attributed to God. Demons serve the purpose of punishing the wicked, especially the Gentiles but also Jews who draw near to Gentiles. Demons do not have power over the righteous or explain unjust suffering. Mastema takes the shame for inciting the Egyptians to pursue the Israelites into the sea, but does not get credit for any successful evil against Israel, such as throwing babies into the Nile. In general, angels are relevant as mediators of a transcendent and omnipotent God. They carry out God's plan, but they do not impinge on human responsibility or interfere in the direct relationship between God and Israel.

Reception of Jubilees in the Second Temple Period

Jubilees was cited and used as authoritative Scripture in the Damascus Document (*see* Damascus Document [CD]) and other texts among the Dead Sea Scrolls. In the subsequent centuries, it would retain this authoritative status only in the Church of Ethiopia. Although echoes of use (more for trivia than as scriptural authority) can be found in other areas of Judaism and Christianity, the book largely fell out of circulation and was lost to Europeans until it was "discovered" by missionaries to Ethiopia. The book would gain scholarly attention in the latter half of the nineteenth century. Europeans rejected the claim of angelic dictation to Moses in Jubilees and placed it in the category "pseudepigrapha" (falsely attributed writings; *see* Overview of Early Jewish Literature).

Even though Jubilees is not used in rabbinic literature, the New Testament, or most Jewish and Christian writings, Jubilees is helpful for understanding the intellectual milieu of Judaism in antiquity. Scholars have often noted the differences between Jubilees and the **Mishnah** on legal rulings, but it could also be noted that many of the questions and methods reflect common discourse. Many of the narrative expansions and interpretations in rabbinic literature are first attested in Jubilees. The rabbinic idea of Oral Torah can be compared to the premise of Jubilees, an expansive testimony given to Moses in addition to the Torah, although the differences are substantial. Similarly, Jubilees seems not to have been used by the authors of the New Testament, but does reflect several theological debates and ideas picked up in the New Testament. For example, Jubilees exemplifies the methods of biblical interpretation found especially in passages such as Stephen's speech in Acts 7. Jubilees casts light on Jewish interpretation of the Book of the Watchers and ideas about the agency of angels and demons. Certain ideas or motifs presumed in the New Testament, such as angelic mediation of the Torah at Sinai, are attested first or only in Jubilees. A work as long and coherent as Jubilees offers invaluable insight into the history of Jewish thought and literature, even if the specific positions proposed were excluded from the forms of Judaism and Christianity that retained dominance.

Jubilees is a prime example of early biblical interpretation. James Kugel describes four assumptions that distinguish early from modern biblical interpretation. The first assumption is that the Bible is *cryptic*—it means more or other than what it appears to mean. For example, Jubilees interprets "on the day you eat of it you will surely die" to mean "in the millennium you eat of it you will surely die." The second assumption is that the Bible is *perfect*. This plays out on multiple levels. Stories are perfect in that they do not contradict themselves. For example, Jubilees explains the apparent contradiction on whether male and female were created at the same time. The woman was created at the same time as the man, even though she was not transformed from a rib into the familiar form until a week later. The Bible as a whole is perfect in that any part of the Bible belongs to the same story as any other part. For example, Psalm 90 can be used to fill in the blanks in Genesis to decode, for example, a day in heaven as the equivalent to a millennium on earth. Characters are perfect examples of virtue or vice, such that Jacob did not really lie to Isaac, and Esau was perfectly wicked. The religious practices of ancient ancestors are perfectly consistent with later religious practices, such as observance of Sabbath, festivals, prayer, and priesthood. The third assumption is that the Bible is *relevant*. A modern interpreter might say that Genesis was written earlier than the crisis of Hellenistic assimilation and the practice of nude athletics, and therefore does not address the issue of public nudity. Jubilees finds relevance to contemporary issues, however, by interpreting the statement that God made garments for Adam and Eve as a prohibition of nakedness. The fourth assumption is that the Bible is *divine*. Whereas Genesis itself makes no claim of authorship or divine inspiration, Jubilees insists that Genesis, along with the testimony of its interpretation, was revealed from the heavenly tablets.

For length, coherence, and antiquity, Jubilees is one of the most significant works of early Jewish literature. It represents a major stage in Jewish history, as Jerusalem emerged from a crisis of confrontation with Hellenistic culture and empire. Jubilees finds a plan for Jewish identity in the interpretation of the traditional books. At the same time, Jubilees solves problems in Genesis and Exodus, particularly when God or national heroes appear in unflattering light. Jubilees reconstructs the heavenly tablets that dictate God's perfect justice and the proper behavior for God's people. Even as most of Judaism and Christianity went on to reject the claim of revelation and many of the teachings, the same basic tools of narrative and legal exegesis continued to thrive. Through those Jews who did accept the heavenly tablets as presented therein, the book would go on to be copied, cited, rewritten, and interpreted as Scripture. Jubilees is therefore essential to understanding the communities that produced the Dead Sea Scrolls. The study of Jubilees can also give us broader insight into the formation of group identity, including early Christianity, based on claims of revelation, biblical interpretation, and legal innovation.

TODD R. HANNEKEN

FURTHER READING

Halpern-Amaru, Betsy. *The Perspective from Mt. Sinai: The Book of Jubilees and Exodus.* Journal of Ancient Judaism Supplements 21. Göttingen: Vandenhoeck & Ruprecht, 2015.

Hanneken, Todd R. *The Subversion of the Apocalypses in the Book of Jubilees.* Early Judaism and Its Literature 34. Atlanta: Society of Biblical Literature, 2012.

Himmelfarb, Martha. *A Kingdom of Priests: Ancestry and Merit in Ancient Judaism.* Jewish Culture and Contexts. Philadelphia: University of Pennsylvania Press, 2006.

Kugel, James L. *The Bible As It Was.* Cambridge, Mass.: Belknap, 1997.

———. *A Walk through Jubilees: Studies in the Book of Jubilees and the World of Its Creation.* Supplements to the Journal for the Study of Judaism 156. Leiden: Brill, 2012.

VanderKam, James C. *The Book of Jubilees: A Critical Text.* 2 vols. Leuven: Peeters, 1989.

———. *The Book of Jubilees.* Guides to the Apocrypha and Pseudepigrapha. Sheffield: Sheffield Academic Press, 2001.

———. *From Revelation to Canon: Studies in the Hebrew Bible and Second Temple Literature.* JSJSup 62. Leiden: Brill, 2000.

———. "The Origins and Purposes of the Book of Jubilees." In *Studies in the Book of Jubilees,* edited by Matthias Albani, Jörg Frey, and Armin Lange, pp. 3–24. Tübingen: Mohr Siebeck, 1997.

Van Ruiten, J. T. A. G. M. *Abraham in the Book of Jubilees: The Rewriting of Genesis 11:26-25:10 in the Book of Jubilees 11:14-23:8.* Supplements to the Journal for the Study of Judaism 161. Leiden: Brill, 2012.

ADVANCED READING

Boccaccini, Gabriele, and Giovanni Ibba, eds. *Enoch and the Mosaic Torah: The Evidence of Jubilees.* Grand Rapids: Eerdmans, 2009.

Endres, John C. *Biblical Interpretation in the Book of Jubilees.* CBQMS 18. Washington, D.C.: Catholic Biblical Association of America, 1987.

García Martínez, Florentino. "The Heavenly Tablets in the Book of Jubilees." In *Studies in the Book of Jubilees,* edited by Matthias Albani, Jörg Frey, and Armin Lange, pp. 243–60. Tübingen: Mohr Siebeck, 1997.

Halpern-Amaru, Betsy. *The Empowerment of Women in the Book of Jubilees.* JSJSup 60. Leiden: Brill, 1999.

Himmelfarb, Martha. "Torah, Testimony, and Heavenly Tablets: The Claim to Authority of the *Book of Jubilees.*" In *A Multiform Heritage: Studies on Early Judaism and Christianity in Honor of Robert A. Kraft,* edited by Benjamin G. Wright, pp. 19–29. Atlanta: Scholars, 1999.

Najman, Hindy. "Interpretation as Primordial Writing: Jubilees and Its Authority Conferring Strategies." *JSJ* 30 (1999): 379–410.

Ruiten, J. T. A. G. M. van. *Primaeval History Interpreted: The Rewriting of Genesis 1–11 in the Book of Jubilees*. JSJSup 66. Leiden: Brill, 2000.

Segal, Michael. *The Book of Jubilees: Rewritten Bible, Redaction, Ideology and Theology*. JSJSup 117. Leiden: Brill, 2007.

VanderKam, James C., and Jozef T. Milik. "Jubilees." In *Qumran Cave 4: Parabiblical Texts*, Part 1, edited by Harold W. Attridge et al., pp. 1–185. Oxford: Clarendon, 1994.

4.5 Jubilees 1–6

Prologue and Setting

These are the words regarding the divisions of the times[a] of the law and of the testimony, of the events of the years, of the weeks of their Jubilees throughout all the years of eternity as he related (them) to Moses on Mt. Sinai when he went up to receive the stone tablets—the law and the commandments—on the Lord's orders as he had told him that he should come up to the summit of the mountain.

1:1 During the first year of the Israelites' exodus from Egypt, in the third month—on the sixteenth of the month[b]—the Lord said to Moses: "Come up to me on the mountain. I will give you the two stone tablets of the law and the commandments which I have written so that you may teach them." 2 So Moses went up the mountain of the Lord. The glory of the Lord took up residence on Mt. Sinai, and a cloud covered it for six days. 3 When he summoned Moses into the cloud on the seventh day, he saw the glory of the Lord like a fire blazing on the summit of the mountain. 4 Moses remained on the mountain for forty days and forty nights while the Lord showed him what (had happened) beforehand as well as what was to come. He related to him the divisions of all the times—both of the law and of the testimony. 5 He said to him: "Pay attention to all the words which I tell you on this mountain. Write (them) in a book so that their offspring may see that I have not abandoned them because of all the evil they have done in straying from the covenant between me and you which I am making today on Mt. Sinai for their offspring. 6 So it will be that when all of these things befall them they will recognize that I have been more faithful than they in all their judgments and in all their actions. They will recognize that I have indeed been with them."

Sin, Punishment, Repentance, and Restoration Predicted[c]

7 "Now you write this entire message which I am telling you today, because I know their defiance and their stubbornness (even) before I bring them into the land which I promised by oath to Abraham, Isaac, and Jacob: 'To your posterity I will give the land which flows with milk and honey.' When they eat and are

---

a. Among the Dead Sea Scrolls and the Ethiopic tradition the book is referred to as the book of the Divisions of the Times, or simply, Divisions.

b. The day after the renewal of the covenant.

c. The language and theology of this section closely resemble that of the book of Deuteronomy, especially 31:16–21.

Translation by James C. VanderKam, *The Book of Jubilees*, CSCO 511, Leuven, 1989, pp. 1–43. Republication of Peeters material courtesy of Peeters Publishers. Notes by Todd R. Hanneken.

full, [8] they will turn to foreign gods—to ones that will not save them from any of their afflictions. Then this testimony will serve as evidence. [9] For they will forget all my commandments—everything that I command them—and will follow the nations, their impurities, and their shame. They will serve their gods, and (this) will prove an obstacle for them—an affliction, a pain, and a trap. [10] Many will be destroyed. They will be captured and will fall into the enemy's control because they abandoned my statutes, my commandments, my covenantal festivals, my Sabbaths, my holy things which I have hallowed for myself among them, my tabernacle, and my temple which I sanctified for myself in the middle of the land so that I could set my name on it and that it could live (there). [11] They made for themselves high places, (sacred) groves, and carved images; each of them prostrated himself before his own in order to go astray. They will sacrifice their children to demons and to every product (conceived by) their erring minds. [12] I will send witnesses to them so that I may testify to them, but they will not listen and will kill the witnesses. They will persecute those also who study the law diligently. They will abrogate everything and will begin to do evil in my presence. [13] Then I will hide my face from them. I will deliver them into the control of the nations for captivity, for booty, and for being devoured. I will remove them from the land and disperse them among the nations. [14] They will forget all my law, all my commandments, and all my verdicts. They will err regarding the beginning of the month, the Sabbath, the festival, the Jubilee, and the decree.

[15] After this they will return to me from among the nations with all their minds, all their souls, and all their strength. Then I will gather them from among all the nations, and they will search for me so that I may be found by them when they have searched for me with all their minds and with all their souls. I will rightly disclose to them abundant peace. [16] I will transform them into a righteous plant with all my mind and with all my soul. They will become a blessing, not a curse; they will become the head, not the tail. [17] I will build my temple among them and will live with them; I will become their God and they will become my true and righteous people. [18] I will neither abandon them nor become alienated from them, for I am the Lord their God."

[19] Then Moses fell prostrate and prayed and said: "Lord my God, do not allow your people and your heritage to go along in the error of their minds, and do not deliver them into the control of the nations with the result that they rule over them lest they make them sin against you. [20] May your mercy, Lord, be lifted over your people. Create for them a just spirit. May the spirit of Belial not rule over them so as to bring charges against them before you and to trap them away from every proper path so that they may be destroyed from your presence. [21] They are your people and your heritage whom you have rescued from Egyptian control by your great power. Create for them a pure mind and a holy spirit. May they not be trapped in their sins from now to eternity."

[22] Then the Lord said to Moses: "I know their contrary nature, their way of thinking, and their stubbornness. They will not listen until they acknowledge their sins and the sins of their ancestors. [23] After this they will return to me in a fully upright manner and with all (their) minds and all (their) souls. I will cut away the foreskins of their minds and the foreskins of their descendants' minds. I will create a holy spirit for them and will purify them in order that they may not

turn away from me from that time forever. ²⁴ Their souls will adhere to me and to all my commandments. They will perform my commandments. I will become their father and they will become my children. ²⁵ All of them will be called children of the living God. Every angel and every spirit will know them. They will know that they are my children and that I am their father in a just and proper way and that I love them."

The Divine Commission of the Book of Jubilees

²⁶ "Now you write all these words which I tell you on this mountain: what is first and what is last and what is to come during all the divisions of time which are in the law and which are in the testimony and in the weeks of their Jubilees until eternity—until the time when I descend and live with them throughout all the ages of eternity."

²⁷ Then he said to an angel of the presence:[a] "Dictate to Moses (starting) from the beginning of the creation until the time when my temple is built among them throughout the ages of eternity. ²⁸ The Lord will appear in the sight of all, and all will know that I am the God of Israel, the father of all Jacob's children, and the king on Mt. Zion for the ages of eternity. Then Zion and Jerusalem will become holy."

²⁹ The angel of the presence, who was going along in front of the Israelite camp, took the tablets (which told) of the divisions of the years from the time the law and the testimony were created—for the weeks of their Jubilees, year by year in their full number, and their Jubilees from [the time of the creation until][b] the time of the new creation when the heavens, the earth, and all their creatures will be renewed like the powers of the sky and like all the creatures of the earth, until the time when the temple of the Lord will be created in Jerusalem on Mt. Zion. All the luminaries will be renewed for (the purpose of) healing, health, and blessing for all the elect ones of Israel[c] and so that it may remain this way from that time throughout all the days of the earth.

Creation in Six Days

²:¹ On the Lord's orders the angel of the presence said to Moses: "Write all the words about the creation—how in six days the Lord God completed all his works,

a. The angel of the presence is modeled on Exod. 14:19, 23:20–23; and Isa. 63:9.

b. VanderKam's reconstruction, following a suggestion by Michael Stone, presupposes that a scribe's eye jumped from the first to the second instance of "the time of." It would be unusual, but possible, to understand the "new creation" as the original creation, when things were newly made. The "until" clause could refer to the creation of the sanctuary in Exodus. "In Jerusalem" could begin a new sentence describing the destiny of that sanctuary. The actual scope of Jubilees in fact covers the original creation up through Exod. 24, just before the commandments for the creation of the sanctuary starting in Exod. 25.

c. The rest of the book emphasizes the unity of all Israel without any mention of an elect group or sect (other than Levi). It seems likely that "all the elect ones of Israel" should be understood as "all the chosen people, Israel."

everything that he had created, and kept Sabbath on the seventh day. He sanctified it for all ages and set it as a sign for all his works. ²For on the first day he created the heavens that are above, the earth, the waters, and all the spirits who serve before him, namely: the angels of the presence; the angels of holiness; the angels of the spirits of fire; the angels of the spirits of the winds; the angels of the spirits of the clouds, of darkness, snow, hail, and frost; the angels of the sounds, the thunders, and the lightnings; and the angels of the spirits of cold and heat, of winter, spring, autumn, and summer, and of all the spirits of his creatures which are in the heavens, on earth, and in every (place).ᵃ [There were also] the depths, darkness and light, dawn and eveningᵇ which he prepared through the knowledge of his mind. ³Then we saw his works and blessed him. We offered praise before him regarding all his works because he had made seven great works on the first day.

⁴On the second day he made a firmament between the waters, and the waters were divided on that day. Half of them went up above and half of them went down below the firmament (which was) in the middle above the surface of the whole earth. This was the only work that he made on the second day.

⁵On the third day he did as he said to the waters that they should pass from the surface of the whole earth to one place and that the dry land should appear. ⁶The waters did so, as he told them. They withdrew from the surface of the earth to one place apart from this firmament, and dry land appeared. ⁷On that day he created for them all the seas—each with the places where they collected—all the rivers, and the places where the waters collected in the mountains and on the whole earth; all the reservoirs, all the dew of the earth; the seed that is sown—with each of its kinds—all that sprouts, the fruit trees, the forests, and the Garden of Edenᶜ (which is) in Eden for enjoyment and for food. These four great types he made on the third day.

⁸On the fourth day the Lord made the sun, the moon, and the stars. He placed them in the heavenly firmament to shine on the whole earth, to rule over day and night, and to separate between light and darkness. ⁹The Lord appointed the sunᵈ as a great sign above the earth for days, Sabbaths, months, festivals, years, Sabbaths of years, Jubilees, and all times of the years. ¹⁰It separates between light and darkness and (serves) for wellbeing so that everything that sprouts and grows on the earth may prosper. These three types he made on the fourth day.

¹¹On the fifth day he created the great sea monsters within the watery depths, for these were the first animate beings made by his hands; all the fish that move about in the waters, all flying birds, and all their kinds. ¹²The sun shone over

a. There are three classes of angels corresponding to three classes of humanity. The angels of the presence are like the Levites in that they serve in the temple (Jub. 31:14). The angels of holiness are like the Israelites in the observance of Sabbath (Jub. 2:18) and circumcision (Jub. 15:27). The angels of nature correspond to the Gentiles (Jub. 15:31), and do not rest on the Sabbath (rivers continue to flow).

b. In Gen. 1 evening and morning seem to occur as by-products of creation, but are not directly willed by God (Gen. 1:5, etc.). Jubilees insists that all creation was directly willed by God. Similarly, in Gen. 1:11, 20, the earth brings forth vegetation and the waters bring forth fish. In Jub. 2:5, 11, God has no assistants in creation.

c. In this and other ways Jubilees combines and reconciles the two creation stories in Genesis.

d. Jubilees removes the moon from any role in determining calendar. See Jub. 6:36.

them for (their) wellbeing and over everything that was on the earth—all that sprouts from the ground, all fruit trees, and all animate beings. These three kinds he made on the fifth day.

¹³ On the sixth day he made all the land animals, all cattle, and everything that moves about on the earth. ¹⁴ After all this, he made humankind—as one man and a woman he made them.ᵃ He made him rule everything on earth and in the seas and over flying creatures, animals, cattle, everything that moves about on the earth, and the entire earth. Over all these he made him rule. These four kinds he made on the sixth day."

The Sabbath

¹⁵ "The total was twenty-two kinds. ¹⁶ He finished all his works on the sixth day:ᵇ everything in heaven, on the earth, in the seas, in the depths, in the light, in the darkness, and in every place. ¹⁷ He gave us the Sabbath day as a great sign so that we should perform work for six daysᶜ and that we should keep Sabbath from all work on the seventh day. ¹⁸ He told us—all the angels of the presence and all the angels of holiness (these two great kinds)—to keep Sabbath with him in heaven and on earth.

¹⁹ He said to us: 'I will now separate a people for myself from among my nations. They, too, will keep Sabbath. I will sanctify the people for myself and will bless them as I sanctified the Sabbath day. I will sanctify them for myself; in this way I will bless them. They will become my people and I will become their God. ²⁰ I have chosen the descendants of Jacob among all of those whom I have seen. I have recorded them as my firstborn son and have sanctified them for myself throughout the ages of eternity. I will tell them about the Sabbath days so that they may keep Sabbath from all work on them.' ²¹ In this way he made a sign on it by which they, too, would keep Sabbath with us on the seventh day to eat, drink, and bless the Creator of all as he had blessed them and sanctified them for himself as a noteworthy people out of all the nations; and to keep Sabbath together with us. ²² He made his commands rise as a fine fragrance that is acceptable in his presence for all times.

²³ There were twenty-two leaders of humanity from Adam until him; and twenty-two kinds of works were made until the seventh day.ᵈ The latter is blessed and holy and the former, too, is blessed and holy. The one with the other served

a. See also Jub. 3:8. Jubilees reconciles the two creation stories by asserting that in the first week God created one being (a combination of male and female), which in the second week was separated into two beings (one male and one female).

b. Compare Gen. 2:2: "And on the *seventh* day God finished the work that he had done."

c. 4Q216 is fragmentary but suggests a longer version of this verse, including the phrases "he ceased" and "were made in six days."

d. There are also twenty-two letters in the Hebrew alphabet (the language of creation, according to Jub. 12:26). Jubilees corresponds to the Septuagint in counting twenty-two generations before Jacob. The Masoretic text has twenty-one, lacking Cainan between Arpachshad and Shelah (Gen. 10:24; Jub. 8:1–5).

(the purposes of) holiness and blessing. [24] It was granted to these that for all times they should be the blessed and holy ones of[a] the testimony and of the first law,[b] as it was sanctified and blessed on the seventh day. [25] He created the heavens, the earth, and everything that was created in six days. The Lord gave a holy festal day to all his creation. For this reason he gave orders regarding it that anyone who would do any work on it was to die; also, the one who would defile it was to die.

[26] Now you command the Israelites to observe this day so that they may sanctify it, not do any work on it, and not defile it for it is holier than all (other) days.[c] [27] Anyone who profanes it is to die and anyone who does any work on it is to die eternally so that the Israelites may observe this day throughout their history and not be uprooted from the earth. For it is a holy day; it is a blessed day. [28] Everyone who observes (it) and keeps Sabbath on it from all his work will be holy and blessed throughout all times like us. [29] Inform and tell the Israelites the law (which relates to) this day and that they should keep Sabbath on it and not neglect it through the error of their minds lest they do (any) work on it—(the day) on which it is not proper to do what they wish, namely: to prepare on it anything that is to be eaten or drunk; to draw water; to bring in or remove on it anything which one carries in their gates—(any) work that they had not prepared for themselves in their dwellings on the sixth day. [30] They are not to bring (anything) out or in from house to house on this day because it is more holy and more blessed than any of the Jubilee of Jubilees. On it we kept Sabbath in heaven before it was made known to all humanity that on it they should keep Sabbath on earth. [31] The Creator of all blessed but did not sanctify any people(s) and nations to keep Sabbath on it except Israel alone. To it alone did he give (the right) to eat, drink, and keep Sabbath on it upon the earth. [32] The Creator of all who created this day blessed it for (the purposes of) blessing, holiness, and glory more than all (other) days. [33] This law and testimony were given to the Israelites as an eternal law throughout their history."

The Second Week

[3:1] "On the sixth day of the second week we brought to Adam, on the Lord's orders, all animals, all cattle, all birds, everything that moves about on the earth, and everything that moves about in the water—in their various kinds and various forms: the animals on the first day; the cattle on the second day; the birds on the third day; everything that moves about on the earth on the fourth day; and the ones that move about in the water on the fifth day. [2] Adam named them all,

---

a. 4Q216 indicates a new sentence, rather than a construct, beginning, "This is the testimony and the first law."

b. The phrase "first law" also appears in Jub. 6:22, where it seems to refer to the Torah (Genesis, Exodus, Leviticus, Numbers, Deuteronomy) given to Moses already written, in contrast to the dictated testimony of the book of Jubilees.

c. Because 364 is divisible by 7, each date falls on the same day of the week every year in the calendar of Jubilees. Consequently, festivals such as the Day of Atonement never conflict with the Sabbath, as they do in other calendars.

each with its own name.[a] Whatever he called them became their name. [3] During these five days Adam was looking at all of these—male and female among every kind that was on the earth. But he himself was alone; there was no one whom he found for himself who would be for him a helper who was like him. [4] Then[b] the Lord said to us: 'It is not good that the man should be alone. Let us make him a helper who is like him.' [5] The Lord our God imposed a sound slumber on him and he fell asleep. Then he took one of his bones for a woman. That rib was the origin of the woman—from among his bones. He built up the flesh in its place and built the woman. [6] Then he awakened Adam from his sleep. When he awoke, he got up on the sixth day. Then he brought (him) to her. He knew her and said to her: 'This is now bone from my bone and flesh from my flesh. This one will be called my wife, for she was taken from her husband.' [7] For this reason a man and a woman are to become one, and for this reason he leaves his father and his mother. He associates with his wife, and they become one flesh.

[8] In the first week Adam and his wife—the rib—were created, and in the second week he showed her to him. Therefore, a commandment was given to keep (women) in their defilement seven days for a male (child) and for a female two (units) of seven days. [9] After forty days had come to an end for Adam in the land where he had been created, we brought him into the Garden of Eden to work and keep it. His wife was brought (there) on the eightieth day. After this she entered the Garden of Eden. [10] For this reason a commandment was written in the heavenly tablets[c] for the one who gives birth to a child: if she gives birth to a male, she is to remain in her impurity for seven days like the first seven days; then for thirty-three days she is to remain in the blood of purification. She is not to touch any sacred thing or to enter the sanctuary until she completes these days for a male. [11] As for a female she is to remain in her impurity for two weeks of days like the first two weeks and sixty-six days in the blood of her purification. Their total is eighty days. [12] After she had completed these eighty days, we brought her into the Garden of Eden because it is the holiest in the entire earth, and every tree which is planted in it is holy. [13] For this reason the law of these days has been ordained for the one who gives birth to a male or a female. She is not to touch any sacred thing or to enter the sanctuary until the time when those days for a male or a female are completed. [14] These are the law and testimony that were written for Israel to keep for all times."

a. Compare Gen. 2:19: "So the Lord God *formed out of the ground* various wild animals and various birds of the air, and *he* brought them to the man *to see* what he would call them." To reconcile the two creation stories Jubilees separates forming the animals in the first week, and bringing them to be named in the second week. Jubilees maintains the transcendence of God by having angels perform the labor of bringing animals. Jubilees maintains the omniscience of God by removing the implication that God needed "to see" what the animals would be called.

b. Gen. 2:18 has God declare intent to find a partner for the man before creating the animals, which might imply that the animals were failed attempts by God to find a mate for Adam.

c. Otherwise found in Lev. 12. Jubilees explains the origin and observance of the commandment from the beginning of creation, and similarly emphasizes eternality in that the law is to be kept for all times, in the future (Jub. 3:14).

The Garden of Eden

[15] "During the first week of the first Jubilee Adam and his wife spent the seven years in the Garden of Eden working and guarding it. We gave him work and were teaching him (how) to do everything that was appropriate for working (it).[a] [16] While he was working (it) he was naked but did not realize (it) nor was he ashamed. He would guard the garden against birds, animals, and cattle. He would gather its fruit and eat (it) and would store its surplus for himself and his wife. He would store what was being kept.

[17] When the conclusion of the seven years which he had completed there arrived—seven years exactly—in the second month, on the seventeenth, the serpent came and approached the woman. The serpent said to the woman: 'Is it from all the fruit of the trees in the garden (that) the Lord has commanded you: "Do not eat from it?"' [18] She said to him: 'From all the fruits of the tree(s) which are in the garden the Lord told us: "Eat." But from the fruit of the tree which is in the middle of the garden he told us: "Do not eat from it and do not touch it so that you may not die."' [19] Then the serpent said to the woman: 'You will not really die because the Lord knows that when you eat from it your eyes will be opened, you will become like gods, and you will know good and evil.' [20] The woman saw that the tree was delightful and pleasing to the eye and (that) its fruit was good to eat. So she took some of it and ate (it). [21] She first covered her shame with fig leaves and then gave it to Adam. He ate (it), his eyes were opened, and he saw that he was naked. [22] He took fig leaves and sewed (them); (thus) he made himself an apron and covered his shame.

[23] The Lord cursed the serpent and was angry at it forever. At the woman, too, he was angry because she had listened to the serpent and eaten. He said to her: [24] 'I will indeed multiply your sadness and your pain. Bear children in sadness. Your place of refuge will be with your husband; he will rule over you.' [25] Then he said to Adam: 'Because you listened to your wife and ate from the tree from which I commanded you not to eat, may the ground be cursed on account of you. May it grow thorns and thistles for you. Eat your food in the sweat of your face until you return to the earth from which you were taken. For earth you are and to earth you will return.'

[26] He made clothing out of skins for them, clothed them, and dismissed them from the Garden of Eden. [27] On that day, as he was leaving the Garden of Eden, he burned incense[b] as a pleasing fragrance—frankincense, galbanum, stacte, and aromatic spices—in the early morning when the sun rose at the time when he covered his shame. [28] On that day the mouths of all the animals, the cattle, the birds, everything that walks and everything that moves about were made incapable of

---

a. Jubilees uses the word "work" four times in this sentence and the next, where Genesis has only "guard." Genesis seems to imply that work was not part of the original plan of creation, but the consequence of sin. Jubilees may be like other texts in suggesting a "back to Eden" eschatology, but describes Eden as a time when Jewish institutions (such as law, temple, and priesthood) and daily life (labor and purity) were already established. Consequently, there would be no eschatological reform of Jewish institutions.

b. Jubilees conceives of Eden as a sanctuary and Adam as a priest.

speaking because all of them used to converse with one another in one language and one tongue.[a] [29] He dismissed from the Garden of Eden all the animate beings that were in the Garden of Eden. All animate beings were dispersed—each by its kind and each by its nature—into the place(s) which had been created for them. [30] But of all the animals and cattle he permitted Adam alone to cover his shame. [31] For this reason it has been commanded in the tablets regarding all those who know the judgment of the law that they cover their shame and not uncover themselves as the nations uncover themselves.[b]

[32] At the beginning of the fourth month Adam and his wife departed from the Garden of Eden. They lived in the land of Elda, in the land where they were created. [33] Adam named his wife Eve. [34] They were childless throughout the first Jubilee; afterward he knew her. [35] He himself was working the land as he had been taught in the Garden of Eden."

The Second Generation

[4:1] "In the third week in the second Jubilee [years 64 to 70],[c] she gave birth to Cain; in the fourth [71 to 77] she gave birth to Abel; and in the fifth [78 to 84] she gave birth to his daughter Awan. [2] During the first (week) of the third Jubilee [99 to 105] Cain killed Abel because we had accepted his sacrifice from him but from Cain we had not accepted (one). [3] When he killed him in a field, his blood cried out from the ground to heaven—crying because he had been killed. [4] The Lord blamed Cain regarding Abel because he had killed him. While he allowed him a length (of time) on the earth because of his brother's blood, he cursed him upon the earth.

[5] For this reason it has been written on the heavenly tablets: 'Cursed is the person who beats his companion maliciously.' All who saw (it) said: 'Let him be (cursed). And let the man who has seen but has not told be cursed like him.' [6] For this reason we report, when we come before the Lord our God, all the sins which take place in heaven and on earth—what (happens) in the light, in the darkness, or in any place.

[7] Adam and his wife spent four weeks of years mourning for Abel. Then in the fourth year of the fifth week [130] they became happy. Adam again knew his wife, and she gave birth to a son for him. He named him Seth because he said: 'The Lord has raised up for us another offspring on the earth in place of Abel' (for Cain had killed him). [8] In the sixth week [134–40] he became the father of his daughter Azura. [9] Cain married his sister Awan, and at the end of the fourth Jubilee [148–96] she gave birth to Enoch for him. In the first year of the first week of the fifth Jubilee [197] houses were built on the earth. Then Cain built a city and named it after his son Enoch. [10] Adam knew his wife Eve, and she gave birth to

---

a. Genesis gives no explanation of the talking serpent or how animals ceased to talk.

b. According to 1 Macc. 1:14, those who endorsed Hellenistic assimilation built a gymnasium in Jerusalem to promote the Greek practice of exercise and athletic competition in the nude (the origin of the word "gymnasium").

c. A Jubilee period is forty-nine years; a week of years is seven years.

nine more children. [11] In the fifth week of the fifth Jubilee [225–31] Seth married his sister Azura,[a] and in its fourth (year) [228] she gave birth to Enosh for him. [12] He was the first to call on the Lord's name on the earth. [13] In the seventh Jubilee, in the third week [309–15] Enosh married his sister Noam. She gave birth to a son for him in the third year of the fifth week [325], and he named him Kenan. [14] At the end of the eighth Jubilee [344–92] Kenan married his sister Mualelit. She gave birth to a son for him in the ninth Jubilee, in the first week—in the third year of this week [395]—and he named him Malalael."

Enoch

[15] "During the second week of the tenth Jubilee [449–55] Malalael married Dinah, the daughter of Barakiel, the daughter of his father's brother. She gave birth to a son for him in the third week, in its sixth year [461]. He named him Jared because during his lifetime the angels of the Lord who were called Watchers descended to earth to teach humankind and to do what is just and upright upon the earth.[b] [16] In the eleventh Jubilee [491–539] Jared took a wife for himself, and her name was Barakah, the daughter of Rasu'eyal, the daughter of his father's brother, in the fourth week of this Jubilee [512–18]. She gave birth to a son for him during the fifth week, in the fourth year, of the Jubilee [522], and he named him Enoch. [17] He was the first of humankind who were born on the earth who learned (the art of) writing, instruction, and wisdom and who wrote down in a book the signs of the sky in accord with the fixed patterns of their months so that humankind would know the seasons of the years according to the fixed patterns of each of their months. [18] He was the first to write a testimony. He testified to humankind in the generations of the earth: The weeks of the Jubilees he related, and made known the days of the years; the months he arranged, and related the Sabbaths of the years, as we had told him. [19] While he slept he saw in a vision what has happened and what will occur—how things will happen for humankind during their history until the day of judgment. He saw everything and understood. He wrote a testimony for himself and placed it upon the earth against all humankind and for their history.[c]

[20] During the twelfth Jubilee, in its seventh week [582–88] he took a wife for himself. Her name was Edni, the daughter of Daniel, the daughter of his father's brother. In the sixth year of this week [587] she gave birth to a son for him, and he named him Methuselah.

[21] He was, moreover, with God's angels for six Jubilees of years. They showed

---

a. Jubilees pays extra attention to the name and lineage of wives, principally to emphasize endogamy and to illustrate a correlation between exogamy and disaster.

b. The Book of Watchers lacks any notion that the angels originally had a good mission before their rebellion (1 En. 6). Jubilees does not introduce the sin until Jub. 5:1.

c. The description of Enoch depends on several parts of 1 Enoch, including the Book of Watchers, the Astronomical Book, and some form of the Book of Dreams. There is special emphasis on Enoch's role in God's perfect justice. Enoch warns of sin and punishment in advance so that sinners can be held fully accountable.

him everything on earth and in the heavens—the dominion of the sun[a]—and he wrote down everything. ²² He testified to the Watchers who had sinned with the daughters of men because these had begun to mix with earthly women so that they became defiled. Enoch testified against all of them.

²³ He was taken from human society, and we led him into the Garden of Eden for (his) greatness and honor. Now he is there writing down the judgment and condemnation of the world and all the wickedness of humankind. ²⁴ Because of him the floodwater did not come on any of the land of Eden because he was placed there as a sign and to testify against all people in order to tell all the deeds of history until the day of judgment. ²⁵ He burned the evening incense of the sanctuary which is acceptable before the Lord on the mountain of incense. ²⁶ For there are four places on earth that belong to the Lord: the Garden of Eden, the mountain of the east, this mountain on which you are today—Mt. Sinai—and Mt. Zion (which) will be sanctified in the new creation for the sanctification of the whole earth. For this reason the earth will be sanctified from all its sins and from its uncleanness into the history of eternity."

Noah

²⁷ "During this Jubilee—that is, the fourteenth Jubilee—Methuselah married Edna, the daughter of Ezrael, the daughter of his father's brother, in the third week in the first year of that week [652]. He became the father of a son whom he named Lamech. ²⁸ In the fifteenth Jubilee, in the third week [701–7], Lamech married a woman whose name was Betanosh, the daughter of Barakiel, the daughter of his father's brother. During this week she gave birth to a son for him, and he named him Noah, explaining: '(He is one) who will give me consolation from my sadness, from all my work, and from the earth the Lord cursed.'

²⁹ At the end of the nineteenth Jubilee, during the seventh week—in its sixth year [930]—Adam died. All his children buried him in the land where he had been created. He was the first to be buried in the ground. ³⁰ He lacked seventy years from one thousand years because one thousand years are one day in the testimony of heaven.[b] For this reason it was written regarding the tree of knowledge: 'On the day that you eat from it you will die.' Therefore he did not complete the years of this day because he died during it.

³¹ At the conclusion of this Jubilee Cain was killed one year after him. His house fell on him, and he died inside his house. He was killed by its stones for with a stone he had killed Abel and, by a just punishment, he was killed with a stone.[c] ³² For this reason it has been ordained on the heavenly tablets: 'By the instrument

---

a. The Astronomical Book describes the movement of the moon as well, but Jubilees rejects any consideration of lunar patterns. See also Jub. 2:9; 6:36.

b. Ps. 90:4: "For a thousand years in your sight are like yesterday when it is past, or like a watch in the night."

c. Cain's death is not mentioned in Genesis. There the punishment for his crime seems to be protection from death, rather than death, which is God's standard of justice prescribed elsewhere (Exod. 21:24; Lev. 24:19).

with which a man kills his fellow he is to be killed. As he wounded him so are they to do to him.'

³³ In the twenty-fifth Jubilee Noah married a woman whose name was Emzara, the daughter of Rakiel, the daughter of his father's brother—during the first year in the fifth week [1205]. In its third year [1207] she gave birth to Shem for him; in its fifth year [1209] she gave birth to Ham for him; and in the first year during the sixth week [1212] she gave birth to Japheth for him."

Perfect Justice

⁵:¹ "When humankind began to multiply on the surface of the entire earth and daughters were born to them, the angels of the Lord—in a certain (year) of this Jubilee—saw that they were beautiful to look at. So they married of them whomever they chose. They gave birth to children for them and they were giants.

² Wickedness increased on the earth. All animate beings corrupted their way— (everyone of them) from people to cattle, animals, birds, and everything that moves about on the ground. All of them corrupted their way and their prescribed course. They began to devour one another, and wickedness increased on the earth. Every thought of all humankind's knowledge was evil like this all the time.

³ The Lord saw that the earth was corrupt, (that) all animate beings had corrupted their prescribed course, and (that) all of them—everyone that was on the earth—had acted wickedly before his eyes. ⁴ He said that he would obliterate people and all animate beings that were on the surface of the earth which he had created. ⁵ He was pleased with Noah alone.

⁶ Against his angels whom he had sent to the earth he was angry enough to uproot them from all their (positions of) authority. He told us to tie them up in the depths of the earth; now they are tied within them and are alone. ⁷ Regarding their children there went out from his presence an order to strike them with the sword and to remove them from beneath the sky. ⁸ He said: 'My spirit will not remain on people forever for they are flesh. Their lifespan is to be 120 years.' ⁹ He sent his sword among them so that they would kill one another. They began to kill each other until all of them fell by the sword and were obliterated from the earth. ¹⁰ Now their fathers were watching, but afterward they were tied up in the depths of the earth until the great day of judgment when there will be condemnation on all who have corrupted their ways and their actions before the Lord. ¹¹ He obliterated all from their places; there remained no one of them whom he did not judge for all their wickedness. ¹² He made a new and righteous nature for all his creatures so that they would not sin with their whole nature until eternity. Everyone will be righteous—each according to his kind—for all time.

¹³ The judgment of them all has been ordained and written on the heavenly tablets; there is no injustice.ᵃ (As for) all who transgress from their way in which it was ordained for them to go—if they do not go in it, judgment has been written down for each creature and for each kind. ¹⁴ There is nothing which is in heaven or

---

a. Jubilees adapts the basic story of the Book of Watchers from an explanation of the origin of evil to an example of perfect justice.

on the earth, in the light, the darkness, Sheol, the deep, or in the dark place—all their judgments have been ordained, written, and inscribed. ¹⁵ He will exercise judgment regarding each person—the great one in accord with his greatness and the small one in accord with his smallness—each one in accord with his way. ¹⁶ He is not one who shows favoritism or one who takes a bribe, if he says he will execute judgment against each person. If a person gave everything on earth he would not show favoritism nor would he accept (it) from him because he is the righteous judge.

¹⁷ Regarding the Israelites, it has been written and ordained: 'If they turn to him in the right way, he will forgive all their wickedness and will pardon all their sins.' ¹⁸ It has been written and ordained that he will have mercy on all who turn from all their errors once each year.^a ¹⁹ To all who corrupted their ways and their plan(s) before the flood no favor was shown except to Noah alone because favor was shown to him for the sake of his children whom he saved from the flood-waters for his sake because his mind was righteous in all his ways, as it had been commanded concerning him. He did not transgress from anything that had been ordained for him."

The Chronology of the Flood

²⁰ "The Lord said that he would obliterate everything on the land—from the people to cattle, animals, birds, and whatever moves about on the ground. ²¹ He ordered Noah to make himself an ark in order to save himself from the flood-waters. ²² Noah made an ark in every respect as he had ordered him during the twenty-seventh Jubilee of years, in the fifth week, during its fifth year [1307].^b ²³ He entered (it) during its sixth (year) [1308], in the second month—on the first of the second month until the sixteenth. He and all that we brought to him entered the ark. The Lord closed it from outside on the seventeenth in the evening.

²⁴ The Lord opened the seven floodgates of heaven and the openings of the sources of the great deep—there being seven openings in number. ²⁵ The flood-gates began to send water down from the sky for forty days and forty nights, while the sources of the deep brought waters up until the whole earth was full of water. ²⁶ The waters increased on the earth; the waters rose fifteen cubits above every high mountain. The ark rose above the earth and moved about on the surface of the waters. ²⁷ The waters remained standing on the surface of the earth for five months—150 days. ²⁸ Then the ark came to rest on the summit of Lubar, one of the mountains of Ararat. ²⁹ During the fourth month the sources of the great deep were closed, and floodgates of heaven were held back. On the first of the seventh month all the sources of the earth's deep places were opened, and the waters started to go down into the deep below. ³⁰ On the first of the tenth month the summits of the mountains became visible, and on the first of the first month the earth became visible. ³¹ The waters dried up from above the earth in the fifth week, in its seventh year [1309]. On the seventeenth day of the second month the

a. The Day of Atonement (Yom Kippur), described especially in Lev. 16.
b. Jubilees matches the date of the flood found in the Samaritan Pentateuch.

earth was dry. [32] On its twenty-seventh (day) he opened the ark and sent from it the animals, birds, and whatever moves about."

The First Earthly Institution of the Festival of the Oath and Covenant

[6:1] "On the first of the third month he left the ark and built an altar on this mountain. [2] He appeared on the earth,[a] took a kid and atoned with its blood for all the sins of the earth because everything that was on it had been obliterated except those who were in the ark with Noah. [3] He placed the fat on the altar. Then he took a bull, a ram, a sheep, goats, salt, a turtledove, and a dove and offered (them as) a burnt offering on the altar. He poured on them an offering mixed with oil, sprinkled wine, and put frankincense on everything. He sent up a pleasant fragrance that was pleasing before the Lord. [4] The Lord smelled the pleasant fragrance and made a covenant with him that there would be no floodwaters which would destroy the earth; (that) throughout all the days of the earth seedtime and harvest would not cease; (that) cold and heat, summer and winter, day and night would not change their prescribed pattern and would never cease.

[5] Now you increase and multiply yourselves on the earth and become numerous upon it. Become a blessing within it. I will put fear of you and dread of you on everything that is on the earth and in the sea. [6] I have now given you all the animals, all the cattle, everything that flies, everything that moves about on the earth, the fish in the waters, and everything for food. Like the green herbs I have given you everything to eat. [7] But you are not to eat animate beings with their spirit—with the blood—(because the vital force of all animate beings is in the blood) so that your blood with your vital forces may not be required from the hand of anyone. From the hand of each one I will require the blood of a human. [8] The blood of the person who sheds the blood of a human will be shed by a human because he made humankind in the image of the Lord. [9] As for you—increase and become numerous on the earth.

[10] Noah and his sons swore an oath not to consume any blood that was in any animate being. During this month he made a covenant before the Lord God forever throughout all the history of the earth. [11] For this reason he told you, too, to make a covenant—accompanied by an oath[b]—with the Israelites during this month on the mountain and to sprinkle blood on them because of all the words of the covenant which the Lord was making with them for all times. [12] This testimony has been written regarding you to keep it for all times so that you may not at any time eat any blood of animals or birds throughout all the days of the earth. (As for) the person who has eaten the blood of an animal, of cattle, or of birds during all the days of the earth—he and his descendants will be uprooted from the earth.

[13] Now you command the Israelites not to eat any blood so that their name

a. Or, "He made atonement for the earth."
b. The Hebrew words for "oaths" and "weeks" are similar in pronunciation and identical in writing. Jubilees places emphasis on the festival or weeks/oaths as the time for the renewal of the same basic covenant sealed on that day (third month, fifteenth day) by Noah, Abraham, Isaac, Jacob, and Israel at Sinai.

and their descendants may continue to exist before the Lord our God for all time. [14] This law has no temporal limits because it is forever. They are to keep it throughout history so that they may continue supplicating for themselves with blood in front of the altar each and every day. In the morning and in the evening they are continually to ask pardon for themselves before the Lord so that they may keep it and not be uprooted.

[15] He gave Noah and his sons a sign that there would not again be a flood on the earth. [16] He put his bow in the clouds as a sign of the eternal covenant that there would not henceforth be floodwaters on the earth for the purpose of destroying it throughout all the days of the earth. [17] For this reason it has been ordained and written on the heavenly tablets that they should celebrate the festival of weeks during this month—once a year—to renew the covenant each and every year. [18] This entire festival had been celebrated in heaven from the time of creation until the lifetime of Noah—for twenty-six Jubilees and five weeks of years [= 1309]. Then Noah and his sons kept it for seven Jubilees and one week of years until Noah's death [= 350 years]. From the day of Noah's death his sons corrupted (it) until Abraham's lifetime and were eating blood. [19] Abraham alone kept (it), and his sons Isaac and Jacob kept it until your lifetime. During your lifetime the Israelites had forgotten (it) until I renewed (it) for them at this mountain.

[20] Now you command the Israelites to keep this festival during all their generations as a commandment for them: one day in the year, during this month, they are to celebrate the festival. [21] because it is the festival of weeks and it is the festival of first fruits. This festival is twofold and of two kinds. Celebrate it as it is written and inscribed regarding it. [22] For I have written (this) in the book of the first law in which I wrote for you[a] that you should celebrate it at each of its times one day in a year. I have told you about its sacrifice so that the Israelites may continue to remember and celebrate it throughout their generations during this month—one day each year."

The Calendar of the Seasonal Festivals

[23] "On the first of the first month, the first of the fourth month, the first of the seventh month, and the first of the tenth month are memorial days and days of the seasons. They are written down and ordained at the four divisions of the year as an eternal testimony. [24] Noah ordained them as festivals for himself throughout the history of eternity with the result that through them he had a reminder. [25] On the first of the first month he was told to make the ark, and on it the earth became dry, he opened (it), and saw the earth. [26] On the first of the fourth month the openings of the depths of the abyss below were closed. On the first of the seventh month all the openings of the earth's depths were opened, and the water began to go down into them. [27] On the first of the tenth month the summits of the mountains became visible, and Noah was very happy.

a. Most scholars understand this to refer to the Pentateuch, which is distinguished from the book of Jubilees (implicitly a second law, or testimony of the law) in that the first was given already written, and the second was dictated for Moses to write down.

28 For this reason he ordained them for himself forever as memorial festivals. So they are ordained, 29 and they enter them on the heavenly tablets. Each one of them (consists of) thirteen weeks; their memorial (extends) from one to the other: from the first to the second, from the second to third, and from the third to the fourth. 30 All the days of the commandments will be fifty-two weeks of days; (they will make) the entire year complete. 31 So it has been engraved and ordained on the heavenly tablets. One is not allowed to transgress a single year, year by year.

32 Now you command the Israelites to keep the years in this number—364 days. Then the year will be complete and it will not disturb its time from its days or from its festivals because everything will happen in harmony with their testimony. They will neither omit a day nor disturb a festival. 33 If they transgress and do not celebrate them in accord with his command, then all of them will disturb their times. The years will be moved from this; they will disturb the times and the years will be moved. They will transgress their prescribed pattern. 34 All the Israelites will forget and will not find the way of the years. They will forget the first of the month, the season, and the Sabbath; they will err with respect to the entire prescribed pattern of the years. 35 For I know and from now on will inform you—not from my own mind because this is the way the book is written in front of me, and the divisions of times are ordained on the heavenly tablets, lest they forget the covenantal festivals and walk in the festivals of the nations,[a] after their error and after their ignorance. 36 There will be people who carefully observe the moon with lunar observations because it is corrupt (with respect to) the seasons and is early from year to year by ten days.[b] 37 Therefore years will come about for them when they will disturb (the year) and make a day of testimony something worthless and a profane day a festival. Everyone will join together both holy days with the profane and the profane day with the holy day, for they will err regarding the months, the Sabbaths, the festivals, and the Jubilee.

38 For this reason I am commanding you and testifying to you so that you may testify to them because after your death your children will disturb (it) so that they do not make the year (consist of) 364 days only. Therefore, they will err regarding the first of the month, the season, the Sabbath, and the festivals. They will eat all the blood with all (kinds of) meat."

a. This point stands out in that it seems to address participating in Gentile festivals, as some Jews embraced and others were forced to do during the reign of Antiochus IV Epiphanes. The primary concern is with those who celebrate the Jewish festivals, but at the improper time. Because of the importance of synchronizing with the festival observance in heaven, the proper timing is essential. The Habakkuk Pesher implies that the Teacher of Righteousness and the Wicked Priest celebrated the Day of Atonement at different times (*see* Habakkuk Pesher).

b. A lunar calendar has 354 days. A luni-solar calendar has a leap month every few years to keep the months correlated with seasons. Luni-solar calendars were used by the Seleucids, Hasmoneans, and rabbis.

4.6 *from* Jubilees 8–50

Distribution of Territories and the Curse of the Canaanites (Jubilees 8–9)

Jubilees 8–9 establishes at length the division of the territories of the earth among Noah's descendants. There is strong emphasis on the legitimacy and permanence of the territorial division, with the consent of an angel, Noah, and all parties. The agreement is sealed with an oath promising destruction for all parties that violate the oath. The details are certainly interesting in that they reflect the geographical knowledge available to the author, but the principal point is to establish that the land of Canaan never really belonged to the Canaanites. It was called Canaan because the Canaanites stole it from the family that includes the Israelites.

> [*Canaan's father and brothers warn him:*] [10:31] Do not settle in Shem's residence because it emerged by their lot for Shem and his sons. [32] You are cursed and will be cursed more than all of Noah's children through the curse by which we obligated ourselves with an oath before the holy judge and before your father Noah. [33] But he did not listen to them. He settled in the land of Lebanon—from Hamath to the entrance of Egypt—he and his sons until the present. [34] For this reason that land was named the land of Canaan.

Consequently, the land was not taken from the Canaanites and given to the Israelites; it was taken back by the Israelites. The slaughter of the Canaanites is the fulfillment of the punishment prescribed by the oath taken by their own ancestors. This detail also fits the larger structure of the book of Jubilees, which sees the exodus and conquest as the fulfillment of the release and return prescribed in Leviticus 25, only in the fiftieth Jubilee of creation rather than the fiftieth year (see below on Jub. 50).

Noah and the Demons (Jubilees 10)

Jubilees 10 presumes the basic idea of the demons known from the Book of Watchers (*see* Book of Watchers [1 Enoch 1–36]), and significantly recasts their importance. In both, the demons are the spirits of the giants, which survive after their bodies die, since they are half-human and half-(rebel) angel. In both, the demons are wicked and cause suffering. In the Book of Watchers, the demons are part of the spread of injustice and affliction of the righteous. Jubilees adapts the demons into a system of perfect justice, in which they serve to punish the wicked, but have no power over the righteous. When the demons begin to afflict Noah's grandchildren, Noah simply asks God that they be removed.

Translation by Todd R. Hanneken.

10:6 "May they not rule the spirits of the living for you alone know their punishment; and may they not have power over the Sons of the Righteous from now and forevermore." 7 Then our God told us to tie up each one. 8 When Mastema, the leader of the spirits, came, he said: "Lord Creator, leave some of them before me; let them listen to me and do everything that I tell them, because if none of them is left for me I will not be able to exercise the authority of my will among [hu]mankind. For they are meant for (the purposes of) destroying and misleading before my punishment because the evil of [hu]mankind is great." 9 Then he said that a tenth of them should be left before him, while he would make nine parts descend to the place of judgment. 10 He told one of us that we should teach Noah all their medicines because he knew that they would neither conduct themselves properly nor fight fairly. 11 We acted in accord with his entire command. All of the evil ones who were savage we tied up in the place of judgment, while we left a tenth of them to exercise power on the earth before Mastema.[a] 12 We told Noah all the medicines for their diseases with their deceptions so that he could cure (them) by means of the earth's plants. 13 Noah wrote down in a book everything (just) as we had taught him regarding all the kinds of medicine, and the evil spirits were precluded from pursuing Noah's children. 14 He gave all the books that he had written to his oldest son Shem because he loved him much more than all his sons.

Only in Jubilees is there any suggestion of a 90 percent reduction of demons. More significantly, they function with divine consent for the particular purpose of punishing wickedness. As Noah requests, they have no power over the righteous. If they do violate their just mandate, they can still be defeated by anyone who studies the ancestral books, which later end up in the hands of the Levites to be taught to all Israel (Jub. 45:16). The demons are particularly associated with the other nations, and explain whatever (destructive) power is seen in idolatry. They punish Israelites who wander into idolatry from the safe haven of divine protection (Jub. 15:31–32). Demons remain a threat to Israelites inasmuch as assimilation is a concern, but Jubilees recasts them into a system of perfect divine justice and an unimpeded relationship between God and Israel.

Mastema first appears in this passage as a member of the heavenly court who is responsible for punishment. Elsewhere in Jubilees, Mastema reappears whenever unbecoming actions are attributed to God in Genesis–Exodus. Mastema illustrates the consequences of the rise of idolatry in the generations before Abraham (Josh. 24:2), and becomes the foil for Abraham's defeat of idolatry. Mastema takes on the role of the accuser in the prologue to Job, and explains the real reason why an omniscient God would propose such a cruel test as the sacrifice of Isaac. Mastema, rather than God, tries and fails to kill Moses on the way to Egypt. Mastema explains why the Egyptian magicians are able to perform some plagues. Mastema, not God, is directly responsible for the hardening of Pharaoh's heart and the massacres attributed to God in Exodus. In all cases, Mastema is put to shame and easily bound whenever his services are not required.

a. One medieval Hebrew fragment reads "Mastema" where the Ethiopic tradition reads "the satan."

Circumcision (Jubilees 15)

The treatment of circumcision in Jubilees 15 illustrates a number of tendencies. The events are drawn from Genesis 17, but the legal implications are expanded. The practice of Abraham is more than a custom; it is an absolute commandment and a nonnegotiable marker of male Jewish identity. It is eternal going forward, but also backward to the first week of creation, when the angels corresponding to Israel were made circumcised, and Israel was elected to be like them.

> [15:25] This law is (valid) for all history forever. There is no circumcising of days,[a] nor omitting any day of the eight days because it is an eternal ordinance ordained and written on the heavenly tablets. [26] Anyone who is born, the flesh of whose private parts has not been circumcised by the eighth day, does not belong to the people of the pact that the Lord made with Abraham but to the people (meant for) destruction. Moreover, there is no sign on him that he belongs to the Lord, but (he is meant) for destruction, for being destroyed from the earth, and for being uprooted from the earth because he has violated the covenant of the Lord our God. [27] For this is what the nature of all the angels of the presence and all the angels of holiness was like from the day of their creation. In front of the angels of the presence and the angels of holiness, he sanctified Israel to be with him and his holy angels.

Also in typical fashion, the event is dated to the middle of the third month, the festival of oaths/weeks on which the eternal covenant is renewed (Jub. 15:1).

Jubilees reflects concern with Hellenistic assimilation, probably the movement described in 1 Maccabees 1 as forgoing circumcision in order to join with the surrounding nations.

> [15:33] I am now telling you that the Israelites will prove false to this ordinance. They will not circumcise their sons in accord with this entire law because they will leave some of the flesh of their circumcision when they circumcise their sons. All the people of Belial will leave their sons uncircumcised just as they were born.

The phrase here translated "people of Belial" is translated in the Septuagint (2 Chron. 13:7) with the same phrase used to describe the renegades in 1 Maccabees 1:11. In addition to polemics against those who forgo circumcision entirely, scholars have also found here an argument with Jews who do practice circumcision, but are more flexible in moving it to another day under extenuating circumstances (Sabbath or illness). The Mishnah holds the more lenient position. This is one of many legal positions in Jubilees that were not widely held in the long term (see also the prohibitions of sex and fighting on the Sabbath in Jub. 50:8, 12). In light of the emphasis on Jewish unity in the rest of the book, it seems unlikely that the author of Jubilees would have considered someone circumcised on the ninth day to be permanently excluded from the Jewish community. It is possible that Jubilees rejects converts who became circumcised as adults. In any case,

---

a. There is a pun here in Hebrew. "Circumcising of days" and "completion of days" sound similar.

circumcision is held up as the requisite marker of male Israelites for purposes of divine protection and mercy.

The issue of circumcision is the occasion for the most theological statement on the difference between Jews and Gentiles.

> 15:28 Now you command the Israelites to keep the sign of this covenant throughout their history as an eternal ordinance so that they may not be uprooted from the earth 29 because the command has been ordained as a covenant so that they should keep it forever on all the Israelites. 30 For the Lord did not draw near to himself either Ishmael, his sons, his brothers, or Esau. He did not choose them (simply) because they were among Abraham's children, for he knew them. But he chose Israel to be his people. 31 He sanctified them and gathered (them) from all [hu]mankind. For there are many nations and many peoples and all belong to him. He made spirits rule over all in order to lead them astray from following him. 32 But over Israel he made no angel or spirit rule because he alone is their ruler. He will guard them and require them for himself from his angels, his spirits, and everyone, and all his powers so that he may guard them and bless them and so that they may be his and he theirs from now and forever.

The idea of angelic princes of nations is upheld, but limited to other nations. The relationship between God and Israel is never mediated. The spirits who rule over Gentiles and lead them away from following God are the spirits of nature created on the first day (Jub. 2:2). This would explain why Gentiles worship nature rather than the Creator. It would also imply that God does not want to be worshiped by nations besides Israel.

Jacob's Blessings (Jubilees 19–22)

If the book of Jubilees has one central hero, it is Jacob. If Genesis leaves any room for seeing Jacob's election as the result of chance or trickery, or Jacob's character as less than perfect at all times, Jubilees more than compensates. The election of Jacob is first emphasized in the first week of creation, twenty-two generations before Jacob is even born. Once Jacob is born, Abraham is the first to recognize and amplify the blessings of Jacob. Abraham's blessings go on at great length, even after the narrator declares the blessings concluded (Jub. 22:25–30). An excerpt gives a sense of the whole.

> 22:10 He summoned Jacob and said to him: "My son Jacob, may the God of all bless and strengthen you to do before him what is right and what he wants. May he choose you and your descendants to be his people for his heritage in accord with his will throughout all time. Now you, my son Jacob, come close and kiss me." 11 So he came close and kissed him. Then he said: "May my son Jacob and all his sons be blessed to the Most High Lord throughout all ages. May the Lord give you righteous descendants, and may he sanctify some of your sons[a] within the

a. See below on the elevation of Levi.

entire earth. May the nations serve you, and may all the nations bow before your descendants. [12] Be strong before people and continue to exercise power among all of Seth's descendants. Then your ways and the ways of your sons will be proper so that they may be a holy people. [13] May the Most High God give you all the blessings with which he blessed me and with which he blessed Noah and Adam. May they come to rest on the sacred head of your descendants throughout each and every generation and forever. [14] May he purify you from all filthy pollution so that you may be pardoned for all the guilt of your sins of ignorance. May he strengthen and bless you; may you possess the entire earth. [15] May he renew his covenant with you so that you may be for him the people of his heritage throughout all ages. May he truly and rightly be God for you and your descendants throughout all the time of the earth."

Abraham's blessing is reinforced by Rebecca, a spirit of prophecy, divine intervention, and Isaac once he comes to his senses. Even Esau recognizes Jacob's merit.

The Jubilees Apocalypse (Jubilees 23)

Jubilees 23 begins with the death of Abraham, and extends the discourse to address the correlation between longevity and righteousness. Although Abraham individually was more righteous than other ancestors who lived longer, he lived a mere 175 years because of the wickedness of the world around him.

> [23:9] For the times of the ancients were nineteen Jubilees for their lifetimes. After the flood, they started to decrease from nineteen Jubilees, to be fewer with respect to Jubilees, to age quickly, and to have their times be completed in view of the numerous difficulties and through the wickedness of their ways—with the exception of Abraham. [10] For Abraham was perfect with the Lord in everything that he did—being properly pleasing throughout all his lifetime. And yet (even) he had not completed four Jubilees during his lifetime when he became old—in view of wickedness—and reached the end of his time.

From there Jubilees "predicts" that lifetimes will continue to decrease to a mere seventy to eighty years and worse before Israel turns to the proper study of the laws. At that point, Israel will live in purity and longevity will gradually return to one thousand years.

The outer framework of the book as a whole is technically that of an apocalypse, but this chapter in particular has been called the Jubilees apocalypse because it concentrates literary features typical of the historical apocalypses. It "predicts" history up to and beyond the actual time of composition. It describes a decline of history culminating in "final woes." It describes a form of divine judgment, followed by a utopian restoration. However, these formal features are significantly adapted to a more Deuteronomistic theology of sin, punishment, repentance, and restoration. The final woes are not a climax of evil against the righteous, but punishment from God for breach of covenant.

23:22 There will be a great punishment from the Lord for the actions of that generation. He will deliver them to the sword, judgment, captivity, plundering, and devouring. 23 He will arouse against them the sinful nations.

The nations are pawns of God, and angels, good or evil, are strikingly absent. The turning point is human repentance, rather than divine intervention. The restoration was gradual, and was probably understood as having already begun.

23:26 In those days the children will begin to study the laws, to seek out the commands, and to return to the right way. 27 The days will begin to become numerous and increase, and [hu]mankind as well—generation by generation and day by day until their lifetimes approach one thousand years and to more years than the number of days (had been).

Jubilees 23 is unusual, to say the least, in its combination of literary features and theology drawn from early apocalypses, Deuteronomy, Psalm 90, and Isaiah.

The chapter also gives a vague clue to the author's position on resurrection of the body or the afterlife of the individual, which seem to have been issues at the time.

23:30 Then the Lord will heal his servants. They will rise and see great peace. He will expel his enemies. The righteous will see (this), offer praise, and be very happy forever and ever. They will see all their punishments and curses on their enemies. 31 Their bones will rest in the earth and their spirits will be very happy. They will know that the Lord is one who executes judgment but shows kindness to hundreds and thousands and to all who love him.

The ones who rise were not necessarily dead, or if they were dead, their rising seems to be for a moment of vindication before returning to a state better described as resting in peace than an afterlife.

The Elevation of Levi (Jubilees 30–32)

If one had to judge from Genesis and the first half of Exodus, it would seem the Levites had no distinction other than morally dubious violence. Indeed, the elevation of the Levites to priestly status under the watch of Moses the Levite might have appeared to be self-serving. Again, Jubilees more than compensates with abundant arguments from merit and divine will for the elevation even before Levi was born. The first hint of the status of Levi appears on the first day of creation, when God establishes a threefold hierarchy of angels, which, it becomes clear, corresponds to the Levites, all Israel, and the other nations. Priestly functions are attributed to the great ancestors Adam, Enoch, Noah, Abraham, and Isaac. When Isaac is no longer able to perform his priestly duty, the status passes directly to Levi. Jubilees gives at least six justifications for the elevation of Levi: the merit of slaughtering the Shechemites in defense of endogamy (Jub. 30:18–24), a prophetic voice through Isaac (Jub. 31:14–15), the testimony of Jacob (Jub. 31:32), the testimony of the angel of the presence (Jub. 31:32), Levi's dream-vision (Jub. 32:1), and application of the law of tithes (Jub. 32:2–3). Among these, Isaac's prophetic blessing may be the most interesting because it enumerates the roles attributed to the Levites.

> ³¹:¹³ He turned to Levi first and began to bless him first. He said to him: "May the Lord of everything—he is the Lord of all ages—bless you and your sons throughout all ages.
>
> ¹⁴ May the Lord give you and your descendants extremely great honor;
> may he make you and your descendants (alone) out of all humanity approach him
> to serve in his temple like the angels of the presence and like the holy ones.
> The descendants of your sons will be like them in honor, greatness, and holiness.
> May he make them great throughout all the ages.
>
> ¹⁵ They will be princes, judges, and leaders of all the descendants of Jacob's sons.
> They will declare the word of the Lord justly
> and will justly judge all his verdicts.
> They will tell my ways to Jacob
> and my paths to Israel.
> The blessing of the Lord will be placed in their mouths,
> so that they may bless all the descendants of the beloved.
>
> ¹⁶ Your mother named you Levi,
> and she has given you the right name.
> You will become one who is joined to the Lord
> and a companion of all Jacob's sons.
> His table is to belong to you;
> you and your sons are to eat (from) it.
> May your table be filled throughout all history;
> may your food not be lacking throughout all ages.
>
> ¹⁷ May all who hate you fall before you,
> and all your enemies be uprooted and perish.
> May the one who blesses you be blessed,
> and any nation who curses you be cursed."

Besides temple service, the Levites have the functions of political leadership, legal judgment, teaching, and blessing.

The praise of the Levites and the overlap between the roles attributed to the Levites and the book of Jubilees itself (interpreting laws, teaching) suggest that the author was a Levite. The author may or may not have been a priest. It is at least somewhat curious that Jubilees makes no distinction between priests and Levites, as is emphasized in what we today call the Priestly Source (but not Deuteronomy). The book of Jubilees is set before the consecration of the sons of Aaron ("until the time when my sanctuary is built"; Jub. 1:27), which somewhat explains why the narratives and themes surrounding Aaron are deferred. However, one might have expected some anticipation of Aaron's distinction, such as in the heavenly hierarchy of angels, or the predictive blessings of Abraham, Isaac, Rebecca, and Jacob. It makes sense that the author viewed the classification "Levite" as more fundamental and theologically significant than the distinctions of priests and priestly families. By the mid-second century BCE, equality among all Levites was apparently no longer an issue, and it would have taken more than silence to argue against the distinction of priests over other Levites. The author may well have been a priest who simply deferred matters of priestly politics in the work at hand.

Jacob and Esau (Jubilees 35–38)

The narratives concerning Jacob and Esau should be understood primarily as addressing interpretive issues in Genesis, especially making Jacob perfectly righteous and his rival perfectly wicked (although his sons are more consistent in their wickedness). Secondarily, the narratives may be mined for hints of the perceived or proposed relationship with the Idumeans (Edomites) in the second century BCE. Whereas Genesis leaves Jacob and Esau with an amicable separation, Jubilees finds more to the story. Esau recognizes Jacob's blessing, but his sons persuade him to attack.

> [38:1] After this Judah spoke to his father Jacob and said to him: "Draw your bow, father; shoot your arrow; pierce the enemy; and kill the foe. May you have the strength because we will not kill your brother, since he is near to you and, in our estimation, he is equal to you in honor." [2] Jacob then stretched his bow, shot an arrow, pierced his brother Esau [on his right breast], and struck him down. [*Esau's allies are routed by Jacob and his sons in verses 3–8.*] Esau's four sons ran away with them. They left their slain father just as he had fallen on the hill that is in Aduram. [9] Jacob's sons pursued them as far as Mount Seir, while Jacob buried his brother on the hill that is in Aduram and then returned to his house. [10] Jacob's sons pressed hard on Esau's sons in Mount Seir. They bowed their necks to become servants for Jacob's sons. [11] They sent to their father (to ask) whether they should make peace with them or kill them. [12] Jacob sent word to his sons to make peace. So they made peace with them and placed the yoke of servitude on them so that they should pay tribute to Jacob and his sons for all time. [13] They continued paying tribute to Jacob until the day that Jacob went down to Egypt. [14] The Edomites have not extricated themselves from the yoke of servitude that Jacob's sons imposed on them until today.

Although it is tempting to look for times in the second century when the relationship or events described best fit, the author may have been less concerned with contemporary politics than issues of interpretation beyond Genesis, such as Numbers 24:17–19.

The Jubilee of Jubilees (Jubilees 50)

Not until the end of the book do we learn what may rightly be considered the real reason for giving a chronology from creation to Moses in terms of Jubilee periods. Leviticus 25 calls for the Israelites to count forty-nine years and proclaim release from slavery and return to ancestral land in the fiftieth year. Jubilees applies the same principle on a macroscale. God counts forty-nine periods of history (i.e., forty-nine Jubilee periods of forty-nine years each), and in the fiftieth period, releases the Israelites from slavery in Egypt and returns them to their ancestral homeland.

> 50:4 For this reason I have arranged for you the weeks of years and Jubilees—forty-nine Jubilees from the time of Adam until today, and one week and two years. It is still forty years off (for learning the Lord's commandments) until the time when he leads (them) across to the land of Canaan, after they have crossed the Jordan to the west of it.

The revelation of the book of Jubilees occurs just after the exodus from Egypt in the fiftieth Jubilee, in the year 2410 of creation (49 × 49 + 7 + 2). After 40 years of wandering in the wilderness, in the year 2450 (50 × 49 years), the Israelites return to their ancestral land and complete the Jubilee of Jubilees.

The Genesis Apocryphon

The discoveries of hundreds of previously unknown Jewish compositions in the Judean Desert from the 1940s until the present have opened up new vistas, and extended old ones, on Second Temple period Jewish thought, literature, and history (*see* Overview of Early Jewish Literature). One of the more surprising and fascinating areas of discovery has been literature related to or dependent on (but not identical with) the canonical books of the Hebrew Bible, or Christian Old Testament—this seems to have been a flourishing industry during the Persian through Roman periods, and has raised new questions for biblical scholars and historians regarding the handling and status of sacred traditions at that time.

1QapGen (Genesis Apocryphon) is a highly creative, entertaining rewriting of portions of the book of Genesis, and a banner example of what scholars have often called "rewritten Scripture" (*see* Introduction to Biblical Interpretation and Rewritten Scripture). Discovered in the initial cache of seven scrolls from Qumran Cave 1, the Genesis Apocryphon was eventually purchased along with three other scrolls by the Syrian metropolitan of Jerusalem, Mar Athanasius Yeshue Samuel. The road to the publication of the Genesis Apocryphon was a wending one, complicated especially by the fact that it was in an advanced state of deterioration and unrolling it was a precarious undertaking. Five of its twenty-three columns were finally published in 1956 (cols. 2 and 19–22), but it took until the 1990s for all remaining portions of the scroll to be published in preliminary form. Additional fragments had been found by excavators of Cave 1 (1Q20; originally named Apocalypse of Lamech) and were eventually identified as belonging to the outer layers of Mar Samuel's scroll; these were then rejoined with the Genesis Apocryphon and now bear the unusual designation "column 0 [zero]." Though incomplete, it was immediately apparent that the Genesis Apocryphon was written in Aramaic (the other six scrolls from Cave 1 are in Hebrew), and that it preserved a rewritten form of Genesis hitherto unknown, though parallels were drawn with 1 Enoch (*see* Introduction to 1 Enoch) and Jubilees (*see* The Book of Jubilees) already at an early stage. The Genesis Apocryphon has been identified in one copy only among the Dead Sea Scrolls, though the fine, well-trained scribal hand and impressively executed manuscript tells us that it was a highly prized scroll by whoever commissioned it. Curiously, the final column of the scroll was cut off in Antiquity just past the sewn seam of two sheets of leather (this column was at the center of the rolled scroll), causing the text to end abruptly in midsentence. No satisfactory explanation has yet been provided for this.

Narrative Description

The extant portions of the Genesis Apocryphon include text from approximately Genesis 5:28 to 15:4. It was once longer at both its beginning and end, though how much so it is now impossible to tell. The preserved narrative may be broken down into three main sections: (1) the pre-Noah, or Enoch/Lamech, section; (2) the Noah section; and (3) the Abram section. Judging by the phrase "A [c]o[p]y of the Book of the Words of Noah" after an unusually large empty space (or *vacat*) in Genesis Apocryphon 5.29, which commences a firsthand account by Noah, it appears that the final composer of the Genesis Apocryphon structured his narrative around a series of such first-person testimonies. Another very large *vacat* in 18.23–24 presumably signals the beginning of the Abram section, though the writing is too disintegrated to read in this column. The deployment of first-person accounts placed in the mouths of figures from the era of the patriarchs marks off the Genesis Apocryphon as **pseudepigraphic,** but there are some notable aspects of this practice in the scroll. First, the story occasionally breaks out of the first person, most conspicuously for the division of the earth among Noah's sons and grandsons (cols. 16–17), and for a long section at the end of the scroll (from 21.34 to the end), but elsewhere as well (e.g., 5.29). Similar vacillations are found in Tobit (*see* The Book of Tobit) and Nehemiah. Second, the author engages in what Loren Stuckenbruck has called "serial pseudepigraphy," as opposed to the more typical, static sort in which one character narrates the entire composition (e.g., Jubilees or the Aramaic Levi Document; *see* Aramaic Levi Document). This could indicate that whoever wrote the Genesis Apocryphon did not intend his pseudepigraphy to be taken seriously, but it is more likely that the scroll was cast in an editorial voice now lost—either third or first person, anonymous or not—that related earlier events through successive first-person accounts claimed to have been recorded in ancient books or on tablets. Hence, it may be that in the Genesis Apocryphon we have both "serial pseudepigraphy" and "layered pseudepigraphy," the latter also being found in Jubilees' use of Moses to narrate the words of the angel of the presence.[1] In fact, in the Genesis Apocryphon, columns 2–5, we may have up to four "layers" of narrative voices: the framework narrator (of Genesis Apocryphon 5.29) is relating the words of Lamech, who is quoting the first-person account of both his father Methuselah and (then) his grandfather Enoch. A literary technique very similar to that of the Genesis Apocryphon is now also discernable in other Aramaic Dead Sea Scrolls, such as the Book of Giants (4Q203; *see* Book of Giants), the Words of Michael (4Q529),

---

1. The angel of the presence was often the guide of apocalyptic visions in Second Temple period literature, with "presence" referring to the presence of YHWH, the God of Israel. In Jubilees, the angel of the presence is responsible for giving Moses the law at Sinai (see, e.g., Jub. 1:27).

and the Visions of Amram (4Q543). We know from these works and others (e.g., 1 Enoch, Jubilees) that recourse to ancient or heavenly books and tablets was a desirable strategy for claiming authority; whether such authority is genuine or feigned is not always clear.

We join the story of the Genesis Apocryphon in progress at column 0, where a singular, plural party ("we") is in the midst of a second-person, singular address ("you"). Based on the content of this section it is nearly certain that those speaking are either the angelic Watchers (*see* Book of Watchers [1 Enoch 1–36]) or their offspring, the giants, known from other Second Temple period works and especially writings associated with Enoch. The general biblical setting for this portion of the scroll is Genesis 6:1–4:

> Now it came about, when humankind began to multiply on the face of the land, and daughters were born to them, that the sons of God saw that the daughters of humanity were beautiful; and they took wives for themselves, whomever they chose. Then the Lord said, "My Spirit will not strive with humankind forever, because it also is flesh; nevertheless its days will be one hundred and twenty years." The Nephilim were on the earth in those days, and also afterward, when the sons of God came in to the daughters of humanity, and they bore children to them. Those were the mighty men who were of old, men of renown.(—trans. Wright)

The episode seems to be a cause of the great flood in Genesis, and was certainly viewed with disdain in later Judaism. The Book of Watchers,[2] the Book of Giants, Jubilees,[3] and the Genesis Apocryphon, columns 0–1, betray an intense interest in the flood generally, and the activities, supplication, and eventual judgment of the Watchers and giants in particular, each preserving extrabiblical stories about them. The Genesis Apocryphon's account is fragmentary, but provides the words of a supplication by the Watchers and/or giants, which is apparently rejected by

---

2. See, for example, 1 En. 6:1–2: "And it happened in those days that humanity increased; there were born to them fair and beautiful daughters. And the angels, the Sons of Heaven ["Watchers"], desired them (humans) and were led astray after them and they said to one another, 'Come, let us choose for ourselves women from among the humans, and we will produce for ourselves children.'" See also 1 En. 7:1–2: "These ones and the remainder like them took for themselves women and they chose one each from all (humanity) and they began to commingle with them and they were promiscuous with them and defiled themselves with them and they (the angels) taught them sorcery and incantations and revealed to them the cutting of roots and the (power of) herbs. And the (women) became pregnant by them (the angels) and they bore for them great giants three thousand cubits high. And the giants bore Napheleim, and to the Napheleim were born Elioud. And they were growing according to their greatness." —trans. Wright

3. Jub. 5:1–2: "When [hu]mankind began to multiply on the surface of the entire earth and daughters were born to them, the angels of the Lord—in a certain (year) of this Jubilee—saw that they were beautiful to look at. So they married of them whomever they chose. They gave birth to children for them and they were giants. Wickedness increased on the earth. All animate beings corrupted their way—(every one of them) from people to cattle, animals, birds, and everything that moves about on the ground. All of them corrupted their way and their prescribed course. They began to devour one another, and wickedness increased on the earth. Every thought of all [hu]mankind's knowledge was evil like this all the time." —trans. VanderKam

the Lord. The closest literary parallel to this episode is 1 Enoch 13:4–7, which reports briefly that the Watchers asked Enoch to approach the Lord on their behalf to read a prepared entreaty, which he does only to be given a stern sentence of judgment to be ferried back to the fretting Watchers:

> And they begged me to write for them a memorial prayer in order that there may be for them a prayer of forgiveness, and so that I may raise their memorial prayer unto the Lord of heaven. For as for themselves, from henceforth they will not be able to speak, nor will they raise their eyes unto heaven as a result of their sins which have been condemned. And then I wrote down their memorial prayers and the petitions on behalf of their spirits and the deeds of each one of them, on account of the fact that they have prayed in order that there may be for them forgiveness (of sin) and a length (of days). And I went and sat down upon the waters of Dan—in Dan which is on the southwest of Hermon—and I read their memorial prayers until I fell asleep. (1 Enoch 13:4–7; trans. E. Isaac, "1 [Ethiopic Apocalypse of] Enoch")

No petition is provided in 1 Enoch, but the Genesis Apocryphon, columns 0–1, seems to fill this gap in what must have been a very entertaining account (as long as you are not a Watcher) and was possibly also provided in the full Book of Giants (see, e.g., cols. 12–13). Though the preserved bits of dialogue in these columns are put in the mouths of either the Watchers/giants or the Lord, 1 Enoch 13 raises the distinct possibility that Enoch is actually the one relating the orations (as Lamech does for Methuselah and Enoch in the following columns).

GENEALOGY OF GENESIS 5

Adam (930 years)
→ Seth (912)
    → Enosh (905)
        → Cainan (910)
            → Mahalaleel (895)
→ Jared (962)
    → Enoch (365)
        → Methuselah (969)
            → Lamech (777)
                → Noah (950)
                    → Shem, Ham, Japheth

The next portion of the scroll (cols. 2–5) deals with the birth of Noah to Lamech, and must be read in light of the preceding columns on the Watchers/ giants and their evil conduct. Due to some astounding traits of Noah at birth (e.g., luminescence; see 5.12–13), Lamech suspects that his wife has been too well acquainted with a Watcher. This she vociferously denies, causing Lamech's "mind to waver," but in the end he asks his father Methuselah to approach Enoch, who is assumed to be inerrant, for the truth. Enoch quells all suspicion in a long, repetitive speech highlighting the special role of salvation Noah will play, and the story is allowed to move forward. These columns have a stark parallel in 1 Enoch 106–7, and less direct connections to 1Q19 (Book of Noah) and 4Q534–4Q536 (Elect of God, or Birth of Noah). All of these texts show a robust interest in the birth story of Noah, and the Genesis Apocryphon and 1 Enoch 106–7 display an apologetic impulse to clear Noah of any possible insalubrious lineage.

Genesis Apocryphon 5.29–18.23 is taken up with the events of Noah's life, in which he is presented as wholly righteous. In contrast to Genesis and Jubilees (though see the Noah segments of 1 Enoch), Noah is presented as a visionary who receives frequent apocalyptic revelations and dreams. Many of these concern the flood and Noah's crucial role in saving humanity and eradicating evil from the earth, though in Genesis Apocryphon 13 we sense a shift toward handing divine knowledge on to his son Shem and the division of the earth among his sons and grandsons. The symbolic dream and interpretation in columns 13–15 presumably take place in the biblical context of Noah's drunken sleep (Gen. 9:21: "He drank some of the wine and became drunk, and he lay uncovered in his tent"), which is a novelty in this Jewish interpretation. Almost all other interpreters, Jewish and Christian alike, view this episode negatively, while the Genesis Apocryphon's approach seems yet another way of asserting Noah's uprightness.

The section dealing with Abram's life begins at 18.25 and continues until the text is cut off at 22.34. As with previous sections, this one includes a host of alterations, additions, omissions, and rearrangements relative to Genesis, though as we progress—and especially for the third-person segment in columns 21–22—the story lines up more and more closely with the biblical account. Armin Lange has suggested that the Abram tale in the Genesis Apocryphon has been shaped and adapted to fit the genre of a "wisdom didactic narrative," in which Abram is presented as the able, virtuous sage whose wisdom allows him success in all his endeavors (cf. Joseph and Daniel in the Hebrew Bible). Wisdom is one important theme in this portrayal of Abram (among others), though it should be stressed that, unlike the other texts cited by Lange, in the Genesis Apocryphon wisdom has its roots in Enochic revelation (see 19.23–29). There are many aspects of the Abram section in particular that are at the same time exegetically valuable and highly entertaining, risqué, and even funny.

Date/Provenance

Based on the factors of language, relationship to other early Jewish works, knowledge of **Hellenistic** science, and other internal elements, it seems safe to say that the Genesis Apocryphon was composed sometime during the third to first centuries BCE, though a few scholars have defended significantly later dates. A minority of scholars have proposed that certain characters or statements in the scroll allude to known historical figures or social concerns (e.g., Hyrcanus the Tobiad, or a Jewish anti-Samaritan bias) (*see* 1 and 2 Maccabees), but these have been rightly rejected as too tenuous and vague. The most recent studies have advocated a date nearer the early end of our spectrum, circa the late third to mid-second centuries BCE.

A wide consensus exists that the Genesis Apocryphon was composed in Judea or at least the land of Israel. The supporting evidence consists of the writer's impressive knowledge of regional geography, as seen, for example, in toponyms such as Ramat-Hazor and Bet-Hakerem. Though the author shows some familiarity with lower Egyptian geography and names (e.g., Hyrcanus, Karmon River), a Palestinian location for his work remains the most compelling option.

Text, Language, Sources, and Transmission

The genre of the Genesis Apocryphon has been a topic of keen interest from the beginning of its modern study. Early suggestions that it should be classified as a *targum* have been widely rejected. In their studies of the relatively fixed formal features of *targum*, A. Samely and others have demonstrated that the Genesis Apocryphon does not have the form of a classical *targum*. An early alternative was to classify it as **midrash,** but this hypothesis too encountered opposition, not least because midrash is regularly used to refer to a specific group of later rabbinic exegetical texts with the very different formal feature of scriptural lemma plus discrete commentary. Though adjectives like "parabiblical" have been suggested for the Genesis Apocryphon and similar texts, the clear winner in the discussion has been a term coined by Geza Vermes in 1961: "rewritten Bible." By this was meant an interpretative text based on what we now, in hindsight, call the biblical account. According to Vermes's definition, a rewritten biblical work follows the narrative flow of Scripture but freely rearranges, harmonizes, subtracts, and adds material that is not formally distinguished from the base text, all in an effort to create a more engaging, comprehensive, and intelligible account. Philip Alexander describes this type of text as centripetal rather than centrifugal because it returns to the biblical narrative again and again. In response to Vermes, experts have proposed a series of qualifiers and adjustments to "rewritten Bible," including "retold Bible" (less committed to the written form), "rewritten Scripture" (less anachronistic), and "biblically allied" (less canonically restricted). These discussions have had the happy result of clarifying how texts like the Genesis Apocryphon relate to their scriptural progenitors: the writer follows the basic storyline of the scriptural text but takes significant interpretative liberties in the process—liberties guided by a complex set of exegetical, theological, and literary concerns. The result is a rewritten account intended to interpret authoritative Scripture from a particular perspective in order to address an equally particular setting. It should be added, however, that this did not exempt the author from paying attention to and interpreting even minute details in the Hebrew text of Genesis—a fact that conveys something about his opinion of the status of the text on which he relied.

Theology

Initially, specialists devoted to study of the Genesis Apocryphon tended to view the scroll as relatively free of theological or ideologically driven exegesis. Later scholars, however, have argued that numerous concerns can be identified in the scroll's handling of Genesis—especially in the added material. Following are some of the most significant areas of interest and concern for the author.

Throughout the Genesis Apocryphon one can sense an acute concern over the issue of who has original rights to the land of Canaan. This is evidenced in Noah's divinely appointed role as apportioner of the earth (3.17); repeated statements of Noah's authority over the earth (7.1–2; 11.9–12, 16–17); Noah's dream in columns 13–15, in which the Shemites and Hamites are juxtaposed; the extensive section about the earth's division among Noah's sons and grandsons (cols. 16–17); and the expanded geographic statements made to Abram regarding his inherited land (19.12–13; 21.8–22). It is notable that, like Jubilees and the War Scroll (*see* 1QM [War Scroll]), the Genesis Apocryphon depends on a prevailing scientific map of its time often called the "Ionian" world map *(mappa mundi)*, which divides the habitable earth into three land masses corresponding to Europe, Asia, and Africa, surrounded by an outer sea and divided by two major rivers (the modern Don and Nile Rivers) and the Great Sea (the Mediterranean Sea) (*see* Map of the World at the Time of 1QapGen, p. 39).

There is also a considerable admixture of apocalyptic thought in the scroll—a factor evident at a number of junctures. It is most prominently displayed in the opening columns of the scroll and in the subsequent visions of Noah (6.11–7.6; 11.15–12.6; and cols. 13–15). At issue in these passages is the transfer of concealed divine matters (e.g., historical, medicinal, ritual, **apotropaic**, and calendrical) to elect, righteous individuals, though the way in which each patriarch interacts with this information is different: Enoch is a direct conduit, Noah a recipient through dreams and visions, and Abram a teacher from books handed down to him. At one point in the scroll Noah is shown what appears to be a cataclysmic, eschatological judgment scene (15.5–18), similar to those so often found in historical apocalypses (*see* Introduction to Apocalyptic Literature). Related to this concern is a keen interest in revelatory dreams as a vehicle for relating privileged, divine instruction or information that aids the reader in understanding the true import of Genesis. Especially significant here is the concept of "mysteries," as in other Aramaic works from this period (e.g. 1 Enoch and Daniel; *see* The Book of Daniel) and later **sectarian** writings (e.g., 1QpHab 7; *see* Habakkuk Pesher [1QpHab]).

An associated theological stance of the author is his belief that spirits influence the course of human events for good or ill (cf. Jub. 10:1–14). The good spirits—the angels of God—reveal all things to Enoch (Jub. 2:21–22),[4] but evil spirits may have a most baneful effect, as Lamech, who feared that his wife was pregnant by one of the "Sons of Heaven" (2.5; cf. 2.1), knew only too well. The passage in which an evil spirit plays the most decisive role is in the episode of Sarai in Pharaoh's harem in column 20.

The Genesis Apocryphon presents the major patriarchs in the story (Enoch, Noah, and Abram) as paradigms of righteousness and faithfulness. Whereas in

---

4. Jub. 2:21–22: "In this way he made a sign on it by which they, too, would keep Sabbath with us on the seventh day to eat, drink, and bless the Creator of all as he had blessed them and sanctified them for himself as a noteworthy people out of all the nations; and to keep Sabbath together with us. He made his commands rise as a fine fragrance that is acceptable in his presence for all times." —trans. VanderKam

Genesis patriarchs act in questionable ways at times, in the Genesis Apocryphon no such impression is given. This is especially clear in the case of Noah, whom the author associates with "righteousness" some eleven times in the extant narrative—perhaps because of outside allegations that he was the offspring of a fallen Watcher (cols. 2–5). Furthermore, it is quite certain that his arboreal dream in columns 13–15 takes place during his inebriated sleep while inside his tent (cf. Gen. 9:20–21). The divine, revelatory nature of the dream erases any doubts surrounding the episode and in addition provides an ingenious explanation for the jarring prophecy uttered by Noah in the following verses of Genesis. A similar scenario unfolds with Abram's dream as he is about to enter Egypt, which neatly clears him of self-preservation at the expense of his wife's better interests.

Like other works from the Second Temple period the scroll portrays the patriarchs as following sacrificial and various other *halakhic* rulings revealed only later in the scheme of the Torah. This is evident in the description of Noah's sacrifice in 10.13–17 and concern over diet and the handling of blood throughout the Noah section. A similar concern is exhibited in 21.1–2, where instead of simply "calling on the Lord" (Gen. 13:4) Abram offers "burnt offerings and a meal offering" reminiscent of Levitical instructions.

While the Genesis Apocryphon does not exhibit the intense interest in calendrical issues that other books do (especially Jubilees), there are clear indications that calendar and biblical chronology held some interest for the author. Noah reckons one point in his life by the calculation of "ten Jubilees" (6.9–10; cf. 7.3), reports that a certain event took "two weeks" (6.18), and scrupulously follows the rule of eating the produce of his vineyard at the beginning of the fifth year after planting (col. 12; cf. Lev. 19:23–25; Deut. 20:6). In addition, the reader is notified of the chronological placement or duration of several key events in Abram's time: Abram's construction of and tenure at Hebron (19.9–10; cf. Num. 13:22), Sarai's captivity in Pharaoh's house (19.23; 20.17–18), and their journey more generally (22.27–28).

George Nickelsburg has highlighted the fact that the author was interested in the psychological and emotional states of characters in a manner that is rarely on display in Genesis or Second Temple period texts. Included are expressions of thoughts, feelings, and even sexual arousal. Along with this we find heightened attention given to female characters. In most cases, they are simply mentioned or named where we find no such information in Genesis, but in some passages they are also given larger roles in the narrative (e.g., the evocative description of Sarai's beauty in 20.1–8).

While the writer obviously accepted the standard monotheistic belief of his religion, he found it important to stress the greatness of God by the multiplicity of the titles that his characters use for the deity. Some of these are drawn from Genesis (e.g., the Most High God [12.17; 20.12, 16; 21.2, 20; 22.15, 16 (twice), 21; cf. 2.4]), but most are added to the text: the Great Holy One (0.11; 2.14; 6.13, 15; 7.7; 12.17); the Mighty Lord (2.4; 15.11); the King of all Ages (2.4, 7; 10.10); the King of Eternity (?) (19.8); the Lord of Eternity (0.17); the Lord of the Ages (21.2); the King of Heaven (2.14); the Lord of Heaven (7.7; 11.12–13 [?]; 12.17); the Lord of Heaven and Earth (22.16, 21); the Lord of All (5.23); Lord and Ruler over Everything (20.13); Lord of All the Kings of the Earth (20.15–16); my Lord (20.12 [for all ages],

14, 15); and my Lord God (22.32). It is notable that the author avoids use of the **Tetragrammaton**, a rule commonly followed in the Aramaic Dead Sea Scrolls.

Reception of the Genesis Apocryphon in the Second Temple Period

Numerous connections between the Genesis Apocryphon and other compositions from the Second Temple period have been noted above, but from the earliest studies of the scroll onward pride of place has been given to 1 Enoch and, especially, Jubilees. In general, we may observe that the first portions of the scroll, from approximately columns 0 to 6, have a close affinity with traditions also present in the Enochic corpus. Connections to the "Birth of Noah" texts (1 En. 106-7, 1Q19, and possibly 4Q534-4Q536) have already been mentioned, along with the plea of the Watchers in the Genesis Apocryphon, columns 0-1 (cf. 1 En. 13 and the Book of Giants). Another point of contact is the three-branched tree from Noah's dream in the Genesis Apocryphon, columns 13-15, which is also present in the Book of Giants (4Q530 and 6Q8) and related later rabbinic and Persian (Zoroastrian) writings. The image of the righteous individual as a tree is relatively widespread in biblical and postbiblical writings (e.g., Ps. 92 and 1QH 16), but the imagery deployed in the Genesis Apocryphon is related more specifically to a tradition preserved in other Jewish sources that tells of the destruction of the flood and Noah's survival by way of a symbolic, arboreal dream given to one of the giants. We should also recall the reference to Abram teaching Enochic wisdom to the Egyptians in Genesis Apocryphon 19.24-29.

As for Jubilees, the most extensive parallel is Noah's division of the earth in the Genesis Apocryphon, columns 16-17, and Jubilees 8:10-9:15; the two passages are so similar that at a few junctures Jubilees may be used as a textual source for reconstructing **lacunae** in the Genesis Apocryphon. Other correspondences are the name of Noah's wife (Batenosh; Genesis Apocryphon 5.3, 8; Jub. 4:28); Noah's expiatory sacrifice following the flood (Genesis Apocryphon 10.13-17; Jub. 6:1-3); the chronology and physical location (Mount Lubar) of Noah's vineyard and agricultural activity (Genesis Apocryphon 12.13-15; Jub. 7:1-2); the construction of Hebron by Abram (Genesis Apocryphon 19.9; Jub. 13:12); and the seven-year chronology of Abram, Sarai, and Lot's sojourn in Egypt (Genesis Apocryphon 22.27-29; Jub. 13:10-12). It is obvious from these parallels why scholars have paid so much attention to the relationship between these two texts.

It is one thing to cite parallels but quite another to determine the precise relationship between the texts that share them. Suffice it to say that the problem has proved to be a vexed one, with a variety of viewpoints being proposed by scholars. In general, early researchers believed the composition of the Genesis Apocryphon (though not necessarily the present copy) antedated Jubilees and even 1 Enoch. This was widely rejected by later scholars, some of whom seem to have assumed that the present copy and the composition of the work were either simultaneous or very close in date to each other (ca. the late first century BCE).[5] Recently, however, a date in the early second or even late third century has been

---

5. This opinion, however, faces a number of difficulties and is almost certainly not the case.

championed on several different grounds by a handful of scholars (e.g., Golda Werman, Hanan Eshel, and Daniel A. Machiela). An introduction of this sort is not the place to enumerate fully the arguments in support of the earlier date, but the reasons for it include the language of the text; its use of Hellenistic science; and analysis of shared passages with Jubilees, especially the section dealing with Noah's division of the earth.

In addition, there are some similarities with the book of Daniel and literature related to it from Qumran. This is certainly true for the language of the scroll, but also obtains for some of the content, such as the visions seen by Noah in columns 6–8 and 13–15. In them we appear to have a historical, or periodized, apocalyptic framework similar to the one in Daniel 2 and 7–12 and symbolic tree imagery reminiscent of Daniel 4 (as well as Ezek. 31 and other passages from the Hebrew Bible). An underexplored area of interconnection is the broader corpus of Aramaic Dead Sea Scrolls, many of which seem to share a similar worldview with the Genesis Apocryphon. Finally, though some have pointed to numerous exegetical parallels with various rabbinic midrashic works and the classical *targumim*, these are typically of a general sort and speak more to a common exegetical outlook and to shared practices than direct influence.

Regarding language, Joseph Fitzmyer has listed some eighteen examples of contributions that Qumran Aramaic makes to the understanding of the New Testament. Of his examples, the following ones from the Genesis Apocryphon may be highlighted here:

1. the title Lord of Heaven and Earth (22.16; Matt. 11:25; Luke 6:7)
2. the phrase "in truth," that is, truthfully (2.5, 7, 10, 18, 22; Matt. 22:16)
3. the verb "to find" used with the meaning "can, be able" (21.13; Luke 6:7)
4. the verb "to do, make" combined with a time word to express the notion of spending time (22.28; Acts 15:33; 18:23; 20:3)
5. the phrase "mystery of evil" (1.3), which resembles the "mystery of lawlessness" in 2 Thessalonians 2:7
6. the phrase "son of man" (21.13) with the meaning "someone" (e.g., Matt. 12:32)

The Genesis Apocryphon contains some of the Genesis stories that figure in the New Testament; the Melchizedek account (*see* Melchizedek [11Q13]) is just one example (22.14–17; note that in the scroll he provides food and drink, not bread and wine). The more important contributions that the Genesis Apocryphon makes to New Testament studies come, however, in the areas of what might be called narrative parallels and language.

Fitzmyer has expressed surprise that scholars have not more fully exploited the paternity discussion in Genesis Apocryphon, column 2, in connection with some of the birth narratives in the Gospels. Like Lamech, Joseph had concerns about Mary's pregnancy and received supernatural information about the facts regarding the conception (Matt. 1:18–21).[6] In contrast to Matthew's story, Noah

---

6. Matt. 1:18–21: "Now the birth of Jesus the Messiah took place in this way. When his mother Mary had been engaged to Joseph, but before they lived together, she was found to be with child from the Holy Spirit. Her husband Joseph, being a righteous man and unwilling to expose her

learned that the wondrous child was actually his, while Joseph was told that the conception was due to the Holy Spirit. The story in the Genesis Apocryphon tells of the special role that the child would play in the future, while Jesus would save his people from their sins. Abram's dream in which he is warned about the danger that will confront them when he and Sarai arrive in Egypt is somewhat reminiscent of the dream that Joseph has and in which he is warned about the danger to the child and the need to flee to Egypt (Matt. 2:13–15).[7]

Another correspondence is the laying on of hands to exorcise evil spirits. Abram provides this ritual service, accompanied by prayer, for Pharaoh in Genesis Apocryphon 20.21, 28–29, while New Testament writings regularly ascribe the expulsion of evil spirits to Jesus and the apostles. An especially close parallel is found in Luke 4:40–41: "Now when the sun was setting, all those who had any that were sick with various diseases brought them to him; and he laid his hands on every one of them and healed them. And demons also came out of many" (note, too, the frequent references to Jesus or the disciples laying hands upon those to be healed [Mark 5:23; 6:5; 7:32; 16:18; Luke 13:13; Acts 9:12, 17; 28:8]).

DANIEL A. MACHIELA

FURTHER READING

Crawford, S. White. *Rewriting Scripture in Second Temple Times.* Grand Rapids: Eerdmans, 2008 (pp. 105–29).

Fitzmyer, J. A. "Genesis Apocryphon." In *Encyclopedia of the Dead Sea Scrolls,* edited by Lawrence H. Schiffman and James C. VanderKam, 1:302–4. 2 vols. Oxford: Oxford University Press, 2000.

Machiela, D. A., and A. B. Perrin. "Tobit and the *Genesis Apocryphon*: Toward a Family Portrait." *JBL* 133.1 (2014): 111–32.

Segal, M. "The Literary Relationship between the Genesis Apocryphon and Jubilees: The Chronology of Abram and Sarai's Descent to Egypt." *Aramaic Studies* 8.1-2 (2010): 71–88.

Vermes, G. "The Genesis Apocryphon from Qumran." In *The History of the Jewish People in the Age of Jesus Christ,* translated, revised, and edited by G. Vermes, F. Millar, and M. Goodman, 3:318–25. 3 vols. Edinburgh: T. & T. Clark, 1986.

———. *Scripture and Tradition in Judaism: Haggadic Studies.* StPB 4. 2nd rev. ed. Leiden: Brill, 1973 (pp. 96–126).

to public disgrace, planned to dismiss her quietly. But just when he had resolved to do this, an angel of the Lord appeared to him in a dream and said, 'Joseph, son of David, do not be afraid to take Mary as your wife, for the child conceived in her is from the Holy Spirit. She will bear a son, and you are to name him Jesus, for he will save his people from their sins.'"

7. Matt. 2:13–15: "Now after they had left, an angel of the Lord appeared to Joseph in a dream and said, 'Get up, take the child and his mother, and flee to Egypt, and remain there until I tell you; for Herod is to search for the child, to destroy him.' Then Joseph got up, took the child and his mother by night, and went to Egypt, and remained there until the death of Herod. This was to fulfill what had been spoken by the Lord through the prophet, 'Out of Egypt I have called my son.'"

ADVANCED READING

Avigad, N., and Y. Yadin. *A Genesis Apocryphon: A Scroll from the Wilderness of Judaea. Description and Contents of the Scroll, Facsimiles, Transcription and Translation of Columns II, XIX–XXII.* Jerusalem: Magnes and Heikhal ha-Sefer, 1956.

Bernstein, M. J. "Divine Titles and Epithets and the Sources of the Genesis Apocryphon." *JBL* 128 (2009): 291–310.

———. "Re-arrangment, Anticipation and Harmonization as Exegetical Features in the Genesis Apocryphon." *Dead Sea Discoveries* 3 (1996): 37–57.

Eshel, E. "The Genesis Apocryphon: A Chain of Traditions." In T*he Dead Sea Scrolls and Contemporary Culture: Proceedings of the International Conference held at the Israel Museum, Jerusalem (July 6-8, 2008)*, edited by A. Roitman et al. STDJ 93. Leiden: Brill, 2011 (pp. 181-94).

Falk, D. K. *The Parabiblical Texts: Strategies for Extending the Scriptures among the Dead Sea Scrolls.* Companion to the Dead Sea Scrolls 8; Library of Second Temple Studies 63. London: T&T Clark, 2007 (pp. 26–106).

Fitzmyer, J. A. *The Genesis Apocryphon from Qumran Cave 1 (1Q20): A Commentary.* 3rd rev. ed. Biblica et Orientalia 18/B. Rome: Pontifical Biblical Institute, 2004.

Kugel, James L. "Which Is Older, Jubilees or the Genesis Apocryphon? An Exegetical Approach." In T*he Dead Sea Scrolls and Contemporary Culture: Proceedings of the International Conference held at the Israel Museum, Jerusalem (July 6-8, 2008)*, edited by A. Roitman et al. STDJ 93. Leiden: Brill, 2011 (pp. 257-94).

Machiela, D. A. *The Dead Sea Genesis Apocryphon: A New Text and Translation with Introduction and Special Treatment of Columns 13–17.* STDJ 79. Leiden: Brill, 2009.

———. "Genesis Revealed: The Apocalyptic Apocryphon from Qumran Cave 1." In *Qumran Cave 1 Revisited: Texts from Cave 1 Sixty Years after Their Discovery. Proceedings of the Sixth Meeting of the IOQS in Ljubljana*, edited by D. K. Falk et al. STDJ 91. Leiden: Brill, 2011.

Machiela, D. A., et al. T*he Dead Sea Scrolls: Hebrew, Aramaic, and Greek Texts with English Translations.* Volume 8A: *The Genesis Apocryphon and Related Documents*, edited by J. H. Charlesworth. Tübingen: Mohr Siebeck/Louisville: Westminster John Knox, 2016.

Peters, D. M. *Noah Traditions in the Dead Sea Scrolls: Conversations and Controversies of Antiquity.* Early Judaism and Its Literature 26. Atlanta: SBL, 2008 (pp. 97–127).

4.7 Genesis Apocryphon (1QapGen)

Column 0

1 [ ] . . . and a[l]l of us from . . .
2 [ ] that in every (way) we might undertake an adulterous act
3 [ ] *vacat*
4 [al]l that you will . . .
5 [ ] . . . you will intensify your anger and will be unrelenting, for who is there
6 [who . . .] . . . the heat of your anger *vacat*
7 [the sim]ple and the humble and the lowly ones quiver and tremble
8 [ ] And now we are prisoners!
9 [ ] . . . this
10 [ ] . . . hasten (?), and [to] relent from your anger [ ] *vacat*
11 [ ] by your anger . . . since we will depart to the house of . . . [ ] the Great [H]oly One
12 [ ] And now your hand has drawn near to strike . . . [ ] and to do away with all
13 [ ] . . . because he ceased his words at the [time] of our imprisonment
[ ] . . . a fire that has appeared
14 [ ] . . . befo[re the Lord of] Heaven . . .
15 [ ] th[em] and attacking from behind them. And no longer
16 [ ] *vacat*
17 [ ] . . . seeking favor and . . . from the Lord of Eternity
18 [ ] . . . before the Lord of Eternity. *vacat*
19–36(?)

Column 1

1 [wer]e descend[in]g, and with the women
2 [ ] . . . and also the mystery of wickedness, which
3 [ ] times, and the mystery that
4 [ ] w[e]did not make known
5 [ ] . . . not
6 . . . [ ] . . . until
7 the day whi[ch] the mystery, whether they
8 are all your sons, and [ ] . . . great . . . ,
9 medicines, acts of sorcery, and divi[nations] . . .

Translation by Daniel A. Machiela.

Column 2

1   Then suddenly it occurred to me that the conception was from Watchers, and the seed from Holy Ones, and to Nephil[in   ]

2   and my mind wavered concerning this infant.   *vacat*

3   Then I, Lamech, was upset, so I approached Batenosh my wife and sa[id to her   ]

4   ... I bear witness by the Most High, by the Mighty Lord, by the King of all A[ges   ]

5   [one of] the Sons of Heaven, until you recount truthfully everything for me, whether [   ]

6   you must recount [truthfully] for me, without lies. The son (born) from you is unique (?) [   ]

7   by the King of all Ages until you will speak truthfully with me, without lies. [   ]

8   Then Batenosh my wife spoke with me very harshly, and wept [   ]

9   and she said, "O my brother and my husband, recall for yourself my pleasure ... [   ]

10 in the heat of the moment, and my panting breath! I [am telling] you everything truthfully ... [   ]

11 [   ] ... entirely." Then my mind wavered greatly within me.   *vacat*

12 Now when Batenosh my wife saw that my demeanor had changed because of [my] ang[er   ]

13 Then she controlled her emotions and continued speaking with me. She was saying to me, "O my husband and my brother, [   ]

14 my pleasure. I swear to you by the Great Holy One, by the King of He[aven   ]

15 that this seed is from you, and from you this conception, and from you the planting of [this] fruit [   ]

16 and not from any stranger, nor from any of the Watchers, nor from any of the Sons of Hea[ven. Why is the appearance of]

17 your face changed and contorted like this, and your spirit ... [   ] upon you like this? [I]

18 am speaking truthfully with you."   *vacat*   [   ]

19 Then I, Lamech, ran to Methuselah my father and [t]ol[d] him everything [to Enoch]

20 his father in order to learn everything from him with certainty, since he is a beloved and ... [and with the Holy Ones]

21 is his lot apportioned, for they make everything known to him.   When Methusel[ah my father] heard [   ]

22 he ran to Enoch his father to learn everything truthfully from him [   ]

23 his will. And he went through the length of the land of Parvain, and there he found the end of [the] ea[rth   ]

24 [and] he said to Enoch his father, "O my father and my lord, I have co[me] to you [   ]

25   [   ] . . . to me, and I say to you, do not be angry that I came here to s[eek]
    you [out   ]
26   fearful of you" [   ]
27–36(?)

Column 5

1   *vacat*   Now to you, Methuselah [my] so[n   ] . . . of this
2   child, for when I, Enoch, . . . [   ] n[ot] from the Sons
3   of Heaven, but from Lamech your son [   ] . . .
4   and in resemblance he is not . . . [   ]
5   Now I am talking to you, my son, and making known to you all th[at   ],
    then truthfully . . . [   ]
6   Go, say to Lamech your son, ["The chi]l[d is t]r[ul]y from you [and]n[ot]
    from the Sons[of Heaven . . ."   ]
7   and his heights (?) on the earth, and every act of judgment I will entrust
    to him . . . [   ]
8   he lifted his face to me and his eyes shone like [the] su[n   ]
9   this child is a light, and he . . . [   ]
10   the seed from a stranger [   ]
11   . . . [   ]
12   Then they will be ensnared and destroyed [   ]
13   forever, giving according to their impurity to . . . . . . [   ]
14   doing much violence, they will act (thus) until [   ]
15   they will boil over, and every path of violence . . . from . . . [   ]
16   And now I am making known to you, my son, . . . [to Lamech]
17   your son make known by this mystery all . . . [that]
18   will be done in his days. And look, . . . [   ]
19   blessing the Lord of All . . . [   ]
20   When Methuselah heard [my] w[ords   ]
21   and he spoke with Lamech his son of a mystery[   ]
22   And when I, Lamech, h[eard   ]
23   rejoicing that from me [the] Lor[d of . . .] had brought forth[   ]
24   *vacat*   [   ]
25   A [c]o[p]y of the book of the words of Noah [   ]

Column 6

1   from iniquity. Through the uterus of she who bore me I burst forth for
    uprightness, and when I emerged from my mother's womb I was planted
    for righteousness.
2   All of my days I conducted myself uprightly, continually walking in the
    paths of everlasting truth. For [the] Holy One had instructed me (?) to
    . . . [   ]
3   in the ways of the paths of truth and to keep myself away from the highway
    of deceit, which lead to everlasting darkness, and to c[ons]ider whether

4   I would . . . the Lord. So I girded my loins in the vision of truth and wisdom, in the robe of supplication, and . . . [   ]

5   [   ] . . . [   ] . . . all the paths of violence.   *vacat*

6   T[h]e[n] I, Noah, became a grown man. I held fast to righteousness and strengthened myself in wisdom . . . [   ]

7   . . . I went and took Emzera his daughter as my wife. She conceived by way of me and gave birth to th[r]ee sons,

8   [and daughters.] Then I took wives for my sons from among the daughters of my brothers, and my daughters I gave to the sons of my brothers, according to the custom of the eternal statute

9   [that] the [Lo]rd of Eternity [gave   ] to humanity.   *vacat*   During my days, when there were completed for me, according to the calculation by which I reckoned,

10   [   ] . . . ten Jubilees.   Then the time of my sons taking women for themselves in marriage came to a close,

11   [and the Lord of] Heaven [appeared to me] in a vision. I looked and was shown and informed about the conduct of Sons of Heaven, and how all

12   [   ] heaven. I hid this mystery within my heart, and did not make it known to anyone.   *vacat*

13   [   ] . . . to me, and the great Watcher to me through an errand, and by an emissary of the great Holy One to me [   ]

14   [   ] he r[ev]ealed, and he spoke with me in a vision. He stood before me and loudly (?) proclaimed, "To you, O No[ah]"

15   [And through an em]issary of the great Holy One to me I was hearing a voice, "To you they are speaking, O Noah, . . ."

16   [   ] . . . before me. So I considered all the behavior of the sons of the earth. I understood and saw all of [   ]

17   [   ] . . .   . . . they would succeed, and they chose among them . . . [   ]

18   [   ] . . . two weeks. Then was sealed up . . . [   ]

19   [   ] bearing witness to the blood that the Nephilin had poured out. I was silent, and waited until . . . [   ] . . .   . . .

20   [   ] . . .   . holy ones, who with the daughters of me[n]

21   [   ] making (it) un[cl]ean by the divinatory arts. And I approached [one] of them and he said, "To you . . ." [   ]

22   [   ] . . .   and examining . . . [   ]

23   [   ] But I, Noah, f[o]und grace, prominence, and justification in the eye[s] of [the] L[ord of . . .   ]

Column 7

1   [   ] . . . [you will r]u[le] over them; the earth and all that is upon it, in the seas and on the mountains

2   [   ] . . .   . . . every heavenly body; the sun, the moon and the stars, and the Watchers

Column 10

1   Then [I] blessed the Lord of All, who from me . . . and kept safe . . . [   ]
8   Then (it) was on the earth . . .   . . . and he took from . . . [   ]
    . . .
9   finding, for in the wa[ter] . . .   . . . upon . . . [   ] the ark
    rested on one of the mountains of Ararat, and the eternal fire . . .
10 . . .   . . . [   ] . . . and I atoned for all the earth in its entirety.
    To begin, the [he-goat] was
11 placed u[pon   ] first, and after it came upon . . . [   ] . . . and I
    burned the fat upon the fire. Second, . . . [   ]
12 [Th]en . . . all of their blood to the base of the altar and [I] poured (it) out,
    and all of their flesh I burned upon the altar. Third, I offered the young
    turtledoves
13 wi[th] them upon the altar; their blood and all (of the rest) of them upon
    it. I gave fine wheat flour, mixed together with oil containing incense, as
    their meal offerings.
14 . . . portion of (?) . . . I said a blessing, and was putting salt on all of them,
    and the scent of my offering rose up to the [he]avens.   *vacat*

Column 11

1   [   ] N[o]w (as) I, Noah, was at the door of the ark the springs
    rec[eded . . .   ]
8   [Then] I, Noah, went out and walked throughout the land, through its
    length and through its breadth, [   ] . . .
9   [   ] upon it; rejuvenation in their leaves and in their fruit. The
    entire land was full of grass, herbs, and grain. Then I blessed the Lord of
10 [Heaven,] whose praise endures forever, and to whom (be) the glory!
    Once again I blessed the one who had compassion on the land, and who
    removed and obliterated from it
11 all those doing violence and wickedness and deceit, but rescued the righ-
    teous man . . . one, and he obtained all for his sake.   *vacat*
12 And . . . a[ppeared] to me from heaven, speaking with me and saying to
    me, "Do not fear, O Noah! I am with you and with those of your sons who
    will be like you forever.
13 [be fr]uitful and multiply, and fill the land. Rule over all of all of
    them; over its seas and over its wildernesses, over its mountains and over
    everything that is in them. I am now
14 [gi]ving to you and to your sons everything for food; that of the vegetation
    and herbs of the land. But you will not eat any blood. The awe and fear of
    you
15 [   ] forever."

Column 12

1   [   ] . . . See, I [hav]e now placed my bow [in a cloud]; it has become a sign for me in the cloud, in order to be . . .

6   ] . . . on the mountains of Ararat. After this, I went down to the base of this mountain, my sons and I, and we built

7   a ci[ty   ] for the devastation on the land was great. Then [son]s[and daugh]ters were born to[my sons] after the flood.

8   To my oldest son [Shem] was first born a son, Arpachshad, two years after the flood. And all the sons of Shem, all together, [wer]e

9   [Ela]m, Asshur, Arpachshad, Lud, and Aram, as well as five daughters. The s[ons of Ham (were) Cush, Mitzrai]n, Put, and Canaan, as well as

10   seven daughters. The sons of Japheth (were) Gomer, Magog, Madai, Javan, Tubal, Meshech, and Tiras, as well as four daughters.

11   [Then] I, along with all of my sons, began to cultivate the earth. I planted a great vineyard on Mount Lubar, and in four years it produced abundant wine

12   for me, and I brought forth all of the wine.   *vacat*   When the first feast came, on the first day of the first feast, which is in the

13   [first] month, [   ] . . . in my vineyard, and inside of my vineyard I opened this vessel, and began to drink from it on the first day of the fifth year

14   [after the planting of] the vineyard. On that day I called together my sons, my grandsons, and all of our wives and their daughters. We gathered together and went

15   [   ] the[altar]. I was blessing the Lord of Heaven, the Most High God, the great Holy One, who saved us from the destruction

16   [   ] . . .   . . . [   ] . . . us, and for all . . . his . . . , which my fathers hid and . . .   until [   ] . . .

17   . . . beautiful . . . [   ] . . . by my righteousness. And I lay down upon my bed and fell asleep [   ] . . .

Column 13

7   [   ] . . . the wood [the bir]ds of the heavens, the wild beasts of the field, the [livesto]ck of the soil, and the creeping things of the dry ground going . . . [   ] . . .

8   [   ] . . . the stones and the clay objects (they) were chopping and taking of it for themselves. As I continued watching, the gold, the sil[ver],

9   the . . . , the iron, and all of the trees (they) were chopping and taking of it for themselves. As I continued watching, the sun, the moon,

10   and the stars (they) were chopping and taking of it for themselves. I kept watching until they brought to an end the swarming creatures of the earth and the swarming creatures of the water.

11   So the water ceased, and it ended.   *vacat*

12   I turned to see the olive tree, and how the olive tree had grown in height!

[This continued] for many hours, with a bursting forth of many branches
. . . [   ] . . .

13 good and beautiful fr[uit] . . . and appearing in them. I was pondering
this olive tree, and the great abundance of its leaves [   ] . . .

14 [   ] everything, and tying ropes (?) onto it. Now I was very greatly
astounded over this olive tree and its leaves. I continued staring in amazement until [   ]

15 the [four] winds of heaven blowing powerfully and violently against this
olive tree, knocking off its branches and breaking it to pieces. First, [a
wind] swelled up from . . .

16 . . . west. It struck it, caused some of its leaves and fruit to fall from it, and
scattered it to the winds. And after this [a wind swelled up] . . .

17 and a northern wind from [   ] . . . and some of its fruit . . .
[   ] . . .

Column 14

4   [its] fruit. You were contemplating the [wo]od, an upper
part being knocked off from

5   [al]l of [the] boughs, and all the fr[ui]t of the foliage

6   [Now] listen and hear! You are the great cedar tree that was standing
before you on top of mountains in your dream,

7   [and] the shoot that emerged from it, gre[w h]igh, and was rising up to
its height (concerns) three sons . . .   . . . water from . . .   the earth.

8   As for the fact that you saw the first shoot adhering to the cedar trunk,
note too the one division branching off, and the wood from it . . .

9   [No]w the first son will not separate from you for all of his days, and
among his seed will your name be recalled. From his division a[l]l your
sons . . .

10 and in him . . .   the [fi]rst son will come forth as a righteous planting for
all . . .   the day, and . . .

11 [   ] . . . standing fast forever. As for the fact that you saw the shoot
adhering to the tr[un]k [of the cedar tree   ] . . .

12 [   ] . . . As for the fact that you saw the branch of the last shoot,
which . . . from it . . . [   ]

13 *vacat*   . . . the darkness, and part of their bough entering into the
midst of the bough of the first one, (concerns) two sons . . . its . . .   . . .
bra[nch]es

14 [   ] . . . one to the south of the earth and one to the north of the earth.
As for the fact that you saw part of their bough entering into the midst of
the bough of the first one

15 [   ] . . . of this shoot were settling in his land and all the coastlands
. . . to the Great Sea, and not . . .   . . . they [se]ttled in the midst of the
[coas]tlands

16 [   ] . . . to comprehend the mystery, there will be for you an end . . .
you will scatter (?) . . .   . . . water that . . .   . . . [   ]

¹⁷ [   ] and the mystery . . .   . . . entering into it, and [the] first one . . . for himself their every god (?) that . . . [   ]

¹⁸ [   ] . . . for himself . . .   . . . in an allotment in Amania, next to Elam . . . the [Gr]eat [S]ea . . . [   ]

¹⁹ [   ] . . . serve; first, exchanging his allotment for an allotment . . . [   ]

Column 15

⁵] from them a profusion of wrongdoing, and settling in your [lan]d . . .

⁶ the ends of the earth. As for the fact that you saw all of them crying out and turning away, the majority of them will be evil. As for the fact that you saw [   ]

⁷ the great warrior coming from the south of the earth, sickle in hand and fire with him, he has crushed all . . . [   ]

⁸ . . . [   ] . . . and the Mighty Lord, he is the one who will come from the south of the earth [   ] . . .

⁹ [   ] the torches (?) and the evil one. And he threw all [the] rebel[lious] ones onto the fire[   ]

¹⁰ and they will seal . . . (?), and . . . [   ] the . . . As for the fact that you saw (that) they plucked up . . . [   ]south

¹¹ . . . [   ] . . . a chain on them, four mighty angels[   ]

¹² *vacat*   You, Noah, do not be amazed at this dream, and may there not be added upon it [   ]

¹³ [   ] I have related everything to you in truth, and thus it is written concerning you [   ]

¹⁴ and I will j[oi]n some of your people to you . . . to you. [Then I], Noah, [awoke] from my sleep. The sun rose, and I, [Noah,   ]

¹⁵ to bless the Everlasting God. And [   ] I[we]nt to Shem, my son, and relat[ed] everything to [him]

Column 16

⁸ [   ] as a spring in [w]est [un]til it reaches [   ] . . .

⁹ of the sea that is between them; the source of (the) Mahaq, up to the Tina [R]iver. It then passes as a spring the length

¹⁰ of the whole land of the north, in its entirety, until it reaches (the) source of [   ] and up to the lan[d   ] . . .

¹¹ This boundary line crosses the waters of the Great Sea until it reaches Ga[de]ra, and . . .

¹² And Noah divided (it) by lot for Japheth and his sons to receive as an everlasting inheritance.

¹³ *vacat*

¹⁴ For Shem emerged the second lot, for him and his sons to receive as [an ever] l[asting inheritance] . . .

15   [   ] the waters of this Tina River emerge, until . . . [   ]
. . . as a spring [   ]

16   [up] to the Tina River, which . . .   . . . the Maeota Sea, which reaches
. . . the gulf of

17   the Great Salt Sea. And this boundary goes as a spring from this gulf,
wh[ich   ] . . .

18   to . . .   . . . [   ] up to the gulf of the sea that faces toward Eg[yp]t.
It then passes . . . [   ]

19   And for Ham [there eme]rged [the thi]rd [share] . . . to inherit for him
[and his sons . . . everlasti]ng

20   [up] to the G[iho]n[River   ] . . . reaches to [the
sou]th (of)

Column 17

6   [And] Shem divided his [po]rtion among his sons. There fell first to
[E]lam (an area) in the north, along the waters of the Tigris River, until
it reaches the Erythrean

7   Sea, to its source that is in the north. And aft[er him](there fell) to Asshur
(the area) toward the west, until it reaches the Tigris . . . [   ] . . .   And
after him

8   (there fell) to Aram the land that is between the two rivers until it reaches
the peak of Mount Ar[arat], in that region. And after him to Lud . . .

9   fell this Mount Taurus. This portion passes to the west until it reaches
Magog; everything al[ong] the . . . gulf that is by the Eastern Sea,

10   in the north, adjoining this gulf—that which is above the three portions
to its south. For Arpachshad (there fell) . . .   . . . un[til] it reaches

11   to . . .   . . . which turns to the south; the entire land irrigated by the Euphrates, and all . . . [   ] . . .

12   [   ] . . . a[l]l of the valleys and the plains that are between them, and the
coastlands that are within this gulf; a[l]l . . . un[til] it reaches . . .[   ] . . .

13   [   ] to Amana, which abuts Mount Ararat, and (from) Amana until
it reaches the Eup[hrates] . . . to [   ] . . . until it re[aches . . .   ]
. . .

14   [   ] the portion that Noah, his father, divided for him and gave to
him.   *vacat*

15   [And] Japheth divided among his sons. First, he gave to Gomer (an area)
in the north, until it reaches the Tina River. And after him (he gave) to
Magog, and after him

16   to Madai, and after him to Javan; all the islands that are alongside Lud,
and (that) between the gulf th[at] is n[ex]t to Lud and the [se]cond gu[lf].
To Tubal (he gave) that which is across

17   [the] second g[ulf]. To Meshech . . . [   ]. To [Tiras] (he gave)
four [island]s, and up to the . . .   alongside it, within

18   [the sea that reaches alongside to the por]tion of the sons of Ham . . .
[for]ever   *vacat*

19 [   ] the sons of Noah [di]vi[ded] th[eir] allotment[s among their sons   ]

Column 19

6   . . . I called there on the na[me of G]o[d], and I said, "You are

7   God . . .   . . . and King of Etern[i]ty." [And] he spoke with me in the night ". . .   and take strength (?) to wander; up to now you have not reached the holy mountain." So I set out

8   to [g]o there. I was going to the south of Moreh . . . , I went until I reached Hebron—now I b[u]ilt Hebron for that region—and I lived

9   [the]re for [two] years.   *vacat*   Now there was a famine in all of this land, but I heard that there wa[s] w[h]eat in Egypt. So I set out

10   to go . . . [   ] to the land that is in Egypt . . .   [   ]   . . . and there was [   ] I [reached] the Karmon River, one of

11   the heads of the river, [I] sai[d] "Enter (?) [   ] . . . [until] now we have been within our land." So I crossed over the seven heads of this river, which

12   af[terward en]ters [int]o the Great Sea [o]f Salt. [After this I said], "Now we have left our land and entered the land of the sons of Ham, the land of Egypt."

13   *vacat*   Now I, Abram, dreamed a dream in the night of my entry into Egypt. I saw in my dream that there was a single cedar and a single date

14   palm, having sprout[ed] together from [one] roo[t]. And m[e]n came seeking to cut down and uproot the [ce]dar, thereby leaving the date palm by itself.

15   But the date palm cried out and said, "Do not cut down the cedar, for the two of us are sp[rung] from o[ne] root!" So the cedar was left on account of the date palm,

16   and they did not cut me down.   *vacat*   Then I awoke in the night from my sleep, and I said to my wife Sarai, "I dreamed

17   a dream, (and) on acco[unt] of this dream I am afraid." She said to me, "Tell me your dream, so that I may know (about it)." So I began to tell her this dream,

18   and I said to [her], ". . .   this dream . . .   . . . that they will seek to kill me, but to spare you. Therefore, this is the entire kind deed

19   th[at you] must do for me: in all cities that [we will ent]er s[a]y of me, 'He is my brother.' I will live under your protection, and my life will be spared because of you.

20   [t]hey [will s]eek to take you away from me, and to kill me." Sarai wept because of my words that night

21   . . . when we en[ter]ed into the dist[ri]ct of E[gypt . . .   ] . . . And Pharaoh Zoa[n   ] . . . t[he]n . . . Sarai to turn toward Zoan

22   . . . [and] she was secretly [v]ery concerned that no man would see her (for) [fiv]e years. Now at the end of those five years

23 ...   ... to me, and three men from nobles of Egypt ... his [   ]
... by Phara[oh] Zoan because of my words and my wisdom, and they
were giving

24 m[e many gifts   They as]ked erudition and wisdom and truth for
themselves, so I read before them the book of the words of Enoch

25 [   ] in the womb in which he had grown. They were not going to
get up until I would clearly expound for them ...   ... the words of

26 [   ] ...   with much eating and much drinking ...
[   ] ... the wine

Column 20

1] ... how irresistible and beautiful is the image of her face; how

2 lovely h[er] foreh[ead, and] soft the hair of her head! How graceful are
her eyes, and how precious her nose; every feature

3 of her face is radiating beauty! How lovely is her breast, and how beautiful
her white complexion! As for her arms, how beautiful they are! And her
hands, how

4 perfect they are! Every view of her hands is stimulating! How graceful are
her palms, and how long and thin all the fingers of her hands! Her legs

5 are of such beauty, and her thighs so perfectly apportioned! There is not
a virgin or bride who enters the bridal chamber more beautiful than she.

6 Her beauty surpasses that of all women, since the height of her beauty
soars above them all! And alongside all this beauty she possesses great
wisdom. Everything about her

7 is lovely! Now when the king heard the words of Herqanos and his two
companions—that the three of them spoke as one—he greatly desired her,
and sent someone

8 to be quick in acquiring her. When he saw her he was dumbfounded at
all of her beauty, and took her for himself as a wife. He also sought to kill
me, but Sarai said

9 to the king, "He is my brother," so that I would be benefited on account
of her. Thus I, Abram, was spared because of her, and was not killed. I,

10 Abram, wept bitterly—I and Lot, my brother's son, with me—on the night
when Sarai was taken from me by force.   *vacat*

11 That night I prayed and entreated and asked for mercy. Through sorrow
and streaming tears I said, "Blessed are you Most High God, my Lord, for
all

12 ages; for you are Lord and Ruler over everything. You are sovereign over
all the kings of the earth, having power to enact judgment on all of them.
So now

13 I lodge my complaint before you, my Lord, concerning Pharaoh Zoan,
king of Egypt, for my wife has been taken from me forcefully. Bring judgment against him on my behalf, and reveal your mighty hand

14 through him and all of his house, that he might not prevail this night in

rendering my wife unclean for me! Thus, they will come to know you, my Lord, that you are Lord over all the kings

15   of the earth." So I wept and was deeply troubled. During that night the Most High God sent a pestilential spirit to afflict him, and to every person of his household an evil

16   spirit. It was an ongoing affliction for him and every person of his household, so that he was not able to approach her, nor did he have sexual relations with her. She was with him

17   for two years, and at the end of two years the afflictions and hardships grew heavier and more powerful over him and every person of his household. So he sent

18   a message to all the wise me[n] of Egypt, and to all the magicians, in addition to all the physicians of Egypt, (to see) if they could heal him and (every) person

19   of his household of this affliction. But all of the physicians and magicians and all of the wise men were not able to succeed in curing him, for the spirit began afflicting all of them (too),

20   so that they fled the scene!   *vacat*   At this point Herqanos came to me asking that I come pray over

21   the king and lay my hands upon him, so that he would live. This was because he had seen [me] in a dream . . . But Lot said to him, "Abram, my uncle, cannot pray over

22   the king while his wife Sarai is with him! Now go and tell the king that he should send his wife away from himself to her husband; then he (Abram) will pray over him so that he might live."

23   *vacat*   Now when Herqanos heard the words of Lot, he went (and) said to the king, "All these afflictions and hardships

24   that are afflicting and troubling my lord the king are due to Sarai, the wife of Abram. Just return Sarai to Abram her husband

25   and this affliction and the spirit of foulness will depart from you." So the [k]i[ng] called me and said to me, "What have you done to me?! Why were you saying

26   to me 'she is my sister' when she was your wife, so that I took her as a wife for myself?! Here is your wife. Take her, go and get yourself out of

27   every district of Egypt! But now pray over me and my household, that this evil spirit may be driven away from us." So I prayed over [hi]m, that I might heal

28   him, and I laid my hands upon his [h]ead. Thus, the affliction was removed from him, and the evil [spirit] driven away [from him]. The king recovered, rose up, and gave

29   to me on t[hat da]y many gift[s], and the king swore to me by an oath that he did not have sexual relations with her, [nor] did he [de]file her. Then he returned

30   Sarai to me, and the king gave to her [m]uch si[lver and g]old and much clothing of fine linen and purple, which . . .   . . . [   ]

31   before her, as well as Hagar. Thus he restored her to me, and appointed

for me a man who would escort me [from Egypt]t to [ ] . . .   to your
people. To you [ ]

32 *vacat*   Now I, Abram, grew tremendously in many flocks and also in
silver and gold. I went up from Egy[p]t, [and] my brother's son

33 [Lot wen]t with me. Lot had also acquired for himself many flocks, and
took a wife for himself from the daughters of Egy[p]t. I was encamping
[with him]

Column 21

1   (at) every place of my (former) encampments until I reached Bethel, the
place where I had built the altar. I built it a second time,

2   . . . and offered upon it burnt offerings and a meal offering to the Most
High God, and I called there on the name of the Lord of the Ages. I praised
the name of God, blessed

3   God, and gave thanks there before God because of all the flocks and good
things that he had given to me, and because he had worked good on my
behalf and returned me

4   to this land in peace.   *vacat*

5   After this day Lot parted from me due to the behavior of our shepherds.
He went and settled in the Jordan Valley along with all of his flocks,

6   and I also added a great deal to his belongings. As he was pasturing his
flocks he reached Sodom, and bought a house for himself in Sodom.

7   He lived in it while I was living on the mountain of Bethel, and it was
disturbing to me that Lot, my brother's son, had parted from me.

8   *vacat*   Then God appeared to me in a vision in the night, and said
to me, "Go up to Ramat-Hazor, which is to the north of

9   Bethel, the place where you are living. Lift up your eyes and look to the
east, to the west, to the south, and to the north, and see this entire

10 land that I am giving to you and to your descendants for all ages." So on
the following day I went up to Ramat-Hazor and I saw the land from

11 this high point: from the River of Egypt up to Lebanon and Senir, and
from the Great Sea to Hauran, and all the land of Gebal up to Kadesh, and
the entire Great Desert

12   that is east of Hauran and Senir, up to the Euphrates. He said to me, "To
your descendants I will give all of this land, and they will inherit it for all
ages.

13 I will make your descendants as numerous as the dust of the earth, which
no one is able to reckon. So too will your descendants be beyond reckon-
ing. Get up, walk around, go

14 and see how great are its length and its width. For I will give it to you and
to you descendants after you unto all the ages."   *vacat*

15 So I, Abram, embarked to hike around and look at the land. I began to
travel the circuit from the Gihon River, and came alongside the sea until

16 I reached Mount Taurus. I then traversed from alo[ng] this Great Sea of

Salt and went alongside Mount Taurus to the east, through the breadth of the land,

17 until I reached the Euphrates River. I journeyed along the Euphrates until I reached the Erythrean Sea, to the east, and was traveling along

18 the Erythrean Sea until I reached the gulf of the Red Sea, which extends out from the Erythrean Sea. I went around to the south until I reached the Gihon

19 River, and I then returned, arriving at my house in safety. I found all of my people safe and went and settled at the Oaks of Mamre, which are near Hebron,

20 to the northeast of Hebron. I built an altar there and offered upon it a burnt offering and a meal offering to the Most High God. I ate and drank there,

21 I and every person of my household. I also sent an invitation to Mamre, Arnem, and Eshkol, three Amorite brothers (who were) my friends, and they ate

22 and drank together with me.   *vacat*

23 Before these days, Chedarlaomer, the king of Elam, Amraphel, the king of Babylon, Arioch, the king of Cappadocia, (and) Tiral, the king of Goiim, which

24 is Mesopotamia, came and waged war with Bera, the king of Sodom, and with Birsha, the king of Gomorrah, and with Shinab, the king of Admah,

25 and with Shemiabad, the king of Zeboiim, and with the king of Bela. All of these banded together for battle at the Valley of Siddim. The king of

26 Elam and the kings who were with him overpowered the king of Sodom and all of his allies, and they imposed a tribute on them. For twelve years they were

27 paying their tributes to the king of Elam, but during the thirteenth year they rebelled against him, so that in the fourteenth year the king of Elam gathered together all

28 of his allies. They went up the Way of the Desert, destroying and plundering from the Euphrates River (onward). They destroyed the Rephaim who were in Ashtera

29 of Karnaim, the Zumzamim, who were in Amman, the Emim, [who were in] Shaveh-Hakerioth, and the Hurrians, who were in the mountains of Gebal, until they reached El-

30 Paran, which is in the desert. They then turned back and destroyed Ein-[Dina   ] . . . , which is in Hazazon-Tamar.   *vacat*

31 Now the king of Sodom went out to meet them along with the king of [Gomorrah, the k]ing of Admah, the king of Zeboiim, and the king of Bela. They engaged in battle

32 in the Valley o[f Siddim] against Chedarla[omer and the kings] who were with him, but the king of Sodom was crushed and fled, while the king of Gomorrah

33 fell, and many from [al]l[   ] . . . [   ] The king of Elam plundered all of the goods of Sodom and of

34 [Go]morrah, [and all] the p[oss]essions [of   and all th]at
they fou[nd there], while Lot, the son of Abram's brother,

Column 22

1 who was living in Sodom together with them along with his flocks, was taken captive. But one of the shepherds

2 of the flock that Abram had given to Lot, who had escaped from the captors, came to Abram. Now at that time Abram

3 was living in Hebron, and he informed him that his brother's son Lot had been captured, along with all of his property, but that he had not been killed. Also that

4 the kings had set out (on) the Way of the Great Valley toward their province, (all the while) taking captives, plundering, destroying, killing, and heading

5 for the city Damascus. Then Abram wept over his brother's son Lot. Having collected himself, Abram got up

6 and chose from his servants three hundred eighteen choice warriors fit for battle. Arnem,

7 Eshkol, and Mamre also set out with him. He chased after them until he reached Dan, where he found them

8 camping in the Valley of Dan. He swooped upon them at night from all four directions, killing

9 among them throughout the night. He crushed them and chased after them, and all of them were fleeing before him

10 until they reached Helbon, which is situated to the north of Damascus. (There) he took away from them everyone they had captured,

11 all that they had plundered, and all of their own goods. Lot, his brother's son, he also saved, along with his property. All

12 those whom they had taken captive he brought back. When the king of Sodom heard that Abram had brought back all of the captives

13 and all of the plunder, he went up to meet him. He came to Salem, which is Jerusalem, and Abram encamped in the Valley

14 of Shaveh, which is the Valley of the King—the Valley of Bet-Hakerem. And Melchizedek, the king of Salem, brought out

15 food and drink for Abram and for all of the men who were with him. He was the priest of the Most High God, and he blessed

16 Abram, saying, "Blessed be Abram by the Most High God, the Lord of heaven and earth! And blessed be the Most High God,

17 who delivered those who hate you into your hand!" So he gave him a tenth of all the property of the king of Elam and his allies.

18 *vacat*   Then the king of Sodom drew near and said to Abram, "My lord, Abram,

19 give me anyone who belongs to me of the captives with you, whom you have rescued from the king of Elam. But as for all the property,

20 it is left to you."   *vacat*   Then Abram said to the king of Sodom, "I lift up

21 my hands this day to the Most High God, the Lord of heaven and earth,
(swearing) that I will take neither string nor sandal strap

22 from all that which belongs to you, lest you should say, 'All the wealth of
Abram (derives) from my

23 property.' (This) excludes that which my young men who are with me have
already eaten, and also the portion of the three men who

24 went with me. (Only) they have authority to give you their portions." So
Abram returned all of the property and all

25 of the captives, and gave (them) to the king of Sodom. Every one of the
captives who were with him from that land he set free

26 and sent all of them away.   *vacat*

27 After these things God appeared to Abram in a vision, and said to him,
"Look, ten years

28 have elapsed since the day you came out of Haran; two years you spent
here, seven in Egypt, and one (has passed)

29 since you returned from Egypt. Now inspect and count all that you have;
see that by doubling they have increased greatly, beyond

30 all that came out with you on the day of your departure from Haran. And
now do not fear; I am with you, and will be for you

31 a support and strength. I am a shield over you, and a buckler for you
against those stronger than you. Your wealth and your property

32 will increase enormously."   Abram said, "My Lord God, I have
wealth and property in great abundance, yet what are

33 all [th]ese things to me while I, when I die, will go stripped bare, without
children. One of my household servants will receive my inheritance;

34 Eliezer, son of Dameseq, he . . .   the one acquiring an inheritance from
me." But he said to him, "This one will not receive your inheritance, but
one who will go forth"

The Reworked Pentateuch

Reworked Pentateuch is the name given to a group of five manuscripts from Cave 4, Qumran: 4Q158, or 4QReworked Pentateuch[a], or 4QRP[a]; 4Q364, or 4QReworked Pentateuch[b], or 4QRP[b]; 4Q365, or 4QReworked Pentateuch[c], or 4QRP[c]; 4Q366, or 4QReworked Pentateuch[d], or 4QRP[d]; and 4Q367, or 4QReworked Pentateuch[e], or 4QRP[e] (*see* Overview of Early Jewish Literature). These manuscripts, which are not copies of one another, are grouped together because of the method by which they transmit the text of the Torah or Pentateuch, the five books of Moses (Genesis, Exodus, Leviticus, Numbers, and Deuteronomy). These five manuscripts are representative of a scribal tradition active in the Second Temple period that intervened in a scriptural text for the purpose of exegesis. This scribal phenomenon is already observable in earlier texts that became part of the Hebrew Bible; for example, Deuteronomy reworks parts of Exodus and Numbers, while Chronicles rewrites Samuel–Kings.

By the fifth century BCE, the Pentateuch as we know it had reached its present shape, and each of the five books within it had reached their respective shapes. However, the text inside each book was still fluid; that is, it was subject to scribal changes and was not fixed. There were two scribal approaches to the transmission of scriptural texts in this period. The first attempted to make exact copies, neither adding nor changing anything. The second approach intervened in the text for exegetical purposes, adding short or long interpretive comments, updating archaic language, harmonizing similar passages, and occasionally rearranging **pericopes**. This second approach can be seen most fully in the Samaritan Pentateuch, the version of the Pentateuch canonical in the Samaritan community. The Samaritans are a religious/ethnic community centered around Mount Gerizim in the present-day West Bank, who claim descent from the Israelites of the northern kingdom of Israel, although this claim is disputed by the Jews. The Samaritans were much more numerous in the Second Temple period, and had their own temple on Mount Gerizim where they worshiped the God of Israel until it was destroyed in 135 BCE. They acknowledge only the Torah as their canonical Scripture (*see* Florilegium [4Q174]).

The Samaritan Pentateuch is characterized by harmonization, that is, smoothing out differences between parallel texts (Text A and Text B) by importing elements from Text B into Text A and content editing. An example of harmonization can be seen in 4Q158, fragment 6, where Deuteronomy 5:28–29 and 18:18–22 are imported in Exodus 20:19–21. This same harmonization occurs in the Samaritan Pentateuch. Thus the Samaritan Pentateuch is longer, or more expanded, than the version known as the **Masoretic Text** (**MT**), which is the version translated in most English Bibles. It is helpful to think of the different texts of the Pentateuch as points along a spectrum, with short, unexpanded texts at one end, and longer, expanded texts farther along. The Reworked Pentateuch manuscripts occupy a point even farther along the spectrum of expansion than the Samaritan Pentateuch because they sometimes insert new material, not from known scriptural sources, into the received text.

It is important to note here that a scribe who altered his received text meant no disrespect to the text by his actions. On the contrary, the scribe saw his role as pivotal in the continuing vitality of the scriptural tradition, updating and explaining it for the next generation. The question of authority may arise here as well: How were these manuscripts viewed or received by the Jewish community, whether at Qumran or elsewhere? Were they considered scriptural or authoritative? The two manuscripts for which we have the most fragments, 4Q364 and 4Q365, certainly intend to present themselves in the same way as other "biblical" manuscripts at Qumran; there is no indication in the physical remains of the manuscripts that they differ in any way from other manuscripts of, say, Exodus or Deuteronomy found in the Qumran caves. It is possible that some of the "new" material in 4Q364 and 4Q365 served as a source for other compositions in the Second Temple period. If that is the case, then these manuscripts had an authoritative status. The evidence, however, is not firm, and the question is still unresolved.

Discussion of Individual Manuscripts

In this section I investigate each individual manuscript separately, discussing the types of scribal intervention found in them. All of the examples are found in the English translations.

4QReworked Pentateuch^a, or 4QRP^a (4Q158)

4QRP^a was copied in the late first century BCE. It consists of fifteen fragments, containing portions of Genesis and Exodus. Fragments 1–2, which contain sections of Genesis 32:25–32[1] and Exodus 4:27–28,[2] demonstrate expansion and the

---

1. Gen. 32:25–32: "When the man saw that he did not prevail against Jacob, he struck him on the hip socket; and Jacob's hip was put out of joint as he wrestled with him. Then he said, 'Let me go, for the day is breaking.' But Jacob said, 'I will not let you go, unless you bless me.' So he said to him, 'What is your name?' And he said, 'Jacob.' Then the man said, 'You will no longer be called Jacob, but Israel, for you have striven with God and with humans, and have prevailed.' Then Jacob asked him, 'Please tell me your name.' But he said, 'Why is it that you ask my name?' And there he blessed him. So Jacob called the place Peniel, saying, 'For I have seen God face to face, and yet my life is preserved.' The sun rose upon him as he passed Peniel, limping because of his hip. Therefore to this day the Israelites do not eat the thigh muscle that is on the hip socket, because he struck Jacob on the hip socket at the thigh muscle."

2. Exod. 4:27–28: "The Lord said to Aaron, 'Go into the wilderness to meet Moses.' So

juxtaposition of distant passages. Lines 7–9 contain "added" material, giving the words of the blessing the angel gives to Jacob after their nocturnal wrestling. Line 14 introduces Exodus 4:27–28. The reason for the juxtaposition of the two passages has not yet been satisfactorily explained. Lines 16–18 contain another addition to the received text, evidently a speech by Moses explaining God's commands to Aaron.

Fragment 6 contains a text of Exodus 20:19–21,[3] which resembles that found in the Samaritan Pentateuch. Exodus 20 is part of the Sinai pericope; Deuteronomy 5:28–29[4] and 18:18–22[5] are inserted into it. The two Deuteronomy passages concerning God's response to the people's fear and his promise to raise up a prophet like Moses are imported into the Exodus passage to harmonize the two accounts, as can be seen here:

1. [   ] you [
2. [Exod. 20:19 But do n]ot let [God] speak to u[s,
3. 20 G[od] has come [and t]o put the fear of [him
4. 21 God was. Deut. 5:28 And the Lord [spoke] to Moses, s[aying,
5. 29 they had such a mind as this, to fear [me
6. My words, sa[y] to them, [Deut. 18:18 "I will raise up for them] a prophet[
7. 19 who does not heed the words [that
8. 20 him [to] speak, or who shall sp[eak"
9. 22 If a [prophet] speaks [

Fragments 7–8 also harmonize Exodus and Deuteronomy; Deuteronomy 5:30–31 ("Go! Say to them, 'Return to your tents!'") is inserted into Exodus 20. Line 5 contains content editing; in the received text, God commands the people to return to their tents (Deut. 5:30), but it is never reported that they actually

---

he went; and he met him at the mountain of God and kissed him. Moses told Aaron all the words of the Lord with which he had sent him, and all the signs with which he had charged him."

3. Exod. 20:19–21: "And [they] said to Moses, 'You speak to us, and we will listen; but do not let God speak to us, or we will die.' Moses said to the people, 'Do not be afraid; for God has come only to test you and to put the fear of him upon you so that you do not sin.' Then the people stood at a distance, while Moses drew near to the thick darkness where God was."

4. Deut. 5:28–29: "The Lord heard your words when you spoke to me, and the Lord said to me: 'I have heard the words of this people, which they have spoken to you; they are right in all that they have spoken. If only they had such a mind as this, to fear me and to keep all my commandments always, so that it might go well with them and with their children forever!'"

5. Deut. 18:18–22: "I will raise up for them a prophet like you from among their own people; I will put my words in the mouth of the prophet, who will speak to them everything that I command. Anyone who does not heed the words that the prophet will speak in my name, I myself will hold accountable. But any prophet who speaks in the name of other gods, or who presumes to speak in my name a word that I have not commanded the prophet to speak—that prophet will die. You may say to yourself, 'How can we recognize a word that the Lord has not spoken?' If a prophet speaks in the name of the Lord but the thing does not take place or prove true, it is a word that the Lord has not spoken. The prophet has spoken it presumptuously; do not be frightened by it."

returned. Line 5 inserts the fulfillment of the command: "So the people returned to their individual tents, but Moses remained before [the Lord.]"

4QReworked Pentateuch*ᵇ*, or 4QRP*ᵇ* (4Q364)

4QRP*ᵇ* was copied in the middle of the first century BCE. It consists of thirty-two fragments (as well as thirty-five small unidentified fragments), containing portions of Genesis, Exodus, Numbers, and Deuteronomy. No fragments of Leviticus were recovered, but there is no reason to suppose that the manuscript did not contain Leviticus when whole. 4QRP*ᵇ* demonstrates an interesting scribal feature: the scribe places two vertical dots before each occurrence of the Divine Name[6] (indicated by a colon [:] in the English translation). This was evidently to warn the reader not to pronounce the Divine Name (*see* Habakkuk Pesher [1QpHab]).

Fragment 1a-b contains a small exegetical insertion. In line 3, Sarah is identified as the mother of Isaac, probably to make certain the reader understood that Isaac, the child of both Abraham and Sarah, was the recipient of God's promise to Abraham.

Fragment 3, column 2, contains an addition of six lines before Genesis 28:6. The addition appears to include a longer speech by Rebekah to Jacob, sending him away after his deception of Esau, and a scene in which Isaac comforts Rebekah after Jacob's departure. This scene is repeated in Jubilees 27:14, 17, using some of the same words. It is possible that 4QRP*ᵇ* served as a source for this scene in Jubilees (*see* The Book of Jubilees).[7] There is also a similar scene in the book of Tobit (*see* The Book of Tobit), in which Anna weeps after the departing Tobias and Tobit attempts to comfort her (Tob. 5:21).

An example of content editing occurs in fragment 4b-e, column 2. Lines 21–26 give an account of Jacob having a dream, in which God commands him to leave Laban and return to Canaan. This is the dream that Jacob has and that he reports to Leah and Rachel in Genesis 31:10–13.[8] But the received text does not portray

---

6. The "Divine Name" refers to the four consonant proper names of God found in the Hebrew Bible (sometimes referred to as the **Tetragrammaton**). The consonants indicate that the Divine Name of God was a form of the verb "to be." Already in the Second Temple period, Jews avoided pronouncing the Divine Name. The Hebrew Bible vocalizes the four consonants as "Adonai," or "Lord"; hence in most English translations the Tetragrammaton is translated as LORD in capital/small capital letters.

7. Jub. 27:13–14: "And it came to pass after Jacob had gone away to Mesopotamia, Rebecca fretted after her son and wept. And Isaac said to Rebecca, 'My sister do not weep on my son Jacob's account; for he has gone in peace, and he will return in peace.'" —trans. R. H. Charles, revised by C. Rabin, *The Apocryphal Old Testament.* Jub. 27:17: "Do not be afraid for him, my sister, because he is just in his way. He is perfect; he is a true man. He will not be abandoned. Do not cry." —trans. VanderKam

Tob. 5:21: "And he said to her, 'Have no concern. Our son will travel safely, and come back to us safely, and your eyes will see him on the day when he comes to you safely. Have no concern, do not be afraid for him, sister.'" —trans. Weeks

8. Gen. 31:10–13: "During the mating of the flock I once had a dream in which I looked up and saw that the male goats that leaped upon the flock were striped, speckled, and mottled. Then

him as actually having it. That gap in the text is remedied here by an anticipatory harmonization, using the same words as in the dream report in chapter 31.

Fragment 14 contains a short addition (lines 1–2) before Exodus 24:12, using some of the language from Exodus 19, which portrayed Moses' earlier trip up the mountain. Because the addition is so fragmentary, its purpose is not clear.

Fragment 23a-b, column 1, demonstrates a harmonization between parallel passages in Deuteronomy and Numbers. Numbers 20 and Deuteronomy 2:2–8 both recount the Israelites' encounter with the Edomites during their wilderness journey. However, Numbers 20:14–18 contains the message that Moses sent to the Edomites; that message does not appear in the parallel passage (Deut. 2:2–8). That gap in the Deuteronomy narrative is rectified by inserting the Numbers passage before Deuteronomy 2:8.

4QReworked Pentateuch^c, or 4QRP^c (4Q365)

4QRP^c was also copied in the middle of the first century BCE. It includes thirty-eight fragments (with twenty-four further unidentified fragments), with remnants from all five books of the Pentateuch. If 4QRP^c was one scroll when whole, it would have been the longest scroll (ca. 25 meters) from the Qumran caves. It too contains many small harmonizations and examples of content editing, but its most interesting remains are two larger blocks of additional material.

The addition now called "The Song of Miriam" appears in fragment 6a-c. Fragment 6b, column 1, preserves some of the Song of Moses found in Exodus 15. After that song is finished, Miriam, Moses' sister, leads the women in a victory song (15:20–21: "Then the prophet Miriam, Aaron's sister, took a tambourine in her hand; and all the women went out after her with tambourines and with dancing. And Miriam sang to them: 'Sing to the Lord, for he has triumphed gloriously; horse and rider he has thrown into the sea'"). In the received text of Exodus, Miriam sings only the first verse of Moses' song (15:1, 21). There seemed to be a gap in the text, leading to speculation in rabbinic sources about the remainder of Miriam's song. But here in 4QRP^c, fragment 6a-c, column 2, lines 1–7, the rest of Miriam's song is supplied. The scribe who constructed the song drew language from Moses' song, but the poem must have been a freestanding composition when complete:

1. with an olive branch (*or:* you despised)[
2. for the pridefulness [   ]
3. You are great, O deliverer [
4. the enemy's hope has perished and he is for[gotten (*or:* has cea[sed)
5. they have perished in the mighty waters, the enemy [
6. Praise him in the heights, he has given salvation [
7. [who has] done glorious things *vacat* [

---

the angel of God said to me in the dream, 'Jacob,' and I said, 'Here I am!' And he said, 'Look up and see that all the goats that leap on the flock are striped, speckled, and mottled; for I have seen all that Laban is doing to you. I am the God of Bethel, where you anointed a pillar and made a vow to me. Now leave this land at once and return to the land of your birth.'"

The second major addition is legal in nature. Fragment 23 preserves the end of Leviticus 23, which contains the festival calendar, that is, the dates and the practices of the festivals that God commanded to Moses. By the Second Temple period, however, additional festivals were being observed by various groups of Jews. An organized offering of wood for the temple service appears already in Nehemiah 10:34 ("We have also cast lots among the priests, the Levites, and the people, for the wood offering, to bring it into the house of our God, by ancestral houses, at appointed times, year by year, to burn on the altar of the Lord our God, as it is written in the law"). Questions about the legitimacy of these additional festivals must have arisen since they were not Mosaic. In fragment 23 that dilemma is resolved for at least two of these festivals, the New Oil and Wood Festivals, by adding their legislation to the end of the festival calendar in Leviticus (lines 5–11). The Wood Festival legislation contains a close parallel to the Temple Scroll, columns 22–23, giving rise to the possibility that 4QRP^c was a source for the Temple Scroll (*see* Temple Scroll [11Q19–20]).

The last example from 4QRP^c, fragment 26a-b, preserves the end of the book of Leviticus (with variants from the received text) and the beginning of the book of Numbers, demonstrating clearly that more than one book of the Pentateuch was copied on this single scroll.

4QReworked Pentateuch^d, or 4QRP^d (4Q366)

4QRP^d, copied in the early to middle first century BCE, contains five fragments preserving parts of Exodus, Numbers, and Deuteronomy. It is uncertain whether it was a complete manuscript of the Pentateuch, or contained only excerpts. Fragment 2 contains the juxtaposition of two passages from Leviticus. The reason for this juxtaposition has not yet been satisfactorily explained. Fragment 4, column 1, brings together two of the Torah texts, Numbers 29:12–38 and Deuteronomy 16:13–15, legislating for the festival of **Sukkot**. Since the fragment is broken, it is possible that the Leviticus passage concerning Sukkot, 23:33–36, was found here as well.

4QReworked Pentateuch^e, or 4QRP^e (4Q367)

4QRP^e, copied in the middle of the first century BCE, contains three fragments (as well as one unidentified fragment) of Leviticus. This manuscript was either a complete or excerpted copy of a scribally reworked text of Leviticus. Both fragments given here demonstrate the juxtaposition of different passages from Leviticus (again for unclear reasons); fragment 3 has a brief addition before 20:13.

Theology

These manuscripts of an expanded and Reworked Pentateuch (or excerpts therefrom) testify to the existence of a scribal tradition in Second Temple Judaism that treated the scriptural text with reverence but also relative freedom. That this scribal tradition was not confined to the Qumran collection is evident in the fact that the Samaritan Pentateuch is also an exemplar of this scribal tradition. Further, the additions that go beyond the received text of the Pentateuch are completely nonsectarian in nature; there is nothing in their language that marks them as belonging to any particular group of Jews in the Second Temple period. These manuscripts were meant to be read and understood by the Jewish community as scriptural texts.

SIDNIE WHITE CRAWFORD

FURTHER READING

Crawford, S. White. *Rewriting Scripture in Second Temple Times*. Grand Rapids: Eerdmans, 2008 (pp. 39-59).

Falk, Daniel K. *The Parabiblical Texts: Strategies for Extending the Scriptures among the Dead Sea Scrolls*. New York: T&T Clark, 2007 (pp. 109-19).

ADVANCED READING

Bernstein, Moshe J. *Reading and Re-Reading Scripture at Qumran*. Vol. 2. Leiden / Boston: Brill, 2013 (pp. 476-97).

Tov, Emmanuel. "From 4QReworked Pentateuch to 4QPentateuch (?)." In *Authoritative Scriptures in Ancient Judaism*. Edited by M. Popovic. JSJSup 141. Leiden: Brill, 2010 (pp. 73-91).

VanderKam, James C. "Questions of Canon Viewed through the Dead Sea Scrolls." In *The Canon Debate*. Edited by Lee Martin McDonald and James A. Sanders. Grand Rapids: Baker Academic, 2002 (pp. 91-109).

Zahn, Molly M. *Rethinking Rewritten Scripture: Composition and Exegesis in the 4QReworked Pentateuch Manuscripts*. Leiden: Brill, 2011.

4.8 *From* Reworked Pentateuch
(4Q158, 4Q364–4Q367)

4QReworked Pentateuch^a, or 4QRPa (4Q158)

Fragments 1–2: Genesis 32:25–33; Exodus 4:27–28

1   [   ] so that [

2   [without] remnant or su[rvivor

3   ^{Gen. 32:25} [J]ac[ob] was left there [a]lone; and [a man] wrestled [with him

4   [   ] as he wrestled with him. [Still,] he held him tight; ²⁷ then the man said, [   ]

5   [   ] me." ²⁸ So he said to him, "What is your name?" And he replied, ["Jacob." ²⁹]

6   [with God and] humans, and have prevailed." ³⁰ J[a]cob then asked him, "Please [te]ll me [your name."

7   [And he bless]ed him [there], saying, "May the Lo[rd] make you fruitful, [and multiply] you [

8   [know]ledge and insight. May he preserve you from all wrongdoing, and [

9   until this day and forever more [

10   Then the man went on his way, having blessed Jacob there. Subsequently [Jacob] ca[lled ?"]

11   ³² The sun rose upon him as he left Penie[l,

12   on that day, and said, "You will not ea[t

13   ³³ on the hip sockets to t[his day,   ]

14   ^{Exod. 4:27} to Aaron saying, "Go to meet [

15   ²⁸ the Lord's words with which he had s[en]t him, and all [the signs   ]

16   "The Lord [has spoken] to me, saying, 'When you have brought the [   ] out [

17   to go as slaves, and consider, they number thir[ty

18   the Lord, God [

Fragment 6: Exodus 20:19–21; Deuteronomy 5:28–29; 18:18–22
(harmonized)

1   [   ] you [

2   [^{Exod. 20:19} But do n]ot let [God] speak to u[s,

3   ²⁰ G[od] has come [and t]o put the fear of [him

4   ²¹ God was. ^{Deut. 5:28} And the Lord [spoke] to Moses, s[aying,

5   ²⁹ they had such a mind as this, to fear [me

6   my words, sa[y] to them, [^{18:18} "I will raise up for them] a prophet [

Translation by Sidnie White Crawford.

7   ¹⁹who does not heed the words [that

8   ²⁰him [to] speak, or who will sp[eak

9   ²²If a [prophet] speaks ["

Fragments 7–8: Exodus 20:12–17; Deuteronomy 5:30–31; Exodus 20:22–21:10 (harmonized)

1   Exod. 20:12 your [father] and your mother, [

2   ¹⁶false witness [against] your [neighbor.] ¹⁷You will not covet [your] nei[ghbor's] wife

3   Deut. 5:30 And the Lord said to Moses, "Go say to them, 'Return to [your tents.'

4   ³¹and the ordinances that you will teach them, so that they may do them in the land that ["

5   So the people returned to their individual tents, but Moses remained before [the Lord.

6   Exod. 20:22 You have seen for yourselves that I spoke with you from heaven. You are not to mak[e

7   ²⁴on it your burnt offerings and offerings of well-being, your sheep [

8   ²⁵you make for me [   ] do not build it of hewn stones; for by [using] a chisel [upon it

9   ²⁶on it. *vacat* ²¹:¹These are the ordinances [that] you will se[t

10   [³if] he came in by himself, he will go out by himself. I[f

11   [   ] ⁴his master's and he [   ]

12   ⁶(?) will br[ing him

13   his ear with an awl [

14   ⁸[then let] her [be re]deemed. To a peo[ple

15   ¹⁰[her marital rights] not

4QReworked Pentateuchᵇ, or 4QRPᵇ (4Q364)

Fragment 1a-b: Genesis 25:18–21

1   Gen. 25:18 as you [go] toward Ass[y]ria. [He settled down before all his brothers. ¹⁹Now these are the generations of]

2   [I]saac son of Abraham. Abraham [was the father of Isaac   ]

3   whom Sarah [his] wife [bore] to him. [²⁰And Isaac was forty]

4   [yea]rs [old] when he took Rebekah, [the daughter of Bethuel the Syrian of Paddan-Aram,]

5   [the sister of Laban to b[e his wife. ²¹And Isaac entreated the Lord]

6   for [his] wife, [because she was barren. And the Lord was entreated by him and Rebekah,] his wife, [conceived.]

Fragment 3, column 2: addition + Genesis 28:6

1   "him you will see [   ]

2   you will see in good health [   ]

3 your death, and unto your eyes [lest I be deprived of even   ]
4 the two of you." and [Isaac] called [Rebekah his wife and he told   ]
5 her all [these] things [   ]
6 after Jacob her son [and she wept.   ]
7 Gen. 28:6 Now Esau saw that [Isaac had blessed Jacob and sent him away]
8 to Pa[ddan] Aram to find from [there a wife] for him [   ]

Fragment 4b–e, column 2: Genesis 30:26–36 + addition

1   [Gen. 30:26 "I have served] you [for them and let me go   ]
2   [for yo]u know [my service with which I served you   ]
3   [fou]rteen y[ears."   ]
4   [27 And Laban said to him,] "If now I have found [favor in your eyes, I have divined that the Lord has blessed me]
5   [on account of you."] 28 And he said, "Name me [your wages and I will give them." 29 And he said]
6   [to him, "Yo]u know ho[w I have served you and how your cattle have fared]
7   [with me. 30 For it was little which] you [had before I came, and it has increased into a multitude and]
8   [the Lord has blessed y]ou [wherever I turned.] Now,[when will I provide for my own house also?"]
9   [31 And he said, "Wh]at will I give to you?" [Jacob said, "You will not give anything to me. If]
10 [you will do] this thing for me, [I will again shepherd your flock and keep it.]
11 [32 I will pass] through all your flock [today, removing from them every sheep that is speckled]
12 [and spotted and ever]y one of the flock that is black [among the sheep and the spotted and speckled among the goats]
13 [and these will be my wages.] 33 So will [my] righteous[ness] answer for me [from this day forward. When you will come]
14 [concerning my wages wi]th you, every one of the flock wh[ich is not speckled or spotted among the goats]
15 [and black among the sh]eep will be counted stolen [if it is with me." 34 And Laban said, "Behold! Let it be]
16 [according to your words." 35 That day, he removed the male goats that were ring-streaked and spotted]
17 [and all the speckled and spotted female goats, every one that]
18 had white [on it. He gave them into the hand of his sons, all the black ones among the sheep. 36 He set]
19 a th[ree days' journey between himself and Jacob, and Jacob shepherded]
20 [the remainder of] Laban's flocks. [*vacat*]
21 And [the angel of God sai]d [to Jacob in a dream, and he said, "Jacob," and he answered,]
22 "He[re am I." He said, "Lift up] your [eyes and see that all the male goats that are mounting]

23 [the flock are ring-streaked and spe]ckled [and grizzled, for I have seen what Laban has done]

24 [to you. I am the God of Bethel wh]ere [you anointed a pillar and where you vowed]

25 [a vow to me there. And now, arise, get out] fr[om this land and return to the land]

26 [of your] fa[thers and I will deal well with you."]

Fragment 14: Exodus 19:17 (?); 24:12–14

1 *vacat* [Exod. 19:17 and they stood]

2 on the lower part of the mountain *vacat*.

3 24:12 The Lord said to Moses, "Com[e up to me] on the mountain and b[e there and I will give to you tablets of stone]

4 and the law and the commandment that I have written in order that you might teach them. *vacat* [13 And Moses arose and Joshua]

5 [his] assistant and he went up to [the mountain] of God. 14 And to [the elders he said, "Wait for us until]

6 we re[turn to you.] Aaron and Hur [are with you. Whoever has a cause, let him approach them."]

Fragment 23a–b, column 1: Numbers 20:17–18; Deuteronomy 2:8–14 (harmonized)

1 [Num. 20:17 We will not]turn aside into a field or through a vineya[rd] and

2 [we will n]ot drink from waters of a spring. We will walk along the King's Highway. We will n[ot] turn aside to the right hand or to the left

3 [until we have passed your border. 18 He said,] "You will not pa[ss through] me, lest

4 [I come out with the sword to meet you.] *vacat*

5 [Deut. 2:8 We passed through our brothers, the children of Esau, who dwe]ll in Seir from the way

6 [of the Arabah from Elath and from Ezion-Geber. We turned and pa]ssed by the way of the wilderness of Moab.

7 [*vacat*? 9 The Lord said] to [me,] "Do not distress

8 [Moab, neither engage in strife for I will not give you this land]

9 [as a possession, because I have given Ar to the children of Lot as a possession." 10 The Emim dwelt there before them,]

10 [a people great, and many, and tall, as the Anakim. 11]

11 [The Moabites called them Emim. 12 The Horites also dwelt in Seir]

12 [before them, but the children of Esau dispossessed them and destroyed them from before] them, and [they dwelt]

13 [there in their stead, just as Israel did to the land] of his [possess]ion, which [the Lord] gave

14 [to them. 13 "Now rise up, and get yourselves to the wadi Zered." Then, we] went over the wad[i]

15 [Zered. ¹⁴ Now the days that we came from Kadesh-Barnea, until] we passed over

16 [the wadi Zered were thirty-eight years; until] all

4QReworked Pentateuch^c, or 4QRP^c (4Q365)

Fragment 6b, column 1 + Fragments 6a, column 2, and 6c: Exodus 15:16– 20; addition + Exodus 15:22–26

Column 1

1   Exod. 15:16 Until [your people pass over, *vacat* O Lord, *vacat* until this people pass over *vacat* whom you have purchased. *vacat* ¹⁷ You will bring them, and plant them]

2   in the mountain of your possession. *vacat* The place that [you made] for yourself to dwell in, [*vacat* O Lord; the sanctuary *vacat* that your hands have established.]

3   ¹⁸ The Lord will reign forever and ever. *vacat* ¹⁹ For [the horses of Pharaoh *vacat*] went in [with his chariots and with his horsemen into the sea, *vacat* and]

4   [the Lo]rd [brought back] the waters of the sea *vacat* upon them *vacat*; [but the children of Israel walked on dry land in the midst of the sea.]

5   [Now the wate]rs were [a wall] for th[em on] their right and on their left. *vacat* ²⁰ [Miriam the prophetess, the sister]

6   [of Aaron,] took [a timbrel in her hand and a]ll the women went out after her with [timbrels and with dances. ²¹ She answered,]

Column 2

1   with an olive branch (*or:* you despised)[

2   for the pridefulness[   ]

3   You are great, O deliverer[

4   the enemy's hope has perished and he is for[gotten (*or:* has cea[sed)

5   they have perished in the mighty waters, the enemy[

6   Praise him in the heights, he has given salvation [

7   [who has] done glorious things *vacat* [

8   Exod. 15:22 Moses led [Isra]el onward from the sea, and they went into the wilderness of Sh[ur three days and they found no water.]

9   ²³ When they came to Marah, they could [not] drink of the waters of Marah, for [they were bit]ter. [Therefore the name of it was called Marah.]

10   ²⁴ And the people murmured again[st Moses, sa]ying, "What will we drink?" ²⁵ Moses cried to [the Lord ? the Lord]

11   a tree, and he cast it into [the water]s, and the waters were made sweet. There he made for them a statute and an [ordinance, and there he tested them. ²⁶ Then he said,]

12   "If [you will] diligent[ly lis]ten[to the voi]ce of the Lord your God, [and] do that which is right in his eyes, and [give ear to his commandments,]

13 [and keep] all his statues, [I will put none] of the diseases [upon you,] which I have put upon the E[gyptians,]

14 [for I am the Lord] your [hea]ler."

Fragment 23: Leviticus 23:42–24:2 + addition

1 Lev. 23:42 ["In bo]oths you will dwell seven days; every citizen of Israel should dwell in booths, 43 so that [your descendants may know]

2 that I made your ancestors live [in b]ooths when I brought them out of the land of Egy[p]t. I am the Lord your God.

3 *vacat* 44 Then Moses spoke concerning the festivals of the Lord to the children of Israel. *vacat*

4 24:1 The Lord spoke to Moses, saying, 2 "Command the children of Israel, saying: 'When you come to the land that

5 I am about to give you as an inheritance, and you dwell upon it securely, bring wood for the whole burnt offering and for all the wor[k of]

6 [the h]ouse that you will build for me in the land, arranging them upon the altar of burnt offering [and] the calve[s]

7 [ ] for Passover sacrifices and for peace offerings and for thank offerings and for freewill offerings and for whole burnt offerings; daily [

8 [ ] and for the d[o]ors and for all the work of the house [they] will brin[g

9 [the fes]tival of new oil, let them bring the two [ ]

10 [ ] those who bring on the first day, Levi [

11 [Reu]ben, and Simeon; [on the] fourth day, ['"

Fragment 26a–b: Leviticus 27:34 (?); Numbers 1:1–5

1 [Lev. 27.34] all the children of Isr[ael

2 [ ] just as [

3 [ ] *vacat* [

4 [Num. 1:1 The Lord spoke to Moses in] the desert of Sinai in the tent of meeting during the firs[t day of the second month]

5 [in the second year after they came out] of the land of Egypt, saying, 2 "Take a census of the congregation of the chil[dren of Israel,]

6 [by their families, by] their [ancestors' houses,] according to the number of the names written of each individual 3 from twen[ty years old and upward,]

7 [all that are able to go out to war in I]srael. You and Aaron will number them by their hosts. 4 Wi[th you]

8 [will be a man of every] tribe; every one head of his ancestors' house. 5 [The]se are [the names"

4QReworked Pentateuch^d, or 4QRP^d (4Q366)

Fragment 2: Leviticus 24:20-22 (?); 25:39-43

1   [^{Lev. 24:20} tooth for a tooth, just as he ca]used [a blemish in a man, so it will
be given to him. ²¹ He that kills an animal will make restitution and he that
kills]

2   [a man will be put to death.] ²² You will have the same [la]w [for the sojourner as for the homeborn, for I am the Lord]

3   [your God.] *vacat*

4   [^{25:39} If] your brother [becomes poor] with you and sells himself to you,
you will not [make him serve as a slave. ⁴⁰ As a hired hand and as a
sojourner,]

5   [he will] be to you. He will serve [you] until the year of Jubilee. [⁴¹ Then
he will depart from you, he and his children with him,]

6   [and will return] to his possession and to his own family, and [will return]
to the po[ssession of his ancestors. ⁴² For they are my servants]

7   [whom] I [br]ought out of the land of Eg[ypt. They will not be sold as
slaves. ⁴³ You will not rule]

8   [over him with ruthlessness, but you will fear your G]o[d

Fragment 4, column 1: Numbers 29:32-30:1 and Deuteronomy 16:13-14

1   [^{Num. 29:32} On the seventh day, seven bulls, t]wo [rams, fourteen] male
la[mbs, one year old, without blemish]

2   [³³ and the meal offering and the drink offerings for the bulls, for the
rams, and for the lamb]s, according to their number, [according to the
ordinance, ³⁴ and] one [male go]at for a sin offering besides

3   [the continual burnt offering, the meal offering, and the drink offering.]
vacat

4   [³⁵ On the eighth day, you will have a solemn assembly.] You will not [work
at] your [occ]upation. ³⁶ But you will offer a burnt offering to the Lord,

5   [an offering made by fire, of a sweet savor, one bull, one ram,] seven [male
lambs, one ye]ar old, without blemish, ³⁷ the meal offering and the drink
offerings

6   [for the bull, for the ram, and for the lambs will be according to their
number, according to the ordinance, ³⁸ and] one [male goat for a si]n
offering, besides the continual burnt offering, and the meal offering

7   [and the drink offering. ³⁹ You will offer these to the Lord during your
appointed feasts, besides] your [vow]s, and your freewill offerings, for
your burnt offerings, and for your meal offerings,

8   [and for your drink offerings, and for your peace offerings. *vacat* ^{30:1} Moses
said] to the children of Israel all that the Lord had commanded

9   [Moses.] *vacat*

10   [^{Deut. 16:13} You will keep the Feast of Booths seven days, after you gathered
in from] your [threshing-floor] and from your winepress. ¹⁴ You will rejoice in your feast, you, and your son . . .

4QReworked Pentateuch^e, or 4QRP^e (4Q367)

Fragment 2a–b: Leviticus 15:14–15; 19:1–4, 9–15

1   Lev. 15:14 to the door of the te[nt of meeting, and give them to the priest.
    15 The priest will offer them, the one]

2   for a sin offering, and the other for a burnt offering. [The priest will make
    atonement for him before the Lord for his emission.]

3   19:1 the Lord [spoke] to Moses, say[ing, 2 "Speak to all the congregation]

4   [of the children of Israel, and] say to them, [You will be holy, for I am
    holy,]

5   [the Lord your God. 3 You will honor,] every one, his mother, [and his
    father; and you will keep my Sabbaths.]

6   [I am the Lord] your [God.] 4 Do not [turn to idols, or make for yourselves
    molten idols. I am]

7   [the Lord yo[ur God.] *vacat* [9 When you reap the harvest]

8   [of your land, do not completely reap the corners] of your field, [neither
    will you gather the gleaning of your harvest. 10 You will not glean]

9   [your vineyard, neither will you gather the fallen fruit of your vineyard.
    You will leave them] for the po[or and for the sojourner. I am]

10 [the Lord your God. 11 You will not steal; neither will you deal] falsely, nor
    li[e to one another.]

11 [12 You will not swear by my name falsely, and thus profane] the name of
    your God. [I am the Lord. 13 You will not oppress]

12 [your neighbor, or rob him. The wages] of a hired servant [will not stay]
    with you [all night] until the mor[ning. 14 You will not curse the deaf,]

13 [or put a stumbling block before the blind, but you will fear] your [G]od.
    I am [the Lord. 15 You will do no unrighteousness]

14 [in judgment. You will not make the poor lose face or defer] to the
    migh[ty, but in righteousness]

Fragment 3: addition (?) + Leviticus 20:13; 27:30–34

1–2 *Addition?*

3   [Lev. 20:13 a man will lie]

4   [with a male as with a woman] both [of them have com]mitted
     a[b]omination,

5   [they will surely be put] to death. Their [blood]guilt is on them. *vacat*

6   [27:30 All the tith]e of the land, whether of the seed of the land, or of the
     fruit *vacat* of the tree,

7   [is the Lord's. I]t is holy to the Lord. 31 If *vacat* [a man] wishes to redeem

8   [some of] his [tith]e, [he will add] a fifth of it *vacat* to it. 32 All

9   [the tithe of the herd] or the flock, what[ever passes *vacat*] under the staff,
     the tenth]

10   [will be holy to] the Lord. [33 He will] n[ot seek *vacat* whether it be good
     or bad,]

11   [neither will he change it. If he change it at all, *vacat* then both] it and that
      for which it is changed
12   [will be holy. It will not be redeemed.] *vacat*
13   [³⁴ These are the commandments, which the Lord commanded *vacat*]
      Moses for the children
14   [of Israel at Mount Sinai   ] *vacat*

The Temple Scroll

There are two problems with the title Temple Scroll. The first is that "Scroll" implies that the text is to be found in one scroll alone. However, it is certainly the case that there are two copies of this composition, and there could be more. Nevertheless, most scholars without further clarification frequently refer to the composition's principal exemplar (11QT^a = 11Q19) when they talk about the Temple Scroll. The second problem concerns the term "Temple." Although the first forty-seven columns do indeed concern the temple, both its architecture and what takes place in each part of the temple, there are nineteen columns of text that are concerned with other matters. As a result, some scholars have tried to rename the composition, particularly as a torah of some sort.[1]

It is very difficult to provide a simple label to define the genre of the Temple Scroll. For several scholars it is like the Genesis Apocryphon (*see* Genesis Apocryphon [1QapGen]), another classic example of "rewritten Scripture" (*see* Introduction to Biblical Interpretation and Rewritten Scripture), but that label has developed as an umbrella term for a very wide range of parascriptural compositions and is not precise. It is a form of torah, or more precisely a reworked torah (akin to Deuteronomy itself), not unlike the so-called Reworked Pentateuch (4Q365) (*see* Reworked Pentateuch [4Q158, 4Q364–4Q367]), though it adjusts the order of its sources in a thoroughgoing fashion, except in the explicitly Deuteronomic section (cols. 52–66).

The composition's initial audience in the second century BCE most likely consisted of priests and Levites who had no direct responsibility in the temple but who were trying to promote their views in the period of cultic restoration and reform between the **Maccabean** (*see* 1 and 2 Maccabees) rededication in 164 BCE and the innovative and centralizing practices of **Jonathan Hyrcanus I** (135–104 BCE; cf. m. Ma'aś. Š. 5:15[2]). The King's Law might be directed against any **Has-**

---

1. Unless otherwise stated, all the references in this chapter are to the principal extant witness of the composition, 11QT^a (11Q19), with column and line numbers following those used in *The Dead Sea Scrolls Reader*.

2. See m. Ma'aś. Š. 5:15: "Jonathan the High Priest did away with the Avowal (declaration) concerning the Tithe. He also made an end to the 'Awakeners' and the 'Stunners.' Until his

monean ruler who combined both political and high priestly offices. The scroll would have subsequently found sympathetic hearers among the Qumran group and the wider movement of which it was a part and been understood as directed against Hasmonean king-priests or Herodian rebuilders of the temple.

Narrative Description

Most scholars observe that there are five main sections to the Temple Scroll. The first two are interwoven editorially: one of them concerns the architecture of the temple, working from the holy of holies outward through the temple courts (cols. 2–13, 30–45), a priestly perspective for certain, and the other concerns what takes place in each part of the temple building, the sacrifices for the various festivals, and other ceremonies (cols. 13–29). Third, there is a collection of purity regulations (cols. 45–51), some concerning the temple and holy city and others that are more general. Fourth, there is an extensive section that is a rewritten form of large sections of Deuteronomy 12–23, the laws given to Israel for when they occupy the land (cols. 52–55). Fifth, as part of the rewritten form of Deuteronomy, there is an extensive section (cols. 56–59) expounding the King's Law of Deuteronomy 17:14–20; this section of the expanded King's Law might have had an independent literary existence. These five sections are woven together with redactional comments and provided with a narrative introduction based on the Sinaitic material in Exodus 34 and Deuteronomy 7.

In many parts of the composition the first-person speaker is God himself, making the text into a divine speech; occasionally, the third person of the source reappears so that God speaks about himself in the third person. God addresses Moses directly; 11QT^a 44.5 mentions "Aaron, your brother." Nevertheless, the legislation is intended for all Israel.

There has been much debate about whether the Temple Scroll is a sectarian composition. In several respects, its affinities with the book of Jubilees (*see* The Book of Jubilees) suggest that it was compiled in similar quasi-sectarian circles. It does not contain any of the explicit sectarian terminology of the writings of the *yaḥad* community, part of which eventually came to reside at Qumran, but it does reflect the 364-day calendar in the way that it portrays the festivals, none of which start or finish on a Sabbath (*see* Overview of Early Jewish Literature).

The literary setting of the text appears to be Mount Sinai and the renewal of the covenant there: "which I relate to you on this mountain" (11QT^a 51.7). God talks in the first-person singular to Moses. The whole work is thus presented as a divine speech and perhaps was intended to be construed by the reader as of greater authority than the Torah itself, which in its larger narrative frame consists only of reported, secondhand divine speeches. Its self-presentation goes against those in late Second Temple period Judaism who had notions of dual or ongoing revelation expressed in the Oral Torah.

The composition's setting in Palestinian Judaism of the second century BCE

---

days, the hammer used to smite in Jerusalem. And in his days none needed to inquire about *demai*-produce." —trans. H. Danby

remains unknown, though its affinities with Jubilees, the **Zadokites**, even proto-Sadducean elements of 4QMMT (*see* Some Works of the Law [4QMMT]), and some features of the Damascus Document (*see* Damascus Document) strongly suggest it was compiled and transmitted in such circles. Given that the Levites are explicitly mentioned twenty times in what is extant of 11QT^a, it is likely that some of them were influential in the selection of topics and the overall compilation.

Author/Provenance

Although for the most part God speaks in the first person, one must take it that the first hearers of the text would assume that a third party in some way had transcribed the divine voice. However, unlike in Jubilees 1:5–6,[3] there is no mention of how the transcription was done. The **halakhic** viewpoint in the composition is one that promotes the Levites and shares many perspectives with Jubilees. The compiler probably belonged to similar priestly or Levitical circles in the second century BCE.

The compilation of sources, some possibly much older, seems to belong in the second half of the second century BCE. There is nothing to suggest that in its complete form it comes from anywhere other than Judea, from the same priestly and Levitical circles from which the Qumran sectarians would eventually emerge. Some of its halakhic positions are close to those of 4QMMT.

Date/Occasion

In the first decades of research of the Temple Scroll, there was considerable disagreement about the date of the composition. On the one hand, it was suggested that it might be from the early Second Temple period when its authority might have stood a chance of being widely recognized alongside the other books of the Torah. On the other hand, it was argued that it was put together to influence **Herod the Great**, both as temple-builder and as king. Although it is most probably a second-century BCE compilation, the range of original suggestions remains relevant. It certainly contains much earlier source material, and also the fact that the two most certain copies come from the turn of the era possibly suggests that it was copied out and reproduced then to assert various views that had both similarities with and differences from those of Herod's architects and priests.

Overall, the purpose of the Temple Scroll seems to have been to re-present large sections of the Torah so as to fill a significant gap in the Torah itself. That gap is the absence of a blueprint for the temple. Although the Torah describes

---

3. Jub. 1:5–6: "He said to him: 'Pay attention to all the words that I tell you on this mountain. Write (them) in a book so that their offspring may see that I have not abandoned them because of all the evil they have done in straying from the covenant between me and you that I am making today on Mount Sinai for their offspring. So it will be that when all of these things befall them they will recognize that I have been more faithful than they in all their judgments and in all their actions. They will recognize that I have indeed been with them.'" —trans. Hanneken

and defines the tabernacle (Exod. 25–31, 35–40), there is no direct description of how the temple itself should be designed, built, and used (cf. 1 Chron. 28:1–21). The author of the Temple Scroll addresses that problem directly and in so doing offers, with divine authority, a wide range of halakhic opinions. These halakhot (plural for halakhah) concern the design of the temple; the calendar of 364 days and its festivals (including those for wine, oil, and wood in a 50-day **pentecontad** sequence); purity regulations of considerable stringency; and an adjusted form of Deuteronomy 12–23, which, among other matters, highlights the rights of the Levites and sanctions crucifixion as a capital punishment. Overall in their interpretations of the Torah, the compilers of the Temple Scroll attempted to present a torah that was more coherent, unified, and homogenized, with difficulties in the plain meaning of the text removed.

Which temple does the Temple Scroll refer to? It is neither any actual temple ever built nor the eschatological temple to which a separate reference is made in column 29. Rather, it is the temple that should have been built in Jerusalem by Solomon or the returnees from the exile, but never was. The composition thus highlights problems in the existing temple and its practices.

Text, Language, Sources, and Transmission

The Temple Scroll is written in Hebrew, the language of divine revelation (cf. 4Q464 3.1.8—*karah lishon hakodesh*—"called the holy tongue [language]"). The use of at least one Persian loanword in the descriptions of the temple architecture indicates that some of the source material might come from the fourth century BCE.

As mentioned, there are at least two copies of the Temple Scroll. The principal scroll to which most reference is made is technically designated 11QTemple[a] (11Q19). It was probably discovered in 1956 but remained in a dealer's hands until 1967. It is a beautiful manuscript with sixty-six columns preserved in nineteen thin sheets; at more than eight meters, it is the longest manuscript to have survived from the Qumran caves. It was penned by two scribes with the largest part (cols. 6–66) in a middle **Herodian** formal hand, likely to date from the second half of the first century BCE or a little later; the hand of the first sheet (cols. 1–5) may be a little later, and since part of the content of column 5 overlaps with the top of column 6, it is likely that the original opening sheet was replaced to repair the manuscript. Though the top of the scroll is extensively damaged, where its contents seem to be close to a known scriptural source, they can sometimes be reconstructed to suggest that the original columns contained between twenty-two (cols. 20–22, 42) and twenty-nine (col. 65) lines of writing. A second extensively preserved copy of forty-two fragments also comes from Qumran Cave 11: 11QTemple[b] (11Q20). There are overlaps between the two copies that correspond with parts of 11QT[a] 15–55. 11QT[b] is in a developed Herodian formal hand, probably from the first century CE.

A number of fragments from Cave 4 have also been identified as containing at least part of the composition. First, one fragment of 4Q365a (*formerly* 4QTemple[a]), actually now reassigned to 4Q365, contains text that overlaps substantially

Figure 10. The late Israeli achaeologist Yigael Yadin excavated numerous Qumran sites. Here he examines a portion of the Temple Scroll, a major focus of his scholarship. Supplied by the Estate of Yigael Yadin.

with parts of 11QT^a 38 and 41–42; perhaps it was a source used by the compilers of that part of the Temple Scroll. Second, fragments 6–22 of 4Q524 (4QTemple^b) correspond to some extent with parts of 11QT^a 59–60, 64, and 66. This is a late-second-century BCE manuscript that represents the **Tetragrammaton** with four dots; largely, as reworked parts of Deuteronomy, it is more likely to contain similar source material to the Temple Scroll than to be an early copy of it. Third, three fragments of 11Q21 (11QTemple^c) have been published; seven letters of fragment 1 overlap with 11QT^a 3 and fragment 2 overlaps with 4Q524. A further two fragments are apparently in private hands.

The principal sources of the Temple Scroll are evident in its several sections: a temple source, a festival source, and the book of Deuteronomy. In those sources, several of the Scriptures as known in the Hebrew Bible or its versions are adjusted and rephrased. Notable among these are the books of Exodus, Leviticus, Numbers, and especially Deuteronomy. Parts of the book of Ezekiel, 1 Kings, and 1–2 Chronicles are also reused in the text, though the overall architectural plan of the temple is other than that which appears in those sources. These adjusted scriptural texts are mediated into the Temple Scroll through the sources it reuses. Further adjustments no doubt took place as the sources were redacted together. Some phraseology echoes or is echoed in Jubilees, 4QMMT, and the Damascus Document.

From all that is known of this composition, it survived only in the Qumran collection. This does not make it sectarian, but it might indicate that it was not in wide circulation.

Theology

There are two very significant features of the Temple Scroll. First, it suggests in an extensive fashion how some Jews in the Second Temple period understood the continuing activity of the divine voice. Perhaps God could no longer be heard directly, but through the adaptation of other authoritative texts that were taken as authentic presentations of the divine voice, that divine first-person voice could be presented afresh and earlier texts extended to include new perspectives. This was not oral Torah but an extended written Torah.

Second, the Temple Scroll discloses in several ways how some priestly Jews understood the law. It was a direct gift from God fresh in each new generation, replete with divine consistency and an inner coherence. It was concerned with both space and time. Spatially, life was to be oriented around the temple and the temple city, but it was also concerned with life in the land more generally, with a stringent but graded holiness reflected in various purity laws. Temporally, life was based on a particular annual calendar and festival cycle.

The Temple Scroll is indirectly relevant to several of the theologies of the New Testament. It is an important attestation of ongoing revelation, particularly as Exodus 34 is used as a starting point (John 1:17: "The law indeed was given through Moses; grace and truth came through Jesus Christ"). It stresses the place of the festivals within the calendar, a concern that might be echoed in the way the author of the Fourth Gospel adjusts the festivals christologically. It stresses the purity of the temple, a feature that can help explain Jesus' ministry of healing those considered impure, inasmuch as he may have intended such ministry to facilitate the inclusion of as many people as possible in temple worship (cf. Luke 17:11–19). It stresses the centrality of the law in Jewish life and has undoubtedly contributed to the revived interest in New Testament scholarship concerning the place of the law in the teaching of Jesus and among his early followers, not least Paul.

Reception of the Temple Scroll in the Second Temple Period

The Temple Scroll is not known in any texts outside the Qumran collection; even there it is apparently not cited as an authority. However, some of its halakhic rules and some of its themes are found in other compositions: for example, halakhic similarities concerning animal hides (11QT^a 47.7–15; 4QMMT B 18–23); the compulsory monogamy of the king (11QT^a 57.17–18; CD 5.2); the subordination of the king to the high priest (11QT^a 58.18; 1QSb 4); the prohibition of uncle-niece marriages (11QT^a 66.16–17: CD 5.7–8); the use of crucifixion as a capital punishment (11QT^a 64.8–11; 4QpNahum 3–4 1. 7–8); the oil festival (11QT^a 21.14–15; 4Q394 1–2 5. 4); and the description of some temple structures (11QT^a 37.4; 2Q24 8 8).

As for the New Testament, the Temple Scroll provides evidence that some Jews understood "hanging on a tree" (= crucifixion) as a divinely approved legitimate form of capital punishment. It may be suggested that the appeal to Deuteronomy 21:22 by Paul (Gal. 3:13) and others (Acts 5:30; 10:39) with reference to the death of Jesus indicates that they knew the law in the form that is also preserved in the Temple Scroll (11QT^a 64.8–12a).[4]

As for the Gospels in particular, the placing of the cleansing of the temple and the concern with festivals in the Gospel of John indicate something of a priestly perspective that is similar to that of the Temple Scroll. The concern with the Levites in a few New Testament texts (Luke 10:32; John 1:19; Acts 4:36) might imply, as also for the Temple Scroll, that their interests were an ongoing issue in some circles. The use of David's example to interpret the law is a feature of the halakhah concerning spoils of war in 11QT^a 43.11–15 (using 1 Sam. 30:24–25) and of the Sabbath halakhah of Mark 2:23–26 (1 Sam. 21:1–6).

Much concerning the Temple Scroll remains unclear. Nevertheless it represents a priestly, especially Levitical, set of concerns, several of which can be seen to correspond more or less with those associated with the Sons of Zadok or proto-Sadducees (not the Sadducees of the New Testament or Josephus), some of whom eventually found their way into the Qumran community.

GEORGE J. BROOKE

FURTHER READING

Brooke, George J., ed. *Temple Scroll Studies: Papers Presented at the International Symposium on the Temple Scroll, Manchester, December 1987.* JSOTSup 7. Sheffield: JSOT, 1989.

Crawford, Sidnie White. *The Temple Scroll and Related Texts.* Companion to the Qumran Scrolls 2. Sheffield: Sheffield Academic Press, 2000.

Garcia Martinez, Florentino. "Temple Scroll." In *Encyclopedia of the Dead Sea Scrolls,* edited by L. H. Schiffman and J. C. VanderKam, 2:927–33. 2 vols. New York: Oxford University Press, 2000.

Maier, Johann. *The Temple Scroll: An Introduction, Translation and Commentary.* JSOTSup 34. Sheffield: JSOT, 1985.

Yadin, Yigael. *The Temple Scroll: The Hidden Law of the Dead Sea Sect.* Westminster, Md.: Random House, 1985.

ADVANCED READING

Charlesworth, James H., ed. *The Dead Sea Scrolls: Hebrew, Aramaic, and Greek Texts with English Translations.* Voume 7: *Temple Scroll and Related Documents.* Princeton

---

4. 11QT^a 64:8–12a: "You will hang him on the tree, and he will die. On the evidence of two witnesses and on the evidence of three witnesses, he will be put to death, and they will hang him on the tree. If a man has committed a crime punishable by death, has fled to the midst of the nations, and has cursed my people, even the people of Israel, you will hang him also on the tree, and he will die. Their body must not remain upon the tree all night, but you will bury them that same day, for those hung on the tree are accursed by God and men." —trans. Brooke. Deut. 21:22: "If there is upon a man a sin worthy of the judgment of death then he will be killed and you will hang him upon a tree." Gal. 3:13: "Christ redeemed us from the curse of the law becoming a curse on our behalf; for it has been written, 'Cursed is the one who hangs upon a tree.'" Acts 5:30: "The God of our fathers raised Jesus whom you put to death by hanging on a tree." Acts 10:39: "And we are witnesses to all which he did in the country of Judea and in Jerusalem, whom also they put to death by hanging on a tree."

Theological Seminary DSS Project. Tübingen: Mohr Siebeck and Louisiville: Westminster John Knox Press, 2011. (New editions of all the relevant manuscripts, mostly by Lawrence H. Schiffman, Andrew D. Gross, and Michael C. Rand.)

Najman, Hindy. *Seconding Sinai: The Development of Mosaic Discourse in Second Temple Judaism.* JSJSup 77. Leiden: Brill, 2003.

Parry, Donald W., and Emanuel Tov, eds. *Texts Concerned with Religious Law, Exegetical Texts and Parabiblical Texts.* Vol. 1 of *The Dead Sea Scrolls Reader.* 2nd edition revised and expanded. Leiden: Brill, 2014 (pp. 622-733).

Qimron, Elisha. *The Dead Sea Scrolls: The Hebrew Writings,* xxxiv–xxxviii, 137–207. Jerusalem: Yad Ben-Zvi, 2010.

Schiffman, Lawrence H. *The Courtyards of the House of the Lord: Studies on the Temple Scroll.* Edited by F. Garcia Martinez. STDJ 75. Leiden: Brill, 2008.

Swanson, Dwight D. *The Temple Scroll and the Bible: The Methodology of 11QT.* STDJ 14. Leiden: Brill, 1995.

Wacholder, Ben-Zion. *The Dawn of Qumran: The Sectarian Torah and the Teacher of Righteousness.* HUCM 8. Cincinnati, Ohio: Hebrew Union College Press, 1983.

Wise, Michael O. *A Critical Study of the Temple Scroll from Qumran Cave 11.* SAOC 49. Chicago: Oriental Institute of the University of Chicago, 1990.

Yadin, Yigael. *The Temple Scroll.* 3 vols. Jerusalem: Israel Exploration Society, Institute of Archaeology of the Hebrew University of Jerusalem, Shrine of the Book, 1983.

4.9 *from* Temple Scroll (11Q19–20)

Column 2.2–12: the extant start of the scroll[a]

2 [Behold, I will clear away before you] the A[morites, the Canaanites,]
3 [the Hittites, the Girgashite]s, the Pe[rizzites, the Hivites, and]
4 [the Jebusites. Take] care not to make a cove[nant with the inhabitants of the land]
5 [to which you are] going or it will become a sn[are among you.]
6 [   ] You will tear down their [alta]rs, [and break their] pillars,
7 [and] cut down their [sacred poles, and] the images of [their] go[ds]
8 [you will burn with fire.] Do [n]ot covet silver and gold, whi[ch is on them.]
9 [. . .] You will [not] take of it, and you will not bri[ng an abominable thing]
10 [into your house or you will be] set apart for destruction like it; you must utterly dete[st and abhor it;]
11 [for] it is set apart for destruction. And you will worship no [other] go[d, for]
12 [your God] is a jealous God.

Column 7.10–13: design for the holy of holies[b]

10   ] . . . its width. And two cherubim . . . [
11   ] . . . the end—the second, spreading their wings [
12   ] . . . above the ark, and their faces, one [to
13   ]   And you will m[a]ke a curtain of gold [

Column 19.11–16: New Wine Festival[c]

11 [And] you will count from the day that you brought the new grain offering to the Lo[rd,]

a. Cf. Exod. 34:10–16; Deut. 7:25–26.
b. The command to make the cherubim and the veil, apparently omitting the table and lampstand at this stage; cf. Exod. 25:17–20; 1 Kings 8:7; 2 Chron. 5:8.
c. Fifty days after Shebuot; there are significant overlaps in this column with 11QT[b] 3–4 that are indicated by underlining.

Translation by George J. Brooke. Whereas Yadin often attempted to provide echoes of the RSV in his English translations, I have tried to reflect some of the idioms of the NRSV where the Temple Scroll depends closely on a scriptural text; I have based most of my translations on Qimron's 2010 edition of the text.

12 [th]e <u>bread of the firstfruits, seven weeks</u>; seven complete Sabbaths
13 [there will be, un]til the day after the <u>seventh</u> Sabbath: <u>you will count fifty</u> days.
14 Then <u>you w</u>[ill bring] new wine for a drink offering, four hins from all the tribes of <u>Israel</u>,
15 <u>a third of a hin for</u> each tribe; and they will offer with the {this}[a] wine on that day
16 [a burnt offering] <u>to the Lord twelve r</u>[a]<u>ms, all</u> the heads of the thousands of Israel . . .

Column 21.12–16: New Oil Festival[b]

12 And [you wi]ll count from <u>that</u> day <u>on seven weeks—seven</u> times, nine
13 and forty days, seven complete Sabbaths there will be—until the <u>morrow of the seventh</u>
14 <u>Sabbath</u> you will count fifty days. Then you will offer new oil from the dwellings
15 of the [tr]ibes of the peo[ple of Is]<u>rael, half a hin</u> from each tribe, newly pressed oil.
16 [They are to offer the first] oil on the altar of the burnt <u>offering, firstfruits</u> before the Lord . . .

Column 29.2–10: an editorial seam[c]

2 These [are the appointed festivals of the Lord, holy convocations (Lev. 23:37) that you will observe for all the people of Is]rael,
3 for burnt offerings and [grain offerings, sacrifices and drink offerings according to the ordinance] in the house upon which I [will cause]
4 my name [to dwell. And they will offer in it] burnt offerings, [day] by day, according to the law of this ordinance,
5 continually from the people of Israel, besides their freewill offerings for all their offerings,
6 for all their drink offerings and all their gifts that they will bring to me that th[ey] may be accepted.
7 And I will accept them, and they will be my people, and I will be theirs forever, and I will dwell

a. The "{this}" inserted here is the translator's suggested reconstruction, i.e. "this" = "new wine" from line 14.

b. Fifty days after the New Wine; again with overlaps with 11QT[b] 5, which are indicated by underlining.

c. From line 7 this is a redactional section looking forward to the eschatological sanctuary to be created by God himself, implying that the Temple Scroll itself contains the design for the temple that should have been built by Israel but never was; cf. Ezek. 37:23; Exod. 15:17 (cited in 4Q174); Lev. 26:42; Jub. 1:17–18.

8   with them forever and ever. And I will consecrate my [t]emple by my glory, on which I will settle

9   my glory, until the day of creation on which I will create my temple

10 and establish it for myself for all times, according to the covenant that I have made with Jacob at Bethel.

Column 39.11–16: temple courtyard architecture[a]

11   And the names of the gates of this court will be after the nam[es]

12 of the people of Is[r]ael: Simeon, Levi, and Judah, in the east; Reuben, Joseph, and Benjamin, to the south;

13 Issachar, Zebulun, and Gad, to the west; Dan, Naphtali, and Asher, to the north. And between the gates

14 the measure: from the northeastern corner to the gate of Simeon, ninety-nine cubits, and the gate (itself)

15 twenty-eight cubits; and from {Simeon} this gate to the gate [   ] of Levi, ninety-nine

16 cubits, and the gate twenty-eight cubits; and from the gate of Levi to the gate of Judah

Column 45.7–14: part of the purity laws[b]

7   And if a m[an] has a nocturnal emission, he will not enter into

8   any part of the temple until [he will com]plete three days. And he will wash his clothes and bathe

9   on the first day, and on the third day he will wash his clothes {and bathe} and when the sun has set, afterward

10 he may come within the temple. And they will not come into my temple in their soiled uncleanness and defile it.

11 And if a man lies with his wife and has an emission of semen, he will not come into any part of the city of

12 the temple, where I will settle my name, for three days.   No blind man

13 will enter it all their days, so that they will not defile the city in which I dwell;

14 for I, the Lord, dwell among the people of Israel forever and ever.

Column 47.7–13: further purity regulations, concerning animal hides[c]

7   No skin of any clean animal that they will slaughter

a. Note the names and order of the tribes, with Levi in the center in the east; cf. 44.3–45.2.

b. Cf. Deut. 23:11–12; Lev. 15:18; 2 Sam. 5:8 (used in 1QM 7.4–5; 1QSa 2.4–11); some minor overlaps with 11QT[b] 11–12, which are indicated by underlining.

c. Cf. 4QMMT B 27–35.

8   within their own cities will they bring into it; for in their own cities they may do

9   with them their work for all their needs. But into the city of my temple they will not bring (them),

10   for their cleanness is according to their flesh. And you will not defile the city in the midst of which

11   I settle my name and my temple; but in the skins that they will slaughter

12   in the temple, in them they will bring their wine and their oil and all

13   their foodstuffs to my temple city. And they will not defile my temple with the skins of

14   their abominable offerings that they will sacrifice in their land.

Column 50.10–19: more purity regulations, concerning a mother carrying a dead fetus[a]

10   And if <u>a woman</u> is pregnant, and the child dies in her womb, all the days for which

11   it is dead inside her, she is <u>unclean like a grave</u>; and every house that she comes into is unclean,

12   and all its vessels, for seven days. And anyone who touches it will be unclean until the evening; and if

13   he enters inside the house with her, he will be unclean seven days. And he will wash his clothes

14   and bathe himself on the first day; and on the third day he will sprinkle and wash his clothes and bathe himself;

15   and on the seventh day he will sprinkle for the second time and wash his clothes and bathe himself, and when the sun sets

16   he will become clean.   <u>And to all the vessels, clothes and skins and all</u>

17   <u>work of goat('s hair)</u> you will do according to the ordinance of this law. And all

18   earthen vessels will be broken, for they are unclean and cannot <u>become</u> <u>clean</u> again

19   forever.

Column 56.3–10: the authority of priestly law[b]

3   And you will do according to the law that they declare to you and according to what

4   they say to you from the book of the law and declare to you truly

5   from that place on which I will choose to settle my name; and you will be careful to do

---

a. (Cf. Num. 19:14–22; Exod. 19:10; Lev. 11:33; some overlaps with 11QT[b] 14, which are indicated by underlining.)

b. (Cf. Deut. 17:9–13; the identity of the "book of the law" is disputed.)

6   according to all that they instruct you; according to the decision that they pronounce to you,

7   you will do; you will not turn aside from the law that they declare to you, either to the right

8   or to the left. The man who does not obey and presumes to

9   disobey the priest appointed to minister there before me, or the

10   judge, that man will die; so you will purge the evil from Israel.

Column 57.7–19: part of the King's Law[a]

7   And all

8   the selected whom he will choose will be men of truth, God-fearing,

9   hating unjust gain and mighty men for war, and they will always be with him,

10   day and night, and they will protect him from every sinful thing

11   and from a foreign people, lest he be taken by them. And the twelve

12   leaders of his people (will be) with him, and from the priests twelve, and from the Levites

13   twelve who will sit together with him for judgment,

14   and for the law. His heart should not be lifted up above them nor should he do anything

15   by any counsel apart from them.   And he will not take a wife from all

16   the daughters of the nations, but from his father's house he will take for himself a wife,

17   from his father's family. And he will not take additionally another wife, for

18   she alone will be with him all the days of her life. But should she die, he may take

19   for himself another from his father's house, from his family.

Column 59.13–21: the closing section of the King's Law[b]

13   And as for the king

14   whose heart and eyes stray lustfully from my commandments, there will be not be found anybody for him to sit on the throne

15   of his fathers all the days, for I will permanently cut off his descendants forever from ruling over Israel.

16   But if he will walk in my statutes, and will observe my commandments, and will do

17   what is right and good in my sight, <u>one of his sons will not be cut off from sitting</u> on the throne of the kingdom of

a. Combining idioms from several sections of the narratives of the historical books with some phraseology from the Torah.

b. Cf. Num. 15:39; Jer. 33:17–18; Deut. 28:7, 13; overlaps with 4Q524 are underlined.

18   Israel forever, and I will be with him, and I will deliver him from the hand of those who hate him, and from the hand

19   of those who would seek to take his life. And <u>I will give up all his enemies before him, and he will</u> rule over them

20   according to his pleasure, and they will not rule over him, and I will make him at the top, and at the bottom, the head,

21   and not the tail, so that he may continue <u>for many days in his kingdom, he and his sons after</u> him.

Column 60.6–15: rules that appear to favor the Levites[a]

6   And to the Levites: one-tenth of the grain and the wine and the oil which

7   they have first dedicated to me, and the shoulder from those sacrificing a sacrifice, and the tribute from

8   the booty and from the spoil and from the hunt of fowl and of beasts and of fishes, one-hundredth;

9   and from the young pigeons and from the tithe of the honey, one-fiftieth. But to the priests:

10   one-hundredth of the young pigeons, for them I have chosen from all your tribes

11   to minister before me and serve and pronounce blessings in my name, he and all his sons always.

12   And if a Levite leaves any of your towns out of all Israel, where

13   he resides—and he may come whenever he wishes—for the place upon which I will choose to settle

14   my name, then he may serve like all his brother-Levites who stand there before me. They will have equal portions

15   to eat, besides what is received from the sale of family possessions.

Column 63.10–15: the beautiful captive woman[b]

10   When you go out to war against your enemies, and I hand them over to you, and you take them captive,

11   suppose you see among the captives a beautiful woman whom you desire and want to marry,

12   and so you bring her home to your house: you will shave her head and pare her nails, and you will discard

13   her captive's garb, and she will remain in your house, mourning for her father and her mother a full

14   month. After that you may go into her and be her husband, and she will be your wife. But she will not touch your pure things for

a. Cf. Deut. 18:3–8; Num. 18:8–11; Neh. 10:38; 13:5; Num. 31:30.
b. Cf. Deut. 21:10–13.

15 seven years, and she will not eat a peace offering sacrifice until seven years pass; afterward she may eat.

Column 64.6–12: the crimes punishable by crucifixion[a]

6   If

7 a man <u>informs against my people</u>, and delivers my people up to a foreign nation, and does harm to my people,

8 you will hang him on the tree, and he will die. On the evidence of two witnesses and on <u>the evidence of three witnesses</u>

9 he will be put to death, and they will hang him on the tree.   If a man has committed a crime punishable by death, and has fled to

10 the midst of the nations, and has cursed <u>my people, even the people of Israel</u>, you will hang him also on the tree,

11 and he will die. And their body must not remain upon the tree all night, but you will bury them that same day, for

12 those hung on the tree are accursed by God and men. You must not defile the land that I am giving you for possession.

Column 66.8–17: rape and incest[b]

8   If a man seduces a

9 virgin who is not engaged, but is fit for him according to the law, and he lies with her

10 and is caught in the act, then the <u>man who lay with her</u> will give fifty shekels of silver to the young woman's father, and she will become his

11 wife. Because he violated her, he will not be permitted to divorce her <u>as long as</u> he lives. A man will not take

12 <u>his father's</u> wife, nor will he uncover his father's skirt. A man will not take

13 <u>his brother's</u> wife, nor will he uncover his brother's skirt, whether it his father's son or <u>his mother's son</u>, for this is impurity.

14 A man will not take his sister, his father's daughter, or his mother's daughter, for this is an abomination. A

15 man <u>will not take</u> his father's sister or his mother's sister, for <u>it is wickedness</u>. A man

16 will not take

17 <u>his brother's daughter</u> or his sister's daughter, for it is an abomination.

a. Cf. Deut. 21:22–23; Lev. 19:16; Exod. 22:27; overlaps with 4Q524 are underlined.

b. Cf. Deut. 22:29; 23:1; Lev. 18:12–13; 20:13–14, 17, 21; CD 5.7–8; overlaps with 4Q524 are underlined.

The Writings of Philo of Alexandria

Philo of **Alexandria** was a Jewish scholar and philosopher who lived his entire life in Alexandria in Egypt (*see* Map of the Roman Empire in the First Century CE, p. 41). Alexandria was founded by Alexander the Great in 331 BCE. It was famous for its great Pharos lighthouse, possibly the first of its kind. During the first century CE, it was a large, thriving metropolis, second only to Rome in population. It was a center of scholarship and included one of the great libraries of the ancient world. It was home not only to Philo but also, in later generations, to the philosopher Plotinus and church fathers Clement of Alexandria, Origen, and Athanasius, among many others.

The exact dates of Philo's life are not known, but it probably spanned the period of 20/15 BCE to 45/50 CE. Hence, he was a contemporary of both Jesus of Nazareth and Paul the apostle. There is little reason, however, to presume that Paul and Philo knew each other or that Philo had any knowledge of the writings now associated with Paul or any other New Testament authors, or vice versa. This does not mean that there are no similarities or even influences between the tendencies and traditions that can be found in the works of Philo and in early Christian literature. Several scholars have used the writings of Philo to illuminate theological concepts found in the writings of the early Christians, and to explain debates and conflicts witnessed in the New Testament. Apart from this alignment with New Testament writings, Philo is also considered a very important witness to the kind of **Diaspora** Judaism that flourished in Egypt in the first century CE.

Philo's Life and Works

Philo's Life

Philo came from a very rich and influential family, and thus belonged to the elite strata of the Jewish communities in Alexandria. It is possible that the family had ties to the **Hasmonean** dynasty in Palestine. His brother, Alexander Lysimachus, was an alabarch in Alexandria, an office most probably concerned with the administration of paying of taxes and customs in the harbor of Alexandria. Josephus (*see* Introduction to Flavius Josephus) says that Alexander "surpassed all his fellow citizens both in ancestry and in wealth" (*Antiquities* 20.100; see *Jewish Antiquities*). One of Alexander Lysimachus's sons, Marcus Julius Alexander, was married to Berenice, the daughter of Agrippa I (*Antiquities* 19.277: "And Marcus Julius Alexander, the son of Alexander the Alabarch of Egypt, married Agrippa's daughter Bernice. Upon the death of Marcus, who had taken her as a virgin, Agrippa gave her to his brother Herod"). However, another son, Tiberius Julius Alexander, is mentioned more often in our sources. Tiberius had a great career in the service of the Romans. In ca. 46–48 CE he was procurator of Judea (*Antiquities* 20.100; *War* 2.220; see *Jewish War*), and in ca. 66–70 CE he was **prefect** of Egypt (*see War* 2.309, 492–98). He also participated actively in the campaigns against Jerusalem in 66–70 CE (*War* 5.45–46; 6.237). Two of Philo's works (*Prov.* and *Anim.*) can be read as discussions with his nephew Tiberius. Sometime during the reign of Emperor Caligula in 37–41 CE, Alexander was imprisoned in Rome during a period of racial tensions in Alexandria. Some suggest that this may have been part of the reason for Philo's embassy to Gaius Caligula in Rome in 38 CE. Apart from this information, very little is known about Philo's closest family, such as his wife or possible children.

As a member of the Jewish elite citizenry of Alexandria, Philo received a thorough Jewish upbringing and education, while at the same time he was introduced to the various aspects of the Greco-Roman culture prevalent during this time. His writings reveal that he was thoroughly acquainted with the Jewish political and religious institutions of the city. It is highly likely that he participated in the Greco-Roman educational institutions, such as the **gymnasium**, and was introduced to Greek philosophy. His attitudes toward the Greco-Roman cultural institutions of Alexandria seem to have been rather friendly and accepting, while he still retained his Jewish identity. According to several sayings in his writings, he knew, through personal experience, various forms of the cultural activities of the city. He describes competitions of wrestling and boxing (*Prob.* 26) as well as horse races (cf. Eusebius, *Praeparatio evangelica* 7.14, 58 [*Hypoth.*]), and it is obvious that he frequented the theater and attended concerts (*Ebr.* 177; *Prob.* 141). In *Allegorical Law* 3.155, he states that he participated several times in friendly gatherings in the city. The attitude of Philo toward the Greco-Roman culture can be illustrated further by his view of the encyclical education, the *encyclia paideia*. It appears that for Philo these institutions represented an issue of *adiaphora*, that is, they were in and of themselves neither good nor bad (cf. *Congr.* 35; *Fug.* 212–13). But according to Philo, they were in fact only preliminary to the study of the real and genuine philosophy represented by the law, that is, the Jewish Torah. But Philo's attitudes toward the Greco-Roman culture are not unhesitatingly positive; he warns against getting into situations in which one would be in danger of losing one's Jewish identity. He offers counsel against assimilating too much into the Greco-Roman culture, and offers some stern admonitions against particular settings and aspects that might induce apostasy from the Jewish faith and communities (e.g., *Spec.* 3.315–18).

It is most plausible that Philo held official positions in the city; for example, in 40/41 CE he was appointed the leader of a Jewish delegation to the Emperor

Gaius Caligula in Rome.[1] Philo describes the work of the delegation and its task before Caligula in his *On the Embassy to Gaius*. It is, however, not obvious what kind of official office he held or for how long. Some scholars suggest that his duties were of a judicial character, but there is no definitive evidence to support this suggestion. An autobiographical section in *Special Laws* 3.1–6 suggests that Philo first had a rather long period in his life in which he was primarily concerned with his philosophy and writing; later he was reluctantly drawn into the political life and the work of the Jewish community in Alexandria. This is a possible interpretation, but the function of *Special Laws* 3.1–6 might also have been to serve as an expression of his frustration over the political work compared with his activities as a philosopher, a task in which he had much more delight (cf. also *Spec.* 2.44).

Philo's Works

The literary production of Philo is impressive. About forty of his works are still extant, but indications in his own works, as well as remarks by some of the church fathers, suggest that he must have written at least twenty additional titles. Following the classification of his works, as set forth by Peder Borgen,[2] Philo's works can be grouped in the categories that follow.

Exposition of the Law of Moses

The "exposition of the law of Moses" is a not a label used by Philo, but one established by scholars in recent times, constituting a comprehensive category that comprises several treatises representing Philo's expositions of the Law (Torah): *On the Creation of the World (Opif.*; see *On the Creation of the World); On the Life of Abraham (Abr.); On the Life of Joseph (Ios.); On the Decalogue (Decal.*; see *On the Decalogue); On the Special Laws* 1–4 *(Spec.* 1–4); *On the Virtues (Virt.); On Rewards and Punishments (Praem.).* In addition, some scholars also place *On the Life of Moses* 1–2 *(Mos.* 1–2; see *On the Life of Moses)* in this group.

The Exegetical Commentaries: Questions and Answers

This category of commentary may have developed from within the setting of Philo's teaching in which he incorporated the process of "question and answer." The writings exhibit how he may have dealt with the biblical text, in this instance, the books of Genesis and Exodus.

Questions and Answers on Genesis 1–2 *(QG* 1–2)
Questions and Answers on Exodus 1–2 *(QE* 1–2)

---

1. Caligula succeeded Tiberius as emperor in 31 CE. For the first two years of his reign, things went quite well until he fell ill in 37 CE. It is unclear what he suffered from, but upon his recovery, he appears to have lost his mental faculties, as his irrational behavior intensified for the next few years. It is believed that because of his insane behavior in 41 CE Caligula was assassinated by members of the Praetorian Guard; they appointed Claudius as emperor in his place.

2. Peder Borgen, "Philo of Alexandria: A Critical and Synthetical Survey of Research since World War II," *ANRW* 33.1:117–18.

The Allegorical Commentaries

This group of writings consists of eighteen titles and twenty-one books; the individual volumes focus on a specific biblical text, but often digress from it in a way sometimes quite frustrating to the uninformed reader.

The Allegorical Laws 1–3 (Leg. 1–3)	Genesis 2:1–17; 2:18–3:1; 3:8b–19
On the Cherubim (Cher.)	Genesis 3:24–4:1
On the Sacrifices of Abel and Cain (Sacr.)	Genesis 4:2–4
That the Worse Attacks the Better (Det.)	Genesis 4:8–15
On the Posterity and Exile of Cain (Post.)	Genesis 4:16–25
On the Giants (Gig.) (see On the Giants)	Genesis 6:1–4a
On the Unchangeableness of God (Deus)	Genesis 6:4b–12
On Agriculture (Agr.)	Genesis 9:20–21
On Noah's Work as a Planter (Plant.)	Genesis 9:20–21
On Drunkenness (Ebr.)	Genesis 9:20–21
On Sobriety (Sobr.)	Genesis 9:24–27
On the Confusion of Tongues (Conf.)	Genesis 11:1–9
On the Migration of Abraham (Migr.)	Genesis 12:1–6
Who Is the Heir of Divine Things? (Her.)	Genesis 15:2–18
On the Preliminary Studies (Congr.)	Genesis 16:1–15
On Flight and Finding (Fug.)	Genesis 16:6b–14
On the Change of Names (Mut.)	Genesis 17:1–5, 16–22
On Dreams 1–2 (Somn. 1–2)	Genesis 37:8–11; 40:9–11, 16–17; 41:17–24

Pentateuchal Principles Applied to Contemporary Issues and Events

Writings in which pentateuchal material is applied to socioreligious factors in the Jewish community:

> *On the Contemplative Life (Contempl.)* Although fragmentary, this work was probably a part of an apology for the Jews, addressed to Gentiles. It should be followed by the remains of what is now called *The Hypothetica (Hypoth.)*, a work that also should be categorized as apologetic, written for a Gentile audience.

Writings in which pentateuchal principles are applied to, or developed in, dialogue with contemporary philosophical issues and religious phenomena:

> *That Every Good Person Is Free (Prob.)* This work is a treatise in which Philo attempts to show that every virtuous man is free.
>
> *On the Eternity of the World (Aet.)* Philo argues, in opposition to the Stoics, that the world is uncreated and indestructible.
>
> *On Providence 1–2 (Prov. 1–2)* This work is a dialogue between Philo and Alexander his nephew in which he argues that God is providential in his concern for the world.
>
> *On Animals (Anim.)* Philo discusses the animals used for sacrifice and the varieties of sacrifices.

Writings in which pentateuchal principles are applied to specific historical events and persons.

> *Against Flaccus (Flacc.)* and *On the Embassy to Gaius (Legat.)* These are the more historical treatises of Philo. These writings from a later period in his life demonstrate how Philo considered the situation of the Jews in the Diaspora and also the role of Israel.

Philo as an Exegete

As can be gathered from the list of texts above, Philo extensively examined the Jewish Scriptures in his work. Furthermore, his main scriptural source is the Pentateuch—the Jewish Torah—with only a few scattered references to other books from the Hebrew Bible included in his writings. All this amounts to the fact that Philo should be considered and read as an exegete of Scripture, particularly an exegete of the laws of Moses. However, the scholarly consensus suggests that Philo knew little Hebrew; hence his version of the Jewish Scriptures was the Greek version(s), what we now have come to call the Septuagint (LXX; *see* Overview of Early Jewish Literature). In *On the Life of Moses* 2.25–45, Philo provides his version of the legend of the origin of the Septuagint in very much the same manner as we find it in the Letter of Aristeas (*see* Letter of Aristeas). To Philo, the Pentateuch is the inspired word of God, which was given to the Jews as his only people, thus representing the constitution of Israel as the people of God.

The most prominent exegetical method in Philo's works, and the one for which he is most famous, is the allegorical method. While most of the corpus of his writings contains allegories and allegorical interpretations of the Jewish Scriptures, they are especially prominent in his so-called allegorical commentaries. That does not mean, however, that Philo always allegorized. He interprets and most often offers a literal understanding of the texts, but on occasion he uses allegory to discover the deeper or symbolic meaning of the biblical text. Living in Alexandria, Philo seems to have been an exegete among other exegetes, and he reveals knowledge of both literalists and allegorists. For his work, he seems to often prefer the middle way (*Migr.* 89–94).

Dating of Philo's Works

Various hypotheses concerning the dating of Philo's works have been set forth, but none seem to have gained a general consensus. Too many unknowns exist in his life to provide us with enough information to make a chronology of his works. Some books, however, can be dated with greater exactness than others: *Against Flaccus* and *On the Embassy to Gaius* must be later than the historical events they deal with. Hence they are probably among his later works. But scholars do not agree on the question of whether his more philosophical works are from his younger years, or if they too are to be placed within the later period of his life.

Sources of Philo's Works

The question of Philo's traditions or sources is complicated. Scholars have generally failed to agree on the origin of the traditions in his work. This fact is to a great extent due to the nature of Philo's writings: they take the form of expositions. As expositions they consist of exegetical paraphrases of words and phrases from the pentateuchal texts together with other words and phrases. Philo himself characterizes his method in his work on Moses' life: "I . . . tell the story of Moses as I have learned it from the sacred books, the wonderful monuments of his wisdom that he has left behind, and from some of the elders of the nation; for I always interwove what I was told with what I read" (*Mos.* 1.4).

Readers and Transmitters of Philo's Texts

Philo likely wrote primarily for his fellow Jews. Some scholars have suggested, however, that *The Expositio* was written for Gentile readers. Others have argued that we can hardly presuppose a Gentile readership at all, and that all of Philo's works were written for a Jewish audience. Nonetheless, the works belonging to *The Expositio*, as well as his more apologetic works, which may be considered his more accessible writing, may have been written for Jews on the fringe of the Jewish communities and even for interested Gentiles. The more advanced and more difficult exegetical and allegorical commentaries were presumably written for the insiders, those well initiated into the Judaism as taught by Philo. In general, one might say that he wrote primarily for his fellow Jews to strengthen them to live as loyal Jews in the Greco-Roman culture of Alexandria. In this way he might try to strengthen the Jewish identity of his readers, while at the same time be looked favorably upon by any Gentiles who would encounter his works. Philo's works can hardly be called missionary, but he was nevertheless very favorable toward the proselytes (cf. *Spec.* 1.51–53; *Virt.* 102–3).

Due to various circumstances, the Jewish communities did not keep and transmit Philo's writings through the first centuries CE; rather, the transmission of his works is primarily due to Christian readers and theologians. Most of the Greek manuscripts preserved are from the tenth to fourteenth centuries CE, but a few papyri have been discovered from the third century. Some of Philo's works are preserved only in an ancient Armenian translation such as *Questions and Answers on Genesis, Questions and Answers on Exodus, On Providence* 1–2, and *On Animals.*

Theology

Philo was a Jew, as is evidenced by a very Jewish profile in all his works. But at the same time, in order to understand his works, the topics he dealt with, and his emphases, we have to take into consideration the fact that he lived in the Diaspora, in the Greco-Roman culture of Alexandria, and not in Palestine.

We know that Philo visited Jerusalem at least once in his life (*Prob.* 64), but in general, we have very little knowledge of his possible contact with Palestinian Judaism. As mentioned previously, he apparently did not read Hebrew, and his social location in Alexandria makes him first of all a representative of Diaspora Judaism. Scholars debate, however, how representative he was of Diaspora Judaism in general. One must examine his predecessors (e.g., Aristobulus), alongside other works like the Letter of Aristeas and the Wisdom of Solomon (*see* Wisdom of Solomon) when considering Philo's theology in context.

As an expositor of the Jewish Scriptures, especially the Torah, Philo deals with the constitutive and foundational documents of Judaism. The Jewish monotheistic concepts of God, as well as other descriptions of God in the Jewish Scriptures, are very important to him. The monotheistic aspect of God is emphasized by various expressions, although not all of them are present in the Jewish Scriptures. Philo knows that according to Exodus 3:14 the name of God was revealed to Moses by the expression "I am who I am" (*Somn.* 1.231; *Mut.* 11; *Det.* 160; *Mos.* 1.75). The expression "God is one" is found several times in his writings (e.g., *Opif.* 100, 171; *Leg.* 3.105; *Sacr.* 190; *Post.* 154), and he is stern in his warnings to his fellow Jews not to depart from this belief: "Let us engrave deep in our hearts this as the first and most sacred of commandments, to acknowledge and honor one God who is above all, and may the idea that gods are many never reach the ears of the man whose rule of life is to seek truth in purity and guilelessness" (*Decal.* 65; cf. *Spec.* 1.54–56). On the other hand, Philo also emphasizes that God is unnamable: no name whatsoever can properly be assigned to him (*Mos.* 1.75) and the names given are given only by license of language. Philo often prefers to characterize God as the "one who really is" (*Congr.* 52; *Ebr.* 83) or the "really existing and true God" (*Decal.* 8), along with other similar expressions probably influenced by contemporary philosophy. In emphasizing that God is unnamable, Philo is advocating a kind of negative theology (*Somn.* 1.67; *Leg.* 6). In addition to his Jewish influences, one can find many aspects in Philo's expositions of God that are influenced by his Greco-Roman environment. God is depicted as the transcendent one, but he also has powers around him that are personifications of the attributes of God.

Additionally, Philo has a very elaborate *Logos* theology. For Philo, *Logos* can be described as the image of God; it is God's force in the world as well as his instrument in creation, for example. It is not possible to set Philo's doctrine of *Logos* in a simple formula. *Logos* is like the beams of the sun: it derives from God, it belongs to God, it makes humanity realize that God exists, and it is thus important in leading the human soul to God. Philo also talks of God's regal power (*kyrios; Abr.* 121; *Conf.* 137) and creative power (*theos*). In this way, Philo manages to keep intact the monotheism of the one God by contending that the relationship of God to his world is mediated by supreme beings that are apprehensible, while God himself remains transcendent. Furthermore, he manages to give an explanation to some of the names used in the Old Testament for God. In all this exposition, scholars find influences from both Judaism (wisdom) and **Platonism, Stoicism**, and **Pythagorean** philosophy.

Philo's view of humanity might be described as heavily influenced by Greek philosophy. In his writings, Philo presents his views on God as a Creator and the creation. God is the Creator of the world, and the human being is the perfect piece of all his creations. However, Platonic aspects are present in many ways; for instance, when God created the visible world, he made it in accordance to the eternal model, present in God's mind, also called the *Logos* of God (*Opif.* 25.29–35). God created the model, the world of the ideas, as an incorporeal and invisible world. Then the visible world was made after the pattern of the incorporeal, and the crown of all creation is the human (*Opif.* 65–88). According to Genesis 1:26,[3]

---

3. Gen. 1:26: "Then God said, 'Let us make humankind in our image, according to our

the human was created in the image of God; for Philo, this does not have to do with human form, but with the human mind, the sovereign element of the human soul that was made after the patterns of the Mind of the universe as an archetype.

The Platonic influence on Philo is also evident when he suggests that the creation of the human mentioned in Genesis 1:27 ("So God created human-kind in his image, in the image of God he created them; male and female he created them"—NRSV) and the one of Genesis 2:7 ("then the Lord God formed man from the dust of the ground, and breathed into his nostrils the breath of life; and the man became a living being"—NRSV) concern the creation of two different humans. The first was an incorporeal ideal human, the second the corporeal molded human, created according to the ideal human of Genesis 1:27 (*Leg.* 1.31ff.). Furthermore, the soul of a human is the higher part of the being, the one most nearly akin to heaven, and the purest thing (*Decal.* 134). The duality of body and soul is one of the cornerstones of Philo's anthropology.

The soul is not, however, at home in its human body. It is as if traveling in a foreign country; it is only to sojourn there (*Her.* 267; *Conf.* 77–78). At death, the soul is set free from the bonds of the flesh (*Virt.* 78); released from the vessel of the body (*Migr.* 197), it is free to enter the truly holy place (*Migr.* 104) and see the Existent One (*Migr.* 170). This process of releasing the soul from the body is to begin early in this life, while still residing in the body; releasing the soul is carried out by mastering the bodily impulses, by loosening the ties to the impulses of the body, and thus being able to see the bright light; the goal is the vision of God. Education plays an important role in this development.

According to Philo, the soul can also be divided into several parts. One division in which the soul is described as two-partite is influenced by Stoic philosophy. The soul is spoken of as having two parts: the rational and the irrational (*Her.* 55; *Congr.* 25–31). The rational part is immortal; the irrational part is mortal. The irrational part is the dwelling place of the passions, which fight against the reasoning part. The real conflict in humans is between the rational and irrational parts of the soul. However, human beings tied to the body, as they are, have to comply with the bodily requirements. The danger involved in this situation must be overcome by means of the virtues. Important to his presentation here is the role of education and the role of philosophy in education. As Judaism is the highest philosophy to Philo, it also demonstrates the prerogatives of those reared in Judaism. In fact, according to Philo, the other philosophers have learned their doctrines from Moses. Hence, according to his view, when Philo is interpreting the law with the help of philosophy he is only fleshing out what is there already in the teachings of Moses.

Philo is thus to be considered as a person very much assimilated to the culture of his time and place, but not totally integrated: he is still a Torah-observing Jew. The Jewish scholar Samuel Sandmel says that "in Philo, the Greek philosophical tradition [was] absorbed to the maximum; on the other hand, Philo was as loyal

---

likeness; and let them have dominion over the fish of the sea, and over the birds of the air, and over the cattle, and over all the wild animals of the earth, and over every creeping thing that creeps upon the earth.'"

to Judaism as any personality in the age with which we deal, and, indeed as any personality in subsequent times."[4]

Reception of Philo of Alexandria in the Second Temple Period

Philo's writings, ideas, and expositions are important for readers of the New Testament. While we are not able to detect any direct quotations from Philo in the various books of the New Testament, it is nevertheless possible—and even plausible—that several of its authors had in some way been acquainted with some of his teachings. The New Testament may also be profitably read in light of some of the traditions and conflicts that are mirrored in Philo's works.

The New Testament writings considered to reveal the clearest evidence of some influence from Philo are the book of Hebrews and the Gospel of John. In the latter, one might think about the use of *Logos* in the Johannine prologue (1:1–18). In reading Hebrews, many have compared its teaching about the heavenly sanctuary (8:1–5; 9:11–14; 11:16) with similar issues in the works of Philo. But he may also be profitably drawn on when investigating aspects and issues inherent in several of the Pauline letters and other New Testament writings.

These influences might be sought in language and genres; in modes of interpretation; in theological issues such as the doctrine of God, humanity, and the heavenly realms; in anthropology; and in issues of ethics, cult, rites, and eschatology. Philo could also be called on when investigating the early Christians' social conditions as minority Diaspora groups struggling to survive in a pluralistic polytheistic world of external antagonism and strife.

TORREY SELAND

FURTHER READING

Borgen, Peder. "Philo of Alexandria: A Critical and Synthetical Survey of Research since World War II." *Aufstieg und Niedergang der römischen Welt II. Geschichte und Kultur Roms im Spiegel der neueren Forschung* (Hellenistisches Judentum in römischer Zeit: Philon und Josephus) 33.1:98–154. Part 2, *Principat*, 33.1. Ed. Wolfgang Haase. Berlin: de Gruyter, 1984.

Goodenough, Erwin R. *An Introduction to Philo Judaeus.* Ed. J. Neusner. Brown Classics in Judaica. Lanham, Md.: University Press of America, 1986 (1940).

Mendelson, Alan. *Philo's Jewish Identity.* Brown Judaic Studies. Atlanta: Scholars, 1988.

Sandmel, Samuel. *Judaism and Christian Beginnings.* Oxford: Oxford University Press, 1978.

———. *Philo of Alexandria: An Introduction.* New York: Oxford University Press, 1979.

Schenk, Kenneth. *A Brief Guide to Philo.* Louisville: Westminster John Knox, 2005.

Seland, Torrey, ed. *Reading Philo: A Handbook to Philo of Alexandria.* Grand Rapids: Eerdmans, 2014.

Sterling, Gregory E. "'Philo Has Not Been Used Half Enough': The Significance of Philo

---

4. Samuel Sandmel, *Judaism and Christian Beginnings* (Oxford: Oxford University Press, 1978), p. 280.

of Alexandria for the Study of the New Testament." *Perspectives in Religious Studies* 30 (2003): 251–69.

ADVANCED READING

Alexandre, Manuel. *Rhetorical Argumentation in Philo of Alexandria*. Brown Judaic Series 322. Studia Philonica Monographs 2. Atlanta: Scholars, 1999.

Birnbaum, Ellen. *The Place of Judaism in Philo's Thought: Israel, Jews, and Proselytes*. Brown Judaic Series 290. Studia Philonica Monographs 2. Atlanta: Scholars, 1996.

Borgen, Peder. *Philo of Alexandria: An Exegete for His Time*. NovTSup 86. Leiden: Brill, 1997.

Deines, R., and K.-W. Niebuhr, eds. *Philo und das Neue Testament: Wechselseitige Wahrnehmungen*. WUNT 172. Tübingen: Mohr Siebeck, 2004.

Feldman, Louis H. *Philo's Portrayal of Moses in the Context of Ancient Judaism*. Christianity and Judaism in Antiquity Series 15. Notre Dame, Ind.: University of Notre Dame Press, 2007.

Goodenough, E. R. *By Light, Light: The Mystic Gospel of Hellenistic Judaism*. New Haven, Conn.: Yale University Press, 1935.

Kamesar, Adam, ed. *The Cambridge Companion to Philo*. Cambridge: Cambridge University Press, 2009.

Leonhardt, Jutta. *Jewish Worship in Philo of Alexandria*. Texts and Studies in Ancient Judaism 84. Tübingen: Mohr Siebeck, 2001.

Niehoff, Maren. *Philo on Jewish Identity and Culture*. Texts and Studies in Ancient Judaism 86. Tübingen: Mohr Siebeck, 2001.

Runia, David T. *Philo in Early Christian Literature: A Survey*. CRINT 3.3. Assen: Van Gorcum, 1993.

Runia, David T., and Gregory E. Sterling, eds. *The Studia Philonica Annual/Studies in Hellenistic Judaism*. Atlanta: SBL Press. Journal published once a year.

Wolfson, H. A. *Philo: Foundations of Religious Philosophy in Judaism, Christianity and Islam*. 2 vols. Cambridge, Mass.: Harvard University Press, 1948.

Introduction to *On the Creation of the World*

Most books produced during the lifetime of Philo (*see* Introduction to Philo of Alexandria) were written on one or more papyri scrolls with a title usually not given before the concluding portion of the scroll. A scroll containing this work would have been about 4 meters long. There is no record as to the title Philo gave this work, but the present Latin title, *De opificio mundi (On the Creation of the World)*, or the Greek *Philonos peri tēs kata Mousea kosmopoiias (Of Philo concerning the Cosmos-Making according to Moses)*, is very much attuned to the initial sections of Philo's work. Here Philo introduces his work by comparing it with how other lawgivers presented their laws, stating that Moses introduced his laws with a most impressive opening section that included an account of the creation of the world.

Narrative Description

As the title indicates, Philo provides an exposition of the creation of the world as set forth by Moses. Hence, this work is closely linked to the creation accounts in Genesis 1–3 of which Philo presents a commentary on selected relevant theological issues. His most comprehensive theme is his use of the seven days of creation scheme (13–130); he goes on to contend with some selected topics inherent in the creation narratives (131–71). I suggest the following outline of *On the Creation of the World*:

1–12 *Introductory comments*

Here Philo describes the excellence of Moses' accounts of the creation, which represent an initial introduction to Philo's presentations of the law of Moses (1–6); in addition he provides some brief comments on the relationship between the world and its Creator.

13–130 *The creation of the cosmos in six days*

According to Philo, the six days of creation are not to be taken literally; rather, the episode should be understood as an indication of order. Order involves number, and the most perfect number is six.

15b–35 First day

God first creates the intelligible world, which is the model of the sensible world. This intelligible world is discernable by the mind alone, and is identified, in fact, with the divine *Logos*:

> Accordingly, when he [Moses] recorded the creation of the human being, in the words that follow, he asserts that the human was made in the image of God, and if the image is a part of the image, then manifestly so is the entire form. Namely, the whole of this world that is perceptible by the external senses is a greater imitation of the divine image than the human form is. It is manifest also, that the archetypal seal, which we call that world that is perceptible only to the intellect, must itself be the archetypal model, the idea of ideas, the *Logos* of God. (25)[1]

36–37 Second day

God creates the sense-perceptible world after the patterns of the incorporeal and intelligible world, beginning with the heavens.

38–44 Third day

God creates the earth, putting it in order by arranging the rivers and lakes, and bidding the herbs of all kinds to spring forth.

45–61 Fourth day

God orders the heaven in its varied beauty (45–52). This section firmly establishes the sovereign power of God in the cosmos. In addition, an excursus is provided on the number four, and then the creation of the heavenly bodies is described, dealing especially with light, "the source of many boons to humankind, but especially to philosophy" (53–61).

62–88 Fifth day

God makes the animal world, and to crown all his creation, he makes the human being. Philo discusses several aspects of the creation of the human, especially what it means that he was created after the image of God:

> So then after all the other things, as has been said before, Moses said that the human was made in the image and likeness of God. He stated well, for nothing that is born on the earth does more resemble God than the human. And let no one think that he is able to judge of this likeness from the characters of the body: for neither is God a being with human form, nor is the human body like the form of

---

1. Unless otherwise noted, all biblical and *On the Creation of the World* translations by Torrey Seland.

God; but the resemblance is spoken of with reference to the most important part of the soul, namely, the mind: for the mind that exists in each individual has been created after the likeness of that one mind that is in the universe. (69)

In addition Philo approaches the questions why it is said "let *us* make" (72–76) and why man was created last (77–88).

89–128 Sixth day
"Now, when the whole world had been brought to completion in accordance with the properties of six, a perfect number, the Father invested with dignity the seventh day which comes next, extolling it and pronouncing it holy" (89).

129–30 Summarizing comments
Philo repeats that the creation account deals with concerns of the manifestation of incorporeal ideas in objects that our senses encounter.

131–33 *Separation of saltwater from freshwater*

Philo describes the earth as a mother, providing springs and streams.

134–47 *On the making of the first human being*

Philo states that there is a vast difference between the human being formed by clay (Gen. 2:7: "Then the Lord God formed the human of the dust from the earth and he breathed in his nostrils the breath of life and the human became a living soul"), and the one made after the image of God (Gen. 1:26–27: "Let us make humankind in our image as our likeness and they may rule over the fish of the sea, and over the fowl of the air, and over the beasts, and over all the land, and over all the creeping things creeping on the earth. And God created humankind in his image; in his image God created him, male and female he created them." The latter was an idea or type, while the former is an object of sense perception, consisting of body and soul, by nature mortal.

148–50 *The giving of names*

The first human names the animals God brings before him.

151–52 *The first woman is made*

God makes the first woman, breaking the solitude of the first man, and a desire for fellowship is kindled—a desire, however, that is also the beginnings of wrongs and violation of law.

153–66 *Life in, and aspects of, the garden*

Philo explains the symbolical meaning of the trees (153–56) and the snake as representing pleasure or being a symbol of pleasure (157–66). The woman is deceived because she represents senses, for the human mind corresponds to the male, the senses to the female.

167–70a Reflections on the punishments

Philo details the wages paid for following pleasure.

170b–71 Final remarks

Through his creation account, Moses teaches five fundamental doctrines concerning God and the world.

Location in the Philo Corpus

In most modern text editions, *De opificio* is placed just before the allegorical commentaries. This might lead to the conclusion that it is a kind of introduction to these commentaries. However, the common view in recent scholarship is that this location is misleading. Rather, *De opificio* should be considered the first book of the exposition of the law of Moses; therefore, it should be placed just before *De Decalogo* and read as a kind of introduction to this work of Philo; it would then be preceded only by *De vita Mosis*.

The authorship of *De opificio* by Philo is not disputed, but it is not possible to determine in what period of his life he wrote *De opificio*. David Runia suggests that it may have been written between 30 and 40 CE.

TORREY SELAND

FURTHER READING

Runia, David T. *Philo in Early Christian Literature: A Survey*. CRINT 3.3. Assen: Van Gorcum, 1993.

————. *Philo of Alexandria. On the Creation of the Cosmos according to Moses: Introduction, Translation and Commentary*. Philo of Alexandria Commentary Series 1. Leiden: Brill, 2001.

ADVANCED READING

Cox, Ronald. *By the Same Word: Creation and Salvation in Hellenistic Judaism and Early Christianity*. Beihefte zur Zeitschrift für die Neutestamentliche Wissenschaft und die Kunde der Älteren Kirche 145. Berlin: de Gruyter, 2007.

Kamesar, Adam, ed. *The Cambridge Companion to Philo*. Cambridge Companions to Philosophy. Cambridge: Cambridge University Press, 2009.

Philo of Alexandria. Vol. 1. Trans. F. H. Colson and G. H. Whitaker. 12 vols. Loeb Classical Library. Cambridge, Mass.: Harvard University Press, 1929.

4.10 *On the Creation of the World*

[Chapter 1] Introduction

[1] If you consider the other lawgivers, you will find that some drew up the regulations that they regarded as just in an unadorned and naked fashion, while others enclothed their thoughts with a mass of verbiage and so deceived the masses by concealing the truth with mythical fictions. [2] Moses surpassed both groups, regarding the former as lacking reflection, indolent, and non-philosophical, the latter as mendacious and full of trickery. Instead, he made a splendid and awe-inspiring start to his laws. He did not immediately state what should be done and what not, nor did he, since it was necessary to form in advance the minds of those who were to make use of the laws, invent myths or express approval of those composed by others. [3] The beginning is, as I just said, quite marvelous. It contains an account of the making of the cosmos, the reasoning for this is that the cosmos is in harmony with the law and the law with the cosmos; the man who observes the law is at once a citizen of the cosmos, directing his actions in relation to the rational purpose of nature, in accordance with which the entire cosmos also is administered.

[4] In celebrating the beauty of the thoughts contained in this creation account, no one, whether writing poetry or prose, can do them true justice. They transcend both speech and hearing, for they are greater and more august than what can be adapted to the instruments of a mortal being. [5] This does not mean, however, that we must keep our peace. No, on behalf of the God-beloved [author] we must dare to speak, even if this goes beyond our ability, presenting nothing from our own supply and stating only a few things instead of many, namely, those to which the human mind can reasonably attain when it is possessed by a love and desire for wisdom. [6] For just as even the tiniest seal when it has been engraved is able to contain the representations of things with colossal dimensions, so it may be that the overwhelming beauties of the making of the cosmos as they have been written in the laws, even if they bedazzle the souls of the readers with their brightness, can be elucidated with delineations on a smaller scale. First a preliminary remark needs to be made, which should not be passed over in silence.

[Chapter 2] A Preliminary Comment on God and the Cosmos

[7] There are some people who, having more admiration for the cosmos than for its Maker, declared the former both ungenerated and eternal, while falsely and

---

Translation by David T. Runia/Brill. Republication of Brill material courtesy of Koninklijke BRILL NV. Both chapter numbers and titles were added by the translator. Section numbers correspond to the editions of PCW and PLCL English words placed in brackets indicate that they are not present in the Greek, but are added for the sake of fluency in English. Relevant Greek words are also placed in brackets.

impurely attributing to God much idleness. What they should have done was the opposite, namely, be astounded at God's powers as Maker and Father, and not show more reverence for the cosmos than is its due.

[8]Moses, however, had not only reached the very summit of philosophy, but was also instructed in the many and most essential doctrines of nature by means of oracles. He recognized that it is absolutely necessary that among existing things there is an activating cause on the one hand and a passive object on the other, and that the activating cause is the absolutely pure and unadulterated intellect of the universe, superior to excellence and superior to knowledge and even superior to the good and the beautiful itself. [9]But the passive object, which of itself was without soul and unmoved, when set in motion and shaped and ensouled by the intellect, changed into the most perfect piece of work, this cosmos. Those who declare that it is ungenerated are unaware that they are eliminating the most useful and indispensable of the contributions to piety, the [doctrine of] providence. [10]Reason demands that the Father and Maker exercise care for that which has come into being. After all, both a father aims at the safety of his children and a craftsman aims at the preservation of what has been constructed, using every means at their disposal to repel all that is injurious and harmful, while desiring to provide in every way that which is advantageous and profitable. But there is no affinity between that which did not come into being and the one who did not make it. [11]It is a worthless and unhelpful doctrine, bringing about a power vacuum in this cosmos, just like [what happens] in a city, because it does not then have a ruler or magistrate or judge, by whom everything is lawfully administered and regulated.

[12]But the great Moses considered that what is ungenerated was of a totally different order from that which was visible, for the entire sense-perceptible realm is in a process of becoming and change and never remains in the same state. So to what is invisible and intelligible he assigned eternity as being akin and related to it, whereas on what is sense-perceptible he ascribed the appropriate name becoming [genesis]. Since, therefore, this cosmos is both visible and sense-perceptible, it must necessarily also be generated. Hence he was not off the mark in also giving a description of its becoming, thereby speaking about God in a truly reverent manner.

[Chapter 3] The Scheme of Six Days

[13]He says that the cosmos was fashioned in six days, not because the Maker was in need of a length of time—for God surely did everything at the same time, not only in giving commands but also in his thinking—but because things that come into existence required order. Number is inherent in order, and by the laws of nature the most generative of numbers is the six.

Of the numbers [proceeding] from the unit, six is the first perfect number. It is equal to [the product of] its parts and is also formed by their sum, namely, the three as its half and the two as its third and the unit as its sixth. It is also, so to speak, both male and female by nature, forming a harmonic union out of the product of each of them, for among existing things the odd is male and the female is even. The first of the odd numbers is the three, of the even numbers it is the two, and the product of both is the six. [14] So it was right that the cosmos, as the most perfect of the things that have come into existence, be built in accordance with the perfect number six; because births resulting from coupling would take place in it, also be formed in relation to a mixed number, the first even-odd number that contains both the form of the male who sows the seed and the form of the female who receives it.

[15] To each of the days he assigned some of the parts of the universe, making an exception for the first, which he himself does not actually call first, in case it be counted together with the others. Instead, he gives it the accurate name one, because he perceived the nature and the appellation of the unit in it, and so gave it that title.

[Chapter 4] Day One: Creation of the Intelligible Cosmos

We must now state as many as we can of the things that are contained in it, since it is impossible to state them all. It contains as preeminent item the intelligible cosmos, as the account concerning it [day one] reveals. [16] For God, because he is God, understood in advance that a beautiful copy would not come into existence apart from a beautiful model, and that none of the objects of sense perception would be without fault, unless it was modeled on the archetypal and intelligible idea. Therefore, when he had decided to construct this visible cosmos, he first marked out the intelligible cosmos, so that he could use it as an incorporeal and most godlike paradigm and so produce the corporeal cosmos, a younger likeness of an older model, which would contain as many sense-perceptible kinds as there were intelligible kinds in that other one.

[17] To state or think that the cosmos composed of the ideas exists in some place is not permissible. We will understand how it has been constituted if we pay careful attention to an image drawn from our own world. When a city is founded, in accordance with the high ambition of a king or a ruler who has laid claim to supreme power and, outstanding in his conception, adds further adornment to his good fortune, it may happen that a trained architect comes forward. Having observed both the favorable climate and location of the site, he first designs within himself a plan of virtually all the parts of the city that is to be completed—temples, gymnasia, public offices, marketplaces, harbors, shipyards, streets, constructions of walls, the establishment of other buildings both private and public. [18] Then, taking up the imprints of each object in his own soul like in wax, he carries around the intelligible city as an image in his head. Summoning up the representations by means of his innate power of memory and engraving their features even more distinctly [on his mind], he begins, as a good builder, to construct the city out of stones and timber, looking at the model and ensuring that the corporeal objects correspond to each of the incorporeal ideas. [19] The conception we have concerning God must be similar to this, namely, that when he had decided to found the great cosmic city, he first conceived its outlines. Out of these he composed the intelligible cosmos, which served him as a model when he completed the sense-perceptible cosmos as well. [20] Just as the city that was marked out beforehand in the architect had no location outside, but had been engraved

in the soul of the craftsman, in the same way the cosmos composed of the ideas would have no other place than the divine *Logos* who gives these [ideas] their ordered disposition. After all, what other place would there be for his powers, sufficient to receive and contain, I do not speak about all of them, but just any single one in its unmixed state?

[21] Among these is also his cosmos-producing power, which has as its source that which is truly good. For if anyone should wish to examine the reason why this universe was constructed, I think he would not miss the mark if he affirmed, what one of the ancients also said, that the Father and Maker was good. For this reason he did not begrudge a share of his own excellent nature to a material that did not possess any beauty of its own but was able to become all things. [22] Of itself it was unordered, devoid of quality, lacking life, dissimilar, full of inconsistency and maladjustment and disharmony; but it received a turning and change to the opposite and most excellent state, order, quality, ensoulment, similarity, homogeneity, sound adjustment, harmony, indeed all the characteristics possessed by the superior idea. [23] With no one to assist him—indeed who else was there?—but relying solely on his own resources, God recognized that he had to confer the unstinting riches of his beneficence on the nature that of itself without divine grace could not sustain any good whatsoever. But he does not confer his blessings in proportion to the size of his own powers of beneficence—for these are indeed without limit and infinitely great—but rather in proportion to the capacities of those who receive them. The fact is that what comes into existence is unable to accommodate those benefits to the extent that God is able to confer them, since God's powers are overwhelming, whereas the recipient is too weak to sustain the size of them and would collapse, were it not that he measured them accordingly, dispensing with fine tuning to each thing its allotted portion.

[24] If you would wish to use a formulation that has been stripped down to essentials, you might say that the intelligible cosmos is nothing else than the *Logos* of God as he is actually engaged in making the cosmos. For the intelligible city too is nothing else than the reasoning of the architect as he is actually engaged in the planning of the foundation of the city. [25] This is the doctrine of Moses, not my own. When describing the genesis of the human being in what follows, he explicitly declares that the human being was in fact formed after God's image.[a] Now if the part is image of an image, it is plain that this is also the case for the whole. But if this entire sense-perceptible cosmos, which is greater than the human image, is a representation of the divine image, it is plain that the archetypal seal, which we affirm to be the intelligible cosmos, would itself be the model and archetypal idea of the ideas, the *Logos* of God.

[Chapter 5] "In the Beginning" Does Not Mean Creation in Time

[26] When he says that in [the] beginning God made the heaven and the earth,[b] he does not take the [term] beginning, as some people think, in a temporal sense.

a. Gen. 1:27.
b. Gen. 1:1.

For there was no time before the cosmos, but rather it either came into existence together with the cosmos or after it. When we consider that time is the extension of the cosmos's movement, and that there could not be any movement earlier than the thing that moves but must necessarily be established either later or at the same time, then we must necessarily conclude that time too is either the same age as the cosmos or younger than it. To venture to affirm that it is older is not philosophical.

²⁷ If beginning[a] in the present context is not taken in the temporal sense, it is likely that its use indicates beginning in the numerical sense; so that the expression "in [the] beginning" he made[b] is equivalent to what he first made—heaven. It is indeed reasonable that heaven should in fact be the first thing to enter into becoming. It is the most excellent of the things that have come into existence and is composed of the purest substance, because it was to be the holiest dwelling-place for the gods whose appearance is perceived by the senses. ²⁸ Even if the Maker proceeded to make all things simultaneously, it is nonetheless true that what comes into a beautiful existence did possess order, for there is no beauty in disorder. Order is a sequence and series of things that precede and follow, if not in the completed products, then certainly in the conceptions of the builders. Only in this way could they be precisely arranged, and not deviate from their path or be full of confusion.

[Chapter 6] The Chief Contents of the Intelligible Cosmos

²⁹ First, therefore, the Maker made an incorporeal heaven, an invisible earth,[c] and a form of air and of the void. To the former he assigned the name darkness,[d] since the air is black by nature, to the latter the name abyss,[e] because the void is indeed full of depths and gaping. He then made the incorporeal being of water[f] and of spirit,[g] and as seventh and last of all of light,[h] which once again was incorporeal and was the intelligible model of the sun and all the other light-bearing stars that were to be established in heaven.

³⁰ Both spirit and light were considered deserving of a special privilege. The former he named of God,[i] because spirit is highly important for life and God is the cause of life. Light he describes as exceedingly beautiful,[j] for the intelligible surpasses the visible in brilliance and brightness just as much, I believe, as sun surpasses darkness, day surpasses night, and intellect, which gives leadership to

a. Gen. 1:1.
b. Gen. 1:1.
c. Gen. 1:1–2.
d. Gen. 1:2.
e. Gen. 1:2.
f. Gen. 1:2.
g. Gen. 1:2.
h. Gen. 1:3.
i. Gen. 1:2.
j. Gen. 1:4.

the entire soul, surpasses its sensible sources of information, the eyes of the body. [31] That invisible and intelligible light has come into being[a] as image of the divine *Logos,* which communicated its genesis. It is a star that transcends the heavenly realm, the source of the visible stars, and you would not be off the mark to call it "all-brightness." From it, the sun and moon and other planets and fixed stars draw the illumination that is fitting for them in accordance with the capacity they each have. However, that unmixed and pure gleam has its brightness dimmed when it begins to undergo a change from the intelligible to the sense-perceptible, for none of the objects in the sense-perceptible realm is absolutely pure. [32] Well said too is the statement that there was darkness above the abyss,[b] for in a way the air is over the void, since it is mounted on and has filled up the entire gaping, empty, and void space that extends from the region of the moon to us.

[33] As soon as the intelligible light, which existed before the sun, was ignited, its rival darkness[c] proceeded to withdraw. God built a wall between them and kept them separate,[d] for he well knew their oppositions and the conflict resulting from their natures. Therefore, in order to ensure that they would not continually interact and be in strife with each other, and that war would not gain the upper hand over peace and bring about disorder [*akosmia*] in the cosmos [*kosmos*], he not only separated light and darkness, but also placed boundaries in the extended space between them, by means of which he kept the two extremes apart. For if they were neighbors, they would produce confusion in the struggle for dominance and would strip in readiness for a great and unceasing rivalry, unless boundaries were fixed in between them to restrain and resolve their confrontation. [34] These [boundaries] are evening and morning[e] of which the latter announces in advance that the sun is about to rise and gradually forces back the darkness, while the evening follows on the setting sun and gently admits the massive onset of the darkness. Mark well, however, that these two, I mean morning and evening, must be placed in the order of incorporeal and intelligible reality. For in that realm there is nothing at all that is sense-perceptible, but everything there is ideas and measures and marks and seals, incorporeal entities required for the genesis of the other bodily realm. [35] So when light came into being, darkness[f] retired and withdrew, while evening and morning were fixed as boundaries in the extended space in between, this necessarily entailed that a measure of time was produced forthwith. The Maker called this measure day,[g] and not the first day, but day one.[h] It was named in this way because of the aloneness of the intelligible cosmos that has the nature of the unit.

a. Gen. 1:3.
b. Gen. 1:2.
c. Gen. 1:4.
d. Cf. Gen. 1:4.
e. Gen. 1:5.
f. Gen. 1:4.
g. Gen. 1:5.
h. Gen. 1:5.

[Chapter 7] Second Day: Creation of the Firmament

³⁶ Now that the incorporeal cosmos had been completed and established in the divine *Logos*, the sense-perceptible cosmos began to be formed as a perfect off-spring, with the incorporeal serving as model. As first of its parts, which indeed was also the very best of all, the Creator proceeded to make the heaven, which he correctly named firmament^a [*stereōma*], inasmuch as it is a bodily object; for the body is by nature solid [*stereon*], because it is extended in three directions. What other conception of what is solid and bodily is there than that which has been extended in all directions? Suitably, therefore, he opposed the sense-perceptible and corporeal heaven to its intelligible and incorporeal counterpart and called it firmament. ³⁷ Then he immediately named it heaven^b [*ouranos*], an apposite and highly appropriate title, either because it is the boundary [*horos*] of all things, or because it came into existence as first of the visible things [*horatōn*]. After its genesis he also names the day second,^c devoting the entire extension and measure of a day to heaven on account of its high value and honor in sense-perceptible reality.

[Chapter 8] Third Day: Creation of the Earth

³⁸ Now the entire body of water had been poured out over all the earth and had penetrated throughout all its parts like a sponge that has absorbed moisture. This meant that there were swamps and deep mud, the result of both elements having been mixed and confounded, in the manner of a paste, into a single indistinct and shapeless nature. God next commands the water that is salty, which would be the cause of infertility to plants and trees, to flow together and assemble from the pores of the entire earth, and the dry land^d to emerge. The moisture of the sweet water was left behind in it for the sake of preservation— for the sweet moisture when measured out acts as a kind of glue for binding together opposed elements—both so that the earth would not be completely parched and become childless and sterile; so that like a mother it would offer not just one kind of nourishment, namely, food, but would furnish, as if to its offspring, both food and drink. For this reason, he proceeded to flood its veins in the manner of breasts, and these, when they had obtained a mouth, would pour forth as rivers and springs. ³⁹ Similarly, he also extended invisible moisture-bearing capillaries throughout the rich and fertile soil, so that it would yield a most copious supply of crops. Having given these [parts] their ordered disposition, he proceeded to impose names on them, calling the dry land earth and the separated water sea.^e

⁴⁰ Then he starts giving the earth its adornment. He commands it to bear green

a. Gen. 1:7.
b. Gen. 1:8.
c. Gen. 1:8.
d. Gen. 1:9.
e. Gen. 1:10.

shoots and crops, and to bring forth all kinds of plants and well-grassed[a] plains and everything that would serve as forage for animals and as food for humans. In addition, he also caused all kinds of trees to grow, not omitting any of the wild or any of the so-called domesticated timber. Immediately on their first creation, these trees were all heavily laden with fruit,[b] contrary to the manner in which this now takes place. [41] For now, plants develop in succession at different times, and not all together at a single opportune time. Everyone knows that first sowing and planting occur, and second the growth of what has been sown and planted. This growth partly extends downward, establishing roots like foundations and partly extends upward, whereby the plants lift themselves to a height and develop stems. Next come shoots and the growth of leaves, and finally the production of fruit takes place. In this case too, the fruit is not [immediately] full grown, but undergoes all manner of changes, both quantitatively in terms of size and qualitatively in many different forms and shapes. When the fruit is first given birth, it resembles tiny specks so small as to be hardly visible. You would not be off the mark in calling them the first perceptibles. After this, in a gradual process, it grows in size and attains a bulk that is fully complete. This occurs both through the channeled nourishment that waters the tree, and through the fine mixture of winds that warm it and nurse it in a combination of cool and milder breezes. And together with its size it also alters its qualitative characteristics, offering varieties of color as if produced with a painter's art. [42] But in the case of the first genesis of the universe, as I just said, God caused all the timber of the plants to rise from the earth complete with fruit that was not imperfect but at its peak, fully ready for the immediate use and enjoyment of the living beings that were very soon to come into existence. [43] He thus gives orders to the earth to generate all these things. The earth, like a woman who has been pregnant for a long time and is now in travail, gives birth to every kind of sown plant, every kind of tree, and countless kinds of fruit. But the fruit was not only ready to serve as food for living beings. It was also equipped for the perpetual genesis of what is similar in kind, containing as it does spermatic[c] substances in which the indistinct and invisible patterns of the entire organisms are found. These patterns become distinct and visible as the cycles of the seasons proceed. [44] For God had decided that nature should run a cyclical race, thereby immortalizing the kinds[d] and giving them a share of eternity. On this account, he not only guided and urged the beginning on toward the end, but also caused the end to turn back toward the beginning. Out of the plants emerges the fruit, as an end out of a beginning, while out of the fruit that encloses the seed[e] within itself the plant emerges again, as a beginning out of an end.

a. Cf. Gen. 1:11.
b. Cf. Gen. 1:11.
c. Gen. 1:12.
d. Cf. Gen. 1:11–12.
e. Gen. 1:12.

[Chapter 9] Fourth Day: A Puzzle and the Significance of Its Number

45 On the fourth day,[a] now that the earth was finished, God proceeded to order the heaven with variegated adornment, not because he placed it behind the earth in rank, thereby giving a privileged position to the inferior nature and considering the superior and more divine deserving of the second position only, but rather in order to give a very clear demonstration of the might of his sovereignty. He understood in advance what the humans who had not yet come into existence would be like in their thinking. They would focus their aim on what is likely and convincing and contains much that is reasonable, but not on the unadulterated truth, and they would put their trust in appearances rather than on God, thereby showing admiration for sophistry rather than wisdom. Moreover, when they observe the revolutions of the sun and moon, by means of which summer and winter and the solstices of spring and autumn occur, they would suppose that it was the circuits of the heavenly bodies that were responsible for the emergence and growth of things out of the earth each year. Not wishing that some people, either out of shameless insolence or through overwhelming ignorance, would dare to attribute the first causes to any created being, he says: 46 Let them turn back in their minds to the first coming into existence of the universe, when, before the sun and moon even existed, the earth bore all manner of plants and all manner of fruits. Reflecting on these matters in their minds, let them expect that the earth will once again bring forth such produce at the command of the Father, whenever it seems appropriate to him. He does not stand in need of his heavenly offspring. He has given them powers, but these certainly do not mean full autonomy. Just like a charioteer who takes hold of the reins or a pilot who grasps the rudder, he guides each process according to law and just desert in whichever direction he wishes, not needing anyone else's help. After all, for God all things are possible. 47 This is the reason why the earth sprouted and brought forth verdure earlier [than the heaven].

But the heaven in its turn was ordered with a perfect number, the four. You would not go astray in affirming that it is the principle and source of the all-perfect number ten; for what the ten is in actuality, the four, it would seem, is potentially. If the numbers from the unit to the four are added up, they will produce the ten. It forms the boundary for the infinitude of numbers, which wind around it like a turning post and turn back. 48 The four also contains the ratios that produce the musical accords, namely, the quart, the quint, the octave, and the double octave. Out of these the most perfect system [of music] is generated. For the quart the ratio is one plus a third, for the quint one plus a half, for the octave double, for the double octave quadruple. The four contains all of these: one plus a third in the ratio four to three, one plus a half in the ratio three to two, double in the ratio two to one, quadruple in the ratio four to one. 49 There is also another capacity of the four that is really marvelous to describe and understand. It is the first number that has revealed the nature of the solid, the numbers before it being devoted to the incorporeal realm. Under the one is aligned what in geometry is called the point; under the two the line, because the two is constituted through

a. Gen. 1:19.

extension of the one and the line through extension of the point. A line is length without breadth. When breadth is added, surface arises, which is aligned under the three. For surface to attain to the nature of the solid it requires just one thing [more], depth; if this is added to the three, the four arises. Hence, this number in fact has great significance: it has led us from the incorporeal and intelligible substance to a conception of three-dimensional body, which is by nature the first object to be perceived by the senses. [50] If someone does not grasp what has been said, he will understand by taking notice of a very common game. People playing with nuts are in the habit of laying out three nuts on a plane and placing one more on top, thereby producing a pyramidal figure. The triangle in a plane thus stops at the three, while the unit placed on top produces the four in the realm of numbers and the pyramid in the realm of shapes, and then you already have a solid body. [51] In addition, another fact must be not ignored, namely, that four is the first of the numbers that is square, the product of two equal factors, and so is a measure of fairness and equality. Moreover, it alone has the ability to be produced from the same factors by both addition and multiplication, by addition from two plus two, by multiplication in turn from two times two. It thus demonstrates a splendid form of concord, which in fact is not possessed by any other number. For example, six is produced by adding together two threes, but if these are multiplied not six but another number results, namely, the nine. [52] The four possesses many other capacities, which should be further demonstrated in more detail in the account especially devoted to it. It will suffice to add the following. It was also a principle for the genesis of the entire heaven and cosmos. The four elements, out of which this universe was constructed, flowed forth, as from a source, from the four in the realm of numbers. Moreover, the annual seasons that are responsible for the birth of animals and plants are four, the year having received a fourfold division into winter and spring and summer and autumn.

[Chapter 10] Fourth Day: Creation of the Heavenly Bodies

[53] Since the above-mentioned number had been considered worthy of such a privileged position in the nature of reality, it was inevitable that the Maker would proceed to order the heaven with the four, decorating it with a splendid and most godlike adornment, the light-bearing heavenly bodies. Knowing that light was the most excellent of things that exist, he produced it as an instrument for the most excellent of the senses, sight; for what the intellect is in the soul, this is what the eye is in the body; each of them sees, in the one case the objects of thought, in the other the objects of perception. The intellect requires science in order to gain knowledge of the incorporeal realities; the eye has need of light in order to gain apprehension of bodies. For humans it is the cause of many other benefits, but especially of the greatest of them, love of wisdom. [54] Through light, sight had its attention drawn upward. It observed the nature of the heavenly bodies and their harmonious motion, the well-ordered circuits of fixed stars and planets, the former circling in the one and same manner, the latter following a double revolution, each differently and in the opposed direction. When sight observed the concordant choral dances of all these, ordered in accordance with the laws

of perfect musicality, it instilled in the soul unspeakable delight and pleasure. Feasting on a succession of spectacles, the one following after the other, the soul was filled with an insatiable desire for contemplation. Then, as is its inclination, it started to busy itself with further inquiries: What is the substance of these objects of sight? Are they by nature uncreated, or did they obtain a beginning of genesis? What is the manner of their movement, and what are the causes by means of which each thing is administered? From inquiry into these matters, the pursuit of philosophy arose. No more perfect good than this has entered into human life.

55 Using as his model that form of intelligible light, which was discussed in connection with the incorporeal cosmos, he proceeded to create the sense-perceptible heavenly bodies, divine images of exceeding beauty. These he established in heaven, as in a temple made of the purest part of bodily substance, for many reasons: firstly to give light,[a] secondly for signs, then to give the right times for the annual seasons, and finally for days and months and years,[b] which indeed have come into existence as the measures of time and also have generated the nature of number. 56 The value and usefulness of each of the above-mentioned tasks is quite self-evident, but for a more accurate understanding, it is perhaps not out of place to track down the truth in a reasoned account as well. Since the whole of time has been divided into two sections, day and night, the Father proceeded to give authority over the day to the sun, like to a great king, while authority over the night was given to the moon and the multitude of the remaining stars.[c] 57 The greatness of the power and sovereignty[d] possessed by the sun is most clearly proven by what was just said: though a single entity and quite alone all by itself, it has nevertheless been allotted the day, which constitutes half of the whole of time, whereas all the other heavenly bodies, together with the moon, received the other part, which was called night.[e] And when the sun rises, the appearances of all those heavenly bodies not only become dim, but even disappear completely through the outpouring of bright light, but when it sets, they all begin together to disclose their own qualities. 58 They have come into existence, as he himself said, not only for the purpose of sending forth light onto the earth, but also in order to reveal in advance signs[f] of future events. By observing their risings or settings, or eclipses, or their appearances or occultations, or other variations in their movements, humans make predictions about what will happen, the supply or lack of crops, the births and deaths of animals, clear weather and cloudiness, wind-still weather and violent winds, river torrents and dried-up riverbeds, calm and stormy seas, alterations in the annual seasons, whether in the form of a wintry summer or a scorching winter, a spring that feels like autumn or an autumn that feels like spring. 59 There are also people who have based conjectures on heavenly movements and have given indications in advance that tremors and earthquakes would occur, as well as numerous other more unusual phenomena, so that it was

a. Cf. Gen. 1:14.
b. Gen. 1:14.
c. Gen. 1:16.
d. Cf. Gen. 1:16, 18.
e. Gen. 1:16, 18; cf. Genesis 1:5.
f. Gen. 1:14.

most truly said that the heavenly bodies have come into existence for [serving as] signs.[a] Moreover [the phrase] for [indicating] right times[b] was also added. By right times he understood the annual seasons, and this is surely reasonable. For what else is the notion of right time than the time when a right result is achieved? The seasons bring everything to fruition and achieve a right result, whether it be sowing and planting of crops or births and growth of livestock. [60] They have also come into existence to serve as measures of time, for by the ordered revolutions of the sun and moon and other heavenly bodies days and months and years[c] have been constituted. And immediately that most useful thing, the nature of number, was revealed because time makes it manifest. For from a single day the number one is derived, from two days two, from three days three, and from a month thirty, from a year the number equivalent to the days produced by twelve months, and from infinite time the number that is infinite.

[61] This is how great and how indispensable the benefits are which the natures of the heavenly bodies and their movements supply. I am sure that there are many others that are unclear to us—for not everything is known to the human race—but contribute to the preservation of the whole. These are fully and invariably achieved in accordance with the ordinances and laws that have been immutably established in the universe by God.

[Chapter 11] Fifth Day: Creation of the Animal World

[62] Now that the earth and the heaven had been ordered with the adornment appropriate to them, the one by means of the three, the other, as has been explained, by means of the four, he proceeded to undertake the formation of the kinds of mortal living beings. He started with the aquatic creatures on the fifth day, considering that nothing bears such a family resemblance to anything else as the five does to living beings. The chief difference between living beings with and without soul is the possession of sense perception. Sense perception is divided fivefold, into sight, into hearing, into taste, into smell, into touch. To each of these the Maker distributed special materials and its own criterion by which it would judge what falls under its notice. For sight, there were colors, for hearing sounds, for taste flavors, for smell aromas, while for touch there were things soft and hard, hot and cold, smooth and rough. [63] He therefore commands all manner of kinds of fishes and sea creatures[d] to be constituted, differing in both size and characteristics according to [their] location, for in the various seas various types are found, but sometimes also the same ones. Nevertheless, he did not proceed to form all the kinds in every location, and this was surely reasonable. Some feel at home in willow water and not in the very deep sea; others love bays and harbors, being able neither to creep on land nor to swim far from it; yet others spend their time right out in the depths of the sea, avoiding headlands that jut out or islands

a. Gen. 1:14.
b. Gen. 1:14.
c. Gen. 1:14.
d. Gen. 1:21.

or rocks. Some thrive in a clear and calm sea, others are fond of storms and huge waves, for they are conditioned by the continual buffeting, and the strong effort involved in moving around makes them more powerful and sleek. Immediately thereafter he proceeded to create the kinds of birds,[a] because these are related to the creatures in the water—both sorts are in fact floaters—not leaving any form of airborne creatures unachieved.

[64] Now that the water and air had received the kinds of living beings that were appropriate to them as a kind of native allotment, he once again called on the earth to produce the part [of its task] that remained—after the plants, the land animals had still been left to do—and says: let the earth bring forth livestock and wild beasts and reptiles after each kind.[b] The earth then immediately releases what it had been commanded, animals varying in build and strength and the possession of powers that can harm or give benefit.

[65] To crown all he proceeded to make the human being.[c] How he did this I will say a little later. But first I want to show that he [Moses] employed a truly excellent sequence of succession in describing the birth of the animal realm. The most sluggish and least delineated type of soul has been allotted to the kind of the fishes, the most developed and in every respect best type has been assigned to the kind of the human beings. The type of soul bordering on these both is found in the living beings that inhabit the land and the air, for it is more sensitive than the soul found in fishes, but feebler than that found in humans. [66] For this reason, as the first of all ensouled beings, he produced fishes, which share in more of the substance of body than of soul. In a sense they both are and are not living beings. They move, yet do not really have soul. The soul principle has been sown in them in order to preserve their bodies, just like they say salt is added to meat, so that it will not easily go bad. After the fish come the birds and land animals. These are already more sensitive and in their makeup they reveal more clearly the characteristics of being ensouled. To crown all, as was said, he produced the human being, whom he endowed with intellect as special gift, a kind of soul of [the] soul just like the pupil in the eye. Indeed, those who carry out more accurate research into the nature of reality call this eye of [the] eye. [67] At that time, everything was constituted simultaneously. But, even though everything was constituted together, it was still necessary that the ordered sequence should be outlined in an account, because in the future beings would originate from each other. When individual beings come into existence, the following ordered sequence takes place: nature begins with what is most insignificant and ends with what is best of all. What this sequence is I should now show. It is a fact that for living beings seed is the starting point of the process of genesis. It is common knowledge that seed is something very insignificant, similar to foam. But when it has been deposited in the womb and has established itself there, it immediately obtains movement and is turned into natural growth. Natural growth is superior to seed, since movement is superior to quiescence in the realm of becoming. Like an artisan, or to put it more accurately, like an irreproachable art, nature molds living beings by distributing

a. Cf. Gen. 1:21.
b. Gen. 1:24, 25.
c. Cf. Gen. 1:27.

the moist substance to the limbs and organs of the body, and the life-giving sub-stance to the faculties of the soul, namely, nourishment and sense perception. The faculty of reasoning should be set aside for the moment because of those who affirm that, as something divine and eternal, it enters the living being from the outside. [68] Therefore nature began from seed, something of little value, and ended with what is most precious, the structure of an animal and of a human being. The same was also the case when the universe came into existence. When the Creator decided to form the living beings, the first in the ordered sequence were insignificant, namely, the fishes, while the last were the best, human beings. The other [kinds] are situated in between the extremes, being superior to the first group but inferior to the other, namely, land animals and birds.

[Chapter 12] Why Is the Human Being Created after God's Image?

[69] After all these other creatures, as has been stated, he says that the human being has come into existence after God's image and after his likeness.[a] This is most excellently said, for nothing earthborn bears a closer resemblance to God than the human being. However, no one should infer this likeness from the characteristics of the body, for God does not have a human shape and the human body is not godlike. The term image[b] has been used here with regard to the director of the soul, the intellect.

On that single intellect of the universe, as on an archetype, the intellect in each individual human being was modeled. In a sense, it is a god of the person who carries it and bears it around as a divine image. For it would seem that the same position that the Great Director holds in the entire cosmos is held by the human intellect in the human being. It is itself invisible, yet it sees all things. Its own nature is unclear, yet it comprehends the natures of other things. By means of the arts and sciences it opens up a vast network of paths, all of them highways, and passes through land and sea, investigating what is present in both realms. [70] Next, it is lifted on high and, after exploring the air and the phenomena that occur in it, it is borne further upward toward the ether and the revolutions of heaven. Then, after being carried around in the dances of the planets and fixed stars in accordance with the laws of perfect music, and following the guidance of its love of wisdom, it peers beyond the whole of sense-perceptible reality and desires to attain the intelligible realm. [71] And when the intellect has observed in that realm the models and forms of the sense-perceptible things that it had seen here, objects of overwhelming beauty, it then, possessed by a sober drunkenness, becomes enthused like the Corybants. Filled with another longing and a higher form of desire, which has propelled it to the utmost vault of the intelligibles, it thinks it is heading toward the Great King himself. But as it strains to see, pure and unmixed beams of concentrated light pour forth like a torrent, so that the eye of the mind, overwhelmed by the brightness, suffers from vertigo.

Since, however, not every single image resembles its archetypal model, but

a. Gen. 1:26, 27.
b. Gen. 1:26, 27.

many are dissimilar, he added to the words after the image as an extra indication the words after his likeness,[a] in order to emphasize that it is an accurate and clearly marked casting.

[Chapter 13] Why Was the Human Being Not Created by God Alone?

[72] It would not be off the mark to raise the difficulty as to why only in the case of the human being he attributed his coming into existence not to a single Creator as in the case of the other creatures, but as if to a plurality. For he introduces the Father of the universe as saying these words: let us make a human being after our image and likeness.[b] Surely, I would say, he to whom all things are subject would not be in need of anyone whatsoever. Alternatively, is it likely that when he made heaven, earth, and sea, he did not need any collaborator, but that in the case of such a tiny and perishable creature as the human being, he was unable to fashion it all by himself without the assistance of others? Of necessity, only God knows the truest reason for this, but we should not conceal the answer that seems to be convincing and reasonable, based on a likely conjecture. It is the following.

[73] Of the creatures that exist, some share neither in goodness nor in evil, such as plants and animals without reason, the former because they do not possess soul and are regulated by a nature without imagination, the latter because they have been excluded from intellect and reason. Intellect and reason may be regarded as the home where goodness and evil naturally reside. Other beings have taken part in goodness only and are without share in any form of wickedness, such as the heavenly beings. These are said not only to be living beings, but living beings with intelligence, or rather each of them is an intellect, excellent through and through and not susceptible to any kind of wickedness. But there are also creatures of a mixed nature, such as the human being, who admits opposite characteristics, wisdom and foolishness, self-control and lack of restraint, courage and coward-ice, justice and injustice, and—to summarize—good deeds and evil deeds, fine behavior and foul, goodness and wickedness.

[74] Now for God the universal Father it was highly appropriate to make the virtuous beings on his own because of their family relationship with him, and in the case of the indifferent beings, it was not alien to him to do so, since these too have no part in the wickedness that is hateful to him. In the case of the mixed natures, however, it was partly appropriate and partly inappropriate, appropriate on account of the better kind mixed in with them, inappropriate on account of the kind that was opposite and inferior. [75] For this reason it is only in the case of the genesis of the human being that he states that God said "let us make,"[c] which reveals the enlistment of others as collaborators, so that whenever the human being acts rightly in decisions and actions that are beyond reproach, these can be assigned to God's account as universal Director, whereas in the case of their opposite they can be attributed to others who are subordinate to him. After all,

a. Gen. 1:26.
b. Gen. 1:26.
c. Gen. 1:26.

it must be the case that the Father is blameless of evil in his offspring, and both wickedness and wicked activities are certainly something evil.

⁷⁶ Most excellently, after he had called the genus human being, he separated its species and stated that it was created male and female,ᵃ even though the individuals had not yet taken shape. This is because the most proximate of the species are present in the genus and become apparent as if in a mirror to observers with sharp vision.

[Chapter 14] Why Was the Human Being Created Last of All?

⁷⁷ You might inquire for what reason the human being was the final item in the creation of the cosmos, for, as the Holy Scriptures indicate, the Maker and Father produced him after all the others.

Now those who have made a profounder study of the law and have elucidated its contents to the best of their ability with much attention to detail assert that, when God granted to the human being kinship to himself through the possession of reason, which is the best of all gifts, he also did not begrudge him other benefits. So for the living being that was dearest and closest to him in nature he made everything ready in advance, it being his will that once the human being had come into existence, he would lack nothing that was required both for life and for the good life, the former furnished by the abundant supply of things that give enjoyment, the latter by contemplation of the heavenly realm, which strikes the intellect with wonder and engenders in it the passionate desire to gain knowledge of what it observes. This is what caused the pursuit of philosophy to spring up, enabling humankind, though mortal, to achieve immortality. ⁷⁸ Just as those who give a banquet do not invite their guests to the meal until all the preparations for the feast have been completed, and those who organize athletic or dramatic contests, before they assemble the spectators in the theaters and the stadiums, first have a vast number of competitors and spectacles and sound effects to get ready, in the same way the Director of the universe too, like an organizer of games and a holder of a banquet, when he was about to invite the human being to a lavish feast and a spectacle, first brought into readiness what was required for both kinds of entertainment, so that, when the human being entered into the cosmos, he would immediately encounter both a festive meal and a most sacred theater, the former replete with all the things that earth and rivers and sea and air supply for his use and enjoyment, the latter filled with all manner of things to see, absolutely stunning in their essential natures, absolutely stunning in their features, revealing the most wonderful motions and rhythmic dances performed in harmonic sequences by means of numerical proportions and concordant revolutions. You would not be mistaken if you said that in all these movements the original and true and paradigmatic science of music was embodied. The human beings who came later inscribed the images of this music on their souls, and so handed down to human life a most indispensable and useful art.

⁷⁹ This was the first reason, it appears, why the human being was created after

a. Gen. 1:27.

all the other creatures. It will not be off the mark to mention a second. When the human being first came into existence, he found all the equipment required for living. This was meant to teach those humans who would be born later a lesson. Nature was all but shouting aloud that, if they follow the example of the original ancestor of their race, they would lead a life without toil or trouble amid a most lavish supply of the necessary goods. This will take place when unreasoning pleasures fail to gain the upper hand by constructing gluttony and lust as battle stations in the soul, when the desire for fame and money and power fails to gain control over life, when grief does not constrict and distract the mind, when that bad advisor fear does not upset the impulses toward virtuous deeds, when foolishness and cowardice and injustice and the enormous number of other vices do not mount their assault. ⁸⁰ At the present time, however, when all these vices that have just been mentioned flourish and human beings have unconditionally surrendered themselves to the passions and to uncontrolled and blameworthy desires that it is unlawful even to mention, they are confronted with punishment as rightful retribution for their unholy practices. This punishment is that the necessities of life are difficult to obtain. With difficulty, humans plow the plains and channel the streams of springs and rivers. They sow and plant, and continually by day and by night they take upon themselves the labor of working on the land. So throughout the year they gather together the supplies that they need, but these are often meager and quite insufficient because for various reasons they are damaged. The produce has either been swept away by continuous torrents of rain or been crushed by the accumulated weight of hailstorms or become frozen by snowfall or been torn up roots and all by the violence of the winds; for water and air have many violent means to bring about the unproductivity of crops. ⁸¹ If, however, self-control were to alleviate the immoderate impulses of the passions, a sense of justice were to do the same for the ambitions and inclinations to injustice, and in short the virtues and deeds in accordance with these virtues were to put an end to the vices and the never-ending evil deeds they bring about, and if then the war in the soul, which is truly the harshest and most burdensome of wars, were to cease and peace would gain the upper hand, calmly and gently bringing the powers within us to good order, then we might entertain the hope that God, who is a lover of virtue and fine behavior and is moreover well disposed to humankind, will cause the good things of life to be supplied to the race spontaneously and ready for consumption. After all, it is obviously easier to bestow lavishly a good supply of produce from what already exists without the intervention of the farmer's art than to bring what does not yet exist at all into existence.

⁸² Let this be said as the second reason. A third is as follows. God, having reasoned that the beginning and end of creation should be harmonized together in a necessary and loving relationship, proceeded to make heaven as its beginning and the human being as its end, the former as the most perfect of immortal beings in the sense-perceptible realm, the latter as the best of earthborn and mortal creatures. Indeed, if the truth be said, he is a miniature heaven who carries around in himself numerous starlike beings as divine images, taking the form of arts and sciences and noble theories corresponding to each excellence. Since the mortal and the immortal are by nature opposite, he assigned the finest example of each

kind to the beginning and the end, respectively, to the beginning heaven, as has been said, to the end the human being.

[83] Last of all, however, the following is also stated as a necessary reason. The human being had to emerge as last of all creation so that, when he finally came and all of a sudden appeared before the other living beings, he would instill astonishment in them. On first seeing him, they would be amazed and would worship him as their natural director and master. For this reason, when they saw him, they became thoroughly tame, and those who had the wildest natures on the first glance in his direction immediately became manageable. They still demonstrated their savage aggression against each other, but toward the human being alone, their behavior was compliant. [84] For this reason the Father, when he brought him into existence as the living being who was by nature dominant, not only in fact but also by means of a pronouncement[a] appointed[b] him king of all the creatures in the sublunary realm, those on land and in the sea and borne on the air. All the mortal creatures in the three elements earth, water, and air he subjected to his rule,[c] excluding the creatures in heaven because they have obtained a portion that is more divine. Of this sovereignty, our experience furnishes the clearest proof. It can happen that vast flocks of animals are led by a single ordinary human being, who does not wear armor or carry a weapon of iron or bear any other kind of defensive instrument, but only has a leather jacket for protection and a staff for pointing the direction and for leaning on if he grows weary during his wanderings. [85] Thus flocks consisting of numerous sheep, goats, and cattle are led by a shepherd, a goatherd, or a cowherd, men who are not so physically robust and energetic that through their bodily condition they instill astonishment in those who look at them. The combined strength and power of so many well-armed creatures—for they are endowed by nature with equipment to defend themselves—stand in awe of him like slaves before their master and carry out his commands. Oxen are yoked for plowing the earth. Cutting deep furrows during the day and sometimes also at night, they make a long track under the direction of a single farmer. Rams, weighed down in springtime by their thick coats of wool, at the command of a shepherd remain quietly standing or even calmly lie down, allowing their fleece to be shorn. Like cities they are accustomed to presenting their annual tribute to him who is by nature their king. [86] Another example is the most spirited of animals, the horse, who is easily harnessed and led along so that he does not refuse the reins and jump away. He hollows his back and so offers an excellent seat to his rider. Lifting him on high, he moves at a swift pace, doing his best to bring and convey his charge to the places where his mount would have him go. The latter sits up there quite peacefully without getting tired, and by making use of another's body and limbs completes his ride. [87] Much more could be said if anyone wishes to extend this account and offer more examples in order to demonstrate that no creature has gained its freedom and been exempted from the rulership of humankind. Let what has been said suffice by way of example.

It is important, however, to be aware that the human being was not created last

a. Cf. Gen. 1:28.
b. Cf. Ps. 8:7.
c. Cf. Ps. 8:7.

of all as an indication of inferior rank. [88] As witnesses, we can call on charioteers and pilots. The former come after their team and have their place behind it. They guide it wherever they wish with the reins in their hands, sometimes loosening them for a fast trot, at other times restraining it if it races along faster than is required. Pilots in turn take up their position on the stern at the very end of the ship, but they are, so to speak, the best of all those sailing, because they hold in their hands the safety of the ship and the people on it. The Maker thus proceeded to fashion the human being after all the others as a kind of charioteer and pilot, so that he could guide and steer earthly affairs, taking on the care of animals and plants like a governor acting on behalf of the first and great King.

[Chapter 15] The Seventh Day: Excursus on the Hebdomad

[89] When the entire cosmos had been completed[a] in accordance with the nature of the perfect number six,[b] the Father proceeded to honor the seventh day that followed by praising it and calling it holy.[c] For this day is a festival, not of a single city or country, but of the universe, the only day that rightly deserves to be called universal and the birthday of the cosmos.

[90] I do not know whether anyone can give sufficient praise to the nature of the seven. It is superior to every form of speech. Nevertheless, even though it is more wonderful than the words used to describe it, this does not mean that we should keep our peace. Even if we are unable to tell everything or even the most important aspects, we should still be bold enough to elucidate at least those features that are accessible to our minds.

[91] The seven is spoken of in two ways. In the former case it is confined within the ten. It is measured by taking the unit on its own seven times and consists of seven units. In the latter case it falls outside the ten, a number whose starting point in each case is the unit in accordance with the double or the triple or with numbers generally corresponding to these, such as 64 and 729, the former attained by doubling [seven times] from the unit, the latter by tripling.

[92] Each kind should not be just incidentally investigated. The second kind possesses a distinction that is very apparent. Every time that a number, beginning from the unit, is doubled or tripled or generally multiplied analogously, the resultant seventh number is both a cube and a square. This number contains the kinds of both incorporeal and corporeal being, the former through the surface produced by squares, the latter through the solidity produced by cubes. [93] A very clear proof of this is given by the numbers just mentioned. To start with, the seventh number attained from the unit by doubling, the 64, is a square if eight is multiplied eight times, and is a cube if four times four is multiplied four times. In addition, in the other case the seventh number attained from the unit in the triple relation, the 729, is a square if the 27 is multiplied by itself and a cube if nine times itself is multiplied nine times. [94] Moreover, invariably if you take the seventh

a. Gen. 2:1.
b. Cf. Gen. 2:2.
c. Gen. 2:3.

number as starting point instead of the unit and you increase it according to the same procedure until you reach the seven, you will find that the number attained in each case is both a cube and a square. Therefore, if you multiply from 64 by doubling you will generate the seventh number 4,096, which is at the same time a square and a cube, a square which has a side of 64, and a cube with a side of 16.

[95] We should now move on to the other kind of the seven that is contained within the ten. It reveals a marvelous nature not inferior to the kind just dealt with. To start with, the seven consists of one, two, and four, and so possesses two most harmonious ratios, the double and the quadruple, the former producing the chord of the octave, the quadruple the chord of the double octave. The seven also contains other divisions that as it were form yoked pairs when taken together, for it is divided first into the one and the six, then into the two and the five, and finally into the three and the four. [96] The relationship between these numbers is also highly musical. Six to one has a sixfold ratio, and the sixfold ratio produces the greatest distance among things that exist, the distance that separates the highest from the lowest sound, as we will demonstrate when we move on from numbers to harmonic theory. The ratio five to two demonstrates considerable harmonic power, almost rivaling that of the octave, as is shown very clearly in the mathematical theory of music. The ratio four to three produces the prime harmony of one plus a third, which is the quart. [97] The seven also demonstrates another of its beauties, a most sacred object of knowledge. Consisting as it does of the three and the four, it supplies that which among existents is by nature perpendicular and straight. How this happens should be made clear. The right-angle triangle, which is the starting point of the qualities, consists of the numbers three, four, and five. The three and the four, which make up the substance of the seven, produce the right angle. The obtuse and the acute angles reveal irregularity, disorder, and inequality, because there are various degrees of acuteness and obtuseness. The right angle, however, does not admit comparison, nor can the one be more upright than the other can, but it remains unaltered and never changes the nature it possesses. If the right-angled triangle is indeed the starting point of shapes and qualities, and its most indispensable feature, the right angle, is furnished by the nature of the seven as formed by the three and the four together, the seven may be reasonably considered to be the source of every shape and every quality. [98] In addition to what has been said, another aspect needs to be mentioned. Three is the number of the surface's shape—since the point is ordered under the one, the line under the two, the surface under the three—while four is the number of solid shape through the addition of the one, depth being added to surface. From this it is apparent that the being of the seven is the starting point of geometry and stereometry and—to summarize—of both incorporeal and bodily reality.

[99] So sacred is the nature inherent in the seven that it possesses a special feature not shared by all the other numbers in the ten. Of these numbers the first group generate but are not generated themselves, a second group are generated but do not themselves generate, while a third group do both, generating and being generated. Only the seven is not observed in any of these categories. This assertion should be confirmed by a demonstration. Now the one generates the entire succession of numbers, and is not generated by any of them at all. Eight is generated by twice four, but generates none of the numbers in the ten. Four

in turn falls under the categories of both parents and offspring: it generates the eight by being doubled, while it is generated by twice two. [100] Only the seven, as I said, has the nature neither to generate nor be generated. For this reason the rest of the philosophers liken this number to motherless Victory and to the Maiden, who according to the account appeared out of the head of Zeus, but the Pythagoreans liken it to the Director of the universe. For that which neither generates nor is generated remains unchanged. Generation involves change, since [both that which generates] and that which is generated cannot do without change, in the one case so that it can generate, in the other case so that it can be generated. The only being who neither changes nor is changed is the very ancient Ruler and Director, of whom the seven would fittingly be called an image. As a witness for this account, I can call on Philolaus when he says, "There exists the Director and Ruler of all things, God who is one, always existent, abiding, unchanged, himself identical to himself and differing from all others."

[101] In the realm of intellect, therefore, the seven demonstrates what is unchanging and not subject to action, but in the realm of sense perception it demonstrates a great and most essential power, [in the seven planets and the Great Bear and the choir of the Pleiades], by which all things on earth are able to make progress, and also in the revolutions of the moon. How this occurs should be investigated. If the numbers in succession starting from the unit are added up, the seventh number generates the 28, a perfect number that is equal to its own parts. The generated number restores the moon back to its original shape, from which it began visibly to increase and to which it returns through diminution. From the first appearance of the crescent shape it waxes to the half-moon in seven days, then in another such period it becomes full moon. From here it turns back again and follows the same route along the back part of the track, from the full moon to the half-moon in another seven days, and then from this stage to the crescent shape in the same number. Out of these four [periods] the above-mentioned number is completed.

[102] The seven is also called by those who are in the habit of using names correctly the "completion bringer," since by means of this number all things are brought to completion. Evidence for this may be gained from the fact that all bodies with instrumental force possess three dimensions, length, breadth, and depth, as well as four limits, point, line, surface, and solid body. When these are added together the seven is produced. It would have been impossible to measure bodies with the seven in accordance with the addition of the three dimensions and four limits, were it not the case that the ideas of the first numbers, one, two, three, and four, which form the foundation of the ten, contain the nature of the seven; for the numbers just mentioned have four boundaries, the first, the second, the third, and the fourth, as well as three intervals, the first from one to two, the second from two to three, the third from three to four. [103] Aside from what has already been said, the clearest manifestation of the completion-bringing power of the seven is also furnished by the stages of life of human beings from infancy to old age. These stages are measured by the number seven. During the first period of seven years the growth of the teeth takes place. During the second the right time occurs for being able to emit fertile seed. In the third the beard develops and in the fourth the progress to full strength occurs. In the fifth it is the right season for marriage, in the sixth the peak of intelligence is attained. In the sev-

enth improvement and increase in both the powers of intellect and speech take place, while in the eighth perfection in both departments is reached. During the ninth there is a time of mildness and serenity, as the passions are considerably moderated. In the tenth the end of life that one has prayed for occurs, when the bodily parts are still in working condition; for advanced age has the habit of tripping each of them up and removing their force. [104] These stages of life have been described by Solon, the lawgiver of the Athenians, when he composed the following elegiac verses:

> The young child, still an infant, grows a line of teeth,
>> and expels them in the first seven years.
> But when God has made complete another set of seven years,
>> the signs of advancing youth become manifest.
> In the third period, while the limbs still lengthen,
>> the chin grows downy and the complexion loses its bloom.
> In the fourth period of seven each person is at the very peak
>> of strength, which men possess as marks of excellence.
> In the fifth it is time for a man to be mindful of marriage,
>> and to seek a family of children for hereafter.
> In the sixth a man's intellect gains mastery in all things,
>> and no longer wishes to perform reckless deeds.
> In the seventh seven he is best in intellect and speech,
>> and the eighth too, fourteen years for both periods.
> In the ninth he is still capable, but for great achievement
>> his speech and wisdom have less power.
> If he reach the tenth in completion of due measure,
>> he would obtain his allotment of death not unseasonably.

[105] Solon thus enumerates human life by means of the ten sevens just outlined. But the doctor Hippocrates says that there are seven stages of life: child, boy, youth, young man, man, older man, old man. These are measured by sevens, he says, but not in direct succession. He writes as follows, "In human nature there are seven seasons, which are called stages of life: child, boy, youth, young man, man, older man, old man. A human being is a child up to the age of seven and the expulsion of teeth; a boy up to the growth of seed, until twice seven; a youth up to the growth of down on the chin, until three times seven; a young man up to the maturity of the entire body, until four times seven; a man up to one short of fifty years, until seven times seven; a older man up to fifty-six, until seven times eight; from then on he is an old man." [106] Another feature of the seven that is mentioned in order to introduce it as having a wonderful position in nature depends on the fact that it consists of three and four. If you start doubling, you will find that the third number from the one is a square, the fourth number a cube, while the seventh number formed from both is both a cube and a square. Thus the third number from the one in the double ratio, four, is a square, the fourth number, eight, is a cube, and the seventh number, 64, is both a cube and a square. It may be concluded that the seventh number is truly a completion bringer, because it proclaims both kinds of equality, of the surface by means of the square, based on

the affinity with the three, and of the solid by means of the cube, based on the close connection with the four. From the three and the four the seven results.

[107] The seven is not only a "completion bringer," but is also so to speak harmonious in the highest degree and in a sense source of the most beautiful table, which contains all the accords—the quart, the quint, the octave—as well as all the proportions—arithmetical, geometrical, and also harmonic. This "brick" consists of the following numbers: six, eight, nine, twelve. Eight to six is in a ratio of a one plus a third , which is the accord of the quart; nine to six is in a ratio of a one plus a half, which is the accord of the quint; twelve to six is a double ratio, which is the accord of the octave. [108] It also contains, as I said, all the proportions. The arithmetical consists of six, nine, and twelve; by the same number that the middle term exceeds the first term, namely, three, the final term exceeds the middle term. The geometrical consists of four numbers; the same ratio that eight has to six, also occurs in the case of twelve to nine; this is the ratio of one plus a third. The harmonic consists of three numbers, six, eight, and twelve. [109] There are two ways of determining whether you have a harmonic proportion. The first is whenever the ratio of the final term to the first term is the same as the ratio that the excess by which the final term exceeds the middle term has to the excess by which the first term is exceeded by the middle term. You may obtain a very clear proof of this from the numbers set out before us, six, eight, and twelve. The final number is double the first, while the excess is also double: twelve exceeds eight by four, eight exceeds six by two; four is the double of two. [110] The other test for determining whether you have a harmonic proportion is whenever the middle term both exceeds and is exceeded by the same fraction of the end terms. Eight is the middle term and exceeds the first by the fraction of a third; for if you subtract six from it, two remains, which is a third of the first term. It is exceeded by the final term by the same fraction; for if eight is subtracted from twelve, four remains, which is a third of the final term.

[111] Let these remarks suffice as explanation of the august nature possessed by the table or "brick" or however it should be called. All these features and still more the seven demonstrates in the incorporeal realm that is the object of intellect. But its nature also extends to the whole of visible reality, reaching as far as heaven and earth, the limits of the universe. After all, what section of the cosmos is not philhebdomadic, overpowered by love and desire for the seven?

[112] To start with, they say the heaven is girdled by seven circles, the names of which are: arctic, Antarctic, summer solstice, winter solstice, equator, zodiac, and in addition the Milky Way. The horizon should be excluded because it is a matter of our own experience, depending on whether we have clear vision or not, the sense of sight sometimes marking off a smaller and sometimes a larger circumference. [113] As for the planets, that army which forms a counterweight to the sphere of the fixed stars, they are ordered in seven ranks, which display a very close affinity with the air and the earth. The air they convert and change into the annual seasons, as they are called, bringing about numerous changes for each: wind-still weather, clear skies, clouds, extremely violent storms. In addition they cause rivers to swell and to diminish, and plains to become marshy and—the opposite—to become parched. They also bring about the alternation of low and high tides. It can happen that broad bays, when the sea recedes in the ebb tide,

quite suddenly form an extended beach, yet a little later, when the sea flows back, they become very deep stretches of water, navigable not only for small craft but even for large cargo ships. Moreover, they cause all things on earth to grow, both living beings and fruit-bearing plants, and bring them to completion, enabling the nature in each of them to run the full cycle, so that new fruits bloom and reach maturity on old plants, furnishing a lavish supply of necessary goods. [114] The Great Bear, which they call the sailors' escort, consists of seven stars. By keeping their gaze directed toward it, skippers have opened up countless routes, applying themselves to an incredible task that goes beyond human nature, for by targeting the above-mentioned stars they discover hitherto undisclosed lands, those who live on the mainland discovering islands, islanders in their turn finding continents. It was indeed fitting that the living being that is most God-beloved, the race of human beings, be shown the distant parts of both land and sea by the purest form of being, the heaven. [115] In addition to what has been said, the starry choir of the Pleiades is also made complete by the seven. The risings and settings of these stars are the cause of great boons for everyone. When they set, the furrows are cut open for sowing. When they are about to rise, they announce the harvest time, and when they have risen, they wake up the farmers who are glad to gather in the necessities of life. Joyfully they store away the supplies of food for daily use. [116] The great ruler over the day, the sun, in completing two equinoxes each year, in the spring and autumn—the spring equinox in the Ram, the autumn equinox in the Balance—gives the clearest proof of the majesty of the seven. For each of these equinoxes occurs in the seventh month, and in both cases it is prescribed by law that the largest and most popular public festivals be celebrated, because at both times the products of the earth reach full growth, in spring the produce of corn and all the other things that are sown, in the autumn the produce of the vine and most other fruit-bearing trees.

[117] Since things on earth are dependent on the heavenly realm through a natural affinity, the principle of the seven, which began on high, has also come down to us and made its presence felt among the mortal kinds. To start with, the part of our soul separate from the directive part is divided sevenfold, into the five senses, the organ of speech, and finally the reproductive part. Just like in puppet shows, all these are manipulated by the ruling element through the nerves. Sometimes they are at rest, at other times they move, each producing its own appropriate disposition and movement. [118] Similarly, if you were to undertake to examine the external and internal parts of the body, you will find seven in each case. Those that are visible are: head, chest, abdomen, two hands, two supports. The parts within, called internal organs, are: stomach, heart, lungs, spleen, liver, two kidneys. [119] Moreover the most directive part of the living being, the head, has seven highly essential parts: two eyes, the same number of ears, two nostrils, and as seventh the mouth, through which, as Plato has said, mortal things have their entry and immortal things have their exit. Food and drink enter inside by way of the mouth, perishable foods for a perishable body. But what goes out is speech, immortal laws of an immortal soul, by means of which the life of reason is guided. [120] The objects discriminated by the best of the senses, sight, share in this number according to kind, for there are seven sorts of things we see: body, extension, shape, size, color, movement, rest, and no others besides these. [121] It

is certainly the case that the modulations of the voice too are seven in all: acute, grave, circumflex, as fourth the aspirated sound, the unaspirated as fifth, the long as sixth, and the short as seventh. [122] But it is also the case that there are seven motions: upward, downward, to the right, to the left, forward, backward, circular. These are demonstrated above all by people who make a display of dancing. [123] It is also said that the secretions of the body are restricted to the above-mentioned number. Through the eyes, tears flow forth, through the nostrils the filtrations of the head, through the mouth the saliva that is spat out. There are also two discharges for drawing off what remains after the digestion of food and drink, one at the front and one at the back. The sixth occurs all over the body, a profusion in the form of sweat, while the seventh is the emission of seed through the reproductive parts, which is very much a part of nature. [124] Hippocrates too, the authority on what happens in nature, states that in seven days the fixing of the seed and the formation of flesh is secured. Moreover, in the case of women the menstrual flow continues for at most seven days. It is natural for the fetus in the womb to reach full development in seven months, which results in a highly paradoxical fact: seven-month-old fetuses are viable, whereas those of eight months are generally unable to survive. [125] Serious illnesses of the body, especially when we are wracked by unremitting fevers resulting from the bad mixing of our powers, are mostly resolved on the seventh day. This day adjudicates the struggle for life, allotting recovery to some and death to others.

[126] The power of the seven has not only made its presence felt in the areas just mentioned, but also in the best of the sciences, grammar, and music. The seven-stringed lyre produces renowned harmonies, similar to what occurs in the choral dance of the planets, giving it virtually the leading position in the entire instrumental production of music. As far as the elements in grammar are concerned, the vowels [or "vocals"] are seven in number. These are named in conformity with their nature, because they plainly sound of their own accord, and when aligned with the others [the consonants] they produce articulated sounds. In the case of the semivowels, they fill in what is lacking and bring about complete tones, while in the case of the voiceless consonants they change and convert their nature by breathing in some of their own power, so that what was unspeakable can now be spoken.

[127] It seems to me, therefore, that those who in the beginning conferred names on things, because they were wise, called this number seven [*hepta*], because of its venerability [*sebasmos*] and the august nature [*semnotēs*] that it possesses. The Romans indicate this even more clearly by adding the letter S, which the Greeks leave out. They call the number *septem* and this name, which, as was just said, comes from *semnos* [august] and *sebasmos* [venerable], conforms more closely to its true nature.

[128] All this and even more has been stated and philosophized about the seven. For these reasons it has obtained the highest honors in nature, and is also honored by Greeks and foreigners of the highest reputation who practice the science of mathematics. But it has been especially honored by that lover of excellence, Moses, who recorded its beauty in the most holy tables of the law and also imprinted it on the minds of his followers. He commanded them after every period of six days to keep the seventh day holy, refraining from all the work required for the

pursuit and provision of a livelihood, and keeping themselves free to concentrate on one thing only, practicing philosophy for the improvement of their character and the examination of their conscience, which has been established in the soul and like a judge is not at all bashful about administering rebukes, making use both of threats that are rather forceful and of warnings that are more moderate. The former it applies to those unjust deeds that appear to be deliberate, whereas it uses the latter for involuntary acts done through lack of foresight, in order that a similar lapse will not happen again.

[Chapter 16] A Summarizing Reflection

[129] Reflecting on his account of the creation [so far] with a summarizing statement, Moses says, This is the book of the genesis of heaven and earth when it occurred, on the day that God made the heaven and the earth, and all the green of the field before it came into being on the earth and all the grass of the field before it rose up.[a] Does he not clearly present here the incorporeal and intelligible ideas, which are in fact the seals of the completed products perceived by the senses? For before the earth became green, this green itself was present in the nature of things, he says, and before grass rose up, there was grass[b] that was not visible.

[130] It should be understood that for each of the other things that the senses judge, anterior forms and measures also preexisted, by means of which the things that come into being are given form and measured. For even if he has not gone through the partial things all together, being as concerned as anyone ever was to attain brevity of speech, nevertheless the few things mentioned are indications of the nature of the whole of reality, which brings none of the things that are sense-perceptible to completion without an incorporeal model.

[Chapter 17] The Separation of the Freshwater from the Saltwater

[131] Holding on to the sequence of thought and preserving the series of what follows in relation to what precedes, he next states a spring went up from the earth and watered all the face of the earth.[c] Other philosophers say that the entirety of water is one element of the four from which the cosmos was fashioned. Moses, accustomed as he is to sharply observing and understanding even distant things with a more penetrating gaze, regards the great sea as an element, a fourth part of the entirety of things, which those who came after him called the Ocean, considering the seas that we traverse as having the size of harbors. The sweet and drinkable water, however, he proceeded to separate off from the seawater. He assigned it to the earth and understood it to be part of it and not of the [element] water for the reason mentioned earlier, namely, so that the earth would be held together by a sweet quality as if by a bond in the manner of a unifying glue. For if it had been

a. Gen. 2:4–5a.
b. Gen. 2:5.
c. Gen. 2:6.

left behind as dry earth, and the moisture had not sunk in and penetrated through its pores by multiple divisions, it would have fallen apart. Now its contents are held together and continue to exist partly through the force of the unificatory spirit, and partly through the moisture that does not allow it to dry out and be broken into small and large clumps.

132 This was one explanation, but we should also state another that aims at the truth like a target. Nothing of what grows on earth can gain its structure without moist substance. This is shown by the deposition of seed. Either it is moist itself, as in the case of animals, or it does not grow without moisture, as in the case of plants. From this it is clear that the above-mentioned moist substance has to be part of the earth that gives birth to all things, just as in the case of women there has to be the menstrual flow. For it is said by men of science that this is the bodily substance of fetuses.

133 What I now will state is also in harmony with what has been said so far. Nature has equipped every mother with a highly essential [bodily] part in the form of breasts like fountains,[a] and so has prepared food in advance for the child that will be born. It seems that the earth too is a mother. For this reason, the first humans decided to call her Demeter, combining the words for mother [*mētēr*] and earth [*gē*]. For, as Plato has said, it is not earth who has imitated woman, but rather woman who has imitated earth. The race of poets are quite correct in calling it "mother of all" and "crop-bearer" and "giver of all" [Pandora], since for all living beings and plants alike it is the cause of birth and continuing existence. It was quite reasonable, therefore, that nature equipped the earth, as oldest and most fertile of mothers, with flowing rivers and springs like breasts, so that it could both water the plants and provide a generous supply of drink for all living beings.

[Chapter 18] Creation of the First Human Being from the Earth

134 After this he says that God molded the human being, taking clay from the earth, and he inbreathed onto his face the breath of life.[b] By means of this text too he shows us in the clearest fashion that there is a vast difference between the human being who has been molded now and the one who previously came into being after the image of God.[c] For the human being who has been molded as sense-perceptible object already participates in quality, consists of body and soul, is either man or woman, and is by nature mortal. The human created after the image as a kind of idea or genus or seal, is perceived by the intellect, incorporeal, neither male nor female,[d] and is immortal by nature.

135 He says that the sense-perceptible and individual human being has a structure that is composed of earthly substance and divine spirit, for the body came into being when the Craftsman took clay and molded[e] a human shape out of it,

a. Cf. Gen. 2:6.
b. Gen. 2:7.
c. Gen. 1:27.
d. Gen. 1:27.
e. Gen. 2:7.

whereas the soul obtained its origin from nothing that has come into existence at all, but from the Father and Director of all things. What he breathed in was nothing else than the divine spirit[a] that has emigrated here from that blessed and flourishing nature for the assistance of our kind, in order that, even if it is mortal with regard to its visible part, at least with regard to its invisible part it would be immortalized. For this reason it would be correct to say that the human being stands on the borderline between mortal and immortal nature. Sharing in both to the extent necessary, he has come into existence as a creature, which is mortal, and at the same time immortal, mortal in respect of the body, immortal in respect of the mind.

[Chapter 19] The Excellence of the First Human Being

[136] That first human being who was born from the earth, the original ancestor of our entire kind, seems to me to have come into existence as most excellent in both body and soul, superior by far in both respects to those who came later. He was indeed truly a noble person. Evidence for the excellent form of his body can be gained from three considerations, of which the first is this. Since the earth[b] was newly established, having just appeared when the great body of water that was named sea[c] was separated out, it was the case that the material for those things that came into being was unmixed and undefiled and pure, as well as receptive and easy to work with. Products made from it would surely be beyond reproach. [137] Secondly, it is not likely that God took clay from any part of the earth which he happened to come across when he wished to mold this statue in the form of a human being with the utmost care, but rather that he separated out the best part from the entire mass, taking from pure matter the purest and utmost refined part that was especially suited for the construction. For it was built as a home or holy temple for the rational soul, which it was to carry around as the most godlike of images. [138] The third argument, which bears no comparison with what has been said so far, is the following. As in other things, the Creator also excelled in knowledge, so that each of the parts of the body received individually the proportions it required and was carefully fashioned to fit in harmoniously with the whole. And, in addition to this symmetry, he proceeded to model it with a beauty of flesh and embellish it with a beauty of color, because he decided that the first human being should possess the most beautiful appearance possible. [139] That he was also excellent in respect of his soul, is obvious. For it is fitting that for his construction God used no other model belonging to the realm of becoming, but only, as I said, his own *Logos*. For this reason he says that the human being has come into existence as its likeness and representation by being inbreathed into the face,[d] which is the location of the senses. By means of these the Creator gave soul to the body, but as for reason, having established it as king in the directive

a. Gen. 2:7.
b. Gen. 1:10; 2:5, 7.
c. Gen. 1:10.
d. Gen. 2:7.

part, he arranged for it to be flanked with bodyguards for the apprehension of colors and sounds and tastes and smells and related sensations, which on its own without sense perception it was unable to grasp. The representation of a splendid model must be splendid itself. The *Logos* of God is even superior to the beauty that is beauty as it occurs in nature. It is not adorned with beauty, but, if the truth be told, is itself beauty's preeminent adornment.

140 Such was the nature, it seems to me, of the first human being in body and soul, surpassing all those living now and all our predecessors as well, for our origin is from other human beings, whereas he was created by God. The greater the superiority of the maker, the greater is the excellence of what comes into being. For just as that which is at its peak is always better than that which is past its prime, whether it concerns a living being or a plant or a fruit or whatever else might be found in nature, so it is likely that the first molded human being was the acme of our entire species, while those who came later were no longer at the same peak, since generation by generation they obtained both outward appearance and capabilities which were ever inferior. 141 I have seen this happen in the arts of sculpture and painting. Copies are deficient when compared to the originals, while those [products] that are painted and sculpted based on the copies are even more so, because they stand at a great remove from the origin. A similar phenomenon is demonstrated by the magnetic stone. The iron ring that touches the stone itself is most powerfully affected; the ring next to the one touching is affected less, while the third hangs from the second, the fourth from the third, the fifth from the fourth, and so forth in a long series. They are held together by a single attractive force, but not to the same degree, for the rings, which are suspended farther away from the origin, are held less and less tightly, the reason being that the attractive force weakens and is no longer able to constrain them in equal measure. Something similar also appears to have happened to the race of human beings. In each generation they receive capabilities and qualities of both body and soul that are fainter and fainter.

142 If we describe that original ancestor not only as the first human being, but also as the only real citizen of the cosmos, we will be telling the absolute truth. The cosmos was his home and city, since no handmade constructions built out of materials of stone and wood were yet present. He resided in the cosmos with complete safety like in his native land, wholly without fear, because he had been found worthy to exercise dominion over earthly affairs and all mortal creatures stood in awe of him, having either been trained or compelled to obey him as master. Therefore, he lived in the enjoyment of peace without conflict. 143 Nevertheless, since every well-governed city has a constitution, it was the case that the citizen of the world necessarily made use of the constitution that belonged to the entire cosmos. This is the right reason of nature, which is named with a more appropriate title "ordinance" [*thesmos*], a divine law, according to which obligations and rights have been distributed to each creature. This city and its constitution must have had citizens before the human being. These might justly be called citizens of the great city, since they have obtained the greatest precinct to dwell in and have been enrolled in the community which is greatest and most complete. 144 Who else would these be than the rational and divine natures, some of whom are incorporeal and intelligible beings, while others have bodies of the

kind that the stars in fact possess? Consorting and having fellowship with these beings, the first man surely passed the time in undiluted well-being. He was closely related and akin to the Director, because the divine spirit had flowed into him in ample measure, and so all his words and actions were undertaken in order to please the Father and King, in whose footsteps he followed along the highways that the virtues mark out; because only those souls are permitted to approach him who consider the goal of their existence to be assimilation to the God who brought them forth.

[145] Our description of the beauty, both in soul and in body, of the firstborn human being has been given to the best of our ability, even if it falls far short of the truth. His descendants, who partake of his form, necessarily still manage to preserve the marks of the family relationship with their ancestor, even if these have become rather faint. [146] What does this family relationship consist of? Every human being, as far as his mind is concerned, is akin to the divine *Logos* and has come into being as a casting or fragment or effulgence of the blessed nature, but in the structure of his body, he is related to the entire cosmos. For it is a compound made from the same things, earth and water and air and fire, each of the elements making the required contribution for the completion of an entirely sufficient material, which the Creator had to take to hand in order to fabricate this visible image. [147] In addition he resides in all the above-mentioned elements as locations that are most congenial and familiar to him, alternating and spending time in different places, so that the human being can most justifiably be said to be everything at once, a being of the earth, of the water, of the air, and of the heavens. For inasmuch as he dwells and walks on the earth, he is a land animal. Inasmuch as he frequently dives and swims and sails, he is a water creature—merchants and sailors and divers and those who hunt after oysters and fish are the clearest proof of what has been said. Inasmuch as his body moves around lifted up and raised from the earth, he might rightly be called an airborne creature. Finally, he is also heavenly, because through sight, the most directive of the senses, he draws near to the sun and moon and each of the other planets and fixed stars.

[Chapter 20] The Giving of Names

[148] Most excellently, he also ascribed the imposition of names[a] to the first human being. This is a task involving wisdom and kingship. That person was wise with a self-taught and self-instructed wisdom, having come into existence through divine beneficence. Moreover, he was king, and it is fitting for a ruler to address each of his subjects by name. The power of the authority attached to that first human being was surely exceedingly strong. God had molded him with care and considered him worthy of the second rank, establishing him subordinate to himself but as ruler over all other creatures. Even those who are born so many generations later, when the race has become feeble through the long revolutions of time, still manage to rule over the creatures without reason, preserving a torch— as it were—of rule and authority handed down from the first human being.

a. Gen. 2:20.

[149] He says therefore that God led all the living beings to the human being, wishing to see which[a] titles he would impose on each of them, not because he was in any doubt—for nothing is unknown to God—but because he knew that he had fashioned the rational nature in the mortal being with freedom of movement, so that he himself would have no share in wickedness. He proceeded to test him, as a teacher tests a pupil, inciting his innate disposition and inviting him to demonstrate the appropriate actions, so that he would of his own accord produce epithets that were not inappropriate or unfitting, but would reveal in an excellent fashion the individual characteristics of their subjects. [150] After all, the rational nature in his soul was still uncorrupted, and not a single weakness or disease or passion had found its way in. So he took in wholly unblemished impressions of things material and immaterial, and made appellations that were accurate, taking aim in excellent fashion at what was revealed, so that their natures were pronounced and understood at the very same time.

In this way he distinguished himself with every fine attribute, attaining the very limit of human well-being.

[Chapter 21] Woman Appears on the Scene

[151] However, since nothing is stable in the world of becoming and mortal beings necessarily undergo reverses and changes, the first human being too had to enjoy some ill fortune. The starting point of a blameworthy life becomes for him woman.[b] As long as he was single, he resembled God and the cosmos in his solitariness, receiving the delineations of both natures in his soul, not all of them but as many as a mortal constitution could contain. But when woman too was molded,[c] he observed a sisterly form and a kindred figure. Rejoicing at the sight, he came up to her and gave her a greeting. [152] She, seeing no other living creature that looked more like herself than he, was glad and modestly responded to his greeting. The love that ensues brings together the two separate halves of a single living being as it were, and joins them into unity, thereby establishing in both a desire for union with the other in order to produce a being similar to themselves. Nevertheless, this desire also gave rise to bodily pleasure, which is the starting point of wicked and law-breaking deeds, and on its account they exchange the life of immortality and well-being for the life of mortality and misfortune.

[Chapter 22] Events in the Garden of Delights and Their Interpretation

[153] While the man was still leading his solitary life and the woman had not yet been molded, it is related that a garden of delights was planted by God,[d] which bears no resemblance to those in our experience. For these have timber without

---

a. Gen. 2:20.
b. Gen. 2:23.
c. Cf. Gen. 2:19, 22.
d. Gen. 2:8.

soul, filled with all manner of trees. Some bloom all the time and give continuous visual pleasure, others blossom and grow leaves in the spring season; some bear domesticated fruit for human beings, not only supplying the necessary nourishment but also the additional enjoyment of luxurious living, while others bear a different sort, which of necessity has been apportioned to wild animals. But in the case of the divine garden of delights all the plants in fact possess soul and reason, bearing fruit in the form of the virtues and in addition neutral understanding and keenness of mind—by which what is good and what is evil is recognized[a]—as well as life without disease and indestructibility and whatever is of a similar kind to these. [154] These themes, it seems to me, are philosophized symbolically rather than in the proper sense of the words. No trees of life[b] or understanding have ever appeared on earth in the past or are ever likely to appear in the future. Rather, it would seem that with the garden of delights he hints at the ruling part of the soul, which is filled with countless opinions just like plants, while with the tree of life he hints at the most important of the virtues, reverence for God, through which the soul is immortalized, and with the tree that makes known good and evil things[c] at intermediate practical insight, through which things that are opposite by nature are discriminated.

[155] Once he had placed[d] these boundaries in the soul, he proceeded like a judge to observe in which direction it would incline. When he saw it leaning toward cunning and having little regard for piety and holiness, from which immortal life results, he expelled it,[e] as might be expected, and banished it from the garden of delights.[f] He did not offer any hope of future return to a soul, which was going incurably and irremediably astray, since the reason for the deception,[g] too was in no small measure blameworthy. This subject deserves not to be passed over in silence.

[156] It is said that in ancient times, the venomous and earthborn reptile,[h] the snake,[i] could project a human voice, and that one day he approached the first man's wife and reproached her for being slow and excessively cautious, because she delays and postpones picking a fruit that is highly attractive to behold[j] and most pleasant to taste, and moreover is extremely advantageous for enabling one to discern what is good and what is evil.[k] Without further reflection, as the result of an unstable and unsettled conviction, she consented to the idea, ate of the fruit, and shared it with her husband. This was the event that suddenly changed them both from innocence and simplicity of character to cunning. The Father was outraged by this act, for it was a deed deserving to give rise to anger. They

a. Cf. Gen. 2:9, 17.
b. Gen. 2:9.
c. Gen. 2:9.
d. Cf. Gen. 2:8, 15.
e. Gen. 3:24.
f. Gen. 3:23.
g. Cf. Gen. 3:13.
h. Cf. Gen. 1:24, 30.
i. Gen. 3:1.
j. Gen. 3:6.
k. Cf. Gen. 3:5.

had passed by the tree of immortal life,[a] perfection of excellence, through which they could have enjoyed the fruits of an agelong life of well-being, and made the choice for that ephemeral and mortal existence, not a life but a time span full of misfortune. Therefore, he determined the punishments against them that they deserved.

[Chapter 23] Interpretation of the Snake

[157] These are not the fabrications of myth, in which the race of poets and sophists rejoice, but indications of character types that invite allegorical interpretation through the explanation of hidden meanings. You will follow a reasonable conjecture if you say that the above-mentioned snake is suitable as a symbol for pleasure, firstly because it is a legless creature that lies face forward on its stomach, secondly because it takes clumps of earth[b] as food, and thirdly because it carries poison in its teeth, by which it able to kill those whom it bites. [158] None of the above-mentioned traits are missing in the lover of pleasure. Only with difficulty can he raise his head, burdened and dragged downward as he is by the lack of self-control that throws him forward and trips him up. He does not feed on the heavenly food that wisdom extends to lovers of contemplation by means of words and doctrines, but rather on what is provided from the earth according to the annual seasons, from which arise indulgence in wine and love of delicacies and gluttony. These stimulate the appetites of the stomach to break loose and become inflamed and enslaved to excessive eating, as well as making the lusts of the lower parts burst forth. Greedily he desires after the labors of caterers and chefs de cuisine. Moving his ugly head in a circle, he longs to partake of the smells of the delicious food. Whenever he sees a well-supplied table, he hurls himself and spreads out full-length onto what has been laid out, hastening to fill himself with everything all at once and making his aim not to reach satiety but to make sure that nothing of what has been laid out is left behind. [159] Hence this person, no less than a snake, carries poison in his teeth. Teeth are the servants and assistants of insatiable appetite. Everything to do with food they chop up and grind, first handing it over to the tongue that examines the flavors for approval, then to the throat. A lack of moderation in food is deadly by nature and poisonous, because it does not allow digestion on account of the influx of new food that occurs before the previous lot has been absorbed.

[160] The snake is said to project a human voice because pleasure makes use of countless defenders and champions, who have taken its care and advocacy upon themselves and go so far as to teach that the power of pleasure attaches itself to all things great and small, without any exception whatsoever. [161] Certainly, the first intercourse of the male with the female has pleasure as its guide. Impregnation and birth take place through its agency. The offspring naturally first feel an affinity to nothing else but it, rejoicing in pleasure and disliking its opposite pain. For this reason babies cry when they are born, feeling pain, it would seem, because

a. Gen. 2:9.
b. Gen. 3:5.

of the chill around them. After spending a long time in the extremely warm and fiery location of the womb, they all of a sudden emerge into the air, a chilly and unaccustomed place. It gives them a fright and their cries are the clearest evidence of their distress and the fact that they dislike pain. [162] Every living being, they say, strives after pleasure as its most necessary and essential goal, but this applies especially to the human being. Other living beings seek it through taste and the genital organs only, but the human being does so through the other senses as well, pursuing all the sights and sounds that give delight to ears and eyes. [163] A vast number of other assertions are made in praise of this passion, arguing that it is something highly native and akin to living beings. But what has been said so far is sufficient to demonstrate the reason why the snake appeared to project a human voice. For this reason, it seems to me, in the detailed laws too, when he wrote about which animals should be offered as food and which not, he gave special praise to the animal named the snake-fighter.[a] This is a reptile that has legs above his feet,[b] enabling it to jump from the earth and be lifted in the air just like the species of the grasshoppers.[c] [164] The snake-fighter, it seems to me, is nothing but a symbol of self-control, which engages in an unrelenting battle and unremitting war against lack of self-control and pleasure. Self-control especially welcomes simplicity and frugality and whatever is required for an austere and holy life, whereas pleasure loves luxury and extravagance, which cause soul and body to grow soft and decadent, and result in a life that in the view of sensible people is in fact blameworthy and harsher than death.

[165] Pleasure does not dare to offer her tricks and deceits[d] to the man,[e] but rather to the woman[f] and through her to him. This is said quite suitably and appropriately, for in us the intellect has the role of man, while sense perception has that of woman. Pleasure encounters and consorts with the senses first, and through them she deceives the ruling intellect as well. Each of the senses is seduced by her charms. They rejoice in what is set before them, sight responding to varieties of color and shape, hearing to melodious sounds, taste to the sweetness of flavors, and smell to the fragrances of exhaled vapors. On receiving these gifts, in the manner of female servants, they offer them to reason as their master, taking persuasion along as their advocate so that none of the offerings whatsoever would be rejected. He is immediately ensnared. Instead of being a ruler he becomes a subject, a slave instead of a lord, an exile instead of a citizen, a mortal instead of an immortal being. [166] In short, one should be aware that, like a shameless prostitute, pleasure desires to get hold of a lover and seeks out pimps that can help her lure him. It is the senses that act as pimps for her and solicit the lover. Once she has ensnared them, she will easily bring the intellect under her sway. They convey the external appearances inside, announce and display them, imprinting the characteristics of each thing on it and activating the passion that corresponds

a. Lev. 11:22.
b. Lev. 11:21.
c. Lev. 11:22.
d. Cf. Gen. 3:13.
e. Gen. 3:6.
f. Gen. 3:1.

to them. For, just like in wax, the intellect receives the impressions via the senses. It needs them in order to comprehend bodily reality, not being able on its own to do this, as I have said already.

[Chapter 24] The Consequences of Wickedness

[167] The consequences of pleasure were immediately discovered by those who first became slaves of a passion that is harsh and difficult to heal. The woman obtained the strong labor pains and the grief that occurred successively during the rest of her life, especially those to do with the birth of children[a] and their upbringing and sickness and health and good fortune and misfortune, to which was added the loss of freedom and the absolute mastery of the husband[b] at her side, whose commands she had to obey. The man in turn obtained toil, hardships, and the sweat[c] of continual hard labor in order to obtain a supply of the necessities of life. He was deprived of the spontaneous good things, which the earth had been taught to bear without the mediation of agricultural science, but had to take part in unremitting labors in order to find the means of living and food and not perish through starvation. [168] I believe in fact that, just as the sun and the moon always shine forth after they had once been commanded to do so at the first genesis of the universe and continue to keep the divine command for no other reason than that wickedness has been exiled far away from the borders of heaven, in the same way the fertile and crop-bearing soil of the earth would have continued to bear a lavish supply [of goods] in accordance with the annual seasons without the art and assistance of farmers. But now that wickedness has begun to abound at the expense of the virtues, the ever-flowing fountains of God's grace have been blocked, lest they be lavished on those who do not deserve to receive them. [169] Indeed, if the human race had undergone the punishment that was appropriate, it would have been wiped out because of the ingratitude that it showed toward God its benefactor and savior. But he, being merciful by nature, took compassion and moderated the punishment. He allowed the race to survive, but no longer provided food ready to hand in the same way as before, lest they, by indulging in two forms of wickedness, laziness and overindulgence, go astray and become insolent in their behavior. [170] Such was the life of those who in the beginning[d] enjoyed innocence and simplicity, but then preferred evil deeds, from which one should abstain, to virtue.

[Chapter 25] Moses Teaches Five Vital Lessons

By means of the creation account, which we have discussed, he [Moses] teaches us among many other things five lessons that are the most beautiful and excellent

a. Gen. 3:16.
b. Gen. 3:16.
c. Cf. Gen. 3:19.
d. Cf. Gen. 1:1.

of all. The first of these is that the divinity is and exists, on account of the godless, some of whom are in doubt and incline in two directions concerning his existence, while others are more reckless and brazenly assert that he does not exist at all, but is only said to exist by people who overshadow the truth with mythical fictions. [171] The second lesson is that God is one, on account of those who introduce the polytheistic opinion, feeling no shame when they transfer the worst of political systems, rule by the mob, from earth to heaven. The third lesson is, as has already been said, that the cosmos has come into existence, on account of those who think it is ungenerated and eternal, attributing no superiority to God. The fourth lesson is that the cosmos too is one, since the Creator is one as well and he has made his product similar to himself in respect of its unicity, expending all the available material for the genesis of the whole. After all, it would not have been a complete whole if it had not been put together and constituted of parts that were themselves whole. There are those who suppose there to be multiple cosmoi, and there are others who think their number is boundless, whereas they themselves are the ones who are boundlessly ignorant of what it is fine to know. The fifth lesson is that God also takes thought for the cosmos, for that the maker always takes care of what has come into existence is a necessity by the laws and ordinances of nature, in accordance with which parents too take care of their children.

[172] He, then, who first has learned these things not so much with his hearing as with his understanding, and has imprinted their marvelous and priceless forms on his own soul, namely, that God is and exists, and that he who truly exists is one, and that he made the cosmos and made it unique, making it, as was said, similar to himself in respect of its being one, and that he always takes thought for what has come into being, this person will lead a blessed life of well-being, marked as he is by the doctrines of piety and holiness.

Introduction to *On the Giants*

On the Giants (De gigantibus) belongs to the corpus of writings of the Jewish exegete and philosopher Philo of Alexandria (*see* Introduction to Philo of Alexandria), and is one of three primary treatises in which he discusses (among other topics) the material of Genesis 6:1–4. The two other writings in which he undertakes this task are *On the Unchangeableness of God (Quod Deus sit immutabilis)* and *Questions and Answers on Genesis (Quaestiones et solutiones in Genesin)*. Philo's purpose for writing *On the Giants* is to describe the spiritual position of humanity in relation to the heavens and holiness. The nature of angels, *daemons*, and souls is examined through allegorizing the tradition found in Genesis 6:1–4:

> And it came about that humanity began to multiply upon the face of the earth and daughters were born to them. And the Sons of God saw that the daughters of humanity were good to behold and they took for themselves women from whomever they chose. And God said: "My spirit will not remain in humanity forever in that it [humanity] also is flesh, and the days in which it [humanity] will have to repent will be 120 years." The Fallen Ones were on the earth in those days, and after, when the Sons of God went into the daughters of humanity. And there were born to them [the angels and women] the mighty men who were from the days of old, men of renown. —trans. Wright

At the same time, Philo is perhaps writing a polemic against the Fallen Watcher tradition of 1 Enoch (*see* Book of Watchers [1 Enoch 1–36]), Jubilees (*see* The Book of Jubilees), and other Jewish texts.[1]

Narrative Description

Philo's *On the Giants* presents a detailed discussion of anthropology through the lens of the story of the Sons of God and the daughters of humanity. In the Genesis

---

1. See Archie T. Wright, "Some Observations on Philo's de Gigantibus and Evil Spirits in Second Temple Judaism," *JSJ* 36 (2005): 471–88.

account, the Sons of God (angels) mate with human women to produce giant offspring, thus the title, *On the Giants*. The title of the treatise gives the reader the impression that Philo's focus is on the giant offspring; however, as one reads through the text it becomes apparent that he is offering a discussion of a dualistic approach to anthropology in first-century CE Judaism. From the very beginning of the treatise in 1, Philo implies that there is an ethical **dualism** (*see* Rule of the Community [1QS]) within humanity as he compares the righteous Noah to the humans of Genesis 6:1. Based on the narrator's introduction of Noah and his sons in Genesis 5:32 ("After Noah was five hundred years old, Noah fathered Shem, Ham, and Japheth"—trans. Wright; cf. Jub. 4:33: "In the twenty-fifth jubilee Noah married a woman whose name was Emzara, the daughter of Rakiel, the daughter of his father's brother—during the first year in the fifth week. In its third year, she gave birth to Shem for him; in its fifth year, she gave birth to Ham for him; and in the first year during the sixth week, she gave birth to Japheth for him"—trans. VanderKam), Philo suggests that the multiplication of humanity in Genesis 6:1 is an evil act (cf. *QG*).[2] It is through this wrongdoing of humanity that evil enters the cosmos, thus allowing Philo to separate God from the responsibility of evil. As such, *On the Giants* describes the journey of the human soul as one of personal responsibility for the decisions and actions of the individual. Accordingly, these personal choices govern the purity of one's soul and determine the person's opportunity to return to the heavenly realm upon death.

Philo begins his study of anthropology in *Gig.* 6, in which he argues that Moses gave the name of angels to what Greek philosophers called *daemons*. Philo explains that "these are spirits flying down from the upper regions" (6)[3] and are just one type of being that fill every division of the universe; the earth contains living beasts, the fire contains the fireborn, and heaven contains the stars (7). The angels and *daemons* are living beings that fill the air and, although invisible to natural senses, can be perceived by the mind (9; see Plato's description of *daemons* in *Symposium* 236).[4]

---

2. *QG* 89: "Why from the time that the deluge drew near, the human race is said to have increased so as to become a multitude? Divine mercies do always precede judgment; since the first work of God is to do good, and to destroy follows afterwards; but he himself (when terrible evils are about to happen) loves to provide and is accustomed to provide that previously an abundance of many and great blessings will be produced. On this principle also Egypt, when there was about to be a barrenness and famine for seven years as the prophet himself says, was for an equal number of years continuously made exceedingly fertile by the beneficent and saving power of the Creator of the universe. And in the same way in which he showers benefits upon men, he also teaches them to depart and to abstain from sin; that these blessings may not be turned into the contrary. And on this account now, by the freedom of their institutions, the cities of the world have increased in generous virtue, so that if any corruption supervenes subsequently they may disapprove of their own acts of wickedness as extraordinary and irremediable; not at all looking upon the divinity as the cause of them, for that has no connection with wickedness or misery, for the task of the Deity is only to bestow blessings." —trans. R. Marcus

3. Unless otherwise noted, all translations from *On the Giants* are by Archie T. Wright.

4. Plato, *Symposium* 236: "Eros is neither beautiful nor ugly, neither good nor evil. He is an intermediate state, a demon, half man, half god; he is like opinion (intermediate between ignorance and episteme). Love is a link, a demon. He is the true lover of wisdom because wis-

On the Giants 11 notes that the air is able, through divine direction, "to bring forth living beings . . . through the special gift of the Creator." Philo argues that the air contains a variety of bodiless souls, mighty beings, composed of at least two groups. The first group is predisposed to seek a human body in which to reside, while the second group has a "divine makeup" that does not entertain the desire to enter the physical realm. These latter beings are the "heroes" of the Greek philosophers[5] and the "angels" of Moses. These angels are described as messengers between humanity and the divine (12: "These ones being consecrated and devoted to the service of the Father. The Creator has been accustomed to using handmaidens and servants in the affairs of mortals"). The identification of both groups of beings indicates that Philo is very much aware of the spiritual forces at work in the heavenly realm.

One finds two categories within Philo's description of the human soul; these two classes are based on his ethical dualism (13–14). The first category of soul descends to the earth to take on human flesh but it is caught up in the rushing torrent of human passions, which, in turn, results in the corruption of the soul, leaving it no longer able to return to the heavenly realm. Such a soul does not seek wisdom to overcome the passions of the flesh but, rather, abandons itself to things of chance, which have nothing to do with the noblest part of humanity, the soul or mind. The second category of human soul is the one who descends to the earth to take on a human body, but is able to rise above the torrent of passions. This soul seeks the wisdom of "genuine philosophy" (Judaism) in order to regain the immortal and incorporeal existence in the presence of the divine (14).

Philo continues his theme of ethical dualism in 16–17, in which he argues that angels, *daemons,* and souls are different names for the same principal being, which one must assume is the soul. Each of these three beings has dualistic characteristics; there are good and bad angels, *daemons,* and souls.[6] To support his argument, Philo draws on Psalm 78:49 (LXX 77:49: "He sent among them his

---

dom is beautiful and beauty is the object of love. Men are lovers of the good, which they want to possess perpetually. Perpetuity achieved through procreation. Thus, Eros is procreation: physical, spiritual, and philosophical (that of wisdom)."

5. Hesiod, *Theogeny* 176: "Great Ouranos came, bringing the night, and spread out around Gaia, desiring *philotēs,* and was extended. His son reached out from ambush with his left hand, and in his right, he held the sickle, long and serrated, and the genitals of his father he quickly reaped and threw them behind his back to be carried away. But they did not flee from his hand fruitlessly. As many drops of blood spurted forth, all of them Gaia received. In the revolving years, she bore the powerful Erinyes, and great Giants, gleaming in their armor, holding long spears in their hands, and the nymphs whom they call the Ash Tree Nymphs across endless Gaia." Hesiod, *Theogeny* 207: "Father great Ouranos, quarreling with the children he sired himself, gave them the name Titans, Stretchers. He said that they stretched with a great recklessness to accomplish a huge deed, and for it retribution will be laid up for the future"—trans. Glenn W. Most (Loeb Classical Library 57).

6. There appear to be several connections to the Watcher tradition of 1 Enoch within Philo's discussion of the soul found in *Gig.* 16. See Archie T. Wright, *The Origin of Evil Spirits: The Reception of Genesis 6.1–4 in Early Jewish Literature,* WUNT 2.198 (Tübingen: Mohr Siebeck, 2005), pp. 210–15.

anger's wrath, anger and wrath and affliction, a dispatch of wicked angels") from which he identifies the evil angels of the psalm as human souls. These evil "fallen" angels, accordingly, do not seek to know the daughters of right reason (virtues), but rather they seek out the fleshly desires of humanity (vices). Each person is not entrapped by every vice, but his or her desire can involve the lusts of sight, hearing, eating, sex, or the abnormal (18):

> And they do not all take all the daughters, but some chose some from the great multitude for themselves; some chose through outward appearance and others chose through hearing. And others on account of taste and others by the belly or of sex. And many stretching their inward desires to the limit, taking hold of pleasures lying beyond the outward boundaries; for various kinds of pleasure are diverse out of necessity. Different pleasures are established in different places.

It is for this reason that the Spirit of God will not dwell among humanity forever (Gen. 6:3).

Daemons in Philo's work appear to be in a rather ambiguous class by themselves. The typical Greek classification is that of a divine being that operated in the human realm at the behest of the Olympian gods. Philo, on the other hand, equates the *daemon* with the Jewish concept of angel, a mediator of knowledge between God and humans. As it corresponds to the human desire for rescue or salvation, the *daemon* represents a mediator between the state of unrighteousness and impurity in the cycle of reincarnation and at the same time mediates a state of purity and justification. This intervention allows the individual soul to return to the realm of the divine.

Philo clearly understands the giants of Genesis 6:4 to be distinct from the portrayal presented in the Watcher tradition of 1 Enoch. For Philo, the giants are neither physical nor spiritual entities. They are, in fact, the irrational vices, the fleshly human passions. The task of the giants of Philo (vices), similar to that of the giants in 1 Enoch, is to create discord within the individual and among the community. For Philo, these "giants" result in an internal conflict within the human soul that holds the person beneath the torrent of the stream (the passions of the human nature and flesh). As a result, the person must avoid the pleasures of the flesh and live as a person of virtue. Philo goes on to indicate that the vices are numerous and represent a deadly threat to humans; as he contends, "let us subdue the great and numerous host of her deadly foes" (35).

In *On the Giants* 58, Philo attempts to explain the true meaning of Genesis 6:1–4. He declares it is not a myth about the giants, but rather it is Moses' account of three levels of humanity, the earthborn, the heavenborn, and the God-born. The earthborn are those souls who take part in the pleasures of the fleshly body, not concerning themselves with the virtues of a holy life. The heavenborn are lovers of learning, those who remain in the heavenly realm pursuing the things of the mind. The God-born are priests and prophets who refuse to enter into the worldly sector of humanity, instead choosing to remain in the divine realm (61). As an example of such men of God, Philo offers Abraham who, through his study of the upper world of heaven, was transformed in what can be described as

angelomorphic language. Philo encourages all his readers to follow the examples of Moses and Abraham and seek the transformation into the divine realm, forever in the fullness of God.

Author/Provenance/Date/Occasion

The consensus is that Philo wrote his entire corpus during the first century CE in the Hellenistic Jewish community of Alexandria, Egypt.[7] There is no confirmed date of authorship for *On the Giants* save to say that it was likely written in the early first century CE (*see* Introduction to Philo of Alexandria).

On the Giants is considered part of Philo's exegetical commentaries on Genesis. Some consider this particular portion of the corpus to be Jewish **Midrash**, in this case, one directed at Philo's **Hellenistic** audience. Philo's audience likely includes two distinct groups of people; one that appreciates wisdom and another that Philo identifies as those who are in need of the literal meaning of the biblical text.[8] It may be suggested that the audience had a sophisticated knowledge of Scripture and philosophy. Additionally, this audience may have held two complementary beliefs: (1) Scriptural traditions were written on a level for the philosophically poor; and (2) Scripture could be approached allegorically. As such, Philo wrote to meet the needs of his Alexandrian audience. Some scholars argue that there was little regard for Philo's work during his lifetime and it is possible, as David Runia suggests, that the majority of Jews, in particular the rabbinic community, ignored his work due to its exploitation by Christian authors.[9]

Text, Language, Sources, and Transmission

The extant versions of Philo's work, including *On the Giants,* are thought to be preserved in Greek by the early church fathers. An Armenian translation preserves *Questions and Solutions on Genesis* and *Questions and Solutions on Exodus.* Some Greek fragments preserve these two works plus a similar selection on Leviticus; in addition, a minor portion of *Questions and Solutions on Genesis* survives in Latin. Philo's source for *On the Giants* is the Greek Septuagint (*see* Overview of Early Jewish Literature). However, it is clear that he was familiar with many of the Greek philosophers (in particular Plato) and ethicists (the **Stoics**), as their methods of teaching and thought clearly influence his writings.

It is unclear if what survives today is the original form in which Philo authored the various texts. It is believed that *On the Giants* was originally a part of a larger

---

7. Due to the lack of historical and textual evidence, it is difficult to discuss the issues in this section with specific reference to *On the Giants*. One must offer generalities to which one can only assume the text falls in line.

8. See Alan Mendelson, *Philo's Jewish Identity,* Brown Judaic Studies 161 (Atlanta: Scholars, 1988).

9. David T. Runia, *Philo in Early Christian Literature: A Survey* (Assen: Van Gorcum, 1993), pp. 15–17.

work that contained the text of *On the Unchangeableness of God (Quod Deus sit immutabilis)*; this included an allegorical commentary on Genesis 6:5–12,[10] which considers the claim that God repented and changed his mind.

It is unclear how the writings of Philo were transmitted during their early existence. Due to the virtual extermination of Jewish culture in Alexandria during the second-century **Alexandrian revolt** (115–117 CE), these writings were likely known in a rather limited line of tradition. The works were eventually taken up by Christians of Alexandria, as is noted by Clement of Alexandria and later by Origen. The texts became part of Clement's library upon his move to Caesarea in the third century and were used by the church historian Eusebius. From Clement's work we can determine that there was other material that is no longer extant. The Caesarean manuscripts are likely those used for later manuscripts of Philo's work.

Theology

Philo and the Palestinian Jews held similar views on many significant theological issues but, at times, used very different language to express their views. One of the primary theological issues expressed in *On the Giants* is the concept of angels. Philo followed the tradition of the Pentateuch in which angels perform multiple tasks such as singing praises to God, moving the heavenly bodies, guarding the regions of the cosmos, and performing service in the heavenly sanctuary. Similar to the perspective of 1 Enoch, angels are messengers that pass between the divine and human realms; they inform God of the actions of humanity, and they are intercessors for creation. However, contrary to the teachings of 1 Enoch on the rebellious angels, Philo dismisses the idea of malevolent angels as mere superstition.

A second issue found in *On the Giants* is a contrast between spirit and flesh. This is also a common theme in Pauline texts from the New Testament where the author sees a fairly clear dichotomy of the two aspects of humanity. For Philo the spirit (soul) is something that exists in the heavenly realm and takes on human flesh only if it is drawn into the earthly realm by desires of the flesh. The human soul must then decide to remain above the torrent of temptation and desire a return to the heavenly realm; otherwise, it will remain trapped in the earthly realm and in a human body. On several occasions Paul describes

---

10. Gen. 6:5–12: "The Lord saw that the wickedness of humankind was great in the earth, and that every inclination of the thoughts of their hearts was only evil continually. And the Lord was sorry that he had made humankind on the earth, and it grieved him to his heart. So the Lord said, 'I will blot out from the earth the human beings I have created—people together with animals and creeping things and birds of the air, for I am sorry that I have made them.' But Noah found favor in the sight of the Lord. These are the descendants of Noah. Noah was a righteous man, blameless in his generation; Noah walked with God. And Noah had three sons, Shem, Ham, and Japheth. Now the earth was corrupt in God's sight, and the earth was filled with violence. And God saw that the earth was corrupt; for all flesh had corrupted its ways upon the earth"—trans. Wright.

the human struggle to overcome the flesh and walk in the spirit along the same lines as Philo.

A third issue is the role of human will regarding the choice of evil and sin. The idea that sin has a direct correlation to a person's own desire is quite apparent in the New Testament (Rom. 7:5–7; James 1:14; 4:1–3). Philo sees the human ability to overcome the desires of the flesh as clearly connected to one's study of Torah, while Paul and others frame this possibility in terms of human reliance on the Holy Spirit.

ROMANS 7:5–7	JAMES 1:14	JAMES 4:1–3
While we were living in the flesh, our sinful passions, aroused by the law, were at work in our members to bear fruit for death. But now we are discharged from the law, dead to that which held us captive, so that we are slaves not under the old written code but in the new life of the Spirit. What then should we say? That the law is sin? By no means! Yet, if it had not been for the law, I would not have known sin. I would not have known what it is to covet if the law had not said, "You shall not covet."	But one is tempted by one's own desire, being lured and enticed by it.	Those conflicts and disputes among you, where do they come from? Do they not come from your cravings that are at war within you? You want something and do not have it; so you commit murder. And you covet something and cannot obtain it; so you engage in disputes and conflicts. You do not have, because you do not ask. You ask and do not receive, because you ask wrongly, in order to spend what you get on your pleasures.

Reception of *On the Giants* in Second Temple Period

Philo's writings, although quite distinct from other texts written or discovered in the Second Temple period, fit quite well into the wide variety of Judaisms that existed during the period. This diversity of extant writings from the period is due in part to the various political, social, and cultural settings in which each was authored. *On the Giants* reflects a heavy Hellenistic influence on Philo's thought and his developing anthropology and giantology. Philo took advantage of ideas and concepts from his Greek culture in order to creatively interpret the Jewish Scriptures for his audience.

Philo's *On the Giants* serves as an important treatise on the problem of evil and the role of human responsibility in its perpetuation. Philo draws on various aspects of Greek philosophy and Jewish theology to describe the struggles facing the human soul in its earthly journey. He appears to make a distinct shift from traditions regarding the giants found in the Book of Watchers and other Second Temple period Jewish texts that have rewritten (or expanded) the story of the Sons of God and the daughters of humanity and the **etiology** of evil spirits on the earth.

ARCHIE T. WRIGHT

FURTHER READING

Kamesar, Adam, ed. *The Cambridge Companion to Philo.* Cambridge: Cambridge University Press, 2009.

Runia, David T. *Philo in Early Christian Literature: A Survey.* Assen: Van Gorcum, 1993.

Winston, David. *Philo of Alexandria: The Contemplative Life, The Giants, and Selections.* New York: Paulist, 1981.

ADVANCED READING

Mendelson, Alan. *Philo's Jewish Identity.* Brown Judaic Series 161. Atlanta: Scholars, 1988.

Philo of Alexandria. Trans. F. H. Colson and G. H. Whitaker. Vol. 2. Loeb Classical Library. Cambridge, Mass.: Harvard University Press, 1958.

Winston, David, and John Dillion, eds. *Two Treatises of Philo of Alexandria: A Commentary on De Gigantibus and Quod Sit Immutabilis.* Brown Judaic Series 25. Chico, Calif.: Scholars, 1983.

Wright, Archie T. *The Origin of Evil Spirits.* WUNT 2:198. Tubingen: Mohr Siebeck, 2005.

4.11 *On the Giants*

^{1.1} "And also it happened when humans began to be established numerously upon the earth and daughters were being born to them" (Gen. 6:1). I think this is something worthy of being examined; why, following the birth of Noah and his sons, did our ancestors grow to such a large population. The reason for this is not difficult to explain; for always when the rare appears the opposite is found to be numerous. ² Accordingly, the natural goodness of the one shows clearly the lack of natural goodness of the multitude. Yet actually the things of artful skills and science and virtue and goodness, being few, reveal that many unskillful, unintelligent, unjust, and generally worthless things lie in the shadow. ³ Do you not see that in all things, also the sun, being one body, by its shining forth dissipates the great and deep darkness that is spread upon the earth and sea? Naturally, therefore, the birth of the just Noah and his sons makes evident the many unjust, for it is by the nature of the opposite especially that the opposite is known to exist. ⁴ But no one (or nothing) unjust sows an altogether male spiritual generation, but being unmanly, broken, effeminate in their thoughts, being naturally producers of females; having planted no tree of virtue whose fruit was bound to be good and noble by necessity, but all the trees were of wicked vices and passions, whose offshoots were feminine. ⁵ For this reason, these men are said to have produced daughters and none of them a son; for since the righteous Noah begat male children, indeed being one who follows the perfect, upright, and masculine reason, as such the injustice of the multitude appears in the producing of females. For it is impossible for the same offspring to have opposite parents, but again they must produce the opposite offspring.

^{2.6} "And when the angels of God saw that the daughters of men were beautiful, they took for themselves a woman they chose whoever they wished out of all of them" (Gen. 6:2). Those that the other philosophers call demons, that Moses customarily calls angels (messengers), these are spirits flying down from the upper regions. ⁷ And let no one assume the saying is a myth. For it is a necessity that the entire universe be filled with living things. The primary and elemental portions (of the cosmos) each contain their suitable living creatures; on the one hand the earth has the creatures of the land, and the sea and rivers contain the water creatures, and fire, the fireborn (a saying suggests these exist especially in Macedonia), and heaven contains the stars. ⁸ For these stars are souls throughout the whole universe, completely without blemish and divine, and for which in a circle they are moving, a motion related to the mind. For each of them is a mind unmixed. Therefore it is necessary that the air be filled with living creatures. And to us these are unseen since even the air is not visible to the human eye. ⁹ Rather, the power of sight is not able to envision the outward appearance of souls. On account of this reason there are no souls in the air, but by necessity they are detected by the mind in order that like may be perceived by like. Also what else can be said? ¹⁰ Do not

---

Translation by Archie T. Wright.

all land and sea creatures live by air and breath? Is it not true that when the air is filled with afflictions, pestilences often arise suggesting that air is the animating principle for all? Is it not true that it is harmless and uncorrupted especially when the North Wind prevails? Does not the drawing out of purer air tend toward an abundant and powerful duration of vitality? [11] Is it then natural that this element through which all others, water and land creatures, are given life, is itself desolate and soulless? On the contrary, even if all other living creatures were barren the air by itself would be obligated to produce living creatures, receiving from the Creator the souls through his remarkable grace.

[3.12] Now some of the souls indeed descended into bodies but others desire no portion of the earth when they come in contact with it. These ones being consecrated and devoted to the service of the Father. The Creator has been accustomed to using handmaidens and servants in the affairs of mortals. [13] And those having descended into a body as into a river, on one occasion are swept away as by a violent whirlpool, but on another occasion having been able to resist the rush of the current, initially rising to the surface from where they hasten onward flying back to the place they started. [14] These then are souls of the genuine philosophers who from beginning to the end meditate on dying to the life of the body, in order that they may obtain the incorporeal and incorruptible life in the presence of the uncreated and the incorruptible one. [15] But those who have sunk below the water are the souls of other men as many who disregard wisdom. They have sold themselves to unstable things and matters of chance, none of which are related to the upright portions in us, soul or mind, but all are related to the dead corpse born to us, the body, or related to these lifeless things—glory, wealth, authority, honor, and all other things that are molded and painted in deceitful and false glory by the ones not keeping their eyes upon the truly good things.

[4.16] If then you consider that souls, demons, and angels are indeed differing in name but are the same underlying object, you will cast off this heavy burden of religious superstition. But many speak of good and evil *daemons* and souls also in like manner, and so also they speak of angels as worthy of the calling. Some are ambassadors of men to God and of God to holy and inviolate men through this blameless and noble office. But of others, you will not err if you recognize as unholy and unworthy to take up the title of angel. [17] And bearing witness to my assertion, according to the expression of the psalmist in his song, "He sent out his wrathful anger, rage, anger, and affliction, through the mission of evil angels" (Ps. 77:49). These were the evil ones, who taking on the name of angels, not knowing the daughters of right reason, understanding, and virtue, put pursued the mortal descendants of mortal men, that is, the pleasures that cannot bestow genuine beauty that the mind alone can perceive, but illegitimate beauty through which the insight is deceived. [18] And they do not all take all the daughters, but some chose some from the great multitude for themselves; some chose through outward appearance and others chose through hearing. And others on account of taste and others by the belly or of sex. And many stretching their inward desires to the limit, taking hold of pleasures lying beyond the outward boundaries; for various kinds of pleasure are diverse out of necessity. Different pleasures are established in different places.

5.19 Indeed, in all such beings as these, it is impossible for the breath of God to remain forever, as the lawgiver himself made clear for he said, "The Lord God stated, 'My spirit (breath) will not remain in humanity for eternity because they are flesh'" (Gen. 6:3). **20** For indeed at times it does remain, but it does not remain forever with us. For who is in this manner without reason or is lifeless as never taken hold of the knowledge of the Good either willingly or unwillingly. For even over the ones devoted to evil hovers often a sudden appearance of the Good, but they are unable to take hold and keep it to themselves. **21** For it departs immediately, going elsewhere, having turned away from the inhabitants who have approached those who have turned away from the Law and justice. To whom it would never have come if not for the grace of refuting those who choose what is disgraceful instead of good. **22** But he speaks of the spirit (breath) of God throughout in one sense as air flowing over the earth, carrying a third element, water. For this reason Moses said in the creation story, "The spirit of God moved upon the face of the waters" (Gen. 1:2), since the air, being light, rises and is carried aloft using water as its foundation and in another sense, it is undefiled knowledge that every wise person naturally shares. **23** Even as he reveals this concerning the Creator and Craftsman of the holy works of creation, since "God called up Bezaleel and filled him with a divine spirit, wisdom, insight, understanding to devise every task" (Exod. 31:1). So that it is suggested in these words how the spirit of God is defined.

6.24 Such also is the spirit of Moses that came to the seventy elders so that they might be superior to others and be made better, who could not truly be made elders unless partaking of the spirit of perfect wisdom. For it is spoken (written), "I will remove my spirit which is upon you and I will place (it) upon the seventy elders" (Num. 11:17). **25** But let you not think that this taking away (of the spirit) is accordingly cutting off and making a separation, but rather it is as happens when taking fire from fire; for though it can kindle a myriad of torches, it still remains the same with being diminished. Such too is the nature of knowledge. Of all those who show forth effort and become its students, it makes into people of skill, yet no portion is diminished, but many times it is also is improved, as they say of the drawing of water of a spring for this reason thereafter the water is especially sweet. **26** For the continuous interaction with others entails training and practice and makes for complete perfection. If then the individual spirit of Moses or any other creature were about to be distributed to so large a mass of disciples, if it were divided into small portions, then it would be diminished. **27** But now the spirit that is upon him is the wise, the divine, the indivisible, the undividable, the beautiful, the spirit diffused completely everywhere and in all things, the one that benefits but does not cause harm, neither if shared with others nor added to something is it diminished in knowledge, understanding, and wisdom.

7.28 Now although it is possible for a divine spirit to tarry in a soul, but for it to remain is impossible, as we have said. And why need we wonder? For no other thing whatsoever is stable and secure, since human things sway to and fro, tilting the scale from side to side and liable at various times to various changes. **29** And the greatest cause of ignorance is the flesh and the appropriation of the flesh. And he (Moses) declares (God) stated, "because they are flesh" the divine spirit is not able to remain indwelling. Yet marriage and raising children, furnishing necessary things, disgrace with the want for money and business, both private things and public things, and countless other things cause wisdom to waste away before it flourishes. [30] But nothing in this manner impedes the growth as the fleshly nature. For this, if anything, is the primary and greatest foundation of which ignorance and hatred for learning rest, which of the previously stated things is built upon. [31] For souls that are without flesh and body pass the time in the theater of the universe seeing and hearing divine things of which an insatiable desire for has entered into them, they enjoy them with nothing hindering. But as many who bear the burden of flesh, being weighed down and pressed upon, unable to see above the revolutions of the heavens, but being dragged down, the neck forcibly pressed to the ground like four-footed beasts.

[8.32] And for this reason the lawgiver having determined to put an end to outlawed and illicit intercourse and unions, he begins his abolishment in this manner, "A man, a man will not come near to any member of the household akin to his flesh to uncover his nakedness, I am the Lord" (Lev. 18:6). How could anyone more strongly urge to despise the flesh and what is akin to the flesh than in this manner? [33] And yet he not only urges to turn away from this but also positively asserts that the true man will never approach voluntarily the pleasures that are friend and kindred to the body, but will always make it a practice to estrange himself from them. [34] The idea that he states not once but twice "a man, a man" is a sign this is not the man made up of body and soul but the one who exercises virtue. For indeed he is this true man and for whom one of the ancients lit a candle at midday and said to them who inquired he was seeking a man. And as for the prohibition of a man approaching any who is akin to his flesh, it has a necessary reason. For there are some things that must be admitted, such as the necessities of life themselves through whose use we are able to live sickness-free and healthy. But we should scornfully reject the superfluous things that kindle the lusts, which by a single flare consume every good thing. [35] Then do not let our pleasurable desires be stirred up toward all things, toward the things dear to the flesh. For the undisciplined pleasures oftentimes fawn upon us in the manner of dogs, then turning around and inflicting fatal bites. Therefore, let us welcome the spirit of contentment, the friend of virtue, rather than the things akin to the body, and let us throw down the infinite vast multitude of her irreconcilable enemies. And if some opportune time forces us to receive more than a moderately sufficient measure, let us not approach it ourselves. For he says, "He will not himself go near to uncover shame."

[9.36] And why is this? It is worthwhile to explain these words. Often many not being themselves providers of wealth have had an unlimited abundance, while others who have not pursued glory are considered worthy of public praise and honor. Even the ones not hoping for a little strength have found themselves with abundant vigor. [37] Now let all of these (ones) learn that no one is to approach knowingly the things mentioned. That is, not to admire them and praise them with great measure, judging that each of them is not only not a good thing but rather a great evil—whether the wealth, the glory, the bodily strength—the lovers of these things each makes an "approach," money lovers to money, glory lovers to glory, lovers of athletic and gymnastics to bodily strength. They have abandoned the good soul for the evil soulless. [38] But they who are masters of themselves, they show that the splendor and fight for success are obedient to the mind as to a governor. Indeed, if the evils approach, they are received for improvement of life, but if having remained far away, they do not draw near, but even without them the "masters of themselves" are able to be happy. [39] But the one pursuing philosophy and following its path eagerly defiles it with disgrace on account of he is said "to uncover its nakedness." For how certainly clear is the disgrace of those who say they are wise, but sell wisdom for a bargained price as they say of the ones in the market who hawk their goods sometimes for little profit, sometimes with a pleasing and seductive speech, sometimes with uncertain hope established on nothing firm, and sometimes on promises that are no better than dreams.

[10.40] The words that follow, "I am the Lord," are spoken beautifully and are extremely instructive. Contrast, he says, "O noble man, the good of the flesh to the good of the soul and to the good of the All." The pleasure of the flesh is irrational but the pleasure of the soul and the All is the mind of the whole, God. [41] For the comparison of these two incomparable things is, indeed, a serious match. So close the similarity it may deceive the one alongside unless one will say the living things are like the lifeless things, reasoning with unreasoning, well-adapted with ill-adapted, odd with even, light with darkness, day with night, and all opposites with their contraries. [42] And yet even if it is possible for these things to have something in common, kinship with one another by reason of creation, still God is not in any respect like the best of created beings. Inasmuch as these are created and will suffer in the future, God is uncreated and ever doing. [43] Now it is good not to desert from the ranks of God in which it is established that all must by necessity be brave and to desert to the effeminate and cowardly pleasure that harms its friends and benefits its enemies. For new to itself is its nature; for all to whom it chooses to give its own good things, immediately it inflicts damage. It harms when it bestows and it benefits when it takes away. [44] If therefore, O soul, should the love charms of pleasure beckon you, turn yourself away and direct your gaze on the genuine beauty of virtue. And having gazed upon it, remain until a desire has sunk into you; like a magnet draws you on and brings you near and binds you fast to the object of your desire.

[11.45] But the words "I am Lord" must be understood not only in equality to "I am the perfect one and the incorruptible and the truly good" which whoever takes hold of, he will reject the imperfect and perishable and things attached to the flesh, but also in place of the phrase, "I am the sovereign ruler, and the king, and the master." [46] And neither for the subjects in the presence of the ruler nor the servants in the presence of their masters is it safe to do wrong. For when the punishers are near by, those who lack by nature the ability to reprove themselves are corrected and restrained by fear. [47] For God having filled all things is near at hand, therefore he is present and looking over everything, we being filled with great reverence, but if not that, being fearful of the unconquered power of his sovereignty and fearful and inexorable in its punishment. When he determines to use his power, may we desist from doing wrong in order that the divine spirit of wisdom may not be inclined to swiftly move his dwelling and depart. But may he remain with us for a long time as he did also with Moses the wise one. [48] For whether standing or sitting, Moses acted in the most peaceful way, maintaining a nature that did not change or mutate. For it is said that "Moses and the ark did not move" (Num. 14:44), either because the wise one is not separated from virtue or virtue is immovable or the earnest person is not subject to change, but each of these is steadfastly grounded in right reason. [49] Again in another passage, "But you stand here with me" (Deut. 5:31). This is an oracle given to the prophet. Steadfast and tranquil is the existence of the one alongside the ever-immovable steadfast God. For all that are placed beside a sound standard, they are made straight. [50] On account of this it seems to me also that excessive vanity, named Jethro, was amazed at the unwavering and consistent, unvarying and constant direction of the sage; he was bitter and inquired in this manner, "Why do you sit alone?" (Exod. 18:14). [51] For one who observes in the midst of peace the continual war among men, existing not only according to nations and country and cities, but also according to household and particularly within an individual man and the indescribable heavy storms with the soul; stirred by the violent force of life's events, he can naturally wonder if in such a storm another can enjoy fair weather or in swelling waves of the sea is able to bring calm. [52] You see that not even the High Priest Reason is continually lingering in and devoting himself to the holy decrees, being able with freedom to approach and to examine them at the appointed times, but scarcely once a year (Lev. 16:2, 34). For when something is associated with reason through an utterance it is uncertain, since it is of a dual nature. The one that approaches through no sound, only in the language of the soul, this is to contemplate the existent one, because such stands upon the indivisible One.

12.[53] Accordingly therefore among the many, that is to say, the ones having planned many life goals, the divine spirit does not abide, even though it may return only for a short time. To only one kind of man does it come to dwell in, those having thrown off all things of the creation and the inner curtain and veil of splendor and the unhampered and naked mind will reach God. [54] Thus also Moses built his own tent outside the camp (Exod. 33:7) and the whole host of bodily things, that is, he settled his unwavering judgment. He begins to worship God and entering the darkness, the invisible region, he abides there and fulfills the sacred rites and he becomes not only the one initiated, but also the teacher of the sacred rites and teacher of divine things, which he will impart to those with pure ears. [55] To this therefore the divine spirit is always at his side leading him in every upright way. But from the others, as I said, it quickly disengages itself. These are those whose lifespan is fulfilled at one hundred and twenty years; for he said, "Their days will be one hundred and twenty years" (Gen. 6:3). [56] But also Moses, when he came to the same number of years of his life, migrates to another place (Deut. 34:7). How then are the guilty equal to the wise sage and prophet? For the moment it is sufficient to say this: that things of the same name are not always the same, but many times differ altogether in kind and also that which is bad may have numbers and times that match the good since they are represented in a twin existence but are powers different and widely separated from each other. [57] But the precise discussion of the one hundred and twenty years, we will set aside until the examination of the whole life of the prophet when we may become sufficiently knowledgeable in it. But for now let us discuss what is next.

13.58 "And when the giants were upon the earth in those days" (Gen. 6:4). Some may think the lawgiver is speaking in riddles and alluding to the things equal to the giants of the creators of myths. But he is far removed from mythmaking and thinks it fit to walk on the paths of truth. 59 And for which reason he drove out from his own commonwealth painting and sculpting; despite their good reputation and subtle artistry, they lie about the nature of truth and fabricate fallacy and deceit through the eyes to easily lead astray souls. 60 So then, concerning the giants, he is in no way representing a myth. But desiring to demonstrate this to you that some men are born of the earth, some are born of heaven, and some are born of God. Those of the earth are seekers of the pleasures of the body, practicing the enjoyment of them and providing the necessary means to indulge in each. The heavenborn are great craftsmen, men of skill, lovers of learning. Of the heavenly element of us, the mind, indeed every heavenly being is mind, pursues the various branches of schools and other arts each and every one. Further whetting and sharpening and exercising and training in the intelligible realm. 61 And men born of God are priests and prophets, who have not considered themselves a part of the commonwealth of the world but have turned away from becoming citizens of the world. Also, they have stepped beyond the realm of perception and migrated into the world of the intelligible of the mind and dwell there registered to the commonwealth of ideas, incorporeal and incorruptible.

14.62 Thus as long as Abraham was remaining in the land of the Chaldeans it was their notion that before being called a new name, while still being called Abram, he was a heavenborn man. He was investigating the upper regions and the ethereal nature and all the things that took place and the cause of them and the like. And he received a name suitable for the studies he pursued, for Abram is being interpreted "uplifted father." The name of the "father-mind" that examines every celestial and lofty thing in every respect. For the mind is the father of the composite being, which reaches out to the ether and still even further. 63 But when being improved and about to be called by a new name, he became a man of God according to the oracle delivered to him, "I am your God; be well pleasing before me and be blameless" (Gen. 17:1). 64 But if the God of the world, being the only God is his own God also in a special sense and grace; then of necessity of course he is a man of God. For he is named Abraham, which must be interpreted "the elect father of sound" that is "the good man's reasoning." For such a reason is attached only to the one God which becomes a companion of God and makes straight the pathway of the whole life using the king's way. The one of the only king, the all-powerful one, not turning or deviating to the left or right.

15.65 But the sons of the earth, their minds turning away from contemplation (reason) and having converted it into the soulless and inert nature of the flesh, "for the two became one flesh" (Gen. 2:24), as the lawgiver affirms. They have adulterated the excellent coinage and left behind the rank of their household, deserting to a worse and contrary one. It was Nimrod who began this deed. 66 For the lawgiver says that "this man began to be a giant upon the earth" (Gen. 10:29) and Nimrod means "deserted." For it was not enough for the thoroughly wretched soul to stand neutral, but he crossed over to the enemies (of the soul), taking up arms against his friends and opposing them in open war. And for this reason to

Nimrod Moses attributes the beginning of the kingdom of Babylon, for Babylon means "change." It is kindred to desertion in both name and deed. For the prelude to every act of desertion is a decision to change and transform. [67] It would follow then to say that according to Moses, the holy one, the worthless man is as a man without a home, without a city, and without a settlement, a refugee. But the diligent one is a strong ally. Having said enough for the present concerning the giants, let us now proceed to what follows in the text.[a]

a. The text ends at this point and Philo continues his exegesis of Gen. 6:4 in the treatise *On the Unchangeableness of God (Quod Deus sit immutabilis).*

Introduction to *On the Decalogue*

Philo of Alexandria's *On the Decalogue (De Decalogo)* is not so much an exegesis of the Ten Commandments (Exod. 20; Deut. 5) as a retelling of them in **Hellenistic** terms. Though Philo will interpret texts allegorically at times, he provides a more literal reading that seeks to make "this-worldly" connections between his audience and Torah. In modern editions, the treatise has 178 sections; 1–49 explain where and how the Decalogue was given; 50–153 examine each commandment, investigating "everything that is marked by especial importance or difference in them" (50); 154–74 discuss how each of the ten epitomizes the remainder of the Mosaic law. The concluding 175–78 speak to how the Decalogue is formally and substantively consistent with God's goodness and his objective of "preserving the universe in peace . . . giving at all times, to all people, in all riches and abundance, all the blessings of peace" (178).

Narrative Description

Philo introduces the Ten Commandments first by addressing the question of why they were given in the wilderness with four conjectures: (1) Moses chose to give God's law in an austere rural location since the urban environment is "full of unspeakable evils," especially pride, which divide humans from each other and breed neglect for divine things (2–9); (2) Moses separated the Israelites in order to cleanse them of their impurities to make them better able to receive the food of "divine laws and reasonings" (11–13); (3) Moses recognized that, as sailors know to equip a ship before it sails, it was better to equip the Israelites with laws before inhabiting the land (14); and (4) Moses led them out to where they could not survive on their own physically but only by God's supernatural provision, so they might "see that he, who had given them a sufficiency of the means of life, was now also giving them a means that should contribute to their living well" (15–17).

As to why God spoke only Ten Commandments directly and the rest came by way of Moses, Philo appeals to the numerical and philosophical virtues of the number ten in 20–31.[1] In 32–35 Philo answers the question whether God spoke the commandments by his own voice by saying, "let not such an idea enter your mind," since God is not like a human being. The voice instead was a "holy miracle," an invisible sound, "a rational soul . . . which fashioned the air and stretched it out and changed it into a kind of flaming fire, [sounding] forth so loud and articulate a voice . . . so that those who were at a great distance appeared to hear equally with those who were nearest to it."

Philo next addresses why the Ten Commandments were spoken as if to one person, even though they were given to a multitude (i.e., in the singular and not the plural). He provides three answers (36–43): (1) the individual obedient to the law is worth the same as a whole nation, if not the whole world; (2) speaking to the individual means that everyone will listen, otherwise "he who hears it as if it were only directed to him in common with others is, to a certain degree, rendered deaf to it, making the multitude a kind of veil and excuse for his obstinacy" (39); and (3) this was done to set an example to all human beings, even the mightiest rulers, such that if the uncreated, immortal, and everlasting God should address a lowly individual, no human being should treat others as of lesser importance than themselves. Sections 44–49 provide a rousing description of the scene at Sinai that sets a suitable **theophanic** ambience for a discussion of each of the commandments.

The First Commandment (51–65)

Philo offers an impassioned appeal to honor God by forswearing the deification of any created thing, no matter how great or heavenly (see 58: "Accordingly, to one who understands how to apply himself to philosophy in a genuine, honest spirit, and who lays claim to a guiltless and pure piety, God gives that most beautiful and holy commandment, that he will not believe that any one of the parts of the world is its own master, for it has been created"—trans. Yonge; cf. Exod. 20:2–3; Deut. 5:6–7[2]). After describing at some length the folly of replacing the Creator with created things, Philo makes this appeal:

> Let us, therefore, reject all such impious dishonesty, and not worship those who are our brothers by nature, even though they may have received a purer and more immortal essence than ourselves (for all created things are brothers to one another, inasmuch as they are created; since the Father of them all is one, the Creator of the

1. On Philo's understanding of numbers, which he inherits from the Neo-Pythagoreans, see David T. Runia's discussion of arithmology in *On the Creation of the World according to Moses: Introduction, Translation and Commentary,* Philo of Alexandria Commentary Series (Leiden: Brill, 2001), pp. 25–29; see also Runia's commentary on *On the Creation* 89–128, Philo's forty-paragraph celebration of the number seven. Unless otherwise noted, all *On the Decalogue* translations are by Charles D. Yonge.

2. Exod. 20:2–3: "I am the Lord your God, who brought you out of the land of Egypt, out of the house of slavery; you shall have no other gods before me." Deut. 5:6–7: "I am the Lord your God, who brought you out of the land of Egypt, out of the house of slavery; you shall have no other gods before me." —NRSV

universe); but let us rather, with our mind and reason, and with all our strength, gird ourselves up vigorously and energetically to the service of that Being who is uncreated and everlasting. (64)

In this Philo approximates the positive expression of the First Commandment in Deuteronomy 6:4–5, the *Shema*: "Hear, O Israel: the Lord is our God, the Lord alone. You will love the Lord your God with all your heart, and with all your soul, and with all your might."

The Second Commandment (66–81)

If replacing the Creator with his creations is lamentable, replacing him with the work of one's own hand is utterly reprehensible:

> Exodus 20:4–6: You will not make for yourself an idol, whether in the form of anything that is in heaven above, or that is on the earth beneath, or that is in the water under the earth. You will not bow down to them or worship them; for I the Lord your God am a jealous God, punishing children for the iniquity of parents, to the third and the fourth generation of those who reject me, but showing steadfast love to the thousandth generation of those who love me and keep my commandments.

> Deuteronomy 5:8–10: You will not make for yourself an idol, whether in the form of anything that is in heaven above, or that is on the earth beneath, or that is in the water under the earth. You will not bow down to them or worship them; for I the Lord your God am a jealous God, punishing children for the iniquity of parents, to the third and fourth generation of those who reject me, but showing steadfast love to the thousandth generation of those who love me and keep my commandments.

Idolaters not only "cut away the most beautiful support of the soul, namely, the proper conception of the ever-living God" (67) by failing to recognize "the Creator is better than the creature" (69), they have also honored paintings and sculptures over the painters and sculptors, thus denying the dignity of humanity. Philo suggests that since "the proper object of happiness" is "to attain to a likeness to God," idolaters should seek to become like the mute, deaf, blind, breathless, immobile, and impotent statues that are "confined and guarded in the temple, as if in a prison" (73–74). Saving his greatest invective for the Egyptians who fashion idols in the shape of the most wild and ferocious of animals, Philo perceives a relationship between what one worships and what one becomes, claiming that the Egyptians "in their souls are changed into those very animals, so as to appear to be merely brutes in human form" (80). By enjoining against this idolatry, God has invited humankind to honor him, not that he needs it, but because knowledge of God is the "best end of all things" (81).

The Third Commandment (82–95)

Though it is best not to swear, if one does swear, one must understand all that is involved in such an act (86: "For an oath is the calling of God to give his testimony concerning the matters that are in doubt; and it is a most impious thing to invoke God to be witness to a lie"; cf. Exod. 20:7; Deut. 5:11[3]). In preparing to make an oath, one must fully weigh the worthiness of the matter as well as the quality of one's own character over against the Deity one seeks to involve in the affair, unless one might profane the latter through the impiety of the former, ensuring certain punishment.

The Fourth Commandment (96–105)

God has set the seventh day (Sabbath) aside for contemplation of his creation:

> Exodus 20:8–11: Remember the Sabbath day, and keep it holy. Six days you will labor and do all your work. But the seventh day is a Sabbath to the Lord your God; you will not do any work—you, your son or your daughter, your male or female slave, your livestock, or the alien resident in your towns. For in six days the Lord made heaven and earth, the sea, and all that is in them, but rested the seventh day; therefore the Lord blessed the Sabbath day and consecrated it.

> Deuteronomy 5:12–15: Observe the Sabbath day and keep it holy, as the Lord your God commanded you. Six days you will labor and do all your work. But the seventh day is a Sabbath to the Lord your God; you will not do any work—you, or your son or your daughter, or your male or female slave, or your ox or your donkey, or any of your livestock, or the resident alien in your towns, so that your male and female slave may rest as well as you. Remember that you were a slave in the land of Egypt, and the Lord your God brought you out from there with a mighty hand and an outstretched arm; therefore the Lord your God commanded you to keep the Sabbath day.

Philo paraphrases Exodus 20:8–11:

> Always imitate God; let that one period of seven days in which God created the world, be to you a complete example of the way in which you are to obey the law, and an all-sufficient model for your actions. Moreover, the seventh day is also an example from which you may learn the propriety of studying philosophy; as on that day, it is said, God beheld the works that he had made; so that you also may yourself contemplate the works of nature, and all the separate circumstances that contribute toward happiness. (100)

From these two types of days (the six versus the seventh) Philo perceives two ways of life, the practical and the contemplative. He concludes his discussion of the command by contemplating the number seven.

---

3. Exod. 20:7: "You will not make wrongful use of the name of the Lord your God, for the Lord will not acquit anyone who misuses his name." Deut. 5:11: "You will not make wrongful use of the name of the Lord your God, for the Lord will not acquit anyone who misuses his name."

The Fifth Commandment (106–20)

This commandment bridges the previous four commands about divine-human interactions with the next five about human interrelations since parents are human yet like God (in generating life). So to honor parents is to be both pious and humane:

> Exodus 20:12: Honor your father and your mother, so that your days may be long in the land that the Lord your God is giving you.

> Deuteronomy 5:16: Honor your father and your mother, as the Lord your God commanded you, so that your days may be long and that it may go well with you in the land that the Lord your God is giving you.

The Sixth Commandment (121–31)

Adultery results in dissipation of the adulterer's soul, leads the adulteress into sin, harms the families of all involved, and places children born of adultery in a precarious circumstance.[4]

The Seventh Commandment (132–34)

Murder violates both the law of nature and the dignity of humankind.[5] On the latter, Philo writes that man "in his soul is also most closely related . . . to the Father of the world, inasmuch as he [the human] has received mind, which is of all the things upon the earth the closest copy and most faithful representation of the everlasting and blessed Idea" (134).

The Eighth Commandment (135–37)

The thief is the enemy of society, checked only by his ability.[6] However, habituated thievery is "more powerful than nature; and small things, if they are not checked, increase and grow, becoming gradually greater and greater until they reach a formidable magnitude" (137).

The Ninth Commandment (138–41)

False witnesses corrupt the truth, hide reality, and subvert justice.[7] This last, which involves making false oaths, results in the impiety denounced in the Third Commandment.

---

4. See Exod. 20:14: "You shall not commit adultery"; Deut. 5:18: "Neither shall you commit adultery."

5. See Exod. 20:13: "You shall not murder"; Deut. 5:17: "You shall not murder."

6. See Exod. 20:15: "You shall not steal"; Deut. 5:19: "Neither shall you steal."

7. See Exod. 20:16: "You shall not bear false witness against your neighbor"; Deut. 5:20: "Neither shall you bear false witness against your neighbor."

The Tenth Commandment (142–53)

Desire (i.e., covetousness) is the worst of the passions "since it derives its origins from ourselves, and is wholly voluntary":

> Last of all, the divine legislator prohibits covetousness, knowing that desire is a thing fond of revolution and of plotting against others; for all the passions of the soul are formidable, exciting and agitating it contrary to nature, and not permitting it to remain in a healthy state, but of all such passions the worst is desire. On which account each of the other passions, coming in from without and attacking the soul from external points, appears to be involuntary; but this desire alone derives its origin from ourselves, and is wholly voluntary. (142)[8]

Philo's treatment of desire, like that of idolatry, is his rhetorical flourish at its best. He captures the futility of desire with a reference to the Greek myth of Tantalus: "For Tantalus, whenever he seemed about to lay his hands on any of the objects that he desired, was invariably disappointed, and the man who is overcome by desire, always thirsting for what is not present, is never satisfied, wallowing about among vain appetites" (149). Philo understands desire to be the source of perpetual human conflict:

> For, both among the Greeks and barbarians, the wars between one another, and between their own different tribes, which have been so celebrated by tragedians, have all flowed from one source, namely, desire of money, or glory, or pleasure; for it is on such subjects as these that the race of humankind goes mad. (153)

Author/Provenance

Philo (ca. 20/15 BCE–45/50 CE) was a member of a wealthy, influential Jewish family in Alexandria, Egypt (*see* Introduction to Philo of Alexandria). Brother to a senior city administrator and uncle to the eventual procurator of Judea and prefect of Egypt, Philo himself opted for a life devoted to philosophy (though he led an embassy to appeal directly to the emperor Caligula following a pogrom against Jews in Alexandria in 38 CE).[9] Philo, well versed in his ancestral religion

---

8. See Exod. 20:17: "You shall not covet your neighbor's house; you shall not covet your neighbor's wife, or male or female slave, or ox, or donkey, or anything that belongs to your neighbor"; Deut. 5:21: "Neither shall you covet your neighbor's wife. Neither shall you desire your neighbor's house, or field, or male or female slave, or ox, or donkey, or anything that belongs to your neighbor."

9. Josephus, *Ant.* 18.259: "There was now a tumult arisen at Alexandria, between the Jewish inhabitants and the Greeks; and three ambassadors were chosen out of each party that were at variance, who came to Caius. Now one of these ambassadors from the people of Alexandria was Apion, who uttered many blasphemies against the Jews; and, among other things that he said, he charged them with neglecting the honors that belonged to Caesar; for that while all who were subject to the Roman Empire built altars and temples to Caius, and in other regards universally received him as they received the gods, these Jews alone thought it a dishonorable

and a recipient of an elite Greek education, married these two in his writings and work (he appears to have run a school where the Jewish Scriptures were studied in the light of Hellenistic philosophy).

Text, Language, Sources, and Transmission

On the Decalogue falls under the category "exposition of the law of Moses," those works by Philo that appear to have been written to make Torah more accessible to Hellenistic readers (whether Hellenized Jews or Gentiles is still debated).[10] *On the Decalogue* follows a description of creation according to Moses and the virtuous lives of Abraham and Joseph (whom Philo calls "Unwritten Laws") and precedes examinations of the laws written down by Moses *(On Special Laws 1–4, On Virtues)* and an epilogue *(On Rewards and Punishments)*. This treatise explicates the Ten Commandments as both distinctive from the written laws because the ten come directly from God at Sinai and as a summary of and entrée to the more specific laws set forth by Moses.

Philo's writings and legacy do not appear to have been influential in post–Second Temple (rabbinical) Judaism. Rather, his library found its way into the hands of second- and third-century Christians, first at Alexandria and then in Caesarea. The convergence of philosophy and Scripture in his works paved the way for the development of Christian exegesis and theology for several centuries, implicitly or explicitly influencing so-called **Gnosticism**, allegorical interpretation, *Logos* theology, and mysticism. The value of Philo's works for contemporary readers of ancient Jewish and Christian writings includes (1) what it preserves from and communicates about Hellenistic philosophy (especially **Stoicism** and **Middle Platonism**); (2) what it testifies about the state of biblical interpretation among educated, Greek-speaking Jews of the Diaspora; and (3) how Philo reworks Jewish theological and ethical teachings in Hellenistic terms.

Theology

There is no evidence of any direct influence of *On the Decalogue* on Second Temple Jewish or New Testament writings, although there are a number of theological parallels. Significant among these are the following:

thing for them to erect statues in honor of him, as well as to swear by his name. Many of these severe things were said by Apion, by which he hoped to provoke Caius to anger at the Jews, as he was likely to be. But Philo, the principal of the Jewish embassage, a man eminent on all accounts, brother to Alexander the alabarch, and one not unskillful in philosophy, was ready to betake himself to make his defense against those accusations; but Caius prohibited him, and bid him be gone; he was also in such a rage, that it openly appeared he was about to do them some very great mischief. So Philo being thus affronted, went out, and said to those Jews who were about him, that they should be of good courage, since Caius's words indeed showed anger at them, but in reality had already set God against himself"—trans. Whiston.

10. Editors' note: To locate this text in the wider writings of Philo, the reader is encouraged to consult the Introduction to Philo of Alexandria in this volume.

1. *On the Decalogue* fits under the scholarly construct "rewritten Bible" (*see* Introduction to Biblical Interpretation and Rewritten Scripture), which refers to works that retell a biblical text, via paraphrase or poetic means, and in so doing indirectly reinterpret, explain, and even supplement the biblical material for a later context (some examples include 1–2 Chronicles' retelling of Samuel and Kings, Jubilees' retelling of Genesis [*see* The Book of Jubilees], and Josephus's *Antiquities*' retelling the biblical history from Adam to Saul [see *Jewish Antiquities*]). While *On the Decalogue* is self-consciously an explanation of the Ten Commandments, it does not quote and then exegete the commandments as much as reformulate them in words and concepts accessible to Philo's Hellenistic audience. This is a theological issue since, as Philo extrapolates from the laconic biblical Decalogue lengthy demonstrations of the universal significance and appeal of God and his law, he is also redefining these in more Hellenized terms (e.g., averting **anthropomorphic** accusations by saying God's voice is not a physical but a rational voice; recasting the Sabbath as a day of philosophical contemplation; transforming the Tenth Commandment's coveting proscription into a discourse against the passions, a common Hellenistic **topos**).

2. *On the Decalogue*'s polemic against polytheism and idolatry is very similar to that of other early Jewish and Christian writings. Compare the use of irony and the special mockery of Egyptians in 66–81 (esp. 76)[11] with Wisdom of Solomon 12–14 (esp. 12:23–24)[12] (*see* Wisdom of Solomon), a writing that may also come from turn-of-the-era Alexandria and that has numerous similarities with Philo's work. Or compare Philo's critique of the veneration of the natural order in 58, 65, and especially 69 with the apostle Paul's in Romans 1:25:

> *On the Decalogue* 69: On which account pity is bestowed on the one class as unfortunate, but the other class are justly punished as being wicked, who in conjunction with others have not chosen to recognize that fact which even an infant child would understand, namely, that the creator is better than the creature; for he is both more ancient in point of time, and is also in a manner the father of that which he has made. He is also superior in power, for the agent is more glorious than the patient.

> Romans 1:24–25: Therefore God gave them up in the lusts of their hearts to impurity, to the degrading of their bodies among themselves, because they exchanged

---

11. *Dec.* 76: "Let no one therefore of those beings who are endowed with souls worship anything that is devoid of a soul; for it would be one of the most absurd things possible for the works of nature to be diverted to the service of those things that are made by hand; and against Egypt, not only is that common accusation brought, to which the whole country is liable, but another charge also, which is of a more special character, and with great fitness; for besides falling down to statues and images they have also introduced irrational animals, to the honors due to the gods, such as bulls, and rams, and goats, inventing some prodigious fiction with regard to each of them."

12. Wis. 12:23–24: "Therefore those who lived unrighteously, in a life of folly, you tormented through their own abominations. For they went far astray on the paths of error, accepting as gods those animals that even their enemies despised; they were deceived like foolish infants."—NRSV

the truth about God for a lie and worshiped and served the creature rather than the Creator, who is blessed forever! Amen.

3. Though not as robust as in his other treatises, one does catch a glimpse in *On the Decalogue* of the distinctive place humankind has in Philo's thinking. The dignity of humankind is in their special relationship with the Deity:

> Man, who is the most excellent of all animals, in respect of that predominant part that is in him, namely, his soul, is also most closely related . . . to the Father of the world, inasmuch as he has received mind, which is of all the things that are upon the earth the closest copy and most faithful representation of the everlasting and blessed idea. (134)

4. Above we have noted Philo's eschewing anthropomorphic notions of God, his appeal against polytheism and idolatry on the grounds of God's being the Creator, and his identification of rational soul as the most godlike feature. Lastly, we add here the divine attribute of goodness discussed in *On the Decalogue*'s conclusion. Because God is the "good Lord, the cause of good alone," he is not the cause of evil, which includes even punishment for disobeying his commands; hence the Ten Commandments do not refer to any punishments (unlike the laws delivered by Moses). It is "justice" that will execute punishment, by means of God's ministers and lieutenants (i.e., angels; cf. Philo's *On the Confusion of Languages* 173–78):

> But Moses, perceiving their design, says, "O Lord, Lord, King of the gods" (Deut. 10:17), in order to show the difference between the ruler and those subject to him. And there is also in the air a most sacred company of incorporeal souls as an attendant upon the heavenly souls; for the word of prophecy is accustomed to call these souls angels . . . it becomes the great King that general safety should be ascribed to him, as preserving the universe in peace, and giving at all times, to all people, in all riches and abundance, all the blessings of peace: for, in truth, God is the president of peace.

RONALD R. COX

FURTHER READING

Kamasar, Adam, ed. *The Cambridge Companion to Philo.* Cambridge: Cambridge University Press, 2009.

Nickelsburg, George W. E. *Jewish Literature between the Bible and the Mishnah.* 2nd ed. Minneapolis: Fortress, 2005.

Niehoff, M. "Philo, Exposition of the Law." In *The Eerdmans Dictionary of Early Judaism,* edited by J. Collins and D. C. Harlow, pp. 1076–74. Grand Rapids: Eerdmans, 2010.

Schenck, Kenneth. *A Brief Guide to Philo.* Louisville, Ky.: Westminster John Knox, 2005.

Sterling, G. "Philo." In *The Eerdmans Dictionary of Early Judaism,* edited by J. J. Collins and D. C. Harlow, pp. 1063–70. Grand Rapids: Eerdmans, 2010.

Yonge, C. D. *The Works of Philo Judaeus.* 4 vols. Peabody, Mass.: Hendrickson, 2005 (1854–55).

ADVANCED READING

Philo of Alexandria. Trans. F. H. Colson and G. H. Whitaker. Vol. 7. Loeb Classical Library. Cambridge, Mass.: Harvard University Press, 1958.

Runia, David. *Philo of Alexandria: On the Creation of the World according to Moses: Introduction, Translation and Commentary*. Philo of Alexandria Commentary Series. Leiden: Brill, 2001.

4.12 from *On the Decalogue*

11.44 And, moreover, as was natural, he filled the whole place with miraculous signs and works, with noises of thunder too great for the hearing to support, and with the most radiant brilliancy of flashes of lightning, and with the sound of an invisible trumpet extending to a great distance, and with the march of a cloud, which, like a pillar, had its foundation fixed firmly on the earth, but raised the rest of its body even to the height of heaven; and, last of all, by the impetuosity of a heavenly fire, which overshadowed everything around with a dense smoke. For it was fitting that, when the power of God came among them, none of the parts of the world should be quiet, but that everything should be put in motion to minister to his service. 45 And the people stood by, having kept themselves clean from all connection with women, and having abstained from all pleasures, except those that arise from a participation in necessary food, having been purifying themselves with baths and ablutions for three days, and having washed their garments and being all clothed in the purest white robes, and standing on tiptoe and pricking up their ears, in compliance with the exhortations of Moses, who had forewarned them to prepare for the solemn assembly; for he knew that such would take place, when he, having been summoned up alone, gave forth the prophetic commands of God. 46 And a voice sounded forth from out of the midst of the fire that had flowed from heaven, a most marvelous and awful voice, the flame being endowed with articulate speech in a language familiar to the hearers, which expressed its words with such clearness and distinctness that the people seemed rather to be seeing than hearing it. 47 And the law testifies to the accuracy of my statement, where it is written, "And all the people beheld the voice most evidently." For the truth is that the voice of men is calculated to be heard, but that of God to be really and truly seen. Why is this? Because all that God says are not words, but actions that the eyes determine on before the ears. 48 It is, therefore, with great beauty, and also with a proper sense of what is consistent with the dignity of God, that the voice is said to have come forth out of the fire; for the oracles of God are accurately understood and tested like gold by the fire. 49 And God also intimates to us something of this kind by a figure. Since the property of fire is partly to give light, and partly to burn, those who think fit to show themselves obedient to the sacred commands will live forever and ever as in a light that is never darkened, having his laws themselves as stars giving light in their soul. But all those who are stubborn and disobedient are forever inflamed, and burned, and consumed by their internal appetites, which, like flame, will destroy all the life of those who possess them.

12.50 These, then, were the things that it was necessary to explain beforehand. But now we must turn to the commands themselves, and investigate everything that is marked by especial importance or difference in them. Now God divided them, being ten, as they are, into two tables of five each, which he engraved on

---

Translation by Charles D. Yonge.

two pillars. And the first five have the precedence and preeminence in honor; but the second five have an inferior place assigned to them. But both the tables are beautiful and advantageous to life, opening to men wrought and level roads kept within limits by one end, so as to secure the unwavering and secure progress of that soul which is continually desiring what is most excellent. [51] Now the most excellent five were of this character: they related to the monarchial principle on which the world is governed; to images and statues, and in short to all structures of any kind made by hand; to the duty of not taking the name of God in vain; to that of keeping the holy seventh day in a manner worthy of its holiness; to paying honor to parents both separately to each, and commonly to both. So that of the one table the beginning is the God and Father and Creator of the universe; and the end are one's parents, who imitate his nature, and so generate the particular individuals. And the other table of five contains all the prohibitions against adulteries, and murder, and theft, and false witness, and covetousness. [52] But we must consider, with all the accuracy possible, each of these oracles separately, not looking upon any one of them as superfluous. Now the best beginning of all living beings is God, and of all virtues, piety. And we must, therefore, speak of these two principles in the first place. There is an error of no small importance that has taken possession of the greater portion of [hu]mankind concerning a subject that was likely by itself, or, at least, above all other subjects, to have been fixed with the greatest correctness and truth in the mind of everyone; [53] for some nations have made divinities of the four elements, earth and water, and air and fire. Others, of the sun and moon, and of the other planets and fixed stars. Others, again, of the whole world. And they have all invented different appellations, all of them false, for these false gods put out of sight that most supreme and most ancient of all, the Creator, the ruler of the great city, the general of the invincible army, the pilot who always guides everything to its preservation; [54] for they call the earth Proserpine, and Ceres, and Pluto. And the sea they call Neptune, inventing besides a number of marine deities as subservient to him, and vast companies of attendants, both male and female. The air they call Juno; fire, Vulcan; and the sun, Apollo; the moon, Diana; and the evening star, Venus; Lucifer, they call Mercury; [55] and to every one of the stars they have affixed names and given them to the inventors of fables, who have woven together cleverly contrived imaginations to deceive the ear, and have appeared to have been themselves the ingenious inventors of these names thus given. [56] Again, in their descriptions, they divided the heaven into two parts, each one hemisphere, the one being above the earth and the other under the earth, which they called the *Dioscuri* [Sons of Jupiter, i.e., Castor and Pollux]; inventing, besides, a marvelous story concerning their living on alternate days. [57] For, as the heaven is everlastingly revolving, in a circle without any cessation or interruption, it follows of necessity that each of the hemispheres must every day be in a different position from that which it was on the day before, everything being turned upside down as far as appearance goes, at least; for, in point of fact, there is no such thing as any uppermost or undermost in a spherical figure. And this expression is used only with reference to our own formation and position; that which is over our head being called uppermost, and that which is in the opposite direction being called undermost. [58] Accordingly, to one who understands how to apply himself to philosophy in a genuine, honest spirit, and who lays claim to a guiltless and pure piety, God gives that most beautiful and holy commandment, that he will not believe that any one of the parts of the world is its own master, for it has been created; and the fact of having been created implies a liability to destruction, even though the thing created may be made immortal by the providence of the Creator; and there was a time once when it had no existence, but it is impiety to say that there was a previous time when God did not exist, and that he was born at some time, and that he does not endure forever.

13.59But some persons indulge in such foolish notions respecting their judgments on these points, that they not only look upon the things that have been mentioned above as gods, but as each separate one of them as the greatest and first of gods, either because they are really ignorant of the true living God, from their nature being uninstructed, or else because they have no desire to learn, because they believe that there is no cause of things invisible, and appreciable only by the intellect, apart from the objects of the external senses, and this too, though the most distinct possible proof is close at hand; 60 for though, as it is owing to the soul that they live, and form designs, and do everything that is done in human life, they nevertheless have never been able to behold their soul with their eyes, nor would they be able if they were to strive with all imaginable eagerness, wishing to see it as the most beautiful possible of all images or appearances, from a sight of which they might, by a sort of comparison, derive a notion of the uncreated and everlasting God, who rules and guides the whole world in such a way as to secure its preservation, being himself invisible. 61 As, therefore, if anyone were to assign the honors of the great king to his satraps and viceroys, he would appear to be not only the most ignorant and senseless of men, but also the most foolhardy, giving to slaves what belongs to the master; in the same manner, let the man who honors the Creator, with the same honors as those with which he regards the creature, know that he is of all men the most foolish and the most unjust, in giving equal things to unequal persons, and that too not in such a way as to do honor to the inferior, but only to take it from the superior. 62 There are again some who exceed in impiety, not giving the Creator and the creature even equal honor, but assigning to the latter all honor, and respect, and reverence, and to the former nothing at all, not thinking him worthy of even the common respect of being recollected; for they forget him whom alone they should recollect, aiming, like demented and miserable men as they are, at attaining to an intentional forgetfulness. 63 Some men again are so possessed with an insolent and free-spoken madness, that they make an open display of the impiety that dwells in their hearts, and venture to blaspheme the Deity, whetting an evil-speaking tongue, and desiring, at the same time, to vex the pious, who immediately feel an indescribable and irreconcilable affliction, which enters in at their ears and pervades the whole soul; for this is the great engine of impious men, by which alone they bridle those who love God, as they think it better at the moment to preserve silence, for the sake of not provoking their wickedness further.

14.64 Let us, therefore, reject all such impious dishonesty, and not worship those who are our brothers by nature, even though they may have received a purer and more immortal essence than ourselves (for all created things are brothers to one another, inasmuch as they are created; since the Father of them all is one, the Creator of the universe); but let us rather, with our mind and reason, and with all our strength, gird ourselves up vigorously and energetically to the service of that Being who is uncreated and everlasting, and the Maker of the universe, never shrinking or turning aside from it, nor yielding to a desire of pleasing the multitude, by which even those who might be saved are often destroyed. [65] Let us, therefore, fix deeply in ourselves this first commandment as the most sacred of all commandments, to think that there is but one God, the most highest, and to honor him alone; and let not the polytheistic doctrine ever even touch the ears of any man who is accustomed to seek for the truth, with purity and sincerity of heart; [66] for those who are ministers and servants of the sun, and of the moon, and of all the host of heaven, or of it in all its integrity or of its principal parts, are in grievous error; (how can they fail to be, when they honor the subjects instead of the prince?) but still they sin less grievously than the others, who have fashioned stocks, and stones, and silver, and gold, and similar materials according to their own pleasure, making images, and statues, and all kinds of other things wrought by the hand; the workmanship in which, whether by statuary, or painter, or artisan, has done great injury to the life of man, having filled the whole habitable world. [67] For they have cut away the most beautiful support of the soul, namely, the proper conception of the ever-living God; and therefore, like ships without ballast, they are tossed about in every direction forever, being borne in every direction, so as never once to reach the haven, and never to be able to anchor firmly in truth, being blind respecting that which is worth seeing, and the only object as to which it is absolutely necessary to be sharp-sighted; [68] and such men appear to me to have a more miserable life than those who are deprived of their bodily sight; for these latter have either been injured without their own consent, or else have endured some terrible disease of the eyes, or else have been plotted against by their enemies; but those others by their own deliberate intention, have not only dimmed the eye of their soul, but have even chosen utterly to discard it; [69] on which account pity is bestowed on the one class as unfortunate, but the other class are justly punished as being wicked, who in conjunction with others have not chosen to recognize that fact which even an infant child would understand, namely, that the Creator is better than the creature; for he is both more ancient in point of time, and is also in a manner the father of that which he has made. He is also superior in power, for the agent is more glorious than the patient. [70] And though it would be proper, if they had not committed sins, to deify the painters and statuaries themselves with exceeding honors, they have left them in obscurity, giving them no advantage, but have looked upon the figures that have been made, or the pictures that have been painted by them, as gods; [71] and these artists have often grown old in poverty and obscurity, dying, worn out by incessant misfortunes, while the things that they have fabricated are made splendid with purple, and gold, and all sorts of costly splendor that wealth can furnish, and are worshiped not only by freemen but even by men of noble birth, and of the greatest personal strength and beauty. For the race of priests is scrutinized with the greatest rigor and minuteness, to see whether they are without blemish, and to see whether the whole combination of the parts of their bodies is entire and perfect; [72] and these are not the worst points of all, bad as they are: but this is entirely intolerable, for I have known before now, some of the very men who have made the things, praying and sacrificing to the very things that have been made by them, when it would have been more to their purpose to worship either of their own hands, or, if they feared the reproach of self-conceit, and therefore did not choose to do that, at all events to worship their anvils, and hammers, and graving tools, and compasses, and other instruments, by means of which the materials have been fashioned into shape.

15.73 And yet it is well for us, speaking with all proper freedom, to say to those who have shown themselves so devoid of sense; "My good men, the best of all prayers, and the end, and proper object of happiness, is to attain to a likeness to God. 74 Do you therefore pray to become like those structures of yours, that so you may reap the most supreme happiness, neither seeing with your eyes, nor hearing with your ears, nor respiring, nor smelling with your nostrils, nor speaking, nor tasting with your mouth, nor taking, nor giving, nor doing anything with your hands, nor walking with your feet, nor doing anything at all with any one of your members, but being as it were confined and guarded in the temple, as if in a prison, and day and night continually imbibing the steam from the sacrifices offered up; for this is the only one good thing which can be attributed to any kind of building or structure." 75 But I think that when they hear these things, they will be indignant, as if they were listening not to prayers, but to curses, and that they will take refuge in such defense as chance may furnish them with, bringing retaliatory accusations; which may be the greatest proof of the manifest and undesirable impiety of those men, who look upon those beings as gods, to whom they themselves would never wish to have their own natures assimilated.

16.76 Let no one therefore of those beings who are endowed with souls worship anything that is devoid of a soul; for it would be one of the most absurd things possible for the works of nature to be diverted to the service of those things that are made by hand; and against Egypt, not only is that common accusation brought, to which the whole country is liable, but another charge also, which is of a more special character, and with great fitness; for besides falling down to statues and images they have also introduced irrational animals, to the honors due to the gods, such as bulls, and rams, and goats, inventing some prodigious fiction with regard to each of them; 77 and as to these particular animals, they have indeed some reason for what they do, for they are the most domestic, and the most useful to life. The bull, as a plower, draws furrows for the reception of the seed, and is again the most powerful of all animals to thresh the corn out when it is necessary to purify it of the chaff; the ram gives us the most beautiful garments for the coverings of our persons; for if our bodies were naked, they would easily be destroyed either through heat, or though intense cold, caused at one time by the blaze of the sun, and at another by the cooling of the air. 78 But as it is they go beyond these animals, and select the most fierce, and untamable of all wild animals, honoring lions, and crocodiles, and of reptiles the poisonous asp, with temples, and sacred precincts, and sacrifices, and assemblies in their honor, and solemn processions, and things of that kind. For if they were to seek out in both elements, among all the things given to man for his use by God, searching through earth and water, they would never find any animal on the land more savage than the lion, or any aquatic animal more fierce than the crocodile, both of which creatures they honor and worship; 79 they have also deified many other animals, dogs, ichneumons, wolves, birds, ibises, and hawks, and even fish, taking sometimes the whole, and sometimes only a part; and what can be more ridiculous than this conduct? [80] And, accordingly, the first foreigners who arrived in Egypt were quite worn out with laughing at and ridiculing these superstitions, until their minds had become impregnated with the conceit of the natives; but all those who have tasted of right instruction are amazed and struck with consternation at their system of ennobling things that are not noble, and pity those who give into it, thinking the men, as is very natural, more miserable than even the objects that they honor, since they in their souls are changed into those very animals, so as to appear to be merely brutes in human form, now returning to their original nature. [81] Therefore, God, removing out of his sacred legislation all such impious deification of undeserving objects, has invited men to the honor of the one true and living God; not indeed that he has any need himself to be honored; for being all-sufficient for himself, he has no need of anyone else; but he has done so, because he wished to lead the race of [hu]mankind, hitherto wandering about in trackless deserts, into a road from which they should not stray, so that by following nature it might find the best end of all things, namely, the knowledge of the true and living God, who is the first and most perfect of all good things; from whom, as from a fountain, all particular blessings are showered upon the world, and upon the things and people in it.

28.142 Last of all, the divine legislator prohibits covetousness, knowing that desire is a thing fond of revolution and of plotting against others; for all the passions of the soul are formidable, exciting and agitating it contrary to nature, and not permitting it to remain in a healthy state, but of all such passions the worst is desire. On which account each of the other passions, coming in from without and attacking the soul from external points, appears to be involuntary; but this desire alone derives its origin from ourselves, and is wholly voluntary. [143] But what is it that I am saying? The appearance and idea of a present good, or of one that is accounted such, rouses up and excites the soul that was previously in a state of tranquility, and raises it to a high degree of elation, like a light suddenly flashing before the eyes; and this passion of the soul is called pleasure. [144] But the contrary to good is evil, which, when it forces its way in, and inflicts a mortal wound, immediately fills the soul against its will with depression and despondency; and the name of the passion is sorrow. [145] But when the evil presses upon the soul, when it has not as yet taken up its habitation in it, but when it is only impending, being about to come and to agitate it, it sends before it agitation and suspense, as express messengers, to fill the soul with alarm; and this passion is denominated fear. [146] And when anyone, having conceived an idea of some good that is not present, hastens to lay hold of it, he then drives his soul forward to a great distance, and extending it in the greatest possible degree, from his anxiety to attain the object of his desires, he is stretched as it were upon the rack, being anxious to lay hold of the thing, but being unable to reach it, and being in the same condition with those who are pursuing people who are running away, following with an inferior speed, but with unrivaled eagerness. [147] And something of the same kind appears to happen, also, with respect to the external senses; for very frequently the eyes, hastening to come to the comprehension of something that is removed to a great distance, strain themselves, exerting themselves to the very fullest extent of and even beyond their power, are unsuccessful, and grow dim in the empty space between themselves and their object, wholly failing in attaining to an accurate knowledge of the subject before them, and moreover impairing and injuring their sight by the exceeding intensity of their efforts and steady gaze. [148] And, again, sometimes when an indistinct noise is borne toward us from a long distance, the ears are excited, and feeling as it were a fair breeze, are eager and hasten to approach nearer to it if possible, from a desire that the sound should be distinctly apprehended by the sense of hearing. [149] But the noise, for it is still obscure as it seems, strikes the ear but faintly, not giving forth any more distinct tone by which it may be understood, so that the desire of comprehending it, being unsuccessful and unsatisfied, is excited more and more, the desire causing a Tantalus-like kind of punishment. For Tantalus, whenever he seemed about to lay his hands on any of the objects that he desired, was invariably disappointed, and the man who is overcome by desire, being always thirsting for what is not present, is never satisfied, wallowing about among vain appetites, [150] like those diseases that would creep over the whole body, if they were not checked by excision or cautery, and that would overrun and seize upon the whole composition of the body, not leaving a single part in a sound state; in like manner, unless discourse in accordance with philosophy did not, like a good physician, check the influx of appetite, all the affairs of life would of necessity be set in motion in a manner contrary to nature; for there is nothing exempt from such an affliction, nothing that can escape the dominion of passion, but, when once it has obtained immunity and license, it devours everything and becomes by itself everything in every part. [151] Perhaps it is a piece of folly to make a long speech on matters that are so manifest, as to which there is no individual and no city that is ignorant, that they are not only every day, but even every hour, as one may say, supplying a visible proof of the truth of my assertion. Is the love of money, or of women, or of glory, or of any one of the other efficient causes of pleasure, the origin of slight and ordinary evils? [152] Is it not owing to this passion that relationships are broken asunder, and change the goodwill that originates in nature into an irreconcilable enmity? And are not great countries and populous kingdoms made desolate by domestic seditions, through such causes? And are not earth and sea continually filled with novel and terrible calamities by naval battles and military expeditions for the same reason? [153] For, both among the Greeks and barbarians, the wars between one another, and between their own different tribes, which have been so celebrated by tragedians, have all flowed from one source, namely, desire of money, or glory, or pleasure; for it is on such subjects as these that the race of [hu]mankind goes mad.

Introduction to *On the Life of Moses*

Philo of Alexandria's *On the Life of Moses (De vita Mosis)* is a two-volume biography of the Israelite lawgiver that appears to serve as an introduction to the
Mosaic law for a general audience, possibly Greek-speaking Jews or interested
Gentiles or both. In *Moses,* Philo is doing more than simply retelling the story;
the details of the exodus, wilderness wandering, and arrival at Canaan are in
many ways re-presented so as to emphasize the essential roles Moses played in
the life of Israel, namely, the roles of king, lawgiver, priest, and prophet. Philo
advocates for the importance of the divine law by celebrating the unique and
distinguished nature of the lawgiver, "the greatest and most perfect man who
ever lived" (*Moses* 1.1).[1]

Narrative Description

Philo's *On the Life of Moses* is not so much an explanation or exegesis of the
Pentateuch as it is a reworking of that source material into a *bios,* a **Hellenistic**
biography wherein the life and qualities of a great individual are extolled. In the
manner of such Hellenistic biographies, the first part of Philo's treatise (*Moses*
1) provides a chronological description of Moses' career while the second part
(*Moses* 2) provides a series of topical studies on Moses' character. The first volume
establishes the kingly nature of Moses through a telling of his life story, from his
miraculous rescue as an infant to his ascent as "god and king of the whole nation"
(*Moses* 1.158) to his delivering the people to the cusp of the promised land at the
end of his earthly life. Although volume 1 follows closely the narrative materials
of Exodus and Numbers, it is not difficult to see how Philo shifts the emphasis
to Moses. It is easiest to observe this shift in the biographical information Philo
supplies that does not come from the biblical source. In *Moses* 1.18–33 Philo takes
the liberty of describing Moses' education as an Egyptian prince who had the
best tutors not just from that country but from Greece and Assyria, and yet he
quickly surpassed them, "anticipating all their lessons by the excellent natural

1. Unless otherwise noted, all *On the Life of Moses* translations are by Charles D. Yonge.

684

endowments of his own genius; so that everything in his case appeared to be a recollecting rather than a learning, while he himself also, without any teacher, comprehended by his instinctive genius many difficult subjects" (*Moses* 1.21). These passages make clear both that Moses is the beneficiary of a premium Hellenistic education and that his innate intellectual and ethical abilities exemplify the value of that instruction rather than benefit from it.

At the outset of the exodus as the Israelites depart Egypt, Philo again steps away from his scriptural source to provide a reflection on Moses' authority in *Moses* 1.148–62. Here Philo describes how Moses is an ideal ruler because he did not grasp at leadership but was granted it by God because of his virtue, excellence, and benevolence toward all men (148). Moses' "nobleness of soul" is apparent in his stalwart resolve (150) and in his refusal to use the power he received for his own financial gain (152). Philo anticipates the crossing of the sea as well as the other provisions in the wilderness by noting that since "all the property of friends is common," God makes Moses God's friend (cf. Exod. 33:11: "Thus the Lord used to speak to Moses face to face, as one speaks to a friend. Then he would return to the camp; but his young assistant, Joshua son of Nun, would not leave the tent"), heir to the whole world so that the elements obeyed him as master (155–56). Thus Philo credits Moses as much as God for these events, and it is in this section that Philo refers to the Sinai theophany in order to highlight not the divine law but the divine status of Moses. Tying together Exodus 7:1 ("The Lord said to Moses, 'See, I have made you like God to Pharaoh, and your brother Aaron will be your prophet'"), 20:21 ("Then the people stood at a distance, while Moses drew near to the thick darkness where God was"), and 25:9 ("In accordance with all that I show you concerning the pattern of the tabernacle and of all its furniture, so you will make it"), Philo says Moses was called "the god and king of the whole nation, and he is said to have entered into the darkness where God was; that is to say, into the invisible, and shapeless, and incorporeal world, the essence, which is the model of all existing things, where he beheld things invisible to mortal nature." In doing so, Moses sets himself up as "a most beautiful and godlike work, to be a model for all those who were inclined to imitate him" (158).

Philo's retelling of the biblical narrative, even when he stays close to his source material, nevertheless recenters the focus on Moses. Exodus 13:17–21 describes God's active role in deciding which route the Israelites will take to the land:

> When Pharaoh let the people go, God did not lead them by way of the land of the Philistines, although that was nearer; for God thought, "If the people face war, they may change their minds and return to Egypt." So God led the people by the roundabout way of the wilderness toward the Red Sea. The Israelites went up out of the land of Egypt prepared for battle. And Moses took with him the bones of Joseph who had required a solemn oath of the Israelites, saying, "God will surely take notice of you, and then you must carry my bones with you from here." They set out from Succoth, and camped at Etham, on the edge of the wilderness. The Lord went in front of them in a pillar of cloud by day, to lead them along the way, and in a pillar of fire by night, to give them light, so that they might travel by day and by night. Neither the pillar of cloud by day nor the pillar of fire by night left its place in front of the people.

Moses 1.163–66 credits Moses with discerning the best route (one that will keep the Israelites safe as well as test them to "see how obedient they would be when they were not surrounded by any necessities" [164]). Repeatedly, Philo takes actions attributed to God in Scripture and attributes them to Moses (e.g., contrast Num. 13:1 with 220 or Num. 31:25 with 315–16). Further, those actions Philo does ascribe to God are often for Moses' benefit. So when the people rebel out of hunger and Moses entreats God on their behalf (cf. Exod. 16), God provides manna "partly by reason of his natural love and compassion for man, and partly because he desired to honor the commander whom he had appointed to govern them, and still more to show his [the commander's = Moses'] great piety and holiness in all matters whether visible or invisible" (198). The cumulative results of these and several other "minor" changes to the narrative is that Philo, in effect, creates a new story in which Moses has a much more significant role than he does in the Bible.

NUMBERS 13:1–2 / *LIFE OF MOSES* I.220	NUMBERS 31:25–26 / *LIFE OF MOSES* I.315
[1] The Lord said to Moses, [2] "Send men to spy out the land of Canaan, which I am giving to the Israelites; from each of their ancestral tribes you will send a man, every one a leader among them."	[25] The Lord spoke to Moses, saying, [26] "You and Eleazar the priest and the heads of the ancestral houses of the congregation make an inventory of the booty captured, both human and animal."
§220 After this battle he (Moses) considered that it was proper to reconnoiter the country into which the nation was now being led as a colony.	§315 However, after no long lapse of time he (Moses) divided the booty among those who had taken part in the expedition.

Philo begins his second volume making the case that Moses is the lawgiver par excellence. After noting that Moses evinces all the virtues expressed in his law (*Moses* 2.8–11), Philo then provides in 12–65 several examples of how Moses' law is universally admired and applicable, illustrating that the "beauty and dignity of the legislation of Moses is honored not among the Jews only, but also by all other nations" (25). Most noteworthy of these is Philo's recounting of the legend where **Ptolemy II Philadelphus**, greatest of the rulers of Hellenistic Egypt, out of deep admiration and love for Moses' laws, "conceived the idea of having our laws translated into the Greek language" (31; *see* Letter of Aristeas). The greatest translators assembled on the island of Pharos, near Alexandria, and working in isolation one from another they arrived at exactly the same translation. This showed that the laws were like universal mathematical principles and that these were not simply translators "but hierophants and prophets to whom it had been granted in their honest and guileless minds to go along with the most pure spirit of Moses" (40) (*see* Overview of Early Jewish Literature). Also worth mentioning is Philo's brief discussion of Genesis (45–65), wherein Moses begins "his history of the giving of the law" with the creation account and the stories of Lot and Noah, so as to illustrate that the divine laws aim "at the harmony of the universe . . . corresponding to the law of eternal nature" (52).

Philo treats Moses as the ultimate priest in *Moses* 2.66–186, describing his role in the construction of the tabernacle, the making of liturgical vessels and clothing, and the appointment of priests to facilitate worship. Philo claims that Moses attained his priestly status when, as a reward for his philosophical acumen, he ascended Sinai and there "was instructed by the sacred oracles of God in everything that related to the sacred offices and ministrations" (67). This philosophical acumen is necessary because Moses does more than serve as a cipher for God's commands; he receives instruction about the tabernacle and its accouterments by "contemplating with his soul the incorporeal patterns" so that he might have fashioned a "sense-perceptible" imitation "of an archetypal sketch and pattern appreciable only by the intellect" (74). Philo goes so far as to say that the "general form of the model was stamped upon the mind of the prophet" (76). Accessing the intelligible realm (Philo is clearly drawing from **Platonic** thought here) alters Moses (69) and, more significantly, affords a philosophical way of understanding Moses' instructions about how to worship God. For example, after Philo recounts Moses' description of the priestly vestments (cf. Exod. 28), he then provides a lengthy allegorical interpretation of those vestments, providing a cosmological understanding of what the priest wears as he enters the holy of holies (109–35). This interpretation is not Philo's own contrivance but such "are the figurative meanings that he [Moses] desires to indicate by the sacred vestments of the high priest" (131).

The final portion of the second volume (187–291) treats Moses' role in delivering God's prophecies, of which there are three types: (1) those that come directly from God through the prophet and are meant to encourage God's people; (2) those where God answers an inquiry by the prophet to clarify a matter where he and the people are at an impasse; and (3) those where God has given the prophet "a share of his prescient power, by means of which he will be able to foretell the future" (190). Philo does not discuss the first but uses the latter two prophecy types to assemble examples where Moses does much more than simply relate God's message. In retelling episodes where Moses inquires of the Lord, Philo adds to the scriptural accounts explanations of Moses' motivation. So in the instance where a half-Israelite, half-Egyptian man blasphemes the Lord, Leviticus 24:12 reads only "they put him in custody until the decision of the Lord should be made clear." Philo adds:

> Wherefore Moses, marveling at his insanity and at the extravagance of his audacity, although he was filled with a noble impetuosity and indignation, and desired to slay the man with his own hand, nevertheless feared lest he should be inflicting on him too light a punishment; for he conceived that no man could possibly devise any punishment adequate to such enormous impiety. (197)

Philo demonstrates here Moses' astuteness in turning to God for the proper punishment (which in this case will be stoning since the lawbreaker has a "stony and hardened heart" and since only stoning could allow the whole community to express their justifiable wrath toward him). In all his examples of this type of prophecy, Philo wants to show that Moses turns to God not because he is indecisive but because he asks the right question, his good instincts being at odds with each other. With the third type of prophecy, Philo is able to provide a common context and purpose for distinct episodes such as the deliverance at the Red Sea (Exod. 14), the provision of manna (Exod. 16), the calling of the Levites (Num. 1–3), the judgment of the Korah rebellion (Num. 16), and the death of Moses (Deut. 34; cf. 32:48–52), namely, to attest that God has given Moses God's own power of foreknowledge and by this Moses is able to reveal future events.

Moses' last prophecy is of his own death, the description of which provides the conclusion of Philo's biography. Yet Philo perceives in Moses' death not the cessation of life but a mystical transformation, describing "how he had died when he was not as yet dead, and how he was buried without anyone being present so as to know of his tomb, because in fact he was entombed not by mortal hands, but by immortal powers, so that he was not placed in the tomb of his forefathers, having met with particular grace that no man ever saw." Philo aptly shrouds the mystery of the great hierophant's departure, noting simply that he "he fl[ies] away and complete[s] his journey to heaven" (291).

Author/Provenance

Philo (20/15 BCE–45/50 CE) was a member of a wealthy, influential Jewish family in Alexandria, Egypt (*see* Introduction to Philo of Alexandria). Brother to a senior city administrator and uncle to the eventual procurator of Judaea and prefect of Egypt, Philo himself opted for a life devoted to philosophy (though he led an embassy to appeal directly to the emperor Caligula following a pogrom against Jews in Alexandria in 38 CE; *see* Josephus, *Jewish Antiquities*). Philo, well-versed in his ancestral religion and a recipient of an elite Greek education, married these two in his writings and work (he appears to have run a school where the Jewish Scriptures were studied in the light of Hellenistic philosophy).

Text, Language, Sources, and Transmission

Moses has strong affinities in style with the expositions of the law of Moses, those Philonic treatises that seek to make Torah more accessible to Hellenistic readers.[2] Yet, while in modern editions of Philo, *Moses* is often placed after *On Abraham* and *On Joseph* and before *On the Decalogue,* it is not, like them, an explanation of Moses' writings but an introduction to the man himself.[3] One plausible explanation is that *Moses* serves as an introduction to the expositions (or perhaps to Philo's interpretative enterprise more generally). Gregory Sterling suggests, given similarities with the Hellenistic *bios* genre, that *Moses* functions in a fashion similar to Arrian's biography of Epictetus or Porphyry's *Life of Plotinus,* both of which

---

2. Editors' note: To locate this text in the wider writings of Philo, the reader is encouraged to consult the Introduction to Philo of Alexandria in this volume.

3. The last treatise of the category "exposition of the law of Moses," *On Rewards and Punishments,* lends to this ambiguity since it seems to mention *Moses* in 52–56, but not in its summary of the series in 1–2.

were written by disciples to introduce and celebrate the works of their masters.[4] Certainly, Philo's adjustments to his biblical source material to represent Moses as a great philosopher who enters into the divine darkness and has his soul stamped with archetypal patterns that substantiate a spiritual understanding of his laws pave the way to better understand the Alexandrian's own allegorical interpretations of the Scriptures. More generally, Philo describes Moses as in himself "a living and reasonable law" (*Moses* 1.162) and as such "a model to all those who were inclined to imitate him."

Theology

In some fashion an entrée into Philo's understanding of the Mosaic law, *Moses* provides the life of the divine lawgiver as a lens to understand Torah. The reader who grasps the extent that Moses embodied philosophical excellence and attained spiritual ascendency will perceive the universal applicability and divine authority of the Jewish Scriptures. What is more, *Moses* is an overture to Hellenistic thought and culture, an invitation to see that the good that the prevailing culture values found distinct expression already at the heart of Judaism, in its law and in its lawgiver. By locating the impetus for the law's distinctiveness in the man Moses, Philo shows that Judaism has appeal for all humans (not just those who are Jewish); yet by demonstrating that Moses is the "greatest and most perfect man who ever lived" Philo shows that his religion provides unique access to God.

Reception of Life of Moses in the Second Temple Period

While Philo's writings and legacy do not appear to have been influential in post–Second Temple (rabbinical) Judaism, *Moses* was read by other Jews of the first century (see, e.g., Josephus's interpretation of the priestly vestments in *Antiquities* 3.179–87). Philo's works, including *Moses,* found their way into the hands of second- and third-century Christians first at Alexandria and then in Caesarea. The convergence of philosophy and Scripture in his works paved the way for the development of Christian exegesis and theology for several centuries, implicitly or explicitly influencing so-called **Gnosticism**, allegorical interpretation, *Logos* theology, and mysticism. While patristic authors often refer to Philo's works, *Moses* has the distinction of being the impetus for a treatise with the same title and subject matter, namely, *Life of Moses* by **Gregory of Nyssa** (ca. 338–ca. 395 CE).[5] However, while Gregory draws from Philo's *Moses,* the two works have

---

4. G. Sterling, "Philo," in *Eerdmans Dictionary of Early Judaism,* ed. John J. Collins and Daniel C. Harlow (Grand Rapids: Eerdmans, 2010), p. 1068.

5. Gregory, *Life of Moses* 2.162–63, 525: "What does it mean that Moses entered the darkness and then saw God in it [Exod. 20:21]? What is now recounted seems somehow to be contradictory to the first theophany [the burning bush], for then the Divine was beheld in light but now he is seen in darkness. . . . Scripture teaches by this that religious knowledge comes at first to those who receive it as light. Therefore what is perceived to be contrary to religion is

considerable differences, which reflect their different audiences (Philo's general readers versus Gregory's ascetics), approaches (Philo only occasionally employs allegory while it is central to Gregory's *Moses*), and especially contexts (Philo's Greek-speaking Judaism and Gregory's fourth-century Christianity).[6] Still, that Gregory's *Moses* draws its format from Philo's *Moses* and its allegorical approach from Philo's more technical writings provides some vindication to Philo's effort at rendering Moses as a philosopher worthy of emulation whose laws reflect the spiritual heights he himself achieved. The value of Philo's works for contemporary readers of ancient Jewish and Christian writings also includes what it preserves from and communicates about Hellenistic philosophy (especially **Stoicism** and **Middle Platonism**); what it testifies about the state of biblical interpretation among educated, Greek-speaking Jews of the **Diaspora**; and how Philo reworks Jewish theological and ethical teachings in Hellenistic terms.

RONALD R. COX

FURTHER READING

Burridge, R. A. *What Are the Gospels? A Comparison with Greco-Roman Biography*. Society for New Testament Studies Monograph Series 70. Cambridge: Cambridge University Press, 1992.

Sandmel, Samuel. *Philo of Alexandria: An Introduction*. Oxford: Oxford University Press, 1979.

Schenck, Kenneth. *A Brief Guide to Philo*. Louisville, Ky.: Westminster John Knox, 2005.

Sterling, G. "Philo." In *The Eerdmans Dictionary of Early Judaism*, edited by J. J. Collins and D. C. Harlow, pp. 1063–70. Grand Rapids: Eerdmans, 2010.

Yonge, C. D. *The Works of Philo Judaeus*. 4 vols. Peabody, Mass.: Hendrickson, 2005 (1854–55).

ADVANCED READING

Borgen, P. *Philo, John and Paul: New Perspectives on Judaism and Early Christianity*. Brown Judaic Studies 131. Atlanta: Scholars, 1987.

---

darkness, and the escape from darkness comes about when one participates in light. But as the mind progresses and, through an ever greater and more perfect diligence, comes to apprehend reality, as it approaches more nearly to contemplation, it sees more clearly what of the divine nature is uncontemplated. For leaving behind everything that is observed, not only what sense comprehends but also what the intelligence thinks it sees, it keeps on penetrating deeper until by the intelligence's yearning for understanding it gains access to the invisible and the incomprehensible, and there it sees God. This is the true knowledge of what is sought; this is the seeing that consists in not seeing, because that which is sought transcends all knowledge, being separated on all sides by incomprehensibility as by a kind of darkness. So Moses, who eagerly seeks to behold God, is now taught how he can behold him: to follow God wherever he might lead is to behold God. His passing by signifies his guiding the one who follows, for someone who does not know the way cannot complete his journey safely in any other way than by following behind his guide. He who leads, then, by his guidance shows the way to the one following. He who follows will not turn aside from the right way if he always keeps the back of his leader in view." —trans. Abraham J. Malherbe and Everett Ferguson.

6. David Runia, *Philo in Early Christian Literature: A Survey* (Assen: Van Gorcum, 1993), pp. 256–61 (p. 257).

Feldman, L. H. *Philo's Portrayal of Moses in the Context of Ancient Judaism.* Christianity and Judaism in Antiquity. Notre Dame, Ind.: University of Notre Dame Press, 2007.

Holladay, Carl. *"Theios Aner."* In *Hellenistic Judaism: A Critique of the Use of This Category in New Testament Christology.* Society of Biblical Literature Dissertation Series 40. Missoula: Scholars, 1977.

Malherbe, A. J., and E. Ferguson. *Gregory of Nyssa: The Life of Moses: Translation, Introduction and Notes.* New York: Paulist, 1978.

Philo of Alexandria. Trans. F. H. Colson and G. H. Whitaker. Vol. 6. Loeb Classical Library. Cambridge, Mass.: Harvard University Press, 1958.

Runia, David T. *Philo in Early Christian Literature: A Survey.* Assen: Van Gorcum, 1993.

4.13 from *On the Life of Moses*

Volume 1

2.5And I will begin first with that with which it is necessary to begin. Moses was by birth a Hebrew, but he was born, and brought up, and educated in Egypt, his ancestors having migrated into Egypt with all their families on account of the long famine that oppressed Babylon and all the adjacent countries; for they were in search of food, and Egypt was a champagne country blessed with a rich soil, and very productive of every thing that the nature of man requires, and especially of corn and wheat,

⁶ for the river of that country at the height of summer, when they say that all other rivers that are derived from winter torrents and from springs in the ground are smaller, rises and increases, and overflows so as to irrigate all the lands, and make them one vast lake. And so the land, without having any need of rain, supplies every year an unlimited abundance of every kind of good food, unless sometimes the anger of God interrupts this abundance by reason of the excessive impiety of the inhabitants.

⁷ And his father and mother were among the most excellent persons of their time, and though they were of the same time, still they were induced to unite themselves together more from an unanimity of feeling than because they were related in blood; and Moses is the seventh generation in succession from the original settler in the country who was the founder of the whole race of the Jews.

3.8And he was thought worthy of being bred up in the royal palace, the cause of which circumstance was as follows. The king of the country, inasmuch as the nation of the Hebrews kept continually increasing in numbers, fearing lest gradually the settlers should become more numerous than the original inhabitants, and being more powerful should set upon them and subdue them by force, and make themselves their masters, conceived the idea of destroying their strength by impious devices, and ordered that of all the children that were born the females only should be brought up (since a woman, by reason of the weakness of her nature, is disinclined to and unfitted for war), and that all the male children should be destroyed, that the population of their cities might not be increased, since a power that consists of a number of men is a fortress difficult to take and difficult to destroy.

⁹ Accordingly as the child Moses, as soon as he was born, displayed a more beautiful and noble form than usual, his parents resolved, as far as was in their power, to disregard the proclamations of the tyrant. Accordingly they say that for three months continuously they kept him at home, feeding him on milk, without its coming to the knowledge of the multitude;

¹⁰ but when, as is commonly the case in monarchies, some persons discovered

---

Translation by Charles D. Yonge.

what was kept secret and in darkness, of those persons who are always eager to bring any new report to the king, his parents being afraid lest while seeking to secure the safety of one individual, they who were many might become involved in his destruction, with many tears exposed their child on the banks of the river, and departed groaning and lamenting, pitying themselves for the necessity that had fallen upon them, and calling themselves the slayers and murderers of their child, and commiserating the infant too for his destruction, which they had hoped to avert.

[11] Then, as was natural for people involved in a miserable misfortune, they accused themselves as having brought a heavier affliction on themselves than they need have done. "For why," said they, "did we not expose him at the first moment of his birth?" For people in general do not look upon one who has not lived long enough to partake of salutary food as a human being at all. "But we, in our superfluous affection, have nourished him these three entire months, causing ourselves by such conduct more abundant grief, and inflicting upon him a heavier punishment, in order that he, having at last attained to a great capacity for feeling pleasures and pains, should at last perish in the perception of the most grievous evils."

[4.12] And so they departed in ignorance of the future, being wholly overwhelmed with sad misery; but the sister of the infant who was thus exposed, being still a maiden, out of the vehemence of her fraternal affection, stood a little way off watching to see what would happen, and all the events that concerned him appear to me to have taken place in accordance with the providence of God, who watched over the infant.

[13] Now the king of the country had an only daughter, whom he tenderly loved, and they say that she, although she had been married a long time, had never had any children, and therefore, as was natural, was very desirous of children, and especially of male offspring, which should succeed to the noble inheritance of her father's prosperity and imperial authority, which was otherwise in danger of being lost, since the king had no other grandsons.

[14] And as she was always desponding and lamenting, so especially on that particular day was she overcome by the weight of her anxiety, that, though it was her ordinary custom to stay indoors and never to pass over the threshold of her house, yet now she went forth with her handmaidens down to the river, where the infant was lying. And there, as she was about to indulge in a bath and purification in the thickest part of the marsh, she beheld the child, and commanded her handmaidens to bring him to her.

[15] Then, after she had surveyed him from head to foot, and admired his elegant form and healthy vigorous appearance, and saw that he was crying, she had compassion on him, her soul being already moved within her by maternal feelings of affection as if he had been her own child. And when she knew that the infant belonged to one of the Hebrews who was afraid because of the commandment of the king, she herself conceived the idea of rearing him up, and took counsel with herself on the subject, thinking that it was not safe to bring him at once into the palace;

[16] and while she was still hesitating, the sister of the infant, who was still looking out, conjecturing her hesitation from what she beheld, ran up and asked her

whether she would like that the child should be brought up at the breast by some one of the Hebrew women who had been lately delivered;

¹⁷ and as she said that she wished that she would do so, the maiden went and fetched her own mother and that of the infant, as if she had been a stranger, who with great readiness and willingness cheerfully promised to take the child and bring him up, pretending to be tempted by the reward to be paid, the providence of God thus making the original bringing up of the child to accord with the genuine course of nature. Then she gave him a name, calling him Moses with great propriety, because she had received him out of the water, for the Egyptians call water "mos."

⁵·¹⁸ But when the child began to grow and increase, he was weaned, not in accordance with the time of his age, but earlier than usual; and then his mother, who was also his nurse, came to bring him back to the princess who had given him to her, inasmuch as he no longer required to be fed on milk, and as he was now a fine and noble child to look upon.

¹⁹ And when the king's daughter saw that he was more perfect than could have been expected at his age, and when from his appearance she conceived greater goodwill than ever toward him, she adopted him as her son, having first put in practice all sorts of contrivances to increase the apparent bulk of her belly, so that he might be looked upon as her own genuine child, and not as a supposititious one; but God easily brings to pass whatever he is inclined to effect, however difficult it may be to bring to a successful issue.

²⁰ Therefore the child being now thought worthy of a royal education and a royal attendance, was not, like a mere child, long delighted with toys and objects of laughter and amusement, even though those who had undertaken the care of him allowed him holidays and times for relaxation, and never behaved in any stern or morose way to him; but he himself exhibited a modest and dignified deportment in all his words and gestures, attending diligently to every lesson of every kind that could tend to the improvement of his mind.

²¹ And immediately he had all kinds of masters, one after another, some coming of their own accord from the neighboring countries and the different districts of Egypt, and some being even procured from Greece by the temptation of large presents. But in a short time he surpassed all their knowledge, anticipating all their lessons by the excellent natural endowments of his own genius; so that everything in his case appeared to be a recollecting rather than a learning, while he himself also, without any teacher, comprehended by his instinctive genius many difficult subjects;

²² for great abilities cut out for themselves many new roads to knowledge. And just as vigorous and healthy bodies that are active and quick in motion in all their parts release their trainers from much care, giving them little or no trouble and anxiety, and as trees that are of a good sort, and that have a natural good growth, give no trouble to their cultivators, but grow finely and improve of themselves, so in the same manner the well-disposed soul, going forward to meet the lessons that are imparted to it, is improved in reality by itself rather than by its teachers, and taking hold of some beginning or principle of knowledge, bounds, as the proverb has it, like a horse over the plain.

²³ Accordingly he speedily learned arithmetic, and geometry, and the whole

science of rhythm and harmony and meter, and the whole of music, by means of the use of musical instruments, and by lectures on the different arts, and by explanations of each topic; and lessons on these subjects were given him by Egyptian philosophers, who also taught him the philosophy that is contained in symbols, which they exhibit in those sacred characters or hieroglyphics, as they are called, and also that philosophy that is conversant about that respect which they pay to animals which they invest with the honors due to God. And all the other branches of the encyclical education he learned from Greeks; and the philosophers from the adjacent countries taught him Assyrian literature and the knowledge of the heavenly bodies so much studied by the Chaldeans.

²⁴ And this knowledge he derived also from the Egyptians, who study mathematics above all things, and he learned with great accuracy the state of that art among both the Chaldeans and Egyptians, making himself acquainted with the points in which they agree with and differ from each other—making himself master of all their disputes without encouraging any disputatious disposition in himself—but seeking the plain truth, since his mind was unable to admit any falsehood, as those are accustomed to do who contend violently for one particular side of a question, and who advocate any doctrine that is set before them, whatever it may be, not inquiring whether it deserves to be supported, but acting in the same manner as those lawyers who defend a cause for pay, and are wholly indifferent to the justice of their cause.

⁶·²⁵ And when he had passed the boundaries of the age of infancy he began to exercise his intellect; not, as some people do, letting his youthful passions roam at large without restraint, although in him they had ten thousand incentives by reason of the abundant means for the gratification of them which royal places supply; but he behaved with temperance and fortitude, as though he had bound them with reins, and thus he restrained their onward impetuosity by force.

²⁶ And he tamed, and appeased, and brought under due command every one of the other passions that are naturally and as far as they are themselves concerned frantic, and violent, and unmanageable. And if any one of them at all excited itself and endeavored to get free from restraint he administered severe punishment to it, reproving it with severity of language; and, in short, he repressed all the principal impulses and most violent affections of the soul, and kept guard over them as over a restive horse, fearing lest they might break all bounds and get beyond the power of reason that ought to be their guide to restrain them, and so throw everything everywhere into confusion. For these passions are the causes of all good and of all evil; of good when they submit to the authority of dominant reason, and of evil when they break out of bounds and scorn all government and restraint.

²⁷ Very naturally, therefore, those who associated with him and everyone who was acquainted with him marveled at him, being astonished as at a novel spectacle, and inquiring what kind of mind it was that had its abode in his body, and that was set up in it like an image in a shrine; whether it was a human mind or a divine intellect, or something combined of the two; because he had nothing in him resembling the many, but had gone beyond them all and was elevated to a more sublime height.

²⁸ For he never provided his stomach with any luxuries beyond those necessary tributes that nature has appointed to be paid to it, and as to the pleasures of the

organs below the stomach he paid no attention to them at all, except as far as the object of having legitimate children was concerned.

29 And being in a most eminent degree a practicer of abstinence and self-denial, and being above all men inclined to ridicule a life of effeminacy and luxury (for he desired to live for his soul alone, and not for his body), he exhibited the doctrines of philosophy in all his daily actions, saying precisely what he thought, and performing such actions only as were consistent with his words, so as to exhibit a perfect harmony between his language and his life, so that as his words were such also was his life, and as his life was such likewise was his language, like people who are playing together in tune on a musical instrument.

30 Therefore men in general, even if the slightest breeze of prosperity does only blow their way for a moment, become puffed up and give themselves great airs, becoming insolent to all those who are in a lower condition than themselves, and calling them dregs of the earth, and annoyances, and sources of trouble, and burdens of the earth, and all sorts of names of that kind, as if they had been thoroughly able to establish the undeviating character of their prosperity on a solid foundation, though, very likely, they will not remain in the same condition even until tomorrow,

31 for there is nothing more inconstant than fortune, which tosses human affairs up and down like dice. Often has a single day thrown down the man who was previously placed on an eminence, and raised the lowly man on high. And while men see these events continually taking place, and though they are well assured of the fact, still they overlook their relations and friends, and transgress the laws according to which they were born and brought up; and they overturn their national hereditary customs to which no just blame whatever is attached, dwelling in a foreign land, and by reason of their cordial reception of the customs among which they are living, no longer remembering a single one of their ancient usages.

7.32 But Moses, having now reached the very highest point of human good fortune, and being looked upon as the grandson of this mighty king, and being almost considered in the expectations of all men as the future inheritor of his grandfather's kingdom, and being always addressed as the young prince, still felt a desire for and admiration of the education of his kinsmen and ancestors, considering all the things that were thought good among those who had adopted him as spurious, even though they might, in consequence of the present state of affairs, have a brilliant appearance; and those things that were thought good by his natural parents, even though they might be for a short time somewhat obscure, at all events akin to himself and genuine good things.

33 Accordingly, like an uncorrupt judge both of his real parents and of those who had adopted him, he cherished toward the one a goodwill and an ardent affection, and he displayed gratitude toward the others in requital of the kindness that he had received at their hands, and he would have displayed the same throughout his whole life if he had not beheld a great and novel iniquity wrought in the country by the king;

34 for, as I have said before, the Jews were strangers in Egypt, the founders of their race having migrated from Babylon and the upper satrapies in the time of the famine, by reason of their want of food, and come and settled in Egypt, and having in a manner taken refuge like suppliants in the country as in a sacred

asylum, fleeing for protection to the good faith of the king and the compassion of the inhabitants;

^{35} for strangers, in my opinion, should be looked upon as refugees, and as the suppliants of those who receive them in their country; and, besides, being suppliants, these men were likewise sojourners in the land, and friends desiring to be admitted to equal honors with the citizens, and neighbors differing but little in their character from original natives.

$^{27.148}$ Of all these men, Moses was elected the leader; receiving the authority and sovereignty over them, not having gained it like some men who have forced their way to power and supremacy by force of arms and intrigue, and by armies of cavalry and infantry, and by powerful fleets, but having been appointed for the sake of his virtue and excellence and that benevolence toward all men that he was always feeling and exhibiting; and, also, because God, who loves virtue, and piety, and excellence, gave him his authority as a well-deserved reward. ^{149} For, as he had abandoned the chief authority in Egypt, which he might have had as the grandson of the reigning king, on account of the iniquities that were being perpetrated in that country, and by reason of his nobleness of soul and of the greatness of his spirit, and the natural detestation of wickedness, scorning and rejecting all the hopes that he might have conceived from those who had adopted him, it seemed good to the Ruler and Governor of the universe to recompense him with the sovereign authority over a more populous and more powerful nation, which he was about to take to himself out of all other nations and to consecrate to the priesthood, that it might forever offer up prayers for the whole universal race of [hu]mankind, for the sake of averting evil from them and procuring them a participation in blessings. ^{150} And when he had received this authority, he did not show anxiety, as some persons do, to increase the power of his own family, and promote his sons (for he had two) to any great dignity, so as to make them at the present time partakers in, and subsequently successors to, his sovereignty; for as he always cherished a pure and guileless disposition in all things both small and great, he now subdued his natural love and affection for his children, like an honest judge, making these feelings subordinate to his own incorruptible reason; ^{151} for he kept one most invariable object always steadily before him, namely, that of benefiting those who were subjected to his authority, and of doing everything in both word and deed, with a view to their advantage, never omitting any opportunity of doing anything that might tend to their prosperity. ^{152} Therefore he alone of all the persons who have ever enjoyed supreme authority, neither accumulated treasures of silver and gold, nor levied taxes, nor acquired possession of houses, or property, or cattle, or servants of his household, or revenues, or anything else that has reference to magnificence and superfluity, although he might have acquired an unlimited abundance of them all. ^{153} But as he thought it a token of poverty of soul to be anxious about material wealth, he despised it as a blind thing, but he honored the far-sighted wealth of nature, and was as great an admirer as anyone in the world of that kind of riches, as he showed himself to be in his clothes, and in his food, and in his whole system and manner of life, not indulging in any theatrical affectation of pomp and magnificence, but cultivating the simplicity and unpretending affable plainness of a private individual, but a sumptuousness that was truly royal, in those things that it is becoming for a ruler to desire and to abound in; [154] and these things are temperance, and fortitude, and continence, and presence of mind, and acuteness, and knowledge, and industry, and patience under evil, and contempt of pleasure, and justice, and exhortations to virtue and blame, and lawful punishment of offenders, and, on the contrary, praise and honor to those who did well in accordance with law.

28.155 Therefore, as he had utterly discarded all desire of gain and of those riches that are held in the highest repute among men, God honored him, and gave him instead the greatest and most perfect wealth; and this is the wealth of all the earth and sea, and of all the rivers, and of all the other elements, and all combinations whatever; for having judged him deserving of being made a partaker with himself in the portion that he had reserved for himself, he gave him the whole world as a possession suitable for his heir: [156] therefore, every one of the elements obeyed him as its master, changing the power that it had by nature and submitting to his commands. And perhaps there was nothing wonderful in this; for if it be true according to the proverb—"That all the property of friends is common"—and if the prophet was truly called the friend of God, then it follows that he would naturally partake of God himself and of all his possessions as far as he had need; [157] for God possesses everything and is in need of nothing; but the good man has nothing that is properly his own, no, not even himself; but he has a share granted to him of the treasures of God as far as he is able to partake of them. And this is natural enough; for he is a citizen of the world; on which account he is not spoken of as to be enrolled as a citizen of any particular city in the habitable world, since he very appropriately has for his inheritance not a portion of a district, but the whole world. [158] What more will I say? Has he not also enjoyed an even greater communion with the Father and Creator of the universe, being thought unworthy of being called by the same appellation? For he also was called the god and king of the whole nation, and he is said to have entered into the darkness where God was; that is to say, into the invisible, and shapeless, and incorporeal world, the essence, which is the model of all existing things, where he beheld things invisible to mortal nature; for, having brought himself and his own life into the middle, as an excellently wrought picture, he established himself as a most beautiful and godlike work, to be a model for all those who were inclined to imitate him. [159] And happy are they who have been able to take, or have even diligently labored to take, a faithful copy of this excellence in their own souls; for let the mind, above all other parts, take the perfect appearance of virtue, and if that cannot be, at all events let it feel an unhesitating and unvarying desire to acquire that appearance; [160] for, indeed, there is no one who does not know that men in a lowly condition are imitators of men of high reputation, and that what they see, these last chiefly desire, toward that do they also direct their own inclinations and endeavors. Therefore, when the chief of a nation begins to indulge in luxury and to turn aside to a delicate and effeminate life, then the whole of his subjects, or very nearly the whole, carry their desire for indulging the appetites of the belly and the parts below the belly beyond all reasonable bounds, except that there may be some persons who, through the natural goodness of their disposition, have a soul far removed from treachery, being rather merciful and kind. [161] If, on the other hand, the chief of a people adopts a more austere and dignified course of life, then even those of his subjects, who are inclined to be very incontinent, change and become temperate, hastening, either out of fear or out of shame, to give him an idea that they are devoted to the same pursuits and inclinations that he is; and, in fact, the lower orders will never, no, nor will mad men even, reject the customs and habits of their superiors: [162] but, perhaps, since Moses was also destined to be the lawgiver of his nation, he was himself long previously, through the providence of God, a living and reasonable law, since that providence appointed him to be the lawgiver, when as yet he knew nothing of his appointment.

Volume 2

[23.109] After these things the architect of the tabernacle next prepared a sacred dress for him who was to be appointed high priest, having in its embroidery a most exceedingly beautiful and admirable work; and the robe was twofold; one part of which was called the underrobe, and the other the robe over the shoulders. [110] Now the underrobe was of a more simple form and character, for it was entirely of hyacinthine colors, except the lowest and exterior portions, and these were ornamented with golden pomegranates, and bells, and wreaths of flowers; [111] but the robe over the shoulders or mantle was a most beautiful and skillful work, and was made with most perfect skill of all the aforesaid kinds of material, of hyacinth color, and purple, and fine linen, and scarlet, gold thread being entwined and embroidered in it. For the leaves were divided into fine hairs, and woven in with every thread, [112] and on the collar stones were fitted in, two being costly emeralds of exceeding value, on which the names of the patriarchs of the tribes were engraved, six on each, making twelve in all; and on the breast were twelve other precious stones, differing in color like seals, in four rows of three stones each, and these were fitted in what was called the *logeum* [113] and the *logeum* was made square and double, as a sort of foundation, that it might bear on it, as an image, two virtues, manifestation and truth; and the whole was fastened to the mantle by fine golden chains, and fastened to it so that it might never get loose; [114] and a golden leaf was wrought like a crown, having four names engraved on it which may only be mentioned or heard by holy men having their ears and their tongues purified by wisdom, and by no one else at all in any place whatever. [115] And this holy prophet Moses calls the name, a name of four letters, making them perhaps symbols of the primary numbers, the unit, the number two, the number three, the number four: since all things are comprised in the number four, namely, a point, and a line, and a superficies, and a solid, and the measures of all things, and the most excellent symphonies of music, and the *diatessaron* in the *sesquitertial* proportion, and the chord in fifths, in the ratio of one and a half to one, and the diapason in the double ratio, and the double diapason in the fourfold ratio. Moreover, the number four has an innumerable list of other virtues likewise, the greater part of which we have discussed with accuracy in our dissertation on numbers. [116] And in it there was a miter, in order that the leaf might not touch the head; and there was also a *cidaris* made, for the kings of the eastern countries are accustomed to use a *cidaris* instead of a diadem.

24.117 Such, then, is the dress of the high priest. But we must not omit to mention the signification that it conceals beneath both in its whole and in its parts. In its whole it is a copy and representation of the world; and the parts are a representation of the separate parts of the world. 118 And we must begin with the long robe reaching down to the feet of the wearer. This tunic is wholly of the color of a hyacinth, so as to be a representation of the air; for by nature the air is black, and in a measure it reaches down from the highest parts to the feet, being stretched from the parts about the moon, as far as the extremities of the earth, and being diffused everywhere. On which account also, the tunic reaches from the chest to the feet, and is spread over the whole body, 119 and unto it there is attached a fringe of pomegranates round the ankles, and flowers, and bells. Now the flowers are an emblem of the earth; for it is from the earth that all flowers spring and bloom; but the pomegranates (*rhoiskoi*) are a symbol of water, since, indeed, they derive their name from the flowing (*rhysis*) of water, being very appropriately named; and the bells are the emblem of the concord and harmony that exist between these things; for neither is the earth without the water, nor the water without the earthly substance, sufficient for the production of anything; but that can be effected only by the meeting and combination of both. 120 And the place itself is the most distinct possible evidence of what is here meant to be expressed; for as the pomegranates, and the flowers, and the bells are placed in the hem of the garment that reaches to the feet, so likewise the things of which they are the symbols, namely, the earth and water, have had the lowest position in the world assigned to them, and being in strict accord with the harmony of the universe, they display their own particular powers in definite periods of time and suitable seasons. 121 Now of the three elements, out of which and in which all the different kinds of things that are perceptible by the outward senses and perishable are formed, namely, the air, the water, and the earth, the garment that reached down to the feet in conjunction with the ornaments that were attached to that part of it which was about the ankles have been plainly shown to be appropriate symbols; for as the tunic is one, and as the aforesaid three elements are all of one species, since they all have all their revolutions and changes beneath the moon, and as to the garment are attached the pomegranates, and the flowers; so also in certain manner the earth and the water may be said to be attached to and suspended from the air, for the air is their chariot. 122 And our argument will be able to bring forth twenty probable reasons that the mantle over the shoulders is an emblem of heaven. For in the first place, the two emeralds on the shoulder blades, which are two round stones, are, in the opinion of some persons who have studied the subject, emblems of those stars that are the rulers of night and day, namely, the sun and moon; or rather, as one might argue with more correctness and a nearer approach to truth, they are the emblems of the two hemispheres; for, like those two stones, the portion below the earth and that over the earth are both equal, and neither of them is by nature adapted to be either increased or diminished like the moon. 123 And the color of the stars is an additional evidence in favor of my view; for to the glance of the eye the appearance of the heaven does resemble an emerald; and it follows necessarily that six names are engraved on each of the stones, because each of the hemispheres cuts the zodiac in two parts, and in this way comprehends within itself six animals. 124 Then the twelve stones on the breast, which are not like one another in color, and which are divided into four rows of three stones in each, what else can they be emblems of, except of the circle of the zodiac? For that also is divided into four parts, each consisting of three animals, by which divisions it makes up the seasons of the year, spring, summer, autumn, and winter, distinguishing the four changes, the two solstices, and the two equinoxes, each of which has its limit of three signs of this zodiac, by the revolutions of the sun, according to that unchangeable, and most lasting, and really divine ratio that exists in numbers; [125] on which account they attached it to that which is with great propriety called the *logeum*. For all the changes of the year and the seasons are arranged by well-defined, and stated, and firm reason; and, though this seems a most extraordinary and incredible thing, by their seasonable changes they display their undeviating and everlasting permanence and durability. [126] And it is said with great correctness, and exceeding beauty also, that the twelve stones all differ in their color, and that no one of them resembles the other; for also in the zodiac each animal produces that color which is akin to and belongs to itself, in the air, and in the earth, and in the water; and it produces it likewise in all the affections that move them, and in all kinds of animals and of plants.

[25.127] And this *logeum* is described as double with great correctness; for reason is double, both in the universe and also in the nature of [hu]mankind. In the universe there is that reason which is conversant about incorporeal species that are like patterns as it were, from which that world which is perceptible only by the intellect was made, and also that which is concerned with the visible objects of sight, which are copies and imitations of those species above mentioned, of which the world that is perceptible by the outward senses was made. Again, in man there is one reason that is kept back, and another that finds vent in utterance: and the one is, as it were a spring, and the other (that which is uttered) flows from it; and the place of the one is the dominant part, that is, the mind; but the place of the one that finds vent in utterance is the tongue, and the mouth, and all the rest of the organs of the voice. [128] And the architect assigned a quadrangular form to the *logeum,* intimating under an exceedingly beautiful figure, that both the reason of nature, and also that of man, ought to penetrate everywhere, and ought never to waver in any case; in reference to which, it is that he has also assigned to it the two virtues that have been already enumerated, manifestation and truth; for the reason of nature is true, and calculated to make manifest, and to explain everything; and the reason of the wise man, imitating that other reason, ought naturally, and appropriately to be completely sincere, honoring truth, and not obscuring anything through envy, the knowledge of which can benefit those to whom it would be explained; [129] not but what he has also assigned their two appropriate virtues to those two kinds of reason that exist in each of us, namely, that which is uttered and that which is kept concealed, attributing clearness of manifestation to the uttered one, and truth to that which is concealed in the mind; for it is suitable to the mind that it should admit of no error or falsehood, and to explanation that it should not hinder anything that can conduce to the most accurate manifestation. [130] Therefore there is no advantage in reason that expends itself in dignified and pompous language, about things that are good and desirable, unless it is followed by consistent practice of suitable actions; on which account the architect has affixed the *logeum* to the robe that is worn over the shoulder, in order that it may never get loose, as he does not approve of the language being separated from the actions; for he puts forth the shoulder as the emblem of energy and action.

26.131 Such then are the figurative meanings that he desires to indicate by the sacred vestments of the high priest; and instead of a diadem he represents a *cidaris* on the head, because he thinks it right that the man who is consecrated to God, as his high priest, should, during the time of his exercising his office be superior to all men, not only to all private individuals, but even to all kings; [132] and above this *cidaris* is a golden leaf, on which an engraving of four letters was impressed; by which letters they say that the name of the living God is indicated, since it is not possible that anything that is in existence, should exist without God being invoked; for it is his goodness and his power combined with mercy that is the harmony and uniter of all things. [133] The high priest, then, being equipped in this way, is properly prepared for the performance of all sacred ceremonies, that, whenever he enters the temple to offer up the prayers and sacrifices in use among his nation, all the world may likewise enter in with him, by means of the imitations of it which he bears about him, the garment reaching to his feet, being the imitation of the air, the pomegranate of the water, the flowery hem of the earth, and the scarlet dye of his robe being the emblem of fire; also, the mantle over his shoulders being a representation of heaven itself; the two hemispheres being further indicated by the round emeralds on the shoulder blades, on each of which were engraved six characters equivalent to six signs of the zodiac; the twelve stones arranged on the breast in four rows of three stones each, namely, the *logeum*, being also an emblem of that reason which holds together and regulates the universe. [134] For it was indispensable that the man who was consecrated to the Father of the world, should have as a *paraclete,* his son, the being most perfect in all virtue, to procure forgiveness of sins, and a supply of unlimited blessings; [135] perhaps, also, he is thus giving a previous warning to the servant of God, even if he is unable to make himself worthy of the Creator, of the world, at least to labor incessantly to make himself worthy of the world itself; the image of which he is clothed in, in a manner that binds him from the time that he puts it on, to bear about the pattern of it in his mind, so that he will be in a manner changed from the nature of a man into the nature of the world, and, if one may say so (and one may by all means and at all times speak the plain truth in sincerity), become a little world himself.

27.136 Again, outside the outer vestibule, at the entrance, is a brazen laver; the architect having not taken any mere raw material for the manufacture of it, as is very common, but having employed on its formation vessels that had been constructed with great care for other purposes; and which the women contributed with all imaginable zeal and eagerness, in rivalry of one another, competing with the men themselves in piety, having determined to enter upon a glorious contest, and to the utmost extent of their power to exert themselves so as not to fall short of their holiness. [137] For though no one enjoined them to do so, they, of their own spontaneous zeal and earnestness, contributed the mirrors with which they had been accustomed to deck and set off their beauty, as the most becoming firstfruits of their modesty, and of the purity of their married life, and as one may say of the beauty of their souls. [138] The maker then thought it well to accept these offerings, and to melt them down, and to make nothing except the laver of them, in order that the priests who were about to enter the temple might be supplied from it, with water of purification for the purpose of performing the sacred ministrations that were appointed for them; washing their feet most especially, and their hands, as a symbol of their irreproachable life, and of a course of conduct that takes itself pure in all kinds of praiseworthy actions, proceeding not along the rough road of wickedness that one may more properly call no road at all, but keeping straight along the level and direct path of virtue. [139] Let him remember, says he, let him who is about to be sprinkled with the water of purification from this laver, remember that the materials of which this vessel was composed were mirrors, that he himself may look into his own mind as into a mirror; and if there is perceptible in it any deformity arising from some agitation unconnected with reason or from any pleasure that would excite us, and raise us up in hostility to reason, or from any pain that might mislead us and turn us from our purpose of proceeding by the straight road, or from any desire alluring us and even dragging us by force to the pursuit of present pleasures, he seeks to relieve and cure that, desiring only that beauty that is genuine and unadulterated.

Glossary of Biographical Names

Aeneas The protagonist of Virgil's *Aeneid*. The Romans traced their ancestry back to him.

Aeschylus (525–456 BCE) A Greek dramatist and the founder of Greek tragedy.

Agrippa I Agrippa I (12 BCE–44 CE), originally named Marcus Julius Agrippa, is known as Herod or Herod Agrippa. He was the grandson of Herod the Great and son of Aristobulus IV and Berenice. He is the King Herod who is identified in Acts 12:1–23. Agrippa ruled over the territory of Israel, including Judea, Galilee, Batabaea, and Perea. He is known to have intervened for the Jews of Alexandria before his friend Emperor Caligula. At the time Caligula was attempting to set up his statue (the Abomination of Desolation) in the Jerusalem temple. Agrippa I would die a violent and painful death in which he was eaten by worms for five days—the same death his grandfather Herod the Great suffered.

Alexander I Balas (d. 145 BCE) Claimed to be the son of Antiochus IV Ephiphanes and Laodice IV and thus the heir to the Seleucid throne. He ruled the Greek Seleucid kingdom from 150 BCE until his defeat in the Battle of Antioch (145 BCE).

Alexander Jannaeus (d. 76 BCE) A Hasmonean ruler who reigned from 103 to 76 BCE. He was the son of Jonathan Hyrcanus I. His rule involved constant military conflict. He was the first of the Hasmonean rulers to style himself as king on his coins.

Anaxagoras (ca. 510–428 BCE) A pre-Socratic Greek philosopher of nature and science.

Antiochus IV Epiphanes (215–164 BCE) The Seleucid king of Syria and its territories, which included Judea, from 175 BCE to 163 BCE. He was the younger son of Antiochus III and a descendant of Seleucus, a general of Alexander the Great who inherited a portion of the vast Macedonian Empire after the young emperor's death in 323 BCE. As the younger son, Antiochus IV Epiphanes was not in line for the throne, but ascended after arranging the death of his young nephew. He seems to have coined the name "Epiphanes," or "God Manifest," for himself as a nickname. Indeed, his arrogance, along with his looting of the Jerusalem temple and his bloody suppression of Jewish practices in Jerusalem from 167 to 164 BCE, provoked resistance from many groups, including the scribes responsible for Daniel's visions and those militant groups that were part of the Maccabean Revolt.

Antiochus V (172–162 BCE) The son of Antiochus IV. He succeeded his father at the age of nine and reigned from 163 to 162 BCE. He, like many other kings in the Seleucid Empire, had a regent, named Lysias. Lysias had full control of the powerful army and set out against Judea to do battle with Judas Maccabee. Lysias overwhelmed the Jews in a battle near Beth Zechariah; Beth Zur was captured and Jerusalem was under siege. However, the political situation in the empire would bring hope for the Jews. In an effort to retain power over a rival, Lysias granted full religious freedom to the Jews. This victory would not be enjoyed for long by Lysias or Antiochus V, as they were both killed by Demetrius I in 162 BCE.

Antiochus VI (148–142 BCE) Proclaimed king of Syria while still a minor (ca. 146 BCE) by Trypho, the former general of Alexander I Balas. He never actually ruled as king and was assassinated by Trypho, who took the throne himself.

Antony (83–30 BCE) A Roman politician, also called Marc Antony, who played a critical role in the transformation of the Roman Republic into the Roman Empire.

Aristobulus Probably the earliest known Jewish philosopher. He lived in Alexandria, Egypt, in the second century BCE. He wrote *Explanations of the Book of Moses,* of which only five fragments are preserved as quotations in the works of the fourth-century CE church historian Eusebius. Aristobulus's work consisted of exegetical discussions written in the form of a dialogue. He applied allegorical interpretations, trying to correlate Greek wisdom with the biblical tradition. He was attempting to establish the legitimacy of allegorical interpretation to demonstrate that the Torah, properly understood, could be intelligible to educated Greeks. In fact, according to Aristobulus, Plato and other ancient philosophers had followed the traditions of the Torah as known by the Jews. Philo might be understood as a successor of Aristobulus. Philo does not, however, quote or refer to Aristobulus, but he probably knew his works and drew on them.

Augustus (63 BCE–14 CE) Founder of the Roman Empire and its first emperor (r. 40 BCE–14 CE).

Brutus (85–42 BCE) Roman senator and one of the conspirators in the assassination of Julius Caesar.

Caligula (12–41 CE) was a first-century Roman emperor who ruled from 37 to 41 CE.

Cassius Cassius (d. 43 BCE) Roman senator and one of the conspirators in the assassination of Julius Caesar.

Cleopatra VII Philopater (69–30 BCE) Better known as simply Cleopatra, she was the last active pharaoh in ancient Egypt in the first century BCE. She was romantically linked to both Julius Caesar and Marc Antony.

Demetrius II (161–125 BCE) Succeeded in gaining the Syrian throne four years after the death of his father Demetrius (Soter). Jonathan Maccabeus, remaining faithful to Alexander I Balas to the end, had opposed the succession of Demetrius II. Demetrius II's viceroy, Apollonius, who ruled over Coele-Syria, held Joppa and Ashdod for his king, but was expelled by Jonathan, who destroyed Ashdod and brought the plunder to Jerusalem. Jonathan tried to throw off Syrian rule altogether and besieged the fortress of Jerusalem. He eventually faced Demetrius II at Ptolemais. He demanded an extension of territory and several privileges for the Jews, and supported his demand by costly gifts. Demetrius II did not dare to refuse, and agreed to turn over three Samaritan districts, Ephraim, Lydda, and Ramathaim, to Judea; he freed Judea from all taxes and confirmed Jonathan's position. Demetrius II had thus escaped further danger from his Jewish vassal but soon after encountered Trypho, a former general of Alexander I Balas.

Dio Cassius (155–235 CE) Of Greek origin, he was a Roman consul and historian. He wrote in Greek, and is best known for his *Roman History.*

Dio Chrysostom (40–120 CE) A Greek rhetorician, author, philosopher, and historian of the Roman Empire.

Diodorus of Sicily (90–30 BCE) A Greek historian. He is best known for his *Library of History.*

Dionysius of Halicarnassus (b. 60 BCE) A Greek historian and teacher of rhetoric. He is best known for his *Roman Antiquities.*

Domitian (51–96 CE) Roman emperor from 81 to 96 CE. He was the third and final emperor of the Flavian dynasty.

Eleazar High priest in Jerusalem during the period of the collision of Jewish and Hellenistic cultures that resulted from Alexander the Great's conquests.

Epaphroditus An individual to whom Josephus dedicated his late works. He has not been clearly identified, but was probably one of two scholars by that name living in Rome when Josephus was there.

Eusebius (263–339 CE) Roman bishop of Caesarea and the first major church historian.

Gregory of Nyssa (ca. 338–ca. 395 CE) Bishop of Nyssa from 372 to 376 CE and from 378 CE until his death. He was the most philosophically adept of the Cappadocians (Gregory of Nyssa, Basil the Great, and Gregory of Nazianzus).

Hadrian (76–138 CE) Roman emperor from 117 to 138 CE. He is primarily known for his building projects, especially Hadrian's Wall.

Herod the Great (d. 4 BCE) Appointed king of the Jews by the Roman Senate. With the help of Rome, in 37 or 36 BCE he captured Jerusalem and executed Antigonus, thus establishing the Herodian dynasty. Herod is well known for his building projects throughout Jerusalem and Judea. He undertook several sizable projects, including the reconstruction/remodeling of the temple in Jerusalem. In addition, he ordered the construction of the harbor and surrounding facilities at Caesarea. To fund these enormous undertakings, Herod instituted a taxation system that proved to be a heavy burden on the Jews. Although he was king of the Jews, many Jews doubted whether he was truly Jewish due to his Idumean lineage. However, it is thought that he largely acknowledged traditional Jewish observances in his public life. For instance, he minted coins without human images to be used in Jewish areas and recognized the holiness of the Second Temple by employing priests in the construction of the temple.

Herodotus (484–425 BCE) Greek historian, recognized as the "father of history." He is best known for his *Histories.*

Irenaeus (130–202 CE) Early church father and apologist, primarily known for his refutation of Gnosticism in his major work *Against Heresies;* he was the bishop of Lugdunum in Gaul.

John of Gischala Leader of the Jewish revolt against Rome that resulted in the destruction of Jerusalem in 70 CE. Josephus denounced him in his *Life* (87–88).

Jonathan Hyrcanus I Hasmonean ruler who reigned from 135 to 104 BCE. He was the son of Simon Maccabeus and the nephew of Judas Maccabeus. His truce with the Seleucid Antiochus VII caused the loss of support among the Judean population. After Antiochus VII was killed in battle, Hyrcanus's military conquests made Judea a significant power in Syria.

Jonathan Maccabeus (d. 143 BCE) Son of Mattathias and brother of Judas Maccabeus; he was the leader of the Jews following the Maccabean Revolt from 161 to 142 BCE. He is also called Apphus ("the dissembler") based on his character portrayal in 1 Maccabees 2:5.

Judas Maccabeus Jewish priest and son of the priest Mattathias who led the Jewish resistance fighters in the Maccabean Revolt against the Seleucid Empire from 167 to 160 BCE.

Julius Caesar (100–44 BCE) Roman statesman, general, and author who was made dictator for life in February 44 BCE; he was assassinated by Roman senators a month later.

Lucian of Samosata (125–180 CE) Second-century Greco-Syrian author and satirist who wrote more than seventy dialogues and treatises.

Mani of the Manicheans (b. ca. 216 CE) Lived parts of his life in Babylon and Persia. He is described as the founder and prophet of Manicheism, which was a Gnostic religion that was widespread in Late Antiquity. Six of his major works were written in Aramaic and a seventh survives in Middle Persian. He is thought to have died in Gundeshapur, Persia (ca. 276 CE), in what is now modern-day Iran. The teachings of Mani, similar to those of Zoroastrianism, were based on a rigid dualism of good and evil, which were locked in eternal struggle. He claimed that salvation could come about through education, self-denial, fasting, and chastity. One of the writings closely connected to Mani is the Manichean *Book of Giants*. Remnants of seven copies of the work survive. Fragments of the work have been recovered in medieval manuscripts in various languages, including Middle Persian. The identification of the Qumran fragments of the *Book of the Giants* is based on this Manichean *Book of Giants*.

Mattathias Founder of the Hasmonean dynasty, not mentioned in 2 Maccabees, but the center of attention in 1 Maccabees 2. Here his "zealous" murder of a Seleucid official and of a Jew who was willing to knuckle under to the Seleucid decrees against Judaism are portrayed as the opening of the rebellion and, by comparison to Phineas's act portrayed in Numbers 25, offered as justification for the dynasty's claim to the high priesthood. Mattathias is not mentioned in 2 Maccabees since it has no interest in the Hasmonean dynasty. The standard Jewish prayer for Hanukkah, 'Al Hanissim, opens by placing the events "In the days of Mattathias."

Nicanor Second Maccabees 8 assumes that the Nicanor who campaigned against Judas and who had his ups and downs with Judas in chapters 14–15 is the same person (paralleled by the latter half of 1 Macc. 7). The sobriquet "thrice-accursed" is used of him in both contexts (2 Macc. 8:34; 15:3) and Nicanor is the central figure in both episodes. In its version of the earlier episode, 1 Maccabees 3–4 only briefly mentions Nicanor (3:38) and instead focuses on another general, Gorgias, who is not even mentioned by 2 Maccabees. Thus, it is not clear that the two Nicanors are one and the same, and it is in any case apparent that 2 Maccabees has emphasized his role as part of its case for the celebration of Nicanor's Day.

Onias III (Hebrew: Johanan) was, just as his father Simon II, high priest in Jerusalem when Antiochus IV Epiphanes came to power. According to 2 Maccabees 4, he was supplanted by his brother Jason, and when Jason was supplanted by Menelaus, the latter had Onias murdered in Antioch. Others, however, follow a tradition preserved by Josephus that Onias fled to Egypt and founded a temple there that competed with the one in Jerusalem.

Plutarch (45–120 CE) Greek historian, biographer, and author. He is best known for his *Parallel Lives* and the *Moralia*.

Polybius (200–118 BCE) Greek historian, best known for his *Histories*.

Pompey (106–48 BCE) Roman general whose forces invaded Jerusalem in 63 BCE, removed the Hasmonean monarchy, and reinstated Jonathan Hyrcanus II as high priest.

Ptolemy I (367–283 BCE) Macedonian general under Alexander the Great who became ruler of Egypt (323–283 BCE) and founder of the Ptolemaic dynasty.

Ptolemy II Philadelphus (309–246 BCE) Son of Ptolemy I Soter and Berenice, he ruled Ptolemaic Egypt from 283 to 246 BCE. During his reign, the Alexandrian court was at its material and literary height.

Ptolemy VI (Greek: Philometor, literally "loving his mother") (186–145 BCE) Macedonian king of Egypt from 180 to 145 BCE. His attempted invasion of Coele-Syria led to the occupation of Egypt by the Seleucids.

Pythagoras (571–495 BCE) Greek philosopher and mathematician, best known for the Pythagorean theorem and often described as the first pure mathematician.

Seleucus I (359–281 BCE) Macedonian general under Alexander the Great who assumed the title of *basileus* and founded the Seleucid Empire, which he ruled from 305 to 280 BCE.

Sennacherib (Sennacherim) (d. 681 BCE) King of Assyria (r. 705–681 BCE), best known for his military campaigns against Judea and Babylon and his building programs, especially in his capital city Nineveh.

Simon Maccabeus Second son of Mattathias and the first prince of the Hasmonean dynasty. He ruled as high priest from 142 to 135 BCE.

Suetonius (70–130 CE) Roman biographer and antiquarian. He is best known for his *Concerning Illustrious Men* and *Lives of the Caesars*.

Tacitus (56–117 CE) Senator and historian of the Roman Empire. He is best known for his *Germania, Histories,* and *Annals.*

Thales (ca. 624–ca. 546 BCE) Pre-Socratic Greek philosopher and mathematician, renowned as one of the legendary Seven Sages or Seven Wise Men of Antiquity.

Theognis (fl. sixth century BCE) Greek elegiac poet.

Thucydides (460–395 BCE) Historian, regarded as the first "scientific" historian. He is best known for his *History of the Peloponnesian War.*

Titus (39–81 CE) Roman emperor from 79 to 81 CE. He was the first emperor to come to the throne after his biological father (Vespasian).

Trajan (53–117 CE) Roman emperor from 98 to 117 CE. He is best known for his military success and philanthropic rule.

Trypho Military commander of Syria and the regent of Antiochus VI. Following the victories of the Hasmoneans, Trypho was considering the removal of Antiochus VI and planning to take the throne for himself. However, he suspected that Jonathan Maccabeus would oppose him on moral and political grounds. Trypho convinced Jonathan of his allegiance but betrayed and murdered him in 142 BCE. A year later Trypho murdered Antiochus VI and took the Seleucid throne.

Vespasian (9–79 CE) Roman emperor from 69 to 79 CE and founder of the Flavian dynasty.

Xenophon (430–354 BCE) Greek historian and philosopher. He is best known for his *Anabasis, Memorabilia,* and *Apology* (the latter two dealing with Socrates).

Xerxes (519–465 BCE) King of Persia (r. 485–465 BCE) who took Athens in 480 BCE but was eventually defeated by the Greeks in the last of the major Persian Wars.

Glossary of Terms

Acherusian Sea A lake into which the Acheron River flowed and which was believed to be connected to the underworld. It had prominent mythic significance as the locale where the god of the underworld river and lake of pain transported the souls of the dead to the afterlife.

Ahiqar Probably composed originally in the seventh or eighth century BCE in Syria, this work tells the fictional story of an Assyrian royal counselor, Ahiqar, who is betrayed by his nephew, Nadin, whom he had adopted as a son. He is saved from execution by a soldier whom he had earlier helped, and eventually restored to his former station, enabling him to exact revenge on Nadin. The story serves as a vehicle for a long collection of sayings, and it was adapted into many different languages over many centuries. Its great popularity gave it considerable influence, and there were various imitations. In some respects, the book of Tobit is just such an imitation, using another story of rescue as a vehicle for its own prayers and advice. The debt is acknowledged, moreover, with direct reference made to the Ahiqar story in Tobit 14:10. With a certain *chutzpah,* the writer even introduces Ahiqar as Tobit's nephew, making him Jewish (see 1:21–22; 2:10; 11:18).

Ahriman The evil spirit in Zoroastrianism.

Ahura Mazda Supreme god in Zoroastrianism, thought to be responsible for all the good in the world.

alabarch Magistrate responsible for handling customs in Alexandria during the rule of the Ptolemies and the Roman Empire.

Alexandria Alexandria, Egypt, was founded by Alexander the Great in 331 BCE. It was famous for its great Pharos lighthouse, possibly the first of its kind. During the first century CE, it was a large, thriving metropolis, second only to Rome in population. It was a center of scholarship and included one of the great libraries of the ancient world. It was not only home to Philo but also in later generations, the philosopher Plotinus and church fathers Clement of Alexandria, Origen, and Athanasius, among many others. Alexandria is mentioned four times in the Bible, all in the book of Acts (6:9; 18:24; 27:6; 28:11).

Alexandrian revolt Positive Jewish relations with the Greco-Roman world were perhaps on greatest display in Alexandria, Egypt, in the second and first centuries BCE. However, by the late first century CE, high tension between Jews and the Greco-Roman world, resulting from the Jewish revolt (66–70 CE), disintegrated even further into the Diaspora revolts of 115/116–117 CE. Beginning in Cyrene and Cyprus, uprisings among Jewish communities spread to Alexandria in Egypt. This effectively ended the long history of Jewish intellectual and cultural flourishing in that Egyptian city.

allegorization Exegetical technique in which a hidden or symbolic meaning *(hyponoia)* is looked for under or behind the obvious connotations of a text.

allegory Sustained metaphor in which objects, persons, and actions in a narrative are equated with symbolic meanings.

angelomorphic Having the form of an angel.

antediluvian Of or belonging to the time before the biblical flood.

anthropomorphic Ascribing human characteristics to a nonhuman thing or being, especially a deity.

apocalypse Lit. "unveiling" or "revelation." A vision, dream, or enlightened (even ecstatic) experience communicated in written (literary) form, most often with the help of a mediating being (angel) and frequently including a "heavenly journey." Common among certain early Jewish, and then Christian, circles, apocalypses addressed the circumstances (often crises) of their audiences and sought to shape attitudes and behavior accordingly.

apocalyptic Of or relating to the cataclysmic events, characteristics, and qualities of the end-time (often presented either as the final throes of the present age or the anticipated future age); or, characteristic of the genre "apocalypse."

Apocrypha (Old Testament) Books written by Jewish authors between ca. 300 and 100 BCE that are included as an appendix to the Old Testament Septuagint and the Latin Vulgate but are not in the Hebrew Bible.

apotropaic From the Greek verb *apotrepein,* "to ward off," apotropaic is defined as "intending to ward off evil"; an apotropaic prayer generally involved the use of the name of the person's god in order to ward off the evil spirit.

Archaizing Hebrew Consisted of the imitation of the style of biblical Hebrew by post-biblical scribes in an attempt to make a composition appear to be from the prior era. Contemporary scholars occasionally debate whether or not a scribe from the Second Temple period imitated the conventions of ancient Hebrew successfully.

Armageddon Transliterated from Hebrew "Har-Megiddo" (lit. "mountain of Megiddo") into Greek by the author of Revelation (16:16). Presented as the site of the gathering of armies for a final battle during the end-time, the term may have reflected traditions that developed from the Hebrew Bible in the Second Temple period since no such mountain exists (but the town of Megiddo in the plain of Esdraelon was a historical site of such hostilities).

atomization Exegetical technique in which each word (and sometimes letters or parts of letters) is interpreted as a hermeneutic unit.

Atticism Style or idiom of Attic Greek (Greek dialect spoken in ancient Attica) occurring in another dialect or language, especially in the Hellenistic period.

autographs Reference to the original (first) version of an ancient document of which now only fragments, copies, versions, and variants are available.

basilisk Mythical creature that may have its origins in legendary Egyptian descriptions of the cobra snake (first mentioned in Pliny the Elder's *Natural History*). Eventually came to represent evil (or even the devil) in later Christian tradition and iconography.

Beelzebul One of many terms thought to be related to the Christian tradition of the Satan figure. Possible similar names are given to a leader of evil spirits in other Second Temple period literature, although we cannot be sure the same figure is intended in any of the instances. The names include Melki-resha, the Angel of Darkness, Satan, Mastema, and Belial/Beliar. He is further identified as Satan or the evil one in the Gospel traditions.

Belial In Jewish apocryphal literature an actual evil being with a backstory. The term "Belial" is generally used as a personal name and at times as a synonym of "Satan"; some go as far as to identify it with the personification of evil. The Hebrew Bible renders it as a common noun meaning "wickedness" or "worthlessness." The phrase "sons of Belial" in Judges 19:22 would be understood as worthless individuals. Another rendering in the Hebrew Bible is "Sheol," which may have further developed into "darkness" or "prince of darkness," often used in this manner in the first century CE. This may have emerged from an understanding of 2 Corinthians 6:15 in which Belial is identified as the Prince of Darkness over against the Christ. The name plays an important role in the Testaments of the Twelve Patriarchs, the Ascension of Isaiah, and the Sibylline Oracles.

Berakhot Literally "blessings." Hebrew work from Qumran that contains blessings, curses, and a series of laws. It is preserved in five manuscripts dated paleographically from 1 to 50 CE (4QBerakhot^{a-e}/4Q286–4Q290). The work is a liturgy concerning the ceremony of the renewal of God's covenant with Israel. The event appears to have involved a time of communal confession, followed by a series of blessings addressed to God and curses against Belial and his lot. These blessings and curses are recited by heavenly and earthly participants and are followed by responses by the community. Thus, this work continues the dualistic ideas at Qumran of good and evil. This ceremony appears to work toward the expelling of a willful sinner from the community. Finally, it concludes with an eschatological hope in which all wickedness will vanish.

bicola See below on **cola**.

Book of Hagu Book mentioned in the Dead Sea Scrolls, usually translated as "Book of Meditation"; its identity and contents are unclear.

catechetical Relating to religious instruction by means of questions and answers.

Chaldeans Semites whose nation, located on the far southeastern corner of Mesopotamia, emerged between the late tenth and early ninth centuries BCE and survived until the mid-sixth century BCE. The Chaldeans were an influential and highly educated group of people.

chiasm Literary technique that uses the repetition of similar ideas in the reverse sequence (A-B-C/C'-B'-A' pattern) for emphasis.

codices (sg. codex) Bound editions of edited or collated biblical texts that appeared alongside the New Testament with the advent of full-scale Christian Bibles, of which the best attested are *Codex Vaticanus* (B), *Codex Sinaiticus* (S), and *Codex Alexandrinus* (A).

codicology Study of the codex form.

cola Refers to the parts of a line or sentence in a poetic structure. When two, three, or four parts match in length and rhythm they are identified as bicola, tricola, or tetracola.

conflagration Extensive and destructive fire that is part of God's enactment of judgment and doom in the eschaton.

cosmology Study of the origin and structure of the universe.

covenantal liturgy Liturgy in the *Rule of the Community* that was celebrated annually for the renewal of the covenant with the introduction of new members.

Cronos and Titan In the *Sibylline Oracles* Book 3 Cronos and Titan are two of the three sons of Ouranus and Gaia (along with Iapetus).

cult System of religious beliefs and rituals.

Cynics Members of the ancient school of Greek philosophy founded in Athens by Antisthenes (ca. 445 BCE–ca. 365 BCE).

***Decretum Gelasianum* (Gelasian Decree)** Five-part text written between 519 and 553 CE by an anonymous author; it was formerly ascribed to Pope Gelasius (r. 494–496 CE).

Delphi Archaeological site in upper central Greece renowned for its oracle whose advice was sought by peoples far and near.

descensus ad inferos Reference to the Christian concept of Christ's descent into hell (Hades).

determinism Concept that God has preordained all of history and nothing can happen outside God's plan. It is often associated at Qumran with predestination, the idea that God has chosen who will be saved and who will be damned. In this view, the omnipotent plan of God ranges from the creation and order of history to events in the life of the individual. First, God has decided who will be part of his covenant community (Israel/the community). However, even within the community, God has decided each person's rank and/or gifts. These are based on the spirits that God has put in each person. While the preexistent plan of God cannot be changed, the community does leave room for the free will of the individual. Even entrance into the community itself is based on a voluntary decision. This tension is difficult to resolve, but it appears that the community believed that God had determined history and predestined individuals, yet there was a constant call in many works at Qumran exhorting its members to choose to walk in the ways of God.

deuterocanonical Term referring to biblical books in the Septuagint (a "second canon") that are not in the Hebrew canon.

Deuteronomistic Referring to writers who modeled their theology on the book of Deuteronomy.

Diaspora Dispersion of Jews among Gentiles outside the land of Israel.

diatribe Informal method of argumentation that simulates dialogue with an imaginary opponent, often utilizing rhetorical questions and hypothetical objections.

didactic Designed or intended to teach.

dittograph Letters or words inadvertently repeated in copying.

dramatis personae Characters of a narrative or poetic presentation.

dualism Philosophical theory that envisions an inherent conflict between two antagonistic forces, such as good and evil or light and darkness.

editio princeps First printed edition of a text that had only existed in manuscript form until that time.

el Early Semitic word meaning "god"; its base meaning is "strength" or "power."

elohim Word most often used for God in the Hebrew Bible; it refers to the true God as well as gods, goddesses, and divine or mighty things.

emic From the perspective of an insider.

endogamy Marriage within a specific local community, clan, or tribe.

Endzeit ist Uhrzeit Idiomatic German phrase belonging to the descriptive vocabulary of those eschatological (often apocalyptic) visions that anticipate the future kingdom of God (*Endzeit*) as a restoration/re-creation of the biblical descriptions of original creation (*Uhrzeit*; cf. Gen. 1–2).

Enochic Judaism In the closing centuries BCE, there was an ongoing struggle over control of the Jerusalem temple cult. Several groups attempted to challenge the ruling party; this opposition is reflected primarily in the pseudepigrapha. One particular opposition group finds its voice in the figure of Enoch and a group of texts known as Enochic literature, that is, 1 Enoch, including the Book of Watchers and the Astronomical Book, among others. This movement is identified as Enochic Judaism, although there is considerable debate surrounding the defining characteristics. Primarily the literature is characterized by its apocalyptic and judgment motifs.

Epicureans Members of the ancient school of Greek philosophy founded in Athens by Epicurus ca. 307 BCE.

epistle Literary work in the form of a letter addressed to a person or a group of persons.

epitomator Term for the editor who produced 2 Maccabees (since 2 Macc. 2:19–32 presents the book as an epitome, or abridgment of a longer original work).

eponymous Relating to the person for whom something is named.

eschatological Of or relating to the future age (lit. "last, final things").

eschaton The future age (sometimes called "end-time"), during which the evil and corruption on the earth will be brought to an end by the intervention of YHWH.

Essenes Second Temple period Jewish sect whose members practiced a simple, communal lifestyle.

etic From the perspective of an outsider.

etiology Cause or source of something; also refers to investigation into the origins of something with the goal of providing some historical, social, or mythic explanation for this origin.

evil inclination Congenital inclination to do evil in violation of God's will; the phrase derives from the Hebrew *yetser hara*. The expression is found twice in the Hebrew Bible (Gen. 6:5; 8:21).

ex eventu Prophecy or foretelling after events have taken place. *Ex eventu* prophecies are frequently found in Jewish apocalyptic literature. They can also be identified in such pagan oracles as the (Egyptian) Potter's Oracle that may date as early as the third century BCE. *Ex eventu* prophecies were not only useful to anchor genuine predictions, but they also allowed an author to reinterpret past events as well.

exogamy Marriage outside a social group, especially as required by custom or law.

Festival of Weeks Also known as Shavuot, this is the second of three major Israelite festivals with both historical and agricultural significance (the other two are Passover and Sukkot). Agriculturally, it commemorates the time when the firstfruits were harvested and brought to the temple, and is also known as the Festival of the Firstfruits (Hag ha-Bikkurim), later as Pentecost. In addition, historically, it celebrates the giving of the Law at Mount Sinai. Its scriptural origins are found in Exodus 23:16, 34:22; Leviticus 21:15–16, 21; Numbers 28:26; and Deuteronomy 16:10.

flashback Narrative device in which an event or scene from the past is inserted into the chronology of a work.

Flavians Family dynasty of three Roman emperors (Vespasian, Titus, and Domitian) whose rule of the Roman Empire began in 69 CE and ended in 96 CE.

Gallic Wars (sometimes called the *War Commentaries of Caesar*) Written by Julius Caesar, this work details his military campaigns in the land that is today occupied by the nations of France (except the southern portion), the Netherlands, Germany (the western part), Belgium, and most of Switzerland. This area was generally referred to as Gaul, and the people as Gauls or Celts. Caesar spent nearly nine years of his life, from 58 to 49 BCE, in Gaul as governor of Transalpine Gaul. Even though the *Gallic Wars* comprises eight volumes (or chapters), only the first seven were written by Caesar.

Geʿez Semitic language of the Southern Peripheral group; the ancestor of the modern Tigrinya and Tigré languages of Eritrea and Ethiopia. Commonly identified as Ethiopic, the language developed in the region of the Horn of Africa. Currently the language is used only in the liturgy of the Ethiopian Orthodox and Catholic Churches. The language, or some version of it, is thought to have been in use since approximately 2000 BCE. Some Geʿez inscriptions have been identified from the fifth century BCE and possibly in an earlier form of the script from the eighth century BCE. The Ethiopian Church is primarily responsible for the transmission of 1 Enoch and the book of Jubilees (among other Deuterocanonical books), which are in the Ethiopic canon.

genizah Storage space in a Jewish synagogue or cemetery for discarded documents.

gnosis Greek term for knowledge that came to refer primarily to esoteric spiritual knowledge.

Gnosticism Religious and philosophical movement that emphasized the dualistic contrast between the evil god of this world (the Demiurge) and the higher God revealed by Jesus Christ. Gnosticism became a sophisticated theological system in the middle of the second century CE, inheriting many early traditions about salvation and dualism from numerous sources, including Greek, Jewish, and Christian. Gnostics stressed a dualism in which some individuals have *gnosis* (the Greek word for "knowledge") and others do not. Those with knowledge learn their origins and by introspection (and at times with the help of a redeemer) can return to a heavenly abode.

Gog and Magog In the Judeo-Christian tradition, legendary or evil powers who wage war against God and the righteous in the end-time (based on Ezek. 38–39 and Rev. 20; cf. Gen. 10:2).

Greek Chester Beatty-Michigan Papyrus Important Greek papyrus, dated to the fourth century CE, that preserves a sermon by Melito, *On the Passover* (late second century CE), and part of The Epistle of Enoch (1 En. 97:6–107:3). Hastily produced, this copy demonstrates the ongoing importance of the Enochic tradition in Greek during Late Antiquity and demonstrates by comparison the significance of the Ethiopic version of the Epistle of Enoch for recovering an early form of the text.

gymnasium The Greek *gymnasion* was the location in a city in which the physical and intellectual education of young men took place. The word is defined as a "place to be naked"; this meant that all activities, including exercise, bathing, and study, were performed naked. In the Hellenistic world, the physical aspects of learning were considered as important as cognitive learning. Many of the gymnasiums included libraries for study.

Hades Greek translation of the Hebrew *Sheol;* in the New Testament, Hades is both the underworld and the personification of evil that it represents.

hagiographical Of or relating to the biography of a saint or a venerated person. Rooted in the Greek term *hagios* (meaning "holy" or "other"), this can refer pejoratively to an overinflated report or opinion of the person being described.

halakhah "Jewish Law" or the "path that one walks"; collective body of Jewish religious laws derived from the Written and Oral Torah.

Hasidim (Hebrew: "pious ones") A sect of Jews that developed between 300 and 175 BCE; they maintained the highest standards of Jewish religious observance and moral action. They led the resistance against the Hellenizing efforts of Antiochus IV Epiphanes and played an important role in the Maccabean Revolt.

Hasmoneans Ancient Judean dynasty; descendants of the Maccabee family who established a semi-independent state under the Seleucid kings in the region of Judea between ca. 140 and ca. 63 BCE.

hegemony Dominance of one country or social group over others.

***hekhalot* literature** Derives its name from *hekhal*, a Hebrew word meaning "palace" or "temple." This literature, which overlaps with merkavah literature, is a specific genre of Jewish mysticism that developed in the rabbinic period and typically features ascents into heavenly palaces.

Hellenistic An adjective rooted in the self-descriptive Greek term *Hellas* and referring to Greek activity and influence.

Hellenization The process of Greek influence across the world in political, social, cultural, and religious contexts beginning with Alexander the Great's death (323 BCE) and ending with the defeat of the Ptolemaic Empire (Egypt) at the Battle of Actium (31 BCE).

Herodian period Period of political rule in Palestine beginning with Herod the Great and ending with Agrippa II, when Rome assumed full power over Agrippa's domain (37 BCE–70 CE).

Herodian script Form of Hebrew or Aramaic handwriting prominent during the reign of Herod the Great; many of the Dead Sea Scrolls were written in this script.

Herodium Herod's palace-fortress built to commemorate his victory over his Hasmonean and Parthian enemies in 40 BCE. It is located on a hill 12 kilometers south of Jerusalem and 5 kilometers southeast of Bethlehem in the Judean Desert.

Hexapla A "parallel Bible" in which six translation traditions appear alongside one another; the term especially applies to Origen's edition of the Old Testament.

hyperbaton Inversion of normal word order, especially for emphasis.

idiosyncratic Of or relating to peculiarity or eccentricity.

Idumeans Greek for Edomites. The Edomites were the reputed descendants of Jacob's brother Esau. They inhabited the region south of Judea. Jonathan Hyrcanus I forced their conversion to Judaism ca. 130 BCE.

interpolation Passage inserted into a text that was not written by the original author.

Isis Ancient Egyptian goddess who was the archetypal mother and patron goddess of childbirth and motherhood; she was also a skillful queen and powerful sorceress.

Karaite Term describing Jews who reject the authority of the rabbis and of classical rabbinic texts such as the Talmuds and Midrashim, and who formulate a system of Jewish law without primary reference to those documents. They have consequently tended to stress the authority of Scripture. Their beginnings may be traced to the eighth century CE in Babylonia, and they grew in numbers in the Middle Ages.

Khirbet Qumran Archaeological site south of modern Jericho on the northwestern shore of the Dead Sea where the Dead Sea Scrolls were discovered.

Kittim Originally appearing in the Hebrew Bible (see Num. 24:24 and Dan. 11:30), this is a coded reference to an external enemy that gained particular focus in the Dead Sea Scrolls. Generally, "Kittim" translates as "Westerners," but in Jewish literature from the mid-first century BCE onward most likely refers to the Romans (see also 1 Macc. 1:1 as an earlier reference to Greece and the rule of Alexander the Great).

lacuna Place in an ancient text in which part of the text has been lost and is usually re-constructed; lacunae in the Dead Sea Scrolls are generally marked out with bracketed ellipses […].

Leitmotif German term for a recurrent theme in a literary composition.

lemma Canonical or citation form of a word.

Levant Geographical region in southwest Asia bounded by the Taurus Mountains to the north, the Mediterranean Sea to the west, the Arabian Desert to the south, and Mesopotamia to the east.

Lilith Female demon found in early Jewish and other ancient Near Eastern traditions. The role of Lilith as a feminine demon dates back to the third millennium BCE in the Sumerian Epic of Gilgamesh. She is also a figure in Persian magical incantation bowls. Within Judaism, there is one potential reference to Lilith in Isaiah 34:14, although this reading is debated since it is the only place in the Hebrew Bible where this word is used. Regardless of the original intent of Isaiah, Songs of the Sage specifically mentions Lilith in a similar context within a list of demons. In later Jewish literature, the traditions about Lilith grow. The Talmud portrays her as a demon who seduces men (Erub. 100b; Nid. 24b; Shab. 151b). In the Alphabet of Ben Sira, dating from 800 to 1000 CE, a tradition develops that Lilith was the first wife of Adam. In the Middle Ages, Lilith becomes the grandmother of the Devil or the Devil himself, and also the mother of witchcraft.

lingua franca Language of commerce used in common by speakers of different vernaculars.

Maccabean Referring to the Maccabees, a Jewish family of priests who organized a successful revolt against the Seleucid ruler Antiochus IV Epiphanes (ca. 164–160 BCE).

Machaerus Fortified hilltop palace (Herod the Great's Black Fortress) in Jordan 24 kilometers southeast of the mouth of the Jordan River on the eastern side of the Dead Sea.

Man of the Lie Coded reference in the Dead Sea Scrolls to an internal enemy who is accused of trying to discredit the Teacher of Righteousness and the Torah.

mantic Relating to prophecy or divination.

Masada Mountaintop fortress in the Judean Desert constructed by Herod the Great between 37 and 31 BCE; Masada is where a group of Jewish rebels and Zealots took their last stand against the Romans before committing mass suicide in 73 CE.

maskilim Lit. "wise ones"; cf. Dan. 12:3. Probably a scribal group among the elite of Judean society that was employed either by the aristocracy or by the local governing bureaucracy prior to Antiochus IV Epiphanes's reign.

Masoretes Scribes who preserved the texts of the Hebrew Bible, copying and adding marks to the text to instruct readers in the precise ways of reading Hebrew. The work of the Masoretes culminated in the medieval period, but these tasks were a continuation of a longer process of preservation going back to the Second Temple period. The base text of the Hebrew Bible, as it survives today, was preserved by the Masoretes and is called the Masoretic Text, or MT.

Masoretic Text (MT) Traditional text of the canon of the Hebrew Bible.

Mastema Personification of the Hebrew word *mastemah* (hostility); according to the book of Jubilees, he is the chief of the evil spirits and the tester of humans (with God's permission). The term "Mastema" originates from the Hebrew root *satam,* which is a derivative of *satan.* The origins of this personification are found in the Hebrew Bible. The LXX uses the term *diabolos* to translate the Hebrew *hasatan* ("the adversary") as a proper name in the following passages: Job 1:6, 7(2), 8, 9, 12(2); 2:1, 2(2), 3, 4, 6, 7; Zechariah 3:1, 2(2); and 1 Chronicles 21:1. In these instances, it could be implied that *hasatan* is a member of the *bene elohim* (sons of God; angelic beings in the heavenly court); however, it could be understood that he has been singled out, thus leaving room to recognize him as some other type of being. The Hebrew *satan* is transliterated three times (1 Kings 11:14, 23, 25) and is translated as *epiboulos* (adversary) in 1 Kings 5:18. In these four instances, *satan* is portrayed as a human adversary. Mastema appears in Hosea 9:7–8 as a noun that is translated "hostility." It has likely evolved from the concept of hostility or adversarial conduct to the personification of this concept in postbiblical Judaism in the figure of Satan, Mastema (Jubilees), Belial (Dead Sea Scrolls), and other designations in the New Testament. In Jubilees 10:8, he is seen as the "chief of the spirits" and is identified as *satan* in 10:11. 11QPs[a] 19.15 appears to be identifying *satan* as the Mastema figure of Jubilees 10 along with the evil spirits of the giants: "Let not *satan* rule over me, nor an evil spirit." 1QSb 1.8 identifies the enemy of holiness as *satan* in a general manner. It seems likely that the origin of Mastema as the leader of the demonic realm began in Jubilees and the Qumran literature.

mēbîm An "understanding" or "discerning" person.

merkavah **literature** Derives its name from the ascent of Elijah in a chariot in 1 Kings 2; *merkavah* is the Hebrew word for "chariot." This literature, which overlaps with *hekhalot* literature, is a specific genre of Jewish mysticism that developed in the rabbinic period, typically featuring revelatory experience in heavenly palaces.

messianism Belief in a Messiah (savior or redeemer).

Middle Platonism Stage in the development of Plato's philosophy beginning with Antiochus of Ascalon's rejection of the skepticism of the New Academy ca. 90 BCE and ending with the development of Neo-Platonism under Plotinus in the third century CE.

midrashic Referring to a rabbinic method of interpretation by which gaps found in the Torah could be filled in with commentary or explanatory material.

midrashim (**sing.** *midrash*) Post-Second Temple period rabbinical commentaries on the Torah.

Mishnah Authoritative collection of rabbinic exegetical material codifying the Oral Torah and comprising the first part of the Talmud.

neologism Newly invented word or phrase.

Nineveh Ancient Mesopotamian city on the eastern bank of the Tigris River; it was the capital of the Neo-Assyrian Empire.

nomen regens The first noun in a simple two-noun construction. In Semitic languages, the *status constructus* indicates a genitive-case relationship between nouns. The first noun *(nomen regens)* is in a phonetically abbreviated state while the second noun *(nomen rectum)* occurs in its phonetically full form *(status absolutus)*.

non-Masoretic reading A variant reading of a Hebrew Bible (OT) text that is different from the Masoretic Text.

Old Greek Early version of the Septuagint that was revised in three later translations by Aquila, Symmachus, and Theodotion. Aquila produced a very accurate translation that was close to his Hebrew text in about 130 CE. The other two were produced in the later second century: by Symmachus (a more idiomatic and elegant rendering) and by Theodotion (a version much closer than the others to the Septuagint).

Orphic Resembling music attributed to the Greek god Orpheus.

orthography Study of letters and how they are used to express sounds and form words.

otot Text listing the order of the priestly service according to the 364-day solar calendar; it may be the earlier stage of the tradition (still linked with the temple service) that could later be replaced by a text reflecting the order of prayer within the community, thus separating it from the temple service.

Oxyrhynchus Papyri Papyrus texts discovered by archaeologists (including Bernard Pyne Grenfell and Arthur Surridge Hunt) at an ancient garbage dump in Egypt in the nineteenth and twentieth centuries.

paleography Study of ancient handwriting in documents and inscriptions.

parallelism Use of grammatically similar components in a sentence to form a consistent pattern.

parallelismus membrorum Technical term used to describe a complex and pervasive feature of Hebrew poetry, whereby themes, phrases, and expressions are set alongside one another in parallelism. Thus a poetic line may consist of two or three sections, the second and third balancing the first by repeating its sentiments in slightly different language, or presenting an explicit or implicit contrast to it. A whole poetic line, itself consisting of two or three parallel items, may further be set in parallel with lines that precede it to create a balanced sense-unit.

parenesis Ethical instruction.

paronomasia A play on words that sound alike but have different meanings.

parousia Greek word in the New Testament translated as the "coming" or "presence" of an individual. The term is found twenty-four times in the New Testament: it is used seventeen times to speak of the "coming (or return) of Jesus (or the Son of Man)" from his heavenly abode (Matt. 24:3, 27, 37, 39; Phil. 1:26; 2 Thess. 2:1, 8; James 5:7, 8; 2 Pet. 1:16; 3:4; 1 Thess. 2:19; 3:13; 4:15; 5:23; 1 Cor. 15:23; 1 John 2:28); it is once used to describe of the coming of the "Day of God" in 2 Peter 3:12; it is once used to speak of the coming of the "Man of Lawlessness" in 2 Thessalonians 2:9; three references speak of the coming of a "missionary" (1 Cor. 16:17; 2 Cor. 7:6, 7); and the final two references are understood as the "presence of an individual" (2 Cor. 10:10; Phil. 2:12).

Parthian Empire Major Iranian cultural and political power in the ancient Near East that ruled from 247 BCE to 224 CE.

patrimony Estate inherited from one's father or male ancestors.

pentecontad Referring to an ancient Semitic agricultural calendar thought to be of Amorite origin in which the year is broken down into seven periods of seven days each.

pericope Extract or selection from Scripture that forms one coherent unit of thought.

pesharim (sing. ***pesher***) Distinctive commentaries on specific biblical books composed in Hebrew by anonymous members of the Qumran community.

Peshitta Translation of the Hebrew Scriptures into Syriac for use in the Syriac (eastern) churches, probably done around the second century CE. Eventually, the New Testament would also be translated into Syriac.

Pharisees Jewish sect or group during the Second Temple period that scrupulously observed the Law as interpreted by the scribes. They operated in opposition to the priestly Sadducees. Following the destruction of the Second Temple in 70 CE, their beliefs became the basis for rabbinic Judaism.

physiognomic Of, or relating to, the activity of judging or determining a person's character based on outward (physical) appearance (often emphasis is on facial features).

Platonism Ancient Greek school of philosophy from the Socratic period founded ca. 387 BCE by Plato; it is best known for its theory of forms.

pleonastically To express ideas using more words than necessary; redundancy.

polyvalence The multiplicity of meanings embedded within a text and beyond it.

postdiluvian Of or belonging to the time after the biblical flood.

prefect Governing official thought to be appointed by the emperor for a fixed period or to accomplish a particular task (generally military in nature).

primeval Of or relating to the first age or ages.

prophylactic Preventive or protective.

propitiate To ease/appease the anger (especially a divine being in religious texts); to avert the effects of a superior being's wrath. "Propitiation" also refers to an outcome of sacrificial activity in which sins or wrongdoings are addressed.

protreptic discourse Type of ancient philosophical treatise with a specific, sustained focus that utilized a variety of literary elements to persuade the listener or reader to embrace a particular approach to life to the exclusion of others.

prosopopoeial Figure of speech in which an imagined or absent person is depicted as speaking.

pseudepigrapha Pseudonymous Jewish writings ascribed to various biblical patriarchs and prophets composed ca. 200 BCE to 200 CE (see **pseudonmity**).

pseudonymity Use of a pseudonym (usually the falsely ascribed name of an ancient biblical figure) by unidentified authors of certain ancient texts such as early Jewish apocalypses and testaments, certain Jewish and Christian epistles, Gospel traditions, and extrabiblical Christian literature.

Pseudo-Eupolemos Fragment cited in Eusebius of Caesarea's *Praeparatio evangelica* that suggests that Enoch was the discoverer of astrology through the revelation of angels, which he later passed on to his son Methuselah.

Ptolemies Macedonian dynasty founded by Ptolemy, a general under Alexander the Great, which ruled in the region of ancient Egypt from 323 to 30 BCE.

Pythagoreans Members of the ancient school of Greek philosophy founded in Samos by Pythagoras in the fifth century BCE.

recension Revision of an existing translation; in textual criticism, selection of the most trustworthy evidence on which to base a text; a family of manuscripts with common traits (e.g., the Alexandrian recension).

redaction Editing process in which multiple texts are combined (redacted) and changed to make a single text; a version of a text such as a new edition or an abridged edition.

redaction criticism Method of criticism that examines how an author or editor edited (redacted) source materials in the process of creating a final literary work.

romanticized narrative Literary subgenre of history or localized history that was read or understood as stories that were grounded in real events.

Sadducees Jewish sect or group active in the Second Temple period; they were conservative in outlook and accepted only the written Mosaic Law.

Samaritan Pentateuch The Samaritan Pentateuch is the form of the Pentateuch or Torah, the first five books of the Hebrew Bible, accepted by the Samaritan community as canonical. The Samaritans, a community still in existence today, acknowledge only the Pentateuch as their Bible.

Samaritans Ethnoreligious group in the Levant with a mixed Jewish and pagan ancestry; they accepted only the Pentateuch as canonical, and their temple was on Mount Gerizim instead of Mount Zion.

sapiential Of or relating to wisdom.

Scythians An ancient people whose kingdom was located in southern Russia; they had a reputation for cruelty and barbarity.

sectarian Of or relating to a sect or sects.

sectarianism Of or related to the characteristics and behaviors of groups or individuals identified with a given sect, especially as they promote exclusivity and specific expressions of devotion.

Seleucids Macedonian dynasty founded by Seleucus, a general under Alexander the Great, which ruled in the region of ancient Syria from 198 to 63 BCE.

Sheol Hebrew word of uncertain etiology used to connote the miserable underworld where the departed souls continue a shadowy existence.

Sicarii Jewish "bandits" operating primarily during the revolts against Rome in 66–74 CE; it is generally thought that the group originated in Jerusalem and that it was named for the weapons it used—curved daggers.

sons of Zadok Priests in the Hebrew Bible of the Zadokite lineage, including Ezra and Joshua the high priest.

soteriological Of or relating to salvation.

source criticism Method of criticism that seeks to establish sources used by authors and redactors of a text.

stichometric format Special poetic format of text. In the printed Hebrew Bible, the Psalms are laid out stichometrically, that is, in poetic format, with each line called a stich and groupings within lines called cola (sing. colon). At least ten Psalms scrolls are arranged in stichometric format, twenty-one in prose format, and one in prose with a single piece written stichometrically.

Stoics Members of the ancient school of Greek philosophy founded in Athens by Zeno of Citium in the early third century BCE.

Sukkot Biblical Jewish festival of giving thanks for the fall harvest celebrated on the fifteenth day of Tishri, the fifth day after Yom Kippur; it is also known as Feast of Booths or Feast of Tabernacles.

synchrisis Elaborate series of contrasts in Greek rhetoric.

targumim **(sing.** *targum***)** Explanatory translations, paraphrases, and expansions of the Hebrew Bible (excluding Ezra, Nehemiah, and Daniel) in Aramaic.

Tartarus In Greek mythology both a deity and a region of the underworld.

Teacher of Righteousness Coded reference in the Dead Sea Scrolls to one who has received revelation of the Torah and provides accurate interpretation of it. While the identity of the Teacher remains elusive, his influence on the Qumran community is apparent in a number of texts preserved there. The Teacher figures most prominently in the Damascus Document, which recounts his initial appearance, his importance as a teacher and interpreter, and his death; he is also mentioned in a few *pesharim*. Some scholars believe the Teacher authored one or more of the Qumran scrolls. The most prominent opponent of the *moreh haṣṣedeq* (the Teacher of Righteousness or the Righteous Teacher) is the Wicked Priest, an epithet that presumably refers to one of the Hasmonean high priests.

tekamim Unique term in sectarian texts for bodily members or entrails.

terminus ad quem The point at which something ends or finishes.

terminus ante quem The latest possible date for something.

terminus post quem The earliest possible date for something.

Testament of Moses Text sometimes also called the Assumption of Moses, which was originally composed in Aramaic or Hebrew during the reign of the persecutor Antiochus IV Epiphanes, just before the Maccabean Revolt (early 160s BCE). Surviving only in a Latin translation of a Greek text, it retells the content of Deuteronomy 31–34, containing some of Moses's hidden instructions to Joshua, his successor, and anticipates that eschatological events of divine punishment and deliverance will follow the martyred Taxo and his sons (chap. 10). The work underwent revisions during the time of Herod the Great at the turn of the Common Era and then toward the beginning of the second century CE.

Testament of Qahat Text that survives in three Aramaic fragments among the Dead Sea Scrolls (4Q542). The fragments are given the title because in them, Qahat, the son of Levi, while speaking in first person, blesses and gives instruction to his children. This work is closely related to Aramaic literature composed during the third or early second century BCE, such as the Aramaic Levi Document and the Visions of Amram (Amram being Qahat's son in the biblical tradition).

Tetragrammaton The term used to identify the name of the God of Israel in the Hebrew Bible—YHWH. It comes from the Greek for four (*tetra*), and letters (*grammat*).

theocracy A governmental structure whereby a deity is believed to be the highest civic ruler, and laws are established and maintained by religious leaders. Josephus coined the term in *Against Apion* for the Judean kind of aristocracy, elevating it to a unique level.

theodicy Attempt to answer why a good God permits the manifestation of evil.

theophany Manifestation or appearance of God to a human being.

topos Literary theme or motif.

treatise A formal and systematic work on a given subject.

Uhrzeit als Endzeit Literary technique in which an author directs readers to a future goal by presenting a picture of an ideal past in which these qualities were already present (see also ***Endzeit ist Uhrzeit***).

Urim and Thummim A kind of divine oracle connected with the breastplate of the high priest (Lev. 8:7–8). The LXX translates Urim and Thummim with *delosis* and *aletheia,* "revelation" and "truth." Exodus 28:13–30 describes the high priestly ephod and the breastplate with the Urim and Thummim. It is called a "breastplate of judgment" in Exodus 28:30. When Moses consecrated Aaron and his sons as priests, he placed the breastplate containing the Urim and Thummim on Aaron.

vacat Meaning "empty"; indicates a line of text without surviving content.

virtue Moral excellence.

Vorlage From the German for prototype or template, a *Vorlage* is the original-language version of a text that a translator works into a translation. Several of the biblical scrolls found at Qumran confirm that the translator's Semitic *Vorlage* often differed from the Hebrew Masoretic Text that is used by scholars today.

Watchers Class of angel that is compared with the archangels (1 En. 12:3). They are the "Watchers from eternity" (14:1) whose place was in the "highest heaven, the holy and eternal one" (15:3). These angels once stood before the Great Lord and King of Eternity (14:23). They "do not sleep," but "stand before your glory and bless and praise and exalt" (39:12; 61:12; 71:7).

Wicked Priest Coded reference in the Dead Sea Scrolls to an external enemy who is the opponent of the Teacher of Righteousness. He is accused of corruption, oppression of the poor, and violation of the Torah.

wisdom In the Hebrew Bible, especially the book of Proverbs, the ability on the part of a person to exercise covenant faithfulness and avoid sinful or ungodly ways.

yaḥad Lit. "unity." Generally thought to be the men of the community that occupied Khirbet Qumran who held to a very dualistic worldview. The *yaḥad* divided humanity between the righteous and the wicked—the Sons of Light and the Sons of Darkness—and asserted that human nature and the events of the world have been predestined by God.

Yahwist One of the sources thought to comprise the Torah (Pentateuch); it gets its name from the fact that it uses the term YHWH for God rather than Elohim.

Yom Kippur Most important holiday of the Jewish year. It means "Day of Atonement"—it is a day set aside to "afflict the soul" by atoning for the sins of the previous year. It is celebrated on the tenth day of Tishri.

Zadokites A family of priests who descended from Eleazar the son of Aaron. Zadok was the first of the family to serve as high priest in Solomon's temple in Jerusalem. Zadok apparently earned this right by helping David during the rebellion of Absalom. It was during this time that Zadok served as high priest (with Abiathar) when David had to flee Jerusalem. The sons of Zadok played a central role as priests at the Qumran community; in addition, 1QS suggests that the Zadokites were the leaders in the community.

Zealots Revolutionary political party established by Judas the Galilean ca. 6 CE in opposition to Roman rule in Palestine. Referred to by Josephus as the "fourth sect," in 64–66 CE they rebelled against Florus and the "treacherous" Jerusalem population.

zoomorphic Having or representing animal forms.

Contributors

Martin Abegg (Professor of Religious Studies, Trinity Western University): The Qumran Messianic Texts, Introduction to the Aramaic Apocalypse, Aramaic Apocalypse (4Q246) (trans.), Introduction to the Messianic Apocalypse, Messianic Apocalypse (4Q521) (trans.), Introduction to The Book of War, Book of War (4Q285 and 11Q14) (trans.)

John Barclay (Lightfoot Professor of Divinity, Durham University): from *Against Apion* (trans.)

Leslie Baynes (Associate Professor of New Testament and Second Temple Judaism, Missouri State University): Introduction to the Similitudes of Enoch

Christopher T. Begg (Katherine Drexel Chair of Religious Studies, Catholic University of America): from *Jewish Antiquities* (trans.)

George J. Brooke (Rylands Professor of Biblical Criticism and Exegesis, University of Manchester): The Temple Scroll, *from* Temple Scroll (11Q19–20) (trans.)

Jared C. Calaway (Visiting Assistant Professor, Department of Religion, Illinois Wesleyan University): Songs of the Sabbath Sacrifice

James H. Charlesworth (George L. Collord Professor of New Testament Language and Literature, Director of the Princeton Dead Sea Scrolls Project, Princeton Theological Seminary): *from* Rule of the Community (1QS) (trans.), *from* Odes of Solomon (trans.)

Randall D. Chesnutt (William S. Banowsky Chair in Religion, Pepperdine University): Joseph and Aseneth, *from* Joseph and Aseneth (trans.)

Ronald R. Cox (Associate Professor of Religion, Pepperdine University): Introduction to *On the Decalogue*, Introduction to *On the Life of Moses*

Sidnie White Crawford (Willa Cather Professor of Classics and Religious Studies, University of Nebraska-Lincoln): The Reworked Pentateuch, Reworked Pentateuch (4Q158, 4Q364–4Q367) (trans.)

James Davila (Professor of Jewish Studies, University of St. Andrews): Songs of the Sabbath Sacrifice (4QShirShab) (trans.)

C. J. Patrick Davis (Sessional Instructor Trinity Western University): Additions to Daniel and Other Danielic Literature, The Prayer of Azariah in the Fiery Furnace and the Song of the Three Young Men, Introduction to Susanna, Introduction to Bel and the Dragon, Introduction to the Prayer of Nabonidus (4Q242), Introduction to Pseudo-Daniel A and B (4Q243–4Q245)

James D. G. Dunn (Emeritus Lightfoot Professor of Divinity, Durham University): Some Works of the Law, Some Works of the Law (4QMMT) (trans.)

Brad Embry (Associate Professor of Hebrew Bible and Old Testament Studies, Regent University): Preface; Introduction to Scriptural Texts and Traditions; The Letter of Aristeas; Introduction to Wisdom Literature, Psalms, Hymns, and Prayers; The Psalms of Solomon; *from* Psalms of Solomon (trans.)

Louis H. Feldman (late Abraham Wouk Family Chair in Classics and Literature, Professor of Classics, Yeshiva University): from *Jewish Antiquities* (trans.)

Peter W. Flint (late Canada Research Chair in Dead Sea Scrolls Studies, Professor of Biblical Studies, Trinity Western University): Additions to Daniel and Other Danielic Literature, The Prayer of Azariah in the Fiery Furnace and the Song of the Three Young Men, The Prayer of Azariah in the Fiery Furnace and the Song of the Three Young Men (trans.), Introduction to Susanna, *from* Susanna (trans.), Introduction to Bel and the Dragon, Bel and the Dragon (trans.), Introduction to the Prayer of Nabonidus (4Q242), The Prayer of Nabonidus (4Q242) (trans.), Introduction to Pseudo-Daniel A and B (4Q243–4Q245), Pseudo-Daniel A (4Q243–4Q244) (trans.), Pseudo-Daniel B (4Q245) (trans.), The Great Isaiah Scroll and the Interpretation of Isaiah at Qumran, *from* Great Isaiah Scroll (1QIsa^a) (trans.), Psalms and Psalters at Qumran, The Eschatological Hymn (4QPsf = 4Q88 9:5–13) (trans.), Apostrophe to Judah (4QPs^f = 4Q88 10:5–15) (trans.), Hymn to the Creator (11QPs^a = 11Q5 27) (trans.), *from* David's Compositions (11QPs^a = 11Q5 27) (trans.), Third Song (or Incantation) against Demons (11QapocrPs = 11Q11 5) (trans.)

Jörg Frey (Professor of New Testament and Early Judaism and Hermeneutics, Theological Faculty, University of Zürich): The Rule of the Community

Michael Fuller (Associate Professor of Early Judaism and Biblical Studies): Sibylline Oracles; Introduction to Sibylline Oracles, Book 3; Sibylline Oracles, Book 3 (trans.); Introduction to Sibylline Oracles, Book 4; Sibylline Oracles, Book 4 (trans.); Introduction to Sibylline Oracles, Book 5; Sibylline Oracles, Book 5 (trans.)

Matthew E. Gordley (Dean of the College of Learning and Innovation, Carlow University): The Wisdom of Solomon, *from* Wisdom of Solomon (trans.)

Todd R. Hanneken (Associate Professor of Theology, St. Mary's University): The Book of Jubilees, *from* Jubilees 8–50 (trans.)

Angela Kim Harkins (Associate Professor, Department of Religious Studies, Boston College): Hodayot

Rebecca L. Harris (Ph.D. Candidate, Rice University): The Aramaic Levi Document, Aramaic Levi Document (trans.)

C. T. Robert Hayward (Professor Emeritus of Hebrew, Department of Theology and Religion, Durham University): The Wisdom of Sirach

Ronald Herms (Dean of the School of Humanities, Religion, and Social Sciences and Associate Professor of Biblical Studies, Fresno Pacific University): Overview of Early Jewish Literature, Introduction to Apocalyptic Literature, Introduction to Interpretive History, Introduction to the Animal Apocalypse, Animal Apocalypse (1 Enoch 85–90) (trans.), *from* War Scroll (1QM) (trans.), Fourth Ezra, Introduction to Testamentary Literature, The Testament of Moses

Robert Kugler (Paul S. Wright Professor of Religious Studies and Classics, Lewis & Clark College): The Testaments of the Twelve Patriarchs, Testament of Levi (trans.), The Testament of Abraham, Testament of Abraham (trans.)

John R. (Jack) Levison (W. J. A. Power Professor of Old Testament Interpretation and Biblical Hebrew, Perkins School of Theology, Southern Methodist University): The Life of Adam and Eve, Life of Adam and Eve (trans.)

Daniel A. Machiela (Associate Professor of Religious Studies, Early Judaism, McMaster University): The Genesis Apocryphon, Genesis Apocryphon (1QapGen) (trans.)

Steve Mason (Distinguished Professor in Ancient Mediterranean Religions and Cultures, University of Groningen): The Writings of Flavius Josephus, Introduction to the *Life*, from *Life* (trans.), Introduction to the *Jewish Antiquities*, from *Jewish Antiquities* (trans.), Introduction to *Against Apion*, Introduction to the *Jewish War*, from *Jewish War* (trans.)

Bruce Metzger (late George L. Collord Professor Emeritus of New Testament Language and Literature, Princeton University): *from* 4 Ezra (2 Esdras 3–14) (trans.)

George W. Nickelsburg (Daniel J. Krumm Emeritus Distinguished Professor of New Testament and Reformation Studies, University of Iowa): Similitudes of Enoch (1 Enoch 37–71) (trans.)

R. Steven Notley (Program Director in Ancient Judaism and Christian Origins, Nyack College): The Melchizedek Scroll, *from* Melchizedek (11Q13) (trans.)

Lidija Novakovic (Associate Professor of Religion, Baylor University): The *Pesharim*, Introduction to the Habakkuk Pesher

Gerbern S. Oegema (Professor of Biblical Studies, Faculty of Religious Studies, McGill University): Second Baruch

Chad T. Pierce (Pastor, Faith Christian Reformed Church, Holland, Michigan): Songs of the Sage, Incantation and Exorcism

Elisha Qimron (Professor of Hebrew Language, Ben Gurion University): *from* Rule of the Community (1QS) (trans.)

Brian Schultz (Associate Professor of Biblical Studies, Fresno Pacific University): The War Scroll

Daniel R. Schwartz (Professor of Jewish History, Hebrew University of Jerusalem): The Books of the Maccabees, from *Jewish Antiquities* (trans.)

Torrey Seland (Professor Dr.Art., Dean of Studies, School of Mission and Theology, Norway): The Writings of Philo of Alexandria, Introduction to *On the Creation of the World*

Kevin L. Spawn (Associate Professor of Old Testament, Regent University School of Divinity): LXX Psalm 151, LXX Psalm 151 (trans.)

Loren T. Stuckenbruck (Professor of New Testament and Judaism in Antiquity, Faculty of Protestant Theology, Ludwig-Maximilians-Universität München): The Exhortation of Enoch and the Epistle of Enoch, *from* Exhortation of Enoch (1 Enoch 91:1-10, 18-19) (trans.), *from* Epistle of Enoch (1 Enoch 92:1-5; 93:11-105:2) (trans.), Introduction to the Apocalypse of Weeks, Apocalypse of Weeks (1 Enoch 93:1-10 and 91:11-19) (trans.)

Eibert Tigchelaar (BOF Research Professor, Faculty of Theology and Religious Studies, Katholieke Universiteit, Leuven): Instruction, Instruction (4Q418) (trans.), Beatitudes and Wiles of the Wicked Woman, *from* Beatitudes (4Q525) (trans.), *from* Wiles of the Wicked Woman (4Q184) (trans.)

Marc Turnage (Director of Holy Land Studies): Hodayot (1QHa) (trans.)

Eugene Ulrich (John A. O'Brien Professor of Theology, Emeritus, University of Notre Dame): *from* Great Isaiah Scroll (1QIsaᵃ) (trans.)

James C. VanderKam (John A. O'Brien Professor of Hebrew Scriptures, Emeritus, University of Notre Dame): Jubilees 1-6 (trans.)

Ben Zion Wacholder (late Freehof Professor Emeritus of Talmud and Rabbinics, HUC-JIR/Cincinnati): Damascus Document (CD) (trans.)

Cecilia Wassen (Associate Professor of New Testament Exegesis, Uppsala University): The Damascus Document

Stuart Weeks (Professor in Old Testament and Hebrew, Department of Theology and Religion, Durham University): The Book of Tobit, Tobit (trans.)

Ethan R. White (Independent Scholar, Regent University): Testament of Moses (trans.)

Amy C. Merrill Willis (Associate Professor of Religious Studies, Lynchburg College): The Book of Daniel, *from* Daniel (trans.)

Benjamin Wold (Assistant Professor in New Testament, Trinity College Dublin): Florilegium and Testimonia, Florilegium (4Q174) (trans.), Testimonia (4Q175) (trans.)

Archie T. Wright (Associate Professor of Ancient Judaism and Christian Origins, Regent University): Overview of Early Jewish Literature, History of the Second Temple Period, Introduction to Romanticized Narrative, Introduction to Biblical Literature and Rewritten Scripture, Habakkuk Pesher (1QpHab) (trans.), Introduction to *On the Giants*, *On the Giants* (trans.), First Enoch, Introduction to the Book of Watchers, Book of Watchers (1 Enoch 1–36) (trans.), Introduction to the Book of Giants, Book of Giants (1Q23, 6Q8, 4Q203, 4Q530, 4Q531) (trans.), War Scroll (1QM) (trans.), Songs of the Sage (4Q510 and 4Q511) (trans.), Incantation (4Q444) (trans.), Exorcism (4Q560) (trans.), Testament of Moses (trans.), The Aramaic Levi Document, Aramaic Levi Document (trans.)

Charles D. Yonge (late Professor of History and English Literature, Queens College Belfast): from *On the Decalogue* (trans.), from *On the Life of Moses* (trans.)